THEORETICAL AND APPLIED ECONOMETRICS

ECONOMISTS OF THE TWENTIETH CENTURY

General Editors: Mark Perlman, *University Professor of Economics, Emeritus, University of Pittsburgh* and Mark Blaug, *Professor Emeritus, University of London, Professor Emeritus, University of Buckingham and Visiting Professor, University of Exeter*

This innovative series comprises specially invited collections of articles and papers by economists whose work has made an important contribution to economics in the late twentieth century.

The proliferation of new journals and the ever-increasing number of new articles make it difficult for even the most assiduous economist to keep track of all the important recent advances. By focusing on those economists whose work is generally recognized to be at the forefront of the discipline, the series will be an essential reference point for the different specialisms included.

A list of published and future titles in this series is printed at the end of this volume.

Theoretical and Applied Econometrics

The Selected Papers of Phoebus J. Dhrymes

Phoebus J. Dhrymes

Professor of Economics
Columbia University in the City of New York

ECONOMISTS OF THE TWENTIETH CENTURY

Edward Elgar
Aldershot, UK • Brookfield, US

Published by
Edward Elgar Publishing Limited
Gower House
Croft Road
Aldershot
Hants GU11 3HR
UK

Edward Elgar Publishing Company
Old Post Road
Brookfield
Vermont 05036
US

British Library Cataloguing in Publication Data
Dhrymes, Phoebus J.
Theoretical and Applied Econometrics:
Selected Papers of Phoebus J. Dhrymes. –
(Economists of the Twentieth Century
Series)
I. Title II. Series
330.015195

Library of Congress Cataloguing in Publication Data
Dhrymes, Phoebus J., 1932–
Theoretical and applied econometrics : the selected papers of
Phoebus J. Dhrymes / Phoebus J. Dhrymes.
p. cm. — (Economists of the twentieth century)
Includes index.
1. Dhrymes, Phoebus J., 1932—Contributions in econometrics.
2. Economists—United States. I. Title. II. Series.
HB139.D487 1995
330′.01′5193—dc20 94–48416
CIP

ISBN 1 85898 092 5

Printed and bound in Great Britain by
Hartnolls Limited, Bodmin, Cornwall

To Beatrice

Contents

Acknowledgements

The publishers wish to thank the following who have kindly given permission for the use of copyright material.

American Economic Association for article: 'On the Measurement of Price and Quality Changes in Some Consumer Capital Goods', *American Economic Review*, **57**, 1967, 501–18.

American Finance Association for articles: 'A Critical Reexamination of the Empirical Evidence on the Arbitrage Pricing Theory' with Irwin Friend and N. Bulent Gultekin, *Journal of Finance*, **39**, 1984, 323–46; 'New Tests of the APT and Their Implications', with Irwin Friend, Mustafa N. Gultekin and N. Bulent Gultekin, *Journal of Finance* **XL**(3), 1985, 659–74.

American Statistical Association for article: 'Asymptotic Properties of an Iterate of the Two-Stage Least Squares Estimator' with Vishwanath Pandit, *Journal of the American Statistical Association*, **67**(338), 1972, 444–7.

Australian Economic Papers for articles: 'On the Game of Maximising $\bar{R}^2$', **14**, 1970, 177–85; 'Equivalence of Iterative Aitkin and Maximum Likelihood Estimators for a System of Regression Equations', **15**, 1971, 20–24.

Blackwell Publishers for article: 'On Optimal Advertising Capital and Research Expenditures under Dynamic Conditions', *Economica*, NS **29**, 1962, 275–9.

The Brookings Institute for article: 'A Model of Short Run Labor Adjustment', Chapter 5 in *The Brookings Model: Some Further Results*, (eds J.S. Duesenberry et al.), North Holland Publishing, 1969, 111–49.

The Econometric Society for articles: 'Restricted and Unrestricted Reduced Forms: Asymptotic Distribution and Relative Efficiency', *Econometrica*, **41**(1), 1973, 119–34; 'Small Sample and Asymptotic Relations between Maximum Likelihood and Three Stage Least Squares Estimators', *Econometrica*, **41**(2), 1973, 357–64; 'A Comparison of Some Limited Information Estimators for Dynamic Simultaneous Equations Models with Autocorrelated Errors' with R. Berner and D. Cummins, *Econometrica*, **42**(2), 1974, 311–32; 'On Devising Unbiased Estimators for the Parameters of the Cobb-Douglas Production Function', *Econometrica*, **30**(2), 1962, 297–304; 'Technology and Scale in Electricity Generation', *Econometrica*, **32**(3), 1964, 287–315; 'Estimation of Joint Production Functions' with B.M. Mitchell, *Econometrica*, **37**(4), 1969, 732–6.

Elsevier Science Publishers for articles: 'Asymptotic Properties of Full Information Estimators in Dynamic Autoregressive Simultaneous Equation Models' with H. Erlat, *Journal of Econometrics*, **2**, 1974, 247–59; 'A Note on an Efficient Two-Step Estimator', *Journal of Econometrics*, **2**, 1974, 301–4; 'A Comparison of the Forecasting Performance of WEFA and ARIMA Time Series Methods' with Stavros C. Peristiani, *International Journal of Forecasting*, **4**, 1988, 81–101; 'A Comparison of Productivity Behavior in Manufacturing and Service Industries', *Review of Economics and Statistics*, **45**, 1963, 64–9; 'Some Extensions and Tests for the CES Class of Production Functions', *Review of Economics and Statistics*, **XLVII**(4), 1965, 357–66; 'A Comment on CES Production Functions', *Review of Economics and Statistics*, **49**, 1967, 610–11; 'Elasticities of Substitution for Two-Digit Manufacturing Industries: A Correction' with P. Zarembka, *Review of Economics and Statistics*, **LII**(2), 1970, 115–17; 'An Empirical Examination of the Implications of Arbitrage Pricing Theory' with Irwin Friend, N. Bulent Gultekin and Mustafa N. Gultekin, *Journal of Banking and Finance*, **9**, 1985, 73–99; 'Financial Stringency and the Probability of Homeownership', *Studies of Banking and Finance*, **5**, 1988, 27–47.

Greek Economic Review for articles: 'On the Invariance of Estimators for Singular Systems of Equations' with Samuel Schwarz, **9**(1), 1987, 88–107; 'On the Estimation of the Polynomial Lag Hypothesis', **3**(1), 1981, 18–24.

International Investor Inc. for article: 'The Empirical Relevance of Arbitrage Pricing Models', *Journal of Portfolio Management*, **10**, 1984, 35–44.

John Wiley & Sons Ltd for article: 'On the Existence of Generalized Inverse Estimators in a Singular System of Equations' with Samuel Schwarz, *Journal of Forecasting*, **6**, 1987, 181–92.

National Bureau of Economic Research for article: 'Criteria for Evaluation of Econometric Models', *Annals of Economic and Social Measurement*, **1**(3), 1972, 291–324.

Review of Economic Studies for articles: 'Alternative Asymptotic Tests of Significance and Related Aspects of 2SLS and 3SLS Estimated Parameters', **36**(2), 1969, 213–26; 'On a Class of Utility and Production Functions Yielding Everywhere Differentiable Demand Fucntions', **XXXIV**(4), 1967, 399–408.

Southern Economic Association for article: 'On the Treatment of Certain Recurrent Non-linearities in Regression Analysis', *Southern Economic Journal*, **33**(2), 1966, 187–96.

Statistical Associaiton of Australia for article: 'A Simplified Structural Estimator for Large-Scale Econometric Models', *Australian Journal of Statistics*, **13**(3), 1971, 168–75.

University of Pennsylvania Press for articles: 'An Identity Between Double k-class and Two Stage Least Squares Estimators', *International Economic Review*, **10**(1), 1969, 114–17; 'Asymptotic Properties of Simultaneous Least Squares Estimators', *International Economic Review*, **13**(2), 1972, 201–11; 'On an Efficient Two-Step Estimator for Dynamic Simultaneous Equations Models with Autoregressive Errors' with John B. Taylor, *International Economic Review*, **17**(2), 1976, 362–76; 'Efficient Estimation of Distributed Lags with Autocorrelated Errors', *International Economic Review*, **10**(1), 1969, 47–67; 'Estimation of Distributed Lags' with Lawrence R. Klein and Kenneth Steiglitz, *International Economic Review*, **11**(2), 1970, 235–50; 'On the Strong Consistency of Estimators for Certain Distributed Lag Models with Autocorrelated Errors', *International Economic Review*, **12**(2), 1971, 329–43; 'Adjustment Dynamics and the Estimation of the CES Class of Production Functions', *International Economic Review*, **8**(2), 1967, 209–17; 'On the Theory of the Monopolistic Multiproduct Firm Under Uncertainty', *International Economic Review*, **5**(3), 1964, 239–57.

Western Economic Association for article: 'A Simple Proof of the Asymptotic Efficiency of 3SLS Relative to 2SLS Estimators', *Western Economic Journal*, **XI**(2), 1973, 187–90.

Every effort has been made to trace all the copyright holders but if any have been inadvertently overlooked the publishers will be pleased to make the necessary arrangements at the first opportunity.

Preface

This book contains 42 of my papers, written over a period of approximately 30 years, and is roughly divided into six parts. The first part, comprised of 14 papers, deals with topics in the theory of simultaneous equations, and includes a paper that compares the forecasting performance of an econometric model of the US economy (the Wharton Mark III model) to that of a Box-Jenkins type model for 23 macro variables. The second part, consisting of six papers, deals with the theory of single or multiple equation regression models. The third part deals with the econometric theory of distributed lags and consists of four papers. The fourth part deals with empirical applications and with issues related to production functions, technical change, productivity, the decomposition of price movements into quality improvement and pure price components, and related issues. It consists of ten papers, including a hitherto unpublished paper, entitled 'The Structure of Production Technology: Productivity and Aggregation Effects'. The fifth part consists of five papers dealing with econometric investigations in Finance, chiefly in connection with the arbitrage pricing theory for risky assets. The sixth and final part consists of three of my early papers dealing with topics in general economic theory.

Many of the papers included in this volume are the product of collaboration with students and friends as well as former colleagues, to whom I acknowledge a debt of gratitude for their insights and contributions.

The nature and scope of the work brought together in this volume reflects my deeply held view that applied work has to be informed not only by underlying economic but also econometric theory and that the latter serves primarily the role of solving problems encountered in applications and ought not to be an end in itself.

I have excluded from this collection papers that are of a survey nature and current papers in the process of being published by scholarly journals.

Phoebus J. Dhrymes
Bronxville, NY

PART I

ECONOMETRIC THEORY: SIMULTANEOUS EQUATIONS

Reprinted from THE REVIEW OF ECONOMIC STUDIES, Vol. XXXVI (2), April, 1969, P. J. DHRYMES, pp. 213-226.

Alternative Asymptotic Tests of Significance and Related Aspects of 2SLS and 3SLS Estimated Parameters[1]

INTRODUCTION AND SUMMARY

The purpose of this paper is to put forth an alternative derivation of the two-stage (2SLS) and three-stage (3SLS) least squares estimators.

In this context 2SLS and 3SLS emerge, respectively, as ordinary least squares (OLS) and Aitken estimators in a suitably transformed system. Indeed, it will be shown that 2SLS estimation is (asymptotically) equivalent to the estimation of parameters in the framework of the classical general linear model.

A by-product of this approach is a straightforward proof of the efficiency of 3SLS relative to 2SLS and the derivation of necessary and sufficient conditions for (strict) efficiency to materialize.

Beyond that we shall motivate and derive alternative asymptotic tests of significance for 2SLS estimated parameters based on the *t*-distribution with well-defined degrees of freedom parameter.

The results herein will be developed under the restrictive assumption that all predetermined variables of the model are *exogenous*; although it is conjectured that such results are applicable to the case where the model contains lagged endogenous variables, this extension will be postponed to a later paper.

1. ASSUMPTIONS AND NOTATION

Consider the model

$$y_{.i} = Y_i\beta_{.i} + X_i\gamma_{.i} + u_{.i} \quad i = 1, 2, ..., m. \qquad ...(1)$$

where $y_{.i}$ is the $(T\times 1)$ vector of observations on the current endogenous variable y_i, Y_i and X_i are respectively the $(T\times m_i)$, $(T\times G_i)$ matrices of observations on the current endogenous and predetermined variables appearing (as explanatory variables) in the ith structural equation, and $u_{.i}$ is the $(T\times 1)$ vector of error terms. In (1), $\beta_{.i}$ and $\gamma_{.i}$ are the vectors of unknown parameters in the ith equation which are to be estimated. Thus, our convention is that the ith equation contains G_i+m_i structural parameters. Finally, let

$$Y = (y_{.1}, y_{.2}, ..., y_{.m}), \quad X = (x_{.1}, x_{.2}, ..., x_{.G}), \qquad ...(1a)$$

be respectively the $(T\times m)$ and $(T\times G)$ matrices of observations on all the current endogenous and predetermined variables contained in the system of equations (1).

Let us agree to the following numbering convention: The variable "explained" by the first structural equation will be taken to be y_1; the current endogenous variables appearing in the first structural equation are designated as $y_1, y_2, y_3, ..., y_{m_1+1}$; the

[1] The research on which this paper is based was supported in part by NSF grant GS 571 at the University of Pennsylvania.

I wish to thank H. Theil and A. Zellner for their helpful comments on an earlier version of this paper.

predetermined variables appearing therein will be designated as $x_1, x_2, \ldots, x_{G_1}$. As a matter of notation, we put

$$Y_1 = (y_{.2}, y_{.3}, \ldots, y_{.m_1+1}), \quad X_1 = (x_{.1}, x_{.2}, \ldots, x_{.G_1}), \qquad \ldots(2)$$

where the notation $x_{.r}$ will always denote a *column* vector. Define, further,

$$B^* = (\beta^*_{.1}, \beta^*_{.2}, \ldots, \beta^*_{.m}), \quad C^* = (\gamma^*_{.1}, \gamma^*_{.2}, \ldots, \gamma^*_{.m}), \qquad \ldots(2a)$$

In (2*a*) B^* is $(m \times m)$ and C^* is $(G \times m)$, both being the matrices containing the unknown parameters. Their component vectors $\beta^*_{.i}$, $\gamma^*_{.i}$ differ from those in (1) only to the extent that zeros have been inserted in the appropriate positions—signifying the *a priori* restrictions—so that we can write

$$Y = YB^* + XC^* + U, \qquad \ldots(3)$$

where, of course,

$$U = (u_{.1}, u_{.2}, \ldots, u_{.m}). \qquad \ldots(3a)$$

We shall make the following assumptions:

(A. 1). The *rows* of U, $u_{t.}$,[1] $t = 1, 2, \ldots, T$ obey

$$u'_{t.} \sim N(0, \Sigma), \quad \operatorname{cov}(u'_{t.}, u'_{t'.}) = \delta_{tt'}\Sigma, \quad \text{all } t, t', \qquad \ldots(4)$$

$\delta_{tt'}$ being the Kronecker delta.

(A. 2). The structural error terms are independent of the predetermined variables. Thus, in particular,

$$E(u_{t.}X) = 0 \quad \text{all } t. \qquad \ldots(4a)$$

(A. 3). The matrix $I - B^*$ is nonsingular and thus, the reduced form

$$Y = XC^*(I-B^*)^{-1} + U(I-B^*)^{-1} \qquad \ldots(4b)$$

is uniquely defined.

(A. 4). The probability limit

$$\operatorname*{plim}_{T\to\infty} \frac{Z'Z}{T} = M^* \qquad \ldots(4c)$$

exists as a nonsingular matrix of nonstochastic (and finite) elements, where

$$Z = (Y, X). \qquad \ldots(4d)$$

2. AN ALTERNATIVE DERIVATION OF 2SLS AND 3SLS ESTIMATORS, AND THEIR RELATIVE EFFICIENCY

It is customary in discussing 2SLS estimation to proceed as follows, concentrating for the sake of definiteness on the first *structural* equation.

Transforming the equation by the matrix of predetermined variables, one obtains

$$X'y_{.1} = X'Z_1\delta_{.1} + X'u_{.1}, \qquad \ldots(5)$$

where

$$Z_1 = (Y_1, X_1), \quad \delta_{.1} = \begin{pmatrix} \beta_{.1} \\ \gamma_{.1} \end{pmatrix}. \qquad \ldots(5a)$$

[1] This somewhat cumbersome notation is necessitated by the fact that we are interested in both the columns *and* rows of U. The former give the T observations on the error term of a *given* equation, while the latter give the *error terms* appearing in all the *equations of the system* at a given " time ". Thus, if we are interested in the joint distribution of the error terms of the system, we must consider the distribution of $u_{t.}$ which is a row vector containing all such errors at time t. If we fix attention on the ith equation, then we need consider only the *marginal distribution* of the error terms it contains. Such errors constitute the column vector $u_{.i}$.

While this convention might at first appear cumbersome, in fact it is indispensable when one wishes to consider both aspects.

It is then argued that 2SLS is Aitken estimation taking into account the fact that asymptotically

$$\lim_{T\to\infty} \operatorname{cov}\left(\frac{X'u_{.1}}{\sqrt{T}}\right) = \sigma_{11} \operatorname*{plim}_{T\to\infty}\left(\frac{X'X}{T}\right). \qquad \text{...(5}b\text{)}$$

Finally, 3SLS is also presented as an Aitken estimator in a somewhat different context. This approach, however, does not make quite clear the distinction between 2SLS and 3SLS estimation and, moreover, it does not lead to a particularly fruitful view of the problem.

Consider instead the following approach. By assumption (A. 4), the probability limit

$$M^*_{xx} = \operatorname*{plim}_{T\to\infty} \frac{X'X}{T} \qquad \text{...(6)}$$

exists as a positive definite matrix (with finite nonstochastic elements). Since for finite samples, $X'X$ is a positive definite symmetric matrix—at least it is so with probability one—then there exists a nonsingular matrix R, such that

$$RR' = X'X. \qquad \text{...(6}a\text{)}$$

From (6*a*) we see that

$$(\sqrt{T}R'^{-1})(\sqrt{T}R^{-1}) = \left(\frac{X'X}{T}\right)^{-1}. \qquad \text{...(6}b\text{)}$$

In virtue of (6) we conclude that

$$\operatorname*{plim}_{T\to\infty} \sqrt{T}R^{-1} = \bar{R}^{-1} \qquad \text{...(7)}$$

exists as a $(G\times G)$ nonsingular matrix with finite nonstochastic elements, and indeed

$$\bar{R}'^{-1}\bar{R}^{-1} = M^{*-1}_{xx}. \qquad \text{...(7}a\text{)}$$

Instead of (5), consider then, the alternative transformation

$$R^{-1}X'y_{.1} = R^{-1}X'Z_1\delta_{.1} + R^{-1}X'u_{.1}, \qquad \text{...(8)}$$

and let

$$w_{.1} = R^{-1}X'y_{.1}, \quad Q_1 = R^{-1}X'Z_1, \quad r_{.1} = R^{-1}X'u_{.1}. \qquad \text{...(8}a\text{)}$$

If we employ the same transformation for all the structural equations of (1), we have, using an obvious extension of the notation in (8) and (8*a*),

$$w_{.i} = Q_i\delta_{.i} + r_{.i} \quad i = 1, 2, \dots, m. \qquad \text{...(9)}$$

Finally, putting

$$w = \begin{pmatrix} w_{.1} \\ w_{.2} \\ \vdots \\ w_{.m} \end{pmatrix}, \quad Q = \operatorname{diag}(Q_1, Q_2, \dots, Q_m), \quad \delta = \begin{pmatrix} \delta_{.1} \\ \delta_{.2} \\ \vdots \\ \delta_{.m} \end{pmatrix}, \quad r = \begin{pmatrix} r_{.1} \\ r_{.2} \\ \vdots \\ r_{.m} \end{pmatrix}, \qquad \text{...(9}a\text{)}$$

we can write the *sample* on the *entire model* as

$$w = Q\delta + r. \qquad \text{...(10)}$$

Remark 1. The transformation in (8) converts the data into a finite dimensional form for all possible samples. Thus, notice that $w_{.i}$ is $G\times 1$, Q_i is $G\times(G_i+m_i)$, and $r_{.i}$ is $G\times 1$, *irrespective of how large T is.*

Implicit in the above is the convention that the *i*th structural equation contains G_i exogenous and m_i jointly dependent " explanatory " variables.

Let us now determine the distribution of the transformed error vector, as it appears in (10). We have

Lemma 1. *The distribution of r is given by*

$$r \sim N(0, \Sigma \otimes I_G). \qquad ...(11)$$

Proof. By construction, r can be expressed as

$$r = Fu, \qquad ...(12)$$

where

$$F = (I_m \otimes R^{-1}X'), \quad u = \begin{pmatrix} u_{.1} \\ u_{.2} \\ \vdots \\ u_{.m} \end{pmatrix}. \qquad ...(12a)$$

In virtue of assumption (A. 1)

$$u \sim N(0, \Sigma \otimes I_T). \qquad ...(13)$$

The conditional distribution of r given F is obviously normal in virtue of (13). The moments of that distribution are given by

$$E(r) = FE(u) = 0,$$
$$\text{cov}(r) = (I_m \otimes R^{-1}X')(\Sigma \otimes I_T)(I_m \otimes XR'^{-1}) = \Sigma \otimes I_G. \qquad ...(13a)$$

Since the conditional distribution of r does *not* depend on X, it follows that the unconditional distribution of r is given by (11). Q.E.D.

Moreover, we have

Lemma 2. *Asymptotically the error vectors of the system* (8) *are uncorrelated with the " explanatory " variables.*

Proof. We need to show that [1]

$$\lim_{T \to \infty} E\left(\frac{Q'r}{\sqrt{T}}\right) = 0. \qquad ...(14)$$

Now, consider the ith subvector of $Q'r$, which is given by

$$Q_i'r_{.i} = \frac{Z_i'X}{T}\left(\frac{X'X}{T}\right)^{-1} X'u_{.i}. \qquad ...(14a)$$

But it is apparent that in virtue of assumptions (A. 1), (A. 2), and Cramer's theorem [5, p. 254], we have

$$\lim_{T \to \infty} E\frac{[Q'r_{.i}]}{\sqrt{T}} = \underset{T \to \infty}{\text{plim}}\left[\frac{Z'X}{T}\left(\frac{X'X}{T}\right)^{-1}\right] \lim_{T \to \infty} E\left(\frac{X'u_{.i}}{\sqrt{T}}\right) = 0. \qquad ...(14b)$$

From (14b) the validity of (14) follows directly. Q.E.D.

Remark 2. It is an obvious consequence of Lemma 1 that

$$\text{cov}(r_{.i}) = \sigma_{ii} I_G. \qquad ...(15)$$

Remark 3. In view of (15) and Lemma 2, it follows that every equation of the transformed structural system as exhibited in (9) obeys asymptotically the classical assumptions of the general linear model. One would conjecture, then, that the techniques applicable therein are applicable in the case of simultaneous equations (structural) systems as well.

In pursuit of the conjecture in Remark 3, we now prove

Theorem 1. *Let assumptions* (*A.* 1) *through* (*A.* 4) *be valid and consider the model in* (1). *If the model is transformed as in* (9) *or* (10), *then the* 2SLS estimator of the parameters

[1] This convenient, but somewhat imprecise notation indicates that the joint asymptotic distribution of $\frac{Q}{\sqrt{T}}$ and r is such that the two quantities are uncorrelated.

of, say, the first structural equation, is given by the ordinary least squares (OLS) estimator of the parameters in (9) for $i = 1$. *Moreover, the* 2SLS *estimator for the parameters of the* entire *system is given by the OLS estimator of the parameters of the system as exhibited in* (10).

Proof. The OLS estimator of $\delta_{.1}$ may be obtained from (9) as

$$\tilde{\delta}_{.1} = (Q_1'Q_1)^{-1}Q_1'w_{.1}, \qquad \text{...(16)}$$

where

$$Q_1'Q_1 = Z_1'XR'^{-1}R^{-1}X'Z_1. \qquad \text{...(16a)}$$

Further

$$Q_1'w_{.1} = Z_1'XR'^{-1}R^{-1}X'y_{.1} = Z_1'X(X'X)^{-1}X'y_{.1}. \qquad \text{...(16b)}$$

But $(Z_1'X(X'X)^{-1}X'Z_1)^{-1}Z_1'X(X'X)^{-1}X'y_{.1}$. is exactly the 2SLS estimator of $\delta_{.1}$.

Finally, we observe

$$\tilde{\delta} = (Q'Q)^{-1}Q'w = \begin{bmatrix} (Q_1'Q_1)^{-1}Q_1'w_{.1} \\ (Q_2'Q_2)^{-1}Q_2'w_{.2} \\ \vdots \\ (Q_m'Q_m)^{-1}Q_m'w_{.m} \end{bmatrix}, \qquad \text{...(17)}$$

which is thus recognized as the 2SLS estimator for the parameters of the entire system. Q.E.D.

Remark 4. It is implicit in the argument above that the structural system *does not contain identities*; if it does, then the discussion applies to the system resulting after the identities have been removed by substitution.

Definition 1. Consider the general linear model

$$y = X\beta + u, \qquad \text{...(18)}$$

and suppose that

$$E(u) = 0, \text{cov}(u) = \Sigma, \qquad \text{...(18a)}$$

Σ being a (general) positive definite matrix. Then the *Aitken* estimator of β is given by

$$\tilde{\beta} = (X'\Sigma^{-1}X)^{-1}X'\Sigma^{-1}y. \qquad \text{...(18b)}$$

The *feasible Aitken estimator* of β is given by

$$\hat{\beta} = (X'\hat{\Sigma}^{-1}x)^{-1}X'\hat{\Sigma}^{-1}y. \qquad \text{...(18c)}$$

Remark 5. The definition is only necessary since in general Σ is not known; in the equation (18*c*), $\hat{\Sigma}$ is a consistent estimator of Σ.

We may now prove

Theorem 2. *The* 3*SLS estimator of the parameters of the system in* (1) *is* the (feasible) Aitken estimator *of parameters of the system as exhibited in* (10).

Proof. Let

$$\Phi = \Sigma \otimes I_G, \quad \hat{\Phi} = \hat{\Sigma} \otimes I_G, \qquad \text{...(19)}$$

where $\hat{\Sigma}$ is a consistent estimator of Σ. Then the (feasible) Aitken estimator of δ in (8) is

$$\hat{\delta} = (Q'\hat{\Phi}^{-1}Q)^{-1}Q'\hat{\Phi}^{-1}w. \qquad \text{...(19a)}$$

It is easily verified by comparison of (19*a*) with the 3SLS estimator given in [9] that the two are identical. Q.E.D.

In this framework the following are almost immediately apparent.

Corollary 1. *If it is known* a priori *that* Σ *of* (4) *is diagonal, i.e. if error terms in distinct structural equations are independent, then* 2*SLS and* 3*SLS are identical.*

Proof. From (19*a*) we observe that under the hypothesis of the Corollary, i.e. if $\sigma_{ij} = 0, i \neq j$,

$$(Q\hat{\Phi}^{-1}Q)^{-1} = \text{diag}\,[\hat{\sigma}_{11}(Q_1'Q_1)^{-1}, \ldots, \hat{\sigma}_{mm}(Q_m'Q_m)^{-1}], \qquad \ldots(20)$$

$$Q'\hat{\Phi}^{-1} = \text{diag}\left[\frac{Q_1'}{\hat{\sigma}_{11}}, \ldots, \frac{Q_m'}{\hat{\sigma}_{11}}\right]. \qquad \ldots(20a)$$

Thus

$$\hat{\delta} = (Q'Q)^{-1}Q'w. \qquad \ldots(20b)$$

A comparison with (17) completes the proof of the Corollary.

Corollary 2. *If every equation in the system satisfies the condition for* just identifiability, *i.e., if*

$$G_i + m_i = G \quad i = 1, 2, \ldots, m, \qquad \ldots(21)$$

then with probability one 2SLS and 3SLS are identical.

Proof. By definition

$$Q_i = R^{-1}X'Z_i. \qquad \ldots(21a)$$

In virtue of (21) Q_i is a $G \times G$ matrix and thus by assumption (A. 4) nonsingular with probability one. Thus,

$$\hat{\delta} = (Q'\hat{\Phi}^{-1}Q)^{-1}Q'\hat{\Phi}^{-1}w = Q^{-1}\hat{\Phi}Q'^{-1}Q'\hat{\Phi}^{-1}w = Q^{-1}w. \qquad \ldots(21b)$$

From (16*a*) we see that the 2 SLS estimator obeys:

$$\tilde{\delta} = (Q'Q)^{-1}Q'w = Q^{-1}Q'^{-1}Qw = Q^{-1}w. \qquad \ldots(21c)$$

Q.E.D.

The conclusions of the two corollaries lead naturally to the question: Under what conditions is the 3SLS estimator more efficient than the 2SLS one? This is answered by

Theorem 3. *Let the conditions of Theorem* 1 *hold and consider the 2SLS and 3SLS estimators as developed in Theorems* 1 *and* 2. *Let C_2, C_3 be respectively the covariance matrices of the asymptotic distribution of the 2SLS estimator as exhibited in* (17) *and the 3SLS estimator as exhibited in* (19*a*).[1] *Then the matrix*

$$C = C_2 - C_3 \qquad \ldots(22)$$

is positive semidefinite.

Proof. We first observe that (as is well known), the asymptotic distribution of $\sqrt{T}(\tilde{\delta}-\delta) \sim N(0, C_2)$, $\sqrt{T}(\hat{\delta}-\delta) \sim N(0, C_3)$, where

$$C_2 = \operatorname*{plim}_{T\to\infty}\left[\left(\frac{Q'Q}{T}\right)^{-1}\frac{Q'\Phi Q}{T}\left(\frac{Q'Q}{T}\right)^{-1}\right],$$

$$C_3 = \operatorname*{plim}_{T\to\infty}\left(\frac{Q'\Phi^{-1}Q}{T}\right)^{-1}.$$

Now define a matrix A by

$$(Q'Q)^{-1}Q' = (Q'\Phi^{-1}Q)^{-1}Q'\Phi^{-1} + A, \qquad \ldots(24)$$

and note that

$$AQ = 0. \qquad \ldots(24a)$$

Further,

$$\sqrt{T}A = \left[\frac{Q'Q}{T}\right]^{-1}\frac{Q'}{\sqrt{T}} - \left[\frac{Q'\Phi^{-1}Q}{T}\right]^{-1}\frac{Q'}{\sqrt{T}}\Phi^{-1}. \qquad \ldots(24b)$$

[1] These matrices are popularly referred to, somewhat inaccurately, as the asymptotic covariance matrices, when they are in fact the covariance matrices of the respective asymptotic distributions.

Since the probability limits of the matrices in the right-hand side of (24*b*) are known to exist,[1] especially in view of assumption (*A*. 4), it follows that

$$\operatorname*{plim}_{T\to\infty} \sqrt{T}\,A = \bar{A} \qquad \ldots(24c)$$

exists as a well defined matrix of (finite) constants.

Now, in view of (24), we have

$$\left(\frac{Q'Q}{T}\right)^{-1}\frac{Q'\Phi Q}{T}\left(\frac{Q'Q}{T}\right)^{-1}$$

$$= \left[\left[\frac{Q'\Phi^{-1}Q}{T}\right]^{-1}\frac{Q'}{\sqrt{T}}\Phi^{-1}+\sqrt{T}\,A\right]\Phi\left[\Phi^{-1}\frac{Q}{\sqrt{T}}\left[\frac{Q'\Phi^{-1}Q}{T}\right]^{-1}+\sqrt{T}\,A'\right]. \qquad \ldots(25)$$

Taking the probability limits and noting (23*b*) and (24*a*), we conclude

$$C_2 = C_3+\bar{A}\Phi\bar{A}'. \qquad \ldots(25a)$$

Since Φ is by assumption nonsingular, we conclude that

$$C = \bar{A}\Phi\bar{A}' \qquad \ldots(26)$$

is positive semidefinite.

In virtue of (25*a*), we then have

$$C_2-C_3 = C. \qquad \ldots(26a)$$

Remark 6. The matrix A, and hence $\bar{A}$, is of dimension $\sum_{i=1}^{m}(G_i+m_i)\times mG$, which is certainly finite.

Remark 7. Since Φ is positive definite, we note that

$$\operatorname{rank}(C) = \operatorname{rank}(\bar{A}). \qquad \ldots(27)$$

Corollary 3. *The* 3 *SLS is "strictly efficient" relative to the 2SLS estimator in the sense that the generalized variance of the former is strictly less than that of the latter if and only if*

$$\operatorname{rank}(\bar{A})>0. \qquad \ldots(28)$$

Proof. Consider the characteristic roots and vectors of C in the metric of C_3 (which is assumed to be positive definite). Thus, let the non-negative roots, λ_i of

$$|\lambda C_3-C| = 0 \qquad \ldots(28a)$$

be arranged in decreasing order of magnitude as

$$\Lambda = \operatorname{diag}(\lambda_1, \lambda_2, \ldots, \lambda_n), \quad n = \sum_{i=1}^{m}(m_i+G_i), \qquad \ldots(28b)$$

Let P be the (orthogonal) matrix of associated characteristic vectors. Thus, we may write

$$CP = C_3P\Lambda, \qquad \ldots(29)$$

and using (26*a*) we see that

$$C_2P = C_3P(I+\Lambda). \qquad \ldots(29a)$$

Since $|P| = \pm 1$, taking determinants in (29*a*), we have

$$|C_2| = |C_3|\prod_{i=1}^{n}(1+\lambda_i). \qquad \ldots(30)$$

Thus

$$|C_2|>|C_3| \qquad \ldots(30a)$$

unless *all* $\lambda_i = 0$. Q.E.D.

[1] Notice that the *i*th diagonal block of $\frac{Q'}{\sqrt{T}}$ is given by $\frac{Q_i'}{\sqrt{T}} = \frac{Z_i'X}{T}(\sqrt{T}R'^{-1})$ and in virtue of (A. 4) and (7), the probability limit of the quantity can easily be shown to exist.

Corollary 4. *The 3SLS is " strictly efficient " relative to the 2SLS estimator in the sense that for at least one element, say the* sth,

$$\text{Asy. var}(\hat{\delta}_s) < \text{Asy. var}(\tilde{\delta}_s) \qquad ...(31)$$

if and only if

$$\text{rank}(\bar{A}) > 0 \qquad ...(31a)$$

where, e.g., $\hat{\delta}_s$ *is the* sth *element of* $\hat{\delta}$.

Proof. Since

$$\text{rank}(C) = \text{rank}(\bar{A}). \qquad ...(32)$$

we may argue in terms of C. But the latter is a positive semi-definite matrix and thus its roots are non-negative. If c_{ss} is the sth diagonal element of C, then we have

$$\text{Asy. var}(\tilde{\delta}_s) = \text{Asy. var}(\hat{\delta}_s) + c_{ss}. \qquad ...(32a)$$

Thus, (31) *must* be valid for *at least one* index s, unless

$$c_{ss} = 0, \quad s = 1, 2, ..., n. \qquad ...(32b)$$

Since

$$\text{tr}\, C = \sum_{i=1}^{n} \mu_i, \qquad ...(32c)$$

the μ_i being the (non-negative) characteristic roots of C, the conclusion of the corollary follows immediately.

Remark 8. Although it is not formally correct, one might conjecture that in any concrete estimation problem

$$\text{rank}(\bar{A}) = 0 \qquad ...(33)$$

only if $\bar{A}$ is the zero matrix. This, however, will not in general be true unless A is the *zero matrix*. Hence, we may expect that a gain in efficiency will always be obtained by the use of 3SLS unless this estimator coincides with that obtained by 2SLS techniques as, e.g., under the conditions given in Corollaries 1 and 2.

3. ASYMPTOTIC TESTS OF SIGNIFICANCE FOR 2SLS ESTIMATED PARAMETERS

In applied econometric research, it has been, by now, a long tradition that the " significance " of 2SLS estimated parameters of an equation in the system (1) is tested by the use of the t-statistic; in applying such tests one takes the appropriate diagonal element of the asymptotic covariance matrix as chi-square distributed and independent of the corresponding parameter. In this context the degrees of freedom parameter of the resulting " t-ratio " is quite ambiguous. If one is dealing with, say, a parameter in the first equation estimated on the basis of T observations, one is rather prone to base the test on the t-distribution with $T - G_1 - m_1$ degrees of freedom.

Unfortunately, *there is nothing in the preceding theory to justify this practice.*

On the basis of the asymptotic distribution of the 2SLS estimator one can only assert that in this context the relevant " t-ratio " is, under the null hypothesis,[1] asymptotically distributed as a *normal* variable with *mean zero and variance one.* Thus tests of significance, properly understood, must be based on the standard normal distribution if one is to rely only on the preceeding theory. This is an asymptotic result. The theory, however, *does not support the practice of relying on the t-distribution for small samples.*

On the other hand, in the context of limited information maximum likelihood estimation, certain tests of identifiability have been developed. In particular, the likelihood ratio test statistic for the identifiability of (the parameters of) a structural equation obtained by

[1] The null hypothesis is, of course, that the relevant parameter is zero.

Anderson and Rubin [1, 2] is shown by them to be *asymptotically chi-square distributed with degrees of freedom equal to the extent to which the given equation is overidentified under the null hypothesis.*

In this section we shall formulate rigorously a t-test of significance for 2SLS estimated parameters of an *identified* structural equation; it will be seen that in the framework developed in the previous section this will be a natural consequence of the interpretation of 2SLS as OLS estimators.

Interestingly, the degrees of freedom for our test will be exactly the same as in the case of the identifiability test statistic given in [1, 2].

Thus, consider again one of the structural equations in (1), say, the first. In terms of the notation of Theorem 1, the 2SLS estimator of its structural parameter $\delta_{.1}$, is given by

$$\tilde{\delta}_{.1} = (Q_1Q_1)^{-1}Q_1'w_{.1} = \delta_{.1} + (Q_1'Q_1)^{-1}Q_1'r_{.1}. \qquad \text{...(34)}$$

We may now prove

Lemma 3. *Let the conditions of Theorem* 1 *hold; let* $\tilde{\delta}_{.1}$ *be the 2SLS estimator as exhibited in* (34) *and let*

$$\tilde{r}_{.1} = w_{.1} - Q_1\tilde{\delta}_{.1}. \qquad \text{...(35)}$$

Then

$$\tilde{\sigma}_{11} = \frac{1}{G - G_1 - m_1}\tilde{r}'_{.1}\tilde{r}_{.1} \qquad \text{...(35}a\text{)}$$

is an asymptotically unbiased estimator of σ_{11} *and moreover, asymptotically*

$$\frac{\tilde{r}'_{.1}\tilde{r}_{.1}}{\sigma_{11}} \sim \chi^2_{G-G_1-m_1}. \qquad \text{...(35}b\text{)}$$

Proof. In view of (34) and the definition of $w_{.1}$, we have

$$\tilde{r}_{.1} = r_{.1} - Q_1(Q_1'Q_1)^{-1}Q_1'r_{.1} = (I - N_1)r_{.1} \qquad \text{...(36)}$$

where, obviously, I is the identity matrix of order G and

$$N_1 = Q_1(Q_1'Q_1)^{-1}Q_1' \qquad \text{...(36}a\text{)}$$

is a $G \times G$ idempotent matrix. Clearly $I - N_1$ is also a $G \times G$ idempotent matrix for every sample size. Moreover,

$$\text{rank}\,(I - N_1) = \text{tr}\,(I - N_1) = G - \text{tr}\,[Q_1(Q_1'Q_1)^{-1}Q_1']$$
$$= G - \text{tr}\,[(Q_1'Q_1)^{-1}Q_1'Q_1] = G - G_1 - m_1. \qquad \text{...(37)}$$

We further observe that

$$N_1 = Q_1(Q_1'Q_1)^{-1}Q_1' = \frac{Q_1}{\sqrt{T}}\left[\frac{Q_1'Q_1}{T}\right]^{-1}\frac{Q_1'}{\sqrt{T}} \qquad \text{...(38)}$$

which, in virtue of asumption (A. 4), shows that the matrix N_1 has a well defined probability limit as an idempotent matrix with nonstochastic (and finite) elements.

Thus,

$$\underset{T\to\infty}{\text{plim}}\,\frac{\tilde{r}'_{.1}\tilde{r}_{.1}}{\sigma_{11}} = \frac{1}{\sigma_{11}}r'_{.1}[\underset{T\to\infty}{\text{plim}}\,(I - N_1)]r_{.1}. \qquad \text{...(39)}$$

We recall from [6, p. 168] that if the probability limit of a sequence exists, then the sequence converges in distribution to the distribution of the probability limit.

Since, for every sample size

$$\frac{r_{.1}}{\sqrt{\sigma_{11}}} \sim N(0, I_G), \qquad \text{...(39}a\text{)}$$

and $\operatorname{plim}_{T\to\infty} (I-N_1)$ is a nonstochastic idempotent matrix of rank $G-G_1-m_1$, we conclude

$$\frac{\tilde{r}'_{.1}\tilde{r}_{.1}}{\sigma_{11}} \sim \chi^2_{G-G_1-m_1}. \quad ...(40)$$

Hence the asymptotic expectation of (35*a*) is σ_{11}. Q.E.D.

Corollary 5. *Asymptotically the estimators* $\tilde{\delta}_{.1}$ *and* $\bar{\sigma}_{11}$ *are mutually independent.*

Proof. We observe that the identity

$$r'_{.1}r_{.1} \equiv r'_{.1}N_1r_{.1} + r'_{.1}(I-N_1)r_{.1} \quad ...(41)$$

is valid for every sample size. Moreover,

$$\bar{\sigma}_{11} = \frac{1}{G-G_1-m_1}[r'_{.1}(I-N_1)r_{.1}]. \quad ...(41a)$$

Now, by definition, the 2SLS estimator obeys

$$(\tilde{\delta}_{.1}-\delta_{.1}) = (Q_1'Q_1)^{-1}Q_1'r_{.1}. \quad ...(42)$$

Thus

$$(\tilde{\delta}_{.1}-\delta_{.1})'(Q'Q_1)(\tilde{\delta}_{.1}-\delta_{.1}) = r'_{.1}N_1r_{.1}. \quad ...(42a)$$

By the arguments of the preceding Lemma, we have that asymptotically

$$\frac{r'_{.1}N_1r_{.1}}{\sigma_{11}} \sim \chi^2_{G_1+m_1}, \quad \frac{r'_{.1}(I-N_1)r_{.1}}{\sigma_{11}} \sim \chi^2_{G-G_1-m_1}. \quad ...(43)$$

Since, for every sample size

$$N_1(I-N_1) = 0, \quad \operatorname{rank} N_1 = G_1+m_1, \quad \operatorname{rank}(I-N_1) = G-G_1-m_1, \quad ...(43a)$$

the conclusion of the corollary follows immediately from Cochran's theorem [8, p. 420].

Remark 9. It should be noted that the statistic in (35*a*) is a *quadratic form in the 2SLS residuals* of the structural equation. This is so since the vector of 2SLS residuals for the first (structural) equation is given by

$$\tilde{u}_{.1} = y_{.1} - Z_1\tilde{\delta}_{.1}. \quad ...(44)$$

But

$$\tilde{u}'_{.1}XR'^{-1}R^{-1}X'\tilde{u}_{.1} = \tilde{r}'_{.1}\tilde{r}_{.1} \quad ...(44a)$$

and the assertion follows directly.

Theorem 4. *Let the conditions of Theorem* 1 *hold and let* $\tilde{\delta}_{.1}$ *be the 2SLS estimator of* $\delta_{.1}$ *as exhibited in* (16). *Let* $\tilde{\delta}^{(s)}_{.1}$ *be a subvector of* $\tilde{\delta}_{.1}$ *consisting of* $s(<m_1+G_1)$ *elements. Let* $C_{(s)}$ *be the submatrix of* $\left[\frac{Q_1'Q_1}{T}\right]^{-1}$ *corresponding to the elements of* $\tilde{\delta}^{(s)}_{.1}$. *Then, asymptotically,*

$$\frac{T(\tilde{\delta}^{(s)}_{.1}-\delta^{(s)}_{.1})'C^{-1}_{(s)}(\tilde{\delta}^{(s)}_{.1}-\delta^{(s)}_{.1})}{\tilde{r}'_{.1}\tilde{r}_{.1}}\cdot\frac{G-G_1-m_1}{s} \sim F_{s,\,G-G_1-m_1}, \quad ...(45)$$

where $\delta^{(s)}_{.1}$ *is the vector of parameters corresponding to* $\tilde{\delta}^{(s)}_{.1}$ *and* $F_{s,\,G-G_1-m_1}$ *is a central F variable with s and* $G-G_1-m_1$ *degrees of freedom.*

Proof. It is well known that, under the conditions of the theorem, asymptotically

$$T^{\frac{1}{2}}(\tilde{\delta}_{.1}-\delta_{.1}) \sim N\left[0,\ \sigma_{11}\operatorname*{plim}_{T\to\infty}\left[\frac{Q_1'Q_1}{T}\right]^{-1}\right]. \quad ...(45a)$$

Thus, asymptotically

$$T^{\frac{1}{2}}(\tilde{\delta}^{(s)}_{.1}-\delta^{(s)}_{.1}) \sim N[0,\ \sigma_{11}\operatorname*{plim}_{T\to\infty} C_{(s)}]. \quad ...(45b)$$

Moreover, in virtue of Corollary 5, $T^{\frac{1}{2}}(\tilde{\delta}_{.1}-\delta_{.1})$ and hence $T^{\frac{1}{2}}(\tilde{\delta}^{(s)}_{.1}-\delta^{(s)}_{.1})$ are asymptotically independent of $\tilde{r}'_{.1}\tilde{r}_{.1}$.

From (45*b*) it follows that asymptotically

$$\frac{1}{\sigma_{11}}\left\{(\tilde{\delta}^{(s)}_{.1}-\delta^{(s)}_{.1})'\left[\frac{C_{(s)}}{T}\right]^{-1}(\tilde{\delta}^{(s)}_{.1}-\delta^{(s)}_{.1})\right\}\sim\chi^2_s. \qquad ...(46)$$

In view of Corollary 5, the conclusion of the Theorem is now obvious.

Corollary 6. *A test of the hypothesis*

$$H_0:\ \delta^{(s)}_{.1}=0 \qquad ...(47)$$

as against the alternative

$$H_1:\ \delta^{(s)}_{.1}\neq 0, \qquad ...(47a)$$

where $\delta^{(s)}_{.1}$ *is as in Theorem* 4 *can be based on the central F-distribution with s and* $G-G_1-m_1$ *degrees of freedom.*

In particular, if $s = 1$ *and the vector* $\delta^{(s)}_{.1}$ *consists of a single element, say* δ_{k1}, *then a test of the hypothesis*

$$H_0:\ \delta_{k1}=0 \qquad ...(48)$$

as against the alternative

$$H_1:\ \delta_{k1}\neq 0 \qquad ...(48a)$$

can be based on the Student t-distribution with $G-G_1-m_1$ *degrees of freedom.*

Proof. Under the null hypothesis (47) we have that

$$\frac{\tilde{\delta}^{(s)\prime}_{.1}\left[\frac{C_{(s)}}{T}\right]^{-1}\tilde{\delta}^{(s)}_{.1}}{\tilde{r}'_{.1}\tilde{r}_{.1}}\cdot\frac{G-G_1-m_1}{s}\sim F_{s,\,G-G_1-m_1} \qquad ...(49)$$

is a statistic, i.e., it contains no unknown parameters and thus can serve as a test statistic for the null hypothesis in (47).

If $s = 1$ and we are dealing with the test of the null hypothesis in (48), let q_{kk} be the (k, k) element of $(Q_1'Q_1)^{-1}$. In view of Theorem 4, under (48) we have—asymptotically—

$$\frac{\tilde{\delta}^2_{k1}}{q_{kk}\tilde{r}'_{.1}\tilde{r}_{.1}}\,\frac{G-G_1-m_1}{1}\sim F_{1,\,G-G_1-m_1}. \qquad ...(50)$$

But then it is apparent that

$$\frac{\tilde{\delta}_{k1}}{\sqrt{\tilde{\sigma}_{11}q_{kk}}}\sim t_{G-G_1-m_1}.\quad \text{Q.E.D.} \qquad ...(50a)$$

Remark 10. If will be noticed that, as is the case with the Anderson-Rubin identifiability test, the distributions of the statistics in Corollary 5 are ***not defined when the equation under consideration is just identified.*** This is so since in that case

$$G-G_1-m_1 = 0. \qquad ...(51)$$

The degrees of freedom parameter in (50*a*) is *the extent to which the equation under consideration is overidentified,*[1] and if (51) holds, then the test will be based on zero degrees of freedom:

Even though the condition in (51) represents the most obvious way in which this aspect becomes noticeable, a more complete explanation of this phenomenon rests on the following little known property of just-identified equations, summarized in

[1] It is interesting that Bassman [3] appears to claim on the basis of some special models that the small sample distribution of 2SLS estimators possesses finite moments of order at most equal to the extent to which the given equation is *over-identified*, i.e., of order at most $G-G_1-m_1$ in this context.

Proposition 1. Let the conditions of Theorem 1 hold and suppose the first structural equation satisfies the condition for just identifiability. Then, with probability one, *the vector of 2SLS residuals of that equation is orthogonal to the matrix of predetermined variables of the system.*

Proof. The 2SLS estimator of the parameters as exhibited in (16) is

$$\tilde{\delta}_{\cdot 1} = (Q_1'Q_1)^{-1}Q_1'w_{\cdot 1}. \qquad \text{...(52)}$$

If the equation satisfies the condition for just identifiability, then in view of assumption (A. 4) Q_1 is nonsingular with probability one. Hence we may rewrite (52) as

$$\tilde{\delta}_{\cdot 1} = Q_1^{-1}w_{\cdot 1} = (X'Z_1)^{-1}X'y_{\cdot 1}. \qquad \text{...(52}a\text{)}$$

Thus, the vector of 2SLS residuals is given by

$$\tilde{u}_{\cdot 1} = y_{\cdot 1} - Z_1\tilde{\delta}_{\cdot 1} = y_{\cdot 1} - Z_1(X'Z_1)^{-1}X'y_{\cdot 1} \qquad \text{...(52}b\text{)}$$

and

$$X'\tilde{u}_{\cdot 1} = X'y_{\cdot 1} - (X'Z_1)(X'Z_1)^{-1}X'y_{\cdot 1} = 0. \qquad \text{Q.E.D.} \qquad \text{...(52}c\text{)}$$

Corollary 7. *If the conditions of Theorem* 1 *hold and if the first structural equation of the system in* (1) *satisfies the condition for just identifiability, then with probability one*

$$\tilde{r}_{\cdot 1} = 0 \qquad \text{...(53)}$$

and thus the statistic $\tilde{\sigma}_{11}$ *of* (41*a*) *is not defined.*

Proof. In view of (52*a*), we have

$$\tilde{r}_{\cdot 1} = w_{\cdot 1} - Q_1\tilde{\delta}_{\cdot 1} = w_{\cdot 1} - Q_1Q_1^{-1}w_{\cdot 1} = 0. \qquad \text{...(53}a\text{)}$$

The conditions of the corollary imply

$$G - G_1 - m_1 = 0, \qquad \text{...(53}b\text{)}$$

and the statistic $\tilde{\sigma}_{11}$ is of the form $\frac{0}{0}$ and, thus, not defined. Q.E.D.

Remark 11. It may be thought that the discussion of this section establishes, even in the case of a structural equation, a goodness of fit criterion with well-defined distributional properties—at least asymptotically. Thus, e.g., if all variables are measured as deviations from respective sample means then

$$\frac{\tilde{\delta}'_{\cdot 1}(Q_1'Q_1)\tilde{\delta}_{\cdot 1}}{\tilde{r}'_{\cdot 1}\tilde{r}_{\cdot 1}} \cdot \frac{G - G_1 - m_1}{G_1 + m_1} \sim F_{G_1+m_1,\, G-G_1-m_1} \qquad \text{...(54)}$$

is a statistic analogous to $\frac{R^2}{1-R^2}$ used to test the goodness of fit of a general linear model, where, of course, R^2 is the coefficient of determination (unadjusted for degrees of freedom) This, however, *is not so unless we are interested in the fit of the transformed equation*

$$w_{\cdot 1} = Q_1\delta_{\cdot 1} + r_{\cdot 1}. \qquad \text{...(54}a\text{)}$$

Nonetheless, (54) continued to serve the purpose—as its analogue would in the context of the general linear model—of providing a statistic for the test of the hypothesis

$$\delta_{\cdot 1} = 0. \qquad \text{...(54}b\text{)}$$

Remark 12. The asymptotic tests obtained in this section are best viewed as taking advantage of the overidentifying restrictions in order to define alternative tests of significance. Such alternative tests *are not applicable to a just identified equation*, much as the Anderson-Rubin identifiability test is not applicable in this case as well.

The alternative proposed here is asymptotic in character. Asymptotically it is an exact test based on the t-distribution.

The standard theory would motivate a normal test which is also asymptotically exact. One would conjecture that, in finite samples, the convergence to exactitude of the test proposed here would be faster than that of the standard test based on normal (asymptotic) theory. This is so since here we are employing a *quadratic form* in the 2SLS residuals in estimating the parameter σ_{11}, while in the standard case we should be using the sum of squares of the 2SLS residuals which is, of course, a rather special quadratic form.

Thus, notice that the estimator $\bar{\sigma}_{11}$ proposed here is

$$\bar{\sigma}_{11} = \frac{1}{G-G_1-m_1}\tilde{u}'_{.1}[X(X'X)^{-1}X']\tilde{u}_{.1}, \qquad \text{...(55)}$$

while the standard estimator of σ_{11} is

$$\tilde{\sigma}_{11} = \frac{1}{T}\tilde{u}'_{.1}\tilde{u}_{.1}, \qquad \text{...(55}a\text{)}$$

$\tilde{u}_{.1}$ being the vector of 2SLS residuals of the first structural equation.

In addition, observe that expressing the 2SLS residuals in terms of the basic disturbance vector, we have

$$\tilde{u}_{.1} = [I - Z_1(Q_1'Q_1)^{-1}Z_1'X(X'X)^{-1}X']u_{.1}. \qquad \text{...(56)}$$

Thus

$$\tilde{u}'_{.1}\tilde{u}_{.1} = u'_{.1}[I - X(X'X)^{-1}X'Z_1(Q_1'Q_1)^{-1}Z_1' - Z_1(Q_1'Q_1)^{-1}Z_1'X(X'X)^{-1}X' + Z_1(Q_1'Q_1)^{-1}Z_1']u_{.1}, \qquad \text{...(56}a\text{)}$$

and the matrix of this quadratic form is certainly not idempotent. On the other hand, observe that the quadratic form involved in (55) is

$$\tilde{u}'_{.1}X(X'X)^{-1}X'\tilde{u}_{.1} = u'_{.1}[X(X'X)^{-1}X' - XR'^{-1}Q_1(Q_1'Q_1)^{-1}Q_1'R^{-1}X']u_{.1}. \qquad \text{...(56}b\text{)}$$

Its matrix is easily shown to be idempotent. Moreover, one would expect (56*b*) to provide more rapid convergence than (56*a*).

An interesting topic for further research might be a Monte Carlo comparison of the performance of the tests proposed here and those properly based on (asymptotic) normal theory.

4. CONCLUSION

We have developed, in this paper, an alternative formulation of the problem of 2SLS and 3SLS estimation of structural parameters in a simultaneous equations system.

In this framework it emerges quite clearly that 2SLS estimation is OLS estimation of parameters in a transformed system which is asymptotically equivalent to a classical general linear model. The covariance matrix of the error terms in the transformed system will, in general, be a nondiagonal positive definite matrix. Then, 3SLS estimation emerges as (feasible) Aitken estimation of parameters in the context of the transformed system. A byproduct of this approach is a direct proof of the efficiency of 3SLS relative to 2SLS estimation and the derivation of necessary and sufficient conditions for the former to be strictly efficient relative to the latter.

A further byproduct, exploiting the formal equivalence (asymptotically) between 2SLS estimators and OLS estimators in the context of the general linear model, is the formulation of asymptotic tests of significance on 2SLS estimated parameters, the tests being based on central F- and t-distributions. In the case of the latter, the degrees of freedom parameter equals the extent to which the equation under consideration is *over-identified.*

This test is akin to the identifiability test developed by Anderson and Rubin [1, 2] in that both tests share the same degrees of freedom parameter and in that both tests are not well defined when the equation under consideration is just identified.

University of Pennsylvania P. J. DHRYMES

First version received 3.10.67; *final version received* 8.8.68

REFERENCES

[1] Anderson, T. W., and Rubin, H. " Estimation of Parameters of a Single Equation in a Complete System of Stochastic Equations ", *Annals of Mathematical Statistics*, **20** (1949), 46.

[2] Anderson, R. W., and Rubin, H. " Asymptotic Properties of Estimates of the Parameters of a Single Equation in a Complete System of Stochastic Equations ", *Annals of Mathematical Statistics*, **21** (1950), 570.

[3] Bassman, R, L. " A Note on the Exact Finite Sample Frequency Functions of Generalized Classical Linear Estimators in Two Leading Overidentified Cases ", *Journal of the American Statistical Association*, **56** (1961), 619.

[4] Bassman, R. L. " On the Application of the Identifiability Test Statistic in Predictive Testing of Explanatory Economic Models ", *Indian Economic Journal* (Econometric Annual), **12**, No. 3, p. 387.

[5] Cramer, H. *Mathematical Methods of Statistics* (Princeton University Press, 1946).

[6] Loeve, M. *Probability Theory* (second edition) (D. Von Nostrand, Princeton, 1960).

[7] Madansky, A. " On the Efficiency of Three Stage Least Squares ", *Econometrica*, **32** (1964), 51.

[8] Scheffe, H. *The Analysis of Variance* (John Wiley & Sons, Inc., New York, 1959).

[9] Zellner, A., and Theil, H. " Three Stage Least Squares: Simultaneous Estimation of Simultaneous Equations ", *Econometrica*, **30** (1962), 54.

INTERNATIONAL ECONOMIC REVIEW
Vol. 10, No. 1, February, 1969

AN IDENTITY BETWEEN DOUBLE k-CLASS AND TWO STAGE LEAST SQUARES ESTIMATORS*

BY PHOEBUS J. DHRYMES[1]

1. INTRODUCTION

IN THIS NOTE we derive an identity between double k-class and two stage least squares (2SLS) estimators, of which the identities given in Maeshiro [1] and Oi [2] are special cases.[2]

2. THE PROBLEM

Consider the general (structural) simultaneous equations model

$$Y_{\cdot i} = Y_i\beta_{\cdot i} + X_i\beta_{\cdot i} + u_{\cdot i}\,, \qquad i = 1, 2, \cdots, m\,, \tag{1}$$

where Y_i is $(T \times m_i)$, X_i is $(T \times G_i)$ and denote respectively the matrices of observations on the jointly dependent and predetermined variables that appear as explanatory variables in the equation "determining" the i-th jointly dependent variable; $\beta_{\cdot i}$, $\gamma_{\cdot i}$ are, respectively, the $(m_i \times 1)$ and $(G_i \times 1)$ vectors of parameters to be estimated and $u_{\cdot i}$ is the $(T \times 1)$ vector of disturbances. The set in (1) can be written compactly as

$$Y = YB + XC + U\,. \tag{1a}$$

We associate with it the reduced form

$$Y = X\Pi + V \tag{2}$$

where

$$\Pi = CD\,, \qquad V = UD\,, \qquad D = (I - B)^{-1}\,. \tag{2a}$$

Let us, for definiteness, concentrate on the first (structural) equation and so number the variables that in the notation of (1)

$$Y_1 = (y_{\cdot 2}, y_{\cdot 3}, \cdots y_{\cdot m_1+1})\,, \qquad X_1 = (x_{\cdot 1}, x_{\cdot 2}, \cdots x_{\cdot G_1})\,. \tag{3}$$

Corresponding to $y_{\cdot 1}$, we have the reduced form expression

$$y_{\cdot 1} = X\pi_{\cdot 1} + v_{\cdot 1} \tag{3a}$$

and corresponding to Y_1 we have the the reduced form expression

$$Y_1 = X\Pi_1 + V_1\,. \tag{3b}$$

Evidently $\pi_{\cdot 1}$ is the first column of Π, Π_1 is the submatrix of the latter corresponding to its next m_1 columns and the same relation holds between

* Manuscript received May 8, 1968. This manuscript is published ahead of our usual schedule in the belief that our readers will benefit from its appearance in the same issue as the paper on which it comments (Editor).

[1] The research on which this paper is based was in part supported by NSF grant GS-571 at the University of Pennsylvania.

[2] This note owes its origin to the illuminating paper by Oi [2]. In fact, it was an attempt to simplify somewhat his results that give rise to this generalization.

$v_{\cdot 1}$, V_1 and V.

The matrix of all predetermined variables may be written as

$$X = (X_1, X_2) \tag{4}$$

where by convention X_2 is to be a $(T \times G_2)$ matrix such that

$$G_1 + G_2 = G\,, \tag{4a}$$

G being the number of all predetermined variables in the system. Denote by $\tilde{v}_{\cdot 1}$, $\tilde{V}_1$ the reduced form ordinary least squares (OLS) residuals of the relations in (3a) and (3b) and observe that

$$X'\tilde{v}_{\cdot 1} = 0\,, \qquad X'\tilde{V}_1 = 0\,. \tag{5}$$

Let

$$\tilde{y}_{\cdot 1} = X\tilde{\pi}_{\cdot 1}\,, \quad \tilde{Y}_1 = X\tilde{\Pi}_1\,, \quad \tilde{\pi}_{\cdot 1} = (X'X)^{-1}X'y_{\cdot 1}\,, \quad \tilde{\Pi}_1 = (X'X)^{-1}X'Y_1\,. \tag{5a}$$

To proceed with our discussion we require the following useful result which we cite without proof.

LEMMA. *Consider the general linear model*

$$y = X\beta + u \tag{6}$$

and the ordinary least squares estimator

$$\hat{\beta} = (X'X)^{-1}X'y\,. \tag{6a}$$

Partition X by

$$X = (X_1, X_2) \tag{7}$$

and β by

$$\beta = \begin{bmatrix} \beta_1 \\ \beta_2 \end{bmatrix} \tag{7a}$$

so that X_i is $(T \times G_i)$, $i = 1, 2$ and β_i is $(G_i \times 1)$, $i = 1, 2$. Then, independently of the properties of the error terms in (6), *the regression coefficients in the the regression of y on X_1, denoted by $\tilde{\beta}_1$ and defined by*

$$\tilde{\beta}_1 = (X_1'X_1)^{-1}X_1'y \tag{8}$$

obey the identity

$$\tilde{\beta}_1 = \hat{\beta}_1 + S_{12}\hat{\beta}_2 \tag{9}$$

where

$$S_{12} = (X_1'X_1)^{-1}X_1'X_2 \tag{9a}$$

and $\hat{\beta}_i$, $i = 1, 2$ are subvectors of $\hat{\beta}$ in (6a) *corresponding to the partition in* (7a).

What is the import of this Lemma relative to the present discussion? It is simply this: One can show that the 2SLS estimator of the parameters $\beta_{\cdot 1}$, $\gamma_{\cdot 1}$ is the OLS estimator of the (appropriate) parameters in

$$y_{\cdot 1} + \tilde{w}_{\cdot 1} = (\tilde{Y}_1 + \tilde{W}_1)\beta_{\cdot 1} + X_1\gamma_{\cdot 1} + \tilde{W}_1 d_{\cdot 1} + \text{error} \tag{10}$$

while the double k-class estimator of $\beta_{\cdot 1}, \gamma_{\cdot 1}$ is the OLS estimator of parameters in

$$\text{(10a)} \qquad y_{\cdot 1} + \tilde{w}_{\cdot 1} = (\tilde{Y}_1 + \tilde{W}_1)\beta_{\cdot 1} + X_1\gamma_{\cdot 1} + \text{error}$$

where

$$\text{(10b)} \qquad \tilde{W}_1 = h_1 \tilde{V}_1 , \qquad \tilde{w}_{\cdot 1} = h_2 \tilde{v}_{\cdot 1}$$

and the h_i are as yet unspecified constants.

Let us verify these assertions. The OLS estimator of parameters in (10a) is defined by

$$\text{(11)} \qquad \begin{bmatrix} \tilde{\beta}_{\cdot 1}(h_1, h_2) \\ \tilde{\gamma}_{\cdot 1}(h_1, h_2) \end{bmatrix} = \begin{bmatrix} \tilde{Y}_1' \tilde{Y}' + \tilde{W}_1' \tilde{W}_1 & Y_1' X_1 \\ X_1' Y_1 & X' X_1 \end{bmatrix}^{-1} \begin{bmatrix} (\tilde{Y}_1' + \tilde{W}_1')(y_{\cdot 1} + \tilde{w}_{\cdot 1}) \\ X_1' y_{\cdot 1} \end{bmatrix}$$

On the other hand

$$\text{(11a)} \qquad \tilde{Y}_1' \tilde{Y}_1 + \tilde{W}' \tilde{W} = Y_1 Y_1 - (1 - h_1^2) \tilde{V}_1' \tilde{V}_1$$

$$\text{(11b)} \qquad (\tilde{Y}_1' + \tilde{W}_1')(y_{\cdot 1} + \tilde{w}_{\cdot 1}) = (Y_1' - [1 - h_1(1 + h_2)] \tilde{V}_1')y_{\cdot 1} .$$

Effecting the identification

$$\text{(11c)} \qquad k_1 = 1 - h_1^2 , \qquad k_2 = 1 - h_1(1 + h_2) ,$$

we see that indeed (11) gives the double k-class estimator of the parameters of the first structural equation.

To prove the validity of the first assertion we note that the equations defining the OLS estimators of parameters in (10) are

$$\text{(12)} \qquad \begin{aligned} (\tilde{Y}_1' \tilde{Y}_1 + \tilde{W}_1' \tilde{W}_1)\tilde{\beta}_{\cdot 1} + Y_1' X_1 \tilde{\gamma}_{\cdot 1} + \tilde{W}_1' \tilde{W}_1 \tilde{d}_{\cdot 1} &= (\tilde{Y}_1' + \tilde{W}_1')(y_{\cdot 1} + \tilde{w}_{\cdot 1}) \\ X_1' Y_1 \tilde{\beta}_{\cdot 1} + X_1' X_1 \tilde{\gamma}_{\cdot 1} \qquad &= X_1' y_{\cdot 1} \\ \tilde{W}_1' \tilde{W}_1 \tilde{\beta}_{\cdot 1} \qquad + \tilde{W}_1' \tilde{W}_1 \tilde{d}_{\cdot 1} &= \tilde{W}_1'(y_{\cdot 1} + \tilde{w}_{\cdot 1}) . \end{aligned}$$

Subtracting the last from the first set of equations in (12), we obtain a recursive system, so that the first two sets determine $\tilde{\beta}_{\cdot 1}$ and $\tilde{\gamma}_{\cdot 1}$ while the last set determines $\tilde{d}_{\cdot 1}$ as

$$\text{(12a)} \qquad \tilde{d}_{\cdot 1} = (\tilde{W}_1' \tilde{W}_1)^{-1} \tilde{W}_1'(y_{\cdot 1} + \tilde{w}_{\cdot 1}) - \tilde{\beta}_{\cdot 1} .$$

But the first two sets in (12) (as modified) yield exactly the 2SLS estimators of $\beta_{\cdot 1}$ and $\gamma_{\cdot 1}$.

Now, from (10) and (10a) we observe that the latter commits the "misspecification" of omitting certain variables. In view of the Lemma we immediately conclude

$$\text{(13)} \qquad \begin{bmatrix} \tilde{\beta}_{\cdot 1}(h_1, h_2) \\ \tilde{\gamma}_{\cdot 1}(h_1, h_2) \end{bmatrix} = \begin{bmatrix} \tilde{\beta}_{\cdot 1} \\ \tilde{\gamma}_{\cdot 1} \end{bmatrix} + S_{12} \tilde{d}_{\cdot 1} ,$$

where S_{12} is the matrix of regression coefficients in the regression of $\tilde{W}_1$ on $\tilde{Y}_1 + \tilde{W}_1$ and X_1, *i.e.*,

$$\text{(13a)} \qquad S_{12} = h_1 \begin{bmatrix} Y_1' Y_1 - (1 - h_1^2) \tilde{V}_1' \tilde{V}_1 & Y_1' X_1 \\ X_1' Y_1 & X_1' X_1 \end{bmatrix}^{-1} \begin{bmatrix} (Y_1' - (1 - h_1) \tilde{V}_1') \tilde{V}_1 \\ 0 \end{bmatrix} .$$

Notice that

(13b) $$\tilde{d}_{\cdot 1} = \frac{1 + h_2}{h_1} (\tilde{V}_1' \tilde{V}_1)^{-1} \tilde{V}_1' \tilde{v}_{\cdot 1} - \tilde{\beta}_{\cdot 1} \, ,$$

where of course $\tilde{\beta}_{\cdot 1}$ (and $\tilde{\gamma}_{\cdot 1}$) is the 2SLS estimator of $\beta_{\cdot 1}$(and $\gamma_{\cdot 1}$).

Notice further that if

(14) $$h_2 = 0$$

then (7a) yields the h-class estimator; if

(14a) $$h_2 = h_1 - 1$$

then (7a) yields the general k-class estimator; if in addition to (14a) h_1 is pure imaginary then (7a) yields the Limited Information Maximum Likelihood estimator; if

(14b) $$h_2 = 0 \, , \qquad h_1 = 1$$

then (7a) yields the OLS estimator, and of course if

(14c) $$h_1 = 0$$

then (7a) yields the 2SLS estimator. Thus, the identity in (13) connects a wide variety of well known estimators to the 2SLS estimator for structural parameters.

We have therefore established

THEOREM. *Consider the structural system in* (1); *then the double k-class estimator of the parameters, say, of the first structural equation, denoted by* $\tilde{\beta}_{\cdot 1}(h_1, h_2)$, $\tilde{\gamma}_{\cdot 1}(h_1, h_2)$, *and the 2SLS estimator of such parameters, denoted by* $\tilde{\beta}_{\cdot 1}$, $\tilde{\gamma}_{\cdot 1}$, *are connected by the following identity*

(15) $$\begin{bmatrix} \tilde{\beta}_{\cdot 1}(h_1, h_2) \\ \tilde{\gamma}_{\cdot 1}(h_1, h_2) \end{bmatrix} = \begin{bmatrix} \tilde{\beta}_{\cdot 1} \\ \tilde{\gamma}_{\cdot 1} \end{bmatrix} + \begin{bmatrix} Y_1'Y_1 - (1 - h_1^2) \tilde{V}_1' \tilde{V}_1 & Y_1'X_1 \\ X_1'Y_1 & X_1'X_1 \end{bmatrix}^{-1} \begin{bmatrix} (Y_1' - (1 - h_1) \tilde{V}_1') \tilde{V}_1 \\ 0 \end{bmatrix} \cdot ((1 + h_2)(\tilde{V}_1' \tilde{V}_1)^{-1} \tilde{V}_1' \tilde{v}_{\cdot 1} - h_1 \tilde{\beta}_{\cdot 1}) \, .$$

University of Pennsylvania, U.S.A.

REFERENCES

[1] MAESHIRO, A., "A Simple Mathematical Identity Among k-Class Estimators," *Journal of the American Statistical Association*, Vol. LXI (June, 1966), 368-74.

[2] OI, WALTER, "On the Relationship Among Different Members of the k-Class," *International Economic Review*, this issue.

[3]

Reprinted from *The Australian Journal of Statistics*, Vol. 13, No. 3, pages 168–175. November, 1971

A SIMPLIFIED STRUCTURAL ESTIMATOR FOR LARGE-SCALE ECONOMETRIC MODELS[1, 2]

PHOEBUS J. DHRYMES
University of Pennsylvania

0. Introduction

It is well known that for many economy-wide models the number of predetermined variables far exceeds the number of observations. This renders infeasible estimation of the parameters of the unrestricted reduced form by the usual method of ordinary least squares (OLS). Since this aspect is essential to both limited information maximum likelihood (LIML) and two-stage least squares (2SLS), it follows that in such cases these well-known techniques are not directly applicable.

A number of alternatives designed to circumvent this problem have been proposed. One has been to use a subset of the principal components of the predetermined variables and obtain an estimate of the reduced form by regressing the current endogenous variables of the system on this subset of principal components. This proposal was, in effect, put forth by Kloek and Mennes (1960) and later modified and elaborated upon in Dhrymes (1970). Whereas it is pointed out in Dhrymes (1970) that this is, indeed, a consistent estimator, one ought to bear in mind the peculiar nature of the argument involved. Specifically, it is observed in Dhrymes (1970) that as *the sample size increases one ought to take more and more principal components into account until one ultimately uses all.* Thus, when the number of observations exceeds the number of predetermined variables the "first" stage will, indeed, estimate the unrestricted reduced form by OLS, and hence the estimator will be nothing but the 2SLS one.

Now one might interject that asymptotic properties are extremely important for two reasons. First, they are relatively easily obtained in comparison with the difficulties one has in establishing small sample distributions. Second, they are useful approximations to small sample properties, at least for samples of reasonable size. Indeed, a number of Monte Carlo studies, e.g. Cragg (1967), bear directly on this aspect. However, in the present case the second point applies only with severely diminished force. For, as the sample size increases, not only do we have the working of various laws of large numbers, *but also the nature of the estimator changes from one which neglects some of the information conveyed by the sample to one that ultimately uses all information—i.e. one that uses all of the principal components.*

While, to the best of my knowledge, this point has not, hithertofore, been made in the literature, it no doubt was part of the reason for the vague dissatisfaction with the use of principal components.

[1] The research on which this paper is based was, in part, supported by N.S.F. grant GS 2289 at the University of Pennsylvania.
[2] Manuscript received July 16, 1970; revised November 24, 1970.

In this connection Fisher (1965) and Mitchell and Fisher (1970) suggested the use of structurally ordered instrumental variables (SOIV) as a solution to this vexing problem. While their suggestion is not free of criticism regarding "arbitrariness," it is a highly ingenious proposal that utilizes the à priori information pertaining to the structure of the model in a fairly systematic way. Unfortunately, for practical application, it necessitates a system that may be decomposed into a number of reasonably small subsystems. If not, the technique is an enormously cumbersome one. Thus, while the principal component approach has been employed in the estimation of the Wharton and Brookings models it is unlikely that SOIV will be employed in connection with large-scale models, since the models extant are not decomposable to any appreciable extent. The recent work of Mitchell (1970) is an exception. Another useful addition to these approaches was one put forth by Cooper and Jorgenson (1967) as well as, subsequently, Cooper (1969).[3] When first proposed, it was thought that it had the same asymptotic properties as 2SLS. Unfortunately, as shown by Dhrymes and Pandit (1970), this is not so. For the purposes of testing the prediction performance of the various econometric models now extant—which was the object of the studies by Jorgenson and Cooper—it is important that a certain uniformity in sample periods, data and estimation techniques be preserved. In this fashion, differences observed in the predictive performance of models will reflect correctness of specification, i.e. the adequacy of the economic "theories" embodied in them. Thus one would not want to proclaim model A better than model B in terms of the predictive test above if one knew that model B is correctly specified from an economic theoretic point of view, but it has been so inefficiently estimated that model A, although misspecified, performed better simply by virtue of a "better" estimation technique. The results of Dhrymes and Pandit (1970) show that the efficiency of the first iterate of I2SLS relative to 2SLS is structure-dependent, i.e. it depends on the nature of the matrix of coefficients of the jointly-dependent variables as well as the covariance matrix of the system's disturbances. The present paper is an attempt to provide a constructive alternative which is equivalent to that referred to in footnote 2 of Dhrymes and Pandit (1970). This alternative estimator is computationally far simpler to obtain. The demonstration of equivalence is given in the Appendix.

1. A Simplified Estimator

We shall follow here the conventions and notation of Dhrymes and Pandit (1970). Thus we are dealing with a model consisting of m simultaneous equations and thus containing m current endogenous variables. These are contained in the data matrix Y and appear as its (T element) columns. Similarly, there are G predetermined variables which are contained in the data matrix X and appear as its (T element) columns. A normalization convention has been employed and identities have been removed by substitution, if necessary. Thus the sample (T) observations on the model may be written as

$$Y = YB + XC + U. \tag{1}$$

[3] In substance, this estimator is the first iterate of the iterated 2SLS estimator (I2SLS).

In (1) U is the matrix of the system's disturbances. We assume that, if u_t is the tth row of U, then

$$\text{(A.1)} \qquad E(u'_{t.})=0, \text{ Cov }(u'_{t.})=\Sigma$$

Σ being a *non-singular matrix*. It is further assumed that

$$\{u'_{t.}: \ t=1, 2, \ldots\}$$

is a sequence of mutually independent identically distributed random variables.

$$\text{(A.2)} \qquad T<G.$$

Certain assumptions on the existence of second moments of the current endogenous and predetermined variables are also necessary, but those will be invoked as they are necessitated in the course of the argument.

In Dhrymes and Pandit (1970) the problem was to find the asymptotic distribution of the first iterate of I2SLS. The salient results were that such estimators are uniformly neither efficient nor inefficient relative to 2SLS.

Remark 1. In Dhrymes and Pandit (1970) it was shown that if all equations were just identified then, asymptotically, the first iterate of I2SLS and 2SLS were equivalent, i.e. they had the same asymptotic distribution. It was further conjectured that they would be computationally equivalent—except possibly for differences in round-off errors. A little reflection will show that this conjecture is, indeed, correct. This is so since under just identifiability indirect least squares and 2SLS estimators of the structural parameters of (1) are identical; consequently, the restricted and non-restricted reduced forms utilized by I2SLS and 2SLS will coincide. But even more is true. For, suppose that the *current endogenous* variables which appear as *explanatory variables in a given equation*, in fact, are dependent (left hand) variables *in just identified equations*. It would then be apparent that the *restricted and unrestricted reduced form estimators corresponding to these parameters* will coincide. Hence, the first iterate of I2SLS and 2SLS estimators above will coincide.

Returning now to (1), we observe that if the à priori zero restrictions are imposed then we can write

$$\text{(3)} \qquad y_{.i}=Y_i\beta_{.i}+X_i\gamma_{.i}+u_{.i}, \quad i=1, 2, \ldots, m$$

where $y_{.i}$ is the vector of T observations on the ith endogenous variable y_i; Y_i, X_i are the submatrices of Y and X respectively containing the current endogenous and predetermined explanatory variables entering the ith equation. In (3) $\beta_{.i}$, $\gamma_{.i}$ are, respectively, subvectors of the ith columns of B and C resulting when elements known to be zero are suppressed. They contain, respectively, m_i and G_i elements.

The proposed limited information estimator is as follows: By instrumental variables or other means, obtain initial consistent estimators of the structural parameters. This will always be possible, for even though $T<G$ we would typically have a situation in which m_i+G_i will be small relative to G and hence

$$\text{(4)} \qquad m_i+G_i<T.$$

A SIMPLIFIED STRUCTURAL ESTIMATOR

This procedure will result in a consistent estimator of the structural matrices, say $\tilde{B}$, $\tilde{C}$. The efficiency of this estimator will not be known unless the precise nature of the instruments is specified.

Now, however, we can compute the *restricted reduced form* and obtain

$$\tilde{Y}=X\tilde{C}(I-\tilde{B})^{-1}. \tag{5}$$

For this purpose we require

(A.3) The matrix I–B is non-singular.

Remark 2. Here the question would arise whether I–$\tilde{B}$ would be singular if $T<m$. I have not examined this question. On the other hand, while exact singularity could probably be ruled out by the condition $T\geq m$, near singularity could be handled by using something like the Gauss-Seidel method to solve, for $\tilde{Y}$, the system

$$\tilde{Y}=\tilde{Y}\tilde{B}+X\tilde{C}. \tag{6}$$

which will ameliorate serious error in accuracy resulting from possible near singularity of I–$\tilde{B}$.

Consider now the estimator

$$\tilde{\delta}_{.i}=(\tilde{Z}_i'Z_i)^{-1}\tilde{Z}_i'y_{.i} \qquad i=1, 2, \ldots, m \tag{7}$$

where

$$\tilde{Z}_i=(\tilde{Y}_i,X_i), \quad Z_i=(Y_i,X_i). \tag{8}$$

Remark 3. The estimator in (7) is simply an instrumental variables (I.V.) estimator using as instruments the included predetermined variables and the estimated systematic component of the explanatory current endogenous variables as computed from the *restricted reduced form.* For this reason it will be termed the limited information iterated instrumental variables (L.I.I.V.) estimator.

Notice, also, that the usual 2SLS estimator is of the same form, *provided* $\tilde{Y}_1$ *is interpreted as being derived from the unrestricted reduced form obtained by OLS.*

The difference in the two cases is that

$$\tilde{Y}_i'Y_i\neq\tilde{Y}_i'\tilde{Y}_i \tag{9}$$

if $\tilde{Z}_i$ is interpreted according to (5) and (8). On the other hand, if $\tilde{Y}_i$ is obtained from the unrestricted reduced form, estimated by OLS, then equality will hold in (9).

Now rewrite the system in (3) as

$$y=Z\delta+u \tag{10}$$

where

$$y=\begin{pmatrix} y_{.2} \\ y_{.2} \\ \vdots \\ y_{.m} \end{pmatrix}, \quad Z=\text{diag }(Z_1, \; Z_2, \; \ldots, \; Z_m), \quad \delta=\begin{pmatrix} \delta_{.1} \\ \delta_{.2} \\ \vdots \\ \delta_{.m} \end{pmatrix}, \quad u=\begin{pmatrix} u_{.1} \\ u_{.2} \\ \vdots \\ u_{.m} \end{pmatrix} \tag{11}$$

PHOEBUS J. DHRYMES

The L.I.I.V. estimator for the parameters of the entire system is, thus, given by

(12) $$\tilde{\delta}=(\tilde{Z}'Z)^{-1}\tilde{Z}'y.$$

This immediately suggests a full information iterated instrumental variables estimator (F.I.I.V.) as follows

(13) $$\hat{\delta}=(\tilde{Z}'\tilde{\Phi}^{-1}Z)^{-1}\tilde{Z}'\tilde{\Phi}^{-1}y$$

where

(14) $$\Phi=\Sigma\otimes I,\ \tilde{\Phi}=\tilde{\Sigma}\otimes I,\ \tilde{\Sigma}=(\tilde{\sigma}_{ij})$$

and

(15) $$\tilde{\sigma}_{ij}=\frac{\tilde{u}_{.i}'\tilde{u}_{.j}}{T}.$$

Remark 4. We observe that the residual vectors $\tilde{u}_{.i}$ may be obtained using the initial consistent estimator or using the L.I.I.V. estimator. One would conjecture that, asymptotically, it makes no difference which is used. We shall postpone discussion of this aspect until we consider the question of the asymptotic distribution of such estimators.

Remark 5. One need examine, particularly in this case, the question of whether the inverse in (13) will exist. Observe that the matrix in question is of order $\sum_{i=1}^{m}(m_i+G_i)$. The same is true of (12), but in that case the problem does not arise in acute form since $\tilde{Z}'Z$ is block diagonal. As a minimum requirement for the existence of the F.I.I.V. estimator, we must have $T>m$.

2. Asymptotic Equivalence of L.I.I.V. and F.I.I.V. to 2SLS and 3SLS Respectively

We deal first with the estimator in (12). Substituting from (10) we find

(16) $$\tilde{\delta}=\delta+(\tilde{Z}'Z)^{-1}\tilde{Z}'u.$$

We now require the assumption

(A.4) The matrix

$$\underset{T\to\infty}{\text{plim}}\ \frac{1}{T}\begin{bmatrix}\overline{Y}'\overline{Y} & \overline{Y}'X\\ X'\overline{Y} & X'X\end{bmatrix}=\overline{M}$$

exists and is non-stochastic of rank G.

From the above we conclude that

(17) $$\underset{T\to\infty}{\text{plim}}\ \frac{\tilde{Z}_i'Z_i}{T}=\underset{T\to\infty}{\text{plim}}\ \tilde{Q}_i'\frac{X'X}{T}\tilde{Q}_i$$

exists as a non-singular matrix, where

(18) $$\tilde{Z}_i=(X\tilde{\Pi}_{.i},X_i)=X\tilde{Q}_i \qquad i=1,2,\ldots,m,$$

A SIMPLIFIED STRUCTURAL ESTIMATOR

$\tilde{\Pi}_i$ being the appropriate submatrix of $\tilde{C}(I-\tilde{B})^{-1}$, provided

(A.5) All equations of the system obey the rank condition for identifiability.

To see why in (17) we have a non-singular matrix, consider the case $i=1$ and partition

$$X=(X_1,X^*) \tag{19}$$

where X^* contains the columns of X not contained in X_1.

$$\tilde{Z}_1=(X\tilde{\Pi}_1,X_1)=X\begin{pmatrix}\tilde{\Pi}_1 & I \\ & 0\end{pmatrix}=X\begin{bmatrix}\tilde{\Pi}_{G_11} & I \\ \tilde{\Pi}_{G^*1} & 0\end{bmatrix}=X\tilde{Q}_1 \tag{20}$$

which provides an implicit definition of $\tilde{Q}_1$.

But

$$\text{rank}\begin{bmatrix}\Pi_{G_11} & I \\ \Pi_{G^*1} & 0\end{bmatrix}=\text{rank}\begin{bmatrix}I & \Pi_{G_11} \\ 0 & \Pi_{G^*1}\end{bmatrix}=G_1+m_1 \tag{21}$$

since

$$\text{rank } \Pi_{G^*1}=m_1 \tag{22}$$

where $G^*=G-G_1$.

If the equation is *just identified*, then $G^*=m_1$ and the matrix Q_1 is *non-singular*. A similar argument may be made with respect to Q_i for *any* i.

Defining

$$\bar{Z}_i=(X\Pi_{i},X_{i}),\quad \bar{Z}=\text{diag}\,(\bar{Z}_1,\bar{Z}_2,\ldots,\bar{Z}_m) \tag{23}$$

we conclude, in view of the consistency of $\tilde{C}(I-\tilde{B})^{-1}$ as an estimator of $C(I-B)^{-1}$ $(=\Pi)$, that asymptotically

$$\sqrt{T}(\tilde{\delta}-\delta)\ \left(\frac{\bar{Z}'\bar{Z}}{T}\right)^{-1}\frac{\bar{Z}'u}{\sqrt{T}} \tag{24}$$

But the right member of (24) is exactly what determines the asymptotic distribution of the 2SLS estimator of the parameters of the entire system. We therefore conclude that L.I.I.V. and 2SLS are asymptotically equivalent.

Let us now turn to the F.I.I.V. estimator of (13), assuming that the matrices inverted there are, in fact, invertible. If a consistent estimator of $\delta_{.i}$ and $\delta_{.j}$ is used in obtaining $\tilde{\sigma}_{ij}$, then

$$\operatorname*{plim}_{T\to\infty}\tilde{\Sigma}=\Sigma. \tag{25}$$

Consequently, asymptotically

$$\sqrt{T}(\hat{\delta}-\delta)\sim\left(\frac{\bar{Z}'\Phi^{-1}\bar{Z}}{T}\right)^{-1}\frac{\bar{Z}'\Phi^{-1}u}{\sqrt{T}} \tag{26}$$

and the reader easily verifies that the right member of (26) has, in fact, the same asymptotic distribution as the 3SLS estimator under the conditions customarily imposed in the literature.

This discussion also answers the query raised in Remark 4 whether the $\tilde{\sigma}_{ij}$ are to be obtained at the " first " or " second " stage. Asymptotically, it makes no difference.

3. Conclusion and Caveats

We have shown in the preceding that the L.I.I.V. and F.I.I.V. estimators have the same asymptotic distributions as 2SLS and 3SLS respectively. Thus, on that account, they are particularly suitable for use when one is interested in comparing the predictive performance of econometric models which are differently structured, particularly so when for some models the number of predetermined variables (G) exceeds the number of observations (T).

There is, however, one question which is yet to be answered. How are the initial consistent estimators of the structural parameters to be chosen? The manner of their choice will no doubt affect the small sample properties of the resulting L.I.I.V. and F.I.I.V. estimators. In principle, here, one must acknowledge an element of arbitrariness that exists in all techniques stated in the Introduction, as well as in L.I.I.V. and F.I.I.V.

One useful rule of thumb would be to choose as instruments, at the initial stage, those predetermined variables that appear in the " own " equations of the jointly dependent variables they replace and which exhibit the highest correlation. More specifically, if X is the set of all possible instruments, then the initial instrumental matrix for, say, the first equation, is to be chosen as

$$P_1=(X_1^*,X_1) \tag{27}$$

where X_1^* is a submatrix of X *distinct* from X_1 and such that the (sample) coefficient of vector correlation between the variables in P_1 and Z_1 is maximized. This keeps the choice of instruments relatively simple and at the same time insures reasonably " efficient " initial estimators.[4]

Appendix

Here we make explicit the equivalence of the L.I.I.V. estimator and that referred to in footnote 2 of Dhrymes and Pandit (1970). The latter estimator is obtained as follows: As with L.I.I.V., obtain initial instrumental variables estimators, $\tilde{B}$, $\tilde{C}$, and compute the restricted reduced form

$$\tilde{Y}=X\tilde{C}(I-\tilde{B})^{-1}. \tag{A.1}$$

Estimators of the parameters of the ith structural equation are given by

$$\approx{\delta}_{.i}=(\approx{Z}_i'\approx{Z}_i)^{-1}\approx{Z}_i'y_{.i}, \qquad i=1, 2, \ldots, m \tag{A.2}$$

where

$$\approx{Z}_i=(\approx{Y}_i,X_i), \quad \approx{Y}_i=\tilde{Z}_i(\tilde{Z}_i'\tilde{Z}_i)^{-1}\tilde{Z}_i'Y_i \tag{A.3}$$

and $\tilde{Z}_i$ is defined in equation (8).

[4] After this paper was completed it has been brought to my attention that in a recent unpublished paper E. Lyttkens has proposed an estimator similar to L.I.I.V.

A SIMPLIFIED STRUCTURAL ESTIMATOR

We observe that we may write

$$\text{(A.4)} \qquad \tilde{\tilde{Z}}_i=\tilde{Z}_i S_i, \quad S_i=(\tilde{Z}_i'\tilde{Z}_i)^{-1}\tilde{Z}_i'Z_i$$

and that S_i is a non-singular matrix, $i=1, 2, \ldots, m$. Since $\tilde{\tilde{Z}}_i'\tilde{\tilde{Z}}_i=\tilde{\tilde{Z}}_i'Z_i$, we see that

$$\text{(A.5)} \qquad \tilde{\tilde{\delta}}_{.i}=(\tilde{\tilde{Z}}_i'\tilde{\tilde{Z}}_i)^{-1}\tilde{\tilde{Z}}_i'y_{.i}=(\tilde{Z}_i'Z_i)^{-1}\tilde{Z}_i'y_{.i}=\tilde{\delta}_{.i}$$

which shows the equivalence of the two estimators.
The procedure implicit in (A.2) may be extended to the full information case as well. Thus we would define

$$\text{(A.6)} \qquad \hat{\hat{\delta}}=(\tilde{\tilde{Z}}'\tilde{\Phi}^{-1}\tilde{\tilde{Z}})^{-1}\tilde{\tilde{Z}}'\tilde{\Phi}^{-1}y$$

where $\tilde{\tilde{Z}}=\text{diag}\,(\tilde{\tilde{Z}}_1, \tilde{\tilde{Z}}_2, \ldots, \tilde{\tilde{Z}}_m)$. We note that

$$\text{(A.7)} \qquad \tilde{\tilde{Z}}=\tilde{Z}S, \; \tilde{Z}=\text{diag}\,(\tilde{Z}_1, \tilde{Z}_2, \ldots, \tilde{Z}_m), \; S=\text{diag}\,(S_1, S_2, \ldots, S_m).$$

Since $\tilde{\tilde{Z}}'\tilde{\Phi}^{-1}\tilde{\tilde{Z}}=\tilde{\tilde{Z}}'\tilde{\Phi}^{-1}Z$, we have

$$\text{(A.8)} \qquad \hat{\hat{\delta}}=(\tilde{\tilde{Z}}'\tilde{\Phi}^{-1}\tilde{\tilde{Z}})^{-1}\tilde{\tilde{Z}}'\tilde{\Phi}^{-1}y=(\tilde{Z}'\tilde{\Phi}^{-1}Z)^{-1}\tilde{Z}'\tilde{\Phi}^{-1}y=\hat{\delta}$$

which shows equivalence of the estimator in (A.6) and F.I.I.V.

References

Cooper, R. (1969). "The predictive performance of quarterly econometric models of the united states." Paper presented at the N.B.E.R. Conference on Econometric Models of Cyclical Behavior, Boston, Mass., November.

Cooper, R., and Jorgenson, D. W. (1967). "The predictive performance of quarterly econometric models of the U.S." Working paper in Mathematical Economics and Econometrics No. 113, University of California, Berkeley, August.

Cragg, J. C. (1967). "On the relative small sample properties of several structural equation estimators." *Econometrica*, 35, 89–110.

Dhrymes, P. J. (1970). *Econometrics : Statistical Foundations and Applications.* Harper and Row, New York.

Dhrymes, P. J., and Pandit, V. (1970). "Asymptotic properties of an iterate of the two-stage least squares estimator." Discussion Paper No. 154, University of Pennsylvania, February.

Fisher, F. M. (1965). "On the choice of instrumental variables in the estimation of economy-wide econometric models." *International Economic Review*, 6, 245–274.

Kloek, T., and Mennes, L. B. M. (1960). "Simultaneous equations estimation based on principal components of predetermined variables." *Econometrica*, 28, 45–61.

Mitchell, B. M. (1970). "Estimation of large econometric models." Unpublished Ph.D. thesis, Massachusetts Institute of Technology, January.

Mitchell, B. M., and Fisher, F. M. (1970). "The choice of instrumental variables in the estimation of economy-wide models : Some further thoughts." *International Economic Review*, 11, 226–234.

AUSTRALASIAN MEDICAL PUBLISHING CO. LTD.
71-79 ARUNDEL ST., GLEBE, SYDNEY, N.S.W., 2037

© Journal of the American Statistical Association
June 1972, Volume 67, Number 338
Theory & Methods Section

Asymptotic Properties of an Iterate of the Two-Stage Least Squares Estimator

PHOEBUS J. DHRYMES and VISHWANATH PANDIT*

In this article we obtain the asymptotic distribution of the first iterate of iterated two stage least squares; we demonstrate that this distribution is different from that of the usual two stage least squares estimator. Moreover, we show that the difference in the covariance matrices of their respective asymptotic distributions is, generally, neither positive nor negative semidefinite. In particular, we produce examples in which for some parametric configurations this difference is positive semidefinite while for others it is negative semidefinite.

1. INTRODUCTION

In this article we examine the distribution and other asymptotic properties of the first iterate of the iterated two stage least squares (I2SLS) estimator. The latter was first suggested in Theil [9] and attributed to H. S. Houthakker. An empirical experiment was carried out by A. L. Nagar [8]. The fix point estimator of Wold [10], as modified by Lyttkens [7], is akin but not identical to I2SLS.

More recently, however, a variant of the estimator considered in this paper has been employed by Cooper and Jorgenson [3] and Cooper [2] in the context of evaluating the predictive performance of various econometric models. Here, we shall show that the asymptotic distribution of the first iterate of I2SLS, does not, generally, coincide with that of 2SLS; whether it is efficient or inefficient, relative to the latter, is structure-dependent.

* Phoebus J. Dhrymes is professor, Department of Economics, University of Pennsylvania, Philadelphia, Penn. 19104. Vishwanath Pandit is reader, Delhi School of Economics, Delhi University, Delhi 7, India. The research on which this article is based was supported in part by NSF Grant GS 2289 at the University of Pennsylvania.

Thus, this estimator is not particularly suitable for the purposes to which it has been put since it may be efficient or inefficient relative to 2SLS depending on the structural configuration of the model to be estimated.

2. FORMULATION OF THE PROBLEM

Consider the general linear structural econometric model

$$y_{.i} = Z_i\delta_{.i} + u_{.i},\ Z_i = (Y_i, X_i)\ \delta_{.i} = (\beta'_{.i}, \gamma'_{.i})', \qquad i = 1.2, \cdots, m \tag{2.1}$$

In dealing with this model we shall follow the standard conventions and assumptions as given, for example, in [5].

The model may be written more compactly as

$$Y = YB + XC + U \tag{2.2}$$

where

$$Y = (y_{.1}, y_{.2}, \cdots, y_{.m}),\ X = (x_{.1}, x_{.2}, \cdots, x_{.G}),$$
$$U = (u_{.1}, u_{.2}, \cdots, u_{.m}) \tag{2.3}$$

and $y_{.j}$, $u_{.i}$, $x_{.j}$ denote, respectively, the (T) observations on the ith jointly dependent variable, the error term in the ith equation and the jth predetermined variable. The ith column of B, $b_{.i}$, consists of the elements of $\beta_{.i}$ with zeros inserted at appropriate places, reflecting *a priori* restrictions. Similarly, with respect to the ith column of C and $\gamma_{.i}$. Finally, Y_i, X_i are appropriate submatrices of Y and X, respectively. The estimator we are concerned with is as follows:

a. Obtain the usual 2SLS estimator of the unknown parameters in B and C, say $\hat{B}$, $\hat{C}$, and compute the *restricted* reduced form parameters

$$\tilde{\Pi} = \hat{C}\hat{D}, \qquad \hat{D} = (I - \hat{B})^{-1}. \tag{2.4}$$

b. Define

$$\tilde{Y} = X\tilde{\Pi} \tag{2.5}$$

c. Obtain the first iterate of I2SLS (for the ith structural equation)[1] as

$$\delta_{.i} = (\tilde{Z}_i'\tilde{Z}_i)^{-1}\tilde{Z}_i'y_{.i}, \qquad \tilde{Z}_i = (\tilde{Y}_i, X_i). \tag{2.6}$$

---

[1] In the experiment carried out by Nagar [8] the corresponding iterate was defined by

$$\hat{\delta}_{.i} = Q_i^{-1}\tilde{Z}_i'y_{.i} \quad \text{where} \quad Q_i = \begin{bmatrix} Y_i'Y_i - \tilde{V}_i'\tilde{V}_i & Y_i'X_i \\ X_i'Y_i & X_i'X_i \end{bmatrix}$$

We shall be concerned with the asymptotic properties of the estimator in (2.6) for a given structural equation, say, the first. We shall employ the following convention.

Convention: The system contains no identities. There are m current endogenous and G predetermined variables. In the first structural equation the variable to be "explained" is y_1; the "explanatory" current endogenous variables are $y_2, y_3, \cdots, y_{m_1+1}$; the explanatory predetermined variables are $x_1, x_2, \cdots, x_{G_1}$.

It has been conjectured that the preceding estimator would be more "efficient" than 2SLS since "it takes into [444] account the restrictions on the entire system and not merely those of the given equation under consideration."

3. PROPERTIES OF THE ITERATE

In the course of the argument below, we shall require certain assumptions. Thus,

- A.1 The equations of the system satisfy the rank and order conditions for identifiability and the reduced form exists.
- A.2 If $u_{t\cdot}$ is the tth row of U, then $\{u_{t\cdot}: t=1, 2, \cdots\}$ is a sequence of mutually independent, identically distributed (i.i.d.) random vectors with mean zero and (nonsingular) covariance matrix $\sum$.
- A.3 The predetermined variables of the system, i.e., the columns of X, are *entirely* exogenous, linearly independent and moreover they are nonstochastic uniformly bounded, and $\lim_{T\to\infty} (X'X/T)$ exists as a nonsingular matrix.

Remark 1: Assumption A.3 is somewhat restrictive. The restrictive aspects are that no *lagged endogenous* variables are admitted and that the elements of X are required to be uniformly bounded. These assumptions can be easily removed at the cost of considerable analytical complications. The conclusions reached under the present set of assumptions will remain valid. If lagged endogenous variables are admitted the consequence is that we shall have to invoke a *central limit theorem on m-dependent random variables, provided the resulting dynamic system is asserted to be stable.*

The boundedness of the remaining (exogenous) variables is not a problem. For practical purposes it rules

---

and $\tilde{V}_i = Y_i - \tilde{V}_i$. Thus, Nagar's iteration differs from the straightforward iteration of 2SLS since it is not necessarily true that $\tilde{V}'X = 0$, when the residual matrix $\tilde{V}$ is obtained from the 2SLS induced restricted reduced form. All such iterates have the same asymptotic distribution as 2SLS.

out the consideration of time trends. While we do not seriously consider these trends as *bona fide* variables in this context, still this aspect can be covered by certain other boundedness conditions on them. If time trends are admitted, it should be pointed out, Assumption A.3 cannot generally be valid.

Finally if exogenous variables are allowed to be random we have to assume that they are *independent* of the error vector of the system and moreover they are intertemporally independent. All these qualifications apply to the customary discussions of the simultaneous equations model, and not merely to the one under discussion here.

From the definition of the estimator in (2.6)—and its natural extention to subsequent iterations—we have, in view of Assumptions A.1, A.2, A.3, the following lemma.

Lemma 1: The iterates of the I2SLS estimator of the parameter vector $\delta_{.1}$ are consistent.

We now establish the asymptotic distribution of the first iterate. First, observe that

$$Z_1 = \tilde{Z}_1 + (\tilde{V}_1, 0) \tag{3.1}$$

where $\tilde{V}_1$ is defined by

$$Y_1 = \tilde{Y}_1 + \tilde{V}_1. \tag{3.2}$$

Thus (2.6) may be rewritten as

$$\tilde{\delta}_{.1} - \delta_{.1} = (\tilde{Z}_1' \tilde{Z}_1)^{-1} \tilde{Z}_1' (\tilde{V}_1 \beta_{.1} + u_{.1}). \tag{3.3}$$

Remark 2: The expression in (3.3) makes clear the difference between the I2SLS and 2SLS estimators. In the latter the residual matrix, $\hat{V}_1$ is orthogonal to $\hat{Z}_1 = (\hat{Y}_1, X_1)$, where $\hat{V}_1 = [I - X(X'X)^{-1}X']Y_1$.
Since

$$\operatorname*{plim}_{T\to\infty} \frac{\hat{Z}_1' \hat{Z}_1}{T} = \operatorname*{plim}_{T\to\infty} \frac{\tilde{Z}_1' \tilde{Z}_1}{T}, \tag{3.4}$$

it follows that the only difference, asymptotically, between the two estimators is the nonorthogonality bebetween $\tilde{Z}_1$ and $\tilde{V}_1$.
Noting that

$$\begin{aligned} \tilde{V} = Y - \tilde{Y} &= V - X(\hat{C}\hat{D} - CD), \\ Y = X\Pi + V, \quad \Pi &= CD, \quad V = UD \end{aligned} \tag{3.5}$$

and

$$\hat{C}\hat{D} - CD = [\hat{C}\hat{D}(\hat{B} - B) + \hat{C} - C]D, \tag{3.6}$$

we see that

$$
\begin{aligned}
&\frac{1}{\sqrt{T}}\tilde{Z}_1'(\tilde{V}_1\beta_{.1}+u_{.1}) \\
&= \frac{1}{\sqrt{T}}\tilde{Z}_1'\{u_{.1}+[U-X(\hat{C}\hat{D}(\hat{B}-B)+\hat{C}-C)]D_1\beta_{.1}\} \\
&= \frac{1}{\sqrt{T}}\tilde{Z}_1'\{u_{.1}+\textstyle\sum_{i=1}^{m}[u_{.i}-\tilde{Z}_i(\hat{\delta}_{.i}-\delta_{.i})]s_{i1}\},
\end{aligned}
\tag{3.7}
$$

where s_{i1} is the ith element of $D_1\beta_{.1}$ and $\hat{\delta}_{.i}$ is the usual 2SLS estimator of the parameter vector $\delta_{.i}$.

Noting, further, that

$$\hat{\delta}_{.i}-\delta_{.i}=(\hat{Z}_i'\hat{Z}_i)^{-1}\hat{Z}_i'u_{.i} \tag{3.8}$$

and that the asymptotic distribution of the last number of (3.7) is precisely the same as when we replace $\tilde{Z}_i$ or $\hat{Z}_i$ by $\bar{Z}_i=(X\Pi_{i}, X_i)$ we conclude that

$$
\begin{aligned}
\frac{1}{\sqrt{T}}\tilde{Z}_1'(\tilde{V}_1\beta_{.1}+u_{.1}) \sim \frac{1}{\sqrt{T}}\Big\{&\bar{Z}_1'u_{.1} \\
&+\textstyle\sum_{i=2}^{m}\Big[\bar{Z}_1'-\Big(\frac{\bar{Z}_1'\bar{Z}_i}{T}\Big)\Big(\frac{\bar{Z}_i'\bar{Z}_i}{T}\Big)^{-1}\bar{Z}_i'\Big]u_{.i}s_{i1}\Big\}.
\end{aligned}
\tag{3.9}
$$

We have,

Lemma 2: If $\bar{Z}_1$ lies in the intersection of vector spaces spanned by the vectors in $\bar{Z}_i$, $i=2, \cdots, m$, then the asymptotic distributions of the first iterate of I2SLS and the 2SLS estimator of $\delta_{.1}$ are identical.

Proof: Obvious from (3.3) and (3.9).

Corollary: If all equations of the system are just identified, I2SLS and 2SLS estimators have the same asymptotic distribution.

Proof: The rank and order conditions for just identifiability imply

$$\bar{Z}_i(\bar{Z}_i'\bar{Z}_i)^{-1}\bar{Z}_i'\bar{Z}_1=\bar{Z}_1 \tag{3.10}$$

and the conclusion follows easily from (3.3) and (3.9). [445]

To determine the asymptotic distribution of the first iterate, define

$$
\begin{aligned}
R_j &= s_{j1}[I-\bar{Z}_j(\bar{Z}_j'\bar{Z}_j)^{-1}\bar{Z}_j'] \qquad & j=2,3,\cdots,m \\
&= I & j=1
\end{aligned}
\tag{3.11}
$$

and observe that the right member of (3.9) can be rendered as

$$\frac{1}{\sqrt{T}} \sum \overline{Z}_1' R_j u_j = \frac{1}{\sqrt{T}} \sum_{i=1}^{T} Q_r u_r'. \qquad (3.12)$$

where

$$Q_r = (\overset{(1)}{q}_{.r}, \overset{(2)}{q}_{.r}, \cdots, \overset{(m)}{q}_{.r}, \qquad (3.13)$$

$q_{.r}^{(i)}$ being the rth column of $\overline{Z}_1' R_r$ and $u_{r.}$ the rth row of U. It is easily verified that the conditions of the Lindeberg-Feller theorem (see [1] or [6]) hold and thus the right member of (3.12), asymptotically, obeys

$$\frac{1}{\sqrt{T}} \sum_{r=1}^{T} Q_r u_{r.}' \sim N(0, \Phi) \qquad (3.14)$$

where

$$\Phi = \lim_{T\to\infty} \frac{1}{T} \sum_{r=1}^{T} \Phi_r, \qquad \Phi_r = Q_r \sum Q_r'. \qquad (3.15)$$

More explicitly,

$$\Phi = \sigma_{11}\overline{M}_{11} + \Phi^* \qquad (3.16)$$

$$\begin{aligned}\Phi^* = 2 \sum_{j=2}^{m} s_{j1}\sigma_{1j}(\overline{M}_{11} - \overline{M}_{1j}\overline{M}_{jj}^{-1}\overline{M}_{j1}) \\ + \sum_{i=2}^{m} \sum_{j=2}^{m} s_{i1}s_{j1}\sigma_{ij}(\overline{M}_{11} - \overline{M}_{1j}\overline{M}_{jj}^{-1}\overline{M}_{j1} \\ - \overline{M}_{1i}\overline{M}_{ii}^{-1}\overline{M}_{i1} + \overline{M}_{1j}\overline{M}_{jj}^{-1}\overline{M}_{ji}\overline{M}_{ii}^{-1}\overline{M}_{i1}),\end{aligned}$$

where

$$\overline{M}_{ij} = \lim_{T\to\infty} \frac{1}{T} \overline{Z}_i' \overline{Z}_j, \qquad i,j = 1, 2, \cdots, m. \qquad (3.17)$$

Consequently,

$$\sqrt{T}\,(\tilde{\delta}_{.1} - \delta_{.1}) \sim N(0, \sigma_{11}\overline{M}_{11}^{-1} + \overline{M}_{11}^{-1}\Phi^*\overline{M}_{11}^{-1}). \qquad (3.18)$$

The question next arises as to whether such iterated estimators are efficient relative to the usual 2SLS ones. The answer, unfortunately, is that this is not necessarily so. To establish this claim it is sufficient to produce cases in which such iterated estimators are inefficient and cases in which they are efficient relative to 2SLS. This is accomplished simply by considering a two equation model. In such a case the covariance matrix of the asymptotic distribution reduces to

$$\sigma_{11}\overline{M}_{11}^{-1} + \overline{M}_{11}^{-1}\Phi^*\overline{M}_{11}^{-1} = \sigma_{11}\overline{M}_{11}^{-1} + (s_{21}^2\sigma_{22} + 2\sigma_{12}s_{21}) \cdot \overline{M}_{11}^{-1}(\overline{M}_{11} - \overline{M}_{12}\overline{M}_{22}^{-1}\overline{M}_{21})\overline{M}_{11}^{-1}. \tag{3.19}$$

The difference between the covariance matrices of the asymptotic distribution of the first iterate of I2SLS and 2SLS estimators of the parameters of the first structural equation is given by

$$(s_{21}^2\sigma_{22} + 2\sigma_{12}s_{21})\overline{M}_{11}^{-1}(\overline{M}_{11} - \overline{M}_{12}\overline{M}_{22}^{-1}\overline{M}_{21})\overline{M}_{11}^{-1}.$$

Since matrix in (3.19) is, at least, positive semidefinite, the question of the asymptotic efficiency of such iterated estimators hinges on the sign of the scalar. The latter, however, depends on the structural coefficients, as they enter s_{21}, and the covariance parameters σ_{12}, σ_{22}. Thus, for some parametric configurations 2SLS will be efficient while for others it will be inefficient relative to the first iterate of I2SLS.

We have, therefore, proved the following:

Theorem: Consider the model in (2.1) under the usual convention and assumptions, in particular A.1, A.2, A.3. Then, the first iterate of the I2SLS estimator of the first structural equation obeys:

a. It is consistent. Indeed, all subsequent iterates are as well.
b. Its asymptotic distribution is given by $\sqrt{T}(\tilde{\delta}_{\cdot 1} - \delta_{\cdot 1}) \sim N(0, \overline{M}_{11}^{-1}\Phi\overline{M}_{11}^{-1})$
c. If all equations of the system are just identified the asymptotic distributions of all iterates of I2SLS and 2SLS estimators coincide.
d. There exist cases in which the first iterate of the I2SLS is, asymptotically, efficient and cases where it is inefficient relative to the 2SLS estimator.

4. CONCLUSION

In this article we have derived the distribution of the first iterate of the iterated two stage least squares estimator and have shown that, in general, this estimator cannot be ranked with respect to the 2SLS estimator in terms of relative asymptotic efficiency. One may proceed to obtain an expression for the distributional aspects *for all the structural parameters* of the system—and not merely those of one equation. This may shed some additional light on its properties *vis-à-vis* those of the 2SLS estimator.

Another aspect that deserves to be developed is the derivation of the distribution of the (converging) iterated 2SLS estimator and an elucidation of the conditions under which convergence is obtained. This will have a bearing on the distributional aspects of the "fix point" estimator of Wold provided again, that the latter converges independently of "initial conditions."

Finally, it would be useful to investigate the properties of this iterate in the case of models exhibiting certain simple nonlinearities of the type found in most currently researched economy wide models.

In view of the greater sensitivity of the iterated estimator to misspecification errors, it is useful to examine such problems before this estimator is employed widely.

[*Received November 1970. Revised October 1971.*] [446]

REFERENCES

[1] Chung, K. L., *A Course in Probability Theory*, New York: Harcourt, Brace and World Inc., 1968.

[2] Cooper, R., "The Predictive Performance of Quarterly Econometric Models of the United States," paper presented at the NBER Conference on Econometric Models of Cyclical Behavior, Boston, Massachusetts, November 1969.

[3] ——— and Jorgenson, D. W., "The Predictive Performance of Quarterly Econometric Models of the U. S.," Working paper in Mathematical Economics and Econometrics No. 113, University of California, Berkeley, August 1967.

[4] Cramer, H., *Mathematical Methods of Statistics*, Princeton: Princeton University Press, 1947.

[5] Dhrymes, P. J., *Econometrics: Statistical Foundations and Applications*, New York: Harper and Row, 1970.

[6] ———, "A Simplified Structural Estimator for Large Scale Econometric Models," *The Australian Journal of Statistics*, (November 1971).

[7] Lyttkens, E., "Non-iterative Estimation of a Special Interdependent System by CREID-Specification," Paper presented at Ken Blaricum meetings of the Econometric Society, January 1967.

[8] Nagar, A. L., "Simultaneous Equations Estimation: Iterative Two Stage Least Squares," Report 5821, Netherlands: Econometric Institute, School of Economics, July 1958.

[9] Theil, H., *Economic Forecasts and Policy*, Amsterdam: North Holland Publishing Co., 1957.

[10] Wold, H. O. A., "A Fix-Point Theorem with Econometric Background," *Arkiv für Mathematik*, 6, No. 6 (1965), 209–40. [447]

[5]

INTERNATIONAL ECONOMIC REVIEW
Vol. 13, No. 2, June, 1972

ASYMPTOTIC PROPERTIES OF SIMULTANEOUS LEAST SQUARES ESTIMATORS*

BY PHOEBUS J. DHRYMES[1]

1. INTRODUCTION

IN AN INTERESTING PAPER [2], over a decade ago, Brown suggested an estimation procedure for the standard simultaneous equations model which he termed simultaneous least squares (SLS). A paper by Nakamura [7] showed its consistency. Since that time, however, no systematic attempt has been made to study the efficiency of this estimator *vis-a-vis* other commonly employed estimators. An exception to this is the brief discussion of SLS by Malinvaud [6] in the context of the class of minimum distance estimators.

Contrary to assertions in [2] SLS is not a full information procedure and this despite the fact that it takes into account *all* a priori restrictions on the coefficient matrices of the system. What is overlooked in this connection is that by failing to take into account the stochastic dependence of the system's structural errors it fails to utilize all of the relevant information provided by the sample. This is made clear below when the minimands of SLS and full information maximum likelihood (FIML) are compared.

Perhaps the simplest way of understanding the relationship of SLS to two stage least squares (2SLS) and three stage least squares (3SLS) estimators is in the context of the general linear model.

$$(1) \qquad y = X\beta + u\,, \qquad E(u) = 0\,, \qquad \mathrm{Cov}\,(u) = \Sigma\,.$$

If in (1) we obtain the estimator

$$(2) \qquad \tilde{\beta} = (X'RX)^{-1}X'Ry$$

where R is a symmetric nonsingular matrix which, if nonstochastic it is not necessarily Σ^{-1}, and again if stochastic it is not necessarily true that plim $R = \Sigma^{-1}$, then one has an exact analog of the relation between SLS and 2SLS, 3SLS. Clearly the estimator in (2) may or may not be efficient relative to the ordinary least squares (OLS) estimator of β depending on the proximity of R (or its probability limit) to Σ^{-1}. This is exactly the relation of SLS to 2SLS. Thus SLS would be (asymptotically) inefficient relative to 3SLS, except in very special circumstances, and cannot be uniformly ranked relative to the 2SLS estimator in terms of (asymptotic) efficiency.

* Manuscript received June 17, 1971; revised December 7, 1971.

[1] The research on which this paper is based was in part supported by NSF grant GS 2289 at the University of Pennsylvania and was completed during the author's visit at the University of California, Los Angeles. I am indebted to T. M. Brown for helpful comments on an earlier version.

2. ASYMPTOTIC PROPERTIES OF THE SLS ESTIMATOR

Consider the standard structural econometric model

$$y_{t\cdot} = y_{t\cdot}B + x_{t\cdot}C + u_{t\cdot}\,, \qquad t = 1, 2, \ldots, T, \tag{3}$$

where $y_{t\cdot} = (y_{t1}, y_{t2}, \ldots, y_{tm})$, $x_{t\cdot} = (x_{t1}, x_{t2}, \ldots, x_{tG})$ are, respectively, the vectors of observation on the m current endogenous and G predetermined variables of the system; the matrices B, C contain the structural parameters of the problem. The system is assumed to be identified through a priori restrictions so that it will be known that some elements of B and C are zero.

The sequence $\{u_{t\cdot}: = 1, 2, \ldots\}$ is assumed to be one of independent identically distributed (i.i.d.) random variables obeying

$$E(u'_{t\cdot}) = 0\,, \qquad \operatorname{Cov}(u'_{t\cdot}) = \Sigma\,. \tag{4}$$

It is convenient, but not necessary, to assume that the predetermined variables are nonstochastic and that the second moment matrices of the variables of the problem possess nonsingular limits.

If we impose the a priori restrictions, the observations on the ith structural equation may be written as

$$y_{\cdot i} = Y_i\beta_{\cdot i} + X_i\gamma_{\cdot i} + u_{\cdot i}\,, \tag{5}$$

where $y_{\cdot i}$ is the ith column of

$$Y = (y_{\cdot 1}, y_{\cdot 2}, \ldots, y_{\cdot m}) = (y_{ti})\,, \qquad t = 1, 2, \ldots, T;\ i = 1, 2, \ldots, m. \tag{6}$$

If we put

$$X = (x_{\cdot 1}, x_{\cdot 2}, \ldots, x_{\cdot G}) = (x_{tj})\,, \qquad t = 1, 2, \ldots, T; j = 1, 2, \ldots, m, \tag{7}$$

then Y_i, X_i in (5) are appropriate submatrices of Y, X respectively; $\beta_{\cdot i}, \gamma_{\cdot i}$ are the ith columns of B, C, respectively after suppression of elements known to be zero. Finally $u_{\cdot i}$ is the ith column of

$$U = (u_{\cdot 1}, u_{\cdot 2}, \ldots, u_{\cdot m}) = (u_{ti})\,, \qquad t = 1, 2, \ldots, T;\ i = 1, 2, \ldots, m. \tag{8}$$

The model in (3) may be written more completely as

$$Y = YB + XC + U\,, \tag{9}$$

from which we can obtain the reduced form

$$Y = X\Pi + V\,, \qquad \Pi = C(I - B)^{-1}\,, \qquad V = U(I - B)^{-1}\,. \tag{10}$$

The SLS estimator is obtained by minimizing

$$\sum_{t=1}^{T} (y_{t.} - x_{t.}\Pi)(y_{t.} - x_{t.}\Pi)' = \operatorname{tr}(Y - X\Pi)'(Y - X\Pi)\,, \tag{11}$$

with respect to the unknown elements of C and B.

A slight rearrangement of (11) yields the alternative expression

$$\operatorname{tr}(Y - X\Pi)'(Y - X\Pi) = \operatorname{tr} K^{-1}A'Z'ZA\,, \tag{12}$$

where

$$A = \begin{pmatrix} I - B \\ -C \end{pmatrix}, \qquad Z = (Y, X), \qquad K = (I - B')(I - B).$$

At this stage it is enlightening to compare the minimands of 3SLS, 2SLS and FIML to that of SLS. The minimands of the first two estimating procedures are given, respectively, by tr $\Sigma^{-1}A'\tilde{Z}'\tilde{Z}A$ and tr $A'\tilde{Z}'\tilde{Z}A$, where

$$\tilde{Z} = (\tilde{Y}, X), \qquad \tilde{Y} = NY, \qquad N = X(X'X)^{-1}X'.$$

The concentrated likelihood function, after elimination of Σ by partial maximization is given by

$$L(A;\ Y, X) = -\frac{mT}{2} \ln[(2\pi) + 1] + \frac{T}{2} \ln|(I - B')(I - B)| - \frac{T}{2} \ln|A'Z'ZA|. \tag{13}$$

Thus FIML obtains estimators of B, C by *minimizing*

$$\ln|K^{-1}A'Z'ZA| = \ln|(1 - B')^{-1}A'Z'ZA(1 - B)^{-1} = \ln|(Y - X\Pi)'(Y - X\Pi)|, \tag{14}$$

where the definition $\Pi = C(1 - B)^{-1}$ is taken into account and the restrictions on C and B are respected. Thus, the minimands of FIML and SLS, are, respectively the determinant and the trace of the matrix $(Y - X\Pi)'(Y - X\Pi)$, which in the face of the restrictions on Π, again demonstrates the limited information character of SLS.

It would appear that a full information version of SLS would have to be obtained from

$$\text{tr}\, \Omega^{-1}(Y - X\Pi)'(Y - X\Pi), \tag{15}$$

where Ω is the covariance matrix of reduced form errors[2]

$$\Omega = (I - B')^{-1}\Sigma(I - B)^{-1}.$$

[2] It is interesting that in the discussion of minimum distance estimators, when specialized to the case under consideration Malinvaud [6, (Chapter 9)] observes that the estimatorminim izing

$$\text{tr}\, \hat{\Omega}^{-1}(Y - X\Pi)'(Y - X\Pi)$$

is asymptotically efficient when the structural errors are joinltly normal. In the above $\hat{\Omega}$ is a consistent estimator of the reduced form error covariance matrix and Π is estimated subject to the constraint that

$$\Pi(I - B) = C.$$

If we operate with (15) and make use of the definition of Ω, it is easy to see that the estimators of B, C obtained by minimizing

$$\text{tr}\, \tilde{\Sigma}^{-1}A'Z'ZA$$

are inconsistent, where $\tilde{\Sigma}$ is a (prior) consistent estimator of Σ.

In obtaining the normal equations for the SLS estimator it is more convenient to group the unknown parameters according to

$$(16) \qquad \delta = (\gamma', \beta')', \quad \gamma = (\gamma'_{.1}, \gamma'_{.2}, \ldots, \gamma'_{.m})', \quad \beta = (\beta'_{.1}, \beta'_{.2}, \ldots, \beta'_{.m})'$$

instead of the customary grouping, $\delta = (\delta'_{.1}, \delta'_{.2}, \ldots, \delta'_{.m})'$, $\delta_{.i} = (\beta'_{.i}, \gamma'_{.i})'$. Observations on the model in (3) or (5) may then be written in the compact form

$$(17) \qquad y = Z^*\delta + u,$$

where

$$(18) \qquad \begin{aligned} y &= (y'_{.1}, y'_{.2}, \ldots, y'_{.m})', & X^* &= \operatorname{diag}(X_1, X_2, \ldots, X_m), \\ Y^* &= \operatorname{diag}(Y_1, Y_2, \ldots, Y_m), & Z^* &= (X^*, Y^*), \\ u &= (u'_{.1}, u'_{.2}, \ldots, u'_{.m})'. \end{aligned}$$

The normal equations for the SLS estimator are obtained as

$$(19) \qquad \begin{aligned} f(\delta) = Z^{*\prime}(K^{-1} \otimes I_T)Z^*\delta &= Z^{*\prime}(K^{-1} \otimes I_T)y \\ &+ \begin{pmatrix} 0 \\ V^{*\prime} \end{pmatrix}(K^{-1} \otimes I_T)(y - Z^*\delta), \end{aligned}$$

where

$$(20) \qquad V^* = \operatorname{diag}(V_1, V_2, \ldots, V_m), \quad V_i = Y_i - X\Pi_i, \qquad i = 1, 2, \ldots, m.$$

Remark 1. Equation (19) suggests a possibly efficient algorithm for obtaining the SLS estimator—as a solution of the equation $f(\delta) = 0$—by iteration. Thus, suppose an initial consistent estimator is available for δ, say $\tilde{\delta}_{(0)}$. We thus compute the quantities $\tilde{K}^{-1}$, $\tilde{V}_i = Y_i - \tilde{Y}_i$, $\tilde{Y}_i = X\tilde{\Pi}_i$ and obtain the first iterate

$$(21) \qquad \tilde{\delta}_{(1)} = [\tilde{Z}^{*\prime}(\tilde{K}^{-1} \otimes I_T)Z^*]^{-1}[\tilde{Z}^{*\prime}(\tilde{K}^{-1} \otimes I_T)y],$$

where

$$(22) \qquad \tilde{Z}^* = (X^*, \tilde{Y}^*), \qquad \tilde{Y}^* = \operatorname{diag}(\tilde{Y}_1, \tilde{Y}_2, \ldots, \tilde{Y}_m).$$

It is then clear that given $\tilde{\delta}_{(1)}$ we can obtain $\tilde{\delta}_{(2)}$ and continue until convergence is attained. Of course, the conditions under which convergence holds will have to be established. *It is clear that the converging iterate is the SLS estimator.*

Remark 2. It is evident from (21) that all iterates—beyond the initial consistent estimator $\tilde{\delta}_{(0)}$—have an interpretation as instrumental variables (I.V.) estimators with instrumental matrix $\tilde{Z}^{*\prime}(\tilde{K}^{-1} \otimes I)$.

Remark 3. The expression in (21) elucidates the comments made at the end of Section 1. Thus, we see that SLS proceeds analogously with the 3SLS estimator except that it uses the irrelevant matrix $\tilde{K}^{-1}$ instead of $\tilde{\Sigma}^{-1}$ and "purges" the current endogenous variables in each equation by using the *restricted reduced form residuals*. We remind the reader that 3SLS has an interpretation as an I.V. estimator obeying a relation like (21) in which $\tilde{K}^{-1}$ is replaced by $\tilde{\Sigma}^{-1}$ and $\tilde{Y}^*$

is obtained from the *unrestricted reduced form* by ordinary least squares. Thus, although SLS has the appearance (and the computational burden) of a full information estimator, it is essentially a limited information one.

Remark 4. The initial consistent estimator $\tilde{\tilde{\delta}}_{(0)}$ may be easily obtained from equations (5) by using as instruments, in addition to the included predetermined variables, other (excluded) predetermined variables. In view of the identifiability condition it will always be possible to obtain $\tilde{\tilde{\delta}}_{(0)}$. In fact there is a multiplicity of such estimators. For the reasons above, perhaps SLS is more aptly named the restricted reduced form iterated instrumental variables (RRFIIV) estimator.

From (21) we immediately have

LEMMA 1. *The iterates of the RRFIIV estimator are consistent provided*

$$\text{(23)} \qquad \lim_{T\to\infty} \frac{\bar{Z}^{*\prime}(K^{-1} \otimes I_T)\bar{Z}^*}{T} = \Psi$$

exists as a nonsigular matrix, where

$$\text{(24)} \qquad \bar{Z}^* = (X^*, \bar{Y}^*), \quad \bar{Y}^* = \operatorname{diag}(\bar{Y}_1, \bar{Y}_2, \ldots, \bar{Y}_m), \quad \bar{Y}_i = X\Pi_i, \quad i = 1, 2, \ldots, m.$$

PROOF. It will be sufficient to prove the consistency of $\tilde{\tilde{\delta}}_{(1)}$. Thus,

$$\text{(25)} \qquad \tilde{\tilde{\delta}}_{(1)} - \delta^0 = [\tilde{Z}^{*\prime}(\tilde{K}^{-1} \otimes I_T)Z^*]^{-1}\tilde{Z}^{*\prime}(\tilde{K}^{-1} \otimes I_T)u,$$

and the result follows immediately from the consistency of $\tilde{\tilde{\delta}}_{(0)}$ and the nonstochastic character of the predetermined variables.[3]

COROLLARY 1. *If the RRFIIV (SLS) estimator can be obtained through the iteration of* (21), *then it is consistent.*

PROOF. Obvious from Lemma 1.

Remark 5. Although Corollary 1 qualifies the consistency property, in fact Brown [2] assumes iterative convergence beginning from an unspecified initial condition. Nakamura [2] takes convergence of the Brown process as given or, at any rate, assumes that the minimizing solution has been somehow obtained. Thus, the corollary above may be viewed as an alternative proof of consistency.

LEMMA 2. *All iterates have the same asymptotic distribution.*

PROOF. It is clear that for any $i \geq 1$

$$\text{(26)} \qquad \operatorname*{plim}_{T\to\infty} \sqrt{T}(\tilde{\tilde{\delta}}_{(i)} - \delta^0) = \psi^{-1} \operatorname*{plim}_{T\to\infty} \frac{1}{\sqrt{T}} \bar{Z}^{*\prime}(K^{-1} \otimes I_T)u.$$

Thus, asymptotically,

$$\sqrt{T}(\tilde{\tilde{\delta}}_{(i)} - \delta^0) \sim \sqrt{T}(\tilde{\tilde{\delta}}_{(1)} - \delta^0), \qquad i = 2, 3, \ldots.$$

[3] Actually independence of, or even uncorrelatedness with the elements of u would be sufficient to establish consistency. In (25) δ^0 is the "true" parameter vector.

Remark 6. Lemma 2 does not imply that "iteration does not matter." It states that it does not matter for "large samples." Evidently, small sample properties will differ according as the estimator we obtain satisfies $f(\hat{\delta}) = 0$ or not. *What we my deduce, however, is that, if we terminate the iteration after k steps, the resulting estimator has the same properties as the converging iterate, if one exists.*

The asymptotic distribution is given by

LEMMA 3. *The RRFIIV (SLS) estimator has, asymptotically, the distribution*

$$\sqrt{T}\,(\hat{\delta} - \delta^0) \sim N(0, \Phi)\,, \tag{27}$$

where

$$\Phi = \Psi^{-1}\left[\lim_{T\to\infty} \frac{\bar{Z}^{*\prime}(K^{-1} \otimes I_T)(\Sigma \otimes I_T)(K^{-1} \otimes I_T)\bar{Z}^*}{T}\right]\Psi^{-1}\,. \tag{28}$$

PROOF. Utilizing the result in (26) it will be sufficient to obtain the asymptotic distribution of $(1/\sqrt{T})\bar{Z}^{*\prime}(K^{-1} \otimes I_T)u$. To this effect see, for example, [**3**, (254)] or [**4**, (Chapter 3)]. Now define the matrices

$$R_s^{(i)} = {}_i x'_{s\cdot} k^*_{i\cdot}\,, \qquad Q_s^{(i)} = {}_i \bar{y}'_s k^*_{i\cdot}\,, \qquad i = 1, 2, \ldots, m;\ s = 1, 2, \ldots, T, \tag{29}$$

where ${}_i x'_{s\cdot}$ is sth column of X'_i, ${}_i \bar{y}'_{s\cdot}$ is sth column of $\bar{Y}_i$ and each contains, respectively, G_i and m_i elements; evidently, $k^*_{i\cdot}$ is the ith row of K^{-1}. Let

$$R_s = \begin{bmatrix} R_s^{(1)} \\ \vdots \\ R_s^{(m)} \end{bmatrix}, \qquad Q_s = \begin{bmatrix} Q_s^{(1)} \\ \vdots \\ Q_s^{(m)} \end{bmatrix}, \qquad P_s = \begin{bmatrix} R_s \\ Q_s \end{bmatrix}. \tag{30}$$

Noting that P_s is a matrix of dimension $\sum_{i=1}^m (m_i + G_i)xm$ we may thus write

$$\frac{1}{\sqrt{T}}\,\bar{Z}^{*\prime}(K^{-1} \otimes I_T)u = \frac{1}{\sqrt{T}} \sum_{s=1}^{T} P_s u'_s\,. \tag{31}$$

But $\{P_s u'_{s\cdot} : s = 1, 2, \ldots\}$ is a sequence of mutually independent nonidentically distributed random variables with mean zero and covariance matrix $P_s \Sigma P'_s$. We further note that

$$\lim_{T\to\infty} \frac{1}{T} \sum_{s=1}^{T} P_s \Sigma P'_s = \lim_{T\to\infty} \frac{1}{T}\,[\bar{Z}^{*\prime}(K^{-1} \otimes I_T)(\Sigma \otimes I_T)(K^{-1} \otimes I_T)\bar{Z}^*] \tag{32}$$

which we may assert to be a nonsingular matrix with finite elements. It may also be shown that the Lindeberg-Feller condition (see [**4**, (Chapter 3)]) is satisfied and thus

$$\frac{1}{\sqrt{T}}\,\bar{Z}^{*\prime}[K^{-1} \otimes I_T]u \sim N\left(0,\ \lim_{T\to\infty} \frac{1}{T} \sum_{s=1}^{T} P_s \Sigma P'_s\right). \tag{33}$$

From (26) it then follows immediately that

$$\sqrt{T}\,(\hat{\delta} - \delta^0) \sim N(0, \Phi)\,. \tag{34}$$

q.e.d.

The proof above, strictly speaking, applies to the iterates of equation (21) and would give the distribution of the SLS estimator only when the iteration converges. If the equation $f(\delta) = 0$ has a consistent solution—which must be obtained by a procedure other than the one given in (21)—then an alternative argument can establish the asymptotic distribution of the estimator. Thus, by the mean value theorem, write

$$f(\hat{\delta}) = f(\delta^0) + \frac{d}{d\delta} f(\delta^*)(\hat{\delta} - \delta^0), \tag{35}$$

where δ^* lies between δ^0 and $\hat{\delta}$. One can then show that

$$\operatorname*{plim}_{T\to\infty} \frac{1}{T} \frac{d}{d\delta} f(\delta^*) = \Psi. \tag{36}$$

Moreover, by establishing the asymptotic distribution of $(1/\sqrt{T})f(\delta^0)$ one obtains the result given in Lemma 3.

Remark 7. If we waive the condition that the predetermined variables are nonstochastic and, in particular, if we admit lagged endogenous variables a certain complication will arise. Thus in (31) we would no longer be dealing with a sequence of independent random vectors. However, if we obtain the final form of the model—see [**4**, (Chapter 12)]—we can express the lagged endogenous variables in terms of the exogenous variables and a certain rational lag in the structural errors. Because we shall impose a stability condition on the model it will be possible to deduce *mutatis mutandis*, exactly the same results as in Lemma 3 by the application of a central limit theorem on m-dependent variables. For extensive applications of this approach, see [**5**].

We have therefore established

THEOREM 1. *Consider the model in* (3) *subject to the assumptions and conditions given in Section* 2. *Then*

i. The RRFIIV (*SLS*) *estimator has and interpretation as an instrumental variables estimator.*

ii. It may be obtained by iteration, as given in equation (21), *provided the iteration converges.*

iii. If we begin the process with an initial consistent estimator then all subsequent iterates are consistent.

iv. All iterates have the same asymptotic distribution.

v. The asymptotic distribution of the converging iterate (*if one exists*), *in fact of every iterate, is given by* $\sqrt{T}(\hat{\delta} - \delta^0) \sim N(0, \Phi)$ where Φ *is as given in* (28).

3. COMPARISON WITH 2SLS AND 3SLS ESTIMATORS

Having obtained the asymptotic distribution of RRFIIV it is now rather simple to appraise its efficiency relative to that of 3SLS or full information maximum likelihood (FIML) estimators. The asymptotic distribution of 3SLS is given by

$$\sqrt{T}(\hat{\delta}_{3SLS} - \delta^0) \sim N(0, C_3) \tag{37}$$

where

$$C_3 = \lim_{T\to\infty}\left[\frac{\bar{Z}^{*\prime}(\Sigma^{-1}\otimes I_T)\bar{Z}^*}{T}\right]^{-1}. \tag{38}$$

We have

LEMMA 4. *RRFIIV (SLS) estimators are asymptotically inefficient relative to 3SLS.*

PROOF. We show that the difference of the two covariance matrices is positive semidefinite. Now, define D by

$$\begin{aligned}&[\bar{Z}^{*\prime}(K^{-1}\otimes I_T)\bar{Z}^*]^{-1}\bar{Z}^{*\prime}(K^{-1}\otimes I_T)\\ &\quad= [\bar{Z}^{*\prime}(\Sigma^{-1}\otimes I_T)\bar{Z}^*]^{-1}\bar{Z}^{*\prime}(\Sigma^{-1}\otimes I_T) + D,\end{aligned} \tag{39}$$

and observe that $D\bar{Z}^* = 0$. Multiply both sides of (39) by $(\Sigma\otimes I_T)$ to obtain

$$\begin{aligned}&[\bar{Z}^{*\prime}(K^{-1}\otimes I_T)\bar{Z}^*]^{-1}\bar{Z}^{*\prime}(K^{-1}\otimes I_T)(\Sigma\otimes I_T)\\ &\quad= [\bar{Z}^{*\prime}(\Sigma^{-1}\otimes I_T)\bar{Z}^*]^{-1}\bar{Z}^{*\prime} + D(\Sigma\otimes I_T).\end{aligned} \tag{40}$$

Postmultiply (40) by T times the transpose of (39) and take limits to obtain

$$\Phi = C_3 + \lim_{T\to\infty} TD(\Sigma\otimes I_T)D', \tag{41}$$

which establishes the desired result.

COROLLARY 2. *3SLS is strictly efficient relative to RRFIIV (SLS), in the sense that for at least one element of $\hat{\delta}$ the asymptotic 3SLS variance is strictly less than the corresponding SLS variance, unless*

$$\lim_{T\to\infty} TD(\Sigma\otimes I_T)D' = 0. \tag{42}$$

PROOF. Obvious from the Lemma.

LEMMA 5. *RRFIIV (SLS) has the same asymptotic distribution as 3SLS if*
i. $K = \Sigma$
ii. All equations of the system are just identified.

PROOF. Obvious from (39) since, under either *i.* or *ii.*, $D = 0$.

Remark 8. Since 3SLS and FIML have the same asymptotic distribution, under normality of the structural errors, Lemmas 4, 5 and Corollary 2 hold with respect to FIML estimators as well.

The relation of RRFIIV (SLS) to 2SLS and limited information maximum likelihood (LIML) estimators is established by

LEMMA 6. *RRFIIV (SLS) estimators are asymtotically*

i. equivalent to 2SLS if the equations of the system are just identified, or if K^{-1} is a diagonal matrix.

ii. efficient relative to 2SLS if $K = \Sigma$, or (by contiunity) if $K^{-1} = \Sigma^{-1} + \varepsilon R$, for suitably small ε, R being some $m \times m$ matrix such that $\Sigma^{-1} + \varepsilon R$ is nonsingular.

iii. inefficient relative to 2SLS if Σ is a diagonal matrix.

PROOF. To prove *i.* we observe first that

$$\sqrt{T}\,(\hat{\delta}_{2SLS} - \delta^0) \sim N(0, C_2)\,, \tag{43}$$

where

$$C_2 = \lim_{T\to\infty}\left[\left(\frac{\bar{Z}^{*\prime}\bar{Z}^{*}}{T}\right)^{-1} \frac{\bar{Z}^{*\prime}(\Sigma\otimes I_T)\bar{Z}^{*}}{T}\left(\frac{\bar{Z}^{*\prime}\bar{Z}^{*}}{T}\right)^{-1}\right]. \tag{44}$$

When K^{-1} is a diagonal matrix, then

$$[\bar{Z}^{*\prime}(K^{-1}\otimes I_T)\bar{Z}^{*}]^{-1}\bar{Z}^{*\prime}(K^{-1}\otimes I_T) = (\bar{Z}^{*\prime}\bar{Z}^{*})^{-1}\bar{Z}^{*\prime}\,, \tag{45}$$

and it is easily verified that

$$\Phi = C_2\,. \tag{46}$$

When the system is just identified 2SLS coincides with 3SLS and thus the first part of *i.* follows from Lemma 4.

To prove *ii.* we note that if $K = \Sigma$ then $\Phi = C_3$; the second part of *ii.* follows easily by continuity and the arguments given in [**1**, (Chapter 4)].

To prove *iii.* we note that when Σ is diagonal, then

$$C_2 = C_3\,. \tag{47}$$

The result then follows from Lemma 4.

Remark 9. Since LIML has the same asymptotic distribution as 2SLS Lemma 6 applies to LIML estimators as well. It is possible to give more precise conditions under which 2SLS is inefficient or efficient relative to RRFIIV (SLS) estimators in terms of the relation between the characteristic roots of K^{-1} and those of Σ. It does not seem worthwhile to do so, however, since our inability to rank RRFIIV (SLS) relative to 2SLS is well established by Lemma 6.

We have therefore established

THEOREM 2. *RRFIIV (SLS) estimators are inefficient relative to* 3*SLS or FIML in the sense that the difference of the covariance matrices of their respective asymptotic distributions—in the order stated—is a positive semidefinite matrix. Thus, FIML and* 3*SLS dominate RRFIIV (SLS).*

It is not possible to rank, uniformly, RRFIIV (SLS) and 2*SLS or LIML estimators in terms of relative asymptotic efficiency. They are equivalent if K^{-1} is a diagonal matrix,* 2*SLS (or LIML) dominates if Σ is a diagonal matrix, and RRFIIV (SLS) dominates if $K = \Sigma$.*

4. CONCLUSION

In this paper we have studied extensively the properties of the SLS estimator proposed by Brown [2]. We have given it an iterated instrumental variables estimator interpretation and have shown that if we begin the iteration with a consistent estimate then all subsequent iterates are consistent. Moreover we have established that SLS is (asymptotically) dominated by 3SLS (or FIML) estimators and that it neither dominates nor is dominated by 2SLS (or LIML) estimators. Which of the two situations holds depends on the parametric configuration of the problem.

University of Pennsylvania, U.S.A.

APPENDIX

Here we give the results of a very limited Monte Carlo experiment.[1] Its purpose is to illustrate the properties of RRFIIV (SLS) relative to 2SLS and to give some indication about the properties of the iteration procedure described in equation (21) of the text.

The model utilized was

$$y_{t1} = -0.3y_{t2} + 3 + 0.5x_{t1} - 0.8x_{t2} \qquad\qquad + u_{t1}$$

$$y_{t2} = -0.5y_{t1} + 2 \qquad\qquad + 0.6xt_3 + 1.5x_{t4} + u_{t2}\,.$$

The error vectors (u_{t1}, u_{t2}), were generated from a zero mean multivariate normal process with covarianc matrix

$$\Sigma_u = \begin{bmatrix} 1 & 1 \\ 1 & 3.56 \end{bmatrix}.$$

The exogenous variables were generated by a zero mean multivariate normal process with covariance matrix.

$$\Sigma_x = \begin{bmatrix} 16 & 4 & 4 & 8 \\ 4 & 10 & 4 & 2 \\ 4 & 4 & 6 & 4 \\ 8 & 2 & 4 & 21 \end{bmatrix}.$$

We have generated 100 samples, each with 100 "observations." Initial consistent estimators were obtained by using as instruments for the first equation, (x_{t1}, x_{t2}, x_{t4}) and for the second equation (x_{t2}, x_{t3}, x_{t4}).

Convergence of the iteration is summarized in the table below

TABLE 1

CONVERGENCE CHARACTERISTICS OF THE ITERATION

Iteration No.	1	2	3	4	5	6	7	8	9	10
Frequency of Convergence	0	2	26	59	11	0	1	0	1	0

[1] All computations were carried out by Taku Yamamoto, to whom I am indebted for very able research assistance.

The criterion of convergence employed was

$$\left| \frac{\delta_i^{(k)} - \delta_i^{(k+1)}}{\delta_i^{(k)}} \right| < .0001 \text{ for all } i$$

where δ_i is the ith structural parameters to be estimated. Other characteristics of the two procedures are given below.

TABLE 2

BIAS CHARACTERISTICS

True Parameter	3.0	0.5	−0.8	−0.3	2.0	0.6	1.5	−0.5
SLS	−0.00231	−0.00055	−0.00378	0.00498	0.00253	−0.00783	−0.00334	0.00043
2 SLS	−0.00216	0.00023	−0.00494	0.00590	0.00062	−0.00854	−0.00262	0.00044

TABLE 3

MEAN SQUARED ERRORS

SLS	.99422	.09271	.18000	.45696	6.39732	.75260	.45796	.02220
2 SLS	.93208	.07726	.18038	.44586	6.19943	.90809	.45427	.02132

If we consider the matrix difference $MSE_{SLS} - MSE_{2SLS}$ we find that the characteristic roots of this matrix are

$$-0.194, -0.020, -0.002, -0.0003, 0.00003, 0.001, 0.088, 0.262.$$

The results above can be summarized as follows:

i. Convergence is obtained rapidly; in 87% of the cases we have convergence in 4 or fewer iterations.

ii. Of the two procedures, SLS and 2SLS none can be said to dominate, much as one is led to expect from the discussion in the text. In particular, the difference in the mean squared error matrices of the two estimators is indefinite.

REFERENCES

[1] BELLMAN, R., *Introduction to Matrix Analysis* (New York: McGraw-Hill, 1960).

[2] BROWN, T. M., "Simultaneous Least Squares: A Distribution-free Method of Equation System Structure Estimation," *International Economic Review*, I (September, 1960), 173–191.

[3] CRAMER, H., *Mathematical Methods of Statistics* (Princeton: Princeton University Press, 1964).

[4] DHRYMES, P. J., *Econometrics: Statistical Foundations and Applications* (New York: Harper and Row, 1970).

[5] ———, *Distributed Lags: Problems of Estimation and Formulation* (San Francisco: Holden-Day, 1971).

[6] MALINVAUD, E., *Statistical Methods of Econometrics* (Chicago: Rand McNally and Company, 1966).

[7] NAKAMURA, M., "A Note on the Consistency of Simultaneous Least Squares Estimation," *International Economic Review*, I (September, 1960), 192–197.

[6]

Annals of Economic and Social Measurement, 1/3, 1972

CRITERIA FOR EVALUATION OF ECONOMETRIC MODELS*

BY PHOEBUS J. DHRYMES, E. PHILIP HOWREY, SAUL H. HYMANS, JAN KMENTA, EDWARD E. LEAMER, RICHARD E. QUANDT, JAMES B. RAMSEY, HAROLD T. SHAPIRO AND VICTOR ZARNOWITZ

This multi-authored article develops a framework for systematically evaluating large scale econometric models. Reasonably self-contained aspects of model evaluation include parametric evaluation prior to the "release" of the model (model selection, parameter estimation, and pseudo-forecasts and structural stability tests) and evaluation after "release" of the model. Many operational procedures for parametric evaluation are noted; alternative, ad hoc procedures are necessary in some cases, given the present state of the art. Non-parametric "validation" procedures are then outlined. These include single-variable measures, tracking measures, error decomposition, and cyclical and dynamic properties. A statistical appendix sketches some of the theoretical results used in the paper.

I. INTRODUCTION

For purposes of this paper an econometric model is considered to be an analytical representation of one or more statements about economic behavior, which representation relies upon statistical implementation for the purposes of hypothesis testing, parameter estimation, or use in prediction or simulation circumstances. A model in this sense may be anything from a single linear equation to a complicated set of simultaneous, non-linear equations. The term "model evaluation" is here used to encompass a broad set of tests to which a model can and should be subjected at many different stages during the process of construction and subsequent use.

During the past decade econometric models have come in for increasingly widespread use by government (for policy analysis and forecasting), by industry (largely as a forecasting tool), and by universities (for instructional use and a wide variety of research purposes). Despite the growing importance of such models in various decision-making situations, the process of systematic model evaluation has—with some noteworthy exceptions—lagged seriously behind the process of multi-model proliferation. Within the past few years, however, a handful of significant attempts have been made—with respect to large scale econometric models—to conduct serious cross-model comparisons. Building on a series of pioneering efforts by Carl Christ [10], Irma Adelman [1], Henri Theil [50], and others, the studies of Zarnowitz, Boschan and Moore [57], and Evans, Haitovsky and Treyz [21] are examples of current research work in this area. Particular model builders, of course, have also subjected their own models to careful "audits" both on sample and post-sample data. At the level of subsector and single equation

* This paper is a joint effort of the authors listed and was undertaken as a project of the Seminar on Criteria for the Evaluation of Econometric Models (S. H. Hymans and H. T. Shapiro, co-chairmen) of the Conference on Econometrics and Mathematical Economics, sponsored by the National Bureau of Economic Research and the National Science Foundation. An earlier version of this paper was presented at the Brookings Model Conference, Washington, D.C. February 11–12, 1972. The authors are grateful to Professors C. Christ, R. A. Gordon, L. R. Klein and L. D. Taylor for their continuing help during many stages of the writing of this paper.

models recent work by Bischoff [7], Hymans [37], [38], and Jorgenson, Hunter, and Nadiri [39] may be cited as examples of cross-model evaluations. What stands out most clearly from all these evaluation exercises is that, aside from the simplest single-equation cases we suffer the lack of a clear and accepted analytical basis for the selection of proper criteria for model evaluation. This is true with respect to the criteria by which a single model should be evaluated and holds a-fortiori in the case of cross-model evaluations. This state of affairs has been the motivation for several recent papers, [21] [36], and is the *raison-d'etre* for the NBER-NSF sponsored seminar which has led to this paper.

In the next section of this paper, we shall outline a framework which decomposes the evaluation set into fairly natural subsets, and thus permits the orderly discussion of reasonably self-contained aspects of model evaluation. These are discussed in turn in succeeding sections of the paper.

It has been our aim to suggest operational procedures for evaluation whenever possible, and to compare alternative procedures whenever our knowledge permits. To this end, a number of statistical derivations and proofs have been relegated to an appendix in order that the flow of discussion in the body of the paper may be more easily digested. While we have succeeded in arriving at some useful "recipes" for particular evaluation circumstances, there are still gaping holes in our knowledge. For some evaluation problems we simply have nothing to suggest for a "best practice" procedure, and we have had to be content with a brief and general enumeration of the alternative, often ad hoc, procedures which are in current use or under current study. Most of what we have to say is in direct reference to time series econometric models, but much of what follows applies to cross-section models with perhaps minor rephrasing.

II. Aspects of Model Evaluation

What we (as builders, users or judges of models) choose to do in the process of evaluating an econometric model is heavily dependent on what we have chosen to axiomatize. At an early stage in the life of a model we may regard its functional form as "up for grabs," as something yet to be determined. At a later stage, after the model has already been "certified" with respect to functional form, we may choose to test hypotheses about parameter values within the confines of the functional form already settled upon or axiomated.[1] Alternatively, we may take the approach which one of the authors has called "Sherlock Holmes inference," a process of data analysis in which Sherlock the econometrician weaves together all the bits of evidence into a plausible story. In this view, it is taken as axiomatic that the process being modeled is far too complicated and the data available far too weak to be able to specify and implement a structurally and behaviorally sound representation. Such notions as parametric hypothesis testing, best linear unbiased estimators, and the like are then wholly irrelevant, if not dangerously misleading. Nearly all that remains is a series of evaluative measurements specified in the light of the particular uses to which it is desired to put the model. At best,

[1] This is the basic set-up in the classical statistical procedures based on the work of Fisher, Neyman, Pearson and others.

the model can tentatively be certified as a reasonable tool for specific uses until it errs seriously and is found to have a fatal uncorrectable flaw, or until it is replaced by a better "untrue" model.[2] Sherlock Holmes' inference leads naturally to evaluation procedures heavily geared to the specific potential uses of the model, that is, to the calculation of performance statistics with generally unknown probability characteristics (and a strong presumption of stochastic dependence which even eliminates the possibility of conducting distribution-free statistical tests). Procedures of this kind have also had to be employed in the evaluation of models originally constructed under a strong stochastic axiomatization. This has been necessitated, for example, by the fact that we have not yet succeeded in identifying a uniquely proper way to evaluate a matrix of dynamically generated time series forecasts of all the endogenous variables in a macroeconometric model. Nor do we fully understand the stochastic properties of such a matrix,[3] a necessary first step in the generation of any statistically valid inference procedure.

To break this formidable evaluation process down into a series of manageable problems, we propose first a binary split into categories which we shall refer to as *parametric* and *non-parametric* evaluation. An evaluation procedure is said to be parametric if it relies on a formal statistical test based on the stochastic specification assumed to apply to the econometric model. Non-parametric evaluation is concerned with specialized and descriptive procedures such as those mentioned in the previous paragraph. Such procedures are not derived from the stochastic assumptions of the model, and they rarely depend on formal tests of significance. It is our view that non-parametric evaluation can be important and valid under many different axiomatizations, and we shall discuss this matter more fully in section V below. Our discussion of parametric evaluation will proceed according to the following outline:

Parametric Evaluation

1. Prior to "release" of the model
   (a) Model selection
   (b) Hypothesis tests and parameter estimation
   (c) Pseudo-forecasts and structural stability tests
2. Subsequent to "release" of the model
   (a) Availability of a small post-sample data set: predictive testing, pooling of sample and post-sample data.
   (b) Availability of a large post-sample data set.

III. Parametric Evaluation: Prior to Model Release

In this section we discuss a number of aspects of evaluation which are considered as taking place during the process of model construction and continuing through to the first time the model builder actually "puts his money" on the results generated by the model.

[2] This is not the first time that economists have heard such arguments.
[3] Except possibly for some very simple cases.

(a) Model Selection

The term "model selection" here refers to the problem of choosing between alternative functional representations of an economic relation. The classical statistical procedures which most economics graduate students are required to internalize depend very heavily on a specification axiom. These procedures yield likelihood ratio tests, minimum variance estimators and predictors, and other such munificent benefits all under the assumption that $Y = X\beta + \varepsilon$ and its familiar accompanying probability statements accurately reflect the true state of affairs. As practicing economists we are well aware that a logically prior problem exists. Economic theory gives preciously few clues as to the functional forms appropriate to the specification of economic relationships, and the presence of random error terms in stochastically specified equations adds an additional element of functional ambiguity. In certain cases, known in the literature as situations of "nested hypotheses," classical statistical techniques provide sound discriminating procedures limited in power "only" by the quantity and richness of the sample evidence. Classical techniques are woefully silent in the case of non-nested hypotheses, or disparate families of hypotheses, but research is being done in this area and there is also the possibility of a useful Bayesian approach to such problems.

Techniques for the handling of pairs of nested hypotheses in a linear econometric model are by now second nature in the profession. They are well-documented in our standard textbooks and there is little to be gained by any review here. Let us turn directly to the less understood problem of selecting among alternative model specifications which cannot be represented in the framework of nested hypotheses.

Ramsey has made an interesting beginning in the analysis of non-nested linear models [46]. Suppose we consider two alternative specifications of a linear-in-the-parameters model to explain the dependent variable Y:

$$H_0: E[Y X] = X\beta$$

$$H_A: E[Y|Z] = Z\gamma,$$

where $Z = g(X)$, and the function g represents a non-stochastic, non-linear transformation. H_0 is the maintained hypothesis, while H_A is the alternative hypothesis. If H_A is true, then the regression calculated under H_0 has used an incorrect functional form for the regressors. Letting u denote the vector of residuals from the least squares regression of Y on X, it is easily shown [46; pp. 353–354] that

$$E[u|X, H_0] = 0,$$

and

$$E[u|X, H_A] = MZ\gamma$$

where $M = [I - X(X'X)^{-1}X']$. Using $Z = g(X)$, the second relation can be written as

$$E[u|X, H_A] = Mg(X)\gamma = h(X)\gamma,$$

where $h(X) = Mg(X)$.

Ramsey reasons[4] that

(i) $h(X)$ can be approximated as a multivariate power series in the X variables,

(ii) The predicted values of Y from the regression of Y on X, say $\hat{Y}$, are linear functions of X, and therefore,

(iii) It should be possible to approximate $h(X)$ by a power series in $\hat{Y}$. It is therefore approximately true that

$$E[u|X, H_A] \cong \sum_{j=2}^{J} \hat{Y}^j \alpha_j,$$

where

(i) the number J represents a Jth degree power series approximation to $h(X)$,

(ii) the index j begins with $j = 2$ since the least squares residuals are uncorrelated with $\hat{Y}$, and

(iii) $\hat{Y}^j$ refers to the jth power of $\hat{Y}$, element by element.

Under H_0, all the α_j should be zero; under H_A at least some of the α_j should be non-zero. Ramsey's idea, then, is to regress the residuals on powers of $\hat{Y}$ and test the hypothesis that the vector $\alpha = (\alpha_2, \alpha_3, \ldots, \alpha_J)'$ is null. Rejecting the null hypothesis on α is equivalent to rejecting H_0 in favor of some hypothesis of the form H_A.[5] In point of fact, Ramsey carries out the above test, not on the least squares residuals, but on Theil's BLUS residuals [51; chapter 5]. The idea is the same, but the BLUS residuals yield more convenient stochastic properties which permit the test on the vector α to be carried out by the usual multiple regression F-test, provided one begins with the assumption of (conditional) normality of the vector Y.[6]

An alternative approach to the problem, one not limited to the linear model framework and not requiring any condition analogous to the $Z = g(X)$ requirement in the Ramsey approach, may be formulated as follows. Let two alternative specifications of an economic relation be represented by the hypotheses H_f and H_g. According to H_f the random variable Y has probability density function (p.d.f.) $f(y; \alpha)$, with the parameter α specified to be an element of the space Ω_α. According to H_g, Y has p.d.f. $g(y; \beta)$ with $\beta \in \Omega_\beta$, and furthermore

$$\Omega_\alpha \cap \Omega_\beta \neq \Omega_\alpha,$$

$$\Omega_\alpha \cap \Omega_\beta \neq \Omega_\beta.$$

In such a case the usual (variants of) likelihood ratio tests are not available and the asymptotic chi-square test on $-2 \ln \lambda$ (where λ is the likelihood ratio) cannot

[4] The reader is referred to the Ramsey paper [46] for a more rigorous discussion.

[5] Note that the test depends only on the alternative hypothesis that the X variables should have been transformed via *some* $g(X)$ before running the regression. The function g is not used specifically in carrying out the test. The test is therefore quite general, but probably sacrifices power relative to a test which might have been constructed for a specific alternative such as $Z_i = \ln X_i$.

[6] In [46] Ramsey reports the results of several applications of his test procedure. An entirely similar procedure can be used to obtain tests for heteroskedasticity, omitted variables, and simultaneity, as Ramsey indicates, but such tests do not necessarily pinpoint the cause of rejection of the maintained hypothesis.

be performed. Problems of this type have been studied by D. R. Cox [14] [15] who has suggested various procedures—within the framework of classical statistics—for testing H_f against H_g.

One possibility is to transform the problem into a more familiar framework by introducing a new parameter γ. The probability density function of the random variable can then be written as

$$h(y;\alpha,\beta) = k[f(y;\alpha)]^{\gamma}[g(y;\beta)]^{1-\gamma},$$

where the factor of proportionality required for h to be a p.d.f. is given by

$$\frac{1}{k} = \int_{-\infty}^{\infty} [f(y,\alpha)]^{\gamma}[g(y,\beta)]^{1-\gamma}\,dy.$$

Employing $h(y;\alpha,\beta)$ one can, at least in principle, obtain maximum likelihood estimators for α, β and γ. Because of the presence of the factor k, the maximization of the likelihood function may pose considerable numerical problems. It appears possible to use the asymptotic theory of likelihood ratio tests for testing hypotheses about γ. Clearly, confirmation that γ is (close to) zero or unity supports one hypothesis and tends to discredit the other; intermediate values of γ are ambiguous and awkward in economics since the two hypotheses may be incompatible. Perhaps such an outcome suggests the interpretation that both hypotheses are suspect.[7]

Cox's main procedure is based on the (generalized) likelihood ratio

$$e^{l_{fg}} = \frac{\sup_{\alpha\in\Omega_\alpha} L_f^*(\alpha)}{\sup_{\beta\in\Omega_\beta} L_g^*(\beta)}$$

where $L_f^*(\alpha)$ and $L_g^*(\beta)$ are the sample likelihoods under H_f and H_g respectively. Since it is not true in the present case that $\Omega_\alpha \subset \Omega_\beta$, it is not true in general that $l_{fg} \leq 0$; hence standard procedures cannot be applied. Let $\hat{\alpha}$ and $\hat{\beta}$ be the maximum likelihood estimators under H_f and H_g respectively. The natural logarithm of the generalized likelihood ratio is

$$\begin{aligned} l_{fg} &= \ln L_f^*(\hat{\alpha}) - \ln L_g^*(\hat{\beta}) \\ &= L_f(\hat{\alpha}) - L_g(\hat{\beta}) \\ &= \{L_f(\alpha) - L_g(\beta_\alpha)\} + \{L_f(\hat{\alpha}) - L_f(\alpha)\} - \{L_g(\hat{\beta}) - L_g(\beta_\alpha)\} \end{aligned}$$

where

$$\beta_\alpha = \text{plim}\,\hat{\beta},$$

the probability limit taken on the assertion that H_f is true. That a large value for l_{fg} constitutes evidence against H_g may be seen as follows. Under H_f and the usual regularity conditions,

$$\text{plim}\,[L_f(\hat{\alpha}) - L_f(\alpha)] = \text{plim}\,[L_g(\hat{\beta}) - L_g(\beta_\alpha)] = 0,$$

[7] Recent work by Atkinson [5], elaborates the results given by Cox. Moreover, it shows that in instances where multiple hypotheses (exceeding two) are employed, or when the exponential combination of the distributions involves two parameters, γ_1, γ_2 (instead of γ, $1-\gamma$) it may not be possible to identify the "mixing" parameters.

while

$$\text{plim}\,[L_f(\alpha) - L_g(\beta_\alpha)] > 0,$$[8]

and therefore a "large" l_{fg} renders evidence against H_g.

The test statistic considered by Cox is a variant of l_{fg}, namely

$$\begin{aligned} S_f &= l_{fg} - E_{\hat{\alpha}}\{L_f(\hat{\alpha}) - L_g(\hat{\beta})\} \\ &= \{L_f(\hat{\alpha}) - L_g(\hat{\beta})\} - E_{\hat{\alpha}}\{L_f(\hat{\alpha}) - L_g(\hat{\beta})\}, \end{aligned}$$

where $E_{\hat{\alpha}}$ denotes the expectation operator conditional on the hypothesis H_f.

It is shown by Cox that S_f is asymptotically normally distributed and its variance is obtained. Clearly the test is not symmetric and the roles of H_f and H_g can be interchanged. The results of the test on S_f may indicate consistency with H_f, departure from H_f in the direction of H_g or departure away from H_g. If the test is performed on both S_f and S_g (obtained by interchanging the roles of H_f and H_g), there are nine possible outcomes and care must be taken to employ the correct qualitative interpretation. In appendix section A.1 we give an example of an application of this procedure. Unfortunately, the test cannot be performed routinely since, as we show in the appendix, the form of the test statistic depends crucially on the nature of the hypotheses to be tested and can easily involve nuisance parameters. Further, carrying out the test requires computations of substantial analytical difficulty.

Finally, we turn to a Bayesian approach to the problem of model selection. While the classical approach of Cox uses the generalized likelihood ratio

$$e^{l_{fg}} = \frac{\sup_{\alpha \in \Omega_\alpha} L_f^*(\alpha)}{\sup_{\beta \in \Omega_\beta} L_g^*(\beta)}$$

as a measure of whether the data generally favor hypothesis f relative to hypothesis g, the Bayesian approach considers, instead, a weighted likelihood ratio of the form

$$R = \int_\alpha L_f^*(y;\alpha)W(\alpha, f)\,d\alpha \Big/ \int_\beta L_g^*(y;\beta)W(\beta, g)\,d\beta,$$

where $W(\alpha, f)$ and $W(\beta, g)$ are "appropriately" defined weights relating to the parameters (α, β) and hypotheses (H_f, H_g) under consideration. It is perhaps simplest to illustrate the meaning of such weights in the likelihood function in the following way.

Let $\tilde{\omega}_f$ and $\tilde{\omega}_g(=1 - \tilde{\omega}_f)$ represent the model builder's "prior probabilities" attaching to (initial degrees of belief in) H_f and H_g respectively. Let $p_f(\alpha)$ be the prior density on α, given that H_f is true; similarly let $p_g(\beta)$ be the prior density on β given that H_g is true. Let $w_f(\alpha)$ be the "cost" of rejecting H_f when true and $w_g(\beta)$ the "cost" of rejecting H_g when it (H_g) is true. The (expected) cost of rejecting H_f, on the basis of information y, when in fact H_f is true, is

$$\tilde{\omega}_f \int_\alpha L_f^*(y;\alpha)p_f(\alpha)w_f(\alpha)\,d\alpha.$$

[8] Recall that the probability limits are taken conditional on H_f.

Similarly the (expected) cost of rejecting H_g when it is, in fact, true is

$$\tilde{\omega}_g \int_\beta L_g^*(y;\beta)p_g(\beta)w_g(\beta)\,d\beta.$$

In this context the weight $W(\alpha, f)$ is given by $\tilde{\omega}_f p_f(\alpha) w_f(\alpha)$, and similarly for $W(\beta, g)$. The usual rule derived from minimizing expected loss is:

$$\text{Accept } H_f \text{ if } \tilde{\omega}_f \int_\alpha L_f^*(y;\alpha)p_f(\alpha)w_f(\alpha)\,d\alpha \geq \tilde{\omega}_g \int_\beta L_g^*(y;\beta)p_g(\beta)w_g(\beta)\,d\beta,$$

otherwise reject.

Now if $w_f(\alpha) = w_g(\beta) = c$, a constant independent of α and β, then the rule reduces to:

Accept H_f (on the basis of information y) if:

$$\frac{\tilde{\omega}_f \int_\alpha L_f^*(y;\alpha)p_f(\alpha)\,d\alpha}{\tilde{\omega}_g \int_\beta L_g^*(y;\beta)p_g(\beta)\,d\beta} \geq 1.$$

The left-hand quantity, of course, is the usual definition of posterior odds.

Current activity in this area of Bayesian research, e.g., Geisel [24], Zellner [58], Leamer [41], Dickey [19], is aimed at exploring the implications of alternative weighting functions (prior densities). There are several important substantive implications of the Bayesian literature on this topic, including (a) Minor differences in R^2's among the competing models allow considerable discriminatory power depending on the degrees-of-freedom, (b) An appropriate criterion statistic for choice among models is (roughly) an average of the sample R^2 and an "*a priori*" R^2 computed using *a priori* likely values of the parameters. (That is, it does not matter if an R^2 is high if it implies absurd values of the parameters.)

Economic model builders rarely view themselves in the role of decision maker. Generally, the model builder concentrates on the estimation of many parameters and the pure testing of relatively few hypotheses.[9] But here, in the crucial area of model selection, is a circumstance clearly defined as a decision problem, whether to select H_f or H_g as the axiom on which to proceed in subsequent analysis.[10] And this clearly represents an area for which Bayesian analysis

[9] In current practice, most of the pure statistical tests carried out by model builders involve either the omitted variables specification analysis of Theil [50], or the test for structural change discussed by Chow [9], or various tests for the presence of autocorrelation. These major exceptions aside, it seems clear that far more time and attention is given to estimation than to the statistical testing of hypotheses.

[10] We recognize a logical problem here; having chosen H_f on the basis of the data available, subsequent estimates of parameters, tests of hypotheses etc. are to be understood as conditional on the "truth" of H_f. But given that the choice of H_f is itself the outcome of a statistical test the probabilistic properties of the subsequent estimators, the levels of significance, *are not the stated (nominal) ones*. The latter would hold only if H_f were in fact true, and would be valid in the present case conditionally on H_f. Indeed, empirical research ought to differentiate sharply between the test and "discovery" of hypotheses. Thus, if after a long "data mining" process one decides that a given model fits the data well, this exercise ought not to be understood as a test of the hypothesis that the world is described by such a model; at least not at the stated level of significance. It may, however, and indeed ought to be thought of as the discovery or the formulation of a hypothesis to be subsequently tested on an independent body of data. An early reference to this problem is T. A. Bancroft [6].

is tailor-made. After all, we do approach model selection with strong prior attachments even now. Only we tend—as a group—to apply these attachments in rather ad hoc, if not haphazard, and surely not reproducible ways. There may be a great deal to be gained by formalizing these procedures along Bayesian lines.

(*b*) *Estimation and Testing*

At this point we assume that some model selection procedure has gotten the researcher to the point at which it is appropriate to seek optimal parameter estimates (or to test hypotheses) under the usual specification axiom regarding appropriateness of the form of the model being analyzed. The existing econometric literature is more explicit in this area and in recent years econometricians have begun to pay increasing attention to the estimation of parameters which are subject to constraints [33] [52] and to various problems involving non-linear estimation [18] [26]. There would seem to be little purpose in our reviewing this literature which is quite familiar to most of those who engage in the construction (and testing) of econometric models. Rather, we have chosen to call attention to two strands of thought which exist in the literature of mathematical statistics, which seem to us to be potentially useful in economic problems, and which are on the whole not at all well-known to econometric model builders. We refer to two different situations involving restrictions on parameter values. The first—to which we now turn—is a case of intermediate hypotheses involving successively more severe restrictions on the admissable parameter space.[11] Here the problem has not yet been satisfactorily solved and we mention it briefly to draw attention to a research area which could yield a substantial payoff for econometric model building.

Suppose it is desired to test

$$H_0 : \theta \varepsilon \omega$$

against

$$H_1 : \theta \varepsilon (\Omega - \omega)$$

where θ is a vector of parameters, Ω is the admissable parameter space, and $\omega \subset \Omega$. It may be meaningful to conduct a sequence of tests on the intermediate hypotheses $\omega_1, \omega_2, \ldots, \omega_n$, where

$$\Omega = \omega_0 \supset \omega_1 \supset \omega_2 \supset, \ldots, \supset \omega_n = \omega,$$

in order to be able to pinpoint the reason, say, for the failure of hypothesis H_0 above.[12]

Suppose, in other words, that we employ the following procedure: Test ω_1 against $\omega_0 - \omega_1$. If ω_1 is not rejected, text ω_2 against $\omega_1 - \omega_2$. If ω_2 is not

[11] Economists are familiar with a special case of this problem involving a *single* subset hypothesis, and Chow [9] has provided a useful method for dealing with a two-sample problem within the subset hypothesis framework.

[12] Thus, a Chow test [9] may lead to the inference of structural change either because the coefficient vector, β, in the model $Y = X\beta + \varepsilon$ differs between the two sample periods under investigation, *or* because the variance of ε has changed (or both). It would therefore be desirable to be able to handle an intermediate hypothesis regarding the stability of the variance of ε.

rejected, test ω_3 against $\omega_2 - \omega_3$, and so on. If no rejections occur, then $H_0(\theta\varepsilon\omega = \omega_n)$, is accepted. If, however, some subhypothesis is rejected, say we reject $\theta\varepsilon\omega_k$ and thus accept $\theta\varepsilon(\omega_{k-1} - \omega_k)$, $0 < k < n$, we know that $\theta \notin \bigcup_{i=k}^{n} \omega_i$ and $\theta\varepsilon(\omega_{k-1} \cap \bar{\omega}_k)$, $\bar{\omega}_k$ being the complement of ω_k (in Ω). Since the sequence of intermediate hypotheses represents successively more severe restrictions upon the parameter space, the test tells us at what point the severity of the restriction becomes incompatible with the sample and, consequently, we know "why" H_0 is rejected.

Problems of this type have been discussed extensively by, among others, Darroch and Silvey [16], Hogg [31], Larson and Bancroft [40], and Seber [47]. To this point no easy solutions have yet been identified, a principal stumbling block involving the problem of statistical dependence of the successive hypothesis tests.

A more satisfactory result can be displayed in the case, to which we now turn, involving a Lagrange multiplier approach to the testing of a set of restrictions on the parameters being estimated. In general terms, the problem can be stated as follows. Let Y be a random variable (or vector) with p.d.f. $f(y; \theta)$ depending on a k-dimensional vector of parameters denoted by θ. It is asserted that certain restrictions hold, say $h(\theta) = 0$, where $h(\theta)$ is an r-dimensional vector valued function with $r < k$. The parameters can, in general, be estimated by first imposing the restrictions on the vector θ or, alternatively, by maximizing the expression

$$\mathscr{L}(\theta, \lambda) = L(y; \theta) + \lambda' h(\theta)$$

with respect to θ and λ, where $L(y; \theta)$ is the log likelihood corresponding to a sample on Y and λ is an r-dimensional vector of Lagrange multipliers.

The latter approach can be shown to yield a test of the validity of the restrictions, while the former does not. One could, of course, estimate unrestricted parameters and then derive statistics appropriate to testing the restrictions. If the restrictions are thereby rejected, then the unrestricted parameter estimates are the appropriate ones. On the other hand, if the hypothesis $h(\theta) = 0$ is accepted one would want to have the estimates obtained from a procedure which observes the restrictions—presumably on grounds of efficiency. The Lagrangian procedure yields both restricted parameters *and* the estimated Lagrange multipliers. In this case the test on the validity of the restrictions may be carried out on the Lagrange multipliers. If the restrictions are, in fact, valid the Lagrange multipliers should be zero since the restrictions imposed on the procedure are not binding—the data already incorporate such restrictions. Thus, a test on the estimated multipliers should lead to acceptance of the hypothesis that they are "insignificantly different from zero."

On the other hand, if the restrictions are invalid then the restrictions imposed by the procedure are, in fact, binding and a test based on the estimates of the Lagrange multipliers should yield the conclusion that they are "significantly different from zero." Thus, insignificance of Lagrange multipliers leads to *acceptance* of the restricted model, while significance leads to *rejection* of the restricted model and thus *acceptance* of the unrestricted model. If the unrestricted model is accepted, however, the restricted estimates are no longer appropriate—on grounds of possible inconsistency due to misspecification.

Such problems have been investigated by Aitchison and Silvey [2], [3], [48], who have shown that under the usual regularity conditions underlying maximum likelihood estimation, the appropriate test statistic for the hypothesis

$$H_0 : \lambda = 0$$

is

$$A = -\frac{1}{T}\hat{\lambda}' D^{-1}\hat{\lambda} = \frac{1}{T}\left(\frac{\partial L(y;\theta)}{\partial\theta}\right)' V^{-1}\left(\frac{\partial L(y;\theta)}{\partial\theta}\right),$$

where T is the sample size,

$$D^{-1} = -(RV^{-1}R')$$

$$R' = \left[\frac{\partial h(\theta)}{\partial\theta}\right]$$

and V is the so-called "information matrix,"

$$V = -\frac{1}{T}E\left[\frac{\partial^2 L(y;\theta)}{\partial\theta\partial\theta'}\right].$$

In the test statistic A all unknown parameters have been replaced by their *restricted* maximum likelihood estimates. If the statistic is "small" we accept the restricted model; if "large" we reject. Notice that if the restricted model were, in fact, valid then we would expect the restricted estimates to be "close" to the unrestricted ones. But the unrestricted estimates imply $\partial L/\partial\theta = 0$; thus, if both are close then for the restricted estimates we would have $\partial L/\partial\theta \cong 0$. Such considerations make this test intuitively quite attractive. Aitchison and Silvey have shown that the statistic A is, asymptotically, distributed as Chi-square with r degrees-of-freedom under the hypothesis $\lambda = 0$.

It is instructive to specialize the Aitchison–Silvey test to the linear model framework and compare it with the more familiar F-test based on the unrestricted estimates. Suppose

$$Y = X\beta + \varepsilon,$$

where Y is $(T \times 1)$; X is $(T \times K)$, nonstochastic, and of rank K; β is $(K \times 1)$; and ε is a $(T \times 1)$ multivariate normal vector with mean zero and covariance matrix $\sigma^2 I$. The log-likelihood function is

$$L = -\frac{T}{2}\ln(2\pi) - \frac{T}{2}\ln\sigma^2 - \frac{1}{2\sigma^2}\varepsilon'\varepsilon,$$

and, for subsequent reference, we note that $\partial^2 L/\partial\beta\partial\beta' = -(1/\sigma^2)(S)$, where $S = (X'X)$. The restrictions on β are given by

$$R\beta = r,$$

where r is a $J \times 1$ vector of known constants; R is a $(J \times K)$ matrix of known constants with the rank of R equal to $J < K$. We then form the Lagrangean function,

$$\mathscr{L} = L + \lambda'(R\beta - r).$$

Maximizing $\mathscr{L}$ with respect to β, σ^2, and λ yields the estimators (see [25, pp. 256–258]:

$$\hat{\beta} = b + S^{-1}R'(RS^{-1}R')^{-1}(r - Rb) \tag{1}$$

$$\hat{\lambda} = \frac{1}{\hat{\sigma}^2}(RS^{-1}R')^{-1}(r - Rb) \tag{2}$$

and

$$\hat{\sigma}^2 = \frac{\hat{\varepsilon}'\hat{\varepsilon}}{T}, \tag{3}$$

where b is the unrestricted Least Squares estimator, $b = S^{-1}X'Y$; and $\hat{\varepsilon}$ is the (restricted estimator) residual vector, $\hat{\varepsilon} = (Y - X\hat{\beta})$.

The Aitchison–Silvey test-statistic, A, is

$$A = -\frac{1}{T}\hat{\lambda}'D^{-1}\hat{\lambda}. \tag{4}$$

In this case D^{-1} is given by $-T\sigma^2(RS^{-1}R')$, since R' is itself the derivative of the constraint function with respect to the parameter vector β, and the information matrix is given by

$$\begin{aligned} V &= -\frac{1}{T}E\left[\frac{\partial^2 L}{\partial\beta\partial\beta'}\right] = -\frac{1}{T}E\left(-\frac{1}{\sigma^2}S\right) \\ &= \frac{1}{T\sigma^2}E(S) \\ &= \frac{S}{T\sigma^2}, \end{aligned}$$

since S is a non-stochastic matrix. Thus,

$$\begin{aligned} D^{-1} &= -(RV^{-1}R') \\ &= -\left[R\left(\frac{S}{T\sigma^2}\right)^{-1}R'\right] \\ &= -T\sigma^2(RS^{-1}R'). \end{aligned}$$

Substituting the latter into A in equation (4) yields:

$$A = \sigma^2\hat{\lambda}'(RS^{-1}R')\hat{\lambda}. \tag{5}$$

This statistic is asymptotically distributed as (central) chi-square with J degrees-of-freedom under the hypothesis $\lambda = 0$, as shown in [48]. With σ^2 unknown, $\hat{\sigma}^2$ can be substituted, yielding the observable test-statistic

$$\hat{A} = \hat{\sigma}^2\hat{\lambda}'(RS^{-1}R')\hat{\lambda} \tag{6}$$

which converges in distribution to the asymptotic distribution of A (since $\hat{\sigma}^2$ is consistent for σ^2) and is therefore also asymptotically chi-square with J degrees-of-freedom, if $\lambda = 0$.

The common test of the hypothesis $R\beta = r$ is based on an F-distributed statistic the derivation of which may be motivated as follows. The specification of the model implies that the unrestricted Least Squares estimator, b, is distributed multivariate $\mathcal{N}(\beta, \sigma^2 S^{-1})$, so that

$$R(b - \beta) = (Rb - R\beta) \sim \mathcal{N}(0, \sigma^2 RS^{-1}R').$$

But if $R\beta = r$, it follows that

$$(Rb - r) \sim \mathcal{N}(0, \sigma^2 RS^{-1}R'),$$

and therefore the statistic

$$\text{(7)} \qquad C = (Rb - r)'[\sigma^2 RS^{-1}R']^{-1}(Rb - r) = \frac{1}{\sigma^2}(Rb - r)'(RS^{-1}R')^{-1}(Rb - r)$$

is distributed as (central) chi-square with J degrees-of-freedom. The statistic C contains the nuisance parameter σ^2, but

$$\frac{e'e}{\sigma^2} = \frac{(Y - Xb)'(Y - Xb)}{\sigma^2} = \frac{T\mathcal{S}^2}{\sigma^2}$$

is independent of the estimator b and is distributed as (central) chi-square with $(T - K)$ degrees-of-freedom. Thus,

$$\text{(8)} \qquad \mathcal{F} = \frac{C/J}{T\mathcal{S}^2/\sigma^2(T - K)} = \frac{(Rb - r)(RS^{-1}R')^{-1}(Rb - r)}{\mathcal{S}^2} \frac{(T - K)}{TJ}$$

is distributed as (central) F with J and $(T - K)$ degrees-of-freedom, if $R\beta = r$.

To compare the latter with the Aitchison–Silvey test, substitute the expression for $\hat{\lambda}$ from (2) into the expression for A given in (5) to yield

$$A = \frac{\sigma^2}{\hat{\sigma}^2} \frac{1}{\hat{\sigma}^2}(r - Rb)'(RS^{-1}R')^{-1}(r - Rb).$$

Suppose now that σ^2 is known and does not have to be estimated, then A becomes

$$\text{(9)} \qquad A = \frac{1}{\sigma^2}(r - Rb)'(RS^{-1}R')^{-1}(r - Rb) = \frac{1}{\sigma^2}(Rb - r)'(RS^{-1}R')^{-1}(Rb - r),$$

which is precisely the statistic C given in (7). Thus, if σ^2 were known, the Aitchison–Silvey test would coincide with the usual test on the unrestricted estimators, for the latter would then be based on the statistic C, there being no need to employ $T\mathcal{S}^2/\sigma^2$ to get rid of any nuisance parameter. From this we obtain the conclusions that, within the linear model framework as specified

(i) the two tests are (mathematically) equivalent if σ^2 is known,

and

(ii) the Aitchison–Silvey test is a valid small sample test under the normality assumption on ε, provided σ^2 is known.

If σ^2 is unknown, we then have the choice between the small sample F-test and the asymptotic chi-square test. Two additional results can be proven for the case of unknown σ^2:

(iii) the two tests are asymptotically equivalent in the sense that $J\mathscr{F}$ and $\hat{A}$ have the same asymptotic distribution (see appendix section A.2),

(iv) If ε is normally distributed, then the usual F-test is the appropriate test because the other is only asymptotically valid, while the F-test is valid for any sample size, enjoys the properties of a "Neyman-Structure" test [42; chapter 4] and so on. Furthermore, although

$$\frac{T\hat{\sigma}^2}{\sigma^2}$$

is distributed as chi-square with $(T - K + J)$ degrees-of-freedom, it is not independent of the estimator b, and thus *cannot* be used to convert A into an F-statistic with more denominator degrees-of-freedom (hence higher power) than $\mathscr{F}$ (see appendix section A.2).

Finally, and probably most important from an econometric model point of view, it appears that in the *absence* of a normality assumption on ε the Aitchison–Silvey test based on $\hat{A}$ is preferable to the test based on $\mathscr{F}$ for the following considerations. If ε is not normally distributed, the statistic C given in equation (7) will be distributed as chi-square with J degrees-of-freedom asymptotically, since it is mathematically equivalent to A.[13] Further the asymptotic distribution of C will be unaffected if the σ^2 in (7) is replaced by *any* consistent estimator. In effect, the standard statistic $\mathscr{F}$ results from replacing σ^2 by $\mathscr{S}^2$, a consistent estimator derived from b, while the Aitchison-Silvey statistic $\hat{A}$ results from replacing σ^2 by $\hat{\sigma}^2$, a consistent estimator derived from $\hat{\beta}$ which contains the restrictions $R\beta = r$. If the restrictions are valid then $\hat{\sigma}^2$ should be preferable to $\mathscr{S}^2$ (on grounds of efficiency), in the same way that any full information estimator is to be preferred to its corresponding limited information estimator. Although it does not matter asymptotically, for any finite sample size the estimator $\mathscr{S}^2$ can be considered to be based on a sample of size $(T - K)$ while $\hat{\sigma}^2$ can be considered to be based on a sample of size $(T - K + J) > (T - K)$.[14]

[13] This could be proven directly without appealing to the equivalence of C and A. If ε is not normally distributed, we can consider a quasi-maximum likelihood estimation problem, as though ε were normally distributed, or simply minimize the residual sum of squares subject to $R\beta = r$ and still obtain the same results including asymptotic normality.

[14] If the test is to be based on asymptotic principles, there is no purpose to running the test on $\mathscr{F}$ in any case. One should use either

$$\hat{C} = \frac{1}{\mathscr{S}^2}(Rb - r)'(RS^{-1}R')(Rb - r)$$

or

$$\hat{A} = \frac{1}{\hat{\sigma}^2}(Rb - r)'(RS^{-1}R')^{-1}(Rb - r),$$

each of which is asymptotically χ^2_J if $R\beta = r$. We are arguing that $\hat{A}$ is preferable because $\hat{\sigma}^2$ is a "better" fixed sample estimator of σ^2 by virtue of its using more information about the structural model.

The reader will have noted that the discussion in this section has been predicated on a single-equation approach with non-stochastic regressors. In the case of stochastic regressors little difficulty is introduced if the regressors are fully independent of the error term ε. The small-sample F-test based on equation (8) would become a conditional F-test (conditional on the observed X's). In the Aitchison–Silvey test, the information matrix would be given by

$$V = \frac{ES}{T\sigma^2} = \frac{E(T^{-1}S)}{\sigma^2}.$$

This results in

$$\hat{A} = \frac{1}{T}\hat{\sigma}^2\hat{\lambda}'[R\{E(T^{-1}S)\}^{-1}R']\hat{\lambda},$$

which can be consistently estimated by

$$\hat{\hat{A}} = \frac{1}{T}\hat{\sigma}^2\hat{\lambda}'[R(T^{-1}S)^{-1}R']\hat{\lambda}$$

$$= \hat{\sigma}^2\hat{\lambda}'[RS^{-1}R']\hat{\lambda}, \tag{10}$$

precisely as in equation (6). The Aitchison–Silvey Test is thus completely unaffected by the presence of random regressors if they are independent of ε.[15] If the regressors include a lagged dependent variable (and we maintain the assumption of independent error terms) it becomes necessary to rely on a central limit theorem for dependent random variables to establish the asymptotic distribution of the Aitchison–Silvey statistic. Theil [51 ; p. 487] refers to one such central limit theorem which would apparently justify use of the Aitchison–Silvey test in the case of a lagged dependent variable.

Finally, suppose we are dealing with a simultaneous-equations model. If β is a vector of reduced-form parameters, then all of the foregoing applies. We are more apt, however, to be concerned about restrictions applying to behavioral (structural) parameters of the model. In that case, suppose the regressors in the equation for Y contain predicted values of some endogenous variables obtained from a directly estimated reduced form, so that b and $\hat{\beta}$ become, respectively, unrestricted and restricted $2SLS$ estimators of the structural parameters β. If the structural error terms are serially independent and the predetermined variables are either non-stochastic or fully independent of the structural error terms, then the Aitchison–Silvey test can be performed on the $2SLS$ estimators with unchanged asymptotic justification, precisely as discussed in the immediately preceding paragraph.[16]

[15] $\sqrt{T}(\hat{\lambda}/T)$ would still be asymptotically normally distributed, or—equivalently—$\sqrt{T}(b - \beta)$ would be asymptotically normally distributed with zero mean and covariance matrix $\sigma^2 \operatorname{Plim}(T^{-1}X'X)^{-1}$, which would again result in the statistic C in (7) being asymptotically χ^2_J if $R\beta = r$.

[16] The Aitchison–Silvey test-statistic would still be consistently estimated by the $\hat{\hat{A}}$ of equation (10), which would still yield the statistic

$$\frac{1}{\hat{\sigma}^2}(Rb - r)'(RS^{-1}R')^{-1}(Rb - r)$$

upon substitution for $\hat{\lambda}$, though b is now the unrestricted $2SLS$ estimator. It is shown in [14; pp. 190–191] that under the conditions stated above,

$$\sqrt{T}(b - \beta) \text{ is asymptotically } \mathcal{N}\left(0, \sigma^2 \operatorname{plim}\left(\frac{X'X}{T}\right)^{-1}\right),$$

where X contains "predicted" endogenous variables. This is all that is needed to establish that the above statistic is asymptotically χ^2_J (if $R\beta = r$), with $\hat{\sigma}^2$ being the variance estimator based upon $\hat{\beta}$ (the restricted $2SLS$ estimator of β).

The presence of lagged endogenous variables would again lead to the need for a central limit theorem for dependent variables.

(c) *Pseudo-Forecasts and Structural Stability Tests*

We assume now that an econometric model has been estimated and is ready for a "forecasting" evaluation prior to actual use as an operating model. A number of evaluation methods are available and several will be discussed in section V below. Here we should like to concentrate on the use of a data set which could have been pooled with the sample used to estimate the model, but was instead "saved" for a post-construction test of the model. We are well aware that under strong specification axioms it makes more sense to use all the available data in estimation, than to save some of it for later testing. This view is argued persuasively by Christ [11; pp. 546–548]. But in a realistic situation in which model selection procedures, hypothesis tests of various kinds, and a number of other "experiments" all amount to considerable data-mining, it would seem wise to have saved some data on which to evaluate the resulting model.[17]

Suppose, then, that the model-builder has available a set of m observations on each of the independent and dependent variables of the model. These data are assumed to lie outside the sample used to estimate the model, and it is further assumed that the m observations are too few in number to permit re-estimation of the model.[18] The model is to be used along with the m observations on the independent variables to generate m forecasts of the dependent variable(s) which can then be compared with the m *known* values of the dependent variable(s). For the case of a single equation and $m = 1$, a normality assumption on the error term (plus serial independence of the error term) permits the familiar t-test which can be considered equivalently either as a predictive test of the model or as a test of structural stability. For the single equation case with $m > 1$, it is possible to calculate a root mean squared error of forecast (the square root of the average of the squared forecasting errors) and it is tempting to think that such a statistic should be approximately the same as the standard error of estimate of the fitted equation if the structure has not changed. That this is not so, is alluded to in a recent paper by Jorgenson, Hunter and Nadiri [39].

Suppose the relation $Y = X\beta + \varepsilon$, with the same assumptions as previously given (including normality), is estimated by Least-Squares. The residual vector, say e, is given by

$$e = M\varepsilon,$$

where

$$M = I - XS^{-1}X',$$

and $e'e/(T - K)$ has expectation σ^2. The standard error of estimate is, of course, the square root of $e'e/(T - K)$. Now suppose that X_0 is the $(m \times K)$ matrix of

[17] Obviously if the model builder "knows" the data set which has been saved, he may find it impossible to prevent it from influencing his specification of the model. To that extent, a test on saved data is biased in favor of the model being tested. Subsequent testing on data which could not have been known at the time of model construction is clearly more desirable.

[18] In section IV we discuss the case in which there are enough new data to re-estimate the model on the new data set.

observations to be used in the predictive test of the model. If the structure of the model is correct, then

$$Y_0 = X_0\beta + \varepsilon_0$$

and the vector of forecast errors, say e_0, is given by

$$e_0 = Y_0 - X_0 b,$$

where $b = S^{-1}X'Y$. It is well known that under the stated assumptions e_0 is distributed as multivariate Normal with mean zero and covariance matrix $\sigma^2(I_m + X_0S^{-1}X_0')$, where I_m is an $(m \times m)$ identity matrix. Denoting the matrix $(I_m + X_0S^{-1}X_0')$ by Q, it follows that

$$\frac{e_0'(I_m + X_0S^{-1}X_0')^{-1}e_0}{\sigma^2} = \frac{e_0'Q^{-1}e_0}{\sigma^2}$$

is distributed as (central) chi-square with m degrees-of-freedom. Thus

$$E[e_0'Q^{-1}e_0/m] = \sigma^2.$$

The mean squared error of forecast, however, is given by $e_0'e_0/m$, not $e_0'Q^{-1}e_0/m$, and the difference between these two measures is

$$e_0'e_0/m - (e_0'Q^{-1}e_0/m = e_0'(I_m - Q^{-1})e_0/m.$$

It can be shown (see appendix section A.3) that $(I_m - Q^{-1})$ is a positive definite matrix. Thus $e_0'(I_m - Q^{-1})e_0/m$ is always positive which implies that

$$E(e_0'e_0/m) > E(e_0'Q^{-1}e_0/m) = \sigma^2.$$

The root mean squared error of forecast, which is the square root of $e_0'e_0/m$, should thus be *expected* to exceed the standard error of estimate of the fitted equation. Intuitively, this result is due to the fact that the variance of the forecast error arises not only from the residual variance, σ^2, but also from the discrepancy between b and β. The proper predictive test involves the ratio

$$\text{(11)} \qquad \frac{e_0'Q^{-1}e_0/m}{e'e/(T-K)} = \frac{e_0'(I_m + X_0S^{-1}X_0')^{-1}e_0/m}{e'e/(T-K)}$$

which "corrects" for the component of the prediction error due to imprecision in the estimation of β, and is distributed as (central) F with m and $(T - K)$ degrees-of-freedom, if the structure is unchanged [40].

It is interesting that this predictive testing procedure can be generalized to the situation in which the reduced form of a linear simultaneous equations model is used to forecast m new observations on each of G endogenous variables. We make the following assumptions:

(i) the predetermined variables are non-stochastic,

(ii) the reduced form error terms are Normally distributed, serially independent, but contemporaneously dependent with contemporaneous covariance matrix denoted by Σ.

(iii) the reduced form parameters are estimated by ordinary least squares.

The covariance matrix Σ is estimated by $\hat{\Sigma}$ with typical element $e_i'e_j/(T-K)$ where e_i is the vector of residuals from the reduced form equation corresponding to the ith endogenous variable, e_j is the residual vector corresponding to the reduced form equation of the jth endogenous variable, and K is the number of predetermined variables (the same, of course, in all G reduced form equations). Now define e_0^G as an $(mG \times 1)$ vector of forecast errors, where the first m elements correspond to the first endogenous variable, the second m elements correspond to the second endogenous variable, and so on. We show in appendix section A.3 that the statistic

$$(12) \qquad (e_0^G)'[\hat{\Sigma}^{-1} \otimes (I_m + X_0 S^{-1} X_0')^{-1}](e_0^G)\frac{(T-K-G+1)}{mG(T-K)},$$

where $\otimes$ represents the Kronecker product, is distributed as (central) F with mG and $(T-K-G+1)$ degrees-of-freedom if the structure is unchanged. It is obvious that for $G = 1$ the expression in (12) collapses to the single equation statistic given in (11).[19]

The assumption of non-stochastic predetermined variables can be relaxed in two ways. If the predetermined variables are stochastic but fully independent of the reduced form error terms, then the test-statistic given in (12) is appropriate for an F-test conditional on *both* X and X_0. More interesting is the case of predetermined variables which include lagged endogenous variables. Suppose we make a series of m one-period forecasts, that is, always using *actual* values for the lagged endogenous variables. It is then possible to consider the forecasts to be conditional on the observed matrix X_0, even though X_0 contains lagged endogenous variables. In this case, *if T is large* (the size of m does *not* matter)

$$(13) \qquad (e_0^G)'[\hat{\Sigma}^{-1} \otimes (I_m + X_0 S^{-1} X_0')^{-1}](e_0^G)$$

can be considered to have an *approximate* chi-square distribution with mG degrees-of-freedom if the structure is unchanged (see Appendix section A.3).[20] Unfortunately, we do not at this time know of any analogous statistical test for a sequence of dynamic forecasts in which the model generates its own lagged endogenous variables. We conclude this section by observing that if the model passes its predictive test evaluation, the m saved observations should then presumably (but see footnote 10) be incorporated into the data set to reestimate the model on all $(T + m)$ observations. If the model fails, then, of course, it's "back to the drawing board."

[19] Except for a recursive model, it makes little sense to assume that Σ is diagonal, for each reduced form error term is, in general, a linear combination of all the structural error terms. On the other hand, if we consider the set of G equations to be "seemingly unrelated regressions," Σ might be diagonal in which case (12) can be simplified to

$$\sum_{i=1}^{G}\left\{\frac{e_{0,i}'(I_m + X_0 S^{-1} X_0')^{-1} e_{0,i}/m}{e_i'e_i/T-K}\right\}\frac{(T-K-G+1)}{G(T-K)},$$

where $e_{0,i}$ is the set of m forecast errors corresponding to the ith dependent variable. In this case, the test-statistic is proportional to the sum of the single-equation test-statistics as given in (11).

[20] The statistic in (12) yields a small sample test and would be proportional to a χ^2 if Σ were known. The F distribution arises because $\hat{\Sigma}$ has been used as a Wishart-distributed estimator of Σ. In equation (13), which is only approximately valid for large samples, no such correction is appropriate. If Σ itself were in (13) the statistic would still be only an approximate χ^2, and since $\hat{\Sigma}$ is a consistent estimator of Σ, the same should hold for the statistic containing $\hat{\Sigma}$.

IV. Parametric Evaluation: Subsequent to Model Release

In this section we present a brief set of comments related to the evaluation of econometric models which are already at an operating stage. This section is quite brief for two primary reasons. First, the procedures discussed in this section depend on a sufficiently strong axiomatization to permit statistical testing in the familiar classical sense; there is not a great deal of scope for discussion here because our current knowledge is not terribly extensive. Secondly, much of what there is to say can be said by referring the reader back to discussions already presented in the previous section.

(a) *Availability of a Small Data Set*

Here we have reference to the continual flow of new data which, in the case of time series models, accrues a point at a time. Existing models can be checked against small sets of new data very frequently. Indeed, most of the operating macro forecasting models are subjected to a "residual analysis" check at least once per calendar quarter as new national income account data are issued by the government. These and other models, however, could in principle be put through a regularly scheduled predictive testing procedure along the lines discussed in section III, part (*c*). The only differences lie in the fact that the test procedure would be conducted on a data set which, obviously, could not have been incorporated into the original sample. Such predictive testing is especially valuable because it involves data successively further separated from the sample data used in the initial specification of the model.

A clearly useful procedure would be to incorporate each new data set into the model's estimation sample each time a predictive test is passed.[21] Most model-builders stop far short of such a procedure and re-estimate, indeed re-build, their models on a much looser schedule. It is not quite so obvious whether failure to pass a given predictive test, based on a small data set, should be grounds for immediate rejection of a model, for a number of reasons. Newly released data are frequently subject to substantial subsequent revision; it may be the new data which have failed the test, not the model. Small data sets can be heavily dominated by unique events which are outside the model's specified structure. Such circumstances have to be recognized as a *limitation* of the model, not as an indication that those processes which *are* represented within the model have been proven to be inadequately specified.

(*b*) *Availability of a Large Data Set*

Some econometric models are constructed in order to test hypotheses, not to be in continual use as forecasting or policy-analysis models. In such cases, they may well lie dormant over periods of time long enough for substantial new bodies of data to emerge. In the case of cross-section models, large sets of new data continually appear or can be obtained. In these circumstances it is possible to use the new data set, by itself, to re-estimate the model. This, of course, puts the model-builder (or someone else, for that matter) into the position of being able to conduct

[21] Ray Fair, for example, is one of the few model operators who actually re-estimates his model each quarter. See [22].

a rather powerful test of structural change. Economists are quite familiar with the use of the analysis of variance test discussed by Gregory Chow [9] for this situation. Here, especially, it would be useful if the series-tests on successively more restrictive nested hypotheses[22] were to become operational.

The predictive tests as discussed above are not, of course, limited in application to small data sets and are therefore alternatives to the Chow test. The latter, however, is a more powerful test when the new data set is large enough to be used by itself to re-estimate the model. Indeed, the Chow test is the classical likelihood ratio test for this situation.[23]

V. Non-Parametric Evaluation

In view of the nature of the preceding discussion, it is useful to remind the reader once again that no pejorative intent is to be inferred from our use of the term non-parametric evaluation, or its connection with the process of Sherlock Holmes inference which we identified earlier. Indeed, we firmly believe that the need for somewhat descriptive kinds of evaluation procedures points as much to the richness of the areas of application of econometric models as it does to any inability of economists to put forth a strong axiomatization for their models. The spirit of our discussion here may be stated as follows. In the current state of our knowledge and analytical needs, to concentrate our attention solely on proving or disproving the "truth" of an econometric model is to choose an activity virtually guaranteed to suppress the major benefits which can flow from the proper use of econometric models. Having constructed the best models of which we are capable,[24] we ought to concern ourselves directly with whether or not particular models can be considered to be reliable tools for particular uses, regardless of the strict faithfulness of their specification.

In this context, "validation" becomes a problem-dependent or decision-dependent process, differing from case to case as the proposed use of the model under consideration changes. Thus a particular model may be validated for one purpose and not for another. In each case the process of validation is designed to answer the question: Is this model fulfilling the stated purpose? We can then speak of the evaluation of these models as the process of attempting to validate them for a series of purposes.[25] Thus the motivation of model-builders or users becomes directly relevant to the evaluation of the models themselves. The "success" of a model can then be measured by the extent to which it enables its user to decrease the frequency and consequences of wrong decisions. As Zarnowitz [55] has pointed

[22] See section III, part (*b*).

[23] The Chow test is a fixed sample F-test based on the same strict axiomatization as the predictive test discussed in section III, part (*c*). We have not here concerned ourselves with generalizations in the direction of lagged dependent variables, reduced-forms vs. structural models, and so on. Presumably this could be done along the lines of our previous discussions, with substantial benefits accruing to the process of econometric model evaluation.

[24] And while continuing the search for ever closer approximations to economic reality.

[25] Howrey et. al. [36] have pointed out that the method of estimation itself may also be partially a function of the use to which the model is to be put. The evaluation of any model should, of course, include an evaluation of the estimating procedures used. We do not comment on this aspect of the evaluation process here. For an interesting discussion of this issue, see Howrey [36].

out, however, the full application of even this more limited goal still poses very high informational requirements, namely: (i) the errors must be identifiable, (ii) the preferences of the decision maker and the constraints under which he operates must be available, (iii) the cost of providing the model must be ascertained. Large macroeconometric models, for example, are frequently used for both forecasting and policy analysis. In the role of a forecasting instrument, a model's usefulness is directly related to the accuracy of its *ex ante* forecasts. In the case of the policy analysis role, the main criterion is how well the model performs with respect to conditional forecasts based on particular configurations of policy options. In this case, especially, the user of the model typically possesses some—at least qualitative—knowledge about the policy maker's preferences concerning growth rates, inflation, unemployment, and so on. Such knowledge provides a natural set of criteria by which to judge the model's adequacy as a tool of policy analysis.[26]

But even here it is dangerous to polarize the evaluation too strongly onto specific use-oriented criteria. Our tests or evaluation procedures should—initially at least—center on the ability of the model to generate "historical" simulations which conform to the actual data. These simulations might be either deterministic or stochastic, and either static (one period) or dynamic (multi-period) in nature. A minimal requirement would involve a broad consistency of the data generated by a deterministic single-period simulation with the data from the actual historical record (both within and outside the sample period).[27]

However, even if a model "passed" a more demanding test of its ability to "track" the historical record (e.g., a deterministic multi-period historical simulation), economists would normally also want to investigate whether or not the model responded to various types of stimuli in the fashion anticipated or suggested by economic theory or independent empirical observation. Quite aside from the individual hypotheses underlying particular equations in the system, economists have certain (not entirely independent) "*reduced form*" *hypotheses* to which they would demand "acceptable" models to conform. That is, as a profession we seem to have developed some more or less vague ideas about the magnitudes of various impact, dynamic and steady-state multipliers as well as some prior notions about other dynamic characteristics that the model "should" exhibit. Despite Haavelmo's early warning [27], however, we have, at least until the recent work of Howrey [34], failed to realize just how difficult such tests are to design and carry out. This set of issues was finally confronted again at a recent NBER conference concerned with whether or not an existing set of models adequately reproduced the cyclical swings observed in our economic system.[28] It is difficult to catalogue what seems to be a

[26] Thus, a model which accurately predicts the employment effects of alternative tax policies may be considered "successful" even if its prediction of the composition of GNP is poor by the standards for other uses of a model.

[27] Especially, perhaps, in the simulation of historical episodes which involve policy changes or initial conditions relevant to current interests and decisions. It should be emphasized, however, that consistency of the data generated by a deterministic multi-period simulation with historical data is in general too strong a requirement. Howrey and Kalejian [35] have shown that under certain circumstances the dynamic deterministic simulation path of a correctly specified non-linear model may differ substantially from the historical time path.

[28] Conference on Research in Income and Wealth, Harvard University, November 14–15, 1969. For a summary introduction to these issues as they arose at this conference see Hickman [30].

minimal set of demands of this sort as needs and requirements vary according to the preferences and prejudices of the researcher and the actual needs of the user. In any case, the constraints imposed by these demands are, given the current state of knowledge, not overly stringent. Even if we consider the case of the government expenditure multiplier—where a relatively large amount of evidence has accumulated, "acceptable" estimates of its magnitude (both impact and steady state) vary widely among different "accepted" models of the U.S. economy.

We should also briefly consider whether in all types of experiments the simulated data should be generated by stochastic or non-stochastic simulation procedures. Certainly stochastic simulation, if we have the necessary extra information (in practice we often ignore the problem of obtaining good estimates of the variance-covariance matrix of the disturbance process), will yield a more informative characterization of the model being used and thus increase the quality of the evaluation procedure. Further, if the model is non-linear, and most macroeconometric models are these days, then the reduced form of the model *cannot* be inferred from the results of a non-stochastic solution [35]. That is, the application of non-stochastic simulation procedures yields results that should be expected to differ from those implied by the properties of the actual reduced form of the model. Although some preliminary experiments with the Wharton model suggested that the differences were not large, the results of the more extensive multi-model study by Haitovsky and Wallace [29] suggest a strong contrary conclusion regarding the ability of non-stochastic simulations to represent the reduced form properties of existing non-linear models.

The evaluation of the predictive ability of a model is essentially a goodness-of-fit problem. Because the statistical techniques available for this purpose normally require a strong axiomatization of the structure, econometric model builders have often found themselves restricted to simple graphical techniques (the fit "looks good") or simple summary measures (root mean square error, Theil's U-Statistic . . . , etc.),[29] of the performance of certain key variables. In a recent paper, Haitovsky and Treyz [28] have proposed an interesting descriptive decomposition of the forecast error for an endogenous variable in a large econometric model. The decomposition identifies error components involving: (a) the structural equation explaining the variable in question, (b) the rest of the estimated structural system, (c) incorrect values of lagged endogenous variables (in the case of dynamic simulations), (d) incorrect guesses about exogenous variables (in the case of an *ex ante* forecast), and (e) failure to make serial correlation "adjustments" for observed errors. Some attention has also been given to the development of a statistic analogous to the single-equation R^2, to be used to test the hypothesis that $\beta = 0$, where β is the coefficient vector of the system of equations under consideration. An interesting and complete discussion of this issue can be found in Dhrymes [17; Ch. 5]. Dhrymes defines such a statistic, but finds that it is dependent on the unknown covariance parameters of the joint distribution of the error terms of the system. Dhrymes [17] also derives an alternate test procedure

[29] Howrey et. al. [36] have recently suggested some difficulty with the root mean square error statistic (where small sample properties are unknown), particularly when used to compare structural versus autoregressive models, or sample versus post sample performance of a given model. See also our section III, part (*b*), and the discussion of Theil's U-Statistic in Jorgenson et. al. [39].

regarding the goodness-of-fit of the reduced form model (the fraction of the generalized variance of the jointly dependent variables explained by the reduced form), but this procedure involves the restriction that the number of variables in the model (endogenous plus predetermined) be less than the total number of observations—a restriction not generally fulfilled by large econometric models. The trace *correlation* statistic suggested by Hooper (based on the estimates of the canonical correlations) is closely related to the statistic discussed by Dhrymes, but its distribution seems quite intractable—although Hooper has given an approximate expression for the asymptotic variance of the statistic [32]. Perhaps this is an area of research that holds some promise.

Many interesting applications with large econometric models involve what is known as a "multiple response problem." That is we are interested in more than one characterization of the outcome of the experiment. This raises the question of whether to treat the outcome as one of many experiments each with a single response, or to combine all the responses (endogenous variables of interest) into a single response. This latter procedure, of course, involves the explicit formulation of the utility function of the user—a difficult situation.[30]

Other techniques which are in common use in the evaluation of a model's predictive performance are regression analysis and spectral analysis. In the former case we simply regress actual values on the predicted values of a series and test whether the resulting equations have zero intercepts and slopes not significantly different from unity (see Cohen and Cyert [12] and Hymans [37]). This general technique has also been used extensively by Theil [50], but as usual he has extended it and forced it to yield additional information. By regressing predicted values on actual values and actual values lagged one period, Theil is also able to investigate whether or not predicted changes tend to be biased toward recent actual changes. Theil's inequality coefficient and its decomposition into elements of bias, variance and covariance is very closely related to this type of analysis (although it refers to a regression of actual *changes* on predicted *changes*) and offers a great deal more information including some information on the tendency of the model to make turning point errors. Mincer and Zarnowitz [43] have provided some further development of Theil's procedure and have also suggested an additional measure of forecast error: the relative mean squared error. The latter is particularly interesting by virtue of its attempt to compare the costs and benefits of forecasts derived from alternative models of the economic process.

Spectral (cross-spectral) analysis is a statistical technique that can be used to obtain a frequency decomposition of the variance (covariance) of a univariate (bivariate) stochastic process. There are several ways in which spectrum analytic techniques might be used in the evaluation of econometric models. Naylor et al. [44] suggest that the spectra estimated from simulation data be compared with the spectra estimated directly from actual data. Howrey [34] has pointed out that for linear models the implied spectrum can be derived directly from the model and the stochastic simulation of the model is therefore not needed to make this comparison. Another application of spectral techniques is to test estimates of the

[30] For an interesting attempt to solve the multiple response problem see Fromm and Taubman [23] and Theil [49], [50].

structural or reduced-form disturbances for serial correlation, an important step in the Box–Jenkins modeling procedure [8].[31]

Cross-spectral analysis can also be used to investigate the relationship between predicted and actual values. That is, the Theil procedures can be extended to the frequency domain using cross-spectral analysis. This permits statistical testing of some more general hypotheses about the relationship of actual and predicted values.

An important advantage of spectral analysis is that it is a nonparametric approach to data analysis. Thus it is a particularly useful device in situations involving a weak axiomatization of the relationships under investigation. In addition, spectral methods do not depend on the statistical independence of the generated data points; they require only that the process generating the data be stationary to the second order. The significance tests that are available, however, depend on the assumption of Normality of the underlying process or on a sample size that is large enough that a form of the central limit theorem can be invoked. What little empirical experience has been accumulated in connection with the use of spectral analysis to investigate econometric models suggests that the technique can be used quite effectively to investigate certain dynamic properties of econometric models.

By way of tieing up the strands of this necessarily broad discussion, we should like to sketch, in outline form, the range of descriptive measures which have been found to yield useful insights into the performance and realiability characteristics of large scale econometric models. While some of these measures can be subjected to classical statistical tests, many are—at this stage of our knowledge—merely descriptive and geared to specialized model uses. A large number of these procedures can be traced to the writings of Zarnowitz and his co-workers [53], [54], [56], [57], Evans, Haitovsky and Treyz [21], Box and Jenkins [8], and Theil [50].

An Outline of Non-Parametric Measures

A. *Single-Variable Measures*
   1. Mean forecast error (changes and levels)
   2. Mean absolute forecast error (changes and levels)
   3. Mean squared error (changes and levels)
   4. Any of the above relative to
      (a) the level or variability of the variable being predicted
      (b) a measure of "acceptable" forecast error for alternative forecasting needs and horizons

B. *Tracking Measures*
   1. Number of turning points missed
   2. Number of turning points falsely predicted

[31] If one is primarily interested in forecasting (as opposed to explaining the behavior of the economic system) the conceptual simplicity of the Box-Jenkins procedure (essentially a battery of sophisticated smoothing techniques) has some appeal. This is particularly so if there is only one variable of interest as these procedures do not treat the output variables as being "tied" together in a system of interdependent relationships. Thus, forecasts of output, employment and prices, for example, need have no particular relatlonship to each other. Further, since the procedures are void of economic theory, they cannot, of course, be used to test hypotheses. Currently research is being done on developing procedures for building more information and constraints (exogenous and policy variables) into these models [8] [20] [45]. These investigations, if successful, may prove fruitful to econometricians.

3. Number of under- or overpredictions
4. Rank correlation of predicted and actual changes (within a subset of "important" actual movements)
5. Various tests of randomness
   (a) of directional predictions
   (b) of predicted turning points

C. *Error Decompositions*
1. Bias and variance of forecast error
2. Errors in start-up position vs. errors in the predicted changes
3. Identification of model subsectors transmitting errors to other sectors

D. *Comparative Errors*
1. Comparison with various "naive" forecasts[32]
2. Comparison with "judgmental," "consensus," or other non-econometric forecasts
3. Comparison with other econometric forecasts

E. *Cyclical and Dynamic Properties*
1. Impact and dynamic multipliers
2. Frequency response characteristics

The measures just outlined have been found to be suitable for a wide variety of purposes, and—surely—a user's confidence in any particular model would grow in proportion to the number of positive results yielded by such of these measures as seem relevant to the use in question. Several recent studies, [29], [39], and especially the Cooper–Jorgenson study [13], have made a valuable contribution by standardizing both the period of fit and the technique of estimation across alternative models prior to conducting inter-model comparisons. While model builders have in some measure tended to resent such activity on the part of "outsiders,"[33] the controversy certainly shows signs of producing improved procedures on all sides.

Models will be used for decision making, and their evaluation, therefore, ought to be tied to optimization of these decisions. The question we have to ask ourselves, then, is what series of tests and/or procedures will be sufficient to achieve a particular level of confidence in the use of a model for a certain specified purpose? What model builders have done, to date, is to catalogue the properties of their models, concentrating on those aspects of the system which seemed useful to them. There are two difficulties. First, model *users* may or may not find these properties to be relevant to their decision making. Second, we have not yet standardized the "list" of properties studied. A remedy for the latter situation would be most helpful to all users, is certainly feasible, and ought to receive high priority. The former issue is much more formidable and requires a greater degree of cooperation and candid communication than has to date taken place between model builders and the growing population of model users.

[32] The procedures of Box and Jenkins [8] may be particularly powerful in helping to identify the autoregressive procedures which would best serve as "Naive" alternatives to a structural model.

[33] See Howrey, Klein and McCarthy [36] who present arguments regarding the controls needed in such standardization attempts.

Appendix

This appendix serves to *sketch* some of the less familiar theoretical results which are the basis for statements made in the body of the paper.

A.1 An Illustration of the Cox Procedure for Non-Nested Hypotheses

Hypothesis H_f:

$$L_f(y;\alpha) = -\frac{T}{2}\ln(2\pi) - \frac{T}{2}\ln\sigma^2 - \frac{1}{2\sigma^2}(y - X\alpha)'(y - X\alpha),$$

where

$$y = (y_1, y_2, \ldots, y_T)', \qquad X = (e, x), \qquad x = (x_1, x_2, \ldots, x_T)',$$

$$\alpha = (\alpha_1, \alpha_2), \qquad e = (1, 1, \ldots, 1)'.$$

Hypothesis H_g:

$$L_g(y:\beta) = -\frac{T}{2}\ln(2\pi) - \frac{T}{2}\ln\sigma^2 - \frac{1}{2\sigma^2}(y - X^*\beta)'(y - X^*\beta)$$

where

$$X^* = (e, x^*), \qquad x^* = (x_1^*, x_2^*, \ldots, x_T^*)', \qquad \beta = (\beta_0, \beta_1)'.$$

Define

$$\hat{\sigma}_f^2 = \frac{1}{T}y'[I - N]y, \qquad N = X(X'X)^{-1}X'$$

$$\hat{\sigma}_g^2 = \frac{1}{T}y'[I - N^*]y, \qquad N^* = X^*(X^{*\prime}X^*)^{-1}X^{*\prime}.$$

Then

$$l_{fg} = -\frac{T}{2}[\ln\hat{\sigma}_f^2 - \ln\hat{\sigma}_g^2]$$

$$\beta_\alpha = \operatorname{plim}(X^{*\prime}X^*)^{-1}X^{*\prime}[X\alpha + u] = \operatorname{plim}\left(\frac{X^{*\prime}X^*}{T}\right)^{-1}\left(\frac{X^{*\prime}X}{T}\right)\alpha$$

on the assumption that H_f is true and that accordingly

$$y = X\alpha + u,$$

$u = (u_1, u_2, \ldots, u_T)'$, $\{u_t : t = 1, 2 \ldots\}$ being a sequence of identically and independently distributed random variables with mean zero and variance σ^2. In the preceding it is assumed that the x's are either a sequence of fixed constants or if they are random variables they are distributed independently of u.

We observe that, under H_f,

$$\frac{1}{T}L_f(\hat{\alpha}) = \tfrac{1}{2}[\ln(2\pi) + 1] - \tfrac{1}{2}\ln\hat{\sigma}_f^2$$

$$\frac{1}{T}L_f(\alpha) = -\tfrac{1}{2}\ln(2\pi) - \tfrac{1}{2}\ln\sigma^2 - \frac{1}{2\sigma^2}\frac{u'u}{T}.$$

Because $\hat{\sigma}_f^2$ is a consistent estimator of σ^2 and so is $u'u/T$, we conclude that

$$\operatorname{plim}\frac{1}{T}[L_f(\hat{\alpha}) - L_f(\alpha)] = 0.$$

Further, since $\operatorname{plim}[L_g(\hat{\beta})|H_f] = L_g(\beta_\alpha)$,

$$\operatorname{plim}\frac{1}{T}[L_g(\hat{\beta}) - L_g(\beta_\alpha)] = 0.$$

Moreover,

$$\frac{1}{T}L_g(\beta_\alpha) = -\frac{1}{2}\ln(2\pi) - \frac{1}{2}\ln\sigma^2 - \frac{1}{2\sigma^2}\frac{(y - X^*\beta_\alpha)'(y - X^*\beta_\alpha)}{T}.$$

But we see that

$$\operatorname{plim}\frac{1}{T}(y - X^*\beta_\alpha)'(y - X^*\beta_\alpha) = \sigma^2 + \operatorname{plim}\left[\frac{1}{T}\alpha'X'(I - N^*)X\alpha\right].$$

Thus

$$\operatorname{plim}\frac{1}{T}[L_f(\alpha) - L_g(\beta_\alpha)] = \frac{1}{2\sigma^2}\operatorname{plim}\left[\frac{1}{T}\alpha'X'(I - N^*)X\alpha\right] \geq 0.$$

In general we would expect a strict inequality except for special x-sequences.

Turning now to the test statistic $(1/T)S_f$ (as defined in the text, supra), we obtain

$$\frac{1}{T}S_f = -\tfrac{1}{2}[\ln\hat{\sigma}_f^2 - \ln\hat{\sigma}_g^2] + \tfrac{1}{2}E_{\hat{\alpha}}[\ln\hat{\sigma}_f^2 - \ln\hat{\sigma}_g^2].$$

Under H_f, $(T\hat{\sigma}_f^2/\sigma^2)$ is (central) chi-square with $(T - 2)$ degrees of freedom, and $(T\hat{\sigma}_g^2/\sigma^2)$ is non-central chi-square with $(T - 2)$ degrees of freedom. Thus, in principle, this expectation may be carried out. In general, it will involve the unknown parameter α and for purposes of the test we would have to insert the maximum likelihood estimate (MLE) $\hat{\alpha}$, in its stead. Further, such tests require specification of the distribution of the data under consideration and the derivation of the MLE under the two alternatives.

A.2 The Aitchison–Silvey Test

1. *$J\mathscr{F}$ and $\hat{A}$ have the same asymptotic distribution*

$$J\mathscr{F} = \frac{(Rb - r)'(RS^{-1}R')^{-1}(Rb - r)}{\mathscr{S}^2}\frac{(T - K)}{T},$$

while

$$\hat{A} = \frac{1}{\hat{\sigma}^2}(Rb - r)'(RS^{-1}R')^{-1}(Rb - r).$$

Hence

$$(J\mathscr{F} - \hat{A}) = \hat{A}\left[\frac{\hat{\sigma}^2}{\mathscr{S}^2}\frac{(T - K)}{T} - 1\right]$$

$$= \hat{A}\left[\frac{\hat{\sigma}^2}{\mathscr{S}^2}\left(1 - \frac{K}{T}\right) - 1\right].$$

Since $\hat{A}$ has an asymptotic distribution,

$$\hat{A}\left[\frac{\hat{\sigma}^2}{\mathscr{S}^2}\left(1 - \frac{K}{T}\right) - 1\right] = (J\mathscr{F} - \hat{A})$$

will have a zero probability limit if

$$\operatorname{plim}\left[\frac{\hat{\sigma}^2}{\mathscr{S}^2}\left(1 - \frac{K}{T}\right) - 1\right] = 0.$$

But

$$\operatorname{plim}\left[\frac{\hat{\sigma}^2}{\mathscr{S}^2}\left(1 - \frac{K}{T}\right) - 1\right] = \left[\operatorname{plim}\frac{\hat{\sigma}^2}{\mathscr{S}^2}\lim\left(1 - \frac{K}{T}\right) - 1\right]$$

$$= (1 - 1) = 0,$$

since $\hat{\sigma}^2$ and $\mathscr{S}^2$ are both consistent estimators of σ^2. Hence, plim $(J\mathscr{F} - \hat{A}) = 0$, and since $\hat{A}$ has an asymptotic distribution this condition implies that $J\mathscr{F}$ has the same asymptotic distribution as $\hat{A}$. Q.E.D.

1. *$T\hat{\sigma}^2$ is not independent of b*

$$T\hat{\sigma}^2 = \hat{\varepsilon}'\hat{\varepsilon}.$$

$$\hat{\varepsilon} = Y - X\hat{\beta}$$

$$= (M + N)\varepsilon,$$

where

(i) $M = I - XS^{-1}X'$, idempotent of rank $(T - K)$,
(ii) $N = XS^{-1}R'(RS^{-1}R')^{-1}RS^{-1}X'$, idempotent of rank J, and therefore
(iii) $M + N$ is idempotent of rank $(T - K + J)$.
It follows that

$$T\hat{\sigma}^2 = \varepsilon'(M + N)\varepsilon.$$

$$b = S^{-1}X'Y = \beta + S^{-1}X'\varepsilon,$$

hence, $$b - \beta = S^{-1}X'\varepsilon.$$

Thus $(b - \beta)$ is a linear form in the Normally distributed vector ε, and $T\hat{\sigma}^2$ is an idempotent quadratic form in ε. Independence of the linear and quadratic forms requires $S^{-1}X'(M + N) = 0$. But

$$\begin{aligned} S^{-1}X'(M + N) &= S^{-1}(X'M + X'N) \\ &= S^{-1}[X'(I - XS^{-1}S') + X'(XS^{-1}R'(RS^{-1}R')^{-1}RS^{-1}X')] \\ &= S^{-1}[0 + R'(RS^{-1}R')^{-1}RS^{-1}X'] \\ &= S^{-1}R'(RS^{-1}R')^{-1}RS^{-1}X' \neq 0. \end{aligned}$$

Hence b and $T\hat{\sigma}^2$ are not independent. Q.E.D.

A.3 Predictive Testing

1. *$(I_m - Q^{-1})$ is a positive definite matrix*

$$Q = I_m + X_0S^{-1}X_0'.$$

Clearly, I_m is positive definite. Q is positive definite if $X_0S^{-1}X_0'$ is positive definite. Let z be any nonzero m-dimensional vector, then $z'X_0S^{-1}X_0'z = (z'X_0)S^{-1}(z'X_0)' > 0$, by virtue of S^{-1} being positive definite.

Since Q is positive definite, so is its inverse, thus I_m and Q^{-1} are positive definite and we can apply the theorem given in [17; pp. 581–583] which implies that $(I_m - Q^{-1})$ will be positive definite if and only if the roots of Q^{-1} are smaller than unity.

But the roots of Q^{-1} are the inverses of the roots of Q. Denote a root of Q by $(1 + \alpha)$, so that

$$\begin{aligned} 0 &= [Q - (1 + \alpha)I_m]z \\ &= [I_m + X_0S^{-1}X_0' - (1 + \alpha)I_m]z \\ &= [X_0S^{-1}X_0' - \alpha I_m]z. \end{aligned}$$

Thus α is a root of $X_0S^{-1}X_0'$ and must be positive since $X_0S^{-1}X_0'$ is positive definite. But $\alpha > 0$ implies $(1 + \alpha) > 1$, which implies $(1 + \alpha)^{-1} < 1$.

Q.E.D.

2. *The Distribution of*

$$(e_0^G)'[\hat{\Sigma}^{-1} \otimes (I_m + X_0S^{-1}X_0')^{-1}](e_0^G)\frac{(T - K - G + 1)}{mG(T - K)}$$

The vector of forecast errors, say $e_{0,g}$, corresponding to the gth endogenous variable is given by

$$e_{0,g} = X_0(b_g - \beta_g) - \varepsilon_{0,g},$$

where

(i) β_g is the vector of reduced form coefficients corresponding to the gth endogenous variable.
(ii) b_g is the Least Squares estimator of β_g.
(iii) $\varepsilon_{0,g}$ is the gth reduced form disturbance vector in the forecast period.

Then

$$\begin{pmatrix} e_{0,1} \\ e_{0,2} \\ \vdots \\ e_{0,G} \end{pmatrix} = \begin{pmatrix} X_0 & 0 & \cdots & 0 \\ 0 & X_0 & \cdots & 0 \\ \vdots & & & \\ 0 & \cdots & \cdots & X_0 \end{pmatrix} \begin{pmatrix} b_1 - \beta_1 \\ b_2 - \beta_2 \\ \vdots \\ b_G - \beta_G \end{pmatrix} + \begin{pmatrix} \varepsilon_{0,1} \\ \varepsilon_{0,2} \\ \vdots \\ \varepsilon_{0,G} \end{pmatrix}$$

or

$$(e_0^G) = Z_0(b - \beta) + (\varepsilon_0^G).$$

Conditional on X and X_0, e_0^G is clearly normally distributed with mean zero and the following covariance matrix.

$$E[(e_0^G)(e_0^G)'|X, X_0] = Z_0[\text{cov}\,(b - \beta)]Z_0' + \text{cov}\,(\varepsilon_0^G),$$

where

(i) cov $(b - \beta)$ is the covariance matrix of $(b - \beta)$ conditional on X and X_0;

$$\text{cov}\,(b - \beta) = \Sigma \otimes S^{-1},$$

(ii) cov (ε_0^G) is the covariance matrix of (ε_0^G);

$$\text{cov}\,(e_0^G) = \Sigma \otimes I_m,$$

and

(iii) Σ is the contemporaneous covariance matrix of ε.
Combining terms above yields

$$\begin{aligned} \text{cov}\,(e_0^G) &= E[(e_0^G)(e_0^G)'|X, X_0] \\ &= Z_0(\Sigma \otimes S^{-1})Z_0' + \Sigma \otimes I_m \\ &= \Sigma \otimes X_0 S^{-1} X_0' + \Sigma \otimes I_m \\ &= \Sigma \otimes (I_m + X_0 S^{-1} X_0'). \end{aligned}$$

Thus, $(e_0^G) \sim \mathcal{N}[0, \Sigma \otimes (I_m + X_0 S^{-1} X_0')]$,
which implies that

$$(e_0^G)'[\Sigma^{-1} \otimes (I_m + X_0 S^{-1} X_0')^{-1}](e_0^G)$$

is distributed as χ^2_{mG}.

Now $\hat{\Sigma}$, as defined in the body of the paper, is based only on the residuals in the period of fit which, it can be shown, are independent of e_0^G.

It follows [4; pp. 105–107, 181–183] that

(i) $(T - K)\hat{\Sigma}$ is a Wishart distributed matrix, independent of (e_0^G), with $(T - K)$ degrees-of-freedom, and

(ii) $$(e_0^G)'[\hat{\Sigma}^{-1} \otimes (I_m + X_0 S^{-1} X_0')^{-1}](e_0^G)\frac{(T - K - G + 1)}{mG(T - K)}$$

is distributed as $F_{mG, (T - K - G + 1)}$.

3. The Approximate Distribution of $(e_0^G)'[\hat{\Sigma}^{-1} \otimes (I_m + X_0 S^{-1} X_0')^{-1}](e_0^G)$ *for Large T, for Static Forecasting with Lagged Endogenous Variables.*

Again $(e_0^G) = Z_0(b - \beta) + (\varepsilon_0^G)$, but Z_0 contains lagged endogenous variables.

Since b can be written as $b = \beta + (Z'Z)^{-1}Z'\varepsilon^G$, where ε^G and Z are the fit period analogues of (ε_0^G) and Z_0 respectively, it follows that

$$(e_0^G - \varepsilon_0^G) = Z_0(Z'Z)^{-1}Z'\varepsilon$$
$$= Z_0(T^{-1}Z'Z)^{-1}T^{-1}Z'\varepsilon.$$

assuming that the observed moment matrix of the predetermined variables in the fit period converges in probability to their population moments, i.e., plim $(T^{-1}Z'Z)$ exists and is non-zero, then

$$\text{plim}\,[\sqrt{T}(e_0^G - \varepsilon_0^G)|Z_0]$$
$$= Z_0\,\text{plim}\,(T^{-1}Z'Z)^{-1}\,\text{plim}\,\sqrt{T}(T^{-1}Z'\varepsilon).$$

But plim $\sqrt{T}(T^{-1}Z'\varepsilon)$ is asymptotically distributed as Normal with mean zero and covariance matrix $\Sigma \otimes M_X^*$, where M_X^* is the matrix of population moments of the predetermined variables. (See [51; p. 487].) Further, by the definition of Z,

$$\text{plim}\,(T^{-1}Z'Z)^{-1} = I_{GK} \otimes (M_X^*)^{-1},$$

where I_{GK} is a $(GK \times GK)$ identity matrix. Thus, $\sqrt{T}(e_0^G - \varepsilon_0^G)$, conditional on Z_0, is asymptotically distributed as $\mathcal{N}(0, H)$, where

$$H = Z_0[I_{GK} \otimes (M_X^*)^{-1}](\Sigma \otimes M_X^*)[I_{GK} \otimes (M_X^*)^{-1}]Z_0'$$
$$= \Sigma \otimes X_0(M_X^*)^{-1}X_0'.$$

For large T, it should therefore be approximately true that

$$(e_0^G - \varepsilon_0^G) \text{ is approximately } \mathcal{N}(0, T^{-1}H).^1$$

Since e_0^G and ε_0^G are independent (e_0^G depending only on ε's prior to the fit period),

$$e_0^G \text{ is approximately } \mathcal{N}[0, (T^{-1}H) + (\Sigma \otimes I_m)],$$

for large T. But

$$(T^{-1}H) + (\Sigma \otimes I_m) = (T^{-1}\Sigma \otimes X_0(M_X^*)^{-1}X_0') + (\Sigma \otimes I_m)$$
$$= \Sigma \otimes [I_m + T^{-1}X_0(M_X^*)^{-1}X_0']$$
$$= \Sigma \otimes [I_m + X_0(TM_X^*)^{-1}X_0'].$$

Hence, for large T,

$$(e_0^G)'[\Sigma^{-1} \otimes (I_m + X_0(TM_X^*)^{-1}X_0')^{-1}](e_0^G)$$

is approximately χ^2_{mG}.

Since

$$\text{plim}\,\hat{\Sigma}^{-1} = \Sigma^{-1}$$

[1] $(e_0^G - \varepsilon_0^G)$ has of course a degenerate limiting distribution. We are arguing here that as T increases $(e_0^G - \varepsilon_0^G)$ "degenerates" through the normal limiting distribution of $\sqrt{T}(e_0^G - \varepsilon_0^G)$.

and plim $(T^{-1}S)$ = plim $(T^{-1}X'X) = M_X^*$, the above statistic can be consistently estimated by

$$(e_0^G)'[\hat{\Sigma}^{-1} \otimes (I_m + X_0S^{-1}X_0')^{-1}](e_0^G)$$

which, for large T, is also approximately χ^2_{mG}.

REFERENCES

[1] Adelman, I. and F. Adelman, "The Dynamic Properties of the Klein–Goldberger Model," *Econometrica*, Vol. 27 (1959).

[2] Aitchison, J. "Large Sample Restricted Parametric Tests," *JRSS* (series B), Vol. 24, 1962.

[3] Aitchison, J. and S. D. Silvey. "Maximum Likelihood Estimation of Parameters Subject to Restraints," *Annals of Mathematical Statistics*, Vol. 29, 1958.

[4] Anderson, T. W. *An Introduction to Multivariate Statistical Analysis*, J. Wiley and Sons, 1958.

[5] Atkinson, A. C. "A Method for Discriminating Between Models," *JRSS* (Series B) Vol. 32, 1970.

[6] Bancroft, T. A. "On Biases in Estimation Due to the Use of Preliminary Tests of Significance," *Annals of Mathematical Statistics*, Vol. 15, 1944.

[7] Bischoff, Charles W. "Business Investment in the 1970's: A Comparison of Models," *Brookings Papers on Economic Activity*, 1 : 1971.

[8] Box, G. and G. Jenkins, *Time Series Analysis*, Holden-Day, 1970.

[9] Chow, Gregory. "Tests of the Equality Between Two Sets of Coefficients in Two Linear Regressions," *Econometrica*, Vol. 28 (1960).

[10] Christ, Carl F. "A Test of an Econometric Model for the U.S., 1921–1947," in Universities—National Bureau Committee for Economic Research *Conference on Business Cycles*, New York, National Bureau of Economic Desearch, 1951, pp. 35–107.

[11] Christ, Carl F. *Econometric Models and Methods*, J. Wiley and Sons, 1966.

[12] Cohen, Kalman J. and R. M. Cyert. "Computer Models in Dynamic Economics," *QJE*, February 1961.

[13] Cooper, Ronald L. and D. W. Jorgenson. "The Predictive Performance of Quarterly Econometric Models of the United States," in *Econometric Models of Cyclical Behavior*, B. Hickman, Editor, Conference on Research in Income and Wealth, Vol. 36, National Bureau of Economic Research, 1972.

[14] Cox, D. R. "Further Results on Tests of Separate Families of Hypotheses," *JRSS* (Series B), Vol. 24 (1962).

[15] Cox, D. R. "Tests of Separate Families of Hypotheses," *Proceedings of the Fourth Berkeley Symposium on Mathematical Statistics and Probability*, Vol. 1, University of California Press, Berkeley, 1961.

[16] Darroch, N. N. and S. D. Silvey. "On Testing More than One Hypothesis," *Annals of Mathematical Statistics*, Vol. 34 (1963).

[17] Dhyrmes, Phoebus J. *Econometrics*, Harper and Row, 1970.

[18] Dhrymes, Phoebus J. "On the Treatment of Certain Recurrent Nonlinearities in Regression Analysis," *SEJ*, October 1966.

[19] Dickey, J. M. "Bayesian Alternatives to the F Test," Research Report No. 50, SUNY at Buffalo.

[20] Dunn, D. M., W. H. Williams, and A. Spivey, "Analysis and Prediction of Telephone Demand in Local Geographic Areas," *The Bell Journal of Economics and Management Science*, Vol. 2, No. 2, Autumn 1971, p. 561.

[21] Evans, Michael K., Y. Haitkovsky, and G. Treyz. "An Analysis of the Forecasting Properties of U.S. Econometric Models," in *Econometric Models of Cyclical Behavior*, B. Hickman, Editor, Conference on Research in Income and Wealth, Vol. 36, National Bureau of Economic Research, 1972.

[22] Fair, Ray C. *A Short-Run Forecasting Model of the U.S. Economy*, Heath and Co., Lexington, Mass., 1971.

[23] Fromm, Gary and P. Taubman. *Policy Simulations with an Econometric Model*. Washington, The Brookings Institution, 1968.

[24] Geisel, M. S. Comparing and Choosing Among Parametric Statistical Models: A Bayesian Analysis with Microeconomic Applications, Unpublished Ph.D. Dissertation, University of Chicago, 1969.

[25] Goldberger, Arthur S. *Econometric Theory*, J. Wiley and Sons, 1964.

[26] Goldfeld, Stephen M., R. E. Quandt, and H. F. Trotter. "Maximization by Quadratic Hill Climbing," *Econometrica*, July 1966.

[27] Haavelmo, T. "The Inadequacy of Testing Dynamic Theory by Comparing Theoretical Solutions and Observed Cycles," *Econometrica*, October 1940.

[28] Haitovsky, Yoel, and G. Treyz. "The Decomposition of Econometric Forecast Error," Mimeo.

[29] Haitovsky, Yoel, and N. Wallace. "A Study of Discretionary and Nondiscretionary Fiscal and Monetary Policies in the Context of Stochastic Macro-Econometric Models," in V. Zarnowitz, ed., *The Business Cycle Today*, N.B.E.R., 1972.

[30] Hickman, Bert G. "Introduction and Summary," in *Econometric Models of Cyclical Behavior*, B. Hickman, editor, Conference on Research in Income and Wealth, Vol. 36, National Bureau of Economic Research, 1972.

[31] Hogg, R. B. "On the Resolution of Statistical Hypotheses," *Journal of American Statistical Association*, Vol. 56 (1961).

[32] Hooper, J. W. "Partial Trace Correlations," *Econometrica*, Vol. 30 (1962).

[33] Houthakker, Hendrik S. and L. D. Taylor. *Consumer Demand in the United States*, Second edition, Harvard University Press, 1970.

[34] Howrey, E. Philip, "Dynamic Properties of a Condensed Version of the Wharton Model," *Econometric Models of Cyclical Behavior*, B. Hickman, editor, Conference on Research in Income and Wealth, Vol. 36, National Bureau of Economic Research, 1972.

[35] Howrey, E. Philip and H. H. Kalejian. "Computer Simulation Versus Analytical Solutions," in T. H. Naylor, ed., *The Design of Computer Simulation Experiments*, Duke University Press, 1969.

[36] Howrey, E. Philip, L. R. Klein, and M. D. McCarthy. "Notes on Testing the Predictive Performance of Econometric Models," Discussion Paper No. 173, Wharton School, Department of Economics, University of Pennsylvania, Philadelphia, 1970.

[37] Hymans, Saul H. "Consumption: New Data and Old Puzzles," *Brookings Papers on Economic Activity*, 1:1970.

[38] Hymans, Saul H. "Prices and Price Behavior in Three U.S. Econometric Models," Paper prepared for the Conference on the Econometrics of Price Determination, October 30–31, 1970. Washington, D.C.

[39] Jorgenson, Dale, W., J. Hunter, and M. Nadiri. "The Predictive Performance of Econometric Models of Quarterly Investment Behavior," *Econometrica*, March 1970.

[40] Larson, H. J. and T. A. Bancroft. "Sequential Model Building for Prediction in Regression Analysis," *Annals of Mathematical Statistics*, Vol. 34 (1963).

[41] Leamer, Edward E. "Model Selection Searches: A Bayesian View," Discussion Paper 151, Harvard Institute of Economic Research, December 1970.

[42] Lehmann, E. L. *Testing Statistical Hypotheses*, J. Wiley and Sons, 1959.

[43] Mincer, Jacob and V. Zarnowitz. "The Evaluation of Economic Forecasts," in J. Mincer, ed., *Economic Forecasts and Expectations: Analyses of Forecasting Behavior and Performance*, N.B.E.R., 1969.

[44] Naylor, Thomas H., K. Wertz and T. H. Wonnacott. "Spectral Analysis of Data Generated by Simulation Experiments with Econometric Models," *Econometrica*, April 1969.

[45] Pierce, D. A. "Fitting Dynamic Time Series Models: Some Considerations and Examples," Federal Reserve Bank of Cleveland, Mimeo.

[46] Ramsey, J. B. "Tests for Specification Errors in Classical Least-Squares Regression Analysis," *Journal of the Royal Statistical Society*, Series B, 1969, pt. 2, pp. 350–371.

[47] Seber, G. A. F. "Linear Hypotheses and Induced Tests," *Biometrika*, Vol. 51 (1964).

[48] Silvey, S. D. "The Lagrangian Multiplier Test," *Annals of Mathematical Statistics*, Vol. 30, 1959.

[49] Theil, Henri. *Applied Economic Forecasting*, Rand-McNally, 1966.

[50] Theil, Henri. *Economic Forecasts and Policy*, North-Holland Publishing Co., 1961.

[51] Theil, Henri. *Principles of Econometrics*, John Wiley and Sons, 1971.

[52] Theil, Henri and A. S. Goldberger, "On Pure and Mixed Statistical Estimation in Economics," *IER*, Vol. 2 (1961).

[53] Zarnowitz, Victor. "Forecasting Economic Conditions: The Record and the Prospect," in V. Zarnowitz, editor, *The Business Cycle Today*, National Bureau of Economic Research, 1972.

[54] Zarnowitz, Victor. *An Appraisal of Short-Term Economic Forecasts*, N.B.E.R., 1967.

[55] Zarnowitz, Victor. "New Plans and Results of Research in Economic Forecasting," *Fifty-First Annual Report*, National Bureau of Economic Research, 1971, pp. 53–70.

[56] Zarnowitz, Victor. "Prediction and Forecasting: Economic," *International Encyclopedia of the Social Sciences*, The Macmillan Co. and the Free Press, 1968.
[57] Zarnowitz, Victor, C. Boschan, and G. H. Moore, with the assistance of Josephine Su. "Business Cycle Analysis of Econometric Model Simulations," in *Econometric Models of Cyclical Behavior*, B. Hickman, Editor, Conference on Research in Income and Wealth, Vol. 36, National Bureau of Economic Research, 1972.
[58] Zellner, Arnold. *An Introduction to Bayesian Inference in Econometrics*, John Wiley and Sons, New York, 1971.

[7]

Econometrica, Vol. 41, No. 1 (January, 1973)

RESTRICTED AND UNRESTRICTED REDUCED FORMS: ASYMPTOTIC DISTRIBUTION AND RELATIVE EFFICIENCY[1]

BY PHOEBUS J. DHRYMES

This paper derives the asymptotic distribution of restricted and unrestricted reduced form estimators and compares their asymptotic efficiency. It also shows that the same techniques yield the asymptotic distribution of dynamic multipliers.

1. INTRODUCTION AND SUMMARY

IN THIS PAPER we derive the asymptotic distribution of the restricted reduced form, when the underlying parameters have been estimated by two stage least squares (2SLS) and three stage least squares (3SLS) methods. Since a number of other estimators such as limited information maximum likelihood (LIML) and full information maximum likelihood (FIML) have the same asymptotic distribution, under proper distributional assumptions, as 2SLS and 3SLS, we have also determined the asymptotic distribution of the restricted reduced form when the underlying parameters have been estimated by maximum likelihood methods, the structural errors being jointly normally distributed.

An interesting finding is that 2SLS induced restricted reduced form estimators are not necessarily (asymptotically) efficient relative to unrestricted reduced form estimators. This conflicts with the widely held view that "the more restrictions we take into account the more efficient the resulting estimators." What this statement overlooks is that in identifying the structural parameters of an econometric model we make use of two types of information: sample information and a priori information. Unrestricted reduced form estimators use all of the sample information, and none of the a priori information; 2SLS induced restricted reduced form estimation, on the other hand, uses all a priori information but, typically, only some of the relevant sample information, unless all of the system's equations are just identified.

In appropriately designed Monte Carlo experiments, Yamamoto [**5**] obtains mean square errors for unrestricted reduced form estimators which are appreciably smaller than corresponding mean square errors of 2SLS induced restricted reduced form estimators.

Some of the results of this paper have been obtained, previously, in the literature through somewhat heuristic arguments. In the basic Goldberger, Nagar, and Odeh [**2**] paper which first gave the (asymptotic) covariance matrix of 2SLS induced restricted reduced forms, the authors use a heuristic argument based on a Taylor series expansion. In fact, however, a Taylor series expansion is unnecessary and the desired result may be obtained by simple rearrangement.

The important paper by Klein [**4**] which deals with the efficiency of restricted reduced forms proceeds in a highly ingenious but rather heuristic manner and

[1] The research on which this paper is based was in part supported by National Science Foundation Grant GS 2289 at the University of Pennsylvania and was completed during the author's visit at the University of California, Los Angeles. I wish to thank P. Schmidt for helpful comments on an earlier version.

uses a definition of limited information restricted reduced forms which is at variance with what has become standard in the literature. Thus, it is easy to obtain the erroneous impression, not intended by the author, that limited information restricted reduced forms are necessarily efficient (asymptotically) relative to unrestricted reduced form estimators.

2. FORMULATION OF THE PROBLEM

In this, and subsequent discussion, we shall use the notation and conventions given in Dhrymes [**1**]. Thus let

$$y_{.i} = Y_i\beta_{.i} + X_i\gamma_{.i} + u_{.i} \qquad (i = 1, 2, \ldots, m) \tag{1}$$

be the econometric model under consideration. All identities have been removed by substitution[2] and the vectors $\beta_{.i}, \gamma_{.i}$ contain only those structural parameters not known a priori to be zero. The model contains m jointly dependent and G predetermined variables and all equations obey the rank condition for identifiability. The ith equation contains m_i unknown parameters in $\beta_{.i}$ and G_i unknown parameters in $\gamma_{.i}$. The error terms $u_{t.} = (u_{t1}, u_{t2}, \ldots, u_{tm})$, $t = 1, 2, \ldots$, are assumed to be a sequence of independent identically distributed (i.i.d.) random variables with finite second moments; in particular we have

$$E(u'_{t.}) = 0, \qquad \operatorname{cov}(u'_{t.}) = \Sigma \tag{2}$$

where Σ is assumed nonsingular. In (1) $y_{.i}$ is a T element vector of observations on the ith jointly dependent variable and $u_{.i}$ is a T element vector in the structural error of the ith equation; $x_{.i}$ is defined to be the vector of T observations on the ith predetermined variable. If we define

$$Y = (y_{.1}, y_{.2}, \ldots, y_{.m}), \qquad X = (x_{.1}, x_{.2}, \ldots, x_{.G}), \qquad Z = (Y, X), \tag{3}$$

we assume that

$$\operatorname*{plim}_{T\to\infty} \frac{1}{T} X'X = \overline{M} \tag{4}$$

exists as a nonsingular matrix with finite elements.[3] Put

$$B = (b_{.1}, b_{.2}, \ldots, b_{.m}), \qquad C = (c_{.1}, c_{.2}, \ldots, c_{.m}). \tag{5}$$

[2] This assumption is introduced only because we shall be dealing with full information estimators. It is clear that it need not be invoked when dealing with limited information estimators such as LIML or 2SLS.

[3] This assumption appears to rule out time trends as explanatory variables; however a slightly different set of assumptions can accommodate such variables. To give an example, for the scalar case we might impose the conditions

$$d_T^2 = \sum_{t=1}^{T} x_t^2, \qquad \lim_{T\to\infty} d_T^2 = \infty, \qquad \lim_{T\to\infty} \frac{\max_{t\le T} x_t^2}{d_T^2} = 0.$$

Then, instead of considering the asymptotic distribution of estimators centered about the true parameters and normalized by $\sqrt{T}$, we would normalize by $\sqrt{d_T^2}$.

In (5) $b_{.i}$ differs from $\beta_{.i}$ in that zeros have been appropriately inserted so that it is an m-element vector. Similarly $c_{.j}$ differs from $\gamma_{.j}$ in that zeros have been inserted, appropriately rendering it a G-element vector.

The matrix of reduced form coefficients is given by

$$\Pi = CD, \qquad D = (I - B)^{-1}. \tag{6}$$

Let the elements of C, B, not known a priori to be zero, be estimated by some consistent method and let $\tilde{C}$, $\tilde{B}$ be the matrices resulting when for the unknown parameters we insert their consistent estimators. Define

$$\tilde{\Pi} = \tilde{C}\tilde{D}, \qquad \tilde{D} = (I - \tilde{B})^{-1}. \tag{7}$$

Consider[4]

$$\tilde{\Pi} - \Pi = \tilde{C}\tilde{D} - CD = [\tilde{\Pi}(\tilde{B} - B) + \tilde{C} - C]D = (\tilde{\Pi}, I)\begin{pmatrix} \tilde{B} & -B \\ \tilde{C} & -C \end{pmatrix} D. \tag{8}$$

After some rearrangement, and writing in one column successive columns of $\tilde{\Pi} - \Pi$, we find

$$\tilde{\pi} - \pi = D^*\tilde{P}(\tilde{\delta} - \delta) \tag{9}$$

where

$$\begin{aligned} \pi &= (\pi'_{.1}, \pi'_{.2}, \ldots, \pi'_{.m})', \qquad D^* = D' \otimes I_G, \\ \tilde{P} &= \operatorname{diag}(\tilde{P}_1, \tilde{P}_2 \ldots, \tilde{P}_m), \qquad \delta = (\delta'_{.1}, \delta'_{.2}, \ldots, \delta'_{.m})', \\ \delta_{.i} &= (\beta'_{.i}, \gamma'_{.i})', \ \tilde{P}_i = (\tilde{\Pi}_i, L_i), \end{aligned} \tag{10}$$

L_i is a selection matrix such that

$$XL_i = X_i \qquad (i = 1, 2, \ldots, m), \tag{11}$$

and the $\pi_{.i}$ are the columns of Π. To understand the meanings of the matrices $\tilde{P}_i$, consider $\tilde{P}_1$. Partition

$$X = (X_1, X^*), \tag{12}$$

X_1 being the matrix appearing in (11) for $i = 1$. Partition

$$\Pi = \left(\pi_{.1}, \begin{matrix} \Pi_{G_1 m_1} \\ \Pi_{G_1^* m_1} \end{matrix} \ \Pi_{Gm^*} \right) \tag{13}$$

such that $\pi_{.1}$ is a column vector, $\Pi_{G_1 m_1}$ is a $G_1 \times m_1$ matrix, $\Pi_{G_1^* m_1}$ is $G_1^* \times m_1$ ($G_1^* = G - G_1$), Π_{Gm^*} is $G \times m^*(m^* = m - m_1 - 1)$, and observe that $\Pi_{G_1 m_1}$ is the submatrix of Π_1 corresponding to X_1 in the reduced form expression for Y_1, the latter being the matrix appearing in (11) for $i = 1$; similarly $\Pi_{G_1^* m_1}$ is the matrix of coefficients corresponding to X^* in the reduced form expression for Y_1.

Given initial consistent estimates $\tilde{B}, \tilde{C}$, we can determine $\tilde{\Pi}$ and, thus, the matrices $\tilde{P}_i$, $i = 1, 2, \ldots, m$.

[4] The second equality follows easily if we add and subtract $\tilde{C}D$.

By the consistency of $\tilde{\Pi} = \tilde{C}(I - \tilde{B})^{-1}$ as an estimator of Π, we have

(14) $$\bar{P}_i = \operatorname*{plim}_{T\to\infty} \tilde{P}_i = (\Pi_{\cdot i}, L_i) \qquad (i = 1, 2, \ldots, m).$$

The rank condition for identifiability, thus, easily implies that the matrices above are of full rank. We illustrate this for $i = 1$. We have, for arbitrary vectors α and β,

(15) $$\begin{bmatrix} \Pi_{G_1 m_1} & I \\ \Pi_{G_1^* m_1} & 0 \end{bmatrix} \begin{bmatrix} \alpha \\ \beta \end{bmatrix} = \begin{bmatrix} \Pi_{G_1 m_1} & \alpha + \beta \\ \Pi_{G_1^* m_1}\alpha & \end{bmatrix}.$$

But the vector on the right member of (15) can be the zero vector only if $\alpha = 0$ and $\beta = 0$ due to the rank condition

(16) $$\operatorname{rank} \Pi_{G_1^* m_1} = m_1 .$$

From (9) we then see that the asymptotic distribution of the restricted form coefficients is given by

(17) $$\sqrt{T}(\tilde{\pi} - \pi) \sim D^*\bar{P}\sqrt{T}(\tilde{\delta} - \delta), \qquad \bar{P} = \operatorname{diag}(\bar{P}_1, \bar{P}_2, \ldots, \bar{P}_m).$$

Since the asymptotic distribution of the quantity $\sqrt{T}(\tilde{\delta} - \delta)$ has been determined for a variety of estimating techniques, the problem of finding the asymptotic distribution of the quantity $\sqrt{T}(\tilde{\pi} - \pi)$ is thereby solved.

The following lemma is an immediate consequence of (17).

LEMMA 1: *Unless every equation in the structural system* (1) *obeys the rank and order conditions for just identifiability the restricted reduced form coefficients have a singular asymptotic distribution.*

PROOF: Let S be the covariance matrix of the asymptotic distribution of $\sqrt{T}(\tilde{\delta} - \delta)$. For the case of 2SLS and 3SLS estimated structural parameters, this is given explicitly in [**1**, ch. 4]. Under the conditions of this paper S is a nonsingular matrix of order K, where

(18) $$K = \sum_{i=1}^{m} (m_i + G_i).$$

But D^* is a nonsingular matrix of order mG while $\bar{P}$ is $mG \times K$ and its rank is, thus, at most K. Now, the identifiability conditions imply

(19) $$K \leqslant mG$$

and

(20) $$K = mG$$

if every equation is just identified; consequently the result follows immediately since from (17) we have that, asymptotically,

$$(21) \qquad \sqrt{T}(\tilde{\pi} - \pi) \sim N(0, D^* \bar{P} S \bar{P}' D^*).$$

REMARK 1: In Goldberger, Nagar, and Odeh [**2**] it would appear that the asymptotic covariance matrix derivation is valid even though the identifiability conditions are not valid. This is, however, incorrect. The authors operate essentially with

$$\operatorname{vec}\begin{bmatrix} \tilde{B} & -B \\ \tilde{C} & -C \end{bmatrix}$$

which will contain a number of zero elements. Consequently the matrices Σ_{ii} of their equation (4.2) will contain zero blocks, and in general the matrix Σ will be singular.

REMARK 2: In the very ingenious paper by Klein [**4**] it is not clear under what conditions the inverse in his equation (16) will exist. It is clear, however, *that if the inverse exists and if* $\hat{A}$, *in the notation of* [**4**], *is the asymptotic covariance matrix of the restricted reduced form coefficients*, then $\hat{A}$ must be singular.

3. ASYMPTOTIC EFFICIENCIES

DEFINITION 1: Let Θ^i, $i = 1, 2$, be two estimators of a parameter Θ such that, asymptotically,

$$(22) \qquad \sqrt{T}(\Theta^i - \Theta) \sim N(0, \Sigma_i), \qquad i = 1, 2.$$

Then, Θ^1 is said to be, asymptotically, efficient relative to Θ^2 if and only if

$$(23) \qquad \Sigma = \Sigma_2 - \Sigma_1$$

is positive semidefinite.

From the definition we deduce the following lemma.

LEMMA 2: *The 3SLS induced restricted reduced form estimator is asymptotically efficient relative to the 2SLS induced estimator.*

PROOF: By the results of the previous section the 3SLS induced estimator has the distribution given in (21) with

$$(24) \qquad S = S_3$$

where, in the notation of [**1**],

$$S_3 = \operatorname*{plim}_{T\to\infty}\left(\frac{Q'\Phi^{-1}Q}{T}\right)^{-1}, \qquad Q = \operatorname{diag}(Q_1, Q_2, \ldots, Q_m),$$

(25)

$$Q_i = R^{-1}X'Z_i, \qquad Z_i = (Y_i, X_i), \qquad X'X = RR', \qquad \Phi = \Sigma \otimes I_G,$$

and R is nonsingular. The 2SLS induced estimator has the asymptotic distribution given in (21) with

$$S = S_2 = \operatorname*{plim}_{T\to\infty}\left[\left(\frac{Q'Q}{T}\right)^{-1}\frac{Q'\Phi Q}{T}\left(\frac{Q'Q}{T}\right)^{-1}\right]. \tag{26}$$

Consequently, the positive semidefiniteness of

$$D^*\bar{P}S_2\bar{P}'D^{*\prime} - D^*\bar{P}S_3\bar{P}'D^{*\prime} = D^*\bar{P}(S_2 - S_3)\bar{P}'D^{*\prime}$$

follows immediately from the positive semidefiniteness of $S_2 - S_3$.

REMARK 3: Since single equation LIML and FIML estimators have the same asymptotic distribution as 2SLS and 3SLS respectively, the lemma above applies to the restricted reduced form estimators induced by these maximum likelihood methods.

We now turn to the question of whether restricted reduced form estimators of the type noted above are efficient relative to unrestricted ones.

We first note that the ordinary least squares (OLS) estimator of the unrestricted reduced form has, under the condition set forth in Section 2, the asymptotic distribution:

$$\sqrt{T}(\tilde{\pi} - \pi)_{\text{un}} \sim N(0, \Omega \otimes \bar{R}'^{-1}\bar{R}^{-1}) \tag{27}$$

where

$$\Omega = D'\Sigma D, \qquad \bar{R}'^{-1}\bar{R}^{-1} = \operatorname*{plim}_{T\to\infty}\left(\frac{X'X}{T}\right)^{-1} = \operatorname*{plim}_{T\to\infty}(\sqrt{T}R'^{-1})(\sqrt{T}R^{-1}). \tag{28}$$

We also note that

$$\Omega \otimes \bar{R}'^{-1}\bar{R}^{-1} = (D' \otimes \bar{R}'^{-1})(\Sigma \otimes I_G)(D \otimes \bar{R}^{-1}), \tag{29}$$

and moreover

$$\bar{P}_i = \bar{R}'^{-1}\operatorname*{plim}_{T\to\infty}\frac{Q_i}{\sqrt{T}} = \bar{R}'^{-1}\bar{Q}_i. \tag{30}$$

Consequently, we can write

$$D^*\bar{P}S_2\bar{P}'D^* = D^*(I_m \otimes \bar{R}'^{-1}) \times \operatorname*{plim}_{T\to\infty}\left[\frac{Q}{\sqrt{T}}\left(\frac{Q'Q}{T}\right)^{-1}\frac{Q'\Phi Q}{T}\left(\frac{Q'Q}{T}\right)^{-1}\frac{Q'}{\sqrt{T}}\right](I_m \otimes \bar{R}^{-1})D^{*\prime}, \tag{31}$$

and we thus find

$$\Omega \otimes \bar{R}'^{-1}\bar{R}^{-1} - D^*\bar{P}S_2\bar{P}'D^* = (D' \otimes \bar{R}'^{-1}) \times [\Sigma \otimes I_G - A(\Sigma \otimes I_G)A](D \otimes \bar{R}^{-1}) \tag{32}$$

where

$$A = \bar{Q}(\bar{Q}'\bar{Q})^{-1}\bar{Q}', \qquad \bar{Q} = \operatorname*{plim}_{T\to\infty}\frac{Q}{\sqrt{T}}. \tag{33}$$

We note that

$$\frac{Q}{\sqrt{T}} = (I_m \otimes \sqrt{T}R^{-1})\operatorname{diag}\left(\frac{X'Z_1}{T}, \frac{X'Z_2}{T}, \ldots, \frac{X'Z_m}{T}\right) \tag{34}$$

and thus A as exhibited in (33) is a well defined $Gm \times Gm$ matrix with finite nonstochastic elements. Before we deal with the problem of the efficiency of restricted relative to unrestricted reduced forms we require the following general result.

LEMMA 3: *Let B be an $n \times n$ positive definite matrix and A be an $n \times n$ symmetric idempotent matrix of rank $r \leqslant n$; let T be the matrix of the* (orthonormal) *characteristic vectors of A and define*

$$B^* = T'BT = \begin{bmatrix} B^*_{11} & B^*_{12} \\ B^*_{21} & B^*_{22} \end{bmatrix} \tag{35}$$

such that B^*_{11} is $r \times r$. Let

$$C = B - ABA. \tag{36}$$

Then (i) C is the zero matrix iff $r = n$, or equivalently iff $A = I$; (ii) C is positive semidefinite iff $B^*_{12} = B^{*\prime}_{21} = 0$; and (iii) C is an indefinite matrix iff $B^*_{12} \neq 0$.

PROOF: For (i) we note if A is of rank n, then from

$$AA = A \tag{37}$$

we conclude $A = I$. Thus, suppose $C = 0$; this implies

(38) $$\text{rank}(A) = n, \qquad A = I.$$

Conversely, suppose (38) to be true. Then it is obvious that $C = 0$.

For (ii) we observe that

(39) $$T'CT = B^* - \begin{bmatrix} I_r & 0 \\ 0 & 0 \end{bmatrix} B^* \begin{bmatrix} I_r & 0 \\ 0 & 0 \end{bmatrix} = \begin{bmatrix} 0 & B_{12}^* \\ B_{21}^* & B_{22}^* \end{bmatrix}.$$

If $B_{12}^* = 0$, it is obvious that $T'CT$, and hence C, is a positive semidefinite matrix. Conversely, suppose C is positive semidefinite; hence, so is $T'CT$. Consider the vector

(40) $$z = (x_1', x_2' - x_1' B_{12}^* B_{22}^{*-1})'$$

where x_1 has r elements and x_2 $n - r$, and observe that

(41) $$z'T'CTz = -x_1' B_{12}^* B_{22}^{*-1} B_{21}^* x_1 + x_2' B_{22}^* x_2.$$

For this quadratic form to be positive semidefinite the first term in the right member of (41) must be zero for all nonnull x_1. For if not, take $x_2 = 0$ and note that the quadratic form assumes a negative value which is a contradiction. This implies, however, that $B_{12}^* = B_{21}^{*\prime} = 0$.

Finally, for (iii) we note that if $B_{12}^* \neq 0$, then choosing a vector as in (40), we find for $x_2 = 0$ and x_1 such that $x_1' B_{12}^* \neq 0$,

(42) $$z'T'CTz < 0,$$

while for $x_1 = 0$ and $x_2 \neq 0$,

(43) $$z'T'CTz > 0$$

which establishes that $T'CT$, and hence C, is an indefinite matrix. To show the latter, choose z as in (40) and consider Tz with regard to the matrix C.

Conversely, suppose $T'CT$ is indefinite; then it is obvious that $B_{12}^* \neq 0$ for, if it were, then for any vector $x = (x_1', x_2')$,

(44) $$x'T'CTx = x_2' B_{22}^* x_2,$$

which shows that $T'CT$ is not an indefinite matrix, thus concluding the proof of the lemma.

COROLLARY 1: *If*

(45) $$B = kI, \qquad k > 0,$$

and A is as in Lemma 3, then

(46) $$C = B - ABA$$

is positive semidefinite.

PROOF:

$$T'CT = kI - k\begin{bmatrix} I_r & 0 \\ 0 & 0 \end{bmatrix} \tag{47}$$

which is obviously positive semidefinite.

COROLLARY 2: *Suppose*

$$B = \Sigma \otimes I_G, \qquad \Sigma = diag\,(\sigma_{11}, \sigma_{22}, \ldots, \sigma_{mm}), \tag{48}$$

and A is of the form

$$A = diag\,(A_1, A_2, \ldots, A_m), \tag{49}$$

the A_i, $i = 1, 2, \ldots, m$, *being symmetric idempotent matrices of dimension G and rank* $0 < r_i \leqslant G$. *Then*

$$C = B - ABA \tag{50}$$

is positive semidefinite.

PROOF: Since A_i is an idempotent matrix we may write

$$A_i = T_i\begin{bmatrix} I_{r_i} & 0 \\ 0 & 0 \end{bmatrix}T'_i = T_i I^*_{r_i} T'_i \qquad (i = 1, 2, \ldots, m). \tag{51}$$

Define

$$T = \text{diag}\,(T_1, T_2, \ldots, T_m), \qquad I^*_r = \text{diag}\,(I^*_{r_1}, I^*_{r_2}, \ldots, I^*_{r_m}), \tag{52}$$

and observe

$$T'CT = B^* - I^*_r B^* I^*_r. \tag{53}$$

We note, however, that

$$B^* = T'BT = B \tag{54}$$

is a diagonal matrix. Thus the condition for (ii) of the lemma is satisfied, and C is a positive semidefinite matrix.

LEMMA 4: 3*SLS induced restricted reduced form estimators are, asymptotically, efficient relative to unrestricted reduced form estimators.*

PROOF: We must show that

$$\begin{aligned}(\Omega \otimes \bar{R}'^{-1}\bar{R}^{-1}) - D^*\bar{P}S_3\bar{P}'D^{*\prime} &= (D' \otimes \bar{R}'^{-1}) \\ &\quad \times [\Phi - \bar{Q}(\bar{Q}'\Phi^{-1}\bar{Q})\bar{Q}'](D \otimes \bar{R}^{-1})\end{aligned} \tag{55}$$

is a positive semidefinite matrix. It will suffice to show that

$$\Phi - \bar{Q}(\bar{Q}'\Phi^{-1}\bar{Q})^{-1}\bar{Q}'$$

is positive semidefinite.

Postmultiplying by $\bar{Q}(\bar{Q}'\bar{Q})^{-1}$ and premultiplying by $(\bar{Q}'\bar{Q})^{-1}\bar{Q}'$, we find

$$(\bar{Q}'\bar{Q})^{-1}\bar{Q}'\Phi\bar{Q}(\bar{Q}'\bar{Q})^{-1} - \bar{Q}'\Phi^{-1}\bar{Q})^{-1} = S_2 - S_3 \tag{56}$$

which establishes the conclusion of the lemma.[5]

COROLLARY 3: *If all equations of the system obey the rank and order condition for just identifiability, then 3SLS induced 2SLS induced restricted reduced form and unrestricted reduced form estimators are asymptotically equivalent.*

PROOF: Proof is obvious from (55), (56) and the fact that under just identifiability

$$S_2 = S_3. \tag{57}$$

REMARK 4: Under conditions of just identifiability all reduced form estimators considered in the preceding discussion are numerically equivalent as well. This is due to the fact that in such a case 2SLS, 3SLS, and indirect least squares estimators of structural parameters coincide numerically.

The question of relative efficiency of 2SLS induced restricted reduced forms requires a lengthier argument to establish. We have the following lemma.

LEMMA 5: *Unless (a) the covariance matrix of the structural errors is diagonal, or (b) all equations of the system are just identified, 2SLS induced restricted reduced form are, asymptotically, neither efficient nor inefficient relative to unrestricted (OLS) reduced form estimators.*

PROOF: We have to show that

$$\begin{aligned}(\Omega \otimes \bar{R}'^{-1}\bar{R}^{-1}) - D^*\bar{P}S_2\bar{P}'D^{*\prime} &= (D' \otimes \bar{R}'^{-1}) \\ &\times [\Sigma \otimes I_G - A(\Sigma \otimes I_G)A](D \otimes \bar{R}^{-1})\end{aligned} \tag{58}$$

[5] An alternative, more direct proof, is as follows: Consider the characteristic roots of $\bar{Q}(\bar{Q}'\Phi^{-1}\bar{Q})\bar{Q}'$ in the metric of Φ. Thus we note

$$|\lambda\Phi - \bar{Q}(\bar{Q}'\Phi^{-1}\bar{Q})^{-1}\bar{Q}| = 0$$

iff

$$|\lambda I_{Gm} - \Psi\bar{Q}(\bar{Q}'\Phi^{-1}\bar{Q})^{-1}\bar{Q}'\Psi'| = 0$$

where $\Phi = \Psi^{-1}\Psi'^{-1}$. But the nonzero characteristic roots above are exactly those of

$$|\lambda I_K - (\bar{Q}'\Phi^{-1}\bar{Q})^{-1}\bar{Q}'\Psi'\Psi\bar{Q}| = |\lambda I_K - I_K| = 0$$

which shows immediately the validity of the assertion of the lemma.

is an indefinite matrix, unless Σ is diagonal or all equations are just identified. Since $D \otimes \bar{R}^{-1}$ is a nonsingular matrix it will suffice to do so for the bracketed matrix.

Let

$$(59) \qquad A_i = \bar{Q}_i(\bar{Q}_i'\bar{Q}_i)^{-1}\bar{Q}_i', \qquad A = \operatorname{diag}(A_1, A_2, \ldots, A_m),$$

$\bar{Q}_i$ being as defined in (30). Note that A_i is a $G \times G$ symmetric idempotent matrix and

$$(60) \qquad \operatorname{rank}(A_i) = m_i + G_i = r_i \qquad (i = 1, 2, \ldots, m).$$

Let T_i be the orthogonal matrix of the characteristic vectors of A_i. Partition

$$(61) \qquad T_i = (T_{i1}, T_{i2}) \qquad (i = 1, 2, \ldots, m)$$

such that T_{i1} is $G \times r_i$ and corresponds to the unit characteristic roots of A_i. Thus,

$$(62) \qquad A_i = T_i\begin{bmatrix} I_{r_i} & 0 \\ 0 & 0 \end{bmatrix}T_i = T_{i1}T_{i1}'.$$

Because T_i is orthogonal, we also have

$$(63) \qquad T_{i1}'T_{i1} = I_{r_i}, \qquad T_{i1}'T_{i2} = 0, \qquad T_{i2}'T_{i2} = I_{G-r_i} \qquad (i = 1, 2, \ldots, m).$$

Define now the matrix

$$(64) \qquad T = \begin{bmatrix} T_{11} & & 0 & T_{12} & & 0 \\ 0 & & \vdots & & & \vdots \\ & \ddots & \vdots & \ddots & & \vdots \\ \vdots & & 0 & & \ddots & 0 \\ 0 & & 0 & T_{m1} & 0 & 0 & T_{m2} \end{bmatrix}$$

and note that it is an orthogonal matrix of dimension mG. Moreover, we can write

$$(65) \qquad A = T\begin{bmatrix} I_r & 0 \\ 0 & 0 \end{bmatrix}T', \qquad r = \sum_{i=1}^{m} r_i.$$

Let $B = \Sigma \otimes I_G$. Then we must show that

$$(66) \qquad C = B - ABA$$

is indefinite unless Σ is diagonal or all equations of the system are just identified. By Lemma 3, C is not indefinite if and only if

$$(67) \qquad T'CT = \begin{bmatrix} 0 & 0 \\ 0 & B_{22}^* \end{bmatrix}$$

In view of the definition of T and B we have that

(68) $$B^* = \begin{bmatrix} B^*_{11} & B^*_{12} \\ B^*_{21} & B^*_{22} \end{bmatrix}$$

where

(69) $$B^*_{11} = [\sigma_{ij}T'_{i1}T_{j1}], \qquad B^*_{22} = [\sigma_{ij}T'_{i2}T_{j2}], \qquad (i, j = 1, 2, \ldots, m).$$
$$B^*_{12} = [\sigma_{ij}T'_{i1}T_{j2}], \qquad B^*_{21} = [\sigma_{ij}T'_{i2}T_{j1}]$$

Notice that T_{i1} is $G \times r_i$, $i = 1, 2, \ldots, m$, and consequently that B^*_{11} is an $r \times r$ matrix. Since T_{i2} is $G \times (G - r_i)$ it follows that B^*_{22} is $(Gm - r) \times (Gm - r)$. Finally B^*_{12} is $r \times (Gm - r)$.

By Lemma 3, the matrix in (66) is indefinite if and only if $B^*_{12} \neq 0$. Notice, that in view of (63) the block elements corresponding to the case $i = j$ vanish, i.e., we have

(70) $$\sigma_{ii}T'_{i1}T_{i2} = 0.$$

Consequently when Σ is diagonal, i.e., when $\sigma_{ij} = 0$, $i \neq j$ we conclude

(71) $$B^*_{12} = B^{*\prime}_{21} = 0$$

and thus C is positive semidefinite. If Σ is not diagonal, however, $B^*_{12} = 0$ if and only if

(72) $$T'_{i1}T_{j2} = 0 \qquad (i, j = 1, 2, \ldots, m).$$

We shall now show that this can occur only if all the system's equations are just identified. Noting that

(73) $$T_iT'_i = T_{i1}T'_{i1} + T_{i2}T'_{i2} = I,$$

we conclude that

(74) $$A_i = I - T_{i2}T'_{i2}.$$

In view of (72) and (62) we have, for all i

(75) $$\begin{aligned} A_iA_1 &= (I - T_{i2}T'_{i2})T_{11}T'_{11} = T_{11}T'_{11} = A_1 \\ &= T_{i1}T'_{i1}(I - T_{12}T'_{12}) = T_{i1}T'_{i1} = A_i, \end{aligned}$$

whence we conclude

(76) $$A_i = A_1 \qquad \text{for all } i.$$

In view of (30) we can write

$$A_i = P^*_i(P^{*\prime}_iP^*_i)^{-1}P^{*\prime}_i, \qquad P^*_i = \bar{R}\bar{P}_i = \bar{R}(\Pi_i, L_i),$$

and thus conclude

(77) $$(I - A_1)\bar{R}(\bar{P}_1, \bar{P}_2, \ldots, \bar{P}_m) = 0.$$

But the matrix $(L_1, L_2, \ldots, L_m)$ contains G linearly independent G-element vectors; this is so since every predetermined variable appears in at least one equation. In fact by rearranging columns we can write the matrix above as (I, L^*). Thus (77) implies, in part,

$$(I - A_1)\bar{R} = 0$$

whence we conclude

$$A_i = A_1 = I \qquad \text{for all } i. \tag{78}$$

Since I in (78) is of order G we have

$$\text{rank}\,(P_i^*) = \text{rank}\,(\bar{P}_i) = G \qquad \text{for all } i \tag{79}$$

which shows that every equation in the system must be just identified. Thus, we have proved that $B_{12}^* = 0$, in general, requires either that $\sigma_{ij} = 0$, $i \neq j$, or that every equation in the system be just identified.

REMARK 5: When Σ is diagonal

$$B_{22}^* = \text{diag}\,(\sigma_{11} I, \ldots, \sigma_{mm} I)$$

so that 2SLS induced restricted reduced form are asymptotically efficient relative to unrestricted reduced form estimates, as is also obvious from Lemma 4. On the other hand when all equations of the system are just identified, the matrix A of (58) is the identity, because the two covariance matrices are identical. Of course, we would expect this since in such a case indirect least squares and 2SLS estimates of structural parameters coincide, numerically as well.

REMARK 6: It is still possible to have $B_{12}^* = 0$ even though $\sigma_{ij} \neq 0$, $T'_{i1} T_{j2} \neq 0$ for some pairs (i, j). This could occur, e.g., if whenever $\sigma_{ij} \neq 0$, $T'_{i1} T_{j2} = 0$, and whenever $T'_{i1} T_{j2} \neq 0$, $\sigma_{ij} = 0$. Thus for certain types of models and certain types of data—since A_i and hence T_i depend *inter alia* on the matrix X—it is possible to have relative efficiency of 2SLS induced restricted reduced forms. These occurrences stress the fact that in terms of the criterion of relative asymptotic efficiency 2SLS induced restricted reduced form cannot, generally, be ranked with respect to unrestricted (OLS) restricted reduced form estimators.

REMARK 7: It is a generally held, intuitive, view that "the more restrictions are taken into account" the more efficient the resulting estimators. The result of Lemma 5 appears to run counter to this view. Is there a reconciliation? The answer appears to lie in the observation that $\hat{\pi}_{\text{un}}$ is an "efficient" estimator of the unrestricted reduced form, while $\hat{\pi}_{\text{2SLS}}$ is an "inefficient" estimator of the restricted reduced form. The intuitive basis of this observation is as follows. In the estimation of reduced (or structural) forms we have two types of information. The information conveyed by the sample (embodied in the predetermined variables) and the over-identifying restrictions (a priori information).

In estimating the "unrestricted" reduced form, we bring to bear on the estimation of each of the elements of the matrix Π *all sample information but no a priori information whatever.*

In obtaining 2SLS induced reduced forms we bring to bear *all a priori information*, but, generally, *only part of the sample information that may be utilized in this connection*. This is so since in estimating the elements of the columns of B and C we only use the predetermined variables actually appearing in the structural equation under consideration, plus certain linear combinations of all the predetermined variables of the system.

But unless we deal with a just identified equation (or the entire system is just identified) or the covariance matrix of the structural errors is diagonal, information that is conveyed by other equations, and which is relevant, is not utilized.

Thus, both estimating procedures leave something out of the maximal information set that may be utilized.

Since what they leave out is different, it is not surprising that some parameters may be estimated "better" by one method and others "better" by another. This is the meaning of indefiniteness in this context.

By contrast 3SLS induced restricted reduced forms use the maximal information set relevant and, for that "reason," are necessarily efficient (weakly) relative to 2SLS induced and unrestricted reduced form estimators.

REMARK 8: It might appear that Lemma 5 runs counter to the theorem given in Klein [**4**, p. 226]. This, however, is not so. Strictly speaking, that theorem refers to FIML induced restricted reduced forms when in obtaining the FIML estimators restrictions on the matrix C are taken into account in varying degrees.

Thus, the definition of "limited information" estimators employed in that paper is very different from what has become accepted usage in the literature.

The estimators commented on in [4] are, indeed, limited information in that the covariance structure of the error terms of the system is taken into account, restrictions on the matrix B are fully taken into account, but only part of the restrictions on the matrix C are observed, say those pertaining to the first m^* equations. However, in the standard usage of the literature, this is not what we mean by the 2SLS or LIML induced estimator of the restricted reduced form.

It is also possible to operate with only a subset of the system. In that case one uses the (marginal) likelihood function pertaining to that subset alone and takes into account all (relevant) restrictions on the matrix B and part or all of the (relevant) restrictions on the matrix C. In this interpretation, however, the restricted reduced form for the entire system is not well defined.

REMARK 9: The results of the lemma imply that there is no particularly compelling reason why 2SLS induced restricted reduced forms are to be preferred, for forecasting purposes, over unrestricted reduced forms. If we wish to gain predictive efficiency over OLS estimated unrestricted reduced forms, then we are assured of this only if we use 3SLS induced restricted reduced forms.

We have therefore proved the following theorem.

THEOREM: *Consider the structural econometric model*

$$y_{t.} = y_{t.}B + x_{t.}C + u_{t.} \qquad (t = 1, 2, \ldots, T), \tag{80}$$

where $y_{t.}$ *is an m-element row vector and* $x_{t.}$ *a G-element row vector of observations on the jointly dependent and predetermined variables respectively. The sequence* $\{u'_{t.} : t = 1, 2, \ldots\}$ *is one of i.i.d. random vectors obeying* (2). *Suppose that* (4) *holds,* $I - B$ *is nonsingular,* (80) *contains no identities and all equations are identifiable. If* (80) *is a dynamic model, i.e., if it contains lagged endogenous variables, the system is assumed to be stable. Then the following statements are true.*

(i) *If* δ *is the vector of unknown structural coefficients as defined in* (16) *and* $\tilde{\delta}$ *is a consistent estimator for it, the restricted reduced form estimator,* $\tilde{\pi}$, *of the vector* π *defined in* (16) *behaves, asymptotically, as*

$$\sqrt{T}(\tilde{\pi} - \pi) \sim D^* \bar{P} \sqrt{T}(\tilde{\delta} - \delta) \tag{81}$$

where D^* *is as defined in* (16) *and* $\bar{P} = \text{plim}_{T \to \infty} \tilde{P}$, $\tilde{P}$ *being as defined in* (16).

(ii) *If* $\tilde{\delta}$ *is the 2SLS estimator of* δ, *then*

$$\sqrt{T}(\tilde{\pi} - \pi)_{2SLS} \sim N(0, D^* \bar{P} S_2 \bar{P}' D^{*\prime}) \tag{82}$$

where S_2 *is as defined in* (26). *If* $\tilde{\delta}$ *is the 3SLS estimator of* δ, *then*

$$\sqrt{T}(\tilde{\pi} - \pi)_{3SLS} \sim N(0, D^* \bar{P} S_3 \bar{P}' D^{*\prime}) \tag{83}$$

where S_3 *is as defined in* (25).

(iii) *If* $\hat{\pi}$ *is the unrestricted estimator of* π, *then*

$$\sqrt{T}(\hat{\pi} - \pi) \sim N[0, D^*(\Sigma \otimes \bar{R}'^{-1} \bar{R}^{-1}) D^{*\prime}] \tag{84}$$

where $\bar{R}^{-1}$ *is as defined in* (28).

(iv) *The estimator in* (83) *is asymptotically efficient relative to the estimator in* (82) *and* (84).

(v) *The estimator in* (82) *is, asymptotically, neither efficient nor inefficient relative to that in* (84), *except in special circumstances.*

(vi) *The estimator in* (82) *is, asymptotically, equivalent to that in* (83), *i.e., both have the same asymptotic distribution, if the off diagonal elements of* Σ *in* (2) *vanish. In such case the two estimators are also numerically equivalent for every sample size.*

(vii) *The estimators in* (82), (83), *and* (84) *are asymptotically equivalent if and only if every equation in* (80) *obeys the rank and order condition for just identifiability. When this condition is satisfied then the three estimators are also numerically equivalent for every sample size.*

(viii) *Restricted reduced form estimators induced by single equation LIML, or FIML estimated structural parameters have, respectively, the same properties as those given in* (82) *and* (83).

REMARK 10: An interesting byproduct of the preceding result is that it affords us an asymptotic distribution theory for dynamic multipliers. Consider, for instance, the particular model

$$(85) \qquad y_{t.} = y_{t.}B + y_{t-1.}C_0 + w_{t.}C_1 + u_{t.}$$

where $(y_{t-1.}, w_{t.}) = x_{t.}$ and $(C_0', C_1')' = C$, in terms of the notation above, x_{t}. being the tth row of the matrix X, and $w_{t.}$ being the vector of *exogenous* variables.

Using lag operator methods we can solve the model to obtain

$$(86) \qquad y_{t.}' = (I - \Pi_0'L)^{-1}\Pi_1'w_{t.}' + (I - \Pi_0'L)^{-1}v_{t.}'$$

where

$$(87) \qquad \Pi_0 = C_0(I - B)^{-1}, \qquad \Pi_1 = C_1(I - B)^{-1}, \qquad v_{t.}' = (I - B')^{-1}u_{t.}'$$

and L is the usual lag operator. The dynamic multiplier matrix (see [**1**, ch. 12]) is given by

$$\Pi_1(I - \Pi_0)^{-1}$$

provided Π_0 is a stable matrix.

In the preceding we have shown how the (asymptotic) joint distribution of the elements of $\tilde{C}(I + \tilde{B})^{-1}$ can be inferred from the distribution of the elements of $\tilde{C}$, $\tilde{B}$. We have thus established the distribution of the matrix estimators $\tilde{\Pi}_0$, $\tilde{\Pi}_1$. It is, then, an easy modification of the procedure above to obtain the joint distribution of the elements of $\tilde{\Pi}_1(I - \tilde{\Pi}_0)^{-1}$. It is obvious that the result extends in the same manner to the case where the model contains additional lags in the endogenous variables, provided the model remains stable.

University of California

Manuscript received December, 1971.

REFERENCES

[1] DHRYMES, P. J.: *Econometrics: Statistical Foundations and Applications*. New York: Harper and Row, 1970.

[2] GOLDBERGER, A. S., A. L. NAGAR, AND H. S. ODEH: "The Covariance Matrices of Reduced Form Coefficients and of Forecasts for a Structural Econometric Model," *Econometrica*, 29 (1961), 556–573.

[3] HYMANS, S.: "Simultaneous Confidence Intervals in Econometric Forecasting," *Econometrica*, 36 (1968), 18–30.

[4] KLEIN, L. R.: "The Efficiency of Estimation in Econometric Models," in R. W. Pfouts, Ed., *Essays in Economics and Econometrics*. Chapel Hill: University of North Carolina Press, 1960.

[5] YAMAMOTO, T.: "Sampling Experiments of Predictive Ability," Mimeo, University of Pennsylvania, 1971.

[8]

Econometrica, Vol. 41, No. 2 (March 1973)

SMALL SAMPLE AND ASYMPTOTIC RELATIONS BETWEEN MAXIMUM LIKELIHOOD AND THREE STAGE LEAST SQUARES ESTIMATORS[1]

BY PHOEBUS J. DHRYMES

This paper deals with similarities and differences in the equations defining the full information maximum likelihood and three stage least squares estimators. It shows that the two sets of equations are similar, the difference being that the two estimators "purge" the jointly dependent variables differently. Hence, even if three stage least squares is iterated, it will not give an estimator which is the same as the maximum likelihood one. On the other hand, it is quite apparently asymptotically equivalent to full information maximum likelihood. A number of other results are also obtained.

1. INTRODUCTION

THE RELATIONSHIP BETWEEN full information maximum likelihood (FIML) and three stage least squares (3SLS) estimators has received considerable attention in the literature. In particular, Madansky [**5**], Sargan [**7**], and Rothenberg and Leenders [**6**] have shown that, asymptotically, the two procedures are equivalent in the sense of having the same asymptotic distribution under a given set of assumptions. Chow [**1**] examines such relations by comparing the minimands of the two procedures, but his derivation of the 3SLS estimator appears to be in error. The present author [**3**, **4**] has shown that the maximand of the FIML procedure can be decomposed into two components, one of which converges to zero in probability upon division by the sample size. It is then shown that 3SLS may be viewed as maximizing the first component given a prior consistent estimate of the covariance matrix of the system's structural errors. Hence, it was argued, iterating 3SLS until convergence is obtained will not yield the FIML estimator, because we disregard the second component. On the other hand, this approach makes clear the asymptotic equivalence of the two procedures. An objection may be raised, an unfounded one as it turns out, that in such arguments one ought to be dealing with the estimators themselves, not with their associated maximands.

In this paper we establish the nature of the small sample difference between 3SLS and FIML estimators, which makes it absolutely transparent why the two estimators have the same asymptotic distribution. The difference between the two estimators reduces essentially to the manner in which the explanatory current endogenous variables are "purged" of their stochastic component. We also point out how the Chow [**1**] derivation of the 3SLS estimator is in error and indeed we obtain a "linearized" FIML estimator similar in motivation to the one given in Chow [**2**]. This "linearized" estimator requires little additional computation over that required for 3SLS and has the same asymptotic distribution as FIML and 3SLS. Indeed, 3SLS may be viewed as a kind of "linearized" FIML.

[1] The research on which this paper is based was in part supported by National Science Foundation Grant GS 2289 at the University of Pennsylvania and was completed during the author's visit at the University of California, Los Angeles.

2. SPECIFICATIONS, ASSUMPTIONS, AND NOTATION

The standard simultaneous equations model may be written in the notation and conventions of [**3**] as

$$(1)\qquad Y = YB + XC + U$$

where

$$(2)\qquad \begin{aligned} Y &= (y_{\cdot 1}, y_{\cdot 2}, \ldots, y_{\cdot m}), \\ X &= (x_{\cdot 1}, x_{\cdot 2}, \ldots, x_{\cdot G}), \\ U &= (u_{\cdot 1}, u_{\cdot 2}, \ldots, u_{\cdot m}), \end{aligned}$$

the $y_{\cdot i}$, $x_{\cdot j}$, $u_{\cdot i}$ being, respectively, the T element (column) vectors of observations on the ith jointly dependent variable, the jth predetermined variable, and the structural error of the ith equation. It is assumed that all identities have been substituted out and that all equations obey the rank condition for identifiability. If lagged endogenous variables are included among the predetermined variables the system is, in addition, assumed to be stable. Moreover, the second order moment matrices of the current endogenous and predetermined variables are assumed to have well defined nonsingular probability limits.

The tth observation on the system in (1) may be written as

$$(3)\qquad y_{t\cdot} = y_{t\cdot}B + x_{t\cdot}C + u_{t\cdot} \qquad (t = 1, 2, \ldots, T)$$

where

$$\begin{aligned} y_{t\cdot} &= (y_{t1}, y_{t2}, \ldots, y_{tm}), \\ x_{t\cdot} &= (x_{t1}, x_{t2}, \ldots, x_{tG}), \\ u_{t\cdot} &= (u_{t1}, u_{t2}, \ldots, u_{tm}), \end{aligned}$$

it being implied that the system contains m jointly dependent and G predetermined variables.

Concerning the error structure we assume that the vectors $\{u'_{t\cdot} : t = 1, 2, \ldots\}$ are mutually independent, identically distributed, and moreover

$$(4)\qquad u'_{t\cdot} \sim N(0, \Sigma)$$

Σ being a positive definite matrix. No restrictions are imposed on Σ. The identifiability conditions exclude some variables from each equation, so that we may write, for example,

$$(5)\qquad y_{\cdot i} = Y_i\beta_{\cdot i} + X_i\gamma_{\cdot i} + u_{\cdot i} \qquad (i = 1, 2, \ldots, m).$$

The vectors $\beta_{\cdot i}$, $\gamma_{\cdot i}$ contain, respectively, m_i and G_i elements not known a priori to be zero.

3. THE RELATION BETWEEN FIML AND 3SLS ESTIMATORS

Given the assumptions in (4) we can write the (log) likelihood function of the sample as

$$
\begin{aligned}
L(A, \Sigma; Y, X) = & -\frac{mT}{2}\ln(2\pi) - \frac{T}{2}\ln|\Sigma| + \frac{T}{2}\ln|(I-B)'(I-B)| \\
& -\frac{T}{2}\operatorname{tr}\left\{\Sigma^{-1}A'\frac{Z'Z}{T}A\right\}
\end{aligned} \tag{6}
$$

where

$$
Z = (Y, X), \qquad A = [I - B', -C']'. \tag{7}
$$

Partially maximizing the function with respect to the elements of Σ, which are assumed to be unrestricted, we find $\Sigma(A) = A'Z'ZA/T$ and concentrating the likelihood function we have

$$
\begin{aligned}
L(A; Y, X) = & -\frac{mT}{2}[\ln(2\pi) + 1] - \frac{T}{2}\ln\left|A'\frac{Z'Z}{T}A\right| \\
& + \frac{T}{2}\ln|(I-B)'(I-B)|.
\end{aligned} \tag{8}
$$

Defining

$$
N = X(X'X)^{-1}X', \qquad \tilde{V} = (I - N)Y, \tag{9}
$$

we can rewrite (8) more suggestively as

$$
\begin{aligned}
L(A; Y, X) = & -\frac{mT}{2}[\ln(2\pi) + 1] - \frac{T}{2}\ln\left|\frac{\tilde{V}'\tilde{V}}{T}\right| - \frac{T}{2}\ln\left|\frac{A'Z'Z'A}{T}\right| \\
& + \frac{T}{2}\ln\left|(I-B)'\frac{\tilde{V}'\tilde{V}}{T}(I-B)\right|.
\end{aligned} \tag{10}
$$

Differentiating successively with respect to the columns of A, after a priori restrictions have been imposed, we find

$$
\begin{aligned}
& [Z^{*\prime}(\Sigma^{-1} \otimes I_T)Z^* - V^{*\prime}(S^{-1} \otimes I_T)V^*]\delta \\
& \quad = Z^{*\prime}(\Sigma^{-1} \otimes I_T)y - V^{*\prime}(S^{-1} \otimes I_T)v
\end{aligned} \tag{11}
$$

where

$$
\begin{aligned}
& Z^* = \operatorname{diag}(Z_1, Z_2, \ldots, Z_m), \qquad && \delta = (\delta'_{\cdot 1}, \delta'_{\cdot 2}, \ldots, \delta'_{\cdot m})', \\
& Z_i = (Y_i, X_i), && \delta_{\cdot i} = (\beta'_{\cdot i}, \gamma'_{\cdot i})',
\end{aligned}
$$

and

$$
V^* = \operatorname{diag}(\tilde{V}_1^*, \tilde{V}_2^*, \ldots, \tilde{V}_m^*), \qquad v = (\tilde{v}'_{\cdot 1}, \tilde{v}'_{\cdot 2}, \ldots, \tilde{v}'_{\cdot m})', \qquad \tilde{V}_i^* = (\tilde{V}_i, 0). \tag{12}
$$

$\tilde{V}_i$ is a submatrix of $\tilde{V}$ and bears the same relationship to the latter as Y_i bears to Y; the $\tilde{v}_{\cdot i}$ are the columns of $\tilde{V}$. In addition

$$S = (I - B)' \frac{\tilde{V}'\tilde{V}}{T}(I - B). \tag{13}$$

Since Σ in (11) is as defined in (4) and S is as defined in (13), it follows that (11) is a highly nonlinear function of δ and can only be solved by iteration. On the other hand the preceding discussion affords a particularly simple method of "linearizing" the FIML estimator.

Let $\tilde{\Sigma}$, $\tilde{S}$ be the matrices resulting when for the unknown parameter δ we substitute its 2SLS estimator $\tilde{\delta}$ in Σ and S respectively. The "linearized" FIML estimator of δ is then easily obtained as

$$\begin{aligned}\hat{\delta} = [Z^{*\prime}(\tilde{\Sigma}^{-1} \otimes I_T)Z^* - V^{*\prime}(\tilde{S}^{-1} \otimes I_T)V^*]^{-1}[Z^{*\prime}(\tilde{\Sigma}^{-1} \otimes I_T)y \\ - V^{*\prime}(\tilde{S}^{-1} \otimes I_T)v].\end{aligned} \tag{14}$$

It is now simple to verify that the estimator above has the same asymptotic distribution as the FIML estimator. Since the distribution of the latter is well known we shall confine ourselves to a very brief demonstration. To this effect define

$$\tilde{V}_i = (I - N)Y_i, \qquad Y_i^* = (Y_i, 0), \qquad Y^* = \operatorname{diag}(Y_1^*, Y_2^*, \ldots, Y_m^*). \tag{15}$$

and note that

$$\begin{aligned}V^* &= [I_m \otimes (I - N)]Y^*, \\ v &= [I_m \otimes (I - N)]y, \\ y &= (y'_{\cdot 1}, y'_{\cdot 2}, \ldots, y'_{\cdot m})'.\end{aligned} \tag{16}$$

Consequently, (14) may be written as

$$\begin{aligned}\hat{\delta} = [Z^{*\prime}(\tilde{\Sigma}^{-1} \otimes I_T)Z^* - Y^{*\prime}[\tilde{S}^{-1} \otimes (I - N)]Y^*]^{-1}[Z^{*\prime}(\tilde{\Sigma}^{-1} \otimes I_T) \\ - Y^{*\prime}[\tilde{S}^{-1} \otimes (I - N)]]y.\end{aligned} \tag{17}$$

Since $y = Z^*\delta + u$, $u = (u'_{\cdot 1}, u'_{\cdot 2}, \ldots, u'_{\cdot m})'$, it follows that

$$\begin{aligned}\hat{\delta} - \delta = [Z^{*\prime}(\tilde{\Sigma}^{-1} \otimes I_T)Z^* - Y^{*\prime}[\tilde{S}^{-1} \otimes (I - N)]Y^*]^{-1}[Z^{*\prime}(\tilde{\Sigma}^{-1} \otimes I_T) \\ - Y^{*\prime}(\tilde{S}^{-1} \otimes (I - N)]u.\end{aligned} \tag{18}$$

The desired result is then immediate if we note that, asymptotically,

$$\begin{aligned}\sqrt{T}(\hat{\delta} - \delta) \sim \left[\frac{(Z^* - V^*)'(\Sigma^{-1} \otimes I_T)(Z^* - V^*)}{T}\right]^{-1} \\ \times \frac{1}{\sqrt{T}}[(Z^* - V^*)'(\Sigma^{-1} \otimes I_T)]u\end{aligned} \tag{19}$$

which yields exactly the asymptotic distribution of the 3SLS estimator, and hence that of the FIML estimator.

REMARK 1: The expression in (17) affords a convenient iteration scheme for obtaining FIML estimators. Thus, the $(k + 1)$st iterate, $\hat{\delta}_{k+1}$, it given by

$$\text{(20)}\quad \begin{aligned}\hat{\delta}_{k+1} = {} & [Z^{*\prime}(\tilde{\Sigma}_k^{-1} \otimes I_T)Z^* - Y^{*\prime}[\tilde{S}_k^{-1} \otimes (I - N)]Y^*]^{-1}[Z^{*\prime}(\tilde{\Sigma}_k^{-1} \otimes I_T) \\ & - Y^{*\prime}[\tilde{S}_k^{-1} \otimes (I - N)]]y\end{aligned}$$

where $\tilde{\Sigma}_k$, $\tilde{S}_k$ are defined in terms of the kth iterate, $\hat{\delta}_k$.

If we put

$$\text{(21)}\quad \begin{aligned}Q_k &= Z^{*\prime}(\tilde{\Sigma}_k^{-1} \otimes I_T)Z^* - Y^{*\prime}[\tilde{S}_k^{-1} \otimes (I - N)]Y^*, \\ f_k &= [Z^{*\prime}(\tilde{\Sigma}_k^{-1} \otimes I_T) - Y^{*\prime}[\tilde{S}_k^{-1} \otimes (I - N)]]y,\end{aligned}$$

the iteration scheme above becomes

$$\text{(22)}\quad Q_k(\hat{\delta}_{k+1} - \hat{\delta}_k) = f_k - Q_k\hat{\delta}_k.$$

Alternatively if we follow a variant of the method of scoring we may use, instead, the iteration scheme

$$\text{(23)}\quad (\hat{\delta}_{k+1} - \hat{\delta}_k) = \bar{Q}^{-1}[f_k - Q_k\hat{\delta}_k], \qquad \bar{Q} = Z^{*\prime}(\tilde{\Sigma}^{-1} \otimes N)Z^*,$$

$\tilde{\Sigma}$ being an initial consistent estimate of Σ. Which of these two iterations, or other variants thereof, converges faster is an open question. The advantage of the scheme in (23) is that $\bar{Q}$ need be inverted only once, and it is, in addition, a consistent estimate of the covariance matrix of the asymptotic distribution of FIML (or 3SLS) estimated structural parameters.

Now, what is the small sample relation between FIML and 3SLS estimators? The answer is readily determined from (17). First we note that the 3SLS estimator may be written as

$$\text{(24)}\quad \begin{aligned}\hat{\delta}_{3SLS} = {} & [Z^{*\prime}(\tilde{\Sigma}_3^{-1} \otimes I_T)Z^* - Y^{*\prime}[\tilde{\Sigma}_3^{-1} \otimes (I - N)]Y^*]^{-1}[Z^{*\prime}(\tilde{\Sigma}_3^{-1} \otimes I_T) \\ & - Y^{*\prime}[\tilde{\Sigma}_3^{-1} \otimes (I - N)]]y\end{aligned}$$

where

$$\text{(25)}\quad \tilde{\Sigma}_3 = \frac{\tilde{A}'Z'Z\tilde{A}}{T}$$

and $\tilde{A}$ has been obtained by 2SLS methods. If we iterate 3SLS, and the iteration converges, we shall obtain an estimator obeying (24) *but in this case $\tilde{\Sigma}_3$ of* (25) *will be computed with $\tilde{A}$ as obtained by 3SLS methods.*

On the other hand if we iterate (17) and the iteration converges, then the FIML estimator will obey (17) but with

$$\text{(26)}\quad \tilde{\Sigma} = \frac{\tilde{A}_{ML}'Z'Z\tilde{A}_{ML}}{T}, \qquad \tilde{S} = (I - \tilde{B}_{ML})'\frac{\tilde{V}'\tilde{V}}{T}(I - \tilde{B}_{ML}).$$

In general, a converging iteration of 3SLS *will not* produce the FIML estimator. Intuitively, the essential difference between the two estimators is that FIML employs the quantities

$$\tilde{\sigma}^{ij}Y_i'Y_j - \tilde{s}^{ij}\tilde{V}_i'\tilde{V}_j, \qquad \tilde{\sigma}^{ij}Y_i'y_{\cdot j} - \tilde{s}^{ij}\tilde{V}_i'\tilde{v}_{\cdot j},$$

while the 3SLS estimator operates with the quantities

$$\tilde{\sigma}^{ij}(Y_i - \tilde{V}_i)'(Y_j - \tilde{V}_j), \qquad \tilde{\sigma}^{ij}(Y_i - \tilde{V}_i)'(y_{\cdot j} - \tilde{v}_{\cdot j}).$$

The "reason" the two estimators are asymptotically equivalent in terms of their asymptotic distribution is that

$$(27) \qquad \operatorname*{plim}_{T\to\infty} \tilde{\Sigma} = \operatorname*{plim}_{T\to\infty} \tilde{S} = \Sigma$$

where $\tilde{\Sigma}$, $\tilde{S}$ are defined as in (26) in the case of the FIML estimator, and $\tilde{\Sigma}$ is defined as in (25) in the case of the 3SLS estimator. Notice that $\tilde{S}$ is the estimator of Σ obtained from the residuals of the *unrestricted reduced form*, as modified in (26). On the other hand, $\tilde{\Sigma}$ in (26) and Σ_3 in (25) are estimators of Σ obtained from the residuals of the *restricted* reduced form, the former as induced by the FIML estimator of δ, the latter as induced by the 2SLS estimator of δ. Are there any conditions under which, for every sample size, FIML and 3SLS estimators will coincide? The answer appears to be yes, and the condition is that all equations of the system obey the rank (and order) condition for just identifiability. If in (17) we commence the iteration with $\hat{\delta}_{2SLS}$, then $\tilde{S}$ and $\tilde{\Sigma}$, thus computed, would be identical, since indirect least squares and 2SLS estimated structural parameters will coincide. Consequently, the first iterate would be simply the 3SLS estimate. But under just identifiability conditions 3SLS and 2SLS estimators coincide. Thus, nothing will be gained by further iteration. *Indeed under conditions of just identifiability (for all equations of the system) it would appear that 2SLS, 3SLS, and FIML estimators are identical for every sample size.*

The preceding discussion has therefore established the following:

THEOREM: *Consider the model in* (3) *and* (4) *together with the conditions customarily assumed for such simultaneous equations models. Then* (i) *iterating 3SLS until convergence is obtained does not yield the FIML estimator,* (ii) *the "linearized" FIML estimator exhibited in* (17) *has the same asymptotic distribution as the FIML estimator, and* (iii) *under conditions of just identifiability for all the equations of the system, FIML and 3SLS estimators coincide for every sample size.*

4. CHOW'S DERIVATION

In his interesting paper [**1**], Chow claims that 3SLS is obtained by minimizing

$$(28) \qquad |\Sigma^*| = |A'\tilde{Z}'\tilde{Z}A|$$

where

$$(29) \qquad \tilde{Z} = (\tilde{Y}, X), \qquad \tilde{Y} = NY,$$

and it is contrasted to the FIML estimator which minimizes

$$\frac{|A'Z'ZA|}{|(I - B)'(I - B)|}.$$

Unfortunately, it is not true that 3SLS is obtained by minimizing the expression in (28). If we did follow this procedure, then we would obtain either an inconsistent estimator or one that would not be defined in the limit. This is easily verified if one notes that in the process of minimizing $|\Sigma^*|$ of (28) we obtain a nonlinear expression in the elements of A. In 3SLS practice we use a prior estimate for these whenever they occur in Σ^{*-1}, thus obtaining a "linearized" version. But if $\tilde{A}$ is any consistent estimator of A, we see that

$$\text{(30)} \qquad \operatorname*{plim}_{T \to \infty} \frac{\tilde{A}'\tilde{Z}'\tilde{Z}\tilde{A}}{T} = 0.$$

In addition, if the ith equation is just identified, then it may be shown [**3**, p. 198] that the 2SLS residuals are orthogonal to the predetermined variables of the system. Consequently $\tilde{\sigma}^*_{ij} = 0, j = 1, 2, \ldots, m$, and the inverse Σ^{*-1} does not exist. As is easily verified, 2SLS is obtained by minimizing tr $A'\tilde{Z}'\tilde{Z}A$ while 3SLS is obtained by minimizing tr $\Sigma^{-1}A'\tilde{Z}'\tilde{Z}A$. In order to obtain 3SLS by minimizing a determinant we must operate *not* with (28) but rather with

$$\text{(29)} \qquad |\Sigma^*| = |(y_{\cdot i} - \tilde{Z}_i\delta_{\cdot i})'(y_{\cdot j} - \tilde{Z}_j\delta_{\cdot j})| \qquad (i, j = 1, 2, \ldots, m).$$

Thus, in Chow's framework 3SLS is obtained by minimizing (29) while FIML is obtained by minimizing

$$\frac{|(y_{\cdot i} - Z_i\delta_i)'(y_{\cdot j} - Z_j\delta_{\cdot j})|}{|(I - B)'(I - B)|} \qquad (i, j = 1, 2, \ldots, m).$$

5. CONCLUSION

In this paper we have elucidated the small sample relation between 3SLS and FIML estimators. Moreover, we have established that iteration of 3SLS does not yield FIML estimates. An interesting byproduct of this approach is the result that under just-identifiability conditions for all the equations of the system FIML and 3SLS estimators coincide for every sample size. Since it is known that 2SLS and 3SLS also coincide under such conditions, it is therefore established that in such a case all commonly employed limited and full information estimators yield identical estimates, apart from roundoff errors.

University of Pennsylvania

Manuscript received March, 1971; revision received July, 1971.

REFERENCES

[1] CHOW, G. C.: "A Comparison of Simultaneous Estimators for Simultaneous Equations," *Econometrica*, 32 (1964), 532–553.
[2] ———: "Two Methods of Computing Full Information Maximum Likelihood Estimates in Simultaneous Stochastic Equations," *International Economic Review*, 9 (1968), 100–112.
[3] DHRYMES, P. J.: *Econometrics: Statistical Foundations and Applications*. New York: Harper & Row, 1970.
[4] ———: "A Relation Between Three Stage Least Squares and Full Information Maximum Likelihood Estimators," Discussion Paper No. 83, University of Pennsylvania, Department of Economics, 1968.
[5] MADANSKY, A.: "On the Efficiency of Three Stage Least Squares Estimation," *Econometrica*, 32 (1964), 51–56.
[6] ROTHENBERG, T., AND C. T. LEENDERS: "Efficient Estimation of Simultaneous Equation Systems," *Econometrica*, 32 (1964), 57–76.
[7] SARGAN, J. D. "Three Stage Least Squares and Full Maximum Likelihood Estimates," *Econometrica*, 32 (1964), 77–81.

Reprinted for private circulation from Western Economic Journal
Vol. XI, No. 2, June 1973 • Copyright 1973 • Printed in U.S.A.

A SIMPLE PROOF OF THE ASYMPTOTIC EFFICIENCY OF 3SLS RELATIVE TO 2SLS ESTIMATORS

PHOEBUS J. DHRYMES
University of California, Los Angeles

I. INTRODUCTION

In this note we provide a simple proof that the 3SLS is asymptotically efficient relative to 2SLS estimator by showing that the appropriate difference of the covariance matrices of their asymptotic distribution is positive semidefinite. The proof is novel and simple in that it utilizes exactly the procedure for showing the efficiency of Aitken relative to ordinary least squares estimators in the context of the general linear model.

Previous proofs of this fact [1], [2], [3], [4] are unduly complicated.

II. FORMULATION OF THE PROBLEM

Utilizing the notation in [1], we deal with the model

$$Y = YB + XC + U \tag{1}$$

where $Y = (y_{\cdot 1}, y_{\cdot 2}, \ldots, y_{\cdot m}), X = (x_{\cdot 1}, x_{\cdot 2}, \ldots, x_{\cdot G})$ are the matrices (of T observations) on the m current endogenous and G pre-determined variables, respectively. It is further assumed that

$$\{ u_{t\cdot}' : t = 1, 2, \ldots \}$$

is a sequence of independent identically distributed random variables such that

$$E(u_{t\cdot}') = 0, \text{Cov}\,(u_{t\cdot}') = \Sigma \tag{2}$$

Σ being positive definite; i.e., for simplicity we assume that the model contains no identities. It is also assumed that

$$\underset{T \to \infty}{\text{plim}}\,(X'X)/T = M \tag{3}$$

is a positive definite matrix.

Imposing the a priori restrictions on the elements of B, C and multiplying on the left by $R^{-1}X'$ we have, for the i-th structural equation

$$w_{\cdot i} = Q_i \delta_{\cdot i} + r_{\cdot i} \qquad i = 1, 2, \ldots, m \tag{4}$$

where R is a nonsingular matrix such that $X'X = RR'$ and

(5) $$w_{\cdot i} = R^{-1}X'y_{\cdot i},\ Q_i = R^{-1}X'Z_i,\ Z_i = (Y_i, X_i),\ \delta_{\cdot i} = (\beta_{\cdot i}', \gamma_{\cdot i}')',$$
$$r_{\cdot i} = R^{-1}X'u_{\cdot i}$$

the $u_{\cdot i}$ being the T element columns of U.

The system may then be written in the compact notation

(6) $$w = Q\delta + r$$

where

(7) $$w = (w_{\cdot 1}', w_{\cdot 2}', \ldots, w_{\cdot m}')',\ Q = \text{diag}(Q_1, Q_2, \ldots, Q_m),$$
$$\delta = (\delta_{\cdot 1}', \delta_{\cdot 2}, \ldots, \delta_{\cdot m}')',\ r = (r_{\cdot 1}', r_{\cdot 2}', \ldots, r_{\cdot m}')'.$$

It is shown in [1] that

(8) $$(\tilde{\delta} - \delta)_{2SLS} = (Q'Q)^{-1}Q'r,\ (\dot{\delta} - \delta)_{3SLS} = (Q'\tilde{\Phi}^{-1}Q)^{-1}Q'\tilde{\Phi}^{-1}r$$

where

$$\tilde{\Phi} = \tilde{\Sigma} \otimes I_G$$

and $\tilde{\Sigma}$ is a consistent estimator of Σ.

We now observe that if we write the reduced form as

(9) $$Y = X\Pi + V$$

and obtain

(10) $$\tilde{\Pi} = (X'X)^{-1}X'Y$$

then

(11) $$Q_i'Q_i = Z_i'X(X'X)^{-1}X'Z_i = \tilde{S}_i'X'X\tilde{S}_i$$

where

(12) $$\tilde{S}_i = (\tilde{\Pi}_i, P_i)$$

such that $\tilde{\Pi}_i = (X'X)^{-1}X'Y_i$ and P_i is a selection matrix such that $X_i = XP_i$. It follows then that

(13) $$(Q'Q)/T = \tilde{S}'[I_m \otimes (X'X)/T]\tilde{S},\quad \tilde{S} = \text{diag}(\tilde{S}_1, \tilde{S}_2, \ldots, \tilde{S}_m)$$

and moreover

(14) $$(Q'r)/\sqrt{T} = \tilde{S}'(1/\sqrt{T})(I_m \otimes X')u,\quad u = (u_{\cdot 1}', u_{\cdot 2}', \ldots, u_{\cdot m}')'$$

Moreover

(15) $$(Q'\tilde{\Phi}^{-1}Q)/T = \tilde{S}'[\tilde{\Sigma}^{-1} \otimes (X'X)/T]\tilde{S}$$

(16) $$(Q'\tilde{\Phi}^{-1}r)/\sqrt{T} = \tilde{S}'(\tilde{\Sigma}^{-1} \otimes I_G)(1/\sqrt{T})(I_m \otimes X')u$$

Since $\tilde{S}_i$ converges in probability to $S_i = (\Pi_i, P_i)$ we see that, asymptotically,

(17) $$\sqrt{T}(\tilde{\delta} - \delta)_{2SLS} \sim (S^{*\prime}S^*)^{-1}S'(1/\sqrt{T})(I_m \otimes X')u$$

(18) $$\sqrt{T}(\dot{\delta} - \delta)_{3SLS} \sim (S^{*\prime}\Phi^{-1}S^*)^{-1}S'\Phi^{-1}(1/\sqrt{T})(I_m \otimes X')u$$

An important implication of (17) and (18) is *that the arguments establishing the asymptotic distribution of* 2SLS *are exactly those establishing the asymptotic distribution of* 3SLS *estimators*. In (17) and (18),

$$S^* = \text{diag}\,(S_1^*, S_2^*, \ldots, S_m^*),\ S_i^* = \bar{R}S_i, \qquad i = 1, 2, \ldots, m$$

and $\bar{R}$ is a nonsingular matrix such that

$$M = \bar{R}\bar{R}'$$

Under the standard assumptions we have that, asymptotically,

(19) $$1/\sqrt{T}(I_m \otimes X')u \sim N(0, \Sigma \otimes \bar{R}\bar{R}')$$

whence it is seen, immediately, that

(20) $$\sqrt{T}(\tilde{\delta} - \delta)_{2SLS} \sim N(0, C_2),\ \sqrt{T}(\dot{\delta} - \delta)_{3SLS} \sim N(0, C_3)$$

where

(21) $$C_2 = (S^{*\prime}S^*)^{-1}S^{*\prime}\Phi S^*(S^{*\prime}S^*)^{-1},\ C_3 = (S^{*\prime}\Phi^{-1}S^*)^{-1}$$

But showing that $C_2 - C_3 \geqslant 0$ involves exactly the elementary arguments one uses in establishing the efficiency of Aitken relative to ordinary least squares estimators in the context of the general linear model. Precisely, write

(22) $$(S^{*\prime}S^*)^{-1}S^{*\prime} = (S^{*\prime}\Phi^{-1}S^*)^{-1}S^{*\prime}\,\Phi^{-1} + F.$$

Note that $FS^* = 0$; post multiply by Φ, transpose and post multiply by it the two members of (22) to obtain

(23) $$(S^{*\prime}S^*)^{-1}S^{*\prime}\Phi S^*(S^{*\prime}S^*)^{-1} = (S^{*\prime}\Phi^{-1}S^*)^{-1} + F\Phi F', \text{ q.e.d.}$$

REFERENCES

1. P. J. Dhrymes, *Econometrics: Statistical Foundations and Applications*, New York 1970.
2. A. Madansky, "On the Efficiency of Three Stage Least Squares Estimation," *Econometrica*, 1964, *32*, 51-56.
3. T. J. Rothenberg and C. T. Leenders, "Efficient Estimation of Simultaneous Equation Systems," *Econometrica*, 1964, *32*, 57-76.
4. J. D. Sargan, "Three Stage Least Squares and Full Maximum Likelihood Estimates," *Econometrica*, 1964, *32*, 77-81.

Econometrica, Vol. 42, No. 2 (March, 1974)

A COMPARISON OF SOME LIMITED INFORMATION ESTIMATORS FOR DYNAMIC SIMULTANEOUS EQUATIONS MODELS WITH AUTOCORRELATED ERRORS[1]

BY PHOEBUS J. DHRYMES, R. BERNER, AND D. CUMMINS

In this paper we consider a number of estimators for the linear structural simultaneous equations model containing lagged endogenous variables and autocorrelated errors. The special case is considered in which the matrix of autocorrelation coefficients of the (vector) structural error process is *diagonal*.

We consider the two stage least squares analogue (C2SLA) in this case, its relation to the estimators proposed earlier by Fair, the estimator obtained when the autocorrelation matrix is known, and a number of instrumental variables estimators, as well as a modification of the method of scoring which yields an estimator that is asymptotically equivalent to the C2SLSA estimator.

The asymptotic distributions of such estimators are obtained and we determine their relative asymptotic efficiencies.

1. INTRODUCTION

WHILE MOST ECONOMETRIC models extant contain lagged endogenous variables among their predetermined variables, relatively little attention has been paid to the complications entailed by the, possibly, autoregressive character of structural errors. Indeed, most such models are estimated by some variant of two stage least squares (2SLS). The problem has been examined, first by Sargan [**15**] and later by Amemiya [**1**] and Fair [**9**]. Sargan operates in a very general context and Amemiya assumes in his models the absence of lagged endogenous variables. The present paper has been stimulated by Fair's contribution which, while an interesting addition to the literature of such models, leaves a number of questions unanswered.

In a previous version of this paper [**8**] we considered a simple two step estimator whose asymptotic distribution was invariant to iteration. Here we shall examine systematically the problem of limited information estimation in the context of a model containing first order lags in the endogenous variables and an autoregressive error process of the first order. Extension to higher order lags in the dependent variables and higher order autoregressions is rather routine.

We shall show that one of the procedures suggested by Fair is similar, but not identical to the limited information variant of the estimators discussed in Dhrymes [**4**]. We shall also show how a modified method of scoring approach yields estimators that are asymptotically equivalent to the converging iterate of the two stage least squares estimator (C2SLSA) as discussed in [**4**].

Finally, having produced the asymptotic distributions of the estimators above, we shall obtain a ranking of the various alternatives based on the covariance matrices of the appropriate asymptotic distributions.

[1] The research on which this paper is based was, in part, supported by National Science Foundation Grant GS2289 at the University of Pennsylvania (Dhrymes), the National Defense Education Act, Title IV (Berner), and the S. S. Huebner Foundation (Cummins).

2. FORMULATION OF THE PROBLEM

Consider the standard linear dynamic structural econometric model for which we have a sample of size T. It may be written, compactly, as

$$(1) \qquad Y = YB + XC + U,$$

where Y is $T \times m$, X is $T \times G$, and U is $T \times m$, being, respectively, the matrices of current endogenous variables, predetermined variables, and error terms of the system. The matrices B and C are $m \times m$ and $G \times m$ and comprise, subject to certain identifiability restrictions, the unknown structural parameters of the problem.

Following the practice in Amemiya [**1**] and Fair [**9**], we write the error specification as

$$(2) \qquad U = U_{-1}R + E,$$

where

$$(3) \qquad R = \operatorname{diag}(\rho_1, \rho_2, \ldots, \rho_m), \qquad |\rho_i| < 1 \qquad (i = 1, 2, \ldots, m).$$

It is assumed that the rows of E, i.e., $\varepsilon_{t\cdot} = (\varepsilon_{t1}, \varepsilon_{t2}, \ldots, \varepsilon_{tm})$, $t = 1, 2, \ldots, T$, constitute a random sample, or more generally $\{\varepsilon'_{t\cdot} : t = 0, \pm 1, \pm 2, \ldots\}$ is a sequence of independent identically distributed (i.i.d.) random variables. In addition, it is assumed that

$$(4) \qquad E(\varepsilon'_{t\cdot}) = 0, \qquad \operatorname{cov}(\varepsilon'_{t\cdot}) = \Sigma,$$

Σ being a general (unrestricted) positive definite matrix, and that the equations of the system are identifiable.

REMARK 1: The fact that R is assumed to be a diagonal matrix in no way implies that the error terms of the system are uncorrelated or mutually independent across equations. One may, quite easily, show that

$$(5) \qquad \Omega = R\Omega R + \Sigma, \qquad \Omega = \operatorname{cov}(u'_{t\cdot}).$$

Consequently, the u_{ti}, $i = 1, 2, \ldots, m$, are *not* generally uncorrelated (or in the case of normality independent).

Let us now focus on one of the equations of the system, say the first. We may write

$$(6) \qquad y_{\cdot 1} = Y_1\beta_{\cdot 1} + X_1\gamma_{\cdot 1} + u_{\cdot 1},$$

where $y_{\cdot 1}, u_{\cdot 1}$ are, respectively, the first columns of Y and U; $\beta_{\cdot 1}, \gamma_{\cdot 1}$ are the first columns of B and C after elements known to be zero have been suppressed; and Y_1 and X_1 are, thus, appropriate submatrices of Y and X.

For simplicity we assume that the system contains only first order lags.[2]

[2] Higher order lags can be easily accommodated at the cost of some analytical complications. No essentially new problem, however, is introduced.

Consequently, partition

$$X_1 = ({}_1Y^*_{-1}, W_1), \tag{7}$$

where ${}_1Y^*_{-1}$ is an appropriate submatrix of Y_{-1}, and W_1 is an appropriate submatrix of W, a $T \times s$ matrix containing all the exogenous variables of the system.

To conclude this section it seems appropriate to restate Fair's proposal in the context of our notation. This will elucidate at least one of the alternatives with which he has dealt and indicate the similarities and differences of his procedure relative to the estimators to be discussed below.

While a number of suggestions are put forth, perhaps the most clearly enunciated of Fair's procedures is the following:

(i) Regress the variables in Y_1 on a set of variables that, at least, *includes*[3] $Y_{1,-1}$, the variables in Y_1 lagged one period, the variables in ${}_1Y^*_{-1}$ as well as their one period lags, and the variables in W_1 as well as their one period lags, and obtain the "predicted" matrix $\hat{Y}_1$.

(ii) Regress $(y_{t1} - \rho_1 y_{t-1,1})$ on the variables contained in the matrices $(\hat{Y}_1 - \rho_1 Y_{1,-1})$, $({}_1Y^*_{-1} - \rho_{11} Y^*_{-2})$, and $(W_1 - \rho_1 W_{1,-1})$ repeatedly, with ρ varying over the interval, say, $[-.99, .99]$, and select that regression which minimizes the sum of squared residuals. From that regression one, thus, obtains estimators of $\delta_{\cdot 1}, \rho_1$, say $\tilde{\delta}_{\cdot 1}, \tilde{\rho}_1$.

A difficulty with this procedure is that the list of regressors is not specified and no attempt is made to determine precisely how the properties of the structural estimators are affected by the choice of regressors at the first stage. Moreover, if we follow the procedure not merely for one equation of the system but for all, we would expect to have a situation in which a variable in Y_1 is "explained" (at the first stage) by different specifications depending on which structural equation is considered at the moment.

3. A TWO STEP ALTERNATIVE

Consider again, under the standard assumptions, the model in (1), whose first equation is as exhibited in (6). Let W be the $T \times s$ matrix of exogenous variables in the entire system, of which W_1 is an appropriate submatrix. Using W_1 and as many other columns of W (and W_{-1}, if necessary) as there are columns in Y_1 and ${}_1Y^*_{-1}$, estimate[4] $\delta_{\cdot 1}$ by instrumental variables. More precisely, let P_1 be the matrix of instruments so selected. The first stage estimator of $\delta_{\cdot 1}$ is then

$$\tilde{\delta}_{\cdot 1} = (P_1' Z_1)^{-1} P_1' y_{\cdot 1}. \tag{8}$$

Under the standard assumptions (a matter we shall examine at greater length below) the estimator in (8) is consistent.

[3] This is the aspect of the procedure that makes it ill specified.

[4] It is assumed that the model contains enough exogenous variables for this to be feasible.

Do this for every equation and thus estimate consistently the parameters of B and C not known a priori to be zero. Partition conformably,

$$(9) \qquad X = (Y_{-1}, W), \qquad \Pi = \begin{pmatrix} \Pi_0 \\ \Pi_1 \end{pmatrix}, \qquad \Pi = C(I - B)^{-1},$$

and note that the tth row of the reduced form is given by

$$(10) \qquad y_{t\cdot} = y_{t-1\cdot}\Pi_0 + w_{t\cdot}\Pi_1 + v_{t\cdot}, \qquad v_{t\cdot} = u_{t\cdot}(I - B)^{-1},$$

$u_{t\cdot}$ being the tth row of U, $y_{t\cdot}$ the tth row of Y, and $w_{t\cdot}$ the tth row of W.

Since $\tilde{B}$ and $\tilde{C}$ have been estimated consistently we can obtain "predictions" of $y_{t\cdot}$, recursively, from

$$(11) \qquad \tilde{y}_{t\cdot} = \tilde{y}_{t-1\cdot}\tilde{\Pi}_0 + w_{t\cdot}\tilde{\Pi}_1$$

given some fixed initial condition, the simplest of which is $\tilde{y}_{0\cdot} = 0$.

REMARK 2: The initial condition $\tilde{y}_{0\cdot} = 0$ is, of course, quite arbitrary and the particular estimates are likely, in small samples, to be sensitive to this requirement, i.e., the numbers one obtains in any given application are likely to vary as we alter the specification. The properties of the *estimators*, however, are unaffected by such practices if the model is *stable*, as one customarily assumes. For alternative ways of handling this aspect, see Pesaran [**14**]. Such alternatives, proposed in the context of single equation models, entail specific assumptions on the sequence of exogenous variables $\{w_{t\cdot} : t = 0, \pm 1, \pm 2, \ldots\}$.

In this connection, it should be pointed out that Monte Carlo studies, in a single equation context, indicate that small sample "bias" and "mean square errors" are not materially affected by whether we "estimate" initial conditions or set them equal to zero (see, for example, Morrison [**13**]). On the other hand such "estimates" of initial conditions are not consistent.

From (11) we thus obtain the matrix $\tilde{Y}$ of "predictions," and lagging every element once we obtain $\tilde{Y}_{-1\cdot}$.

In addition, from the first stage estimators we have

$$(12) \qquad \tilde{u}_{\cdot 1} = y_{\cdot 1} - Z_1\tilde{\delta}_{\cdot 1},$$

and from these residuals we obtain, by the usual methods, $\tilde{\rho}_1$. Define the matrices

$$(13) \qquad \tilde{V}_1^{-1} = \begin{vmatrix} 1 & -\tilde{\rho}_1 & 0 & 0\ldots 0 \\ -\tilde{\rho}_1 & 1+\tilde{\rho}_1^2 & -\tilde{\rho}_1 & 0\ldots 0 \\ 0 & -\tilde{\rho}_1 & 1+\tilde{\rho}_1^2 & \ldots 0 \\ & \ldots & -\tilde{\rho}_1 1 + \tilde{\rho}_1^2 & -\tilde{\rho}_1 \\ 0 & \ldots & -\tilde{\rho}_1 & 1 \end{vmatrix}, \qquad \tilde{Z}_1 = (\tilde{Y}_1, \tilde{Y}^*_{-1}, W_1),$$

and obtain the instrumental variables estimator

$$(14) \qquad \tilde{\delta}_{\cdot 1} = (\tilde{Z}_1'\tilde{V}_1^{-1}Z_1)^{-1}\tilde{Z}_1'\tilde{V}_1^{-1}y_{\cdot 1}.$$

Evidently, this procedure may be applied to every equation yielding, in the obvious notation,

$$(15) \qquad \tilde{\delta}_{\cdot i} = (\tilde{Z}_i'\tilde{V}_i^{-1}Z_i)^{-1}\tilde{Z}_i'\tilde{V}^{-1}y_{\cdot i} \qquad (i = 1, 2, \ldots, m).$$

REMARK 3: It may be thought that the estimator above is equivalent to the limited information maximum likelihood estimator when the structural errors are jointly normal. This conjecture may be prompted by the similarity of the procedure above to the interpretation given by Amemiya and Fuller [2] to the distributed lag estimator proposed by Hannan [**10**]. This, however, is not so. Perhaps the simplest way of noting the differences and similarities is to revert to the single equation model. If we write

$$(16) \qquad y_t = \alpha w_t + \lambda y_{t-1} + u_t, \qquad u_t = \rho u_{t-1} + \varepsilon_t,$$

the estimation procedure we suggest in the preceding amounts to the following: Estimate α and λ by instrumental variables, obtain the residuals, and estimate ρ. Compute

$$(17) \qquad \tilde{y}_{t-1} = \tilde{\alpha} \sum_{i=0}^{t-2} \tilde{\lambda}^i w_{t-1-i}.$$

Define

$$(18) \qquad \tilde{X} = (\tilde{y}_{-1}, w)$$

in the obvious notation, and obtain

$$(19) \qquad \begin{pmatrix} \hat{\alpha} \\ \hat{\lambda} \end{pmatrix} = (\tilde{X}'\tilde{V}^{-1}X)^{-1}\tilde{X}'\tilde{V}^{-1}y.$$

If

$$(20) \qquad \operatorname*{plim}_{T\to\infty} \frac{(\tilde{X}'\tilde{V}^{-1}X)}{T} = Q$$

exists as a nonsingular nonstochastic matrix, and if

$$(21) \qquad \operatorname*{plim}_{T\to\infty} \frac{1}{T} \sum_{t=1}^{T} u_t w_{t+\tau} = 0 \qquad \text{for all } \tau,$$

then the asymptotic distribution of (19) is given by

$$(22) \qquad \sqrt{T}\left[\begin{pmatrix} \hat{\alpha} \\ \hat{\alpha} \end{pmatrix} - \begin{pmatrix} \alpha \\ \lambda \end{pmatrix}\right] \sim N(0, \Phi_{\text{IIV}}), \ \Phi_{\text{IIV}} = \sigma^2 \operatorname*{plim}_{T\to\infty} \left(\frac{\bar{X}'V^{-1}\bar{X}}{T}\right)^{-1},$$

where

$$(23) \qquad \bar{X} = (\bar{y}_{-1}, w), \qquad \bar{y}_{-1} = (\bar{y}_1, \bar{y}_2, \ldots, \bar{y}_{T-1}), \qquad \bar{y}_t = \alpha \sum_{i=0}^{\infty} \lambda^i w_{t-i}.$$

On the other hand the maximum likelihood (ML) (or in case of nonnormality, the minimum chi square) estimator of α and λ has the distribution (see, e.g., [**6**, Ch. 7])

$$\sqrt{T}\left[\begin{pmatrix}\hat{\alpha}\\ \hat{\lambda}\end{pmatrix}_{\mathrm{ML}} - \begin{pmatrix}\alpha\\ \lambda\end{pmatrix}\right] \sim N(0, \Phi_{\mathrm{ML}}), \tag{24}$$

where

$$\Phi_{\mathrm{ML}}^{-1} = \sigma^2\left[\lim_{T\to\infty}\frac{\bar{X}'V^{-1}\bar{X}}{T} + S\right], \qquad S = \begin{bmatrix} 0 & 0 \\ 0 & \dfrac{(\rho-\lambda)^2}{(1-\lambda^2)\quad(1-\lambda\rho)^2}\end{bmatrix}. \tag{25}$$

It is thus easy to see that

$$\Phi_{\mathrm{IIV}} - \Phi_{\mathrm{ML}} \geqslant 0 \tag{26}$$

in the sense that the difference is positive semidefinite.

In the Amemiya and Fuller problem we have

$$y_t = \alpha\sum_{i=0}^{\infty}\lambda^i w_{t-i} + u_t, \qquad u_t = \rho u_{t-1} + \varepsilon_t. \tag{27}$$

Here λ is a parameter that enters only the *mean* of the dependent variable, *but not its variance.* For this "reason" the estimators of λ and ρ (by ML methods) are asymptotically independent. "Hence," the asymptotic properties of the ML estimators of α and λ are independent of the properties of the consistent estimator of ρ. If we solve the difference equation in (16) we find

$$y_t = \alpha\sum_{i=0}^{\infty}\lambda^i w_{t-i} + \sum_{i=0}^{\infty}\lambda^i u_{t-i}. \tag{28}$$

Thus, in (28), we have a second order autoregressive error process and λ is *both a mean and a variance parameter*. "Consequently," the estimators of λ and ρ are not independent even asymptotically. Thus, how well λ is estimated will depend on how well we estimate ρ in the "first" stage since we treat these two parameters asymmetrically.

The point of using the iterated instrumental variables (IIV) approach instead of the direct maximum likelihood is that the IIV estimator does not depend, in its asymptotic distribution, on anything but the consistency of the "first stage" estimator of ρ.

4. PROPERTIES OF THE ESTIMATOR

Consider again the model as exhibited in (10). We make the following assumptions.

ASSUMPTION 1: *The matrix Π_0 is stable, in the sense that its roots are less than unity, in modulus.*

ASSUMPTION 2: *The sequence* $\{\varepsilon'_{t\cdot}: t = 0, \pm 1, \pm 2, \ldots\}$ *is one of mutually i.i.d. random variables with mean zero and covariance matrix* Σ, *and the matrix* R, *in* (3), *is stable.*

ASSUMPTION 3: *The exogenous variables are (uniformly) bounded, nonstochastic,*[5] *and*

$$\lim_{T\to\infty} \frac{1}{T}(\bar{Z}'_1 V^{-1} \bar{Z}_i) = \Phi_{ii}^{-1} \qquad (i = 1, 2, \ldots, m) \tag{29}$$

exist as nonsingular matrices, where

$$\bar{Z}_i = (\bar{Y}_i, {}_i\bar{Y}^*_{-1}, W_i)$$

and $\bar{Y}_i$, ${}_i\bar{Y}^*_{-1}$ *are obtained from the systematic part of the final form*

$$y'_t = (I - \Pi'_0 L)^{-1} \Pi'_1 w'_{t\cdot} + (I - \Pi'_0 L)^{-1} v'_{t\cdot}. \tag{30}$$

REMARK 4: Assumption 3 entails some restrictions, when it so happens that the columns of $\bar{Z}_i$ are linearly dependent (at least asymptotically). This will occur, e.g., when the system contains only two exogenous variables, the two being a sine and a cosine.[6] When this is so, $\bar{Y}_i, {}_i\bar{Y}^*_{-1}$ contain only linear combinations of sines and cosines, thus rendering Assumption 3 invalid. The same is true when the only exogenous variables of the system are polynomials of various degrees in "time." In most applications, however, these limitations are innocuous since the various columns of $\bar{Y}_i, {}_i\bar{Y}^*_{-1}$ are (infinite) linear combinations of all the predetermined variables *and* all their lags. In general we would not expect such linear dependencies to materialize, and Assumption 3 rules out explicitly the case where the tth row of $\bar{Y}_i$, $\bar{Y}^*_{-1}$ consists of linear combinations of the tth observations on the exogenous variables of the system.

If we define

$$\begin{aligned} \tilde{Z}^* &= \operatorname{diag}(\tilde{Z}_1, \tilde{Z}_2, \ldots, \tilde{Z}_m), & \delta &= (\delta'_{\cdot 1}, \delta'_{\cdot 2}, \ldots, \delta'_{\cdot m})', \\ \tilde{V}^{-1} &= \operatorname{diag}(\tilde{V}_1^{-1}, \tilde{V}_2^{-1}, \ldots, \tilde{V}_m^{-1}), & y &= (y'_{\cdot 1}, y'_{\cdot 2}, \ldots, y'_{\cdot m})', \end{aligned} \tag{31}$$

then the IIV estimator of the system as a whole is given by

$$\tilde{\delta} = (\tilde{Z}'^* \tilde{V}^{-1} Z^*)^{-1} \tilde{Z}'^* \tilde{V}^{-1} y. \tag{32}$$

We have the following lemma.

LEMMA 1: *Given Assumptions* 1–3 *and the conventions of the model as exhibited in* (1), *the estimator in* (32) *is consistent.*

[5] This assumption may be relaxed at the cost of some analytical complications, as will be indicated below.

[6] This limitation was pointed out to us by a reader of an earlier version of this paper.

PROOF: After substitution for y we obtain

$$(33)\qquad \tilde{\delta} - \delta = (\tilde{Z}'^{*}\tilde{V}^{-1}Z)^{-1}\tilde{Z}'^{*}\tilde{V}^{-1}u, \qquad u = (u'_{\cdot 1}, u'_{\cdot 2}, \ldots, u'_{\cdot m})'.$$

It will suffice to show that

$$(34)\qquad \operatorname*{plim}_{T\to\infty} \frac{\tilde{Z}'^{*}\tilde{V}^{-1}u}{T} = 0.$$

This is so, since

$$(35)\qquad \operatorname*{plim}_{T\to\infty} \frac{\tilde{Z}'\tilde{V}^{-1}Z}{T} = \Phi^{*}, \qquad \Phi^{*} = \operatorname{diag}(\Phi^{*}_{11}, \Phi^{*}_{22}, \ldots, \Phi^{*}_{mm}),$$

and the Φ^{*}_{ii} are nonsingular by Assumption 3.

Consider the ith subvector of (34). We observe that

$$(36)\qquad \operatorname*{plim}_{T\to\infty} \frac{\tilde{Z}_i'\tilde{V}_i^{-1}u_{\cdot i}}{T} = \operatorname*{plim}_{T\to\infty} \frac{\bar{Z}_i'V_i^{-1}u_{\cdot i}}{T} = 0.$$

The last equality follows easily from Assumption 2 and the fact that the exogenous variables of the system are bounded non-stochastic.

LEMMA 2: *The asymptotic distribution of the estimator in* (32) *is given by*

$$(37)\qquad \Phi^{*}_{\text{IIV}} = \lim_{T\to\infty} \frac{(\bar{Z}^{*\prime}V^{-1}Z^{*})^{-1}}{T}\,\frac{\bar{Z}^{*\prime}M^{*\prime}(\Sigma\otimes I_T)M^{*}\bar{Z}^{*}}{T}\,\frac{(\bar{Z}^{*\prime}V^{-1}Z^{*})^{-1}}{T},$$

$$\bar{Z}^{*} = \operatorname{diag}(\bar{Z}_1, \bar{Z}_2, \ldots, \bar{Z}_m), \qquad M_i'M_i = V_i^{-1},$$

$$M^{*} = \operatorname{diag}(M_1, M_2, \ldots, M_m).$$

PROOF: First, we observe that

$$(38)\qquad \operatorname*{plim}_{T\to\infty} \frac{\tilde{Z}_i'(\tilde{V}_i^{-1} - V_i^{-1})u_{\cdot i}}{\sqrt{T}}$$

$$= \operatorname{plim} \sqrt{T}(\tilde{\rho}_i - \rho_i)\frac{1}{T}\tilde{Z}_i' \begin{bmatrix} 0 & -1 & 0 & \cdots & & 0 \\ -1 & \tilde{\rho}_i + \rho_i & -1 & & & \\ 0 & -1 & \tilde{\rho}_i + \rho_i & -1 & & 0 \\ 0 & & \vdots & & & \\ \vdots & & -1 & \tilde{\rho}_i + \rho_i & & -1 \\ 0 & 0 & \cdots & 0 & -1 & 0 \end{bmatrix} u_{\cdot i} = 0,$$

since $\sqrt{T}(\tilde{\rho}_i - \rho_i)$ has a well defined asymptotic distribution as $T \to \infty$. Next, by similar arguments, we see that

$$(39)\qquad \operatorname*{plim}_{T\to\infty} \frac{(\tilde{Z}_i - \bar{Z}_i)'V_i^{-1}u_{\cdot i}}{\sqrt{T}} = 0.$$

Thus, we need be concerned only with

$$(40) \qquad \frac{\bar{Z}^{*\prime}V^{-1}u}{\sqrt{T}} = \frac{\bar{Z}^{*\prime}M^{*\prime}\varepsilon^{*}}{\sqrt{T}},$$

where $\varepsilon^{*} = (\varepsilon_{\cdot 1}^{*\prime}, \varepsilon_{\cdot 2}^{*\prime}, \ldots, \varepsilon_{\cdot m}^{*\prime})'$, $\varepsilon_{\cdot i} = (\varepsilon_{1i}, \varepsilon_{2i}, \ldots, \varepsilon_{Ti})'$, and $\varepsilon_{\cdot i}^{*} = \varepsilon_{\cdot i}$ with the exception that $\varepsilon_{1i}^{*} = \sqrt{1 - \rho_i^2}\, u_{t1}$, $i = 1, 2, \ldots, m$. Let ${}_i\bar{z}_{s\cdot}^{*}$ be the sth row of $M_i\bar{Z}_i$ and note that

$$(41) \qquad \frac{Z^{*\prime}V^{-1}u}{\sqrt{T}} = \frac{1}{\sqrt{T}}\begin{bmatrix} {}_1\bar{z}_{1\cdot}^{*\prime} \\ \\ {}_m\bar{z}_{1\cdot}^{*\prime} \end{bmatrix}\varepsilon_{1\cdot}^{*\prime} + \frac{1}{\sqrt{T}}\sum_{s=2}^{T}\begin{bmatrix} {}_1\bar{z}_{s\cdot}^{*\prime} \\ {}_2\bar{z}_{s\cdot}^{*\prime} \\ {}_m\bar{z}_{s\cdot}^{*\prime} \end{bmatrix}\varepsilon_{s\cdot}',$$

where $\varepsilon_{s\cdot} = (\varepsilon_{s1}, \varepsilon_{s2}, \ldots, \varepsilon_{sm})$.

But the first term in the right member of (41) vanishes in probability with T; moreover in view of Assumptions 1–3 the Lindeberg-Feller Theorem [**3**, Ch. 3] applies, and thus we conclude

$$(42) \qquad \frac{\bar{Z}'V^{-1}u}{\sqrt{T}} \sim N\left(0, \lim_{T\to\infty}\frac{\bar{Z}^{*\prime}M^{*\prime}(\Sigma \otimes I_T)M^{*}\bar{Z}^{*}}{T}\right).$$

It is then immediate from (32) that

$$(43) \qquad \sqrt{T}(\tilde{\delta} - \delta) \sim N(0, \Phi_{\text{IIV}}^{*}) \qquad Q.E.D.$$

COROLLARY 1: *Iterating the estimator in* (32) *will not alter its asymptotic properties.*

Proof is obvious from Lemmas 1 and 2.

REMARK 5: The motivation for the two step alternative considered here may be seen from (38). It is evident that the asymptotic distribution in (43) *does not depend on the distribution of the "first step" estimators of the autoregressive parameters* ρ_i, $i = 1, 2, \ldots, m$.

This is so since the vector multiplying $\sqrt{T}(\tilde{\rho}_i - \rho_i)$ in the right member of (38) vanishes asymptotically. *It is in order to effectuate this property that we have defined both* $\tilde{Y}_i$ *and* ${}_i\tilde{Y}_{-1}^{*}$ *in terms of the final form of the system.*

The estimator we shall consider in the next section will lack this simplicity since its distribution will be shown to depend on the properties of the quantities $\sqrt{T}(\tilde{\rho}_i - \rho_i)$ as obtained from the "first stage."

5. TWO AND THREE STAGE LEAST SQUARES VARIANTS IN THE AUTOREGRESSIVE ERRORS CASE

In this discussion it is useful, but not necessary, in motivating the estimators to assume, in addition to Assumption 2, that

$$\varepsilon_{t\cdot}' \sim N(0, \Sigma). \tag{44}$$

It may be shown (see, e.g., [**4**]) that the log likelihood function of the observations may be written as

$$\begin{aligned} L(A, R, \Sigma; Y, W) = & -\frac{Tm}{2}\ln(2\pi) - \tfrac{1}{2}\ln|\Omega| - \tfrac{1}{2}z_{1\cdot}A\Omega^{-1}A'z_{1\cdot}' \\ & - \frac{T}{2}\ln\frac{|\tilde{V}'\tilde{V}|}{T} - \frac{T-1}{2}\ln|\Sigma| \\ & + \frac{T}{2}\ln\ (I-B)'\frac{\tilde{V}'\tilde{V}}{T}(I-B) \\ & - \tfrac{1}{2}\operatorname{tr}\{\Sigma^{-1}(ZA - Z_{-1}AR)'(ZA - Z_1AR)\}. \end{aligned} \tag{45}$$

In (45) the symbols have a slightly different meaning than was the case earlier; in particular, we have put

$$Y = YB + Y_{-1}C_0 + WC_1 + U, \qquad ZA = U, \tag{46}$$

where, of course,

$$Z = (Y, Y_{-1}, W), \qquad A = (I - B', -C_0' - C_1')', \tag{47}$$

and the observation corresponding to $t = 2$ is eliminated from the definition of Z in (47). This observation appears separately as the row z_1. Further, it is clear that the terms $-\frac{1}{2}[\ln|\Omega| + z_{1\cdot}A\Omega^{-1}A'z_{1\cdot}']$ play no role in obtaining the (asymptotic) properties of the ML estimators; this is so since the relative weight of such terms vanishes as $T \to \infty$.

It is shown in [**4**] that the three stage least squares (3SLS) analogue in the present model is obtained by minimizing, with respect to the unknown elements of A,

$$\Lambda = \operatorname{tr}\Sigma^{-1}(\tilde{Z}A - Z_{-1}AR)'(\tilde{Z}A - Z_{-1}AR) \tag{48}$$

subject to a prior estimate of Σ and R. In the preceding,

$$\tilde{Z} = (\tilde{Y}, Y_{-1}, W), \tag{49}$$

and Y is the projection of Y on the space spanned by the columns of $Y_{-1}, Y_{-2}, W, W_{-1}$.

If $\tilde{A}$ is a prior estimate of A, then the prior estimates of Σ and R are given by

$$\begin{aligned} &\tilde{\Sigma} = \frac{1}{T}\tilde{E}'\tilde{E}, \qquad \tilde{R} = (\tilde{U}_{-1}'\tilde{U}_{-1})^{-1}\tilde{U}_{-1}'\tilde{U}, \\ &\tilde{U} = Z\tilde{A}, \qquad \tilde{E} = \tilde{U} - \tilde{U}_{-1}\tilde{R}. \end{aligned} \tag{50}$$

It is further conjectured in [**4**] that if we iterate this procedure (with respect to $\tilde{A}$, $\tilde{\Sigma}$, and $\tilde{R}$) until it converges, then the resulting estimators have the same asymptotic distribution as the ML estimators of A, Σ, and R. *While this is not shown directly, what is shown is that these two sets of estimators satisfy asymptotically the same set of equations.*

We specialize these results to the case under consideration, i.e., to the case where R is diagonal.

Before proceeding to this task it will be useful to introduce a more convenient notation to overcome the confusion arising from the many subscripts one has to employ in such situations. Thus, introduce the selection matrices S_{i1}, S_{i2}, and S_{i3} such that

$$YS_{i1} = Y_i, \qquad Y_{-1}S_{i2} = {}_iY^*_{-1}, \qquad WS_{i3} = W_i \qquad (i = 1, 2, \ldots, m). \tag{51}$$

Putting

$$S_i = \begin{bmatrix} S_{i1} & 0 & 0 \\ 0 & S_{i2} & 0 \\ 0 & 0 & S_{i3} \end{bmatrix}, \qquad S = \operatorname{diag}(S_1, S_2, \ldots, S_m), \tag{52}$$

we have that

$$\begin{aligned} Z_i &= ZS_i, \qquad Z^* = (I_m \otimes Z)S, \\ Z^*_{-1} &= (I_m \otimes Z_{-1})S, \qquad y = Z^*\delta + u. \end{aligned} \tag{53}$$

At any rate, minimizing Λ of (48) with respect to the unknown elements of A, we find

$$\begin{aligned} &[\tilde{Z}^* - (\tilde{R}' \otimes I)Z^*_{-1}]'(\tilde{\Sigma}^{-1} \otimes I)[\tilde{Z}^* - (\tilde{R}' \otimes I)Z^*_{-1}]\tilde{\delta} \\ &\qquad = [\tilde{Z}^* - (\tilde{R}' \otimes I)Z^*_{-1}]'(\tilde{\Sigma}^{-1} \otimes I)[y - (\tilde{R}' \otimes I)y_{-1}], \end{aligned} \tag{54}$$

where y is as defined in (31) (except that observations for $t = 2$ are omitted), and y_{-1} is obtained by reducing the time subscript of the elements of y by one.

It is clear that the 2SLS variant of this estimator is obtained by neglecting the stochastic dependence of the system's errors across equations, which means, operationally, that we set, in (54), $\tilde{\Sigma}^{-1} = I$. Thus, substituting for y in (54) we find

$$\begin{aligned} \hat{\delta} - \delta = &\{[\tilde{Z}^* - (\tilde{R} \otimes I)Z^*_{-1}]'[\tilde{Z}^* - (\tilde{R}' \otimes I)Z^*_{-1}]\}^{-1} \\ &\times [\tilde{Z}^* - (\tilde{R}' \otimes I)Z^*_{-1}]'[u - (\tilde{R}' \otimes I)u_{-1}]. \end{aligned} \tag{55}$$

REMARK 6: The relations in (54) and (55) show that it is not necessary to define the $\tilde{Y}$ component of $\tilde{Z}$ as the projection of Y on the space spanned by the columns of Y_{-1}, Y_{-2}, W, and W_{-1}. This is necessary only in order to obtain orthogonality between the matrix of residuals and Z^*_{-1} and thus justify the transition from (54) to (55). It is interesting that an (asymptotically) equivalent procedure can be derived that makes repeated use of instrumental variables estimators. To be precise, if $\tilde{Y}$ is not obtained by projection, then *it is necessary that it be obtained* *from the relationship*

$$(56)\qquad \tilde{Y} = Y_{-1}\tilde{F}_1 + Y_{-2}\tilde{F}_2 + W\tilde{F}_3 + W_{-1}\tilde{F}_4,$$

where

$$\tilde{F}_1 = \tilde{C}_0(I - \tilde{B})^{-1} + (I - \tilde{B})\tilde{R}(I - \tilde{B})^{-1}, \qquad \tilde{F}_2 = \tilde{C}_0\tilde{R}(I - B)^{-1},$$
$$\tilde{F}_3 = \tilde{C}_1(I - \tilde{B})^{-1}, \qquad \tilde{F}_4 = \tilde{C}_1\tilde{R}(I - \tilde{B})^{-1}.$$

The alternative, but asymptotically equivalent procedure is as follows: Estimate, by instrumental variables methods, the vectors $\beta_{\cdot i}, \gamma_{\cdot i}$ $(i = 1, 2, \ldots, m)$ using the relations in (6) and thus obtain the estimates $\tilde{B}$, $\tilde{C}_0$, and $\tilde{C}_1$. Using these estimates we can compute the residual matrix $\tilde{U}$ and obtain an estimate of R by computing

$$(57)\qquad \tilde{\rho}_i = \left(\sum \tilde{u}_{t-1,i}\tilde{u}_{ti}\right)/\left(\sum \tilde{u}^2_{t-1,i}\right) \qquad (i = 1, 2, \ldots, m).$$

This is all that is required to obtain the matrices $\tilde{F}_1$, $\tilde{F}_2$, $\tilde{F}_3$, and $\tilde{F}_4$ and thus $\tilde{Y}$. The estimator that is (asymptotically) equivalent to the one in (55) is

$$(58)\qquad \hat{\delta} = \{[\tilde{Z}^* - (\tilde{R}' \otimes I)Z^*_{-1}]'[Z^* - (\tilde{R}' \otimes I)Z^*_{-1}]\}^{-1}$$
$$\times [\tilde{Z}^* - (\tilde{R}' \otimes I)Z^*_{-1}]'[y - (\tilde{R}' \otimes I)y_{-1}].$$

Note that it is *not necessary to recompute the* $\tilde{F}_i$, $i = 1, 2, 3, 4$, since *iteration would rely only on* (57) *and* (58) *and would not involve* (56).

REMARK 7: It is shown in [**4**] that the asymptotic properties of the estimator in (54) do not depend on any of the properties of $\tilde{\Sigma}$ *beyond consistency*: they do, however, depend rather crucially on the estimator of R. Provided Σ and R are initially estimated consistently, all subsequent iterates are shown to be consistent as well.

REMARK 8: The procedure discussed in connection with (58) is the exact analogue, in the autoregressive errors case, of the LIIV estimator given in Dhrymes [7]; when the estimator is modified to take into account the covariance matrix Σ, i.e., when it is based on (54) rather than on (55), then it is the exact analogue of the FIIV estimator, also given in [7]. One difference ought to be noted, however. While in the absence of autocorrelated errors the LIIV and FIIV estimators are asymptotically equivalent to 2SLS and 3SLS estimators respectively, this is not so here. The estimator in (58) (and its full information analogue) would have to be iterated until convergence is obtained. *Only the convergent iterate is asymptotically equivalent to the autoregressive* 2SLS *and* 3SLS *estimators.*

To establish the asymptotic properties of the estimator in (54) and (55) we put

$$(59)\qquad \tilde{G}(\tilde{\Sigma}) = \frac{1}{T}[\tilde{Z}^* - (\tilde{R}' \otimes I)Z^*_{-1}]'[\tilde{\Sigma}^{-1} \otimes I][\tilde{Z}^* - (\tilde{R}' \otimes I)Z^*],$$

and slightly expand Assumption 3 to read, in the relevant part:

ASSUMPTION 3′:

$$\operatorname*{plim}_{T\to\infty} \frac{1}{T}[\bar{Z}^* - (R' \otimes I)Z^*_{-1}]'(\Sigma^{-1} \otimes I)[\bar{Z}^* - (R' \otimes I)Z^*_{-1}]$$

exists as a nonstochastic nonsingular matrix, we conclude that

$$G(\Sigma) = \operatorname*{plim}_{T\to\infty} \frac{1}{T}[\tilde{Z}^* - (\tilde{R}' \otimes I)Z^*_{-1}](\tilde{\Sigma}^{-1} \otimes I)[\tilde{Z}^* - (\tilde{R}' \otimes I)Z^*_{-1}] \tag{60}$$

exists as a nonstochastic nonsingular matrix.

It is then easy to show that the asymptotic distribution of the estimator in (54) is given by

$$\sqrt{T}(\hat{\delta} - \delta)_{3SLSA} \sim [G(\Sigma)]^{-1} \frac{1}{\sqrt{T}}[\bar{Z}^* - (R' \otimes I)Z^*_{-1}]'(\Sigma^{-1} \otimes I) \times \{\varepsilon - [(\tilde{R} - R)' \otimes I]u_{-1}\}, \tag{61}$$

where, we remind the reader,

$$\bar{Z}^* = (I_m \otimes \bar{Z})S, \qquad \bar{Z} = (\bar{Y}, Y_{-1}, W), \qquad \bar{Y} = Y_{-1}F_1 + Y_{-2}F_2 + WF_3 + W_{-1}F_4, \tag{62}$$

the F_i being the probability limits of the quantities $\tilde{F}_i$, $i = 1, 2, 3, 4$, defined in (57).

We now proceed to find the distribution of the limited information estimator as exhibited in (55). Clearly, this is given by

$$\sqrt{T}(\hat{\delta} - \delta)_{2SLSA} \sim [G(I)]^{-1} \frac{1}{\sqrt{T}}[\bar{Z}^* - (R' \otimes I)Z^*_{-1}]' \times \{\varepsilon - [(\tilde{R} - R) \otimes I]u_{-1}\}. \tag{63}$$

Let $\bar{z}^{(i)}_{t\cdot}$ be the tth row of $\bar{Z}_i = \bar{Z}S_i$ $(i = 1, 2, \ldots, m)$; $z^{(i)}_{t\cdot}$ is, obviously, the tth row of $Z_i = ZS_i$ $(i = 1, 2, \ldots, m)$. We remind the reader that, in this context, $t = 3, 4, \ldots, T$. Let

$$\bar{z}^{*(i)}_{t\cdot} = \bar{z}^{(i)}_{t\cdot} - \rho_i z^{(i)}_{t-1\cdot}, \qquad z^*_t = \operatorname{diag}(\bar{z}^{*(1)\prime}_{t\cdot}, \bar{z}^{*(2)\prime}_{t\cdot}, \ldots, \bar{z}^{*(m)\prime}_{t\cdot}). \tag{64}$$

Let

$$\operatorname*{plim}_{T\to\infty} \frac{1}{T}[\bar{Z}^* - (R' \otimes I)Z^*_{-1}]u_{-1} = \begin{bmatrix} \xi_{11} \\ \xi_{22} \\ \vdots \\ \xi_{mm} \end{bmatrix}, \tag{65}$$

ξ_{ii} being the probability limit of $(1/T)(\bar{Z}_i - \rho_{i\,i}Z_{-1})'u_{\cdot i,-1}$. Similarly,

$$\operatorname*{plim}_{T\to\infty}\frac{1}{T}[Z^* - (R'\otimes I)Z^*_{-1}]'u_{-1} = \begin{bmatrix}\zeta_{11}\\ \zeta_{22}\\ \vdots\\ \zeta_{mm}\end{bmatrix}, \tag{66}$$

and

$$\xi = \operatorname{diag}(\xi_{11}, \xi_{22}, \ldots, \xi_{mm}), \qquad \zeta = \operatorname{diag}(\zeta_{11}, \zeta_{22}, \ldots, \zeta_{mm}), \tag{67}$$

and define ξ^* to be the matrix in which ξ_{ii} is replaced by $((1 - \rho_i^2)/\sigma_{ii})\xi_{ii}$. Finally, letting

$$u_t^* = \operatorname{diag}(u_{t1}, u_{t2}, \ldots, u_{tm}), \tag{68}$$

we see that we may rewrite (63) as

$$\sqrt{T}(\hat{\delta} - \delta)_{2SLSA} \sim G^{-1}\left[\frac{1}{\sqrt{T}}\sum_{t=3}^{T} z_t^*\varepsilon_{t\cdot}' - \frac{1}{\sqrt{T}}\xi^*\sum_{t=3}^{T} u_{t-1}^*\varepsilon_{t\cdot}' + \xi^*\zeta'\sqrt{T}(\tilde{\delta} - \delta)\right], \tag{69}$$

where $\tilde{\delta}$ is the initial estimator of the structural parameters on the basis of which we estimate the autoregressive parameters ρ_i $(i = 1, 2, \ldots, m)$ and $G(I)$ is written, for simplicity, as G. This third term in the right member of (69), thus, shows quite clearly how the estimator of the autoregressive parameters affects, in this context, even the asymptotic properties of the system's (other) structural parameter estimators.

To complete the problem we must obtain an explicit expression for the ξ_{ii} and ζ_{ii}. To this effect define

$$\zeta_i = \begin{bmatrix}(\Pi_0' - \rho_i I)(I - \rho_i\Pi_0')^{-1}(I - B)^{-1}(I - \rho_i R)^{-1} + (I - B')^{-1}(I - \rho_i R)^{-1}\\ (1 - \rho_i^2)(I - \rho_i\Pi_0')^{-1}(I - B)^{-1}(I - \rho_i R)^{-1}\end{bmatrix}\sigma_{\cdot i}, \tag{70}$$

where $\sigma_{\cdot i}$ is the ith column of Σ. We note, then, that

$$\zeta_{ii} = S_i'\zeta_{i\cdot}, \qquad \xi_{ii} = \zeta_{ii}. \tag{71}$$

Instead of obtaining the distribution of $\sqrt{T}(\hat{\delta} - \delta)_{2SLSA}$ for arbitrary estimator $\tilde{\delta}$, we obtain the distribution of the converging iterate of such an estimator.

Asymptotically, this estimator behaves as

$$(G - \xi^*\zeta')\sqrt{T}(\hat{\delta} - \delta)_{C2SLSA} \sim \frac{1}{\sqrt{T}}\left[\sum_{t=3}^{T}(z_t^* - \xi^* u_{t-1}^*)\varepsilon_{t\cdot}'\right]. \tag{72}$$

Unfortunately, the right member of (72) is not the sum of independent random vectors. Thus, the Lindeberg-Feller Theorem invoked in Section 4 is not applicable here. The random vectors in (72) are dependent; because of the special character of the autoregression from which this dependence arises, it is possible to use the results of Mann and Wald [**12**] to convert the problem to one involving n dependent variables. We illustrate this for the case

$$(73) \qquad \frac{1}{\sqrt{T}}\xi^* \sum_{t=3}^{T} u^*_{t-1\cdot}\varepsilon'_{t\cdot} = \frac{1}{\sqrt{T}}\xi^* \sum_{t=3}^{T} u^{*n}_{t-1}\varepsilon'_{t\cdot} + \frac{1}{\sqrt{T}}\xi^* R^n \sum_{t=3}^{T} u^*_{t-n-1}\varepsilon'_{t\cdot}.$$

It is clear that the second term in the right member of (73) can be made arbitrarily small in probability by appropriate[7] choice of n, since its expectation is identically zero. Thus, the asymptotic behavior of the left member of (73) is determined, essentially, by the first term in the right member. Evidently, we may apply the same reasoning to both terms of the right member of (72). This is perfectly feasible since the (stochastic) components of z^*_t may be expressed in terms of the final form; the latter, however, represents a rational lag in the exogenous variables and a rational lag in the ε-process.

Having used this truncation argument in (72) we do, in effect, find the asymptotic distribution of a random vector which differs from $\sqrt{T}(\hat{\delta} - \delta)_{\mathrm{C2SLSA}}$ by an arbitrarily small quantity with probability as close to unity as desired. This is essentially the meaning of Lemma 1 in Mann and Wald [**12**].

Now, there are many variants of central limit theorems for n dependent variables. If the process is assumed to be Gaussian, then, in view of Assumption 3, the conditions of the Hoeffding-Robbins Theorem [**11** or **6**] will hold[8] and thus we conclude that, asymptotically,

$$(74) \qquad \frac{1}{\sqrt{T}} \sum_{t=3}^{T} (z^*_t - \xi^* u^*_{t-1})\varepsilon'_{t\cdot} \sim N(0, A_1 + A_2 - A_3),$$

where

$$(75) \qquad A_1 = \operatorname*{plim}_{T\to\infty} \frac{1}{T}[\bar{Z}^* - (R' \otimes I)Z^*_{-1}]'(\Sigma \otimes I)[\bar{Z}^* - (R' \otimes I)Z^*_{-1}],$$

$$(76) \qquad A_2 = \left[r^2_{ij}\frac{(1-\rho_i^2)(1-\rho_j^2)}{1-\rho_i\rho_j}\zeta_{ij}\zeta'_{jj} \right], \qquad r^2_{ij} = \frac{\sigma^2_{jj}}{\sigma_{ii}\sigma_{jj}} \qquad (i,j = 1, 2, \ldots, m),$$

$$(77) \qquad A_3 = [\sigma_{ij}(\xi^*_{ii}\zeta'_{ji} + \zeta_{ij}\xi^{*\prime}_{jj})],$$

[7] To see this, note that for an arbitrary (conformable) vector of constants α,

$$\operatorname{var}\left[(1/\sqrt{T})\alpha'\xi^* R^n \sum_{t=3}^{T} u^*_{t-n-1}\varepsilon'_{t\cdot} \right]$$

can be made arbitrarily small by proper choice of n; apply, then, Chebyshev's inequality.

[8] The Hoeffding-Robbins Theorem is usually stated for scalar random variables; its application to vector random variables is possible by the following result (see Dhrymes [**3**, Ch. 3]). Let $\{x_T : T = 1, 2, \ldots\}$ be a sequence of random vectors and α an arbitrary real conformable vector. If $\{z_T : z_T = \alpha' x_T, T = 1, 2, \ldots\}$ converges in distribution to $N(\alpha'\mu, \alpha'\Sigma\alpha)$ for all real α, then $\{x_T : T = 1, 2, \ldots\}$ converges in distribution to a $N(\mu, \Sigma)$ random vector.

and

(78) $$\zeta_{ji} = \underset{T\to\infty}{\text{plim}} \frac{1}{T}(\bar{Z}_j - \rho_{j\,j}Z_{-1})'u_{\cdot i,-1} = S_j'\zeta_i,$$

the ζ_i being as defined in (70). It follows immediately that

(79) $$\sqrt{T}(\hat{\delta} - \delta)_{\text{C2SLSA}} \sim N(0, \Phi_{\text{C2SLSA}}),$$

where

(80) $$\Phi_{\text{C2SLSA}} = (G - \xi^*\zeta')^{-1}(A_1 + A_2 - A_3)(G - \zeta\xi^{*\prime})^{-1}.$$

We have, therefore, proved:

LEMMA 3: *Consider the linear structural econometric model as given in* (1) *and* (2) *subject to Assumptions* 1–3 *and the additional requirements that the sequence* $\{\varepsilon_{t\cdot}' : t = 0, \pm 1, \pm 2, \dots\}$ *have finite sixth order absolute moments and that*

(81) $$G = \underset{T\to\infty}{\text{plim}} \frac{1}{T}[\tilde{Z}^* - (\tilde{R}' \otimes I)Z^*_{-1}]'[\tilde{Z}^* - (\tilde{R}' \otimes I)Z^*_{-1}]$$

exist as a nonsingular matrix with nonstochastic elements. Then the converging iterate of the limited information dynamic autoregressive (LIDA) estimator as exhibited in (72) *has the asymptotic distribution*

(82) $$\sqrt{T}(\hat{\delta} - \delta)_{\text{C2SLSA}} \sim N(0, \Phi_{\text{C2SLSA}})$$

where

(83) $$\Phi_{\text{C2SLSA}} = (G - \xi^*\zeta')^{-1}(A_1 + A_2 - A_3)(G - \zeta\xi^{*\prime})^{-1},$$

the $A_i, i = 1, 2, 3$ *being as defined in* (75), (76), *and* (77), *respectively.*

COROLLARY 2: *The kth (nonconvergent) iterate of the LIDA estimator does not have the same asymptotic distribution as the* $(k + 1)$*st (nonconvergent) iterate or the convergent iterate* $\sqrt{T}(\hat{\delta} - \delta)_{\text{C2SLSA}}$.

Proof is obvious from (69).

REMARK 9: It is interesting that we can give a two step estimator that is asymptotically equivalent to the C2SLSA estimator, by using a modified form of the method of scoring [**3**, Ch. 3]. It ought to be noted that this is a general procedure applicable to all problems that obtain estimators by extremizing some function. To this effect, note that the C2SLSA estimator is obtained by minimizing the function

(84) $$\Lambda = \text{tr}\,(\tilde{Z}A - Z_{-1}AR)'(\tilde{Z}A - Z_{-1}AR)$$

with respect to the unknown elements in A and R. If we put

(85) $$\delta^* = (\delta, \rho^{*\prime})', \qquad \rho^* = (\rho_1, \rho_2, \dots, \rho_m)',$$

then the C2SLSA estimator is a consistent root of $\partial\Lambda/\partial\delta^* = 0$.

Now, let $\tilde{\delta}^*$ be *any* consistent estimator of δ^* and consider the estimator

$$(86) \qquad \hat{\delta}^* = \tilde{\delta}^* - \left[\frac{\partial^2 \Lambda}{\partial \delta^* \, \partial \delta^*}(\tilde{\delta}^*)\right]^{-1} \frac{\partial \Lambda}{\partial \delta^*}(\tilde{\delta}^*).$$

Clearly, this estimator can always be obtained given the initial estimator $\tilde{\delta}^*$ and is easily recognized as a modified form of the first iterate involved in the application of the method of scoring.

Now expand

$$(87) \qquad \frac{\partial \Lambda}{\partial \delta^*}(\delta^*) = \frac{\partial \Lambda}{\partial \delta^*}(\delta_0^*) + \frac{\partial^2 \Lambda}{\partial \delta^* \partial \delta^*}(\delta^{**})(\delta^* - \delta_0^*),$$

where $|\delta^{**} - \delta_0^*| < |\tilde{\delta}^* - \delta_0^*|$, δ_0^* being the true value of the vector δ_0^*. Substituting (87) in (86), we obtain

$$(88) \qquad \sqrt{T}(\hat{\delta}^* - \delta_0^*) = \sqrt{T}(\tilde{\delta}^* - \delta_0^*) - \left[\frac{1}{T}\frac{\partial^2 \Lambda}{\partial \delta^* \partial \delta^*}(\tilde{\delta}^*)\right]^{-1}$$
$$\times \left[\frac{1}{\sqrt{T}}\frac{\partial \Lambda}{\partial \delta^*}(\delta_0^*) + \frac{1}{T}\frac{\partial^2 \Lambda}{\partial \delta^* \partial \delta^*}(\delta^{**})\sqrt{T}(\tilde{\delta}^* - \delta_0^*)\right].$$

Given the usual regularity conditions and the fact that, if $\operatorname{plim} \tilde{\delta}^* = \delta_0^*$, then $\operatorname{plim} \delta^{**} = \delta_0^*$ as well, we conclude that, asymptotically,

$$(89) \qquad \sqrt{T}(\hat{\delta}^* - \delta_0^*) \sim -M^{-1}\frac{\partial S}{\partial \delta^*}(\delta_0^*),$$

where

$$(90) \qquad M = \operatorname*{plim}_{T \to \infty} \frac{1}{T}\frac{\partial^2 \Lambda}{\partial \delta^* \partial \delta^*}(\delta_0^*).$$

But the asymptotic distribution of the right member of (89) is that of the consistent root of the equation $(\partial \Lambda / \partial \delta^*) = 0$. Since the C2SLSA estimator gives a consistent solution of this equation, the (asymptotic) equivalence claimed above is demonstrated.[9] Finally, it should be pointed out that, in our derivation in (82) we have given the *marginal* asymptotic distribution of the δ component of δ^*, as the latter is defined in (85).

6. DESCRIPTION AND COMPARISON OF ALTERNATIVE ESTIMATORS

There are a number of limited information estimators for problems similar to the one dealt with in this paper. However, no distribution theory exists except in cases which are far more restrictive than those considered here. Thus, e.g., Amemiya [**1**] deals with a model *not containing lagged endogenous variables*. We could, if we wished, specialize our results and compare them with what he calls MS2SLS

[9] A certain uniqueness condition is clearly involved in this claim.

estimators. In Fair [9] a problem entirely similar to ours is considered, but the distribution theory of his proposed estimators is not adequately developed. His search and iterated estimators are similar to the C2SLSA estimator developed in this model, although it is not clear what effect, if any, the selection of regressors in the first stage might have on the properties of the resulting estimators.

It will be helpful before we undertake a comparison to give an outline of the various procedures considered here.

1. Fair's procedure was outlined at the end of Section 2 and need not be repeated here.

2. Converging iterate two stage least squares autoregressive (C2SLSA): First obtain the reduced model

$$Y = Y_{-1}F_1 + Y_{-2}F_2 + WF_3 + W_{-1}F_4 + E$$

and regress Y on Y_{-1}, Y_{-2}, W, and W_{-1}, thus obtaining the projection $\tilde{Y}$ of Y on the space spanned by the columns of Y_{-1}, Y_{-2}, W, and W_{-1}. Obtain by instrumental variables (or other) methods an initial consistent estimate of C_0, C_1, and B, and using these obtain an initial consistent estimate of ρ_i $(i = 1, 2, \ldots, m)$ as indicated in equation (57). Using these estimates (of the ρ_i), estimate δ as in (54) (putting $\tilde{\Sigma} = I$). From the new estimates of δ obtain the residual matrix $\tilde{U}$ and recompute the ρ_i as in (57). Using these, recompute estimates of δ as in (54) and continue until convergence is obtained.[10]

3. The instrumental variables version of the C2SLSA estimator: This is essentially the same as under 2 above, except that $\tilde{Y}$ is *not* the projection of Y on the space spanned by the columns of Y_{-1}, Y_{-2}, W, and W_{-1}. Rather, given the initial consistent estimates of C_0, C_1, and B, we compute $\tilde{Y}$ as

$$\tilde{Y} = Y_{-1}\tilde{F}_1 + Y_{-2}\tilde{F}_2 + W\tilde{F}_3 + W_{-1}\tilde{F}_4,$$

the $\tilde{F}_i$ $(i = 1, 2, 3, 4)$ being as defined just below equation (56). This version obtains estimators for δ and ρ_i $(i = 1, 2, \ldots, m)$ by iterating, until convergence, equations (57) and (58). Here the initial consistent estimate of C_0, C_1, and B serves both in defining $\tilde{Y}$ as well as in obtaining the initial estimates of the ρ_i.

4. The modified method of scoring version of C2SLSA estimators: Here, from an initial consistent estimate of δ and ρ^*, say $\tilde{\delta}^*$, we evaluate $(\partial\Lambda/\partial\delta^*)(\partial^2\Lambda/\partial\delta^*\partial\delta^*)$ at the point $\tilde{\delta}^*$ and obtain the desired estimator as in equation (86). In the present case Λ is defined in (84), and the $\tilde{Y}$ component of $\tilde{Z}$ is the projection of Y on Y_{-1}, Y_{-2}, W, and W_{-1}.

5. When the ρ_i $(i = 1, 2, \ldots, m)$ are known, we may operate with the reduced model

$$y_{\cdot i} - \rho_i y_{\cdot i,-1} = (Z_i - \rho_{1\,i}Z_{-1})\delta_{\cdot i} + \varepsilon_{\cdot 1} \qquad (i = 1, 2, \ldots, m),$$

treating $y_{\cdot i} - \rho_i y_{\cdot i,-1}$ and $Z_i - \rho_{i\,i}Z_{-1}$ as known data. Here, operating analogously with the 2SLS procedure means that we use the estimator

$$[(\tilde{Z}_i - \rho_{i\,i}Z_{-1})'(\tilde{Z}_i - \rho_{i\,i}Z_{-1})]^{-1}(\tilde{Z}_i - \rho_{i\,i}Z_{-1})'(y_{\cdot i} - \rho_i y_{\cdot i,-1}) \qquad (i = 1, 2, \ldots, m),$$

[10] It should be noted that no theorem has been produced giving the precise conditions under which convergence will obtain.

the $\tilde{Y}_i$ component of $\tilde{Z}_i$ being obtained from the projection of Y on the space spanned by the columns of Y_{-1} and W.

6. The iterated (two step) instrumental variables estimator developed in Section 3 is obtained as follows: From an initial (instrumental variables) estimator of C_0, C_1, and B compute $\tilde{Y}$ *from the final form as indicated in* (11), and the $\tilde{\rho}_i$ as indicated in (57). The estimator is then as defined in (32) *where the Y component of Z^* is obtained from the final form*, i.e., for the ith structural equation we use the matrix of instruments $\tilde{Z}_i'\tilde{V}_i^{-1}$, for the $\tilde{Y}_i$ component of $\tilde{Z}_i$ being an appropriate submatrix of $\tilde{Y}$, as defined immediately above.

Fair has not explicitly derived the asymptotic distribution of his estimator and thus direct comparison is not possible in this case. On the other hand we may extend one of Fair's suggestions so that it becomes the C2SLSA estimator.[11]

The procedures under 2, 3, and 4 above are asymptotically equivalent, provided in the first two we employ an iterative scheme and the iteration converges.

Thus, effectively, the comparison is to be carried out with respect to C2SLSA (item 2), the obvious modification of 2SLS when the autocorrelation parameters are known (item 5), and the iterated (two step) instrumental variables estimator (item 6).

Inspection of the matrices Φ^*_{IIV} and Φ_{C2SLSA} reveals that comparison in terms of the estimators of all the parameters of the model is rather cumbersome. Thus, we confine ourselves to a comparison of the marginal *asymptotic distribution* of the parameters of, say, the ith structural equation.

Extracting the appropriate submatrix from (83), we find

$$\sqrt{T}(\hat{\delta}_{\cdot i} - \delta_{\cdot i})_{\mathrm{C2SLSA}} \sim N(0, \Phi_{ii}) \tag{91}$$

and

$$\Phi_{ii} = \sigma_{ii}(G_{ii} - \xi^*_{ii}\zeta'_{ii})^{-1}, \tag{92}$$

where G_{ii} is the ith block diagonal element of G.

Examining now the iterated instrumental variables estimator of Section (4), we see that the (marginal) asymptotic distribution of $\sqrt{T}(\tilde{\delta}_{\cdot i} - \delta_{\cdot i})_{\mathrm{IIV}}$ is normal with covariance matrix[12]

$$\Phi^*_{ii} = \operatorname*{plim}_{T\to\infty}\left[\frac{(\bar{Z}_i - \rho_{i\,i}\bar{Z}_{-1})'(\bar{Z}_i - \rho_{i\,i}\bar{Z}_{-1})}{T}\right]^{-1}. \tag{93}$$

Here, however, $\bar{Z}_i = (\bar{Y}_i, {}_i\bar{Y}^*_{-1}, W_i)$ and $\bar{Y}_i, {}_i\bar{Y}^*_{-1}$ are obtained from the *systematic part* of the final form.

We observe that G_{ii} is defined by

$$G_{ii} = \operatorname*{plim}_{T\to\infty}\frac{1}{T}(\bar{Z}_i - \rho_{i\,i}Z_{-1})'(\bar{Z}_i - \rho_{i\,i}Z_{-1}), \tag{94}$$

[11] This would be the case, e.g., when at the first stage all jointly dependent variables are regressed on Y_{-1}, Y_{-2}, W, and W_{-1}, and iteration is carried out until convergence is obtained.

[12] Strictly speaking this is not the expression given in Section 4: it differs from the former only in excluding from $\bar{Y}_i$ and W_i observations corresponding to $t = 2$ and from ${}_i\bar{Y}^*_{-1}$ observations corresponding to $t = 1$. Clearly, in a limiting context this is of no consequence.

where now

(95) $\bar{Z}_i = (\bar{Y}_i, {}_iY^*_{-1}, W_i), \qquad {}_iZ_{-1} = (Y_{i,-1}, {}_iY^*_{-2}, W_{i,-1}),$

and the rows of $\bar{Y}_i$ as given in (95) consist of subvectors of

(96) $\bar{y}_{t\cdot} = y_{t-1\cdot}\Pi_0 + w_{t\cdot}\Pi_1 + u_{t-1\cdot}R(I-B)^{-1}.$

By contrast, $\bar{Z}_i$ as it appears in (95) differs from the quantity defined in (93); the difference is twofold. First the $\bar{Y}_i$ component of the former consists of subvectors of

(97) $\bar{y}'_{t\cdot} = (I - \Pi'_0 L)^{-1}\Pi'_1 w'_{t\cdot} \qquad (t = 1, 2, \ldots),$

and second, the Y^*_i component of the former consists of subvectors of

(98) $\bar{y}'_{t-1\cdot} = (I - \Pi'_0 L)^{-1}\Pi'_1 w'_{t-1\cdot}.$

In both cases the parameters Π_0 and Π_1 have been estimated consistently by instrumental variable or other methods. Consequently,

(99) $$G_{ii} = \Phi^{*\,-1}_{ii} + S'_i Q\left[\operatorname*{plim}_{T\to\infty}\frac{1}{T}\sum_{t=3}^{T}\begin{bmatrix}u'_{t-1\cdot}\\ v^{*\prime}_{t-1\cdot}\\ v^{*\prime}_{t-2\cdot}\end{bmatrix}[u_{t-1\cdot}, v^*_{t-1\cdot}, v^*_{t-2\cdot}]\right]Q'S_i,$$

where

(100) $$Q = \begin{bmatrix}(I-B')^{-1}R' & (\Pi'_0 - \rho_i I) & 0\\ 0 & I & -\rho_i I\\ 0 & 0 & 0\end{bmatrix},$$

and $v^*_{t-1\cdot}$ is the row vector of final form disturbances for the system as a whole.

We observe (see, for example, the arguments given in Dhrymes [**5**]) that the sum whose probability limit is taken in (99) converges to its limit with probability one as well; thus, the probability limit in question may be determined as the expectation of the matrix under the summation sign. Denote this probability limit by N. Comparing with (66) and using the Schwarz inequality for integrals, we conclude

(101) $S'_i\zeta_i\zeta'_i S_i \leqslant S'_i QNQ'S_i\sigma_{ii}$

in the sense that the difference of the two matrices is negative semidefinite. Thus,

(102) $$G_{ii} - \xi^*_{ii}\zeta'_{ii} - \Phi^{*\,-1}_{ii} = S'_i QNQ'S_i - \frac{1-\rho_i^2}{\sigma_{ii}}S'\zeta_i\zeta'_i S_i,$$

which is *positive semidefinite* by (101). Consequently,

(103) $\Phi^*_{ii} - (G_i - \xi^*_{ii}\zeta'_{ii})^{-1} \geqslant 0,$

which shows the relative (marginal) asymptotic efficiency of the C2SLSA estimator relative to the IIV estimator examined earlier.

Finally, it is easy to show that if ρ_i is known, then operating with the reduced model,

$$(104) \qquad y_{\cdot 1} - \rho_i y_{\cdot 1,-1} = (Z_i - \rho_{i\,i} Z_{-1})\delta_{\cdot i} + \varepsilon_{\cdot i},$$

and applying the usual 2SLS procedure, the asymptotic distribution of the resulting estimator is given by

$$(105) \qquad \sqrt{T}(\hat{\delta}_{\cdot i} - \delta_{\cdot i})_{\rho_i = \rho_{io}} \sim N(0, \sigma_{ii} G_{ii}^{-1}).$$

Since

$$(106) \qquad G_{ii} \geqslant G_{ii} - \xi_{ii}^{*} \zeta_{ii}' \geqslant \Phi_{ii}^{*-1},$$

we conclude that the relative (marginal) asymptotic efficiency rankings are as follows: The estimator in (105) is asymptotically efficient relative to the C2SLSA and the latter is asymptotically efficient relative to the IIV estimator.

The substance of our results may be summarized in the following theorem.

THEOREM: *Consider the linear structural econometric model exhibited in* (46), *its error process obeying* (2), *and subject to Assumptions* 1, 2, 3, 3′, *and the usual identifiability conditions. Then*:

(*i*) *The iterated* (*two step*) *instrumental variables estimator in* (31) *is consistent and its asymptotic distribution is given in* (36). *Moreover, iterating this estimator further will not alter its asymptotic properties.*

(*ii*) *If the autocorrelation parameters* ρ_i ($i = 1, 2, \ldots, m$) *are known, then applying the usual 2SLS procedure to the reduced model in* (104) *yields an estimator which is consistent and has the asymptotic distribution given in* (105).

(*iii*) *If an initial consistent estimator of the structural parameters is used to obtain the estimator in* (55), *then all successive iterates are consistent. Successive iterates have, generally, different asymptotic distributions. The asymptotic distribution of the converging iterate* (*C2SLSA*), *if one exists, is given by* (82).

(*iv*) *The instrumental variables version of the convergent iterate two stage least squares autoregressive* (*C2SLSA*) *estimator and the modified method of scoring version* (*items* 3 *and* 4) *are, asymptotically, equivalent to C2SLSA.*

(*v*) *Employing the criterion of marginal* (*relative*) *asymptotic efficiency, the estimator in* (*ii*) *dominates those in* (*i*) *and* (*iii*); *the converging iterate of* (*iii*) *dominates the estimator in* (*i*).

REMARK 10: It is conjectured that the $(k+1)$st iterate of the estimator in (ii) is, asymptotically, efficient relative to the kth iterate.

Columbia University,
Federal Reserve System,
and
University of Pennsylvania

Manuscript received August, 1972; revision received December, 1972.

REFERENCES

[1] AMEMIYA, T.: "Specification Analysis in the Estimation of Parameters of a Simultaneous Equations Model with Autoregressive Residuals," *Econometrica*, 34 (1966), 283–306.

[2] AMEMIYA, T., AND W. FULLER: "A Comparative Study of Alternative Estimators in a Distributed Lag Model," *Econometrica*, 35 (1967), 509–529.

[3] DHRYMES, P. J.: *Econometrics: Statistical Foundation and Applications*. New York: Harper and Row, 1970.

[4] ———: "Full Information Estimation of Dynamic Simultaneous Equations Models with Autoregressive Errors," Discussion Paper No. 203, University of Pennsylvania, March, 1971.

[5] ———: "On the Strong Consistency of Estimators for Certain Distributed Lag Models with Autocorrelated Errors," *International Economic Review*, 12 (1971), 329–343.

[6] ———: *Distributed Lags: Problems of Estimation and Formulation*. San Francisco: Holden-Day, 1971.

[7] ———: "A Simplified Structural Estimator for Large-Scale Econometric Models," *Australian Journal of Statistics*, 13 (1971), 168–175.

[8] DHRYMES, P. J., R. BERNER, AND D. CUMMINS: "Limited Information Estimation of Simultaneous Equations Models with Lagged Endogenous Variables and Autocorrelated Errors," Discussion Paper No. 183, University of Pennsylvania, October, 1970.

[9] FAIR, R. C.: "The Estimation of Simultaneous Equations Models with Lagged Endogenous Variables and First Order Serially Correlated Errors," *Econometrica*, 38 (1970), 507–516.

[10] HANNAN, E. J.: "The Estimation of Relationships Involving Distributed Lags," *Econometrica*, 33 (1965), 409–418.

[11] HOEFFDING, W., AND H. ROBBINS: "The Central Limit Theorem for Dependent Variables," *Duke Mathematical Journal*, 15 (1948), 773–780.

[12] MANN, H. B., AND A. WALD: "On the Statistical Treatment of Linear Stochastic Difference Equations," *Econometrica*, 11 (1943), 173–220.

[13] MORRISON, J. L.: "Small Sample Properties of Selected Distributed Lag Estimators: A Monte Carlo Experiment," *International Economic Review*, 11 (1970), 13–23.

[14] PESARAN, M. H.: "The Small Sample Problem of Truncation Remainders in the Estimation of Distributed Lag Models with Auto-Correlated Errors," mimeographed, undated.

[15] SARGAN, J. D.: "The Maximum Likelihood Estimation of Economic Relationships with Autoregressive Residuals," *Econometrica*, 29 (1961), 414–426.

Journal of Econometrics 2 (1974) 247–259 © North-Holland Publishing Company

ASYMPTOTIC PROPERTIES OF FULL INFORMATION ESTIMATORS IN DYNAMIC AUTOREGRESSIVE SIMULTANEOUS EQUATION MODELS

Phoebus J. DHRYMES and H. ERLAT*

Columbia University, New York, N.Y. 10027, U.S.A.

Received February 1973, revised version received February 1974

1. Introduction

In a previous paper [Dhrymes (n.d.)] the first author examines the problem of estimating, by maximum likelihood (ML) and three-stage least squares-like methods, the parameters of the model,

$$y_{t\cdot} = y_{t\cdot}B + y_{t-1\cdot}C_0 + w_{t\cdot}C_{1\cdot} + u_{t\cdot}; \qquad t = 1, 2, \ldots, T, \tag{1}$$

where $\{w_t : t = 0, \pm 1, \pm 2, \ldots\}$ is a sequence of s-element vectors of exogenous variables (which are uniformly bounded and nonstochastic), the error process obeys

$$u_{t\cdot} = u_{t-1\cdot}R + \varepsilon_{t\cdot}, \tag{2}$$

where R is a stable matrix, $\{\varepsilon'_{t\cdot} : t = 0, \pm 1, \pm 2, \ldots\}$ is a sequence of independent identically distributed (i.i.d.) random variables such that

$$E(\varepsilon_{t\cdot}) = 0, \qquad \operatorname{cov}(\varepsilon'_{t\cdot}) = \Sigma, \tag{3}$$

Σ being positive definite, and $y_{t\cdot}$ is the m-element vector of jointly dependent variables.

As is shown in Dhrymes (n.d.), the three-stage squares-like procedure – termed there the full information dynamic autogressive (FIDA) – satisfies, asymptotically, the same set of normal equations as the ML estimator, the difference being in the manner in which the jointly dependent variables are 'purged' of their stochastic components.

In this paper we further explore the asymptotic properties of the FIDA estimator and establish its asymptotic distribution. Because of the relative inaccessibility of the above mentioned paper we give a brief account of its contents.

*The authors wish to express their thanks to C. Sims for useful comments on an earlier draft of this paper.

D

2. Formulation of the problem

In connection with eqs. (1) and (2) we observe that we require that:

(A1) $(I-B)$ is non-singular.
(A2) $C_0(I-B)^{-1}$, R are both stable matrices.

Certain other assumptions will be invoked as the need for them arises.

We also observe that

$$E(u'_{t\cdot}) = 0, \qquad \operatorname{cov}(u'_{t\cdot}) = \sum_{i=0}^{\infty} R'^{i}\Sigma R^{i} = \Omega, \tag{4}$$

and we assert that Ω is non-singular.
The reduced form of eq. (1) can be written as

$$y_{t\cdot} = y_{t-1\cdot}\Pi_0 + w_{t\cdot}\Pi_1 + v_{t\cdot}, \tag{5}$$

where

$$\Pi_0 = C_0(I-B)^{-1},$$
$$\Pi_1 = C_1(I-B)^{-1},$$
$$v_{t\cdot} = u_{t\cdot}(I-B)^{-1}, \tag{6}$$

and the final form is

$$y'_{t\cdot} = (I-\Pi'_0 L)^{-1}\Pi'_1 w'_{t\cdot} + (I-\Pi'_0 L)^{-1} v'_{t\cdot}, \tag{7}$$

where L is the usual lag operator.
If we add the distributional assumption

$$\varepsilon'_{t\cdot} \sim N(0, \Sigma),$$

we can conclude that

$$u'_{*} \sim N(0, \Phi),$$

where

$$u_{*} = (u_{1\cdot}, u_{2\cdot}, \ldots, u_{T\cdot}),$$

and Φ is a block matrix defined as follows

$$\Phi_{ii} = \Omega; \qquad i = 1, 2, \ldots, T,$$
$$\Phi_{ij} = \Omega R^{j-i}; \qquad \text{for } j \geqq i,$$
$$= R'^{i-j}\Omega; \qquad \text{for } i \geqq j,$$

each block, Φ_{ij}, being a square matrix of order m.

Moreover, we have that

$$\Phi^{-1} = [\Phi^{ij}],$$

where

$$\Phi^{ii} = \Omega^{-1} + R\Sigma^{-1}R\,; \qquad \text{for } i = 1,$$
$$= \Sigma^{-1}; \qquad \text{for } i = T,$$
$$= \Sigma^{-1} + R\Sigma^{-1}R'; \qquad \text{for } i = 2, 3, \ldots, T-1,$$

and

$$\Phi^{ij} = -R\Sigma^{-1}; \qquad \text{for } i = j-1,$$
$$= -\Sigma^{-1}R'; \qquad \text{for } i = j+1,$$
$$= 0; \qquad \text{otherwise.}$$

Finally, Φ^{-1} can be decomposed by the upper triangular matrix Ψ, i.e.,

$$\Phi^{-1} = \Psi\Psi',$$

where Ψ is again a block matrix such that

$$\Psi_{ii} = \Omega^{-\frac{1}{2}}; \qquad \text{for } i = 1,$$
$$= \Sigma^{-\frac{1}{2}}; \qquad \text{for } i = 2, 3, \ldots T,$$

and

$$\Psi_{ij} = -R\Sigma^{-\frac{1}{2}}; \qquad \text{for } i = j-1,$$
$$= 0; \qquad \text{otherwise.}$$

In the above, $\Sigma^{\frac{1}{2}}$ and $\Omega^{\frac{1}{2}}$ are, respectively, the 'square roots' of Σ and Ω. The relations above can be verified directly, the only additional fact needed for this purpose being the relation between Σ and Ω, which is

$$\Sigma = \Omega - R'\Omega R,$$

a fact that follows directly from the definition of Ω. Assuming that the process generating the data has been in operation indefinitely far into the past, and treating the initial conditions as fixed, we can write the log likelihood function of the observations as

$$L(A, R, \Sigma; Y, W) = -\frac{Tm}{2}\ln(2\pi) - \tfrac{1}{2}\ln|\Omega| - \frac{T-1}{2}\ln|\Sigma| + \frac{T-1}{2}\ln(I-B)'(I-B) - \tfrac{1}{2}z^*\Phi^{-1}z^{*\prime}. \tag{8}$$

In the above

$$z_{t\cdot} = (y_{t\cdot}, y_{t-1\cdot}, w_{t\cdot}),\ z^* = (z_{1\cdot}A, z_{2\cdot}A, \ldots, z_{T\cdot}A),\ A = \begin{bmatrix} I-B \\ -C_0 \\ -C_1 \end{bmatrix}. \tag{9}$$

What is required for the validity of eq. (8) is to note that the Jacobian of the transformation from u^* to z^* is $\{|I-B|^2\}^{(T-1)/2}$ – treating initial conditions as fixed–and that

$$\Phi^{-1} = |\Omega^{-1}|\,|\Sigma^{-1}|^{T-1}.$$

It follows from the decomposition of Φ^{-1} that

$$z^*\Phi^{-1}z^{*\prime} = z_{1\cdot}A\Omega^{-1}A'z_{1\cdot} + \sum_{t=2}^{T}(z_{t\cdot}A - z_{t-1\cdot}AR)\Sigma^{-1}(z_{t\cdot}A - z_{t-1\cdot}AR)'.$$

We note that the first term in the right member above does not vary with T and thus, in deriving the maximum likelihood (ML) estimator, we may safely ignore it. The same may be said of the term $-\frac{1}{2}\ln|\Omega|$. Consequently, we may operate, instead, with

$$L(A, R, \Sigma;\ Y, W) = -\frac{Tm}{2}\ln(2\pi) - \frac{T-1}{2}\ln\left|\frac{\tilde{V}'\tilde{V}}{T-1}\right| - \frac{T-1}{2}\ln|\Sigma| + \frac{T-1}{2}\ln\left|(I-B)'\frac{\tilde{V}'\tilde{V}}{T-1}(T-B)\right| - \tfrac{1}{2}\operatorname{tr}\Sigma^{-1}(ZA - Z_{-1}AR)'(ZA - Z_{-1}AR), \quad (10)$$

where

$$Z = (y_{t\cdot}, y_{t-1\cdot}, w_{t\cdot}), \quad Z_{-1} = (y_{t-1\cdot}, y_{t-2\cdot}, w_{t-1\cdot}); \quad t = 2, 3, \ldots, T,$$

i.e., Z is the $(T-1)$-row matrix whose rows are $z_{t\cdot}$ of eq. (9). Similarly, Z_{-1} is the $(T-1)$-row matrix whose rows are $z_{t-1\cdot}$. Moreover, the matrix $\tilde{V}$ is obtained as follows:
Reducing the lag structure in the error process of eq. (1), we have

$$y_{t\cdot} = y_{t\cdot}B + y_{t-1\cdot}(C_0 + R - BR) - y_{t-2\cdot}C_0R + w_{t\cdot}C_1 - w_{t-1\cdot}C_1R + \varepsilon_{t\cdot},$$

and obtaining the 'reduced form' above, we find

$$y_{t\cdot} = y_{t-1\cdot}F_1 + y_{t-2\cdot}F_2 + w_{t\cdot}F_3 + w_{t-1\cdot}F_4 + \varepsilon^*;\ t = 3, 4, \ldots, T, \quad (11)$$

where, obviously,

$$F_1 = \Pi_0 + (I-B)R(I-B)^{-1}, \qquad F_2 = -C_0R(I-B)^{-1},$$
$$F_3 = \Pi_1, \qquad F_4 = -C_1R(I-B)^{-1}. \quad (12)$$

Let

$$q_{t\cdot} = (y_{t-1\cdot}, y_{t-2\cdot}, w_{t\cdot}, w_{t-1\cdot}), \quad Q = (q_{t\cdot}); \quad t = 3, 4, \ldots, T.$$

The matrix $\tilde{V}$ is then the OLS matrix of residuals, i.e., its rows are given by

$$\tilde{v}_{t\cdot} = y_{t\cdot} - q_{t\cdot}\tilde{F}, \qquad \tilde{F} = (Q'Q)^{-1}Q'Y. \quad (13)$$

Remark 1. It might appear that we have a different stability requirement for the model in eq. (11) than that given in assumption (A2). This is, however, illusory. Stability in eq. (11) is determined by the roots of

$$0 = |\rho^2 I - \rho F_1 - F_2| = |(\rho I - \Pi_0)|\ |(\rho I - (I-B)R(I-B)^{-1}|, \quad (14)$$

which consist of the roots of

$$|\rho I - \Pi_0| = 0,$$

and the roots of

$$|\rho I - (I-B)R(I-B)^{-1}| = |\rho I - R| = 0.$$

Consequently, (A2) does, indeed, insure that eq. (11) is a stable model.

Generally, identification requirements will dictate that certain variables be absent from certain equations, i.e., that some elements in B, C_0, C_1 are known a priori to be null. Giving expression to these requirements will be greatly facilitated by introducing the selection matrices S_{ij}, $i = 1, 2, \ldots, m$; $j = 1, 2, 3$, such that

$$YS_{i1} = Y_i, \; Y_{-1}S_{i2} = {}_iY_{-1}, \; WS_{i3} = W_i; \quad i = 1, 2, \ldots, m, \quad (15)$$

where Y_i, ${}_iY_{-1}$, W_i are, respectively, the matrices of observations on the jointly dependent, lagged endogenous and exogenous variables appearing in the right member of the ith equation. Putting

$$S_i = \operatorname{diag}(S_{i1}, S_{i2}, S_{i3}), \qquad S = \operatorname{diag}(S_1, S_2, \ldots, S_m), \quad (16)$$

we see that the ith equation of (1), after having imposed the a priori restrictions, may be written as

$$y_{\cdot i} = ZS_i\delta_{\cdot i} + u_{\cdot i}; \quad i = 1, 2, \ldots, m, \quad (17)$$

and the entire model may be written as

$$y = Z^*\delta + u, \quad (18)$$

where

$$Z^* = (I_m \otimes Z)S, \quad \delta = (\delta'_{\cdot 1}, \delta'_{\cdot 2}, \ldots, \delta'_{\cdot m})', \quad u = (u'_{\cdot 1}, u'_{\cdot 2}, \ldots, u'_{\cdot m})',$$

$$\delta_i = (\beta'_{\cdot 1}, \gamma^{*\prime}_{\cdot i}, \gamma'_{\cdot i})', \quad y = (y'_{\cdot 1}, y'_{\cdot 2}, \ldots, y'_{\cdot m})', \quad (19)$$

and $\beta_{\cdot i}$, $\gamma^*_{\cdot i}$, $\gamma_{\cdot i}$ are the ith columns of B, C_0, C_1, respectively, after the elements known to be zero have been suppressed, while $y_{\cdot i}$, $u_{\cdot i}$ are, respectively, the ith columns of $Y = (y_{ti})$, $u = (u_{ti})$, $t = 2, \ldots, T$; $i = 1, 2, \ldots, m$.

For ML estimation we may write the likelihood function more conveniently as

$$L^*(A, R, \Sigma; Y, W) = -\frac{Tm}{2}\ln(2\pi) - \frac{T-1}{2}\ln\left|\frac{\tilde{V}'\tilde{V}}{T-1}\right|$$

$$-\frac{T-1}{2}\ln|\Sigma| + \frac{T-1}{2}\ln|S| - \tfrac{1}{2}\varphi, \quad (20)$$

where

$$S = (I-B)'\frac{\tilde{V}'\tilde{V}}{T-1}(I-B),$$

$$\varphi = [y-(R' \otimes I_{T-1})y_{-1} - \{Z^* - (R' \otimes I_{T-1})Z^*_{-1}\}\delta]'$$
$$\times (\Sigma^{-1} \otimes I_{T-1})[y-(R' \otimes I_{T-1})y - \{Z^* - (R' \otimes I_{T-1})Z^*_{-1}\}\delta].$$

The equations defining the ML estimators are:

$$\tilde{\Sigma} = \frac{1}{T-1}(ZA - Z_{-1}AR)'(ZA - Z_{-1}AR), \tag{21}$$

$$\tilde{R} = (A'Z'_{-1}Z_{-1}A)^{-1}A'Z'_{-1}ZA, \tag{22}$$

$$\begin{aligned}\tilde{\delta} = {} & [\{Z^* - (R' \otimes I_{T-1})Z^*_{-1}\}(\Sigma^{-1} \otimes I_{T-1})\{Z^* - (R' \otimes I)Z^*_{-1}\} \\ & - \tilde{V}^{*\prime}(S^{-1} \otimes I_{T-1})\tilde{V}^*]^{-1} \\ & \times [\{Z^* - (R' \otimes I_{T-1})Z^*_{-1}\}(\Sigma^{-1} \otimes I_{T-1})\{y - (R' \otimes I_{T-1}\}Y_{-1}] \\ & - \tilde{V}^{*\prime}(S^{-1} \otimes I_{T-1})y,\end{aligned} \tag{23}$$

where

$$V^* = \operatorname{diag}(\tilde{V}_1^*, \tilde{V}_2^*, \ldots, \tilde{V}_m^*), \quad \tilde{V}_i^* = (\tilde{V}_i, 0, 0), \quad \tilde{V}_i = \tilde{V}S_{i1},$$

the zeros in the definition of $\tilde{V}_i^*$ corresponding to $Y_{-1}S_{i2}$ and WS_{i3}.

The equations defining the FIDA estimators are obtained by minimizing

$$\operatorname{tr} \Sigma^{-1}(\tilde{Z}A - Z_{-1}AR)'(\tilde{Z}A - Z_{-1}AR)$$

with respect to the unknown parameters of A subject to prior estimates of Σ and R. The equations are

$$\{\tilde{Z}^* - (\tilde{R}' \otimes I_{T-1})Z^*_{-1}\}'(\tilde{\Sigma}^{-1} \otimes I_{T-1})\{y - (\tilde{R}' \otimes I_{T-1})y_{-1}\} = \tilde{M}\tilde{\delta}. \tag{24}$$

In the above we have

$$\tilde{M} = \{\tilde{Z}^* - (\tilde{R}' \otimes I_{T-1})Z^*_{-1}\}'(\tilde{\Sigma}^{-1} \otimes I_{T-1}) \times \{\tilde{Z}^* - (\tilde{R}' \otimes I_{T-1})Z^*_{-1}\},$$

$$\tilde{Z}^* = (I_m \otimes \tilde{Z}), \quad \tilde{Z} = (\tilde{Y}, Y_{-1}, W), \quad \tilde{Y} = Q(Q'Q)^{-1}Q'Y.$$

Of course, in order to complete the estimation scheme we have to provide a procedure for estimating R and Σ. But this is easily given, by analogy with eqs. (21) and (22) as

$$\tilde{R} = (\tilde{A}'Z'_{-1}Z_{-1}\tilde{A})^{-1}\tilde{A}'Z'_{-1}Z\tilde{A}, \tag{25}$$

$$\tilde{\Sigma} = \frac{1}{T-1}(Z\tilde{A} - Z\tilde{A}\tilde{R})'(Z\tilde{A} - Z\tilde{A}\tilde{R}).$$

Remark 2. As in Dhrymes (1973), we see that the basic difference between the ML and FIDA estimator of δ – apart from considerations relating to estimators of R and Σ – lies in the way in which the current endogenous variables are 'purged' of their 'stochastic components', as is obvious by comparing eqs. (23) and (24). It is, thus, conjectured that the converging iterate of the FIDA estimator in eq. (24) – in conjunction with eq. (25) – will have the same asymptotic distribution as the ML estimator since both will satisfy, asymptotically, the same equation. This aspect will not be pursued here. Instead, we derive the asymptotic distribution of the *converging iterate of the FIDA estimator of* δ. We assume that an initial *consistent* estimate of A is available – say $\tilde{A}_0$; this enables us to obtain $\tilde{R}_0$, $\tilde{\Sigma}_0$ from eq. (25) and hence enables the iteration scheme to commence. We iterate only on A and R. As we shall see below it does not matter, asymptotically, whether we iterate on Σ or not provided $\tilde{\Sigma}_0$ is consistent for Σ.

Noting that no prior restrictions are imposed on R, writing $r_{\cdot i}$, $i = 1, 2, \ldots, m$, for its ith column and letting

$$r = (r_{\cdot 1}', r_{\cdot 2}', \ldots, r_{\cdot m}')',$$

we conclude[1] that, asymptotically, the converging iterated FIDA estimator of δ and r obeys

$$\begin{bmatrix} M & P_1 \\ P_2 & I \end{bmatrix} \sqrt{T} \begin{pmatrix} \tilde{\delta} - \delta \\ \hat{r} - r \end{pmatrix} \sim \begin{bmatrix} I & 0 \\ 0 & I_m \otimes \Omega^{-1} \end{bmatrix} \frac{1}{\sqrt{T}} \times \begin{bmatrix} \{\bar{Z}^* - (R' \otimes I) Z_{-1}^*\}' (\Sigma^{-1} \otimes I) \\ I_m \otimes U_{-1} \end{bmatrix} \varepsilon, \tag{26}$$

where $\bar{Z}^* = (I_m \otimes \bar{Z})$, $\bar{Z} = (\bar{Y}, Y_{-1}, W)$, $\bar{Y} = QF$;

$$M = \operatorname*{plim}_{T\to\infty} \frac{1}{T} [\bar{Z}^* - (R' \otimes I) Z_{-1}^*]' (\Sigma^{-1} \otimes I) [\bar{Z}^* - (R' \otimes I) Z_{-1}^*],$$

$$P_1 = \operatorname*{plim}_{T\to\infty} \frac{1}{T} [\bar{Z}^* - (R' \otimes I) Z_{-1}^*]' (\Sigma^{-1} \otimes I)(I_m \otimes U_{-1}), \tag{27}$$

$$P_2 = \operatorname*{plim}_{T\to\infty} \frac{1}{T} (I_m \otimes \Omega^{-1})(I_m \otimes U_{-1}')[Z^* - (R' \otimes I) Z_{-1}^*]$$

$$= (\Sigma \otimes \Omega^{-1}) P_1',$$

and ε is defined analogously with u in eq. (19).

If we put

[1] For details, of the derivation see the appendix. Also in what follows the subscript $T-1$ in the notations $(R' \otimes I_{T-1})$ and $\Sigma^{-1} \otimes I_{T-1}$ will be suppressed for typographical convenience.

$$h_{\cdot t}^{\prime(i)} = (\delta_{i1}\bar{z}_{t\cdot}^{(1)} - r_{i1}z_{t-1}, \delta_{i2}\bar{z}_{t\cdot}^{(2)} - r_{i2}z_{t-1\cdot}^{(2)}, \ldots, \delta_{im}\bar{z}_{t\cdot}^{(m)} - r_{im}z_{t-1\cdot}^{(m)}),$$

where δ_{ij} is the Kronecker delta, $\bar{z}_{t\cdot}^{(i)}$ is the row corresponding to the tth observation (row) vector in $\bar{Z}S_i$, and $z_{t-1\cdot}^{(i)}$ is analogously defined for $Z_{-1}S_i$, then we can write compactly

$$\begin{bmatrix} M & P_1 \\ P_2 & I \end{bmatrix} \sqrt{T}\begin{pmatrix} \tilde{\delta}-\delta \\ \hat{r}-r \end{pmatrix} \sim \begin{bmatrix} I & 0 \\ 0 & I_m \otimes \Omega^{-1} \end{bmatrix} \frac{1}{\sqrt{T}} \sum_{t=2}^{T} \begin{pmatrix} H_t \\ I_m \otimes u_{t-1\cdot}' \end{pmatrix} \varepsilon_{t\cdot}', \tag{28}$$

where

$$H_t = (H_t^{\prime(1)}, \ldots, H_t^{\prime(m)})', \quad H_t^{(i)} = h_{\cdot t}^{(i)}\sigma^{i\cdot};$$

$\sigma^{i\cdot}$ is the ith row of Σ^{-1} and $\varepsilon_{t\cdot} = (\varepsilon_{t1}, \varepsilon_{t2}, \ldots, \varepsilon_{tm})$ is the vector of structural errors at 'time' t.

The vectors of the sum in the right member of eq. (28) do not represent a sequence of independent random vectors. If in addition to assumptions (A1) and (A2), we also assume:

(A3) The sequence $\{\varepsilon_{t\cdot}' : t = 0, \pm 1, \ldots\}$ has finite sixth-order moments.
(A4) The exogenous variables are uniformly bounded non-stochastic.

then it can be shown that the conditions of the Hoeffding–Robbins (1943) theorem or Dhrymes (1971) on m-dependent variables apply to a truncated vector sequence. The truncation may be determined by using the results in Mann and Wald (1943), especially[2] Lemma 1. We, thus, conclude that, asymptotically,

$$\frac{1}{\sqrt{T}} \sum_{t=2}^{T} \begin{pmatrix} H_t \\ I_m \otimes u_{t-1\cdot}' \end{pmatrix} \varepsilon_{t\cdot}' \sim N(0, C^*),$$

where

$$C^* = \begin{bmatrix} M & P_2' \\ P_2 & \Sigma \otimes \Omega^{-1} \end{bmatrix}.$$

Consequently, in view of eq. (27), we have

$$\sqrt{T}\begin{pmatrix} \hat{\delta}-\delta \\ \hat{r} \quad r \end{pmatrix} \sim N(0, \Phi_{\text{FIDA}}),$$

where

$$\Phi_{\text{FIDA}} = \begin{bmatrix} M & P_1' \\ P_1' & \Sigma^{-1} \otimes \Omega \end{bmatrix}^{-1}. \tag{29}$$

[2] A somewhat more general theorem, i.e., one that utilizes assumptions less restrictive than (A3) and (A4), may be obtained by using the results in Billingsley (1968). Such results, however, are unfamiliar in the literature of econometrics and are not utilized here.

We have therefore proved:

Theorem 1. Consider the model in eqs. (1), (2), (3) subject to the following conditions:

(A1) $(I-B)$ is non-singular.

(A2) $C_0(I-B)^{-1}$, R are both stable matrices.

(A3) The sequence $\{\varepsilon'_{t\cdot} : t = 0, \pm 1, \pm 2, \ldots\}$ is one of i.i.d. random variables having finite sixth-order moments.

(A4) The exogenous variable sequence $\{w'_{t\cdot} : t = 0, \pm 1, \pm 2, \ldots\}$ is non-stochastic uniformly bounded.

(A5) Σ as defined in eq. (4) is an unrestricted positive definite matrix.

(A6) The matrix M, defined in eq. (27), exists as a non-singular non-stochastic probability limit of the right member of eq. (27).

Then, the FIDA estimators of the parameter vector $(\delta', r')'$ have the asymptotic distribution which is given by

$$\sqrt{T}\begin{pmatrix}\hat{\delta}-\delta\\ \hat{r}-r\end{pmatrix} \sim N(0, \Phi_{\text{FIDA}}), \tag{30}$$

where Φ_{FIDA} is defined in eqs. (29) and (27).

Corollary 1. The marginal asymptotic distribution of the vector $\sqrt{T}(\hat{\delta}-\delta)$ is given by

$$\sqrt{T}(\hat{\delta}-\delta \sim N(0, C_{\text{FIDA}}), \tag{31}$$

where

$$C_{\text{FIDA}} = [M - P_1(\Sigma^{-1} \otimes \Omega)P'_1]^{-1}. \tag{32}$$

Proof. Obvious from the theorem.

Corollary 2. If $R = 0$, but this fact is not utilized in the estimation process, then there is asymptotic loss of efficiency in estimating δ.

Proof. If the information is utilized then the asymptotic distribution of $\sqrt{T}(\hat{\delta}-\delta)_{R=0}$ is normal with mean zero and covariance matrix M_0^{-1}, where M_0 is the matrix defined in eq. (27) for the special case where $R = 0$. We observe that $P_1 \neq 0$, when $R = 0$. This immediately implies the corollary.

Remark 2. Thus, here we incur a certain cost when autoregression in the errors is assumed, when in fact it is absent. This is to be contrasted to the case where the model contains no lagged endogenous variables. In such a case no loss in (asymptotic) efficiency results, when one assumes a higher order of autoregression, than is, in fact, true. To see that this is so, observe that when the model *does not contain lagged endogenous variables* and $R = 0$ – even though this fact is not utilized in estimation – we have that

$$P_1 = \operatorname*{plim}_{T\to\infty} \frac{1}{T}(\Sigma^{-1} \otimes \bar{Z}' U_{-1}),$$

where

$$\bar{Z} = (QF, W),$$

and

$$F = \operatorname*{plim}_{T\to\infty} \tilde{F},$$

where, mutatis mutandis, $\tilde{F}$ is as defined in eq. (13).

In the case under consideration and using, for comparability, the notation of eq. (12), we have

$$F = (F_1', F_2', F_3', F_4')' = (0, 0, \Pi_1, 0).$$

The first two elements are zero because $C_0 = 0$ – whether this fact is used in estimation or not – and the last element is zero because $R = 0$. Of course if $C_0 = 0$ and this fact is not utilized in estimation, the resulting M matrix would differ as compared to the case where this fact *is* utilized. This, however, is a result that persists independently of whether or not autocorrelation in the residuals is assumed when, in fact, it is absent.

Remark 3. It is easily verified that the results of Theorem 1 specialize, in the case where we deal with a single-equation 'system' containing a lagged endogenous variable and first-order autoregressive error, to the result contained in Theorem 7.1 of Dhrymes (1971, ch. 7). In many ways the contents of this paper represent a generalization of the treatment of the model,

$$y_t = \sum_{j=1}^{n-1} \beta_j x_{tj} + \beta_n y_{t-1} + u_t; \qquad u_t = \rho u_{t-1} + \varepsilon_t,$$

considered in Dhrymes (1971, ch. 7).

Remark 4. It appears that no additional complications are entailed by the introduction of additional lags in the jointly dependent variables, or a higher-order autoregression in the errors, except for the obvious computational burden of obtaining an expression for the covariance matrix of the structural errors.

Remark 5. It should be observed that, although we routinely commence the iteration of the FIDA estimator from an initial consistent estimator – presumably obtained through instrumental variables – there do exist models in which such estimators may not be available. In such cases we have exactly the same convergence problems as we do with maximum likelihood procedures, i.e., we have to prove which of the possibly many roots of the non-linear equations defining the FIDA estimator is consistent and how this root is to be obtained computationally.

Appendix

Here we make explicit the transition from eq. (18) to eq. (24) and hence to eq. (26).

Substituting from eq. (18) into eq. (24) we obtain, for the $(k+1)$st iterate

$$(\tilde{\delta}-\delta)_{k+1} = [\{\tilde{Z}^*-(\tilde{R}_k' \otimes I)Z^*_{-1}\}'(\tilde{\Sigma}^{-1} \otimes I)\{\tilde{Z}^*-(\tilde{R}_k' \otimes I)Z^*_{-1}\}]^{-1} \times [\{\tilde{Z}-(\tilde{R}_k' \otimes I)Z^*_{-1}\}'(\tilde{\Sigma}^{-1} \otimes I) - [\varepsilon - \{(\tilde{R}_k'-R') \otimes I\}u_{-1}]], \tag{33}$$

where in computing $\tilde{R}_k$ we have used the kth iterate $\tilde{\delta}_k$.

Now we have

$$\tilde{R}-R = (\tilde{U}'_{-1}\tilde{U}_{-1})^{-1}\tilde{U}_{-1}[\tilde{U}-\tilde{U}_{-1}R]. \tag{34}$$

But by definition

$$\tilde{U} = Y-Z\tilde{A}^* = U-Z(\tilde{A}^*-A^*), \quad A^* = \begin{bmatrix} I \\ 0 \\ 0 \end{bmatrix} - A. \tag{35}$$

Hence

$$\tilde{U}-\tilde{U}_{-1}R = E-Z(\tilde{A}^*-A^*)+Z_{-1}(\tilde{A}^*-A^*)R. \tag{36}$$

Writing eq. (34) in column form we find

$$(\tilde{r}-r)_k = [I_m \otimes (\tilde{U}'_{-1}\tilde{U}_{-1})^{-1}\tilde{U}'_{-1}][\varepsilon-\{Z^*-(R' \otimes I)Z^*_{-1}\}(\tilde{\delta}-\delta)_k]. \tag{37}$$

Moreover, we note that

$$[(\tilde{R}-R)_k' \otimes I]u_{-1} = (I_m \otimes U_{-1})(\tilde{r}-r)_k. \tag{38}$$

Hence, the iteration scheme in eq. (24) can be written more conveniently as

$$\tilde{M}_k(\tilde{\delta}-\delta)_{k+1} = [\tilde{Z}^*-(\tilde{R}_k' \otimes I)Z^*_{-1}]'(\tilde{\Sigma}^{-1} \otimes I)\varepsilon - [\tilde{Z}^*-(\tilde{R}_k' \otimes I)Z^*_{-1}]'(\tilde{\Sigma}^{-1} \otimes I)(I_m \otimes U_{-1})(\hat{r}-r)_k, \tag{39}$$

$$(\tilde{r}-r)_k = [I_m \otimes (\tilde{U}'_{-1}\tilde{U}_{-1})^{-1}\tilde{U}'_{-1}]\varepsilon - [I_m \otimes (\tilde{U}'_{-1}\tilde{U}_{-1})^{-1}\tilde{U}'_{-1}]\{\tilde{Z}^*-(R' \otimes I)Z^*_{-1}\}(\tilde{\delta}-\delta)_k. \tag{40}$$

For the converging iterate, we can then write

$$\sqrt{T}\begin{pmatrix}\hat{\delta}-\delta\\ \hat{r}-r\end{pmatrix}=\begin{bmatrix}\left(\dfrac{\tilde{M}}{T}\right)^{-1}\dfrac{1}{\sqrt{T}}[\tilde{Z}^{*}-(\tilde{R}'\otimes I)Z_{-1}^{*}]'(\tilde{\Sigma}^{-1}\otimes I)\\ I_m\otimes\left(\dfrac{\tilde{U}'_{-1}\tilde{U}_{-1}}{T}\right)^{-1}\dfrac{\tilde{U}'_{-1}}{\sqrt{T}}\end{bmatrix}\varepsilon$$

$$-\begin{bmatrix}0 & \dfrac{1}{T}\left(\dfrac{\tilde{M}}{T}\right)^{-1}[\tilde{Z}^{*}-(\tilde{R}'\otimes I)Z_{-1}^{*}]'(\tilde{\Sigma}^{-1}\otimes I)(I_m\otimes U_{-1})\\ \left[I_m\otimes\left(\dfrac{\tilde{U}'_{-1}\tilde{U}_{-1}}{T}\right)^{-1}\dfrac{\tilde{U}'_{-1}}{T}\right][\tilde{Z}^{*}-(R'\otimes I)Z_{-1}^{*}] & 0\end{bmatrix}$$

$$\times\sqrt{T}\begin{pmatrix}\hat{\delta}-\delta\\ \hat{r}-r\end{pmatrix}. \tag{41}$$

Multiplying through, on the left, by

$$\begin{bmatrix}\dfrac{\tilde{M}}{T} & 0\\ 0 & I\end{bmatrix},$$

and rearranging terms we find

$$\begin{bmatrix}\dfrac{\tilde{M}}{T} & \dfrac{1}{T}[\tilde{Z}^{*}-(\tilde{R}'\otimes I)Z_{-1}^{*}]'(\tilde{\Sigma}^{*-1}\otimes I)(I_m\otimes U_{-1})\\ I & \left[I_m\otimes\left(\dfrac{\tilde{U}'_{-1}\tilde{U}_{-1}}{T}\right)^{-1}\dfrac{\tilde{U}'_{-1}}{T}\right][\tilde{Z}^{*}-(R'\otimes I)Z_{-1}^{*}]\end{bmatrix}\sqrt{T}\begin{pmatrix}\hat{\delta}-\delta\\ \hat{r}-r\end{pmatrix}$$

$$=\frac{1}{\sqrt{T}}\begin{bmatrix}[Z^{*}-(\tilde{R}'\otimes I)Z_{-1}^{*}]'(\tilde{\Sigma}^{-1}\otimes I)\\ I_m\otimes\left(\dfrac{\tilde{U}'_{-1}\tilde{U}_{-1}}{T}\right)^{-1}\tilde{U}'_{-1}\end{bmatrix}\varepsilon. \tag{42}$$

It is, thus, easily verified that the solution vector in eq. (42), i.e.,

$$\sqrt{T}\begin{pmatrix}\hat{\delta}-\delta\\ \hat{r}-r\end{pmatrix}$$

behaves asymptotically according to the relation given in eq. (30).

References

Billingsley, P., 1968, Convergence of probability measures (Wiley, New York).

Dhrymes, P.J., 1971, Distributed lags: Problems of estimation and formulation (Holden-Day, San Francisco).

Dhrymes, P.J., n.d., Full information estimation of dynamic simultaneous equations models with autoregressive errors, in: V.K. Srivastava, ed., Proceedings of All India Seminar on Statistics and Demography (in press).

Dhrymes, P.J., 1973, Small sample and asymptotic relations between maximum likelihood and three stage least squares estimators, Econometrica 41, 357–364.

Hoeffding, W. and H. Robbins, 1943, The central limit theorem for dependent variables, Duke Mathematical Journal 15, 773–780.

Mann, H.B. and A. Wald, 1943, On the statistical treatment of linear stochastic difference equations, Econometrica 11, 173–220.

[12]

Journal of Econometrics 2 (1974) 301–304. © North-Holland Publishing Company

A NOTE ON AN EFFICIENT TWO-STEP ESTIMATOR

Phoebus J. DHRYMES

Columbia University, New York, N.Y. 10027, U.S.A.

Received April 1974

1. Introduction

This note was motivated by the interesting preceding paper of Hatanaka, and its aim is to connect Hatanaka's contribution more explicitly to the discussion in Dhrymes (1971, ch. 7) and to provide a more transparent motivation.

2. Formulation of the problem

Consider the standard dynamic model with autoregressive errors

$$y_t = \alpha x_t + \lambda y_{t-1} + u_t, \qquad t = 1, 2, \ldots, T. \tag{1}$$

Compactly, we write

$$y = X\beta + u, \quad X = (x, y_{-1}), \quad \beta = (\alpha, \lambda)', \tag{2}$$

the notation having the obvious meaning.

Moreover,

$$u_t = \rho u_{t-1} + \varepsilon_t,$$

the sequence $\{\varepsilon_t : t = 0, \pm 1, \pm 2, \ldots\}$ being one of independent identically distributed (i.i.d.) random variables. The parameters λ, ρ are assumed to lie in a closed subset of $(-1, 1) \times (-1, 1)$, and the true parameter point $\gamma_0 = (\alpha_0, \lambda_0, \rho_0)'$ is assumed to lie in the interior of the admissible parameter set.

Consider

$$S = (y - X\beta)' V^{-1} (y - X\beta), \tag{3}$$

where

$$\mathrm{Cov}\,(u) = \sigma^2 V.$$

The minimum chi square (MCS) estimator of γ, say $\hat{\gamma}$, obeys

$$\partial S / \partial \gamma(\hat{\gamma}) = 0. \tag{4}$$

This estimator was obtained by a non-linear (search) procedure in Dhrymes (1971). Hatanaka's objective is to obtain an efficient two-step estimator that is computationally simple. He terms this the 'residual-adjusted Aitken' estimator. An alternative derivation, however, that gives a transparent motivation and shows it immediately to have the same asymptotic distribution as the MCS (or in case of normality of the ε-process the maximum likelihood) estimator is obtained through the following argument:

Consider the estimator $\hat{\gamma}$ obeying (4). We may write

$$\begin{aligned} 0 &= \partial S/\partial\gamma\,(\hat{\gamma}) \\ &= \partial S/\partial\gamma\,(\gamma_0)+\partial^2 S/\partial\gamma\partial\gamma\,(\gamma^*)\,(\hat{\gamma}-\gamma_0), \end{aligned} \tag{5}$$

where

$$|\gamma^*-\gamma_0| < |\hat{\gamma}-\gamma_0|.$$

Consequently, if $\hat{\gamma}$ is shown to be consistent, its asymptotic distribution is determined through

$$\sqrt{T}\,(\hat{\gamma}-\gamma_0) \sim -[(1/T)\,\partial^2 S/\partial\gamma\partial\gamma\,(\gamma_0)]^{-1}\,(1/\sqrt{T})\,\partial S/\partial\gamma\,(\gamma_0). \tag{6}$$

What I called the modified method of scoring obtains a two-step estimator as follows: By instrumental variables methods obtain a consistent estimator of β, say $\tilde{\beta}$. From the residual vector

$$\tilde{u} = y - X\tilde{\beta}$$

compute

$$\tilde{\rho} = \tilde{u}'\tilde{u}_{-1}/\tilde{u}'_{-1}\tilde{u}_{-1},$$

and thus derive the two-step estimator

$$(\hat{\gamma}-\tilde{\gamma}) = -[\partial^2 S/\partial\gamma\partial\gamma\,(\tilde{\gamma})]^{-1}\,\partial S/\partial\gamma\,(\tilde{\gamma}), \qquad \tilde{\gamma} = (\tilde{\beta}', \tilde{\rho})'. \tag{7}$$

It is easy to show that the estimator $\hat{\gamma}$ in (7) has the same asymptotic distribution as the estimator in (6). Thus, note,

$$\sqrt{T}(\hat{\gamma}-\gamma_0) = \sqrt{}(\tilde{\gamma}-\gamma_0)-[1/T\,\partial^2 S/\partial\gamma\partial\gamma\,(\tilde{\gamma})]^{-1}(\sqrt{1/T})\partial S/\partial\gamma\,(\tilde{\gamma}). \tag{8}$$

Expand

$$\partial S/\partial\gamma\,(\tilde{\gamma}) = \partial S/\partial\gamma\,(\tilde{\gamma}_0)+\partial^2 S/\partial\gamma\partial\gamma\,(\bar{\gamma})\,(\tilde{\gamma}-\gamma_0), \tag{9}$$

where

$$|\bar{\gamma}-\gamma_0| < |\tilde{\gamma}-\gamma_0|.$$

We note that under the standard assumptions

$$\begin{aligned} \operatorname*{plim}_{T\to\infty}(1/T)\,\partial^2 S/\partial\gamma\partial\gamma\,(\bar{\gamma}) &= \operatorname*{plim}_{T\to\infty}(1/T)\,\partial^2 S/\partial\gamma\partial\gamma\,(\gamma_0) \\ &= \Omega, \end{aligned}$$

with Ω positive definite, for any consistent $\bar{\gamma}$. Consequently, we see that the estimator in (8) obeys, asymptotically,

$$\sqrt{T}(\hat{\gamma}-\gamma_0) \sim \sqrt{T}(\tilde{\gamma}-\gamma_0)-\Omega^{-1}\frac{1}{\sqrt{T}}\partial S/\partial\gamma\,(\gamma_0)-\sqrt{T}(\tilde{\gamma}-\gamma_0)$$

$$= -\Omega^{-1}\frac{1}{\sqrt{T}}\,\partial S/\partial\gamma\,(\gamma_0). \tag{10}$$

A careful look at (6), however, readily shows that the two asymptotic distributions are identical.

Now that this aspect is understood *we note that in* (7) *we can use in lieu of* $\partial^2 S/\partial\gamma\partial\gamma\,(\tilde{\gamma})$ *any other matrix having the same probability limit.* In particular, this argues for suppressing any components of the matrix above having null probability limits.

We note that

$$\operatorname*{plim}_{T\to\infty}(1/T)\,\partial^2 S/\partial\gamma\partial\gamma\,(\tilde{\gamma})$$
$$= \operatorname*{plim}_{T\to\infty}(2/T)\begin{bmatrix}(X-\rho X_{-1})'(X-\rho X_{-1}) & (X-\rho X_{-1})'u_{-1}\\ u'_{-1}(X-\rho X_{-1}) & u'_{-1-}u_1\end{bmatrix}.$$

This is so since, for example, the off-diagonal block can be written, approximately, as

$$(2/T)X'(\partial\tilde{V}/\partial\rho)\tilde{u} = (2/T)[(X-\tilde{\rho}X_{-1})'\tilde{u}_{-1}+X'_{-1}(\tilde{u}-\tilde{\rho}\tilde{u}_{-1})],$$

and the second term above vanishes in probability. Consequently, the modified method of scoring estimator is also equivalent to the estimator obeying

$$(X-\tilde{\rho}X_{-1})'(X-\tilde{\rho}X_{-1})(\hat{\beta}-\tilde{\beta})+(X-\tilde{\rho}X_{-1})'\tilde{u}_{-1}(\hat{\rho}-\tilde{\rho})$$
$$= (X-\tilde{\rho}X_{-1})'[(y-\tilde{\rho}y_{-1})-(X-\tilde{\rho}X_{-1})\tilde{\beta}],$$
$$\tilde{u}'_{-1}(X-\tilde{\rho}X_{-1})(\hat{\beta}-\tilde{\beta})+\tilde{u}'_{-1}\tilde{u}_{-1}(\hat{\rho}-\tilde{\rho}) = \tilde{u}'_{-1}\big|(y-\tilde{\rho}y_{-1})$$
$$-(X-\tilde{\rho}X_{-1})\tilde{\beta}\big|. \tag{11}$$

This further simplifies to

$$(X-\tilde{\rho}X_{-1})'(X-\tilde{\rho}X_{-1})\hat{\beta}+(X-\tilde{\rho}X_{-1})'\tilde{u}_{-1}(\hat{\rho}-\tilde{\rho})$$
$$= (X-\tilde{\rho}X_{-1})'(y-\tilde{\rho}y_{-1}),$$
$$\tilde{u}'_{-1}(X-\tilde{\rho}X_{-1})\hat{\beta}+\tilde{u}'_{-1}\tilde{u}_{-1}(\hat{\rho}-\tilde{\rho}) = \tilde{u}'_{-1}(y-\tilde{\rho}y_{-1}). \tag{12}$$

But this estimator, which is equivalent, asymptotically, to that yielded by the modified method of scoring and hence to the MCS (or the ML as the case may be) estimator, is easily recognized as the 'residual-adjusted Aitken' estimator of Hatanaka.

The arguments establishing its consistency and asymptotic normality were given in Dhrymes (1971), and are also proved under somewhat more general assumptions in Hatanaka's paper. The key to the derivation of such estimators (and they may be extended to many other cases) is the observation in (7) that the matrix and vector in the right member can be replaced by any other such quantities that have the same probability limits. The choice is immaterial in terms of asymptotic properties and thus is to be made, perhaps, on the criterion of computational simplicity. Nothing is implied by the above regarding small sample properties but this aspect was addressed by Hatanaka through a Monte Carlo study.

References

Dhrymes, P.J., 1971, Distributed lags: Problems of estimation and formulations (Holden-Day, San Francisco).

Hatanaka, M., 1974, An efficient two-step estimator for the dynamic adjustment model with autocorrelated errors, Journal of Econometrics 2, 199–220.

INTERNATIONAL ECONOMIC REVIEW
Vol. 17, No. 2, June, 1976

ON AN EFFICIENT TWO-STEP ESTIMATOR FOR DYNAMIC SIMULTANEOUS EQUATIONS MODELS WITH AUTOREGRESSIVE ERRORS*

BY PHOEBUS J. DHRYMES AND JOHN B. TAYLOR[1]

1. INTRODUCTION

WE CONSIDER THE MODEL:

$$y_{t\cdot} = y_{t\cdot}B + y_{t-1\cdot}C_0 + w_{t\cdot 1} + u_{t\cdot}, \qquad t = 1, 2, \cdots T \tag{1}$$

where $y_{t\cdot}$ is an m-element vector of the dependent variables of the system and $w_{t\cdot}$ is an s-element vector of *exogenous* variables; the error term obeys

$$u_{t\cdot} = u_{t-1\cdot}R + \varepsilon_{t\cdot} \tag{2}$$

where R is a stable matrix and $\{\varepsilon'_{t\cdot}: t = 0, \pm 1, \pm 2, \cdots\}$ is a sequence of independent identically distributed (i.i.d.) random variables having mean zero and nonsingular covariance matrix Σ.

It is assumed that whatever the process generating $\{w'_{t\cdot}: t = 0, \pm 1, \pm 2, \cdots\}$ the latter sequence is independent of $\{\varepsilon'_{t\cdot}: t = 0, \pm 1, \pm 2, \cdots\}$.

In Dhrymes [**1**] under the additional assumption of normality for the ε-process the full information maximum likelihood (ML) estimator wasobtai ned as well as the three-stage-least-squares-like estimator, termed there the full information dynamic autoregressive (FIDA). The converging iterate of the latter (CIFIDA) was compared with the ML estimator and it was determined that the difference between the two lies in the way in which the (jointly) dependent variables of the system are purged of their stochastic component.

In Dhrymes and Erlat [**3**] the asymptotic distribution of the converging iterate of FIDA was obtained.

The purpose of this paper is twofold: First, to show that the asymptotic distributions of the converging iterate of FIDA and the ML estimator are identical and second, to provide a simple two step procedure which is fully as efficient as CIFIDA and ML estimators. This is a natural extension of the results in Dhrymes [**2**] and Hatanaka [**5**].

2. EQUIVALENCE OF ML AND CIFIDA ESTIMATORS

Write the Equation (1) compactly as

$$ZA = U$$

* Manuscript received April 3, 1975; revised October 28, 1975.

[1] The research on which this paper is based was in part supported by NSF grant SOC 74-18671. Results similar to the ones reported in this paper were independently derived by Hatanaka in [**6**].

where

$$Z = (Y, Y_{-1}, W), \quad W = (w_{tj}) \quad t = 2, 3, \cdots, T, \ j = 1, 2, \cdots, s$$

$$Y = (y_{ti}), \quad Y_{-1} = (y_{t-1,i}), \quad U = (u_{ti})$$

$$t = 2, 3, \cdots, T, \ i = 1, 2, \cdots, m$$

$$A = (I - B', -C_0', -C_1')' .$$

Making use of the zero restrictions, we can write the i-th equation as

$$y_{\cdot i} = Z_i \delta_{\cdot i} + u_{\cdot i} \tag{3}$$

where $y_{\cdot i}$, $u_{\cdot i}$ are the i-th columns, respectively, of Y and U

$$Z_i = (Y_i, {}_iY_{-1}, W_i), \quad \delta_{\cdot i} = (\beta_{\cdot i}', \gamma_{\cdot i}^{*\prime}, \gamma_{\cdot i}')'$$

Y_i, ${}_iY_{-1}$, W_i being submatrices of Y, Y_{-1}, W, respectively, corresponding to the included right hand variables and $\beta_{\cdot i}$, $\gamma_{\cdot i}^*$, $\gamma_{\cdot i}$ being the i-th columns of B, C_0, C_1 respectively after elements known to be zero have been suppressed. The system may be written also as

$$y = Z^* \delta + u$$

where

$$y = \text{Vec}\,(Y), \quad u = \text{Vec}\,(U), \quad Z^* = \text{diag}\,(Z_1, Z_2, \cdots, Z_m)$$

$$\delta = (\delta_{\cdot 1}', \delta_{\cdot 2}', \cdots \delta_{\cdot m}')'$$

the notation Vec (A) denoting a column vector whose i-th subvector is the i-th column of A.

Using the representation above, it is shown in [**1**] that the converging iterate of FIDA is given as the solution (in δ and R) of the following equation system

$$\begin{aligned} \tilde{M}\tilde{\delta} &= \tilde{P}'(\tilde{\Sigma}^{-1} \otimes I)[y - (\tilde{R}' \otimes I)y_{-1}] \\ R &= (\tilde{A}'Z_{-1}'Z_{-1}\tilde{A})^{-1}\tilde{A}'Z_{-1}'Z\tilde{A} \end{aligned} \tag{4}$$

where

$$\begin{aligned} \tilde{P} &= \tilde{Z}^* - (\tilde{R}' \otimes I)Z_{-1}^*, \quad \tilde{M} = \tilde{P}'(\tilde{\Sigma}^{-1} \otimes I)\tilde{P} \\ \tilde{Z} &= (\tilde{Y}, Y_{-1}, W), \quad \tilde{Y} = Q\tilde{F}, \quad Q = (Y_{-1}, Y_{-2}, W, W_{-1}) \\ \tilde{F} &= (Q'Q)^{-1}Q'Y \\ \tilde{Z}_i &= (\tilde{Y}_i, {}_iY_{-1}, W_i), \quad \tilde{Z}^* = \text{diag}\,(\tilde{Z}_1, \tilde{Z}_2, \cdots, \tilde{Z}_m) \end{aligned} \tag{5}$$

and $\tilde{\Sigma}$ is a prior consistent estimator of $\tilde{\Sigma}$.

The ML estimator is shown to be a solution of

$$\begin{aligned} \tilde{M}_*\tilde{\delta} &= [\tilde{P}_*'(\tilde{\Sigma}^{-1} \otimes I) - \tilde{V}^{*\prime}(S^{-1} \otimes I)][y - (\tilde{R}' \otimes I)y_{-1}] \\ \tilde{R} &= (\tilde{A}'Z_{-1}'Z_{-1}\tilde{A})^{-1}\tilde{A}'Z_{-1}'Z\tilde{A} \end{aligned} \tag{6}$$

$$\tilde{\Sigma} = \frac{1}{T}\tilde{E}'\tilde{E}, \quad \tilde{E} = Z\tilde{A} - Z_{-1}\tilde{A}\tilde{R}$$

where

$$\tilde{P}_* = [Z^* - (\tilde{R}' \otimes I)Z^*_{-1}],$$

(7)
$$\tilde{M}_* = \tilde{P}'_*(\tilde{\Sigma}^{-1} \otimes I)\tilde{P}_* - \tilde{V}^{*\prime}(S^{-1} \otimes I)\tilde{V}^*$$

$$S = \left(\frac{1}{T}\right)(I - \tilde{B}')\tilde{V}'\tilde{V}(I - \tilde{B}), \quad \tilde{V} = Y - Q\tilde{F}$$

$$\tilde{V}^*_i = (\tilde{V}_i, 0, 0), \quad \tilde{V}^* = \text{diag}\,(\tilde{V}^*_1, \tilde{V}^*_2, \cdots, \tilde{V}^*_m)$$

the zeros in the definition of $\tilde{V}^*_i$ corresponding, in dimension, to ${}_iY_{-1}$, W_i.

It is also shown in [**1**] that the asymptotic distribution of the ML estimator of δ and R does not depend on any properties of the asymptotic distribution of the estimator of Σ, so long as the latter is estimated consistently.

Thus, for the purposes of comparison we shall consider only the first two sets of Equations in (6).

On the assumption that, in both Equations (4) and (6), a solution can be found by iteration *beginning with initial consistent estimators for* δ *and* R*, the solution is a consistent estimator of* δ *and* R*, and moreover, after slight rearrangement, we can write for the solution vector of CIFIDA*

(8)
$$\left(\frac{1}{T}\right)\begin{bmatrix} \tilde{M} & \tilde{P}'(\tilde{\Sigma}^{-1} \otimes U_{-1}) \\ (\tilde{\Sigma}^{-1} \otimes \tilde{U}'_{-1})\tilde{P} & \tilde{\Sigma}^{-1} \otimes \tilde{U}'_{-1}\tilde{U}_{-1} \end{bmatrix} \sqrt{T}\begin{pmatrix} \tilde{\delta} - \delta \\ \tilde{r} - r \end{pmatrix} = \left(\frac{1}{\sqrt{T}}\right)\begin{bmatrix} \tilde{P}'(\tilde{\Sigma}^{-1} \otimes I) \\ \tilde{\Sigma}^{-1} \otimes \tilde{U}'_{-1} \end{bmatrix}\varepsilon$$

where

$$\tilde{U}_{-1} = Z_{-1}\tilde{A}, \ \varepsilon = \text{Vec}\,(E), \ E = (\varepsilon_{ti})$$
$$t = 2, \cdots, T \text{ and } i = 1, 2, \cdots m\,.$$

The equations defining the ML estimator, on the other hand, are

(9)
$$\left(\frac{1}{T}\right)\begin{bmatrix} \tilde{M}_* & (\tilde{P}^{*\prime}(\tilde{\Sigma}^{-1} \otimes I) - \tilde{V}^{*\prime}(S^{-1} \otimes I))(I \otimes U_{-1}) \\ (\tilde{\Sigma}^{-1} \otimes \tilde{U}'_{-1})N & \tilde{\Sigma}^{-1} \otimes \tilde{U}'_{-1}\tilde{U}_{-1} \end{bmatrix} \sqrt{T}\begin{pmatrix} \tilde{\delta} - \delta \\ \tilde{r} - r \end{pmatrix} = \frac{1}{\sqrt{T}}\begin{bmatrix} \tilde{P}'_*(\tilde{\Sigma}^{-1} \otimes I) - \tilde{V}^{*\prime}(S^{-1} \otimes I) \\ \tilde{\Sigma}^{-1} \otimes U'_{-1} \end{bmatrix}\varepsilon$$

where

$$N = [Z^* - (R' \otimes I)Z^*_{-1}]\,.$$

To show the equivalence of the two estimators, we proceed somewhat formally giving in the form of Lemmata a number of preliminary required results. We begin by showing that the matrices in the left member of Equations (8) and (9) have identical probability limits. Thus,

LEMMA 1. *Under the standard assumptions*

$$\operatorname*{plim}_{T\to\infty} S = \Sigma \,.$$

PROOF. By definition

$$\tilde{V} = Y - Q\tilde{F} = [I - Q(Q'Q)^{-1}Q']E(I - B)^{-1} \,.$$

Thus

$$\left(\frac{1}{T}\right)\tilde{V}'\tilde{V} = \left(\frac{1}{T}\right)(I - B')^{-1}E'[I - Q(Q'Q)^{-1}Q']E(I - B)^{-1} \,.$$

Since

$$\operatorname*{plim}_{T\to\infty}\left(\frac{1}{T}\right)E'Q(Q'Q)^{-1}Q'E = 0, \quad \operatorname*{plim}_{T\to\infty}\left(\frac{1}{T}\right)E'E = \Sigma$$

we have, by the consistency of $\tilde{B}$

$$\operatorname*{plim}_{T\to\infty} S = \Sigma \,. \qquad \text{Q.E.D.}$$

LEMMA 2.

$$\operatorname*{plim}_{T\to\infty}\left(\frac{1}{T}\right)\tilde{P}'(\tilde{\Sigma}^{-1} \otimes U_{-1}) = P_1'(\Sigma^{-1} \otimes I)$$

where

$$P_1 = \operatorname*{plim}_{T\to\infty}\left(\frac{1}{T}\right)\bar{P}'(I \otimes U_{-1}), \quad \bar{P} = \bar{Z}^* - (R' \otimes I)Z^*_{-1}$$

$$\bar{Z}_i = (QF_i, {}_iY_{-1}, W_i), \quad \bar{Z}^* = \operatorname{diag}(\bar{Z}_1, \cdots, \bar{Z}_m) \,,$$

$$F = \operatorname*{plim}_{T\to\infty} \tilde{F} \,.$$

PROOF. Obvious.

LEMMA 3.

$$\operatorname*{plim}_{T\to\infty}\left(\frac{1}{T}\right)[\tilde{P}_*'(\tilde{\Sigma}^{-1} \otimes I) - \tilde{V}^{*\prime}(S^{-1} \otimes I)][I \otimes U_{-1}] = P_1'(\Sigma^{-1} \otimes I) \,.$$

PROOF. By definition

$$\tilde{P}_* = Z^* - (\tilde{R}' \otimes I)Z_{-1} = \bar{Z}^* - (\tilde{R}' \otimes I)Z_{-1} + V^* \,.$$

We also note that since

$$V = E(I - B)^{-1}, \quad \tilde{V} = [I - Q(Q'Q)^{-1}Q']V$$

and

$$\operatorname*{plim}_{T\to\infty}\left(\frac{1}{T}\right)V'U_{-1} = 0$$

we have

$$\operatorname*{plim}_{T\to\infty}\left(\frac{1}{T}\right)\tilde{V}^{*\prime}(S^{-1}\otimes I)(I\otimes U_{-1}) = 0$$

and consequently

$$\operatorname*{plim}_{T\to\infty}\left(\frac{1}{T}\right)[\tilde{P}_*'(\tilde{\Sigma}^{-1}\otimes I) - \tilde{V}^{*\prime}(S^{-1}\otimes I)](I\otimes U_{-1})$$

$$= \operatorname*{plim}_{T\to\infty}\left(\frac{1}{T}\right)\tilde{P}'(\Sigma^{-1}\otimes I)(I\otimes U_{-1}) = P_1'(\Sigma^{-1}\otimes I)\,. \quad \text{Q.E.D.}$$

LEMMA 4.

$$\operatorname*{plim}_{T\to\infty}\left(\frac{1}{T}\right)(\tilde{\Sigma}^{-1}\otimes \tilde{U}_{-1}')\tilde{P} = \operatorname*{plim}_{T\to\infty}\left(\frac{1}{T}\right)(\tilde{\Sigma}^{-1}\otimes \tilde{U}_{-1}')\tilde{P}_* = (\Sigma^{-1}\otimes I)P_1\,.$$

PROOF. Obvious from Lemma 3.

Finally, letting

$$\Omega = \operatorname*{plim}_{T\to\infty}\frac{1}{T}\tilde{U}_{-1}'\tilde{U}_{-1}$$

and

$$M = \operatorname*{plim}_{T\to\infty}\frac{\tilde{M}}{T}$$

we have

LEMMA 5. *The matrices in the left members of Equations (8) and (9) have the same probability limit, which is given by*

$$C = \begin{bmatrix} M & P_1'(\Sigma^{-1}\otimes I) \\ (\Sigma^{-1}\otimes I)P_1 & \Sigma^{-1}\otimes\Omega \end{bmatrix}. \tag{11}$$

PROOF. Obvious from Lemmata 2, 3 and 4.

Thus, to establish the identity of the asymptotic distribution of the two estimators it will be sufficient to establish that the right members converge in distribution to the same limit. To this effect note that since

$$\tilde{\Sigma}^{-1}\otimes\tilde{U}_{-1}' = \tilde{\Sigma}^{-1}\otimes\tilde{A}'Z_{-1}' = (\tilde{\Sigma}^{-1}\otimes\tilde{A}')(I\otimes Z_{-1}')$$

we have that

$$\frac{1}{\sqrt{T}}[(\tilde{\Sigma}^{-1}-\Sigma)\otimes(\tilde{A}'-A')](I\otimes Z_1')\varepsilon$$

$$= \sqrt{T}(\tilde{\Sigma}-\Sigma)\otimes\sqrt{T}(\tilde{A}'-A')\left(\frac{1}{T}\right)^{3/2}(I\otimes Z_{-1}')\varepsilon$$

which converges in distribution to the degenerate random variable zero. Consequently in both (8) and (9) we can replace

$$(\tilde{\Sigma}^{-1} \otimes \tilde{U}'_{-1})$$

by

$$(\Sigma^{-1} \otimes A')(I \otimes Z_{-1})\,.$$

Thus, the identity of the two asymptotic distributions depends only on the comparison between

$$\left(\frac{1}{\sqrt{T}}\right)\tilde{P}'(\tilde{\Sigma}^{-1} \otimes I)\varepsilon$$

and

$$\frac{1}{\sqrt{T}}[\tilde{P}'_{*}(\tilde{\Sigma}^{-1} \otimes I) - \tilde{V}^{*\prime}(S^{-1} \otimes I)]\varepsilon\,.$$

Consider first the quantity

$$\left(\frac{1}{\sqrt{T}}\right)[\tilde{P}'_{*}(\tilde{\Sigma}^{-1} \otimes I) - \tilde{V}^{*\prime}(\tilde{\Sigma}^{-1} \otimes I)]\varepsilon$$

and define

$$\left(\frac{1}{\sqrt{T}}\right)[\tilde{P}'_{*}(\tilde{\Sigma}^{-1}\otimes I) - \tilde{V}^{*\prime}(S^{-1}\otimes I) - \tilde{P}'_{*}(\tilde{\Sigma}^{-1}\otimes I) + \tilde{V}^{*\prime}(\tilde{\Sigma}^{-1}\otimes I)]\varepsilon$$
$$= \left(\frac{1}{\sqrt{T}}\right)\tilde{V}^{*\prime}[(\tilde{\Sigma}^{-1} - S^{-1}) \otimes I]\varepsilon\,.$$

If we show that

$$\sqrt{T}\,(\tilde{\Sigma}^{-1} - S^{-1})$$

converges in distribution to the degenerate random variable zero, we immediately conclude that

$$\left(\frac{1}{\sqrt{T}}\right)\tilde{V}^{*\prime}[(\tilde{\Sigma}^{-1} - S^{-1}) \otimes I]\varepsilon$$

similarly converges to the degenerate random variable zero. This is so since

$$\operatorname*{plim}_{T\to\infty}\left(\frac{1}{T}\right)\tilde{V}'E = (I - B')^{-1}\Sigma\,.$$

We have

LEMMA 6.

$$\sqrt{T}\,(\tilde{\Sigma}^{-1} - S^{-1})$$

is asymptotically a degenerate random variable.

PROOF.

$$\tilde{\Sigma}^{-1} - S^{-1} = \tilde{\Sigma}^{-1}(S - \tilde{\Sigma})S^{-1}$$

and thus

$$\sqrt{T}(\tilde{\Sigma}^{-1} - S^{-1}) \sim \Sigma^{-1}[\sqrt{T}(S - \tilde{\Sigma})]\Sigma^{-1}.$$

Now

$$\tilde{\Sigma} = \frac{1}{T}\tilde{E}'\tilde{E} = (I - \tilde{B}')(I - \tilde{B}')^{-1}\frac{\tilde{E}'\tilde{E}}{T}(I - \tilde{B})^{-1}(I - \tilde{B})$$

so

$$\sqrt{T}(S - \tilde{\Sigma}) = (I - \tilde{B}')\sqrt{T}\left[\frac{\tilde{V}'\tilde{V}}{T} - (I - \tilde{B}')^{-1}\frac{\tilde{E}'\tilde{E}}{T}(I - \tilde{B})^{-1}\right](I - \tilde{B}).$$

We observe that

$$\tilde{V} = Y - Q\tilde{F}$$

where $\tilde{F}$ is the unrestricted estimator of F. Similarly, we observe that

$$\tilde{E}(I - \tilde{B})^{-1} = Y - Q\hat{F}$$

where $\hat{F}$ is the restricted estimator of F derived from the ML estimator of the elements of A. Thus

$$\sqrt{T}(S - \tilde{\Sigma}) = (I - \tilde{B}')\Big[\sqrt{T}(\hat{F} - \tilde{F})'\frac{Q'Y}{T} + \frac{Y'Q}{T}\sqrt{T}(\hat{F} - \tilde{F})$$
$$- \sqrt{T}(\hat{F} - \tilde{F})\frac{Q'Q}{T}\hat{F} - \tilde{F}'\frac{Q'Q}{T}\sqrt{T}(\hat{F} - \tilde{F})\Big](I - \tilde{B}).$$

Provided $\sqrt{T}(\hat{F} - \tilde{F})$ has a well defined limiting distribution

$$\sqrt{T}(S - \tilde{\Sigma}) \sim (I - B)'[\sqrt{T}(\hat{F} - \tilde{F})'M_{QQ}F + F'M_{QQ}\sqrt{T}(\hat{F} - \tilde{F})$$
$$- \sqrt{T}(\hat{F} - \tilde{F})M_{QQ}F - FM_{QQ}\sqrt{T}(\hat{F} - \tilde{F})](I - B) = 0$$

where

$$M_{QQ} = \operatorname*{plim}_{T\to\infty}\frac{Q'Q}{T}.$$

Thus $\sqrt{T}(S - \tilde{\Sigma})$ converges in distribution to the zero random variable.

Q.E.D.

COROLLARY.

$$\frac{1}{\sqrt{T}}[\tilde{P}'_*(\tilde{\Sigma}^{-1} \otimes I) - \tilde{V}^{*\prime}(S^{-1} \otimes I)]\varepsilon$$

and

$$\frac{1}{\sqrt{T}}[\tilde{P}'_*(\tilde{\Sigma}^{-1} \otimes I) - \tilde{V}^{*\prime}(\tilde{\Sigma}^{-1} \otimes I)]\varepsilon$$

have the same limiting distribution.

PROOF. Obvious.

We now observe that

$$\tilde{P}'_*(\tilde{\Sigma}^{-1} \otimes I) - \tilde{V}^{*\prime}(\tilde{\Sigma}^{-1} \otimes I) = \tilde{P}(\tilde{\Sigma}^{-1} \otimes I)$$

where, *mutatis mutandis*, $\tilde{P}$ is the same matrix as that appearing in the CIFIDA estimator. We now have the following obvious results applying to both the CIFIDA and ML estimators.

LEMMA 7. Asymptotically,

$$\frac{1}{\sqrt{T}}\tilde{P}'(\tilde{\Sigma}^{-1} \otimes I)\varepsilon \sim \frac{1}{\sqrt{T}}\tilde{P}'(\Sigma^{-1} \otimes I)\varepsilon .$$

PROOF.

$$\frac{1}{\sqrt{T}}\tilde{P}[(\tilde{\Sigma}^{-1} - \Sigma^{-1}) \otimes I]\varepsilon = \frac{1}{T}\tilde{P}'[\sqrt{T}(\tilde{\Sigma}^{-1} - \Sigma^{-1}) \otimes I]\varepsilon$$

which obviously converges in distribution to the degenerate random variable zero.

LEMMA 8. *Asymptotically,*

$$\frac{1}{\sqrt{T}}\tilde{P}'(\Sigma^{-1} \otimes I)\varepsilon \sim \frac{1}{\sqrt{T}}\bar{P}'(\Sigma^{-1} \otimes I)\varepsilon .$$

PROOF.

$$\tilde{P} - \bar{P} = \tilde{Z}^* - (\tilde{R}' \otimes I)Z_{-1} - \bar{Z}^* + (R' \otimes I)Z_{-1} .$$

But we note

$$\tilde{Z} - \bar{Z} = (\tilde{Y} - \bar{Y}, 0, 0) = (-Q(\tilde{F} - F), 0, 0) .$$

The desired result is then obtained if we note that $\sqrt{T}(\tilde{F} - F)$ has a well behaved limiting distribution and moreover that

$$\operatorname*{plim}_{T\to\infty} \frac{Q'E}{T} = 0, \quad \operatorname*{plim}_{T\to\infty} \frac{Z'_{-1}E}{T} = 0 .$$

Using the results in Dhrymes and Erlat [3] we observe

LEMMA 9. *Asymptotically*

$$\frac{1}{\sqrt{T}}\begin{bmatrix}\bar{P}'(\Sigma^{-1} \otimes I) \\ \Sigma^{-1} \otimes A'Z'_{-1}\end{bmatrix}\varepsilon \sim N(0, C) .$$

PROOF. See [3].

We have therefore proved

THEOREM 1. *Consider the model in (1) and (2) subject to the following conditions:*

(i) $I - B$ *is nonsingular.*
(ii) $R, C_0(I - B)^{-1}$ *are both stable.*
(iii) $\operatorname{plim}_{T\to\infty} (Q'Q/T)$ *exists and is nonsingular.*
(iv) *The sequence* $\{w'_{t\cdot} : t = 0, \pm 1, \pm 2, \cdots\}$ *is independent of the error process* $\{\varepsilon'_{t\cdot} : t = 0, \pm 1, \pm 2, \cdots\}$.
(v) *The process* $\{\varepsilon'_{t\cdot} : t = 0, \pm 1, \pm 2, \cdots\}$ *is one of independent i.i.d. (normal) random vectors with zero mean and nonsingular covariance matrix* Σ.
(vi) *The ML estimators* $\sqrt{T}(\tilde{\Sigma} - \Sigma)$, $\sqrt{T}(\tilde{A} - A)$ *have well behaved limiting distinctions.*

Then, the converging iterate of the full information dynamic autoregressive (CIFIDA) and ML estimators of δ have the same asymptotic distribution which is

$$N(0, C^{-1})$$

where

$$C = \begin{bmatrix} M & P_1'(\Sigma^{-1} \otimes I) \\ (\Sigma^{-1} \otimes I)P_1 & \Sigma^{-1} \otimes \Omega \end{bmatrix}.$$

PROOF. Lemmata 5, 6, 7, 8, 9.

3. A SIMPLIFIED TWO STEP ESTIMATOR

In demonstrating the asymptotic equivalence of a simplified estimator to the CIFIDA and ML estimators the following lemma is quite useful:

LEMMA 10. *Let* θ^* *be a consistent estimator of a parameter vector* θ_0 *obtained by minimizing some function, say* $S(\theta)$, *and suppose that* $\sqrt{T}(\theta^* - \theta_0)$ *has a limiting distribution. Let* $\tilde{\theta}$ *be a consistent estimator of* θ_0 *such that* $\sqrt{T}(\tilde{\theta} - \theta_0)$ *has a limiting distribution and let* $\Gamma(\tilde{\theta})$ *be a matrix such that*

$$\Gamma(\tilde{\theta}) = \frac{\partial^2 S}{\partial\theta\partial\theta}(\tilde{\theta}) + o_p(T)$$

where T *is the sample size. Define the estimator* $\hat{\theta}$ *by*

$$\hat{\theta} = \tilde{\theta} - \Gamma^{-1}(\tilde{\theta})\frac{\partial S}{\partial\theta}(\tilde{\theta}). \tag{12}$$

Then $\hat{\theta}$ *has the same asymptotic distribution as* θ^*.

PROOF. By the mean value theorem

$$\frac{\partial S}{\partial \theta}(\tilde{\theta}) = \frac{\partial S}{\partial \theta}(\theta_0) + \frac{\partial^2 S}{\partial \theta \partial \theta}(\bar{\theta})(\tilde{\theta} - \theta_0) \tag{13}$$

where θ_0 is the true parameter vector and $\bar{\theta}$ obeys

$$|\bar{\theta} - \theta_0| < |\tilde{\theta} - \theta_0|.$$

Substituting (13) into (12), we have

$$\sqrt{T}(\hat{\theta} - \theta_0) = \left[I - \left(\frac{\Gamma(\tilde{\theta})}{T}\right)^{-1}\left(\frac{1}{T}\frac{\partial^2 S}{\partial \theta \partial \theta}(\bar{\theta})\right)\right]\sqrt{T}(\tilde{\theta} - \theta_0) - \left(\frac{\Gamma(\tilde{\theta})}{T}\right)^{-1}\frac{1}{\sqrt{T}}\frac{\partial S}{\partial \theta}(\theta_0). \tag{14}$$

Under the assumptions of the lemma the first term above converges (in distribution) to the degenerate random variable zero. Since it can be shown that, asymptotically,

$$\sqrt{T}(\theta^* - \theta_0) \sim -\left(\frac{\Gamma(\theta_0)}{T}\right)^{-1}\frac{\partial S}{\partial \theta}(\theta_0)$$

we immediately conclude

$$\sqrt{T}(\theta^* - \theta_0) \sim \sqrt{T}(\hat{\theta} - \theta_0). \qquad \text{Q.E.D.}$$

To obtain the simplified estimator using Lemma 10, recall that the CIFIDA estimator is obtained by minimizing

$$S(\theta) = tr\tilde{\Sigma}^{-1}(\tilde{Z}A - Z_{-1}AR)'(\tilde{Z}A - Z_{-1}AR) \tag{15}$$

with

$$\theta = (\delta', r')'.$$

A matrix satisfying the properties of Γ in Lemma 10, has been determined in the Appendix—Equation (A. 9). Moreover, we observe that

$$\begin{aligned} \frac{\partial S}{\partial \delta}(\tilde{\theta}) &= -2\tilde{P}'(\tilde{\Sigma}^{-1} \otimes I)[y - (\tilde{R}' \otimes I)y_{-1} - \tilde{P}\tilde{\delta}] \\ \frac{\partial S}{\partial r}(\tilde{\theta}) &= -2(I \otimes \tilde{U}'_{-1})(\tilde{\Sigma}^{-1} \otimes I)[y - (\tilde{R}' \otimes I)y_{-1} - \tilde{P}\tilde{\delta}]. \end{aligned} \tag{16}$$

In view of (16) we can write (12)—after minor rearrangement, as

$$\begin{aligned} \tilde{P}'(\tilde{\Sigma}^{-1} \otimes I)\tilde{P}(\hat{\delta} - \tilde{\delta}) + \tilde{P}'(\tilde{\Sigma}^{-1} \otimes I)(I \otimes \tilde{U}_{-1})(\hat{r} - \tilde{r}) &= \tilde{P}'(\tilde{\Sigma}^{-1} \otimes I)[y - (\tilde{R}' \otimes I)y_{-1} - \tilde{P}\tilde{\delta}] \\ (I \otimes \tilde{U}_{-1})(\tilde{\Sigma}^{-1} \otimes I)\tilde{P}(\hat{\delta} - \tilde{\delta}) + (I \otimes \tilde{U}'_{-1})(\tilde{\Sigma}^{-1} \otimes I)(I \otimes \tilde{U}_{-1})(\hat{r} - \tilde{r}) &= (I \otimes \tilde{U}'_{-1})(\tilde{\Sigma}^{-1} \otimes I)[y - (\tilde{R}' \otimes I)y_{-1} - \tilde{P}\tilde{\delta}] \end{aligned}$$

or, upon cancellation of terms involving $\tilde{P}\tilde{\delta}$ on both sides, as

$$\begin{bmatrix} \tilde P'(\tilde\Sigma^{-1}\otimes I)\tilde P & \tilde P'(\tilde\Sigma^{-1}\otimes I)(I\otimes \tilde U_{-1}) \\ (I\otimes \tilde U'_{-1})(\tilde\Sigma^{-1}\otimes I)\tilde P & (I\otimes \tilde U'_{-1})(\tilde\Sigma^{-1}\otimes I)(I\otimes\tilde U_{-1})\end{bmatrix}\begin{bmatrix}\hat\delta \\ \hat r - \tilde r\end{bmatrix} = \begin{pmatrix}\tilde P' \\ I\otimes \tilde U'_{-1}\end{pmatrix}(\tilde\Sigma^{-1}\otimes I)\cdot[y-(\tilde R\otimes I)y_{-1}]. \tag{17}$$

We have therefore proved

THEOREM 2. *Consider the model stated in Theorem 1; an estimator which is asymptotically equivalent to the ML and the converging iterate of FIDA can be obtained as follows:*

(i) *form a consistent estimator, say by instrumental variables, of the unknown elements of A. Denote this by $\tilde A$.*

(ii) *Compute the residual matrix*

$$\tilde U = Z\tilde A .$$

(iii) *Obtain the estimator*

$$\tilde R = (\tilde A' Z'_{-1} Z_{-1}\tilde A)^{-1}\tilde A Z'_{-1} Z\tilde A .$$

(iv) *Compute*

$$\tilde E = \tilde U - \tilde U_{-1}\tilde R .$$

(v) *Estimate*

$$\tilde\Sigma = \left(\frac{1}{T}\right)\tilde E'\tilde E .$$

(vi) *Form the quantities*

$$\tilde Z^* - (\tilde R'\otimes I)Z^*_{-1},\quad I\otimes\tilde U_{-1},\quad y-(\tilde R\otimes I)y_{-1} .$$

(vii) *Obtain the feasible Aitken type estimator by regressing $y-(\tilde R'\otimes I)y_{-1}$ on $\tilde Z^* - (\tilde R'\otimes I)Z^*_{-1}$, $(I\otimes\tilde U_{-1})$ using $(\tilde\Sigma^{-1}\otimes I)$ as the estimated covariance matrix.*

(viii) *Add to the solution vector* $(0, \tilde r')'$.

Remark 1. The theorem above outlines an estimating procedure which involves estimation of the structural parameters by instrumental variables, computation of the residuals and the elements of the autocorrelation matrix R, followed by transformation of the data and another regression. No iteration is involved, although as a practical matter one might wish to iterate at least once in order to reduce the dependence of the procedure on the initial choice of instruments—which is rather arbitrary.

Remark 2. Even though $\tilde Z$ as it appears in (iv) of Theorem 2 was earlier defined with the $\tilde Y$ component given by $\tilde Y = Q\tilde F$, $\tilde F = (Q'Q)^{-1}Q'Y$, it is clear that we can define $\tilde Y$ by $Q\hat F$ where $\hat F$ is the *restricted reduced form* obtained from $\tilde A$ and $\tilde R$ as given in (i) and (iii) respectively. *Thus, we only need an initial instrumental variables estimator and a feasible Aitken procedure to obtain this two-step estimator.*

Remark 3. The limited information analogue may be obtained by setting $\tilde{\tilde{\Sigma}} = I$ and then minimizing

$$tr(\tilde{Z}A - Z_{-1}AR)'(\tilde{Z}A - Z_{-1}AR)$$

with respect to the unknown elements of A and R. The analogue in the two-step procedure will occur if in (17) we set $\tilde{\tilde{\Sigma}} = I$. Needless to say unless R is a *diagonal* matrix this is *not* a single equation procedure.

Remark 4. Outside the almost tautological condition that the matrix M be invertible, it is not clear what corresponds precisely to the rank and order condition (in the standard model) in setting forth the identifiability characteristics of the model.

Remark 5. The instrumental variables procedure given in Fair [**4**] is not an efficient one unless it is iterated to convergence. What Fair proposes, using the notation of this paper, is to write the model as

$$y - (R' \otimes I)y_{-1} = [Z^* - (R' \otimes I)Z^*_{-1}]\delta + \varepsilon$$

and obtain instrumental variables estimators using the instrumental matrix

$$\tilde{P}'(\tilde{\tilde{\Sigma}}^{-1} \otimes I)$$

substituting for R a prior consistent estimate thereof. It can be shown that the resulting estimator will depend on the asymptotic distribution properties of the particular estimate of R and will, in general, be inefficient unless the procedure is iterated with a new estimate of R until convergence.

Columbia University, U.S.A.

APPENDIX

In the discussion of the paper we have used a number of results involving matrix differentiation. For completeness we give a summary derivation here.

In particular we have to obtain the matrix of partial derivatives of

$$S = tr\tilde{\tilde{\Sigma}}^{-1}(\tilde{Z}A - Z_{-1}AR)'(\tilde{Z}A - Z_{-1}AR)$$

with respect to the unknown elements of A and R. No restrictions are assumed to be placed on R and certain zero restrictions are known to hold with respect to the elements of A. We first observe that, using the restrictions on A we can write, in the notation of the text,

$$\text{(A.1)} \quad S = [y - (R' \otimes I)y_{-1} - (\tilde{Z}^* - (R' \otimes I)Z^*_{-1})\delta]'(\tilde{\tilde{\Sigma}}^{-1} \otimes I) \times [y - (R' \otimes I)y_{-1} - (\tilde{Z}^* - (R' \otimes I)Z^*_{-1})\delta].$$

From this we easily establish

(A.2) $$\frac{\partial S}{\partial \delta} = -2(\tilde{Z}^* - (R' \otimes I)Z^*_{-1})'(\tilde{\Sigma}^{-1} \otimes I) \times [y - (R' \otimes I)y_{-1} - (\tilde{Z}^* - (R' \otimes I)Z^*_{-1})\delta]$$

and thus

(A.3) $$\frac{\partial^2 S}{\partial \delta \partial \delta} = [2\tilde{Z}^* - (R' \otimes I)Z^*_{-1}]'(\tilde{\Sigma}^{-1} \otimes I)[\tilde{Z}^* - (R' \otimes I)Z^*_{-1}] .$$

To establish the other derivatives it is convenient to proceed as follows. We first observe that

(A.4) $$\frac{\partial S}{\partial R} = -2[A'Z_{-1}\tilde{Z}A - A'Z'_{-1}Z_{-1}AR]\tilde{\Sigma}^{-1}$$

and as a matter of notation we define

$$\frac{\partial S}{\partial r} = \mathrm{Vec}\left(\frac{\partial S}{\partial R}\right).$$

where for any matrix D, Vec (D) denotes the vector whose i-th subvector is the i-th column of D. Thus,

$$\frac{\partial^2 S}{\partial r \partial \delta} = \frac{\partial\, \mathrm{Vec}\, (\partial S/\partial R)}{\partial\, \mathrm{Vec}\, (A)} .$$

We note, for compatible matrices B_1, B_2, B_3, that

$$\mathrm{Vec}\, (B_1 B_2 B_3) = (I \otimes B_1)(I \otimes B_2)b_3$$

where

$$b_3 = \mathrm{Vec}\, (B_3) .$$

Moreover,

$$(I \otimes B_2)b_3 = (B_3' \otimes I)b_2 .$$

Using these results we easily see

(A.5) $$\mathrm{Vec}\, (A'Z'_{-1}\tilde{Z}A\tilde{\Sigma}^{-1}) = (\tilde{\Sigma}^{-1} \otimes I)(I \otimes A'Z'_{-1}\tilde{Z})a$$

(A.6) $$\mathrm{Vec}\, (A'Z'_{-1}Z_{-1}AR\tilde{\Sigma}^{-1}) = (\tilde{\Sigma}^{-1} \otimes I)(R' \otimes I)(I \otimes A'Z'_{-1}Z_{-1})a .$$

To differentiate (A.5) w.r.t. a, we note that one component can be obtained immediately as

$$(\tilde{\Sigma}^{-1} \otimes I)(I \otimes A'Z'_{-1}\tilde{Z}) .$$

The other component is obtained by noting that the i-th subvector is given by

$$A'Z'_{-1}\tilde{Z} \sum_{j=1}^{m} \sigma^{ji} a_{\cdot j} = A'Z'_{-1}\tilde{Z}A\tilde{\sigma}^{\cdot i}$$

which yields upon differentiation with respect to *a as it enters the component*

$A'Z'_{-1}\tilde{Z}$,

$$(I \otimes \tilde{\sigma}^{i\cdot})(I \otimes A'\tilde{Z}'Z_{-1}), \qquad i = 1, 2, \cdots m$$

where $\tilde{\sigma}^{i\cdot}$ is the i-th row of $\tilde{\Sigma}^{-1}$. Differentiating (A.6) similarly we obtain

$$(\tilde{\Sigma}^{-1} \otimes I)(R' \otimes I)(I \otimes A'Z'_{-1}Z_{-1})$$

and

$$(I \otimes \tilde{\sigma}^{i\cdot})(I \otimes R'A'Z'_{-1}Z_{-1}), \qquad i = 1, 2, \cdots m.$$

Writing

$$\tilde{\Sigma}_i^* = (I \otimes \tilde{\sigma}^{i\cdot}), \quad \tilde{\Sigma}^* = (\tilde{\Sigma}_1^{*\prime}, \tilde{\Sigma}_2^{*\prime}, \cdots \tilde{\Sigma}_m^{*\prime})'$$

we can express the derivative compactly as

$$\frac{\partial \operatorname{Vec}(\partial S/\partial R)}{\partial a} = -2(\tilde{\Sigma}^{-1} \otimes I)(I \otimes A'Z'_{-1})[(I \otimes \tilde{Z}) - (R' \otimes Z_{-1})]$$
$$- 2\tilde{\Sigma}^*(I \otimes (\tilde{Z}A - Z_{-1}AR)'Z_{-1}).$$

Noting that upon division by T the second member above has a null probability limit and imposing the condition that some elements of A are null, we can write equivalently

$$\text{(A.7)} \qquad \frac{\partial^2 S}{\partial r \partial \delta} = -2(\tilde{\Sigma}^{-1} \otimes I)(I \otimes U'_{-1})(\tilde{Z}^* - (R' \otimes I)Z^*_{-1}) + o_p^{(T)}.$$

Finally, to find $(\partial^2 S)/(\partial r \partial r)$ we note that

$$\text{(A.8)} \qquad \operatorname{Vec}(A'Z'_{-1}Z_{-1}AR\tilde{\Sigma}^{-1}) = (\tilde{\Sigma}^{-1} \otimes I)(I \otimes A'Z'_{-1}Z_{-1})r$$

and we conclude immediately

$$\frac{\partial^2 S}{\partial r \partial r} = 2(\tilde{\Sigma}^{-1} \otimes I)(I \otimes A'Z'_{-1}Z_{-1}A).$$

Thus, the Hessian of (A.1), setting to zero all elements which converge to zero in probability when divided by T, can be written

$$\text{(A.9)} \qquad \begin{bmatrix} \dfrac{\partial^2 S}{\partial \delta \partial \delta} & \dfrac{\partial^2 S}{\partial \delta \partial r} \\ \dfrac{\partial^2 S}{\partial r \partial \delta} & \dfrac{\partial^2 S}{\partial r \partial r} \end{bmatrix} = 2 \begin{bmatrix} A_{11} & A_{12} \\ A_{21} & A_{22} \end{bmatrix}$$

where

$$A_{11} = [\tilde{Z}^* - (R' \otimes I)Z^*_{-1}]'(\tilde{\Sigma}^{-1} \otimes I)[\tilde{Z}^* - (R' \otimes I)Z^*_{-1}]$$
$$A_{12} = [\tilde{Z}^* - (R' \otimes I)Z^*_{-1}]'(\tilde{\Sigma}^{-1} \otimes I)(I \otimes Z_{-1}A)$$
$$A_{21} = (I \otimes A'Z'_{-1})(\tilde{\Sigma}^{-1} \otimes I)[\tilde{Z}^* - (R' \otimes I)Z^*_{-1}]$$
$$A_{22} = (I \otimes A'Z'_{-1})(\tilde{\Sigma}^{-1} \otimes I)(I \otimes Z_{-1}A).$$

A more illuminating representation of the right member of the Hessian is

$$[\tilde{Z}^* - (R'\otimes I)Z^*_{-1}, I\otimes Z_{-1}A]'(\tilde{\Sigma}^{-1}\otimes I)[\tilde{Z}^* - (R'\otimes I)Z^*_{-1}, I\otimes Z_{-1}A].$$

REFERENCES

[1] DHRYMES, P. J., "Full Information Estimation of Dynamic Simultaneous Equations Models with Autoregressive Errors" in V. K. Srivastava, ed., *Proceedings of the All-India Seminar on Demography and Statistics*, forthcoming.

[2] ———, "A Note on an Efficient Two-Step Estimator," *Journal of Econometrics*, II (September, 1974), 301–304.

[3] ——— AND H. ERLAT, "Asymptotic Properties of Full Information Estimation in Dynamic Autoregressive Simultaneous Equations Models," *Journal of Econometrics*, II (September, 1974), 247–260.

[4] FAIR, R. C., Efficient Estimation of Simultaneous Equations with Autoregressive Errors by Instrumental variables," *Review of Economics and Statistics*, LV (November, 1972), 444–449.

[5] HATANAKA, M., "An Efficient Two-Step Estimator for the Dynamic Adjustment Model with Autoregressive Errors," *Journal of Econometrics*, II (September, 1974), 199–220.

[6] ———, *Several Efficient Two Step Estimators for the Dynamic Simultaneous Equations Model with Autoregressive Disturbances*, IV (May, 1976), 189–204.

[14]

International Journal of Forecasting 4 (1988) 81–101
North-Holland

A COMPARISON OF THE FORECASTING PERFORMANCE OF WEFA AND ARIMA TIME SERIES METHODS *

Phoebus J. DHRYMES
Columbia University, New York, NY 10027, USA

Stavros C. PERISTIANI
City University of New York, New York, NY 10021, USA

Abstract: This paper examines the forecasting performance of the Wharton model (MARK III) over the period 1973 through 1975 and compares it with that of ARIMA models' performance over the same period. Despite strong intimation in the literature to the contrary, we find that this econometric model, at least, exhibits greater accuracy in every respect relative to ARIMA methods, in terms of its forecasts cum constant adjustments. When constant adjustments are disallowed then its forecasts are still more accurate than ARIMA forecasts over a 4- and 8-quarter forecasting horizon, but less accurate over a 1-quarter horizon. The comparison was carried out over twenty three macrovariables, under a slight handicap for the Wharton Model, in that the latter's parameters were estimated over a sample ending in 1969.3 while the ARIMA models were reidentified and reestimated as of the quarter immediately preceding the forecast.

Keywords: Forecasting accuracy, Wharton model, Forecasting horizon, Exogenous variables, Parametric stability, Comparative accuracy, causal, time series.

1. Introduction

The purpose of this paper is to examine the forecasting performance of WEFA, a large scale econometric model, vis-a-vis that of Box–Jenkins (BJ) time series procedures. A number of papers in the literature deal with the general problem of forecast evaluations, for example, Naylor et al. (1972), Nelson (1972), Narasimham et al. (1974), Levenbach et al. (1974), and Hirsch et al. (1974). More recently issues of forecasting with econometric models have been dealt with in Longbottom and Holly (1985) and extensive reviews of the subject have been published in Armstrong (1978) and Fildes (1985). A definitive exposition of the Mark III version of the Wharton model is found in McCarthy (1972). Nelson, Narasimham and Naylor find that time series ARIMA forecasts do better than forecasts made by using the FMP, BEA and WEFA models, respectively. In particular, Nelson examines some dozen or so macrovariables and claims [that] 'the results of the comparison of FMP and ARIMA model prediction accuracy reported in the study indicate that the former were more accurate for most of the variables during the sample period over which both models were fitted'.

* The research on which this paper was based was, in part, supported by NSF grant SOC 74-18761. We would like to thank the Editor and an anonymous referee for helpful suggestions on a previous draft.

Naylor et al. examine only four macrovariables, investment, the rate of inflation, GNP and the unemployment rate; their conclusions are based solely on a comparison of one period ahead forecasts. Narasimham et al., although they consider only a limited number of macrovariables, base their comparisons on forecasts of up to four quarters ahead. More recently, Longbottom and Holly returning to the same topic make the point that differences in forecasting performance may indicate misspecification errors; it should be noted, however, that this is a rather overreaching conclusion unless such differences are prolonged and systematic, since occasional (random) deviations in the accuracy of forecasts are to be expected even when one model is known to be 'correct' and the other 'misspecified'. Finally, there exist in the literature a large number of papers that touch on one or another aspect of our subject; the interested reader is referred to the recent reviews by Makridakis et al. (1985), Makridakis and Wheelwright (1978) and Fildes (1985).

A continuing record of the forecasting performance of commercial models is available in McNees (1981, 1985a, 1986). The latter work, however, compares mainly the 'published' forecasts from these models and as such it tends to commingle the performance of models qua models with such performance when combined with the astuteness of the model operator. Indeed, this difference is an important motivating factor for our work. A great deal of the published work on the forecasting performance of econometric models, beginning, say, with Cooper (1972) generates model forecasts not quite under the same conditions as the model operators do and, frequently, not using quite the same model. This is not due to any inclination on the part of the investigator to be unfair to the model, but rather to the fact that the investigator does not have access to the modules used by the model operators and is forced to reestimate some version of the model, not necessarily the version used at the time the forecasts were generated. This feature was amply discussed in the case of Cooper's work. The unique aspect of this paper is that it uses an interesting set of data, consisting of the internal records of the Wharton model and the forecasts that it generates over the period 1972.4 through 1973.4, using the Mark III version. Thereafter the Mark III version was retired and the records of the successor version were not generally accessible. Thus, the data set on which we operate is uniquely free of the criticisms noted above. Another very attractive aspect of our data set is that the period over which we have forecasts from Mark III covers one of the more turbulent periods of the postwar era, spanning the imposition and aftermath of the oil embargo and the subsequent abrubt rise in the price of oil. Thus, it offers the opportunity for a particularly stringent test of the 'robustness' of various forecasting methods in the face of drastic change. Our data set contains a record of the assumptions made by the model operators in generating their forecasts, as well as a record of the controversial 'constant adjustments', common to large scale commercially available macromodels. Thus, it is possible for us to reproduce exactly the conditions under which the forecaster operated at the time of the forecast and consequently makes it possible to carry our various types of 'experiments' without doing violence to the structure of the model.

In sections 2 and 3 we briefly review the Wharton model and BJ ARIMA time series models. In section 4 we present our empirical findings. Finally, most tables are relegated to the appendix.

2. Issues in forecasting comparisons

The typical econometric macromodel is generally a stochastic vector difference equation with forcing function. The model operator specifies and estimates the model and thereafter uses various assumptions regarding the path of exogenous variables over the forecasting horizon in order to generate the model's forecasts. In addition to this fairly straighforward feature, a controversial practice has arisen in the case of forecasting with the large commercially available models. This involves the so called 'constant adjustments' or 'add factors' which simply add a constant to each equation prior to forecasting. The practice has been defended by model operators as reflecting information they possess, regarding the variables 'explained' by the equation in question or data revisions of a particular type, see for example, Klein (1971). The forecasting operation, by ARIMA methods, on the other hand is comparatively simple, and indeed, the forecaster need not be a trained economist in order to operate such schemes. Still the choice of the appropriate order of the autoregressive or moving average part of the specification, or the degree of differencing involve a fair amount of discretion; however, more recently, certain rules which can be incorporated in the relevant software might make individual discretion the exception rather than the rule, see for example Harmon (1985).

To just list the process of forecasting in the two contexts is to raise a question as to what is an appropriate comparison between the two methods. The comparison that receives most frequent attention is one involving the published forecasts generated by the various model operators. However, such comparisons do not help us understand the strengths and weaknesses of each approach. They merely answer the following, commercially very relevant, question: if I am to buy forecasting services from a vendor that uses the Wharton model or one that uses ARIMA methods would I get more accurate forecasts from the first or second vendor? Precisely because operators of large macromodels have been sensitive to this type of consideration they have set great store by the provision of 'accurate' forecasts. There is, however, no simply available method for producing 'accurate' forecasts in the long run, save through careful reexamination of the specification, the data base and perhaps the estimation of macromodels. In the short run, however, one could conceivably gain by other methods such as 'add factoring' and 'constant adjustments', which despite the protestations of their proponents are best viewed as procedures for incorporating the model operators' 'insights' into the forecast. The use of ARIMA methods has also been suggested by critiques such as those of Sims (1980) which intimate that we do not know enough to justify the a priori restrictions placed on 'structural models'. Despite our alleged ignorance the evolution from Sims' critique seems to have led us to vector autoregressive systems which are really rather special cases of the unrestricted reduced from of a rather constrained General Linear Structural Econometric Model (GLSEM).

Thus, it is quite appropriate to ask whether a large macro model like that of WEFA, over a turbulent period of the US, forecasts better or worse than ARIMA methods; to examine this comparison not merely in terms of the published WEFA forecasts, but also in terms of the forecasts the model would have generated had the (future) exogenous variables been known with certainty and without benefit of 'add factoring' or 'constant adjustments'. Finally, we should note that despite the rather tenuous evidence presented by the major comparison studies of Naylor et al. (1972) and Nelson (1972) the impression is quite widespread that econometric models do rather poorly in comparison with ARIMA methods; see, for example, Pindyck and Rubinfeld (1976, pp. 534ff) or Makridakis and Wheelwright (1978, pp. 582ff).

3. Box–Jenkins, ARIMA and econometric model based forecasts

Let $y_{t\cdot}$ be a vector of m elements containing a set of macro-variables whose behavior we are interested in forecasting (a dot on the second subscript means that $y_{t\cdot}$ is row vector, hence, $y_{\cdot i}$ $(i=1,\dots,m)$ is column vector of T elements); at our disposal we have a set of observations

$$(y_{t\cdot}, x_{t\cdot}), \quad t=1,2,\dots,T. \tag{1}$$

where $x_{t\cdot}$ is a set of predetermined variables. Using as the expositional paradigm the GLSEM, forecasts based on econometric models involve the specification of a model

$$y_{t\cdot}B^* = w_{t\cdot}C_0 + y_{t-1\cdot}C_1 + \ldots + y_{t-k\cdot}C_k + u_{t\cdot}, \tag{2}$$

where $w_{t\cdot}$ is an s-element row vector containing the exogenous variables and the matrices B^*, C_i, $i = 0, 1, \ldots, k$ contain the unknown structural parameters of the model. Having estimated the model by an appropriate technique we then forecast outside the sample period by means of the (restricted) reduced form

$$\hat{y}_{t\cdot} = w_{t\cdot}\hat{\Pi}_0 + y_{t-1\cdot}\hat{\Pi}_1 + \ldots + y_{t-k\cdot}\hat{\Pi}_k,$$

where $\hat{\Pi}_i$, $i = 0, 1, \ldots, k$ are estimates of the corresponding unknown parameter matrices, i.e.,

$$\hat{\Pi}_i = \hat{C}_i\hat{B}^{*-1}, \qquad i = 0, 1, \ldots, k.$$

Thus, forecasting with an econometric model requires estimation of the structural parameter matrices B^*, C_i, $i = 0, 1, 2\ldots, k$ as well as knowledge or estimation of future values of the exogenous variables. The required lagged dependent variables for the multiple period forecasting are generated pari passu.

ARIMA forecasting is based on the work of Box and Jenkins (1970) and exposited more recently in Chatfield (1975); essentially it involves fitting an autoregressive and error driven model to suitably differenced time series. Thus, the only information required in order to forecast a macrovariable, say y_{ti}, is the sequence of observations

$$\{y_{ti}: t = 1, 2, \ldots T\}.$$

This essential simplicity of the procedure has held great appeal for many applied economists. Indeed, one need not have any economic training whatsoever in order to engage in forecasting economic phenomena by ARIMA methods, see, for example, Anderson and King (1985).

Recently an attempt has been made by Zellner and Palm (1974) to combine the two procedures; further work is also found in Wallis (1977). It should be noted, however, that the work by Zellner and Palm merely provides a convenient way of carrying out a likelihood ratio test for (some of) the a priori restrictions employed by structural (econometric) models; moreover, other works suggesting a transfer function formulation of the basic BJ scheme, do not constitute a particularly novel approach to forecasting, since they are, in effect, special cases of the autoregressive final form of the standard general linear structural econometric model, see, for example, Dhrymes (1974, Ch. 12). Thus, the transfer function formulation destroys the essential simplicity of ARIMA procedures, while at the same time does essentially what econometric models attempt to do, but without access to the structural form. That is, it relies on the unrestricted reduced form and the autoregressive final form and uses various conventions and pre-test rules for deciding the order of the lags. Thus, while useful as a vehicle for testing some of the a priori restrictions in the fashion suggested by Zellner and Palm it does not offer a substantively different forecasting alternative.

4. Empirical results

As indicated earlier the WEFA model (Mark III) was used to generate forecasts beginning with 1972.4; forecasts for WEFA are typically generated with an 8-quarter horizon and we have followed this practice in our experiments. Thus, beginning with 1972.4 we have 8-quarter ahead forecasts. The last (initial) period for which we have a forecasting horizon of 8-ahead quarters is 1973.4. Hence, the last quarter actually forecast by WEFA model is 1975.3 and for the quarters 1973.1 through 1975.2 we have multiple forecasts; this period is one of the most turbulent in the recent economic history of the US and, consequently, provides a very demanding environment in which the performance of the structural models is to be appraised.

ARIMA forecasts are generated from a suitably identified and estimated model using data up to the first quarter in the forecasting horizon of the experiment. We remind the reader that the WEFA model is estimated with data up to 1969.3 and is not reestimated prior to each forecasting episode.

The procedure is fairly straight forward: from each model an 8-quarter ahead forecasting sequence is obtained beginning, consecutively, with 1972.4, 1973.1 and so until 1973.4.

There are many criteria in terms of which the accuracy of the forecasts are to be compared; mainly for simplicity of interpretation, we have chosen the percent root mean squared error criterion.

The results are given in exhaustive detail in the tables of the appendix; here we shall confine ourselves to a discussion of the salient features of these findings. A thorough and objective comparison ought to involve more than just a comparison between the published forecasts of WEFA and their ARIMA counterparts, but we begin with it.

Comparison: Published WEFA vs. ARIMA

For 8-quarter ahead ARIMA does uniformly better only for one variable, real output per manhour. It is unambigously superior, i.e., in four out of the five forecasting episodes it does better, only for one variable, real non-durable consumption. On the other hand, WEFA forecasts are clearly better, i.e., in three out of five forecasting episodes, WEFA forecasts dominate for five variables and for the remaining sixteen variables WEFA's forecasts are overwhelmingly more accurate.

For 4-quarter ahead ARIMA does not do uniformly better for any variable; it is unambigously superior (i.e., it does better in four out of five forecasting episodes) in one variable, real nondurable consumption and is clearly superior (i.e., it does better in three out of five forecasting episodes) for three variables, nominal personal consumption expenditures, real output per manhour and in wage rate (Manufacturing and Mining). In the other nineteen variables WEFA's forecasts are either clearly superior (seven variables), unambiguously superior (three variables) or uniformly superior (nine variables).

For 1-quarter ahead ARIMA is uniformly superior for only one variable, real nondurable consumption; it is unambiguously superior for two variables private compensation per hour and wage rate (for Manufacturing and Mining); it is clearly superior for four variables, nominal residential investment, real output per manhour, nominal nondurable consumption, deflator (Manufacturing). For the remaining sixteen variables WEFA's forecasts were either clearly superior (four variables), unambiguously superior (two variables) or uniformly superior (ten variables).

The preceding discussion makes it abundantly clear that, in terms of published records, the widespread belief that BJ ARIMA methods do better than forecasts from econometric models is certainly called into question given our empirical findings. Moreover, one thing is quite clear from this comparison: the structural WEFA model and its operators must incorporate in their forecasting procedures some (and evidently quite substantial) knowledge of the economy which is clearly lacking, by design or otherwise, in the forecasting procedures that are based on ARIMA methods. The obvious response to this claim, is to ask what 'part' of this knowledge is to be attributed to the 'scientific' aspect of the discipline (economics) and what part is to be attributed to the personal insights of the operators; this latter part is profoundly subjective and hence not easily reproducible by other researchers. Although one cannot possibly expect to obtain an unambiguous separation of the two components one may attempt to gauge their magnitudes by examining the question of 'constant adjustments' or 'add factors'. To the extent that the latter is objectively defined in terms of a computable rule that is based on sample observations such practices, although clumsy, may be reasonably considered as part of the model specification. To the extent, however, that such rules are not prespecified prior to forecasting they can only be considered highly subjective and be interpreted as the incorporation of the operators' personal insights. This is evidently the case with WEFA's 'constant adjustments' for the period under consideration.

Owing to the fact that we have access to the internal records and data sets employed by WEFA at the time of the forecasts it is possible for us to reconstruct the forecasts that would have resulted at the relevant time had 'constant adjustments' not been employed. We may thus compare these forecasts with those generated by ARIMA methods. The results are summarized in table 2 in the appendix. The salient features of this comparison are given below.

Comparison: WEFA without constant adjustment vs. ARIMA

For 8-quarters ahead ARIMA is uniformly superior for five variables, unemployment, private compensation per hour, real nondurable consumption, employment and wage rate (both for Manufacturing and Mining) and clearly superior for three variables, real GNP, real gross private domestic investment and real investment in Manufacturing and Mining. For the remaining sixteen variables WEFA's forecasts are uniformly superior for nine variables and clearly superior for the remaining six variables. In this connection it should be noted that ARIMA is given far more credit than is appropriate. Notice, for example, that BJ dominates real GNP while WEFA dominates nominal GNP as well as the (GNP) implicit price deflator. On the other hand the BJ model does not obey the obvious identity that real GNP times price deflator equals nominal, while WEFA's model does. When we similarly obtain the third variable through the appropriate identity in the BJ context as well, this superiority disappears. This is a feature that has been overlooked in previous comparisons, and relates generally to the fact that provision for the obvious identities is not made when one compares ARIMA and structural model induced forecasts.

For 4-quarters ahead ARIMA forecasts are uniformly superior for six variables, unemployment, nominal residential investment, real nondurable consumption, manufacturing (implicit price) deflator, government expenditures deflator and employment in Manufacturing and Mining; unambiguously superior for four variables and clearly superior for four variables. For the remaining nine variables WEFA is uniformly superior for six variables, unambiguously superior for two variables and clearly superior for one variable.

For 1-quarter ahead ARIMA forecasts are uniformly superior for six variables, unambiguously superior for four variables and clearly superior for three variables. For the remaining ten variables WEFA's forecasts are uniformly superior for one variable, unambiguously superior for four variables and clearly superior for five variables.

Thus, even in the absence of correct information on the values of exogenous variables over the forecasts horizon, the WEFA based forecasts outperform ARIMA forecasts, in the sense that they are more accurate more frequently for more macrovariables. In particular, for 8-quarters ahead WEFA does better for sixteen macrovariables; for 4-quarters ahead it does better for nine macrovariables while for 1-quarter ahead it does better for ten macrovariables. On the other hand when the correct exogenous variables are employed, then, even in the absence of constant adjustments,

WEFA's forecasts are more accurate than ARIMA, for 4- and 8-quarter ahead and worse only for 1-quarter ahead. To be precise (see table A.4 in the appendix) WEFA forecasts are better in 13 of the 23 macrovariables for 4- and 8-quarters ahead and only 8 for 1-quarter ahead. It is also interesting to observe in this connection that while the use of the 'correct' explanatory variables does not improve WEFA's performance for one quarter ahead, it does produce improvements for 4- and 8-quarters ahead forecasts.

The major conclusion one may derive from the experimentation reported in this work is that ARIMA methods have been more accurate for 1-quarter ahead forecasts only when 'constant adjustments' have been omitted from WEFA's model. On the other hand ARIMA methods have been accorded the 'benefit' of reidentification and reestimation prior to each forecasting episode, while WEFA's models was estimated with data as of 1969.3 and thereafter remained intact. Despite that, it clearly dominates ARIMA induced forecasts for this group of 23 macrovariables over 4- and 8-quarter horizons, whether 'constant adjustments' are used or not used and whether we employ the 'correct' or assumed values for the exogenous variables required over the forecasting horizon. A brief exercise, not reported herein, also shows that whether we use ARIMA methods or simply a fourth order autoregressive scheme, forecast accuracy over 1-, 4- and 8-quarter horizons remains basically the same, although ARIMA does slightly better.

Finally, the fact that we have identified and estimated ARIMA models for a number of macrovariables offers us an opportunity to compare our findings with those Nelson's (1972), whose work is frequently cited as having demonstrated the 'superiority' (complete or near) of ARIMA to structural model based forecasts. The identification and parameter estimates for our work appear in table A.5 while those from Nelson's work have been obtained directly from Nelson (1972) (identifications appear in the appendix of the original paper). This discussion is best understood as an obiter dictum rather than as a serious examination of the stability of parameters in an ARIMA context. We remind the reader that Nelson's results are based on the sample 1947.1–1966.4 while ours are based on the period 1955.1–1973.3 thus producing an overlap of about 12 years, in addition, Nelson's results are based on data that, almost certainly, have since been revised. There are five common

Table 1
Comparison of structures and parameters.

	Model identification						
	Ours			Nelson's [a]			
Nominal GNP	ARIMA(1, 1, 0)	0.618 (6.26)		ARIMA(1, 1, 0)	0.615		
Nominal non-res. invest. (Exp. on Prod. structures in Nelson)	ARIMA(2, 1, 0)	0.279 (2.3)	0.063 (0.9)	ARIMA(0, 1, 1)	0.347		
Nominal residential inv. (Housing exp. in Nelson)	ARIMA(1, 1, 0)	0.635 (5.2)		ARIMA(3, 1, 0)	0.639	0.076	−0.286
Unemployment	ARIMA(2, 0, 0)	1.58 (17.4)	−0.68 (−7.4)	ARIMA(2, 0, 1)	1.46	0.612	0.284
Deflator cons. exp. (Cons. goods price index in Nelson)	ARIMA(1, 1, 0)	0.750 (9.9)		ARIMA(1, 1, 0)	0.414		

[a] Numbers in parentheses represent t-ratios; no t-ratios are given in Nelson's work.

variables and a comparison is made in table 1. Even a casual inspection of the comparison above shows that while GNP is a very 'stable' process, the other variables evidently represent rather 'unstable' processes; which shows that parameter instability is not a problem confined exclusively to the estimation of parameters of structural models.

5. Conclusion

This paper has examined the forecasting performance of WEFA's model (MARK III) over the period 1973–1975 and has compared it to that of models obtained by 'purely statistical', in particular Box–Jenkins ARIMA, methods. The salient findings are

(i) Forecasts based on econometric models decisively outperform those based on ARIMA models, when the forecasting horizon is either 4- or 8-quarters ahead; this is true whether constant adjustments are or are not used and whether we employ the correct or the assumed exogenous variables over the forecasting horizon.

(ii) For a 1-quarter ahead horizon WEFA's forecasts dominate by an overwhelming margin, if constant adjustments are employed. If constant adjustments are not employed then ARIMA forecasts dominate by a moderate margin (over a 1-quarter horizon) and this is true whether the 'true' or the assumed exogenous variables are employed over the forecasting horizon.

(iii) As an aside, we compared the results of our ARIMA indentification and estimation with those of Nelson's, whenever there was an overlap of variables; there were five such variables. Of these two produced the same structure and roughly similar parameters; for the other three we identified an entirely different structure.

The major inference to be drawn from this study is that the dedeficiencies of structural models, real and substantial as they are, have been exaggerated in the literature and that ARIMA models do not necessarily make for a better alternative except perhaps in a very limited mechanical and extremely short term forecasting context.

Appendix

This appendix contains the comparison statistics for the various experiments reported in the body of the paper. An extensive summary of all numerical results may be found in Dhrymes and Peristiani (1983). Tables A.1–A.4 contain all the appropriate comparisons. The symbols have the following meanings:

S ARIMA's forecasts have approximately (relative difference is less than 0.01) the same PRMSE as WEFA's forecasts.

B ARIMA's forecasts have PRMSE that are smaller, but not less than one half ($\frac{1}{2}$) of WEFA's forecasts.

BB ARIMA's forecasts have PRMSE which are between one quarter ($\frac{1}{4}$) and one half ($\frac{1}{2}$) of WEFA's forecasts.

BBB ARIMA's forecasts have PRMSE which are at most one quarter ($\frac{1}{4}$) of those of WEFA's forecasts.

W ARIMA's forecasts have PRMSE which are larger than (at most twice) those of WEFA's forecasts.

Table A.1
Comparison of PRMSE of 1.4 and 8-quarter forecasts; WEFA model, with constant adjustments, 'old' exogenous variables; BJ ARIMA reestimated up to quarter immediately predeeding forecasts.

Variable	Periods	1972.4	1973.1	1973.2	1973.3	1973.4
Nominal GNP	1	W	W	S	W	W
	4	W	W	W	WW	W
	8	WW	WW	W	WW	W
Real GNP	1	W	W	W*	WWW	W*
	4	W	W	B	B*	W*
	8	WW	B	B	WW	W
Implicit price deflator	1	W	W	W	S	W
	4	W	W	W	W	W
	8	W	W	W	W	W
Unemployment	1	W	WW	W	W	W
	4	W	B	W	W	W
	8	B	B	W	W	W
Nominal personal consumption expenditures	1	W	W	WW	W	WWW
	4	W	W	B	B	B
	8	W	W	B	W	B
Nominal non-auto durables consumption	1	W	W	WWW	W	W
	4	W	W	W	W	WW
	8	WW	WW	WW	WWW	WW
Nominal gross domestic investment	1	WW	WWW	BBB	BB	W
	4	WW	WW	W	W	W
	8	WWW	W	W	W	WW
Nominal nonresidential investment	1	WW	WW	BB	WWW	B
	4	WWW	WWW	WW	WW	WW
	8	WWW	WWW	WWW	WW	W
Nominal resdential investment	1	W	BB	BB	WW	BB
	4	B	WW	WW	WW	WW
	8	W	W	WW	W	W
Imports	1	W	W	WWW	W	W
	4	W	WW	WW	WW	W
	8	W	WW	WW	WW	WWW
Real gross private domestic investment	1	WWW	BBB	BBB	WWW	W
	4	WWW	W	BB	B	W
	8	W	BB	BB	W	W
Real output/hour	1	B	B	S	B	W
	4	B	B	W	B	W
	8	B	B	B	B	B
Private compensation/ hour	1	BBB	WWW	B	BB	BB
	4	WWW	WWW	BB	W	W
	8	WW	WW	WW	WW	WW
Nominal nondurable consumption	1	W	WW	BB	BBB	BB
	4	WW	WW	B	W	B
	8	WW	W	B	W	B

Table A.1

Variable	Periods	1972.4	1973.1	1973.2	1973.3	1973.4
Nominal consumer	1	W	W	W	B	W
services	4	W	W	W	W	W
	8	W	B	W	B	W
Real nondurable	1	B	B	B	B	B
consumption	4	BB	BB	B	B	W
	8	WWW	BB	B	B	B
Real consumer	1	W	W	W	W	W
services	4	WW	WW	W	W	W
	8	WWW	WW	WW	WW	WW
Real investment in	1	B	W	B	W	WWW
Mining and Manufacturing	4	WW	WW	BBB	B	WW
	8	WWW	WWW	B	WW	WWW
Deflator, consumer	1	W	W	W	W	W
expenditures	4	W	W	W	W	W
	8	W	W	W	W	W
Deflator, Manufacturing	1	B	B	W	B	W
	4	B	B	W	W	WW
	8	B	B	W	W	W
Deflator, Government	1	WW	W	W	WW	WWW
expenditures	4	WWW	W	W	W	W
	8	B	B	W	W	WW
Employment, Mining	1	W	W	W	B	WWW
and Manufacturing	4	W	WW	B	B	WWW
	8	WW	B	W	W	W
Wage rate, Mining and	1	B	W	B	B	B
Manufacturing	4	WW	WWW	B	B	B
	8	WW	WW	WW	W	W

WW ARIMA's forecasts have PRMSE which are between two (2) and four (4) times those of WEFA's forecasts.

WWW ARIMA's forecasts have PRMSE which are more than four (4) times larger than those of WEFA's forecasts.

W*, B* Same as defined above, however, their counterparts have PRMSE which is very small, hence, both methods provide rather accurate forecasts.

Table A.5 gives the identification and estimation of ARIMA processes. Parameters are given as follows: first the autoregressive parameters beginning with the lowest lag and then the moving average parameters also beginning with the lowest lag. Table A.6 contains some general quantitative information by providing the median PRMSE of all five forecasting time periods.

Table A.2
Comparison of PRMSE of 1.4 and 8-quarter forecasts; WEFA model; without constant adjsustments, 'old' exogenous variables; BJ ARIMA reestimated up to quarter immediately preceeding forecasts.

Variable	Periods	1972.4	1973.1	1973.2	1973.3	1973.4
Nominal GNP	1	W	W	B	B	B
	4	WW	WW	B	W	W
	8	WWW	WW	WW	WW	WW
Real GNP	1	W	B	W*	W*	B*
	4	W	W	BB	BBB	BBB
	8	WW	W	B	B	B
Implicit price deflator	1	W	W	B	B	B
	4	WWW	WWW	B	B	B
	8	WWW	WWW	W	W	W
Unemployment	1	B	BBB	BBB	BB	B
	4	BB	BBB	BB	BB	BB
	8	BBB	BBB	BB	BBB	BB
Nominal personal consumption expenditures	1	W	W	B	B	WW
	4	W	WW	B	B	B
	8	WW	WW	S	W	W
Nominal non-auto durables consumption	1	W	W	B	WWW	WWW
	4	WW	WW	W	W	WW
	8	WW	WW	WW	WW	W
Nominal gross domestic investment	1	W	WW	BBB	WW	W
	4	W	S	W	W	B
	8	B	BB	W	WW	W
Nominal nonresidential investment	1	W	W	BB	WW	W
	4	WW	W	WW	WW	W
	8	W	B	W	W	B
Nominal residential investment	1	BB	BBB	BBB	B	BB
	4	BB	B	B	B	B
	8	W	W	W	B	B
Imports	1	W	W	W	W	WW
	4	W	W	W	WW	WWW
	8	W	WW	WW	WW	WWW
Real gross private domestic investment	1	W	B	B	WWW	BBB
	4	W	BB	B	B	BBB
	8	B	BB	BB	W	W
Real output/hour	1	W	WWW	W	B	B
	4	WW	WWW	W	W	W
	8	WW	WW	W	W	W
Private compensation/hour	1	BBB	B	B	BBB	BB
	4	B	W	BBB	BB	BB
	8	B	B	BBB	BB	BB
Nominal nondurable consumption	1	B	W	B	BBB	B
	4	B	WW	BB	B	B
	8	W	WW	WW	BB	BB

Table A.2

Variable	Periods	1972.4	1973.1	1973.2	1973.3	1973.4
Nominal consumer	1	B	B	B	BB	B
services	4	W	W	W	B	B
	8	WW	W	WW	W	W
Real nondurable	1	B	B	B	B	B
consumption	4	BB	B	B	BB	B
	8	BBB	BB	BB	BB	BB
Real consumer	1	W	B	W	W	W
services	4	WWW	W	WW	W	WW
	8	WWW	WW	WW	WW	W
Real investment in	1	B	BB	WWW	WW	W
Mining and Manufacturing	4	B	W	BBB	B	W
	8	W	W	BB	BB	B
Deflator, consumer	1	W	W	W	B	B
expenditures	4	WWW	W	W	W	W
	8	WWW	WW	WW	W	W
Deflator, Manufacturing	1	BB	B	B	BBB	BB
	4	BBB	BB	BB	B	W
	8	WW	B	W	B	W
Deflator, Government	1	B	WW	BBB	BB	B
expenditures	4	B	B	B	B	B
	8	W	B	W	W	S
Employment, Mining	1	B	WWW	B	BB	B
and Manufacturing	4	B	BB	BBB	BBB	BBB
	8	B	BB	BBB	BBB	BBB
Wage rate, Mining and	1	BBB	W*	B	B	B
Manufacturing	4	BB	W	BB	BB	BB
	8	BB	B	BBB	BBB	BBB

Table A.3
Comparison of PRMSE of 1, 4 and 8-quarter forecasts; WEFA model, with constant adjustments, 'correct' exogenous variables; BJ ARIMA, reestimated up to quarter immediately preceeding forecasts.

Variable	Periods	1972.4	1973.1	1973.2	1973.3	1973.4
Nominal GNP	1	WW	WWW	WWW	WWW	WWW
	4	WWW	WW	W	W	B
	8	WW	W	B	B	BBB
Real GNP	1	WWW	W	W*	W*	B*
	4	WWW	WW	W	B	BBB
	8	WWW	W	B	BB	BBB
Implicit price deflator	1	W	W	W	WWW	WWW
	4	WW	W	W	WW	WW
	8	W	W	W	WW	WWW
Unemployment	1	BBB	BBB	BBB	BBB	B
	4	BB	BBB	B	B	W
	8	BB	BB	W	W	W
Nominal personal consumption expenditures	1	W	W	W	WW	WWW
	4	W	WW	B	W	W
	8	WW	WW	B	B	B
Nominal non-auto durables consumption	1	W	W	W	B	B
	4	WW	WW	W	W	W
	8	WW	WWW	WW	WW	W
Nominal gross domestic investment	1	B	BBB	BBB	BB	BBB
	4	WW	W	WW	B	BB
	8	W	B	B	B	B
Nominal nonresidential investment	1	WW	WW	B	B	WW
	4	WW	WW	B	W	WW
	8	WWW	WWW	W	W	S
Nominal residential investment	1	W	B	WW	WW	BB
	4	B	W	WWW	WW	WW
	8	S	W	W	WW	W
Imports	1	W	WW	W	W	B
	4	W	WW	W	W	W
	8	W	WW	W	W	B
Real gross private domestic investment	1	B	BBB	BBB	B	BBB
	4	W	BB	BB	BB	BBB
	8	B	BB	BB	B	B
Real private output/hour	1	B	B	B	B	B
	4	B	B	B	B	W
	8	B	BB	B	B	B
Private compensation/hour	1	B	W	B	B	B
	4	W	WWW	B	W	W
	8	WWW	WW	B	W	W
Nominal nondurable consumption	1	W	W	B	BBB	BBB
	4	W	W	B	B	W
	8	WWW	WW	B	W	B

Table A.3

Variable	Periods	1972.4	1973.1	1973.2	1973.3	1973.4
Nominal consumer	1	W	B	W	B	W
services	4	W	B	W	B	W
	8	W	W	W	B	W
Real nondurable	1	B	B	B	B	B
consumption	4	BBB	BB	B	B	W
	8	BBB	BB	B	B	B
Real consumer	1	W	W	W	W	W
services	4	WW	WW	W	WW	W
	8	WW	WW	WW	WW	WW
Real investment in	1	BB	W	W	WW	WWW
Mining and Manufacturing	4	W	W	BBB	BB	B
	8	W	B	BBB	BBB	BB
Deflator, consumer	1	W	W	W	W	W
expenditures	4	W	W	W	W	WW
	8	W	W	WW	W	WW
Deflator, Manufacturing	1	B	B	B	B	W
	4	BB	BB	B	B	WW
	8	B	B	WW	WW	WWW
Deflator, Government	1	B	BB	W	W	W
expenditures	4	B	B	WW	WW	W
	8	B	B	WWW	W	W
Employment, Mining	1	W	WWW	W	BB	WW
and Manufacturing	4	WWW	W	B	B	W
	8	WW	W	BB	BB	B
Wage rate, Mining and	1	B	B	BB	B	B
Manufacturing	4	WW	WWW	B	B	B
	8	WW	WW	WW	W	W

Table A.4
Comparison of PRMSE of 1, 4 and 8-quarter forecasts; WEFA model, without constant adjustments, 'correct' exogenous variables; BJ ARIMA reestimated up to quarter immediately preceeding forecasts.

Variable	Periods	1972.4	1973.1	1973.2	1973.3	1973.4
Nominal GNP	1	WW	WWW	W	W	W
	4	WWW	WWW	W	W	B
	8	WWW	WWW	W	W	W
Real GNP	1	WW	WW	WWW	W*	B
	4	WWW	W	B*	W*	B
	8	WWW	S	S	B	B
Implicit price deflator	1	W	W	B	B	B
	4	WWW	WW	W	W	B
	8	WWW	WWW	W	W	W
Unemployment	1	B	BB	BBB	BBB	B
	4	BBB	BBB	BB	BB	BB
	8	BBB	BBB	BB	BB	BB
Nominal personal consumption expenditures	1	W	W	B	B	WW
	4	WW	WW	B	B	B
	8	WWW	WW	W	W	W
Nominal non-auto durables consumption	1	W	W	W	W	W
	4	WW	WWW	W	W	W
	8	WW	WW	WW	WW	WW
Nominal gross domestic investment	1	W	BB	BBB	BB	BBB
	4	W	BB	BB	B	BBB
	8	B	B	W	W	B
Nominal nonresidental investment	1	W	W	B	B	B
	4	W	W	B	W	W
	8	W	W	WW	W	W
Nominal residential investment	1	BB	BBB	BBB	B	BB
	4	BB	W	W	WW	B
	8	W	WW	W	W	B
Imports	1	W	W	B	W	W
	4	W	WW	W	W	W
	8	W	WW	W	W	W
Real gross private domestic investment	1	B	BBB	BB	B	BBB
	4	B	BB	BB	BB	BBB
	8	BB	BBB	BB	B	B
Real private output/ hour	1	B	B	B	B	B
	4	B	W	W	B	W
	8	W	B	W	S	S
Private compensation/ hour	1	BBB	WWW	B	BBB	BBB
	4	W	W	B	BB	W
	8	B	BB	B	BB	W
Nominal nondurable consumption	1	B	S	B	BBB	BBB
	4	B	B	BBB	B	W
	8	W	B	BBB	B	B

Table A.4

Variable	Periods	1972.4	1973.1	1973.2	1973.3	1973.4
Nominal consumer services	1	B	S	B	BB	W
	4	W	W	W	B	W
	8	W	W	W	B	W
Real nondurable consumption	1	BB	BB	B	B	B
	4	B	BB	BB	BB	B
	8	BBB	BBB	BB	BB	B
Real consumer services	1	W	W	W	W	W
	4	W	WW	WW	WW	W
	8	WW	WW	W	WW	W
Real investment in Mining and manufacturing	1	BBB	B	WWW	WW	WWW
	4	B	B	BBB	BB	B
	8	B	B	BBB	BB	BB
Deflator, consumer expenditures	1	W	W	W	W	W
	4	W	W	W	W	W
	8	WW	WW	WW	W	W
Deflator, Manufacturing	1	B	B	BB	BBB	W
	4	BB	BBB	BB	BB	WW
	8	BBB	B	BB	B	WWW
Deflator, Government expenditures	1	B	BBB	BBB	BBB	W
	4	B	BB	BB	B	W
	8	B	BB	B	W	W
Employment, Mining and Manufacturing	1	W	B	B	B	WW
	4	B	BB	BB	BB	W
	8	B	BBB	BBB	BBB	B
Wage rate, Mining and Manufacturing	1	B	W	B	B	B
	4	B	B	B	B	B
	8	B	B	BBB	BBB	W

Table A.5
BJ identification of the economic time series (1955.1–1973.3). [a]

Variable	Model	Coefficient estimates (t-ratio)			
Nominal GNP	ARIMA(1, 1, 0)	0.618			
		(6.26)			
Real GNP	ARIMA(1, 1, 0)	0.430			
		(3.88)			
Implicit price	ARIMA(4, 1, 0)	0.425	0.211	−0.019	0.029
deflator		(3.54)	(1.58)	(−0.12)	(2.07)
Unemployment	ARIMA(2, 0, 0)	1.578	−0.6852		
		(17.3)	(−7.3)		
Nominal personal	ARIMA(2, 1, 0)	0.325	0.458		
consumption expenditures		(2.95)	(3.98)		
Nominal non-auto	ARIMA(1, 1, 0)	0.248			
durables consumption		(2.10)			
Nominal gross domestic	ARIMA(1, 1, 1)	−0.636	−1.64		
investment		(−0.77)	(−2.4)		
Nominal nonresidential	ARIMA(2, 1, 0)	0.279	0.063		
investment		(2.29)	(0.91)		
Nominal residential	ARIMA(1, 1, 0)	0.635			
investment		(5.19)			
Imports	ARIMA(1, 1, 0)	0.286			
		(2.69)			
Real gross private	ARIMA(1, 0, 0)	0.965			
domestic investment		(38.1)			
Real private output/	ARIMA(2, 1, 0)	0.060	0.072		
hour [b]		(0.51)	(0.60)		
Private compensation/	ARIMA(2, 1, 0)	0.396	0.411		
hour		(3.48)	(3.59)		
Nominal nondurable	ARIMA(2, 1, 0)	0.299	0.573		
consumption		(2.84)	(5.21)		
Nominal consumption	ARIMA(2, 1, 0)	0.663	0.336		
services		(5.73)	(2.78)		
Real nondurable	ARIMA(2, 0, 0)	0.958	−0.10		
consumption		(75.3)	(−1.4)		
Real consumption	ARIMA(1, 1, 0)	0.441			
services		(3.85)			
Real investment in	ARIMA(2, 1, 1)	1.483	−0.533	0.984	
Mining and Manufacturing		(14.1)	(−5.39)	(11.2)	
Deflator, consumer	ARIMA(1, 1, 0)	0.750			
expenditures		(9.85)			

Table A.5 (continued)

Variable	Model	Coefficient estimates (t-ratio)			
Deflator, Manufacturing	ARIMA(1, 1, 1)	0.974 (24.4)	0.676 (6.71)		
Deflator, Government expenditures	ARIMA(4, 1, 0)	0.091 (0.85)	0.062 (0.62)	0.136 (1.28)	0.554 (5.14)
Employment, Mining and Manufacturing	ARIMA(2, 0, 0)	1.609 (16.8)	−0.606 (−6.42)		
Wage rate, Mining and manufacturing	ARIMA(3, 1, 0)	0.320 (2.85)	0.194 (1.65)	0.396 (3.19)	

[a] These identified models were used to create forecasts for the period 1973.4–1975.3. Since identification of the other time periods gave similar processes with similar coefficients, the above table is representative of all time periods.

[b] Although the coefficients of this model are insignificant, it was chosen because it was the better forecasting model.

Table A.6
Median PRMSE for periods 1972.4–1973.4 (A = ARIMA, B = WEFA with constant adjustments "old" exogenous variables, C = WEFA without constant adjustments "old" exogenous variables, D = WEFA with constant adjustments "correct" exogenous variables, E = WEFA without constant adjustments "correct" exogenous variables).

Variables	Period	A	B	C	D	E
Nominal GNP	1	0.0308	0.0251	0.0354	0.0091	0.0133
	4	0.0451	0.0282	0.0304	0.0256	0.0317
	8	0.0864	0.0419	0.0282	0.0604	0.0420
Real GNP	1	0.0090	0.0040	0.0262	0.0048	0.0074
	4	0.0062	0.0101	0.0208	0.0099	0.0072
	8	0.0196	0.0154	0.0312	0.0255	0.0223
Implicit price deflator	1	0.0200	0.0183	0.0373	0.0113	0.0205
	4	0.0440	0.0286	0.0503	0.0205	0.0347
	8	0.0696	0.0530	0.0479	0.0383	0.0358
Unemployment	1	0.0298	0.0142	0.0814	0.2254	0.0998
	4	0.0843	0.0594	0.3410	0.1271	0.2952
	8	0.1606	0.1137	0.5768	0.1985	0.5423
Nominal personal consumption expenditures	1	0.0464	0.0211	0.0359	0.0221	0.0268
	4	0.0262	0.0316	0.0288	0.0261	0.0259
	8	0.0462	0.0452	0.0252	0.0444	0.0274
Nominal non-auto durables consumption	1	0.0198	0.0152	0.0233	0.0382	0.0179
	4	0.0494	0.0175	0.0292	0.0263	0.0284
	8	0.0883	0.0427	0.0382	0.0306	0.0372
Nominal gross domestic investment	1	0.0281	0.0190	0.0217	0.1148	0.0958
	4	0.0365	0.0209	0.0329	0.0785	0.0895
	8	0.0834	0.0407	0.0908	0.0951	0.0966
Nominal nonresidential investment	1	0.0370	0.0279	0.0318	0.0188	0.0517
	4	0.0723	0.0110	0.0446	0.0487	0.0454
	8	0.1092	0.0237	0.0862	0.0408	0.0589
Nominal residential investment	1	0.0474	0.0491	0.1610	0.0432	0.1531
	4	0.2197	0.0784	0.1652	0.0796	0.1433
	8	0.1910	0.0933	0.1543	0.1319	0.1335
Imports	1	0.1089	0.0729	0.0783	0.0914	0.0835
	4	0.1454	0.0557	0.0942	0.1017	0.1071
	8	0.2056	0.0667	0.872	0.1433	0.1442
Real gross private domestic investment	1	0.0143	0.0107	0.0252	0.1003	0.0847
	4	0.0286	0.0337	0.0677	0.0684	0.0815
	8	0.0562	0.0517	0.0696	0.0901	0.0897
Real output/hour	1	0.0411	0.0446	0.0412	0.0598	0.0581
	4	0.0486	0.0483	0.0346	0.0624	0.0491
	8	0.0615	0.0671	0.0408	0.0853	0.0612
Private compensation /hour	1	0.0041	0.0104	0.0196	0.0104	0.0148
	4	0.0205	0.0156	0.0480	0.0142	0.0245
	8	0.0574	0.0159	0.1163	0.0148	0.1066
Nominal nondurable consumption	1	0.0105	0.0132	0.0155	0.0301	0.0302
	4	0.0227	0.0190	0.0261	0.0198	0.0487
	8	0.0460	0.0449	0.0736	0.0310	0.0930

Table A.6

Variables	Period	A	B	C	D	E
Nominal consumer services	1	0.0581	0.0535	0.0619	0.0538	0.0622
	4	0.0656	0.0553	0.0548	0.0517	0.0522
	8	0.0811	0.0718	0.0481	0.0566	0.0434
Real nondurable consumption	1	0.0338	0.0392	0.0596	0.0536	0.0653
	4	0.0458	0.0558	0.0897	0.0709	0.0847
	8	0.0522	0.0754	0.1246	0.0972	0.1308
Real consumer services	1	0.0340	0.0279	0.0200	0.0264	0.0181
	4	0.0447	0.0216	0.0116	0.0157	0.0132
	8	0.0581	0.0159	0.0202	0.0147	0.0189
Real investment in Mining and Manufacturing	1	0.0239	0.0311	0.0244	0.0126	0.0100
	4	0.0545	0.0256	0.0621	0.1179	0.1178
	8	0.0969	0.0277	0.1453	0.1755	0.2041
Deflator, consumer expenditures	1	0.0539	0.0412	0.0508	0.0370	0.0400
	4	0.0774	0.0512	0.0519	0.0399	0.0391
	8	0.1134	0.0915	0.0559	0.0544	0.0410
Deflator, Manufacturing	1	0.0290	0.0196	0.0662	0.0361	0.0688
	4	0.0387	0.0374	0.0869	0.0609	0.1072
	8	0.1160	0.0851	0.0926	0.0586	0.1516
Deflator, Government expenditures	1	0.0084	0.0053	0.0473	0.0114	0.0493
	4	0.0312	0.0130	0.0427	0.0211	0.0550
	8	0.0431	0.0214	0.0327	0.0275	0.0520
Employment, Mining and Manufacturing	1	0.0193	0.0123	0.0302	0.0139	0.0311
	4	0.0248	0.0272	0.0897	0.0200	0.0939
	8	0.0401	0.0263	0.1881	0.0476	0.1708
Wage Rate, Mining and Manufacturing	1	0.0089	0.0156	0.0327	0.0193	0.0184
	4	0.0192	0.0255	0.0598	0.0247	0.0330
	8	0.0527	0.0247	0.1546	0.0226	0.1260
Average median	1	0.0312	0.0257	0.0402	0.0454	0.0487
	4	0.0544	0.0335	0.0679	0.0493	0.0699
	8	0.0841	0.0502	0.1012	0.0662	0.1056
Overall average median		0.0566	0.0365	0.0698	0.0536	0.0747

References

Anderson, O.D., ed., 1985, Time series analysis: Theory and practice, Vol. 7 (North-Holland, Amsterdam).

Armstrong, J., 1978, Forecasting with econometric methods: Folklore versus fact, Journal of Business, 549–564.

Box, G. and G. Jenkins, 1970, Time series analysis: Forecasting and control (Holden-Day, New York).

Chatfield, C., 1975, The analysis of time series: Theory and practice (Chapman and Hall, London).

Cooper, R., 1972, The predictive performance of quarterly econometric models of the United States, in: B. Hickman, ed., Econometric models of cyclical behaviour, Vol. 2 (Columbia University Press, New York).

Dhrymes, P., 1974, Econometrics, statistical foundations and applications (Springer-Verlag, New York).

Dhrymes, P. and S. Peristiani, 1983, The predictive performance of WEFA versus Box–Jenkins ARIMA models, discussion paper no. 514 (Department of Economics, Columbia University, New York).

Fildes, R., 1985, Quantitative forecasting the state of art: Econometric models, Journal of the Operations Research Society 36, 549–580.

Harmon, P. and D. King, 1985, Expert systems: Artificial intelligence in business (Wiley, New York).

Hirsch, A., T. Grimm and G. Narasimham, 1974, Some multiplier and error characteristics of the BEA quarterly model, International Economic Review 16, 616–631.

Klein, L. 1971, An essay on the theory of economic prediction (Markham, Chicago, IL).

Levenbach, H., J. Clearly and D. Fryck, 1974, A comparison of ARIMA and econometric models for telephone demand, Ameri-Statistical Association, Proceedings of the Business and Economic Statistics Section, 448–450.

Longbottom, J. and S. Holly, 1985, The role of time series analysis in the evaluation of econometric models, Journal of Forecasting 4, 75–87.

McCarthy, M., 1981, The Wharton quartely econometric forecasting model III (Economics Research Unit, University of Pennsylvania, Philadelphia, PA).

McNees, S., 1981, The recent record of thirteen forecasters, New England Economic Review, 5–17.

McNees, S., 1982, The role of macroeconometric models in forecasting and policy analysis in the United States, Journal of Forecasting 1, 37–48.

McNees, S., 1986, Forecasting accuracy of alternative techniques: A comparison of U.S. macroeconomic forecasts, Journal of Business and Economic Statistics 4, 5–15.

Makridakis, S. and S. Wheelwright, 1978, Forecasting methods and application (Wiley, New York).

Markridakis, S., A. Andersen, R. Carbone, R. Fildes, M. Hibon, R. Lewandowski, J. Newton, E. Parzen, and R. Winkler, 1985, The forecasting accuracy of major time series methods (Wiley, Chichester).

Narasimham, G., G. Castellino and N. Singpurwalla, 1974, On the predictive performance of the BEA quarterly model and Box–Jenkins ARIMA models, American Statistical Association, Proceedings of the Business and Economic Statistics Section, 501–504.

Naylor, T., T. Seaks and D. Wichern, 1972, Box–Jenkins methods: An alternative to econometric models, International Statistical Review 40, 123–137.

Nelson, C., 1976, The prediction performance of the FRB-MIT-PENN model of the U.S. economy, American Economic Review 62, 902–917.

Pindyck, R. and D. Rubinfeld, Econometric models and economic forecasts (McGraw-Hill, New York).

Sims, C., 1980, Macroeconomics and reality, Econometrica 48, 1–48.

Wallis, K., 1977, Multiple time series analysis and final form of econometric models, Econometrica 45, 1481–1497.

Zellner, A., 1979, Statistical analysis of econometric models, Journal of the American Statistical Association 74, 631–651.

Zellner, A. and F. Palm, 1974, Time series analysis and simultaneous equation econometric models, Journal of Econometrics 14, 17–54.

Biography: P.J. DHRYMES is a Professor in the Department of Economics at Columbia University. His research interests include theoretical and applied econometrics. He is the author of *Distributed Lags: Problems of Estimation and Formulation* (Holden-Day, 1971), *Econometrics: Statistical Foundations and Applications* (Springer-Verlag, 1974) and *Introductory Econometrics* (Springer-Verlag, 1978).

S. PERISTIANI is an Assistant Professor in the Department of Economics at Queens College-CUNY. His research interest include theoretical and applied econometrics.

PART II

ECONOMETRIC THEORY: SINGLE AND MULTIPLE EQUATIONS REGRESSION MODELS

Econometrica, Vol. 30, No. 2 (April, 1962)

ON DEVISING UNBIASED ESTIMATORS FOR THE PARAMETERS OF THE COBB-DOUGLAS PRODUCTION FUNCTION[1]

BY PHOEBUS J. DHRYMES

1.

IN MANY empirical investigations the geometric mean of observed factor shares serves as an estimator of the factor exponents in a Cobb-Douglas[2] production function. This particular estimator is due to Klein [**7**, p. 194]. It is here shown that such an estimator is biased. Under certain conditions an alternative estimator is derived which is unbiased, sufficient, efficient, and consistent.

2.

The following description for the production process of a firm, sector, or economy is often employed:

$$Q(t) = A(t) \prod_{i=1}^{n} X_i^{\alpha_i}(t)\, e^{u(t)} \qquad (t = 1, 2, \ldots, T) \tag{1}$$

where $Q(t)$, $X_i(t)$ are respectively the output and ith input at time t, $A(t)$ is some positive function of time, $\alpha_i > 0$, and $\sum_{i=1}^{n} \alpha_i = 1$, this latter preserving the condition imposed on (1) when $u(t) \equiv 0$, i.e., when it is nonstochastic, due to the requirements of competitive theory. By virtue of the latter assumption, we may also write:

$$P_i(t) = P_Q(t) \frac{\partial Q^*(t)}{\partial X_i(t)} e^{v_i(t)} (i = 1, 2, \ldots, n\,;\, t = 1, 2, \ldots, T) \tag{2}$$

where $P_i(t)$, $P_Q(t)$ are, respectively, the prices of the ith factor and of output at time t and $Q^*(t) = Q(t)e^{-u(t)}$, i.e., it is the nonstochastic part of (1). A variant of this formulation is given, e.g., by Wolfson [**13**]. What (2) implies

[1] This is a revised version of part of my Thesis submitted at the Massachusetts Institute of Technology. During its preparation I had the benefit of helpful advice by Professors E. Kuh and R. M. Solow. I have also benefited from several suggestions by the referee of this paper. To all I wish to express my gratitude. Acknowledgment is also due to the Ford Foundation which partially financed this investigation through a Doctoral Dissertation Fellowship and to the Cowles Foundation at which the present version was completed during my visit there in the summer of 1961.

[2] The name "Cobb-Douglas" traditionally given to such functions is somewhat inappropriate. Wicksell derives these functions from elementary economic considerations in the course of his analysis of Akerman's problem. (Wicksell, K, *Lectures on Political Economy*, Vol. II, Routledge and Kegan Paul, Ltd., London, 1951, pp. 285–286.)

is that decisions on factor employment are made on the basis of the anticipated output $Q^*(t)$ and not on the basis of the output actually materializing.

The term $u(t)$ in (1) and $v_i(t)$ in (2) are assumed to be serially uncorrelated and to be distributed (the latter marginally) normally with mean zero and variance σ^2 and $\sigma^2_{v_1}$, respectively. We may also assume that $u(t)$ and $v_i(t)$ are independent.

Manipulating (1) and (2) it is then an easy matter to show that

$$\text{(3)} \qquad \frac{P_i(t)\,X_i(t)}{P_Q(t)Q(t)} = \alpha_i(t) = \alpha_i e^{w_i(t)} (i=1,2,\ldots,n\,;\, t=1,2,\ldots,T)$$

where $w_i(t) = u(t) - v_i(t)$. Under the assumption made above, the $w_i(t)$ are (marginally) normal with mean zero and variance $\sigma^2_i = \sigma^2 + \sigma^2_{v_i}$; they are also serially uncorrelated.

Now, if the $\alpha_i(t)$ are interpreted as observed factor shares, then the factor exponents in (1) can be estimated by first transforming into logarithms. Thus:

$$\text{(4)} \qquad \log \alpha_i(t) = \log \alpha_i + w_i(t) \quad (i=1,2,\ldots,n\,;\, t=1,2,\ldots,T).$$

From (4), minimizing the second moment of estimated disturbances gives

$$\text{(5)} \qquad \widehat{\log \alpha_i} = \frac{1}{T} \sum_{t=1}^{T} \log \alpha_i(t) \qquad (i = 1, 2, \ldots, n)$$

where T is the sample size.

On the hypotheses maintained, the estimators (5) are unbiased, efficient, and consistent. This is due to the Markov theorem. Because of the (marginal) normality of the $w_i(t)$, the estimators (5) are also sufficient, since they are maximum likelihood estimators.

Now it is obvious that equations (5) imply a certain set of estimators for the α_i, *viz.*,

$$\text{(6)} \qquad \hat{\alpha}_i = \left[\prod_{t=1}^{T} \alpha_i(t)\right]^{1/T} \qquad (i = 1, 2, \ldots, n).$$

Thus a rather convenient estimator is deduced which requires only readily available information, obviating or at least ameliorating the problems involved in obtaining accurate information concerning, in particular, capital inputs.

It is also occasionally claimed in the literature, e.g., Hoch [**4**, p. 567] and Walters [**11**, p. 26] that the estimators (6) are, on the hypotheses maintained except for normality, "best linear unbiased." This "result" is attributed to Klein [**7**, p. 193]. The ascription, however, is not correct in that Klein nowhere explicitly claims this.

The claim concerning the estimators (6) results presumably from the properties that the Markov theorem under the classical assumptions ascribes to (5) as estimators of log α_i.

Now, although the estimators (6) are transforms of (5) under a homeomorphism (i.e., a continuous one-one correspondence whose inverse is also (one-one and) continuous), yet not all properties ascribed to (5) can be ascribed to (6) as well.

It is a simple matter to show that the estimators (6) are sufficient essentially because of the Fisher-Neyman criterion for sufficient statistics [**5**, p. 101] and the homeomorphism involved in obtaining (6) from (5).

Consistency could also be shown to be preserved using the following heuristic argument which can be made rigorous:

$$\hat{\alpha}_i = e^{\log \hat{\alpha}_i} = f(\log \hat{\alpha}_i) \ . \tag{7}$$

Then we have

$$\operatorname*{plim}_{T\to\infty} \hat{\alpha}_i = f(\operatorname*{plim}_{T\to\infty} \log \hat{\alpha}_i) = f(\log \alpha_i) = \alpha_i \ .$$

Unbiasedness, however, is not necessarily preserved under a homeomorphism; in fact, since $f(\log \hat{\alpha}_i)$ obeys $f''(\widehat{\log \alpha_i}) > 0$ and is everywhere analytic, we have by using the finite form of Taylor's theorem (with remainder after two terms) about log α_i:

$$E[f(\log \hat{\alpha}_i)] \geq f[E(\log \hat{\alpha}_i)] = f(\log \alpha_i) = \alpha_i \quad (i = 1, 2, \ldots, n) \ . \tag{8}$$

In (8) the equality holds if and only if $\operatorname{var}(\widehat{\log \alpha_i}) = 0$.

This suggests that the estimators (6) are asymptotically unbiased. By virtue of the asymptotic unbiasedness and sufficiency of the estimators (6), it follows that they are asymptotically efficient. The term "efficient" here means the property of being unbiased and of minimum variance within the class of unbiased estimators of the parameter in question.

The asymptotic efficiency of (6) is essentially due to the completeness[3] of the density function of the mean of a sample derived from a normal parent.

In the present case we may show asymptotic unbiasedness directly by utilizing the fact that $E(\alpha_i) = \varphi_i(1)$ where $\varphi_i(1)$ is the moment generating function of $\widehat{\log \alpha_i}$ with parameter 1:

$$E(\hat{\alpha}_i) = \alpha_i e^{\frac{1}{2T}\sigma_i^2} > \alpha_i \qquad (i = 1, 2, \ldots, n) \ . \tag{9}$$

The result in (9) points out another difficulty with this particular formulation, *viz.*,

$$E\left[\sum_{i=1}^{n} \hat{\alpha}_i\right] > \sum_{i=1}^{n} \alpha_i = 1 \ . \tag{10}$$

[3] For an elementary development of the notion of completeness, see Hogg and Craig [**5**, p. 106]. For a full development see Lehmann and Scheffé [**8**, p. 305 ff.].

We may wish to preserve the requirement $\sum_{i=1}^{n} \alpha_i = 1$ so that the model would remain a true generalization of the nonstochastic model of production and distribution. This may be accomplished by treating one of the factors, say the nth, asymmetrically by requiring its share to accrue residually.

This has the following consequences: In (2) we do not have n conditions, but rather $n-1$, so that optimization occurs only with respect to $n-1$ factors; in (5) and consequently in (6) we have only $n-1$ independent estimators, so that we always put by definition:

$$\hat{\alpha}_n \equiv 1 - \sum_{i=1}^{n-1} \hat{\alpha}_i . \tag{11}$$

What follows then should be interpreted in the light of (11). From (9) it is easily seen that the inverse of the relative bias of (6) is given by:

$$e^{-\frac{1}{2T}\sigma_i^2} = \sum_{k=0}^{\infty} \left(-\frac{\sigma_i^2}{2T}\right)^k / k! \qquad (i = 1, 2, \ldots, n-1). \tag{12}$$

Bearing this in mind we have:

LEMMA 1: *There exist unbiased estimators for the* α_i, $i = 1, 2, \ldots, n-1$.

Proof. We proceed constructively: Since $\widehat{\log \alpha_i}$ and S_i^2 (the sample mean and variance of the logarithms of $\alpha_i(t)$) are distributed independently, and since

$$E(S_i^{2k}) = \frac{2^k \sigma_i^{2k}\, \Gamma\left(\frac{T-1}{2} + k\right)}{T^k\, \Gamma\left(\frac{T-1}{2}\right)}, \tag{12a}$$

it will suffice to determine a function $f(S_i^2)$ such that $E[f(S_i^2)] = e^{-\frac{1}{2T}\sigma_i^2}$. Writing formally

$$f(S_i^2) = \sum_{k=0}^{\infty} a_k S_i^{2k} \qquad (i = 1, 2, \ldots, n-1), \tag{13}$$

then taking the expectation of (13) with respect to the density function of S_i^2 and equating coefficients of like powers of σ_i^2 in (12) we find

$$f(S_i^2) = \sum_{k=0}^{\infty} (-\tfrac{1}{4})^k \frac{B\left(\frac{T-1}{2}, k\right)}{\Gamma(k)\, k!} S_i^{2k} \quad (i = 1, 2, \ldots, n-1). \tag{13a}$$

It follows[4] that:

$$\bar{\alpha}_i = \hat{\alpha}_i f(S_i^2) \qquad (i = 1, 2, \ldots, n-1) \tag{14}$$

are unbiased estimators of the α_i, *q.e.d.*

LEMMA 2: *The estimators $\bar{\alpha}_i$ in* (14) *are sufficient.*

Proof. This follows from the fact that the $\bar{\alpha}_i$ are simple functions of the (jointly) sufficient statistics $\log \hat{\alpha}_i$ and S_i^2 alone, i.e., not involving unknown parameters.

LEMMA 3: *The estimators $\bar{\alpha}_i$ in* (14) *are efficient.*

Proof. The joint density function of $\log \hat{\alpha}_i$ and S_i^2 is complete;[5] due to a

[4] Expectation of (13) is justified since it is uniformly convergent for $S_i^2 < \infty$; further $f(S_i^2)$ is an analytic function of S_i^2, hence independent of $\hat{\alpha}_i$, so that $E[\hat{\alpha}_i f(S_i^2)] = E(\hat{\alpha}_i) E[f(S_i^2)] = \alpha_i$.

[5] It will be noted that the properties ascribed to the estimators $\bar{a}_i$ are deduced from the characteristics of the marginal distribution of the $w_i(t)$, $i = 1, 2, \ldots, n-1$, and not from those of the joint distribution of the $w_i(t)$. This is in a sense the logical consequence of the fact that the problem as it naturally arises involves the marginal distribution of the $v_i(t)$, $i = 1, 2, \ldots, n-1$, exhibited in equation (2). It is not, however, difficult to derive the joint distribution of the $w_i(t)$. This is seen as follows:

Let the joint distribution of the $v_i(t)$, $i = 1, 2, \ldots, n-1$, be multivariate normal with mean vector 0 and covariance matrix Σ. We still retain the assumption that the $v_i(t)$ are serially uncorrelated but we shall not insist on the independence of the $v_i(t)$ for different indices i. Then consider the transformation:

$$w_i^*(t) = u(t) - v_i(t) = w_i(t) \qquad (i = 1, 2 \ldots, n-1),$$

$$w_n^*(t) = u(t),$$

or for simplicity

$$W^* = AV^*,$$

where W^* is a vector whose components are the $w_i^*(t)$, $i = 1, 2, \ldots, n$, and V^* is the vector whose first component is $u(t)$ and whose remaining $n-1$ components are the $v_i(t)$, $i = 1, 2, \ldots, n-1$, A being the matrix of the transformation. Since $u(t)$ is independent of the $v_i(t)$, it follows that V^* has the multivariate normal distribution with mean vector 0 and covariance matrix Σ^*, where

$$\Sigma^* = \begin{bmatrix} \Sigma & \begin{matrix} 0 \\ \vdots \\ 0 \end{matrix} \\ 0 \ldots 0 & \sigma^2 \end{bmatrix}.$$

Hence, since A is nonsingular, W^* has the (proper) multivariate normal distribution with mean vector 0 and covariance matrix $A\ \Sigma^*\ A'$. But then it is obvious, by "integrating out" $w_n^*(t)$, that the $w_i(t)$, $i = 1, 2, \ldots, n-1$, have the joint multivariate normal distribution with mean vector zero and covariance matrix obtained by deleting the last row and column from $A\ \Sigma^* A'$. It then, of course, follows that the $w_i(t)$ have

result by Rao [**9**, p. 86] if an efficient estimator exists it must be an explicit function of the (jointly) sufficient statistics $\log \hat{\alpha}_i$ and S_i^2 alone. Thus, if another continuous[6] estimator

$$\varrho_i = \varrho_i(\log \hat{\alpha}_i, S_i^2) \qquad (i = 1, 2, \ldots, n-1) \tag{15}$$

exists which is also unbiased, then

$$E[\bar{\alpha}_i - \varrho_i] = 0\,. \tag{15a}$$

Due to the completeness of the joint density function of $\log \hat{\alpha}_i$ and S_i^2 it follows that $\bar{\alpha}_i \equiv \varrho_i$, *q.e.d.*

LEMMA 4: *The estimators* $\bar{\alpha}_i$ *in* (14) *are consistent.*

Proof. Had efficiency been defined by the Cramer-Rao equation, [**2**, p. 481] the proof would have been immediate. Since we have not employed this definition, it seems simpler to give a direct argument from the variance of the $\bar{\alpha}_i$. Thus:

$$\text{Var}(\bar{\alpha}_i) = e^{2\log \alpha_i}\left[e^{\frac{2\sigma_i^2}{T}} V_i(f) - 1\right] \qquad (i = 1, 2, \ldots, n-1) \tag{16}$$

where

$$V_i(f) = E[f(S_i^2)]^2 \qquad (i = 1, 2, \ldots, n-1)\,. \tag{16a}$$

It can be shown that

$$\lim_{T\to\infty} V_i(f) = 1\,. \tag{16b}$$

Hence (16b) together with Lemma 1 and Chebyshev's inequality imply consistency, *q.e.d.*

We may conclude this section by formally stating the theorem:

THEOREM: *Under the hypotheses* (1) *and* (2) *as modified by* (11) *the estimators* (6) *are biased; the estimators given in* (14) *are unbiased, sufficient, efficient, and consistent.*[7]

---

individually the univariate normal (marginal) distribution as claimed earlier. One could if one wished characterize the properties of the $\bar{a}_i$ on the basis of their joint distribution, or derive appropriate estimators by first transforming the $w_i(t)$ so that they become independent. This, however, would represent a departure from the natural way in which the problem is posed.

[6] Continuity is assumed only in order to disallow the possibility that $\bar{a}_i \neq \varrho_i$ on a set of measure zero.

[7] In the interest of completeness one should remark that these attributes are derived from the properties of the marginal distribution of the $v_i(t)$ — and hence of the $w_i(t)$. Of course if $u(t) \equiv 0$ and the $v_i(t)$ are independent, then this qualification would be unnecessary.

3. CONCLUSION

We give below an indication of the size of the bias in estimating the α_i from share-of-capital data in various sectors of the American Economy for the postwar period (1945–1958). The entries in Table I are computed values of $f(S_i^2)$ truncated after 8 terms.

TABLE I

Sector	truncated $f(S_i^2)$
Manufacturing	.996
Transportation	.976
Services	.999

As is apparent from (9) the relative bias will be small if the variance of $\log \hat{\alpha}_i(t)$ is also small.

We may be concerned with unbiasedness, however, if we wish to use estimators of the α_i in obtaining an estimator of a productivity parameter as follows:

It will be noted that the term $A(t)$ in (1) has not appeared in subsequent developments. If a specific functional from were to be employed, say, $A(t) = Ae^{\lambda t}$, then using the estimators $\bar{\alpha}_i$ we easily find:

$$Q(t) \prod_{i=1}^{n} X_i^{-\bar{\alpha}_i}(t) = A\,e^{\lambda t} \prod_{i=1}^{n} X_i^{-(\bar{\alpha}_i - \alpha_i)}(t)\,e^{u(t)} \quad (t = 1, 2, \ldots, T)\,. \tag{17}$$

The right member of (17) involves the random term

$$\prod_{i=1}^{n} X_i^{-(\bar{\alpha}_i - \alpha_i)}(t)\,e^{u(t)}\,.$$

Hence we could derive an estimator for λ and study its properties. In this context it would be desirable to have unbiased estimators for the α_i. An application of this will be made in a subsequent paper.

This procedure gives a statistical counterpart to the method suggested by Solow [**10**, p. 312] and provides a rather simple means of testing a statistical hypothesis on the "rate of change" of productivity as between two economies, firms, or sectors whose productive processes are characterized by a relation such as (1).

Harvard University

REFERENCES

[1] Aitchison, J., and J. A. C. Brown: *The Lognormal Distribution*, Cambridge: University Press, 1957.

[2] Cramer, H.: *Mathematical Methods of Statistics*, Princeton: Princeton University Press, 1946.

[3] Finney, D. J.: "On the Distribution of a Variate Whose Logarithm is Normally Distributed," *Journal of the Royal Statistical Society*, Supplement I, Vol. VII, No. 2, 1941, p. 155.

[4] Hoch, I.: "Simultaneous Equation Bias in the Context of the Cobb-Douglas Function," *Econometrica*, Vol. 29, 1958, p. 566.

[5] Hogg, R. V., and A. T. Craig: *Introduction to Mathematical Statistics*, New York: The Macmillan Co., 1959.

[6] ———: "Sufficient Statistics in Elementary Distribution Theory," *Sankhya*, Vol. 17, 1956–57, p. 209.

[7] Klein, L. R.: *A Textbook of Econometrics*, Evanston: Row, Peterson and Co., 1953.

[8] Lehmann, E. L., and H. Scheffé: "Completeness, Similar Regions and Unbiased Estimation," Part I, *Sankhya*, Vol. 10, 1950, p. 305.

[9] Rao, C. Radhakrishna: "Information and Accuracy Attainable in the Estimation of Statistical Parameters," *Bulletin of the Calcutta Mathematical Society*, Vol. 37, 1945, p. 81.

[10] Solow, R. M.: "Technical Change and the Aggregate Production Function," *Review of Economics and Statistics*, Vol. 39, 1957, p. 312.

[11] Walters, A. A.: *Some Notes on Simultaneous Equations and the Cobb-Douglas Function*, Series A, No. 17, University of Birmingham, Faculty of Commerce and Social Science, June, 1960.

[12] ———: *A Survey of Statistical Production and Cost Functions*, Series A, No. 20, University of Birmingham, Faculty of Commerce and Social Science, June, 1960.

[13] Wolfson, R. J.: "An Econometric Investigation of Regional Differentials in American Agricultural Wages," *Econometrica*, 1959, pp. 225–257.

Reprinted from THE SOUTHERN ECONOMIC JOURNAL
Vol. XXXIII, No. 2, October, 1966
Printed in U.S.A.

ON THE TREATMENT OF CERTAIN RECURRENT NON-LINEARITIES IN REGRESSION ANALYSIS*

PHOEBUS J. DHRYMES

University of Pennsylvania

I. PRELIMINARIES

Consider the problem of estimating the parameters of

$$(1) \quad y_t = \sum_{i=0}^{n} \beta_i x_{it} + u_t \qquad t = 1, 2, \cdots, T$$

where the β_i are bounded parameters, $x_{0t} \equiv 1$, the x_i, $i \neq 0$, are explanatory fixed variates and the error term has the following stochastic structure:

$$(1a) \quad \begin{aligned} u_t &= \rho u_{t-1} + \epsilon_t \\ \epsilon_t &\sim N(0, \sigma^2) \qquad \text{all } t. \end{aligned}$$

If the autoregressive structure of the error term is eliminated by a suitable transformation, there results a model whose error term has the classical properties, but which is nonlinear in its parameters.

Consider, further, the model

$$(2) \quad y_t = \alpha_0 + \alpha \sum_{i=0}^{\infty} \lambda^i x_{t-i} + u_t$$

where α_0, α, λ are bounded parameters, x_t a fixed variate and the error term has the specification

$$(2a) \quad u_t \sim N(0, \sigma^2) \qquad \text{all } t.$$

By a suitable transformation the model becomes

$$(2b) \quad y_t = \beta_0 + \beta_1 y_{t-1} + \beta_2 x_t + v_t$$

where

$$(2c) \quad \begin{aligned} \beta_0 &= (1 - \lambda)\alpha_0, \qquad \beta_1 = \lambda, \\ \beta_2 &= \alpha v_t = u_t - \lambda u_{t-1}. \end{aligned}$$

This problem, originally investigated by Koyck [10], is slightly more complicated than the first, but yields essentially to the same techniques. A variant of this problem, and considerably more realistic, is the following

$$(3) \quad y_t = \alpha_0 + \alpha \sum_{i=0}^{k} \lambda^i x_{t-i} + u_t$$

where u_t has the specification in (2a). Such models invariably occur in studies involving the "permanent income" or "permanent something else" hypothesis. We shall deal mostly with the model (2) generalizing it further to include more than one explanatory variable. Thus, we shall work with

$$(3a) \quad y_t = \alpha_0 + \alpha_1 \sum_{i=0}^{\infty} \lambda^i x_{1t-i} + \sum_{i=2}^{n} \alpha_i x_{it} + u_t.$$

The model in (1) was first investigated by Cochrane and Orcutt [1], who, however, did not produce an analytic solution. A two stage procedure is suggested by Durbin [2] in the context of a far more general investigation. The estimating procedure as exposited in [2] is rather complex but it is shown to be consistent and asymptotically efficient. In the face of the specification (1a) it is not, however, a maximum likelihood estimator.

The same problem was also investigated by Hildreth and Lu [5]. The estimator provided by them, however, is not shown to have any other property besides consistency. Finally, Sargan [15] provides a proof of the convergence of the Cochrane-Orcutt procedure.

In addition to Koyck, the second problem has been investigated by Klein [8], who, however, did not obtain asymptotically efficient estimators of the parameters of (2)

* This research was completed during the author's tenure of a John Simon Guggenheim Memorial Fellowship (1965–1966).

under the specification (2a). Leviatan [11], obtains consistent but clearly inefficient estimators for the parameters of the same model. Finally Hannan [4] provides an interesting application of spectral analysis technique to a problem for which the model in (2) is a special case.

The chief merit of the procedure to be presented in this paper is that in the face of the specification (1a) and (2a) the estimators will be maximum likelihood ones possessing the properties of consistency and asymptotic efficiency and sufficiency. They are in addition computationally simple, and fully capable of being executed on the standard regression computer programs.

II. ESTIMATION OF THE MODELS

Consider (1) first. Solving (1a) we find

$$u_t = \sum_{i=0}^{\infty} \rho^i \epsilon_{t-i} = \left(\frac{I}{I - \rho Z}\right) \epsilon_t \tag{4}$$

where Z is the lag operator defined by

$$\begin{aligned} Z^k \epsilon_t &= \epsilon_{t-k}, \quad k > 0, \\ Z^0 \epsilon_t &\equiv I \epsilon_t = \epsilon_t . \end{aligned} \tag{4a}$$

It is clear from (4) that if we regard u_t as having finite variance for all t we must assume

$$|\rho| < 1. \tag{4b}$$

It may be shown that under (1a) and (4b), we have

$$u \sim N(0, \Sigma) \tag{4c}$$

where

$$\Sigma = \frac{\sigma^2}{1 - \rho^2}$$

$$\begin{bmatrix} 1 & \rho & \rho^2 & \cdots & \rho^{T-1} \\ \rho & 1 & \rho & \rho^2 \cdots & \rho^{T-2} \\ \vdots & & & & \\ \rho^{T-1} & \rho^{T-2} & \cdots & & 1 \end{bmatrix} = \sigma^2 V \tag{4d}$$

and $u = (u_1, u_2, \cdots, u_T)'$. Further, that V^{-1} is given by

$$V^{-1} = \begin{bmatrix} 1 & -\rho & 0 & \cdots & 0 \\ -\rho & 1 + \rho^2 & -\rho & \cdots & 0 \\ \cdot & & \cdot & & \vdots \\ \cdot & & \cdot & 1 + \rho^2 & -\rho \\ \cdot & & \cdot & & \\ 0 & \cdots & & -\rho & 1 \end{bmatrix} \tag{4e}$$

and that

$$\begin{aligned} s'V^{-1}s = \sum_{i=1}^{T-1} (s_i - \rho s_{i+1})^2 \\ + s_T^2(1 - \rho^2) \end{aligned} \tag{4f}$$

for any vector $s \in R^T$. Hence Σ is positive definite for $|\rho| < 1$.

Finally, note that

$$V^{-1} = M'M \tag{5}$$

where

$$M' = \begin{bmatrix} \sqrt{1 - \rho^2} & -\rho & 0 & \cdots & 0 \\ 0 & & 1 & -\rho \cdots & 0 \\ \vdots & & & \cdot 1 & -\rho \\ 0 & \cdots & & \cdots & 1 \end{bmatrix} \tag{5a}$$

Transforming (1) through premultiplying by M[1] we have, in matrix notation

$$W = Q\beta + \epsilon \tag{6}$$

where

$$\begin{aligned} W = My, \quad Q = MX \quad \text{and} \\ \epsilon = (\epsilon_1, \epsilon_2, \cdots, \epsilon_T)' \end{aligned} \tag{6a}$$

y and X being respectively the vector and matrix of observations on the dependant and explanatory variables. Now (6) satisfies all the classical assumptions and thus

[1] This of course is not a unique transformation. Thus, the transforming matrix might as well be taken to be

$$M = \begin{bmatrix} 1 & 0 & 0 & \cdots & 0 \\ -\rho & 1 & 0 & \cdots & 0 \\ 0 & -\rho & 1 & \cdots & 0 \\ \vdots & & & & \\ 0 & & & -\rho & \sqrt{1 - \rho^2} \end{bmatrix}$$

conditionally on ρ, maximum likelihood estimators of β,σ^2 can be obtained by maximizing

$$L(\beta,\sigma^2 \mid \rho,X,y) = -\frac{T}{2}\ln(2\pi) - \frac{T}{2}\ln\sigma^2 - \frac{1}{2\sigma^2}(W - Q\beta)'(W - Q\beta). \tag{7}$$

Notice that the estimators so obtained, say $\tilde{\beta}$, $\tilde{\sigma}^2$ are functions of ρ and satisfy

$$L(\tilde{\beta},\tilde{\sigma}^2 \mid \rho) \geq L(\beta,\sigma^2 \mid \rho) \tag{7a}$$

for all admissible β,σ^2 but for fixed ρ. The estimators so obtained are

$$\begin{aligned} \tilde{\beta} &= (Q'Q)^{-1}Q'W \\ &= (X'V^{-1}X)^{-1}X'V^{-1}y \\ \tilde{\sigma}^2 &= \frac{1}{T}W'[I - Q(Q'Q)^{-1}Q']W \end{aligned} \tag{7b}$$

so that, in terms of the original variables, the estimator for the regression coefficients is the Aitken estimator. One perhaps should write more appropriately $\tilde{\beta}(\rho)\tilde{\sigma}^2(\rho)$, to stress the dependence of (7b) on ρ.

Finally, if we insert (7b) in (7) we obtain the "concentrated" likelihood as

$$L^*(\rho) = -\frac{T}{2}[\ln(2\pi) + 1] - \frac{T}{2}\ln\tilde{\sigma}^2(\rho). \tag{7c}$$

This suggests that we can obtain the maximum of (7c) by simply scanning the range of admissible values for the autocorrelation coefficient. More precisely the procedure is as follows: Select a number of trial values for ρ as dense as dictated by the degree of accuracy required. For each trial value compute the maximum likelihood estimator for β (the Aitken estimator) and σ^2. Then select that set of values for β, σ^2 and ρ corresponding to the regression exhibiting *the smallest standard error of the estimate*. It will be shown in the following section that these indeed possess the classical properties of maximum likelihood estimators.

Return now to the model

$$y_t = \alpha_0 + \alpha_1 \sum_{i=0}^{\infty} \lambda^i x_{1t-i} + \sum_{i=2}^{n} \alpha_i x_{it} + u_t \qquad t = 1, 2, \cdots, T \tag{8}$$

where

$$u \sim N(0,\sigma^2 I), \qquad u = (u_1, u_2, \cdots, u_T)'. \tag{8a}$$

Employing the notation of (4a) we may rewrite (8) as

$$y_t = \alpha_0 + \frac{\alpha_1 I}{I - \lambda Z} x_{1t} + \sum_{i=2}^{n} \alpha_i x_{it} + u_t. \tag{8b}$$

Clearing of fractions we obtain

$$y_t - \lambda y_{t-1} = \alpha_0(1 - \lambda) + \alpha_1 x_{1t} + \sum_{i=2}^{n} \alpha_i (x_{it} - \lambda x_{it-1}) + u_t - \lambda u_{t-1}. \tag{8c}$$

If we put

$$\begin{aligned}
y_t^* &= y_t - \lambda y_{t-1} && t = 2, \cdots, T \\
x_{it}^* &= x_{it} - \lambda x_{it-1} && \begin{cases} i = 2, \cdots, n; \\ t = 2, \cdots, T \end{cases} \\
x_{1t}^* &= x_{1t} && t = 1, 2, \cdots, T \\
u_t^* &= u_t - \lambda u_{t-1} && t = 2, \cdots, T \\
\left.\begin{aligned} y_1^* &= y_1 - \lambda y_0, \\ x_{i1}^* &= x_{i1} - \lambda x_{i0} \end{aligned}\right\} && & i = 2, \cdots, n \\
u_1^* &= u_1 - \lambda u_0 \\
\left.\begin{aligned} \beta_0 &= \alpha_0(1 - \lambda) \\ \beta_i &= \alpha_i \end{aligned}\right\} && & i = 1, 2, \cdots, n
\end{aligned} \tag{8d}$$

then we may write (8c) in matrix form as

$$y^* = X^*\beta + v \tag{9}$$

where y^*,X^* give the vector and matrix of (transformed) observations respectively on the dependent and explanatory variables, β is the vector of coefficients to be estimated and v is the vector of (transformed) error terms.

In the preceding y_0, u_0 as well as x_{i0} $i = 2, \cdots, n$ are taken as given exogenously. Alternatively we may interpret the subsequent development as conditioned on u_0.

At any rate, the likelihood of the "sample" in (9) may be written as

$$L(\beta, \sigma^2 \mid y^*, X^*)$$

$$(9a) \qquad = -\frac{T}{2}\ln(2\pi) - \frac{1}{2}\ln|\Lambda| - \frac{T}{2}\ln\sigma^2 - \frac{1}{2\sigma^2}(y^* - X^*\beta)'\Lambda^{-1}(y^* - X^*\beta).$$

In (9a) $\sigma^2\Lambda$ is the covariance matrix of v and Λ is given by

$$(9b) \qquad \Lambda = \begin{bmatrix} 1 & -\lambda & 0 & 0 & \cdots\cdots & 0 \\ -\lambda & 1+\lambda^2 & -\lambda & 0 & \cdots\cdots & 0 \\ 0 & -\lambda & 1+\lambda^2 & -\lambda & 0 \cdots\cdots & \vdots \\ \vdots & & & & & 0 \\ & & & & 1+\lambda^2 & -\lambda \\ 0 & \cdots & \cdots & 0 & -\lambda & 1+\lambda^2 \end{bmatrix}.$$

To render (9a) fully accessible we need to evaluate $|\Lambda|$ and Λ^{-1}. We have

Lemma 1: $|\Lambda| = 1$ and $\Lambda^{-1} = A - S$ where

$$(10) \qquad A = \frac{1}{1-\lambda}\begin{bmatrix} 1 & \lambda & \lambda^2 & \cdots & \lambda^{T-1} \\ \lambda & 1 & \lambda & \cdots & \lambda^{T-2} \\ \vdots & & & & \\ \lambda^{T-1} & \lambda^{T-2} & & \cdots & 1 \end{bmatrix}$$

$$S = \frac{1}{1-\lambda^2}\begin{bmatrix} \lambda^{2T} & \lambda^{2T-1} & \cdots & \lambda^{T+1} \\ \lambda^{2T-1} & \lambda^{2T-2} & \cdots & \lambda^{T} \\ \vdots & & & \\ \lambda^{T+2} & \lambda^{T+1} & \cdots & \lambda^{3} \\ \lambda^{T+1} & \cdots\cdots & & \lambda^{2} \end{bmatrix}$$

Proof: If we multiply the first row of Λ by λ, add to the second and then evaluate the resulting determinant we obtain

$$(10a) \qquad |\Lambda_T| = |\Lambda_{T-1}|$$

where the notation $|\Lambda_k|$ indicates the determinant of a matrix of the type in (9b) of order k. The relation in (10b) holds at least for $T \geq 3$. Evaluating for $T = 2$, we find

$$|\Lambda_2| = \begin{vmatrix} 1 & -\lambda \\ -\lambda & 1+\lambda^2 \end{vmatrix} = 1$$

which proves the first part of the Lemma. The second part of the Lemma follows by direct verification.

In view of the result above (9a) may be rewritten as

$$L(\beta, \sigma^2 \mid y^*, X^*)$$

$$(11) \qquad = -\frac{T}{2}\ln(2\pi) - \frac{T}{2}\ln\sigma^2 - \frac{1}{2\sigma^2}(y^* - X^*\beta)'\Lambda^{-1}(y^* - X^*\beta).$$

One interesting feature may be pointed out at this juncture. Recalling Koyck's development [10] it is seen that he operates essentially with the minimand (for $n = 1$)

$$(11a) \qquad \frac{1}{1+\lambda^2}(y^* - X^*\beta)'(y^* - X^*\beta) = M$$

which yields a rather awkward compromise between a least squares estimator and the Aitken estimator that is indicated by (11).

Since Λ may be shown to be a positive definite (symmetric) matrix (by essentially repeating (4f)) there exists a non-singular matrix V such that

$$V'V = \Lambda^{-1}. \tag{11b}$$

Applying the transformation analogous to (6a) to (11) we obtain the likelihood function

$$L(\beta, \sigma^2 \mid \lambda) = -\frac{T}{2}\ln(2\pi) - \frac{T}{2}\ln\sigma^2 - \frac{1}{2\sigma^2}(y^{**} - X^{**}\beta)'(y^{**} - X^{**}\beta). \tag{11c}$$

Notice that y^{**} and X^{**} depend only on λ amongst the parameters of the problem. Thus, the situation here is entirely analogous to that encountered in (7) and hence the same estimating technique applies, since from economic considerations λ will be restricted by

$$\lambda \in (0,1) \tag{11c}$$

and certainly by

$$\lambda \in (-1,1). \tag{11d}$$

The technique, it will be recalled consists of scanning over the range of λ. Thus having selected a sufficiently dense set of trial values over this range, we compute for each selected value the estimators

$$\begin{aligned} \hat{\beta}(\lambda) &= (X^{*\prime}\Lambda^{-1}X^*)^{-1}X^{*\prime}\Lambda^{-1}y^* \\ \hat{\sigma}^2(\lambda) &= \frac{1}{T}\, y^{*\prime}[(I - \Lambda^{-1}X^*RX^{*\prime})\Lambda^{-1} \cdot (I - X^*RX^{*\prime}\Lambda^{-1})]y^* \end{aligned} \tag{12}$$

and then select that set of estimators for which the standard error of the estimate is minimal.

Before we leave this topic, two aspects are worthy of comment. First, it may be that no information is available on y_0 and x_{i0} $i = 2, \cdots, n$. In that case if we operate with the model (8) the problem may be handled by a dimension "shrinking" transformation. Thus if we transform our observations by the $(T-1) \times T$ matrix

$$M = \begin{bmatrix} -\lambda & 1 & & & \\ 0 & -\lambda & 1 & & 0 \\ 0 & 0 & -\lambda & 1 & \\ \vdots & & & \ddots & \ddots \\ 0 & \cdots & \cdots & -\lambda & 1 \end{bmatrix} \tag{13}$$

and put

$$y^* = My, \quad X^* = MX, \quad v = Mu \tag{13a}$$

we find

$$E(v) = 0 \qquad \text{Cov}(v) = \sigma^2 MM' = \sigma^2 \cdot \begin{bmatrix} 1+\lambda^2 & -\lambda & \cdots & 0 \\ -\lambda & 1+\lambda' & -\lambda \cdots & 0 \\ \vdots & & & \vdots \\ & & & -\lambda \\ 0 & & -\lambda & 1+\lambda^2 \end{bmatrix}. \tag{13b}$$

The covariance matrix of the error term here differs only slightly from that of the error term in (9). In fact the only difference is that the first row and column of the covariance matrix of the former is eliminated in obtaining that of the latter. A byproduct of this transformation is that one of the sample observation is "lost." Note that the matrix in (13b) is of dimension $(T-1) \times (T-1)$.

Otherwise the problem is identical to the one just treated. Secondly, the specification of the model may be

$$y_t = \alpha_0 + \alpha_1 \sum_{i=0}^{k} \lambda^i x_{1t-i} + \sum_{i=2}^{n} \alpha_i x_{it} + u_t \quad t = 1,2,\cdots,T \tag{14}$$

instead of that given in (9). In this case α_0 may be treated either as an intrinsic parameter or as the sum of an intrinsic parameter and the remainder,

$$\alpha_1 \sum_{i=k+1}^{\infty} \lambda^i x_{1t-i},$$

of an infinite lag structure. In the latter case the choice of a proper value of k represents a problem that we do not wish to investigate here and thus we confine ourselves to the case where α_0 is indeed an intrinsic parameter and thus k is known a priori.

Retaining the stochastic specification (8a) and defining

$$x_{1t}^* = \sum_{i=0}^{k} \lambda^i x_{1t-i} \quad x_{jt}^* = x_{jt} \tag{14a}$$
$$j = 2,\cdots,n \quad x_{0t} \equiv 1 \text{ all } t$$

we may write the likelihood function of the "sample" as

$$L(\alpha,\sigma^2 \mid \lambda) = -\frac{T}{2}\ln(2\pi) - \frac{T}{2}\ln\sigma^2 - \frac{1}{2\sigma^2}(y - X^*\alpha)'(y - X^*\alpha). \tag{15}$$

Holding λ fixed and maximizing (15) with respect to α, σ^2 we obtain the estimators

$$\tilde{\alpha}(\lambda) = (X^{*\prime}X^*)^{-1} X^{*\prime}y,$$
$$\tilde{\sigma}^2(\lambda) = \frac{1}{T} y' \cdot [I - X^*(X^{*\prime}X^*)^{-1} X^{*\prime}]y. \tag{15a}$$

Substituting (15a) in (15) we obtain

$$L^*(\lambda) = \frac{T}{2}[\ln(2\pi) + 1] - \frac{T}{2}\ln\tilde{\sigma}^2(\lambda). \tag{15b}$$

It is seen then that the scanning technique employed above is equally applicable here as well. In fact the problem is considerably simpler.

III. PROPERTIES OF THE ESTIMATORS

In this section we shall determine what properties, if any, of those possessed by the maximum likelihood estimators in the context of the classical general linear model are shared by the estimators here proposed. Although the proofs will be offered with respect to the autocorrelated disturbances model, they apply with minor modifications to the infinite lag models as well.

It should be remarked, incidentally, that although the methods of estimation herein proposed are not entirely new, nonetheless in the previous literature little is said about the properties of such estimators. Thus the primary burden of this paper is to elucidate the nature of these estimators.

Lemma 2. Let

$$y_t = \sum_{i=0}^{n} \alpha_i x_{ti} + u_t \qquad t = 1,2,\cdots,T \tag{16}$$

or

$$y = X\alpha + u \tag{16a}$$

where y,X are the vector and matrix of observations on the dependent and explanatory variables respectively,

$$u \sim N(0,\Sigma)$$

where

$$\Sigma = \sigma^2 V \tag{16b}$$

and V is as in (4d).

Then, the estimators (7b) as amplified by the subsequent discussion are those that globally maximize the likelihood function.

Proof: The likelihood function may be written as

$$\bar{L}(\alpha,\rho,\sigma^2 \mid X,y) = (2\pi)^{-T/2} \mid \Sigma \mid^{-1/2} \cdot \exp\left\{-\frac{1}{2}(y - X\alpha)'\Sigma^{-1}(y - X\alpha)\right\}. \tag{17}$$

Let Ω be the admissible domain of the parameters. In particular, $\alpha \in R^{n+1}$, $\sigma' \in (0,\infty)$ and $\rho \in (-1,1)$ and thus Ω is the Cartesian product of these regions.

Since all derivatives of the likelihood function exist and Ω is an open set, the maxima of $\bar{L}$ occur at interior points. There may, however, be more than one maximum —see the examples given in Huzurbazar [6], and Hildreth and Lu [5]—and since a local maximum of the likelihood function need not, e.g., yield consistent estimators, it is important to establish that our procedure yields a global maximun.

Now, for given ρ, the procedure yields a

(conditional on ρ) global maximum since the Hessian of the (log) likelihood function is negative definite, excepting the case of linear dependencies amongst the explanatory variables.

Thus, the estimators in (7b) obey the relation, for $\rho = \bar{\rho}$

$$\text{(17a)} \quad \bar{L}(\hat{\alpha},\hat{\sigma}^2,\bar{\rho} \mid X,y) \geq \bar{L}(\alpha,\sigma^2,\bar{\rho} \mid X,y).$$

The final set of estimators, as the discussion following (7b) suggests, obey the relation

$$\text{(17b)} \quad \bar{L}(\hat{\alpha},\hat{\sigma}^2,\hat{\rho} \mid X,y) = \max_{\bar{\rho} \in (-1,1)} \bar{L}(\hat{\alpha},\hat{\sigma}^2,\bar{\rho} \mid X,y).$$

Hence

$$\text{(17c)} \quad \bar{L}(\hat{\alpha},\hat{\sigma}^2,\hat{\rho} \mid X,y) \geq \bar{L}(\alpha,\sigma^2,\rho \mid X,y) \qquad \text{q.e.d.}$$

Lemma 3: The estimators as described in Lemma 2 are consistent.

Proof: It is more convenient now to employ the notation $\bar{L}(y \mid X,\gamma)$ for the likelihood function, where

$$\text{(18)} \qquad \gamma = \begin{pmatrix} \alpha \\ \rho \\ \sigma^2 \end{pmatrix}.$$

Let γ_0 be the true value of the parameters and let $\gamma \in \Omega$, $\gamma \neq \gamma_0$ be any other value. Then in view of the concavity of the log function we have

$$\text{(18a)} \quad E\left\{\ln \frac{\bar{L}(y \mid X,\gamma)}{\bar{L}(y \mid X,\gamma_0)}\right\} \leq \ln E\left\{\frac{\bar{L}(y \mid X,\gamma)}{\bar{L}(y \mid X,\gamma_0)}\right\}$$

where the expectation is taken with respect to the "true" density of y, i.e., that having parameters γ_0.

Noting that the right hand side of (18a) is zero, we conclude

$$\text{(18b)} \quad E\{\ln \bar{L}(y \mid X,\gamma)\} \leq E\{\ln \bar{L}(y \mid X,\gamma_0)\}.$$

But for any $\gamma \in \Omega$ we have, employing the transformation in (6a)

$$\text{(18c)} \quad \frac{1}{T} \ln \bar{L}(y \mid X,\gamma) = \frac{1}{T} \sum_{t=1}^{T} \ln f(w_t \mid q_t,\beta,\sigma^2)$$

where we have employed the notation of (6a) so that w_t is an element of W and q_t is the tth row of Q.

However, the w_t are identically distributed (normal) random variables with unit variance and hence conditionally on the X's the right hand side of (18c) tends as $T \to \infty$, by the strong law of large numbers, to its expectation.

It follows, therefore, from (18c) that $(1/T) \ln \bar{L}(y \mid X,\gamma)$ also converges to its expectation as $T \to \infty$. Furthermore, employing (18c) we conclude that for given $\delta > 0$ there exists a T^* such that for all $T > T^*$

$$\text{(18d)} \quad \Pr\left\{\frac{1}{T} \ln \bar{L}(y \mid X,\gamma) \leq \frac{1}{T} \ln \bar{L}(y \mid X,\gamma_0)\right\} \geq 1 - \delta.$$

In particular, (18d) holds for the estimators described in Lemma 2, i.e., for $\gamma = \hat{\gamma}$. On the other hand, by Lemma 2, $\hat{\gamma}$ is selected so that for any T and any $\gamma \in \Omega$

$$\text{(18e)} \quad \ln \bar{L}(y \mid X,\hat{\gamma}) \geq \ln \bar{L}(y \mid X,\gamma).$$

Hence, (18e) in conjunction with (18d) yield the result that for given $\delta > 0$ there exists a T^* such that for any $T > T^*$ we have

$$\text{(18f)} \quad \Pr\left\{\frac{1}{T} \ln \bar{L}(y \mid X,\hat{\gamma}) = \frac{1}{T} \ln \bar{L}(y \mid X,\gamma_0)\right\} \geq 1 - \delta.$$

Thus we conclude

$$\text{(18g)} \quad p \lim_{T \to \infty} \hat{\gamma} = \gamma_0 \qquad \text{q.e.d.}$$

Lemma 4: The estimators described in

Lemma 2 are asymptotically normally distributed with mean γ_0 and covariance matrix

$$(19) \quad -M^{-1}(\gamma_0) = -\left[E\left(\frac{\partial^2 L}{\partial\gamma\partial\gamma}\right)\right]^{-1}.$$

Proof: By Lemma 2 the estimator $\hat{\gamma}$ is that root of

$$(19a) \qquad \frac{\partial \ln \bar{L}(\gamma \mid X,y)}{\partial\gamma} = 0$$

which globally maximizes the likelihood function. Denote in $\bar{L}(\gamma \mid X,y)$ by $L(\gamma \mid X,y)$ and expand $\partial L/\partial\gamma$ by Taylor's series about $\gamma = \gamma_0$.

We obtain

$$(19b) \quad \left.\frac{\partial L}{\partial\gamma}\right|_{\gamma} = \left.\frac{\partial L}{\partial\gamma}\right|_{\gamma_0} + \left[\frac{\partial^2 L}{\partial\gamma\partial\gamma}\right]_{\gamma*}(\gamma - \gamma_0)$$

where the notation $(\partial L/\partial\gamma)\,|_{\gamma_0}$, e.g., means the derivative (gradient) evaluated at the point $\gamma = \gamma_0$. $[\partial^2 L/\partial\gamma\partial\gamma]$ is the Hessian of the likelihood function with respect to the parameters, and γ^* is a vector lying between γ and γ_0.

In particular, for $\gamma = \hat{\gamma}$ (19b) becomes

$$(19c) \quad \left.\frac{\partial L}{\partial\gamma}\right|_{\gamma_0} = -\left[\frac{\partial^2 L}{\partial\gamma\partial\gamma}\right]_{\gamma*}(\hat{\gamma} - \gamma_0)$$

where now γ^* lies between $\hat{\gamma}$ and γ_0 and $\gamma^*, \hat{\gamma}, \gamma_0 \in \Omega$.

Consider now any element of the matrix in (19c) or (19b); employing the transformation in (6a) we may write it as

$$(19d) \quad \frac{1}{T}\frac{\partial^2 L}{\partial\gamma_i\partial\gamma_j} = \frac{\partial^2}{\partial\gamma_i\partial\gamma_j}\frac{1}{T}\sum_{t=1}^{T} f(w_t \mid q_t,\beta,\sigma^2)$$

where the w_t are independent identically distributed random variables—conditionally on the X's; moreover, in this case the operations of differentiation and plim commute, and thus by the strong law of large numbers we conclude that with probability one the right hand side of (19d) converges to its expected value and hence that

$$(19e) \quad \underset{T\to\infty}{p\lim}\left[\frac{\partial^2 L}{\partial\gamma\partial\gamma}\right] = M(\gamma) = E\left[\frac{\partial^2 L}{\partial\gamma\partial\gamma}\right].$$

The matrix M is of course by assumption positive definite. Thus, there exists a nonsingular matrix $R(\gamma)$ such that

$$(19f) \qquad M(\gamma) = R'(\gamma)R(\gamma).$$

Now premultiply both sides of (19c) by $R(\gamma_0)M^{-1}(\gamma_0)$ to obtain

$$(19g) \quad R'^{-1}(\gamma_0)\left.\frac{\partial L}{\partial\gamma}\right|_{\gamma_0} = -R(\gamma_0)\cdot M^{-1}(\gamma_0)\left[\frac{\partial^2 L}{\partial\gamma\partial\gamma}\right]_{\gamma*}(\hat{\gamma} - \gamma_0).$$

Consider the left hand side first. Note that since the range of the error terms in (1a) and hence (1) is independent of the parameters it follows that

$$(19h) \qquad E\left[\frac{\partial L}{\partial\gamma}\right] = 0.$$

In particular, employing the transformation (6a) we conclude that $\partial L/\partial\gamma$ is the sum of independent identically distributed random variables (again conditionally on the X's) with mean zero. Moreover, we have the identity

$$(19i) \quad E\left(\frac{\partial L}{\partial\gamma}, \frac{\partial L}{\partial\gamma}\right) = \operatorname{cov}\left(\frac{\partial L}{\partial\gamma}\right) = -E\left[\frac{\partial^2 L}{\partial\gamma\partial\gamma}\right] = -M(\gamma)$$

where the notation $((\partial L/\partial\gamma), (\partial L/\partial\gamma))$ indicates the scalar product of two vectors. In view of (19f) and the multivariate central limit theorem we conclude that the left hand side of (19g) is asymptotically normal with mean zero and unit covariance matrix.

On the other hand since $\hat{\gamma}$ is consistent for γ_0 by Lemma 3 and γ^* lies between $\hat{\gamma}$ and γ_0 we conclude that

$$(19j) \quad \underset{T\to\infty}{p\lim}\, M^{-1}(\gamma_0)\left[\frac{\partial^2 L}{\partial\gamma\partial\gamma}\right]_{\gamma} = I$$

where I is the identity matrix.

Thus we conclude that $\hat{\gamma}$ is asymptotically normal with mean γ_0 and covariance matrix $-M^{-1}(\gamma_0)$. q.e.d.

The following Lemma states a result originally stated by Geary [3] and intimated by Wilks and Daly [17]. Its proof is given here for the sake of completeness. As will be obvious, the assumption of normality of the error terms in (1) and (1a) is not necessary in the present context.

Lemma 5: Within the class of consistent (and asymptotically unbiased) estimators the estimators described in Lemma 2 are asymptotically efficient in the sense of minimizing the generalized variance.

Proof: Let $\hat{\delta}$ be another set of estimators which are consistent (and asymptotically unbiased). Therefore we have, asymptotically

$$(20) \qquad \int \hat{\delta}_i \bar{L}(y \mid X,\gamma)\, dy = \gamma_i \, .$$

Differentiating with respect to γ_j we have

$$(20a) \qquad \int \hat{\delta}_i \frac{\partial \ln \bar{L}}{\partial \gamma_j} \bar{L}\, dy = \begin{matrix} 0 & \text{if} & i \neq j \\ 1 & \text{if} & i = j \end{matrix} .$$

Employing the notation $\ln \bar{L} = L$ and in view of (19h) we have

$$(20b) \qquad E\left(\hat{\delta}, \frac{\partial L}{\partial \gamma}\right) = I.$$

Note that asymptotically (20b) represents the "cross-covariance" matrix of the vectors $\hat{\delta}$ and $\partial L/\partial \gamma$. Now from (19i) the covariance matrix of $\partial L/\partial \gamma$ is the inverse of the asymptotic covariance matrix of $\hat{\gamma}$. Denoting by N the asymptotic covariance matrix of $\hat{\delta}$ we have

$$(20c) \qquad \mathrm{Cov}\begin{pmatrix} \hat{\delta} \\ \dfrac{\partial L}{\partial \gamma} \end{pmatrix} = \begin{bmatrix} N & I \\ I & -M \end{bmatrix}.$$

Since the matrix in (20c) is at least positive semi-definite, we have from the theory of compound matrices [12]

$$(20d) \qquad |N|\,|-M| \geq 1.$$

Hence that

$$(20e) \qquad |N| \geq | >M^{-1} | \qquad \text{q.e.d.}$$

We have therefore proved the

Theorem: Let the model be specified by (1) and (1a); then the estimators described in Lemma 2 are consistent, asymptotically normal, unbiased and efficient.

IV. CONCLUSION

Although the discussion in section 2 relied mainly on the model with autocorrelated disturbances the same procedures with minor modifications would apply to the infinite lag model as well. The chief results of the paper are that the properties of maximum likelihood estimation in the context of the classical general linear model, are equally applicable in the context of the non-linear models here examined. It should be remarked that the assumption of normality was crucial for Lemmas 3 and 4, of some import in Lemma 2, and of no import in Lemma 5.

REFERENCES

1. Cochrane, D. and Orcutt, G. H., "Application of Least Squares Regression to Relationships Containing Auto-correlated Error Terms," *Journal of the American Statistical Assocation*, Vol. 44, 1949, p. 32.
2. Durbin, J., "Estimation of Parameters in Time Series Regression Models," *Journal of the Royal Statistical Society*, Series B, Vol. 22, 1960, p. 139.
3. Geary, R. C., "The Estimation of Many Parameters," *Journal of the Royal Statistical Society*, (A), Vol. 105, p. 213, 1942.
4. Hannan, E. J., "The Estimation of Relationships Involving Distributed Lags," *Econometrica*, Vol. 33, p. 206, 1965.
5. Hildreth, C. and Lu, J. Y., *Demand Relations with Auto-correlated Disturbances*, Michigan State University, Agricultural Experimental Station, Technical Bulletin 276, 1960.
6. Huzurbazar, V. S., "The Likelihood Equation, Consistency and the Maxima of the Likelihood Function," *Annals of Eugenics*, Vol. 14, p. 185, 1947–49.
7. Kendall, M. G. and A. Stuart, *The Advanced Theory of Statistics*, Vol. 2, Charles Griffin & Col. Ltd., London, 1961.
8. Klein, L. R., "The Estimation of Distributed Lags," *Econometrica*, Vol. 26, p. 553, 1958.
9. Koopmans, T. and W. Hood, W. and T. Koopmans (eds.), *Studies in Econometric Method*, (New York: John Wiley and Sons, 1953).
10. Koyck, L. M., *Distributed Lags and Investment*

Analysis (Amsterdam: North Holland Press, 1954).

11. Leviatan, N., "Consistent Estimation of Distributed Lags," *International Economic Review*, Vol. 4, p. 44, 1963.
12. MacDuffee, C. C., *The Theory of Matrices*, Ergebnisse Series, Vol. II. No. 5 (Berlin: Julius Springer, 1933), p. 87.
13. Rao, C. R., *Advanced Statistical Methods in Biometric Research* (London: John Wiley and Sons, 1952).
14. Rao, C. R., "Minimum Variance and the Estimation of Several Parameters," *Proceedings of the Cambridge Philosophical Society*, Vol. 43, p. 280, 1947.
15. Sargan, D. J. in Hart, P. E., et al. (eds.) *Econometric Analysis for National Economic Planning* (London: Butterworths, 1964).
16. Taylor, L. D. and Wilson, T. "Three Pass Least Squares: A Method for Estimating Models with a Lagged Dependent Variable," *Review of Economics and Statistics*, Vol. XLVI, 1964.
17. Wilks, S. S., and J. F. Daly, "An Optimum Property of Confidence Regions Associated with the Likelihood Functions," *Annals of Mathematical Statistics*, Vol. 10, p. 225, 1939.
18. Wald, A., "Note on the Consistency of the Maximum Likelihood Estimate," *Annals of Mathematical Statistics*, Vol. 20, p. 595, 1949.

[17]

ON THE GAME OF MAXIMIZING $\bar{R}^2$*

PHOEBUS J. DHRYMES

University of Pennsylvania

I. Introduction

Practising econometricians often behave as if their objective is to produce an estimated regression equation exhibiting "maximum" $\bar{R}^2$.

Whereas Theil [2, p. 212ff] has shown that if we consider two alternative specifications, one true and the other false, then the true specification will produce a sum of squared residuals having smaller expected value—and smaller probability limit as well—than the corresponding quantity from the false specification, we typically *do not know in practice that of two alternative specifications one is indeed true*. Both may well be false.

Still, disregarding this, many econometricians operate with the rule of thumb that variables should be added or switched, in a regression context, so long as the coefficient of determination adjusted for degrees of freedom—$\bar{R}^2$—is increased thereby.

This entails adding or retaining variables to the extent that their associated t-ratio exceeds unity.[1]

Here we shall demonstrate the validity of this assertion in a rather simple and straightforward fashion and point out certain unfortunate consequences of the rule of thumb alluded to above.

II. Relations Between Conditional Variances, Covariances, and Correlation Coefficients

In the following discussion we shall have occasion to use repeatedly a well known property of determinants of partitioned matrices, cited below without proof.

Lemma: Let

(1) $E = \begin{bmatrix} A & B \\ C & D \end{bmatrix}$

where A is $k \times k$, D is $m \times m$, B is $k \times m$, and C is $m \times k$

* Financial support under NSF grant GS 2289 at the University of Pennsylvania is gratefully acknowledged.

[1] H. Houthakker was the first person to point out this fact to me sometime back. Thus, the main result of this note is known. The simple proof, however, appears to be quite novel.

If D is nonsingular, then

(1a) $|E| = |A - B D^{-1}C||D|$.

If A is nonsingular, then

(1b) $|E| = |D - C A^{-1}B||A|$.

Now let z be an m-element random vector distributed as

(2) $z \sim N(0, \Sigma)$.

We assume the distribution to be nondegenerate, so that Σ is positive definite.

We recall that if we partition z by

(3) $z = \begin{bmatrix} z^{\mathrm{I}} \\ z^{\mathrm{II}} \end{bmatrix}$

so that z^{I} contains k elements, and if we partition Σ conformally by

(3a) $\Sigma = \begin{bmatrix} \Sigma_{\mathrm{I}} & \Sigma_{\mathrm{I,II}} \\ \Sigma_{\mathrm{II,I}} & \Sigma_{\mathrm{II}} \end{bmatrix}$

then the conditional distribution of z^{I} given z^{II} has covariance matrix

(4) $\Sigma_{\mathrm{I,II}} = \Sigma_{\mathrm{I}} - \Sigma_{\mathrm{I,II}}\Sigma_{\mathrm{II}}^{-1}\Sigma_{\mathrm{II,I}}$

We also recall the convention that if $z_i\, z_j \varepsilon z^{\mathrm{I}}$, then their conditional covariance given z^{II} is denoted by $\sigma_{ij\cdot k+1, k+2, \ldots m}$. Their *conditional correlation* given z^{II} is the *correlation coefficient as obtained from the conditional distribution* and is denoted by $\rho_{ij\cdot k+1, \ldots m}$. Such a conditional correlation is said to be a *partial correlation coefficient of order m−k*. Note that the *order* of the correlation coefficient depends on the number of the variables "held constant" and whose numbers appear as secondary subscripts in the notation $\rho_{ij\cdot k+1, k+2, \ldots m}$. It is interesting that the conditional variance of order $k-1$, can be expressed as a product of the unconditional variance and certain simple functions of partial correlation coefficient of various orders.

Let us now see how this may be accomplished. Consider the conditional variance of z_1, given $z_2, z_3, \ldots z_m$. From (4) we see that this is simply

(5) $\sigma_{11\cdot 2,3,\ldots m} = \sigma_{11} - \sigma_{1\cdot} \sum_{22}^{-1} \sigma_{\cdot 1}$

where

(5a) $\sigma_{1\cdot} = (\sigma_{12}, \sigma_{13}, \ldots \sigma_{1m})$, $\sigma_{\cdot 1} = \sigma_{1\cdot}'$.

and the notation $\sum_{ii}$ will always refer to the principal submatrix of $\sum$ containing its $i, i+1, i+2, \ldots m$ columns and corresponding rows.

Now, applying (1a) to $\sum$ partitioned as

(6) $\sum = \begin{bmatrix} \sigma_{11} & \sigma_{1\cdot} \\ \sigma_{1\cdot} & \sum_{22} \end{bmatrix}$

we find

(6a) $|\sum| = (\sigma_{11} - \sigma_{1\cdot} \sum_{22}^{-1} \sigma_{\cdot 1}) | \sum_{22} |$.

Thus we have

(7) $\sigma_{11\cdot 2,3,\ldots m} = \dfrac{|\Sigma|}{|\Sigma_{22}|}$

Consider now the partition

$$(8)\ \Sigma = \left[\begin{array}{cc|ccc} \sigma_{11} & \sigma_{12} & \sigma_{13} & \sigma_{14} & \sigma_{1m} \\ \sigma_{21} & \sigma_{22} & \sigma_{23} & \sigma_{24} & \sigma_{1m} \\ \hline \sigma_{31} & \sigma_{32} & \Sigma_{33} & & \\ \sigma_{41} & \sigma_{42} & & & \\ \sigma_{m1} & \sigma_{m2} & & & \end{array}\right]$$

Applying (1a), again, we find

$$(8a)\ |\Sigma| = \left|\begin{pmatrix} \sigma_{11} & \sigma_{12} \\ \sigma_{21} & \sigma_{22} \end{pmatrix} - \begin{pmatrix} \sigma_{13} & \sigma_{14}\ldots\sigma_{1m} \\ \sigma_{23} & \sigma_{24}\ldots\sigma_{2m} \end{pmatrix} \Sigma_{33}^{-1} \begin{pmatrix} \sigma_{31} & \sigma_{32} \\ \sigma_{41} & \sigma_{42} \\ \vdots & \vdots \\ \sigma_{m1} & \sigma_{m2} \end{pmatrix}\right| |\Sigma_{33}|$$

But the first term in the right member of (8a) represents the *determinant* of the covariance matrix in the conditional distribution of z_1, z_2 *given* $z_3, z_4, \ldots z_m$. Thus, we have

$$(8b)\ \begin{vmatrix} \sigma_{11\cdot 3,\ldots m} & \sigma_{12\cdot 3,\ldots m} \\ \sigma_{21\cdot 3,\ldots m} & \sigma_{22\cdot 3,\ldots m} \end{vmatrix} = (\sigma_{11\cdot 3,\ldots m}\ \sigma_{22\cdot 3,\ldots m})\,(1-\rho^2_{12\cdot 3,\ldots m}).$$

Similarly, partition

$$(9)\ \Sigma_{22} = \left[\begin{array}{c|c} \sigma_{22} & \sigma_{23}\ldots\sigma_{2m} \\ \hline \sigma_{32} & \\ \sigma_{m2} & \Sigma_{33} \end{array}\right]$$

Apply (1a) and thus obtain

$$(9a)\ |\Sigma_{22}| = \left[\sigma_{22} - (\sigma_{23}, \sigma_{24}, \ldots \sigma_{2m})\ \Sigma_{33}^{-1} \begin{pmatrix} \sigma_{32} \\ \sigma_{42} \\ \sigma_{m2} \end{pmatrix}\right] |\Sigma_{33}| =$$

$$= \sigma_{22\cdot 3,4,\ldots m}\,|\Sigma|$$

Thus we see, in view of (8a) and (9a)

$$(10)\ \sigma_{11\cdot 2,3,\ldots m} = \frac{|\Sigma|}{|\Sigma_{22}|} = \sigma_{11\cdot 3,4,\ldots m}, (1-\rho^2_{12\cdot 3,4,\ldots m}).$$

Consider

$$(11)\ \Sigma^* = \left[\begin{array}{c|ccc} \sigma_{11} & \sigma_{13} & \sigma_{14} & \sigma_{1m} \\ \hline \sigma_{31} & & & \\ \sigma_{41} & \Sigma_{33} & & \\ \sigma_{m1} & & & \end{array}\right]$$

and notice that by (1a) we have

$$(11a)\ |\Sigma^*| = \left[\sigma_{11} - (\sigma_{13}\sigma_{14}\ldots\sigma_{1m})\ \Sigma_{33}^{-1} \begin{pmatrix} \sigma_{31} \\ \sigma_{41} \\ \sigma_{m1} \end{pmatrix}\right] |\Sigma_{33}|$$

so that

$$(11b)\ \sigma_{11\cdot 3,4,\ldots m} = \frac{|\Sigma^*|}{|\Sigma_{33}|}$$

Partition now

$$(12)\ \sum{}^{*} = \left[\begin{array}{cc|c} \sigma_{11} & \sigma_{13} & \sigma_{14} \dots \sigma_{1m} \\ \sigma_{31} & \sigma_{33} & \sigma_{34} \dots \sigma_{3m} \\ \hline \sigma_{41} & \sigma_{43} & \\ \vdots & \vdots & \Sigma_{44} \\ \sigma_{m1} & \sigma_{m3} & \end{array}\right]$$

and apply (1a) to obtain

$$(12a)\ |\Sigma^{*}| = \left| \begin{pmatrix} \sigma_{11} & \sigma_{13} \\ \sigma_{31} & \sigma_{33} \end{pmatrix} - \begin{pmatrix} \sigma_{14} & \sigma_{15} \dots \sigma_{1m} \\ \sigma_{34} & \sigma_{35} \quad \sigma_{3m} \end{pmatrix} \sum\nolimits_{44}^{-1} \begin{pmatrix} \sigma_{41} & \sigma_{43} \\ \sigma_{51} & \sigma_{53} \\ \vdots & \vdots \\ \sigma_{m1} & \sigma_{m3} \end{pmatrix} \right| \left| \sum\nolimits_{44} \right|$$

But the first term in the right member of (12a) is the determinant of the co-variance matrix of the *conditional* distribution of z_1, z_3, *given* $z_4, z_5, \dots z_m$. Thus, we have

$$(13) \begin{vmatrix} \sigma_{11\cdot 4,5,\dots m} & \sigma_{13\cdot 4,5,\dots m} \\ \sigma_{31\cdot 4,5,\dots m} & \sigma_{33\cdot 4,5,\dots m} \end{vmatrix} = (\sigma_{11\cdot 4,5,\dots m}\ \sigma_{33\cdot 4,5,\dots m}) \cdot (1-\rho^2_{13\cdot 4,5,\dots m})$$

Similarly partition Σ_{33} by

$$(13a)\ \sum\nolimits_{33} = \left[\begin{array}{c|c} \sigma_{33} & \sigma_{34} \ \ \sigma_{3m} \\ \hline \sigma_{43} & \\ \vdots & \Sigma_{44} \\ \sigma_{m3} & \end{array}\right]$$

and apply (1a) to obtain

$$(14)\ |\Sigma_{33}| = \left[\sigma_{33} - (\sigma_{34}\ \sigma_{35}, \dots \sigma_{3m}) \sum\nolimits_{44}^{-1} \begin{pmatrix} \sigma_{43} \\ \sigma_{53} \\ \vdots \\ \sigma_{m3} \end{pmatrix} \right] |\Sigma_{44}|$$

In view of (12a), (13), and (14) we see that (11b) implies

$$(15)\ \sigma_{11\cdot 3,\dots m} = \sigma_{11\cdot 4,\dots m}(1-\rho^2_{13\cdot 4,\dots m})$$

Continuing in this fashion we easily establish

$$(16)\ \sigma_{11\cdot 2,\dots m} = \sigma_{11}(1-\rho^2_{12\cdot 3,\dots m})(1-\rho^2_{13\cdot 4,\dots m})(1-\rho^2_{14\cdot 5,\dots m}) \cdot \\ \cdot (1-\rho^2_{1m-1\cdot m})(1-\rho^2_{1m}).$$

Thus (16) expresses the ratio of the conditional variance of z_1, given $z_2, \dots z_m$, to its unconditional variance as a simple function of partial correlation coefficients, of various orders, of z_1 and z_i, $i = 2,3, \dots m$.

Now, since the numbering of variables is quite arbitrary let us transform their indices so that $m \to 2$, $(m-1) \to 3$, $\dots$ $2 \to m$ and write (16) in the more convenient form.

$$(17)\ \frac{\sigma_{11\cdot 2,\dots m}}{\sigma_{11}} = (1-\rho^2_{12})(1-\rho^2_{13\cdot 2})(1-\rho^2_{14\cdot 23})(1-\rho^2_{15\cdot 234})\dots(1-\rho^2_{1m\cdot 23,\dots m-1}).$$

III. Application to Ordinary Least Squares (OLS) Estimation

Consider the case where one is interested in estimating the parameters of a general linear model. One has at one's disposal, say, T observations on the dependent variable y, and on k explanatory variables x_i, $i=1,2, \ldots k$. Suppose, for convenience, all variables are measured as deviations from their respective sample means. Thus we have the data matrix

(18) $X^* = (y, x_{\cdot 1}, x_{\cdot 2}, \ldots x_{\cdot k})$

where, of course

(18a) $y = (y_1, y_2, \ldots y_T)'$, $x_{\cdot i} = (x_{1i}, x_{2i}, \ldots x_{Ti})'$, $i = 1,2, \ldots k$.

Now the matrix

(19) $\hat{\Sigma} = \dfrac{X^{*\prime} X^*}{T}$

is the *sample* covariance matrix of the $k+1$ variables under consideration. All operations carried out in the previous section can be carried out here as well. If the $k+1$ variables $(y, x_1, x_2, \ldots x_k)$ *are jointly normally distributed* then the sample analogues of conditional variances, covariances, and partial correlation coefficients may be regarded as consistent estimators of the corresponding parameters.[2]

If a vector of k regression coefficients is estimated by OLS then we have

(20) $\hat{\beta} = (X'X)^{-1}X'y, \; X = (x_{\cdot 1}, x_{\cdot 2}, \ldots x_k)$.

Obtaining the vector of residuals

(20a) $\hat{u} = y - X\hat{\beta}$

we notice that

(20b) $\dfrac{\hat{u}'\hat{u}}{T} = \sigma_{yy\cdot 1,2,\ldots k}$

This is so since applying (1a) to $\hat{\Sigma}$ partitioned as

(21) $\hat{\Sigma} = \dfrac{1}{T}\begin{bmatrix} y'y & y'X \\ X'y & X'X \end{bmatrix}$

yields

(21a) $|\hat{\Sigma}| = \dfrac{1}{T}(y'y - y'X(X'X)^{-1}X'y)\left|\dfrac{X'X}{T}\right|$

Thus we have, from (20a), (20b), (21), and (21a)

(22) $\hat{\sigma}_{yy\cdot 1,2,\ldots k} = \dfrac{|\hat{\Sigma}|}{|X'X/T|}$

This is, of course, perfectly analogous to (7) and applying the sequence of arguments in the preceding section we conclude

[2] The distribution proviso is inserted because the covariance matrix of various conditional distributions would not necessarily have the form employed in the previous section unless the basic joint distribution is normal.

$$(23)\ \frac{\hat{\sigma}_{yy\cdot 1,2,\ldots k}}{\hat{\sigma}_{yy}} = (1-r^2_{y1})(1-r^2_{y2\cdot 1})(1-r^2_{y3\cdot 12})(1-r^2_{y4\cdot 123})\ldots(1-r^2_{yk\cdot 123,\ldots k-1}).$$

where the quantities $r^2_{yi\cdot 12,\ldots i-1}$ are the sample analogues of the partial correlation coefficients of order $i-1$, dealt with in the previous section.

But notice that

$$(23\text{a})\ \frac{\hat{\sigma}_{yy\cdot 1,2,\ldots k}}{\hat{\sigma}_{yy}} = \frac{\hat{u}'\hat{u}/T}{y'y/T} = \frac{\hat{u}'\hat{u}}{y'y} = (1-R^2_k)$$

i.e., it is one minus the (unadjusted) coefficient of determination when the dependent variable is *regressed on all k explanatory variables.* The representation in (23) is, thus, very convenient[3] since we can obviously write

$$(24)\ (1-R^2_k) = (1-R^2_{k-1})(1-r^2_{yk\cdot 12,\ldots k-1}).$$

Now $\bar{R}^2$ is related to R^2 by

$$(25)\ (1-R^2_k) = (1-\bar{R}^2_k)\frac{T-k-1}{T-1}$$

Thus, the relation in (24) implies, in view of (25)

$$(26)\ \frac{(1-\bar{R}^2_k)}{(1-\bar{R}^2_{k-1})} = \frac{T-k}{T-k-1}(1-r^2_{yk\cdot 12,\ldots k-1})$$

For the introduction of the kth explanatory variable to increase the adjusted coefficient we require that the left member of (26) be less than unity.

The question we must now answer is this: What must be the value of the t-ratio associated with $\hat{\beta}_k$ in order for this to eventuate? Thus, we need a relationship between this t-ratio and $r^2_{yk\cdot 123,\ldots k-1}$.

Now partition $\hat{\beta}$ and X of (20) by

$$(27)\ \hat{\beta} = \begin{pmatrix} \hat{\beta}^1 \\ \hat{\beta}_k \end{pmatrix} \qquad X = (X_1, x_{\cdot k})$$

and notice that we have the following relations

$$(28)\ \begin{aligned} X_1'X_1\hat{\beta}^1 + X_1'x_{\cdot k}\hat{\beta}_k &= X_1'y \\ x_{\cdot k}'X_1\hat{\beta}^1 + x_{\cdot k}'x_{\cdot k}\hat{\beta}_k &= x_{\cdot k}'y \end{aligned}$$

From (28) we easily obtain $\hat{\beta}_k$ as[4]

$$(28\text{a})\ \hat{\beta}_k = \frac{\hat{\sigma}_{yk\cdot 1,2,\ldots k-1}}{\hat{\sigma}_{kk\cdot 1,2,\ldots k-1}}$$

[3] This is essentially the reason why the representation in (17) was obtained in lieu of that in (16).

[4] To see this, solve the first equation for $\hat{\beta}^1$ and substitute in the second to obtain

$$\hat{\beta}_k(x_{\cdot k}'x_{\cdot k} - x_{\cdot k}'X_1(X_1'X_1)^{-1}X_1'x_{\cdot k}) = x_{\cdot k}'y - x_{\cdot k}'X_1(X_1'X_1)^{-1}X_1'y.$$

Now the t-ratio for $\hat{\beta}_k$ is defined as

$$(29)\quad t_{(k)} = \frac{\hat{\beta}_k}{\sqrt{\left(\frac{\hat{u}'\hat{u}}{T-k-1}\right) q_{kk}}}$$

where q_{kk} is the kth diagonal element of $(X'X)^{-1}$.

Partitioning X by

$$(30)\quad X = (X_1, x_{\cdot k})$$

and applying (1b) to $|X'X|$ we see that

$$(31)\quad |X'X| = (x'_{\cdot k}x_{\cdot k} - x'_{\cdot k}X_1(X'_1X_1)^{-1}X'_1x_{\cdot k})\,|X'_1X_1|$$

Since

$$(31a)\quad q_{kk} = \frac{|X'_1X_1|}{|X'X|}$$

we conclude that

$$(32)\quad q_{kk} = \frac{1}{T\hat{\sigma}_{kk\cdot 12,\ldots k-1}}$$

Thus, the denominator of (29) yields

$$(32a)\quad \frac{1}{T-k-1}\;\frac{\hat{u}'\hat{u}}{T}\;\frac{1}{\hat{\sigma}_{kk\cdot 12,\ldots k-1}} = \frac{1}{T-k-1}\;\frac{\hat{\sigma}_{yy\cdot 12,\ldots k}}{\hat{\sigma}_{kk\cdot 12,\ldots k-1}}$$

therefore

$$(33)\quad t^2_{(k)} = \frac{(T-k-1)\;(\hat{\sigma}^2_{yk\cdot 12,\ldots k-1})}{(\hat{\sigma}_{kk\cdot 12,\ldots k-1})\,(\hat{\sigma}_{yy\cdot 12,\ldots k})}$$

$$(34)\quad T\hat{\sigma}_{yy\cdot 12,\ldots k} = \frac{|X^{*\prime}X^{*}|}{|X'X|} = \frac{\begin{vmatrix} y'y & y'X_1 & y'x_{\cdot k} \\ X'_1y & X'_1X_1 & X'_1x_{\cdot k} \\ x_{\cdot k}y & x'_{\cdot k}X_1 & x'_{\cdot k}x_{\cdot k} \end{vmatrix}}{|X'X|} =$$

$$= \frac{\left|\begin{array}{cc|c} y'y & y'x_{\cdot k} & y'X_1 \\ x'_{\cdot k}y & x'_{\cdot k}x_{\cdot k} & x'_{\cdot k}X_1 \\ \hline X'_1y & X'_1x_{\cdot k} & X'_1X_1 \end{array}\right|}{|X'X|}$$

The last equality follows from the fact that permuting a number of rows and their corresponding columns leaves the determinant of the matrix unchanged.

Applying (1b) to the (partitioned form of the) last member of (34) we conclude

$$(35)\quad T\hat{\sigma}_{yy\cdot 12,\ldots k} = (T^2\hat{\sigma}_{yy\cdot 12,\ldots k-1}\hat{\sigma}_{kk\cdot 12,\ldots k-1} - T^2\hat{\sigma}^2_{yk\cdot 12,\ldots k-1})\;\frac{|X_1X'_1|}{|X'X|}$$

But in view of (31a) and (32) we conclude

$$(36) \quad \hat{\sigma}_{yy\cdot 12,\ldots k} = \hat{\sigma}_{yy\cdot 12,\ldots k-1} - \frac{\hat{\sigma}^2_{yk\cdot 12,\ldots k-1}}{\hat{\sigma}_{kk\cdot 12,\ldots k-1}}$$

Thus

$$(37) \quad t^2_{(k)} = \frac{(T-k-1) \quad \hat{\sigma}^2_{yk\cdot 12,\ldots k-1}}{(\hat{\sigma}_{kk\cdot 12,\ldots k-1} \; \hat{\sigma}_{yy\cdot 12,\ldots k-1} \quad - \; \hat{\sigma}^2_{yk\cdot 12,\ldots k-1})} =$$

$$= \frac{(T-k-1) \quad r^2_{yk\cdot 12,\ldots k-1}}{(1-r^2_{yk\cdot 12,\ldots k-1})}$$

which establishes the desired relation between the t-ratio and the pertinent partial correlation coefficient.
In particular, (37) implies that

$$(37a) \; (1-r^2_{yk\cdot 12,\ldots k-1}) = \frac{T-k-1}{(T-k-1)+t^2_{(k)}}$$

Substituting in (26) we find

$$(38) \quad \frac{(1-\bar{R}^2_k)}{(1-\bar{R}^2_{k-1})} = \frac{T-k}{(T-k-1)+t^2_{(k)}}$$

For the coefficient of determination to increase when the kth variable is introduced we require that

$$(39) \quad \frac{T-k}{(T-k-1)+t^2_{(k)}} < 1$$

which implies

$$(40) \quad t^2{}_{(k)} > 1$$

The argument above establishes that the (adjusted) coefficient of determination will be maximized if variables having t-ratio in excess of one are retained and those having t-ratio less than one are dropped. Now, what are the implications of this procedure from the point of view of accepting false hypotheses?

In the standard context the procedure entails that we accept the hypothesis $\beta_k \neq 0$ if the t-ratio above is greater than unity. Now if x is t-distributed with r degrees of freedom then

$$(41) \quad x^2 \sim F_{1,r}$$

Thus, the criterion (40) implies that we accept the hypothesis

$$(42) \quad \beta_k \neq 0$$

whenever a certain F-distributed variable with 1 and $T-k-1$ degrees of freedom assumes a value exceeding unity.
Now, if

$$(42a) \quad \beta_k = 0$$

is, in fact, true then $t^2{}_{(k)}$ is distributed as a central $F_{1,T-k-1}$ variable. The probability that this variable exceeds unity is quite large. Unfortunately, tables of the upper α points of the F. distribution do not exist for $\alpha > \cdot 25$. One, however, can use the following relation

(43) $Pr\{F_{1,r} > c^2_a\} = Pr\{|t_r| > c_a\} = \alpha$

and thus obtain the same information from tables of the t-distribution.

We give below the pertinent critical points for $\alpha = \cdot 30$

TABLE I

$Pr\{\ |t_r|\ > c\} = \cdot 30$

r	10	12	15	17	20	22	25	27	30
c	1·093	1·083	1·074	1·069	1·064	1·061	1·058	1·057	1·055

As is apparent from the table the probability of rejecting the true hypothesis in (42a) is rather high, perhaps ·35 for sample sizes typically dealt with in empirical research. Thus, if the procedure examined here is followed routinely we should be led to accept false hypotheses of the type in (42) inordinately often. Hence, we shall be led to the use of irrelevant and erroneous information altogether too frequently.

If we are interested in prediction this procedure may well lead us to commit unnecessarily large errors of prediction. This is clearly undesirable and unless maximizing $\bar{R}^2$ is a desirable end in itself the procedure outlined in this note is an inadmissible one and should not be employed in serious work.

REFERENCES

1 Kendall, M. G. and A. Stuart, *The Advanced Theory of Statistics*, Volume 2 (Third Edition), (New York: Hafner Publishing Company, 1960).

2 Theil, H., *Economic Forecasts and Policy* (Second Revised Edition), (Amsterdam: North Holland Publishing Company, 1965).

[18]

EQUIVALENCE OF ITERATIVE AITKEN AND MAXIMUM LIKELIHOOD ESTIMATORS FOR A SYSTEM OF REGRESSION EQUATIONS

PHOEBUS J. DHRYMES

University of Pennsylvania and Monash University

I. Introduction and Notation

Consider the system of regression equations

$$y_{\cdot i} = X\bar{\pi}_{\cdot i} + u_{\cdot i} \qquad i = 1, 2, \ldots, m. \tag{1}$$

The columns of X, denoted by $x_{\cdot j}$, $j = 1, 2, \ldots, G$ contain the T observations on the explanatory variables x_j, $j = 1, 2, \ldots, G$, it being understood that the system contains G exogenous variables in all. Similarly, $y_{\cdot i}$, $u_{\cdot i}$ are T element column vectors incorporating the observations on the ith dependent variable and the errors associated with the ith equation.

Let

$$U = (u_{\cdot 1}, u_{\cdot 2}, \ldots, u_{\cdot m}) \tag{2}$$

and let $u_{t\cdot}$ be the tth row of U. Suppose that the $u_{t\cdot}$ are mutually independent and distributed as

$$u'_{t\cdot} \sim N(0, \Sigma) \qquad t = 1, 2, \ldots, T. \tag{3}$$

In (1) we would generally know that some elements of $\bar{\pi}_{\cdot i}$ are zero so that not all explanatory variables necessarily enter all equations. In general we shall suppose that the ith equation contains $G_i \leqslant G$ explanatory variables. The vector $\bar{\pi}_{\cdot i}$ contains a number of zeros reflecting these *a priori* restrictions. In fact, taking explicit account of the restrictions we may write

$$X\bar{\pi}_{\cdot i} = X_i \pi_{\cdot i} \tag{4}$$

where now X_i has G_i columns and $\pi_{\cdot i}$ is the subvector of $\bar{\pi}_{\cdot i}$ resulting when zeros are suppressed.

The problem of whether or not iterative Aitken and maximum likelihood estimators coincide is discussed in Kmenta and Gilbert [3]; it is hinted that they do, but no proof is provided. A sketch of a proof, however, based on a computational argument is given in Ruble [4]. In this note we shall show that they coincide provided we begin both procedures in a natural way. We shall also sketch a proof of the coincidence of their asymptotic distribution.

II. Formulation and Inference

In iterative Aitken estimation we proceed by minimizing with respect to π^*

$$S = (y - X^*\pi^*)' (\Sigma^{-1} \otimes I)(y - X^*\pi^*) \tag{5}$$

where

$$y = \begin{bmatrix} y_{\cdot 1} \\ y_{\cdot 2} \\ \vdots \\ y_{\cdot m} \end{bmatrix}, \ X^* = \operatorname{diag}(X_1, X_2, \ldots, X_m), \ \pi^* = \begin{bmatrix} \pi_{\cdot 1} \\ \pi_{\cdot 2} \\ \vdots \\ \pi_{\cdot m} \end{bmatrix}. \tag{6}$$

The result of minimizing (5) is

$$\hat{\pi}^* = (X^{*\prime} \Phi^{-1} X^*)^{-1} X^{*\prime} \Phi^{-1} y \tag{7}$$

where

$$\Phi = \Sigma \otimes I. \tag{8}$$

The quantity in (7), however, is not an estimator since it depends on the unknown parameter Σ.

A natural way of proceeding is to estimate π^* by ordinary least squares (OLS) and to obtain a consistent estimator of Σ by

$$\tilde{\Sigma} = \frac{(Y - X\tilde{\bar{\Pi}})'(Y - X\tilde{\bar{\Pi}})}{T} \tag{9}$$

where $\bar{\Pi} = (\bar{\pi}_{\cdot 1}, \bar{\pi}_{\cdot 2}, \ldots, \bar{\pi}_{\cdot m})$ and the tilde in (9) indicates that the constituent vectors, $\bar{\pi}_{\cdot i}$, have been estimated; Y is the matrix $Y = (y_{\cdot 1}, y_{\cdot 2}, \ldots, y_{\cdot m})$.

Using $\tilde{\Sigma}$ we obtain $\tilde{\Phi}$ and substituting for Φ in (7) we have a feasible estimator; repeating the procedure until convergence, we obtain the *iterated Aitken estimator*.

Thus, to recapitulate, the iterated Aitken estimator is found by the solution—provided the iteration outlined above converges—of the two equations.

$$\hat{\pi}^* = (X^{*\prime} \tilde{\Phi}^{-1} X^*)^{-1} X^{*\prime} \tilde{\Phi}^{-1} y \qquad \tilde{\Sigma} = \frac{(Y - X\tilde{\bar{\Pi}})'(Y - X\tilde{\bar{\Pi}})}{T} \tag{10}$$
$$\tilde{\Phi} = \tilde{\Sigma} \otimes I.$$

In maximum likelihood (ML) we operate by maximizing with respect to Σ and π^*

$$L = -\frac{mT}{2} \; ln(2\pi) + \frac{T}{2} \; ln|\Sigma^{-1}| - \frac{1}{2} tr(Y - X\bar{\Pi})\, \Sigma^{-1}(Y - X\bar{\Pi})' \tag{11}$$

But,

$$tr(Y - X\bar{\Pi})\Sigma^{-1}(Y - X\bar{\Pi})' = T\, tr\, \Sigma^{-1} \frac{(Y - X\bar{\Pi})'\,(Y - X\bar{\Pi})}{T}. \tag{12}$$

Let

$$W = \frac{(Y - X\bar{\Pi})'\,(Y - X\bar{\Pi})}{T}. \tag{13}$$

Differentiate (11) with respect to σ^{ij}, *i.e.*, the *i*, *j* element of $\sum^{-1}$ to obtain

$$\frac{T}{2} \frac{\Sigma^{ij}}{|\Sigma^{-1}|} - \frac{T}{2} w_{ji} = 0 \tag{14}$$

where $\sum^{ij}$ is the cofactor of σ^{ij}.

Equation (14) implies that

$$\hat{\Sigma} = W. \tag{15}$$

Substituting in (11) we obtain the concentrated likelihood which is to be maximized with respect to the unknown elements of $\bar{\Pi}$. Thus, we obtain

$$L = -\frac{mT}{2} [ln(2\pi) + 1] - \frac{T}{2} \; ln|W|. \tag{16}$$

We observe that, imposing explicitly the zero restrictions, the *i*, *j* element of *W* is given by

$$w_{ij} = \frac{1}{T} \; (y._i - X_i\pi._i)'(y._j - X_j\pi._j), \quad |W| = \sum_{j=1}^{m} W_{ij}\, w_{ij} \tag{17}$$

W_{ij} being the cofactor of w_{ij}. Moreover, $\pi._i$ is contained only in the ith row and column of *W*. Consequently,

$$\frac{\partial\, ln|W|}{\partial \pi._i} = \frac{1}{|W|} \frac{\partial |W|}{\partial \pi._i}. \tag{18}$$

But

$$\frac{\partial |W|}{\partial \pi._i} = \sum_{j \neq i} W_{ij}(X_i'X_j\pi._j - X_i'y._j) + \sum_{j \neq i} W_{ji}(X_i'X_j\pi._j - X_i'y._j) + 2W_{ii}(X_i'X_i\pi._i - X_i'y._i). \tag{19}$$

Thus

$$\frac{\partial ln|W|}{\partial \pi_{\cdot i}} = 2\left[\sum_{j=1}^{m} w^{ij} X_i' X_j \pi_{\cdot j} - \sum_{j=1}^{m} w^{ij} X_i' y_{\cdot j}\right] = 0 \tag{20}$$

$$i = 1, 2, \ldots, m$$

implies that estimators for $\pi_{\cdot i}$ may be obtained by solving

$$\begin{bmatrix} w^{11}X_1'X_1 & w^{12}X_1'X_2 & \ldots & w^{1m}X_1'X_m \\ w^{21}X_2'X_1 & w^{22}X_2'X_2 & \ldots & w^{2m}X_2'X_m \\ \vdots & & & \\ w^{m1}X_m'X_1 & w^{m2}X_m'X_2 & \ldots & w^{mm}X_m'X_m \end{bmatrix} \begin{bmatrix} \pi_{\cdot 1} \\ \pi_{\cdot 2} \\ \vdots \\ \pi_{\cdot m} \end{bmatrix} = \begin{bmatrix} \sum_{j=1}^{m} w^{1j}X_1'y_{\cdot j} \\ \sum_{j=1}^{m} w^{2j}X_2'y_{\cdot j} \\ \vdots \\ \sum_{j=1}^{m} w^{mj}X_m'y_{\cdot j} \end{bmatrix} \tag{21}$$

in conjunction with (13) or (15). Notice that the w^{ij} here play the same role as the σ^{ij} in iterative Aitken estimation.

To show equivalence of the two procedures we note that if we begin with a consistent estimator of $\sum$, say $\sum_1$, then from (21) we obtain an iterate $\tilde{\pi}^*_{(1)}$. We can use this to compute $\sum_2$ and thus $\tilde{\pi}^*_{(2)}$ until the procedure converges. At each step the estimators obtained for $\sum$ and π^* are consistent. Hence upon convergence we have formed a consistent root of the equations defining the ML estimator. Such a consistent root is unique, see *e.g.*, Cramer [1] or Dhrymes [2, Chapter 3] and *it is the ML estimator*. It now remains to show that equations (21) and (13) are equivalent to (7) and (9).

But the matrix in the left member of (21) is $X^{*\prime}(W \otimes I)^{-1} X^*$; the vector is π^*. The vector in the right member is $X^*(W \otimes I)^{-1} y$. Thus solving (21) we have

$$\tilde{\pi}^* = [X^{*\prime}(W \otimes I)^{-1} X^*]^{-1} X^{*\prime} (W \otimes I)^{-1} y \tag{22}$$

which is exactly (7).

We have therefore proved equivalence of the two procedures. Because we have commenced the two iterations from the same initial estimate of $\sum$ we have *numerical equivalence* at every step. *Had we used different initial estimates we would not necessarily have numerical equivalence.*

The asymptotic distribution of the estimator in (7) with *any consistent* estimator of Φ substituted in its stead is given in Dhrymes [2, Chapter 4] and need not be repeated here.

Since iterating the Aitken estimator from an initial consistent estimate of $\sum$ yields successively consistent estimators of $\sum$, it follows that if the procedure converges, the asymptotic distribution of the convergent iterate is also known, as is that of the ML estimator. Thus, to conclude, the numerical coincidence reported by Kmenta and Gilbert is a consequence, for finite samples, of the fact that they have employed the same initial estimate for $\sum$ and W, respectively, for Aitken and ML. Whether given different initial conditions the two procedures will converge, *for finite samples*, to the same estimate is an open question. Asymptotically, the distribution of Aitken estimators is exactly that of ML, in the present context, whether one iterates or not.

References

[1] Cramer, H., *Mathematical Methods of Statistics* (Princeton: Princeton University Press, 1946).

[2] Dhrymes, P. J., *Econometrics: Statistical Foundations and Applications* (New York: Harper and Row Inc., 1970).

[3] Kmenta, J. and Gilbert, R. F., "Small Sample Properties of Alternative Estimators of Seemingly Unrelated Regressions", *Journal of the American Statistical Association*, 63, 1968.

[4] Ruble, W. L., "Improving the Computation of Simultaneous and Stochastic Linear Equation Estimates", Agricultural Economics Report 116, Department of Agricultural Economics, Michigan State University, October, 1968.

Journal of Forecasting, Vol. 6, 181–192 (1987)

On the Existence of Generalized Inverse Estimators in a Singular System of Equations

PHOEBUS J. DHRYMES
Columbia University, U.S.A.

SAMUEL SCHWARZ
The College of Staten Island/CUNY, U.S.A.

ABSTRACT

This paper deals with estimation problems in the context of singular systems of equations. It provides the necessary and sufficient conditions for the existence of restricted estimators as a routine extension of the standard theory of restricted least squares estimation. The paper also provides the means for carrying out tests of hypotheses on subsets of restrictions imposed on the system by explicitly providing an expression for the (appropriate) Lagrange multipliers.

KEY WORDS Singular systems Generalized least squares Restricted least squares Generalized inverse

The problem of estimating the parameters of a system in the presence of a singular covariance matrix exists in a wide variety of topics. Thus, if one wishes to forecast, in a consistent fashion, consumer expenditure on a component basis, one would have to consider a set of general linear models (GLM) that explain the allocation of consumer expenditure amongst its components. Indeed, Powell (1969) is concerned with precisely this topic. Other applications in the study of consumer expenditure or consumption functions may be found in Barten (1969, 1977) and Deaton (1975). Similarly, singular systems arise in the context of derived systems of equations from translog utility or production functions (Berndt and Christensen, 1973, 1974; Christensen, Jorgenson and Lau, 1973, 1975); market share analysis (Weiss, 1968; Rao, 1972); in estimating the parameters of a Cobb–Douglas production function (Klein, 1953; Dhrymes, 1962); demand for financial assets (Friend, 1964); and in many other models.

The theory of such systems was first approached, systematically, by Theil (1971), who suggested the use of the generalized inverse in lieu of the ordinary inverse of the covariance matrix when the latter is singular. Theil produced a set of sufficient conditions for the estimator to exist, and provided an explicit representation when appropriate (and implied) restrictions were imposed. Subsequently, Kreijger and Neudecker (1977) provided an axiomatic derivation of the estimator proposed by Theil. We shall refer to this estimator as the TKN estimator, whose essential feature is that it uses the generalized inverse of the (singular) covariance matrix and represents it as an unrestricted Aitken-like estimator plus a correction, much in the manner of the standard restricted least squares model.

The substance of this paper is to show that, in the context of such systems, the unrestricted

0277–6693/87/030181–12$06.00

Received April 1986
Revised February 1987

Aitken-like estimator does not exist, when we admit that different variables may appear in different equations. When all variables appear in all equations, ordinary least squares (OLS) and generalized least squares (GLS) coincide and thus the issue of the singularity of the covariance matrix is not relevant for the unrestricted estimator. In addition, we shall provide necessary and sufficient conditions for the unrestricted estimator to exist; moreover, we shall produce a proper expression for the restricted estimator and the associated Lagrange multipliers, thus making tests of (subsets of) the restrictions perfectly straightforward.

FORMULATION OF THE PROBLEM

Consider the system of GLM's

$$y = X\beta + u, \tag{1}$$

where

$$\begin{aligned} y &= (y'_{\cdot 1}, y'_{\cdot 2}, \ldots, y'_{\cdot m})' & u &= (u'_{\cdot 1}, u'_{\cdot 2}, \ldots, u'_{\cdot m})' \\ X &= \operatorname{diag}(X_1, X_2, \ldots, X_m) & \beta &= (\beta'_{\cdot 1}, \beta'_{\cdot 2}, \ldots, \beta'_{\cdot m})'. \end{aligned} \tag{2}$$

$y_{\cdot i}$ and $u_{\cdot i}$ are T-element (column) vectors containing, respectively, the ith dependent variable and associated error term; X_i is the $T \times G_i$ matrix of explanatory variables appearing in the ith equation; and $\beta_{\cdot i}$ is the G_i (column) vector containing the corresponding parameters.

It is assumed that the system contains G distinct explanatory variables appearing in the matrix

$$X_0 = (x_{\cdot 1}, x_{\cdot 2}, \ldots, x_{\cdot G}) \tag{3}$$

and that X_0 obeys the rank condition

$$r(X_0) = G. \tag{4}$$

Moreover, we have that

$$E(u) = 0 \qquad \operatorname{Cov}(u) = \Omega \otimes I_T. \tag{5}$$

We shall examine chiefly the case where (1) obeys an adding-up restriction, thus inducing the relation

$$(e'_m \otimes I_T)u = 0, \tag{6}$$

where e_m is an m-element (column) vector, all of whose elements are unity. The relation in (6), of course, implies that

$$\Omega e_m = 0$$

and thus

$$r(\Omega) < m. \tag{7}$$

The estimator suggested by the TKN approach is

$$\tilde{\beta} = (X'\Phi_g X)^{-1} X'\Phi_g y, \tag{8}$$

where

$$\Phi_g = \Omega_g \otimes I_T \tag{9}$$

and Ω_g is the g-inverse (generalized inverse) of Ω (see, for example, Dhrymes, 1984, ch. 3).

The estimator in (8) represents an attempt to circumvent the many problems posed by models in which the error terms obey linear dependency restrictions, some of which were referred to in the introduction. Unfortunately in nearly all such models the estimator in (8) will fail to exist.

In what follows we shall characterize the class of models for which the estimator in (8) is inappropriate by giving necessary and sufficient conditions for the nonexistence of the inverse in (8). Before we do so, however, we require a more adequate notation. Thus, recall that

$$X_0 = (x_{\cdot 1}, x_{\cdot 2}, \ldots, x_{\cdot G})$$

is the matrix containing the distinct explanatory variables of the system exhibited in (1); let

$$S_i \qquad i = 1, 2, \ldots, m$$

be selection matrices, i.e. permutations of (subsets of) the columns of I_G, such that S_i is $G \times G_i$ and obeys

$$X_i = X_0 S_i \qquad \operatorname{rank}(S_i) = G_i \qquad i = 1, 2, \ldots, m$$

with the matrices X_i as defined in (2). In this notation the matrix X of (1) is rendered:

$$X = (I \otimes X_0)S \qquad S = \operatorname{diag}(S_1, S_2, \ldots, S_m). \tag{11}$$

The matrix to be inverted in (8) is representable as

$$\Psi = S'(\Omega_g \otimes R'R)S \qquad X_0'X_0 = R'R \tag{12}$$

where R is $G \times G$ and nonsingular, in virtue of (4). We also note that if e_m is an m-element column vector of unities, then it is a characteristic vector of Ω_g corresponding to the latter's (only) zero root.

We then have

PROPOSITION 1. Let Ψ be as in (12) and put

$$N(\Psi) = \{\alpha : \Psi\alpha = 0\}.$$

Then

$$\alpha \in N(\Psi) \quad \text{if and only if} \quad \gamma \in N(\Omega_g \otimes I_G),$$

where

$$\gamma = S\alpha.$$

Proof. We note that

$$e^* = \frac{e_m}{\sqrt{m}}$$

is the normalized characteristic vector corresponding to the zero root of Ω_g. Thus, we have

$$\Omega_g = Q\Lambda Q' \qquad Q = (Q_1, e^*) \qquad \Lambda = \begin{bmatrix} \Lambda_1 & 0 \\ 0 & 0 \end{bmatrix},$$

where Λ_1 is the diagonal matrix containing the positive characteristic roots of Ω_g and Q_1 is the matrix containing the corresponding (orthonormal) characteristic vectors. It is easy to see that

$$\Omega_g = Q_1 \Lambda_1 Q_1'.$$

For the first part of the Proposition, suppose that $\alpha \in N(\Psi)$; then

$$0 = \Psi\alpha = S'(Q_1\Lambda_1 Q_1' \otimes X_0'X_0)\gamma$$

and

$$0 = \alpha'\Psi\alpha = \gamma'(Q_1\Lambda_1 Q_1' \otimes X_0'X_0)\gamma = \operatorname{tr}(RCQ_1\Lambda_1 Q_1'C'R'), \tag{13}$$

where

$$\gamma = (\gamma'_{\cdot 1}, \gamma'_{\cdot 2}, \ldots, \gamma'_{\cdot m})' \qquad \gamma = \text{vec}(C).$$

Since the matrix in the rightmost member of (13) is at least positive semidefinite, the latter implies

$$RCQ_1\Lambda_1 Q_1' C' R' = 0.$$

Since R is nonsingular we must have

$$CQ_1\Lambda_1 Q_1' C' = 0, \tag{14}$$

and since $\Lambda_1 > 0$ we conclude

$$CQ_1 = 0. \tag{15}$$

But then

$$(\Omega_g \otimes I_G)\gamma = (Q_1\Lambda_1 Q_1' \otimes I_G)\gamma = \text{vec}(CQ_1\Lambda_1 Q_1') = 0,$$

which concludes the proof of the first part.

For the second part, suppose that for

$$\gamma = S\alpha$$

we have that

$$(\Omega_g \otimes I_G)\gamma = 0.$$

Then, since

$$\Psi = S'(I \otimes X_0'X_0)(\Omega_g \otimes I_G)S,$$

the conclusion is obvious.

Corollary 1. The following characterization is valid:

$$N(\Omega_g \otimes I_G) = \{\text{vec}(C)\colon C = c \otimes e_m', c \in E_G\},$$

where E_G is the G-dimensional Euclidean space.

Proof. From (15) we conclude that

$$C = c \otimes e_m' \qquad c \in E_G$$

since

$$e_m = \sqrt{(m)}e^*$$

and e^* is the characteristic vector corresponding to the zero root of Ω_g.

Corollary 2. The following characterization is valid:

$$N(\Psi) = \{\alpha\colon S\alpha = e_m \otimes c, c \in E_G\}.$$

Proof. Proposition 1 states that $\alpha \in N(\Psi)$ if and only if

$$\gamma \in N(\Omega_g \otimes I_G) \qquad \gamma = S\alpha.$$

Corollary 1 states that $\gamma \in N(\Omega_g \otimes I_G)$ if and only if

$$\gamma = e_m \otimes c \qquad c \in E_G.$$

Corollary 3. The null space $N(\Psi)$ contains only the null vector if and only if the equations of the system in (1) have no explanatory variables in common, i.e. if and only if there is no explanatory variable that appears in all equations.

Proof. Necessity: Suppose that $N(\Psi) = \{0\}$ and there are explanatory variables in common. Then there exists at least one variable, say x_k, that appears in all equations. This means that each S_i contains a column that has a unity in its kth position; let this be its i_k column and choose $\alpha_{\cdot i}$, $i = 1, 2, \ldots, m$, such that it has a unity in its i_k position and zeros everywhere else. Thus,

$$S_i \alpha_{\cdot i} = e_{\cdot k} \qquad \alpha_{\cdot i} \neq 0 \qquad \text{for all } i. \tag{16}$$

Consequently,

$$S\alpha = (e_m \otimes e_{\cdot k}) \tag{17}$$

implying

$$\Psi\alpha = 0 \qquad \alpha \neq 0, \tag{18}$$

which is a contradiction.

Sufficiency: Suppose no explanatory variable appears in all equations; we show that

$$\Psi\alpha = 0 \quad \text{implies} \quad \alpha = 0.$$

By Corollary 2, $\Psi\alpha = 0$ if and only if $S\alpha = e_m \otimes c$, which implies

$$S_i \alpha_{\cdot i} = c \quad \text{for all } i. \tag{19}$$

Let c_k be the kth element of the vector c above; we show that $c_k = 0$ for all k. Suppose not; this means that every matrix S_i contains a unity in the kth position in one of its columns, which in turn means that the variable x_k appears, as an explanatory variable, in all equations of the system and this is a contradiction. Hence, $c = 0$ and, thus,

$$S_i \alpha_{\cdot i} = 0 \quad \text{for all } i. \tag{20}$$

Since the S_i are of full column rank, we conclude that $S\alpha = 0$ implies $\alpha = 0$. (q.e.d.)

Remark 1. The (unrestricted) TKN estimator while appealing, in that it purports to resolve the symmetry problem in handling systems obeying adding-up requirements, in fact fails to exist unless severe restrictions are imposed on the specification of the system; such restrictions are impossible to observe in the case of the consumer expenditure allocation system.

Remark 2. The conditions stated in Theorem 6.3 of Theil (1971, p. 278) and which are rendered in our notation as

$$r[(Q_1' \otimes I_T)X] = K \qquad K = \sum_{i=1}^{m} G_i \qquad r[(e^{*\prime} \otimes I_T)X] = 0$$

fail to hold in the current context. Actually, the first condition is an existence requirement, while the second is an 'efficiency' requirement. Regarding the first condition, we note that in the case of the consumer expenditure allocation model this condition cannot be satisfied since such systems will invariably contain at least one variable in common, viz. (total) consumption expenditure. This is easily seen by noting that

$$(Q_1' \otimes I_T)X\alpha = (Q_1' \otimes X_0)S\alpha$$

and for α such that

$$S\alpha = e_m \otimes c$$

we have

$$Q_1' e_m \otimes X_0 c = 0$$

so that the matrix $(Q_1' \otimes I_T)X$ cannot be of full (column) rank! The second condition evidently fails to hold as well since it would imply that

$$S'(e^*e^{*\prime} \otimes X_0'X_0)S = 0,$$

which is evidently impossible!

We have therefore proved

THEOREM 1. Consider the system of GLM's given by (1) through (6); then the (unrestricted) TKN estimator exhibited in (8) fails to exist if and only if the equations of the system have at least one explanatory variable in common, i.e. if at least one explanatory variable appears in all equations of the system.

Proof. Obvious from the preceding discussion.

Remark 3. It is possible to modify the TKN estimator so that it would exist in all instances where it fails to exist in its present form, by simply redefining it as

$$\bar{\beta} = (X'\Phi_g X)_g X'\Phi_g y. \tag{21}$$

This, however, solves a problem at the cost of creating another. Defining the TKN estimator as in (21) means that of all solutions of

$$X'\Phi_g X\beta = X'\Phi_g y$$

we choose the one, say $\bar{\beta}$ of (21), having *minimum norm*—see Dhrymes, 1984, ch. 3. One is hard put to articulate the economic meaning of this restriction.

Remark 4. Common practice when estimating an allocation system (see, for example, Deaton (1975) or Powell (1969)) is simply to drop one equation and estimate the remaining nonsingular $(m-1)$-equation system by Generalized Least Squares (GLS), in which case Theorem 1 has no bearing. Recently, Dhrymes and Schwarz (1984) have shown that the estimators thus derived are, generally invariant to the equation dropped *only* when all equations contain the same explanatory variables, in which case OLS and GLS estimators coincide. Where different variables may enter different equations, the results are not necessarily invariant to the equation dropped. Hence, one must resort to uniform estimation of the complete m-equation system.

RESTRICTED ESTIMATION

In the previous section we showed that the TKN estimator fails to exist when the restrictions implicit in (6) have not been imposed. These restrictions are, evidently, given by

$$(e_m' \otimes I_T)y = (e_m' \otimes I_T)X\beta, \tag{22}$$

which may be written more conveniently as

$$R\beta = r, \tag{23}$$

where

$$R = (e_m' \otimes I_T)X \qquad r = (e_m' \otimes I_T)y. \tag{24}$$

The restricted estimator of the system in (1) subject to the restriction in (23) is given, following the TKN procedure, by the solution of

$$\begin{bmatrix} X'\Phi_g X & R' \\ R & 0 \end{bmatrix} \begin{bmatrix} \beta \\ \lambda \end{bmatrix} = \begin{bmatrix} X'\Phi_g y \\ r \end{bmatrix}, \tag{25}$$

where λ is the vector of Lagrange multipliers associated with the restriction in (23).

A careful examination of (25) will reveal that the matrix in the left member is singular, indeed examination of (23) will also reveal that R is not of full (row) rank. This is so since, in effect,

$$R = (e'_m \otimes I_T)(I_m \otimes X_0)S = X_0(S_1, S_2, \dots, S_m) = (X_1, X_2, \dots, X_m),$$

which shows R to be $T \times K(K = \sum_{i=1}^{m} G_i)$ of rank $G < T$.

Remark 5. In the typical 'allocation' problem, let $x_{\cdot G}$ be (total) consumer expenditure; then (22) is rendered as

$$(e'_m \otimes I_T)y = x_{\cdot G} = X_0 \sum_{i=1}^{m} S_i\beta_{\cdot i} = X_0 \sum_{i=1}^{m} b_{\cdot i} \tag{26}$$

which implies the G restrictions

$$(e'_m \otimes I_G)b = e_{\cdot G}, \tag{27}$$

where

$$B = (S_1\beta_{\cdot 1}, S_2\beta_{\cdot 2}, \dots, S_m\beta_{\cdot m}) \qquad b = \text{vec}(B) = S\beta. \tag{28}$$

Thus (23) is now to be reinterpreted as

$$R\beta = r \qquad R = (e'_m \otimes I_G)S \qquad r = e_{\cdot G}. \tag{29}$$

It is evident that in (29) R is $G \times K$ of rank G as required.

Remark 6. For a system of GLM's obeying (1) through (6), we have the redundant set of restrictions in (22); for a system of market shares or Cobb–Douglas exponents or shares deriving from translog utility or production functions, (22) is rendered as

$$e_T = X_0(e'_m \otimes I_G)S\beta,$$

which is a redundant set requiring that X_0 contain, as one of its columns—or a linear combination thereof—the vector e_T. The most natural way in which this is implementable requires X_0 to contain the fictitious variable associated with the constant term, viz. e_T. Thus the minimal linearly independent set of restrictions is

$$R\beta = r,$$

where now

$$R = (e'_m \otimes I_G)S \qquad r = e_{\cdot 1} \qquad e_T = x_{\cdot 1}. \tag{30}$$

With R, r as in (29) or (30), the restricted estimator is found as the solution of (25).

An immediate consequence of the preceding discussion and Theorem 1, is the following:

THEOREM 2. Consider the system of GLM's as given in equations (1) through (6), together with the minimal set of restrictions in (29) or (30). Then the restricted TKN estimator, rendered as

$$\tilde{\beta}_r = \tilde{\beta} + CR'(RCR')^{-1}(r - R\tilde{\beta}), \tag{31}$$

fails to exist, where $\hat{\beta}$ is the unrestricted estimator and

$$C = (X'\Phi_g X)^{-1}$$

if and only if the equations of the system in (1) have at least one explanatory variable in common.

Proof. Obvious from the representation in (31) and Theorem 1, since $\hat{\beta}$ and C are not defined in such a case.

Remark 7. The meaning of Theorem 2 is quite circumscribed; it states that for systems of GLM's as defined therein the right member of (31) is undefined; *it does not state that no meaning can be assigned to a restricted Aitken or GLS estimator in that context.* The situation is analogous to characterizing the number $1/(1-\gamma)$ for $|\gamma| > 1$. In general, this is a perfectly well defined number but it does not have a representation as

$$1/(1-\gamma) = \sum_{i=0}^{\infty} \gamma^i.$$

We now give the necessary and sufficient conditions for the existence of the restricted estimator.

THEOREM 3. Consider the system of GLM's in (1) through (6), together with a minimal linearly independent set of restrictions of the form

$$R\beta = r,$$

where R is $s \times K$ of rank s. Then the appropriate (restricted GLS) estimator exists if and only if the (column) null spaces of

$$\Psi = S'(\Omega_g \otimes X_0'X_0)S \quad \text{and} \quad R$$

have no vector in common beyond the null vector.

Proof. The equations defining the restricted estimator are given by

$$\begin{bmatrix} S'(\Omega_g \otimes X_0'X_0)S & R' \\ R & 0 \end{bmatrix} \begin{bmatrix} \beta \\ \lambda \end{bmatrix} = \begin{bmatrix} S'(\Omega_g \otimes X_0')y \\ r \end{bmatrix}. \tag{32}$$

For notational convenience put

$$P_1 = \begin{bmatrix} S'(\Omega_g \otimes X_0'X_0)S \\ R \end{bmatrix} \qquad P_2 = \begin{bmatrix} R' \\ 0 \end{bmatrix}$$

and note that, by assumption, P_2 is of full column rank. Now if, in (32), the matrix is nonsingular, P_1 is of full rank and thus for nonnull vector α we cannot have

$$\Psi\alpha = S'(\Omega_g \otimes X_0'X_0)S\alpha = 0 \qquad R\alpha = 0,$$

proving the first part. For the second part let the null spaces of Ψ and R have only the null vector in common, and suppose the matrix in (32) is singular, i.e. for vectors δ_1, δ_2 not both null

$$\Psi\delta_1 + R'\delta_2 = 0 \qquad R\delta_1 = 0 \tag{33}$$

so that δ_1 is in the column null space of R; if $\delta_1 = 0$ then the first equation of (33) implies $\delta_2 = 0$, so that we take $\delta_1 \neq 0$. The first equation then implies

$$\Psi\delta_1 = -R'\delta_2$$

for nonnull δ_1. But then (33) implies

$$\delta_1'\Psi\delta_1 = -\delta_2'(R\delta_1) = 0,$$

which states that δ_1 is in the null space of Ψ (owing to the fact that Ψ is at least positive semidefinite). This is a contradiction.

COROLLARY 4. In the context of Theorem 3 the restricted estimator exists as a solution to (32) for the allocation and share models.

Proof. In either case the matrix of restrictions R is given by

$$R = (e_m' \otimes I_G)S.$$

By Theorem 3 we need only show that, apart from the null vector, the null spaces of R and $\Psi = S'(\Omega_g \otimes X_0'X_0)S$ are disjoint. By Corollary 2, the null space of Ψ consists of (nonnull) vectors α such that $S\alpha = e_m \otimes c$. Hence, for nonnull α,

$$\Psi\alpha = 0 \qquad R\alpha = (e_m' \otimes I_G)S\alpha = e_m'e_m \otimes c = mc \qquad c \neq 0.$$

Consequently the inverse in (32) exists and the restricted estimator is uniquely defined.

Remark 8. An explicit representation of the required inverse in equation (32) is given in Dhrymes (1984); thus explicit representations of the restricted estimator and its associated Lagrange multiplier are available. Moreover, Theorem 3 and the representations cited remain valid if additional constraints are imposed beyond those implied by the adding-up condition.

Remark 9. In Theorem 6.6 of Theil (1971, p. 285) two conditions are invoked for the existence of the restricted estimator, which are in the notation of Remark 2:

$$r[(Q_1' \otimes X_0)S] = K \qquad r[(e^{*\prime} \otimes X_0)S] = p < K.$$

The first condition is not necessary, as indicated by Theorem 3. The second condition is not particularly informative since p is not specified. Note that

$$(e^{*\prime} \otimes X_0)S = \frac{1}{\sqrt{m}}(X_1, X_2, \ldots, X_m),$$

which has rank G; but

$$G < \sum_{i=1}^{m} G_i$$

is not a meaningful constraint, since all variables must appear at least in two equations so that

$$\sum_{i=1}^{m} G_i \geqslant 2G.$$

Generalization of the restricted estimator

The results of the previous section can be easily generalized to the case where the system is subject to a general linear restriction and not merely restricted by an adding-up requirement. Let

$$d = (d_1, d_2, \ldots, d_m)' \qquad d_i \neq 0 \quad \text{all } i$$

be an arbitrary nonnull vector and suppose the linear dependency of the error process in (1) arises out of the requirement

$$(d' \otimes I_T)u = 0. \tag{34}$$

Then we have the consequence that

$$\Omega d = 0 \qquad \Omega_g d = 0. \tag{35}$$

Without loss of generality d may be normalized and, thus, may be taken as the characteristic vector corresponding to the (only) zero root of Ω and Ω_g. Setting up the estimation problem as the minimization of

$$F=(y-X\beta)'(\Omega_g \otimes I_T)(y-X\beta) \tag{36}$$

with respect to β, subject to a certain restriction, will generalize the results of the previous section. The restriction in question is

$$(d' \otimes I_T)y=(d' \otimes I_T)X\beta. \tag{37}$$

Put

$$y^*=(d' \otimes I_T)y=\sum_{i=1}^{m} d_i y_{\cdot i} \tag{38}$$

$$(d' \otimes I_T)X=(d' \otimes I_T)(I_m \otimes X_0)S=X_0(e_m' \otimes I_G)SD_1, \tag{39}$$

where

$$D_1=\operatorname{diag}(d_1 I_{G_1}, d_2 I_{G_2}, \ldots, d_m I_{G_m}).$$

The condition in (37), in view of (38) and (39), may be rendered as

$$R\beta=r, \tag{41}$$

where

$$R=(e_m' \otimes I_G)SD_1 \qquad r=(X_0'X_0)^{-1}X_0'y^*. \tag{42}$$

But then the problem is essentially that dealt with in the previous section, and we have the following characterization.

PROPOSITION 2. The matrix

$$\Psi=S'(\Omega_g \otimes X_0'X_0)S$$

is singular if and only if the equations of the system in (1) have at least one explanatory variable in common.

Proof. Suppose that, in fact, they do have an explanatory variable in common and let this be the variable $x_{\cdot s}$; suppose this is the i_sth variable in the ith equation. Taking

$$\alpha_{\cdot i}=d_i e_{\cdot i_s} \tag{43}$$

we find

$$S_i \alpha_{\cdot i}=d_i e_{\cdot s} \qquad i=1,2,\ldots,m. \tag{44}$$

Hence

$$S\alpha=d \otimes e_{\cdot s} \qquad d=(d_1,d_2,\ldots,d_m)'$$

and thus for the choice of $\alpha_{\cdot i} \neq 0$, as in (43), we have

$$\Psi\alpha=S'(\Omega_g \otimes X_0'X_0)(d \otimes e_{\cdot s})=S'(\Omega_g d \otimes X_0'X_0 e_{\cdot s})=0,$$

which shows Ψ to be singular.

Next suppose Ψ to be singular; let $\alpha \neq 0$, $\alpha \in N(\Psi)$; by Proposition 1

$$(\Omega_g \otimes I_G)\gamma=0 \qquad \gamma=S\alpha.$$

But then we must have, by Corollary 2,

$$\gamma=d \otimes c \quad \text{for arbitrary } c \in E_G.$$

This means that (since $d_i \neq 0$ for all i)

$$(1/d_i)S_i\alpha_{\cdot i} = c \qquad i = 1, 2, \ldots, m. \tag{45}$$

By Corollary 3, (45) is valid for $c \neq 0$ only if the equations of the system in (1) have an explanatory variable in common. We therefore have

THEOREM 4. Consider the system in (1) through (5) and (34). Then the unrestricted estimator resulting from minimization of (36) exists if and only if the equations of (1) have no explanatory variable in common.

Proof. Obvious from Proposition 2.

Finally, we have

THEOREM 5. Consider the system in (1) through (5) and (34). The restricted estimator of β, obtained by minimizing (36) subject to (41) and (42) exists as the solution to

$$\begin{bmatrix} \Psi & R' \\ R & 0 \end{bmatrix} \begin{bmatrix} \beta \\ \lambda \end{bmatrix} = \begin{bmatrix} S'(\Omega_g \otimes X_0)y \\ r \end{bmatrix},$$

where r, R are as in (41) and (42).

Proof. We note that R' is of rank G and thus the matrix in the left member above is nonsingular if and only if $N(\Psi)$ and $N(R)$ have only the null vector in common. Let $\alpha \neq 0$ such that

$$\Psi\alpha = 0.$$

Then

$$S\alpha = d \otimes c \qquad c \neq 0 \qquad c \in E_G$$

and

$$R\alpha = (e'_m \otimes I_G)SD_1\alpha = (e'_m \otimes I_G)(\hat{d} \otimes I_G)(d \otimes c) = d'd \otimes c \neq 0$$

$$SD_1 = (\hat{d} \otimes I_G)S \qquad \hat{d} = \operatorname{diag}(d_1, d_2, \ldots, d_m),$$

which shows that if $\alpha \neq 0$, $\alpha \in N(\Psi)$, then $\alpha \notin N(R)$. We can similarly show that if $\alpha \in N(R)$, then

$$(d' \otimes I_G)S\alpha = 0$$

and thus

$$S\alpha = (q'_{\cdot 1}, q'_{\cdot 2}, \ldots, q'_{\cdot m})'$$

so that

$$d'q_{\cdot i} = 0 \qquad i = 1, 2, \ldots, m.$$

But this means that the vectors $q_{\cdot i}$ are linear combinations of the characteristic vectors of Ω_g corresponding to its positive roots; hence

$$\Psi\alpha \neq 0$$

and the theorem is proved.

CONCLUSION

In this paper we have demonstrated that the TKN estimator, if unrestricted, cannot exist for systems of GLM exhibiting linear dependencies in their error process (due to adding-up requirements) if the equations of the system contain one or more explanatory variables in common, i.e. if one or more explanatory variables appear in all equations.

We have also shown that the restricted TKN estimator as exhibited in the literature also does not exist in the context above. The restricted estimator as a solution to a certain equation, however, was shown to exist for such systems and necessary and sufficient conditions for its existence have been obtained.

REFERENCES

Barten, A. P., 'Maximum likelihood estimation of a complete system of demand equations', *European Economic Review*, **1** (1969), 7–73.

Barten, A. P., 'The systems of consumer demand functions approach: a review', *Econometrica*, **45** (1977), 23–51.

Berndt, E. R. and Christensen, L. R., 'Testing for the existence of a consistent aggregate index of labor inputs', *American Economic Review*, **64** (1974), 391–403.

Berndt, E. R. and Christensen, L. R., 'The translog function and the substitution of equipment, structures and labour in U.S. manufacturing, 1929–1968', *Journal of Econometrics*, **1** (1973), 81–113.

Christensen, L. R., Jorgenson, D. W. and Lau, L. J., 'Transcendental logarithmic production frontiers', *Review of Economics and Statistics*, **55** (1973), 28–45.

Christensen, L. R., Jorgenson, D. W. and Lau, L. J., 'Transcendental logarithmic utility functions', *American Economic Review*, **65** (1975), 367–383.

Deaton, A. S., *Models and Projections of Demand in Postwar Britain*, New York: Halstead Press, 1975.

Dhrymes, P. J., 'On devising unbiased estimators for the parameters of a Cobb–Douglas production function', *Econometrica*, **30** (1962), 297–304.

Dhrymes, P. J., *Mathematics for Econometrics* (2nd edition), New York: Springer-Verlag, 1984.

Dhrymes, P. J. and Schwarz, S. (1984), 'On the invariance of estimators for singular systems of equations', Discussion Paper Series No. 238, Department of Economics, Columbia University; forthcoming in *Greek Economic Review*.

Friend, I., 'The effects of monetary policy on nonmonetary financial institutions and capital markets', in *Private Capital Markets, Commission on Money and Credit*, Englewood Cliffs: Prentice-Hall, 1964.

Klein, L. R., *A Textbook for Econometrics*, Evanston: Row, Peterson, 1953.

Kreijger, R. G. and Neudecker, H., 'Exact linear restrictions on parameters in the general linear model with a singular covariance matrix', *Journal of the American Statistical Association*, **72** (1977), 430–432.

Powell, A. A., 'Aitken estimators as a tool in allocating predetermined aggregates', *Journal of the American Statistical Association*, **64** (1969), 913–922.

Rao, V. R., 'Alternative econometric models of sales advertising relationships', *Journal of Marketing Research*, **9** (1972), 177–181.

Theil, H., *Principles of Econometrics*, New York: Wiley, 1971.

Weiss, D. L., 'Determinants of market share', *Journal of Marketing Research*, **5** (1968), 290–295.

Authors' biographies:

Phoebus J. Dhrymes, who is currently Professor of Economics at Columbia University, has received his Ph.D. degree from the Massachusetts Institute of Technology, and previously served as Editor or co-Editor of *International Economic Review* and the *Journal of Econometrics*.

Samuel Schwarz is currently Associate Professor of Economics at the College of Staten Island of the City University of New York and has received his Ph.D. from Columbia University.

Authors' addresses:

Phoebus J. Dhrymes, Department of Economics, Columbia University, New York, NY 10027, U.S.A.

Samuel Schwarz, The College of Staten Island/CUNY, 715 Ocean Terrace, Staten Island, NY 10301, U.S.A.

GREEK ECONOMIC REVIEW
Vol 9, No 1, June 1987

ON THE INVARIANCE OF ESTIMATORS FOR SINGULAR SYSTEMS OF EQUATIONS

By Phoebus J. Dhrymes and Samuel Schwarz

I. *INTRODUCTION*

Linear allocation or share systems, because of a budget or other constraints, require that the error terms exhibit linear dependency; this has raised the problem of how to deal, in a symmetric way, with the estimation of parameters in a general linear model (GLM) when the covariance matrix of the error is singular. *Actually, one is, in fact, dealing with a set of m* GLM'*s whose error terms exhibit linear dependency*, and this is the context in which we shall carry out our analysis.

Although the problem originated in the consumer demand literature – see e.g. Barten (1977) and Brown and Deaton (1972), it is not limited to demand systems. Singular systems also arise in the context of derived systems of equations from translog utility or production functions, Berndt and Christensen (1973, 1974), Christensen, Jorgenson and Lau (1973, 1975); market share analysis, Weiss (1968), Rao (1972); in estimating the parameters of a Cobb-Douglas production function, Klein (1953), Dhrymes (1962); demand for financial assets, Friend (1964), and in many other models.

The solution essentially associated with Barten (1969) entails a rather remarkable procedure that converts the problem to a nonsingular one. It is not clear, however, why such a procedure ought to produce the desired solution and the explanation given in the literature is neither appropriate nor satisfactory. In the sequel we shall examine the Barten procedure and determine "why" it works.

Moreover, the literature has generally dealt with a special case – in which all explanatory variables appear in every equation. In that case, the estimator obtained by the Barten procedure automatically satisfies the adding up condition and, consequently, has properties which do not hold for the general case. Specifically, we shall show that in the unrestricted case where different equations may contain different variables, the Barten estimator while it exists, it is also sensitive to the auxiliary parameter, k, used to "make" the covariance matrix of the errors nonsingular. We shall also show that when the adding up restrictions are imposed, the Barten estimator does not depend on this auxiliary parameter.

A parallel, but hitherto unconnected, development is given in Theil (1971), where a generalization to the Aitken procedure is attemped; unfortunately, even though perfectly applicable to the present context, up to now its connection to Barten's procedure has not elicited any comment. Possibly this is due to the fact that the estimator *as exhibited in Theil* (1971) *fails to exist when the equations of the system contain one or more variables in common.* This, however, does not mean that the estimator does not exist. In Dhrymes and Schwarz (1984) necessary and sufficient conditions are given for its existence. Here we shall show that when the adding up restrictions are imposed, *the estimator proposed by Theil is identical with the Barten estimator.*

II. *FORMULATION OF THE PROBLEM AND NOTATION*

Consider the system of general linear models

$$y_{t\cdot} = x_{t\cdot}B_{t\cdot} + \overset{*}{u}_{t\cdot}, \qquad t = 1, 2, \ldots, T \tag{1}$$

where $y_{t\cdot}$ is an m-element (row) vector of the dependent variables;
$x_{t\cdot}$ is a G-element vector of the independent variables; and
$\overset{*}{u}_{t\cdot}$ is the vector of the error terms.

We may assume that

$$\overset{*\prime}{u}_{t\cdot} : t = 1, 2, \ldots, T$$

is a sequence of i.i.d. random variables such that

$$E(\overset{*}{u}_{t\cdot}) = 0, \qquad \mathrm{Cov}(\overset{*\prime}{u}_{t\cdot}) = \Omega_* \tag{2}$$

It is convenient to think of (1) as a system of expenditure functions and of the Gth element of $x_{t\cdot}$ as

$$x_{tG} = y_{t\cdot}e_m \tag{3}$$

where e_m is an m-element column vector all of whose elements are unity. It is an immediate consequence of (1), (2) and (3) that

$$\overset{*}{u}_{t\cdot}e_m = 0, \qquad Be_m = e_{\cdot G} \tag{4}$$

where $e_{\cdot G}$ is a G-element column vector all of whose members are zero save the Gth, which is unity. If we put

$$X = (x_{t\cdot}), \qquad Y = (y_{t\cdot}), \qquad U^* = (u^*_{t\cdot}) \qquad\qquad t = 1, 2, \ldots, T \tag{5}$$

and denote by $x_{\cdot i}$, $y_{\cdot i}$, $u^*_{\cdot i}$ the ith columns, respectively, of X, Y, and U^*, then the ith General Linear Model (GLM) reads,

$$y_{\cdot i} = Xb_{\cdot i} + u^*_{\cdot i} \qquad\qquad i = 1, 2, \ldots, m \tag{6}$$

which is to be interpreted as representing T observations on the ith expenditure item.

In the literature it is generally assumed that all explanatory variables appear in every equation, possibly because of difficulties associated with alternative specifications. But it is frequently the case that different equations may be judged, a priori, to contain different sets of variables or, for separability reasons the investigator may wish to specify a distinct set of variables for each equation, the specification being such that, in principle, it is capable of satisfying the second equation of (4).

We therefore introduce:

Convention 1: The ith equation contains $G_i \leqslant G$ explanatory variables including the variable x_{tG}.

Convention 2: Every variable of the system is included in at least two equations.

To give effect to Convention 1 define the selection matrices S_i, $i = 1, 2, \ldots, m$, whose columns are permutations of G_i of the columns of an identity matrix of order G, the last column of S_i always being $e_{\cdot G}$.

It follows immediately that

$$Xb_{\cdot i} = X_i\beta_{\cdot i} \tag{7}$$

such that

$$X_i = XS_i, \qquad\qquad b_{\cdot i} = S_i\beta_{\cdot i} \tag{8}$$

where X_i is the $T \times G_i$ matrix of explanatory variables appearing in the ith equation and $\beta_{\cdot i}$ is the $G_i \times 1$ vector of corresponding parameters. Thus, the system as a whole may be written as

$$y = X^*\beta + u^* \tag{9}$$

where

$$y = \text{vec}(Y), \qquad u^* = \text{vec}(U^*)$$

$$X^* = \text{diag}(X_1, X_2, \ldots, X_m), \qquad \beta = (\beta_{\cdot 1}', \beta_{\cdot 2}', \ldots, \beta_{\cdot m}')' \tag{10}$$

Powell (1969), Barten (1969, 1977), Deaton (1975), Deaton and Muellbauer (1980) and others have considered a special case of (9) where

$$X = X, \qquad \text{for all } i. \tag{11}$$

III. *ESTIMATION OF PARAMETERS*

a. *Unrestricted Procedures*

In this section we shall examine the problem of estimating the parameters of (6) as specified in (9) but without imposing the constraints on parameters implied by the second set of conditions in (4).

It will be convenient, in this context, to simplify our notation by writing

$$\overset{*}{u}_{t\cdot} = (u_{t\cdot}, u_{tm}) \tag{12}$$

so that $u_{t\cdot}$ is an $(m - 1)$-element random vector with a nonsingular covariance matrix.

It is an implication of (4) that

$$u_{tm} = -u_{t\cdot}e \tag{13}$$

where now e is an $(m - 1)$-element column vector all of whose elements are unity. Let

$$\Omega = \text{Cov}(u_{t\cdot}') \tag{14}$$

and note that

$$\text{Cov}(\overset{*}{u}_{t\cdot}') = \Omega_* = \begin{bmatrix} \Omega & -\Omega e \\ -e'\Omega & e'\Omega e \end{bmatrix} \tag{15}$$

In this notation the covariance matrix of the error process in (9) is given by

$$\text{Cov}(u^*) = \Omega_* \otimes I_T = \Phi_* \tag{16}$$

Barten's device consists of writing

$$u_{t\cdot}\,\Omega^{-1}u'_{t\cdot} = (u_{t\cdot}, 0)EE^{-1}\begin{bmatrix}\Omega^{-1} & 0\\ 0 & 1/k\end{bmatrix}E^{-1}E\begin{bmatrix}u'_{t\cdot}\\ 0\end{bmatrix} = u^{*}_{t\cdot}\,\bar{\Omega}^{-1}u^{*\prime}_{t\cdot}. \quad (17)$$

where

$$E = \begin{bmatrix} I & -e\\ -e' & -1\end{bmatrix}, \quad E^{-1} = \begin{bmatrix} I - \frac{1}{m}ee' & -\frac{1}{m}e\\ -\frac{1}{m}e' & -\frac{1}{m}\end{bmatrix} \quad (18)$$

$$\bar{\Omega} = E\begin{bmatrix}\Omega & 0\\ 0 & k\end{bmatrix}E = \Omega_{*} + ke_m e'_m \quad (19)$$

and k is an arbitrary (positive) constant. Since, from Proposition 31 in Dhrymes (1984) it is easily seen that

$$|E| = -m, \qquad |\bar{\Omega}| = m^2 k|\Omega| \quad (20)$$

Barten is able to claim that irrespective of the equation implicitly suppressed by (13) the "likelihood function" can be expressed in terms of $\bar{\Omega}$; hence it is argued that the results one gets are invariant to the equation suppressed.[1]

To paraphrase this statement: It is quite immaterial whether the data are generated by a nonsingular process with covariance $\bar{\Omega}$ or by a singular process with covariance Ω_{*}.

One has then the comforting feeling of observing that the maximum likelihood (ML) estimators of the mean parameters (i.e., the elements of B) do not depend on which equation is chosen for elimination nor do they depend on the arbitrary positive parameter k. This is claimed on the basis of the fact that the (log) "likelihood function" is given by:

$$L = \frac{T}{2}[ln(2\pi) + ln(m^2) + lnk] - \frac{mT}{2}ln(2\pi) - \frac{T}{2}ln|\bar{\Omega}|$$
$$- 1/2\sum_{t=1}^{T}(y_{t\cdot} - x_{t\cdot}B)\bar{\Omega}^{-1}(y_{t\cdot} - x_{t\cdot}B)'. \quad (21)$$

See, for example, Deaton (1975, ch. 4).

1. This is, actually, Deaton's (1975) rendition of the Barten procedure.

We note, however, that (21) does not correspond to a likelihood function, since the integral of its exponential is not one, even on the assertion that

$$(y_{t\cdot} - x_{t\cdot}B)' \sim N(0, \bar{\Omega}) \tag{22}$$

unless we were to specify that $k = (2\pi m^2)^{-1}$. Indeed, if we proceed, without further discussion, to maximize (21) partially with respect to the unknown parameters in $\bar{\Omega}$, i.e., the elements of Ω we obtain

$$\hat{\Omega} = (I_{m-1}, 0)E^{-1} QE^{-1} \begin{bmatrix} I_{m-1} \\ 0 \end{bmatrix} \tag{23}$$

where

$$Q = \frac{1}{T}(Y - XB)' (Y - XB) \tag{24}$$

and the sum of the quadratic form in (21) was rewritten as

$$-1/2 \sum_{t=1}^{T} (y_{t\cdot} - x_{t\cdot}B)\bar{\Omega}^{-1}(y_{t\cdot} - x_{t\cdot}B)' = -\frac{T}{2} \operatorname{tr}\bar{\Omega}^{-1}Q \tag{25}$$

Put

$$Q = \begin{bmatrix} Q_{11} & Q_{12} \\ Q_{21} & Q_{22} \end{bmatrix}, \quad Q^* = E^{-1} QE^{-1} \tag{26}$$

such that Q_{11} is $(m - 1) \times (m - 1)$ and note that (23) implies

$$\hat{\Omega} = Q^*_{11}. \tag{27}$$

Substituting (27) in (25) yields

$$-\frac{T}{2} \operatorname{tr}\bar{\Omega}^{-1}Q = -\frac{T}{2}(m - 1) - \frac{T}{2k} Q^*_{22}$$

where

$$Q^*_{22} = \frac{1}{m^2} [e' Q_{11}e + 2e' Q_{12} + Q_{22}]$$

$$Q_{11} = \frac{1}{T}(Y_1 - XB_1)' (Y - XB_1), \quad Q_{12} = \frac{1}{T}(Y_1 - XB_1)'(y_{\cdot m} - Xb_{\cdot m}) \tag{28}$$

$$Q_{22} = \frac{1}{T}(y_{\cdot m} - Xb_{\cdot m})' (y_{\cdot m} - Xb_{\cdot m})$$

Thus, using (27) to concentrate the likelihood function (LF) yields

$$L^* = -\frac{T(m-1)}{2}[ln(2\pi) + 1] - \frac{T}{2} ln \mid Q_{11}^{\bullet} \mid - \frac{T}{2}\frac{1}{k} Q_{22}^{\bullet}. \qquad (29)$$

If this is now to be maximized with respect to the unknown parameters in B, it is by no means clear that the resulting estimators will not depend on the arbitrary parameter k, or on which equation is suppressed!

Remark 1: It is apparent that the Barten technique in writing the (log) LF is not the "reason" why results are invariant to which equation is suppressed or on what value is assigned to k. The assertions may be true enough but their validity does not rest on the justification adduced and, in fact, the justification is quite irrelevant. Moreover, in the special case where

$$X_i = X \qquad \text{for all } i \qquad (30)$$

such arguments are not needed to establish invariance. Thus, for example, note that if equation (30) above holds then the condition

$$\frac{\partial L}{\partial \text{vec}(B)} = 0$$

yields

$$X'(Y - XB) = 0$$

or

$$\hat{b}_{\cdot} = (X'X)^{-1} X'y_{\cdot i}, \qquad i = 1, 2, \ldots, m$$

which in view of the definition of $x_{.G}$ automatically satisfies the adding up condition. Moreover, for any j,

$$\hat{b}_{\cdot j} = e_{\cdot G} - \sum_{i \neq j} \hat{b}_{\cdot i}$$

The heart of the problem is that the conditions on the parameters force the singularity of the covariance matrix – and to a certain degree the converse is true, i.e., the singularity of the covariance matrix implies certain restrictions.

Remark 2: In order that we may bring out clearly the nature of the difficulties we will examine the problem on the assumption that *Ω is known-*

thus restricting our examination to Aitken estimators. At the end we shall make clear how "maximum likelihood" procedures may be employed, if it is so desired.

In view of the preceding discussion consider the minimand

$$F = \sum_{t=1}^{T} (y_{t\cdot} - x_{t\cdot}B)\bar{\Omega}^{-1} (y_{t\cdot} - x_{t\cdot}B)' = tr\bar{\Omega}^{-1}(Y - XB)' (Y - XB) \quad (31)$$

Incorporating in (31) the restrictions implied by Conventions 1 and 2 yields the form

$$F = (y - X^*\beta)' (\bar{\Omega}^{-1} \otimes I_T) (y - X^*\beta) \quad (32)$$

The estimator suggested by the Barten approach is

$$\hat{\beta} = (X^{*\prime}\bar{\Phi}^{-1}X^*)^{-1}X^{*\prime}\bar{\Phi}^{-1}y \quad (33)$$

where

$$\bar{\Phi} = \bar{\Omega} \otimes I_T \quad (34)$$

We shall now show, unambiguously, that the estimator in (33) does depend on the arbitrary parameter k. Before we do so we require a number or results.

Lemma 1 : The g-inverse of Ω_* as defined in (15) is given by

$$\Omega_{*g} = E^{-1} \begin{bmatrix} \Omega^{-1} & 0 \\ 0 & 0 \end{bmatrix} E^{-1}. \quad (35)$$

Proof: We verify that

$$\Omega_* \, \Omega_{*g} \, \Omega_* = E \begin{bmatrix} \Omega & 0 \\ 0 & 0 \end{bmatrix} E = \Omega_*$$

$$\Omega_{*g} \, \Omega_* \, \Omega_{*g} = E^{-1} \begin{bmatrix} \Omega^{-1} & 0 \\ 0 & 0 \end{bmatrix} E^{-1} = \Omega_{*g}$$

$$\Omega_* \, \Omega_{*g} = E \begin{bmatrix} I & 0 \\ 0 & 0 \end{bmatrix} E^{-1}$$

$$\Omega_{*g} \, \Omega_* = E^{-1} \begin{bmatrix} I & 0 \\ 0 & 0 \end{bmatrix} E.$$

From the definitions of E and E^{-1} in (18) it is easily seen that the last two matrix products above are symmetric. q.e.d.

Moreover,

Lemma 2 : The matrices $\bar{\Omega}^{-1}$ and Ω_{*g} are connected by

$$\bar{\Omega}^{-1} = \Omega_{*g} + \frac{1}{m^2 k} e_m e_m'.$$

Proof: We note that

$$\bar{\Omega}^{-1} = E^{-1}\left\{\begin{bmatrix} \Omega^{-1} & 0 \\ 0 & 0 \end{bmatrix} + \begin{bmatrix} 0 & 0 \\ 0 & \frac{1}{k} \end{bmatrix}\right\} E^{-1} = \Omega_{*g} + \frac{1}{m^2 k} e_m e_m' \qquad \text{q.e.d.}$$

Finally,

Lemma 3 : Put

$$\tilde{C} = \left(\frac{X^{*\prime}\bar{\Phi}^{-1}X^*}{T}\right)^{-1} = \left[S'\left(\bar{\Omega}^{-1} \otimes \frac{X'X}{T}\right)S\right]^{-1}, \quad q = \frac{X^{*\prime}\bar{\Phi}^{-1}y}{T}$$

Then

$$\frac{\partial \tilde{C}}{\partial k} = \frac{1}{m^2 k^2}\tilde{C}D'\frac{X'X}{T}D\tilde{C}, \qquad \frac{\partial q}{\partial k} = -\frac{1}{m^2 k^2}D'\left(\frac{X'x_{\cdot G}}{T}\right)$$

where

$$D = (e_m' \otimes I_G)S.$$

Proof: From Dhrymes (1984), Corollary 2 and Proposition 105

$$\frac{\partial \text{vec}(\tilde{C})}{\partial k} = \frac{\partial \text{vec}(\tilde{C})}{\partial \text{vec}(\tilde{C}^{-1})}\frac{\partial \text{vec}\tilde{C}^{-1}}{\partial k}.$$

But

$$\frac{\partial \text{vec}(\tilde{C})}{\partial \text{vec}(\tilde{C}^{-1})} = -[\tilde{C} \otimes \tilde{C}]$$

and using Lemma 2, we also find

$$\frac{\partial \text{vec}(\tilde{C^{-1}})}{\partial k} = \frac{1}{m^2 k^2}\text{vec}\left[S'\left(e_m e_m' \otimes \frac{X'X}{T}\right)S\right] = -\frac{1}{m^2 k^2}\text{vec}\left[D'\frac{X'X}{T}D\right].$$

Rematricizing, we have

$$\frac{\partial \tilde{C}}{\partial k} = \frac{1}{m^2k^2}\,\tilde{C}D'\,\frac{X'X}{T}\,D\tilde{C}.$$

Next, we easily find

$$\frac{\partial q}{\partial k} = \frac{1}{T}\,S'\left(-\,\frac{1}{m^2k^2}\,e_m e_m' \otimes X'\right)y = -\left(\frac{1}{m^2k^2}\right)\frac{1}{T}\,S'(e_m \otimes I_G)X'(e_m' \otimes I_T)y =$$

$$-\left(\frac{1}{m^2k^2}\right)D'\,\frac{X'x_{\cdot G}}{T} \qquad \text{q.e.d.}$$

We are now in a position to prove

Theorem 1 : Consider the model in equations (1) through (10), and let Conventions 1 and 2 hold. Then, the unrestricted (Barten) estimator as exhibited in (33) depends on the auxiliary parameter, k, introduced in (17) unless all equations contain the same set of variables, in which case it is simply the OLS estimator.

Proof: If all equations contain the same set of variables then

$$X^* = I \otimes X$$

and (33) reduces to

$$\hat{\beta} = [I \otimes (X'X)^{-1}X']\,y.$$

Since, evidently, the matrix $\bar{\Omega}$ does not play a role the estimator does not depend on k; but the expression above is simply the OLS estimator in which case this result is well known. So let us suppose that in Convention 1, $G_i < G$ for at least one i. Then

$$\hat{\beta} = \tilde{C}q$$

and $\tilde{C}$ is a *nonsingular* matrix. Now,

$$\frac{\partial \hat{\beta}}{\partial k} = \frac{\partial \tilde{C}}{\partial k}\,q + \tilde{C}\,\frac{\partial q}{\partial k}\,.$$

From Lemma 3 we find

$$\frac{\partial \hat{\beta}}{\partial k} = \frac{1}{m^2k^2}\tilde{C}\left[D'\frac{X'X}{T}D\hat{\beta} - D'\frac{X'x_{.G}}{T}\right] \tag{36}$$

Consequently, if

$$\frac{\partial \hat{\beta}}{\partial k} = 0 \tag{37}$$

then, since $\tilde{C}$ is nonsingular, (37) implies that in (36) we must have

$$D'X'XD\hat{\beta} = D'X'x_{.G}. \tag{38}$$

Since D is $G \times \left(\sum_{i=1}^{m} G\right)$ of rank G (38) implies

$$D\hat{\beta} = (X'X)^{-1}X'x_{.G} = e_{.G}. \tag{39}$$

But this is a contradiction, for we have ruled out the case where all variables appear in all equations. To see why this is so, note that from (33) we find, using (39)

$$e_{.G} = D\hat{\beta} = D\beta + \frac{1}{T}D\tilde{C}S'(\bar{\Omega}^{-1} \otimes X')u$$

which implies that

$$\frac{1}{T}D\tilde{C}S'(\bar{\Omega}^{-1} \otimes X')u = 0.$$

In particular, the covariance matrix of the vector above must obey

$$\frac{1}{T}\left[D\tilde{C}D' - \frac{1}{m^2k}D\tilde{C}D'\frac{X'X}{T}D\tilde{C}D'\right] = 0.$$

In view of the nonsingularity of $D\tilde{C}D'$, we must have

$$\frac{X'X}{T} = m^2k(D\tilde{C}D')^{-1} \tag{40}$$

which is impossible since Ω is an arbitrary positive definite matrix; note that the left member of (40) does not depend on Ω while the right member does! Consequently, (39) implies a contradiction and, thus, (37) cannot hold! q.e.d.

Remark 3: We have shown in this section that for unrestricted estimators the procedure introduced by Barten is either irrelevant, when all equations contain the same set of variables, or the estimator obtained depends on k.

Thus, it is natural now to examine estimators that explicitly impose on the parameters the restriction implied by the adding up requirement.

b. *Restricted Procedures*

It is implicit in the discussion of the preceding section that the restrictions we have in mind are the adding up restrictions – although the procedure, obviously, will accommodate additional restrictions as well.

More precisely, in terms of the model as exhibited in (9) the restrictions are

$$(e'_m \otimes I_T)y = (e'_m \otimes I_T)X^*\beta + (e'_m \otimes I_T)u = x_{\cdot G} \tag{41}$$

Since

$$(e'_m \cdot I_T)X^*\beta = (e'_m \cdot I_T)\,(I_m \cdot X)S\beta = X(e'_m \cdot I_G)S\beta \tag{42}$$

it is clear that (42) in conjuction with (41) imply not only

$$(e'_m \otimes I_T)u = 0 \tag{43}$$

but, more importantly, that

$$D\beta = e_{\cdot G} \qquad D = (e'_m \otimes I_G)S. \tag{44}$$

For the estimator considered in the preceding section,

$$(e'_m \otimes I_T)\hat{y} = (e'_m \otimes I_T)X^*\hat{\beta} \neq x_{\cdot G}$$

and, consequently,

$$(e'_m \otimes I_T)\,(y - X^*\hat{\beta}) \neq 0$$

so that it violates both (41) and (43).

To ensure that estimators do obey the equivalent of (41) and (43) we impose the conditions (44) in the estimation phase.

The resulting estimator is

$$\hat{\beta}_r = \beta + (I - Q)\,(X^{*\prime}\bar{\Phi}^{-1}X^*)^{-1}X^{*\prime}\bar{\Phi}^{-1}u \tag{45}$$

where

$$Q = \left(\frac{X^{*\prime}\overline{\Phi}^{-1}X^*}{T}\right)^{-1} D' \left[D\left(\frac{X^{*\prime}\overline{\Phi}^{-1}X^*}{T}\right)^{-1} D'\right]^{-1} D. \tag{46}$$

We shall now show analytically that the estimator defined in (45) is independent of the parameter k. Before we do so, however, we require the following auxiliary result.

Lemma 4 *:* Putting

$$\tilde{P} = [D\tilde{C}D']^{-1}$$

we have

$$\frac{\partial \tilde{P}}{\partial k} = -\frac{1}{m^2k^2}\left(\frac{X'X}{T}\right).$$

Proof: Again using Dhrymes (1984), Corollary 2 and Proposition 105 we have

$$\frac{\partial \mathrm{vec}(\tilde{P})}{\partial k} = \frac{\partial \mathrm{vec}(\tilde{P})}{\partial \mathrm{vec}(\tilde{P}^{-1})}\,\frac{\partial \mathrm{vec}(\tilde{P}^{-1})}{\partial \mathrm{vec}(\tilde{C}^{-1})}\,\frac{\partial \mathrm{vec}(\tilde{C}^{-1})}{\partial k}.$$

Hence

$$\frac{\partial \mathrm{vec}(\tilde{P})}{k} = -\frac{1}{m^2k^2}[(D\tilde{C}D')^{-1}\otimes(D\tilde{C}D')^{-1}]\,(D\otimes D)\cdot(\tilde{C}\otimes\tilde{C})\mathrm{vec}\left[D'\frac{X'X}{T}D\right]$$

$$= -\frac{1}{m^2k^2}\,\mathrm{vec}\left[(D\tilde{C}D')^{-1}D\tilde{C}D'\frac{X'X}{T}D\tilde{C}D'(D\tilde{C}D')^{-1}\right]$$

$$= -\frac{1}{m^2k^2}\,\mathrm{vec}\left(\frac{X'X}{T}\right)$$

Rematricizing we have

$$\frac{\partial \tilde{P}}{\partial k} = -\frac{1}{m^2k^2}\left(\frac{X'X}{T}\right). \qquad \text{q.e.d.}$$

We are now in a position to prove

Theorem 2 *:* Consider the model in equations (1) through (10) obeying Conventions 1 and 2. Then, the restricted Barten-like estimator as exhibited in (45) is independent of the auxiliary parameter k.

Proof: Using Lemma 2 we note that

$$X^{*\prime}\bar{\Phi}^{-1}u = S'(I \otimes X')\,[(\Omega_{*g} + \frac{1}{m^2k}\,e_m e_m') \otimes I_T]\,u$$
$$= S'(I \otimes X')\,(\Omega_{*g} \otimes I_T)u$$

owing to the fact that in such a model

$$(e_m' \otimes I_T)\,u = 0.$$

Hence

$$\hat{\beta}_r = \beta + \frac{1}{T}\,WX^{*\prime}\Phi_{*g}u$$

where

$$W = \tilde{C} - \tilde{C}D'\tilde{P}D\tilde{C}$$

is the only component of $\hat{\beta}_r$ that can possibly depend on k. We shall show that

$$\frac{\partial W}{\partial k} = 0$$

thus completing the proof.

But

$$\frac{\partial W}{\partial k} = \frac{\partial \tilde{C}}{\partial k} - \frac{\partial \tilde{C}}{\partial k}\,D'\tilde{P}D\tilde{C} - \tilde{C}\,D'\tilde{P}D\,\frac{\partial \tilde{C}}{\partial k} - \tilde{C}\,D'\,\frac{\partial \tilde{P}}{\partial k}\,D\tilde{C}.$$

Using Lemmata 3 and 4 we easily see that

$$\frac{\partial W}{\partial k} = 0. \qquad \text{q.e.d.}$$

Remark 4 : The result of Theorem 2 makes abundantly clear why Barten's procedure works. Its efficacy in solving the problem really has nothing to do with the manner in which we write the LF. Rather, its success hinges on the fact that, if the adding up constraints are imposed, *the matrix defining the restricted estimator does not depend on the arbitrary parameter k*! This is rather felicitous since it affords us a routine way in which we may impose all sorts of specifications and be assured that, provided the adding up restrictions are imposed as well, the results of the Theorem will hold.

Thus, suppose we impose the restrictions

$$R\beta = r \tag{47}$$

where

$$R = \begin{bmatrix} R_1 \\ R_2 \end{bmatrix}, \quad R_1 = D, \quad r = \begin{bmatrix} r_1 \\ r_2 \end{bmatrix}, \quad r_1 = e_{\cdot G} \tag{48}$$

and R_2, r_2 are a suitable matrix and vector, respectively, reflecting other, appropriate, restrictions. Proceeding as in the proof of Theorem 2, the matrix W therein is now given by

$$W = \tilde{C} - \tilde{C}R'\tilde{P}R\tilde{C}$$

where $\tilde{C}$ is as before; now, however,

$$\tilde{P} = [R\tilde{C}R']^{-1}.$$

Noting that in this case

$$\frac{\partial \tilde{P}}{\partial k} = -\frac{1}{m^2k^2}\begin{bmatrix} \frac{X'X}{T} & 0 \\ 0 & 0 \end{bmatrix}$$

and that

$$D = (I, 0)R$$

we conclude again that

$$\frac{\partial W}{\partial k} = 0.$$

The preceding discussion has proved

Corollary 1 *:* Consider the model of Theorem 2, but subject to the general linear restrictions of (47) and (48). Then the restricted Barten-like estimator does not depend on the auxiliary parameter k.

Remark 5 *:* It is clear that even if Ω is not known the feasible Barten-like estimator can be obtained either by a two-step procedure or by iterative methods as follows: Let $\tilde{\beta}$ be an initial consistent estimator that is obtained, say, by restricted least squares, i.e., by minimizing

$$(y - X^*\beta)'(y - X^*\beta)$$

subject to

$$D\beta = e_{\cdot G}.$$

Obtain the residual matrix

$$\tilde{U} = \Upsilon - X\tilde{B} \tag{49}$$

using the relations in equation (8), i.e., the fact that

$$\tilde{b}_{\cdot i} = S_i \tilde{\beta}_{\cdot i}, \qquad i = 1, 2, \ldots, m.$$

Note that, in a perfectly symmetric fashion

$$\frac{1}{T} \tilde{U}' \tilde{U} = \tilde{\Omega}_* \tag{50}$$

is a consistent estimator of Ω_*; in particular, note that

$$\tilde{\Omega}_* e_m = \frac{1}{T} (\Upsilon - X\tilde{B}) (\Upsilon e_m - X\tilde{B} e_m) = 0$$

owing to the fact that

$$\Upsilon e_m = x_{\cdot G}$$

$$\text{vec}(\tilde{B} e_m) = (e_m' \otimes I) S\tilde{\beta} = D\tilde{\beta} = e_{\cdot G}.$$

Define the "estimator"

$$\hat{\tilde{\Omega}}^{-1} = \tilde{\Omega}_{*g} + \frac{1}{m^2 k} e_m e_m' \tag{51}$$

and the Barten-like estimator

$$\hat{\beta}_r = \frac{1}{T} W X^{*\prime} \tilde{\Phi}_{*g} y + \tilde{C} D' \tilde{P} e_{\cdot G}. \tag{52}$$

Thus, given (51) we can compute (52); given (52) we can recompute (51) and so on until convergence is obtained. Actually, convergence is not required for the limiting (asymptotic) properties of the estimator in (52).

Remark 6 : If one insists on using the normality assumption essentially, one can also have recourse to "maximum likelihood" procedures as well.

In such a case we would maximize the "likelihood function" in (21) subject to the condition

$$D\beta = e_{\cdot G}$$

thus obtaining the normal equations as in (52) and

$$\hat{\hat{\Omega}} = \frac{1}{T} \hat{U}' \hat{U} + k e_m e_m' = \hat{\Omega}_* + k e_m e_m'$$

where

$$\hat{U} = Y - X\hat{B}, \quad \hat{b}_{\cdot i} = S_i \hat{\beta}_{\cdot i}, \qquad i = 1, 2, \ldots, m.$$

But this is exactly the iterative procedure described in (50), (51) and (52) in connection with the feasible Aitken estimator.

IV. *RELATION OF THE RESTRICTED BARTEN TO THE GENERALIZED INVERSE TYPE RESTRICTED ESTIMATORS*

The preceding discussion has clarified the nature and the limitations of the estimator produced by the remarkable procedure invented by Barten. It has not, however, explained, in any understandable way, why it works. It works "because" it does not really depend on the auxiliary parameter. But what are we, in effect, doing?

At about the same time as this estimator was developed, Theil (1971) suggested another procedure based on the generalized inverse (g-inverse) of the covariance matrix.

As we point out in another paper, Dhrymes and Schwarz (1984), for systems of expenditure equations this estimator fails to exist in the form exhibited by Theil (1971) or in the later paper by Kreijger and Neudecker (1977). Perhaps for this reason it has received little attention and has not been employed in empirical work.

Even though, in the form exhibited, the estimator does not exist for the models examined in this paper, *this does not mean that it does not exist at all*!

In fact, the necessary and sufficient conditions for its existence are given in Dhrymes and Schwarz (1984); it turns out that if the adding up restrictions are imposed the g-inverse estimator will always exist; if, however, these restrictions are not imposed this estimator (i.e., the unrestricted estimator) will not exist.

The question is: what, if any, is the connection between the g-inverse restricted estimator and the restricted version of the estimator produced by the Barten procedure. The answer is given in

Theorem 3: Consider the model in equations (1) through (10) together with Conventions 1 and 2. Then the two Aitken like estimators

(a) using $\bar{\Omega}^{-1}$ as the "inverse" of Ω_*
(the Barten estimator)

(b) using the g-inverse, Ω_{*g}, of Ω_*
(the Theil estimator)

obeying the restrictions

$$R\beta = r, \quad R = (R_1', R_2')', \quad R_1 = D, \quad r = (r_1', r_2')', \quad r_1 = e_{\cdot G}$$

where R is $s \times \sum_{r=1}^{m} G_i$, of rank s, *are identical.*

Proof: The estimator according to (a) (i.e., that involving Barten's procedure obeys

$$\begin{bmatrix} X^{*\prime}\bar{\Phi}^{-1}X^* & R' \\ R & 0 \end{bmatrix} \begin{bmatrix} \beta \\ \lambda \end{bmatrix} = \begin{bmatrix} X^{*\prime}\bar{\Phi}^{-1}y \\ r \end{bmatrix} \tag{53}$$

The estimator according to (b) is obtained as the solution of

$$\begin{bmatrix} X^{*\prime}\Phi_{*g}X^* & R' \\ R & 0 \end{bmatrix} \begin{bmatrix} \beta \\ \lambda \end{bmatrix} = \begin{bmatrix} X^{*\prime}\Phi_{*g}y \\ r \end{bmatrix} \tag{54}$$

where, evidently, β is the vector of the parameters to be estimated and λ is the vector of Lagrange multipliers. Recall from equations (18), (34) and Lemma 2 that

$$\bar{\Phi}^{-1} = \Phi_{*g} + \frac{1}{m^2 k}(e_m e_m' \otimes I_T).$$

Consequently, we find

$$X^{*\prime}\bar{\Phi}^{-1}X^* = X^{*\prime}\Phi_{*g}X^* + \frac{1}{m^2 k} D'X'XD,$$

$$X^{*\prime}\bar{\Phi}^{-1}y = X^{*\prime}\Phi_{*g}y + \frac{1}{m^2 k} D'X'x_{\cdot G}.$$

Now transform the system in (54) by multiplication on the left by the non-singular matrix

$$H = \begin{bmatrix} I & \frac{1}{m^2 k} D'X'X & 0 \\ 0 & I & 0 \\ 0 & 0 & I \end{bmatrix}$$

and verify that the result is the system in (53); hence the systems in (53) and (54) *are equivalent* and, thus, yield identical estimators for the parameter vector β – and the Lagrange multiplier vector, λ. q.e.d.

V. *CONCLUSION*

This paper has accomplished a number of objectives. First, it has demonstrated that in a system of expenditure equations (or similar models) the unrestricted Aitken estimator suggested by the use of Barten's auxiliary parameter k, does indeed depend on k so that it is an arbitrary estimator of unknown properties; moreover such estimators will observe the restrictions implied by the adding up requirement only when they are irrelevant, i.e., when all variables appear in all equations so that in fact they are identical to OLS procedures.

Second, it has shown analytically that when the restrictions implied by the adding up requirement are imposed – and possibly other relevant restrictions as well – the estimator does not depend on k, in the sense that its derivative with respect to k is zero, identically.

Finally, it was shown that this restricted estimator is derived from a redundant set of equations implied by that which defines the restricted Aitken estimator based on the g-inverse of the system's (singular) covariance matrix.

Columbia University, New York,
The College of Staten Island, CUNY, New York, U.S.A.

REFERENCES

Barten, A.P. (1969): "Maximum Likelihood Estimation of a Complete System of Demand Equations", *European Economic Review*, Vol. 1, pp. 7-73.

—— (1977): "The Systems of Consumer Demand Functions Approach: A Review", *Econometrica*, Vol. 45, pp. 23-51.

BERNDT, E.R. AND CHRISTENSEN, L.R. (1973) : "The Translog Function and the Substitution of Equipment, Structures and Labor in U.S. Manufacturing, 1929-1986", *Journal of Econometrics*, Vol. 2.

— (1974) : "Testing for the Existence of a Consistent Aggregate Index of Labor Inputs", *American Economic Review*, Vol. 64, pp. 391-403.

BROWN, A. AND DEATON, A. (1972): "Surveys in Applied Economics : Models of Consumer Behavior", *The Economic Journal*, Vol. 82, pp. 1145-1236.

CHRISTENSEN, L.R., JORGENSON, D.W. AND LAU, L.J. (1973) : "Transcendental Logarithmic Production Frontiers", *Review of Economics and Statistics*, Vol. 55, pp. 28-45.

— (1975) : "Transcendental Logarithmic Utility Functions", *American Economic Review*, Vol. 65, pp. 367-383.

DEATON, A.S. (1975) : *Models and Projections of Demand in Postwar Britain*, Halstead Press, New York.

— AND MUELLBAUER, J. (1980) : *Economics and Consumer Behavior*, Cambridge University Press, Cambridge.

DHRYMES, P. J. (1962) : "On Devising Unbiased Estimators for the Parameters of a Cobb-Douglas Production Function", *Econometrica*, Vol. 30, pp. 297-304.

— (1984) : *Mathematics for Econometrics*, (2nd edition), Springer-Verlag, New York.

— AND SCHWARZ, S. (1984) : "On the Existence of Generalized Inverse Estimators in a Singular System of Equations", Discussion Paper Series No. 237, Department of Economics, Columbia University.

FRIEND, I. (1964): "The Effects of Monetary Policy on Nonmonetary Financial Institutions and Capital Markets", in *Private Capital Markets*, Commission on Money and Credit, Prentice-Hall.

KLEIN, L.R. (1953) : *A Textbook for Econometrics*, Row, Peterson and Co, Evanston.

KREIJGER, R.G. AND NEUDECKER, H. (1977) : "Exact Linear Restrictions on Parameters in the General Linear Model with a Singular Covariance Matrix", *Journal of the American Statistical Association*, Vol. 72, pp. 430-432.

POWELL, A.A. (1969) : "Aitken Estimators as a Tool in Allocating Predetermined Aggregates", *Journal of the American Statistical Association*, Vol. 64, pp. 913-922.

RAO, J. R. (1972) : "Alternative Econometric Models of Sales Advertising Relationships", *Journal of Marketing Research*, Vol. 9, pp. 171-181.

THEIL, H. (1971) : *Principles of Econometrics*, John Wiley and Sons, New York.

WEISS, D. L. (1968) : "Determinants of Market Share", *Journal of Marketing Research*, Vol. 5, pp. 290-295.

PART III

ECONOMETRIC THEORY: DISTRIBUTED LAGS

INTERNATIONAL ECONOMIC REVIEW
Vol. 10, No. 1, February, 1969

EFFICIENT ESTIMATION OF DISTRIBUTED LAGS WITH AUTOCORRELATED ERRORS*

BY PHOEBUS J. DHRYMES[1]

1. PRELIMINARIES

THE NOTION THAT an economic variable registers its impact on another not instantaneously but through some specified lag structure is a very old one. It is, however, accurate to say that this hypothesis was first introduced and systematically exploited in an econometric context by Koyck [9]. I have commented on Koyck's procedure in another context [4] and this need not be repeated here.

Subsequently Klein [8] presents an interesting reinterpretation of Koyck's scheme in terms of an error in variables model. In both instances, however, the authors fail to treat the case where the error structure is subject to an autoregressive process.

Liviatan [10] tackles this problem and suggests the use of instrumental variables, in fact the lagged values of the exogenous variables appearing in the equation to be estimated. However, when dealing with economic time series, reliance on the lagged values of endogenous and exogenous variables as explanatory variables is a rather unsatisfactory procedure.

Thus although Liviatan's procedure formally solves the problem of obtaining consistent estimators its empirical implementation is a rather delicate matter. In addition, as Hannan [5] has shown, Liviatan's estimator is inefficient. Hannan proposes an estimator derived by spectral analysis techniques, which is shown to be asymptotically efficient. Finally Amemiya and Fuller [1] show that Hannan's estimator is essentially an Aitken estimator where the relevant covariance matrix employed is consistently estimated. The authors then propose an alternative estimator which converges asymptotically to the maximum likelihood estimator. Since, if the error terms are normally distributed Hannan's estimator is asymptotically equivalent to the maximum likelihood estimator, the procedure suggested by Amemiya and Fuller is simply another way of arriving at the same result obtained by Hannan.

One should remark that in the cases of Hannan and Amemiya and Fuller the error term structure is taken to be a general moving average process of infinite extent, i.e., the error term is taken to be

$$u_t = \sum_{j=0}^{\infty} \rho_j \varepsilon_{t-j} \tag{1}$$

* Manuscript received May 25, 1966, revised December 30, 1966.

[1] The research on which this paper is based was initiated during the author's tenure of a John Simon Guggenheim Memorial Fellowship (1965-1966) and was partially supported by NSF grant GS 571 at the University of Pennsylvania. I wish to thank L.R. Klein and T.W. Anderson for helpful comments on an earlier draft.

where the ε-process consists of orthogonal variables with common variance and mean zero. In the case of Amemiya and Fuller the ε-process is further assumed to be normal.

Typically, however, in econometric research a less general specification than (1) is found to be quite adequate. Thus, one frequently deals with the first order Markov process

$$u_t = \sum_{j=0}^{\infty} \rho^j \varepsilon_{t-j} , \qquad 0 < |\rho| < 1 . \tag{1a}$$

We shall obtain in this paper maximum likelihood estimators for the parameters of the lag structure model when the specification (1a) is employed. The procedure will be considerably simpler than the ones outlined above, and in addition, the estimators derived will globally maximize the likelihood function for every sample size.

2. THE MODEL

We shall consider here a model which is slightly more general than the one customarily employed, in that we shall allow several exogenous variables. However, only one of them will be specified to be subject to an infinite lag structure, say the first.

Thus, we have the model

$$y_t = \alpha_1 \sum_{j=0}^{\infty} \lambda^j x_{t-j,1} + \sum_{i=2}^{n} \alpha_i x_{ti} + u_t . \tag{2}$$

In (2) we assume in addition that

$$u_t = \rho u_{t-1} + \varepsilon_t , \qquad 0 < |\lambda| < 1,\ 0 < |\rho| < 1 , \tag{2a}$$

and further that

$$\varepsilon_t \sim N(0, \sigma^2) , \qquad E(\varepsilon_t \varepsilon_{t'}) = \delta_{tt'} \sigma^2 . \tag{2b}$$

Following Klein [8] we truncate the infinite sum at $j = t - 1$ and rewrite (2) in the alternative form

$$y_t = \alpha_1 \lambda^t \sum_{s=0}^{\infty} \lambda^s x_{-s,1} + \alpha_1 \sum_{j=0}^{t-1} \lambda^j x_{t-j,1} + \sum_{i=2}^{n} \alpha_i x_{ti} + u_t , \qquad t = 1, 2, \cdots, T . \tag{3}$$

This particular approach necessitates that we estimate the unobservable quantity $\sum_{s=0}^{\infty} \lambda^s x_{-s,1}$.

Of course, if we were to specify *ab initio* in (2) that x_1 exerts an influence on y only over a finite number of periods, k, then (2) may be written in the alternative form

$$y_t = \alpha_1 \sum_{j=0}^{k} \lambda^j x_{t-j,1} + \sum_{i=2}^{n} \alpha_i x_{ti} + u_t , \qquad t = 1, 2, \cdots, T . \tag{3a}$$

While this specification would simplify the estimation problem somewhat, the difficulty alluded to above, viz., the estimation of an exponentially weighted sum of unobserved values of x_1 will not be totally absent, although it would be considerably attenuated. Thus, if k is small relative to T we might simply dispense with the first k sample observations and then handle the problem routinely in the manner to be explored below.

In what follows we shall use the formulation in (3) although the results would be equally applicable under the specification (3a) with k known.

Now consider the contribution of the neglected terms in the infinite lag structure of x_1. It is given by

$$\sum_{j=t}^{\infty} \lambda^j x_{t-j,1} = \lambda^t \sum_{s=0}^{\infty} \lambda^s x_{-s,1} = \lambda^t \eta_0 \,. \tag{3b}$$

We shall call η_0 the "truncation remainder." Let

$$\begin{aligned} \alpha_0 &= \alpha_1 \eta_0 \,, \\ x_{t0}^* &= \lambda^t \,, \\ x_{t1}^* &= \sum_{j=0}^{t-1} \lambda^j x_{t-j,1} \,, \\ x_{ti}^* &= x_{ti} \,, \end{aligned} \qquad \begin{aligned} t &= 1, 2, \cdots, T \,, \\ i &= 2, 3, \cdots, n \,. \end{aligned} \tag{3c}$$

With the aid of this notation we may write (3) in standard form as

$$y_t = \sum_{i=0}^{n} \alpha_i x_{ti}^* + u_t \,, \qquad t = 1, 2, \cdots, T \,. \tag{4}$$

In the reformulated problem above we shall consider the α_i to be independent parameters, although it may appear from (3c) that this is inappropriate. It will be apparent, however, from the development below that in the context of the estimation procedure employed, (3c) represents a simple reparameterization and in that context the α_i are indeed free parameters, α_0 reflecting the "initial conditions" of the system, as incorporated in the "truncation remainder." If we are particularly interested in η_0 we can obtain a consistent estimator for it through

$$\hat{\eta}_0 = \frac{\hat{\alpha}_0}{\hat{\alpha}_1} \tag{4a}$$

where $\hat{\alpha}_0$, $\hat{\alpha}_1$ are respectively estimators for α_0 and α_1. With these preliminaries aside we note that the sample of the model in (4) may be written compactly as

$$y = X^* \alpha^* + u \tag{5}$$

where y, u are respectively the vectors of observation on the dependent variable and the error term; α^* is the vector of parameters to be estimated; and X^* is a $T \times (n+1)$ matrix whose k-th column is $x_{\cdot k}^*$ the latter being the vector of observations on the k-th independent variable of (3c).

The logarithmic likelihood function[2] of the observations is given by

[2] The matrix X in the L-function is defined as $(x_1, x_2, \cdots, x_n)$ where, e.g., $x_i = (x_{1i}, x_{2i}, \cdots, x_{Ti})'$.

$$L(\alpha^*, \lambda, \rho, \sigma^2 \mid y, X) = -\frac{T}{2}\ln(2\pi) - \frac{T}{2}\ln\sigma^2 - \frac{1}{2}\ln|V| - \frac{1}{2\sigma^2}(y - X^*\alpha^*)'V^{-1}(y - X^*\alpha^*)\,. \tag{5a}$$

The matrix V is defined by

$$\operatorname{Cov}(u) = \frac{\sigma^2}{1-\rho^2}\begin{bmatrix} 1 & \rho & \rho^2 & \cdots & \rho^{T-1} \\ \rho & 1 & \rho & \cdots & \rho^{T-2} \\ \rho^2 & \rho & 1 & \cdots & \rho^{T-3} \\ \vdots & \vdots & \vdots & & \vdots \\ \rho^{T-1} & \rho^{T-2} & \rho^{T-3} & \cdots & 1 \end{bmatrix} = \sigma^2 V\,. \tag{5b}$$

The likelihood function contains two nonlinearities, in λ and in ρ. These appear in the covariance matrix of u and in x_{t1}^*—since we have agreed to consider the α_i, $i = 0, 1, 2, \cdots, n$, as independent parameters.

Notice that V^{-1} has the decomposition[3]

$$V^{-1} = M'M \tag{5c}$$

where

$$M = \begin{bmatrix} \sqrt{1-\rho^2} & 0 & \cdot & \cdot & \cdot & \cdot & 0 \\ -\rho & 1 & 0 & \cdot & \cdot & \cdot & 0 \\ 0 & -\rho & 1 & 0 & \cdot & \cdot & 0 \\ \vdots & & & & & & \vdots \\ \vdots & & & & & & 0 \\ 0 & & \cdot & \cdot & \cdot 0 & -\rho & 1 \end{bmatrix} \tag{5d}$$

and carry out the transformations

$$w = My\,, \qquad Z = MX^*\,, \qquad v = Mu\,. \tag{5e}$$

It may be readily verified that

$$v \sim N(0, \sigma^2 I)\,. \tag{5f}$$

In terms of the transformed data, the likelihood function can be written:

$$L(\alpha^*, \lambda, \sigma^2, \rho \mid y, X) = -\frac{T}{2}\ln(2\pi) - \frac{T}{2}\ln\sigma^2 + \frac{1}{2}\ln(1-\rho^2) - \frac{1}{2\sigma^2}(w - Z\alpha^*)'(w - Z\alpha^*)\,. \tag{6}$$

3. MAXIMUM LIKELIHOOD ESTIMATORS OF α^*, λ AND ρ

From (6) it is clear that we can obtain the global maximum of the function, for *fixed* λ and ρ, by simple differentiation.[4] The corresponding estimators

[3] Observe, however, that this decomposition is not unique, since if A is any orthogonal matrix define $M^* = AM$ and then note that $M^{*\prime}M^* = M'A'AM = M'M = V^{-1}$.

[4] As we have remarked earlier, in this context the truncation remainder is simply

(*Continued on next page*)

are easily established as

$$\text{(6a)}\qquad \begin{aligned} \hat{\alpha}^*(\lambda, \rho) &= (Z'Z)^{-1}Z'w \\ \hat{\sigma}^2(\lambda, \rho) &= \frac{(w - Z\hat{\alpha}^*)'(w - Z\hat{\alpha}^*)}{T} \,. \end{aligned}$$

Expressing the estimator of α^* in terms of the original data we find

$$\text{(6b)}\qquad \hat{\alpha}^*(\lambda, \rho) = (X^{*\prime}V^{-1}X^*)^{-1}X^{*\prime}V^{-1}y$$

so that this is simply the Aitken estimator for *given* λ and ρ.

Inserting (6a) in (6) we obtain the "concentrated" likelihood function

$$\text{(6c)}\qquad L^*(\lambda, \rho \mid y, X) = -\frac{T}{2}[\ln(2\pi) + 1] - \frac{T}{2}\ln\left[\frac{\hat{\sigma}^2(\lambda, \rho)}{(1-\rho^2)^{1/T}}\right].$$

Thus, finding the global maximum of (6) is equivalent to finding the global minimum of $\hat{\sigma}^2(\lambda, \rho)/(1-\rho^2)^{1/T}$ over the region

$$\text{(6d)}\qquad S = \{(\lambda, \rho): 0 \leqq |\lambda|, \ |\rho| < 1\} \,.$$ [5]

The following procedure then suggests itself: select a set of points (λ_i, ρ_i) such that $\{\lambda_i: i = 1, \cdots, m\}$ and $\{\rho_i: i = 1, 2, \cdots, m\}$ each cover the interval $(-1, 1)$ as densely as desired. How dense the sets need be depends on what degree of accuracy one desires the estimators to possess.[6]

These sequences will determine a lattice lying in an open rectangle and centered on the origin of R^2 (the two dimensional Euclidean space).

For each lattice point obtain the estimators (6a). The maximum likelihood estimators desired are those that correspond to the lattice point yielding the smallest residual variance. Put more concretely, if $\hat{\lambda}, \hat{\rho}$ minimize $\hat{\sigma}^2(\lambda, \rho)/(1-\rho^2)^{1/T}$ then the maximum likelihood estimator of

$$\text{(6e)}\qquad \theta^* = \begin{bmatrix} \alpha^* \\ \lambda \\ \sigma^2 \\ \rho \end{bmatrix}$$

is

---

a convenient function of the initial conditions $x_{-s,1}$, $s = 0, 1, 2, \cdots$, to be estimated from the data.

[5] Perhaps on economic grounds one could argue strongly that the restriction on λ should be $0 < \lambda < 1$; whether we take this or the restriction given in (6d) as the relevant one the subsequent development remains unaffected.

[6] In several empirical applications, in this and related contexts, the procedure was followed of first employing a coarse net, i.e., successive values of λ and ρ were rather widely spaced. Once the region of the maximum was located then a relatively dense net was employed. When the likelihood function does not display excessive fluctuations such a two step procedure usually economizes on computer time.

(6f) $$\hat{\theta}^* = \begin{bmatrix} \hat{\alpha}^*(\hat{\lambda}, \hat{\rho}) \\ \hat{\lambda} \\ \hat{\sigma}^2(\hat{\lambda}, \hat{\rho}) \\ \hat{\rho} \end{bmatrix}$$

where $\hat{\alpha}^*(\lambda, \rho)$ and $\hat{\sigma}^2(\lambda, \rho)$ are given by (6a).

4. PROPERTIES OF THE ESTIMATORS

The estimators obtained in the previous section represent solutions to the maximum likelihood equations; nonetheless, since the random terms in the basic model are not mutually independent and identically distributed, care must be exercised in attributing to them the classical properties of maximum likelihood estimators [7, (61)]. Thus, such properties need to be proved *ab initio* in this case and to this we now turn.

LEMMA 1. *If $\bar{L}(\theta^*; y, X)$ is the likelihood function*[7] *of the parameters in the model of the previous section where θ^* is as in* (6e) *then*

(7) $$\bar{L}(\hat{\theta}^*; y, X) \geqq \bar{L}(\theta^*; y, X) \qquad \textit{any} \quad \theta^* \in \Omega$$

where Ω is the admissible set of parameters.

PROOF. Obvious from the derivation.

REMARK 1. The Lemma simply states that the estimators yield the *global* maximum of the likelihood function; this is of considerable consequence as we shall see below.

LEMMA 2. *In the model of Section* 3, *let $\hat{\theta}^*$ be an estimator of θ^* such that* (7) *holds; then $\hat{\theta}^*$ is a consistent estimator of θ^*.*

PROOF. Let θ_0^* be the true value of the parameters and let $\theta^* \in \Omega$ be any other value ($\theta_0^* \neq \theta^*$). Thus in view of the concavity of the log function we have

(7a) $$E\left[\ln\left\{\frac{\bar{L}(\theta^*; y, X)}{\bar{L}(\theta_0^*\ ; y, X)}\right\}\right] \leqq \ln E\left[\frac{\bar{L}(\theta^*; y, X)}{\bar{L}(\theta_0^*; y, X)}\right]$$

where the expectation is taken with respect to the "true" density of the observations, i.e., the one having parameter θ_0^*. Thus

(7b) $$E\left[\frac{\bar{L}(\theta^*; y, X)}{\bar{L}(\theta_0^*; y, X)}\right] = \int \frac{\bar{L}(\theta^*; y, X)}{\bar{L}(\theta_0^*; y, X)} \bar{L}(\theta_0^*; y, X)dy = \int \bar{L}(\theta_0^*; y, X)dy = 1 .$$

From (7a) and (7b) we conclude

(7c) $$E\{L(\theta^*; y, X)\} \leqq E\{L(\theta_0^*; y, X)\} .$$

Now for any $\theta^* \in \Omega$ the logarithmic likeliood of the observations obeys

(7d) $$\frac{1}{T} L(\theta^*; y, X) = -\frac{1}{2}\ln(2\pi) - \frac{1}{2}\ln\sigma^2 + \frac{1}{2T}\ln(1-\rho^2) - \frac{1}{2\sigma^2 T} u' V^{-1} u .$$

[7] Notice that here we are *not* dealing with the logarithmic likelihood function $L(\cdot; \cdots)$; hence the overbar.

Since

(7e) $$v = Mu$$

and

(7f) $$v \sim N(0, \sigma^2 I)$$

we conclude

(7g) $$u' V^{-1} u = v'v \, .$$

Thus

(8) $$\frac{1}{2\sigma^2 T} u' V^{-1} u = \frac{1}{2T} \frac{v'v}{\sigma^2} = \frac{1}{2T} \sum_{i=1}^{T} \left(\frac{v_i^2}{\sigma^2} \right)$$

and since the v_i^2/σ^2 are independently chi-square distributed with 1 degree of freedom it follows, by the strong law of large numbers that

(8a) $$\operatorname*{plim}_{T\to\infty} \frac{1}{2\sigma^2 T} u' V^{-1} u = \frac{1}{2} \, .$$

Thus

(8b) $$\operatorname*{plim}_{T\to\infty} \frac{1}{T} L(\theta^*; y, X) = \lim_{T\to\infty} \frac{1}{T} E[L(\theta^*; y, X)] \, .$$

But then, in view of (7c), we conclude that there exists a sample size T^* such that for all $T > T^*$ and $\varepsilon > 0$,

(8c) $$\Pr \{L(\theta^*; y, X) \leqq L(\theta_0^*; y, X)\} \geqq 1 - \varepsilon \, .$$

In particular (8c) holds for $\theta^* = \hat{\theta}^*$; thus

(8d) $$\Pr \{L(\hat{\theta}^*; y, X) \leqq L(\theta_0^*; y, X)\} \geqq 1 - \varepsilon \, .$$

But since $\hat{\theta}^*$ is such that (7) holds, we conclude

(8e) $$\Pr \{\frac{1}{T} L(\hat{\theta}^*; y, X) = \frac{1}{T} L(\theta_0^*; y, X)\} \geqq 1 - \varepsilon$$

for all $T > T^*$. Finally (8e) implies

(8f) $$\operatorname{plim} \hat{\theta}^* = \theta^*. \qquad \text{Q.E.D.}$$

It is apparent from the conditions of the problem that the estimator $\hat{\theta}^*$ of θ^* satisfying (7) satisfies

(9) $$\frac{\partial L}{\partial \theta^*} = 0$$

as well.

In what follows we shall be concerned exclusively with the parameters

(9a) $$\theta = (\alpha_1, \alpha_2, \cdots, \alpha_n, \lambda, \sigma^2, \rho)' \, .$$

Thus we exclude from consideration the truncation remainder η_0, although a consistent estimator for it may be obtained. In this connection we should observe that the term $\alpha_1 \eta_0 \lambda^t$ tends to zero as $t \to \infty$ and thus the model behaves, for large t, essentially according to

$$y_t = \alpha_1 \sum_{j=0}^{t-1} \lambda^j x_{t-j,1} + \sum_{i=2}^{n} \alpha_i x_{ti} + u_t \, . \tag{9b}$$

Thus while for small samples it is quite useful to take the term $\alpha_1 \eta_0 \lambda^t$ into account, this is not so for large samples. Since in the subsequent discussion we shall be concerned with the asymptotic moments of the estimators it would entail little loss of relevance if we proceed as follows. Let

$$x_{t1}^* = \frac{I}{I - \lambda L} x_{t1} = \sum_{i=0}^{\infty} \lambda^i x_{t-i,1} \tag{9c}$$

where L is the usual lag operator and I the identity operator. Notice that (9c) implies

$$x_{t1}^* = x_{t1} + \lambda x_{t-1,1}^* \tag{9d}$$

and that if x_{01}^* is known then x_{t1}^* can be computed recursively. We further note that

$$\eta_0 = x_{01}^* \, . \tag{9e}$$

If we take the most convenient value for x_{01}^*, viz.,

$$x_{01}^* = 0 \, , \tag{9f}$$

then x_{t1}^* can be easily computed from the recursive relation in (9d).

We now consider the modified model

$$y_t = \alpha_1 x_{t1}^* + \sum_{i=2}^{n} \alpha_i x_{ti} + u_t \, , \qquad t = 1, 2, \cdots, T \, . \tag{10}$$

For given (λ, ρ) the maximum likelihood equations of this system are given by

$$X' V^{-1} X \alpha = X' V^{-1} y \tag{10a}$$

where

$$X = (\underline{x}_1^*, \underline{x}_2, \underline{x}_3, \cdots, \underline{x}_n) \, . \tag{10b}$$

If we put

$$\underline{\lambda} = (\lambda, \lambda^2, \cdots, \lambda^T)' \tag{10c}$$

we observe that

$$X^* = (\underline{\lambda}, X) \, . \tag{10d}$$

Hence the estimator of α implied by (6b) satisfies

$$\begin{aligned} \underline{\lambda}' V^{-1} \underline{\lambda} \alpha_0 + \underline{\lambda}' V^{-1} X \alpha &= \underline{\lambda}' V^{-1} y \\ X' V^{-1} \underline{\lambda} \alpha_0 + X' V^{-1} X \alpha &= X' V^{-1} y \, . \end{aligned} \tag{11}$$

Dividing through by T we observe that as $T \to \infty$ the terms $\underline{\lambda}' V^{-1} \underline{\lambda} / T$, $\underline{\lambda}' V^{-1} X / T$, $\underline{\lambda}' V^{-1} y / T$ converge to zero and hence for large T the estimator of α implied by (6b) coincides with the estimator of α obtained from the model in (10).[8]

Let us now write the likelihood function as

$$\begin{aligned} L(\theta; y, X) &= -\frac{T}{2}\ln(2\pi) - \frac{1}{2}\ln\sigma^2 \\ &\quad + \frac{1}{2}\ln(1-\rho^2) - \frac{1}{2\sigma^2}(y - X\alpha)'V^{-1}(y - X\alpha)\,. \end{aligned} \tag{12}$$

and observe that the estimator of θ obtained in Section 3, for large T, maximizes globally the function in (12) and thus obeys $\partial L/\partial\theta = 0$. Employing the notation $\partial L(\bar{\theta})/\partial\theta$—or $\partial^2 L(\bar{\theta})/\partial\theta\partial\theta$—to mean the vector $\partial L/\partial\theta$—or the matrix $\partial^2 L/\partial\theta\partial\theta$—evaluated at the point $\theta = \bar{\theta}$ we have

LEMMA 3. *In the model of Section* 3 *let* $\hat{\theta}$ *be the subvector of* $\hat{\theta}^*$ *satisfying* (7), (9) *and* (9a). *Suppose further that the explanatory variables satisfy*

$$\lim_{T\to\infty}\frac{1}{T}\sum_{t=1}^{T}|x_{ti}x_{tj}| = \xi_{ij}\,, \qquad i, j = 1, 2, \cdots, n \tag{12a}$$

and that the ξ_{ij} *are finite.*

Then

$$\begin{aligned} &\lim_{T\to\infty} E[\sqrt{T}(\hat{\theta} - \theta_0)] = 0 \\ &\lim_{T\to\infty} E[T(\hat{\theta} - \theta_0)(\hat{\theta} - \theta_0)'] = -\lim_{T\to\infty} TM^{-1}(\theta_0) \end{aligned} \tag{12b}$$

where

$$M(\theta_0) = E\left[\frac{\partial^2 L}{\partial\theta\partial\theta}(\theta_0)\right]. \tag{12c}$$

PROOF. For any θ in the admissible parameter space, we have by the mean value theorem

$$\frac{\partial L}{\partial\theta}(\theta) = \frac{\partial L}{\partial\theta}(\theta_0) + \frac{\partial^2 L}{\partial\theta\partial\theta}(\bar{\theta})(\theta - \theta_0) \tag{13}$$

where $\bar{\theta}$ lies between θ and θ_0. In particular, for $\theta = \hat{\theta}$ (13) implies

$$\frac{\partial L}{\partial\theta}(\theta_0) = -\frac{\partial^2 L}{\partial\theta\partial\theta}(\bar{\theta})(\hat{\theta} - \theta_0) \tag{13a}$$

where now $\bar{\theta}$ lies between $\hat{\theta}$ and θ_0.

If we rewrite (13a) as

$$\frac{1}{\sqrt{T}}\frac{\partial L}{\partial\theta}(\theta_0) = -\frac{1}{T}\frac{\partial^2 L}{\partial\theta\partial\theta}(\bar{\theta})\sqrt{T}(\hat{\theta} - \theta_0) \tag{13b}$$

we note that by Cramèr's theorem [2, (254)]

[8] This in fact makes clear why in some Monte Carlo studies (in a somewhat different context) Morrison [11] finds that for small sample size the procedure outlined earlier in which the truncation remainder is explicitly taken into account does somewhat better than an iterative procedure based on the likelihood function as exhibited in (12). This advantage, however, tends to disappear for large sample.

$$\text{(13c)} \qquad \lim_{T\to\infty} \frac{1}{\sqrt{T}} E\left[\frac{\partial L}{\partial \theta}\right] = -\operatorname*{plim}_{T\to\infty} \frac{1}{T}\frac{\partial^2 L}{\partial\theta\partial\theta}(\bar\theta) \lim_{T\to\infty} E[\sqrt{T}(\hat\theta-\theta_0)] .$$

But for any admissible θ

$$\text{(13d)} \qquad E\left[\frac{\partial L}{\partial \theta}\right] = 0 .$$

Moreover, since $\bar\theta$ lies between $\hat\theta$ and θ_0 and $\hat\theta$ is consistent for θ_0 then

$$\text{(13e)} \qquad \operatorname*{plim}_{T\to\infty} \frac{1}{T}\frac{\partial^2 L}{\partial\theta\partial\theta}(\bar\theta) = \operatorname*{plim}_{T\to\infty} \frac{1}{T}\frac{\partial^2 L}{\partial\theta\partial\theta}(\theta_0) .$$

But it is shown in the Appendix that

$$\text{(13f)} \qquad \operatorname*{plim}_{T\to\infty} \frac{1}{T}\frac{\partial^2 L}{\partial\theta\partial\theta}(\theta_0) = \lim_{T\to\infty} \frac{1}{T} M(\theta_0) .$$

Since the matrix in (13f) is assumed to be nonsingular, it follows from (13c) and (13d)

$$\text{(13g)} \qquad \lim_{T\to\infty} E[\sqrt{T}(\hat\theta-\theta_0)] = 0 .$$

Turning now to the asymptotic covariance matrix we note first that for any admissible θ

$$\text{(14)} \qquad \operatorname{Cov}\left(\frac{\partial L}{\partial\theta}\right) = E\left[\left(\frac{\partial L}{\partial\theta}\right)\left(\frac{\partial L}{\partial\theta}\right)'\right] = -E\left[\frac{\partial^2 L}{\partial\theta\partial\theta}\right] = -M(\theta) .$$

Thus, from (13b) we find, using again Cramèr's theorem

$$\text{(14a)} \qquad -\lim_{T\to\infty}\frac{1}{T}M(\theta_0) = \operatorname*{plim}_{T\to\infty} \frac{1}{T}\frac{\partial^2 L}{\partial\theta\partial\theta}(\bar\theta) \lim_{T\to\infty} [TE(\hat\theta-\theta_0)(\hat\theta-\theta_0)'] \cdot \operatorname*{plim}_{T\to\infty} \frac{1}{T}\frac{\partial^2 L}{\partial\theta\partial\theta}(\bar\theta) .$$

From (13f) and (14a) in view of the nonsingularity of $M(\theta_0)$ we conclude

$$\text{(14b)} \qquad \lim_{T\to\infty} [TE(\hat\theta-\theta_0)(\hat\theta-\theta_0)'] = -\lim_{T\to\infty} TM^{-1}(\theta_0) .$$ [9] Q.E.D.

[9] It might be legitimately asked: why have we not invoked the standard theorem on maximum likelihood estimators to show not only the conclusion of the Lemma above but also that $\sqrt{T}(\hat\theta-\theta_0) \sim N(0, -TM^{-1}(\theta_0))$. The answer to this is that the usual proof of such theorems breaks down in this case. Such proofs rest on the fact that when the *error terms are intertemporally* independent then $(1/\sqrt{T})(\partial L/\partial\theta)$ obeys a multivariate central limit theorem. This is so since the components of $\partial L/\partial\theta$ can then be expressed as the sum of (T) mutually independent—but not necessarily identically distributed—random variables with finite moments. In this case this breaks down since the component $\partial L/\partial\rho$ yields

$$\frac{\partial L}{\partial\rho} = -\frac{\rho}{1-\rho^2} - \frac{2}{2\sigma^2}u'\frac{\partial V^{-1}}{\partial\rho}u$$

and this cannot be so expressed. The central limit theorem on dependent variables [5] does not seem to apply either. Thus although it is conceivable that asymptotic normality can be shown to hold, I have not been able to establish this property.

REMARK 2. We shall refer to $-M^{-1}(\theta_0)$ as the asymptotic covariance matrix of the estimator $\hat{\theta}$.

LEMMA 4. *The estimator $\hat{\theta}$ is asymptotically efficient.*

PROOF. Let $\tilde{\theta}$ be any other asymptotically unbiased estimator of θ_0 and let $N(\theta)$ be its asymptotic covariance matrix. We shall show

$$N(\theta) + M^{-1}(\theta_0) = P \tag{15}$$

where P is positive semi-definite and

$$|N(\theta)| \geqq |-M^{-1}(\theta_0)| . \tag{15a}$$

Let $\tilde{\theta}_i$ be the i-th component of $\tilde{\theta}$; for large T we have (approximately)

$$\int \tilde{\theta}_i \bar{L}(\theta; y, X) dy = \theta_i . \tag{15b}$$ [10]

Differentiating (15a) with respect to θ_j we have

$$\int \tilde{\theta}_i \frac{\partial L}{\partial \theta_j} \bar{L}(\theta; y, X) dy = \delta_{ij} \tag{15c}$$

where δ_{ij} is the Kronecker delta.

Since

$$\int \bar{L}(\theta; y, X) dy = 1 \tag{15d}$$

and the range of the y's does not depend on θ, it follows that

$$\int \frac{\partial L}{\partial \theta} \bar{L} dy = 0 , \quad \int \frac{\partial^2 L}{\partial \theta \partial \theta} \bar{L} dy = - \int \left(\frac{\partial L}{\partial \theta}\right)\left(\frac{\partial L}{\partial \theta}\right)' \bar{L} dy . \tag{15e}$$

From (15c) and (15e) we conclude that, for large T,

$$\operatorname{Cov}(\varphi) = \begin{bmatrix} N(\theta) & I \\ I & -M(\theta_0) \end{bmatrix} \tag{16}$$

where

$$\varphi = \begin{bmatrix} \tilde{\theta} \\ \dfrac{\partial L}{\partial \theta} \end{bmatrix} \tag{16a}$$

and $\partial L/\partial \theta$ is evaluated at $\theta = \theta_0$.

Define now the matrix

$$D = \begin{bmatrix} I & M^{-1}(\theta_0) \\ 0 & I \end{bmatrix} . \tag{16b}$$

Noting that $\operatorname{Cov}(\varphi)$ is at least positive semidefinite, we conclude that

$$Q = D \operatorname{Cov}(\varphi) D' = \begin{bmatrix} N(\theta) + M^{-1}(\theta_0) & 0 \\ 0 & -M(\theta_0) \end{bmatrix} . \tag{16c}$$

[10] We remind the reader that $\bar{L}(\theta; y, X)$ is the likelihood function while $L(\theta, y, X)$ is the *logarithm* of the likelihood function.

But this means that $N(\theta) + M^{-1}(\theta_0)$ is also at least positive semidefinite which proves the first part. Now the roots of this matrix in the metric of $-M^{-1}(\theta_0)$ are nonnegative. On the other hand the latter are the solutions of

$$|\lambda M^{-1}(\theta_0) + N(\theta) + M^{-1}(\theta_0)| = 0 . \tag{17}$$

But the above is equivalent to

$$|(1 + \lambda)M^{-1}(\theta_0) + N(\theta)| = 0 . \tag{17a}$$

Thus we may write

$$- M^{-1}(\theta)W(I + \Lambda) = N(\theta)W \tag{17b}$$

where W is the matrix of the (orthogonal) characteristic vectors and

$$I + \Lambda = \text{diag}\,(1 + \lambda_1, 1 + \lambda_2, \cdots, 1 + \lambda_{n+3}) \tag{17c}$$

$1 + \lambda_i$ being the roots of (17a). Upon taking determinants in (17b) we conclude, since $\lambda_i \geqq 0$

$$|N(\theta)| = |-M^{-1}(\theta_0)|\,|I + \Lambda| \geqq |-M^{-1}(\theta_0)| . \tag{17c}$$

Q.E.D.

We have therefore proved the following

THEOREM. *Let*

$$y_t = \alpha_1 \sum_{j=0}^{\infty} \lambda^j x_{t-j,1} + \sum_{i=2}^{n} \alpha_i x_{ti} + u_t , \qquad t = 1, 2, \cdots, T , \tag{18}$$

$$u_t = \rho u_{t-1} + \varepsilon_t , \qquad \varepsilon \sim N(0, \sigma^2 I) \tag{18a}$$

where $\varepsilon = (\varepsilon_1, \varepsilon_2, \cdots, \varepsilon_T)'$, *and suppose that*

$$\lim_{T\to\infty} \frac{1}{T} \sum_{t=1}^{T} |x_{ti}x_{tj}| = \xi_{ij} , \qquad i, j = 1, 2, \cdots, n , \tag{18b}$$

exist as finite quantities and that

$$0 < |\lambda| , \qquad |\rho| < 1 \tag{18c}$$

then the estimator $\hat{\theta}$ *of*

$$\theta = (\alpha_1, \alpha_2, \cdots, \alpha_n, \lambda, \rho, \sigma^2)' \tag{18d}$$

derived in Section 3 globally maximizes the likelihood function for every sample size, is consistent, asymptotically unbiased and efficient in the sense that if $\tilde{\theta}$ *is any other asymptotically unbiased estimator of* θ, *then the difference between the covariance of* $\tilde{\theta}$ *and* $\hat{\theta}$ *is positive semidefinite and the (asymptotic) generalized variance of* $\tilde{\theta}$ *is not less than that of* $\hat{\theta}$.

REMARK 3. If one is willing to sacrifice some observations, the problem can also be handled as follows. Write

$$y_t = \frac{\alpha_1 I}{I - \lambda L} x_{t1} + \sum_{i=2}^{n} \alpha_i x_{ti} + \frac{I\varepsilon_t}{I - \rho L} \tag{19}$$

where L is the usual lag operator and I the identity operator. Clearing "fractions" we obtain

$$y_t - (\lambda + \rho)y_{t-1} + \rho\lambda y_{t-2} = \alpha_1(x_{t1} - \rho x_{t-1,1}) + \sum_{i=2}^{n} \alpha_i[x_{ti} - (\lambda + \rho)x_{t-1,i} + \lambda\rho x_{t-2,i}] + (\varepsilon_t - \lambda\varepsilon_{t-1}) . \tag{19a}$$

This is well defined for $t = 3, 4, \cdots, T$. Put

$$\begin{aligned} y_t^* &= y_t - (\lambda + \rho)y_{t-1} + \rho\lambda y_{t-2} , & t &= 3, 4, \cdots, T , \\ x_{t1}^* &= x_{t1} - \rho x_{t-1,1} , & t &= 3, 4, \cdots, T , \\ x_{ti}^* &= x_{ti} - (\lambda + \rho)x_{t-1,i} + \lambda\rho x_{t-2,i} , & i &= 2, 3, \cdots, n , \\ \varepsilon_t^* &= \varepsilon_t - \lambda\varepsilon_{t-1} , & t &= 3, 4, \cdots, T , \end{aligned} \tag{19b}$$

and observe that the covariance matrix of the ε_t^* is given by

$$\mathrm{Cov}\,(\varepsilon^*) = \sigma^2 \begin{pmatrix} 1+\lambda^2 & -\lambda & 0 & 0 & \cdot & \cdot & \cdot & 0 \\ -\lambda & 1+\lambda^2 & -\lambda & 0 & \cdot & \cdot & \cdot & 0 \\ 0 & -\lambda & 1+\lambda^2 & -\lambda & \cdot & \cdot & \cdot & 0 \\ \cdot & \cdot & \cdot & \cdot & \cdot & \cdot & \cdot & 0 \\ \cdot & \cdot & \cdot & \cdot & \cdot & \cdot & \cdot & \cdot \\ \cdot & \cdot & \cdot & \cdot & \cdot & \cdot & \cdot & -\lambda \\ 0 & \cdot & \cdot & \cdot & \cdot & 0 & -\lambda & 1+\lambda^2 \end{pmatrix} = \sigma^2\Phi . \tag{19c}$$

We shall derive approximately the same estimators as in Section 3 if for fixed λ, ρ we minimize

$$S = (y^* - X^* \alpha)'\Phi^{-1}(y^* - X^*\alpha) \tag{19d}$$

where the vector y^* and the matrix X^* are defined according to (19b).

The inverse of Φ above can be easily obtained from Lemma 1 of Dhrymes [4]. It will then be apparent that for large T the approximation

$$\Phi^{-1} \approx \frac{1}{1 - \lambda^2} \begin{bmatrix} 1 & \lambda & \lambda^2 & \cdot & \cdot & \cdot & \lambda^{T-3} \\ \lambda & 1 & \lambda & \cdot & \cdot & \cdot & \lambda^{T-4} \\ \cdot & \cdot & \cdot & \cdot & \cdot & \cdot & \cdot \\ \cdot & \cdot & \cdot & \cdot & \cdot & 1 & \lambda \\ \lambda^{T-3} & \lambda^{T-4} & \cdot & \cdot & \cdot & \lambda & 1 \end{bmatrix} \tag{19e}$$

is quite reasonable.

But then we can decompose the right hand side of (19e) in a particularly simple way to obtain

$$\Phi^{-1} \approx RR', \quad R = \begin{bmatrix} \varphi & 0 & 0 & 0 & \cdot & \cdot & 0 \\ \varphi\lambda & 1 & 0 & 0 & \cdot & \cdot & \cdot \\ \varphi\lambda^2 & \lambda & 1 & \cdot & \cdot & \cdot & \cdot \\ \cdot & \cdot & \lambda & \cdot & \cdot & \cdot & \cdot \\ \cdot & \cdot & \cdot & \cdot & \cdot & 1 & \cdot \\ \varphi\lambda^{T-4} & \lambda^{T-5} & \lambda^{T-6} & \cdot & \cdot & \lambda & 1 \end{bmatrix}, \quad \varphi = \frac{1}{(1 - \lambda^2)^{1/2}} . \tag{19f}$$

Thus we may subject the data to the simple transformation

$$y^{**} = R'y^* , \qquad x^{**} = R'X^* \tag{19g}$$

and for given λ, ρ obtain by ordinary least squares the estimator for α. Thus

$$\tilde{\alpha}(\lambda, \rho) = (X^{**\prime}X^{**})^{-1}X^{**\prime}y^{**} . \tag{19h}$$

We then estimate σ^2 by

$$\tilde{\sigma}^2(\lambda, \rho) = \frac{1}{T-2-n}(y^{**} - X^{**}\tilde{\alpha})'(y^{**} - X^{**}\tilde{\alpha}) \tag{19i}$$

and by scanning, select the set

$$\tilde{\theta} = \begin{bmatrix} \tilde{\alpha}(\tilde{\lambda}, \tilde{\rho}) \\ \tilde{\lambda} \\ \tilde{\sigma}^2(\tilde{\lambda}, \tilde{\rho}) \\ \tilde{\rho} \end{bmatrix} \tag{19j}$$

which minimizes $\tilde{\sigma}(\lambda, \rho)$ of (19i). The merit of this procedure is that it is somewhat simpler to execute. In particular the search technique is simple since the matrix to be inverted depends on linear combinations of lagged auto cross covariances, the weights of such combinations being various functions of λ and ρ. Thus, only the weights need be altered as between different runs. The disadvantage of the procedure is that it "loses" 2 observations. If end points are felt to be significant then clearly it should not be used.

REMARK 4. If one considers the computations entailed by the maximum likelihood estimator unduly excessive, one can employ a two-step procedure. While the latter may not be equivalent to the maximum likelihood estimator, it is definitely an improvement over the method of instrumental variables. We illustrate here in the case of the special model

$$y_t = \frac{I}{I-\lambda L}x_t + \frac{I}{I-\rho L}\varepsilon_t \tag{20}$$

Eliminating the distributed lag on the explanatory variable, we have

$$y_t = \lambda y_{t-1} + \alpha x_t + w_t \tag{20a}$$

where

$$w_t = u_t - \lambda u_{t-1} , \qquad u_t = \frac{I}{I-\rho L}\varepsilon_t . \tag{20b}$$

Using an instrumental variables approach, we can obtain initial (consistent) estimators, say $\tilde{\alpha}_0$, $\tilde{\lambda}_0$, and thus obtain the residuals of (20a), say $\tilde{w}_t$. In virtue of (20b), consistent estimators of the error term in (20) can be obtained recursively from

$$\tilde{u}_t = \tilde{w}_t + \lambda_0 \tilde{u}_{t-1} \tag{21}$$

provided some assumption is made regarding $\tilde{u}_0$. The most convenient assumption is $\tilde{u}_0 = 0$. Although this is an arbitrary convention and may have serious repercussions for small samples, it becomes relatively innocuous as the sample size becomes large. Now, a consistent estimator for ρ can be obtained as

(21a)
$$\tilde{\rho} = \frac{\sum_{t=2}^{T} \tilde{u}_t \tilde{u}_{t-1}}{\sum_{t=2}^{T} \tilde{u}_{t-1}^2} .$$

Alternatively, we may calculate[11]

(22)
$$x_t^* = x_t + \tilde{\lambda}_0 x_{t-1}^*$$

and obtain the residuals

(22a)
$$y_t - \tilde{\alpha}_0 x_t^* - \lambda_0 y_{t-1} = \tilde{u}_t .$$

From the quantities in (22a), we may obtain a consistent estimator of ρ as in (21a).

Consider now the error vector in (20a).

(23)
$$w = (w_2, w_3, \cdots, w_T)' ,$$

and observe that

(23a)
$$\begin{aligned} E(w_t w_{t-\theta}) &= \frac{\sigma^2}{1-\rho^2}[1 - 2\lambda\rho + \lambda^2] && \text{if } \theta = 0 \\ &= \frac{\sigma^2[(\rho-\lambda)(1-\lambda\rho)]}{(1-\rho^2)\rho}\rho^\theta && \text{if } \theta > 0 \end{aligned}$$

Thus

(23b)
$$\mathrm{Cov}\,(w) = \frac{\sigma^2[(\rho-\lambda)(1-\lambda\rho)]}{(1-\rho^2)} \begin{bmatrix} \phi & \rho & \rho^2 & \cdot & \cdot & \cdot & \rho^{T-2} \\ \rho & \phi & \rho & \cdot & \cdot & \cdot & \rho^{T-3} \\ \cdot & \cdot & \cdot & \cdot & \cdot & \cdot & \cdot \\ \rho^{T-2} & \cdot & \cdot & \cdot & \cdot & \cdot & \phi \end{bmatrix} = \sigma^2 \Phi$$

where

(23c)
$$\phi = \frac{\rho - 2\lambda\rho^2 + \lambda^2\rho}{(\rho-\lambda)(1-\lambda\rho)} .$$

Since we now have consistent estimators, $\tilde{\rho}$ and $\tilde{\lambda}_0$, we can obtain the "Aitken" estimator of the coefficients of (20a) as

(24)
$$\begin{bmatrix} \hat{\alpha} \\ \hat{\lambda} \end{bmatrix} = [X' \tilde{\Phi}^{-1} X]^{-1} X' \tilde{\Phi}^{-1} y$$

where

(24a)
$$X = \begin{bmatrix} x_2 & y_1 \\ x_3 & y_2 \\ \vdots & \vdots \\ x_T & y_{T-1} \end{bmatrix}, \qquad y = \begin{bmatrix} y_2 \\ y_3 \\ \vdots \\ y_T \end{bmatrix}$$

[11] The assumption $x_0^* = 0$ (or $u_0 = 0$) induces an error in (22), or (21), to the extent of the term $\lambda^t x_0^*$ (or $\lambda_0^t u_0$) which is omitted from the quantities calculated therefrom.

TABLE 1

SEARCH TECHNIQUE APPLIED TO ARTIFICAL DATA

($T = 20, \quad \lambda = 0.5, \quad \rho = -0.5$)

	First Stage				
λ	0.99	0.8855	0.7811	0.6766	0.5722
Minimizing ρ	−0.0011	−0.1110	−0.2538	−0.4077	−0.6054
Residual variance	18.916	12.206	7.288	4.015	2.003
	Second Stage				
λ	0.5722	0.5490	0.5258	0.5025	0.4793
Minimizing ρ	−0.6054	−0.6494	−0.6604	−0.6823	−0.6823
Residual variance	2.003	1.733	1.536	1.415	1.371
	First Stage				
λ	0.4677	0.3633	0.2588	0.1544	0.05
Minimizing ρ	−0.6604	−0.4846	−0.3307	−0.2648	−0.2319
Residual variance	1.378	2.181	4.129	7.239	11.550
	Second Stage				
λ	0.4561	0.4329	0.4097	0.3865	0.3633
Minimizing ρ	−0.4561	−0.6274	−0.5835	−0.5285	−0.4846
Residual variance	1.403	1.505	1.672	1.899	2.181

and $\tilde{\Phi}$ is the matrix resulting when we substitute $\tilde{\rho}$, $\tilde{\lambda}_0$ for ρ and λ in Φ of of (23b).

To conclude this section, we give in Table 1 an example of the calculations involved in the application of the technique described above. This is an excerpt from a forthcoming study of the performance characteristics of alternative distributed lag estimators. Here we are dealing with data generated from the model

$$y_t = 2.00 \frac{I}{I - 0.5L} x_{t1} + 5.0\, x_{t2} + u_t \tag{25}$$

where the x_{ti}, $i = 1, 2$, are distributed independently of u_t, and the latter obeys

$$u_t = -\,0.5 u_{t-1} + \varepsilon_t \tag{25}$$

the ε_t being mutually independent $N(0, 1)$ variables. The procedure involves finding the minimizing value of ρ for each λ_i, the latter being varied by 10 equal steps over the interval (0.05, 0.99). From the first stage, we obtain that value of λ_i, say λ_{i_0}, which yields the smallest residual variance. Then, we repeat the procedure over the interval $(\lambda_{i_0 - 1}, \lambda_{i_0 + 1})$. We present in the table only information regarding λ and ρ. We see that the residual variance declines monotonically in the first stage up to $\lambda = 0.4677$ and then rises. The second stage establishes that the global minimum—within this degree of numerical accuracy—occurs for $\hat{\lambda} = 0.4793$ and $\hat{\rho} = -0.6823$.

5. CONCLUSION

We have given in this paper an expression for the estimators of the parameters of an infinite (geometric) lag structure model which globally maximizes the likelihood function, and we have shown that such estimators are consistent asymptotically unbiased and efficient. In doing so we have assumed that the error term of the model is a first order Markov process. Although this is somewhat restrictive, it is often found appropriate in econometric work.

If this is indeed so, then it would seem that the procedure herein described, which can be easily executed on a standard regression (computer) program is to be preferred to others which approximate (linearly) the likelihood function and employ a two step procedure.

University of Pennsylvania, U.S.A.

APPENDIX

The logarithm of the likelihood function is given by

$$L(\theta; y, X) = -\frac{T}{2}\ln(2\pi) - \frac{T}{2}\ln\sigma^2 + \frac{1}{2}\ln(1-\rho^2) - \frac{1}{2\sigma^2}(y - X\alpha)' V^{-1}(y - X\alpha) \tag{A.1}$$

where X was defined in (10b).

Now

$$\begin{aligned}
\frac{\partial^2 L}{\partial\alpha\partial\alpha} &= -\frac{1}{\sigma^2}X'V^{-1}X \\
\frac{\partial^2 L}{\partial\alpha\partial\lambda} &= -\frac{1}{\sigma^2}\left[\alpha_1 X'V^{-1}\frac{\partial x_1^*}{\partial\lambda}\right] \\
\frac{\partial^2 L}{\partial\alpha\partial\sigma^2} &= -\frac{1}{\sigma^4}\left[X'V^{-1}u\right] \\
\frac{\partial^2 L}{\partial\alpha\partial\rho} &= \frac{1}{\sigma^2}\left[X'\frac{\partial V^{-1}}{\partial\rho}u\right] \\
\frac{\partial^2 L}{\partial\lambda\partial\lambda} &= \frac{1}{\sigma^2}\left[\alpha_1\frac{\partial^2 x_1^*}{\partial\lambda}V^{-1}u - \alpha_1^2\frac{\partial x_1^*}{\partial\lambda}V^{-1}\frac{\partial x_1^*}{\partial\lambda}\right] \\
\frac{\partial^2 L}{\partial\lambda\partial\sigma^2} &= -\frac{1}{\sigma^4}\left[\alpha_1\frac{\partial x_1^*}{\partial\lambda}V^{-1}u\right] \\
\frac{\partial^2 L}{\partial\lambda\partial\rho} &= \frac{1}{\sigma^2}\left[\alpha_1\frac{\partial x_1^*}{\partial\lambda}\frac{\partial V^{-1}}{\partial\rho}u\right]
\end{aligned} \tag{A.2}$$

$$\frac{\partial^2 L}{\partial\sigma^2\partial\sigma^2} = \frac{T}{2}\frac{1}{\sigma^4} - \frac{1}{\rho^4}\left(\frac{u'V^{-1}u}{\sigma^2}\right)$$

$$\frac{\partial^2 L}{\partial\sigma^2\partial\rho} = \frac{1}{2\sigma^4}\left[u'\frac{\partial V^{-1}}{\partial\rho}u\right]$$

$$\frac{\partial^2 L}{\partial\rho\partial\rho} = -\frac{1+\rho^2}{(1-\rho^2)^2} - \frac{1}{2\sigma^2}\left[u'\frac{\partial^2 V^{-1}}{\partial\rho\partial\rho}u\right]$$

It is easily seen that since the explanatory variables are nonstochastic then trivially

$$\text{(A.3)}\qquad \begin{aligned} \lim_{T\to\infty}\frac{1}{T}E\left[\frac{\partial^2 L}{\partial\alpha\partial\alpha}\right] &= \operatorname*{plim}_{T\to\infty}\frac{1}{T}\frac{\partial_2 L}{\partial\alpha\partial\alpha} \\ \lim_{T\to\infty}\frac{1}{T}E\left[\frac{\partial^2 L}{\partial\alpha\partial\lambda}\right] &= \operatorname*{plim}_{T\to\infty}\frac{1}{T}\frac{\partial^2 L}{\partial\alpha\partial\lambda} \end{aligned}$$

Since the elements of X and V are nonstochastic and thus trivially $E(X'V^{-1}u) = 0$ it readily follows that

$$\text{(A.4)}\qquad \begin{aligned} \lim_{T\to\infty}\frac{1}{T}E\left[\frac{\partial^2 L}{\partial\alpha\partial\sigma^2}\right] &= \operatorname*{plim}_{T\to\infty}\frac{1}{T}\frac{\partial^2 L}{\partial\alpha\partial\sigma^2} = 0 \\ \lim_{T\to\infty}\frac{1}{T}E\left[\frac{\partial^2 L}{\partial\alpha\partial\rho}\right] &= \operatorname*{plim}_{T\to\infty}\frac{1}{T}\frac{\partial^2 L}{\partial\alpha\partial\rho} = 0 \\ \lim_{T\to\infty}\frac{1}{T}E\left[\frac{\partial^2 L}{\partial\lambda\partial\lambda}\right] &= \operatorname*{plim}_{T\to\infty}\frac{1}{T}\frac{\partial^2 L}{\partial\lambda\partial\lambda} \\ &= -\frac{1}{\sigma^2}\left[\alpha_1^2\lim_{T\to\infty}\frac{1}{T}\left(\frac{\partial x_1^*}{\partial\lambda}\right)'V^{-1}\left(\frac{\partial x_1^*}{\partial\lambda}\right)\right] \\ \lim_{T\to\infty}\frac{1}{T}E\left[\frac{\partial^2 L}{\partial\lambda\partial\sigma^2}\right] &= \operatorname*{plim}_{T\to\infty}\frac{1}{T}\frac{\partial^2 L}{\partial\lambda\partial\sigma^2} = 0 \\ \lim_{T\to\infty}\frac{1}{T}E\left[\frac{\partial^2 L}{\partial\lambda\partial\rho}\right] &= \operatorname*{plim}_{T\to\infty}\frac{1}{T}\frac{\partial^2 L}{\partial\lambda\partial\rho} = 0\,. \end{aligned}$$

If we define

$$\text{(A.5)}\qquad v = Mu$$

where M is given by (5d), then we have

$$\text{(A.6)}\qquad v \sim N(0, \sigma^2 I)\,.$$

and thus

$$\text{(A.7)}\qquad \frac{u'V^{-1}u}{\sigma^2} = \frac{v'v}{\sigma^2} = \sum_{i=1}^{T}\frac{v_i^2}{\sigma^2}$$

is the sum of identically distributed mutually independent chi-square variables with one degree of freedom. Thus

$$\text{(A.8)}\qquad \begin{aligned} \frac{1}{T}E\left(\frac{u'V^{-1}u}{\sigma^2}\right) &= \frac{1}{T}E\left(\sum_{i=1}^{T}\frac{v_i^2}{\sigma^2}\right) = 1 \\ &= \operatorname*{plim}_{T\to\infty}\frac{1}{T}\left(\sum_{i=1}^{T}\frac{v_i^2}{\sigma^2}\right) = 1\,. \end{aligned}$$

Hence

$$\lim_{T\to\infty}\frac{1}{T}E\left[\frac{\partial^2 L}{\partial\sigma^2\partial\sigma^2}\right]=\operatorname*{plim}_{T\to\infty}\frac{1}{T}\frac{\partial^2 L}{\partial\sigma^2\partial\sigma^2} = \frac{1}{2}\frac{1}{\sigma^4}-\frac{1}{\sigma^4}=-\frac{1}{\sigma^2}\left(\frac{1}{2\sigma^2}\right). \tag{A.9}$$

Now, it may be shown that

$$u'\frac{\partial V^{-1}}{\partial\rho}u = 2\rho\sum_{t=2}^{T-1}u_t^2 - 2\sum_{t=2}^{T}u_t u_{t-1}. \tag{A.10}$$

The first term by a suitable orthogonal transformation can be expressed as the sum of independent (but not identically) distributed normal random variables with finite moments. With some manipulation, recalling that $u_t = \rho u_{t-1} + \varepsilon_t$ and that the ε's are mutually independent, we conclude that we can similarly express the second term. Hence, the strong law of large numbers applies again and thus

$$\lim_{T\to\infty}\frac{1}{T}\frac{1}{2\sigma^4}E\left[u'\frac{\partial V^{-1}}{\partial\rho}u\right]=\operatorname*{plim}_{T\to\infty}\frac{1}{T}\frac{1}{2\sigma^4}u'\frac{\partial V^{-1}}{\partial\rho}u = 0. \tag{A.11}$$

Since

$$u'\frac{\partial^2 V^{-1}}{\partial\rho\partial\rho}u = 2\sum_{t=2}^{T-1}u_t^2 \tag{A.12}$$

we conclude

$$\lim_{T\to\infty}\frac{1}{T}E\left[\frac{\partial^2 L}{\partial\rho\partial\rho}\right]=\operatorname*{plim}_{T\to\infty}\frac{1}{T}\frac{\partial^2 L}{\partial\rho\partial\rho} = -\frac{1}{\sigma^2}\left(\frac{\sigma^2}{1-\rho^2}\right). \tag{A.13}$$

We finally note that

$$\begin{aligned} E\left[\frac{\partial^2 L}{\partial\sigma^2\partial\rho}\right] &= -\frac{1}{\sigma^2}\frac{\rho}{1-\rho^2}, \\ E\left[\frac{\partial^2 L}{\partial\rho\partial\rho}\right] &= -\frac{1}{\sigma^2}\left[\frac{\left(\frac{1+\rho^2}{1-\rho^2}+T-2\right)\sigma^2}{1-\rho^2}\right]. \end{aligned} \tag{A.14}$$

From the preceding it is apparent that

$$-M^{-1}(\theta) = \sigma^2\begin{bmatrix} M_1^{-1} & 0 \\ 0 & M_2^{-1}\end{bmatrix} \tag{A.15}$$

where M_1 and M_2 are symmetric matrices given by

$$M_1 = \begin{bmatrix} X'V^{-1}X & \alpha_1 X'V^{-1}\dfrac{\partial x_1^*}{\partial\lambda} \\ & \alpha_1^2\left(\dfrac{\partial x_1^*}{\partial\lambda}\right)'V^{-1}\left(\dfrac{\partial x_1^*}{\partial\lambda}\right)\end{bmatrix} \tag{A.16}$$

$$
M_2 = \begin{bmatrix} \dfrac{T}{2\sigma^2} & \dfrac{\rho}{1-\rho^2} \\ & \dfrac{\left(\dfrac{1+\rho^2}{1-\rho^2} + T - 2\right)\sigma^2}{1-\rho^2} \end{bmatrix}. \tag{A.17}
$$

To the extent that an ordinary regression program is used to obtain the estimators derived in Section 3 we should point out that it will in fact produce a covariance matrix for the estimators $(\hat{\alpha}_1, \hat{\alpha}_2, \cdots, \hat{\alpha}_n, \hat{\alpha}_0)$ given by $\hat{\sigma}^2(\hat{\lambda}, \hat{\rho})M_1^{*-1}$ where now

$$
M_1^{*-1} = \begin{bmatrix} X'\hat{V}^{-1}X & X'\hat{V}^{-1}\hat{\lambda} \\ \hat{\lambda}'\hat{V}^{-1}X & \hat{\lambda}'\hat{V}^{-1}\hat{\lambda} \end{bmatrix}^{-1} \tag{A.18}
$$

and

$$
\hat{\lambda} = \begin{bmatrix} \hat{\lambda} \\ \hat{\lambda}^2 \\ \cdot \\ \cdot \\ \cdot \\ \hat{\lambda}^B \end{bmatrix}. \tag{A.19}
$$

To the extent that

$$
\frac{X'\hat{V}^{-1}\hat{\underline{\lambda}}\underline{\lambda}\hat{V}^{-1}X}{\underline{\lambda}'\underline{\lambda}} \approx \frac{X'\hat{V}^{-1}\left(\dfrac{\partial x_1^*}{\partial\lambda}\right)\left(\dfrac{\partial x_1^*}{\partial\lambda}\right)'\hat{V}X}{\left(\dfrac{\partial x_1^*}{\partial\lambda}\right)'V^{-1}\left(\dfrac{\partial x_1^*}{\partial\lambda}\right)} \tag{A.20}
$$

then the implied estimator of the covariance matrix of the estimators $(\hat{\alpha}_1, \hat{\alpha}_2, \cdots, \hat{\alpha}_n)$ is approximately correct. The asymptotic variance of $\hat{\lambda}$ and $\hat{\rho}$ can be easily obtained as $\hat{\sigma}^2(\hat{\lambda}, \hat{\rho})$ times the last diagonal elements of $\underline{M}_1^{-1}$ and $\underline{M}_2^{-1}$ respectively.

REFERENCES

[1] AMEMIYA, T. AND W. FULLER, "A Comparative Study of Alternative Estimators in a Distributed Lag Model," Technical Report No. 12, Institute for Mathematical Studies in the Social Sciences, Stanford University (June 1965).

[2] CRAMER, H., *Mathematical Methods of Statistics.* (Princeton: Princeton University Press, 1946.)

[3] CRAMER, H., *Random Variables and Probability Distributions* (Second edition). (Cambridge: Cambridg University Press, 1962.)

[4] DHRYMES, P. J., "On the Treatment of Certain Recurrent Non-Linearities in Regression Analysis," *Southern Economic Journal* XXXIII (October, 1966) 187–96.

[5] HANNAN, E. J., "The Estimation of Relations Involving Distributed Lags," *Econometrica*, XXXIII (January, 1965), 206–24.

[6] HOEFFDING, W. AND H. ROBBINS, "The Central Limit Theorem for Dependent Variables," *Duke Mathematical Journal*, XV (1948), 773–80.

[7] KENDALL, M. G. AND A. STUART, *The Advanced Theory of Statistics* II, (New York: Hafner Publishing Co., 1961).

[8] KLEIN, L. R.: "The Estimation of Distributed Lags," *Econometrica*, XXVI (October, 1958), 553–65.

[9] KOYCK, L. H., *Distributed Lags and Investment Analysis*, (Amsterdam: North Holland Publishing Co., 1954).

[10] LIVIATAN, N. "Consistent Estimation of Distributed Lags," *International Economic Review*, IV (January, 1963), 44-52.

[11] MORRISON, J. L., "Small Sample Properties of Selected Distributed Lag Estimators: A Monte Carlo Experiment," Discussion Paper No. 42, Department of Economics, University of Pennsylvania, Philadelphia, Pa.

INTERNATIONAL ECONOMIC REVIEW
Vol. 11, No. 2, June, 1970

ESTIMATION OF DISTRIBUTED LAGS*

BY PHOEBUS J. DHRYMES, LAWRENCE R. KLEIN
AND KENNETH STEIGLITZ[1]

1. PRELIMINARIES

THE USE OF DISTRIBUTED LAGS in econometric research is quite old. However, the current intensive interest in the subject dates back to the relatively recent work of Koyck [9]. Since then, a number of extensions have been made to the basic geometric lag distribution and the associated method of estimation taken up by Koyck. A number of such studies are summarized in Amemiya and Fuller [1]. More recently a search technique has been proposed by Dhrymes [2] for the case of a geometric lag distribution occurring in a relation characterized by a first order Markov process in its error term.

Jorgenson [7] has employed in empirical research rational distributed lags although he has not given a full treatment of the estimation problems of the parameters involved. Dhrymes [3] suggested a technique of estimating in a consistent and asymptotically efficient fashion the parameters of a rational distributed lag by the use of spectral techniques thus extending the results obtained by Hannan [5] in the case of the simple geometric lag structure.

At the same time, however, electrical engineers have been interested in much the same problems. In many instances they have produced the elements of a satisfactory solution to the problem of estimating the parameters of the rational distributed lag although their approach has not always been explicitly grounded on a statistical formulation and thus the properties of the resulting estimator were not clear. The present paper builds on an idea proposed by Steiglitz and McBride [13] in an engineering context.

Our purpose here is to give a rigorous formulation and solution to the problem of estimating, by maximum likelihood techniques, the parameters of a general lag structure, to point out the lines of research and terminology followed in the literature of electrical engineering and thus to make available this literature to econometricians. We believe that such contact will prove quite fruitful.

2. ENGINEERING MOTIVATION AND SOME FORMAL ANALOGIES IN ENGINEERING AND ECONOMETRIC RESEARCH

The determination of the dynamic characteristics of an electrical or mechanical system from observation records has been of interest to engineers for some time, especially with regard to the construction of adaptive or learning control systems. Most of the work in electrical engineering has been con-

* Manuscript received February 5, 1968; revised April 8, 1969.

[1] The work of Kenneth Steiglitz was supported in part by Army Research Office-Durham under Contract DA-HCO4-69-C-0012. Some of the computer facilities used were supported in part by NSF grant GP-579.

cerned with the linear stationary case, since many physical systems are operated in a fixed environment with relatively small excursions from quiescence.

Thus, assume that the postulated linear stationary system can be described completely at any time t by an n-dimensional vector w_t, called *state vector* at time t. Assume also that the system is excited by a single scalar variable x_t, called the *input*, and that the system response is determined by the value of the scalar variable y_t, called the output.[2] We may associate x_t with an exogenous or explanatory variable and w_t, y_t with endogenous variables, the general point of view being that x_t is determined outside the system and affects (or determines) w_t and y_t in a *causal way*.

Finally it will be assumed that output is a *linear combination of the components of the state vector and a scalar random variable* u_t, which represents the effect on the system of nonmeasurable or unknown exogenous variables. We many thus write

$$\begin{aligned} w_t &= Aw_{t-1} + bx_t \\ y_t &= c'w_t + u_t \, . \end{aligned} \tag{1}$$

In (1) A and b are respectively an $(n \times n)$ matrix and $n \times 1$ vector of constants, the assumption being that the transition from w_{t-1} to w_t is accomplished in a simple Markovian scheme, under the excitation induced by bx_t. For this reason the matrix A is called the *transition matrix* of the system, though it need not be a probability matrix.

Let z be complex, of unit modulus, and define

$$W(z) = \sum_{t=0}^{\infty} w_t z^{-t}, \; X(z) = \sum_{t=0}^{\infty} x_t z^{-t}, \; Y(z) = \sum_{t=0}^{\infty} y_t z^{-t}, \; U(z) = \sum_{t=0}^{\infty} u_t z^{-t} \, . \tag{2}$$

The first system of equations in (1) may now be written as

$$W(z) = Az^{-1}W(z) + bX(z) \, . \tag{2a}$$

Solving, we obtain

$$W(z) = (I - Az^{-1})^{-1}bX(z) \, . \tag{2b}$$

Finally substituting in the last equation of (1) we have

$$Y(z) = c'(I - Az^{-1})^{-1}bX(z) + U(z) \, . \tag{3}$$

Clearly $c'(I - Az^{-1})^{-1}b$ is a rational function of z^{-1} and as such it may be represented

$$c'(I - Az^{-1})^{-1}b = \frac{A(z^{-1})}{B(z^{-1})} \tag{3a}$$

where $A(z^{-1})$ and $B(z^{-1})$ are polynomials of suitable order. Clearly, the poles $(I - Az^{-1})^{-1}$ are the zeros of $B(z^{-1})$. Indeed, if λ_i are the roots of A then it can be easily seen that

[2] What follows can easily be extended to the multivariate case; i.e., we can easily deal with the case in which x_t and y_t are vectors of suitable dimensions.

$$A(z^{-1}) / B(z^{-1}) = \sum_{i=1}^{n} \left[\frac{c_i^*}{\left(1 - \frac{\lambda_i}{z}\right)} \right], \tag{4}$$

where c_i^* are suitable constants obtained through the process of expansion of the left hand side of (4) by partial fractions. Since the λ_i, $i = 1, 2, \cdots, n$ are less than unity in absolute value and z lies on the unit circle, we may expand

$$\frac{1}{1 - \frac{\lambda_i}{z}} = \sum_{k=0}^{\infty} \left(\frac{\lambda_i}{z}\right)^k . \tag{4a}$$

Thus the system in (3a) can be written as

$$\begin{aligned} \sum_{t=0}^{\infty} y_t z^{-t} &= \sum_{i=1}^{n} c_i^* \sum_{t=0}^{\infty} z^{-t} \sum_{k=0}^{\infty} \lambda_i^k x_t z^{-k} + \sum_{t=0}^{\infty} u_t z^{-t} \\ &= \sum_{\tau=0}^{\infty} \left(\sum_{i=1}^{n} c_i^* \left(\sum_{k=0}^{\infty} x_{\tau-k} \lambda_i^k \right) z^{-\tau} \right) + \sum_{t=0}^{\infty} u_t z^{-t} , \end{aligned} \tag{4b}$$

where the last member of (4b) is obtained by putting $\tau = t + k$. Equating like powers of z^{-1} on both sides we find

$$y_t = \sum_{i=1}^{n} c_i^* \sum_{k=0}^{\infty} \lambda_i^k x_{t-k} + u_t , \qquad t = 1, 2, \cdots, T , \tag{4c}$$

which shows that the system in (3a) represents a lag distribution. Moreover, this is a weighted sum of n simple geometric lag distributions with parameters λ_i, $i = 1, 2, \cdots, n$. Further, from (4b) we note that z^{-1} plays exactly the same role in engineering literature as the lag operator L in econometric and statistical literature.

In what follows we shall therefore use the lag operator exclusively. By definition

$$L^k x_t = x_{t-k} , \qquad L^0 = I , \qquad I x_t = x_t , \qquad k = 0, 1, 2, \cdots ; \tag{4d}$$

therefore, in virtue of (4) and (4a) we can write (4c) as

$$y_t = \sum_{i=1}^{n} c_i^* \sum_{k=0}^{\infty} (\lambda_i L)^k x_t + u_t = \sum_{i=1}^{n} \frac{c_i^* I}{(I - \lambda_i L)} x_t + u_t = \frac{A(L)}{B(L)} x_t + u_t , \tag{4e}$$

where $A(L)$ and $B(L)$ are polynomials of degree at most $n - 1$ and n respectively. This is, of course, the notation of the standard rational distributed lag model discussed in the literature of econometrics. It is particularly striking, for example, that Jorgenson [7] and Steiglitz and McBride [13] use, in entirely different and unrelated contexts, exactly the same model (4e). This is an extreme instance of research convergence in econometrics and electrical engineering and should suggest to econometricians and electrical engineers the benefits to be derived from familiarity with certain aspects of the research in the two disciplines.

We conclude this section by giving a table of equivalent terminology.

Engineering	*Econometrics*
White-Gaussian error	Nonautocorrelated, normally distributed error
Colored-Gaussian	Autocorrelated, normally distributed error
Plant	Nonstochastic model
Record	Sample
Rational z transform	Rational lag distribution
Prefiltering	exponential weighting
Identification	Specification and estimation of a model

3. ESTIMATION OF THE GENERAL RATIONAL LAG MODEL

A. *Formulation.* In this section we shall deal with the problem of estimating the parameters of

$$y_t = \frac{A(L)}{B(L)} x_t + u_t , \qquad t = 1, 2, \cdots, T , \tag{5}$$

where L is the lag operator defined in (4d) and

$$A(L) = \sum_{i=0}^{\mu} a_i L^i , \qquad B(L) = \sum_{j=0}^{\nu} b_j L^j , \qquad b_0 = 1 , \qquad \mu < \nu . \tag{5a}$$

The independent variable x is assumed to be nonstochastic or, if stochastic, uncorrelated with the random term u_t. The latter has the specification

$$u \sim N(0, \sigma^2 I), \; u = (u_1, u_2, \cdots, u_T)' , \tag{5b}$$

and is assumed to be independent of x for all t. We shall employ maximum likelihood methods. Thus the (log) likelihood function of the observations in (5) is given by

$$L(a, b, \sigma^2; y, x) = -\frac{T}{2}\ln(2\pi) - \frac{T}{2}\ln\sigma^2 - \frac{1}{2\sigma^2}\left(y - \frac{A(L)}{B(L)}x\right)'\left(y - \frac{A(L)}{B(L)}x\right) \tag{6}$$

where

$$y = (y_1, y_2, \cdots, y_T)' , \qquad x = (x_1, x_2, \cdots, x_T)'$$
$$a = (a_0, a_1, \cdots, a_\mu)' , \qquad b = (b_1, b_2, \cdots, b_\nu)' .$$

The first order conditions for a maximum are given by

$$\begin{aligned}
\frac{\partial L}{\partial a_i} &= \frac{1}{\sigma^2}\sum_{t=\mu+\nu+1}^{T}\left(y_t - \frac{A(L)}{B(L)}x_t\right)\frac{L^j}{B(L)}x_t = 0 , && j = 0, 1, 2, \cdots, \mu , \\
\frac{\partial L}{\partial b_j} &= \frac{1}{2}\sum_{t=\mu+\nu+1}^{T}\left(y_t - \frac{A(L)}{B(L)}x_t\right)\frac{A(L)}{B(L)^2}L^s x_t = 0 , && s = 1, 2, \cdots, \nu , \\
\frac{\partial L}{\partial \sigma^2} &= -\frac{T}{2}\frac{1}{\sigma^2} + \frac{1}{\sigma^4}\sum_{t=\mu+\nu+1}^{T}\left(y_t - \frac{A(L)}{B(L)}x_t\right)'\left(y_t - \frac{A(L)}{B(L)}x_t\right) = 0 ,
\end{aligned} \tag{6a}$$

We observe that while the equations in (6a) are highly nonlinear in the a_i and b_j, they are linear in a_i for given b_j and they are linear in σ^2. We can search the parameter space for estimates of a_i, given b_i or we can iterate for all parameter estimates simultaneously. Once we have estimates for a_i and b_j, however, an estimate for σ^2 will be easily obtained.

In what follows we shall concentrate our attention solely on the first two sets of equations which would correspond to the normal equations of least squares, although under the assumption of normality the resulting estimators would be maximum likelihood ones as well.

The strategy of our estimation procedure is to determine a consistent solution of the equations in (6a).

Since by a theorem of Huzurbazar [6], for large T there exists a unique consistent solution, and by a theorem of Wald [15] it corresponds to the global maximum of the likelihood function, we would then have found the maximum likelihood estimators of the parameters a_j, b_s, $j = 0, 1, 2, \cdots, \mu$, $s = 1, 2, \cdots, \nu$, which are asymptotically normal, unbiased, and efficient.

B. *An iterative algorithm.* Define

$$(7) \qquad y_t^* = \frac{I}{B(L)} y_t \,, \qquad x_t^* = \frac{I}{B(L)} x_t \,, \qquad x_t^{**} = \frac{A(L)}{B(L)} x_t^* \,, \qquad t = 1, 2, \cdots, T \,,$$

and note that the first two systems in (6a) may be written as

$$(7a) \qquad \sum_{t=\mu+\nu+1}^{T} [B(L) y_t^* - A(L) x_t^*] x_{t-j}^* = 0 \,, \qquad j = 0, 1, 2, \cdots, \mu \,,$$

$$(7b) \qquad \sum_{t=\mu+\nu+1}^{T} [B(L) y_t^* - A(L) x_t^*] x_{t-s}^{**} = 0 \,, \qquad s = 1, 2, \cdots, \nu \,.$$

The equations in (7a) and (7b) are linear in the parameters provided we deal in the transformed variables y^*, x^*, x^{**}. But this suggests how we can solve the system: if an initial (consistent) estimator is given for $B(L)$ and $A(L)$, say $B^0(L)$, $A^0(L)$, it can be used to construct the variables y_t^*, x_t^*, x_t^{**}; then the system in (7a) and (7b) can be solved to provide another estimator $B^1(L)$, $A^1(L)$, etc., until the iteration converges, say at the k-th step; this would mean that for prescribed $\varepsilon > 0$

$$(7c) \qquad \max_j | a_j^k - a_j^{k+1} | < \varepsilon \,, \qquad \max_s | b_s^k - b_s^{k+1} | < \varepsilon \,.$$

Let us see precisely what this algorithm entails. For computational convenience only, the various cross products involved will not contain the observations at times $r = 1, 2, \cdots, \nu$. To this effect, let

$$(8) \qquad Y^* = \begin{bmatrix} y_{\mu+\nu}^*, & y_{\mu+\nu-1}^*, & \cdots, & y_{\mu+1}^* \\ y_{\mu+\nu+1}^*, & y_{\mu+\nu}^*, & \cdots, & y_{\mu+2}^* \\ \vdots & & & \vdots \\ y_{T-1}^*, & y_{T-2}^*, & \cdots, & y_{T-\nu}^* \end{bmatrix}, \quad X^* = \begin{bmatrix} x_{\mu+\nu+1}^*, & x_{\mu+\nu}^*, & \cdots, & x_{\nu+1}^* \\ x_{\mu+\nu+2}^*, & x_{\mu+\nu+1}^*, & \cdots, & x_{\nu+2}^* \\ \vdots & & & \vdots \\ x_T^*, & x_{T-1}^*, & \cdots, & x_{T-\mu}^* \end{bmatrix},$$

$$X^{**} = \begin{bmatrix} x_{\mu+\nu}^{**}, & x_{\mu+\nu-1}^{**}, & \cdots, & x_{\mu+1}^{**} \\ x_{\mu+\nu+1}^{**}, & x_{\mu+\nu}^{**}, & \cdots, & x_{\mu+2}^{**} \\ \vdots & & & \vdots \\ x_{T-1}^{**}, & x_{T-2}^{**}, & \cdots, & x_{T-\nu}^{**} \end{bmatrix}.$$

$$d = \begin{pmatrix} a \\ -b \end{pmatrix}, \quad c^* = (c_j^*), \quad c_j^* = \sum_{j=\mu+\nu+1}^{T} y_t^* x_{t-j}^*, \qquad j = 0, 1, 2, \cdots, \mu \tag{8a}$$

$$= \sum_{t=\mu+\nu+1}^{T} y_t^* x_{t+\mu-j}^{**}, \quad j = \mu+1, \mu+2, \cdots, \mu+\nu$$

$$W^* = \begin{bmatrix} X^{*\prime}X^* & X^{*\prime}Y^* \\ X^{**\prime}X^* & X^{**\prime}Y^* \end{bmatrix}. \tag{8b}$$

With the aid of the notation in (8), (8a) and (8b), the system in (7a) and (7b) may be written compactly as

$$W^*d = c^* . \tag{9}$$

Remark 1. We should observe that the definitions in (7), involving what engineers call prefiltering, are not as cumbersome as they appear. In particular, they need not involve power series expansions of the operators $I/B(L)$. To see this, note that by virtue of the convention in (5a), we can write

$$B(L) = I + \sum_{j=1}^{\nu} b_j L^j = I - B^*(L), \qquad B^*(L) = -\sum_{j=1}^{\nu} b_j L^j . \tag{10}$$

Thus, the first equation in (7) implies

$$y_t^* = y_t + B^*(L) y_t^* . \tag{10a}$$

If initial conditions for y_t^* are specified, we see that y_t^* can be computed recursively, given b, for as many *values of the index* as y_t is available.

Similar comments apply to x_t^*. In the case of x_t^{**} we see that since x_t^* is defined over the same range of index values as x_t, then clearly x_t^{**} is defined for $t = \mu+1, \mu+2, \cdots$. Thus, y_t^*, x_t^*, x_t^{**} are all defined for $t = \nu, \nu+1, \cdots, T$ which is the range of index values appearing in the matrices Y^*, X^* and X^{**}. Finally, a convenient initial condition for y_t^* and x_t^* is

$$x_{-i}^* = y_{-i}^* = 0 , \qquad i = 0, 1, 2, \cdots, \nu . \tag{10b}$$

Since

$$y_{-i}^* = \frac{I}{B(L)} y_{-i} , \qquad x_{-i}^* = \frac{I}{B(L)} x_{-i} \qquad i = 0, 1, 2, \cdots, \nu , \tag{10c}$$

(10b) is equivalent to stating that

$$x_{-i} = y_{-i} = 0 , \qquad i = 0, 1, 2, \cdots, \nu . \tag{10d}$$

This is not a serious handicap if the sample size T is large.

Remark 2. Observe that W^* and c^* are functions of d. In what follows we shall assume that for any admissible value of d, W^* is nonsingular. Now, it is clear from (9) that if an initial consistent estimator of d exists, say $\tilde{d}_0$, then W^* and c^* can be computed, say $\tilde{W}_0^*, \tilde{c}_0^*$, where the tilde is used to denote the fact that W^* is obtained on the basis of a consistent estimator of d and not on the basis of the true value of the parameter vector d.

In view of the above, we may iterate on d by solving, to obtain

$$\tilde{d}_1 = \tilde{W}_0^{*-1} \tilde{c}_0^* . \tag{11}$$

We may now evaluate W^* and c^* at $\tilde{d}_1$ and complete a second iteration

(11a) $$\tilde{d}_2 = \tilde{W}_1^{*-1}\tilde{c}_1^* .$$

Two questions arise with respect to this procedure.

i. if $\tilde{d}_i$ is a consistent estimator of d, is it also the case that $\tilde{d}_{i+1}$ is a consistent estimator of d?

ii. does the iteration process converge, and, if so, under what circumstances?

To this effect we prove

LEMMA 1. *Under the hypotheses of the model as exhibited in* (5), (5a) *and* (5b), *if* $\tilde{d}_i$ *is a consistent estimator of* d *then so is* $\tilde{d}_{i+1}$, *the latter being defined by*

(12) $$\tilde{d}_{i+1} = \tilde{W}_i^{*-1}\tilde{c}_i^* .$$

PROOF. We note that by definition

(12a) $$y_t^* = \frac{I}{B(L)}y_t = \frac{I}{B(L)}\left[\frac{A(L)}{B(L)}x_t + u_t\right] = x_t^{**} + u_t^*$$

the starred quantities in (12a) having the obvious meaning. Thus

(12b) $$Y^* = X^{**} + U^*$$

where U^* is constructed in exactly the same fashion as Y^*. Define

(12c) $$W^{**} = \begin{bmatrix} X^{*\prime}X^* & X^{*\prime}\,X^{**} \\ X^{**\prime}X^* & X^{**\prime}X^{**} \end{bmatrix}.$$

Since

(12d) $$X^{*\prime}Y^* = X^{*\prime}X^{**} + X^{*\prime}U^* ,$$

then

(12e) $$\operatorname*{plim}_{T\to\infty} \frac{X^{*\prime}Y^*}{T} = \operatorname*{plim}_{T\to\infty} \frac{X^{*\prime}X^{**}}{T}$$

since x_t is nonstochastic (or independent of u_t).

Since $\tilde{d}_i$ is a consistent estimate of d, it follows that

(13) $$\operatorname*{plim}_{T\to\infty}\frac{1}{T}\tilde{W}_1^* = \lim_{T\to\infty}\frac{1}{T}W^{**} .$$

We also note that, by the same argument,

(13a) $$\operatorname*{plim}_{T\to\infty}\frac{1}{T}\tilde{c}_i^* = \lim_{T\to\infty}\frac{1}{T}c^{**}$$

where

(13b) $$\begin{aligned} c^{**} = (c_j^{**}),\ c_j^{**} &= \sum_{j=\nu+1}^{T} x_t^{**}x_{t-j}^* , & j &= 0, 1, 2, \cdots, \mu , \\ &= \sum_{j=\nu+1}^{T} x_t^{**}x_{t+\mu-j}^{**} , & j &= \mu+1, \mu+2, \cdots, \mu+\nu . \end{aligned}$$

Since

(14) $$\tilde{d}_{i+1} = \left(\frac{\tilde{W}_i^*}{T}\right)^{-1} \frac{\tilde{c}_i^*}{T}$$

we conclude

(14a) $$\operatorname*{plim}_{T\to\infty} \tilde{d}_{i+1} = \lim_{T\to\infty}\left[\left(\frac{W^{**}}{T}\right)^{-1} \frac{c^{**}}{T}\right].$$

The model obeys

(15) $$B(L)y_t^* = A(L)x_t^* + u_t\,, \qquad t = 1, 2, \cdots, T\,.$$

Putting

(15a) $$y^\nu = (y_{\nu+1}, y_{\nu+2}, \cdots, y_T)'\,, \qquad u^\nu = (u_{\nu+1}, u_{\nu+2}, \cdots, u$$

we can write (15) in the slightly altered form

(15*b*) $$(X^*, Y^*)d = y^\nu - u^\nu\,.$$

Let

(15c) $$Z = (X^*, X^{**})$$

and consider

(15d) $$Z'(X^*, Y^*)d = Z'y^\nu - Z'u^\nu\,.$$

We note

(16) $$\lim_{T\to\infty} \frac{Z'(X^*, Y^*)}{T} = \lim_{T\to\infty} \frac{W^{**}}{T}\,,$$

(16a) $$\operatorname*{plim}_{T\to\infty} \frac{Z'y^\nu}{T} = \lim_{T\to\infty} \frac{1}{T}c^{**}\,, \qquad \operatorname*{plim}_{T\to\infty} \frac{Z'u^\nu}{T} = 0\,.$$

From (15d) we therefore obtain

(16b) $$\lim_{T\to\infty} \frac{W^{**}}{T}d = \lim_{T\to\infty} \frac{1}{T}c^{**}\,.$$

Comparing (14a) and (16b) we conclude

(16c) $$\operatorname*{plim}_{T\to\infty} d_{i+1} = d\,.$$ Q.E.D.

The question of convergence for this procedure is rather difficult to settle definitively. Since asymptotically W^* converges to a positive definite matrix for every admissible d one would surmise that the iteration process will converge, at least for large T. Assuming that the process above is convergent, we are thus able to locate the consistent root of the maximum likelihood equations. By the theorem of Huzurbazar [6] we have therefore found, for large T, the global maximum of the likelihood function. Since the probability structure of the error term in (5) is regular, we conclude that such estimators are consistent, asymptotically efficient, and distributed as

(17) $$\sqrt{T}(\hat{d} - d) \sim N\left(0, \left[-\frac{1}{T}E\frac{\partial^2 L}{\partial d \partial d}\right]^{-1}\right).$$

One can handle rather easily the case of autocorrelated error terms porvided the autocorrelation is first order Markov. Thus, if

$$u_t = \rho u_{t-1} + \varepsilon_t, \, t = 1, 2, \cdots, T, \, |\rho| < 1, \, \varepsilon \sim N(0, \sigma_\varepsilon^2 I) \tag{17a}$$

where

$$\varepsilon = (\varepsilon_1, \varepsilon_2, \cdots, \varepsilon_T)' \, , \tag{17b}$$

then one can employ a scanning (search) technique. As shown by Dhrymes [2] in a slightly different but relevent context the resulting estimators of $\begin{pmatrix} d \\ \rho \end{pmatrix}$, obtained by the procedure above coupled with a search on ρ, are consistent.

4. A MODEL WITH SEVERAL DISTINCT GEOMETRIC LAGS

It is interesting that the techniques of the previous discussion are easily applicable to the model

$$y_t = \sum_{i=1}^{m} \frac{\alpha_i I}{I - \lambda_i L} x_{ti} + u_t \, . \qquad t = 1, 2, \cdots, T \, , \tag{18}$$

which has been found intractable in previous economic applications. When the number of lags is small, say two, then the search technique given in Dhrymes [2] can easily be extended to produce maximum likelihood estimators in a relatively simple manner. If, however, $m > 2$, then the search technique is, realistically, nonapplicable and should resort to the estimation scheme discussed above.

Let us see precisely what this entails. As before we shall assume

$$u \sim N(0, \sigma^2 I) \, , \qquad u = (u_1, u_2, u_3, \cdots, u_T)' \tag{18a}$$

and that the x_i, $i = 1, 2, \cdots, m$ are either nonstochastic or eventually independent of the error terms of (18). The (log) likelihood function of the observations is

$$L(\alpha, \lambda, \sigma^2; y, X) = -\frac{T}{2}\ln(2\pi) - \frac{T}{2}\ln\sigma^2 - \frac{1}{2}\sum_{t=1}^{T}\left(y_t - \sum_{i=1}^{m}\frac{\alpha_i I}{I - \lambda_i L}x_{ti}\right)^2 . \tag{18b}$$

The maximizing equations with respect to the α_i and λ_i are given by

$$\begin{aligned} \frac{\partial L}{\partial \alpha_k} &= \sum_{t=1}^{T}\left(y_t - \sum_{i=1}^{m}\frac{\alpha_i I}{I - \lambda_i L}x_{ti}\right)\frac{I}{I - \lambda_k L}x_{tk} = 0 \, , \\ \frac{\partial L}{\partial \lambda_k} &= \sum_{t=1}^{T}\left(y_t - \sum_{i=1}^{m}\frac{\alpha_k I}{I - \lambda_i L}x_{ti}\right)\frac{\alpha_i I}{(I - \lambda_k L)^2}x_{t-1,k} = 0 \, . \end{aligned} \qquad k = 1, 2, \cdots, m \, , \tag{19}$$

If we now define

$$x_{ti}^* = \frac{I}{I - \lambda_i L}x_{ti} \, , \qquad x_{ti}^{**} = \frac{I}{I - \lambda_i L}x_{ti}^* \, , \qquad y_{ti}^* = \frac{I}{I - \lambda_i L}y_t \tag{19a}$$

the system in (19) may be written as

$$\sum_{i=1}^{m}\alpha_i\sum_{t=1}^{T}x_{ti}^* x_{tk}^* + \lambda_k\sum_{t=1}^{T}y_{t-1,k}^* x_{tk}^* = \sum_{t=1}^{T}y_{tk}^* x_{tk}^* \tag{19b}$$

$$\sum_{i=1}^{m} \alpha_i \sum_{t=1}^{T} x_{ti}^{*} x_{t-1,k}^{**} + \lambda_k \sum_{t=1}^{T} y_{t-1,k}^{*} x_{t-1,k}^{**} = \sum_{t=1}^{T} y_{tk}^{*} x_{t-1,k}^{**} .$$

Two aspects of (19b) should be pointed out: first as an identity we may write, for any k,

$$y_t = \frac{I - \lambda_k L}{I - \lambda_k L} y_t = (I - \lambda_k L) y_{tk}^{*} = y_{tk}^{*} - \lambda_k y_{t-1,k}^{*} . \tag{19c}$$

Second, although the summation over t has the range $(1, T)$ we take $y_{0k}^{*} = x_{0k}^{*} = 0$ all k so that no problem arises.

The estimation scheme here is exactly the same as in previous sections; thus if consistent initial estimators exist for the λ_i, $i = 1, 2, \cdots, m$, say $\tilde{\lambda}_i^0$, then the quantities $\tilde{x}_{tk}^{*}$, $\tilde{x}_{tk}^{**}$, $\tilde{y}_{tk}^{*}$ can be computed from the expressions in (19a) where in lieu of λ_i we make use of the $\tilde{\lambda}_i^0$. Hence from (19b) we shall obtain estimators, say, $\tilde{\alpha}_i^1$, $\tilde{\lambda}_i^1$; using the $\tilde{\lambda}_i^1$ we can recompute the quantities $\tilde{x}_{tk}$, $\tilde{x}_{tk}^{**}$, $\tilde{y}_{tk}^{*}$ from the expressions in (19a) and from (19b) obtain another set of estimators, say $\tilde{\alpha}_i^2$, $\tilde{\lambda}_i^2$ and so on until convergence is obtained, i.e., until at the s-th step we find

$$\max \{ | \tilde{\lambda}_i^s - \tilde{\lambda}_i^{s-1} | , \quad | \tilde{\alpha}_i^s - \tilde{\alpha}_i^{s-1} | \} < \varepsilon \tag{19d}$$

where ε is a preassigned (small) positive constant.

5. AN ILLUSTRATION

Here we briefly examine the geometric lag distribution which has found extensive applications in econometrics. In this case

$$A(L) = \alpha I , \qquad B(L) = I - \lambda L , \qquad | \lambda | < 1 . \tag{20}$$

The model in (5) becomes

$$y_t = \frac{\alpha I}{I - \lambda L} x_t + u_t , \qquad t = 1, 2, \cdots, T . \tag{20a}$$

The equations in (7a) and (7b) become

$$\begin{aligned} &\sum_{t=1}^{T} [(I - \lambda L) y_t^{*} - \alpha x_t^{*}] x_t^{*} = 0 \\ &\sum_{t-1}^{T} [(I - \lambda L) y_t^{*} - \alpha x_t^{*}] \alpha x_{t-1}^{**} = 0 , \end{aligned} \tag{20b}$$

where

$$y_t^{*} = \frac{I}{I - \lambda L} y_t , \qquad x_t^{*} = \frac{I}{I - \lambda L} x_t , \qquad x_t^{**} = \frac{\alpha I}{I - \lambda L} x_t^{*} . \tag{20c}$$

After some rearrangement we can rewrite (20b) as

$$\begin{aligned} &\alpha \sum_{t=2}^{T} x_t^{*2} + \lambda \sum_{t=2}^{T} x_t^{*} y_{t-1}^{*} = \sum_{t=2}^{T} x_t^{*} y_t^{*} \\ &\alpha \sum_{t=1}^{T} x_{t-1}^{**} x_t^{*} + \lambda \sum_{t=2}^{T} x_{t-1}^{**} y_{t-1}^{*} = \sum_{t=2}^{T} x_{t-1}^{**} y_t^{*} . \end{aligned} \tag{21}$$

If we take an initial consistent estimator of λ and α, say $\tilde{\lambda}_0$, $\tilde{\alpha}_0$, then we can compute the prefiltered variables y_t^*, x_t^* and x_t^{**} recursively as follows:

$$\text{(21a)} \qquad y_t^* = y_t + \tilde{\lambda}_0 y_{t-1}^* , \qquad x_t^* = x_t + \tilde{\lambda}_0 x_{t-1}^* , \qquad x_t^{**} = \alpha x_t^* + \tilde{\lambda}_0 x_{t-1}^{**} .$$

We can then solve the system in (21) to obtain another estimator, say $\tilde{\lambda}_1$, $\tilde{\alpha}_1$. We again compute the prefiltered variables in (20c) using the new estimators and continue until the iteration process converges, i.e., until

$$\text{(21b)} \qquad \max \{ | \tilde{\lambda}_{i+1} - \tilde{\lambda}_i | , \quad | \tilde{\alpha}_{i+1} - \tilde{\alpha}_i | \} < \varepsilon ,$$

where ε is some preassigned small quantity. An initial consistent estimator for α and λ can be obtained by instrumental variable techniques. In particular we can take the estimator proposed by Liviatan [10] which is obtained by solving

$$\text{(21c)} \qquad \begin{aligned} \tilde{\alpha}_0 \sum_{t=2}^{T} x_t^2 + \tilde{\lambda}_0 \sum_{t=2}^{T} x_t y_{t-1} &= \sum_{t=2}^{T} x_t y_t \\ \tilde{\alpha}_0 \sum_{t=2}^{T} x_t x_{t-1} + \tilde{\lambda}_0 \sum_{t=2}^{T} x_{t-1} y_{t-1} &= \sum_{t=2}^{T} x_{t-1} y_t . \end{aligned}$$

Efficient estimation of the geometric lag distribution has been the subject of extensive research; a part of this literature was referred to in the introduction. In this connection, it should be noted that a recent Monte Carlo study by Morrison [12] compares a number of proposed estimators of the parameters of the model (20a) where the error terms are assumed to have the classical properties. He finds that the estimator proposed by Liviatan [10] and Hannan [5], as interpreted in the time domain by Amemiya and Fuller [1], on the whole do not do very well. The estimators proposed by Steiglitz and McBride [13], a variant of which was discussed above, does extremely well for large samples (50 observations); that proposed by Dhrymes [4], [2] performs relatively better than the Steiglitz and McBride estimator for smaller sample size, although for larger samples the two estimators perform equally well.

Finally, this is a convenient juncture to consider Malinvaud's comments [11] on the estimation of the geometric lag in the face of autocorrelated errors. Thus, suppose our model is

$$\text{(22)} \qquad y_t = \frac{\alpha I}{I - \lambda L} x_t + u_t , \qquad u_t = \sum_{i=1}^{k} \rho_i u_{t-i} + \varepsilon_t , \qquad t = 1, 2, \cdots T .$$

where

$$\text{(22a)} \qquad \varepsilon \sim N(0, \sigma^2 I) , \qquad \varepsilon = (\varepsilon_1, \varepsilon_2, \cdots, \varepsilon_T)' .$$

We note that

$$\text{(22b)} \qquad y_t - \sum_{i=1}^{k} \rho_i y_{t-i} = \frac{\alpha I}{I - \lambda L} \left(x_t - \sum_{i=1}^{k} \rho_i x_{t-i} \right) + \varepsilon_t .$$

We may then put

$$\text{(22c)} \qquad y_t' = \frac{\alpha I}{I - \lambda L} x_t' + \varepsilon_t , \qquad y_t' = y_t - \sum_{i=1}^{k} \rho_i y_{t-i} , \qquad x_t' = x_t - \sum_{i=1}^{k} \rho_i x_{t-i} .$$

Malinvaud then claims that if we estimate α and λ by the method given in Klein [8] with y'_t, x'_t replacing y_t and x_t respectively, then the resulting estimators of α and λ are inconsistent. The iteration considered by Malinvaud begins with an inconsistent estimator of the parameters α, λ, ρ. It is simple enough to use Liviatan-type or other consistent estimators to start the interations.

Suppose that we have consistent estimators of the ρ_i, say $\hat{\rho}_{i0}$. Then we may define

$$y'_t = y_t - \sum_{i=1}^{k} \hat{\rho}_{i0} y_{t-i} , \qquad x'_t = x_t - \sum_{i=1}^{k} \hat{\rho}_{i0} x_{t-i} . \tag{23}$$

If an initial consistent estimator of α and λ are also available, then we can apply the scheme of this section with $\tilde{y}'_t$ and $\tilde{x}'_t$ replacing y_t and x_t in (20a). Thus we obtain estimators $\tilde{\alpha}_1, \tilde{\lambda}_1$. Using these we can compute

$$\tilde{u}_t - \tilde{\lambda}_1 \tilde{u}_{t-1} = y_t - \tilde{\lambda}_1 y_{t-1} - \tilde{\alpha}_1 x_t . \tag{23a}$$

From the left hand side of (23a) we can obtain recursively the $\tilde{u}_t$, $t = 1, 2, \cdots, T$, on the assumption, say, that

$$\tilde{u}_0 = 0 . \tag{23b}$$

The consequences of this assumption are minimal if the sample is at all large. Then we can regress $\tilde{u}_t$ on $\tilde{u}_{t-i}$, $i = 1, 2, \cdots, k$, to obtain another set ρ_{i1}, $i = 1, 2, \cdots, k$, and repeat the process. It is easily verified that this procedure will yield consistent estimators. Actually, in the empirically relevant case $k = 1$, one easily obtains a rather simply executed estimator which is consistent, asymptotically unbiased, and efficient. An alternative procedure if $k > 1$ may be as follows: Disregard the specification on u_t in (20) and obtain consistent estimators for α and λ by searching on λ. This may be done by using the form given in Klein [8]

$$y_t = \lambda^t \eta_0 + \alpha \sum_{i=1}^{t-1} \lambda^i x_{t-i} + u_t , \tag{24}$$

and employing ordinary least squares.

The resulting estimators of α, λ, say $\tilde{\alpha}_0, \tilde{\lambda}_0$, are consistent. Use the scheme of equations (23a) and (23b) to obtain the residuals $\tilde{u}_1, \tilde{u}_2, \cdots, \tilde{u}_T$. Then regress $\tilde{u}_t$ on $\tilde{u}_{t-i}$, $i = 1, 2, \cdots, k$, to obtain initial estimators of ρ_i say, $\hat{\rho}_{i0}$, $i = 1, 2, \cdots, k$. These are consistent estimators. Compute the quantities $\tilde{y}'_t, \tilde{x}'_t$ of (23) using the estimator $\hat{\rho}_{i0}$ above. Then consider

$$\tilde{y}'_t = \lambda^t \eta_0 + \alpha \sum_{i=1}^{t-1} \lambda^i \tilde{x}'_{t-i} + \tilde{\varepsilon}_t . \tag{24a}$$

This is asymptotically equivalent to

$$y_t - \sum_{i=1}^{k} \rho_i y_{t-i} = \lambda^t \eta_0 + \alpha \sum_{i=1}^{t-1} \lambda^i \Big(x_t - \sum_{i=1}^{t-1} \rho_i x_{t-i} \Big) + \varepsilon_t . \tag{24b}$$

Thus applying the search technique to (24a) in a least squares context yields asymptotically the maximum likelihood estimators of α and λ. One may, of course, iterate the procedure.

6. AN EXAMPLE

Here we shall apply the techniques developed in the previous sections to the problem of estimating the parameters of an investment function. Our purpose is not to give yet another theory of investment but rather to illustrate that the procedures developed have useful applications, and to indicate the extent of the variation in empirical results one might expect due to differences in estimation procedures. The example also demonstrates feasibility and convergence of the computational methods suggested. To this effect, we have chosen the investment function suggested by Jorgenson[2] with respect to the durable manufacturing sector. Our data are somewhat different from his, chiefly in that our sample period is 1948 (first qurater) to 1965 (fourth quarter) while his begin with 1948 and end with 1959. Aside from this both sets of data are comparable, and our results should be compared with the first row of Jorgenson's Table 2.2 in the work cited above. In Table 1 below I_t is Jorgenson's variable, investment at time t minus .0279 times capital stock at time $t-1$, and X_t is Jorgenson's variable $\Delta[p_t x_t / c_t]$, i.e., the change in the value of output divided by user cost.

TABLE 1

ESTIMATED INVESTMENT FUNCTION DURABLE MANUFACTURING, 1948.I-1965.IV

OLS:	$I_{t+3} = \dfrac{.007906 + .007944L + .0003197L^2}{1 - 1.541705L + .575882L^2} X_t$
Jorgenson*:	$I_{t+3} = \dfrac{.00096 + .00080L + .00034L^2}{1 - 1.29501L + .42764L^2} X_t$
Modified M. L.**+ (Instrumental variable) estimators	$I_{t+3} = \dfrac{.0023863 - .0007789L - .0012922L^2}{1 - 1.965438L + .972074L^2} X_t$
Maximum likelihood+ estimators	$I_{t+3} = \dfrac{.0018426 + .0001095L - .0015530L^2}{1 - 1.945464L + .952775L^2} X_t$

* Jorgenson's sample covers only 1948–1959.

** We shall explain the meaning of this below.

\+ The criterion of convergence employed in these computations has been the insensitivity of the residual sum of squares about its minimum.

The point estimates of the parameters of the hypothesized model might appear from Table 1 to be quite close no matter how we estimate them. However, their implications in terms of meaningful economic theoretic constructs are rather substantially different. Before we explore this let us stress again that we do not advance our new estimates above as alternative empirical characterizations of investment behavior, rather as illustrations how alternative estimation techniques can lead to substantially differing conclusions.

[2] Jorgenson, D. W., "Anticipations and Investment Behavior" in J. S. Duesenberry, G. Fromm, L. R. Klein, E. Kuh eds., *The Brookings Quarterly Econometric Model of the U. S.* (Chicago: Rand McNally, 1965).

First let us ask: What is the long run response of investment to the independent variable X_t? The answer is obtained by evaluating the rational functions of the table after replacing L by unity. The conclusions are: OLS: .05573, Jorgenson: .01583, Modified M. L.: .04749, M. L.: .05458. Without trying to explain the magnitude of these numbers—which in part reflect the units in which the variables are measured—we observe that simply by changing the sample period we obtain a more than threefold increase in this quantity. This is so since our OLS estimator is exactly like Jorgenson's eatimator, the only difference being the sample period. On the other hand, OLS, modified M. L. and M. L. procedures yield roughly comparable quantities.

Now, if the denominator polynomial is written as

$$B(L) = I + b_1L + b_2L^2 = (I - \lambda_1 L)(I - \lambda_2 L) \tag{25}$$

we have the identification

$$\lambda_1 + \lambda_2 = -b_1 \qquad \lambda_1\lambda_2 = b_2 \,. \tag{25a}$$

The four sets of results given in Table 1 imply the following estimators for λ_1, λ_2 respectively. OLS: .9043, .6347; Jorgenson: $.6475 \pm .1825i$ ($|\lambda|^2 = .4525$); Modified M. L.: $.9827 \pm .1234i$ ($|\lambda|^2 = .9809$); M. L.: $.9727 \pm .1616i$ ($|\lambda|^2 = .9722$). These results indicate considerable variation in the conclusions to be derived from the four sets of estimators. First, by enlarging the period of the sample we do not have oscillations in the lag coefficients, i.e., OLS yields real roots while Jorgenson results yield complex roots. Second the modified M. L. and M. L. estimators yield complex roots; moreover their modulus is very close to unity. In addition to that, in the last two sets we may well obtain *negative lag coefficients* due to the negative point estimators in the numerator polynomials. Of course, we have not appraised the statistical significance of these results, nor have we experimented with the order of the numerator polynomial so as to obtain the "best fitting" result as was the case with Jorgenson's study.

Finally, if we standardize the lag coefficients so that they add to unity we can obtain the implied mean lag as follows: Let

$$W(s) = \frac{\sum_{i=0}^{\mu} a_i s^i}{\sum_{j=0}^{\nu} b_j s^j} = \frac{A(s)}{B(s)} \tag{26}$$

be the lag generating function; it is apparent that

$$W(1) = \frac{A(1)}{B(1)} \tag{26a}$$

represents the sum of the lag coefficients. If *all lag coefficients are positive,* as must be the case in Jorgenson's model, then it makes perfectly good sense to divide the lag coefficients by $W(1)$ so that they lie in the interval $[0, 1]$ and sum to unity. Thus, they have all the characteristics of a set of probabilities, and we may define the mean lag in the same way as we define the mean of a random variable. In this case we obtain

(26b) $$\text{Mean lag} = \frac{A'(1)}{A(1)} - \frac{B'(1)}{B(1)}$$

where $A'(1)$, $B'(1)$ indicate respectively the derivatives of $A(s)$, $B(s)$ evaluated at $s = 1$. This measure is not useful in the case of the modified M. L. and M. L. estimators—at least not in the present case.

The mean lag for OLS is 15.16 quarters; for Jorgenson it is 7.02 quarters. This is indeed a very substantial variation and one that we might not expect to materialize simply by the enlargement of the sample period. However, it is not our purpose here to comment on this substantive aspect.

To conclude our discussion let us elucidate two aspects. First, by modified M. L. estimators we mean the following. The maximum likelihood (M. L.) estimators are obtained by (iteratively) solving the equations (7a) and (7b). If, however, we replace the quantities x^{**}_{t-s} by y^*_{t-s} then, in fact, we lighten the computational burden without losing consistency. Indeed, in view of the assumptions we make concerning the error term, the quantities y^*_{t-s} are not correlated with the error term and thus the estimators obtained (by iteration) from

(27) $$\begin{bmatrix} X^{*\prime}X^* & X^{*\prime}Y^* \\ Y^{*\prime}X^* & Y^{*\prime}Y^* \end{bmatrix} d = \bar{c}^*$$

where X^*, Y^* are as defined in (8) and

(27a) $$\bar{c}^* = (\bar{c}^*_j) , \quad \bar{c}^*_j = \sum_{t=\mu+\nu+1}^{T} y^*_t x^*_{t-j} , \qquad j = 0, 1, 2, \cdots, \mu$$
$$= \sum_{t=\mu+\nu+1}^{T} y^*_t y^*_{t+\mu-j} , \qquad j = \mu + 1, \mu + 2, \cdots, \mu + \nu ,$$

have an interpretation as instrumental variable estimators.[3] The advantage of making calculations with y^*_{t-s} instead of x^{**}_{t-s} is that the moment matrices of unknown coefficients (see equation (27)) are for each iteration symmetric and positive definite.

Second, we may obtain initial consistent estimators by an obvious extension of Liviatan-type methods or by using as initial instruments a suitable number of the principal components of *a set of lags in the independent variables*. This will have the effect of ameliorating the multicollinearity problems that are induced by using as instruments successive lags of the independent variable as Liviatan's method would suggest.

University of Pennsylvania and Princeton University, USA

REFERENCES

[1] AMEMIYA, T. AND W. FULLER, "A Comparative Study of Alternative Estimators in a Distributed Lag Model," *Econometrica*, XXXV (July-October, 1967), 509–29.

[3] It should, of course, be noted that this is a less efficient estimator than the M. L. one.

[2] DHRYMES, P. J., "Efficient Estimation of Distributed Lags with Autocorrelated Error," *International Economic Review*, X (February, 1969), 41-67.

[3] ———, "Estimation of the General Rational Lag Structure by Spectral Techniques," Discussion Paper No. 35, Department of Economics, University of Pennsylvania.

[4] ———, "On the Treatment of Certain Recurrent Nonlinearities in Regression Analysis," *Southern Economic Journal*, XXXII (October, 1966), 187-96.

[5] HANNAN, E. J., "The Estimation of Relationships Involving Distributed Lags," *Econometrica*, XXXIII (January, 1965), 206-24.

[6] HUZURBAZAR, V. S., "The Likelihood Function, Consistency and the Maxima of the Likelihood Functions," *Annals of Eugenics*, XIV (1948), 185.

[7] JORGENSON, D. W., "Rational Distributed Lag Functions," *Econometrica*, XXXIV January, 1966), 135-49.

[8] KLEIN, L. R., "The Estimation of Distributed Lags," *Econometrica*, XXVI October, 1958), 553-65.

[9] KOYCK, L. M., *Distributed Lags and Investment Analysis* (Amsterdam: North Holland Publishing Company, 1954).

[10] LIVIATAN, N., "Consistent Estimation of Distributed Lags," *International Economic Review*, IV (January, 1963), 44-52.

[11] MALINVAUD, E., "The Estimation of Distributed Lags: A Comment," *Econometrica*, XXIX (July, 1961), 430-3.

[12] MORRISON, J. L., "Small Sample Properties of Selected Distributed Lag Estimators: A Monte Carlo Experiment," *International Economic Review*, IX (February, 1970), 13-32.

[13] STEIGLITZ, K. AND L. E. MCBRIDE, "A Technique for the Identification of Linear Systems," *IEEE Transactions on Automatic Control* Vol. AC-10, No. 4 (October, 1965), 461-4.

[14] ———, "Iterative Methods for Systems Identification," Technical Report No. 15, June, 1966, Department of Electrical Engineering, Princeton University.

[15] WALD, A., "Note on the Consistency of the Maximum Likelihood Estimate," *The Annals of Mathematical Statistics*, XX (1949), 595-601.

INTERNATIONAL ECONOMIC REVIEW
Vol. 12, No. 2, June, 1971

ON THE STRONG CONSISTENCY OF ESTIMATORS FOR CERTAIN DISTRIBUTED LAG MODELS WITH AUTOCORRELATED ERRORS*

BY PHOEBUS J. DHRYMES[1]

1. INTRODUCTION

IN A PREVIOUS PAPER [3], the author presented a maximum likelihood procedure for estimating the parameters of the model

$$y_t = \alpha_0 \sum_{i=0}^{\infty} \lambda_0^i x_{t-i} + u_t, \quad u_t = \rho_0 u_{t-1} + \varepsilon_t\,, \qquad t = 1, 2, \cdots, T \tag{1}$$

where a zero subscript on a parameter symbol will always indicate its true value. In the above, $\{\varepsilon_t: t = 0, \pm 1, \pm 2, \cdots\}$ was taken to be a sequence of mutually independent identically distributed (i.i.d.) $N(0, \sigma_0^2)$ variables. It was further assumed that $\lambda \in (0, 1)$, $\rho \in (-1, 1)$ and that the sequence of explanatory variables $\{x_t: t = 0, \pm 1, \pm 2, \cdots\}$ was bounded nonstochastic and such that

$$\lim_{T\to\infty} \frac{1}{T} \sum_{t=1}^{T} x_t^2 = c$$

is well defined with $c > 0$.

If we define

$$a = \sum_{i=0}^{\infty} \lambda_0^i x_{-i} \tag{2}$$

it was asserted in [3] that a may be consistently estimated by the procedure given there. This claim is false. Lack of consistency is, formally, a consequence of the fact that the "variable" to which it corresponds, *viz.*, λ^t, $t = 1, 2, \cdots, T$ has the property

$$\sum_{t=1}^{\infty} \lambda^{2t} < \infty\,. \tag{3}$$

Intuitively, a represents the (nonstochastic) initial conditions of the model in (1). Thus, in view of the stability requirements, it is clear that the farther we are removed from the origin the "less" the position of the system depends on initial conditions. Consequently, additional observations as $T \to \infty$ convey

* Manuscript received March 17, 1971.

[1] The research on which this paper is based was in part supported by NSF grant GS 2289 at the University of Pennsylvania and was completed during the author's visit at the University of California, Los Angeles. It is a pleasure for me to express my gratitude to Thomas M. Liggett for invaluable advice at some stages of the preparation of this paper. I would also like to thank E. Malinvaud for critical comments on an earlier draft.

less and less information regarding α.

Consistency for the other parameters, however, is preserved as was asserted in [3]. The proof given there is in many ways deficient. In the following we shall show that, under slightly more restrictive conditions, the estimators obtained by the search procedure given in [3] converge to the true parameters, *not only in probability but with probability one*[2] *as well*.

An interesting by-product of the argument used to establish this result is its applicability to problems of estimating, by minimum chi-square methods, the parameters of nonlinear models whose error processes are finite order autoregressions. Such problems are occurring with increasing frequency in econometric research.

2. CONVERGENCE OF ESTIMATORS

Here we shall consider the model in (1) with the stochastic specifications given there but subject to the following additional conditions.

(A. 1) If we put $\omega = (\alpha, \lambda, \rho)'$, then $\omega \in \Omega$, where Ω is a closed bounded set and in particular $\lambda \in [0, 1 - \delta_1]$, $\rho \in [-1 + \delta_2, 1 - \delta_2]$, $\delta_1, \delta_2 > 0$ but small.

(A. 2) The explanatory sequence $\{x_t : t = 0, \pm 1, \pm 2, \cdots\}$ obeys, for all t, $|x_t| < K$, for some constant K and

$$\lim_{T\to\infty} \frac{1}{T} \sum_{t=1}^{\infty} x_t x_{t+\tau} = c(\tau)$$

the $c(\tau)$ being well defined constants and $c(0) > 0$.

(A. 3) The true parameter, ω_0, is an interior point of Ω, and $1/T\ \partial^2 L/\partial\omega\partial\omega$ converges to a nonsingular matrix for ω_0, L being a concentrated log likelihood function to be defined below.

Remark 1. The restrictions imposed by (A. 1) are empirically innocuous. In practice we would be searching over an interval, say, [0, .999] for λ and [−.999, .999] for ρ. The results we shall obtain would, thus, be inapplicable to models in which $|\lambda_0| \geqq .999$ and/or $|\rho_0| \geqq .999$. It is clearthat such restrictions are inconsequential. The condition in (A. 3) is needed only in order to establish the asymptotic normality of the resulting estimators. We shall not derive such results here since they have been obtained in [5].

If we partially maximize the (log) likelihood function of the model in (1) with respect to σ^2 we obtain, upon division by T, the concentrated (log) likelihood function

$$L_T(\omega; y, x) = -\frac{1}{2}[\ln(2\pi) + 1] + \frac{1}{2T}\ln(1-\rho^2) - \frac{1}{2}\ln S_T(\omega; y, x) \tag{4}$$

where

$$S_T(\omega; y, x) = \frac{1}{T}(y - \alpha x^*)' V^{-1}(y - \alpha x^*)\,, \qquad y = (y_1, y_2, \cdots, y_T)'\,,$$
$$x^* = (x_1^*, x_2^*, \cdots, x_T)'\,, \qquad x_t^* = \sum_{i=0}^{\infty} \lambda^i x_{t-i}\,. \tag{5}$$

[2] For a definition of this term see [4, (Chapter 3)]; *convergence with probability one is what we mean by strong consistency.*

The function L referred to in (A. 3) is simply $TL_T(\omega; y, x)$. We observe that $S_T(\cdot; y, x)$ is bounded away from zero, for $\omega \in \Omega$. The plan of the argument is as follows:

i. First, we show that $S_T(\omega; y, x)$ converges to its limit, say $S(\omega)$, with probability one uniformly in ω. Hence that $L_T(\omega; y, x)$ converges to its limit, say $L(\omega)$, with probability one uniformly in ω.

ii. Second, we show that the sequence of estimators defined by

$$L_T(\hat{\omega}_T; y, x) \geqq L_T(\omega; y, x)\ , \ \forall \omega \in \Omega$$

has at least one limit point, say ω_*, and that $w_0 = w_*$. Thus, we conclude that $\hat{\omega}_T$ converges to ω_0 with probability one since ω_* is *any* limit point.

In the course of the argument we shall use a number of results not generally employed in the literature of econometrics, and for that reason we state them as theorems giving appropriate references for their proofs.

THEOREM 1. (*Bolzano-Weierstrass*). *Every bounded infinite set has at least one limit point and there exists a subsequence that converges to it.*

PROOF. See [**1**, (10)] and [**10**, (38)].

THEOREM 2. (*Arzelà-Ascoli*). *Let $\{f_n\}$ be a sequence of equi-continuous functions from a compact topological space X to a metric space Y which converge at each point of X to a function f. Then $\{f_n\}$ converges to f uniformly on X.*

PROOF. For a discussion of a number of variations of this result see [**9**, (153–155)].

THEOREM 3. (*Borel-Cantelli*). *Let Γ be a set of points γ, F be a σ-field, i.e., a collection of subsets of Γ such that if $A_n \in F$ then $A_n^c \in F$, $A_n \cap A_{n'} \in F$, $\bigcup_1^\infty A_n \in F$, A_n^c being the complement of A_n, and* P$(\cdot)$ *be a probability measure over F. If $A_n \in F$, then*

$$\sum_{n=1}^{\infty} P(A_n) < \infty$$

implies

$$P(A_n, \text{ infinitely often}) = 0\ .$$

PROOF. [**2**, (41)].

THEOREM 4. (*Birkhoff-Khinchin*). *Let $\{x_n: n = 0, \pm 1, \pm 2, \cdots\}$ be a strictly stationary process*[3] *and suppose that*

$$E|x_0| < \infty$$

then, with probability one

$$\lim_{n\to\infty} \frac{1}{n} \sum_{k=m}^{n+m} x_k = y^*$$

exists and moreover $E(y^*) = E(x)$.

[3] For an explanation of this term, see [**4**, (Chapter 9)].

PROOF. This is given as Corollary 2 to the Birkhoff-Khinchin theorem in [**6**, (129)].

In order to show convergence of $L_T(\omega; y, x)$ to $L(\omega)$ with probability one, uniformly in ω, it will suffice to show the same for $S_T(\omega; y, x)$ and $S(\omega)$.

Remark 2. Proceeding as above would also show that minimum chi-square estimators, obtained by the condition

$$S_T(\hat{\omega}_T: y, x) \leqq S_T(\omega; y, x), \quad \forall \omega \in \Omega \tag{6}$$

have the same (asymptotic) properties as maximum likelihood estimators in this context.

Remark 3. Note that in (5), ω enters only through α, x^* and V, but *not* through y, since the latter depends only on ω_0.

We have

$$\begin{aligned} S_T(\omega; y, x) = {} & \frac{1}{T}(\alpha_0 x_0^* - \alpha x^*)' V^{-1}(\alpha_0 x_0^* - \alpha x^*) + \frac{2}{T}(\alpha_0 x_0^* - \alpha x^*)' V^{-1} u \\ & + \frac{1}{T} u' V^{-1} u \end{aligned} \tag{7}$$

where x_0^* is a T-element vector whose t^{th}-element is $\sum_{i=0}^{\infty} \lambda_0^i x_{t-i}$. It will suffice to show that, as $T \to \infty$, each of the three terms in the right member of (7) converges to its limit uniformly in ω, and when the occasion requires it, with probability one.

Consider the third term first. Thus,

$$\frac{1}{T} u' V^{-1} u = \frac{1}{T} \sum_{t=1}^{T} u_t^2 - 2\rho \frac{1}{T} \sum_{t=2}^{T} u_t u_{t-1} + \rho^2 \frac{1}{T} \sum_{t=2}^{T-1} u_t^2 . \tag{8}$$

But since $\{u_t: t = 0, \pm 1, \pm 2, \cdots\}$ is a *strictly stationary process*, by virtue of the i.i.d. assumption regarding $\{\varepsilon_t: t = 0, \pm 1, \pm 2, \cdots\}$, so are $\{u_t^2\}$ and $\{u_t u_{t-1}\}$. We note that

$$\begin{aligned} & E(u_0^2) = \frac{\sigma_0^2}{1 - \rho_0^2} < \infty , \qquad E| u_0 u_{-1} | < \infty \\ & \operatorname*{plim}_{T \to \infty} \frac{1}{T} \sum_{t=1}^{T} u_t^2 = \frac{\sigma_0^2}{1 - \rho_0^2} , \qquad \operatorname*{plim}_{T \to \infty} \frac{1}{T} \sum_{t=2}^{T} u_t u_{t-1} = \frac{\sigma_0^2 \rho_0}{1 - \rho_0^2} . \end{aligned} \tag{9}$$

Consequently, by Theorem 4,

$$\frac{1}{T} \sum_{t=1}^{T} u_t^2 , \qquad \frac{1}{T} \sum_{t=2}^{T} u_t u_{t-1} ,$$

converge with probability one to some limits, say ξ_0, ξ_1 respectively. But convergence with probability one implies convergence in probability and we conclude

$$\xi_0 = \frac{\sigma_0^2}{1 - \rho_0^2} , \qquad \xi_1 = \rho_0 \xi_0 . \tag{10}$$

Therefore, in view of the particularly simple way in which ρ enters (8), we conclude that

$$\frac{1}{T}u'V^{-1}u \to \sigma_0^2 + \frac{\sigma_0^2}{1-\rho_0^2}(\rho - \rho_0)^2$$

with probability one uniformly in ω.

Remark 4. It is worth noting that in the argument above the normality of the $\{u_t\}$ process has not been employed. Indeed, it will never be employed, except in defining the likelihood function. The results follow from the fact that $\{\varepsilon_t: t = 0, \pm 1, \pm 2, \cdots\}$ is a sequence of i.i.d. random variables with zero mean and finite (absolute) moments of certain orders.

We now turn to the second term. We have

$$\frac{1}{T}(\alpha_0 x_0^* - \alpha x^*)'V^{-1}u = \frac{1}{T}\alpha_0 x_0^{*\prime} V^{-1}u - \frac{1}{T}\alpha x^{*\prime} V^{-1}u \,. \tag{11}$$

It will suffice to show that the second term in the right member of (11) converges to its limit with probability one, uniformly in ω. The first term depends only on ρ *but not on* α *or* λ.

We may write the tth element of x^* as

$$x_t^* = a\lambda^t + \sum_{i=0}^{t-1} \lambda^i x_{t-i} \,, \qquad t = 1, 2, \cdots, T \tag{12}$$

where a was defined in (2), and note that for all $\omega \in \Omega$

$$|a| < \frac{K}{\delta_1} \,.$$

Using (12) we can write

$$\frac{1}{T}\alpha x^{*\prime} V^{-1}u = \frac{1}{T}\alpha a \underline{\lambda}' V^{-1}u + \frac{1}{T}\alpha x^{**\prime} V^{-1}u \tag{13}$$

where x^{**} is a T-element vector the tth element of which is given by $\sum_{i=0}^{t-1} \lambda^i x_{t-i}$, $t = 1, 2, \cdots, T$ and $\underline{\lambda} = (\lambda, \lambda^2, \cdots, \lambda^T)'$. We observe that

$$\frac{1}{T}\underline{\lambda}' V^{-1}u = \frac{1}{T}\sum_{t=1}^{T} \lambda^t u_t - \rho\frac{1}{T}\sum_{t=2}^{T} \lambda^{t-1} u_t - \rho\frac{1}{T}\sum_{t=2}^{T} \lambda^t u_{t-1} + \rho^2 \frac{1}{T}\sum_{t=2}^{T-1} \lambda^t u_t \,. \tag{14}$$

It will suffice to show that $1/T \sum_{t=1}^{T} \lambda^t u_t$ converges to its limit with probability one uniformly in λ. Convergence of the other terms is proved similarly and uniformity of convergence with respect to ρ is obvious from the representation in (14). But

$$u_t = \rho_0^t u_0 + \sum_{i=0}^{t-1} \rho_0^i \varepsilon_{t-i} \,, \qquad t = 1, 2, \cdots$$

and we note that u_0 (the observation on the u-process at "time" zero) is a finite valued random variable. Thus, we may write

$$\frac{1}{T}\sum_{t=1}^{T} \lambda^t u_t = \frac{u_0}{T}\sum_{t=1}^{T} (\lambda\rho_0)^t + \sum_{t=1}^{T} \lambda^t \left[\frac{1}{T}\sum_{i=0}^{t-1} \rho_0^i \varepsilon_{t-i}\right] \tag{15}$$

and observe that $\sum_{t=1}^{T} (\lambda\rho_0)^t$ is bounded by some constant independently of λ

or T. Since u_0 is a finite valued random variable u_0/T converges to zero with probability one. Hence we need be concerned only with the second term. Define

$$W_{T,t} = \frac{1}{T}\sum_{i=0}^{t-1}\rho_0^i \varepsilon_{t-1} \tag{16}$$

and observe that

$$\left|\sum_{t=1}^{T}\lambda^t W_{T,t}\right| \leqq \sum \lambda^t \sup_t |W_{T,t}| \leqq \frac{1}{\delta_1}\sup_t |W_{T,t}| . \tag{17}$$

Then, to show convergence with probability one, uniformly in λ, we must show that $\sup_t |W_{T,t}| \to 0$ with probability one. If $\varphi_1 > 0$ we have, using the Chebyshev inequality for fourth moments, for a random variable, z, having mean zero and finite fourth moment

$$\Pr\{|z| > \varphi_1\} \leqq \frac{E(z^4)}{\varphi_1^4} .$$

If the ε-sequence has finite fourth order moments, we have, in view of the definition of $W_{T,t}$ in (16)

$$\Pr\{|W_{T,t}| > \varphi_1\} \leqq \frac{E(W_{T,t})^4}{\varphi_1^4} < \frac{K_1}{\varphi_1^4}\frac{1}{T^4} \tag{18}$$

where K_1 is some constant not depending on t, T or ρ_0. Since

$$\sum_{T=1}^{\infty}\sum_{t=1}^{T} E(W_{T,t}^4) < K_1 \sum_{T=1}^{\infty}\frac{1}{T^3} < \infty \tag{19}$$

we conclude, by Theorem 3,

$$\sup_{t \leqq T} |W_{T,t}| \to 0$$

with probability one. Hence, that $\sum_{t=1}^{T}\lambda^t W_{T,t}$ converges to zero with probability one uniformly in λ. We must now deal with

$$\begin{aligned}\frac{1}{T}\alpha x^{**\prime}V^{-1}u = \frac{1}{T}\alpha\Bigg[&\sum_{t=1}^{T}\sum_{i=0}^{t-1}\lambda^i x_{t-i}u_t - \rho\sum_{t=2}^{T}\sum_{i=0}^{t-2}\lambda^i x_{t-1-i}u_t \\ &- \rho\sum_{t=2}^{T}\sum_{i=0}^{t-1}\lambda^i x_{t-i}u_{t-1} + \rho^2\sum_{t=2}^{T-1}\sum_{i=0}^{t-2}\lambda^i x_{t-i}u_t\Bigg] .\end{aligned} \tag{20}$$

It will suffice to show that

$$\frac{1}{T}\sum_{t=1}^{T}\sum_{i=0}^{t-1}\lambda^i x_{t-i}u_t$$

converges to zero with probability one uniformly in λ; uniform convergence with respect to α and ρ is obvious from (20) in view of the fact that the set Ω is bounded (and closed). Using the representation $u_t = \rho_0^t u_0 + \sum_{i=0}^{t-1}\rho_0^i\varepsilon_{t-i}$, as before, it will suffice to show that

$$\frac{1}{T}\sum_{t=1}^{T}\sum_{j=0}^{t-1}\sum_{i=0}^{t-1}\lambda^i\rho_0^j x_{t-i}\varepsilon_{t-j} = \sum_{i=0}^{T-1}\sum_{j=0}^{T-1}\lambda^i\rho_0^j\frac{1}{T}\sum_{t=\max(i,j)+1}^{T} x_{t-i}\varepsilon_{t-j} \tag{21}$$

converges to zero uniformly in λ. Let

$$W_{T,i,j} = \frac{1}{T} \sum_t x_{t-i} \varepsilon_{t-j} . \tag{22}$$

We observe that, provided the ε-sequence has finite eighth order moments,

$$E(W_{T,i,j}^8) < K_2 \frac{1}{T^4} \tag{23}$$

where K_2 is some constant not depending on λ, ρ_0, i, j, T or x_t. Since

$$\sum_{T=1}^{\infty} \sum_{i=0}^{T-1} \sum_{j=0}^{T-1} E(W_{T,i,j}^8) < K_2 \sum_{T=1}^{\infty} \frac{1}{T^2} < \infty \tag{24}$$

we conclude, by Theorem 3,

$$\sup_{i,j} | W_{T,i,j} | \to 0$$

with probability one, and hence that

$$\frac{1}{T} \alpha x^{**\prime} V^{-1} u \to 0$$

with probability one uniformly in ω.

Remark 5. The construction above proves more than is needed, since it shows convergence to zero with probability one uniformly *in* ω *and* ρ_0. Notice also that the bound in (23) uses the fact that the sequence of explanatory variables $\{x_t: t = 0, \pm 1, \pm 2, \cdots\}$ *is bounded*. This may be relaxed, however, if we assert, instead, that

$$\lim_{T\to\infty} d_T^2 = \infty , \qquad \lim_{T\to\infty} \frac{\max_{t \le T} | x_t |}{d_T} = 0 , \qquad d_T^2 = \sum_{t=1}^{T} x_t^2 ,$$

and in the definition of $S_T(\omega; y, x)$ we divide by d_T instead of T.

Finally, we must show that

$$\frac{1}{T} (\alpha_0 x_0^* - \alpha x^*)' V^{-1} (\alpha_0 x_0^* - \alpha x^*)$$

converges to its limit uniformly in ω. Notice that the quadratic form above does not contain random variables.

Let

$$g_t(\omega) = \alpha_0 \sum_{i=0}^{\infty} \lambda_0^i x_{t-i} - \alpha \sum_{i=0}^{\infty} \lambda^i x_{t-i} \tag{25}$$

and note that

$$\begin{aligned} &\frac{1}{T} (\alpha_0 x_0^* - \alpha x^*)' V^{-1} (\alpha_0 x_0^* - \alpha x^*) \\ &= \frac{1}{T} \left[\sum_{t=1}^{T} g_t^2(\omega) - 2\rho \sum_{t=2}^{T} g_t(\omega) g_{t-1}(\omega) + \rho^2 \sum_{t=2}^{T-1} g_t^2(\omega) \right] . \end{aligned} \tag{26}$$

It will suffice to show that $1/T \sum_{t=1}^{T} g_t^2(\omega)$ converges to its limit uniformly in ω.

We note that

$$|g_t(\omega)| < \frac{\alpha_0 K}{1-\lambda_0} + \frac{K_3}{\delta_1} \tag{27}$$

for all t, where K_3 is some constant independent of t and ω. Moreover, let $\omega_1, \omega_2 \in \Omega$, then for all t,

$$\begin{aligned} &|g_t(\omega_1) - g_t(\omega_2)| \\ &= \left|(\alpha_2 - \alpha_1)\sum_{i=0}^{\infty} \lambda_2^i x_{t-i} + \alpha_1(\lambda_2 - \lambda_1)\sum_{i=1}^{\infty}\left(\sum_{j=0}^{i-1}\lambda_2^{i-j-1}\lambda_1^j\right)x_{t-i}\right| \\ &\leqq |\alpha_2 - \alpha_1|\frac{K}{\delta_1} + |\lambda_2 - \lambda_1|\frac{K_4}{\delta_1^2} \end{aligned} \tag{28}$$

where K_4 is a constant not depending on ω or t. What (27) and (28) show is that $\{g_t\}$ is a family of continuous functions defined on the compact set Ω which are uniformly bounded and equicontinuous.

Noting that

$$|g_t^2(\omega_2) - g_t^2(\omega_1)| = |g_t(\omega_2) + g_t(\omega_1)|\,|g_t(\omega_2) - g_t(\omega_1)| \tag{29}$$

we see that $\{g_t^2\}$ is also a family of uniformly bounded equicontinuous functions, continuous on the compact set Ω.

Define now

$$f_{t,T}(\omega) = \frac{1}{T}g_t^2(\omega)\,, \qquad f_T(\omega) = \sum_{t=1}^{T} f_{t,T}(\omega) \tag{30}$$

and note that $\{f_T\}$ is a family of continuous functions on Ω, which is uniformly bounded and equicontinuous. In view of assumption (A. 2) $f_T(\omega)$ converges pointwise (in ω) to a function $f(\omega)$, We then conclude, in view of Theorem 2 that $\{f_T\}$ converges to its limit uniformly in ω.

We have therefore proved

LEMMA 1. *Let $S_T(\omega; y, x)$ be as defined in* (5). *Then $S_T(\omega; y, x)$ converges to its limit with probability one, uniformly in ω and its limit is given by*

$$S(\omega) = \lim_{T\to\infty}\frac{1}{T}(\alpha_0 x_0^* - \alpha x^*)' V^{-1}(\alpha_0 x_0^* - \alpha x^*) + \sigma_0^2 + \frac{\sigma_0^2}{1-\rho_0^2}(\rho - \rho_0)^2\,. \tag{31}$$

Moreover, $L_T(\omega; y, x)$, as defined in (4), *converges to its limit with probability one, uniformly in ω, and its limit is given by*

$$L(\omega) = -\frac{1}{2}[\ln(2\pi) + 1] - \frac{1}{2}\ln S(\omega)\,. \tag{32}$$

Remark 6. It is important to recapitulate what role the various assumptions have played in establishing Lemma 1. The fact that $\{\varepsilon_t: t = 0, \pm 1, \pm 2, \cdots\}$ is a sequence of i.i.d. random variables with finite (absolute) moments of certain order was used in showing that $\{u_t^2\}$, $\{u_t u_{t-1}\}$ were strictly stationary and in invoking certain (ergodic) theorems regarding the convergence with probability one of sample means of processes having finite (absolute) first order moment (Birkhoff-Khinchin theorem). The properties of the ε-sequence were also employed in invoking the Borel-Cantelli lemma (Theorem 3) to show that terms of the form $1/Tx^{*\prime}V^{-1}u$ converge to zero with probability one uniformly in ω. In this connection we have also employed the boundedness of the sequence of explantory variables. The compactness of the set Ω, of admissible parameters, was utilized in invoking Theorem 2 (Ascoli-Arzelà), as was the boundeness of the explanatory variables. Compactness for α is not essential since we may eliminate it by partial maximization, as was done in [5]. This, however, would lead to more involved, but conceptually identical, arguments.

Remark 7. Introducing into the model additional variables, i.e., considering

$$y_t = \alpha_0 \sum_{i=0}^{\infty} \lambda_0^i x_{t-i,1} + \sum_{j=2}^{n} \alpha_{0j} x_{tj} + u_t \tag{33}$$

does not change anything substantially. Essentially the same arguments will go through if similar boundedness conditions are placed on the x_{tj}, $j = 2, 3, \cdots, n$ and on the additional parameters α_{0j}, $j = 2, 3, \cdots, n$.

Remark 8. Increasing the order of autoregression, i.e., if we consider, for finite m,

$$u_t = \sum_{i=1}^{m} \rho_{0i} u_{t-i} + \varepsilon_t \tag{34}$$

will complicate the argument by forcing us to deal with more involved formulae but will leave the essential features of the proof unaltered.

Let us now show that the estimators defined by

$$L_T(\hat{\omega}_T; y, x) \geqq L_T(\omega; y, x), \ \forall \omega \in \Omega \tag{35}$$

converge with probability one to ω_0. It will suffice to do so for the minimum chi-square estimators defined by

$$S_T(\hat{\omega}_T; y, x) \leqq S_T(\omega; y, x), \ \forall \omega \in \Omega \, . \tag{36}$$

We first note that

$$S(\omega_0) = \sigma_0^2, \ S(\omega) \geqq S(\omega_0), \ \forall \omega \in \Omega \, . \tag{37}$$

Let $\{\hat{\omega}_T\}$ be the sequence of estimators obeying (36). For each sequence $\{u_t\}$ this forms an infinite bounded set and by Theorem 1 it has at least one limit point; let ω_* be such limit point and $\{\hat{\omega}_{T_i}\}$ be a subsequence converging to ω_*.

Because $S_T(\omega; y, x)$ converges to $S(\omega)$ *with probability one uniformly in* ω; for almost all sequences $\{u_t\}$, we have

$$S(\omega_*) \leqq S(\omega_0) \, . \tag{38}$$

But (37) then implies

$$S(\omega_*) = S(\omega_0) \, . \tag{39}$$

For the parameters of the model to be identified it is necessary that (39) imply that $\omega_* = \omega_0$. This is an identifiability condition, else the estimator would not be able to discriminate between ω_* and ω_0. Let us postpone the verification of this condition for the model under consideration and first complete the argument, assuming that (39) implies

$$\omega_* = \omega_0 \,. \tag{40}$$

Since ω_* is *any* limit point of $\{\hat{\omega}_T\}$, (40) implies that the sequence, therefore, converges to ω_0. Since (38) and (39) hold with probability one—i.e., for almost all sequences $\{u_t\}$—we conclude that

$$\Pr\{\lim_{T\to\infty} \hat{\omega}_T = \omega_0\} = 1 \tag{41}$$

which states that the estimator, $\hat{\omega}_T$, converges to the true parameter, ω_0, with *probability one.*

Let us now obtain the conditions under which the model under consideration is identifiable. What we must show is that (39) implies (40). In view of (31), we have

$$\lim_{T\to\infty} \frac{1}{T}(\alpha_0 x_0^* - \alpha_* x^*)' V^{-1}(\alpha_0 x_0^* - \alpha_* x^*) + \sigma_0^2 + \sigma_0^2 \frac{(\rho_* - \rho_0)^2}{1-\rho_0^2} = \sigma_0^2 \,. \tag{42}$$

This clearly implies

$$\rho_* = \rho_0, \ \lim_{T\to\infty} \frac{1}{T}(\alpha_0 x_0^* - \alpha_* x^*)' V_0^{-1}(\alpha_0 x_0^* - \alpha_* x^*) = 0 \,. \tag{43}$$

What we must determine is the following: Under what conditions on the sequence $\{x_t\}$ does the second equation in (43) imply $\lambda_* = \lambda_0$, $\alpha_* = \alpha_0$.

It is clear that this is not a vacuous exercise. Consider, for instance, the sequence $x_t = c + \gamma^t$, $t = 1, 2, \cdots$ and zero otherwise, for some constant c and $|\gamma| < 1$. It is easy to see that this obeys (*A.* 2) and that all arguments leading to (39) remain perfectly valid. For this sequence the second equation in (43) becomes

$$(1-\rho_0)^2\left(\frac{\alpha_0}{1-\lambda_0} - \frac{\alpha_*}{1-\lambda_*}\right)^2 = 0 \,.$$

This, unfortunately, *does not imply* $\alpha_* = \alpha_0$, $\lambda_* = \lambda_0$. Thus, for this type of sequence we cannot infer that $\{\hat{\omega}_T\}$ converges to ω_0, nor that (41) is valid.

So, let us see what restrictions we need impose on the x-sequence in order to render the model identifiable. Using the representation in (25) we can write the second equation of (43) as

$$\begin{aligned} &\lim_{T\to\infty} \frac{1}{T}\left[\sum_{t=1}^{T} g_t^2(\omega) - 2\rho_0 \sum_{t=2}^{T} g_t(\omega) g_{t-1}(\omega) + \rho_0^2 \sum_{t=2}^{T} g_{t-1}^2(\omega)\right] \\ &= \sum_{j=0}^{\infty} \varphi(0, j)c(0, j) + \sum_{i=1}^{\infty} \varphi(i, 0)c(i, 0) + \sum_{i=1}^{\infty}\sum_{j=1}^{\infty} \varphi(i, j)c(i, j) \end{aligned} \tag{44}$$

where

$$\varphi(0,0) = \alpha_0^2 + \alpha_*^2 - 2\alpha_0\alpha_* \tag{45}$$

$$\begin{aligned}\varphi(0,j) &= \alpha_0^2\lambda_0^{2j} + \alpha_*^2\lambda_*^{2j} - (\alpha_0\alpha_*)(\lambda_0^j + \lambda_*^j)\\ &\quad - \rho_0[\alpha_0^2\lambda_0^{2j-1} + \alpha_*^2\lambda_*^{2j-1} - \alpha_0\alpha_*(\lambda_*^{j-1} + \lambda_0^{j-1})] \qquad j = 1, 2, \cdots,\\ \varphi(i,0) &= \alpha_0^2\lambda_0^{2i} + \alpha_*^2\lambda_*^{2i} - (\alpha_0\alpha_*)(\lambda_0^i + \lambda_*^i)\\ &\quad - \rho_0[\alpha_0^2\lambda_0^{2i-1} + \alpha_*^2\lambda_*^{2i-1} - (\alpha_0\alpha_*)(\lambda_0^{i-1} + \lambda_*^{i-1})] \qquad i = 1, 2, \cdots,\end{aligned} \tag{46}$$

$$\begin{aligned}\varphi(i,j) = {} & [\alpha_0^2\lambda_0^{2i+j} + \alpha_*^2\lambda_*^{i+j} - \alpha_0\alpha_*(\lambda_0^i\lambda_*^j + \lambda_*^i\lambda_0^j)]\\ & - \rho_0[2\alpha_0^2\lambda_0^{2i-1+j} + 2\alpha_*^2\lambda_*^{i-1+j} - (\alpha_0\alpha_*)(\lambda_0^{i-1}\lambda_*^j + \lambda_*^{i-1}\lambda_0^j + \lambda_0^i\lambda_*^{j-1} + \lambda_0^{i-1}\lambda_*^i)]\\ & + \rho_0^2[\alpha_0^2\lambda_0^{2i+j-2} + \alpha_*^2\lambda_*^{i+j-2} - \alpha_0\alpha_*(\lambda_0^{i-1}\lambda_*^{j-1} + \lambda_*^{i-1}\lambda_0^{j-1})],\\ & \qquad\qquad i, j = 1, 2, 3, \cdots,\end{aligned} \tag{47}$$

and

$$c(i,j) = \lim_{T\to\infty} \frac{1}{T} \sum_{t=1}^{T} x_{t-i}x_{t-j}\,. \tag{48}$$

For the bounded x-sequences we consider here, it is apparent that

$$c(i,j) = c(i-j) = c(j-i)\,. \tag{49}$$

Denote, then, the "autocovariance" function of the x-sequence by

$$c(\tau) \qquad \tau = 0, 1, 2, \cdots.$$

Notice that we previously required that $c(0) > 0$.

If $c(\cdot)$ is *not* a constant function and has the property, say, $c(\tau) = 0$, $\tau \neq 0$, then the identifiability condition holds. To that end the coefficient of $c(0)$ in (44), must vanish. But we observe that for the coefficient of $c(0)$ we must have

$$\sum_{i=0}^{\infty} \varphi(i,i) = (\alpha_0 - \alpha_*)^2 + \sum_{i=1}^{\infty} [(\alpha_0\lambda_0^i - \alpha_*\lambda_*^i) - \rho_0(\alpha_0\lambda_0^{i-1} - \alpha_*\lambda_*^{i-1})]^2 = 0 \tag{50}$$

which immediately implies

$$\alpha_0 = \alpha_*,\ \alpha_0\lambda_0^i - \alpha_*\lambda_*^i = \rho_0(\alpha_0\lambda_0^{i-1} - \alpha_*\lambda_*^{i-1})\,, \qquad i = 1, 2, \cdots. \tag{51}$$

But the second condition in (51) requires

$$\lambda_0 = \lambda_*\,. \tag{52}$$

We have therefore proved

THEOREM 5. *Consider the model*

$$y_t = \alpha_0 \sum_{i=0}^{\infty} \lambda_0^i x_{t-i} + u_t\,,\quad u_t = \rho_0 u_{t-1} + \varepsilon_t\,,\quad t = 1, 2, 3, \cdots, T\,. \tag{53}$$

for i.i.d. $N(0, \sigma_0^2)$ ε_t *and subject to the assumptions* (A. 1), (A. 2); *then the maximum likelihood and minimum chi-square estimators of the parameters* $\omega = (\alpha, \lambda, \rho)'$ *defined by* (35) *and* (36), *respectively, converge with probability one to* ω_0*—the true parameter vector—provided the identifiability condition that* (39) *implies* (40) *is satisfied. To this end it will suffice to place certain restrictions on the "autocovariance function,"* $c(\cdot)$, *of the x-sequence. In particular if* $c(\tau) = 0$, $\tau \neq 0$ *identifiability is obtained.*

COROLLARY 1. *The estimator of σ_0^2 given by $S_T(\hat{\omega}_T; y, x)$ converges to σ_0^2 with probability one.*

PROOF. Obvious by the uniform convergence of $S_T(\omega; y, x)$ to $S(\omega)$ the ω-continuity of the latter and the fact that $\hat{\omega}_T$ converges to ω_0 with probability one.

Remark 9. If we consider the model of Remark 7 with or without the error specification of Remark 8, nothing of substance will change in the argument leading to Theorem 5, except that the verification of the identifiability condition will be rendered more cumbersome.

Remark 10. The preceding theorem and the argument leading to it are extremely useful in dealing with nonlinear (single equation) estimation problems. Such models may be formulated as

$$y_t = g(x_t, \theta) + u_t \qquad t = 1, 2, \cdots, T \tag{54}$$

where $\{x_t\}$ is the explanatory sequence and θ is a parameter vector constrained to lie in a compact set C. The error process may be specified to be strictly stationary. A typical specification in econometrics may be

$$u_t = \sum_{i=1}^{m} \rho_i u_{t-i} + \varepsilon_t \tag{55}$$

where $\{\varepsilon_t : t = 0, \pm 1, \pm 2, \cdots\}$ is a sequence of i.i.d. random variables with zero mean and finite (absolute) moments of order, say, r.

In the model of (54), since the explanatory sequence is one of fixed numbers, it is notationally convenient to write $g(x_t, \theta)$ as $g_t(\theta)$. In this more suggestive notation we have

$$y_t = g_t(\theta) + u_t \qquad t = 1, 2, \cdots, T\,. \tag{56}$$

The functions $g_t(\cdot)$ may be quite nonlinear (in θ). If Φ is the convariance matrix of $u = (u_1, u_2, \cdots, u_T)'$, the minimum chi-square estimator may be defined as that which (globally) minimizes

$$S_T(\theta; y, x) = \frac{1}{T}[y - g(\theta)]'\Phi^{-1}[y - g(\theta)] \tag{57}$$

where

$$g(\theta) = (g_1(\theta), g_2(\theta), \cdots, g_T(\theta))'\,, \quad y = (y_1, y_2, \cdots, y_T)'\,.$$

Thus the estimator, say $\hat{\theta}_T$, is defined by the condition

$$S_T(\hat{\theta}_T; y, x) \leqq S_T(\theta; y, x), \ \forall \theta \in C\,. \tag{58}$$

In order to show that

$$\Pr\left\{\lim_{T\to\infty} \hat{\theta}_T = \theta_0\right\} = 1 \tag{59}$$

where θ_0 is the true parameter vector one must show the following:

i. $(1/T)[g(\theta_0) - g(\theta)]'\Phi^{-1}[g(\theta_0) - g(\theta)]$ converges to its limit uniformly in θ, as $T \to \infty$

ii. $(1/T)[g(\theta_0) - g(\theta)]'\Phi^{-1}u$ converges to zero with probability one uniformly in θ

iii. $(1/T)u'\Phi^{-1}u$ converges to its (constant) limit with probability one uniformly in θ

iv. The model satisfies an identifiability condition, i.e., if $S(\theta)$ is the limit of $S_T(\theta; y, x)$, then $S(\theta_*) = S(\theta_0)$, $\theta_* \in C$ implies $\theta_* = \theta_0$.

Theorems 1 through 4 should be sufficient to establish the validity of the statements in i., ii. and iii. in the case of bounded explanatory variables. It would be an interesting research problem to determine the minimal conditions on the explanatory sequence that insure convergence with probability one of nonlinear minimum chi-square estimators.

Remark 11. The case of nonlinear least squares, i.e., the special case where, in (57), $\Phi = \sigma_0^2 I$ and the $\{u_t\}$ are i.i.d. random variables with mean zero and variance σ_0^2, has been treated in two important papers by Jennrich [7] and Malinvaud [8]. Thus, Jennrich and Malinvaud have given a solution to the problem of nonlinear least squares for models with i.i.d. disturbances. Unfortunately, the procedure employed does not readily extend to the case of dependent random variables. The approach taken in this paper, however, holds the promise that we may find an equally general solution to the problem posed by the model in (54) and (55), the estimator being defined by (57). Asymptotic normality of the resulting estimates will require the additional assumptions that (a) θ_0 is an interior point of C and (b) $(\partial^2 S_T(\theta; y, x))/\partial\theta\partial\theta$ has a *nonsingular limit*, for $\theta = \theta_0$. It is for this reason that (A. 3) was stated at the beginning at Section 2. Such requirements are quite apparent from the standard mean value theorem applied to $(\partial S_T(\theta; y, x))/\partial\theta$, which is typically employed in establishing the asymptotic distribution of such estimators.

3. CONCLUSION

In this paper we have shown that the maximum likelihood and minimum chi-square estimators in the context of the model in (1) converge with probability one to the true parameters, under certain conditions on the explanatory sequence. Moreover, we have indicated how the argument we have employed may be modified in order to show that (nonlinear) minimum chi-square estimators in the context of the model in (54) and (55) converge to the true parameters with probability one, and that their asymptotic distribution is normal.

Finally, it is interesting to note that in the Monte Carlo study reported in [5], using the procedure examined in this paper, for the model

$$y_t = \alpha_1 \sum_{i=0}^{\infty} \lambda_0^i x_{t-i,1} + \alpha_2 x_{t2} + u_t\,, \quad u_t = \rho_0 u_{t-1} + \varepsilon_t$$

one obtains, among other results, the following. For $\lambda_0 = .5$, $\rho_0 = .9$, $\alpha_1 = 2.00$, $\alpha_2 = 5.00$ and 100 replications the mean square error for $\hat{\lambda}_T$ is .002 for sample size 100, .003 for sample size 50. For $\hat{\rho}_T$ the corresponding quantities are .003 and .004. For α_1, they are .009, .010. For α_2, .006, .007.

University of Pennsylvania, U.S.A.

APPENDIX

In this appendix we give a simple argument, justifying the transition from our equation (19) in the text, to the statement that $\sup_{t \leqq T} | W_{T,t} | \to 0$ with probability one. Thus, let (Γ, F, P) be a probability space as in Theorem 3. Define, for any $\varphi > 0$,

$$A^{\varphi}_{T,t} = \{\gamma: | W_{T,t} | > \varphi, \gamma \in F\}$$
$$A^{\varphi}_{T} = U^{T}_{t=1} A^{\varphi}_{T,t} .$$

By the result exhibited in (18) and Theorem 3 we conclude that for any $\varphi > 0$

$$P(A^{\varphi}_{T}, i \cdot o) = 0$$

Let

$$A^{*\varphi}_{T} = \left\{\gamma: \sup_{t \leqq T} | W_{T,t} | > \varphi, \gamma \in F\right\}$$

Then $A^{*\varphi}_{T} \subset A^{\varphi}_{T}$ and therefore we conclude, for any $\varphi > 0$,

$$P(A^{*\varphi}_{T}, i \cdot o) = 0 .$$

Let

$$w = \lim \sup \left\{\sup_{t \leqq T} | W_{T,t} |\right\}$$

and note that w is a nonnegative random variable. Also observe that

$$\Pr \{w > \varphi\} \leqq P(A^{*\varphi}_{T} i \cdot o) = 0 .$$

Consequently conclude that

$$\sup_{t \leqq T} | W_{T,t} | \to 0$$

with probability one, as claimed.

A similar argument will establish the transition from equation (24) to the statement

$$\sup_{i,j} | W_{T,i,j} | \to 0$$

with probability one.

REFERENCES

[1] BUCK, R. C., *Advanced Calculus* (New York: McGraw-Hill, 1956).

[2] BREIMAN, L., *Probability* (Reading, Massachusetts: Addison-Wesley, 1968).

[3] DHRYMES, P. J., "Efficient Estimation of Distributed Lags with Autocorrelated Errors," *International Economic Review*, X (February, 1969), 47-67.

[4] ———, *Econometrics: Statistical Foundations and Applications*, (New York: Harper and Row, 1970).

[5] ———, *Distributed Lags: Problems of Formulation and Estimation* (San

Francisco: Holden-Day, 1971), in press.

[6] GIKHMAN, I. I. AND A. V. SKOROKHOD, *Introduction to the Theory of Random Processes* (Philadelphia: W. B. Saunders, 1969).

[7] JENNRICH, R. J., "Asymptotic Properties of Non-Linear Least Squares," *Annals of Mathematical Statistics*, XL (April, 1969), 633-643.

[8] MALINVAUD, E., "The Consistency of Nonlinear Regressions," *Annals of Mathematical Statistics*, XLI (June, 1970), 956-969.

[9] ROYDEN, H. L., *Real Analysis* (New York: MacMillan, 1963).

[10] RUDIN, W., *Principles of Mathematical Analysis* (New York: McGraw-Hill, 1958).

GREEK ECONOMIC REVIEW
Vol. 3, No 1, April 1981

ON THE ESTIMATION OF THE POLYNOMIAL LAG HYPOTHESIS

By Phoebus J. Dhrymes*

I. Introduction

The purpose of this brief note is to provide a concise discussion of the various strands that have, over the years, emerged in this literature such as those typified in Almon (1965), Dhrymes (1971), Shiller (1973) to mention but a few. While the major results contained herein certainly have been part of the oral tradition of econometrics I am not aware of any systematic exposition of them.

II. Formulation of the problem.

We take the formulation of the problem as that in Dhrymes [Dhrymes (1971), ch. 8]. Thus, we have the model

$$y_t = \sum_{\tau=0}^{n} w_\tau x_{t-\tau} + u_t, \qquad t = 1,2,\ldots, T$$

which can be written compactly as

$$y = Xw + u \tag{1}$$

and it is assumed that

$$u \sim N(0,\sigma^2 I) \tag{2}$$

independently of the elements of X.

The polynomial lag hypothesis (PLH) introduced by Almon [Almon (1965)] relies on the Lagrange Interpolation polynomials

$$s_j(t) = \frac{\prod_{i \neq j} (t-t_i)}{\prod_{i \neq j} (t_j-t_i)}, \qquad j = 0,1,2,\ldots, k$$

* Columbia University.

for arbitrary, fixed, points t_i, $i = 0,1,2,\ldots,k$. Defining

$$S^* = [\underline{s}_0(\tau),\ldots,\underline{s}_k(\tau)] \tag{3}$$

where

$$\underline{s}_j(\tau) = (s_j(0), s_j(1),\ldots, s_j(n))' \tag{4}$$

We assert that

$$w_j = P^*(j) \qquad j = 0,1,2,\ldots,n \tag{5}$$

where

$$P^*(t) = \sum_{j=0}^{k} b_j s_j(t) \tag{6}$$

so that $P^*(.)$ is a polynomial of known degree k. This leads to parametrization of (1) as

$$y = Z_* b + u \tag{7}$$

where

$$Z_* = XS^* \tag{8}$$

and the lag estimator

$$\hat{w}^{(1)} = S^*\hat{b}, \qquad \hat{b} = (Z_*'Z_*)^{-1} Z_*'y = (S^{*\prime}X'XS^*)^{-1} S^{*\prime}X'y \tag{9}$$

The PLH as exposited in Dhrymes [Dhrymes (1971)], specifies that

$$w_j = P(j) \tag{10}$$

where

$$P(t) = \sum_{i=0}^{k} \beta_i t^i \tag{11}$$

Defining

$$S = (s_{.0}, s_{.1},\ldots, s_{.k}) \tag{12}$$

where

$$s_{.0} = (1,1,\ldots,1)', \quad s_{.r} = (0,1,2^r, 3^r,\ldots,n^r)', \quad r = 1,2,\ldots,k, \tag{13}$$

we have the reparametrization

$$y = Z\beta + u \tag{14}$$

where

$$Z = XS$$

and the lag estimator

$$\hat{w}^{(2)} = S\hat{\beta}, \quad \hat{\beta} = (Z'Z)^{-1} Z'y = (S'X'XS)^{-1}S'X'y \tag{15}$$

Finally, one can formulate the PLH as a standard restricted least squares (RLS) problem —an approach implicit in Shiller [Shiller (1973)], although the thrust of that paper is in an entirely different direction.

This can be motivated by noting that

$$\Delta^k t^s = 0 \qquad k > s \tag{16}$$

where

$$\Delta = I - L$$

Hence

$$\Delta^{k+1} = (I - L)^{k+1} = \sum_{r=0}^{k+1} (-1)^r \binom{k+1}{r} L^r = \sum_{r=0}^{k+1} b_r L^r \tag{17}$$

Now define the $(n\text{-}k)x(n+1)$ matrix

$$R_k = [r_{ij}] \qquad i = 0,1,2,\ldots,n-k-1; \qquad j = 0,1,2,\ldots,n. \tag{18}$$

such that

$$\begin{aligned} r_{ij} &= 0 & i > j \\ &= b_{k+1-(j-i)} & j = i, i+1,\ldots,i+k+1 \\ &= 0 & j = i+k+2,\ldots,n \end{aligned} \tag{19}$$

Then the problem can be formulated as

$$y = Xw + u \tag{20}$$

subject to

$$R_k\, w = 0 \tag{21}$$

The resulting RLS estimator is

$$\tilde{w} = [(X'X)^{-1} - (X'X)^{-1} R_k' \,(R_k\,(X'X)^{-1} R_k' \,)^{-1} R_k\,(X'X)^{-1}]X'y \tag{22}$$

We have:

Proposition 1: Consider the model in (1) subject to the PLH degree k. Then

$$\hat{w}^{(1)} = \hat{w}^{(2)} = \tilde{w}$$

Proof: We first consider the question of whether

$$\hat{w}^{(1)} = \hat{w}^{(2)}$$

Evidently,

$$\hat{w}^{(1)} = A_1 X'y \qquad \hat{w}^{(2)} = A_2 X'y$$

where

$$A_1 = S^*(S^{*\prime}X'XS^*)^{-1}S^{*\prime}, \qquad A_2 = S(S'X'XS)^{-1}S' \tag{23}$$

We note that the columns of S contain the "ordinates", respectively, of the polynomials, $1,t,t^2,\ldots,t^k$. Thus, the column space of S contains the vectors encompassing the ordinates of all polynomials up to degree k, at $0,1,2,\ldots,n$. Consequently there exists a nonsingular matrix C such that

$$S^* = SC \tag{24}$$

Indeed, it is easy to see that the jth column of C, $c_{\cdot j}$, contains the coefficients of the polynomial $s_j(t)$. Thus,

$$A_1 = SCC^{-1}(S'X'XS)^{-1}C'C'^{-1}S' = S(S'X'XS')^{-1}S' = \mathrm{A}_2$$

For the second part, put

$$B = (X'X)^{-1} - (X'X)^{-1}\, R_k' \,(R_k(X'X)^{-1}R_k')^{-1} R_k(X'X)^{-1} \tag{25}$$

Now, there exists a nonsingular matrix H such that

$$X'X = H'H \tag{26}$$

Consequently, we have

$$B = H^{-1}(I - B_*)H'^{-1}, \qquad B_* = H'^{-1}R_k'(R_k(X'X)^{-1}R_k')^{-1}R_kH^{-1} \tag{27}$$

Put

$$A_* = HA_2H'$$

and observe that A^*, B^* are symmetric, idempotent matrices such that

$$A_*B_* = 0 \tag{28}$$

Hence, by Proposition 53 in Dhrymes [Dhrymes (1978a)], there exists an orthogonal matrix Q such that

$$A_* = QD_A Q', \qquad B_* = QD_B Q' \tag{29}$$

the matrices D_A, D_B being diagonal and containing the characteristic roots of A_* and B_* respectively. Note that, in view of (28)

$$D_A D_B = 0, \qquad I - D_B = D_A \tag{30}$$

and, thus,

$$B = H^{-1}(I - B_*)H'^{-1} = H^{-1}(I - QD_B Q')H'^{-1} = H^{-1}QD_A Q'H'^{-1} = A_2 \text{ q.e.d.}$$

It is often suggested that the first (Almon) formulation of the PLH is extremely useful in terms of imposing end point restrictions, while in the other contexts such restrictions are cumbersome. In many ways the RLS version of the PLH is the most convenient when imposing end point restrictions. We note that under the PLH

$$w = S\beta$$

while an end point restriction is a statement to the effect

$$P(a) = \underline{a}\beta = 0$$

where

$$\underline{a} = (1, a, a^2, \ldots, a^k).$$

Thus, if we desire to specify that the polynomial has roots, say, at a_1, a_2 we simply define

$$r_{(i)} = \underline{a}_i (S'S)^{-1}S', \qquad i = 1,2 \tag{31}$$

and estimate the parameters of (20) subject to

$$R_k^* w = 0, \qquad R_k^* = \begin{bmatrix} R_k \\ r_{(1)} \\ r_{(2)} \end{bmatrix} \tag{32}$$

III. Compatibility Tests

Once the PLH with or without end point constraints is put in the RLS context all procedures of the general linear hypothesis, see, for example,

Dhrymes (1978) ch.2 become available. Let SSR_i be the sum of squared residuals for

$i = 0$ OLS

$= 1$ PLH no end point constraints

$= 2$ PLH one (near) end point constrained

$= 3$ PLH one (far) end point constrained

$= 4$ PLH both end points constrained.

Then, in view of the normality assumption in (2), we have the following likelihood ratio test statistics

$$\text{Test 1:}\quad \left(\frac{SSR_1 - SSR_0}{SSR_0}\right)\frac{T-2n-1}{n-k} \sim F_{n-k,\, T-2n-1}$$

$$\text{Test 2:}\quad \left(\frac{SSR_2 - SSR_0}{SSR_0}\right)\frac{T-2n-1}{n-k+1} \sim F_{n-k+1,\, T-2n-1}$$

$$\text{Test 3:}\quad \left(\frac{SSR_3 - SSR_0}{SSR_0}\right)\frac{T-2n-1}{n-k+1} \sim F_{n-k+1,\, T-2n-1}$$

$$\text{Test 4:}\quad \left(\frac{SSR_4 - SSR_0}{SSR_0}\right)\frac{T-2n-1}{n-k+2} \sim F_{n-k+2,\, T-2n-1}$$

$$\text{Test 5:}\quad \left(\frac{SSR_2 - SSR_1}{SSR_1}\right)\frac{T-n-k-1}{1} \sim F_{1,\, T-n-k-1}$$

$$\text{Test 6:}\quad \left(\frac{SSR_3 - SSR_1}{SSR_1}\right)\frac{T-n-k-1}{1} \sim F_{1,\, T-n-k-1}$$

$$\text{Test 7:}\quad \left(\frac{SSR_4 - SSR_1}{SSR_1}\right)\frac{T-n-k-1}{2} \sim F_{2,\, T-n-k-1}$$

$$\text{Test 8:}\quad \left(\frac{SSR_4 - SSR_2}{SSR_2}\right)\frac{T-n-k}{1} \sim F_{1,\, T-n-k}$$

$$\text{Test 9:}\quad \left(\frac{SSR_4 - SSR_3}{SSR_3}\right)\frac{T-n-k}{1} \sim F_{1,\, T-n-k}$$

In Tests 1 through 4 the PLH is treated as a testable hypothesis (in various forms) against the alternative of no restrictions.

In Tests 5, 6, 7 the PLH is taken as a maintained hypothesis and what is tested is the validity of the point restrictions.

In Tests 8,9 one of the end point restrictions is taken as the maintained hypothesis and the other as a testable one.

REFERENCES

ALMON, S. (1965) "The Distributed Lag Between Capital Appropriations and Expenditures", *Econometrica*, vol. 33, pp. 178-196.

DHRYMES, P. J. (1971) *Distributed Lags: Problems of Estimation and Formulation*, San Francisco, Holdn-Day Inc.

——(1978) *Introductory Econometrics*, New York, Springer-Verlag.

——(1978a) *Mathematics for Econometrics*, New York, Springer-Verlag.

SHILLER, R. J. (1973) "A Distributed Lag Estimator Derived from Smoothness Prior", *Econometrica*, vol. 41, pp. 775-788.

PART IV

EMPIRICAL APPLICATIONS: PRODUCTION FUNCTIONS, TECHNICAL CHANGE, PRODUCTIVITY, DECOMPOSITION OF PRICE MOVEMENTS INTO QUALITY AND PURE PRICE EFFECTS, AND RELATED ISSUES

A COMPARISON OF PRODUCTIVITY BEHAVIOR IN MANUFACTURING AND SERVICE INDUSTRIES*

Phoebus J. Dhrymes

FOLLOWING a pioneering article by Solow [7] the problem of measuring "technical change" has been investigated by many authors, viz., Hogan [4], Massell [5], Pasinetti [6], Solow [7].

What almost all the papers above attempt to do is to construct a series which indexes or measures "technical change." The term is slightly inaccurate in that the series really purport to describe the time profile of that part of output which is not "explained" by the specified inputs, viz., capital and labor. It may be preferable to employ the term "productivity" in accounting for such variations in observed output, a terminology which will be adhered to below.

We shall provide a simple method of estimating a productivity parameter in a firm or sectoral or global production function. We shall then apply this method in estimating the appropriate parameter for the Manufacturing and Service Sector of the United States post-war economy. Finally, we shall indicate a method for testing a statistical hypothesis on the equality of two parameters so estimated. It will be found that the data does not warrant the conclusion that the "rate of change" of productivity differs significantly as between the two sectors.

The Model

Let the production process in a certain sector be characterized by:

$$Q(t) = A\ e^{\lambda t}\ K^{\alpha}(t)\ L^{\beta}(t)\ e^{u(t)} \qquad (1)$$

where: A, α, β are some real (positive) constants such that $\alpha + \beta = 1$; λ is the productivity parameter which purports to describe the manner in which changes in output occur apart from changes in the specified inputs, $u(t)$ is a random variable with respect to which we make the following specifications.

$$u(t) \text{ is } N(0, \sigma^2) \text{ and } E[u(t) \cdot u(t')] \begin{array}{l} = 0 \ \text{ if } t \neq t' \\ = \sigma^2 \text{ if } t = t' \end{array}$$

If this sector is also assumed to behave as if it obeyed the rules of perfect competition then we may write:

$$\begin{aligned} p_k(t) &= \frac{\partial\ Q^*(t)}{\partial K\ (t)}\ p_Q\ (t)\ e^{v_1(t)} \\ p_L(t) &= \frac{\partial\ Q^*(t)}{\partial\ L\ (t)}\ p_Q\ (t)\ e^{v_2(t)} \end{aligned} \qquad (2)$$

The equation (2) may be interpreted as stating that factor prices behave as if they were random variables in part, rather than as determining the observed capital and labor inputs; this strains the plausibility of the model somewhat in that it implies that factors are attached to sectors and are not free to move intersectorally. But for brief periods of observation this may not be unreasonable. In (2) we have the following definition and specifications:

$Q^*(t) = Q\ (t)\ e^{-u(t)}$, $v_i(t)\ i = 1,2$ are $N(0, \sigma^2_{v_i})$ and $p_k(t)$, $p_L(t)$, $p_Q(t)$ are input and output prices respectively at time t.

Now if we have observations for $t = 1, 2, \ldots T$, then it is shown elsewhere, Dhrymes [3], that there exist best (that is; unbiased and of minimum variance) estimators $\tilde{\alpha}$, $\tilde{\beta}$ for α, and β, respectively.

Having obtained those by the method suggested there we find easily from (1):

$$\begin{aligned} &Q(t)\ K^{-\tilde{\alpha}}(t) L^{-\tilde{\beta}}(t) = \\ &\quad A\ e^{\lambda t}\ K^{-(\tilde{\alpha}-\alpha)}_{(t)}\ L^{-(\tilde{\beta}-\beta)}_{(t)}\ e^{u(t)} \\ &t = 1,2, \ldots T \end{aligned} \qquad (3)$$

* This investigation is a revised version of part of the author's Ph.D Thesis submitted at the Massachusetts Institute of Technology. The present version was completed during the author's visit with the Cowles Foundation. I wish to take this opportunity to express my gratitude to Professors E. D. Domar who suggested this topic and offered helpful advice and J. W. Kendrick for making available to me part of his then unpublished work.

Thanks are also due to Mrs. Maude Peck of the National Bureau of Economic Research and to Mr. Alan Strout of the Harvard Economic Research Project for their help in obtaining the detailed data that is available.

Finally, I wish to thank the Ford Foundation which partially financed this investigation through a Doctoral Dissertation Fellowship.

which may be rewritten — upon taking logarithms — as:

$$y\ (t) = a + \lambda\ (t) + z\ (t)\ t = 1, 2, \ldots T \quad (3a)$$

where $y\ (t) = \ln Q(t) - \tilde{\alpha} \ln K\ (t) - \tilde{\beta} \ln L\ (t)$, $a = \ln A$, $z(t) = u(t) - (\tilde{\alpha} - \alpha) \ln K(t) - (\tilde{\beta} - \beta) \ln L(t)$.

On the hypotheses maintained one easily obtains:

$$E\ [z\ (t)] = E\ [u\ (t)] - E\ [\tilde{\alpha} - \alpha]\ \ln K(t) - E\ [\tilde{\beta} - \beta]\ \ln L\ (t) = 0 \quad (4)$$

provided $\ln K\ (t)$, $\ln L(t)$ remain bounded. It will be noted that (3a) displays a rather simple structure from which λ — the parameter of productivity or "technical change" — can be easily estimated by minimizing the second moment of estimated disturbances.

It is instructive and simpler to write (3a) and conduct the argument in matric form. Thus:

$$y = X\ \gamma + z \quad (5)$$

where y and z are column matrices with obvious meaning,

$$\gamma = \begin{bmatrix} a \\ \lambda \end{bmatrix} \text{ and } X = \begin{bmatrix} 1 & 1 \\ 1 & 2 \\ \cdot & \cdot \\ \cdot & \cdot \\ \cdot & \cdot \\ 1 & T \end{bmatrix}$$

The least squares estimator in (5) is given by:

$$\hat{\gamma} = (X'\ X)^{-1}\ X'y \quad (6)$$

In virtue of (4) it is a simple consequence that (6) is an unbiased estimator.

The variance of (6) is easily found to be:

$$\text{Var}\ (\hat{\gamma}) = \sigma^2\ (X'\ X)^{-1} + \hat{\Pi}\ \text{Var}\ (\tilde{\Theta})\ \hat{\Pi}' - \hat{\Pi}\ \text{Cov}(\tilde{\Theta}, u')\ R' - R\ \text{Cov}(u\ \tilde{\Theta}')\ \hat{\Pi}' \quad (7)$$

where $R = (X'\ X)^{-1}\ X'$, $\tilde{\Theta} = \begin{bmatrix} \tilde{\alpha} \\ \tilde{\beta} \end{bmatrix}$ and $\hat{\Pi} = (X'\ X)^{-1} X'\ [K, L]'$ with:

$$K = [\ln K\ (1), \ln K\ (2), \ldots \ln K\ (T)],$$
$$L = [\ln L\ (1), \ln L\ (2), \ldots \ln L\ (T)].$$

Thus $\hat{\Pi}$ is nothing more than a matrix of least squares estimators of the parameters, in the (linear) regression of the logarithm of capital and labor inputs on time. Hence, the last — second — row of Π consists of the "estimated" exponential rates of growth of the capital and labor inputs.

The device employed herein is somewhat akin to Durbin's extraneous estimators, although here the covariance terms do not vanish, since the estimators $\tilde{\alpha}$, $\tilde{\beta}$ are not independent of the random term in (1). It follows also from the method of constructing the series $y(t)$ that the random terms $z(t)$ are autocorrelated. We may now discuss the properties of the estimator $\hat{\gamma}$, in particular of $\hat{\lambda}$.

Because the terms $u(t)$, $v_i(t)$, $t = 1, 2, \ldots T$ are supposed to be a "realization" of a stationary stochastic process it readily follows from the unbiasedness of $\tilde{\alpha}$ and $\tilde{\beta}$ that $\hat{\gamma}$ is unbiased. Hence, in particular, the estimator of the "productivity" or "technical change" parameter is unbiased.

The consistency of (6) is obtained in the following rather curious way. Note that:

$$\underset{T \to \infty}{p \lim}\ z(t) = u\ (t) \quad (8)$$

provided $\ln K(t)$, $\ln L\ (t)$ do not grow "too rapidly," that is, not faster in t than is the convergence of $\tilde{\alpha}$, $\tilde{\beta}$ to α, β respectively.

It may also be remarked that in view of the hypotheses maintained concerning $u(t)$, the estimator $\hat{\gamma}$ of (6) is also asymptotically sufficient and efficient in virtue of (8) due to the Markov theorem and the assumed normality of $u(t)$. But this is perhaps an unneccesary refinement. It should be pointed out none the less that in all finite samples the estimator (6) is not efficient, since in the case of autocorrelated disturbances the minimality of variance property is possessed by Aitken's generalized least squares estimator.

The Data

It is apparent from the model that there are two stages of estimation. During the first we estimate α and β and during the second phase utilizing the estimates of α, β so obtained we produce an estimate of λ.

For the first stage we require observations on factor shares. We have relied for this exclusively on Department of Commerce data.

Here, returns to labor have been taken to be the category "Compensation of Employees," which consists of Wages, Salaries and Supplements, in Department of Commerce terminology.

Following Solow [7] we have augmented this by 65 per cent of proprietors' income, on the assumption that this approximates the division between returns to labor and returns to capital in this classification.

Output was taken to be "Gross Value Added" in real terms, except that we have not deflated when computing factor shares. "Gross Value Added" is a category compounded of Value Added as defined by the Department of Commerce, plus depreciation.

It is apparent that in the context of the model given in section II, this is the appropriate measure of output. Of course this excludes indirect business taxes. Now, whether we do or do not include indirect business taxes in the measure of output, will tend to have a perceptible effect on the estimates of α and β, as will be seen presently. But the question of "incidence" of such taxation is not clear, nor to my knowledge do there exist data on payment of such taxes by industrial classification, so it was felt best to leave indirect business taxes completely out, and hence no attempt was made to impute such payments to the sectors considered here.

Now from the data described above it is simple to compute the share of labor in the output (income) of the sector.

Then the share of capital was taken to be 1 minus the share of labor, that is, it was defined residually. Note, that due to the nature of the accounts, if we proceed to compute directly the share of capital by the method just given and then obtain as a residue the share of labor we should obtain identical results.

Something should be said about the extent of the sectors involved. Manufacturing was taken to be identically the sector so labelled by the Department of Commerce. The Service sector was taken to comprise the following Department of Commerce classifications: Contract Construction, Wholesale and Retail Trade, Finance Insurance and Real Estate, Services, except that from the latter we have eliminated the subcategories Commercial and Trade Schools and Nonprofit Membership Organizations not elsewhere classified.

To indicate the rough orders of magnitude involved it may be remarked that in the postwar period, Manufacturing accounted for about 35 per cent of the Gross Value Added of the Private Non-Farm Sector, while the sector we have labelled Service Industries accounted for approximately 50 per cent. The remainder is due to Transportation, Communications, and Public Utilities.

For the labor inputs, we have utilized the Department of Commerce series on Full-time Employee equivalent. In the case of the capital series we have not been so fortunate. For manufacturing we have utilized the series given by the Department of Commerce on end of year real capital stock, that is, Equipment, Structures, and Inventories.

For the Service industries, however, the capital series is a rather heroically concocted amalgam obtained as follows:

In Leontief [11] a set of capital coefficients is given; from these it is possible to compute the implied (fixed) capital stock for the Service industries in the year 1947, in 1947 prices. Now, the Department of Commerce publishes a series on depreciation (original cost) and on Expenditure on New Plant and Equipment. Neither of the two series is satisfactory for the use we shall make of them, but it did not appear advisable to "doctor them up."

From these last two series we obtain the annual investment in the fixed capital stock of the Service industries. This implies that we take depreciation in original cost to index "accurately" the economic loss due to obsolescence and use of the capital stock, and expenditures as indexing gross addition to the stock. If we state the difference in 1947 prices the fixed capital stock of the sector can be computed from:

$$K(t+1) = K(t) + \triangle K(t)$$

using the "initial" condition $K(1947)$ which we obtain from Leontief's data. We may interpret $K(t)$ as meaning either capital stock at beginning of period t or at the end of the period $(t-1)$. We have chosen the latter interpretation, partially to conform to the usage of the Department of Commerce in computing the capital stock in Manufacturing.

Using a bench mark provided by Professor Kendrick, for end of year "stock of inventories" for Wholesale and Retail Trade and information on changes in inventories given by the Department of Commerce, we may obtain a "real inventories held" series. The sum of this and the preceding series on real fixed capital yields a series on Structures, Equipment, and Inventories, which is precisely the series required. The sample period for both phases of estimation is 1945–1958.

Results

First Phase of Estimation. As remarked above, the sample period extends over 1945–1958. The reasons for this restriction are to be found in the procedure of estimation and limitations due to lack of data. Firstly, since a decision was reached to "doctor up" the series only as little as possible, the period under consideration is one of reasonably full employment with relatively mild recessions so that the problem of underutilization of the capital stock does not arise acutely, thus obviating the necessity for correction due to idle capacity. Clearly the war and depression periods preceding would not accurately fit the hypotheses underlying the model herein presented.

In actually estimating α and β a rather weak test of lognormality was employed with respect to observed factor shares; the test simply consists in counting the number of observations falling within one sample standard deviation of the sample mean of the logarithms of observed shares.

The results are summarized in Table 1 below, the numbers in parentheses being standard deviations.

the stability of factor shares, however, it makes little difference whether we deduce $\tilde{\alpha}$ from $1 - \tilde{\beta}$ or whether we take the independent estimate given in Table 1. It may also be surmised from the table that the hypothesis of lognormality is not severely contradicted by the data, in that 64–71 per cent of the observations (9 and 10 respectively) fall within the prescribed interval.

Second Phase of Estimation. The residual series determined by the procedure given in equation (3) shows some interesting contrasts and similarities between the Manufacturing and Service sectors. We give the series in Chart I below stating them in different units (that is, the Manufacturing residual is computed with indices of Q, K, L, all based on 1929 = 100.0, while that for Services is based on 1945 = 100.0) in order to facilitate visual comparison.

CHART 1. — SECTOR RESIDUALS

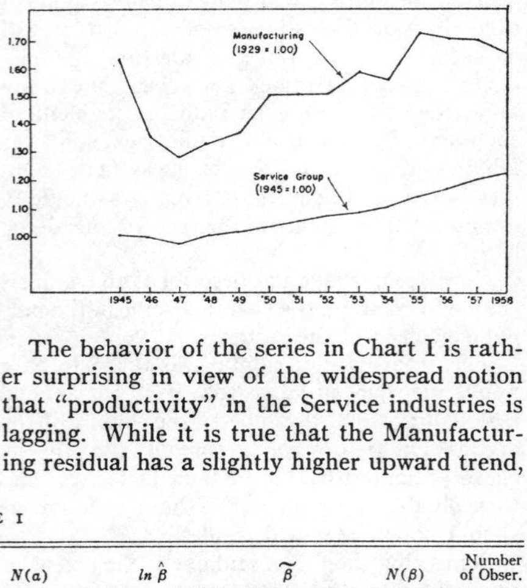

The behavior of the series in Chart I is rather surprising in view of the widespread notion that "productivity" in the Service industries is lagging. While it is true that the Manufacturing residual has a slightly higher upward trend, yet its behavior is not strikingly different from that of the Service industries' residual. What is radically different as between the two series is the rather erratic behavior of the Manufac-

TABLE 1

Sector	$ln\ \hat{\alpha}$	$\tilde{\alpha}$	$N(\alpha)$	$ln\ \hat{\beta}$	$\tilde{\beta}$	$N(\beta)$	Number of Obser.
Manufacturing	−1.2409 (0.0885)	0.2890	9	−0.3435 (0.0370)	0.7092	9	14
Service Industries	−1.0721 (0.0205)	0.3422	10	−0.4191 (0.0107)	0.6576	10	14

As implied by Table 1, we have obtained two independent estimates, one for α and one for β. In fact, as pointed out elsewhere, for example, Dhrymes [3], only one is independent. Due to

turing series. One perhaps ought to point out that the unusual drop in this residual from 1945 to 1946 is due chiefly to two reasons, easily borne out by an examination of the (deflated) output and capital stock series for Manufacturing. The partial lifting of controls, the drop in war materials production has brought about on the one hand the virtual abandonment of double shifts and on the other a rush to replenish a badly impaired capital stock. The result was a drop of the (real) output of the sector and a concomitant increase in the capital stock. Perhaps on these grounds one could have excluded the 1945 observation. It was felt, however, that the sample was already small enough so that it ought not to be reduced further. In addition, as may be rather easily verified, the exclusion of the 1945 observation would not materially affect the nature of the conclusion obtained.

Even neglecting the odd observation for 1945, the erratic behavior of the Manufacturing residual over the ensuing years would tend to weaken the confidence attaching to our model and/or the accuracy of our data, since we would not expect such erratic behavior if we had accurate observations and if our model were tolerably descriptive of reality.

With these reservations we offer the results of the second phase of estimation in Table 2 below:

TABLE 2

Sector	$\hat{\lambda}$	r
Manufacturing	0.0173 (0.0051)	0.7327
Service Group	0.0161 (0.0014)	0.9657

As was to be expected, the numerical esticates confirm the visual impression that productivity behavior in the two sectors is not extremely dissimilar. If we wish to investigate formally whether productivity behavior is "really" similar in the two sectors, then we could resort to testing the hypothesis $\lambda_1 - \lambda_2 = 0$ where λ_1, λ_2 are respectively the productivity parameters in Manufacturing and Service industries.

The test about to be conducted is to be taken rather as an illustration of the method, since already the standard errors strongly suggest that the hypothesis will be accepted.

This procedure is offered, however, in order to exhaust this particular aspect of the investigation.

The test to be employed was originally proposed by B. L. Welch (8), (9), and later elaborated upon by Chernoff (2). Tables for the statistics utilized are given in Aspin (1).

The test in question deals with the equality of means of two independent normal populations whose variance need not be the same. The test is only asymptotically precise. In finite samples it is only approximate.

In order to employ this test we must first show that we may think of λ as the mean of a normal population. But it is easily seen from (3a) that:

$$y(t) - y(t-1) = y^*(t) = \lambda + [z(t) - z(t-1)] \qquad (9)$$

and from (4) it easily follows

$$E[y^*(t)] = \lambda \qquad (9a)$$

while $z(t)$ are asymptotically normally and independently distributed under the hypotheses maintained. It does not seem much worth investigating whether $z(t)$ converges to normality at the same "rate" as the test to be employed converges to exactitude. So in the present context it is not clear that we make things much worse by employing the test in the face of the non-normality of $z(t)$. If we wish to be duly precise we face formidable problems, but probably little will be lost if we neglect covariance terms and take the variance of $y^*(t)$ to be approximately twice that of $z(t)$. This introduces also inaccuracies due to differences between $ln\ K(t)$, $ln\ L(t)$ and $ln\ K(t-1)$. In order to perform the test we require the quantities:

$$v = \frac{(\hat{\lambda}_1 - \hat{\lambda}_2) - (\lambda_1 - \lambda_2)}{\sqrt{(s_1^2/n_1) + (s_2^2/n_2)}} \qquad (10)$$

$$s = \frac{s_1^2/n_1}{(s_1^2/n_1) + (s_2^2/n_2)}$$

where n_i gives the degrees of freedom in the ith sample, $i = 1, 2$, $\hat{\lambda}_i$ are the estimated productivity parameters and s_i^2 are the estimated variances of the two populations.

The assumption of different variances in the two populations is a step in the direction of greater realism; the assumption of independence, however, may not be completely justified.

If we choose to perform a two-tailed test with size of critical region 0.1 we find that the acceptance region is given by $(-1.73, 1.73)$; that is, we will accept the null hypothesis of identical productivity behavior if we find that the computed value of v lies in $(-1.73, 1.73)$. In the present case we obtain $v = -0.6$ which lies well within the region of acceptance.

Conclusion

The investigation herein presented leads to the conclusion that on the basis of the meager available information, we cannot accept the assertion that the two largest components in the post-war Private Non-Farm sector of the American economy display a sharp dichotomy in productivity behavior as we have defined it. In particular we cannot conclude that the rate of change of productivity in Manufacturing exceeds that of the Service sector.

There are many reservations to be made in utilizing this method, both methodological and empirical, that is, relating to the degree of accuracy with which our series describe the economic variables to which they correspond. Not the least of the latter class of reservations is the one relating to the method used to obtain the capital stock in the Service sector.

Some of the drawbacks would disappear if we were to employ this method in making international productivity comparisons amongst reasonably similar countries, for example, among the United States, Canada, the United Kingdom, Scandinavia, and the like. Then the question of dependence of the disturbances in the residuals, remarked upon in the Section discussing the results of the second phase of estimation, will almost surely not arise.

So if it is found that the Wicksell-Douglas function with trend has descriptive validity in several such economies, this method will allow us to arrive at some inference relating to comparative productivity behavior, with due reservations, of course.

REFERENCES

1. Aspin, A. A., "Tables for Use in Comparisons Whose Accuracy Involves Two Variances, Separately Estimated," *Biometrika*, XXVI (June 1949), 290.
2. Chernoff, H., "Asymptotic Studentization in Testing of Hypotheses," *Annals of Mathematical Statistics*, XX (June 1949), 268.
3. Dhrymes, P. J., "On Devising Unbiased Estimators for the Parameters of a Cobb-Douglas Production Function," *Econometrica*, XX (April 1962).
4. Hogan, W. P., "Technical Progress and Production Functions," this REVIEW, XL (Nov. 1958), 407.
5. Massell, B. F., "Capital Formation and Technological Change in United States Manufacturing," this REVIEW, XLII (May 1960), 182.
6. Pasinetti, L., "On Concepts and Measures of Changes in Productivity," this REVIEW, XLI (August 1959), 270.
7. Solow, R. M., "Technical Progress and the Aggregate Production Function," this REVIEW, XXXIX (August 1957), 312.
8. Welch, B. L., "On the Studentization of Several Variances," *Annals of Mathematical Statistics*, XVIII (March 1947), 118.
9. ———., "The Generalization of Student's Problem when Several Different Population Variances are Involved," *Biometrika*, XXXIV (January 1947), 28.

Sources of Data

10. *U.S. National Income and Output*, U.S. Department of Commerce (1959).
11. Leontief, W., "Factor Proportions and the Structure of American Trade," this REVIEW, XXVIII (Nov. 1956), 386.

Econometrica, Vol. 32, No. 3 (July, 1964)

TECHNOLOGY AND SCALE IN ELECTRICITY GENERATION[1]

BY PHOEBUS J. DHRYMES[2] AND MORDECAI KURZ

The question of returns to scale in public utilities is a much debated issue. In this study, the productive process of electricity generation is examined and a modified substitution model is employed, permitting differentiation between returns to scale to labor and to other factors.

The method employed here allows us to isolate the impact of technological progress on (steam) electricity generation. We find that increasing returns to scale prevail throughout, and that the main impact of technology was registered during the 1950's.

This study covers the period 1937–59.

1. INTRODUCTION

IN THIS PAPER we undertake an econometric investigation of the impact of technology and size on the characteristics of production in the (steam) electric generating industry.

Previous studies of similar problems include those of Lomax [13] and Nordin [16] of over a decade ago, as well as those of Johnston [11]. These studies, however, are concerned exclusively with the cost functions of electric generating firms. Recently, studies of the nature of the production function itself have been made by Komiya [12] and Nerlove [15].

Nerlove studies the question of returns to scale for United States (steam) electric generating *firms*. He assumes the productive process to be characterized by a Cobb-Douglas production function and proceeds to estimate its parameters via the implied cost function under the hypothesis that firms act so as to minimize cost under an output constraint. In an Appendix he demonstrates a rather interesting fact, viz., that although a firm may enjoy increasing returns to scale in the production of electricity, yet when viewed as a unit it may operate in a region of decreasing returns; this is due to transmission (power) losses. However, no use is made of this fact in subsequent analysis since he investigated only the production aspect of electricity supply.

[1] This work was supported in part by Office of Naval Research Contract Nonr-225(50) and National Science Foundation Grant 16114 at Stanford University. Reproduction in whole or in part is permitted for any purpose of the United States Government. Most of the computations were performed at the Western Data Processing Center at UCLA.

We wish to acknowledge our gratitude to Professors K. J. Arrow and R. M. Solow for helpful comments on an earlier draft, and to Professor M. Nerlove for stimulating our interest in the subject. We are also grateful to Professors A. S. Manne, V. L. Smith, H. Uzawa, M. Yaari, and the referees of this paper for several suggestions.

In addition, we would like to thank Kwan-Ho Kim and Bridger Mitchell for their competent research assistance.

[2] The work of Dhrymes was supported by a National Science Foundation Post-Doctoral Fellowship held at Stanford University.

Nerlove uses a cross-section sample, his observations being taken on firms for the year 1955. Although the plant is the more basic unit of production and hence the notion of a production function is more meaningful when applied to plants, Nerlove prefers to conduct his analysis on the firm level. This choice is related to the assumption one has to make regarding the market conditions under which the economic unit operates. Nerlove neglects transmission and distribution and finds that the generating aspect of electricity supply is uniformly characterized by increasing returns to scale, the degree of such returns being a decreasing function of the output level.

Komiya's work is more closely related to this study since it deals with the productive process characteristic of (steam) electric generating plants in the United States. His sample covers newly constructed plants over the period 1930–56. He begins by assuming a "substitution model," i.e., he assumes the productive process to be characterized by a Cobb-Douglas production function whose parameters he then proceeds to estimate by regressing the logarithms of capital, labor, and fuel (the inputs) on the logarithm of output. No optimization behavior is assumed on the part of the producing unit. This attempt to fit the Cobb-Douglas function to his observations is essentially a failure, quite likely because of multicollinearity of the inputs. Following this, he introduces a (logarithmic) Leontief model. Komiya's technique is to stratify his sample by technological subclasses and then to conduct an analysis of covariance, treating technology (essentially the time of construction of a plant) as the factor level.

In Komiya's work, size enters in a rather peculiar manner through the average size of units in a given plant and the number of such units. This has a consequence which is hard to accept: Komiya measures capital in terms of the (deflated) cost of the generating unit. So the dollar cost of a plant is explained (loglinearly) through the size of units and their number. Hence, if a firm purchases a number of units simultaneously and gets quantity discounts in the process, Komiya's procedure will interpret this as indicative of increasing returns to scale in the generation of electricity.

By and large, Komiya finds uniformly increasing returns to scale, although the term, as indicated above, may have ambiguous interpretation in his framework. The impact of technology is assumed to register on the multiplicative constants of his input requirements equations since he employs the standard analysis of covariance model.

Finally, we should, perhaps, mention a recent study by Iulo [**10**]. His work is mainly concerned with finding the determinants of unit cost differences among electric utility firms. He does not aim, however, at connecting these differences with differences in the underlying productive processes of the firms in his sample.

In our analysis the neoclassical model of production is used, and we employ a generalized version of the constant-elasticity-of-substitution production function recently proposed by Arrow, Chenery, Minhas, and Solow [**2**], hereafter referred to as ACMS. In this work, we combine the cost minimization hypothesis of Nerlove and the sample stratification technique of Komiya.

Using data relating to newly constructed plants in the United States over the period 1937–59, our analysis aims to isolate the impact of technological progress on the characteristics of (steam) electric generation, to investigate the question of returns to scale in electricity supply, and to assess the effects of technological change on returns to scale. In the process we shall estimate the parameters of the production function assumed.

2. THE ECONOMETRIC MODEL

A. *Preliminaries*

The model presented below is quite general in scope and is not specific to (steam) electric generating plants. Thus, proceeding generally, suppose the output generating process in a firm, industry, or economy is given by

$$(1) \qquad Q=A\Big(\sum_{i=1}^{n} \alpha_i X_i^{\beta_i}\Big)^{1/\gamma}=F(X_1, X_2, \dots, X_n),$$

where $\alpha_i \geqslant 0$, $A \geqslant 0$, and Q, X_i denote the output and ith input, respectively.

The relation (1) represents a generalization of the constant elasticity of substitution production function recently proposed by ACMS, in the sense that (1) need not be a homogeneous function and, if it were, it need not be homogeneous of degree one. In fact, the constant elasticity of substitution production function proposed by ACMS is a special case of (1), with $n=2$, and $\beta_i=\gamma$, $i=1, 2, \dots, n$. Several obvious facts are noted:

i. Suppose we change the units of measuring inputs through the transformation:

$$(2) \qquad X_i=c_i X_i', \quad c_i>0 \qquad (i=1, 2, \dots, n).$$

Then (1) is transformed to

$$(2a) \qquad Q=A\Big(\sum_{i=1}^{n} \alpha_i^* X_i^{\beta_i}\Big)^{1/\gamma},$$

where

$$\alpha_i^*=c_i^{\beta_i}\alpha_i, \qquad (i=1, 2, \dots, n).$$

Consequently, the coefficients, α_i, depend on the units in which inputs are measured, provided, of course, that $\beta_i \neq 0$ for at least one index i.

ii. Suppose further that the coefficients, α_i, are required to satisfy some normalization scheme. In the case of ACMS, the normalization was $\Sigma_{i=1}^{n}\alpha_i=1$.

In the competitive context in which they operate, this is more or less the natural normalization to impose, since then the α_i may be given the interpretation of distribution parameters. In our case, we are not bound by the usual competitive model so we have chosen a normalization which is more suitable for our purposes. Let

$$(3)\qquad S=\prod_{i=1}^{n}\alpha_i\,,\qquad \alpha_i=S^{1/n}\alpha_i'\,.$$

It is seen then that the coefficients, α_i', satisfy $\Pi_{i=1}^{n}\alpha_i'=1$ and that (1) is transformed to

$$(3a)\qquad Q=A^*\Big(\sum_{i=1}^{n}\alpha_i'X_i^{\beta_i}\Big)^{1/\gamma},$$

where $A^*=A\,S^{\gamma/n}$. Hence, it is seen that the parameter A, the efficiency parameter in the ACMS terminology, depends both on the units of measuring inputs and on the particular normalization scheme imposed.

iii. Consider now the case, $\beta_i=\beta$, $i=1, 2, \ldots, n$. Then (1) is homogeneous of degree β/γ. If we define the quantity ε_{ij} by

$$(4)\qquad \varepsilon_{ij}=\frac{d\ln(X_i/X_j)}{d\ln\left(\dfrac{\partial Q/\partial X_j}{\partial Q/\partial X_i}\right)},$$

then we see that it has the specific form:

$$(4a)\qquad \varepsilon_{ij}=\frac{1}{(1-\beta_i)+(\beta_i-\beta_j)/\left[1+\dfrac{\alpha_j\beta_j}{\alpha_i\beta_i}\,\dfrac{X_j^{\beta_j}}{X_i^{\beta_i}}\right]},$$

which, in this case, reduces to the constant

$$(4b)\qquad \varepsilon_{ij}=\frac{1}{1-\beta}\,.$$

This agrees with Meade's **[14]** definition of the (partial) elasticity of substitution between the *i*th and *j*th factors. Note in the case $n=2$ it reduces to the standard notion of the elasticity of substitution. When $n>2$, this concept of substitution differs from that given in Allen **[1]** or Uzawa **[18]**. Since in our application we shall ultimately deal with the case $n=2$, this does not represent any substantive departure from the standard usage of the term.

iv. As noted above, the function given in (1) is homogeneous of degree β/γ whenever $\beta_i=\beta$, $i=1, 2, \ldots, n$. If $\beta_i\neq\beta_j$, however, the function is not homogeneous of any degree; we may, nonetheless, make the following statements:

Let $\beta^*=\max_i\{\beta_i\}$; if $(\beta^*/\gamma)<1$, we have decreasing returns to scale. Further, let $\beta^{**}=\min_i\{\beta_i\}$; then if $(\beta^{**}/\gamma)>1$, we have increasing returns to scale. Otherwise, the question of returns to scale cannot be unambiguously determined. We present below diagrammatic illustrations in the case $n=2$. In Figure 1a, we have drawn the isoquants of a homogeneous function of degree one (constant returns to scale). No matter along which ray expansion takes place, a proportional increase

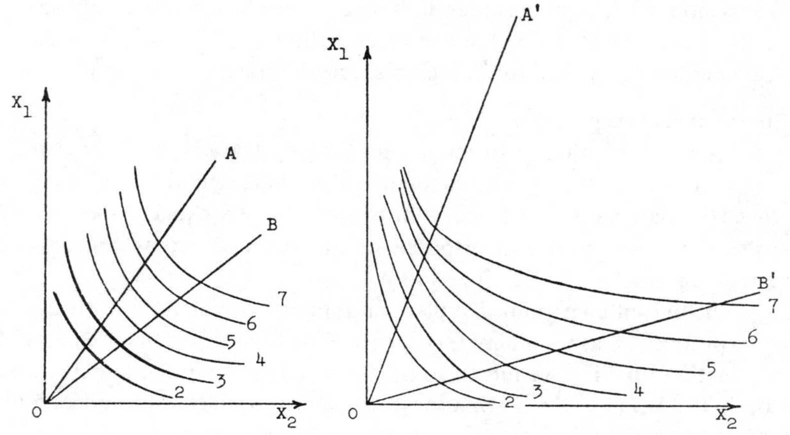

FIGURE 1a FIGURE 1b

in both inputs leads to a proportional increase in output (indicated by the number on the isoquants). In Figure 1b, this is not the case. If we expand along OA′, we shall experience increasing returns to scale, while if we expand along OB′, we shall experience decreasing returns to scale indicated by the increasing distances between the points of intersection of the isoquants with the line OB′. Of course, Figure 1b depicts the isoquants of a nonhomogeneous function.

v. In ACMS, one obtains various limiting results in terms of the behavior of the elasticity of substitution parameter. In our case, analogous results do not, in general, hold because we admit non-constant returns to scale. Thus, suppose $\beta_i=\beta$, all i and $n=2$, so that the elasticity of substitution as defined here reduces to the standard one. Then it is *not*, in general, true that as the elasticity of substitution tends to zero, the functional form (1) reduces to a Leontief type production function. Thus, let $\gamma<0$, γ fixed, and $\beta\rightarrow-\infty$. The elasticity of substitution parameter behaves as

$$\text{(4c)} \qquad \lim_{\beta\rightarrow-\infty}\frac{1}{1-\beta}=0\,.$$

In general, however, we obtain

$$\text{(4d)} \qquad \lim_{\beta\rightarrow-\infty} Q=\begin{cases}0 & \text{if } \min(X_1,X_2)<1\,,\\ m & \text{if } X_1=X_2=1,\ m>0\,,\\ +\infty & \text{if } \max(X_1,X_2)>1\,.\end{cases}$$

This is due to the fact that in our case the expression (4c) does not involve the parameter γ and, hence, its limiting behavior cannot determine the limiting behavior of the functional form (1). Other similar calculations will not be pursued here. They are, however, routine.

The essential thing to note is that limiting processes are considerably more complicated in functions of more than one variable because the result depends on how the variables, here (β,γ), approach their respective limits.

B. *Formulation of the problem*

The purpose of this study is to conduct an econometric analysis of the productive process in (steam) electric generating plants. The fundamental behavior hypothesis employed is that plants are faced with a more or less exogenously determined quantity to be produced and disposed of at the price set by the appropriate regulatory agency.[3]

Given the output constraint, the plant entrepreneur (manager) is assumed so to organize production as to minimize cost in a sense to be made precise below. Since the production function we intend to fit to the data permits input substitution, it may be desirable to explain in what sense this substitution is to be understood.

It may be true that, in electric generation, once a plant is established, little substitution is permitted among the various inputs. Yet it may not be unrealistic to suppose that, in the planning stage at least, the entrepreneur is confronted with the possibility of choosing from a variety of input combinations. In the traditional theory of production this choice is to be made conditionally upon factor prices, and the commitment to one technique of production is to be revised following a change in factor prices. Here, such a mechanism may not be realistic since once a plant is built a firm commitment is being made to a certain technique of production from which it may be difficult (costly) to depart. Hence, the production function we envisage is to be understood as a frontier of technological possibilities in the ex ante sense. This particular interpretation of our point of departure should then clarify the nature of our sample.

Let the cost function be given

$$(5) \qquad C = \sum_{i=1}^{n} p_i X_i ,$$

[3] Since it is quite admissible to take the price of the factors used (here labor and fuel) as given exogenously, the hypothesis allows us to treat output, its price, and all factor prices as exogenous quantities. The assumed exogeneity of the price of output may be received with some reservation since it is well known that it is set by the appropriate regulatory agency in negotiation with the electric utility. It is, however, reasonable in this context for two reasons. The process of rate setting is extremely complex and permeated by political considerations which can hardly be quantified; in addition there are substantial differences in the practices of the various (state) regulatory agencies so that no assumption of comparable simplicity can represent reality equally well. Secondly, the assumption is related to plant operations and is moreover an assumption needed only in the short run. What is necessary for our purposes is that the plant entrepreneur (or, for that matter, the firm) does not expect his investment activity *as such* to influence rate setting in the immediate future. Typically rate increases are related to the pressure of inflation and not to the specific activities of the plant or the firm. It is also the case that electric utility management seems to operate on this premise. With regard to this the reader is referred to the very enlightening discussion given in [3], especially p. 304ff.

where p_i denotes the price of the ith input, which is here considered to be given exogenously. The problem is to minimize (5) subject to a fixed output constraint obeying (1). Thus, we have to minimize

$$\sum_{i=1}^{n} p_i X_i + \lambda[Q_o - F(X_1, \ldots, X_n)] \,. \tag{6}$$

First order conditions are given by:

$$p_j - \lambda \frac{\partial F}{\partial X_j} = 0 \qquad (j=1, \ldots, n) \,. \tag{7}$$

The Lagrangian multiplier, λ, may be interpreted as the marginal cost at the equilibrium point. This is easily seen by taking the total differential of the cost function (5) then substituting in (7) after multiplying the jth equation by dX_j and summing over all j.

Sufficient conditions involve the negative (semi) definiteness of

$$H = \begin{bmatrix} 0 & F_1 & \ldots & F_n \\ F_1 & F_{11} & \ldots & F_{1n} \\ \vdots & \vdots & & \vdots \\ F_n & F_{n1} & \ldots & F_{nn} \end{bmatrix} . \tag{8}$$

This implies certain restrictions on the coefficients β_i, viz., $\beta_i < 1$, since we require the second order conditions to hold for all possible price configurations. From general considerations, we also have that β_i, all i, and γ must be of the same sign. For if $\beta_i \gamma < 0$, for some factor, then this implies that the ith factor will not be used, or that formally, the minimization procedure outlined above breaks down. Also, in the special case $\beta_i = \beta$, all i, then $\beta\gamma < 0$ implies that we have "negative returns to scale," which is inadmissible.

Developing the equations in (7), we find:

$$\ln X_i = \frac{1}{\beta_i - 1} \ln \frac{\alpha_n \beta_n}{\alpha_i \beta_i} + \frac{1}{\beta_i - 1} \ln \frac{p_i}{p_n} + \frac{\beta_n - 1}{\beta_i - 1} \ln X_n \qquad (i=1, \ldots, n) \,. \tag{9}$$

If we substitute (9) in (1), we obtain an implicit relation between the price ratios p_i/p_n, output Q, and the nth input X_n. It can be shown that the resulting equation may be solved for X_n.[4] Thus, a set of inputs optimal for cost minimization can be selected, and the problem is solved.

C. *The Estimation Procedure*

Let the explicit relation between the nth input, output, and the price ratios be given by:

$$X_n = G(\pi_1, \ldots, \pi_{n-1}, Q) \,, \tag{10}$$

where $\pi_i = p_i/p_n$, $i = 1, 2, \ldots, n-1$.

[4] If, for all i, we have $\beta_i < 1$, then, since the partial derivative of the implicit relation with respect to X_n never vanishes in the relevant subspace, we have that such solution indeed exists.

We shall suppose that $\ln X_n$ has a valid Taylor's series expansion in terms of $\ln \pi_i$, and $\ln Q$, which is sufficiently closely approximated by, at most, linear terms. Thus, we may write:

$$\ln X_n = a_0 + \sum_{i=1}^{n-1} a_i \ln \pi_i + a_n \ln Q\,. \tag{11}$$

If we consider (11) as well as (9) as stochastic relations, then the following sequence of estimations may be employed to identify the parameters of (1).[5]

First note that our system, viz., the relations (9), together with (11), constitutes a group to which the two-stage least-squares technique is evidently applicable. Equations (9), except for $\ln X_n$, constitute a diagonal system to which single equation least-squares is immediately applicable. The problem is to substitute for $\ln X_n$ an estimate for its nonstochastic part. But from (11) we note that $\ln X_n$ appears as a function of the exogenous parameters π_i, and of output Q, which is here taken as exogenous.[6] Hence, an estimate for the nonstochastic part of $\ln X_n$ is obtained as soon as we estimate the a_i, $i = 0, 1, 2, \ldots, n$.[7] If this is now inserted into (9), each equation could be estimated individually. The resulting estimates for the parameters under the usual assumptions are known to be asymptotically unbiased and consistent.

The estimators so obtained imply estimators for some, but not all, of the parameters of (1), as follows:

[5] We are about to give a rather informal estimating procedure. To be precise, we should proceed as follows: Let

$$Q = F(X)e^u, \tag{1'}$$

where X is the vector of inputs and u a random term. Let the relation (7) be rewritten as

$$p_j = \lambda \frac{\partial F}{\partial X_j} e^{v_j} \qquad (j = 1, \ldots, n)\,. \tag{7'}$$

We may interpret (7) as indicating imperfect knowledge on the part of the entrepreneur concerning factor prices or imperfections in the process of cost minimization. Then, employing the same sequence of operations outlined above, we shall arrive at a stochastic relation like (11), except that now the a_i, $i = 0, 1, 2, \ldots, n$, are understood to be functions of the random variables $w_j = v_j - v_n$, $j = 1, 2, \ldots, n-1$, and u. Since we know of no instance in the literature where such an estimation problem is handled, we prefer to give the informal formulation above.

[6] This is a somewhat weak assumption because of the existence of multiplant firms and interconnected systems. How much output is allocated to a given firm or plant may be related to its actual or prospective production structure. We noted earlier that Nerlove preferred to assume exogenously given demand for the firm. We tend to believe that this assumption is as applicable to the plant as to the firm. In our judgment the advantages of conducting the analysis on the plant level outweigh these considerations.

[7] It is to be understood that a qualification here is in order, because of the approximate character of (11). This qualification is to be borne in mind throughout this section.

Let

$$(12) \qquad s_{0i} = \frac{1}{\beta_i - 1} \ln \frac{\alpha_n \beta_n}{\alpha_i \beta_i}, \qquad s_{1i} = \frac{1}{\beta_i - 1}, \qquad s_{2i} = \frac{\beta_n - 1}{\beta_i - 1}$$

$$(i = 1, 2, \ldots, n-1).$$

It is obvious that the implied estimators for β_i, $i = 1, 2, \ldots, n-1$, are given by

$$(13) \qquad \hat{\beta}_i = (1/\hat{s}_{1i}) + 1\,.$$

The estimator implied for β_n is given by

$$(14) \qquad \hat{\beta}_n = (\hat{s}_{2i}/\hat{s}_{1i}) + 1\,.$$

This points up a rather interesting statistical consequence caused by the use of the functional type given in (1); namely, that in parameter estimation one is forced to estimate a given parameter, say β_n, $n-1$ times. This is an unwarrantably stringent test on the validity of the model. Note that the same problem besets the CES production function proposed by ACMS.

The implied estimators for the α_i/α_n are given by

$$(15) \qquad \left(\frac{\hat{\alpha}_i}{\alpha_n}\right) = \exp\left[(\hat{s}_{0i}/\hat{s}_{1i}) - \ln(\hat{s}_{2i} + \hat{s}_{1i})/(1 + \hat{s}_{1i})\right] \qquad (i = 1, 2, \ldots, n-1).$$

This, together with the normalization $\prod_{i=1}^{n} \alpha_i = 1$, identifies the parameters α_i, $i = 1, 2, \ldots, n$.

Thus, we have completed the application of the two-stage least-squares technique to our problem, and we have identified the parameters α_i and β_i, $i = 1, 2, \ldots, n$. However, there still remain to be estimated the parameters γ and A. We may proceed as follows:[8] insert the estimates $\hat{\alpha}_i$ and $\hat{\beta}_i$ in (1). Then estimate γ and A by another application of single equation least-squares. More precisely, compute

$$(16) \qquad Z = \sum_{i=1}^{n} \hat{\alpha}_i X_i^{\hat{\beta}_i}$$

and then note that we may write:

$$(17) \qquad Q = AZ^{1/\gamma}\,.$$

Manipulating, we find

$$(18) \qquad \ln Z = \gamma_0 + \gamma_1 \ln Q$$

where $\gamma_0 = -\gamma \ln A$, $\gamma_1 = \gamma$. Since, by hypothesis, $\ln Q$ is exogenous, the parameters of (18) can be estimated; these yield implied estimators for γ and A as follows:

$$(19) \qquad \hat{\gamma} = \hat{\gamma}_1, \qquad \hat{A} = \exp\left(-\frac{\hat{\gamma}_0}{\hat{\gamma}_1}\right).$$

[8] This procedure resembles, but is not identical with, the extraneous estimation procedure of Durbin [6]. For a similar application, see also Dhrymes [5]. In the context of a stochastic model such as is given in footnote 5, the estimators to be obtained can be studied quite rigorously provided we are prepared to consider them as conditional on the particular values $\hat{\alpha}_i$ and $\hat{\beta}_i$, $i = 1, 2, \ldots, n$, inserted in (1).

Some remarks are now in order concerning the properties of the implied estimators. First note that since the α_i and β_i are homeomorphisms of the s_{kj}, it follows that they will inherit certain properties of the s_{kj}. The latter are known to be asymptotically unbiased and consistent. Consistency is preserved under homeomorphisms, hence they are consistent.[9] In general, however, no statement can be made concerning their (small sample) bias characteristics.

Finally, we note that if we wish, we can determine confidence intervals rather easily for the estimators β_i, $i=1, \ldots, n-1$, as follows: $|1/(\hat{\beta}_i-1)| \leqslant \delta$ if and only if $1-(1/\delta) \leqslant \hat{\beta}_i \leqslant 1+(1/\delta)$, hence $\Pr\{1-(1/\delta) \leqslant \hat{\beta}_i \leqslant 1+(1/\delta\} = \alpha$ if and only if $\Pr\{|1/(\hat{\beta}_i-1)| \leqslant \delta\} = \alpha$. But the latter is easily ascertained from the estimated standard error of the parameters of equation (9).

The same procedure, however, cannot be applied to β_n or the α_i because any probability statement concerning them must involve the s_{1i} *and* the s_{2i}.

3. APPLICATION TO (STEAM) ELECTRIC GENERATING PLANTS

There are three specific objectives to our empirical study:

1. to evaluate the degree of factor substitution in the (steam) electric generating industry;
2. to characterize the impact of technological change on the (assumed) production function; and
3. to investigate the question of returns to scale.

The production function (assumed) is the generalized version of the production function recently proposed by ACMS, which is best understood as holding in an ex ante[10] sense, as amplified in Section 2B. Because we are interested in studying

[9] Somewhat heuristically this may be shown as follows: Consistency means convergence in probability. Let $S_{kj}(n)$ be the estimator based on n observations. This is a random variable converging to S_{kj} in probability; i.e., for any $\varepsilon > 0$, $\delta > 0$, there exists N, such that for $n > N$, $\Pr\{|S_{kj}(n) - S_{kj}| \leqslant \varepsilon\} > 1 - \delta$. Consider one of the relations (12), e.g., S_{1i}. Let g be defined by $g(S_{1i}) = \beta_i$. Then g is a homeomorphism provided the range of the β_i is $(-\infty, 1)$. For any sequence of real numbers $S_{1i}(n) \rightarrow S$, $g(S_{1i}(n)) \rightarrow g(S)$. Hence, $|g(S_{1i}(n)) - g(S)| \leqslant \varepsilon$ iff $|S_{1i}(n) - S| \leqslant \mu(\varepsilon)$, and the convergence of $g(S_{1i}(n))$ can be deduced from that of the $S_{1i}(n)$.

[10] Although we interpret our model as being primarily one of ex ante substitution, several ex post substitution possibilities may be noted. First, a plant may consist of more than one generating unit; thus, in our sample, about 50 of the plants have two or more generating units. These units may be operated at different levels of intensity and this permits some measure of substitution between capital and fuel, even in existing plants. Second, although substitution may be a costly process, it is not impossible and may be carried out whenever relative prices warrant it. Note, however, that, as will become apparent later in this article, our procedure of measuring capital obscures the following form of substitution: Suppose two plants have the same rated (nameplate) capacity and operate for the same number of hours. One is, however, more efficient than the other by economizing on the use of fuel, while the cost of its generators is higher. It is intuitively appealing to consider the more efficient plant as using "more" capital than the less efficient one. Our measure, however, will not allow this.

the generation aspects of electricity supply, as distinct from the transmission and distribution aspects, it was felt that the data relevant for this problem are observations on (steam) electric generating plants, since the latter constitute the basic units of production. In view of the ex ante interpretation of the production function (1), we have confined our sample to newly constructed plants in the United States over the period 1937–59. Our sample consists of 362 new plants constructed over this period. It is safe to assume that our sample is almost coextensive with the population of new plants constructed over this period, since our source [7] claims a coverage ranging from 73 per cent in 1937 to 94 per cent in 1959 of all operating plants in Continental U.S., excluding Alaska. In all likelihood the coverage of new plants is complete, at least in the more recent years.

Each plant appears in our sample only once, the year of observation being taken as the year following construction of the plant. This was done since a year is usually a sufficient time for a newly constructed plant to attain its "normal" level of operation—the level for which it was designed.

For the purpose of analysis our sample was stratified, employing the following two-way classification: (i) technological period, (ii) size of plant. We should, perhaps, give a brief explanation of the motivation for, and meaning of, our classification scheme. Plants constructed during a given year embody the latest technological advances, and hence, we could simply choose as the technological level the year of construction of plants. The technological periods chosen were 1937–45, 1946–50, 1951–54, and 1955–59. This particular stratification was motivated by (a) conversations with electrical engineers regarding technological changes in the industry, (b) Cootner's **[4]** findings relating to changes in thermal efficiency in (steam) electricity generation, and (c) the density of observations per classification cell.

The classification by size is simply classification by the rated (nameplate) capacity of the plant.

Table I indicates the size of the sample and the density of observations per cell. The appearance of the table itself warrants some comment. Note that while in the first two technological periods, 1937–45 and 1946–50, a rather substantial number of small (0–40 MGW (megawatts) plants were constructed, in subsequent periods this number declines steadily. Note also that while practically no new plants in the range 201–449 MGW were constructed between 1937 and 1950, yet in the subsequent two periods numerous such plants were constructed. This may be interpreted as indicative of one impact of technology on this industry. Technology apparently operated in the direction of permitting large units to be constructed (it made the operation of such units economical).

Finally, another comment: Between 1953 and 1958, eighteen very large plants were built. These plants have rated capacity between 450 and 1440 MGW. Since their construction straddles two technological periods, we have decided to regard them as an independent group.

TABLE I

THE SAMPLE STRATIFICATION

Size \ Technology	1937–45	1946–50	1951–54	1955–59
I	(0–40 MGW) 28	(0–39 MGW) 42	(0–40 MGW) 26	(0–39 MGW) 3
II	(41–120 MGW) 19	(40–99 MGW) 33	(41–99 MGW) 32	(40–100 MGW) 29
III	(120–200 MGW) 3	(100–200 MGW) 17	(100–200 MGW) 31	(101–200 MGW) 28
IV	—	(201–449 MGW) 4	(201–449 MGW) 25	(201–449 MGW) 27
			(Large-scale group: 450 MGW+) 18	

The technique employed in dealing with our problem, as defined specifically at the beginning of this section, is as follows: for each technology-size cell we shall estimate the parameters of a production function of the type given in (1). Specific conclusions may then be derived by comparing the parameters so estimated for the various cells.

4. EMPIRICAL FINDINGS

A. *Evaluation of the Substitution Model*

Using a production relation like (1) for $n=3$, we have considered three inputs: labor, fuel, and capital. Fuel was measured in BTU (British Thermal Units) equivalents, labor was indicated by the (average) number of employees, while for capital an index was constructed designed to measure the input of capital services in the production process as follows: the rated (nameplate) capacity of a plant was accepted as an index of the capital available to the plant for the generation of electricity. In order to account, however, for the fact that a given generator may not be in use at all times, we have corrected for the fraction of the time during which the generator was actively engaged in generating electricity. Since the generator capacity is stated in MGW, we have constructed an index of capital input in terms of MGW hours of generator service.[11] The source of the data and

[11] The question of overcapacity calls for a few words. In cases of rapidly growing regions, the industry tends sometimes to build "ahead of demand." What happens, in fact, is that new plants are usually lower-cost plants. Hence there is a tendency to use them optimally while using old and medium-age plants as standby plants which also satisfy the increasing demand. When demand reaches a certain level, a new plant will be added, scrapping some old units. In general, we can

the precise nature of this index will be explained in the Appendix below. Finally, output was stated in KWH (kilowatt hours).

Using these data, two equations of the system have been estimated corresponding to labor and fuel. Note that in the estimating procedure the equations (9) may be regarded as the derived demand functions for the inputs.

The results of parameter estimation of the labor equation appear in Table II below.

TABLE II

THE LABOR EQUATION

$$\ln L = 1/\beta_L - 1 \ln(\alpha_K\beta_K/\alpha_L\beta_L) + 1/\beta_L - 1 \ln(P_L/P_K) + \beta_K - 1/\beta_L - 1 \ln[K^*],$$

or

$$\ln L = \delta_0 + \delta_1 \ln(P_L/P_K) + \delta_2 \ln[K^*].$$

Size \ Technology	1937–45	1946–50	1951–54	1955–59
I	$\delta_0 =$ 5.1209 $\delta_1 =$ −.2399 (.1609) $\delta_2 =$ .7514 (.1199) $R =$ .8402	$\delta_0 =$ 5.9895 $\delta_1 =$ −.2232 (.1028) $\delta_2 =$ .6321 (.0885) $R =$ .7547	$\delta_0 =$ 6.2442 $\delta_1 =$ −.0882 (.1015) $\delta_2 =$ .5215 (.0709) $R =$ .8427	
II	$\delta_0 =$ 9.3472 $\delta_1 =$ .2646 (.1442) $\delta_2 =$ .1415 (.2167) $R =$ .4489	$\delta_0 =$ 5.3970 $\delta_1 =$ −.1860 (.0917) $\delta_2 =$ .6856 (.1849) $R =$ .5743	$\delta_0 =$ 7.2132 $\delta_1 =$ −.1954 (.0848) $\delta_2 =$ .4488 (.2059) $R =$ .5466	$\delta_0 =$ 8.4108 $\delta_1 =$ −.1471(.1321) $\delta_2 =$ .2827(.2041) $R =$ .3393
III		$\delta_0 =$ 1.1381 $\delta_1 =$ −.4207 (.2908) $\delta_2 =$ 1.1897 (.4774) $R =$ .5571	$\delta_0 =$ 5.0475 $\delta_1 =$ .3990 (.1987) $\delta_2 =$ .7372 (.1414) $R =$ .7506	$\delta_0 =$ 1.0742 $\delta_1 =$ −.4051(.1336) $\delta_2 =$ 1.1513(.3544) $R =$ .6602
IV			$\delta_0 =$ 5.0756 $\delta_1 =$ −.2369 (.1573) $\delta_2 =$ .7001 (.2601) $R =$ .6693	$\delta_0 =$ 12.1131 $\delta_1 =$ −.4325(.1670) $\delta_2 =$ .0118(.3718) $R =$ .4729
			(Large-scale group: capacity 450 MGW+) $\delta_0 =$ 4.6038 $\delta_1 =$ .0447 (.1529) $\delta_2 =$ .7037 (.2379) $R =$ .6141	

Numbers in parentheses are standard deviation of corresponding estimates.

expect new plants to be used optimally, at least for a few years after their construction. The correction by the number of hours of operations is needed to take into account regional differences in optimal capacity utilization due to different demand patterns. Such differences may result in different optimal numbers of hours of operations. Such patterns of demand are assumed to be known; hence, the effective capital services as measured by us are, in fact, those that were expected.

We denote by $\ln[K^*]$ the estimate of the nonstochastic part of $\ln[K]$, i.e., the output of the first stage of the estimation procedure. There are two disturbing features of these results: (a) the correlation coefficients are uniformly small and hence the explanatory power of the substitution model is very weak with respect to labor; (b) the coefficients, δ_1, which measure the sensitivity of labor input to changes in the relative prices, are essentially insignificant. In only one out of thirteen cases are the δ_1 significantly different from zero at the 1 per cent level of significance if a two-tailed t-test is employed (as we shall do throughout, unless otherwise indicated). In one case (1937–45, size 41–120), δ_1 has the wrong sign.

The empirical results found here were supported very strongly by engineering observations. The engineering explanation for the observed failure of the substitution model runs as follows: steam electric generation is a highly automated process and labor inputs enter the productive process in three ways: (1) operation and supervision of the plant which entails work of control and adjustment; (2) maintenance, and (3) clerical and office work. These operations are more or less *supplementary to the major operations of turning fuel into electricity*. For these reasons the labor requirements move more or less with the output and number of units. It is pointed out that for small plants there is some room for the same worker to perform more than one specialized task; i.e., the worker involved in supervision may also do some maintenance work. This is why we do find that, for small plants, the coefficient δ_1 does in some cases exhibit statistical significance. As we move to larger plants, these possibilities of flexibility disappear and we are essentially in a world of fixed proportions.

For all these reasons the attempt was abandoned to account for the production feasibilities of (steam) electric generating plants in terms of a pure substitution model. In place of (1), the mixed relation is introduced:

$$(20) \qquad Q = \min[g(L)\,, \quad (\alpha_f F^{\beta_f} + \alpha_K K^{\beta_K})^{1/\gamma}]\,.$$

This is a mixture of Leontief and neoclassical ingredients having the following interpretation: in order to produce output Q, a certain quantity of labor, $g^{-1}(Q)$, must be employed. Thus, no optimization can take place with respect to labor. On the other hand, subject to the employment of the quantity of labor, $g^{-1}(Q)$, optimization can take place with respect to capital and fuel. Consequently the structure of the econometric model presented in Section 2 remains valid, with $n=2$.

We shall defer analyzing the results of the alternative labor equation. The estimates obtained for the parameters of the fuel equation appear in Table III. The results show that the fuel equation is indeed highly successful.

The smallest multiple correlation coefficient is .9614, and in nine out of thirteen cases it is greater than .98.

The coefficients, ξ_1, which indicate the sensitivity of the fuel input to relative prices, are uniformly negative and highly significant except for the cell (1946–50, size 100–200 MGW) where the ξ_1 turns out to be insignificantly different from zero.

TABLE III

THE FUEL EQUATION

$$\ln F = 1/(\beta_f - 1)\ln(\alpha_K\beta_K/\alpha_f\beta_f) + 1/(\beta_f - 1)\ln(P_f/P_K) + \beta_K - 1/\beta_f - 1\ln[K^*],$$
$$\ln F = \xi_0 + \xi_1 \ln(P_f/P_K) + \xi_2 \ln[K^*]\,.$$

Size \ Technology	1937–45	1946–50	1951–54	1955–59
I	$\xi_0 =$ 2.6057	$\xi_0 =$ 2.7584	$\xi_0 =$ 2.8895	
	$\xi_1 =$ −.1232 (.0249)	$\xi_1 =$ −.1977 (.0290)	$\xi_1 =$ −.1921 (.0272)	
	$\xi_2 =$ 1.0296 (.0266)	$\xi_2 =$ 1.0556 (.0303)	$\xi_2 =$ 1.0361 (.0205)	
	$R =$ .9926	$R =$ .9843	$R =$ .9957	
II	$\xi_0 =$ 3.1394	$\xi_0 =$ −.2254	$\xi_0 =$ 1.0979	$\xi_0 =$ 2.7020
	$\xi_1 =$ −.1201 (.0189)	$\xi_1 =$ −.1506 (.0275)	$\xi_1 =$ −.0662 (.0218)	$\xi_1 =$ −.1069(.0200)
	$\xi_2 =$ .9566 (.0370)	$\xi_2 =$ 1.3665 (.0722)	$\xi_2 =$ 1.1639 (.0568)	$\xi_2 =$ .9837(.0374)
	$R =$ .9885	$R =$ .9614	$R =$ .9734	$R =$ .9840
III		$\xi_0 =$ .7543	$\xi_0 =$ 2.1935	$\xi_0 =$ −.6918
		$\xi_1 =$ −.0184 (.0261)	$\xi_1 =$ −.1292 (.0238)	$\xi_1 =$ −.2832(.0238)
		$\xi_2 =$ 1.1487 (.0845)	$\xi_2 =$ 1.0605 (.0243)	$\xi_2 =$ 1.4229(.0625)
		$R =$ .9720	$R =$ .9928	$R =$ .9768
IV			$\xi_0 =$ −.5501	$\xi_0 =$ .5317
			$\xi_1 =$ −.0683 (.0279)	$\xi_1 =$ −.1258(.0179)
			$\xi_2 =$ 1.2955 (.0409)	$\xi_2 =$ 1.2058(.0446)
			$R =$ .9912	$R =$ .9841
			(Large-scale group: capacity 450 MGW+)	
			$\xi_0 =$ 1.7327	
			$\xi_1 =$ −.0813 (.0160)	
			$\xi_2 =$ 1.0723 (.0241)	
			$R =$ .9967	

The contrast between the results of the fuel and labor equations constitutes a sufficient justification for employing the revised production relation (20).

To complete this phase of estimation, we specialize the function $g^{-1}(Q)$ to:

$$L = g^{-1}(Q) = BQ^{\beta}\,, \tag{21}$$

which is a logarithmic version of the ordinary Leontief functions of fixed proportionality. This function was estimated over the entire range of outputs without the breakdown by size. The classification by technological periods, however, was retained. Further, due to climatological conditions, labor input requirements may differ in different parts of the country. Thus, in the South and most of the Pacific Coast, electric plants are usually of the outdoor type, while in the North they are chiefly indoor type plants. This in itself would create differences in the labor requirements for operation, as well as for maintenance. For this reason the country was divided into three regions: (A) Southern Pacific Coast and the South, (B) The Northeast, and also Washington and Oregon, (C) The rest of the Continental United States, excluding Alaska. Introducing the (dummy) regional variables in (21), the following equation was estimated:

$$\ln L = \ln B + a_1 Z_1 + a_2 Z_2 + \beta \ln Q\,, \tag{22}$$

where

$$Z_1 = \begin{cases} 1 & \text{if observation belongs to region } B, \\ 0 & \text{otherwise}; \end{cases}$$

$$X_2 = \begin{cases} 1 & \text{if observation belongs to region } C, \\ 0 & \text{otherwise}. \end{cases}$$

Thus, ln B may be interpreted as the intercept of (22) when restricted to plants in region A, $\ln B + a_1$ as the intercept when (22) is restricted to region B, and $\ln B + a_2$ as the intercept when (22) is restricted to region C. The results of estimation appear in Table IV below.

TABLE IV

ESTIMATES OF THE MODIFIED LABOR (INPUT) EQUATION

1937–45	1946–50	1951–54	1955–59
$\ln B = .3580\ (.2754)$	$\ln B = .6307\ (.1899)$	$\ln B = -.0165\ (.1834)$	$\ln B = -.3577(.4075)$
$a_1 = .3473\ (.1367)$	$a_1 = .1547\ (.0876)$	$a_1 = .1491\ (.0851)$	$a_1 = .2561(.1080)$
$a_2 = .1759\ (.1466)$	$a_2 = .1322\ (.0886)$	$a_2 = .1427\ (.0912)$	$a_2 = .4042(.1219)$
$\beta_1 = .5927\ (.0494)$	$\beta_2 = .5323\ (.0318)$	$\beta_3 = .5970\ (.0271)$	$\beta_4 = .6006(.0579)$
$R = .8894$	$R = .8803$	$R = .9045$	$R = .7810$
$\alpha_1 = \ln B + a_1$	$\alpha_1 = \ln B + a_1$	$\alpha_1 = \ln B + a_1$	$\alpha_1 = \ln B + a_1$
$= .7053\ (.2872)$	$= .7852\ (.1949)$	$= .1326\ (.2038)$	$= .1016(.4227)$
$\alpha_2 = \ln B + a_2$	$\alpha_2 = \ln B + a_2$	$\alpha_2 = \ln B + a_2$	$\alpha_2 = \ln B + a_2$
$= .5339\ (.2580)$	$= .7629\ (.1687)$	$= .1262\ (.1863)$	$= .0465(.3869)$

There are several things to be noted in these results:

1. The results show uniformly increasing returns to scale with respect to labor of the order of 1.7. In other words, a 10 per cent increase in output would require only a 6 per cent increase in labor inputs. The estimates of the parameter β_i over the four technological periods do not suggest that technology has had any significant impact on returns to scale. If we treat these estimates as independently distributed normal variables and conduct a t-test on the quantity $(\max_i \beta_i - \min_i \beta_i)$[12], the hypothesis that this quantity is equal to zero will be accepted at the 1 per cent level of significance.

[12] This statistic is related to the "studentized range." See Scheffé [17, p. 28].

2. The impact of technology on the constant terms of the equation is far more pronounced. First note that we may interpret a_1 and a_2 as differences between the intercept of the equation when the latter is restricted to regions B and C, respectively, relative to the intercept obtained when restricting (22) to region A. The estimates of a_1 and a_2 turn out to be uniformly significantly different from zero when a one-tailed t-test with significance level at least 10 per cent is employed (two turn out to be significant at the 1 per cent level). This indicates that regional differences in labor input requirements do indeed exist and are of considerable import. For example, consider the last technological period in which a_1 and a_2 are both significant at the 1 per cent level. Our point estimates imply that for comparable outputs, labor inputs in region B would be 30 per cent higher than those of region A; in the case of region C, the figure is 48 per cent.

3. If we follow these point estimates by technological period we note the following: the point estimates of the intercepts behave in a perverse direction between the first and second technological periods. This seems to indicate that technological change has operated in the direction of increased labor requirements, which is a rather implausible result. Fortunately, however, this difference does not turn out to be statistically significant. Further, there is perhaps a ready explanation for the behavior of the point estimates. Recall that our measure of labor input consists of the average number of employees engaged in a given plant. It does not attempt to take into account the length of the work week, the operation of double shifts, and similar practices. Hence, the behavior of the point estimates between the periods 1937–45 and 1946–50 may in large measure be merely indicative of the great labor shortage during the war years which forced upon the plant management overtime work and consequently the lengthening of the work week. On the other hand, after the war this was largely eliminated so that a given number of man-hours required the employment of a larger number of employees. Aside from this, it is seen that, for given output, the labor input was at least halved in all three regions between the second and third or fourth technological periods. The result suggests a rather striking impact of technological improvement on the degree of mechanization in electric generation, and the reduction in labor requirements due to these changes is very substantial.

B. *Capital Fuel Substitution*

Returning now to the results presented in Table III, we recall from (4a) that the elasticity of substitution in our model reduces to a constant whenever $n=2$ and $\beta_1=\beta_2$. In order to test the hypothesis of constancy of the elasticity of substitution, we may test the hypothesis $(\beta_K-1)/(\beta_f-1)=1$, where β_K, β_f are the exponents of capital and fuel, respectively, in the relation (1), with $n=2$.

Using a two-tailed t-test, it is seen that the hypothesis is to be accepted at the 5 per cent level of significance in six cases. In the 1937–45 period it is accepted for both size groups, in the 1946–50 period it is accepted for the first and third size groups, while for 1951–54 and 1955–59 it is accepted for the smallest size groups (i.e., 0–40 and 41–100 MGW, respectively). The result is interesting since it shows the hypothesis to be accepted for small size plants. The elasticity of substitution, however, cannot be considered as independent of output in large plants.

For each cell the median elasticity of substitution has been computed by inserting into (4a) the median quantities of capital and fuel. These results are presented in Table V. Note first that in the six cases where we have accepted the hypothesis of constancy of the elasticity substitution, the latter quantity is merely $-\xi_1$, and hence the standard error of this estimate is available and is given in parentheses.

TABLE V

THE MEDIAN ELASTICITIES OF SUBSTITUTION

Size \ Technology	1937–45	1946–50	1951–54	1955–59
I	.1232 (.0249)	.1977 (.0290)	.1921 (.0272)	—
II	.1201 (.0189)	.1109	.0672	.1069 (.0200)
III	—	.0184 (.0261)	.1381	.1988
IV	—	—	.0526	.1041
			.0749	

Two general observations may be made with respect to this table.

1. The elasticity of substitution tends to fall with size. This conclusion, however, does not hold uniformly; in particular, the middle size groups (100–200 MGW, 1951–54 and 1955–59) constitute an exception. There the elasticity of substitution appears to be higher than in neighboring cells. This phenomenon may be given a partial explanation as follows: in our study we have ignored the number of generating units in a plant. The fact is, however, that practically all plants of size less than 150 MGW have only one unit. About 50 per cent of plants with capacity over 150 MGW have at least two units. It is possible that the addition of a second unit creates a new type of factor substitution in the sense of different degrees of utilization of the units. Apparently as size becomes still larger the fundamental fact that the elasticity of substitution falls with size is sufficient to overcome the additional substitution possibilities offered by the multiple unit setup.

2. Technology does not seem to have a significant effect on the elasticity of substitution of *small* (0–100 MGW) plants. It does, however, have a significant effect on larger plants. Thus, in the 1946–50 period note that the size group 100–200 MGW shows essentially no possibilities for substitution. In subsequent technological periods substitution possibilities have appreciably increased. The elasticity of substitution for this group has increased from .0184 (1946–50) to .1381 (1951–54) and to .1988 (1955–59). The same phenomenon is found in the 200–449 MGW

group. There the elasticity of substitution increased from .0526 (1951–54) to .1041 (1955–59).

C. *Returns to Scale and Technical Progress*

In this section we shall obtain estimates for the parameters of the relation (1), $n=2$, which are, in part, implied by the results presented in the preceding section. The implied estimates of β_f, β_K, α_f and α_K are presented in Table VI. These estimates are not of great interest in themselves. They do, however, warrant the following comment. In Section 2B it was observed that one of the (necessary) conditions imposed by the existence of an (interior) solution to the cost minimization problem therein posed is that $\beta_i<1$. Table VI indicates that this holds uniformly.

TABLE VI

THE IMPLIED COEFFICIENTS

NORMALIZATION: $\ln \alpha_K + \ln \alpha_f = 0$

Size \ Technology	1937–45	1946–50	1951–54	1955–59
I	$\beta_f = -7.1169$ $\beta_K = -7.3562$ $\ln\alpha_K = .1085$	$\beta_f = -4.0581$ $\beta_K = -4.3393$ $\ln\alpha_K = 2.0119$	$\beta_f = -4.2056$ $\beta_K = -4.3952$ $\ln\alpha_K = 1.9686$	—
II	$\beta_f = -7.3263$ $\beta_K = -6.9649$ $\ln\alpha_K = .6459$	$\beta_f = -5.6401$ $\beta_K = -8.0737$ $\ln\alpha_K = -.7018$	$\beta_f = -14.1057$ $\beta_K = -16.5815$ $\ln\alpha_K = 2.9710$	$\beta_f = -8.3545$ $\beta_K = -8.2020$ $\ln\alpha_K = .5082$
III	—	$\beta_f = -53.3478$ $\beta_K = -61.4293$ $\ln\alpha_K = 26.7289$	$\beta_f = -6.7399$ $\beta_K = -7.2082$ $\ln\alpha_K = -.2824$	$\beta_f = -2.5310$ $\beta_K = -4.0243$ $\ln\alpha_K = -1.1859$
IV	—	—	$\beta_f = -13.6412$ $\beta_K = -17.9677$ $\ln\alpha_K = 7.0522$	$\beta_f = -6.9491$ $\beta_K = -8.5843$ $\ln\alpha_K = 1.6677$
			$\beta_f = -11.3001$ $\beta_K = -12.1893$ $\ln\alpha_K = 2.7050$	

It should be further observed that the unusually large (implied) point estimates for β_f and β_K for the cell 100–200 MGW, 1946–50, are the result of the fact that in this case the elasticity of substitution is insignificantly different from zero and hence the point estimates obtained are subject to very large standard errors. We therefore neglect them in subsequent discussions.

TABLE VII

RESULTS OF THE THIRD STAGE

Let $Z = \alpha_f F^{\beta_f} + \alpha_K K^{\beta_K}$.

The computed regression: $\ln Z = -\gamma \ln A + \gamma \ln Q$.

Size \ Technology	1937–1945	1946–1950	1951–1954	1955–1959
I	$-\gamma \ln A =$ 37.0748 (.7137)	$-\gamma \ln A =$ 23.1879 (.4087)	$-\gamma \ln A =$ 25.1960 (.3844)	
	$\gamma = -5.8733$ (.1501)	$\gamma = -3.5781$ (.0889)	$\gamma = -3.8341$ (.0794)	
	$R =$ .9916	$R =$ .9879	$R =$ .9949	
II	$-\gamma \ln A =$ 43.2753 (1.7111)	$-\gamma \ln A =$ 35.1492 (1.0954)	$-\gamma \ln A =$ 79.1528 (3.7759)	$-\gamma \ln A =$ 47.9420 (1.7119)
	$\gamma = -6.6333$ (.2739)	$\gamma = -5.5330$ (.1831)	$\gamma = -13.0479$ (.6232)	$\gamma = -7.6570$ (.2797)
	$R =$ .9858	$R =$ .9835	$R =$ .9674	$R =$ .9825
III		$-\gamma \ln A =$ 263.1211 (34.6922)	$-\gamma \ln A =$ 43.6278 (1.0409)	$-\gamma \ln A =$ 16.3229 (.6983)
		$\gamma = -46.4874$ (5.0234)	$\gamma = -6.8305$ (.1544)	$\gamma = -2.3796$ (.1023)
		$R =$ .9225	$R =$ .9927	$R =$ .9768
IV			$-\gamma \ln A =$ 79.1869 (2.8694)	$-\gamma \ln A =$ 39.8430 (1.6930)
			$\gamma = -13.4745$ (.3764)	$\gamma = -6.5356$ (.2226)
			$R =$ .9911	$R =$ .9858
			$-\gamma \ln A =$ 65.2125 (1.8302)	
			$\gamma = -10.7432$ (.2178)	
			$R =$ .9967	

As indicated in Section 2C, the point estimates, α_K, α_f, β_K, β_f, are needed in order to complete the estimation of parameters of (1) by obtaining the conditional estimates for γ and A.

It is clear that the results of this third stage can give us an additional test of the validity of our model. Note that except for the approximation of the first stage, in which the nonstochastic part of $\ln K$ was estimated, output data, Q, were not used. Hence, if the estimation of the parameters of (18) yields a high correlation coefficient, this would be reassuring. For this reason the results of this stage of estimation are presented in Table VII.

Two observations may be made with respect to these estimates. Recall again the necessary condition on the parameters, β_i and γ, given in Section 2B; viz., $\beta_i \gamma > 0$. We note that $\gamma < 0$, which is what is required, in view of the results in Table VI. Note further that in ten out of thirteen cases we obtain $R > .98$.

TABLE VIII

THE MEASURE OF RETURNS TO SCALE AND THE CONSTANT

Size \ Technology	1937–45	1946–50	1951–54	1955–59
I	$\beta_f/\gamma =$ 1.211* $\beta_K/\gamma =$ 1.252* $\hat{A} =$ 551.41	$\beta_f/\gamma =$ 1.134* $\beta_K/\gamma =$ 1.213* $\hat{A} =$ 652.27	$\beta_f/\gamma =$ 1.096* $\beta_K/\gamma =$ 1.146* $\hat{A} =$ 714.54	—
II	$\beta_f/\gamma =$ 1.104* $\beta_K/\gamma =$ 1.050* $\hat{A} =$ 681.27	$\beta_f/\gamma =$ 1.019 $\beta_K/\gamma =$ 1.459 $\hat{A} =$ 573.99	$\beta_f/\gamma =$ 1.081 $\beta_K/\gamma =$ 1.270 $\hat{A} =$ 431.084	$\beta_f/\gamma =$ 1.091* $\beta_K/\gamma =$ 1.071* $\hat{A} =$ 523.85
III	—	$\beta_f/\gamma =$ 1.147* $\beta_K/\gamma =$ 1.321* $\hat{A} =$ 287.16	$\beta_f/\gamma =$ .986 $\beta_K/\gamma =$ 1.055 $\hat{A} =$ 594.20	$\beta_f/\gamma =$ 1.063 $\beta_K/\gamma =$ 1.691 $\hat{A} =$ 952.84
IV	—	—	$\beta_f/\gamma =$ 1.012 $\beta_K/\gamma =$ 1.333 $\hat{A} =$ 356.67	$\beta_f/\gamma =$ 1.063 $\beta_K/\gamma =$ 1.313 $\hat{A} =$ 444.20
			$\beta_f/\gamma =$ 1.051 $\beta_K/\gamma =$ 1.134 $\hat{A} =$ 432.72	

* The hypothesis $\beta_K = \beta_f$ accepted (5%).

In Table VIII the ratios, β_f/γ and β_K/γ, were computed along with the implied estimate of A. The latter permits us to make some judgments concerning the neutral component of technical change simply by comparing the size of A across technological periods for given size group.[13] This is so since the units of measurement of the inputs and the normalization $\alpha_f \alpha_K = 1$, are held fixed.

Perhaps the term, "neutral component of technical change," requires some explanation. The impact of technology on the production function (1) may take various forms; i.e., it may affect the parameters β_i, α_i, or γ. Such changes do not, in general, leave the marginal rate of substitution among various factors unchanged. On the other hand, the impact of technology may take the form of modifying the parameter A. It is easily verified that such a change will leave the marginal rate of substitution unchanged. We shall call this type of impact the "neutral component," while the former type shall be termed the "non-neutral component" of technical change.

In this framework, then, it is certainly not true that technical change has been neutral in the electric generating industry, since, as was observed earlier, it had a significant impact on the elasticity of substitution. Observe, however, that the neutral component is equally significant in its size; note that, except for the group 40–100 MGW, the estimate $\hat{A}$ displays a monotone (increasing) behavior. This shows that the neutral component has operated in the direction of increasing the overall productivity in electric (steam) generation.

No clear effect, however, can be observed on the middle-sized group (40–100 MGW) where the estimate $\hat{A}$ behaves somewhat erratically.

We turn now to the question of returns to scale. Recall that when the hypothesis $\beta_f = \beta_K$ is accepted, the function (1) is homogeneous of degree β/γ, and β_f/γ or β_K/γ denotes the rate of returns to scale (degree of homogeneity of the function). Recall also that whenever $\min(\beta_f/\gamma, \beta_K/\gamma) > 1$, we can state that increasing returns to scale will prevail, although the rate of such returns will depend on the level of the inputs.

From Table VIII we conclude that increasing returns to scale is the prevailing phenomenon in (steam) electric generation. The rate of returns to scale with respect to fuel and capital is certainly less than that of labor but the case is quite clear qualitatively. It is true, however, that no specific number can be assigned to the rate of returns to scale where the hypothesis, $\beta_f = \beta_K$, was not accepted, and Table VIII shows seven such cases.

In order to deal summarily with this question and to facilitate discussion and comparison, we have applied the following simulation technique which is designed to approximate the non-homogeneous function estimated in the seven cases by a homogeneous function. Thus, let the production function estimated in the kth cell be given by

$$Q = G_k(K, F). \tag{23}$$

[13] The comparison of A across size groups, for a given technological period, is not very meaningful since we are estimating segments of a production function by a suitable approximation which does not have to yield the same constant, A, for each segment. Hence, changes in A will reflect, in part, the approximation procedure.

TABLE IX

THE SIMULATED COEFFICIENTS OF $r = \mu_0 + \mu_1 \lambda$

Size \ Technology	1937–45	1946–50	1951–54	1955–59
I	$\hat{\mu}_0 =$ 1.21250 (.00094) $\hat{\mu}_1 = -$.00011 (.00108) *	$\hat{\mu}_0 =$ 1.13460 (.00168) $\hat{\mu}_1 = -$.00005 (.00141) *	$\hat{\mu}_0 =$ 1.09716 (.00114) $\hat{\mu}_1 = -$.00002 (.00099) *	—
II	$\hat{\mu}_0 =$ 1.11400 (.00106) $\hat{\mu}_1 = -$.00111 (.00110) *	$\hat{\mu}_0 =$ 1.08418 (.02734) $\hat{\mu}_1 = -$.00904 (.00412)	$\hat{\mu}_0 =$ 1.26541 (.02961) $\hat{\mu}_1 = -$.01660 (.00539)	$\hat{\mu}_0 =$ 1.09452 (.01027) $\hat{\mu}_1 = -$.00097 (.00336) *
III	—	$\hat{\mu}_0 =$ 1.27690 (.00428) $\hat{\mu}_1 =$ .00218 (.00211) *	$\hat{\mu}_0 =$ .99162 (.00023) $\hat{\mu}_1 = -$.00019 (.000015)	$\hat{\mu}_0 =$ 1.07293 (.00728) $\hat{\mu}_1 = -$.00026 (.00039)
IV	—	—	$\hat{\mu}_0 =$ 1.39547 (.00558) $\hat{\mu}_1 = -$.00322 (.00017)	$\hat{\mu}_0 =$ 1.12626 (.04418) $\hat{\mu}_1 = -$.00088 (.00102)
			$\hat{\mu}_0 =$ 1.08414 (.00347) $\hat{\mu}_1 = -$.000088 (.000026)	

* The hypothesis of homogeneity was accepted earlier.

Suppose some fixed pair, $(\bar{K},\bar{F})$, is chosen and the following series is generated:

$$Q(\lambda_i)=G_k(\lambda_i\bar{K},\ \lambda_i\bar{F}) \qquad (i=1,2,\ldots,m). \tag{24}$$

Using the least-squares principle, we may now fit to the points $(Q(\lambda_i),\lambda_i)$ a function of the form:

$$H(\lambda)=B\lambda^r. \tag{25}$$

We may interpret $H(\lambda)$ as being a homogeneous approximation for $G_k(.,.)$ over an appropriate region. The latter depends on the values chosen for the λ_i. In our case, we have chosen a series of 100 equi-spaced values for λ, such that the range of validity of the function is essentially covered. (This is not always possible since the range of K and F may differ considerably.)

In actually fitting H, we have specialized r by:

$$r=\mu_0+\mu_1\lambda. \tag{26}$$

Equation (26) may be interpreted as stating that we permit returns to scale to depend on size. Note also that this procedure yields a valid approximation for some fixed capital-fuel proportion. To this effect, recall the brief discussion of Section 2A.iv.

The application of this procedure has yielded a highly successful fit, the correlation coefficients being uniformly higher than .999. Of course, it is to be understood that the terms "correlation coefficient" or "standard error" in this context have no probability content and merely indicate the goodness of fit or the importance of the computed coefficient in the particular approximation at hand. The results of this simulation are presented in Table IX. It is clear from this table that in all cases where the homogeneity hypothesis ($\beta_f=\beta_K$) was accepted earlier, the coefficient μ_1 turned out to be insignificant, as it should.[14]

For all other cells except those of the period 1955–59, μ_1 is negative and significant. This means that within each size group the rate of returns to scale tends to fall with size. This is not the case for the 1955–59 period for which the μ_1 are negative but insignificant.

Using the appropriate range of λ, we can, for each cell, compute the maximum, minimum, and median values for $r=\mu_0+\mu_1\lambda$. These are presented in Table X.

Ignoring the 100–200 MGW group for 1946–50, Table X shows that during the periods 1937–45 and 1946–50 the rate of returns to scale tends to fall with size. Thus, the computed median r falls from 1.212 (0–40 MGW) to 1.109 (41–120 MGW) in the period 1937–45. Similarly, in the period 1946–50 we observe $r=1.134$ for the 0–39 MGW group, and $r=1.046$ for the 40–99 MGW group. If, for given size, we move across the two technological periods, we observe a similar decline for both size groups.

The great technological changes in (steam) electric generation, as observed

[14] In the simulation of (24), the point estimates of β_K and β_f were used.

TABLE X

THE COMPUTED VALUES FOR MAX r, MIN r, MEDIAN r FOR EACH CELL

Size \ Technology	1937–45	1946–50	1951–54	1955–59
I	max r = 1.21248 min r = 1.21228 med. r = 1.21238	max = 1.13458 min = 1.13450 med. = 1.13454	max r = 1.09716 min r = 1.09711 med. r = 1.09714	
II	max = 1.11108 min = 1.10775 med. = 1.10942	max = 1.06168 min = 1.05010 med. = 1.05589	max = 1.22963 min = 1.20952 med. = 1.21957	max = 1.09250 min = 1.09093 med. = 1.09171
III			max = .99097 min = .99010 med. = .99054	max = 1.07197 min = 1.07036 med. = 1.07116
IV			max = 1.37971 min = 1.34139 med. = 1.36055	max = 1.11752 min = 1.11310 med. = 1.11531
			max = 1.08306 min = 1.07924 med. = 1.08115	

earlier, seem to have taken place mostly in the 1950's. Hence, we have chosen to treat the two periods, 1937–45, 1946–50, as a block in comparing them with the two remaining periods.

Tables IX and X show that, despite the fact that within each size group the rate of returns to scale tends to fall in 1951–54, the intercell comparisons for different size groups do not indicate a monotone behavior of r. These comparisons show that the great technological changes in the 1950's had strongly differentiated effects on different size groups.

In comparing the periods 1946–50 and 1951–54, we observe that, although technical change has apparently induced a reduction of r from 1.134 to 1.097 (0–40 MGW), it has brought about an apparent increase from 1.056 to 1.219 (41–99 MGW).

The technology of large plants appearing in sizable numbers beginning with this period is characterized by sharply differing returns to scale. Thus, we note that plants in the range 100–200 MGW operate at essentially constant returns to scale, while plants in the range 201–449 MGW have $r = 1.360$. By and large, returns to scale appear to fall as we move from the period 1951–54 to 1955–59, in much the same fashion observed earlier with respect to the first two technological periods.

It is interesting, however, that the period 1955–59 evidences a much more homogeneous technology with respect to size. We have already observed that even within cells, r does not tend to fall with size (i.e., μ_1 is insignificant). Similarly, as we move along size groups, the computed median r remains relatively stable, varying from 1.071 to 1.115.

Stanford University

APPENDIX

Here we give a rather detailed description of the data used. In order to conduct the analysis, the following basic data are required: Output (Q), Fuel (F), Labor (L), and Capital (K). Output is stated in 10^6 KWH (kilowatt hours) of net generation, Fuel in 10^7 British Thermal Units (BTU). Generating plants typically consume either coal or natural gas. We have not distinguished plants in this respect but have instead stated fuel consumption in BTU equivalents. Labor is stated in number of employes (annual averages). Where a plant in our sample began operation after the beginning of the year, the number of employes was prorated accordingly.

Capital is stated in $10^{1.8}$ megawatt hours and perhaps this deserves some comment. Each generator has a rated capacity stated in megawatts. However, the unit may or may not have been operated fully during the year. To correct for that, we may proceed as follows: for each plant we have data on the number of hours generators were "connected to load," i.e., actively engaged in contributing to electricity supply. We also have data on the number of hours the generators were "hot, not connected to load"; this means that the boilers were fully operated but the generators were not connected to load; rather, they were held in a state of readiness, presumably for peaking purposes. This was not very often a significant phenomenon.

Combining the two, we obtain the portion of the time the generator was in operation. Multiplying this number by capacity, we find the number of megawatt hours of capital services rendered by the generator units. This, then, is our (flow) measure of capital.

All the above data were taken directly from our primary source [7], except that information concerning hours of operation was not published after 1953. Therefore we circulated a questionnaire among the plants in our sample. Response was fairly satisfactory (over 60%). Hence, for the period 1954–1959 our measure of capital may contain an element of error since we have extrapolated in the case of no response.

In addition, we also require observations on the following prices:

The price of labor: this was simply derived by dividing total labor costs (excluding maintenance costs) by the average number of employees. This gives an average annual wage.

The price of fuel: this was similarly computed by dividing total expenditure on fuel by the total energy consumption stated in BTU equivalents. This gives the price of fuel per BTU.

We also require the price of electricity (P) as evaluated implicitly at the plant. This is a rather abstract concept since electricity cannot be stored and hence cannot be the subject of a market transaction unless it is transmitted and distributed. It is clear, however, that since our analysis is confined to electricity generation, the price alluded to is the relevant one. In computing such a price, we have made use of what we shall call, for want of a better term, the residual method. This simply amounts to stating that the returns to capital consist of what is left of total revenue after the other factors of production have been remunerated. The method is logically consistent with the model presented earlier and is necessitated by the fact that no independent observations on capital returns are directly available. By returns to capital we mean, of course, the rental per megawatt hour of capital services.

To find the price of electricity at the plant, the procedure is as follows:

Let Π = total revenue − total operating costs. This measure includes depreciation, taxes, interest payments, and net income, and is interpreted to constitute the return on the total capital stock of the firm. Data were obtained from [**8**] and [**9**].

Let α be the ratio of the (book value of the) capital stock in (steam) generation to the firm's total capital stock (book value). Then $\alpha\Pi$ is taken to be returns to capital in (steam) generation. This involves the assumption that capital resources are allocated "optimally" within the firm in the sense that a dollar's worth of capital stock earns the same return in every facet of the firm's operation. Hence $\alpha\Pi$ + [total (steam generation) operating costs] represents total cost, and, in this context, total revenue attributable to steam generation as well. Dividing this by our measure of output (net steam generation), we find the price of electricity at the "plant." Note that this method has the consequence of assigning the same price to all plants of a multi-plant firm.

The price (rental) of capital (p_K) was obtained more or less by applying the same method in reverse. Thus, take the price of electricity computed above and multiply by net generation of the plant in question. This gives total revenue attributable to the generation activities of the plant. Subtract from it total (plant) operating expenses minus maintenance. This yields returns to capital in the plant. If we divide by our measure of capital (megawatt hours), we find rental per megawatt hour, which is the "price" of capital in our context.

It might appear that the use of the term $\pi_i = p_i/p_n$ (see Equation (11) in the text) vitiates the exogeneity of factor prices, since, as it is explained above, we derive the price (rental) of capital, p_K, by the operation R/K, where R is return to capital obtained residually; thus, R/K contains the terms K, L, F, and hence its exogeneity may be questioned. This is not a valid objection, however. For even if independent observations were available on the price (rental) of capital, then, provided the assumptions made are valid, the procedure just given must yield a rental identical to the observed one. This is so since: Value of output = total costs = $\Sigma_{i=1}^{n} p_i X_i$; then if, as in our application $n = 2$, X_1 = Fuel (F), X_2 = Capital (K), we should have $p_K K$ = (total cost − $p_L L$) − $p_F F$. The random component in total cost comes from K, L, and F. The random component in $p_K K$ comes solely from K; hence, $p_K K/K$ is free of random elements induced by endogeneity of K, L, and F.

We should mention here that operating expenses include expenditure on some minor items, such as water and miscellaneous expenses. These were not treated as factors of production because they are quantitatively very insignificant; in fact, they were excluded from consideration altogether.

Several objections may be raised to the procedure employed in obtaining the price of electricity and the price of capital. They deserve some discussion.

Insofar as we are concerned with the productive process of electric generation, it is clear that the fundamental unit of investigation must be the plant, not the firm. However, no information is available on the purely abstract price of electricity needed here. Thus, we either (1) employ the price of electricity at the point of consumption with the consequence that the measure so adduced will contain elements of cost due to transmission and distribution, (2) abandon all hope of investigation, or (3) try to accommodate ourselves by making some assumptions which are not deemed too abusive of reality. The assumption we have made here is that a dollar's worth of capital earns the same return (on the average) in all phases of the firm's operation. It is rather difficult to take exception to this statement except under strong evidence to the contrary.

This is very much in the spirit of equilibrium analysis under which this study is conducted, and, we might say, under which many econometric investigations are undertaken.

The second point relates to the price (rental) of capital. Two other approaches to the problem are immediately suggested: first, to use the purchase price of a generator, as was done by Komiya, and second, following Nerlove, to use some index on the rental of capital in general, say the yield on long-term bonds issued by the firms in question.

Neither of these approaches seems more proper to us than the procedure employed herein. Clearly the purchase price of a generator is in no way a proper measure in this context. If the market for generators is perfectly competitive, then the price of a unit is the same for all purchasers, and, hence, ipso facto, capital is equally productive everywhere. On the other hand, if there are imperfections or transport costs, then the observed differences will reflect just those factors and, hence, convey no information on the "value" of the contribution of capital in the process of generating electricity. Moreover, the yield of bonds is related to the standing of the firm as a whole, not to the circumstances of the individual plant; and indeed because of the essentially risk-free character of such bonds, the yields display little, if any, variation except in reflecting the state of current monetary policy.

The method employed here is free of such criticisms, and has the merit of being a logical consequence of the assumption of equilibrium. This assumption may not be universally acceptable, but we do maintain that the electric power industry is one of the most stable and tranquil industries in the entire economy. If the notion of equilibrium ever makes sense in econometric work, it should make sense in our case. Thus, what we envisage is roughly the following: the entrepreneur, on the basis of his anticipations, determines the quantities of factors to be employed, given the relevant price milieu. On the basis of these determinations the entrepreneur proceeds with plant construction. Our use of ex post data on the prices of inputs is validated if we assume that entrepreneurial anticipations are, in fact, realized. Our use of data pertaining to the year after construction is prompted by the fact that in many instances plants commence operation in midyear, and, hence, the information on the inputs published does not reflect accurately their magnitude in that they have been utilized only for a fraction of the basic period of observation (a calendar year). In addition, the installation of a new plant is not a "smooth" affair, and a little time must be allowed to elapse before things are properly organized.

If the above is granted, however, and if we further assert that the regulatory agencies are reasonably effective in their functions, then the procedure employed in computing the price (rentral) of capital must be correct. For we deduce the price of capital from the equation

$$C = p_F F + p_L L + p_K K .$$

The argument above does not mean, of course, to suggest that our assumptions correspond with exactitude to reality—only that they do not grossly violate it. It is encouraging to note that the series of capital price (rental) produced displays sufficient variation, that it tends to be high where one might expect it, say in New York, New Jersey, etc., and low in areas where capital would have low productivity, such as Alabama, Arkansas, rural Louisiana, etc. Another feature of the series is that, on the average, the price of capital is about one-half of the computed price of electricity, which more or less conforms to the order of magnitude given to us by electrical engineers.

Finally, we should remark that observations on plants were usually taken only once. A plant may appear more than once in our sample if it experienced a substantial increase in capacity (at least 50%) within the same technological period. Under such circumstances, it was felt that the plant offered new information sufficient to warrant inclusion in the sample for a second time.

We should further note that while, in general, we considered only new plants, there are a few instances of plants built before 1937 which are included in our sample because it is apparent that the old equipment was either retired or was used only for standby purposes. Thus, effective operation of the plant was carried on by equipment installed during the period under consideration (1937–59) and, hence, the plant warranted inclusion.

REFERENCES

[1] ALLEN, R. G. D.: *Mathematical Analysis for Economists.* London: Macmillan and Co., Ltd., 1938.

[2] ARROW, K. J., B. MINHAS, H. CHENERY, AND R. SOLOW: "Capital-Labor Substitution and Economic Efficiency," *The Review of Economics and Statistics*, Vol. XLIII, No. 3 (1961), 225–250.

[3] BONBRIGHT, J. C.: *Principles of Public Utility Rates*. New York: Columbia University Press, 1961.

[4] COOTNER, P.: "A Model for the Estimation of Water Demand for Stream Electric Generation." Resources for the Future, Inc., New York, 1956 (mimeographed).

[5] DHRYMES, P. J.: "A Comparison of Productivity Behavior in Manufacturing and Service Industries," *Review of Economics and Statistics*. XLV, No. 1 (1963), 64–69.

[6] DURBIN, J.: "A Note on Regression when there is Extraneous Information about One of the Coefficients," *Journal of the American Statistical Association*, Vol. XLVIII, No. 4 (1953), 799–808.

[7] FEDERAL POWER COMMISSION: *Steam Electric Plants: Construction Cost and Annual Production Expenses* (Annual Supplements), 1937–1959. Government Printing Office, Washington, D. C.

[8] ———: *Statistics of Electric Utilities in the United States, Classes A and B Privately Owned Companies*, 1937–1959. Government Printing Office, Washington, D. C.

[9] ———: *Statistics of Electric Utilities in the United States, Classes A and B Publicly Owned Companies*, 1945–1959. Government Printing Office, Washington, D. C.

[10] IULO, W.: *Electric Utilities—Costs and Performance*: Bureau of Economic and Business Research. Pullman, Washington: Washington State University Press, 1961.

[11] JOHNSTON, J.: *Statistical Cost Analysis*. New York: McGraw-Hill, 1960.

[12] KOMIYA, R.: "Technological Progress and the Production Function in the United States Steam Power Industry," *Review of Economics and Statistics*. 44, No. 2 (1962), 156–166.

[13] LOMAX, K. S.: "Cost Curves for Electricity Generation," *Economica*, 19, New Series (1952), 193–197.

[14] MEADE, J. E.: *A Neo-Classical Theory of Economic Growth*. New York: Oxford University Press, 1961.

[15] NERLOVE, M.: "Returns to Scale in Electricity Supply," Technical Report No. 96, Institute of Mathematical Studies in the Social Sciences, Serra House, Stanford University, May 25, 1961.

[16] NORDIN, J. A.: "Note on a Light Plant's Cost Curves," *Econometrica*, 15, No. 3 (1947), 231–235.

[17] SCHEFFÉ, H.: *The Analysis of Variance*. New York: John Wiley and Sons, Inc., 1959.

[18] UZAWA, H.: "Production Functions with Constant Elasticities of Substitution," Technical Report No. 104, Institute of Mathematical Studies in the Social Sciences, Serra House, Stanford University, December 15, 1961.

Reprinted from
THE REVIEW OF ECONOMICS AND STATISTICS
Published by Harvard University

Vol. XLVII, No. 4, November 1965

SOME EXTENSIONS AND TESTS FOR THE CES CLASS OF PRODUCTION FUNCTIONS *

Phoebus J. Dhrymes

I Preliminaries

IN a recent pioneering paper Arrow, Chenery, Minhas, and Solow,[1] hereafter referred to as Arrow, et al., have proposed a new class of production functions of great flexibility.

Essentially, they address themselves to the following problem: If it is given that a certain relationship exists between wages and output per man-hour, then what sort of production function rationalizes this relationship. Specifically if it is given that

$$W = A\left(\frac{Q}{L}\right)^{\beta} \tag{1}$$

and if it is postulated that

$$Q = F(K, L), \tag{2}$$

what is the specification of the functional form F? In this notation W, Q, K, and L denote the (product) wage, output, capital, and labor, respectively. In order to solve the problem, the authors make the following assumptions:

i. The unit characterized by the production function in (2) behaves as if it were a perfect competitor in both the product and factor markets.

ii. The function in (2) is homogeneous of degree one. The functional form thus determined is given by

$$Q = F(K, L) = B[a_1 K^{\delta} + a_2 L^{\delta}]^{1/\delta} \tag{3}$$

where $\delta = 1 - \beta$.

It is easily verified that the elasticity of substitution between K and L, for the functional form in (3), is given by

$$\sigma = -\frac{d\,ln\left(\frac{K}{L}\right)}{d\,ln\ M} = \frac{1}{1-\delta} = \frac{1}{\beta} \tag{4}$$

where M is the marginal rate of substitution between capital and labor defined by

$$M = \frac{\partial Q/\partial K}{\partial Q/\partial L}. \tag{4a}$$

From (4) it is seen that the elasticity of substitution parameter is constant, restricted, from more general considerations, to the range $(0, \infty)$. Differently put, this means that δ is restricted by $\delta < 1$. Clearly, the CES production function is a great improvement over either the fixed proportions or the more traditional Cobb-Douglas functions. It is easily shown that these two types of functions are limiting forms of the CES function, obtained by letting δ approach $-\infty$ and 0, respectively. Another observation of interest is the fact that the elasticity of substitution parameter can be estimated quite easily from readily available data under the assumptions of the Arrow, et al. model. This can be readily seen from a simple variant of (1):

$$\frac{Q}{L} = A^{*}W^{1/\beta}. \tag{5}$$

A test of the validity of the model, or better a test of the two fundamental assumptions — homogeneity of degree one and perfect competition — can be conducted in terms of the companion relationship of (5):

$$\frac{Q}{K} = A^{**}\, r^{1/\beta} \tag{5a}$$

where r is the (product) rental of capital. If the model were valid then the elasticity of substitution obtained from (5) should not be significantly different from that obtained through the use of (5a). We give in table 1 the results of the estimation of the elasticity of substitution parameter from the relations (5) and (5a).

Our data pertain to two-digit manufacturing industries for the year 1957. The nature of the sample will be elaborated upon at a later point. In deriving the results of table 1, use was made of the relation

* The research on which this paper is based was partially supported by a Ford Foundation grant to the Department of Economics at Harvard and National Science Foundation grant GS–95, at the Department of Economics, Massachusetts Institute of Technology. Computations were carried out at the Harvard Computation Center by John Brode.

[1] K. J. Arrow, H. B. Chenery, B. S. Minhas, and R. M. Solow, "Capital-Labor Substitution and Economic Efficiency," this REVIEW, XLIII (Aug. 1961), 225.

TABLE 1. — ELASTICITIES OF SUBSTITUTION ON TWO-DIGIT MANUFACTURING INDUSTRIES, UNITED STATES, 1957

$$Q = B\,[\alpha_1 K^{\delta} + \alpha_2 L^{\delta}]^{1/\delta}, \qquad \sigma = \frac{1}{1-\delta}$$

$$\frac{Q}{L} = A^{*}\,W^{\sigma_1} \qquad \frac{Q}{K} = A^{**}\,r^{\sigma_2}$$

Industrial Classification	Industry	σ_1	R^2	σ_2	R^2	Number of Observations
20	Food and Kindred Prods.	.5596 (.1221)	.3558	.9715 (.1315)	.5896	40
22	Textile Mill Products	.6761 (.1149)	.6455	1.0327 (.1533)	.7049	21
23	Apparel and Related Prods.	.5377 (.1338)	.4232	1.0285 (.1809)	.5951	24
24	Lumber and Wood Prods.	.7794 (.0756)	.8349	1.1010 (.1113)	.8233	23
25	Furniture & Fixtures	.6956 (.0788)	.7956	1.3935 (.0601)	.9642	22
26	Pulp Papers & Allied Prods.	.2030 (.0624)	.2754	.6382 (.0780)	.7052	30
27	Printing and Publishing	.6811 (.1252)	.6490	1.1064 (.0611)	.9535	18
28	Chemicals & Allied Prods.	.3091 (.0959)	.2572	1.0301 (.0634)	.8979	32
29	Petroleum & Coal Products	.1125 (.1108)	.0605	1.3108 (.0834)	.9391	18
30	Rubber Prods.	.4003 (.0884)	.5955	1.0371 (.1439)	.7878	16
31	Leather and Leather Goods	.5082 (.1491)	.4365	1.1257 (.1168)	.8610	17
32	Stone, Clay & Glass Products	.4807 (.1095)	.4454	.8873 (.0765)	.8487	26
33	Primary Metal Industries	.0952 (.0612)	.0822	.9680 (.1357)	.6534	29
34	Fabricated Metal Products	.4005 (.1349)	.2212	.9503 (.1487)	.5684	33
35	Machinery except Electrical	.1206 (.0706)	.0944	.2445 (.7016)	.0043	30
36	Electrical Machinery	.1937 (.1092)	.1203	.6200 (.3502)	.8945	24
37	Transportation Equipment	.1310 (.0532)	.1890	.9130 (.1021)	.7547	27

$$r = \frac{Q - WL}{K} \tag{6}$$

as is of course required by the Arrow, et al. model. Two observations are relevant to the results above.

First, the fit provided by the output per unit of capital-rental relation is significantly better than that provided by the output per unit of labor-wage relation. Second, the elasticity of substitution parameter is significantly higher when derived from the first relation. It is possible to give an explanation of these results solely in terms of errors of specification (or errors in variables). Thus, it is possible to argue that because the capital series is substantially adulterated by errors of observation it would follow that the correlation between $\frac{Q}{K}$ and r may be biased in an upwards direction. This is easily demonstrated as follows:

Recall that $r = \frac{Q - WL}{K}$ and assume that Q, W, and L are free of observational errors. Then taking logarithms, let us seek first the covariance between $(\ln Q - \ln K)$ and $[\ln (Q - WL) - \ln K]$. Let the errors be multiplicative so that we can write

$$\ln K = \xi + u_1. \tag{6a}$$

Put

$$\ln Q = x,\ \ln (Q - WL) = y \tag{6b}$$

and assume

$$\operatorname{Cov}(x, u_1) = \operatorname{Cov}(\xi, u_1) = \operatorname{Cov}(y, u_1) = 0. \tag{6c}$$

Then we have

$$\operatorname{Cov}(x - \xi - u_1, y - \xi - u_1) = \operatorname{Cov}(x - \xi, y - \xi) + \operatorname{Var}(u_1) = a_1 + \sigma_{u_1}^2$$

$$\operatorname{Var}(x - \xi - u_1) = \operatorname{Var}(x - \xi) + \operatorname{Var}(u_1 = a_2 + \sigma_{u1}^2$$

$$\operatorname{Var}(y - \xi - u_1) = \operatorname{Var}(y - \xi) + \operatorname{Var}(u_1) = a_3 + \sigma_{u_1}^2: \tag{6d}$$

Further

$$\operatorname{Corr}(x - \xi - u_1, y - \xi - u_1) = \frac{a_1 + \sigma_{u_1}^2}{\sqrt{a_2 a_3 + \sigma_{u_1}^2 (a_2 + a_3) + \sigma_{u_1}^4}}. \tag{7}$$

In the absence of observational errors in K, we should have

$$\operatorname{Corr}(x - \xi, y - \xi) = \frac{a_1}{\sqrt{a_2 a_3}} \tag{7a}$$

thus

$$\operatorname{Corr}(x - \xi - u_1, y - \xi - u_1) - \operatorname{Corr}(x - \xi\ y - \xi) \tag{7b}$$

$$= \frac{a_1}{\sqrt{a_2 a_3}} \left[\frac{1}{\sqrt{1 + \sigma_{u_1}^2 \dfrac{a_2 + a_3}{a_2 a_3} + \dfrac{\sigma_{u_1}^4}{a_2 a_3}}} - 1 \right] + \frac{\sigma_{u_1}^2}{\sqrt{a_2 a_3 + \sigma_{u_1}^2 (a_2 + a_3) + \sigma_{u_1}^4}}.$$

It follows then that

$$\operatorname{Corr}(x - \xi - u_1, y - \xi - u_1) - \operatorname{Corr}(x - \xi, y - \xi) > 0$$

if and only if

$$\frac{\sigma_{u_1}^2}{\sqrt{a_2 a_3 + \sigma_{u_1}^2 (a_2 + a_3) + \sigma_{u_1}^4}} > \frac{a_1}{\sqrt{a_2 a_3}} \left[1 - \frac{1}{\sqrt{1 + \sigma_{u_1}^2 \dfrac{a_2 + a_3}{a_2 a_3} + \dfrac{\sigma_{u_1}^4}{a_2 a_3}}} \right]. \tag{7c}$$

This could conceivably account for the typically smaller R^2 in the output per unit of labor-wage relation. Similarly, we could account for the relatively smaller estimates of the elasticity of substitution parameter obtained from that same relation in terms of errors of specification resulting from the incorrect assumption of perfect competition. Thus, suppose that the marginal productivity condition is in fact

$$\frac{\partial Q}{\partial L} = \frac{1 + \epsilon}{1 + \eta} W = a(t) W \tag{8}$$

where ϵ and η are the inverses, respectively, of the elasticity of the supply of labor and the elasticity of the demand for output, indexed for convenience by t.

Then the correct form of (5) would be using (3),

$$\frac{Q}{L} = B^{-\delta\sigma} a_2^{-\sigma} a(t)^\sigma W^\sigma = B^* a(t)^\sigma W^\sigma \tag{9}$$

where

$$\sigma = \frac{1}{1 - \delta}.$$

By a slight adaptation [2] of the results given by Theil [3] the specification bias in the estimation of σ from (5) when (9) is in fact true is given by,

$$\text{specification bias} = b\sigma \tag{10}$$

where b is the slope of the regression line of $a(t)$ on W. If b is negative, as would be the case where market imperfections are negatively correlated with the wage rate, then it follows that the results of the first set of estimates displayed in table 1 are negatively biased. Since there is very little intuitive insight into the nature of the errors of observation referring to the capital series (this will become sufficiently clear when the nature of the sample is explained) it follows that a promising line of attack would be the investigation of the pos-

[2] This can easily be accomplished as follows. Let the true relation be

$$Y = X\beta + u$$

where

Y is $T \times 1$, X is $T \times k$, and u is $T \times 1$, u being a random vector. Suppose we estimate

$$\beta_1 = (X_1' X_1)^{-1} X_1' y$$

where X_1 is defined by $X = (X_1, x_1)$, x_1 being a column vector. Then $E(\beta_1) = [I, (X_1' X_1)^{-1} X_1' x_1] \beta$.

Here $\beta = \begin{bmatrix} \ln B^* \\ \sigma \\ \sigma \end{bmatrix}$ and x_1 is the unobservable vector,

$$x_1 = \begin{pmatrix} a(1) \\ a(2) \\ \cdot \\ \cdot \\ \cdot \\ a(T) \end{pmatrix}$$

[3] H. Theil, *Economic Forecasts and Public Policy*, second ed. (Amsterdam: North Holland, 1961).

sibility of misspecification due to the perfect competition assumption of Arrow, et al. If this is to be questioned, however, then it becomes interesting to inquire as to whether market imperfections are associated also with nonconstant returns to scale. Thus, it would be desirable to construct a model in which perfect competition and constant returns to scale are not assumed, but rather become testable hypotheses. To this task we now turn.

II The Model

Suppose that for some specified economic unit the following relationship exists among wages, output, and labor:

$$W = A\,Q^{\beta} L^{\gamma}\,. \tag{11}$$

It is assumed that the unit behaves as if it were a profit maximizer, but that the markets in which it operates are not perfect. It is further assumed that the production function characterizing the unit is homogeneous of degree h. Thus:

$$Q = F\,(K,L) = L^{h} F\left(\frac{K}{L}, 1\right) = L^{h} f\left(\frac{K}{L}\right). \tag{12}$$

Then the factor market equilibrium condition is given by

$$\frac{\partial Q}{\partial L} = W\left(\frac{1+\epsilon}{1+\eta}\right)$$
$$\frac{\partial Q}{\partial K} = r\left(\frac{1+\epsilon_1}{1+\eta}\right) \tag{13}$$

where η, ϵ, and ϵ_1 are, respectively, inverses of the elasticity of demand for output, supply of labor, and supply of capital. Because of the product exhaustion requirement, we must have

$$rK + WL = Q. \tag{14}$$

But using (13) we find that (14) implies

$$\left(\frac{1+\eta}{1+\epsilon}\right)\frac{\partial Q}{\partial L}L + \left(\frac{1+\eta}{1+\epsilon_1}\right)\frac{\partial Q}{\partial K}K = Q. \tag{14a}$$

On the other hand, homogeneity of degree h implies

$$\frac{\partial Q}{\partial K}K + \frac{\partial Q}{\partial L}L = h\,Q. \tag{14b}$$

From (14a) and (14b) we must have

$$\frac{\partial Q}{\partial L}\frac{L}{Q} = \frac{1+\eta}{1+\epsilon}\cdot\frac{\epsilon-\epsilon_1}{h+h\,\eta-1-\epsilon_1}. \tag{14c}$$

But (14c) implies that the elasticity of output with respect to labor is completely specified if we specify, say, constant elasticity of demand (for output) and supply functions (for capital and labor). Partly to avoid this rigidity, we shall specify that not both equations of (13) hold. In particular, we shall assume that only the first equation holds. This has the interpretation that capital behaves independently and therefore, that the economic unit "optimizes" only with respect to labor. Further, the distribution theory envisaged in this model is a residual one; the wage bill is essentially determined by the first equation in (13) and capital gets what is left over.

The problem now is to determine, from the foregoing assumptions the precise functional form of F. At this level of generality, however, the problem is not manageable; hence, we must impose some minimal restrictions on the parameters of (11). First rewrite the equation as

$$W = A\left(\frac{Q}{L^{h}}\right)^{\beta} L^{\gamma+\beta h} \tag{15}$$

and as a matter of notation put

$$s(h) = \gamma + h\,\beta. \tag{15a}$$

Now it is desirable that our model be reducible to that of Arrow, et al. whenever $h = 1$ and the perfect competition assumption holds. This requires that

$$s(1) = 0. \tag{15b}$$

Hence, if to s we give the simplest possible functional form we obtain:

$$s(h) = h - 1. \tag{16}$$

Now as a matter of notation put

$$y = \frac{Q}{L^{h}},\quad x = \frac{K}{L},\quad \frac{1+\epsilon}{1+\eta} = a(t) \tag{17}$$

where t is an index to be interpreted later. In this notation our system could be written as follows:

$$w = A y^{\beta} \qquad L^{h-1} \tag{18}$$
$$y = f(x) \tag{19}$$
$$\frac{\partial Q}{\partial L} = a(t)W. \tag{20}$$

Writing $\frac{\partial Q}{\partial L}$ in terms of f and using (18) and (20) we have:

$$hy - y'x = A\,a(t)\,y^{\beta}. \tag{21}$$

This yields

$$\frac{dx}{x} = \frac{dy}{hy - A\,a(t)y^{\beta}} = \frac{dy}{hy} +$$

$$+\frac{\frac{A}{h^2}a(t)y^{\beta-2}\,dy}{1-\frac{A}{h}a(t)y^{\beta-1}}. \tag{21a}$$

Integrating both sides we obtain:

$$\ln x + c_1 = \frac{1}{h}\ln y - \frac{1}{h(\beta-1)}$$
$$\ln\left[1-\frac{A}{h}a(t)y^{\beta-1}\right] \tag{21b}$$

where c_1 is a constant of integration. Now multiply through by $h(\beta-1)$ and exponentiate to find

$$c_2\,x^{h(\beta-1)} = \frac{y^{\beta-1}}{1-\frac{A}{h}(t)\,y^{\beta-1}} \tag{21c}$$

where $c_2 = e^{h(\beta-1)c_1}$.

This can be simplified to

$$Q = C_3\left[K^{h\delta}+\frac{C_2A}{h}a(t)\,L^{h\delta}\right]^{1/\delta} \tag{22}$$

where

$$C_3 = C_2^{-\frac{1}{\delta}},\ \delta = 1-\beta.$$

Note further that (22) can be written in standard form as

$$Q = C(t)\,[a_1(t)K^{h\delta}+a_2(t)L^{h\delta}]^{1/\delta} \tag{22a}$$

where

$$a_1(t)+a_2(t) = 1,\ a_1(t) = \frac{h}{h+C_2A\,a(t)},$$
$$a_2(t) = \frac{C_2A\,a(t)}{H+C_2A\,a(t)}$$

and

$$C(t) = C_3[a_1(t)]^{-1/\delta}.$$

For the moment neglect questions of interpretation and regard (22a) as a production function. Some of its properties are of interest. Clearly the function is homogeneous of degree h in K and L. The elasticity of substitution between capital and labor is given by

$$\sigma = -\frac{d\ln\left(\frac{K}{L}\right)}{d\ln M} = \frac{1}{1-h\delta} = -\frac{1}{\gamma}. \tag{23}$$

For (22a) to serve as a plausible production function its isoquants must be convex. The equation for an isoquant is given (conveniently) by

$$\left[\frac{Q}{C(t)}\right]^{\delta} = a_1(t)\,K^{h\delta}+a_2(t)\,L^{h\delta} = \text{constant}. \tag{24}$$

Convexity for twice differentiable functions is equivalent to

$$\frac{d^2K}{dL^2} > 0. \tag{24a}$$

By implicit differentiation one finds

$$\frac{d^2K}{dL^2} = -\frac{a_1(t)}{a_2(t)}(h\delta-1)\left(\frac{L}{K}\right)^{h\delta}\frac{1}{L}$$
$$\left[\frac{K}{L}-\frac{dK}{dL}\right]. \tag{24b}$$

Since $\frac{dK}{dL} \leqq 0$, it follows that $\frac{d^2K}{dL^2} \geqq 0$ implies

$$h\delta \leqq 1. \tag{24c}$$

For strict convexity we require

$$h\delta < 1. \tag{24d}$$

Hence, in our case, the elasticity of substitution parameter is a constant and its admissible range is given by the positive half-line, i.e., $\sigma \in (0, \infty)$. Holding the homogeneity parameter fixed, the following limiting processes are of interest.

$$\lim_{\sigma\downarrow 0} Q = \lim_{\delta\to-\infty} Q. \tag{25}$$

Applying L'Hospital's rule we easily find

$$\lim_{\delta\to-\infty} Q = C(t)\min[K^h, L^h]. \tag{25a}$$

Further

$$\lim_{\sigma\to 0} Q = \lim_{\delta\to\frac{1}{h}} Q = C(t)[a_1(t)\,K + a_2(t)\,L]^h. \tag{25b}$$

Finally, the case $\sigma \to 1$ is of some interest since the well-known Cobb-Douglas function has the property of unitary elasticity of substitution. We have

$$\lim_{\sigma\to 1} Q = \lim_{\delta\to 0} Q = A(t)\,K^{ha_1(t)}\,L^{ha_2(t)}. \tag{25c}$$

All these limiting forms are sufficiently well-known as not to require further comment.

It may seem curious that we have conducted our limit processes while holding h fixed. This has two motivations. First note that because the substitution parameter, σ, depends on both h and δ, it is not possible to determine the limiting form of the production function unless we explicitly specify the manner in which both h and δ behave. Second, holding h fixed has the following interpretation. The elasticity of substitution parameter indexes the "ease" with which capital can be substituted for labor. Now, in the short run, at least one of the factors (labor) cannot be increased, or at any rate, if we are speaking aggregatively, capital can typically increase more rapidly than labor. From this point of view, the parameter of interest in indexing the ease of substitution is not the homogeneity parameter, h, but rather δ. Note also that the latter is related to the partial elasticity of the wage with respect to output, β, as can be readily seen from (11) and the definition of δ since $\delta = 1 - \beta$. Typically we would expect $0 < \beta < 1$, so that if δ is "large," then β is "small." If a transition from a state of "low" to a state of "high" capital intensity can be made easily, then the increase in the wage accompanying a given increase in output will not be large. Hence, in this context, the choice of δ is a natural one in indexing the elasticity of substitution.

We now return to the question of interpretation of the function in (22) or (22a). Strictly speaking, it cannot be interpreted as a production function of the neoclassical variety since it contains an element, α (t), which originates with the institutional structure of the market and not with the technological conditions of production. It is easily seen that this prevents the identification of the (technologically determined) coefficient of labor in (22) which, as it appears there, is confounded by the institutional aspects discussed above.

Thus, only with this reservation can we interpret (22) or (22a) as functions between output and factors of production rationalizing the postulated (or observed) relation between wages, output, labor, and the assumed institutional structure of the market. There is another bit of interpretation to be made. The ratio of demand and supply elasticities, is to serve as an "index of imperfection." Now the index t could be interpreted variously depending on the sample at hand. Thus if we are dealing with time series we could interpret t as time. The nature of the test would then be simply to test the hypothesis that market imperfections simply depend on the period of observation. Or if the sample is a cross-sectional one, then t could be interpreted as the rank of the size of the given observation, that is, the hypothesis to be tested is that market imperfections faced by the various units differ, depending upon their size. In both cases, the notion is that the demand (for output) and supply (of labor) facing the economic units are functions of constant (price) elasticity, although less restrictive rationalizations are possible. Finally, it should be pointed out that the derivation of the function in (22) and (22a) shows how difficult it is to distinguish (nonneutral or neutral) technical change from market imperfections.

To summarize: A production function like (22) or (22a) will lead to a Cobb-Douglas-type relation between wages, output, and labor which is not homogeneous of degree zero in output and labor except in the linear homogeneous case. Conversely, a relation like (11), together with the assumptions stated in (12) and (13) and as elaborated upon in this section, will yield the production function (22) or (22a) provided that (16) holds as well.

III

A. Estimation and Testing Procedure

Both the admission of the term α (t) in (20) and the form given to the production function in (12) permit us to test the two basic assumptions of Arrow, et al., that markets are competitive and that production takes place under constant returns to scale.

As the preceding discussion implies, the first step is the estimation [4] of the parameters of (11)

$$W = A\,Q^{\beta}\,L^{\gamma} \tag{11}$$

under the constraint that

$$\gamma = h\delta - 1. \tag{26}$$

Hence we have the following estimators for δ and h.

$$\hat{\delta} = 1 - \hat{\beta}, \; \hat{h} = \frac{1+\hat{\gamma}}{1-\hat{\beta}} \tag{27}$$

where $\hat{\beta}$ and $\hat{\gamma}$ are the least squares estimators of β and h, respectively, obtained from the logarithmic transform of (11). If we give a definite functional form to α (t), say,

$$\alpha\,(t) = a_0 + a_1\,t \tag{28}$$

then we can test for the validity of the per-

[4] Since we are interested, *inter alia*, in the elasticity of substitution parameter $\sigma = -\frac{1}{\gamma}$ it seems preferable to derive an estimator for this parameter by using the regression $\ln L = -\frac{1}{\gamma}\ln A + \frac{1}{\gamma}\ln W - \frac{\beta}{\gamma}\ln Q$. Since L, W, and Q are jointly dependent variables the regression will simply yield the conditional expectation of L given W and Q. The parameter estimators will be subject to simultaneous equation bias.

fect competition assumption by testing whether $a_1 = 0$. Clearly this is not always a conclusive test, since if the hypothesis is accepted, this fact does not necessarily imply the absence of imperfections. It could simply mean that there has been no change in the degree of imperfections, i.e., that imperfections do not vary significantly with t, in whatever manner t has been interpreted.

For the purposes of this test it is best to employ functional form (22). Making use of the estimators obtained in the first stage we have

$$Q^{\hat{\delta}} = C_3^{\hat{\delta}} K^{\hat{h}\hat{\delta}} + \frac{C_3^{\hat{\delta}} C_2 A a_0}{h} L^{\hat{h}\hat{\delta}} + C_3^{\hat{\delta}} C_2 A a_1 t L^{\hat{h}\hat{\delta}} \qquad (29)$$

or

$$y = d_1 z_1 + d_2 z_2 + d_3 z_3 \qquad (29a)$$

where the notation has the obvious interpretation. Then the test $a_1 = 0$ is equivalent to the test $d_3 = 0$ since we do not admit $C_2 = 0$ or $A = 0$.

To summarize: From the first stage we obtain estimators of the elasticity of substitution and homogeneity parameters. In the case of the latter, the usual tests of significance are not readily applicable because of the rational operation involved in its derivation from $\hat{\gamma}$ and β. One could of course obtain an approximate form of its variance by using a Taylor's expansion.

In the second phase the estimator of d_3 permits us to test directly the perfect competition assumption. In both cases, the cogency with which we can assert our conclusions is impaired by the presence of simultaneous equation bias.

B. Empirical Implementation

Here we apply this procedure to United States Manufacturing two-digit industries.

The sample for two-digit industries is a cross-sectional one and for this reason it requires some explanation.

The unit of observation is the quadruple, value added (output), wage bill, number of employees, and (net) book value of the capital stock for a given industry in a given state.

Hence, the application is to an industry level production function. Thus, we require the assumption that for each industry the production function is identical between any two states. But we also need the subsidiary assumption that factor prices, or rather factor price ratios vary sufficiently from state to state to permit identification of the postulated function.

The data are obtained from the Census of Manufactures [5] and pertain to 1957.

Value added in the Census usage includes depreciation and is thus a reasonable approximation to the output data required in this type of estimation. The number of employees series refers to the average number of employees reported and hence may be an overstatement of the true labor employment series in the case where part-time employment practices abound.

The capital stock series consists of the net book value of the capital stock as of December 31, 1956 plus (gross) investment in 1957. It is otherwise computed in a straightforward fashion from the given series on gross book value of the capital stock, accumulated depreciation, and investment expenditures. No attempt has been made to express the series in common units — constant dollars. Here, the problem is essentially that of differing investment (time) profiles in the various states — for given industries.

In principle, successive net investment figures should be deflated by appropriate (but which?) price series and then accumulated on some benchmark. Such benchmarks do not yet exist, and furthermore, it is not clear, without further information on the composition of investment, what are the appropriate deflators. On the other hand if the same industry has had a more or less similar history of development in the various states then using the book value of capital stock will not produce any serious distortions. The only other available alternative would have been to use the gross value of the capital stock. This of course would err in the direction of overstating the capital stock and giving disproportionately high weight to older industries. Clearly neither of the two possible alternatives is the "correct" series. None the less, it was felt that the net series (including current investment) was closer to the "truth" than either of the two other alternatives.

[5] *United States Census of Manufactures*, I (Washington: Government Printing Office, 1958).

From these series the average wage was computed simply by dividing the wage bill by the number of employees series.

We give in table 2, the point estimates of the elasticity of substitution and homogeneity parameters. It should be pointed out, that while the homogeneity estimator is obtained from equation (11) using the relations of (27) the elasticity of substitution parameter is estimated from

$$\ln L = A^* - \frac{1}{\gamma} \ln W + \frac{\beta}{\gamma} \ln Q. \qquad (30)$$

The reason is, essentially, that while an estimator of the elasticity of substitution parameter could be obtained from (11) this would require inverting the estimator of γ. In the case of small point estimators with sizeable standard errors this would lead to instability in the estimators of the elasticity of substitution. Hence the alternative procedure indicated in (30) was employed.

TABLE 2. — ELASTICITIES OF SUBSTITUTION AND RETURNS TO SCALE IN TWO-DIGIT MANUFACTURING INDUSTRIES, UNITED STATES, 1957

$$Q = C(t)\,[\alpha_1(t)\,K^{h\delta} + d_2(t)\,L^{h\delta}]^{1/\delta}$$

Industrial Classification	$\sigma = \left(-\frac{1}{\gamma}\right)$	R^2	h
20	.4685 (.1423)	.9838	1.0443
22	.9360 (.1674)	.9947	.9968
23	1.1693 (.2066)	.9847	1.0293
24	1.1085 (.1165)	.9731	1.2182
25	1.0010 (.1587)	.9924	1.0168
26	1.4699 (.4882)	.9707	1.0403
27	.5621 (.1987)	.9968	1.0224
28	.5056 (.2665)	.9705	1.0423
29	.3336 (.8700)	.9652	1.0724
30	1.9839 (.2902)	.9917	1.0919
31	.8530 (.2623)	.9851	1.0108
32	1.0625 (.2319)	.9852	1.0886
33	.9445 (.5997)	.9510	1.0295
34	.4006 (.2060)	.9937	1.0361
35	.0504 (.3577)	.9929	1.0288
36	.1948 (.3908)	.9866	1.0557
37	1.7754 (.8867)	.9763	1.0457

Several remarks are pertinent with respect to table 2. First, note that the homogeneity point estimates are nearly uniformly, but only moderately, greater than unity. But while they suggest the presence of increasing returns to scale their evidence is not very cogent. Thus the hypothesis of homogeneity of degree one cannot be conclusively rejected — nor for that matter the hypothesis of homogeneity of degree 1.02, or 1.04, etc. Second, note that the two-digit industries are not homogeneous relative to their elasticity of substitution parameters. They do exhibit significant variabilities. A comparison of the estimates in table 2 with those in table 1 reveals that the former estimates are qualitatively more akin to those of table 1 as derived from the output per unit capital — rental relationship, although of course there is no exact correspondence between the results reported in table 2 and either of the two sets presented in table 1. Third, there is another significant aspect of the results of table 2. Note that the elasticity of substitution estimates fall naturally into two groups. Group I consists of industries 28, 29, 33, 34, 35, 36, and 37 for which the elasticity of substitution appears to be insignificantly different from zero. Thus it appears that this group is characterized by quite low elasticities of substitution.

Group II consists of industries 20, 22, 23, 24, 25, 26, 27, 30, 31, and 32 for which the elasticity of substitution parameter appears to be significantly greater than zero. Within this group industry 30 apparently exhibits an elasticity of substitution which is significantly greater than unity.

A reference to table 1 shows that group I consists of the following industries: Chemicals and Allied Products, Petroleum and Coal Products, Primary Metal Industries, Fabricated Metal Products, Machinery except Electrical, and Electrical Machinery and Transportation Equipment.

It appears then that the low elasticity of substitution group is the group of investment-oriented industries. On the other hand, group II consists of: Food and Kindred Products, Textile Mill Products, Apparel and Related Products, Lumber and Wood Products, Furniture and Fixtures, Pulp, Paper, and Allied Products, Printing and Publishing, Rubber Products, Leather and Leather Goods, and Stone, Clay and Glass Products. Hence, the higher elasticity of substitution group appears to be the group of consumer-oriented industries.

The simple generalization to be obtained from the first stage of our estimation is that the two-digit manufacturing industries studied here exhibit (possibly) moderately increasing returns to scale and that consumer-oriented industries tend to be characterized by higher elasticities of substitution than do investment-oriented industries. Before we conclude this section we should point out that the usual tests of significance of a coefficient, applied above — essentially the two- or one-tailed t-tests — cannot be considered to be fully valid. In the first place, it is only by invoking certain strong forms of the central limit theorem that we can claim that the elasticity of substitution estimators are normally distributed. In addition, there is the problem of simultaneous equation bias to contend with. For this reason, it is rather pointless to speak rigorously of hypothesis rejection at specified levels of significance. None the less, the impression is unmistakable from table 2 that a clear cut distinction must be made between consumer and investment-oriented industries.

The second phase of the empirical implementation involves a further test of the perfect competition assumption. Recall the discussion of section III A and, in particular, equation (29a) whose parameters we are to estimate. In this particular application the index t was defined as follows: First notice that

$$a(t) = \frac{1 + \epsilon(t)}{1 + \eta(t)}. \tag{31}$$

where $\eta(t)$ and $\epsilon(t)$ are the inverses of the elasticities of demand for output and supply of labor, respectively.

Since we are dealing with a cross-sectional sample, and since there is no compelling reason to suppose that a given industry producing in state i sells only in state i, the parameter $\eta(t)$ can best be assumed constant among observations pertaining to the same industry in different states. This is so because it is permissible to assume that all such industries sell in essentially the same (national) market. But now we are only left with the elasticity of supply of labor parameter.

While mobility of labor across state boundaries is not entirely absent, it does not occur on such a scale as to make untenable the assumption that industries operate essentially with the supply of labor available in a given state. This of course is not quite so in the case of very highly skilled employees such as engineers, scientists, or highly ranked business executives. None the less, the latter group can be neglected at least as a first approximation. This being the case then, it is quite reasonable to make the elasticity of the supply of labor available to an industry within a state depend upon the relative importance of the industry as an employer. Hence, we have taken the index t to measure the proportion of a state's labor force employed by the industry in question.

Thus, if industry i employs Lij workers in state j and Lj is the latter's labor force employed in (total) manufacturing, then t indexes the rank of $\frac{Lij}{Lj}$.

The form given to $a(t)$ in equation (28), that is,

$$a(t) = a_0 + a_1 t \tag{28}$$

can be rationalized through an (incomplete) Taylor's series expansion

$$a(t) = \frac{1 + \epsilon(t)}{1 + \eta} \approx \frac{1 + \epsilon_0}{1 + \eta} + \frac{\epsilon_1}{1 + \eta} t \tag{32}$$

where

$$\epsilon(t) \approx \epsilon_0 + \epsilon_1 t. \tag{32a}$$

Remembering that $\epsilon(t)$ is the inverse of the elasticity of the supply of labor such expansion would be plausibly accurate, if the elasticity in question were rather small, i.e., if labor is nearly inelastically offered.

With these preliminaries, we present in table 3. the results of the second phase of estimation.

The results presented above contain about five cases in which the coefficient of capital is statistically insignificant. Taken at face value

TABLE 3. — IMPERFECTION PARAMETER IN TWO-DIGIT MANUFACTURING INDUSTRIES, UNITED STATES, 1957

$$Q^{\hat{\delta}} = d_1 L^{\hat{h}\hat{\delta}} + d_2 K^{\hat{h}\hat{\delta}} + d_3 t L^{\hat{h}\hat{\delta}}$$

Industrial Classification	d_1	d_2	d_3	R^2
20	1.5290	.5170	.0003	.9862
	(.3069)	(.1387)	(.0028)	
22	1.4068	.1722	.0143	.9960
	(.1622)	(.1115)	(.0026)	
23	1.3645	.9063	−.0061	.9860
	(.1645)	(1.2886)	(.0058)	
24	.3535	.2799	.0026	.9522
	(.0805)	(.0469)	(.0014)	
25	1.7447	.0550	.0066	.9799
	(.2191)	(.2040)	(.0036)	
26	2.9711	.3156	−.0034	.9893
	(.2622)	(.0337)	(.0082)	
27	2.2973	−.0068	−.0068	.9944
	(.1567)	(1.1251)	(.0040)	
28	4.5273	.3501	−.0127	.9811
	(.3719)	(.0556)	(.0110)	
29	6.5614	.0592	−.1197	.9831
	(1.2574)	(.0816)	(.0622)	
30	1.1662	.3920	−.0092	.9883
	(.2445)	(.1356)	(.0091)	
31	1.9138	.1601	.0089	.9855
	(.1617)	(1.2286)	(.0088)	
32	1.3508	.2104	.0056	.9900
	(.1232)	(.0518)	(.0034)	
33	4.4035	.2759	.0080	.9959
	(.3938)	(.0751)	(.0130)	
34	3.0573	.1774	−.0051	.9947
	(.2602)	(.1168)	(.0058)	
35	5.6510	.2858	−.0163	.9884
	(.2252)	(.0781)	(.0071)	
36	1.9933	.9078	.0562	.9942
	(.3852)	(.2078)	(.0143)	
37	3.9708	.2072	−.0339	.9924
	(.1703)	(1.0523)	(.0128)	

this is an unacceptable result, for which the only admissible interpretation is that this particular functional form does not adequately describe the productive process of the industry in question. Statistical insignificance is most cogently suggested for Furniture and Fixtures (25), Printing and Publishing (27), Petroleum and Coal Products (29), and Leather and Leather Goods (31). In the case of industry (29), it was already determined that the elasticity of substitution was low (the estimate for this parameter was insignificantly different from zero) and hence this is not an unexpected result. But the more relevant results of table 3 are those pertaining to the estimators of d_3, the imperfection parameter. Consider first the industries of group I, that is, 28, 29, 33, 34, 35, 36, and 37. There the imperfection parameter appears to be significantly different from zero (at the ten per cent level of significance) for industries 29, 35, 36, and 37. For the industries of group II, the parameter appears to be significantly different from zero (at the ten per cent level of significance) in the case of industries 22, 24, and 25.

The particular sign of the imperfection coefficient is of no great significance if we remember the interpretation given to a_1, of equation (28) in (32a).

Hence, as a gross generalization, we can derive the following proposition from our empirical results.

Consumption-oriented industries tend to be characterized by relatively high elasticities of substitution (between capital and labor) and to be relatively free from market imperfections.

On the other hand investment-oriented industries tend to be characterized by relatively low elasticities of substitution and to operate in a market environment which is not free of imperfections. To this we may add the subsidiary conclusion that the constant elasticity of substitution production function, as developed herein, does not describe uniformly well the productive process of the (two-digit) industries considered. Clearly, these results are to be understood with the qualifications imposed by data inadequacies and a not very rigorous statistical technique.

[28]

A COMMENT ON CES PRODUCTION FUNCTIONS

Phoebus J. Dhrymes

In his note concerning my paper [2] Griliches presents some empirical results derived from his work on a related matter [4], the main thrust of which is that they do not yield a clear-cut dichotomy regarding the size of the elasticity of substitution parameter as between consumer and producer oriented two-digit manufacturing industries.

Part of my results (table 1) quoted by Griliches are designed to show that if one estimates the elasticity of substitution parameter from the output per unit of labor-wage regression one gets one estimate. If one performs another perfectly admissible regression using the output per unit of capital-renal relation then one gets another. The two estimators turn out to be quite divergent. It is the case, in addition, that the explanatory power of the two relations is markedly different. This was the result obtained with respect to two-digit manufacturing industries using a cross-section sample by states, based on the 1958 *Census of Manufactures.*

Thus, the results of table 1 have the sole purpose of pointing up a problem and are in no way to be interpreted as "my estimates" of the elasticity of substitution parameter. In the face of these results one is confronted with a substantial divergence of conclusions depending on which regression one chooses to perform and the matter cannot be logically left unresolved. One, then, has several alternatives. Thus, one might estimate my equations (5) and (5a) simultaneously, imposing the relevant restrictions on the parameters. This necessitates a nonlinear estimation computer program which was not available to me when this research was carried out (Spring 1963) but is available now [3].

The alternative I chose in my paper [2] was to derive a somewhat more general model than that of Arrow, et al., [1], which allows one to test their two fundamental assumptions, viz., that of perfect competition and homogeneity of degree one. My broad (and qualitative) generalizations about the elasticity of substitution characteristics of various industrial groupings in United States manufacturing were based on my table 2, which presents the results of estimation in the context of my generalized version of the Arrow et al. model.

In addition, estimation in the context of the generalized model yields some evidence that the perfect competition assumption may be inappropriate for certain industries, although this is admittedly highly tenuous evidence.

What impresses me in connection with the estimation of the substitution parameter is the proximity rather than the dissimilarity between my results and those of Griliches. Thus it is only in five cases (industries 20, 30, 34, 35 and 36) that Griliches' estimates differ from mine by more than one standard deviation, and in at least two of these the relevance of the CES function as a rationalization of the data is highly questionable (industries 35 and 36).

Finally, I would like to add two specific comments. One concerns Griliches' point 2. In this he dismisses too lightly the possibility of nonconstant returns to scale. While it is true that my estimators of h (the homogeneity parameter) are probably not "significantly" different from unity, also, they are probably not "significantly" different from 1.02 or 1.06. Thus, one cannot really focus on unity in order to serve one's convenience. Moreover, Griliches himself in his point 4 cites approvingly the fact that my estimates of the homogeneity parameter are "very close" to his own; his estimators do indicate mildly increasing returns to scale. It is very gratifying that my estimation techniques were sensitive enough to yield homogeneity parameters similar to the ones obtained by Griliches, who uses an admittedly somewhat better measure of the variables by employing not state aggregates, but rather state aggregates divided by the number of establishments per state.

Further, in this same point Griliches raises the question as to what is the *right way* of estimating the elasticity of substitution and returns to scale parameter. Of course the right way would be to estimate them in the context of an expanded simultaneous equation model. I think it would be granted that in this context, output, labor and the wage rate are jointly dependent variables and as I remark in my footnote 4 what we are estimating is the conditional expectation of one of these variables given the other two. There is no pretense that the estimators are free of simultaneous equation problems. In one case, it is more meaningful in terms of parameter estimation to estimate from one relation; in another, it is more convenient to use a different one. So this point becomes crystal clear, consider the trivial but illustrative case of the density of two jointly normal variables, say x and y.

Now their conditional expectations are given by

$$E(x \mid y) = \mu_x + \frac{\sigma_{xy}}{\sigma_x^2}(y - \mu_y) \quad (1)$$

$$E(y \mid x) = \mu_y + \frac{\sigma_{yx}}{\sigma_y^2}(x - \mu_x) \quad (2)$$

If we are interested in $\frac{\sigma_{xy}}{\sigma^2}$ then we shall obviously use (1), *we would not use* (2) and then estimate separately σ_y^2 and σ_x^2 say, by s_x^2, s_y^2 and then obtain an estimate of $\frac{\sigma_{xy}}{\sigma_x^2}$ as

$$\left(\frac{\hat{\sigma}_{xy}}{\hat{\sigma}_y^2}\right) \cdot \frac{s_y^2}{s_x^2}$$

This is precisely the rationale involved in obtaining h and σ from two different regressions. When operating with small samples it is unwise to obtain estimators of parameters of interest by subjecting estimators of subsidiary parameters to a series of multiplications and divisions. The stability of the resulting estimators would be too sensitive to small variations in the subsidiary estimators.

Concering Griliches' point 3, while I would not wish to be dogmatic about the verbal form of my characterization of the elasticity of substitution parameters of "consumer" and "investment" oriented industries, the fact remains that on the average these two groups of industries display a perceptible divergence in their elasticity of substitution parameters, and my generalization although not absolutely correct, provides a useful way of summarizing my results.[1] Further and more careful investigation may upset this generalization, but this cannot be claimed solely on Griliches' results which embody the assumption of constant returns to scale, an assumption that his subsequent investigation in (4) does not support.

REFERENCES

[1] Arrow, K. J., H. B. Chenery, B. S. Minhas and R. M. Solow, "Capital-Labor Substitution and Economic Efficiency," this REVIEW, XLIII (Aug. 1961), 225.

[2] Dhrymes, P. J., "Some Extension and Tests for the CES Class of Production Functions," this REVIEW, XLVII (Nov. 1965), 357.

[3] Eisenpress, H. and J. L. Greenstadt, "Non-Linear Full Information Estimation" (mimeo).

[4] Griliches, Z., "Production Functions in Manufacturing: Some Preliminary Results," in NBER, *Production Relations, Studies in Income and Wealth*, vol. 31, forthcoming.

[1] In connection with Griliches' footnote 6, I should point out that the difference in the mean elasticity of substitution parameter for the two groups of industries I consider is somewhat more significant than might be indicated by considering the standard errors of the individual estimators, for if the variances of the k (mutually independent) random variables x_i are given by σ_i, then the variance of their mean is given by $\sigma^2 = \frac{\sum_{i=1}^{k} \sigma_i^2}{k^2}$ and this is certainly not greater than $\frac{\max \sigma_i^2}{k}$.

[29]

Reprinted from
THE REVIEW OF ECONOMICS AND STATISTICS
Published by Harvard University
Copyright, 1970, by the President and Fellows of Harvard College
Vol. LII, No. 1, February 1970

ELASTICITIES OF SUBSTITUTION FOR TWO-DIGIT MANUFACTURING INDUSTRIES: A CORRECTION

Phoebus J. Dhrymes and Paul Zarembka *

Sometime ago one of the authors, Dhrymes [3], presented estimates of the elasticities of substitution

* The first author has been supported in part by a Ford Foundation Faculty Research Fellowship. The second author has been supported by the Ford Foundation and the National Science Foundation under the Project for the Explanation and Optimization of Economic Growth, Institute of International Studies, University of California, Berkeley.

in two-digit manufacturing industries based on United States cross-sectional data, 1957. These estimates were quite incidental to the main thrust of that paper, and were only meant to illustrate the fact that if one estimates the elasticity from output per unit of labor-wage rate data and from output per unit of capital-rental data, one obtains quite

TABLE 1. — **ELASTICITIES OF SUBSTITUTION** ON TWO-DIGIT MANUFACTURING INDUSTRIES. UNITED STATES, 1957

$$Q = B[\alpha_1 K^\delta + \alpha_2 L^\delta]^{1/\delta}, \quad \sigma = \frac{1}{1-\delta}$$

$$\frac{Q}{L} = A^* W^{\sigma_1} \qquad \frac{Q}{K} = A^{**} P^{\sigma_2}$$

Industrial Classification	Industry	σ_1	R^2	σ_2	R^2	Number of Observations
20	Food and Kindred Products	0.8222 (0.1636)[a]	0.3966	0.7683 (0.0690)	0.7655	40
22	Textile Mill Products	0.9675 (0.1540)	0.6752	0.8128 (0.0953)	0.7930	21
23	Apparel and Related Products	1.2140 (0.1965)	0.6345	0.7681 (0.0763)	0.8216	24
24	Lumber and Wood Products	0.8750 (0.0694)	0.8833	0.6352 (0.0774)	0.7624	23
25	Furniture and Fixtures	1.1730 (0.1250)	0.8150	0.7427 (0.0309)	0.9665	22
26	Pulp, Paper and Products	1.4321 (0.4541)	0.2626	1.1558 (0.1088)	0.8012	30
27	Printing and Publishing	0.9980 (0.2061)	0.6436	0.8255 (0.0586)	0.9385	15
28	Chemicals and Products	0.8697 (0.2715)	0.2554	0.9059 (0.0481)	0.9219	32
29	Petroleum and Coal Products	0.8915 (0.5491)	0.1500	0.7702 (0.0370)	0.9666	17
30	Rubber Products	1.5625 (0.3491)	0.5888	0.8082 (0.0970)	0.8322	16
31	Leather and Leather Goods	0.8573 (0.2612)	0.4348	0.8170 (0.0825)	0.8751	16
32	Stone, Clay and Glass Products	1.0273 (0.1920)	0.5341	0.9682 (0.0646)	0.9000	27
33	Primary Metal Industries	0.7654 (0.3965)	0.1255	0.8360 (0.0963)	0.7436	28
34	Fabricated Metal Products	0.5570 (0.1982)	0.2043	0.7172 (0.0955)	0.6451	33
35	Machinery, Except Electrical	0.7468 (0.4662)	0.0843	0.3644 (0.1218)	0.2422	30
36	Electrical Machinery	0.5915 (0.3625)	0.1041	0.7294 (0.0596)	0.8667	25
37	Transportation Equipment	1.2428 (0.6367)	0.1281	0.6854 (0.1310)	0.5129	28

[a] Number in parenthesis is the standard error of the estimate.

different results. In view of the fact that both relations are equally admissible under the standard ACMS model [1], Dhrymes proceeded to obtain a generalization of the basic model which permits one to test the two maintained hypotheses of the ACMS framework, viz., constant returns to scale and perfect competition.

Subsequently, however, many authors have taken the estimates given in [3] and compared them with estimates given by other investigators whose primary interest was to estimate the elasticity of substitution parameter.

The second author, Zarembka [5], working on a related topic has computed estimates of the elasticities of substitution based on the same data as in [3] and has obtained appreciably different results. Joint investigation has led us to the discovery that the estimates reported in [3] were based not on the relationship claimed therein, i.e., on the regression of output per unit of labor (capital) on wage rates (rental cost), but rather the other way around.

The first author wishes to apologize for this error in the original paper and to offer this corrected version so that future comparisons with the work of other investigators will be based on accurate results. The following table reproduces correctly the type of information which table 1 of [3] sought to convey. The data are the same in both cases except for minor variations due to revisions.

A few minor comments on this set of results are appropriate. One point Dhrymes sought to make in [3] is also made here, viz., the two versions of the estimator of the elasticity of substitution give different results.[1] By and large the one based on the output per unit of capital-rental exhibits a smaller standard error and the corresponding regression yields, generally, a higher coefficient of determination (R^2). However, the point estimates of the elasticities of the labor-wage rate relation are higher than the capital-rental relation in all but four cases; in [3] the opposite result was reported since that paper was essentially estimating the reciprocal of the elasticity.

This much for the relation of these results to those of table 1 in [3]. Taking the present results as our frame of reference, there is the following interesting conclusion. If one wishes to test the hypothesis

H_0: The elasticity of substitution is unity as against the alternative.

H_1: The elasticity of substitution is not unity, the estimators based on the output per unit of labor-wage rate relation will generally accept H_0, while those based on the output per unit of capital-rental relation will generally reject H_0. However, although the first set of estimators generally accepts H_0, we might add that it would also accept the null hypothesis that $\sigma = 1.1$ or $\sigma = 0.8$ as against the alternative, $\sigma \neq 1.1$ or $\sigma \neq 0.8$ and so on. On the other hand, for the capital-rental relation the more specific hypothesis that the elasticity of substitution is less than unity will be accepted for the overwhelming majority of the industries reported here.

[1] One of the authors has commented on this and related aspects in [2], [4]. The other has investigated direct production function estimates of the elasticity in [5] as well as the labor-wage rate relation.

REFERENCES

[1] Arrow, K. J., H. B. Chenery, B. S. Minhas and R. M. Solow, "Capital-Labor Substitution and Economic Efficiency," this REVIEW, XLIII (Aug. 1961), 225–250.

[2] Dhrymes, P. J., "Adjustment Dynamics and the Estimation of the CES Class of Production Functions, 8, *International Economic Review* (June 1967), 209–217.

[3] Dhrymes, P. J., "Some Extensions and Tests of the CES Class of Production Functions," this REVIEW, XLVII (Nov. 1965), 357–366.

[4] Dhrymes, P. J., and M. Kurz, "Technology and Scale in Electricity Generation," *Econometrica*, XXXII (July 1964), 287–315.

[5] Zarembka, P., "On the Empirical Relevance of the CES Production Function," this REVIEW, LII (Feb. 1970), 47–53.

INTERNATIONAL ECONOMIC REVIEW
Vol. 8, No. 2, June, 1967

ADJUSTMENT DYNAMICS AND THE ESTIMATION OF THE CES CLASS OF PRODUCTION FUNCTIONS*

BY PHOEBUS J. DHRYMES[1]

1. PRELIMINARIES

EVER SINCE the production relation[2]

$$Q = \left[\sum_{i=1}^{n} \alpha_i X_i^{\beta}\right]^{1/\beta} \tag{1}$$

where $\alpha_i > 0$, $i = 1, 2, \cdots, n$, and $\beta \in (-\infty, 1)$, was first introduced by Arrow, Chenery, Minhas and Solow [1], hereafter referred to as ACMS, for the case $n = 2$ the problem of estimating the elasticity of substitution

$$\sigma = \frac{1}{1-\beta} \tag{1a}$$

was not given a statistically satisfactory solution.

ACMS correctly observed that if product and factor markets are perfectly competitive, then (1) implies the relation

$$\frac{Q}{L} = A_1 w^{\sigma} , \tag{2}$$

where $L = X_1$, $A_1 = \alpha_1^{1/(\beta-1)}$, and w is the product wage.

Apparently from (2) one can estimate α_1 and β. It is, however, equally apparent that (1) with the subsidiary institutional assumptions imply

$$\frac{Q}{K} = A_2 r^{\sigma} , \tag{2a}$$

where $K = X_2$, $A_2 = \alpha_2^{1/(\beta-1)}$, and r is the product rental.

Since generally we have, at least for U.S. Manufacturing components, data on Q, K, L, w, and we can thus derive the appropriate series for r, it follows that we have two estimators for σ, which need not turn out to be insignificantly different from each other. This fact was pointed out in the literature, e.g., in Dhrymes and Kurz [4]. Indeed if one estimates σ from (2) and (2a) one is likely to get diverging results. To this effect see Dhrymes [5].

The difficulty, of course, arises from not making use of the full production model in carrying out parameter estimation and focussing seriatim on particular aspects. By now numerous studies utilizing the CES function have been made with results that are hardly reconcilable with one another. It is

* Manuscript received October 15, 1965, revised January 31, 1966.

[1] The research on which this paper is based was in part carried out during the author's tenure of a John Simon Guggenheim Memorial Fellowship.

[2] We omit the inessential scale parameter multiplying the bracketed expression present in the usual formulations. This has the consequence of releasing the α_i from any constraint other than non-negativity.

certainly not our intention to review the pertinent literature since the excellent survey paper by Nerlove [12] does this quite adequately. We may, however, mention at least two attempts to estimate the CES function by fully utilizing a hypothesized production model, viz., Klein and Bodkin [9] and Kmenta [10]. The former estimates a long run production relation for the U.S. using, *inter alia*, a cost minimization model and fully taking into account the entire model with its attendant nonlinearities.

The latter does not contain any empirical results but estimates the parameter of the function by using a quadratic approximation to the CES about $\sigma = 1$, and thereafter taking fully into account the resulting production model. It is not clear, however, what the value of such approximation is given that nonlinear estimation computer programs are now fully operational and readily accessible. But beyond these purely statistical problems with the estimation of CES production function parameters, there are problems of economic interpretation.

The use of such econometric models requires the condition that our data pertain to an equilibrium situation, or very nearly so. If not, it is not clear that we estimate the parameters we claim to.

Although this condition is generally a dubious one, nonetheless it has been repeatedly employed by econometricians, including on occasion myself, because of its simplicity. There are of course exceptions. Thus, Brown and deCani [2] and Brown [3] employ a weighted sum of past factor prices. This may be rationalized in terms of a rejection of the equilibrium assertion, although it appears that the immediate motivation was related to entrepreneurial expectation regarding factor prices. In a different context, Dhrymes [6] abandons the equilibrium assertion in favor of an adjustment process applied to the problem of estimating a labor employment function.

Adjustment processes are not new to economics. Indeed, Haavelmo [8] puts forth such a view by making the rate of change of factor expenditure a simple function of the divergence between the (value) marginal product of the factor and the latter's price.

The well-known accelerator model of investment essentially makes use of the same formulation, although optimal capital stock is not always linked explicitly to a production function, and the objective is not to estimate the parameters of that function.

In what follows we shall see how such a formulation will greatly simplify the problem of constructing a logically consistent econometric model of production and allow the estimation of the parameters of the CES production function in a context that will free us from reliance on excessively long time series.

2. THE MODEL

Consider an economic unit characterized by

$$Q = \left[\sum_{i=1}^{n} \alpha_i X_i^{\beta}\right]^{1/\gamma} e^{u} , \tag{3}$$

where in addition to the other restrictions imposed in connection with (1) we must have that β and γ be of the same sign; u is a random variable. It may be verified that the elasticity of substitution in (3) is $1/(1-\beta)$ and that the function is homogeneous of degree β/γ in the X_i conditionally on u. Define

$$Q^* = Qe^{-u} \,. \tag{3a}$$

We may assume the unit to behave as if it minimized costs subject to the constraint in (3a). Thus, if desired, one might think of the model as envisaging the entrepreneurs as forming expectations about their output demand and then proceeding to determine optimal factor employment—given their expectations about factor prices—as if their production function were nonstochastic. This is similar but not identical to viewing entrepreneurs as maximizing expected profit.

The problem is then to minimize the Lagrangean

$$\Lambda = \sum_{i=1}^{n} p_i X_i + \lambda\left\{\hat{Q} - \left[\sum_{i=1}^{n} \alpha_i X_i^{\beta}\right]^{1/\gamma}\right\}, \tag{4}$$

where p_i is the price of the i-th factor, $\hat{Q}$ is expected output and λ the Lagrangean multiplier. First order conditions for a minimum are

$$p_i = \lambda\alpha_i \frac{\beta}{\gamma} X_i^{\beta-1}\hat{Q}^{1-\gamma} \qquad i = 1, 2, \cdots, n. \tag{4a}$$

Sufficient conditions for a minimum involve the negative definiteness of the Hessian of the function:[3]

$$F(X_1, \cdots, X_n) = \left[\sum_{i=1}^{n} a_i X_i^{\beta}\right]^{1/\gamma}. \tag{4b}$$

At any rate assuming these conditions and dividing each equation in (4a) by the n-th we find[4]

$$\frac{p_i}{p_n} = \frac{\alpha_i}{\alpha_n}\left(\frac{X_i}{X_n}\right)^{\beta-1} \qquad i = 1, 2, \cdots, n-1 \,. \tag{4c}$$

We further find

$$X_i = \left(\frac{\alpha_n}{\alpha_i}\right)^{1/(\beta-1)}\left(\frac{p_i}{p_n}\right)^{1/(\beta-1)} X_n \qquad i = 1, 2, \cdots, n-1 \,. \tag{4d}$$

Using the production constraint we find

$$\hat{Q} = \alpha_n^{-1/\beta}\left[\sum_{i=1}^{n}\left(\frac{\alpha_n}{\alpha_i}\right)^{1/(\beta-1)}\left(\frac{p_i}{p_n}\right)^{\beta/(\beta-1)}\right]^{1/\gamma} X_n^{\beta/\gamma} \,. \tag{4e}$$

Thus

[3] Actually we only need the Hessian of F to be negative definite under a (linear) constraint. This entails the existence of function $S(X_1, \cdots, X_n) = S(X)$ such that $[F_{ij}] + S(X)gg'$ is negative definite where $g = (F_1, F_2, \cdots, F_n)'$ is the gradient of F.

[4] Notice that (4c) holds exactly whether the constraint in (4) holds exactly, or we have assumed, or it is merely a constraint conditioned on u.

$$X_n = \alpha_n^{-1/\beta}\left[\sum_{i=1}^{n}\left(\frac{\alpha_n}{\alpha_i}\right)^{1/(\beta-1)}\left(\frac{p_i}{p_n}\right)^{\beta/(\beta-1)}\right]^{-1/\beta}\hat{Q}^{\gamma/\beta}\,. \tag{4f}$$

Finally, substituting in (4d) we have

$$X_k = \alpha_k^{-1/\beta}\left[\sum_{i=1}^{n}\left(\frac{\alpha_k}{\alpha_i}\right)^{1/(\beta-1)}\left(\frac{p_i}{p_k}\right)^{\beta/(\beta-1)}\right]^{-1/\beta}\hat{Q}^{\gamma/\beta} \qquad k = 1, 2, \cdots, n\,. \tag{4g}$$

Equations (4g) give the equilibrium levels of employment for the n factors of production. If we were to specify that we, in fact, observe equilibrium situations, then we could estimate the relevant parameters from (4g). The difficulty is that expected output, $\hat{Q}$, is not directly observable. We might specify some simple expectational pattern. Thus, if we are dealing with quarterly data, it may not be inappropriate to specify

$$\hat{Q}_t = Q_{t-1}\,. \tag{4h}$$

This would mean that again the system of equations in (4g) holds exactly. But then we face a totally inadmissible and patently false framework for estimation. We should further observe that the problem is not solved by using a more complicated lag structure in (4h) and adding an error term. The consequence of the latter would be to give us a singular system of stochastic relations from which we cannot obtain full information estimators. We are then reduced to estimation of parameters equation by equation. Formally this means that the system's parameters are not identified, since we should have multiple estimators for β and $\gamma - n -$ as well as for the α_i.

Notice, further, that asserting "incomplete" cost minimization, i.e., adding an error term e^{v_i} to the i-th equation of (4a) does not eliminate our predicament. If we did so, then equations (4g) will become

$$X_k = \alpha_k^{-1/\beta}\left[\sum_{i=1}^{n}\left(\frac{\alpha_k}{\alpha_i}\right)^{1/(\beta-1)}\left(\frac{p_i e^{v_i}}{p_k e^{v_k}}\right)^{\beta/(\beta-1)}\right]^{-1/\beta}\hat{Q}^{\gamma/\beta} \qquad k = 1, 2, \cdots, n\,. \tag{4i}$$

It is apparent from (4i) that we face a hopeless estimation problem.

Fortunately, however, we have not yet fully exploited the economics of the model. As remarked earlier, what (4g) indicate are the optimal levels of factor employment. Denote the left-hand side of (4g) by X_{kt}^* to stress this fact. The unit has at the same time certain magnitudes of such factors at its disposal. The adjustment between actual and optimal factor employment need not be instantaneous. Indeed an adjustment model was proposed, in a noneconometric context by Haavelmo [8]. Adjustment models have become standard econometric specifications in investment studies. Okun [13] has argued that labor may also be viewed as a quasi-fixed factor of production, and Kuh [11] has employed a similar explanation in order to account for the cyclical behavior of "productivity," especially in the post-war American economy. Thus, labor is also viewed as being quasi-fixed in that at certain levels at least, it represents a considerable investment in training by the enterprise and thus will not be readily released on the face of short-run fluctuations. By the same token, it could not be hired on the same considerations in view of training and orientation requirements.

On the face of these observations it would seem reasonable to postulate the following model of adjustment[5]

$$\frac{X_{jt}}{X_{jt-1}} = \left[\frac{X_{jt}^*}{X_{jt-1}}\right]^{\delta_j} e^{w_j(t)} \qquad j = 1, 2, \cdots, n , \tag{5}$$

where $0 \leq \delta_j \leq 1$, X_{jt}^* is the quantity given by (4f), and $w_j(t)$ is a random variable whose specification will be given below.

Taking logarithms in (5) and using (4f) we find

$$\begin{aligned} \ln X_{jt} &= -\frac{\delta_j}{\beta} \ln \alpha_j + (1 - \delta_j) \ln X_{jt-1} - \frac{\delta_j}{\beta} \ln \left[\sum_{i=1}^{n} \left(\frac{\alpha_j}{\alpha_i}\right)^{1/(\beta-1)} \left(\frac{p_{it}}{p_{jt}}\right)^{\beta/(\beta-1)}\right] \\ &\quad + \frac{\gamma\delta_j}{\beta} \ln \hat{Q}_t + w_j(t) \qquad j = 1, 2, \cdots, n . \end{aligned} \tag{5a}$$

If we assume that the factor prices p_j are correctly anticipated and that they are given exogenously and we further put for simplicity

$$\hat{Q}_t = Q_{t-1} \tag{5b}$$

and if we specify that the vector

$$w(t) = (w_1(t), w_2(t), \cdots, w_n(t))' \tag{5c}$$

has a nonsingular distribution with mean 0 and covariance matrix Σ; then it is seen that we deal with a nonlinear system of (reduced form) equations.

3. ESTIMATION OF THE MODEL

If it is valid to specify that

$$\text{cov}\,[w(t), w(t')] = \delta_{tt'}\Sigma \tag{6}$$

where $\delta_{tt'}$ is the Kronecker delta, then estimation of the CES parameters can be carried out by the standard full information nonlinear estimation programs. It would, of course, make matters simpler if in Σ we assumed $\sigma_{ij} = 0$ for $i \neq j$ but such assumption may not be a reasonable one. It is perhaps not reasonable even to assume that (6) is valid. This, of course, may be tested but the presence of the lagged endogenous variable in (5a) may cloud this aspect. Especially in applying this model to short-run (quarterly) data, assumption (6) would be patently false. At least a first order Markov scheme would then characterize the error terms $w_j(t)$.[6] Thus suppose

$$w_j(t) = \rho_j w_j(t-1) + \varepsilon_j(t) , \tag{7}$$

where

[5] Such a model has been successfully employed in a similar but not identical context by Dhrymes [6]. Other forms of adjustment processes may, of course, be equally appropriate, or more so.

[6] This at least was the finding of Dhrymes [6] using quarterly data in a similar but not identical context; the w_k are assumed to be uncorrelated with u.

$$\varepsilon(t) = [\varepsilon_1(t), \varepsilon_2(t), \cdots, \varepsilon_n(t)]'$$

is a random vector with properties

$$\text{(7a)} \qquad E[\varepsilon(t)] = 0 , \qquad \text{cov}\,[\varepsilon(t), \varepsilon(t')] = \delta_{tt'}\Phi .$$

It can be shown that

$$\text{(7b)} \qquad w_j(t) = \frac{\varepsilon_j(t)}{I - \rho_j Z} \qquad j = 1, 2, \cdots, n ,$$

where Z is a lag operator defined by

$$\text{(7c)} \qquad Z^k \varepsilon_j(t) = \varepsilon_j(t-k) , \qquad Z^0 \varepsilon_j(t) = \varepsilon_j(t) \qquad j = 1, 2, \cdots, n .$$

Thus, if we transform the j-th equation by $I - \rho_j Z$ we shall find

$$\ln X_{jt} = -\frac{(\delta_j - \rho_j)}{\beta} \ln \alpha_j + (1 - \delta_j + \rho_j) \ln X_{jt-1} - (1 - \delta_j)\rho_j \ln X_{jt-2}$$

$$\text{(7d)} \qquad - \frac{\delta_j}{\beta} \ln v_{tj} + \frac{\delta_j \rho_j}{\beta} \ln v_{t-1_j} + \gamma\delta_j \ln \hat{Q}_t - \gamma\delta_j\rho_j \ln \hat{Q}_{t-1} + \varepsilon_j(t)$$

$$j = 1, 2, \cdots, n ,$$

where

$$\text{(7e)} \qquad v_{tj} = \sum_{i=1}^{n} \left(\frac{\alpha_j}{\alpha_i}\right)^{1/\beta-1} \left(\frac{p_{it}}{p_{jt}}\right)^{\beta/\beta-1} .$$

We may then estimate the parameters of (7d) by application of a full information nonlinear estimation program, e.g., that given in [7]. One could, of course, approximate $\ln v_{tj}$ as a sum of logarithms involving $\ln(p_{it}/p_{jt})$, the α_i and β but this would hardly be a pressing matter in view of the accessibility of available nonlinear computer programs, although the difficulties involved in operating with such programs should not be minimized.

We shall give below an example that illustrates some of the questions discussed earlier, deferring empirical application of simultaneous nonlinear estimation of the entire parameter set to a later paper.

Suppose we are only interested in the elasticity of substitution parameter, and we wish to use quarterly data. To what extent does a nonsimultaneous approach yield reasonable results? We shall apply a variant of the above scheme to the primary metals two digit industrial classification. The data employed are the quarterly observations used in the Brookings model. Labor is measured by the number of employed workers. Capital is deflated value of structures and equipment. Output is real value added. Wages and rentals are real quantities with the output of this industry as the *numéraire*. We shall assume the component firms to behave as profit maximizers and the production function of the industry to be homogeneous of degree one. Thus optimal factor employments are determined by

$$\text{(8)} \qquad \frac{\partial Q^*}{\partial L} = w , \qquad \frac{\partial Q^*}{\partial K} = r .$$

These yield

(8a) $$L_t^* = A_1^* w^{-\sigma} \hat{Q}_t \,, \qquad K_t^* = A_2^* r^{-\sigma} \hat{Q}_t \,,$$

where $\hat{Q}_t$ is expected output; we assume that factor prices are correctly anticipated. If adjustment to optimal factor employment is incomplete then we can put

(8b) $$\frac{L_t}{L_{t-1}} = \left[\frac{L_t^*}{L_{t-1}}\right]^{\delta_1}, \qquad \frac{K_t}{K_{t-1}} = \left[\frac{K_t^*}{K_{t-1}}\right]^{\delta_2}.$$

Finally if expected output is given by

(8c) $$\hat{Q}_t = A_0 Q_t^{\gamma_1} Q_{t-1}^{\gamma_2} \,,$$

then we have an operational two equation system. If, as in the development of Section 3, the error terms are characterized by a first order Markov scheme application of modified maximum likelihood methods [**6**] yields the following estimator for some of the parameters.

TABLE 1

ELASTICITY OF SUBSTITUTION AND RELATED PARAMETERS
PRIMARY METALS, U.S. (1948–1960)

Labor equation	Capital equation	Labor equation	Capital equation
$\hat{\delta}_1 = 0.88$	$\hat{\delta}_2 = 0.053$	$\hat{\rho}_2 = 0.70$	$\hat{\rho}_2 = 0.70$
$\hat{\gamma}_1 = 0.65$	$\hat{\gamma}_1 = 0.80$	$R^2 = 0.950$	$R^2 = 0.998$
$\hat{\gamma}_1 = 0.11$	$\hat{\gamma}_2 = 0.15$	$D.W = 2.014$	$D.W = 2.250$
$\hat{\sigma} = 0.63$	$\hat{\sigma} = 0.51$		

The results in Table 1 show two things. First, the speed of adjustment, as indicated by the parameters δ_1 and δ_2, differs markedly as between labor and capital. Secondly, the parameters γ_1, γ_2 and σ which are common to both equations are reasonably similar when estimated independently. Since such estimators are obtained after a series of rational operations from subsidiary estimators, standard errors are not readily available. But still, given the magnitudes in Table 1, the difference in the elasticity of substitution, 0.63 compared with 0.51, as estimated from the two equations is substantial. Thus, although explicit recognition of the autoregressive properties of the error terms may allow us to obtain reasonable results with quarterly data, considerable discrepancies remain if we operate with the two equations *seriatim* and independently, and thus further investigation is indicated along the lines suggested earlier in this paper.

4. CONCLUSION

In the preceding pages we have provided a method for estimating the parameters of the CES production function in a context of dynamic adjustment to optimal factor employment.

While the notion of a dynamic noninstantaneous adjustment to equilibrium is not novel, its application in the present case is. This approach has at least two attractive features. First, it frees us of the necessity of asserting that our sample pertains to an equilibrium situation. Second, because we are merely asserting an approach to equilibrium, we have greater latitude in the choice of data. Thus, quarterly observations would hardly be acceptable for an equilibrium model. They would, however, be so acceptable in a dynamic adjustment model. In turn, this mitigates a recurrent problem in estimating production function parameters from time series data. The problem is that with annual data a sufficiently large sample to give sharp statistical results requires a relatively large number of observations. But since technical progress may not be so obliging as to be of the smooth Hicks neutral exponential type, the parameters of the function may not remain unaltered over the sampling period. They may not even be altered in a simple smooth way, suitable to be easily incorporated in the econometric specification. Thus the choice is between small samples with statistically obtuse results, or large samples with results that admit only of economically vague interpretations. The dynamic adjustment model, if successful, will permit relatively large numbers of observations to accumulate over a short period of calendar time and thus reduce the ambiguity induced by the incidence of nonsmooth technical change and its consequent impact on the parameters of the production function.

University of Pennsylvania, U.S.A.

REFERENCES

[1] ARROW, K. J., H. B. CHENERY, B. S. MINHAS and R. M. SOLOW, "Capital-Labor Substitution and Economic Efficiency," *Review of Economics and Statistics*, XLIII (August, 1961), 225-50.

[2] BROWN, M. and J. S. DECANI, "Technological Change and the Distribution of Income," *International Economic Review*, IV (September, 1963), 289-309.

[3] BROWN, M., "The Share of Corporate Profits in the Post-war Period," Staff Working Paper in Economics and Statistics No. 11, Office of Business Economics, U. S. Department of Commerce, (1965).

[4] DHRYMES P. J. and M. KURZ, "Technology and Scale in Electricity Generation," *Econometrica*, XXXII (July, 1964), 287-315.

[5] DHRYMES, P. J., "Some Extensions and Tests of the CES Class of Production Functions," *Review of Economics and Statistics*, XLVII (November, 1965), 357-66.

[6] ———, "A Model of Short Run Labor Adjustment," in J. Duesenberry *et al.*, eds., *Brookings Econometric Model of the U.S.* (to be published).

[7] EISENPRESS, H. and J. L. GREENSTADT, "Non-Linear Full-Information Estimation," (mimeographed).

[8] HAAVELMO, T., "A Note on the Theory of Investment," *Review of Economic Studies*, XVI(2), (1949), 78-81.

[9] KLEIN, L. R. and R. BODKIN, "Non-Linear Estimation of Production Functions," (mimeographed).

[10] KMENTA, J., "On Estimation of the CES Production Function," this *Review, this issue*.

[11] KUH, E., "Cyclical and Secular Labor Productivity in U.S. Manufacturing," *Review of Economics and Statistics*, XLVII (February, 1965) 1-13.

[12] NERLOVE M., "Notes on Recent Empirical Studies of the CES and Related Functions," Technical Report No. 13, Institute for Mathematical Studies in the Social Sciences, Stanford University, (July, 1965).

[13] OKUN, A., "Potential GNP: Its Measurement and Significance," *Proceedings of the Economics and Statistics Section of the American Statistical Association*, (1962).

Econometrica, Vol. 37, No. 4 (October, 1969)

ESTIMATION OF JOINT PRODUCTION FUNCTIONS

BY P. J. DHRYMES AND B. M. MITCHELL

1. INTRODUCTION

IN A RECENT PAPER, H. D. Vinod [1] has suggested canonical correlation analysis as a technique of consistently estimating the parameters of joint production functions. While it is not clear that he intends this technique to be applicable to all possible specifications of such functions, it is presumably applicable at least to the explicit formulation he considers in Section 2, viz.,

$$X_i = k_i \prod_{j=1}^{q} Y_j^{c_{ij}} e^{\varepsilon_i} \qquad (i = 1, 2, \ldots, p), \tag{1}$$

where the X_i are the outputs, Y_j the inputs, k_i, c_{ij} the unknown parameters, and ε_i the error terms.

In this note we shall show several things: first, Vinod's formulation contains an error; second, in the case $p = q$, canonical and ordinary least squares (OLS) analyses are equivalent; third, if $p \neq q$, then the canonical estimators cannot be consistent unless OLS estimators are as well.

2. FORMULATION OF THE PROBLEM: $p = q$

Here we shall set down the notation and the basic theory of canonical correlation so as to correspond to Vinod's convention. Thus, let

$$z = \begin{pmatrix} x \\ y \end{pmatrix}$$

be a random vector (normally) distributed, with mean zero and covariance matrix Φ. It is assumed that the elements of z have variance equal to unity. Partition Φ conformally with z to obtain

$$\Phi = \begin{bmatrix} \Phi_{11} & \Phi_{12} \\ \Phi_{21} & \Phi_{22} \end{bmatrix}. \tag{2}$$

The canonical variables associated with x, y are determined as follows. Consider the system

$$\begin{bmatrix} -\lambda\Phi_{11} & \Phi_{12} \\ \Phi_{21} & -\lambda\Phi_{22} \end{bmatrix} \begin{bmatrix} \alpha \\ \beta \end{bmatrix} = 0. \tag{3}$$

Nontrivial solutions exist if and only if

$$\begin{vmatrix} -\lambda\Phi_{11} & \Phi_{12} \\ \Phi_{21} & -\lambda\Phi_{22} \end{vmatrix} = (-\lambda)^{q-p} |\lambda^2\Phi_{11} - \Phi_{12}\Phi_{22}^{-1}\Phi_{21}| |\Phi_{22}| = 0. \tag{4}$$

It is assumed that p, the number of elements of x, does not exceed q, the number of elements of y. The equation (4) has at least $q - p$ zero roots and will have p nonzero roots if Φ_{12} is of rank p. At any rate, let λ_i^2, $i = 1, 2, \ldots, p$, be the (nonzero) roots of (4); the quantities $\pm\lambda_i$ serve to define the vectors $\alpha_{.j}, \beta_{.i}$, which are the solutions of (3) corresponding to the λ_i. Since the $\alpha_{.i}\, \beta_{.i}$ are arbitrary up to a scalar factor, they are conventionally normalized by the requirement

$$\alpha'_{.i}\Phi_{11}\alpha_{.i} = \beta'_{.i}\Phi_{22}\beta_{.i} = 1 \qquad (i = 1, 2, \ldots, p). \tag{5}$$

Let

$$A^* = (\alpha_{.1}, \alpha_{.2}, \ldots, \alpha_{.p}), \qquad B^* = (\beta_{.1}, \beta_{.2}, \ldots, \beta_{.p}), \tag{6}$$

whose constituent vectors are the solutions of (3) corresponding to the positive square roots of λ_i^2. Let

$$u = A^{*\prime}x, \quad v = B^{*\prime}y. \tag{7}$$

Then the pairs (u_i, v_i) are the canonical pairs corresponding to the vectors x, y. Of course A^*, B^* are nonsingular matrices. Now if Φ is not known, the canonical variables cannot be obtained as above. They may, however, be *estimated* from observations on the vectors x and y.

Thus, let $x_{.i}$, $y_{.j}$ be respectively vectors of T observations on the ith and jth elements of x and y. Define

(8) $$X = (x_{.1}, x_{.2}, \ldots, x_{.p}), \qquad Y = (y_{.1}, y_{.2}, \ldots, y_{.q}).$$

Then the T "observations" on the "estimated" canonical variates are given by

(9) $$U = XA, \qquad V = YB,$$

where A, B are matrices analogous to A^*, B^*, and computed as the solutions of

(10) $$\begin{bmatrix} -r\dfrac{X'X}{T} & \dfrac{X'Y}{T} \\ \dfrac{Y'X}{T} & -r\dfrac{Y'Y}{T} \end{bmatrix} \begin{bmatrix} a \\ b \end{bmatrix} = 0.$$

We observe that if r_i, $i = 1, 2, \ldots, p$, are the p nonnegative roots of the determinantal equation corresponding to (10), and

(11) $$R = \operatorname{diag}(r_1, r_2, \ldots, r_p),$$

then the following is true:

(12) $$\frac{U'V}{T} = A'\frac{X'Y}{T}B = R, \qquad \frac{U'U}{T} = A'\frac{X'X}{T}A = I, \qquad \frac{V'V}{T} = B'\frac{Y'Y}{T}B = I.$$

Mr. Vinod's suggestion is that

(13) $$X = YBRA^{-1}$$

should be taken as a representation of the joint production function. This conclusion is arrived at as follows. If $(u_{.i}, v_{.i})$ represent the T observations on the ith canonical pair, then the regression of $u_{.i}$ on $v_{.i}$ could, in view of their standardized nature, result in the relation

(14) $$u_{.i} = r_i v_{.i} \qquad (i = 1, 2, \ldots, p).$$

Thus, (14) implies, according to Vinod,

(15) $$U = VR,$$

which, in view of (9), yields

(16) $$XA = YBR.$$

The fallacy here is that (14) is not a valid expression; the right hand side gives the "predicted" value of the dependent variable, given the independent one. To make (14) valid we need to add a residual.

We shall show next that if we take (13) at face value, then this is equivalent to a regression of X on Y. In view of (9), the matrix of "regression coefficients" of X on Y is given by, since $p = q$,

(17) $$(Y'Y)^{-1}Y'X = \left(B'^{-1}\frac{V'V}{T}B^{-1}\right)^{-1} B'^{-1}\frac{V'U}{T}A^{-1} = BRA^{-1}.$$

Hence, the "predicted" outputs, $\hat{X}$, may be written as

(18) $$\hat{X} = YBRA^{-1},$$

which is Vinod's proposed "joint" production function. Thus, *his suggestion amounts to nothing more than ordinary least squares*. Therefore, it is impossible for his estimators to possess *any* properties not possessed by the ordinary regression coefficients. Indeed, Vinod's suggestion amounts to a very complicated way of performing ordinary least squares.

We conclude this section by giving a numerical illustration. Mr. Vinod was kind enough to supply us with the data he had used in [**1**]. Employing his data, we have carried out the computations required for his Case 1, Table I.

TABLE I

COMPARATIVE PERFORMANCE OF OLS AND CANONICAL ESTIMATORS

	Ours	Vinod's
Canonical	$W = .25299L + .99956K$	$W = .23083L + .80126K$
	$M = -0.04752L + .65824K$	$M = -0.15738L + .44623K$
OLS	$W = .25298L + .99956K$	$W = 1.4148L + .3272K +$ constant
	$M = -0.04752L + .65829K$	$M = -0.0325L + .0263K +$ constant

Our canonical correlation program yields:

$$A = \begin{bmatrix} -1.002995 & -1.410906 \\ 0.003670 & 1.731085 \end{bmatrix}, \quad B = \begin{bmatrix} -0.307373 & -1.487362 \\ -1.210652 & -0.917089 \end{bmatrix}, \tag{19}$$

$$R = \text{diag}\,(0.8261178, 0.2952975).$$

Hand computation yields

$$BRA^{-1} = \begin{bmatrix} .252994 & -0.047521 \\ .999564 & .658244 \end{bmatrix}. \tag{20}$$

Ordinary least squares applied to the *standardized data* yields similar results. For the reader's convenience we present these results in Table I. Regarding this table, it should be remarked that *Vinod's OLS results agree to the fourth decimal with ours after his coefficients are standardized*, i.e., after multiplication by the relevant ratio of standard deviations. Since our canonical and OLS coefficients agree to the fourth decimal, we may further conclude that there was an error in Mr. Vinod's canonical correlation computation.

Thus, the seeming difference between Mr. Vinod's OLS and canonical results is a consequence of the differing units in which he measures his variables in the two cases and an apparent error in his canonical correlation computations. These differences have nothing whatsoever to do with the alleged superiority of canonical over OLS estimators since in the present case we have shown the two to be equivalent.

3. THE CASE $p \neq q$

Consider first $p < q$ in conjunction with the model in (1). Upon taking logarithms we find

$$x_{ti} = \sum_{j=1}^{q} c_{ji} y_{tj} + \varepsilon_{ti} \qquad (t = 1, 2, \ldots, T;\ i = 1, 2, \ldots, p), \tag{21}$$

where lower case x's, y's indicate logarithms and k_i was taken to be zero. Let the vector $\begin{pmatrix} y \\ \varepsilon \end{pmatrix}$ have covariance matrix

$$\Sigma = \begin{bmatrix} \Sigma_{11} & \Sigma_{12} \\ \Sigma_{21} & \Sigma_{22} \end{bmatrix}.$$

Then we can write

$$x_{t.} = y_{t.} C + \varepsilon_{t.}, \tag{22}$$

where

$$C = (c_{ji}) \qquad (i = 1, 2, \ldots, p;\ j = 1, 2, \ldots, q) \tag{23}$$

and $x_{t.}$, $y_{t.}$, $\varepsilon_{t.}$ denote respectively the *row* vector of the dependent, explanatory, and error variables at "time" t.

The matrix Φ of (2) has, in view of the above, the following representation:

(24) $\Phi_{11} = C'\Sigma_{11}C + \Sigma_{22}, \quad \Phi_{12} = C'\Sigma_{11} + \Sigma_{21}, \quad \Phi_{22} = \Sigma_{11}.$

The estimate of C proposed by Vinod is

(25) $\tilde{C} = BRA^{-1},$

which, in view of (12), can also be written as

(26) $\tilde{C} = BB'\left(\frac{Y'Y}{T}\right)\hat{C},$

where $\hat{C}$ is the OLS estimator of C given by

(27) $\hat{C} = (Y'Y)^{-1}Y'X.$

Thus, the canonical estimator is a simple transform of the OLS estimator. Now A, R, B are *consistent* estimators of A^*, Λ, and B^*, respectively. Hence, the probability limit of Vinod's estimator must satisfy the equation

(28) $\operatorname*{plim}_{t\to\infty} \tilde{C} = B^*\Lambda A^{*-1}.$

On the other hand, since A^*, B^*, Λ satisfy the condition (3), we must also have

(29) $\Phi_{22}B^*\Lambda = \Phi_{21}A^*.$

But (24) implies

(30) $\Sigma_{11}B^*\Lambda = (\Sigma_{11}C + \Sigma_{12})A^*.$

Since Σ_{11} (and A^*) is nonsingular, we conclude that

(31) $B^*\Lambda A^{*-1} = (C + \Sigma_{11}^{-1}\Sigma_{12}).$

Hence, Vinod's estimator will be consistent if and only if

(32) $\Sigma_{11}^{-1}\Sigma_{12} = 0,$

which is equivalent to

(33) $\Sigma_{12} = 0.$

When (33) holds, however, OLS yields a consistent estimator as well.

If now $p > q$, then all the argument above holds except that the matrix A cannot now be inverted. Vinod's estimator in this case becomes

(34) $\tilde{C} = BRA^{\#},$

where $A^{\#}$ is the pseudo inverse

(35) $A^{\#} = (A'A)^{-1}A'.$

Since $A^{\#}$ is a left inverse of A, we have

(36) $A^{\#}A = I.$

Thus, Vinod's estimator converges to

(37) $\operatorname*{plim}_{T\to\infty} \tilde{C} = B^*\Lambda A^{*\#}, \qquad A^{*\#} = (A^{*\prime}A^*)^{-1}A^{*\prime}.$

But (29) is still valid, and thus implies, in view of (24),

(38) $B^*\Lambda A^{*\#} = (C + \Sigma_{11}^{-1}\Sigma_{12})A^*(A^{*\prime}A^*)^{-1}A^{*\prime}.$

We first observe that $\tilde{C}A$ is a consistent estimator of CA^* if and only if the OLS estimator of C is consistent; secondly, it is impossible for $\tilde{C}$ to be a consistent estimator (of C). For suppose it is.

Then we should have

$$(C + \Sigma_{11}^{-1}\Sigma_{12})A^*A^{*\#} = C. \tag{39}$$

Postmultiplying by A^* we find

$$\Sigma_{11}^{-1}\Sigma_{12}A^* = 0, \tag{40}$$

which implies

$$\Sigma_{12}A^* = 0. \tag{41}$$

In particular, this must hold for a Σ_{12} as

$$\Sigma_{12} = (S_1, S_2), \tag{42}$$

where S_1 is $q \times q$ of rank q, and S_2 is identically zero. This implies that A^* must be of the form

$$A^* = \begin{pmatrix} 0 \\ A_2 \end{pmatrix}, \tag{43}$$

where 0 is a $q \times q$ matrix. But then A^* cannot be of rank q for the particular choice $q > 1$ and $p = q + 1$. Hence, we obtain a contradiction.

In contrast with the cumbersome nature of the canonical estimator, OLS is easily carried out. The model is

$$X = YC + E, \tag{44}$$

and the OLS estimator is determined as

$$\hat{C} = (Y'Y)^{-1}Y'X = C + (Y'Y)^{-1}Y'E. \tag{45}$$

This estimator is defined for $p = q$ as well as for $p \neq q$. In the case $p \leqslant q$, Vinod's estimator can be consistent if and only if the OLS estimator is; if inconsistent, its inconsistency is exactly that of the latter, since

$$\operatorname*{plim}_{T\to\infty} \hat{C} = C + \Sigma_{11}^{-1}\Sigma_{12}. \tag{46}$$

If $p > q$, then Vinod's estimator cannot possibly be consistent.

Finally, it might well be that canonical estimators are "better" in some other sense, but Vinod's claim to superiority lies only in their alleged consistency.

The case where A is not of full rank—an unlikely event—may be treated similarly.

University of Pennsylvania

and

Stanford University

REFERENCE

[1] VINOD, H. D.: "Econometrics of Joint Production," *Econometrica*, 36 (1968), pp. 322–336.

[32]

ON THE MEASUREMENT OF PRICE AND QUALITY CHANGES IN SOME CONSUMER CAPITAL GOODS

By Phoebus J. Dhrymes
University of Pennsylvania

I. *Introduction*

This paper reports some preliminary and fragmentary findings of an investigation designed to determine whether it is feasible to correct for quality in the price of certain consumer capital goods by the methods suggested by Court [1] and more recently by Griliches *et al.* [2] [3].

If it is feasible to do so, then we can routinely construct price indices "corrected for quality change" and in this fashion provide a clearer indication of the true character of price movements. Price indices uncorrected for "quality" changes may seriously under- or overstate the extent of price movement. Of course, we should declare at the outset that by quality we shall mean the constellation of identifiable characteristics exhibited by a given product. In this study we are dealing with automobiles and refrigerators. Quality in the case of the former means, e.g., the weight, length, brake horsepower, etc., exhibited by a given model. In the case of the latter it means the height, weight, depth, freezer compartment capacity, etc., of the given refrigerator. Although it would be desirable, it is still not possible to include in the measurement of quality, the durability, or frequency of repair record, or the economy of operation of an automobile, or a refrigerator, due to lack of data.

Studies of this type are not new, as we have remarked above. What will particularly engage us is the examination of the question of homogeneity in the price behavior of various manufacturers. This is a problem of some consequence in the automobile industry, where well over 90 percent of the total car sales is accounted for by the output of three manufacturers. If the price decision-making process is appreciably different as between any two manufacturers, then it is clear that in attempting to "correct for quality" due attention must be paid to the division of the market by such manufacturers. Moreover, it would be inadmissible, under such circumstances, to estimate the pricing equation from a single cross-section, in which several manufacturers are represented. Rather we should estimate each manufacturer's decision rule separately. This is a problem that unfortunately has received little attention in the current literature.

II. *The Samples*

The automobile sample is in principle an exhaustive one for a certain subuniverse of models. The data were obtained[1] in the first instance from *Ward's* or *Automotive Industries.* In selecting models for inclusion the following criteria were employed: exclude sports cars, hardtops, convertibles and station wagons; include all two- and four-door models except deluxe versions of a given model not differing from the basic version in cylinders, weight, length, piston displacement, or horsepower. Notice that the criterion in the second criteria refers to standard equipment. Whenever data ambiguities arose the relevant manufacturer was contacted. The samples cover six years: 1953, 1957, 1961, 1962, 1963, and 1964. Two of the manufacturers provided corrections over the entire period, while one provided corrections for only one year.

The refrigerator sample was mainly obtained from *1966 Home Appliance Blue Book* and various issues of *Mart* magazine. By and large we used the entire set available from such publications. Some manufacturers were underrepresented or only incomplete information was available for their products. In such cases they were contacted directly and some information was solicited. Most responded. This sample covers the period 1950–65.

In the automobile sample we deal with 912 models (observations) of which G.M. accounts for 429, Chrysler for 303, and Ford for 180.

In the refrigerator sample we deal with 632 models (observations) of which Frigidaire accounts for 132, G.E. for 144, Hotpoint for 54, Kelvinator for 80, Philco and R.C.A. 38 each, and Westinghouse for 52. Other manufacturers represented are Admiral (9), Amana (4), Gibson (8), etc.

III. *Empirical Findings*

Automobiles. The work of Court [1], Griliches [2], and others has potentially important consequences for the construction of "quality corrected" price indices. The precise details of such application are subsidiary to the question whether it is in fact feasible to undertake quality correction routinely in this fashion. Two questions are of great importance, particularly in the case of automobiles. First, if we deal with a relation between list price and various identifiable physical characteristics of an automobile, then it would appear that such an equation is best interpreted as a cost plus desired markup relation.[2] We may thus

[1] The sample was collected in the first instance by I. Kravis and R. Lipsey. I am indebted to them for making it available to me.

[2] Other researchers have tended to interpret the parameters of such equations as expressions of consumer valuations of the physical characteristics of an automobile and thus as approximations of the implicit price attaching to such features. Of course such an interpretation should imply equality of coefficients in such equations for different manufacturers, provided the latter produce roughly similar products.

ask: is this costing function similar amongst different manufacturers? If not, it would appear that we ought to take into account the division of the market in constructing quality corrected price indices. Beyond that, if the answer to the previous question is no, then this entire procedure of quality correction could be open to serious doubt. Second, we might want to answer the following: is there some well-defined mathematical form that best describes this pricing function? Are the parameters of this function reasonably stable over time? Of course the parameters of such relations cannot be fixed over time since the cost structure of the relevant markets cannot be expected to remain fixed. Nonetheless we would not expect radical changes in the sign and magnitude of such coefficients from year to year.

We shall not be able to answer all these questions in this preliminary version, although some tentative answers can be suggested. Regarding the second problem, we have attempted to fit a linear, semilog or double-log form to the data, the results being reported in Tables 1, 2, 3, 4 (in the Appendix). The results reported there refer to cross-section regressions for the year 1961 for each manufacturer separately and for the entire sample. Since there is some question of confidentiality and the results are still tentative, we shall not identify the manufacturers.

In the tables W indicates weight in 10^2 lbs., L length in 10 inches, DIS displacement in cubic inches, BHP brake horsepower at 3800 revolutions per minute, MOD the number of units produced in the given year for the particular model and C, DOR, ATR, $P.S.$ are dummy variables assuming the value 1 if the model had as standard equipment eight cylinders, four doors, automatic transmission and power steering, respectively, and zero if not. Prices are stated in 10^2 dollars, and numbers in parentheses indicate t ratios. In addition to $\bar{R}^2$ we have given in the tables what we have called "antilog $\bar{R}^2$" in the case of semi- and double-log regressions. By that we mean the following. Let $\widetilde{\ln P}$ be the "predicted" logarithm of price from one of the last two equations of the tables, then obtain

$$\tilde{P} = e^{\widetilde{\ln P}}. \tag{1}$$

Compute the sample correlation between $\tilde{P}$ of (1) and actual price. Thus "antilog $\bar{R}^2$" gives the correlation between actual and predicted price on the basis of the regression coefficients given in the last two columns of the tables. For purposes of comparison of the goodness of fit of the three functional forms this statistic imposes a reasonable degree of uniformity on the measures for all three forms and thus facilitates comparability. The first feature to note in these tables is that while the linear form is perceptibly inferior to the other two there is really not much to choose between the semi- and the double-log forms. Admittedly there is no simple (but rigorous) statistical test by which we could support the contention above, but in terms of operational expediency there is no doubt that we should reject the linear form.

The second feature worth pointing out is that the correlation coefficients are considerably higher when the relation is estimated on the basis of each manufacturer's sample than when the samples are pooled. This of course would lead us to believe that the pricing behavior of the various manufacturers differs appreciably. Fortunately, if we choose a specific functional form, the hypothesis above can be formally tested. For convenience let us choose the semilog form. It might appear that since displacement and *P.S.* enter in the equation for manufacturer 1 and not in that of the others then *ipso facto* the coefficients must be different. However, this is an overhasty conclusion. First, we should note that for the sample of manufacturers 2 and 3 *P.S.*, when standard, was invariably accompanied by automatic transmission so that in fact the coefficient of *ATR* in Tables 2 and 3 measures the effect of both *ATR* and *P.S.* on price. Second, for these same manufacturers *BHP* was highly correlated with displacement the coefficient for 1961 being about .96 and thus again the independent influence of these two characteristics on price could not be established. In fact, Griliches *et al.* [3] report the following relation, for 1961

$$DIS = 73.4 + 1.07BHP, \qquad R^2 = .914 \tag{2}$$

based on a cross-section of 36 models from various manufacturers. Since apparently the relation between displacement and horsepower is neither rigidly fixed nor freely variable, it would seem that some manufacturers in designing their models allow greater variability in the relation between those characteristics than others. For these reasons a formal test of the hypothesis of equality of coefficients should be formally carried out.

It can easily be proved that if we have s subsamples and if it is desired to test the hypothesis that the regression parameters characteristic of each sample are identical, we can proceed as follows.

Let

$$Y_{\cdot i} = X_i\beta_{\cdot i} + u_{\cdot i} \quad i = 1, 2, \cdots, s \tag{3}$$

be the ith subsample; we assume $Y_{\cdot i}$ is $T_i \times 1$ so that each subsample may have a different number of observations; we also assume that

$$u_{\cdot i} \sim N(0, \sigma_{ii}I) \quad E(u_{\cdot i}u'_{\cdot j}) = 0 \quad i \neq j \quad i, j = 1, 2, \cdots, s. \tag{3a}$$

Let Q_i be the sum of squares of the residuals in the ith subsample—its parameters being estimated independently. Let Q_T be the sum of the squared residuals of the pooled sample. Then it can be shown that under the null hypothesis

(3b) $$\cdot_{i} = \beta, \qquad \sigma_{ii} = \sigma^2 \quad i = 1, 2, \cdots, s$$

(4) $$\frac{Q_T - \sum_{i=1}^{s} Q_i}{\sum_{i=1}^{s} Q_i} \cdot \frac{\sum_{i=1}^{s} T_i - sk}{(s-1)k} \sim F_{(s-1)k, \sum_{i=1}^{s} T_i}.$$

In our case $s=3$, $k=9$ and $\sum_{i=1}^{3} T_i = 192$; applying the above to our sample we conclude in the case of all three manufacturers that the F statistic is

(4a) $$F^* = 2.5594.$$

In view of the degrees of freedom involved (18, 167) the hypothesis is to be rejected even at the .5 percent level of significance.[3] It might be thought that manufacturers 2 and 3 may have identical parameters. This, however, is not borne out formally. A similar procedure applied to them alone yields the test statistic

(4b) $$F^* = 4.065.$$

Here the degrees of freedom are (8, 87) and thus the hypothesis is again rejected.

Thus it would appear that there are significant differences in the pricing behavior of the three manufacturers. This in conjunction with the fact that the coefficient of *MOD* turns out to be statistically significant would tend to support the interpretation that the equations estimated are indeed cost plus markup relations, and thus that the coefficients of the variables cannot reasonably be interpreted as approximations to the implicit price of such characteristics in the sense of an implicit consumer valuation. This being so, the question of whether one can use weights derived from such schemes to correct for quality variations becomes a serious one. It should be remarked that Griliches [2] attempted to do so, although his cross-sectional samples were perhaps not large enough to allow him to test the hypotheses we have tested above. Clearly additional work in this area will be needed to determine the general validity of our conclusions above. Such results will be incorporated in the final report of this study.

Let us illustrate the type of use we can make of our results above and the type of conclusions one is likely to arrive at given that the pricing behavior of various manufacturers differs appreciably.

Again, let us confine ourselves to the semilog form.

Let p_{ij} be the (log of the) price of a model with characteristics identi-

[3] Rejection is also implied for the double log and the linear form as well.

cal to those of the mean car in the sample for the jth year evaluated at the ith year's equation. In some sense p_{ij} is the cost (plus markup) of producing in the year i a model with the features of the mean model actually produced in the year j. It is clear that p_{jj} is then the (log of the) actual mean price of the sampled models in year j. Thus $p_{jj}-p_{ij}$ gives approximately that portion of the relative change in mean price between year i and year j which is not due to quality variations. We shall call this the "pure price effect." It is of course clear that $p_{jj}-p_{ii}$ gives the total (actual) relative change in mean price between the years i and j. It seems logical to define the quality effect or quality component of a price change by

$$(p_{jj} - p_{ii}) - (p_{jj} - p_{ij}) = p_{ij} - p_{ii}. \tag{5}$$

Denote by

$$c_0 = p_{jj} - p_{ii}, \qquad c_1 = p_{ij} - p_{ii}, \qquad c_2 = p_{jj} - p_{ij} \tag{5a}$$

so that c_0 indicates the actual price change, c_1 and c_2, respectively, the "quality" and "pure price" components.

The results of Table 5 may be given the following interpretation. The standard (average) model in the sample as a whole has experienced an apparent price decline between 1961 and 1964 of about 2.2 percent. But the intrinsic price behavior of automobiles is given by the "Pure Price" component under c_1. Thus over the same period this shows a decline of 7 percent; the discrepancy is made up by the fact that the quality of the average car has changed and this really should be thought of as equivalent to a 4.8 percent increase in price. The results are similar for manufacturers 1 and 2 but entirely different for manufacturer 3. Of course, we should remark that one of the variables, viz., *MOD*, cannot easily be thought of as a quality indicator, unless one is determined to so consider it; in this case we presumably could argue that the more units of a given model are produced, the less desirable is the car, much in the manner of women's dresses, where the value of the dress to the consumer is in part derived from the fact that there are not many (any?) others like it. In subsequent investigations, it would probably be best if that variable is removed from consideration.

We should further remark that the entries in Table 5 are not directly comparable to the automobile component of various published price indices; e.g., the consumer price index. In Table 5 all models receive equal weight; in the index, models are being weighted, as is sensible to do, by their sales volume or something equivalent. Finally, it should be remarked that the divergent conclusions emerging from consideration of manufacturer 3 or 2 or 1 tend to call into question the feasibility of routinely correcting for quality through the model pursued here and as suggested by others before. But I do not wish to be inflexible on this in view of the fragmentary and tentative character of the results.

Finally, before leaving this topic let us point out that the entries under c_2 in Table 5 may be tested for significance. It is clear that since the decomposition rests on the estimators for the parameters in each year the pure price effect will in truth be zero if the parameters have remained unchanged from year to year; an appropriate test statistic may be obtained and the test carried out.

Refrigerators. As in the case of automobiles we attempted to explain the price of refrigerators by the variation in certain identifiable physical characteristics. The characteristics considered were

CF = cubic footage capacity
FCF = freezer compartment cubic footage
H = height, inches
W = width, inches
D = depth, inches
$D1$ = dummy, 1 if meat drawer is available
$D3$ = dummy, 1 if egg shelf is available
$D4$ = dummy, 1 if butter shelf is available
$D7$ = dummy, 1 if shelves on freezer door are available
$D8$ = dummy, 1 if shelves are available in freezer compartment
$D9$ = dummy, 1 if ice ejector is available
$D13$ = dummy, 1 if shelves are sliding
$D14$ = dummy, 1 if shelves are swing-out
$D18$ = dummy, 1 if semiautomatic defrosting is available
$D19$ = dummy, 1 if automatic defrosting is available
$D20$ = dummy, 1 if automatic defrosting is available in the freezer section but not in the fresh foods section
$D21$ = dummy, 1 if completely frostless in freezer and fresh foods section
$D24$ = dummy, 1 if unit has 2 doors

Again, in this case we have attempted to fit linear, semilog, and double-log forms. We have found that while the linear form was appreciably inferior to the others, there was little basis for choosing between the semi- and double log. Here we shall base our discussion on the double-log form. The empirical results here are farther removed from finality than the automobile results. An analysis of annual cross-sections has not been completed. Furthermore, since no manufacturer had a sufficient number of models to permit identification of the parameters of the pricing equation of each individual manufacturer, we employed instead a mixed time series cross-section sample per manufacturer. The attempt here is to establish whether over the years the average pricing behavior of a given manufacturer differs from that of another.

In addition to that, we have obtained, on the assumption that pricing behavior of manufacturers is homogeneous, estimates of the parameters of a pricing equation over the entire sample. If the hypothesis is correct, then this is indeed a relation reflecting the pricing behavior in this industry; if the hypothesis is not correct, however, the equation has no clear-cut interpretation, although one may be tempted to use it as an indication of average price behavior in the industry over the period in question.

In Table 6 we give the empirical results of this facet of the investigation. Perhaps a few comments will put this table in proper perspective. The first column refers to results obtained by considering the entire sample and is put there for completeness alone. This sample contains firms whose models are represented only at the early years of the sample (Crosley, Montgomery Ward) or only at later years (Gibson). The second column represents the results obtained when the sample considered contains only the manufacturers listed in the remainder of the table. Although the results do not differ markedly as to the magnitude of the coefficients in these two columns, nonetheless the goodness of fit is markedly inferior in the larger sample, and this is already an indication that the price policy of manufacturers will not be homogeneous. This is indeed borne out by examining the estimated parameters for Frigidaire, G.E., Hotpoint, Kelvinator, Philco, and Westinghouse. We note that the fit ($\overline{R}^2$) of these equations varies considerably from .6525 for Westinghouse to .8981 for G.E. There are also other indications of variability; thus for individual firms *FCF* appears to have an insignificant or negative coefficient while for the sample as a whole it appears to have a positive coefficient. Similarly *H* is unambiguously significant and has a positive coefficient in the total sample, while for the various manufacturer's subsamples it appears to be alternately significant with positive coefficient, insignificant or significant with negative coefficient. One can go on in this vein, but it does not particularly illuminate matters to take this view, since it is conceivable that multicollinearity problems may be particularly severe in one subsample and not in another or in the total sample. To this effect we revert to a formal technique and test the hypothesis that the parameters in all equations are identical by the method indicated above.

In this connection we should point out that the fact that zeros appear in the various places in the last six columns of the table does not necessarily indicate that the corresponding coefficients are (insignificantly different from) zero; rather it means that for the particular subsample the corresponding variable was identically zero and thus it was impossible to estimate such a parameter.

The test statistic implied by this sample is

$$F^* = 2.6885 \tag{6}$$

and in view of the degrees of freedom (77,406) the hypothesis is to be rejected unambiguously. Several pairwise tests also lead to rejection of similar hypotheses except in the case of Hotpoint and Westinghouse where the test statistic (1.47) lies within the acceptance region, but very close to its boundary.

We might well try to make some inference regarding the relative importance of quality variation in price changes over the years. However, since we do not have annual cross-sections, this is not quite satisfactory; so we confine our illustration to the total sample. The relevant information is given in Table 7. If the characteristics of the mean refrigerator in each year are evaluated according to the results of Table 6, there results the second column of Table 7; the latter thus gives the price variation over the years which is solely due to quality variation, since cost conditions are fixed. The quality component of price change is derived as the percent change obtained on the basis of this computed (cost constant) price and is given under q_1 in the table. Finally, the "pure price" component given under p_1 in the table is determined residually so that q_1+p_1 equals the percent change in actual (mean) price. All such calculations have 1958 as a base year.

The conclusion emerging from the table is that apparent (actual) price behavior understates the extent to which the price of a quality corrected (average) refrigerator has fallen in recent years. While such calculations are useful as gross indications of the behavior of the relevant quantities, more definitive conclusions will have to be based on a more careful examination of annual cross-sections.

For in addition to other limitations indicated above, the results do not adequately allow for the fact that the general price level has been fluctuating over the sample period. To some extent this can be allowed for in this aggregative context by introducing time as a variable. It is not clear that this is a very satisfactory substitute for annual cross-sections. Due to this as well as time and space limitations, this will not be pursued here.

IV. *Conclusion*

We have attempted in this paper to give a fragmentary account of certain results pertaining to the feasibility of constructing quality corrected price indices on the basis of suggestions that regression of price on various identifiable characteristics of the relevant products adequately represents the effect of quality in price.

Our tentative conclusion is that it is very difficult to apply such techniques routinely. First, there is the problem that the pricing equations for various manufacturers are not homogeneous, so that the same item is differently evaluated in the different pricing equations and thus it is not clear what is its quality contribution to the price of the product. Second, there is some evidence that the parameters of such equations vary significantly from year to year. What, for instance, would be our interpretation if, for a given manufacturer of automobiles, length is significant with a positive coefficient for one year but for the next—and still the same manufacturer—length is insignificant, or significant but with a negative coefficient?

Particularly in the case of automobiles, fads carefully nurtured by the industry's advertising are common, and since we do not allow for them in our estimation procedure, we are likely to be led astray if we are totally objective about our quality correction.

References

1. A. T. Court, "Hedonic Price Indexes with Automobile Examples" in *The Dynamics of Automobile Demand* (New York, 1939).
2. Z. Griliches, "Hedonic Price Indexes for Automobiles; . . ." in *The Price Statistics of the Federal Government* (N.B.E.R., 1961).
3. F. M. Fisher, Z. Griliches, and C. Kaysen, "The Cost of Automobile Model Changes since 1949," *J.P.E.*, 1962, p. 433.

APPENDIX

TABLE 1

ALTERNATIVE FUNCTIONAL FORMS, *Mf* 1, 1961

	Linear $P = \sum_{i=1}^{n} \alpha_i X_i$	Semilog $\ln P = \sum_{i=1}^{n} \beta_i X_i$	Double Log $\ln P = \sum_{i=1}^{n} \gamma_i \ln X_i$
W	.7898 (1.2450)	.0171 (1.5375)	−0.3777 (−0.9555)
L	4.7060 (1.7042)	.0798 (1.6456)	4.1890 (4.2241)
DIS	−0.1114 (−4.8789)	−0.0017 (−4.2320)	−0.5311 (−3.7497)
BHP	0.0477 (2.7863)	0.0012 (3.9164)	.3339 (4.6638)
MOD	−0.0579 (−3.8918)	−0.0013 (−4.9417)	−0.1152 (−6.4716)
C	1.5376 (.6602)	.0337 (.8236)	.0622 (.0492)
DOR	−2.6438 (−1.6201)	−0.0516 (−1.8018)	−0.0678 (−2.3798)
ATR	−1.4994 (−0.7134)	−0.0058 (−0.1562)	.0193 (.5216)
P.S.	12.0165 (3.6087)	.3162 (5.4091)	.3085 (5.3208)
Const.	−71.3150 (−1.9571)	1.3050 (2.0402)	−6.4053 (−3.4792)
$\bar{R}^2$	.8226	.9069	.9093
Antilog $\bar{R}^2$	.8226	.8980	.9135

TABLE 2

ALTERNATIVE FUNCTIONAL FORMS, *Mf* 2, 1961

	Linear $P = \sum_{i=1}^{n} \alpha_i X_i$	Semilog $\ln P = \sum_{i=1}^{n} \beta_i X_i$	Double Log $\ln P = \sum_{i=1}^{n} \gamma_i \ln X_i$
W	.7412 (2.0924)	.0311 (2.1342)	.9882 (2.1421)
L	−1.2551 (−1.1584)	−0.0440 (−0.9881)	−1.1496 (−1.2486)
BHP	.0192 (3.3766)	.0008 (3.3181)	.1609 (2.8456)
MOD	−0.0893 (−3.1684)	−0.0033 (−2.8530)	−0.0915 (−3.5895)
C	−1.7973 (−2.2625)	−0.0693 (−2.2186)	−0.0666 (−1.9375)
DOR	−0.5699 (−1.3910)	−0.0282 (−1.6732)	−0.0298 (−1.7254)
ATR	7.5232 (5.3169)	0.2005 (3.4493)	.2130 (3.5460)
Const.	23.3652 (2.0099)	2.9577 (6.1929)	2.6271 (1.9202)
$\bar{R}^2$	.8645	.8645	.8557
Antilog $\bar{R}^2$	.8645	.8702	.8635

TABLE 3

ALTERNATIVE FUNCTIONAL FORMS, *Mf* 3, 1961

	Linear $P = \sum_{i=1}^{n} \alpha_i X_i$	Semilog $\ln P = \sum_{i=1}^{n} \beta_i X_i$	Double Log $\ln P = \sum_{i=1}^{n} \gamma_i \ln X_i$
N	.7176 (3.1004)	.0326 (3.2060)	.9532 (3.1372)
L	−2.0737 (1.8343)	−0.0868 (−1.7464)	−1.8124 (−1.8424)
BHP	.0027 (.5913)	.0001 (.4771)	.0341 (.7301)
MOD	−0.0189 (−2.8428)	−0.0008 (−2.7072)	−0.0573 (−2.8506)
C	.4287 (.7568)	.0192 (.7703)	.0204 (.7750)
DOR	−0.1516 (−0.3560)	−0.0075 (−0.4009)	−0.0106 (−0.5790)
ATR	21.5954 (6.6018)	.3917 (2.7242)	.2064 (1.0054)
Const.	41.5015 (2.5160)	3.8156 (5.2620)	5.2898 (2.5447)
$\bar{R}^2$	.9731	.9468	.9465
Antilog $\bar{R}^2$	.9731	.9732	.9732

TABLE 4

ALTERNATIVE FUNCTIONAL FORMS, TOTAL 1961

	Linear $P = \sum_{i=1}^{n} \alpha_i X_i$	Semilog $\ln P = \sum_{i=1}^{n} \beta_i X_i$	Double Log $\ln P = \sum_{i=1}^{n} \gamma_i \ln X_i$
W	0.8861 (3.5491)	0.0247 (5.2114)	0.3763 (2.2063)
L	−1.0440 (−1.0123)	−0.0300 (−1.5305)	0.3071 (0.6918)
BHP	−0.0056 (−0.8206)	0.0002 (1.6677)	0.0614 (1.8327)
MOD	−0.0115 (−1.9044)	−0.0003 (−3.0399)	−0.0204 (−2.6775)
C	0.7605 (0.7484)	0.0385 (1.9944)	0.0462 (2.03552)
DOR	−1.7007 (−2.0621)	−0.0430 (−2.7458)	−0.0513 (−3.0666)
ATR	0.2325 (0.1504)	0.0363 (1.2366)	0.0720 (2.3577)
P.S.	20.8004 (9.9473)	0.4453 (11.2165)	0.5067 (12.3957)
Const.	16.3521 (1.9747)	2.8690 (10.8544)	0.6121 (0.7405)
$\overline{R}^2$	.7762	.8823	.8655
Antilog $\overline{R}^2$	.7762	.827	.790

TABLE 5

"QUALITY" AND "PURE PRICE" COMPONENTS OF CUMULATIVE PRICE CHANGES (PERCENTAGES)—U.S. 1953–64

	Total			*Mf* 1			*Mf* 2			*Mf* 3		
	c_0	c_1	c_2	c_0	c_1	c_2	c_0	c_1	c_2	c_0	c_1	c_2
1953	−4.3	4.25	−0.05	−13.1	−10.6	−2.5	4.2	−5.7	9.9	n.a.	n.a.	n.a.
1957	5.2	−2.8	8.0	−0.6	−2.9	2.3	8.9	2.5	6.4	n.a.	n.a.	n.a.
1961	0	0	0	0	0	0	0	0	0	0	0	0
1962	−0.6	5.0	−5.6	2.2	7.9	−5.7	−1.2	4.3	−5.5	−1.7	−3.3	1.6
1963	.3	2.5	−2.2	3.4	7.6	−4.2	−0.1	6.0	−6.1	−3.3	−5.1	1.8
1964	−2.2	4.8	−7.0	−1.6	9.2	−10.8	1.7	10.0	−8.3	−2.6	−6.6	4.0

TABLE 6

PRICING EQUATION
MAJOR MANUFACTURERS
(Double Log) U. S. 1950–65

	622 obs.	500 obs.	Frigidaire 132 obs.	G.E. 144 obs.	Hotpoint 54 obs.	Kelvinator 80 obs.	Philco 38 obs.	Westinghouse 52 obs.
FCF	.0597 (2.653)	.0461 (1.795)	−0.0276 (.412)	.0165 (.441)	.0897 (.994)	.0948 (1.324)	.2178 (1.313)	−0.2724 (−1.7333)
H	.1801 (2.442)	.2460 (3.199)	.5473 (2.565)	.0855 (.626)	.5726 (2.261)	.3853 (2.960)	−1.6334 (−2.652)	.4353 (.543)
W	.5475 (8.117)	.5757 (7.933)	.5138 (2.529)	1.1234 (7.294)	.2700 (.974)	.5046 (4.972)	1.9455 (2.501)	.7548 (1.298)
D	−0.4958 (−5.186)	−0.5981 (−5.511)	−0.9238 (−3.717)	−0.934 (−5.011)	−0.6587 (−1.284)	−0.6853 (−3.570)	.3389 (.633)	−1.0064 (−1.358)
*D*1	.1164 (6.759)	.1020 (5.473)	.0741 (2.112)	.0413 (1.417)	.1891 (2.817)	.1101 (2.698)	.0353 (.367)	.0700 (.715)
*D*3	−0.0690 (−3.241)	−0.0834 (−3.333)	−0.0750 (−1.164)	−0.0950 (−2.792)	−0.0145 (−0.138)	−0.1147 (−1.815)	−0.1287 (−1.517)	−0.1266 (−0.754)
*D*4	.0594 (2.546)	.0645 (2.552)	.1029 (2.122)	.0605 (1.578)	−0.6139 (−0.148)	.0133 (.236)	.1071 (1.153)	.1994 (1.461)
*D*7	−0.1817 (−4.938)	−0.2109 (−5.507)	−0.0953 (−0.623)	−0.2301 (−3.935)	−0.3741 (−3.622)	−0.1738 (−1.959)	−0.1994 (−1.685)	−0.2565 (−1.350)
*D*8	.1783 (7.3555)	0.1925 (7.2111)	.1149 (2.473)	.2237 (5.572)	.0301 (.334)	.1301 (1.874)	.2578 (1.958)	.2947 (2.133)

TABLE 6—CONTINUED

D9	.12309 (3.780)	.1241 (3.824)	.0228 (.536)	−0.1895 (−1.414)	0	0	.2631 (1.270)	.1389 (1.007)
D13	.0414 (2.074)	.0401 (1.817)	.2015 (4.803)	−0.0133 (−0.269)	.1031 (1.464)	.0113 (.276)	−0.0113 (−0.111)	.1420 (1.242)
D14	.2032 (6.272)	.2128 (6.336)	0	.1996 (4.048)	.3976 (3.251)	0	0	0
D18	.1407 (4.315)	.1058 (2.998)	.1010 (1.897)	−0.0337 (−0.433)	0	.1738 (3.002)	0	.4340 (2.504)
D19	.3333 (11.275)	.3225 (9.334)	.2901 (4.281)	.2420 (4.839)	.1472 (1.191)	.2909 (3.952)	.3151 (2.302)	.3385 (2.113)
D20	.2853 (9.158)	.2884 (8.905)	.2501 (5.397)	.1508 (2.493)	.4240 (3.144)	.5489 (17.175)	.1506 (1.165)	.4757 (2.232)
D21	.2804 (6.957)	.3189 (7.635)	.3566 (5.817)	.2896 (4.194)	.4513 (2.703)	.6209 (6.238)	.1624 (.817)	.2920 (1.278)
D22	.1406 (3.536)	.1394 (3.336)	.0867 (.576)	.2482 (3.754)	−0.1479 (−1.177)	−0.1291 (−1.228)	.1929 (1.504)	.2746 (1.030)
R^2	.7756	.8011	.8668	.8981	.6842	.8755	.8032	.6525

TABLE 7

QUALITY AND PRICE BEHAVIOR
REFRIGERATORS, ALL MANUFACTURERS
U.S. 1950–65

	Actual Price	Computed Price	Actual Price Change Relative to 1958 %	q_1	p_1
1950	284.	293.	−34.0	−24.0	−10.0
1951	318.	277.	−22.0	−29.5	7.3
1952	371.	369.	− 6.9	− 8.5	1.6
1953	365.	321.	− 9.9	−13.9	4.0
1954	340.	305.	−16.5	−20.0	3.6
1955	368.	303.	−11.0	−15.1	4.1
1956	375.	341.	− 9.9	− 8.8	− 1.1
1957	407.	356.	− 2.3	−15.6	16.6
1958	418.	371.	0	0	0
1959	377.	338.	−10.5	− 9.6	− 0.9
1960	483.	418.	16.9	11.5	5.4
1961	392.	369.	− 7.2	− 9.5	2.3
1962	356.	329.	−16.2	−11.8	− 4.4
1963	411.	387.	− 1.1	3.1	− 4.2
1964	422.	391.	1.1	5.1	− 4.0
1965	364.	416.	−12.0	11.9	−23.1

5

A MODEL OF SHORT-RUN LABOR ADJUSTMENT

PHOEBUS J. DHRYMES*
University of Pennsylvania, Philadelphia, Pennsylvania

5.1. Introduction

The problem to be studied is the determination of the speed with which short-run labor force adjustments toward optimal employment are made in response to shifts in expected demand, factor prices, and technological constraints. We shall examine, for aggregates at the two-digit, or higher, level, the impact on employment of changes in expected wage rates and output. We shall also be concerned with any possible effects of investment on employment, including the type of lag structure whereby these impacts are registered.

Net, or gross, investment replaces existing capital goods with plant and equipment of different vintages and, possibly, of higher quality. At a minimum, net investment would tend to change the physical and age composition of the capital stock. Thus, it becomes of interest to ascertain whether investment registers a net conserving or augmenting impact on employment requirements.

Unfortunately, a definitive answer to this question cannot be given since the scale of operation of the economy increased appreciably over the sample period of this study, 1948–60. Thus, there is unavoidable intermingling of scale and other investment effects upon the marginal productivity

---

* I would like to express my thanks to L. R. Klein for comments on an earlier version of this paper and to J. S. Duesenberry, F. M. Fisher, and E. Kuh for helpful discussions at the early stages of the research. Thanks also are due to H. Tsurumi and Yoel Haitowsky for assistance on computational matters. Computations were performed at the University of Pennsylvania Computer Center. Financial assistance was in part provided by NSF grant GS 571 at the University of Pennsylvania.

of labor. Assuming that technical change is embodied in investment to some degree, this makes it extremely difficult to identify the parameters of the production function because they depend both on the scale of operations and the age composition of the capital stock.[1] In other words, as investment takes place, it alters the type of capital goods used in the production process and, presumably, also alters the quantity and skills of labor required.

There are many other ramifications of the model proposed in this paper that might be examined. For example, the relationship between capital structure and "productive capacity" might be studied. While capacity is an amorphous concept, it might be defined as that volume of output at which short run marginal costs rise steeply.[2] We shall not, however, pursue this line of inquiry.

Using the model, one could also study the cyclical characteristics of the income share of labor in total real product, particularly as it is affected by output fluctuations or by changes in the composition of the capital stock. This, too, must be left for future research.

5.2. *Structure of the model*

This paper puts into a more general and rigorous framework, essentially in the context of a neoclassical production process, the excellent studies of Edwin Kuh and Charles Schultze and Joseph Tryon.[3] Kuh considered, inter alia, some employment equations derived by inverting a linear approximation to a production function. Schultze and Tryon estimated price mark-up equations which may be interpreted as approximations to the marginal productivity conditions governing labor employment. Both studies assume a distributed lag adjustment process.

[1] The introduction of an infinite lag structure in investment (because capital stock is a function of the historical path of investment outlays) together with the presence of other exogenous variables in the equation whose parameters are to be determined, also creates some novel estimation problems. A satisfactory solution to these difficulties is obtained through a modification of classical maximum likelihood techniques. Of course technical change may be labor embodied as well. While this must be granted, especially as it relates to skill improvements, nonetheless it would appear that capital embodied technical change is, empirically, more significant.

[2] This is the approach taken by Bert G. Hickman in his *Investment Demand and U.S. Economic Growth* (Brookings Institution, 1965). See also L. R. Klein and R. S. Preston, "The Measurement of Capacity Utilization," *American Economic Review*, Vol. 57, No. 1, pp. 34–58.

[3] E. Kuh, "Income Distribution and Employment Over the Business Cycle", and C. L. Schultze and J. L. Tryon, "Prices and Wages", *Brookings, op. cit.*

In this paper, marginal productivity conditions determine *optimal* labor employment. The path of *actual* employment to the optimal position is then given by an explicit adjustment process. In the overall Brookings model, the combination of these functional relationships could be used to replace the employment equations estimated by Kuh.

While a "structural" motivation for the model is presented below, the latter may also be thought of as a reduced form of the true, imprecisely known and relatively flexible structure of the economy. In any event, even given a degree of uncertainty about that structure, our results should provide some insight into the dynamics of labor adjustment.

Thus (ignoring aggregation problems), let the industry under investigation be characterized by the production function:

$$Q = A[aK^{\beta} + bL^{\beta}]^{1/\beta}, \tag{5.1}$$

where Q is output, K is capital, and L is labor. This is the well-known constant elasticity of substitution production function; A, a, and b are positive parameters; $\sigma = 1/(1-\beta)$ is the (constant) elasticity of substitution. We assume that optimal labor employment is determined by the marginal condition:

$$\frac{\partial Q}{\partial L} = S(t)w, \tag{5.2}$$

where $S(t)$ is a well defined function of the elasticity of demand for output and supply of labor, t is some time index, and w is the product wage.

Since the question of market imperfection does not concern us here and we are constructing a short-run model, it is not unreasonable to take $S(t)$ as a time invariant function. Given a residual theory of income distribution (implicit in this model), the labor share in output is determined through some form of equation (5.2), and capital gets the remainder. (Because the process of capital adjustment has been reasonably adequately treated by others, we shall be concerned only with the process of labor adjustment.[4]) Solving (5.2) we get:

$$L^* = A^* w^{1/(\beta-1)} Q b^{1/(1-\beta)}, \tag{5.3}$$

where

$$A^* = A^{\beta/(1-\beta)}[S(t)]^{\beta/(\beta-1)}.$$

Equation (5.3) determines the optimal labor employment of the industry, given the latter's expectations concerning wage rates and real output. It

---

[4] Cf. Dale W. Jorgenson, "Anticipations and Investment Behavior", in *Brookings, ibid.*

would perhaps be proper to denote the expected quantities by $\hat{w}$ and $\hat{Q}$ respectively; but generally this will not be done now in the interest of simplicity of notation and because no confusion will arise at this stage.

For a variety of reasons, the industry may not choose to carry out the actions implied by equation (5.3). In the short run, the adjustment implied may not be fully realized because: (1) expectations with respect to output and wages are clouded with uncertainty; or (2) because there are costs of increasing employment which the industry may not wish to incur fully in view of uncertainty of future employment needs; or (3) because of difficulties involved in carrying out a concurrent adjustment of capital stock. For these, and perhaps other, reasons we may postulate the following adjustment mechanism: [5]

$$\frac{L_t}{L_{t-1}} = \left[\frac{L_t^*}{L_{t-1}}\right]^\alpha . \tag{5.4}$$

We may also assume that expected wages and output are given by:

$$\hat{w}_t = A_1 w_t , \tag{5.5}$$

and

$$\hat{Q}_t = A_2 Q_t^{\lambda_1} Q_{t-1}^{\lambda_2} . \tag{5.6}$$

Equation (5.4) gives a logarithmic version of the usual adjustment process in which only part of a gap between current desired and previous position values is eliminated in a given period. Equations (5.5) and (5.6) state that expected wages are proportional to actual wages, and expected output is logarithmically proportional to a linear combination of actual output in the current and preceding periods.

As to investment, in this paper we wish to explore the dependence of labor employment on the time profile of the capital stock. The reason for this is that one might expect the marginal productivity of labor, in general, to depend on the type of capital equipment utilized. Since capital goods of different vintages embody different levels of technical advance, it seems reasonable, in formalizing this dependence, to have some of the parameters of the production function depend, with an infinite length lag, on investment. This accomplishes our objective in that it allows, rather elegantly, the entire history of capital stock accumulation to exert an influence on the marginal productivity of labor, and hence on optimal labor employment. With this in

---

[5] A similar approach also was suggested by T. Haavelmo, "A Note on the Theory of Investment", *Review of Economic Studies*, Vol. 16(2), 1949–1950.

mind we postulate:

$$b^{1/(1-\beta)} = \prod_{i=0}^{\infty} I_{t-i}^{\beta_i}, \tag{5.7}$$

where I is investment.

Of course this form of the equation is too general to permit estimation. At the cost of a slight loss in generality, we shall particularize it to:

$$\frac{1}{1-\beta} \ln b = \frac{f(Z)}{g(Z)} \ln I_t, \tag{5.8}$$

where f and g are polynomials in the lag operator Z. The latter is defined by:

$$Z^k \ln I_t = \ln I_{t-k}, \qquad k = 0, 1, 2, \ldots \tag{5.9}$$

For $k = 0$ we have the identity operator,

$$Z^0 \ln I_t = \ln I_t. \tag{5.10}$$

It might be noted that one could just as well have formulated the impact of investment on optimal labor employment through the scale parameter A; in the empirical application of this model, it would have made no difference. The formulation used was preferred because it directly ties an investment impact to employment, and thus it is intuitively more appealing given the objectives of this study.

Since, in the empirical applications, certain forms of the polynomials f and g have been found adequate, we shall further particularize (5.8) and conduct the remainder of the argument in this section in terms of the specifications:

$$f(Z) = f_1 Z + f_2 Z^2 + f_3 Z^3 + f_4 Z^4, \tag{5.11}$$

and

$$g(Z) = I + g_1 Z. \tag{5.12}$$

Now, substituting (5.3), (5.5), (5.6), (5.7), (5.11), and (5.12) into (5.4), we have, upon taking logarithms,

$$\ln L_t = c + \frac{\alpha}{\beta - 1} \ln w_t + \alpha\lambda_1 \ln Q_t + \alpha\lambda_2 \ln Q_{t-1} + (1-\alpha) \ln L_{t-1}$$
$$+ \frac{\sum_{i=1}^{4} f_i Z^i}{I + g_1 Z} \ln I_t. \tag{5.13}$$

Clearing fractions and writing a stochastic version, we obtain:

$$\ln L_t = (c+g_1)+\frac{\alpha}{\beta-1}(\ln w_t+g_1 \ln w_{t-1})+\alpha\lambda_1(\ln Q_t+g_1 \ln Q_{t-1})$$
$$+\alpha\lambda_2(\ln Q_{t-1}+g_1 \ln Q_{t-2})+(1-\alpha)[\ln L_{t-1}+g_1 \ln L_{t-2}]-g_1 \ln L_{t-1}$$
$$+\alpha\sum_{i=1}^{4} f_i Z^i \ln I_t+\varepsilon_t, \tag{5.14}$$

where,

$$c = \alpha\left[\ln A^* + \ln A_2 + \frac{1}{\beta-1}\ln A_1\right].$$

In the interest of more manageable notation, let us put: $\rho = -g_1$;

$$\gamma_0 = c+g_1; \quad \gamma_1 = \frac{\alpha}{\beta-1}; \quad \gamma_2 = \alpha\lambda_1; \quad \gamma_3 = \alpha\lambda_2;$$

$$\gamma_4 = 1-\alpha; \quad \gamma_5 = \alpha f_1; \quad \gamma_6 = \alpha f_2; \quad \gamma_7 = \alpha f_3; \quad \text{and} \quad \gamma_8 = \alpha f_4.$$

Therefore:

$$[\ln L_t-\rho \ln L_{t-1}] = \gamma_0+\gamma_1[\ln w_t-\rho \ln w_{t-1}]$$
$$+\gamma_2[\ln Q_t-\rho \ln Q_{t-1}]+\gamma_3[\ln Q_{t-1}-\rho \ln Q_{t-2}]$$
$$+\gamma_4[\ln L_{t-1}-\rho \ln L_{t-2}]+\gamma_5 \ln I_{t-1}+\gamma_6 \ln I_{t-2}+\gamma_7 \ln I_{t-3}$$
$$+\gamma_8 \ln I_{t-4}+\varepsilon_t. \tag{5.15}$$

It is clear from equation (5.15) that, under the usual specification on the random term (ε_t), and if ρ is known, the parameters of the equation can be estimated by standard, linear techniques. If ρ is not known, we are confronted with a nonlinear estimation problem which does not readily yield to standard procedures.

5.3. *Estimation of the model*

The most obvious approach to the estimation problem posed by equation (5.15) is to determine the parameters by minimizing the sum of the squared residuals under an appropriate set of constraints. Another approach would be to employ the method of scoring.[6] However, both these approaches are,

[6] C. R. Rao, *Advanced Statistical Methods in Biometric Research* (John Wiley and Sons, London, 1952), p. 165.

for this problem, unnecessarily ponderous and computationally tedious. Both entail the extraction of roots of nonlinear equations, and thus involve search in ten-dimensional Euclidean space.

Fortunately, there is a much simpler solution. The estimation difficulties arise because the investment lag structure is inherited by the other variables of the model, thereby inducing nonlinearity in the parameters; if straightforward least squares techniques are applied, a multiplicity of estimators for ρ is obtained. But, if ρ is *assumed* fixed, then maximum likelihood techniques can be applied to obtain the estimates quite simply. By varying the fixed value of ρ over its admissible range, estimators corresponding to the global maximum of the likelihood function are obtained.

This can readily be shown. Let $y_t = L_t - \rho L_{t-1}$. Similarly, with ρ given, let the independent variables (including a unit vector for the constant term) be denoted by x's. Therefore, in this notation (5.15) can be written as:

$$\boldsymbol{y} = \boldsymbol{X}\gamma + \boldsymbol{u}, \tag{5.16}$$

where $\boldsymbol{y}$ is a column vector with T observations, $\boldsymbol{X}$ is a $T \times 9$ matrix, γ is a 9 element (parameters) column vector, and $\boldsymbol{u}$ is a column vector of T random disturbances.

The stochastic specification of the model is given by: [7]

$$u \sim N(0, \sigma^2); \tag{5.17}$$

that is, u is normally distributed with mean zero and variance σ^2. The logarithm of the likelihood function of the parameters is given by:

$$\mathscr{L} = -\frac{T}{2}\ln(2\pi) - \frac{T}{2}\ln\sigma^2 - \frac{1}{2\sigma^2}(\boldsymbol{y}-\boldsymbol{X}\gamma)'(\boldsymbol{y}-\boldsymbol{X}\gamma) \tag{5.18}$$

To obtain the maximum likelihood estimators of (γ, ρ, σ^2), we employ step-wise maximization. Thus, fixing ρ, we maximize first with respect to (γ, σ^2) to obtain:

$$\hat{\gamma}(\rho) = (\boldsymbol{X}'\boldsymbol{X})^{-1}\boldsymbol{X}'\boldsymbol{y}; \quad \text{and} \quad \hat{\sigma}^2(\rho) = \frac{(\boldsymbol{y}-\boldsymbol{X}\gamma)'(\boldsymbol{y}-\boldsymbol{X}\gamma)}{T}. \tag{5.19}$$

[7] It might be objected that the error term in (5.16) cannot have the specification given in (5.17) had a stochastic term been introduced *ab initio* in (5.13). In that case if the error terms were nonautocorrelated initially, then the error term resulting after fractions are cleared in (5.14) will in general display serial correlation. While this is true except in highly special circumstances, nonetheless whether the error terms in (5.16) display autocorrelation or not is something for which we can test once the estimation process has been completed; this shall be done in the empirical work to follow.

The notation $\hat{\sigma}^2$, $\hat{\sigma}^2(\rho)$ and $\hat{\gamma}$, $\hat{\gamma}(\rho)$ have identical meanings; the parenthetical variants are used only to emphasize that these are estimators conditioned on ρ. Substituting (5.19) into (5.18), we obtain the concentrated likelihood function:

$$\mathscr{L}^*(\rho) = -\frac{T}{2}[\ln(2\pi)+1]-\frac{T}{2}\ln\hat{\sigma}^2(\rho). \tag{5.20}$$

From (5.20) it is seen that maximizing the likelihood function involves minimizing $\hat{\sigma}^2(\rho)$, with respect to ρ. The problem is, however, that (5.20) is highly nonlinear with respect to ρ.

Fortunately, there is a rather simple solution. Note that ρ cannot be estimated as a completely free parameter. The investment lag structure was specified by:

$$\frac{\gamma_5 Z+\gamma_6 Z^2+\gamma_7 Z^3+\gamma_8 Z^4}{I-\rho Z}\ln I_t. \tag{5.21}$$

Consider the case where at time t, $I_t = 1$, and thereafter investment is zero. Then the long-run effect on labor employment is given by:

$$\gamma_5\sum_{k=1}^{\infty}\rho^k+\gamma_6\sum_{k=2}^{\infty}\rho^k+\gamma_7\sum_{k=3}^{\infty}\rho^k+\gamma_8\sum_{k=4}^{\infty}\rho^k. \tag{5.22}$$

For this to be finite, it is required that,

$$|\rho| < 1. \tag{5.23}$$

We therefore incorporate the restriction that the absolute value of ρ be less than unity into the basic specification of the model.

Consequently, the maximum likelihood estimator of ρ is given by,

$$\hat{\rho} = \mathscr{L}^{*-1}[\max_{|\rho|<1}\mathscr{L}^*(\rho)]; \tag{5.24}$$

that is, it is that value of ρ which maximizes (5.20) or, equivalently, minimizes $\hat{\sigma}^2(\rho)$.

Now the estimation problem is quite routine. The procedure is to select, arbitrarily, a reasonable number of trial values for ρ in the interval $(-1, 1)$. For each value of ρ, using equation (5.16), estimate by ordinary least squares, γ and σ^2. Then select that regression for which the standard error of estimate ($\hat{\sigma}$) is minimal.

One can be as precise in the estimates as is desired by taking a sufficiently dense set of trial values of ρ. Under the maintained hypotheses, such estimators, being maximum likelihood ones, are asymptotically unbiased and efficient; they are also consistent. (The covariance matrix of the estimators is derived in section 5.7.) Nevertheless, it should be remembered that the maintained hypotheses include the assumption that expected wages and output are exogenous.

Finally, the appropriate coefficient of determination of multiple regression for these estimates is given by:

$$\bar{R}^2 = 1 - \frac{\min\limits_{|\rho|<1} [(y - X\hat{\gamma})'(y - X\hat{\gamma})]}{\sum\limits_{t=1}^{T} (\ln L_t - \overline{\ln L})^2} \cdot \frac{T-1}{T-m}, \tag{5.25}$$

where m is the number of elements (i.e. estimated regression coefficients in the vector γ); in our model, at most, $m = 9$. The corresponding statistic yielded by ordinary regression computer programs is:

$$\bar{R}^2 = 1 - \frac{\min\limits_{|\rho|<1} [(y - X\hat{\gamma})'(y - X\hat{\gamma})]}{\sum\limits_{t=1}^{T} (y_t - \bar{y})^2} \cdot \frac{T-1}{T-m+1} \tag{5.26}$$

In the empirical results, $\bar{R}^2$ shall be reported as calculated from (5.25). This may, obviously, differ considerably from the ordinary $\bar{R}^2$ from (5.26).

5.4. Empirical application of the model

5.4.1. Exact definition of variables in the estimated model

Up this point, the variables to be introduced into the model have been defined in general terms. We have spoken of employment, output, wage rates, investment and so forth. Before proceeding any further, it is best to define these more precisely.

Labor input into the production process, for example, is not merely the number of employees, but that quantity multiplied by the number of hours worked. That is, the production function properly is written in terms of manhours.

Output, wage rates, and investment, of course, should be stated in constant dollars. Moreover, output in the context of this model, should be defined on a value added basis. Of course, ideally, capital should be stated in terms of *capital services* rather than *capital stock*. If the rate of utilization varies, the two measures could be appreciably different. Unfortunately no data are available on capital utilization so that capital stock was used. Combining these considerations leads to a restatement of equation (5.15) in the form to be estimated for each industry:

$$\begin{aligned}\ln MH = {} & \gamma_0+\gamma_1\{\ln [RWSS/PX]-\rho \ln [RWSS/PX]_{-1}\} \\ & +\gamma_2\{\ln X^{54}-\rho \ln [X^{54}]_{-1}\}+\gamma_3\{\ln [X^{54}]_{-1}-\rho \ln [X^{54}]_{-2}\} \\ & +\rho \ln [MH]_{-1}+\gamma_4\{\ln [MH]_{-1}-\rho \ln [MH]_{-2}\} \\ & +\gamma_5 \ln [I^{54}_{BUS}]_{-1}+\gamma_6 \ln [I^{54}_{BUS}]_{-2}+\gamma_7 \ln [I^{54}_{BUS}]_{-3} \\ & +\gamma_8 \ln [I^{54}_{BUS}]_{-4}, \qquad (5.27)\end{aligned}$$

where,

ln = natural logarithm

MH = manhours, millions per year

$RWSS$ = compensation of employes per manhour, dollars per hour

PX = implicit price deflator for gross product originating, 1954 = 1.00

X^{54} = gross product originating, billions of 1954 dollars

I^{54}_{BUS} = business gross investment in plant and equipment, billions of 1954 dollars.

This relationship is easily converted to a real labor cost function by adding ln $[RWSS/PX]$ to both sides of the equation. The procedure is valid, however (when using the previously described estimation technique), only if wage rates are a truly exogenous variable.

Another possible use of equation (5.27) is to study the short-run behavior of the functional distribution of income between labor and nonlabor shares. This can be accomplished by adding $\{\ln [RWSS/PX]- \ln X^{54}\}$ to both sides of the relationship.

This is not to suggest that the variation of short-run (labor) costs or distributive shares is best studied in the context herein employed. Nevertheless, our approach is sufficiently flexible to permit some inference about these characteristics. In addition, the long-run response (elasticity) of labor employment to a change in the wage rate is easily calculated from equation (5.27) as $\gamma_1/(1-\gamma_4) = -1/(1-\beta)$. This is simply the negative of the elasticity of substitution in the postulated (static) production function (5.1).

While it is not the purpose of this study to estimate production function parameters, some of these are generated as a by-product of the estimates. To a limited extent, a test of the plausibility of the model is the credibility of the elasticity of substitution parameters so obtained.

5.4.2. *Description of data*

The model described in the preceding section has been applied to selected two-digit U.S. manufacturing industries, as well as to certain nonmanufacturing aggregates. The list of industries appears in table 5.1.

TABLE 5.1

Two-digit U.S. manufacturing industries and nonmanufacturing aggregates

Industry Number	Industry	Industry Number	Industry
2	Mining	27	Stone, clay and glass
7	Railway transportation	31	Food and beverages
8	Nonrail transportation	33	Textile mill products
9	Communication	35	Paper and allied products
10	Public utilities	37	Chemicals
20	Primary metals	38	Petroleum and coal products
22	Nonelectrical machinery	39	Rubber products
23	Electrical machinery	50	Total manufacturing
24	Motor vehicles and parts	51	Durable manufacturing
25	Other transportation equipment	56	Nondurable manufacturing

Essentially, the definitions and data for the two-digit industries were based on the work of Schultze and Tryon (data for the aggregates were supplied by Brookings).[8] Their series were used for real gross product originating, the product price deflator, and employee compensation (wages and salaries plus supplements). However, investment data is not given in their compilation; therefore, Jorgenson's figures were used.[9] Generally, there was an almost exact correspondence between the Jorgenson and Schultze-Tryon industry definitions; a few sectors required the summation of industry components.

The remaining series needed for estimating the model were derived from data compiled by Ross Preston from Bureau of Labor Statistics sources.[10] They provide monthly, seasonally unadjusted data on total employment,

[8] C. L. Schultze and J. L. Tryon, *op. cit.*

[9] D. W. Jorgenson, *op. cit.*, unpublished appendix.

[10] U.S. Bureau of Labor Statistics, *Employment and Earnings Statistics for the United States*, 1909–65, Bulletin 1312–2 (U.S. Government Printing Office, 1965), and earlier monthly bulletins.

TABLE 5.2

Production worker manhours as a fraction of total manhours in manufacturing industries: 1948: 1–1960: 4

Industry	Average Fraction	$MH_P/MH = h+mTIME$			$\ln[M_PH/MH] = h+m\ TIME$		
		$\hat{h}$	$\hat{m}$	$\bar{R}^2$	$\hat{h}$	$\hat{m}$	$\bar{R}^2$
20 Primary metals	0.838	0.873 (30.535)	−0.001 (14.319)	0.800	−0.106 (12.255)	−0.023 (8.449)	0.579
22 Nonelectrical machinery	0.797	0.831 (39.510)	−0.001 (18.413)	0.868	0.155 (20.314)	−0.023 (9.599)	0.641
23 Electrical machinery	0.735	0.789 (14.964)	−0.001 (11.088)	0.705	−0.203 (11.195)	−0.033 (5.828)	0.392
24 Motor vehicles and parts	0.796	0.824 (19.018)	−0.001 (7.876)	0.544	−0.169 (14.976)	−0.019 (5.524)	0.366
25 Other transportation equipment	0.723	0.825 (30.968)	−0.003 (39.854)	0.968	−0.103 (5.519)	−0.070 (11.023)	0.702
27 Stone, clay and glass	0.842	0.875 (66.002)	−0.001 (28.126)	0.939	−0.104 (18.253)	−0.021 (12.014)	0.737
31 Food and beverages	0.717	0.762 (82.863)	−0.001 (56.766)	0.984	−0.219 (31.926)	−0.027 (17.264)	0.853

33 Textile mill products	0.919	0.936 (143.061)	−0.0007 (31.039)	0.949	−0.050 (22.578)	−0.011 (16.322)	0.838
35 Paper and allied products	0.827	0.869 (53.403)	−0.001 (27.666)	0.937	−0.105 (14.936)	−0.027 (11.974)	0.736
37 Chemicals	0.671	0.745 (45.395)	−0.002 (49.089)	0.979	−0.213 (16.157)	−0.060 (14.361)	0.801
38 Petroleum and coal products	0.706	0.779 (39.642)	−0.002 (42.799)	0.972	−0.169 (12.628)	−0.060 (14.037)	0.793
39 Rubber products	0.790	0.814 (40.033)	−0.0009 (13.025)	0.767	−0.184 (31.106)	−0.016 (8.721)	0.595
50 Total manufac-turing	0.790	0.834 (55.271)	−0.001 (33.507)	0.956	−0.140 (17.127)	−0.031 (12.059)	0.739
51 Durable manufacturing	0.791	0.842 (36.747)	−0.001 (24.719)	0.922	−0.130 (12.340)	−0.034 (10.187)	0.668
56 Nondurable manufacturing	0.788	0.825 (91.446)	−0.007 (47.948)	0.978	−0.153 (28.194)	−0.028 (16.401)	0.840

Note t ratios of coefficients are shown parenthetically.

production worker employment, and average hourly earnings of production workers.

The employment data were seasonally adjusted with the Census Method II computer program of the National Bureau of Economic Research. Nonproduction worker employment was then obtained by subtracting production worker from total employment. Multiplying average weekly hours of production workers by their employment, and nonproduction worker employment by an assumed forty hours per week, adding the two components, summing over the three-month period in each quarter, and multiplying by $(4 \times 52/12)$, yields total quarterly manhours, seasonally adjusted at annual rates (SAAR). Manhours (SAAR) for the production and nonproduction worker components can, of course, also be derived separately.

While it is not customary to disaggregate capital or labor in production function and related studies (the recent study by Kuh, *op. cit.*, is a notable exception), and while production workers form the bulk of total employment, nonetheless it was deemed desirable and appropriate to experiment with some forms of disaggregation. Essentially, this involved estimating separate employment functions for production and nonproduction workers and is reported briefly in sections 5.5.3. after exploring the aggregate results. Given the existence of data for the manufacturing sector, the motivation for this attempt at disaggregation stems from the *a priori* view that the characteristics of production and nonproduction employment may differ markedly because they perform appreciably different tasks in the production process.

Furthermore, the proportion of production workers in total employment has been declining over the post-war period. This is clearly shown in table 5.2. In the table, the mean fraction of production manhours (MH_P) to total manhours (MH), as well as the parameters of the simple linear and logarithmic regressions of the fraction of production manhours, (MH_P/MH) against time, are presented. The results leave no doubt of the persistent (and linear) decline in the relative importance of production workers over the post-war period. (The logarithmic relations are clearly inferior and are reported only to show easily the relative rates of decline.) Thus, while production employment is still the largest component of total employment, it is clear that nonproduction employment is increasingly assuming considerable significance; to the extent that the determinants of the two types of employment are appreciably different, aggregation is bound to lead to considerable difficulties.

To obtain wage rates, series for employee compensation (SAAR) were divided by the total manhours, yielding compensation rates per hour. These were then divided by output price indexes to obtain the required product wage series.

5.5. *Empirical results*

5.5.1. *Total manhours: short-run effects*

The results of estimating the parameters of equation (5.27) are given in table 5.3. Three principal types of short-run effects can directly be observed in the table: (1) the speed of response of actual to desired (or optimal) manhours; (2) the short-run elasticity of labor inputs with respect to real wage rates and output; and (3) the short-run impact of real investment on labor demand.

Speed of response The speed of response is given by $1-\gamma_4$. In the nonmanufacturing aggregate group (industries 02, 07, 08, 09, and 10), the point estimate of this parameter ranges from 0.19 for mining to 0.83 for nonrail transportation; but, generally, it is greater than 0.5. On the other hand, in manufacturing, the two-digit durables industries exhibit a higher speed of response than the nondurable industries. For durables as a group (industry 51) this parameter is 0.432, while for all nondurables (industry 56) it is only 0.064. Multicollinearity difficulties in this last equation, however, cast some suspicion on this extremely low value. Nevertheless, it appears, as a first substantive conclusion, that durables industries tend to adjust their labor utilization to an optimal level much more rapidly than nondurable industries.

Because the estimates are based on quarterly data, and because there is a tendency to interpret the speed of response as the fraction of the gap between actual and desired manhours to be eliminated during a quarter, it might seem that responses are inordinately rapid. This interpretation, which is the customary one, would be correct if the adjustment process were linear. However, the model in this paper is nonlinear (although it is linear in the logs). Therefore, it might be of interest to compare the results under the two alternative assumptions: linear, $(x_t - x_{t-1}) = d(x^* - x_{t-1})$; and log-linear, $\ln (x_t/x_{t-1}) = d \ln (x^*/x_{t-1})$, where x^* is the desired value of x.

Table 5.4 presents illustrations of the magnitude of the gap remaining after four quarters for different values of the speed of adjustment (d), and different initial and desired values of x. This is done for both linear and log-

TABLE 5.3

Total manhours equations: parameter estimates.

$$\ln MH = \gamma_0+\gamma_1\{\ln[RWSS/PX]-\rho\ln[RWSS/PX]_{-1}\}+\gamma_2\{\ln X^{54}-\rho\ln[X^{54}]_{-1}\}+\gamma_3\{\ln[X^{54}]_{-1}-\rho\ln[X^{54}]_{-2}\}$$
$$+\rho\ln[MH]_{-1}+\gamma_4\{\ln[MH]_{-1}-\rho\ln[MH]_{-2}\}+\gamma_5\ln[I^{54}_{BUS}]_{-1}+\gamma_6\ln[I^{54}_{BUS}]_{-2}+\gamma_7\ln[I^{54}_{BUS}]_{-3}$$
$$+\gamma_8\ln[I^{54}_{BUS}]_{-4}$$

Industry	γ_0	γ_1	γ_2	γ_3	ρ	γ_4	γ_5	γ_6	γ_7	γ_8	$\bar{R}^2$	Durbin-Watson statistic
02 Mining	−1.717	−0.122	0.384	−0.122	−0.250	0.814		−0.108			0.9491	2.139
	(2.941)	(3.269)	(8.085)	(2.100)	(24.264)	(12.390)		(2.215)				
07 Railway	−0.272	−0.127	0.407	0.222	0.825	0.245	0.035			0.022	0.9881	2.038
transportation	(1.326)	(1.796)	(6.294)	(2.532)	(40.108)	(1.980)	(2.576)			(2.099)		
08 Nonrail	−1.556	−0.734	0.666	0.203	0.125	0.170				0.026	0.9779	1.086
transportation	(2.111)	(9.630)	(5.261)	(1.758)	(8.442)	(2.002)				(1.915)		
09 Communications	1.228	−0.547	0.534	−0.234	0.450	0.434	0.097			−0.047	0.9724	2.055
	(2.114)	(5.308)	(3.253)	(1.576)	(90.734)	(3.987)	(3.751)			(3.231)		
10 Public	2.523	−0.119	0.010	0.121	0.275	0.513				0.020	0.8947	1.770
utilities	(3.447)	(2.289)	(0.126)	(1.969)	(42.941)	(4.457)				(2.214)		
20 Primary	3.049	−0.420	0.518	−0.004	0.050	0.132		0.045			0.9577	1.931
metals	(4.902)	(6.162)	(24.593)	(0.075)	(37.059)	(1.103)		(3.819)				
22 Nonelectrical	0.616	−0.268	0.411	0.109	0.275	0.037				0.010	0.9900	1.695
machinery	(3.035)	(6.457)	(12.077)	(2.380)	(75.208)	(5.310)				(1.290)		
23 Electrical	0.756	−0.265	0.419	0.052	0.325	0.494	−0.026				0.9968	1.840
machinery	(2.768)	(8.526)	(13.201)	(1.200)	(21.462)	(7.905)	(2.270)					

24 Motor vehicles and parts	2.046 (2.597)	−0.431 (5.941)	0.479 (9.055)	−0.118 (1.544)	0.050 (16.627)	0.390 (3.671)	0.040 (2.245)			0.8754	1.985
25 Other transportation equipment	0.223 (2.393)	−0.324 (5.236)	0.567 (10.420)	−0.007 (0.115)	0.775 (66.368)	0.317 (3.315)		−0.18 (3.414)		0.9984	2.104
27 Stone, clay and glass	0.044 (1.375)	−0.226 (7.00)	0.307 (8.740)	−0.041 (0.295)	0.125 (54.032)	0.601 (6.681)	0.001 (0.140)			0.9564	1.753
31 Food and beverages	0.708 (0.747)	−0.093 (2.787)	0.378 (4.694)	−0.300 (4.115)	0.250 (99.930)	0.832 (10.080)	0.013 (1.400)		−0.023 (2.115)	0.7000	1.975
33 Textile mill products	−0.359 (2.565)	−0.052 (2.003)	0.375 (13.478)	−0.160 (5.064)	0.700 (92.032)	0.830 (17.398)			0.019 (3.504)	0.9969	2.468
35 Paper and allied products	0.579 (1.833)	−0.033 (1.943)	0.304 (9.257)	−0.164 (3.543)	0.175 (47.966)	0.780 (11.983)		−0.014 (2.696)		0.9949	1.929
37 Chemicals	0.412 (1.025)	−0.139 (5.728)	0.329 (6.245)	−0.137 (2.298)	0.225 (53.656)	0.713 (10.606)	0.031 (3.386)			0.9928	1.310
38 Petroleum and coal products	0.449 (0.580)	−0.073 (1.920)	0.261 (4.207)	−0.225 (3.370)	−0.025 (35.302)	0.921 (14.057)	0.045 (2.300)		−0.025 (1.809)	0.9298	2.053
39 Rubber products	0.195 (0.340)	−0.108 (2.531)	0.462 (9.134)	−0.291 (4.156)	0.100 (83.262)	0.792 (7.300)			0.019 (1.555)	0.9298	2.010
50 Total manufacturing	−1.013 (4.701)	−0.283 (7.026)	0.462 (16.335)	−0.122 (2.890)	0.425 (91.337)	0.620 (9.656)			0.010 (1.490)	0.9896	1.847
51 Durable manufacturing	−1.292 (6.797)	−0.290 (7.609)	0.483 (19.839)	−0.107 (2.636)	0.300 (23.470)	0.568 (8.833)			0.013 (1.723)	0.9911	2.075
56 Nondurable manufacturing	−0.370 (1.457)	−0.105 (8.313)	0.421 (24.951)	−0.324 (18.199)	0.300 (7.881)	0.936 (30.274)			0.004 (1.711)	0.9970	2.149

Note t-ratios of parameters are shown parenthetically.

linear cases. In the linear case the fraction of a gap remaining after one year (which is independent of the difference between initial and desired positions) is:

$$\frac{x^* - x_t}{x^* - x_0} = (1-d)^t; \tag{5.28}$$

and for the nonlinear case it is,

$$\frac{x^* - x_t}{x^* - x_0} = \left\{1 - \left[\frac{x_0}{x^*}\right]^{(1-d)^t}\right\}\left\{\frac{1}{1 - \frac{x_0}{x^*}}\right\} \tag{5.29}$$

where x_0 is the initial value of x. A derivation of these equations is given n appendix section 5.7.2.

TABLE 5.4

Fraction of gap between desired and initial values remaining after one year.

Quarterly adjustment speed of (d)	Loglinear adjustment Ratio of initial to desired value					Linear adjustment
	0.5	0.6	0.7	0.8	0.9	
0.1	0.7310	0.7130	0.6973	0.6795	0.6680	0.6561
0.2	0.4942	0.4717	0.4536	0.4360	0.4220	0.4096
0.3	0.3062	0.2878	0.2736	0.2605	0.2490	0.2401
0.4	0.1716	0.1602	0.1500	0.1425	0.1355	0.1296
0.5	0.0852	0.0780	0.0726	0.0695	0.0655	0.0625
0.6	0.0350	0.0322	0.0303	0.0280	0.0270	0.0257
0.7	0.0112	0.0102	0.0096	0.0090	0.0088	0.0081
0.8	0.0023	0.0021	0.0020	0.0018	0.0017	0.0016

It is apparent from table 5.4, irrespective of the type of adjustment or the ratio between initial and desired values, that if the speed of adjustment is high, the gap is nearly completely eliminated within a year's time. Applying the $d = (1-\gamma_4)$ parameters of table 5.3, *ceteris paribus*, about 0.92 of the ıelative gap is closed in four quarters for most of the two-digit durable manufacturing industries and approximately 0.6 of the gap for the nondurables industries. For the aggregates, total, durable, and nondurable manufacturing, the corresponding figures are 0.85, 0.9, and 0.35, respectively. For nonmanufacturing aggregates, the figures range from 0.45 for mining to 0.99 for nonrail transportation.

Although the reaction coefficients indicate a generally rapid adjustment to desired labor input conditions, it might be maintained that they should be even higher, if not unity. That is, while there are well-known justifications for only a partial accommodation of capital adjustment to capacity pressures, it could be argued that labor deficiencies should have been made up instantaneously in view of the persistent underemployment characteristic of the postwar U.S. economy. But this ignores certain frictional elements in finding, attracting, hiring and training new workers and limitations on the extent that the work week can be lengthened.

Elasticity with respect to real wages and output In the short-run sensitivity of total manhours to wage rates and output, as measured by the respective elasticity parameters, a sharp difference again appears in the behavior of durable and nondurable manufacturing (cf. table 5.3). Thus, for the two-digit durable industries, the elasticity parameter ranges between 0.226 for stone, clay and glass and 0.431 for motor vehicles and parts. For the two-digit nondurable industries, the range is from 0.330 for paper and allied products to 0.139 for chemicals. Roughly the same dichotomy holds when we examine the short-run elasticity of labor input with respect to output originating.

The identical conclusion emerges from the parameter estimates of the durable and nondurable aggregates. The difference in the wage elasticity of the aggregates is substantial (0.290 as contrasted with 0.105), while the difference in the output elasticity is rather small (0.483 as contrasted with 0.421).

These results are entirely in accord with the findings regarding the speed of adjustment of the component industries of manufacturing. We determined earlier that durable industries in general exhibited a higher speed of adjustment than nondurable industries. Since desired labor manhours in the model depend on wage rates and output, it is encouraging that our results indicate a greater sensitivity of labor employment to wage rates and output for durable industries than nondurable industries.

Impact of investment The effect of real investment on labor inputs has been formalized in the model by an infinite lag structure represented by a weighted sum of simple geometric lags. The effective length of the lag is determined by the magnitude of the parameter ρ. Since ρ is the common ratio of successive terms of the geometric series, the larger it is, the greater the effective length of the lag structure.

Actually, the length of the lag structure does not vary greatly between the individual durable and nondurable two-digit manufacturing industries. In fact, for the durable and nondurable aggregates, it is identical, with $\rho = 0.300$ in both cases.

In contrast, two noteworthy effects appeared in the results for the nonmanufacturing aggregates. First, the investment impact lag for railroad transportation apparently is very long, $\rho = 0.825$. This result may be the consequence of institutional, rather than technological, factors, reflecting the peculiar labor practices in the railroad transportation sector. (It is because of such circumstances that one hesitates to take full advantage of the structural motivation underlying the model, and to make inferences about the dynamic character of the production relations in the sectors under consideration.)

The second noteworthy result is the negativity of ρ for mining. It is hard to account for this phenomenon. One might, if pressed, provide the following explanation: Since the length of the effective lag structure varies directly with the magnitude of ρ, a negative ρ might indicate a "lead" rather than a "lagged" relationship. That is, a negative ρ could mean that the impact of investment on labor employment is anticipated, and the industry "adjusts" to it prior to the investment's taking place. The reader may judge the degree to which this is a contrived interpretation.

We have thus far discussed only the lag structure of the short-run impact of investment on labor inputs. As to the effects themselves, in general they are augmenting, although there are exceptions (for electrical machinery, other transportation equipment, food and beverages, paper and allied products, and rubber products, on balance, the effects appear to be labor conserving). While individual two-digit industries differ in their labor input response to investment, there seems to be no significant difference in the reaction between durables and nondurables. For the durable and nondurable aggregates, the effects are minor (but somewhat stronger for durables). Thus, while investment does affect labor utilization in manufacturing, the impact is not uniform in all industries.

Summary Estimates of the proposed model of total manhour input reveal a high degree of explanatory power, typically accounting for more than 95 per cent of the variance of the logarithm of manhours. Furthermore, with the possible exception of nonrail transportation, there does not seem to be much evidence of (first order) autocorrelation in the residuals, although the presence of lagged values of the dependent variable in the equation tempers this observation.

Based on the model, the speed of adjustment of actual to desired manhours is quite rapid in all the sectors studied; however, durable two-digit industries tend to adjust somewhat faster than nondurable industries. Consistent with this conclusion, it was found that the short-run elasticities of labor input with respect to wage rates and output tend to be somewhat higher for durable than for nondurable two-digit manufacturing industries. No clear-cut generalization can be made in the case of nonmanufacturing aggregates.

Finally, investment exerts a perceptible and significant effect on labor input. While the impact generally is augmenting, there are notable exceptions. Moreover, this effect, although formalized in terms of an infinite lag structure, appears to work itself out fairly rapidly.

5.5.2. *Total manhours: long-run effects*

This section deals with some further structural aspects of the model, but concentrates mainly on the long-run characteristics of the empirical results. The relevant implied parameters are given in table 5.5.

Before turning to these, let us consider the stability characteristics of the model. The estimated equation (5.27) can be written as:

$$\begin{aligned}\ln MH-(\rho+\gamma_4)\ln[MH]_{-1}+\rho\gamma_4\ln[MH]_{-2} &\\ = \gamma_0+\gamma_1\{\ln[RWSS/PX]-\rho\ln[RWSS/PX]_{-1}\} &\\ +\gamma_2\{\ln X^{54}-\rho\ln[X^{54}]_{-1}\}+\gamma_3\{\ln[X^{54}]_{-1}-\rho\ln[X^{54}]_{-2}\} &\\ +\gamma_5\ln[I^{54}_{\mathrm{BUS}}]_{-1}+\gamma_6\ln[I^{54}_{\mathrm{BUS}}]_{-2}+\gamma_7\ln[I^{54}_{\mathrm{BUS}}]_{-3}+\gamma_8\ln[I^{54}_{\mathrm{BUS}}]_{-4}. &\end{aligned} \tag{5.30}$$

The right hand side of equation (5.30) is independent of MH. Since wage rates, output and investment are predetermined in this context, (5.30) may be rewritten as

$$\ln MH-(\rho+\gamma_4)\ln[MH]_{-1}+\rho\gamma_4\ln[MH]_{-2} = h(t), \tag{5.31}$$

where h is a summary representation of the right hand side of (5.30).

The system represented by (5.31) is stable or unstable according to whether the characteristic roots of the homogeneous part of the equation are less than unity in absolute value. It is simple to establish that such roots are given by: $r_1 = \rho$, $r_2 = \gamma_4$. Thus, the stability of the system depends on the effective length of the investment lag structure. as well as on the rapidity with which a gap between actual and desired manhours is closed.

Table 5.5

Some structural parameters and long-run implications of the model: total manhours

Industry	Elasticity of substitution[a]	Expectation weight on		Wage rate elasticity		Output elasticity		Investment elasticity		Fraction of medium run investment impact realized	
		Current output[b]	Lagged output[c]	Short run[d]	Long run[e]	Short run[f]	Long run[g]	Medium run[h]	Long run[i]	Within one year	Within two years
02 Mining	0.656	2.065	0.656	−0.122	−0.656	0.384	1.409	−0.086	−0.462	0.990	0.990
07 Railway transportation	0.168	0.539	0.294	−0.127	−0.168	0.407	0.833	0.326	0.431	0.397	0.721
08 Nonrail transportation	0.884	0.802	0.245	−0.734	−0.884	0.666	1.047	0.030	0.036	0.875	1.000
09 Communications	0.966	0.944	−0.413	−0.547	−0.966	0.534	0.530	0.091	0.161	1.000	1.000
10 Public utilities	0.244	0.621	0.249	−0.119	−0.244	0.010	0.269	0.028	0.057	0.725	0.998
20 Primary metals	0.484	0.577	−0.005	−0.420	−0.484	0.501	0.573	0.046	0.055	0.999	1.000
22 Nonelectrical machinery	0.404	0.620	0.164	−0.268	−0.404	0.411	0.784	0.014	0.021	0.725	0.998
23 Electrical machinery	0.524	0.828	0.103	−0.265	−0.524	0.419	0.931	−0.039	−0.077	0.989	0.999
24 Motor vehicles and parts	0.707	0.785	−0.193	−0.431	−0.707	0.479	0.592	0.042	0.069	1.000	1.000

25 Other transportation equipment	0.474	0.830	−0.103	−0.024	−0.474	0.567	0.820	−0.080	−0.117	0.399	0.783
27 Stone, clay and glass	0.501	0.673	−0.048	−0.228	−0.501	0.306	0.624	0.003	0.007	0.999	1.000
31 Food and beverages	0.554	2.250	−1.786	−0.093	−0.554	0.378	0.464	−0.013	−0.079	0.430	0.998
33 Textile mill products	0.321	2.315	−0.988	−0.052	−0.321	0.375	1.327	0.063	0.039	0.300	0.832
35 Paper and allied products	0.150	1.382	−0.746	−0.033	−0.150	0.304	0.636	−0.017	−0.077	0.969	1.000
37 Chemicals	0.484	1.146	−0.477	−0.139	−0.484	0.329	0.669	0.040	0.139	0.997	1.000
38 Petroleum and coal products	0.924	3.304	−3.000	−0.073	−0.924	0.261	0.456	0.020	0.247	0.969	1.000
39 Rubber products	0.519	2.221	−1.399	−0.108	−0.519	0.462	0.822	−0.021	−0.102	0.900	1.000
50 Total manufacturing	0.745	1.216	−0.321	−0.283	−0.745	0.462	0.895	0.017	0.045	0.575	0.986
51 Durable manufacturing	0.671	1.118	−0.248	−0.290	−0.671	0.483	0.870	0.019	0.044	0.700	0.998
56 Nondurable manufacturing	1.641*	6.578*	−5.063*	−0.105	−1.641	0.421	1.516	0.006	0.089	0.700	0.998

* These inordinately high magnitudes result, in part, from the incidence of multicollinearity, which is especially severe in the estimates for this sector.

Note Symbolically, the quantities in this table are defined as follows:

[a] $\sigma = \dfrac{-\gamma_1}{1-\gamma_4}$; [b] $\lambda_1 = \dfrac{\gamma_2}{1-\gamma_4}$; [c] $\lambda_2 = \dfrac{\gamma_3}{1-\gamma_4}$; [d] γ_1; [e] $-\sigma$; [f] γ_2; [g] $\dfrac{\gamma_2+\gamma_3}{1-\gamma_4}$; [h] $\dfrac{\gamma_5+\gamma_6+\gamma_7+\gamma_8}{1-\gamma_4}$; [i] $\dfrac{\gamma_5+\gamma_6+\gamma_7+\gamma_8}{(1-\rho)(1-\gamma_4)}$.

It will be recalled that *a priori* restrictions were imposed on the parameters of the model constraining ρ to lie in the range $(-1, 1)$ and γ_4 in the range $(0, 1)$. These restrictions are a sufficient condition for the stability of the model. (The results of table 5.3 all reveal stable systems.)

Nevertheless, even though the homogeneous part of the equation is stable, this in no way implies a stationary long-run equilibrium because the system will grow, decline or oscillate depending upon the behavior of $h(t)$. Therefore, since $h(t)$ is exogenously determined, we shall speak of long-run equilibrium as a constant solution of equation (5.31) *given that* $h(t)$ *is a constant function*, i.e., it is independent of t. This constant solution, dropping time lag subscripts, is given by:

$$\ln MH = \frac{\gamma_0}{(1-\rho)(1-\gamma_4)} + \frac{\gamma_1}{(1-\gamma_4)} \ln [RWSS/PX] + \frac{\gamma_2+\gamma_3}{1-\gamma_4} \ln X^{54} + \frac{\gamma_5+\gamma_6+\gamma_7+\gamma_8}{(1-\rho)(1-\gamma_4)} \ln I_{\mathrm{BUS}}^{54}. \tag{5.32}$$

The entries in table 5.5 can be understood in terms of this equation (structural symbol equivalence for the γ's are given above equation (5.15)).

The first column of the table presents elasticity of substitution parameters ($\sigma = -\gamma_1/(1-\gamma_4)$) of the static production functions that characterize the long-run equilibrium of the model. The results appear to support the conjecture that the elasticity of substitution is less than unity. Qualitatively the results are in accord with an earlier cross-section study of U.S. two-digit manufacturing industries by state.[11] There, it was also found that, generally, durable manufacturing industries exhibit lower elasticities of substitution than nondurable industries.

Furthermore, typically (as shown in columns 2 and 3), current output receives greater weight than lagged output in the planning of production inputs. It was earlier postulated that:

$$\hat{Q}_t = A_2 Q_t^{\lambda_1} Q_{t-1}^{\lambda_2}, \tag{5.33}$$

where $\hat{Q}_t$ is the output expected at time t—1 to be produced at time t. Since the coefficient, $\gamma_3 = \lambda_2 \alpha$, frequently is statistically insignificant (see table 5.3), it appears that the hypothesis of correct expectations is not particularly objectionable and would serve quite well in the estimation of short-run models.

---

[11] P. J. Dhrymes, "Some Extensions and Tests of the CES Class of Production Functions", *Review of Economics and Statistics* (November 1965), pp. 357–66.

Consider next the contrast between short- and long-run elasticities of labor input with respect to wage rates and output. We expect, by intuition or the application of Le Chatelier's principle that long-run elasticities should equal or exceed short-run elasticities.[12] The results shown in columns 4 and 5 of table 5.5 are entirely reassuring in this regard. While the short-run wage elasticities range from 0.033 for paper and allied products to 0.431 for motor vehicles and parts, the long-run elasticities range from 0.150 for paper and allied products to 0.924 for petroleum and coal products. (However, the magnitude of the last estimate is subject to a wide confidence interval since it is obtained as the quotient $\gamma_1/(1-\gamma_4) = 0.073/(1-0.921)$ and the standard deviation of γ_4 is approximately 0.07.)

In general, the long-run wage rate elasticities are more uniform between industries than the short-run elasticities. This might indicate that, although in the short run a given wage policy would have differing labor input consequences within a group of industries, in the long run, impact discrepancies are lessened.

An incongruous result is that, for the aggregates, the long-run wage rate elasticity is greater for nondurables than for durables. The position is reversed for short-run elasticities. This incongruity, however, may be more apparent than real, since the long-run elasticity parameter is given by $\gamma_1/(1-\gamma_4)$, and for nondurables we have $\gamma_4 = 0.936$ with standard deviation of 0.031. Even allowing for this, there is substantial reason to assert that the long-run sensitivity of labor input to wage rates is somewhat higher for nondurables than for durables. As to the non-manufacturing aggregates, long-run wage rate elasticities tend to be somewhat higher than for manufacturing.

The situation is similar with respect to the long-run output elasticity of labor inputs. On the whole, the long-run elasticities are greater than their short-run counterparts; the relative differences appear to be higher for non-durable two-digit industries than for durables, and for non-manufacturing aggregates than for total manufacturing.

Comparison of the wage rate and output elasticity results confirms a very widely held belief, Keynesian in origin, that increases in aggregate demand are far more effective in raising labor input than real wage rate

---

[12] P. A. Samuelson, *Foundations of Economic Analysis* (Harvard University Press, Cambridge, 1955). Nevertheless, this would not be true when action in the recent past precludes action in the present or the near future, as in the case of consumer expenditures for durable goods or in the case of wage increases. There, one might expect the short-run to exceed the long-run elasticity; indeed, the findings of C. L. Schultze and J. L. Tryon, *op. cit.*, are exactly of this nature.

reductions. To increase manhours in manufacturing (in the short run) by 2.8 per cent requires a 10 per cent reduction in real (product) wages, but only a 6.1 per cent increase in "effective demand." The long-run relative effectiveness of wage policy is somewhat higher. To raise manhours, *ceteris paribus*, by 7.4 per cent in manufacturing requires a reduction in wage rates by 10 per cent or an increase in "effective demand" by about 8.3 per cent.

Finally, let us deal with the impact of investment on labor input. Investment may have two distinct or combined effects. First, to the extent that it is the carrier of technical advance, it may change the factor intensity or other pertinent characteristics of the production process; second, to the extent that it leads to an increase in capacity, it may change the scale of production.

In the context of this paper, we shall distinguish three "time dimensions" in investment's impact on labor utilization. The short-run impact is measured by the sum of the coefficients $\gamma_5+\gamma_6+\gamma_7+\gamma_8$. This is the investment effect on labor input registered, *ceteris paribus*, within one calendar year. The "medium run" impact is defined by $(\gamma_5+\gamma_6+\gamma_7+\gamma_8)/(1-\rho)$. Although an artificial construct, this could be interpreted as the *ceteris paribus* effect of a permanent investment increase. In the lag structure postulated for the model, this is simply the partial effect of a constant level of investment on manhours. That is, the lag structure was given by:

$$\sum_{i=0}^{\infty} \beta_i \ln I_{t-i} = \frac{f(Z)}{g(Z)} \ln I_t = \frac{\gamma_5 Z+\gamma_6 Z^2+\gamma_7 Z^3+\gamma_8 Z^4}{I-\rho Z} \ln I_t. \quad (5.34)$$

If $\ln I_t = \ln I$ for all t (i.e., I is constant), then we have:

$$\sum_{i=0}^{\infty} \beta_i \ln I_{t-i} = [(\gamma_5+\gamma_6+\gamma_7+\gamma_8) \sum_{k=0}^{\infty} \rho^k] \ln I = \frac{\gamma_5+\gamma_6+\gamma_7+\gamma_8}{1-\rho} \ln I. \quad (5.35)$$

But, there is a further impact of investment on labor input not captured by the short- and medium-run effects given above. Those measures depicted the continuous adjustment of actual to desired manhours. Investment also affects optimal (desired) labor requirements. This effect is conveniently measured by the coefficient of the investment term in the long-run equilibrium solution given in equation (5.32), i.e., $(\gamma_5+\gamma_6+\gamma_7+\gamma_8)/(1-\rho)(1-\gamma_4)$, and shall be referred to as the long-run impact or elasticity.

Now, turning to the empirical results, the short-run impact of investment, although indisputably significant in a statistical sense, is of rather minor economic consequence. This is particularly evident in total manufacturing and the durable and nondurable aggregates. In manufacturing, for example, a 10 per cent increase in investment at any moment of time would lead, within a year, to an increase in manhours of 0.1 per cent. In mining, however, the same increase in investment would reduce employment by 1.0 per cent. The situation for the two-digit industries lies somewhere in between. The impact is labor augmentive, but not substantially so.

Further research is required to confirm or disprove these empirical findings. One might wish, however, to adduce an economic rationale. In the structural interpretation of the model, investment serves to alter production characteristics by affecting the coefficient of labor in a CES production function. Thus, a positive short-run investment impact means that the marginal product of labor increases (holding output and labor input constant); a negative short-run impact means that it decreases. It might be expected that labor displacing effects of investment would be present in sectors characterized by technologies which are intrinsically capital intensive. In a static CES function, factor intensity at (competative) equilibrium is given by,

$$\frac{w}{r}\,\frac{a}{b} = \left[\frac{K}{L}\right]^{|\beta - 1|}, \tag{5.36}$$

where w is the real product wage rate, r is the real rental rate of capital, K is capital, L is labor, and a, b, and β are constant parameters. (The absolute value appears in (5.36) since, for the elasticity of substitution to be positive, $\beta - 1$ must be negative.) But this means that for any two technologies exhibiting the same production function except for possible differences in b, and confronted with the same wage-rental rate ratio, that technology is more capital intensive which displays the *smaller* value of b.

From the results of table 5.5, it would appear that such industries are mining (02), electrical machinery (23), other transportation equipment (25), food and beverages (31) and rubber products (39). While I do not have any first-hand knowledge, the results seem plausible with the possible exception of those for food and beverages. For the remaining industries, investment raises the marginal product of labor and thus leads to increased employment.

The positive and negative investment effects, when aggregated over all two-digit industries, produce an insignificant net result. This, in turn, would seem to argue that there has been a great deal of reshuffling of the labor force between producer and consumer goods industries in the post-war economy. No doubt this implies that the skill characteristics of the labor force must have changed considerably in the process. But such considerations lie decidedly outside the model and this paper.

Aside from the magnitude of the impact, interest centers on the effective length of the process by which investment affects labor input. This question can be partially answered, for the short run, in terms of the parameter ρ. But this is not wholly adequate. The "medium term elasticity" of labor input with respect to investment must also be considered. (The qualitative characteristics of this elasticity do not much differ from those of the short run.) We are concerned with the fraction of the "medium run" effect realized in one or two years.

From table 5.5, it appears that this fraction is quite high. For the non-manufacturing aggregates, over 72.5 per cent of the total medium-term impact of an initial change in investment is registered in one year; railway transportation (07) is an exception, with only about 40 per cent realized in the same period. For the durable two-digit manufacturing industries, the fraction of the total impact realized within a year is slightly higher than for nondurable two-digit industries. There is, however, no difference in the effective length of this process for the durable and nondurable aggregates. For total manufacturing, about 58 per cent of the total impact is realized within one year of initial investment, a slow response when compared with the non-manufacturing aggregates.

Finally, two observations concerning the long-run response of labor input to investment should be made. First, although long-run elasticities are appreciably higher than medium-run elasticities, they are still rather small. Thus, it would appear that the long-run labor input effects of investment are considerably weaker than those resulting from wage or "aggregate demand" policies. For example, a 10 per cent permanent increase in investment yields a 0.45 per cent manhour increase in manufacturing, while a 10 per cent increase in output or decrease in the product wage rates leads to manhour increases of 8.95 and 7.45 per cent, respectively. Second, for the non-manufacturing aggregates, investment appears to have a far more pronounced effect. Here, a 10 per cent permanent increase in investment leads to a reduction of manhours by 4.62 per cent in mining and an increase of 4.31 per cent in railway transportation.

In summary, the results obtained in this section are as follows:

(i) empirically, the labor adjustment model considered here yields a stable system (furthermore, approach to a stationary equilibrium, if one exists, is fairly rapid);

(ii) to the extent that we can infer anything about the production characteristics of the sectors studied, the elasticity of substitution appears to be

slightly higher for nondurable two-digit manufacturing industries than for durable industries;
(iii) both wage and output long-run elasticities are appreciable, and it is generally the case that labor input is more sensitive to output than it is to real wage changes (the communications (09), motor vehicles and parts (24), food and beverages (31), and petroleum and coal products (38) industries are apparent exceptions to this conclusion); and
(iv) labor employment is significantly sensitive to investment, but the magnitude of this dependence is small in the short run. In the medium and long run, this impact is appreciably higher. Thus, it appears that investment affects the characteristics of the production process rather weakly over time. The primary way in which this impact is registered is through an infinite lag structure affecting the capital intensity of production functions, or equivalently, the marginal productivity of labor. Generally, investment tends to raise labor productivity. Nearly the entire impact of these primary effects is realized within a year or two from the time investment takes place.

In addition, there are secondary effects since investment also alters optimal labor requirements. These effects, which may be of considerable significance, are somewhat slower in manifesting themselves.

An indication of the relative speed at which the primary and secondary effects are implemented can be gained by considering the estimates of ρ and γ_4, which are the characteristic roots of the homogenous part of the difference equation describing the model. By primary effects, we mean those yielded by the postulated investment lag structure; by secondary effects, we mean those that relate to the adjustment necessary to equate actual and desired labor input. Primary effects can roughly be indexed by the "medium-run" elasticity of labor input with respect to investment, while secondary effects can be indexed by the difference between the long- and medium-run elasticities.

5.5.3. *Some qualifications due to aggregation: production and nonproduction worker manhours*

In the preceding sections, we have described the empirical characteristics of a labor adjustment model where labor was treated as a homogeneous factor. It might be desirable to see whether the two major categories of labor, now adequately reported only for the manufacturing sector, production and non-production workers, exhibit disparate behavior patterns. Due to limitations, the presentation will be both brief and elliptical.

TABLE 5.6

Production worker manhours equations: parameter estimates.

$$\ln MH_P = \gamma_0 + \gamma_1\{\ln [RWSS/PX] - \rho \ln [RWSS/PX]_{-1}\} + \gamma_2\{\ln X^{54} - \rho \ln [X^{54}]_{-1}\} + \gamma_3\{\ln [X^{54}]_{-1} - \rho \ln [X^{54}]_{-2}\} + \rho \ln [MH_P]_{-1} + \gamma_4\{\ln [MH_P]_{-1} - \rho \ln [MH_P]_{-2}\} + \gamma_5 \ln [I^{54}_{BUS}]_{-2} + \gamma_6 \ln [I^{54}_{BUS}]_{-2} + \gamma_7 \ln [I^{54}_{BUS}]_{-3} + \gamma_8 \ln [I^{54}_{BUS}]_{-4}$$

Industry	γ_0	γ_1	γ_2	γ_3	ρ	γ_4	γ_5	γ_6	γ_7	γ_8	$\bar{R}^2$	Durbin-Watson statistic
20 Primary metals	1.271 (2.306)*	−0.494 (4.908)	0.622 (21.460)	−0.162 (2.740)	0.025 (16.378)	0.366 (3.064)		0.016 (1.410)			0.947	2.093
22 Nonelectrical machinery	−0.318 (1.211)	−0.326 (4.906)	0.467 (9.630)	0.029 (0.559)	0.425 (24.770)	0.591 (9.723)	−0.046 (4.539)				0.956	1.673
23 Electrical machinery	0.180 (1.463)	−0.174 (1.825)	0.458 (7.108)	0.049 (0.701)	0.850 (80.130)	0.501 (6.135)	−0.037 (3.186)				0.988	1.688
24 Motor vehicles and parts	1.553 (1.801)	−0.684 (5.656)	0.399 (4.125)	0.072 (0.919)	0.025 (4.749)	0.390 (3.610)	0.049 (1.622)			−0.031 (1.033)	0.929	1.968
25 Other transportation equipment	0.104 (1.562)	−0.302 (3.877)	0.575 (8.025)	0.025 (0.339)	0.900 (232.764)	0.285 (2.830)			−0.022 (3.805)		0.996	1.877
27 Stone, clay and glass	−0.437 (0.651)	−0.271 (5.390)	0.390 (7.943)	−0.183 (3.372)	0.225 (68.896)	0.826 (9.690)	−0.009 (0.687)				0.918	1.953

31 Food and	0.408	−0.059	0.470	−0.440	0.000	0.936	0.017		−0.027	0.971	1.796
beverages	(0.259)	(1.346)	(4.079)	(4.179)		(10.978)	(1.220)		(1.906)		
33 Textile mill	0.118	−0.064	0.402	−0.077	0.825	0.633			0.026	0.996	2.458
products	(0.937)	(1.704)	(9.566)	(1.492)	(56.189)	(7.429)			(3.792)		
35 Paper and	1.042	−0.052	0.324	−0.176	0.225	0.709		−0.018		0.982	1.799
allied products	(2.289)	(1.930)	(7.359)	(2.954)	(30.520)	(7.802)		(2.915)			
37 Chemicals	−0.118	−0.148	0.440	−0.311	0.300	0.860	0.020		−0.015	0.959	1.471
	(0.257)	(3.769)	(6.850)	(4.218)	(9.315)	(10.330)	(1.732)		(1.918)		
38 Petroleum	−5.688	−0.118	0.271	−0.238	0.025	0.909	0.044		−0.029	0.960	2.053
and coal	(4.831)	(2.265)	(3.348)	(2.739)	(40.990)	(17.186)	(1.833)		(1.715)		
39 Rubber	−0.298	−0.091	0.567	−0.425	0.075	0.0878			−0.031	0.892	2.135
products	(2.188)	(1.571)	(8.970)	(5.299)	(5.076)	(7.748)			(2.188)		
50 Total manufac-	−1.389	−0.279	0.473	−0.144	0.275	0.658	−0.004		0.012	0.989	1.700
turing	(4.852)	(6.903)	(16.499)	(3.205)	(9.585)	(7.821)	(0.349)		(1.572)		
51 Durable	−2.614	−0.426	0.630	−0.260	0.150	0.733	−0.024		0.019	0.985	2.097
manufacturing	(7.267)	(6.860)	(20.534)	(6.430)	(28.652)	(12.278)	(1.761)		(1.843)		
56 Nondurable	−0.416	−0.098	0.429	−0.349	0.350	0.957	−0.015			0.971	1.727
manufacturing [a]	(1.236)	(1.985)	(7.339)	(6.790)	(3.815)	(13.241)	(1.867)				

[a] The estimates of this equation are plagued by multicollinearity difficulties. The minimum variance ($\hat{\sigma}^2 = 2.1 \times 10^{-5}$) actually is obtained with $\rho = 1.0$; but the determinant of the matrix to be inverted at this value of ρ is only 12×10^{-8}. Therefore, ρ was chosen from the estimate with the second lowest variance.

Note t-ratios of coefficients are shown parenthetically.

TABLE 5.7

Nonproduction worker manhour equations: parameter estimates.

$$\ln MH_0 = \gamma_0+\gamma_1\{\ln [RWSS/PX]-\rho \ln [RWSS/PX]_{-1}\}+\gamma_2\{\ln X^{54}-\rho \ln [X^{54}]_{-1}\}+\gamma_3\{\ln [X^{54}]_{-1}-\rho \ln [X^{54}]_{-2}\} +\rho \ln [MH_0]_{-1}+\gamma_4\{\ln [MH_0]_{-1}-\rho \ln [MH_0]_{-2}\}+\gamma_5 \ln [I^{54}_{BUS}]_{-1}+\gamma_6 \ln [I^{54}_{BUS}]_{-2}+\gamma_7 \ln [I^{54}_{BUS}]_{-3} +\gamma_8 \ln [I^{54}_{BUS}]_{-4}$$

Industry	γ_0	γ_1	γ_2	γ_3	ρ	γ_4	γ_5	γ_6	γ_7	γ_8	$\bar{R}^2$	Durbin-Watson statistic
20 Primary metals	−0.640	0.028	0.081	0.012	0.050	0.940		−0.007			0.982	2.110
	(2.546)	(0.497)	(4.414)	(0.655)	(4.466)	(33.320)		(0.837)				
22 Nonelectrical machinery	−0.368	0.024	0.106	−0.013	0.425	0.949				−0.016	0.996	1.947
	(2.640)	(0.506)	(3.030)	(0.355)	(9.858)	(21.732)				(1.636)		
23 Electrical machinery	−0.652	−0.107	0.088	0.081	0.375	0.927	−0.025				0.998	1.833
	(3.529)	(2.441)	(2.152)	(1.922)	(68.577)	(37.386)	(2.227)					
24 Motor vehicles and parts	0.015	0.048	−0.099	0.074	0.075	0.975	−0.017				0.986	1.962
	(0.025)	(0.798)	(3.355)	(2.499)	(5.496)	(37.302)	(2.034)					
25 Other transportation equipment	0.014	−0.012	0.418	−0.354	0.125	0.924			−0.014		0.998	2.118
	(0.068)	(0.312)	(11.136)	(7.664)	(4.518)	(19.103)			(1.420)			

27 Stone, clay and glass	−0.268 (1.225)	0.038 (1.123)	0.097 (2.868)	0.001 (0.023)	0.225 (94.409)	0.892 (29.281)	0.003 (0.427)		0.995	1.697
31 Food and beverages	0.531 (0.787)	−0.038 (1.466)	0.114 (1.255)	−0.031 (0.323)	0.025 (6.472)	0.882 (17.170)		−0.023 (1.752)	0.993	2.325
33 Textile mill products	0.267 (0.420)	−0.052 (3.278)	0.084 (2.679)	0.051 (1.494)	−0.025 (4.335)	0.833 (15.060)	−0.014 (1.683)		0.919	2.361
35 Paper and allied products	−0.775 (4.622)	−0.062 (2.601)	0.126 (3.004)	−0.023 (0.483)	−0.010 (48.439)	0.950 (34.391)	−0.017 (1.775)		0.998	2.193
37 Chemicals	−0.008 (0.036)	0.008 (0.241)	0.205 (3.919)	−0.047 (0.844)	0.125 (24.538)	0.760 (21.590)	0.045 (5.372)		0.998	2.029
38 Petroleum and coal products	−0.003 (0.006)	−0.010 (0.215)	0.217 (2.577)	−0.156 (1.641)	−0.025 (24.680)	0.915 (13.606)	0.049 (2.225)	−0.032 (1.529)	0.988	2.061
39 Rubber products	−0.02[illegible] (0.104)	−0.034 (1.253)	0.183 (4.817)	−0.039 (0.892)	0.075 (8.545)	0.845 (26.105)	0.013 (1.036)		0.990	2.119
50 Total manufacturing	−0.281 (2.939)	−0.041 (1.244)	0.091 (4.754)	0.013 (0.622)	0.675 (90.218)	0.928 (28.777)		−0.008 (1.939)	0.999	2.223
51 Durable manufacturing	−0.606 (3.911)	−0.039 (0.775)	0.100 (4.478)	0.016 (0.653)	0.450 (23.082)	0.926 (22.691)	0.008 (0.880)	−0.016 (2.227)	0.998	1.873
56 Nondurable manufacturing	−0.716 (1.711)	−0.073 (2.329)	0.079 (1.845)	−0.019 (0.401)	0.000	0.993 (24.995)	0.001 (0.184)	−0.014 (1.395)	0.998	2.072

Note t-ratios of coefficients are shown parenthetically.

If the model is applied to production and nonproduction worker manhours separately, some very striking and significant differences are observed. The empirical results are given in tables 5.6 and 5.7.

On the whole, nonproduction manhours are insensitive to wage rates; the γ_1 coefficient is insignificant, with the exception of the electrical machinery (23), textile mill products (33), and paper and allied products (35) industries. This contrasts with the situation presented in table 5.3 for total manhours. On the other hand, production manhours are more sensitive to wage rates than are total manhours, in the sense that the wage rate elasticity for the production manhour equation is somewhat higher than for the total manhour equation. It appears that nonproduction worker employment decisions are akin to capital investment decisions in which more or less long-range commitments are made. Hence, it would be expected that such decisions would not markedly be influenced by short-run considerations.

The impact of investment on employment also differs appreciably for production and nonproduction manhours. The investment impacts appear to be more clearly negative for the latter.[13] On the other hand, frequently they are statistically insignificant. For example, in nonelectrical machinery (22), the investment impact on production workers manhours is highly significant and negative, while it is not very significant for nonproduction manhours.

The effective length of the investment lag structure, as measured by the magnitude of ρ, is shorter for production than for nonproduction manhours. The same is true for the speed of adjustment. Thus, the relevant parameter $(1-\gamma_4)$ is typically higher for production than for nonproduction manhours. No doubt both these results are symptomatic of the same phenomenon, *viz.*, that nonproduction workers, being more closely tied to the size and "technological status" of the economic unit, are adjusted only slowly to its changing economic environment.

A surprising aspect of the above results is that apparently the changing nature of the capital stock in two-digit manufacturing industries has tended to reduce nonproduction manhours more than production manhours. This would indicate that technical change in recent years has tended to automate staff perceptibly more than line functions.

---

[13] This is in apparent conflict with the results obtained by Kuh, *op. cit.*; it should be recalled, however, that in Kuh's study *capital stock* is an explanatory variable for *nonproduction labor employment.* In this context, it is then not surprising that he obtained a positive relationship between these two variables, since capital stock can best be thought of, in this framework, as an index of size, rather than of technical change.

A fuller analysis of the characteristics of production and nonproduction employment will be carried out in a subsequent study. The preceding discussion had the limited objective of indicating the substantial differences in behavior of the two types of employment.

5.6. Summary

In this paper we have studied the characteristics of the labor input function. The empirical results pertain to quarterly data on two-digit manufacturing industries, total, durable and nondurable manufacturing, and certain nonmanufacturing aggregates. The sample period is 1948–1960.

The salient results are that investment affects labor input. Although the impact is not uniform over all industries examined, it appears that investment tends to change some characteristics of the production function. The change is typically in the direction of increasing the marginal product of labor (for given output and labor input).

Labor input is considerably more sensitive in the short run to changes in output than it is to changes in product wage rates. However, in the long run, a given proportional change in wage rates has nearly the same effect on total manhours as a similar proportional change in output.

Adjustment to optimal labor input is fairly rapid; nearly complete adjustment is typically made within four to six quarters. Moreover, the adjustment is appreciably faster in the durable than in the nondurable sector.

Finally, production and nonproduction manhours exhibit perceptible differences of behavior, both with respect to the rapidity of adjustment and the responsiveness to changes in wage rates and output. Although the impact of investment is not uniform, it would appear that investment has a stronger substitution effect on nonproduction worker employment. All these differences seem to argue quite strongly that production and nonproduction labor inputs should be studied separately when feasible.

5.7. Appendix

5.7.1. The covariance matrix of the estimators

Although the small sample distribution theory of the estimators derived in section 5.3 is difficult to obtain, their asymptotic covariance matrix is easily derived upon applying the fundamental theorem of maximum likelihood estimation, the so-called information limit to variance.[14]

[14] C. R. Rao, *Advanced Statistical Methods in Biometric Research* (John Wiley and Sons, London, 1952).

The asymptotic covariance matrix of the maximum likelihood estimator is given by:

$$\boldsymbol{D} = -\left[\mathscr{E}\left(\frac{\partial^2 \mathscr{L}}{\partial \boldsymbol{\Phi}\, \partial \boldsymbol{\Phi}}\right)\right]^{-1}, \tag{5.37}$$

where

$$\boldsymbol{\Phi} = \begin{bmatrix} \gamma \\ \rho \\ \sigma^2 \end{bmatrix}.$$

The matrix to be inverted in (5.37) is simply the expected value of the Hessian of the likelihood function, as a function of the elements of Φ, evaluated at the point corresponding to the maximum likelihood estimator of Φ.

Since at the point of maximum we must have $\partial \mathscr{L}/\partial \gamma = 0$, and $\partial \mathscr{L}/\partial \rho = 0$, it is clear that:

$$\frac{\partial^2 \mathscr{L}}{\partial \gamma \partial \sigma^2} = 0; \quad \text{and} \quad \frac{\partial^2 \mathscr{L}}{\partial \rho \partial \sigma^2} = 0. \tag{5.38}$$

Thus, we need be concerned only with $\partial^2 \mathscr{L}/\partial \gamma \partial \gamma$, $\partial^2 \mathscr{L}/\partial \gamma \partial \rho$, $\partial^2 \mathscr{L}/\partial \sigma^2 \partial \sigma^2$. Based on these conditions, the (symmetric) matrix to be inverted in (5.37) is given by:

$$\boldsymbol{D}^* = -\mathscr{E}\begin{bmatrix} \dfrac{\partial^2 \mathscr{L}}{\partial \gamma \partial \gamma} & \dfrac{\partial^2 \mathscr{L}}{\partial \gamma \partial \rho} & 0 \\ \dfrac{\partial^2 \mathscr{L}}{\partial \rho \partial \gamma} & \dfrac{\partial^2 \mathscr{L}}{\partial \rho \partial \rho} & 0 \\ 0 & 0 & \dfrac{\partial^2 \mathscr{L}}{\partial \sigma^2 \partial \sigma^2} \end{bmatrix}. \tag{5.39}$$

Because we are not concerned with the variance of σ^2, we need only consider the submatrix of D^* resulting after deletion of its last row and column. Therefore, we have: [15]

$$\frac{\partial \mathscr{L}}{\partial \gamma} = -\frac{1}{\sigma^2}[2\boldsymbol{X}'\boldsymbol{X}\gamma - 2\boldsymbol{X}'\boldsymbol{y}],$$

$$\frac{\partial^2 \mathscr{L}}{\partial \gamma \partial \gamma} = -\frac{1}{\sigma^2}[\boldsymbol{X}'\boldsymbol{X}],$$

[15] For clarity, observe that from equation (5.15) the elements of X are of the form $x_{ti} - \rho x_{t-1,i}$. Thus, e.g., the second column of X consists of the elements $\ln w_t - \rho \ln w_{t-1}$, $t = 2, \ldots T$.

$$\frac{\partial^2 \mathcal{L}}{\partial\gamma\partial\rho} = -\frac{1}{\sigma^2}[-\boldsymbol{X}'(\boldsymbol{B}\gamma-\boldsymbol{z})+\boldsymbol{B}'\boldsymbol{u}],$$

$$\frac{\partial^2 \mathcal{L}}{\partial\rho\partial\rho} = -\frac{1}{\sigma^2}(\boldsymbol{B}\gamma-\boldsymbol{z})'(\boldsymbol{B}\gamma-\boldsymbol{z}), \tag{5.40}$$

where, $\boldsymbol{B} = [0 \ln W_{t-1} \ln Q_{t-1} \ln Q_{t-2} \ln L_{t-2}\, 0\,0\,0\,0]$ and $\boldsymbol{z} = [\ln L_{t-1}]'$ (all elements are column vectors of T observations). Now, let $\boldsymbol{P} = \boldsymbol{B}\gamma - \boldsymbol{z}$. Therefore, the asymptotic covariance matrix of the estimators (γ, ρ) is given by the inverse of:

$$\boldsymbol{C} = \frac{1}{\sigma^2}\begin{bmatrix} \boldsymbol{X}'\boldsymbol{X} & -\boldsymbol{X}'\boldsymbol{P} \\ -\boldsymbol{P}'\boldsymbol{X} & \boldsymbol{P}\boldsymbol{P}' \end{bmatrix} = \frac{1}{\sigma^2}\boldsymbol{V}. \tag{5.41}$$

To find the inverse of C, let

$$\boldsymbol{M} = \begin{bmatrix} I & \dfrac{\boldsymbol{X}'\boldsymbol{P}}{\boldsymbol{P}'\boldsymbol{P}} \\ 0 & I \end{bmatrix}, \tag{5.42}$$

and note that,

$$\boldsymbol{M}\boldsymbol{C}\boldsymbol{M}' = \frac{1}{\sigma^2}\begin{bmatrix} \boldsymbol{X}'\boldsymbol{X} - \dfrac{\boldsymbol{X}'\boldsymbol{P}\boldsymbol{P}'\boldsymbol{X}}{\boldsymbol{P}'\boldsymbol{P}} & 0 \\ 0 & \boldsymbol{P}'\boldsymbol{P} \end{bmatrix}. \tag{5.43}$$

Hence,

$$\boldsymbol{M}'^{-1}\boldsymbol{C}^{-1}\boldsymbol{M}^{-1} = \sigma^2\begin{bmatrix} \left[\boldsymbol{X}'\boldsymbol{X} - \dfrac{\boldsymbol{X}'\boldsymbol{P}\boldsymbol{P}'\boldsymbol{X}}{\boldsymbol{P}'\boldsymbol{P}}\right]^{-1} & 0 \\ 0 & (\boldsymbol{P}'\boldsymbol{P})^{-1} \end{bmatrix}. \tag{5.44}$$

Thus,

$$\boldsymbol{C}^{-1} = \sigma^2\boldsymbol{M}'\begin{bmatrix} \left[\boldsymbol{X}'\boldsymbol{X} - \dfrac{\boldsymbol{X}'\boldsymbol{P}\boldsymbol{P}'\boldsymbol{X}}{\boldsymbol{P}'\boldsymbol{P}}\right]^{-1} & 0 \\ 0 & (\boldsymbol{P}'\boldsymbol{P})^{-1} \end{bmatrix}\boldsymbol{M} \tag{5.45}$$

or,

$$\boldsymbol{C}^{-1} = \sigma^2\boldsymbol{M}'\begin{bmatrix} \boldsymbol{R}_{11} & 0 \\ 0 & \boldsymbol{R}_{22} \end{bmatrix}\boldsymbol{M}. \tag{5.46}$$

Carrying out the multiplication in (5.46), we find:

$$\boldsymbol{C}^{-1} = \sigma^2\begin{bmatrix} \boldsymbol{R}_{11} & \dfrac{\boldsymbol{R}_{11}\boldsymbol{X}'\boldsymbol{P}}{\boldsymbol{P}'\boldsymbol{P}} \\ \dfrac{\boldsymbol{P}'\boldsymbol{X}\boldsymbol{R}_{11}}{\boldsymbol{P}'\boldsymbol{P}} & \boldsymbol{R}_{22} \end{bmatrix}, \tag{5.47}$$

which is the asymptotic covariance matrix of our estimators. Thus, the variances of the estimators of γ and ρ are given, respectively, by the diagonal elements of:

$$\sigma^2 R_{11} = \sigma^2 \left[X'X - \frac{X'PP'X}{P'P} \right]^{-1}, \quad \text{and} \quad \sigma^2 R_{22} = \frac{\sigma^2}{P'P}. \tag{5.48}$$

5.7.2. *Derivation of speed of adjustment rates*

Let x_t be an economic variable subject to adjustment. Let x^* be its (constant, for simplicity) optimal level. Consider two alternative adjustment processes linear,

$$x_t - x_{t-1} = d(x^* - x_{t-1}); \tag{5.49}$$

and loglinear,

$$\frac{x_t}{x_{t-1}} = \left[\frac{x^*}{x_{t-1}} \right]^{d'}. \tag{5.50}$$

Solving the two difference equations we find, respectively,

$$\frac{x_t}{x^*} = 1 + (1-d)^t \left[\frac{x_0}{x^*} - 1 \right], \tag{5.51}$$

$$\frac{x_t}{x^*} = \left[\frac{x_0}{x^*} \right]^{(1-d')^t}, \tag{5.52}$$

where x_0 is the initial value of x. To obtain some comparability between the parameters d and d' consider the following question. Let $x_0 < x^*$ and, fixing t, determine the value of d and d' required in order to make the left hand sides of (5.51) and (5.52) equal.

To this effect expand the logarithm of (5.51) and (5.52) by Taylor series to obtain, respectively:

$$\begin{aligned} \ln \left[\frac{x_t}{x^*} \right]_1 &= \ln \left\{ 1 - \left[1 - \frac{x_0}{x^*} \right] (1-d)^t \right\} \\ &= - \left\{ \left[1 - \frac{x_0}{x^*} \right] (1-d)^t + \frac{1}{2} \left[1 - \frac{x_0}{x^*} \right]^2 (1-d)^{2t} \right. \\ &\quad \left. + \frac{1}{3} \left[1 - \frac{x_0}{x^*} \right]^3 (1-d)^{3t} + \ldots \right\}; \end{aligned} \tag{5.53}$$

$$\ln\left[\frac{x_t}{x^*}\right]_2 = (1-d')^t \ln\left[\frac{x_0}{x^*}\right]$$
$$= -(1-d')^t\left\{\left[1-\frac{x_0}{x^*}\right]+\frac{1}{2}\left[1-\frac{x_0}{x^*}\right]^2+\frac{1}{3}\left[1-\frac{x_0}{x^*}\right]^3+\dots\right\}. \tag{5.54}$$

Now, consider,

$$F(d, d') = \ln\left[\frac{x_t}{x^*}\right]_1 - \ln\left[\frac{x_t}{x^*}\right]_2 =$$
$$-\left\{\left[1-\frac{x_0}{x^*}\right][(1-d)^t-(1-d')^t]+\frac{1}{2}\left[1-\frac{x_0}{x^*}\right]^2\{(1-d)^{2t}-(1-d')^t\}\right.$$
$$\left.+\frac{1}{3}\left[1-\frac{x_0}{x^*}\right]^3\{(1-d)^{3t}-(1-d')^t\}\dots\right\}, \tag{5.55}$$

and let d equal any value between 0 and 1, i.e., $d \in (0, 1)$. Then, for $d' = d$, $F(d, d) > 0$ since $(1-d)^{kt} < (1-d)^t$ for all $t > 0$, $k > 1$. In addition, for any $d' \in (0, 1)$ such that $d' < d$, $F(d, d') > 0$ since $(1-d)^{kt} < (1-d')^t$ for all $k, t > 0$.

On the other hand, $F(d, 1) < 0$ for any $d \in (0, 1)$. Since F is continuous in d' (and d), for any fixed $d \in (0, 1)$, there exists a d' such that $d < d' < 1$ and $F(d, d') = 0$. But this shows that for fixed t, elimination of any preassigned portion of the gap $x^* - x_0$ requires a higher parameter value (d') if the process of adjustment is of the form (5.50) than is the case if the process is of the form (5.49).

To pursue the matter further let us ask: Under the process given by (5.50), what is the formula for the fraction of the gap remaining by time t? Elementary calculation shows:

$$\frac{x^*-x_t}{x^*-x_0} = \left\{1-\left[\frac{x_0}{x^*}\right]^{(1-d')^t}\right\}\left\{\frac{1}{\left[1-\frac{x_0}{x^*}\right]}\right\}. \tag{5.56}$$

[34]

THE STRUCTURE OF PRODUCTION TECHNOLOGY: PRODUCTIVITY AND AGGREGATION EFFECTS

Phoebus J. Dhrymes

03/20/91

Abstract

This is a sequel to an earlier paper by the author, Dhrymes (1990). Using the LRD sample, that paper examined the adequacy of the functional form specifications commonly employed in the literature of US Manufacturing production relations. The "universe" of the investigation was the three digit product group; the basic unit of observation was the plant; the sample consisted of **all** "large" plants, defined by the criterion that they employ 250 or more workers. The study encompassed three digit product groups in industries 35, 36 and 38, over the period 1972-1986, and reached one major conclusion: if one were to judge the adequacy of a given specification by the **parametric compatibility of the estimates of the same parameters**, as derived from the various **implications of each specification**, then the three most popular (production function) specifications, Cobb-Douglas, CES and Translog **all fell very wide of the mark.**

The current paper focuses the investigation on **two digit industries** (but retains the plant as the basic unit of observation), i.e., our sample consists of **all** "large" manufacturing plants, in each of Industry 35, 36 and 38, over the period 1972-1986. It first replicates the approach of the earlier paper; the results are basically of the same genre, and for that reason are not reported herein. Second, it examines the extent to which increasing returns to scale characterize production at the two digit level; it is established that returns to scale at the mean, in the case of the translog production function are almost identical to those obtained with the Cobb-Douglas function.[1] Finally, it examines the robustness and characteristics of measures of productivity, obtained in the context of an econometric formulation and those obtained by the method of what may be thought of as the "Solow Residual" and generally designated as Total Factor Productivity (TFP). The major finding here is that while there are some differences in productivity behavior as established by these two procedures, by far more important is the aggregation sensitivity of productivity measures. Thus, in the context of a pooled sample, introduction of time effects (generally thought to refer to productivity shifts) are of very marginal consequence. On the other hand, the introduction of four digit industry effects is of appreciable consequence, and this phenomenon is universal, i.e., it is present in industry 35, 36 as well as 38. The suggestion that aggregate productivity behavior may be largely, or partly, an aggregation phenomenon is certainly not a part of the established literature. Another persistent phenomenon uncovered is the extent to which productivity measures for individual plants are volatile, while two digit aggregate measures appear to be stable. These findings clearly calls for further investigation.

1 Introduction and Summary

The production structure of US Manufacturing has been studied intensively in the sixties and early seventies. Surveys of empirical findings and theoretical developments may be found in Walters (1963), and Nerlove (1967); see, also, Nerlove (1965), for a specific discussion of empirical findings relative to the Cobb-Douglas function. Other surveys are by Griliches (1967), Jorgenson (1974), (1986) among others. The theoretical

[1] The CES function has not been examined in this context; in the previous paper it was found to be slightly inferior to the other two specifications, and this, combined with associated computational complexities has led us to pass it over.

underpinnings of production theory have been well established in microeconomic theory for almost a century now. Duality theory has been an interesting and helpful addition to the formulation and interpretation of empirical studies since it was introduced by Samuelson (1954) and Shephard (1953). In Fuss and McFadden (1978), we have an extensive review of modern production theory.

Thus, a review of the literature would be completely redundant on our part.

A number of issues are routinely examined in the literature on the basis of rather limited samples. Such issues are whether production relations are to be considered from the **value added** or the **gross output** points of view; whether the translog function is an appreciable improvement over the Cobb-Douglas specification and, if appropriate, whether symmetry and separability (of the associated cost function) prevail. In addition, many authors estimate production functions on the basis of **time series observations** on two digit industry aggregates. This practice invites the question, particularly on the issue of increasing or decreasing returns to scale, of whether the composition of output is responsible for the results and, if so, to what extent. Another issue that merits consideration is whether the measure of productivity, currently favored in the literature, is robust relative to the specification of the underlying production function.

An interesting finding that has substantial bearing on a number of time series studies using **two digit industry data** is that while "time effects" do not make appreciable difference in the interpretation of results, "four digit industry effects" are quite significant, econometrically, and quite appreciable in terms of orders of magnitude. Thus, to the extent that the four digit composition of the output of two digit industries varies over time, phenomena that may resemble productivity movements are generated, so that productivity measurements at the two digit level may simply reflect shifts in the compositional effect

Spurred by this finding we have examined the dynamic behavior of the "residual" from the fitted production relations, both with and without "time" and "(four digit) industry effects". Two basic results stand out; first, if we classify plants according to the **magnitude** of their "total factor productivity" (residual) **each** year, the (geometric) mean TFP of the ith decile is more or less flat over the 15 year period, except possibly for that of the tenth decile; second, if we classify plants according to the **magnitude of their TFP during 1972 only**, the behavior of the **(geometric) mean** TFP of nearly all (1972 rank based) deciles is rather erratic. This suggests that the relatively steady behavior of "productivity" at the higher levels of aggregation hides a great deal of movement at more basic levels of production, thus suggesting a new frontier for research.

As in the previous paper, we deal with fifteen cross sections, from 1972 to 1986, and the unit of observation is the plant. We deal with the pooled sample, but we allow for "year effects" and for "four digit industry" effects. We had considered, but rejected, the possibility of arranging our data in the form of a panel. We rejected this alternative since to have worked with a panel (of plants) would have entailed eliminating a very substantial number of observations. Invariably, this must invite considerations of selectivity bias.

2 Model Specifications and Implications

2.1 Duality and Production Theory

The typical (static) model of production theory, and many dynamic models, require (for equilibrium) that certain optimality conditions hold for every time t. Such models entail, typically, the assumption of perfect competition in the product and factor markets and represent the economic agent as a profit maximizer. If

$$\Pi(p, x) = p_0 Q - \sum_{j=1}^{n} p_i^* x_i, \tag{1}$$

is the profit function, where p_0 is the price of output, Q is output obtained through a production function, $F(x)$, with inputs, x, then under perfect competition the economic agent operates according to the rule

$$p_0 \frac{\partial F}{\partial x_i} = p_i^*, \quad \text{or} \quad \frac{\partial F}{\partial x_i} = p_i, \quad p_i = \frac{p_i^*}{p_0}. \tag{2}$$

In the preceding, we have taken output, Q, as the *numeraire* so that all prices are stated relative to the price of output; we shall follow this practice in the remainder of the paper unless otherwise indicated.

A solution to the system in Eq. (2) expresses **the demand** for the factors of production in terms of input prices, i.e., we have a solution, $x_i = x_i(p)$, and the representation $Q = F[x(p)] = G(p)$, is said to be the **indirect production function**. While it is possible to derive from the preceding demand relations as functions of p and Q, this is not generally done in the literature. Rather, the representation of demand as a function of factor prices **and** output is obtained in the context of the mathematical dual of the profit maximization problem posed above. This is the **(cost) minimization problem, subject to an expected output constraint,**

$$\min_x \sum_{j=1}^n p_i x_i, \quad \text{subject to} \quad \bar{Q} = F(x),$$

whose first order conditions are,

$$\lambda \frac{\partial F}{\partial x_i} = p_i, \quad i = 1, 2, \dots, n, \quad \bar{Q} = F(x), \tag{3}$$

where λ is the Lagrange multiplier. Denote the solution to this problem by $x(p, \bar{Q})$, $\lambda(p, \bar{Q})$, and consider the cost function [2]

$$C(p, Q) = \sum_{j=1}^n p_j x_j(p, Q). \tag{4}$$

Thus,

$$\frac{\partial C}{\partial p_j} = x_j(p, Q) + \sum_{i=1}^n p_i \frac{\partial x_i}{\partial p_j}. \tag{5}$$

From the second (constraint) equation of Eq. (3) we find

$$0 = \sum_{i=1}^n \frac{\partial F}{\partial x_i} \frac{\partial x_i}{\partial p_j} = 0. \tag{6}$$

Substituting in Eq. (5), we find, in view of the fact that $\lambda(p, Q) \neq 0$,

$$\frac{\partial C}{\partial p_j} = x_j(p, Q), \tag{7}$$

[2] For ease of notation we have eliminated the overbar on the output symbol Q.

i.e., the equilibrium employment of the jth factor is representable as the partial derivative of the cost function with respect to the jth factor price.

Eq. (7) is a crucial relationship, and establishes the link between alternative representations of econometrically useful relations. Notice, in particular, that if we proceed from the first order conditions of the profit maximization problem, we obtain relations between the share of output accruing to the various factors of production and **factor inputs**, while if we proceed from the cost function derivation, we establish a similar relationship between the shares of cost and **input prices**. This is a particularly prominent feature of the translog specification.

The duality between the cost and production function representation of technology has led to many studies of the characteristics of manufacturing technology through the cost function, but to relatively few such characterizations through the production function. Since a translog production function does not, generally, have a translog cost function for its dual, one is led to wonder whether similar conclusions are obtained from these two venues. A mention of this problem seems to have appeared in Burgess (1975), but to have received little, if any, attention since.

2.2 Cobb-Douglas Production Functions

In the Cobb-Douglas (Cobb-Douglas) case the basic model is

$$Q_t = A \prod_{j=1}^{n} x_{ti}^{\alpha_i} e^{u_t}, \tag{8}$$

where Q_t represents the tth observation on real output, x_{ti} the tth observation on the ith input, u_t is the tth observation on a zero mean i.i.d. random variable with finite variance, and the remaining symbols represent parameters to be estimated. In nearly all applications in the literature, it is assumed that the markets for inputs as well as products are purely competitive, and that the economic agents proceed on the basis of either cost minimization or profit maximization. This, almost invariably, leads to the additional condition of homogeneity of degree one. It is shown in Dhrymes (1962) and Drèze, Kmenta, and Zellner (1966), that under profit maximization the input quantities are independent of the structural error in the production function. The same may be shown when one assumes cost minimization, subject to an expected output constraint.

The implications of these assumptions are several. First, under expected profit maximization, we can estimate the unknown parameters of the production process through the General Linear Model (GLM),

$$\ln Q_t = \ln A + \sum_{j=1}^{n} \alpha_j \ln x_{tj} + u_t. \tag{9}$$

Second, we can estimate all the parameters above, with the exception of $\ln A$, through the relations

$$s_{ti} = \alpha_i \, e^{v_{ti}}, \quad i = 1, 2, \ldots, n, \tag{10}$$

where s_{ti} is the observed share of output accruing to the ith factor. Thus, we can test whether the translog production function is appropriate, relative to the Cobb-Douglas function, either through the production specification directly, or through the share equations. The cost function corresponding to the Cobb-Douglas production function is given by

$$C(p, \ Q) = f(\theta) g(p) h(Q), \tag{11}$$

where

$$\theta = (A, \alpha_1, \alpha_2, \ldots, \alpha_2)', \quad f(\theta) = \alpha A^{-\frac{1}{\alpha}} \left(\prod_{j=1}^{n} \alpha_j^{-\frac{\alpha_j}{\alpha}} \right),$$

$$g(p) = \left(\prod_{j=1}^{n} p_j^{-\frac{\alpha_j}{\alpha}} \right), \quad h(Q) = Q^{\frac{1}{\alpha}}.$$

We note that the cost function is **separable** in factor prices and output and, moreover, if $\alpha = 1$, we have, for given factor prices, **constant marginal costs**; if $\alpha < 1$, we have increasing marginal costs and if $\alpha > 1$ we have decreasing marginal costs. The standard comprehensive model of production **requires the condition that** $\alpha = 1$**, i.e., that the production function is homogeneous of degree one.** This is so since **if, as asserted, factor and product markets are perfectly competitive**, returns to the factors of production are governed by the marginal productivity conditions; thus, what accrues to them (factors of production) is given by

$$\sum_{j=1}^{n} p_j x_j = \sum_{j=1}^{n} \frac{\partial F}{\partial x_j} x_j = hF$$

for functions homogeneous of degree h. Since the Cobb-Douglas function we have employed is homogeneous of degree α, anything different from unity raises the issue of over- or under exhaustion of output. Thus, we have an incomplete and potentially contradictory theory. Besides, in the typical empirical practice, (and in the national income accounts), it **is assumed that the shares sum to unity**, by attributing to capital what is left over, after compensation of all other factors of production.[3] The practice is perfectly admissible but, if we take it up as part of our framework then we **cannot, at the same time, employ the relations implied by the marginal productivity conditions for capital!** This was pointed out in Dhrymes (1965), but the practice of implementing estimation procedures with increasing or decreasing returns to scale and the competitive first order (marginal productivity) conditions still persists to this day!

2.3 Translog Production Functions

The term translog production function is really a misnomer, in that the translog function is not a proper production function over the nonnegative orthant, as is commonly the case with other specifications. Rather, it has the customary properties of production functions only over a restricted subset of the admissible input space. As such, it is not generally viewed as a production function in its own right, but as an "approximation" to a more general, but unspecified functional form. Noting that, if

$$Q = F(x) \tag{12}$$

[3] Other procedures, such as for example Hall (1989), which independently attribute a return to capital, generally do exhibit over- or under-exhaustion of output. One is then left to explain, how in an equilibrium context we can have, systematically, such over- and under-exhaustions.

is an unspecified general function serving as a production function, we may expand it around $\ln x_j^0$, where $x_j^0 = 1$, for all j, by Taylor's series, retaining only linear and quadratic terms.[4] This yields

$$\ln Q = \ln F(x^0) + \frac{\partial F}{\partial x}(x^0)(\ln x) \tag{13}$$

$$+\frac{1}{2}(\ln x)' \begin{bmatrix} \frac{\partial^2 F}{\partial \ln x_1 \partial \ln x_1} & \frac{\partial^2 F}{\partial \ln x_1 \partial \ln x_2} & \cdots & \frac{\partial^2 F}{\partial \ln x_1 \partial \ln x_n} \\ \frac{\partial^2 F}{\partial \ln x_2 \partial \ln x_1} & \frac{\partial^2 F}{\partial \ln x_2 \partial \ln x_2} & \cdots & \frac{\partial^2 F}{\partial \ln x_2 \partial \ln x_n} \\ \vdots & \vdots & \vdots & \vdots \\ \frac{\partial^2 F}{\partial \ln x_n \partial \ln x_1} & \frac{\partial^2 F}{\partial \ln x_n \partial \ln x_2} & \cdots & \frac{\partial^2 F}{\partial \ln x_n \partial \ln x_n} \end{bmatrix} (\ln x).$$

If we replaced, by parameters, all derivatives evaluated at the point $x = x^0 = e$, where e is a vector of unities, then we have the standard translog function

$$\ln Q = \alpha_0 + \alpha' \ln x + \frac{1}{2}(\ln x)' \mathcal{B} (\ln x). \tag{14}$$

Under perfect competition in the product and factor markets, as well as profit maximization, we obtain the share equations,

$$s_{ti} = \alpha_i + \sum_{j=1}^{n} \beta_{ij} \ln x_{tj} + v_{ti}, \quad i = 1, 2, \ldots, n. \tag{15}$$

This is easily verified from Eq. (14), if we note that the right member of Eq. (15) is simply the derivative,

$$\frac{\partial \ln Q}{\partial \ln x_i} = \frac{x_i p_i}{Q}, \quad \text{owing to the fact that} \quad \frac{\partial Q}{\partial x_i} = p_i.$$

Several remarks are in order, regarding Eq. (15). First, all the parameters of the translog function, with the exception of the scale parameter, α_0, may be estimated from the n share equations.[5]

[4] In connection with this development, note that the Cobb-Douglas function can always be thought of as a Taylor series approximation, retaining only linear terms, to an arbitrary underlying production function. The difference is that this approximation is a production function in its own right, while the quadratic approximation is not!

[5] The reader should note that since, in Eq. (15), all share equations contain the same variables, and since the data is such that all shares add up to unity, least squares applied to the share equations produces estimates that obey the condi-

Second, as indicated in the footnote, we are forced to adopt the conditions,

$$\sum_{i=1}^{n} \alpha_i = 1, \quad e'\mathcal{B} = 0, \quad \text{and, since } \mathcal{B} \text{ is symmetric,} \quad \mathcal{B}'e = 0.$$

Collectively, these conditions imply that the approximating (translog) function is homogeneous of degree one. Alternatively, we may estimate the relevant parameters, without any restrictions, or assumptions regarding the nature of product and factor markets. This may be done by simply regressing the logarithm of output on the inputs. The resulting parameter estimates, may then serve as the test statistics for testing the null

$H_0: \; e'\alpha = 1$, and $e'\mathcal{B} = 0$,

as against the alternative that the parameters in question are unrestricted.

Third, this functional form is almost never employed in the literature. Instead, what is employed are share equations **derived from duality theory**, which means that one operates with the associated cost function. Now, **if the cost function is, actually, of the translog type**, i.e.,

$$\ln C = a_0 + a' \ln p + \frac{1}{2}(\ln p)'B(\ln p) + g(\ln Q) + error, \qquad (16)$$

we obtain the relations,

$$\frac{\partial \ln C}{\partial \ln p_i} = \frac{p_{ti}x_{ti}}{C_t} = s_{ti} = a_i + \sum_{j=1}^{n} b_{ij} \ln p_{tj} + v_{tj}, \quad i = 1, 2, \ldots, n. \qquad (17)$$

---

tions,

$$\sum_{i=1}^{n} \hat{\alpha}_i = 1, \quad \sum_{i=1}^{n} \hat{\beta}_{ij} = 0, \quad \text{for all } j.$$

The proof of this is straightforward. Let S, X be the data matrices, i.e., the matrices containing the observations on the n shares and inputs respectively. The least squares estimates of the parameters are

$$(X'X)^{-1}X'S = \begin{pmatrix} \hat{a}' \\ \hat{B}' \end{pmatrix}; \quad \text{hence,} \quad (X'X)^{-1}X'Se = (X'X)^{-1}Xe = e_{\cdot 1},$$

where e is a vector of unities, and $e_{\cdot i}$ is a vector all of whose elements are zero, except the ith, which is unity. But this imposes on us the assumption that the function is homogeneous of degree one!

The representation above is valid, provided the cost function is **separable**, as in the cases of the Cobb-Douglas and CES based cost functions.

If separability is denied, the cost function should be rendered as

$$\ln C = a_0 + a' \ln p + \alpha \ln Q + \frac{1}{2} \begin{pmatrix} \ln p \\ \ln Q \end{pmatrix}' \begin{bmatrix} B & c \\ c' & \gamma \end{bmatrix} \begin{pmatrix} \ln p \\ \ln Q \end{pmatrix} + error. \quad (18)$$

In this context, the share equations above become

$$\frac{p_{ti}x_{ti}}{C_t} = s_{ti} = a_i + \sum_{j=1}^{n} b_{ij} \ln p_{tj} + c_i \ln Q + v_{tj}, \quad i = 1, 2, \ldots, n, \quad (19)$$

and a test of decomposability, or separability, could be carried out in the form of the hypothesis test

$H_0: \quad c = 0,$

as against the alternative

$H_1: \quad c \neq 0.$

Consequently, a test of separability, may be carried out by estimating the parameters of Eq. (19), and testing the hypothesis

$H_0: c = 0,$

as against the alternative

$H_1: c \neq 0,$

while a test of homogeneity of degree one (constant returns to scale), given separability, may be carried out through the hypothesis test

$H_0: \ \gamma = 0, \quad \alpha = 1.$

Since duality implies that the production process exhibits increasing returns to scale if the cost function has the property that an increase in output, by a factor λ, leads to an increase in cost, by a factor less than λ, and conversely for decreasing returns to scale, a simple calculation shows that the cost function in Eq. (18) allows, in principle, for ranges (of output) corresponding to decreasing, constant and increasing returns to scale. The change in the logarithm of cost, following a change in output by factor λ, is given by

$$[\alpha + c' \ln p + \gamma(\ln Q + \frac{1}{2}\ln\lambda)] \ln\lambda.$$

Thus, for $\lambda > 1$,

$$\alpha + c' \ln p + \gamma(\ln Q + \frac{1}{2}\ln\lambda) \leq 1,$$

implies **non decreasing returns to scale**, while

$$\alpha + c' \ln p + \gamma(\ln Q + \frac{1}{2}\ln\lambda) > 1,$$

implies decreasing returns to scale.

2.4 Productivity Measurement

The most widely used measure of productivity, Total Factor Productivity (TFP), derives from the early work of Solow (1957) and we shall refer to it as the "Solow Residual"; the initial formulation assumed a production function

$$Q_t = A(t)F(x), \tag{20}$$

with "Hicks neutral technical change" function $A(t)$ and a production component F. Taking logarithmic derivatives, we find

$$\frac{\dot{Q}}{Q} = \frac{\dot{A}}{A} + \sum_{j=1}^{n} \frac{x_i}{F}\frac{\partial F}{\partial x_i}\frac{\dot{x}_i}{x_i}. \tag{21}$$

Noting that

$$\frac{x_i}{F}\frac{\partial F}{\partial x_i} = \frac{x_i}{Q}\frac{\partial Q}{\partial x_i} = s_i,$$

we may interpret the relation above as designating the **observed share of output accruing as income to the ith** factor of production. This becomes possible by the interpretation of the partial derivative $(\partial Q/\partial x_i)$ as the "wage" of the ith input in units of the output, which is here taken to be the *numeraire*. This, of course, immediately necessitates the assumption that there is perfect competition in the factor markets and that the production function is homogeneous of degree one, otherwise there will be over- or underexhaustion of output. Notice, further, that Eq. (21) may also be rendered as

$$\frac{d}{dt}\ln Q \approx \frac{d}{dt}\ln A + \frac{d}{dt}\sum_{j=1}^{n} s_j \ln x_j,$$

on the assumption that the s_j are nearly constant. Hence, up to an additive constant, we have, approximately,

$$\ln Q \approx \ln A + \sum_{j=1}^{n} s_j \ln x_j, \tag{22}$$

so that we can write

$$\ln A \approx \ln Q - \sum_{j=1}^{n} s_j \ln x_j. \tag{23}$$

Initially, Solow used Eq. (21), thus obtaining the relation between the rate of growth of output and the rates of growth of the inputs plus the rate of growth of "technical change", or productivity, giving rise to a literature of "growth accounting".[6] He then "integrated" the rate of growth of productivity function to obtain what we would call today the Total Factor Productivity (TFP). From Eq. (23), we see that if we insert a time subscript, we shall obtain

$$\ln A_t = \ln Q_t - \sum_{j=1}^{n} s_{jt} \ln x_{jt},$$

where the share, s_{jt}, is computed for each observation (time period) in the sample.

In Dhrymes (1961), (1963), we have an econometric reformulation of this problem in which it is assumed, explicitly,

$$Q_t = A(t) \prod_{j=1}^{n} x_j^{\alpha_j}; \tag{24}$$

obtaining appropriate estimates of the exponents, say $\hat{\alpha}_j$, we obtain the total factor productivity as

$$TFP_t = Q_t \prod_{j=1}^{n} x_j^{-\hat{\alpha}_j}. \tag{25}$$

Notice that the rationale of the Solow approach almost assumes the Cobb-Douglas production function, while the approach in Dhrymes (1961)

[6] This, of course, was in the early innocent days of applied econometrics, when it was firmly believed that empirical relations, once established, would last for eternity, or at least until the next year!

allows for the specification of any production function, since the basic scheme may be described as specifying the relation

$$Q_t = A(t)F(x_{\cdot t}), \tag{26}$$

estimating the parameters of the function F and obtaining

$$TFP_t = \frac{Q_t}{\hat{F}(x_{\cdot t})}. \tag{27}$$

The only issue remaining here is whether the "productivity" or "technical change" function $A(t)$, should include the scale constant, customary in production function specifications. Evidently, in the Solow residual approach, TFP includes the scale constant in question. We shall address this issue when we discuss the empirical results.

3 Data and Empirical Results

3.1 Data Sources

All data employed in this study are taken from the Census' LRD files. They comprise essentially shipments, inventory, inventory change, production worker compensation, nonproduction worker compensation, production workers' hours of work (as well as number of production workers), number of nonproduction workers, investment in plant and equipment, purchases of materials and energy, as well as the associated prices or implicit price deflators. Data were available on an annual basis, for all plants employing 250 workers or more, for SIC industries 35, 36 and 38. From these, plant specific capital stocks were constructed, utilizing the plant and equipment investment available by plant, and the appropriate deflators. In addition, value added was constructed from shipments plus inventory change minus purchases of energy and materials, divided by the shipments deflator. This value added served as the measure of output in most instances. When gross output was taken to correspond to the theoretical notion of output, it was defined as shipments plus inventory change, deflated by the shipments deflator. The implicit price deflators of production worker and nonproduction worker compensation served as a measure of wages, and the returns to capital, divided by the real capital stock we have constructed, served as a measure of the implicit price (rental) of capital. Thus, we have obtained information on: output, production workers, nonproduction workers and capital (we also had experimented with structure and equipment capital treated separately), annually over the period 1972-1986.

4 Empirical Results: Returns to Scale and Aggregation

As noted in the introduction, the basic unit of observation is the plant, and the universe investigated is variably industries 35 (Machinery, Except Electrical), 36 (Electrical Machinery and Electronic Equipment) and 38 (Instruments and Related Products). For industry 35 we have 17,724 observations, for industry 36, 17,126 and for industry 38 we have 5,054 observations.[7]

Generally, the same parameters being estimated from different implications of the production model, as discussed in sections 2.1, 2.2 and 2.3 gave rise to very different point estimates, much in the manner documented in Dhrymes (1990). Thus, nothing will be gained by further discussion, except to confirm that the same phenomenon extends through the two digit level. For that reason, in what follows, we shall report extensively only on the other findings, including the dynamic behavior of productivity, as determined by the residuals of econometrically fitted productions, first given in Dhrymes (1961), as well as productivity determined in the standard fashion of today, and first suggested in Solow (1957), with antecedents in Kendrick (?) and others. Finally, we note that, in this study, we confine our attention to the Cobb-Douglas and Translog production functions.

[7] In point of fact we had available to us 24,187, 22,772 and 6,503 observations on individual plants over the period 1972-1986. A number of observations were then eliminated if they had nonpositive value added, zero shipments, or experienced a more than doubling of their labor employment over the previous period.

4.1 Value Added versus Gross Shipments

In Tables A1 through A3, in the Appendix, we give the estimation results using **Gross Shipments** as the measure of output. Gross shipments means Shipments plus changes in Inventories. In Tables A4 though A6 we give estimation results using Value Added as the measure of output. Value Added is defined as gross shipments minus purchases from other firms classified as Materials and Energy. In the Gross Shipments version we have four inputs, Capital, designated by K, Production Worker hours, designated by L_1, non-Production Workers hours, designated by L_2 and Materials and Energy, designated by M. Each Table gives the results for the Cobb-Douglas and Translog specifications. The numbers in parentheses, under each coefficient estimate, represent the estimated standard errors. The remainder of the notations of the tables are self evident; thus, KK stands for the coefficient of $\ln K^2$, $L_1 L_2$ stands for the coefficient of $\ln L_1 \ln L_2$ etc.; N.D. stands for the "no dummies" version of the specification, T.D. stands for the "time dummies" only specification and T.D. and I.D. stands for the "time dummies and (four digit) industry dummies" specification. Finally, for the **Cobb-Douglas** specification, Test 1, refers for the test of constant returns to scale (homogeneity of degree 1); Test 2, under the heading T.D., refers to the test of the hypothesis that all time dummies are the same (no time effect, or more precisely, zero time contrasts); under the heading "T.D. and I.D.", Test 2 refers to the test of the hypothesis that all **industry dummies** are the same (zero four digit industry contrasts).

In the **Translog** specification, Test 1 is the homogeneity of degree 1 test, Test 2 is a test of whether the Translog is significantly different from the Cobb-Douglas specification, i.e., that all the extra parameters of the translog specification are zero. This designation is the same in all three columns, under the Translog heading. Test 3, under the heading T.D., refers to the test of the hypothesis that all time dummies are the same (no time effect, or more precisely, zero time contrasts); under the heading "T.D. and I.D.", Test 3 refers to the test of the hypothesis that all **industry dummies** are the same (zero four digit industry contrasts). The entries in the row corresponding to Tests 1,2 and 3, give the p-value, i.e., the probability that the test statistic obtained, or a higher value, could have been obtained under the null hypothesis; thus a p-value greater than an appropriate significance level (such as, e.g., .01 or .05 or .1), indicates **acceptance of the null hypothesis**; a value less **than that, indicates rejection.**

4.1.1 Returns to Scale: Gross Shipments

In point of fact, all tests reported in Tables A1 through A6 result in the rejection of the null hypotheses, since the largest p-value obtained in .02, in the case of "time contrasts" for the Translog function. This would indicate that at the .01 level of significance we would accept the hypothesis that, for all years, the time effect is the same.

Since we reject the degree one homogeneity hypothesis in all cases, it would be desirable to comment on the magnitude of this parameter, as estimated from our data. While for the Cobb-Douglas function the parameter estimate is unambiguous we shall report below the sum of the exponents of the various inputs. For the Translog, we shall evaluate returns to scale **at the mean**. The relevant means are given below in Table 1.

TABLE 1

Industry	No. OBS.	K	L_1	L_2	M
35	17,724	8.8823	6.3958	5.6621	8.9211
36	17,126	8.8554	6.5742	5.5296	8.8283
38	5,054	8.7247	6.4022	5.7372	8.6229

The returns to scale estimates are given in Table 2, below. In the case of the Translog production function, the returns to scale parameter is evaluated at the sample mean; sample means and other relevant information were given in Table 1, above.

TABLE 2		
Industry	Returns to Scale	
	C.D.	Translog
35	.994	1.021
36	1.013	1.034
38	1.020	1.021

These point estimates confirm the results given under Test 1, in Tables A1 through A3, viz., that in either the Cobb-Douglas or the Translog specification we cannot reject the hypothesis of nonconstant returns to scale; the magnitude of the scale parameter, however, is rather close to one. We should also note that the results presented above correspond to the specification that includes time and (four digit) industry dummies and that, especially in the Translog specification, we have occasionally point estimates (components of the vector α) which are negative!

The returns to scale parameter is somewhat larger when industry and time dummies are omitted, indicating another important incidence of aggregation effects.

The results presented herein should be tempered by the realization that there has been no correction for possible autocorrelation in plant disturbances, which is a subject that merits further investigation. Of course, one might argue, perhaps with equal justification, that autocorrelation correction is irrelevant, since one may view the "error" or "shock" component of the specification as a central limit theorem cumulation of factors, individually infinitessimal and unaccounted for, which, collectively, constitute the productivity phenomenon.

4.1.2 Other Issues: Gross Shipments

Certain other features of the results stand out and we comment on these below, always in the context of the specification that includes both time and (four digit) industry contrasts.

1. In the Cobb-Douglas case, materials (and energy) dominate the production process, i.e., the elasticity of output with respect to

materials and energy is generally about twice the elasticity with respect to any other input. In industry 35, this elasticity is of the order of .7, while in Industries 36 and 38 it is of the order of .5;

2. The hypothesis that the additional terms (beyond Cobb-Douglas) have nonnull coefficients is invariably accepted; the additional terms, however, do not contribute materially to the explanatory power of the relation.

3. Another persistent finding is that the sum of squared errors is reduced only by the order of 9 - 15 %, when we move from the Cobb-Douglas to the Translog specification, **but there is a very significant reduction when we introduce, in either the Cobb-Douglas or the Translog specification (four digit) industry effects**. This will be further discussed below.

The hypotheses of no time contrasts and no (four digit) industry contrasts are uniformly rejected, meaning that the scale constants in the specifications, whether Cobb-Douglas or Translog, vary according to the time (year) or four digit industry pertaining to a given plant. But perhaps what is far more significant **is the fact that the introduction of time effects** reduces the sum of squared errors **relatively little**, while the **introduction of four digit industry effects** reduces the sum of squared errors **very considerably**. We display the magnitude of these reductions, due to the introduction of four digit industry effects, in Table 3 below.

TABLE 3

Industry	Reduction in SSE C.D.	Reduction in SSE Translog
35	58 %	53 %
36	34 %	31 %
38	14 %	13 %

The preceding represents a "new finding" in the sense that this point has not been made in the literature, and raises a number of issues regarding productivity measurements, the most important of which is whether what is called "Total Factor Productivity", or in earlier times "Technical Change" is, largely or partly, an aggregation phenomenon that has little to do with technical improvements or "productivity" in their very basic meaning.

4.1.3 Returns to Scale: Value Added

We discuss here the same issues as above, for the case where output is defined by Value Added. The pertinent results are given in Tables A4 through A6 in the Appendix. By and large the results are basically those established in the previous case, except that now the returns to scale (point) estimate is somewhat higher, and slightly more uniform across industries, as is clear from the table below.

TABLE 4

Industry	Returns to Scale C.D.	Returns to Scale Translog
35	1.042	1.040
36	1.029	1.039
38	·1.020	1.020

Generally, the returns to scale parameter estimates here are of about the same magnitude as with Gross Shipments, with the possible exception of Industry 35.

4.1.4 Other Issues: Value Added

As in the previous case, the hypothesis that the "extra" terms of the Translog function have null coefficients is uniformly rejected. Again, the introduction of time contrasts reduces the sum of squared errors (SSE) rather slightly, while the introduction of four digit industry contrasts has a more powerful effect. The reductions in SSE are slightly smaller than in the previous case. The relevant results are given in Table 5, below.

TABLE 5		
Industry	Reduction in SSE	
	C.D.	Translog
35	52 %	48 %
36	23 %	22 %
38	07 %	07 %

The results in Table 4, above, show that the introduction of (four digit) industry contrasts results in appreciable reduction in the sum of squared residuals for industries 35 and 36. For industry 38, however, the reduction is only slight, 7 %. Finally, we note that the basic features of the Table are invariant to the production function specification, i.e., the entries under C.D. and Translog are nearly identical. We had noted a similar result, earlier, when we considered the case where output was defined in terms of Gross Value Added.

5 Empirical Results: Productivity Implications

In the preceding sections we had assumed, in effect, parametric homogeneity across all plants in a given **two digit** industry and progressively relaxed that by allowing "time contrasts" and "(four digit) industry contrasts". Either procedure, allows the scale constant for the production function to be different over time, or across four digit classifications. In the relatively long history of productivity studies, **variation over time** has, more or less, been the basis of productivity comparisons. Often, the departure of observed output from the (estimated or hypothesized) specification of inputs has been termed "technical change"; in many instances the variation of this entity over time has been attributed to research and development expenditures, or other manifestations of the change in the applicable technology, such as the number of patents issued, perhaps in some specified field, over a given time period. In equally as many, or perhaps in even more numerous studies, this entity has been "explained" by time; see, for example Solow (1957) or Dhrymes (1961).

In our study we have a unique opportunity to examine several facets of this problem, owing to the particularly rich data base available to us. We begin the **initial exploration** of this topic herein and reserve the study of several other issues for subsequent papers.

One important question that is often asked in cross section studies, is whether all entities follow the best industry practice and, if not, whether we can isolate those that are " most efficient", "average" or "least efficient". In this context, this may be translated as: can we find a classification of plants into those that exhibit least TFP, average TFP and those that exhibit most TFP. A corollary question is: is productivity (TFP or residual) growing over time? Finally, how much difference does it make in the **measurement of productivity**, if the approach is completely econometric, as in Dhrymes (1961), or is only **partially econometric** as in Solow (1957), and most of the work currently carried out. The latter approach, which we term "Solow Residual" in the graphs of the Appendix, is the ratio of observed output to a geometric (weighted) mean of the inputs, the weights being the observed shares accruing to the enumerated factors of production. In a variation of this basic approach, the weights are chosen as a Divisia Index of the shares over two periods. In the econometric approach, TFP is defined as the ratio of observed output and $\hat{F}(K, L_1, L_2)$, the latter being the **estimated production function** in terms of the inputs. Generally, we deal with the logarithm of this entity.

As we have observed in an earlier section, in order to make the two "residuals" have the same interpretation, we can either obtain TFP in the econometric procedure from the version that has **neither time nor industry** contrasts, or we can simply "regress" the Solow residual on time and (four digit) industry dummies, and use the residual of that regression as a measure of TFP. The graphs reflect this last approach.

5.1 Contemporaneous Rank

Graphs A1 through A6, in the Appendix, contain the course of (logarithmic) mean TFP by decile. More precisely, what is done is as follows: having determined the TFP corresponding to a given plant we rank plants in accordance with the magnitude of their TFP, **in each year**. What is plotted on the graph, then, is the logarithm of the geometric mean of TFP or, equivalently, the mean of the logarithm of the TFP of the plants in a given decile; evidently, the lowest graph corresponds to the first decile; the next corresponds to the second decile and so on. Three remarkable features emerge:

i. the qualitative aspects of productivity behavior are **almost completely independent** of the underlying production function specification, i.e., it makes little difference whether the TFP of plants is determined as a residual from a Cobb-Douglas or a Translog production function.

ii. The time profile of productivity **for deciles three through eight is remarkably flat**. One might interject that, perhaps, this was to be expected since we may well have removed any upward time trend by introducing the **time contrasts** in the estimation of the underlying production relation. This, however, cannot be argued very cogently since, as we had seen earlier, these time contrasts are only marginally significant and reduce the sum of squared errors by relatively small magnitudes.

iii. The first and last two (first, second, ninth and tenth) deciles, vary considerably over the 15-year period. Thus, in industry 35, mean TFP for the first decile rises considerably and that for the second declines somewhat so that the diffrence between them, which is large at the beginning of the period is considerably reduced by the end of the period. For industries 36 and 38, however, the first decile profile shows a decline, as does the second; the difference between them remains fairly constant or declines somewhat.

    The ninth and tenth deciles exhibit a rising profile, the ninth only slightly, the tenth very appreciably, so that by the end of the period the difference between the two shows a very substantial increase.

From previous results appearing in the literature one would have expected a stationary or slightly declining productivity in the middle to late seventies, and substantial growth following the 1980-81 recession.

What we find, by contrast, is the essential absence of relatively significant dynamic shifts in productivity behavior, at least from the three two digit industries under consideration, over the years 1972-1986. The major upward shifts are confined to the upper decile and the major downshifts are confined to the first decile; this is hardly a result that supports the hypothesis of vigorous technical change or productivity growth.

5.2 First Year Rank

Since, in the classification scheme of the previous section, the identity of the plants in each decile is constantly changing, we also examined the behavior of mean productivity by deciles, **when the classification of plants is based solely on their rank in their initial year.** To be precise, what is done is to rank plants according to the magnitude of their TFP in 1972; thereafter plants keep this rank, so that, e.g., the entry for the first decile in 1974, is the (logarithmic) mean of TFP, for plants that were ranked in the **first decile in 1972.** These results appear in Graphs A7 through A12. Their salient features are:

i. the results are qualitative quite similar whether derived from the Cobb-Douglas or the Translog residuals;

ii. in industry 35, plants in the first and second decile (as of 1972) exhibit dramatic growth in productivity in subsequent years, and in the 80's they dominate other plants in terms of TFP. This suggests that such plants must have something in common, such as, e.g., their SIC four digit classification, or substantial investment in modernization; plants in other deciles tend to become very closely bunched, indicating increasing similarity in their TFP behavior.

iii. For industry 36, plants in the first decile exhibit enormous growth, but also enormous fluctuations in their TFP behavior; to a lesser degree, the same is true for plants in the second decile. Plants in the second decile exhibit less vigorous, **but fairly steady growth.** The remaining plants exhibit the same compression in their TFP growth as those in industry 35, although they generally tend to keep their original ranking. These results are rather intriguing and require further investigation.

iv. In industry 38, we find increased "entropy", in that the time profile of the first and second deciles is similar to what has been observed in industries 35 and 36; the paths of the other deciles, however, cross much more frequently. Thus, what we find is that the relative placidity of productivity behavior is replaced by considerable dynamic movements of plants in their TFP characteristics. In turn, this suggests that there is a potentially interesting research problem in studying the transition of plants into and out of various TFP classifications.

5.3 The Solow Residual

5.3.1 Contemporaneous Rank

The time profile of Solow residuals, by contemporaneous rank, is given by deciles, in Graphs A13 through A18, first in the manner usually presented in the literature and thereafter by removing "time effects" and "four digit industry" effects. Precisely, the Solow residual is regressed on "time dummies" and "four digit industry dummies" and the **residuals from that regression are taken to be the measure of TFP**. This last measure is the one most comparable with the results obtained through the econometric approach. Their graphs are labelled "Solow Regression". The corresponding TFP will be referred to below as SR TFP. Several aspects of these graphs are worth noting.

i. In the graphs labelled "Solow Residual, Sorted", where the time and four digit industry effects are not removed, mean TFP by decile is substantially higher than is the case for the econometrically derived results, where such effects had been removed.

ii. When such effects are removed, the SR TFP profiles are quite similar to those obtained earlier with Cobb-Douglas and Translog production functions, except that SR TFP is **smoother**. This is generally the consequence of using a great deal more parameters in obtaining SR TFP in the sense that, with the econometric approach, we are using a limited number of share parameters; four or three in the case of the Cobb-Douglas, and nine or fourteen in the case of the Translog function. By contrast, in the SR context we may use upwards of 34,000 **independent** share parameters for industries 35 and 36, and upwards of 10,000 parameters in the case of industry 38. Evidently, in the econometric approach we can also increase the number of share parameters by simply allowing different Cobb Douglas exponents in each year. The question then is: to the extent that the change in the parametric structure leads to different measures of productivity, have we submerged some aspect of "technical change induced TFP" under another category? Or have we attributed to TFP something that is the result of inefficient handling of data?

Since the issue of productivity measures is imbedded in the production technology literature and purports to measure the extend to which "technical change" or other "improvements in technique enhance the productivity" of the factors of production, it is more appropriate to employ the econometrically based approach to productivity measurement. In that context, it may be said that the Solow residual approach gives a **misleadingly smooth** representation to the phenomenon under study.

5.3.2 Initial Rank

In Graphs A19 through A24 we give the time profile of the Solow residual measure of TFP with initial rank designation of plants. The major features are as follows.

i. A general characteristic running through all graphs is that there are fewer crossovers than is the case with econometrically derived TFP. In industry 35, the tenth decile exhibits considerable growth; this growth, however, almost completely disappears when time and four digit industry effects are removed. Since, generally, time effects are quite weak, it would appear that this phenomenon is largely illusory and simply reflects the four digit industry composition of that decile. When the composition effects are removed in Graph A20, we observe the same phenomenon as in the previous section, viz., the strong TFP growth of first decile plants. As we also remarked above, SR TFP is **more smooth** than econometrically derived TFP.

ii. In industry 36, SR TFP shows the consistent decline in the tenth decile and appreciable growth in the first decile, as noted earlier. In fact, the first three deciles exhibit very similar SR TFP in the eighties.

iii. In industry 38, we see the same phenomenon noted above, viz., increased entropy, although the frequency of crossovers is appreciable smaller than in the case of econometrically derived TFP, reflecting the **smoothness** of the Solow residual approach.

6 Conclusions

In this paper we sought to complete the objectives set in Dhrymes (1990) by investigating, at the two digit industry level, the compatibility of estimates of the parametric structure of a given specification. This is attained **by exploiting all implications of that specification.** The results were that none of the popular specifications, such as the Cobb-Douglas, the Translog, or the CES, production functions have a clear advantage over the others. In fact, all of them show great incompatibility. This is vexing and raises grave doubts regarding the theoretical foundations of production studies, either in the specification of technology or in the specification of the institutional milieu in which production is carried out. Since this was extensively documented at the three digit product group level in Dhrymes (1990) we have not reported the results in this paper. Instead, we focused our attention increasingly on issues of returns to scale and productivity measurement. A number of findings stand out.

i. There are mildly increasing returns to scale at the two digit level, at least in the case of industries 35, 36, and 38.

ii. The translog specification is a slightly preferable specification, in the sense that (some of) the non (log)linear terms (may) have nonzero coefficients. On the other hand, all results of interest such as returns to scale, aggregation effects, or productivity measurements, do not seem to be appreciably affected by the specification of the production process. This would argue, in terms of the principle of simplicity, that Cobb-Douglas should be the production specification of choice, despite the great econometric attraction of the Translog.

iii. Allowing for "time" effects improves the fit very slightly, while allowing for (four digit) "industry" effects improves the fit very substantially.

iv. The results above are valid whether output is defined by Gross Shipments or Value Added.

In taking up issues relative to the measurement of productivity, we have relied exclusively on results obtained from the Value Added formulation. The salient conclusions in this phase of the study are:

i. TFP, interpreted as the (within sample) residual of observed output and the estimated relation, is qualitatively almost identical whether computed on the basis of the Cobb-Douglas or the Translog specification. We have followed the practice of computing TFP on the basis of the production function specification that includes "time" and (four digit) "industry" contrasts. While this particular version may evoke some objections, we note that even when these contrasts are suppressed the results do not change very substantially.

ii. Ranking plants according to TFP, in each year, and graphing the mean TFP by decile, i.e., the mean TFP of plants in the first decile, per year; the second decile, per year, and so on, gives the general impression that aside from the first and tenth decile, the time profile of the other deciles is rather flat. This suggests that it is only at the very bottom and at the very top of the productivity scale that "growth" occurs, and that the growth in question is rather slight.

iii. In the observations made under ii. above, it should be noted that the **identity of the plants** within the various deciles is, at least in principle, **constantly shifting**. To gain a different view of the process, we rank plants by their TFP in the **initial year**, 1972, and thereafter follow these same plants in subsequent years. In this framework, quite a different behavior emerges. Dynamic upward growth characterizes some groups of plants, while for others we observe dramatic declines, generally the first decile experiencing the most dynamic movement **upwards** and the tenth decile the most dynamic movement **downwards**.

The findings in this paper lead to a number of questions and suggest a number of topics for further research:

i. what is the nature of the transition process, i.e., the manner in which plants move from one decile (or other classificatory scheme) to another; is it completely random or are there certain commonalities? Are there distinct characteristics for plants that make frequent transitions and those that don't? Indeed, are there stationary plants? Do plants that leave the sample tend to be those with high, medium, or low productivity?

ii. Should productivity include "time" effects and aggregation or "compositional" effects, i.e., should what we wish to call "productivity" consist of the contribution to output of things other than the specified labor and/or capital inputs, or should it be net of predictable compositional and/or "time" effects?

iii. Can we model the transition process, econometricaly, and determine what factors are most potent in effectuating transition to higher or lower states of TFP, or a stationary status?

iii. Does TFP, as defined by the Solow residual method, give unwarrantedly "smooth" time profiles of the phenomenon?

These issues are reserved for later investigation.

BIBLIOGRAPHY

Afriat, S. (1972). "Efficiency Estimation of Production Functions", *International Economic Review*, 13, 568-598. Discussion, 15, 512-521, 1974; 18, 435-444, 1977.

Applebaum, E. (1979). "On the Choice of Functional Forms", *International Economic Review*, 20, 449-458.

Berndt, E. R. (1976). "Reconciling Alternative Estimates of the Elasticity of Substitution", *Review of Economics and Statistics*, 58, 59-68.

——————— and L. R. Christensen (1973). "Internal Structure of Functional Relationships, Separability, Substitution, and Aggregation", *Review of Economic Studies*, 40, 403-410. Reply. R.R. Russell. 42, 79-85.

——————— *et al.* (1977). "Flexible Functional Forms and Expenditure Distributions, An Application to Canadian Consumer Demand Functions", *international Economic Review*, 18, 651-675.

———————, and D. O. Wood (1981). "Engineering and Econometric Interpretation of Energy-Capital Complementarity", *American Economic Review*, 69, 342-354. Discussion, 71, 1100-1110, 1981.

Berndt, R. A., and M. A. Fuss (1986). "Productivity Measurement with Adjustments for Variations in Capacity Utilization and Other Forms of Temporary Equilibrium", *Journal of Econometrics*, 33, 7-29.

Berndt, R. A., and M. S. Khaled (1979). "Parametric Productivity Measurement and Choice among Flexible Functional Forms", *Journal of Political Economy*, 87, 1220-1245.

Bewley, R. A. (1983). "Tests of Restrictions in Large Demand Systems", *European Economic Review*, 20, 257-269.

Binswanger, H. P. (1974). "Measurement of Technical Change Biases with Many Factors of Production", *American Economic Review*, 64, 964-976.

Blackorby, C., D. Primont, and R. Russell (1978). *Duality, Separability and Functional Structures, Theory and Economic Applications*. Amsterdam, North Holland.

Blackorby, C., and R. Russell (1976). "Functional Structure and the Allen Partial Elasticities of Substitution, An Application of Duality Theory", *Review of Economic Studies*, 43, 285-291.

——————— (1981). "Morishima Elasticity of Substitution; Symmetry, Constancy, Separability, and Its Relationship to the Hicks and Allen Elasticities", *Review of Economic Studies*, 48, 147-158.

Blair, R. D., and J. Kraft (1974). "Estimation of Elasticity of Substitution in American Manufacturing Industry from Pooled Cross-Section and Time Series Observations", *Review of Economics and Statistics*, 56, 343-347.

Brown, M. (ed.) (1967). *The Theory and Empirical Analysis of Production*, New York, Columbia University Press.

——————— (1973). "Toward an Econometric Accommodation of the Capital-Intensity-Perversity Phenomenon", *Econometrica*, 41, 937-954.

Brown, R. S., *et al.* (1979). "Modelling the Structure of Cost and Production for Multi-Product Firms", *Southern Economic Journal*, 46, 256-273.

Burgess, D. F. (1975). "Duality Theory and Pitfalls in the Specification of Technologies", *Journal of Econometrics*, 3, 105-121.

Burmeister, E. (1976). "Factor-Price Frontier and Duality with Many Primary Factors", *Journal of Economic Theory*, 12, 496-503, June 1976.

Chambers, R. G. (1984). "Unbiased Determination of Production Technologies", *Journal of Econometrics*, 20, 285-323.

Christensen, L. R., and others (1975). "Transcendental Logarithmic Utility Functions", *American Economic Review*, 65, 367-383.

Clark, P. K., and J. T. Haltmaier (1985). "The Labor Productivity Slowdown in the United States, Evidence from Physical Output Measures", *Review of Economics and Statistics*, 67, 504-508.

Darby, M. R. (1984). "The U. S. Productivity Slowdown, A Case of Statistical Myopia", *American Economic Review*, 74, 301-322.

Dhrymes, P. J. (1961). "Resource Allocation Implications and Measurement of Sectoral Productivity Parameters in a Multi-Sector Economy", Unpublished Ph.D. dissertation, Massachusetts Institute of Technology.

——————— (1962). "On Devising Unbiased Estimators for the Parameters of a Cobb-Douglas Production Function", *Econometrica*, 30, 686-92.

——————— (1963). "A Comparison of Productivity Behavior in Manufacturing and Service Industries", *Review of Economics and Statistics*, 65, 64-69.

——————— (1965). "Some Extensions and Tests for the CES Class of Production Functions", *Review of Economics and Statistics*, 67, 357-366.

——————— (1969). "A Model of Short-Run Labor Adjustment", in *The Brookings Model, Some Further Results*, J.S. Duesenberry, G. Fromm, L.R. Klein, and E. Kuh, (Eds.), Chicago, Rand-McNally.

——————— (1990). "Technology in US Manufacturing: Evidence from the LRD Sample", in Finley, D. (ed.) *Annual Research Conference*, Bureau of Census, Washington, D.C., US Government Printing Office.

Diewert, W. E. (1971). "An Application of the Shephard Duality Theorem, A Generalized Leontief Production Function", *Journal of Political Economy*, 79, 481-507.

——————— (1974). "Functional Forms for Revenue and Factor Requirements Functions", *International Economic Review*, 15, 119-130.

———————, and T.J. Wales (1987). "Flexible Functional Forms and Global Curvature Conditions", *Econometrica*, 55, 43-68.

Douglas, P. H. (1986). "Cobb-Douglas Production Function Once Again, Its History, Its Teaching, and Some New Empirical Values", *Journal of Political Economy*, 84, 903-915.

———————, and L. Samuelson (1987). "Plant Turnover, Employment Growth, and Job Stability in the U.S. Manufacturing Sector 1963-1982", Unpublished manuscript.

Drèze, J., J. Kmenta and A. Zellner (1966). "Specification of Cobb-Douglas Production Function Models", *Econometrica*, 34, 784-95.

Elbadawi, I., and others (1983). "An Elasticity can be Estimated Consistently without A Priori Knowledge of Functional Forms", *Econometrica*, 51, 731-751.

Epstein, L. G. (1981). "Duality Theory and Functional Forms for Dynamic Factor Demands", *Review of Economic Studies*, 48, 81-95.

——————, and A. J. Yatchew (1985). "Non-parametric Hypothesis Testing Procedures and Applications to Demand Analysis", *Journal of Econometrics*, 30, 149-169.

Fare, R., and D. Primont (1986). "On Differentiability of Cost Functions", *Journal of Economic Theory*, 38, 233-237.

Fare, R., and L. Jansson (1975). "On VES and WDI Production Functions", *International Economic Review*, 16, 733-744.

Field, B. C., and C Grebenstein (1980). "Capital-Energy Substitution in U.S. Manufacturing", *Review of Economics and Statistics*, 62, 207-212.

Fishelson, G. (1979). "Elasticity of Factor Substitution in Cross-Section Production Functions", *Review of Economics and Statistics*, 61, 432-436.

Fisher, A. N. P. (1974). "Non-traditional Demand Curves", *American Economist*, 18, 42-47.

Fisher, F. M., *et al.* (1977). "Aggregate Production Functions, Some CES Experiments", *Review of Economic Studies*, 44, 305-320.

Friedman, J. W. (1973). "Concavity of Production Functions and Non-increasing Returns to Scale", *Econometrica*, 41, 981-984.

Fuss, M. A., and V. K. Gupta (1981). "Cost Function Approach to the Estimation of Minimum Efficient Scale, Returns to Scale, and Suboptimal Capacity, With an Application to Canadian Manufacturing", *European Economic Review*, 15, 123-135.

Fuss, M and D. McFadden (eds.) (1978). *Production Economics, A Dual Approach to Theory and Application*. Amsterdam, North Holland.

Gallant, A. R. (1982). "Unbiased Determination of Production Technologies", *Journal of Econometrics*, 20, 285-323.

————————, and G. H. Golub (1984). "Imposing Curvature Restrictions on Flexible Functional Forms", *Journal of Econometrics*, 26, 295-321.

————————, and D. Jorgenson (1979). "Statistical Inference for a System of Nonlinear, Implicit Equations in the Context of Instrumental Variables Estimation", *Journal of Econometrics*, 11, 275-302.

Ginsberg, W. (1974) "Multiplant Firm with Increasing Returns to Scale", *Journal of Economic Theory*, 9, 283-292.

Griliches, Z., (1967). "Producrion Functions in Manufacturing: Some Empirical Results", 275-322 in Brown, M (ed.) *op. cit.*

Guilkey, D. K., and others (1983). "Comparison of the Performance of Three Flexible Functional Forms", *International Economic Review*, 24, 591-616.

Guilkey, D. K., and C. A. K. Lovell (1980). "On the Flexibility of the Translog Approximation", *International Economic Review*, 21, 137-147.

———————— (1975). "Specification Error in Generalized Production Function Models", *International Economic Review*, 16, 161-170.

Hall, B. (1989). "Increasing Returns: Theory and Measurement with Industry Data", *Journal of Political Economy*, 97, 878-902.

Hanoch, G. (1975a). "Elasticity of Scale and the Shape of Average Costs", *American Economic Review*, 65, 492-497.

———————— (1975b). "Production and Demand Models with Direct or Indirect Implicit Additivity", *Econometrica*, 43, 395-419.

———————— and M. Rothschild (1972). "Testing the Assumptions of Production Theory, A Nonparametric Approach", *Journal of Political Economy*, 80, 256-275.

Hildebrand, W. (1981). "Short-run Production Functions Based on Microdata", *Econometrica*, 49, 1095-1125.

Huang, C. J. (1984). "Estimation of Stochastic Frontier Production Function and Technical Inefficiency via the EM Algorithm", *Southern Economic Journal*, 50, 847-856.

Huang, K. S. (1983). "The Family of Inverse Demand Systems", *European Economic Review*. 23, 329-337.

Intrilligator, M.D. and D.A. Kendrick (eds.) (1974). *Frontiers in Quantitative Economics*, Amsterdam, North Holland.

Jorgenson, D. W. (1974). "Investment and Production: A Review", in Intrilligator, M.D. and D. Kendrick (eds.), *op. cit.*

———————— (1986). "Econometric Methods for Modelling Producer Behavior", ch. 31, 1842-1915, in Grilches, Z. and M. D. Intrilligator (eds.) *op. cit.*

———————— and L. J. Lau (1974). "Duality and Differentiability in Production", *Journal of Economic Theory*, 9, 23-42.

———————— (1974). "Duality of Technology and Economic Behavior", *Review of Economic Studies*, 41, 181-200.

Kako, T. (1980). "Application of the Decomposition Analysis of Derived Demand for Factor Inputs in U.S. Manufacturing", *Review of Economics and Statistics*, 62, 300-301.

Kelejian, H. H. (1972). "Estimation of Cobb-Douglas Type Functions with Multiplicative and Additive Errors, A Further Analysis", *International Economic Review*, 13, 179-182. Reply. A. C. Harvey. 17, 506-509, 1976.

Kopp, R. J., and V. K. Smith (1980). "Measuring Factor Substitution with Neoclassical Models, An Experimental Evaluation", *Bell Journal of Economics*, 11, 631-655.

Lau, L. J. (1976). "Note on Elasticity of Substitution Function", *Review of Economic Studies*, 43, 353-358. Reply. H. Kang and G. Brown. 47, 1003-1004, 1980.

Leech, D. (1975). "Testing the Error Specification in Nonlinear Regression", *Econometrica*, 43, 719-725.

Levy, S. (1985). "Factor Demand Functions for Constant Returns to Scale Technologies", *Southern Economic Journal*, 51, 860-867.

Liebowitz, S. J. (1982). "What Do Census Price-Cost Margins Measure?" *Journal of Law and Economics*, 25, 231-246.

Lopez, R. E. (1985). "Structural Implications of a Class of Flexible Functional Forms for Profit Functions", *International Economic Review*, 26, 593-601.

Lundberg, S. (1985). "Tied Wage-Hours Offers and the Endogeneity of Wages", *Review of Economics and Statistics*, 405-410.

Maccini, L. J. (1977). "Empirical Model of Price and Output Behavior", *Economic Inquiry*, 15, 493-512.

Malcomson, J. M. (1977). "Capital Utilization and the Measurement of the Elasticity of Substitution", *Manchester School of Economics and Social Studies*, 45, 103-111.

——————— (1980). "Measurement of Labour Cost in Empirical Models of Production and Employment", *Review of Economics and Statistics*, 62, 521-528.

Mardsen, J., *et al.*, (1974). "Engineering Foundations of Production Functions", *Journal of Economic Theory*, 9, 124-140.

Mark, J.A. (1986). "Problems Encountered in Measuring Single- and Multifactor Productivity", *Monthly Labor Review*, 109, 3-11.

McCarthy, M. D. (1974). "On the Stability of Dynamic Demand Functions", *International Economic Review*, 15, 256-259.

McGuckin, R.H. and S.V. Nguyen (1989), "Public Use Microdata: Disclosure and Usefulness", *Journal of Productivity*, 1, 69-90.

McKenzie, G. (1977). "Complementarity, Substitutability, and Independence", *Oxford Economic Papers*, 29, 430-441.

Meyer, R. A., and K. R. Kadiyala (1974). "Linear and Nonlinear Estimation of Production Functions", *Southern Economic Journal*, 40, 463-472.

Mizon, G. E. (1977). "Inferential Procedures in Nonlinear Models, An Application in a UK Industrial Cross Section Study of Factor Substitution and Returns to Scale", *Econometrica*, 45, 1221-1242.

Morrison, C. J. (1986). "Productivity Measurement with Non-static Expectations and Varying Capacity Utilization, An Integrated Approach", *Journal of Econometrics*, 33, 51-74.

Mortenson, D. T. (1973). "Generalized Costs of Adjustment and Dynamic Factor Demand Theory", *Econometrica*, 41, 657-665.

Mundlak, Y. (1968). "Elasticities of Substitution and the Theory of Derived Demands", *Review of Economic Studies*, 35, 225-235.

Nerlove, M., (1965) *Estimation and Identification of Cobb Douglas Production Functions*, Chicago, Rand McNally.

——————— (1967). "Recent Empirical Results of the CES and Related Production Functions", 55-112, in Brown, M. (ed.), *op. cit.*

Paraskevopoulos, C. C. (1979). "Alternative Estimates of the Elasticity of Substitution, An Inter-Metropolitan CES Production Function Analysis of U. S. Manufacturing Industries", *Review of Economics and Statistics*, 61, 439-442.

Poirier, D. J. (1975). "On the Use of Cobb-Douglas Splines", *International Economic Review*, 16, 733-744.

Ramenofsky, S. D., and A. R. Shepherd (1979). "Note Concerning a Basic Inconsistency between the Theory of Production and the Theory of Costs", *American Economist*, 23, 55-58.

Ramsey, J. B. (1974). "Limiting Forms for Demand Functions, Tests of Some Specific Hypotheses", *Review of Economics and Statistic*, 56, 468-477.

Ray, R. (1986). "Flexibility in Dynamic Demand Modeling and its Implications for Testing Restrictions", *Manchester School of Economics and Social Studies*, 54, 1-21.

——————— (1985). "Specification and Time Series Estimation of Dynamic Gorman Polar Form Demand Systems", *European Economic*

Review, 27, 357-374.

Razin, A. (1974). "Note on the Elasticity of Derived Demand under Decreasing Returns", *American Economic Review*, 64, 697-700.

Ringstad, V. (1974). "Some Empirical Evidence on the Decreasing Scale Elasticity", *Econometrica*, 42, 87-101.

Rose, D. E., and S. Star (1978). "Homotheticity and the Relationship Between Plant Output and Factor Prices under Perfect Competition", *Canadian Journal of Economics*, 11, 92-97.

Samuelson, P. A. (1979). "Paul Douglas's Measurement of Production Functions and Marginal Productivities", *Journal of Political Economy*, 87, 923-939, Part 1.

Sato, R. (1977) "Homothetic and Non-homothetic CES Production Functions", *American Economic Review*, 67, 559-569.

——————— (1980). "Impact of Technical Change on the Homotheticity of Production Functions", *Review of Economic Studies*, 47, 767-776.

——————— (1975). "Most General Class of CES Functions", *Econometrica*, 43, 999-1003.

——————— (1977). "A Note on Factor Substitution and Efficiency", *Review of Economics and Statistics*, 59, 360-366. Reply with rejoinder, L. Sveikauskas. 62, 135-142, 1980.

———————, *et al.* (1975). "Market Behavior and the Types of Production Functions", *European Economic Review*, 6, 331-342.

Schaafsma, J. (1977). "Capital-Labor Substitution and the Employment Function in Manufacturing, A Model Applied to 1949-1972 Canadian Data", *Quarterly Review of Economics and Business*, 17, 33-42.

Shapiro, M.D. (1986). "The Dynamic Demand for Capital and Labor", *Quarterly Journal of Economics*, 101, 513-542.

Shephard, R. W. (1953). *Cost and Production Functions*. Princeton, Princeton University Press.

——————— (1970). *Theory of Cost and Production Functions.* Princeton, Princeton University Press.

———————, and M. Fare (1980). *Dynamic Theory of Production Correspondences.* Cambridge, Mass., Oelgeschlager, Gunn and Harris.

Simmons, P., and D. Weiserbs (1979). "Translog Flexible Functional Forms and Associated Demand Systems", *American Economic Review*, 69, 892-901.

Sosin, K., and L. Fairchild (1984). "Nonhomotheticity and Technological Bias in Production", *Review of Economics and Statistics*, 66, 44-50.

Syrquin, M., and G. Hollender (1982). "Elasticities of Substitution and Complementarity, The General Case", *Oxford Economic Papers*, 34, 515-519.

Thurnsby, J. G., and C. A. K. Lovell (1978). "Investigation of the Kmenta Approximation to the CES Function", *International Economic Review*, 19, 363-377.

Waldman, D. M. (1984). "Properties of Technical Efficiency Estimators in the Stochastic Frontier Model", *Journal of Econometrics*, 25, 353-364.

Walters, A. A. (1963). "Production and Cost Functions: An Econometric Survey", *Econometrica*, 31, 1-66.

Waud, R. N. (1968). "Man-Hour Behavior in U. S. Manufacturing, A Neoclassical Interpretation", *Journal of Political Economy*, 76,407-427.

Weymark, J. A. (1980). "Duality Results in Demand Theory", *European Economic Review*, 14, 377-395.

Wibe, S. (1984). "Engineering Production Functions, A Survey", *Economica*, 51,401-411. Discussion. 53, 529-536, 1986.

Wu, D. M. (1975). "Estimation of the Cobb-Douglas Production Function", *Econometrica*, 43, 739-744.

You, J. K. (1979). "Capital Utilization, Productivity, and Output Gap", *Review of Economics and Statistics*, 61, 91-100, Discussion, 63, 155-160, 1981.

APPENDIX

TABLE A1						
GROSS SHIPMENTS, INDUSTRY 35 1972-1986						
VAR.	COBB-DOUGLAS			TRANSLOG		
	N.D	T.D.	T.D. AND I.D.	N.D.	T.D.	T.D. AND I.D.
Const	1.108	1.086	1.352	2.743	2.747	2.084
	(0.033)	(0.035)	(0.033)	(0.172)	(0.172)	(0.124)
K	0.150	0.121	0.165	-0.084	-0.075	0.123
	(0.007)	(0.007)	(0.005)	(0.053)	(0.053)	(0.037)
L_1	-0.037	-0.010	0.174	1.198	1.179	0.684
	(0.007)	(0.007)	(0.005)	(0.047)	(0.047)	(0.033)
L_2	0.162	0.165	0.086	-0.032	-0.043	0.232
	(0.006)	(0.006)	(0.004)	(0.045)	(0.045)	(0.032)
M	0.762	0.764	0.595	-0.142	-0.142	0.011
	(0.006)	(0.006)	(0.005)	(0.045)	(0.045)	(0.032)
KK				0.092	0.078	0.012
				(0.012)	(0.012)	(0.008)
KL_1				-0.042	-0.038	-0.010
				(0.010)	(0.010)	(0.007)
KL_2				0.031	0.027	0.022
				(0.009)	(0.009)	(0.006)
KM				-0.063	-0.054	-0.016
				(0.008)	(0.008)	(0.006)
L_1L_1				0.384	0.388	0.183
				(0.013)	(0.013)	(0.009)
L_1L_2				-0.103	-0.101	-0.031
				(0.009)	(0.009)	(0.006)
L_1M				0.297	-0.300	-0.156
				(0.008)	(0.008)	(0.006)
L_2L_2				0.139	0.144	0.048
				(0.010)	(0.010)	(0.007)
L_2M				-0.022	-0.021	-0.046
				(0.007)	(0.007)	(0.005)
MM				0.387	0.381	0.222
				(0.009)	(0.009)	(0.006)
SSE	3555.67	3523.05	1451.86	2734.77	2714.44	1296.27
R-SQ	0.845	0.846	0.937	0.880	0.881	0.943
Test1	0.000	0.000	0.000	0.000	0.000	0.000
Test2	n.a.	0.000	0.000	0.000	0.000	0.000
Test3	n.a.	n.a.	n.a.	n.a.	0.000	0.000

TABLE A2						
GROSS SHIPMENTS, INDUSTRY 36 1972-1986						
VAR.	COBB-DOUGLAS			TRANSLOG		
	N.D	T.D.	T.D. AND I.D.	N.D.	T.D.	T.D. AND I.D.
Const	1.534 (0.022)	1.496 (0.023)	1.355 (0.024)	1.919 (0.121)	1.979 (0.120)	1.302 (0.105)
K	0.268 (0.005)	0.256 (0.005)	0.273 (0.004)	-0.194 (0.038)	-0.175 (0.038)	0.075 (0.032)
L_1	0.124 (0.005)	0.137 (0.005)	0.179 (0.004)	0.300 (0.034)	0.254 (0.034)	0.285 (0.029)
L_2	0.134 (0.003)	0.135 (0.003)	0.082 (0.003)	0.399 (0.026)	0.397 (0.025)	0.350 (0.022)
M	0.501 (0.004)	0.498 (0.004)	0.479 (0.004)	0.560 (0.030)	0.548 (0.029	0.428 (0.026)
KK				0.170 (0.009)	0.158 (0.009	0.083 (0.008)
KL_1				0.012 (0.007)	0.018 (0.007)	0.023 (0.006)
KL_2				0.005 (0.005)	0.005 (0.005)	0.001 (0.004)
KM				-0.137 (0.006)	-0.132 (0.006)	-0.083 (0.005)
L_1L_1				0.098 (0.008)	0.103 (0.008)	0.095 (0.007)
L_1L_2				-0.031 (0.005)	-0.033 (0.005)	-0.033 (0.004)
L_1M				-0.083 (0.005)	-0.083 (0.005)	-0.083 (0.005)
L_2L_2				0.109 (0.004)	0.113 (0.004)	0.078 (0.004)
L_2M				-0.079 (0.004)	-0.080 (0.004)	-0.054 (0.004)
MM				0.246 (0.006)	0.242 (0.006)	0.188 (0.005)
SSE	1612.63	1583.13	1052.15	1338.42	1312.89	916.65
R-SQ	0.917	0.918	0.946	0.931	0.932	0.953
Test1	0.000	0.000	0.000	0.000	0.000	0.000
Test2	n.a.	0.000	0.000	0.000	0.000	0.000
Test3	n.a.	n.a.	n.a.	n.a.	0.000	0.000

TABLE A3

GROSS SHIPMENTS, INDUSTRY 38 1972-1986

VAR.	COBB-DOUGLAS			TRANSLOG		
	N.D	T.D.	T.D. AND I.D.	N.D.	T.D.	T.D. AND I.D.
Const	1.617	1.554	1.508	2.645	2.641	2.711
	(0.033)	(0.035)	(0.037)	(0.172)	(0.172)	(0.166)
K	0.284	0.278	0.281	-0.330	-0.306	-0.279
	(0.008)	(0.008)	(0.008)	(0.068)	(0.068)	(0.065)
L_1	0.125	0.130	0.153	0.356	0.349	0.331
	(0.006)	(0.006)	(0.007)	(0.053)	(0.053)	(0.050)
L_2	0.098	0.097	0.086	0.730	0.706	0.699
	(0.006)	(0.006)	(0.006)	(0.052)	(0.052)	(0.049)
M	0.507	0.507	0.500	0.285	0.267	0.238
	(0.007)	(0.007)	(0.007)	(0.058)	(0.058)	(0.055)
KK				0.096	0.082	0.097
				(0.019)	(0.019)	(0.018)
KL_1				0.020	0.019	0.010
				(0.012)	(0.012)	(0.012)
KL_2				-0.032	-0.031	-0.035
				(0.011)	(0.011)	(0.011)
KM				-0.021	-0.010	-0.019
				(0.013)	(0.013)	(0.012)
L_1L_1				0.063	0.068	0.056
				(0.012)	(0.012)	(0.011)
L_1L_2				-0.032	-0.029	-0.025
				(0.009)	(0.009)	(0.009)
L_1M				-0.070	-0.073	-0.054
				(0.009)	(0.009)	(0.009)
L_2L_2				0.092	0.093	0.098
				(0.011)	(0.011)	(0.010)
L_2M				-0.076	-0.077	-0.081
				(0.009)	(0.009)	(0.008)
MM				0.147	0.142	0.143
				(0.013)	(0.013)	(0.012)
SSE	378.39	374.00	327.81	348.09	344.47	301.42
R-SQ	0.930	0.931	0.939	0.936	0.936	0.944
Test1	0.004	0.009	0.000	0.000	0.000	0.000
Test2	n.a.	0.000	0.000	0.000	0.000	0.000
Test3	n.a.	n.a.	n.a.a	n.a.	0.020	0.000

TABLE A4						
VALUE ADDED, INDUSTRY 35 1972-1986						
VAR.	COBB-DOUGLAS			TRANSLOG		
	N.D	T.D.	T.D. AND I.D.	N.D.	T.D.	T.D. AND I.D.
Const	1.561 (0.046)	1.523 (0.049)	1.537 (0.051)	3.990 (0.246)	4.008 (0.246)	2.127 (0.185)
K	0.441 (0.009)	0.424 (0.010)	0.405 (0.007)	-0.581 (0.077)	-0.557 (0.077)	0.073 (0.057)
L_1	0.239 (0.009)	0.253 (0.010)	0.431 (0.007)	1.083 (0.069)	1.040 (0.069)	0.556 (0.050)
L_2	0.406 (0.008)	0.408 (0.008)	0.206 (0.006)	0.191 (0.063)	0.172 (0.063)	0.372 (0.047)
KK				0.189 (0.017)	0.178 (0.017)	0.034 (0.012)
KL_1				-0.147 (0.014)	-0.137 (0.014)	-0.014 (0.011)
KL_2				0.034 (0.012)	0.033 (0.012)	0.018 (0.009)
L_1L_1				0.355 (0.018)	0.350 (0.019)	0.132 (0.014)
L_1L_2				-0.307 (0.012)	-0.306 (0.012)	-0.147 (0.009)
L_2L_2				0.333 (0.015)	0.338 (0.015)	0.109 (0.011)
SSE	7289.01	7255.69	3455.95	6527.6	6501.91	3377.13
R-SQ	0.677	0.678	0.847	0.711	0.712	0.850
Test1	0.000	0.000	0.000	0.000	0.000	0.000
Test2	n.a.	0.000	0.000	0.000	0.000	0.000
Test3	n.a.	n.a.	n.a.	n.a.	0.000	0.000

TABLE A5						
VALUE ADDED, INDUSTRY 36 1972-1986						
VAR.	COBB-DOUGLAS			TRANSLOG		
	N.D	T.D.	T.D. AND I.D.	N.D.	T.D.	T.D. AND I.D.
Const	1.599	1.550	1.296	2.624	2.703	1.602
	(0.031)	(0.033)	(0.036)	(0.182)	(0.181)	(0.168)
K	0.481	0.464	0.497	-0.055	-0.026	0.199
	(0.006)	(0.006)	(0.006)	(0.056)	(0.055)	(0.050)
L_1	0.314	0.327	0.364	0.298	0.217	0.298
	(0.006)	(0.007)	(0.006)	(0.049)	(0.049)	(0.045)
L_2	0.254	0.255	0.168	0.737	0.729	0.601
	(0.004)	(0.004)	(0.005)	(0.039)	(0.038)	(0.035)
KK				0.120	0.107	0.058
				(0.012)	(0.012)	(0.011)
KL_1				-0.019	-0.009	-0.001
				(0.009)	(0.009)	(0.008)
KL_2				-0.082	-0.083	-0.046
				(0.007)	(0.007)	(0.007)
L_1L_1				0.143	0.147	0.117
				(0.011)	(0.011)	(0.010)
L_1L_2				-0.126	-0.130	-0.117
				(0.007)	(0.007)	(0.006)
L_2L_2				0.197	0.202	0.137
				(0.007)	(0.007)	(0.006)
SSE	3513.32	3459.45	2638.55	3256.50	3194.73	2506.82
R-SQ	0.825	0.828	0.869	0.838	0.841	0.875
Test1	0.000	0.000	0.000	0.000	0.000	0.000
Test2	n.a.	0.000	0.000	0.000	0.000	0.000
Test3	n.a.	n.a.	n.a.	n.a.	0.000	0.000

TABLE A6						
VALUE ADDED, INDUSTRY 38 1972-1986						
VAR.	COBB-DOUGLAS			TRANSLOG		
	N.D	T.D.	T.D. AND I.D.	N.D.	T.D.	T.D. AND I.D.
Const	1.628	1.556	1.600	3.141	3.090	3.167
	(0.050)	(0.054)	(0.057)	(0.251)	(0.252)	(0.249)
K	0.569	0.571	0.563	-0.538	-0.515	-0.472
	(0.010)	(0.011)	(0.011)	(0.091)	(0.091)	(0.091)
L_1	0.253	0.251	0.282	0.407	0.395	0.379
	(0.010)	(0.010)	(0.010)	(0.081)	(0.081)	(0.080)
L_2	0.199	0.196	0.177	1.159	1.134	1.075
	(0.009)	(0.009)	(0.009)	(0.077)	(0.077)	(0.075)
KK				0.205	0.200	0.190
				(0.024)	(0.024)	(0.024)
KL_1				-0.012	-0.010	-0.000
				(0.018)	(0.018)	(0.018)
KL_2				-0.113	-0.110	-0.114
				(0.016)	(0.016)	(0.016)
L_1L_1				0.090	0.088	0.080
				(0.018)	(0.018)	(0.018)
L_1L_2				-0.103	-0.103	-0.101
				(0.013)	(0.013)	(0.013)
L_2L_2				0.125	0.123	0.132
				(0.016)	(0.016)	(0.016)
SSE	914.83	908.52	841.78	869.47	864.93	801.81
R-SQ	0.838	0.839	0.851	0.846	0.847	0.858
Test1	0.000	0.000	0.000	0.000	0.000	0.000
Test2	n.a.	0.004	0.000	0.000	0.000	0.000
Test3	n.a.	n.a.	n.a.	n.a.	0.O37	0.000

Fig. A1

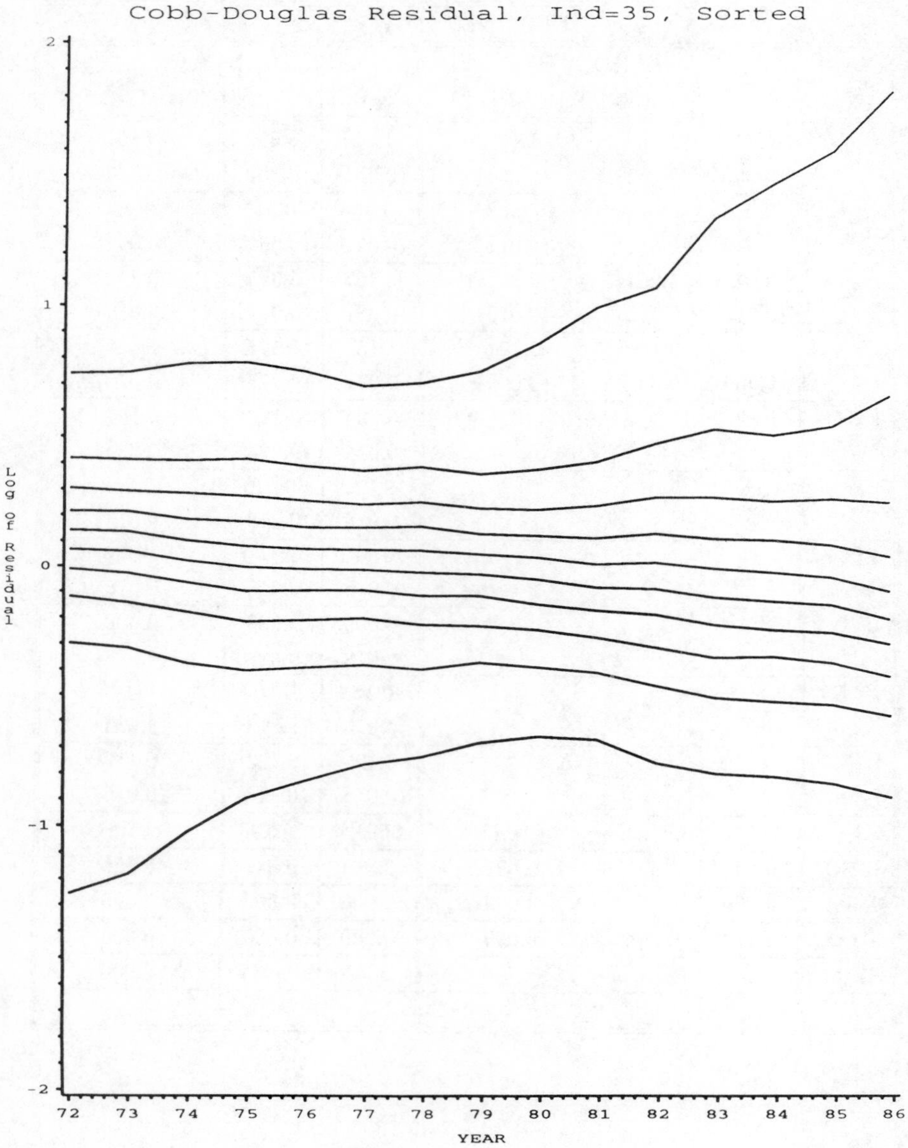
Cobb-Douglas Residual, Ind=35, Sorted
2
1
0
-1
-2
Log of Residual
72
73
74
75
76
77
78
79
80
81
82
83
84
85
86
YEAR

Fig. A2

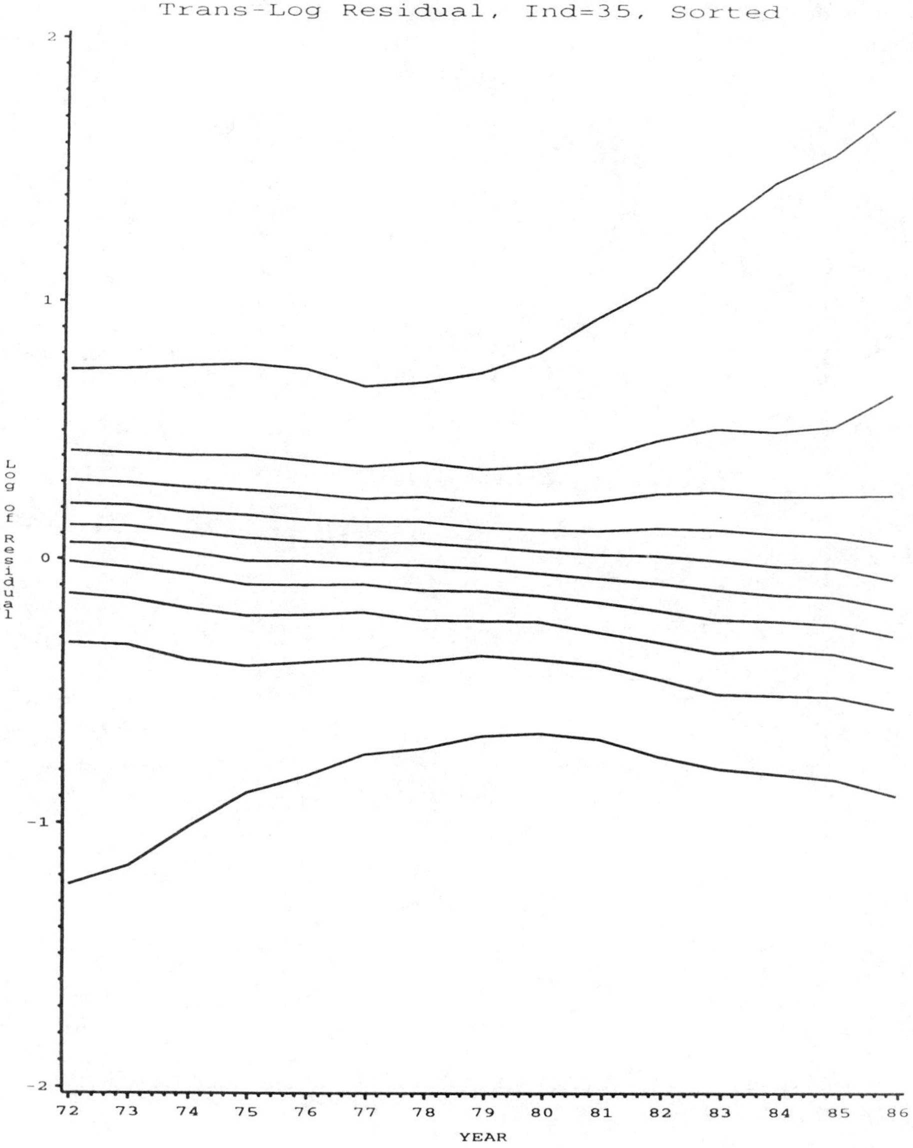
Trans-Log Residual, Ind=35, Sorted
2
1
0
-1
-2
Log of Residual
72
73
74
75
76
77
78
79
80
81
82
83
84
85
86
YEAR

Fig. A3

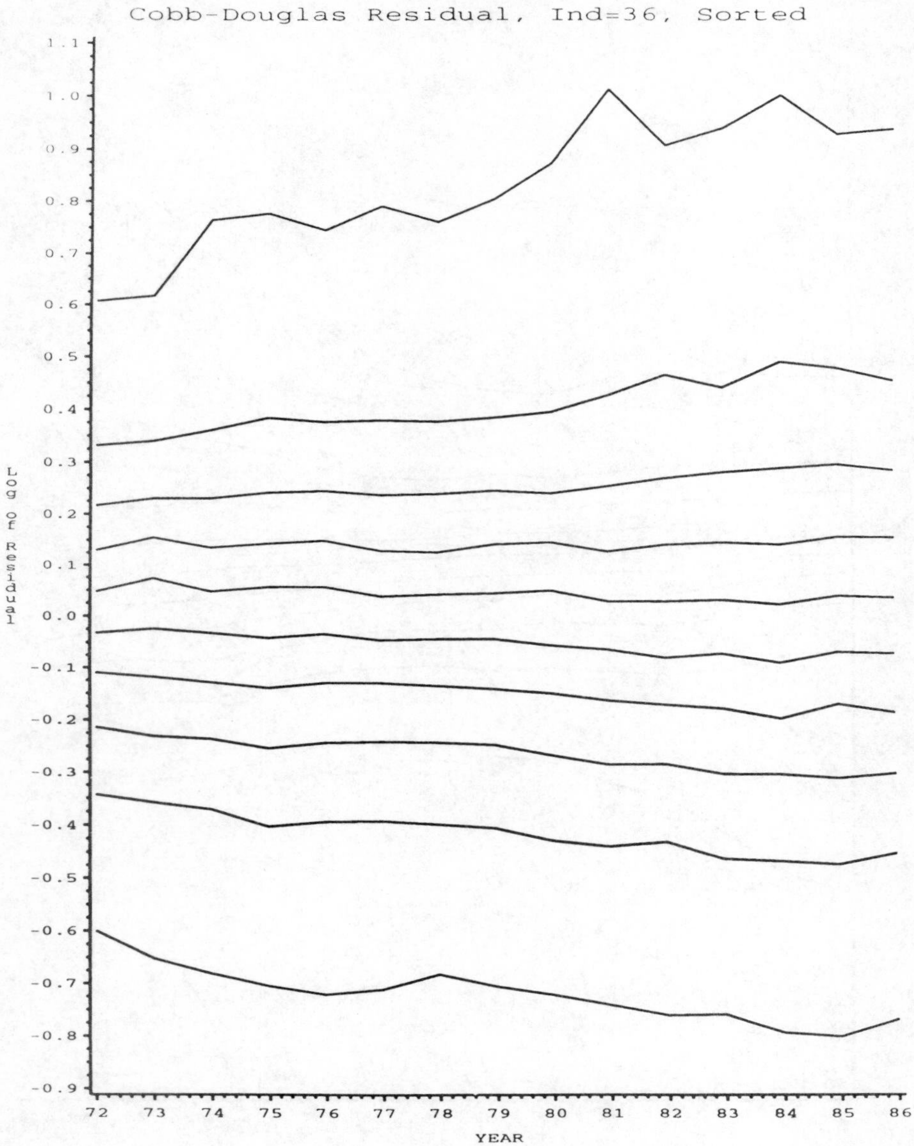
Cobb-Douglas Residual, Ind=36, Sorted
Log of Residual
1.1
1.0
0.9
0.8
0.7
0.6
0.5
0.4
0.3
0.2
0.1
0.0
-0.1
-0.2
-0.3
-0.4
-0.5
-0.6
-0.7
-0.8
-0.9
72
73
74
75
76
77
78
79
80
81
82
83
84
85
86
YEAR

Fig. A4

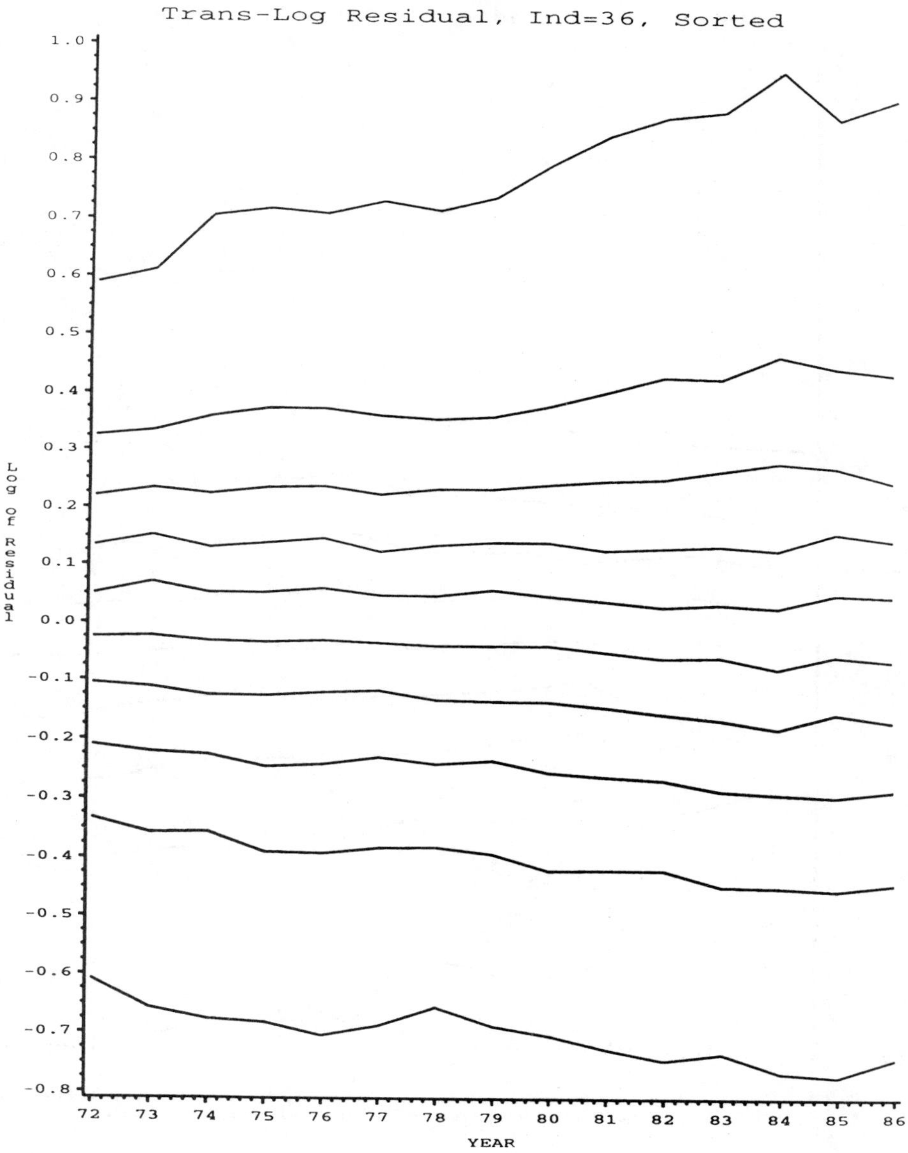
Trans-Log Residual, Ind=36, Sorted
Log Of Residual
1.0
0.9
0.8
0.7
0.6
0.5
0.4
0.3
0.2
0.1
0.0
-0.1
-0.2
-0.3
-0.4
-0.5
-0.6
-0.7
-0.8
72
73
74
75
76
77
78
79
80
81
82
83
84
85
86
YEAR

Fig. A5

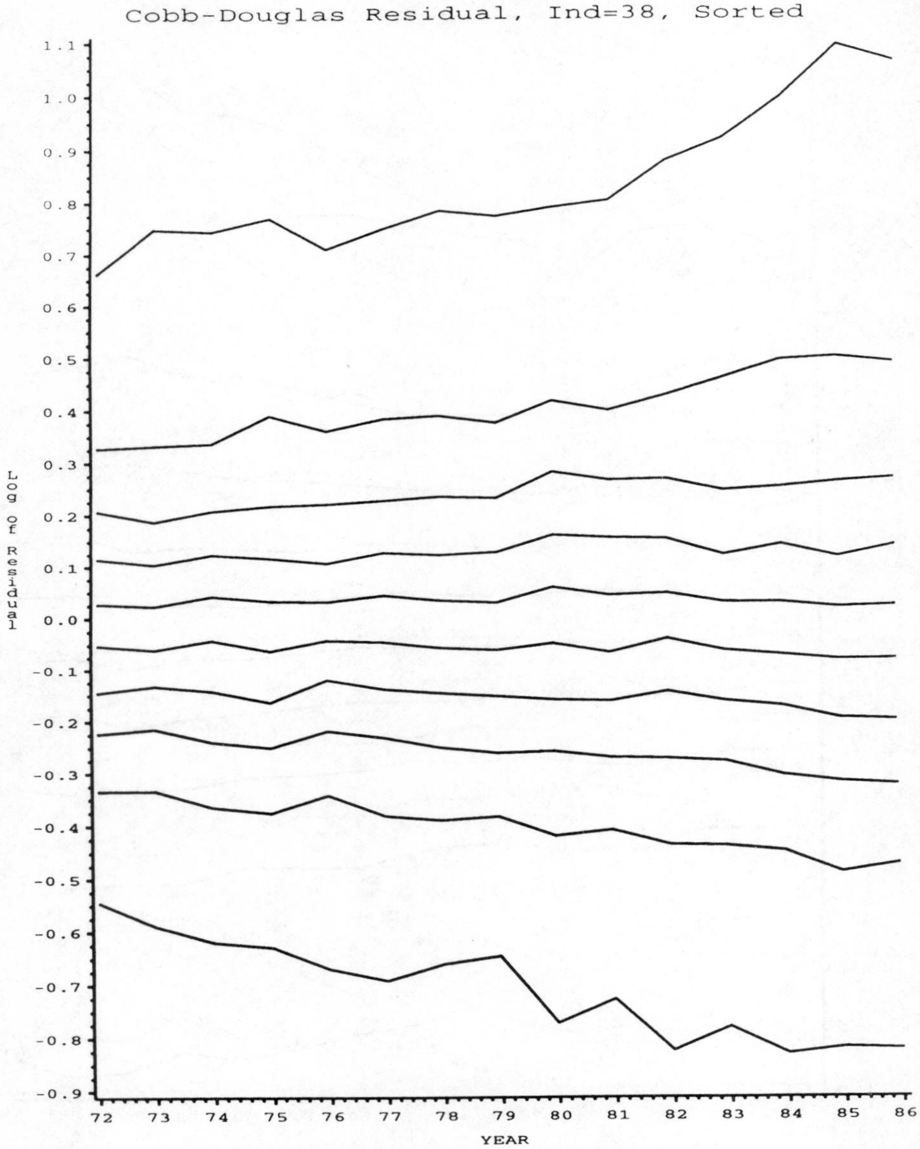
Cobb-Douglas Residual, Ind=38, Sorted
Log of Residual
1.1
1.0
0.9
0.8
0.7
0.6
0.5
0.4
0.3
0.2
0.1
0.0
-0.1
-0.2
-0.3
-0.4
-0.5
-0.6
-0.7
-0.8
-0.9
72 73 74 75 76 77 78 79 80 81 82 83 84 85 86
YEAR

Fig. A6

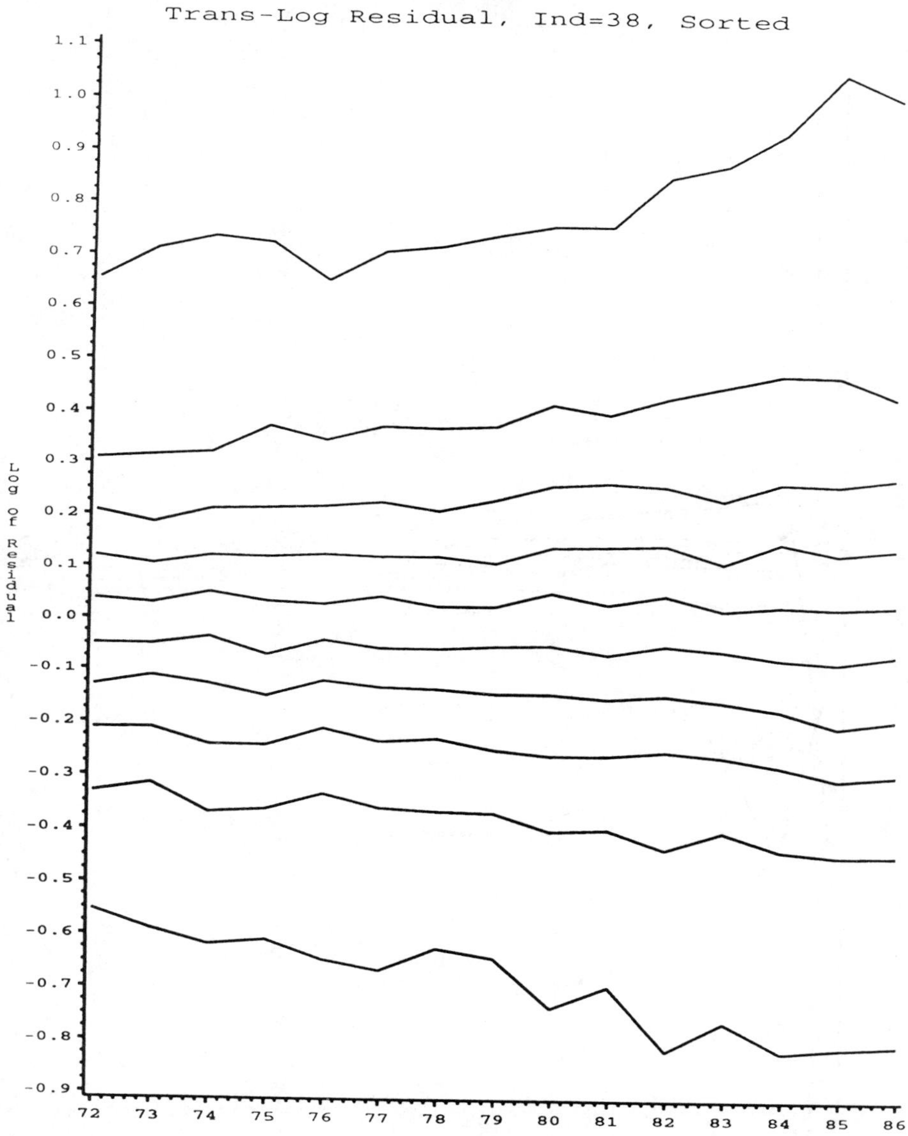
Trans-Log Residual, Ind=38, Sorted
Log of Residual
1.1
1.0
0.9
0.8
0.7
0.6
0.5
0.4
0.3
0.2
0.1
0.0
-0.1
-0.2
-0.3
-0.4
-0.5
-0.6
-0.7
-0.8
-0.9
72 73 74 75 76 77 78 79 80 81 82 83 84 85 86
YEAR

Fig. A7

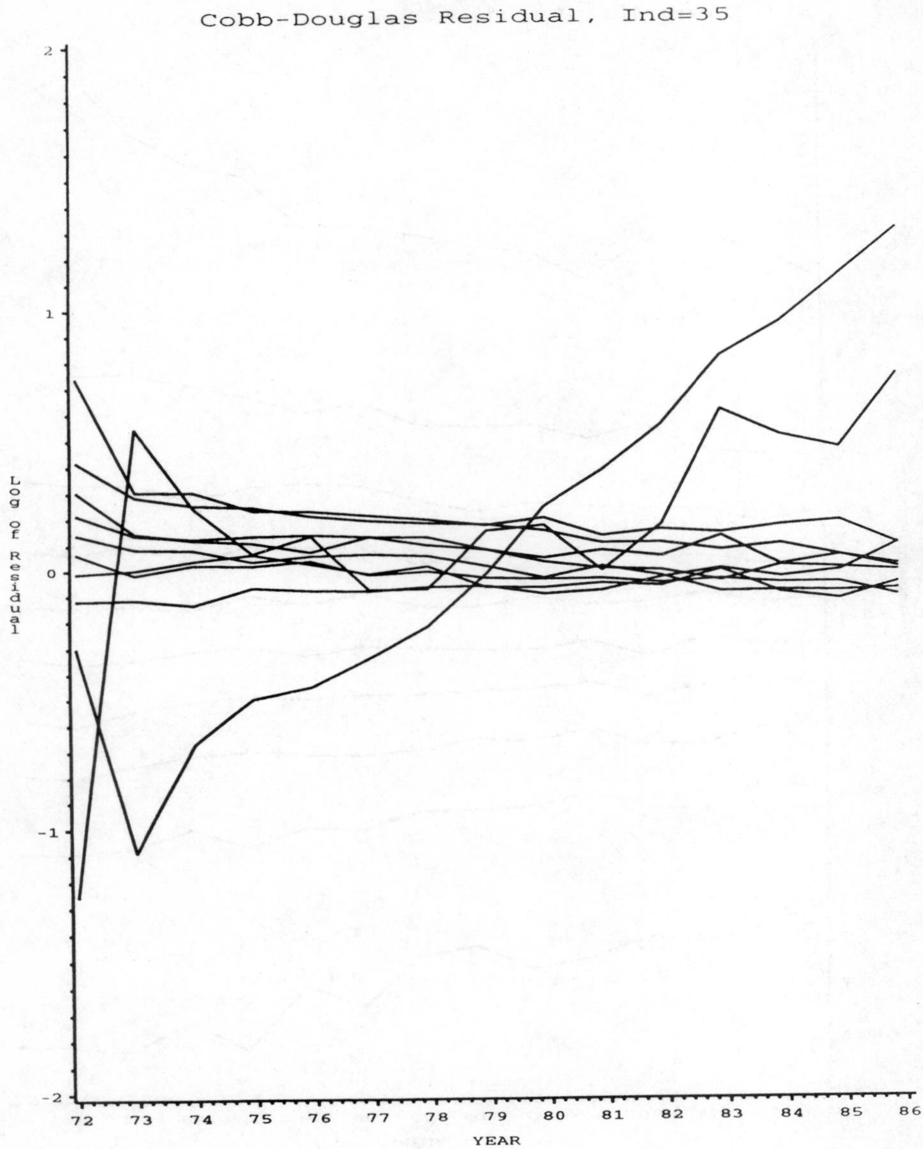
Cobb-Douglas Residual, Ind=35
2
1
0
-1
-2
Log of Residual
72
73
74
75
76
77
78
79
80
81
82
83
84
85
86
YEAR

Fig. A8

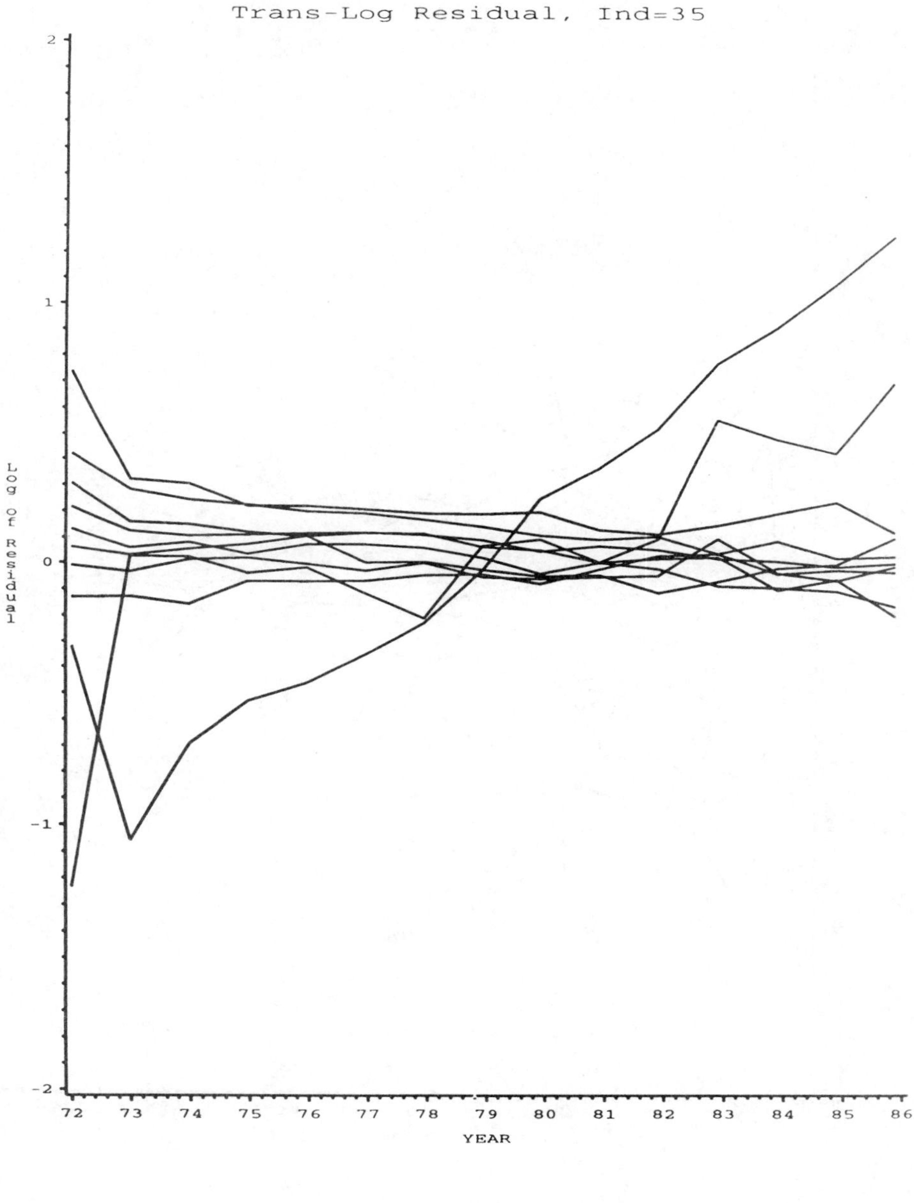
Trans-Log Residual, Ind=35
Log of Residual
2
1
0
-1
-2
72
73
74
75
76
77
78
79
80
81
82
83
84
85
86
YEAR

Fig. A9

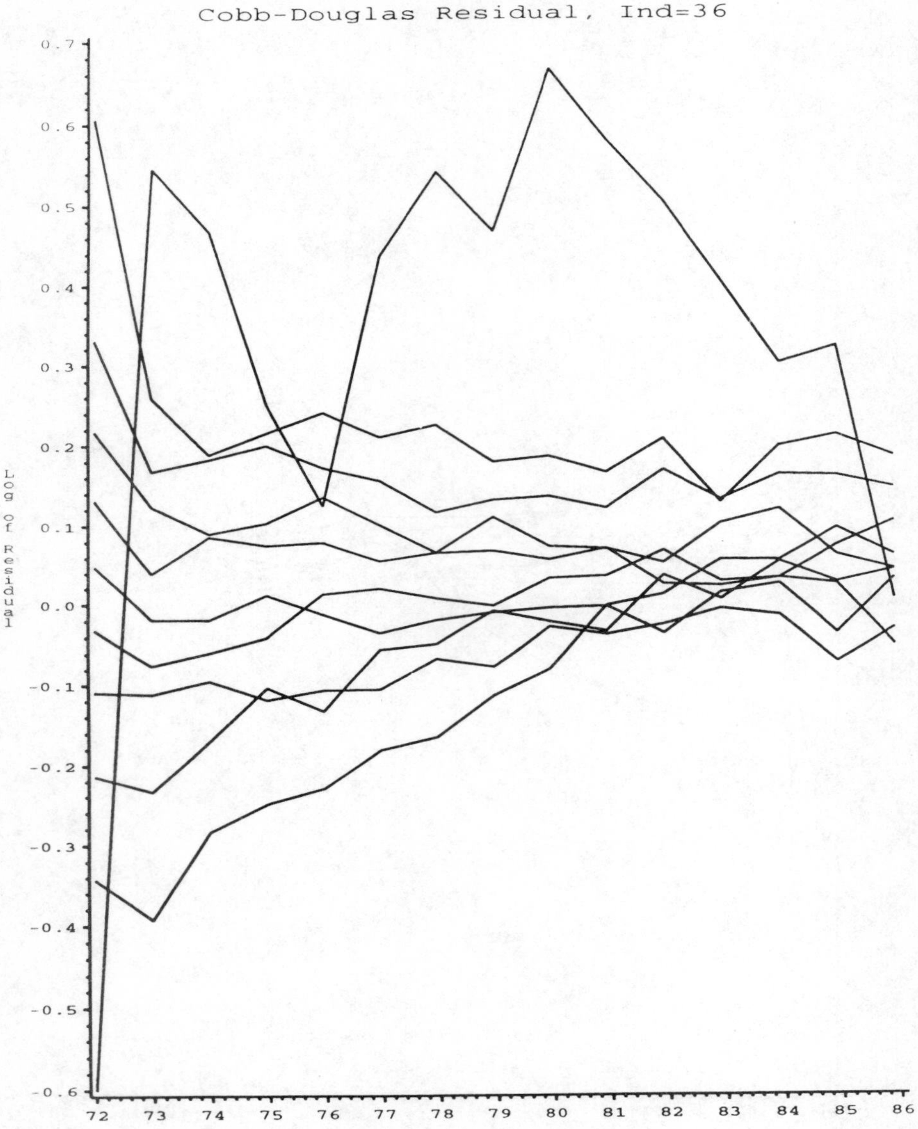
Cobb-Douglas Residual, Ind=36
Log of Residual
0.7
0.6
0.5
0.4
0.3
0.2
0.1
0.0
-0.1
-0.2
-0.3
-0.4
-0.5
-0.6
72
73
74
75
76
77
78
79
80
81
82
83
84
85
86
YEAR

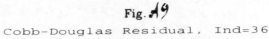

Fig. A10

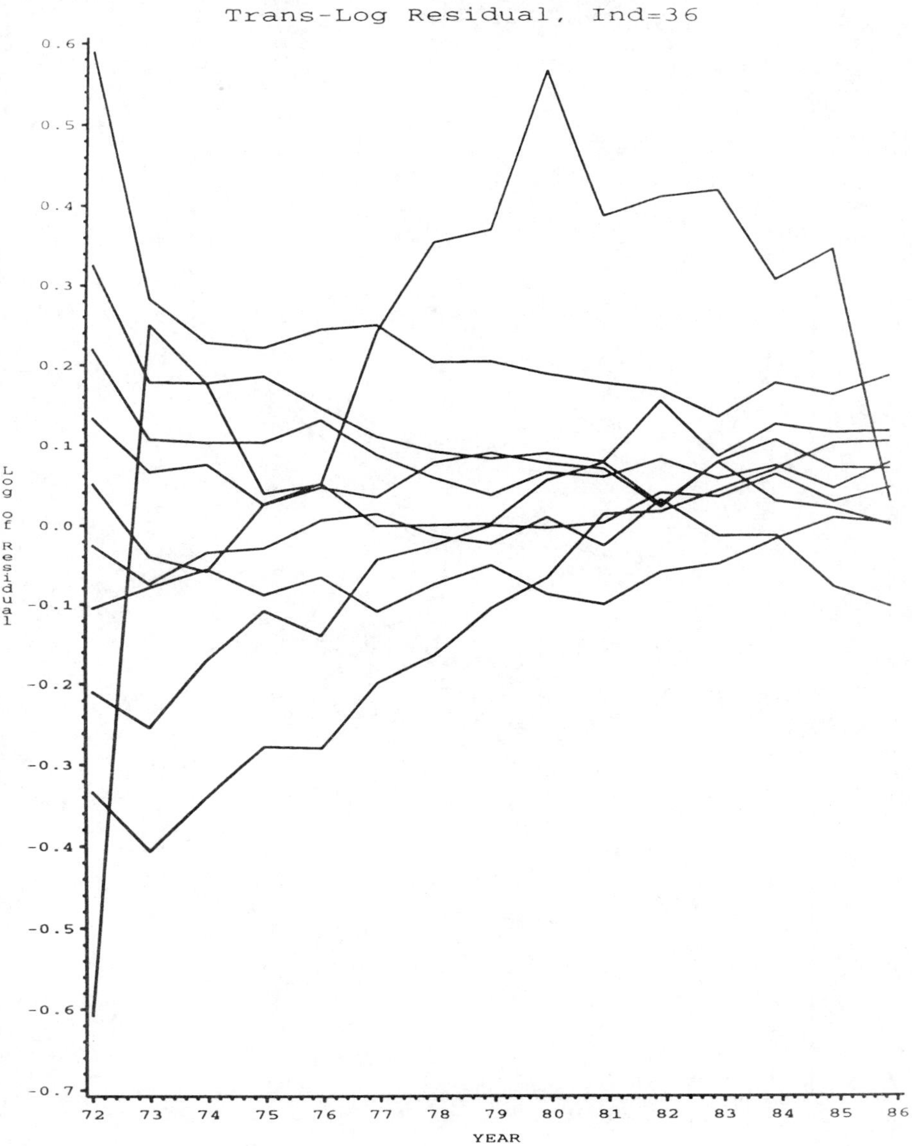
Trans-Log Residual, Ind=36
Log of Residual
0.6
0.5
0.4
0.3
0.2
0.1
0.0
-0.1
-0.2
-0.3
-0.4
-0.5
-0.6
-0.7
72
73
74
75
76
77
78
79
80
81
82
83
84
85
86
YEAR

Fig. A11

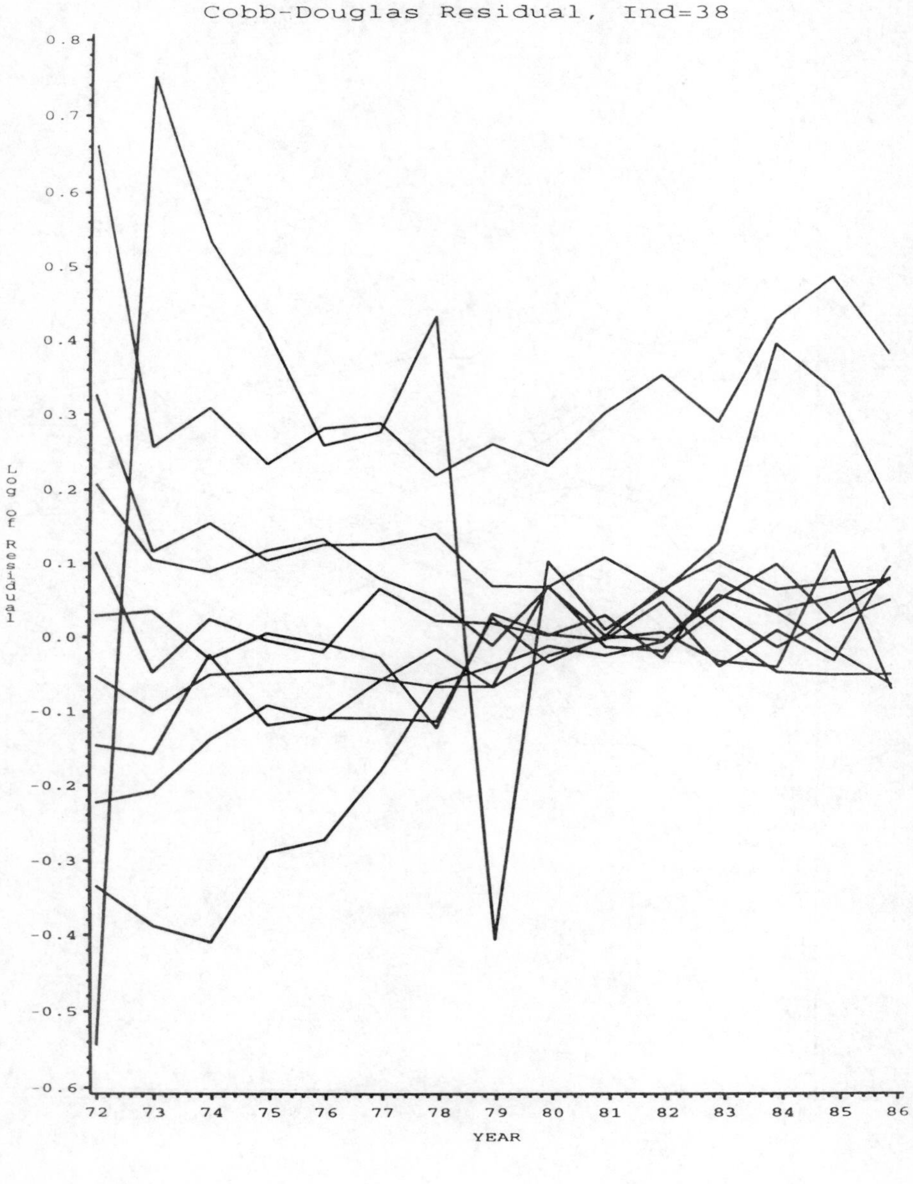
Cobb-Douglas Residual, Ind=38
Log Of Residual
0.8
0.7
0.6
0.5
0.4
0.3
0.2
0.1
0.0
-0.1
-0.2
-0.3
-0.4
-0.5
-0.6
72
73
74
75
76
77
78
79
80
81
82
83
84
85
86
YEAR

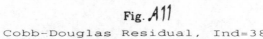

Fig. A12

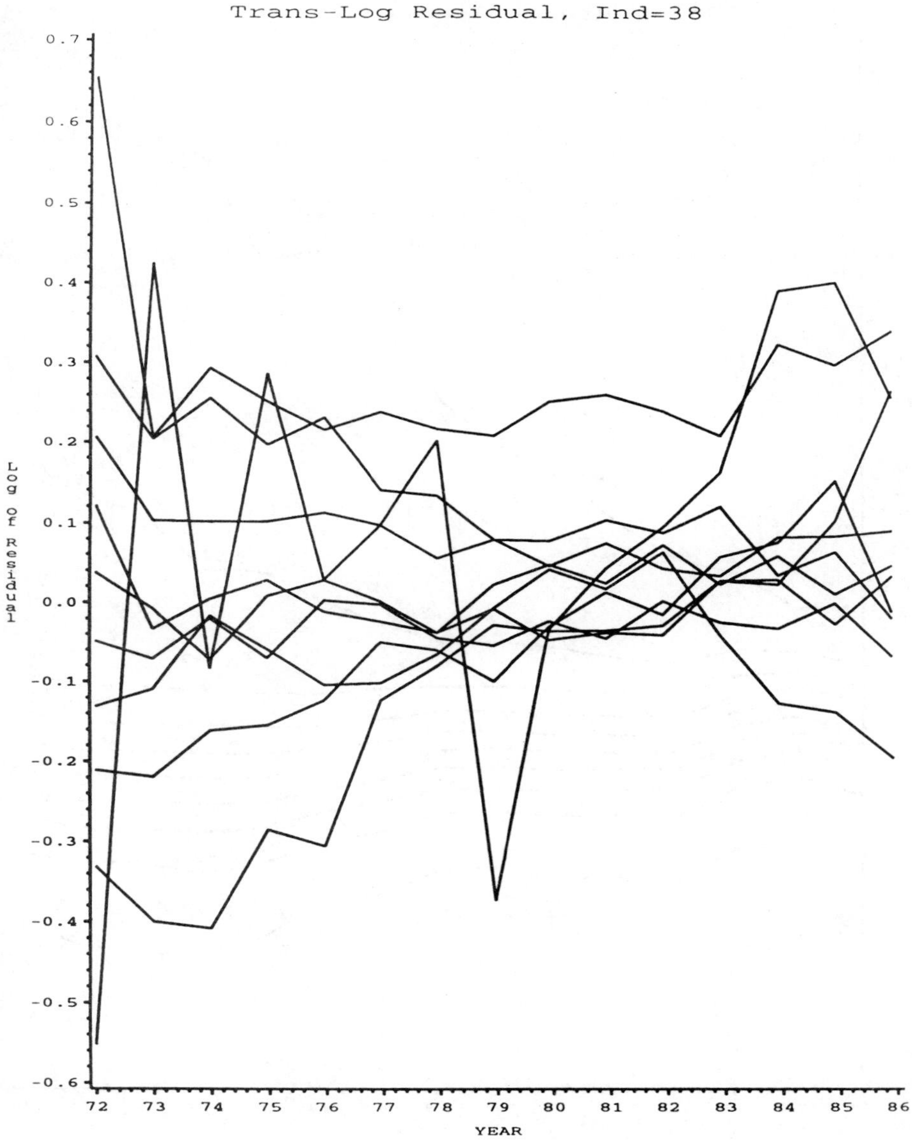
Trans-Log Residual, Ind=38
Log of Residual
0.7
0.6
0.5
0.4
0.3
0.2
0.1
0.0
-0.1
-0.2
-0.3
-0.4
-0.5
-0.6
72 73 74 75 76 77 78 79 80 81 82 83 84 85 86
YEAR

Fig. A13

Solow Residual, Ind=35, Sorted

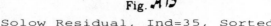

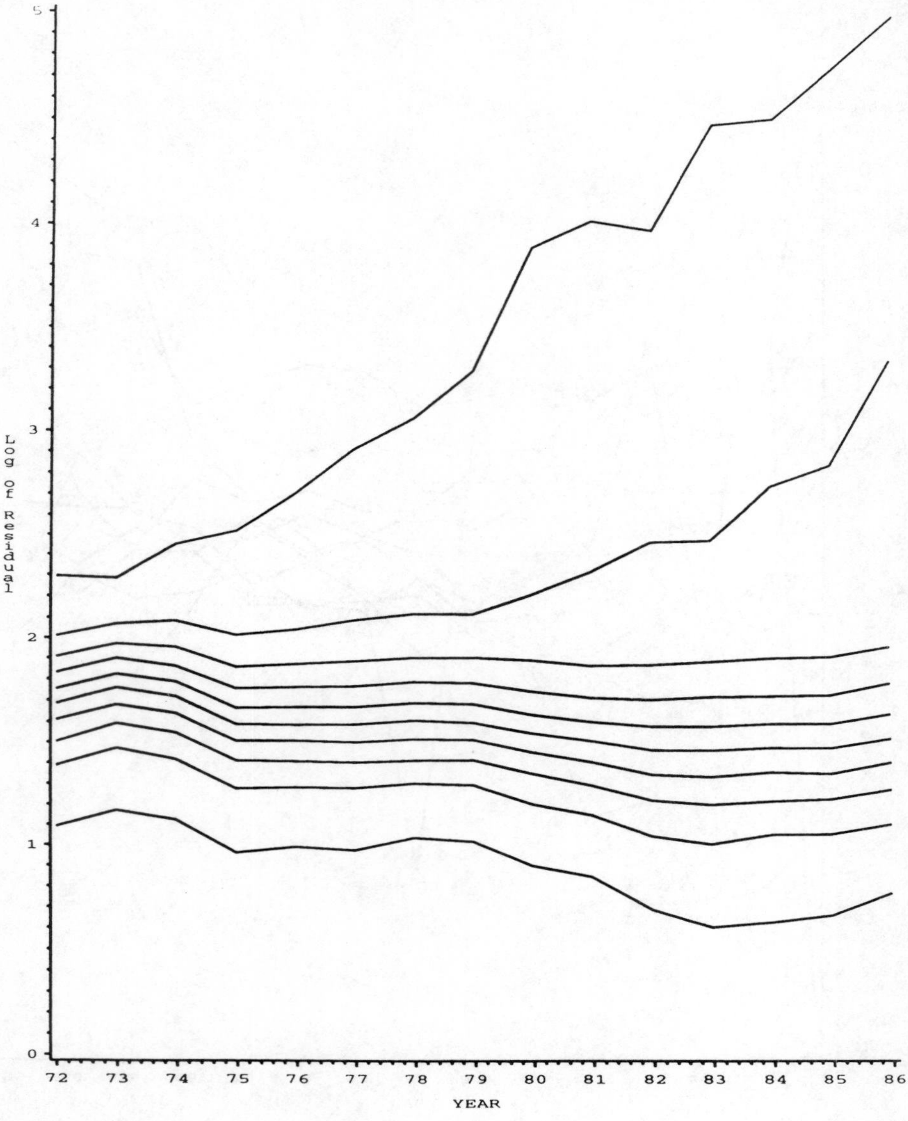

Fig. A14

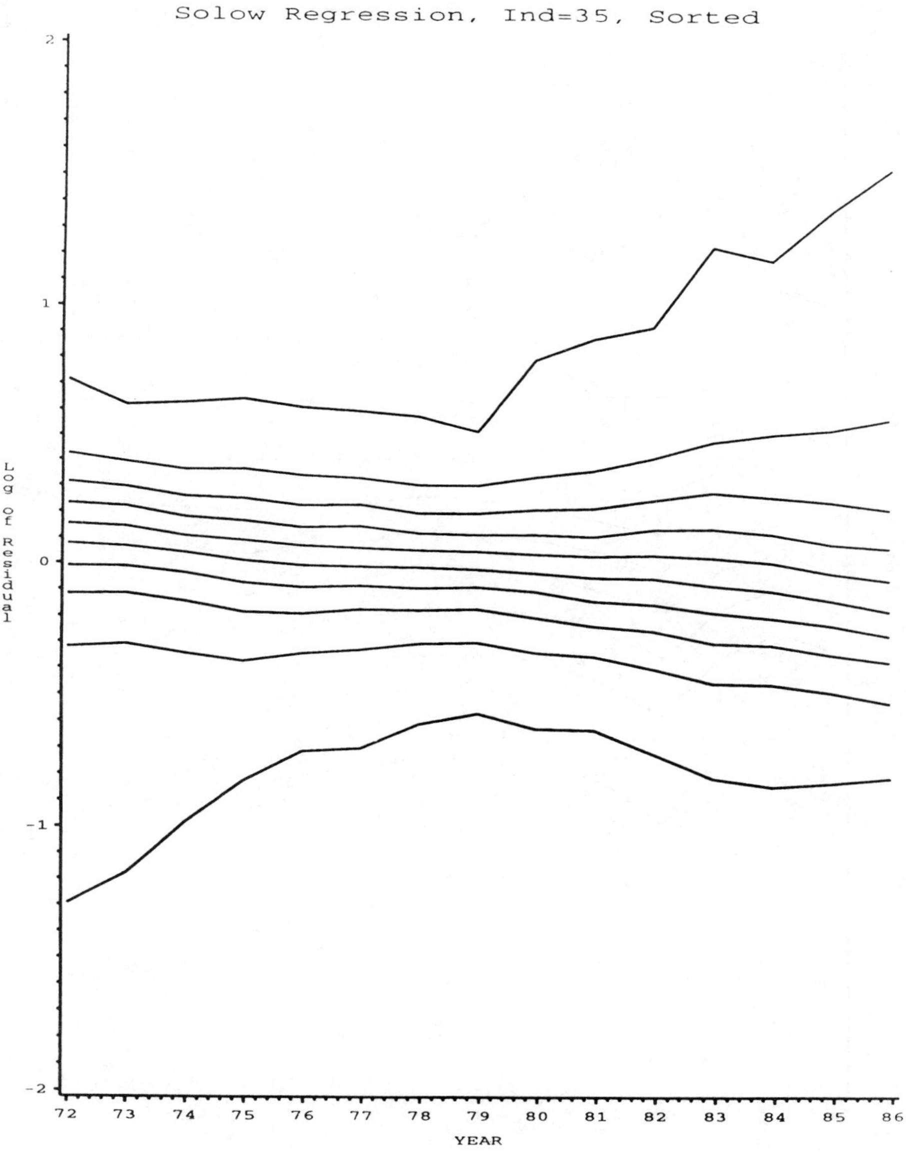
Solow Regression, Ind=35, Sorted
Log of Residual
2
1
0
-1
-2
72
73
74
75
76
77
78
79
80
81
82
83
84
85
86
YEAR

Fig. A15

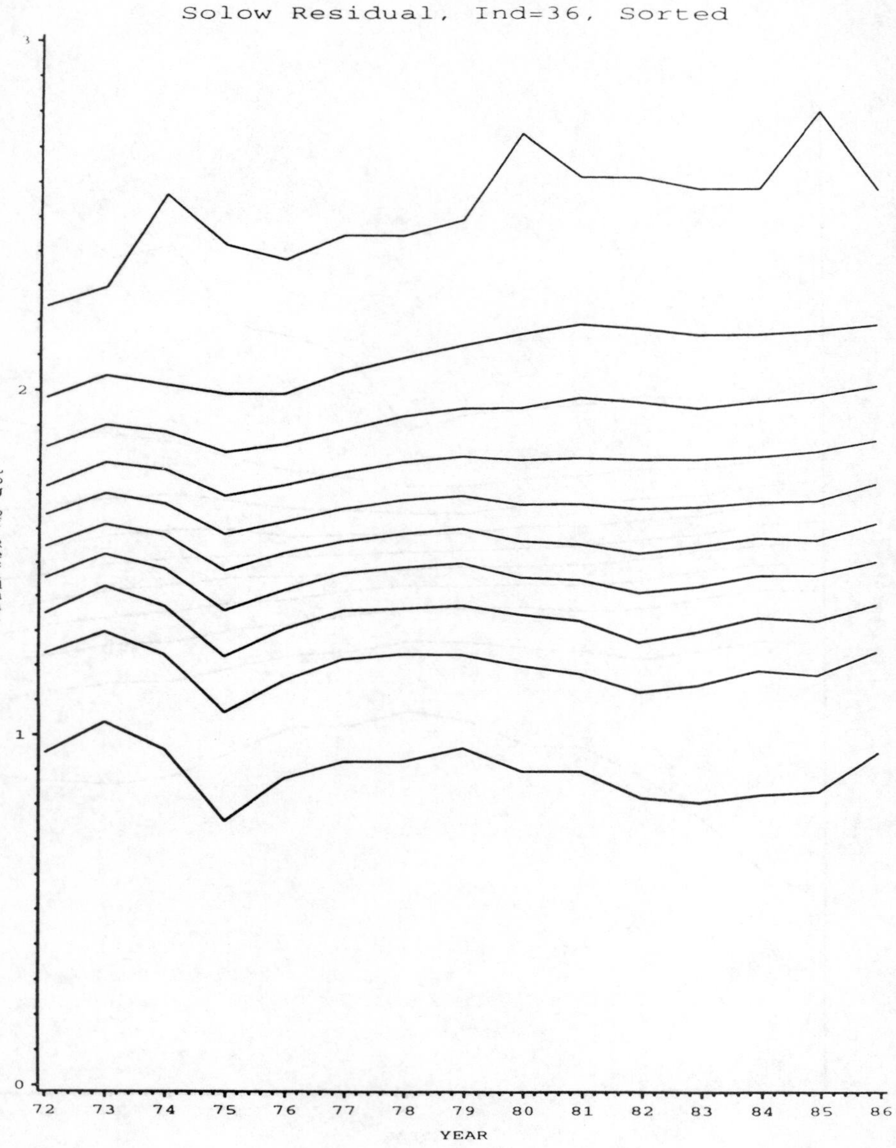
Solow Residual, Ind=36, Sorted
3
2
1
0
Log of Residual
72
73
74
75
76
77
78
79
80
81
82
83
84
85
86
YEAR

Fig. A16

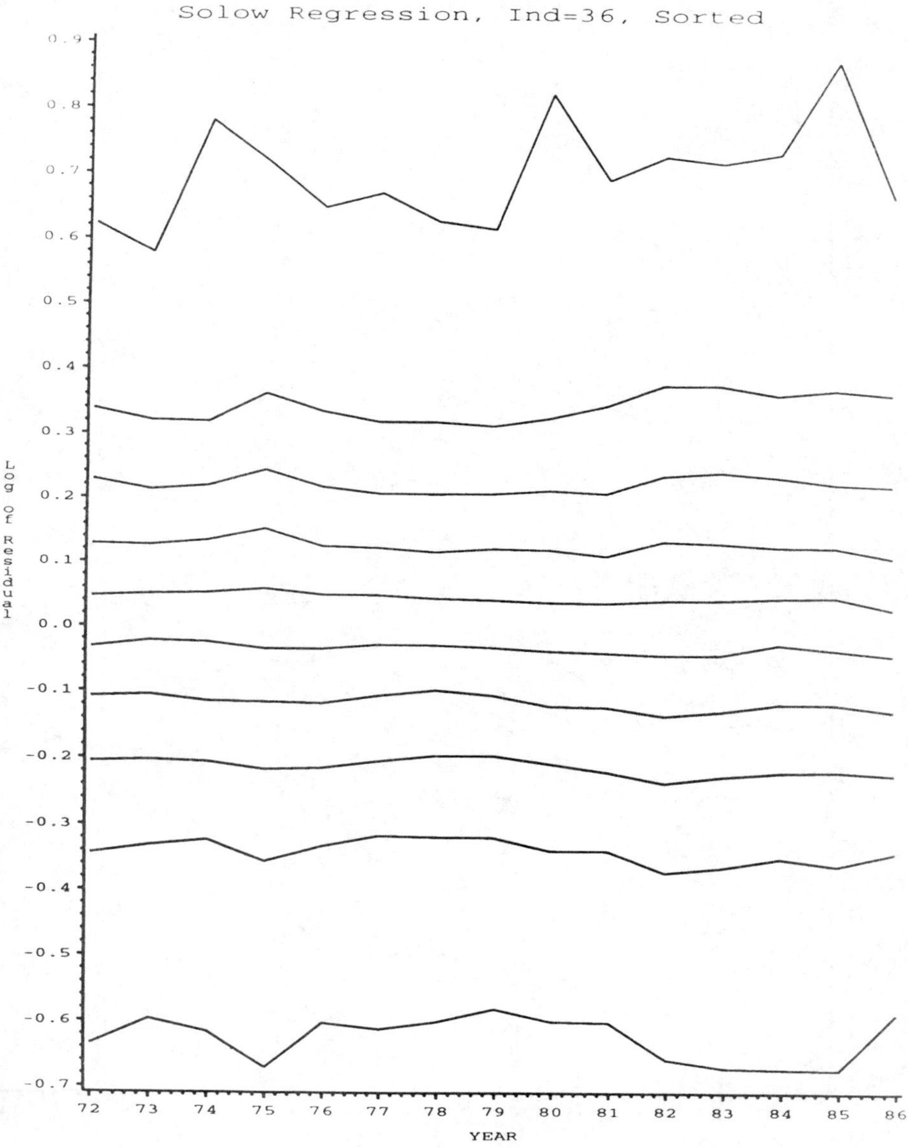
Solow Regression, Ind=36, Sorted
Log of Residual
0.9
0.8
0.7
0.6
0.5
0.4
0.3
0.2
0.1
0.0
-0.1
-0.2
-0.3
-0.4
-0.5
-0.6
-0.7
72 73 74 75 76 77 78 79 80 81 82 83 84 85 86
YEAR

Fig. A17

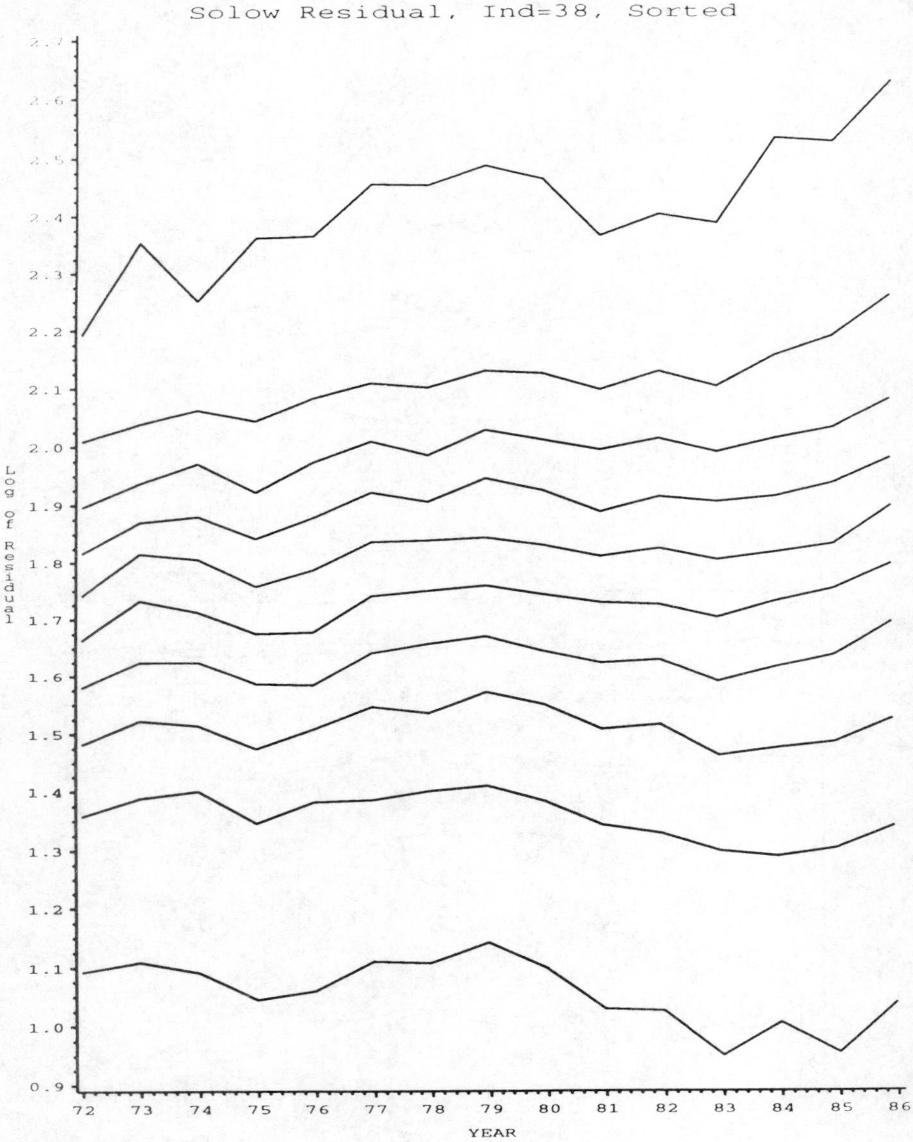
Solow Residual, Ind=38, Sorted
Log of Residual
2.7
2.6
2.5
2.4
2.3
2.2
2.1
2.0
1.9
1.8
1.7
1.6
1.5
1.4
1.3
1.2
1.1
1.0
0.9
72
73
74
75
76
77
78
79
80
81
82
83
84
85
86
YEAR

Fig. A18

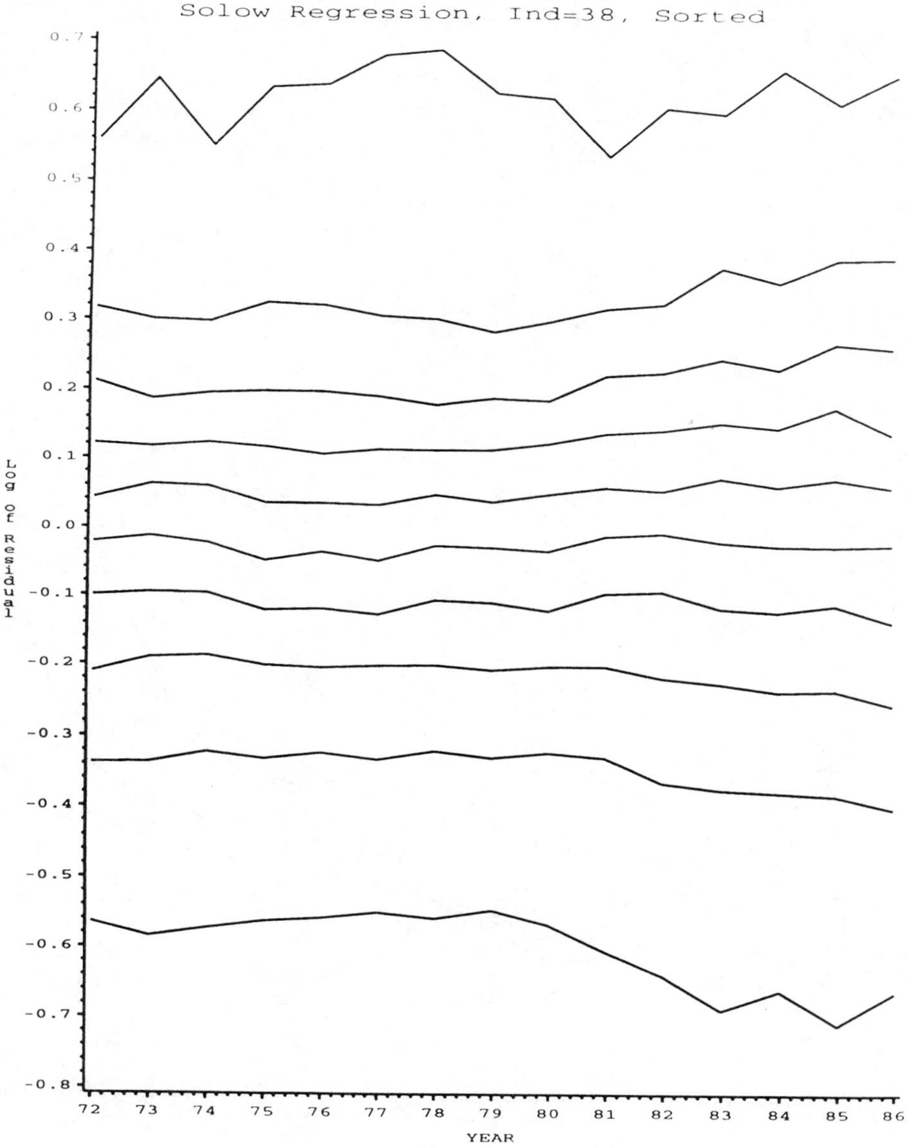
Solow Regression, Ind=38, Sorted
0.7
0.6
0.5
0.4
0.3
0.2
0.1
0.0
-0.1
-0.2
-0.3
-0.4
-0.5
-0.6
-0.7
-0.8
Log of Residual
72
73
74
75
76
77
78
79
80
81
82
83
84
85
86
YEAR

Fig. A19

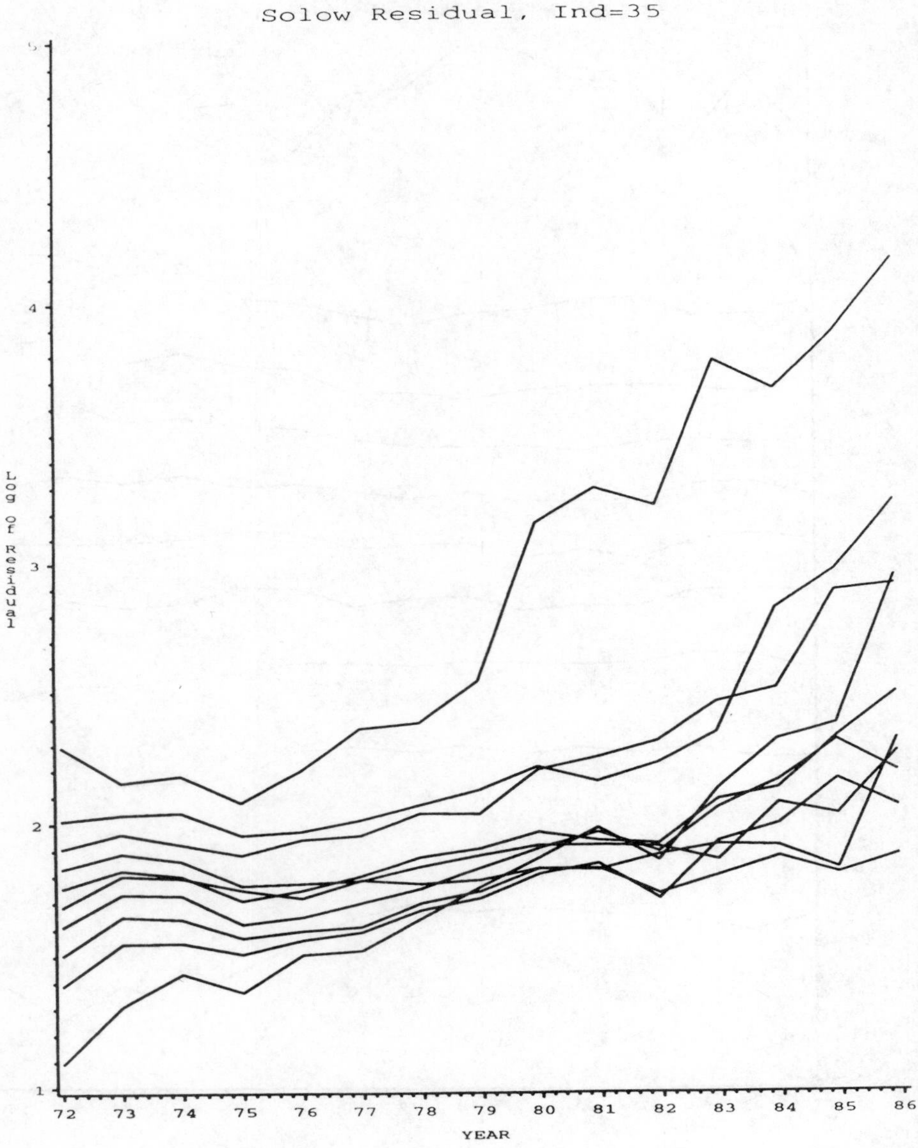
Solow Residual, Ind=35
Log Of Residual
5
4
3
2
1
72
73
74
75
76
77
78
79
80
81
82
83
84
85
86
YEAR

Fig. A20

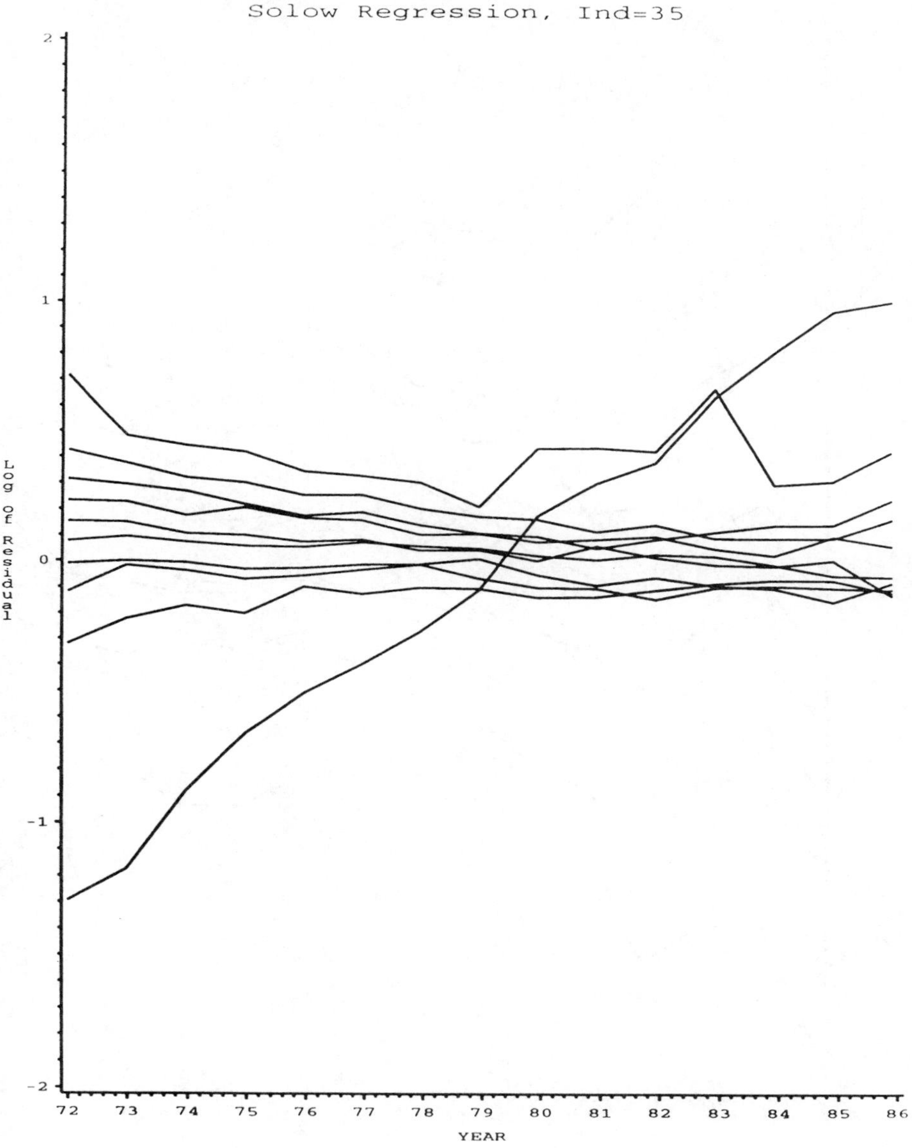

Solow Regression, Ind=35
Log of Residual
2
1
0
-1
-2
72
73
74
75
76
77
78
79
80
81
82
83
84
85
86
YEAR

Fig. A21

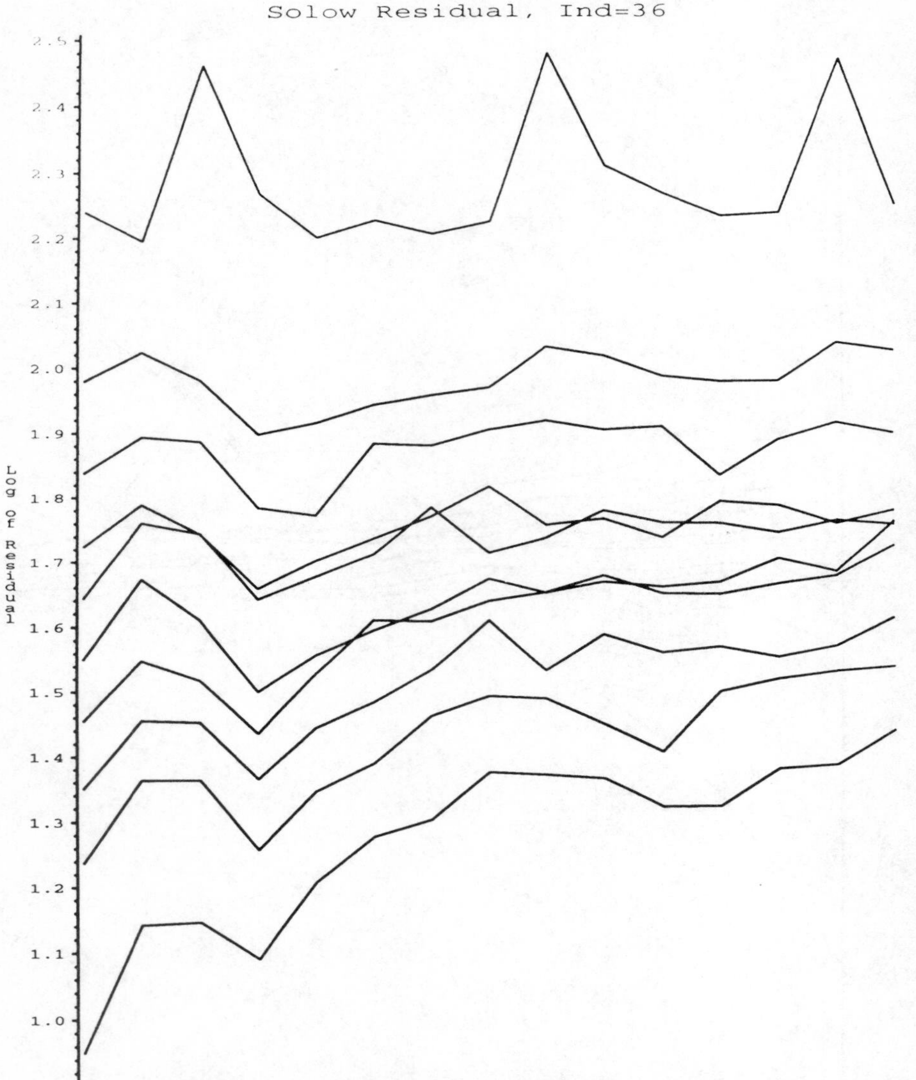
Solow Residual, Ind=36
Log of Residual
2.5
2.4
2.3
2.2
2.1
2.0
1.9
1.8
1.7
1.6
1.5
1.4
1.3
1.2
1.1
1.0
0.9
72
73
74
75
76
77
78
79
80
81
82
83
84
85
86
YEAR

Fig. A22

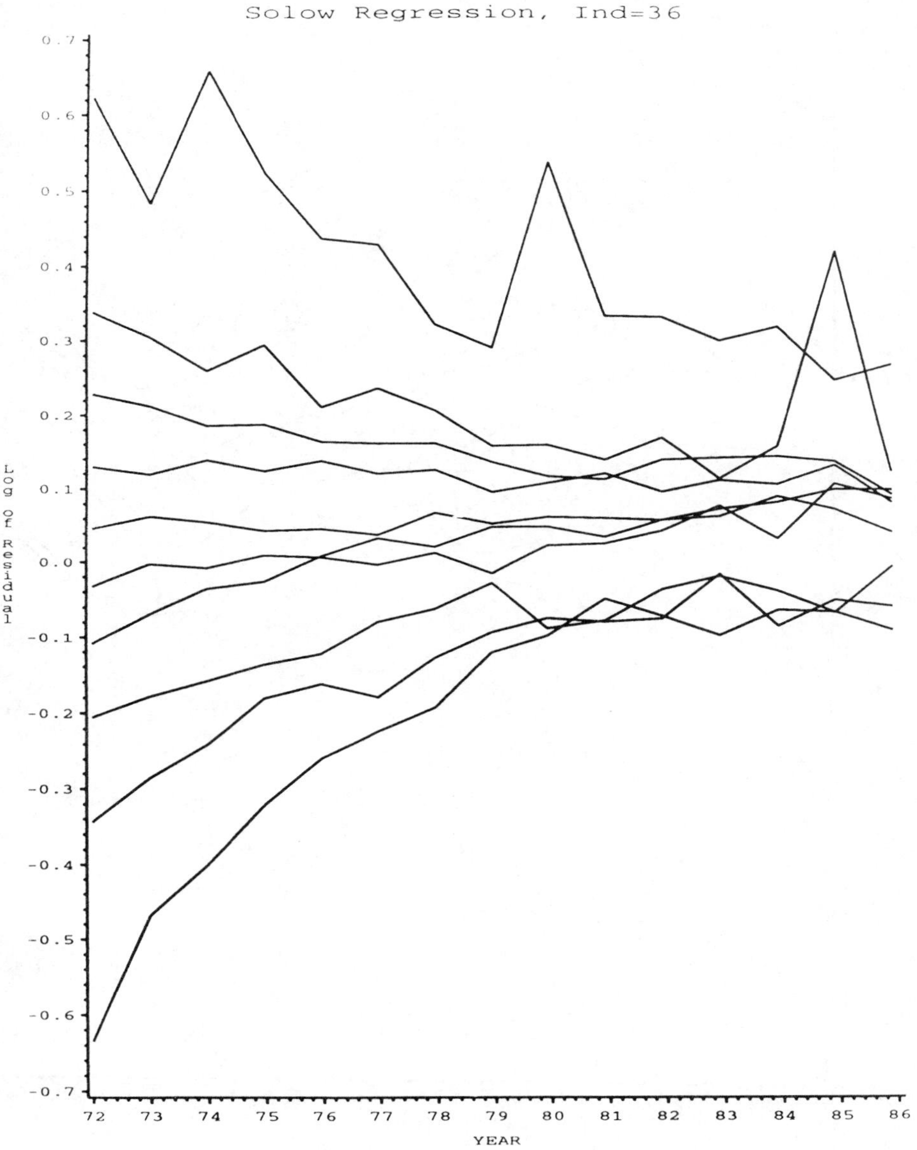
Solow Regression, Ind=36
0.7
0.6
0.5
0.4
0.3
0.2
0.1
0.0
-0.1
-0.2
-0.3
-0.4
-0.5
-0.6
-0.7
Log of Residual
72
73
74
75
76
77
78
79
80
81
82
83
84
85
86
YEAR

Fig. A23

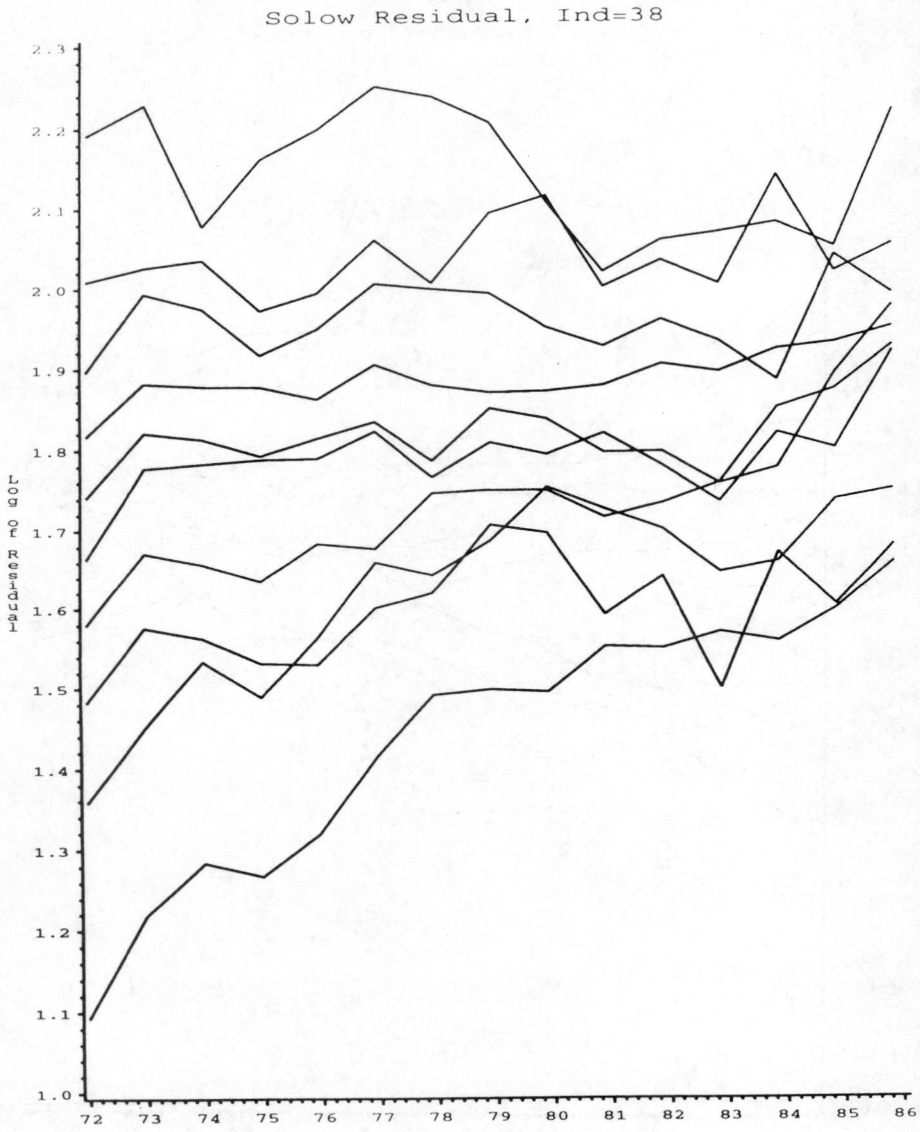
Solow Residual, Ind=38
Log of Residual
2.3
2.2
2.1
2.0
1.9
1.8
1.7
1.6
1.5
1.4
1.3
1.2
1.1
1.0
72
73
74
75
76
77
78
79
80
81
82
83
84
85
86
YEAR

Fig. A24

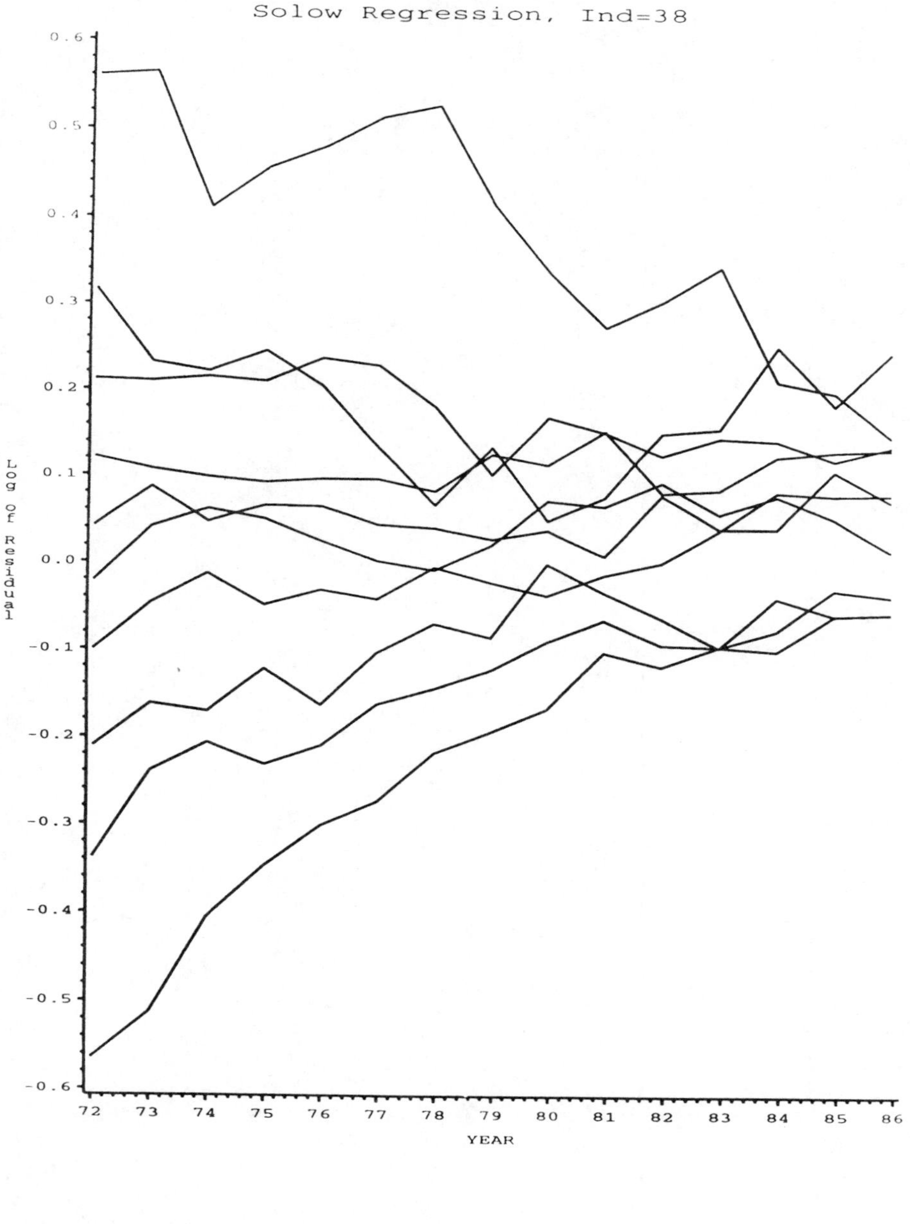
Solow Regression, Ind=38
Log of Residual
0.6
0.5
0.4
0.3
0.2
0.1
0.0
-0.1
-0.2
-0.3
-0.4
-0.5
-0.6
72
73
74
75
76
77
78
79
80
81
82
83
84
85
86
YEAR

PART V

EMPIRICAL APPLICATIONS: ISSUES IN FINANCE

THE JOURNAL OF FINANCE • VOL. XXXIX, NO. 2 • JUNE 1984

A Critical Reexamination of the Empirical Evidence on the Arbitrage Pricing Theory

PHOEBUS J. DHRYMES, IRWIN FRIEND, and N. BULENT GULTEKIN*

ABSTRACT

This paper demonstrates that the Roll and Ross (RR) and other previously published tests of the APT are subject to several basic limitations. There is a general nonequivalence of factor analyzing small groups of securities and factor analyzing a group of securities sufficiently large for the APT model to hold. It is found that as one increases the number of securities, the number of "factors" determined increases. This increase in the number of "factors" with larger groups of securities cannot readily be explained by a distinction between "priced" and "nonpriced" risk factors as it is impermissible to carry out tests on whether a given "risk factor is priced" using factor analytic procedures.

THE APT MODEL as exposited by Ross [17], [18] and extended by Huberman [9] has provided the basis of an extensive literature, as for example, Brown and Weinstein [1], Chen [3], Hughes [10], Ingersoll [11], Jobson [12], Reinganum [15], Roll and Ross (RR) [16] and Shanken [17], to mention but a few. It has also been treated in a more general context by Chamberlain and Rothschild [2].

Our purpose here is not to comment on this collection of papers—many of which are unpublished—but to reexamine the evidence presented by RR and point out major pitfalls involved in the empirical methodology employed by them and others who have followed their lead.

RR claim that, on theoretical and more importantly on empirical grounds, arbitrage pricing theory (APT) is an attractive alternative to the capital asset pricing model (CAPM). The APT, it is argued, requires less stringent and presumably more plausible assumptions, is more readily testable since it does not require the measurement of the market portfolio, and may be better able to explain the anomalies found in the application of the CAPM to asset returns.

The acceptability of the APT, like that of the CAPM or any other theory, ultimately depends on its ability to explain the relevant empirical evidence. Our subsequent discussion will show that many of the problems associated with the CAPM are also present in the APT context and that its ability to explain the relevant empirical evidence is not markedly superior. Moreover, it raises questions not only about the RR and related empirical investigations of the APT but also about the testability of that theory in the present state of the art. A major part of the problem results from the necessity to break down the "universe" being analyzed through the APT model; this is forced upon the investigator by the fact

* Dhrymes from Department of Economics, Columbia University, and Friend and Gultekin from The Wharton School, University of Pennsylvania. We owe a great deal to Mustafa N. Gultekin for his generous help in computer programming and for sharing his expertise in computer applications of factor analytic methods with us.

that computer software does not permit factor analysis involving covariance or correlation matrices of high order (in the case of RR 1260).

Our paper has three major thrusts:

1. It is generally impermissible to carry out tests on whether a given "risk factor is priced"; this is a result that is inherent in the structure of standard factor analytic models, *unless one is prepared a priori to specify that in the "true" structure certain factor loadings are known.*
2. Factor analyzing small groups of (30) securities is not equivalent to factor analyzing a group of securities sufficiently large for the APT model to hold.
3. As one increases the size of the security groups to which the APT/factor analytic procedures are applied, the number of 'factors" determined increases.

I. The APT Model: Implications and the Nature of Empirical Tests

In order to establish notation and make this paper as self-contained as possible, we give a brief exposition of the APT model and discuss some aspects of its empirical implications.

The model begins by postulating the return generating function

$$r_{t\cdot} = E_{t\cdot} + f_{t\cdot}B + u_{t\cdot} \tag{1}$$

where $r_{t\cdot}$ is an m-element row vector containing the observed rates of return at time t for the m-securities under consideration; $E_{t\cdot}$ is similarly an m-element row vector containing the expected (mean) returns at time t. Finally,

$$v_{t\cdot} = f_{t\cdot}B + u_{t\cdot} \tag{2}$$

represents the error process at time t. It is an essential feature of the APT model that the error process has two components: the idiosyncratic component

$$u_{t\cdot}, \qquad t = 1, 2, \cdots$$

and the common component

$$f_{t\cdot}B.$$

It is assumed that

$$\{u'_{t\cdot}: t = 1, 2, \cdots\}$$

is a sequence of independent identically distributed (i.i.d.) random vectors with

$$E(u'_{t\cdot}) = 0, \qquad \mathrm{Cov}(u'_{t\cdot}, f'_{t\cdot}) = 0, \quad \text{and} \quad \mathrm{Cov}(u'_{t\cdot}) = \Omega, \tag{3}$$

the covariance matrix Ω being *diagonal* and such that

$$0 < \omega_{ii} < \infty, \qquad i = 1, 2, \cdots, m. \tag{4}$$

Regarding the common component, we note that the form in which it is stated creates an identification problem, since neither $f_{t\cdot}$ nor B are directly observable. We (partly) eliminate this problem by specifying that

$$\{f'_{t\cdot}: t = 1, 2, \cdots\}$$

is a sequence of k-element i.i.d. random vectors with[1]

$$E(f'_{t\cdot}) = 0, \qquad \mathrm{Cov}(f'_{t\cdot}) = I. \tag{5}$$

It is a consequence of the assertions above that

$$\{(r_{t\cdot} - E_{t\cdot})' : t = 1, 2, \cdots\}$$

is a sequence of i.i.d. random vectors with

$$E[(r_{t\cdot} - E_{t\cdot})'] = 0, \qquad \mathrm{Cov}[(r_{t\cdot} - E_{t\cdot})'] = B'B + \Omega = \Psi. \tag{6}$$

We further note that

$$\begin{aligned} \mathrm{Cov}(r_{ti}, r_{tj}) &= b'_{\cdot i} b_{\cdot j} && i \neq j \\ &= b'_{\cdot i} b_{\cdot i} + \omega_{ii} && i = j \end{aligned} \tag{7}$$

and that indeed the columns of B ($b_{\cdot i}$, which are $k \times 1$) contain information on the covariation of securities.

Finally, since only Ψ can be estimated directly from the data, (6) shows that there is a further identification problem not eliminated by the assertion in (5) and the discussion of footnote 1. For if B is a matrix satisfying (6) and (1) and even if $f_{t\cdot}$ obeys (5), then for any orthogonal matrix Q, QB also satisfies (6) and (1). Hence, B can be identified only up to left multiplication by an orthogonal matrix, unless we are prepared to put *a priori* restrictions on the elements of B.

Now, just what restrictions on empirical evidence are implied by the APT model? First, we should note that the proof of the crucial implication of APT requires the invocation of a strong law of large numbers (SLLN); hence, the universe of securities to which one seeks to apply the model must contain a sufficiently large number of them so that the invocation of the SLLN may be reasonably justified.

Second, the fundamental conclusion of APT requires that there exists a $(k + 1)$-element row vector, $c_{t\cdot}$, such that

$$E_{t\cdot} = c_{t\cdot} B^*, \qquad t = 1, 2, \cdots, T \tag{8}$$

where

$$B^* = \begin{pmatrix} e' \\ B \end{pmatrix}, \tag{9}$$

e being an m-element column of ones.

Thus, the no arbitrage condition characterizing equilibrium rates of return requires that if $x_{t\cdot}$ is such that

$$u_{t\cdot} x'_{t\cdot}$$

is an entity to which the SLLN applies and if $x_{t\cdot}$ belongs to the column null space of B^*, then $E_{t\cdot}$ *must lie in the row space of* B^*.[2] If the number of securities

[1] Note that if $\mathrm{Cov}(f'_{t\cdot}) = \Phi$, $\Phi > 0$ otherwise arbitrary, then $f_{t\cdot}B$ is indistinguishable from $f^0_{t\cdot}B^0$ where, for arbitrary nonsingular C,

$$f^0_{t\cdot} = f_{t\cdot}C, \qquad B^0 = C^{-1}B.$$

[2] See Huberman [9] for a precise definition of arbitrage and a concise yet elegant exposition of the APT model.

(m) is sufficiently large, then for any desired degree of approximation we can rewrite (1) as

$$r_{t\cdot} = c_{t\cdot}B^* + f_{t\cdot}B + u_{t\cdot}, \qquad t = 1, 2, \cdots, T. \tag{10}$$

The restriction on empirical evidence imposed by (10) is rather stringent; in particular, it requires that no other (relevant) economic/financial variables have any bearing on the determination of expected rates of return, once the impact (on the expected rates of return) of the covariation among securities is taken into account.

II. Significance Tests for the "Priced" Risk Factors

The empirical tests of APT carried out by RR and others are based on a two-step factor analytic approach. Factor analytic methods are, in effect, suggested by the formulation in (1) and the composition of the covariance matrix in (6). In the first stage, one determines the number of factors (k) and estimates the elements of B and in the second stage, using the latter as the "independent variables," one estimates the vector $c_{t\cdot}$, whose elements have the interpretation that c_{ti} is the risk premium attached to the ith factor, $i = 1, 2, \cdots, k$, while c_{t0} is the risk-free rate, or possibly the return on a zero-beta asset.

The question often arises as to whether all (common) risk factors are priced or only a subset thereof. In this section, we wish to address the methodological issues bound up with these concerns.

Thus, suppose T is sufficiently large so that these covariance or correlation matrices, Ψ, can be estimated with reasonable accuracy and by factor analysis we estimate B, say by $\tilde{B}$, and Ω, say by $\tilde{\Omega}$. Thus, we have implicitly estimated

$$\tilde{\Psi} = \tilde{B}'\tilde{B} + \tilde{\Omega} \tag{11}$$

which completes the first stage; in the second stage, for each t, we may estimate

$$\tilde{c}'_{t\cdot} = (\tilde{B}^*\tilde{\Psi}^{-1}\tilde{B}^{*\prime})^{-1}\tilde{B}^*\tilde{\Psi}^{-1}r'_{t\cdot}, \qquad t = 1, 2, \cdots, T. \tag{12}$$

If the underlying error process is normal and if T is sufficiently large, it is easy to show that (approximately)

$$(\tilde{c}_{t\cdot} - c_{t\cdot})' \sim N[0, (B^*\Psi^{-1}B^{*\prime})^{-1}]. \tag{13}$$

Thus, we may view the $\{\tilde{c}'_{t\cdot}: t = 1, 2, \cdots, T\}$, approximately, as drawings from a multivariate normal distribution with mean[3]

$$c'_{t\cdot}: t = 1, 2, \cdots, T$$

and covariance matrix

$$(B^*\Psi^{-1}B^{*\prime})^{-1}.$$

Recalling, however, that B is identified by factor analytic procedures only to the extent of left multiplication by an orthogonal matrix, we are led to doubt the

[3] As we point out later at a more appropriate juncture, it is somewhat incongruous that we insist on time stationarity for the distribution of f (the risk "factors") while here we do not insist on the "stationarity," i.e., the constancy, of the risk premia c_{ti}, $i = 1, 2, \cdots, k$.

manner in which tests on individual elements of $c_{t\cdot}$ are typically carried out. General tests, see for example RR, involve the introduction of other explanatory variables and a test of the hypothesis that the corresponding coefficients are zero.

In the remainder of this section, we shall examine the question whether, in the context of the specification,

$$r_{t\cdot} = c_{t\cdot}B^* + d_{t\cdot}P + v_{t\cdot} \tag{14}$$

where P is a matrix of "extraneous" variables and B^* is only identified to within left multiplication by

$$Q^* = \begin{bmatrix} 1 & 0 \\ 0 & Q \end{bmatrix} \tag{15}$$

and Q is orthogonal, it is possible to have unambiguous tests of significance on $d_{t\cdot}$, c_{t0}, and c_{ti}, $i = 1, 2, \cdots, k$. To avoid extraneous issues, *we shall suppose that T is sufficiently large so that the estimates of B obtained by a factor analytic approach have negligible sampling variation and we can deal with them as if they were their probability limits.* Let B_0 be the "true" parameter matrix as initially specified in (1). Then the output of the factor analytic procedure and therefore the set of explanatory variables in (14) is a matrix, say $\bar{H}$, which is related to the true matrix H_0 through

$$\bar{H} = \begin{bmatrix} 1 & 0 & 0 \\ 0 & Q & 0 \\ 0 & 0 & I \end{bmatrix} H_0, \qquad H_0 = \begin{bmatrix} e' \\ B_0 \\ P \end{bmatrix} \tag{16}$$

Note that H_0 is unambiguously specified although B_0 is unknowable; what is knowable is only the transformation

$$\bar{B} = QB_0$$

where Q is an arbitrary orthogonal matrix. Hence, the only unambiguous conclusions that may be derived from such an analysis must be conclusions "modulo" Q, i.e., conclusions that do not in any way depend on Q.

We have

PROPOSITION 1. *Consider the general model in* (14) *and suppose T is sufficiently large so that sampling variation may be ignored. Define*

$$\tilde{h}'_{t\cdot} = (H_0\Psi^{-1}H'_0)^{-1}H_0\Psi^{-1}r'_{t\cdot},$$

$$h_{t\cdot} = (c_{t\cdot}, d_{t\cdot}), \qquad \bar{h}'_{t\cdot} = \bar{Q}h'_{t\cdot}, \qquad \bar{H} = \bar{Q}H_0,$$

$$\tilde{\bar{h}}'_{t\cdot} = (\bar{H}\Psi^{-1}\bar{H}')^{-1}\bar{H}\Psi^{-1}r'_{t\cdot}, \qquad \bar{Q} = \begin{bmatrix} 1 & 0 & 0 \\ 0 & Q & 0 \\ 0 & 0 & I \end{bmatrix} \tag{17}$$

where Q is an orthogonal matrix of order k, I is the identity matrix of order s (s being the number of extraneous explanatory variables—the rows of P), and H_0 as in Equation (16); *then*

$$\tilde{\bar{h}}'_{t\cdot} = \bar{Q}\tilde{h}'_{t\cdot} \tag{18}$$

Proof: Obvious by noting that

$$\bar{Q}'\bar{Q} = I,$$

i.e., $\bar{Q}$ is also an orthogonal matrix (of order $s + k + 1$).

It is evident that the "risk-free" or "zero-beta" rate is uniquely estimated since in the obvious notation

$$\tilde{\tilde{c}}_{t0} = \tilde{c}_{t0}.$$

Moreover, the vector $d_{t\cdot}$ is also uniquely estimated since

$$\tilde{\tilde{d}}_{t\cdot} = \tilde{d}_{t\cdot}.$$

On the other hand

$$(\tilde{\tilde{c}}_{t1}, \tilde{\tilde{c}}_{t2}, \cdots, \tilde{\tilde{c}}_{tk})' = Q(\tilde{c}_{t1}, \tilde{c}_{t2}, \cdots, \tilde{c}_{tk})'$$

which states that, in general,

$$\tilde{\tilde{c}}_{ti} \neq \tilde{c}_{ti}, \qquad i = 1, 2, \cdots, k.$$

Hence, the interpretation of the regression estimates $\tilde{\tilde{c}}_{ti}$ as the "risk premium" for the ith common risk factor is a serious overreaching of the empirical evidence.

In RR as well as Hughes [10], among others, many tests are carried out as to how many factors are being "priced"; in RR tests are also carried out on the "significance" of individual extraneous variables as a "test" of the APT model. To what extent are the results of such tests unambiguous? This is, in part, answered by:

PROPOSITION 2. *Under the conditions of Proposition* 1 *the covariance matrix of the estimator* $\tilde{\tilde{h}}_{t\cdot}'$ *has the following properties.*

1. *The variance of* $\tilde{\tilde{c}}_{t0}$ *is exactly the variance of* $\tilde{c}_{t0}$, *i.e., it does not depend on the matrix Q.*
2. *The covariance matrix corresponding to* $\tilde{\tilde{d}}_{t\cdot}$ *is exactly the covariance matrix of* $\tilde{d}_{t\cdot}$, *i.e., it does not depend on the matrix Q.*
3. *The covariance matrix corresponding to the "risk premia" assigned to the common risk factors does depend on the matrix Q.*

Proof: The covariance matrix of $\tilde{\tilde{h}}_{t\cdot}'$ is evidently given by

$$(\bar{H}\Psi^{-1}\bar{H}')^{-1} = \bar{Q}(H_0\Psi^{-1}H_0')^{-1}\bar{Q}'.$$

Thus the variance of $\tilde{c}_{t0}$ is simply the (1, 1) element of $(H_0\Psi^{-1}H_0')^{-1}$ which is independent of Q. Specifically, it is

$$[e'\Psi^{-1}e - e'\Psi^{-1}H_2^{0\prime}(H_2^0\Psi^{-1}H_2^{0\prime})^{-1}H_2^0\Psi^{-1}e]^{-1}$$

where

$$H_2^0 = \begin{pmatrix} B_0 \\ P \end{pmatrix}.$$

For the second statement of the proposition, we note that the corresponding covariance matrix is

$$[P\Psi^{-1}P' - P\Psi^{-1}B_0^{*\prime}(B_0^*\Psi^{-1}B_0^{*\prime})^{-1}B_0^*\Psi^{-1}P']^{-1}$$

which evidently does not depend on Q; B_0^* is the true parameter matrix, B_0, augmented by a (row) vector of ones as in (9). For the last part of the statement, we note that the relevant covariance matrix is

$$\Phi_{22} = Q[B_0\Psi^{-1}B_0' - B_0\Psi^{-1}P^{*\prime}(P^*\Psi^{-1}P^{*\prime})^{-1}P^*\Psi^{-1}B_0']^{-1}Q' \qquad (19)$$

or

$$\Phi_{22} \neq Q\Phi_{22}^0 Q'$$

where

$$P^* = \begin{pmatrix} e' \\ p \end{pmatrix}$$

and Φ_{22}^0 has the obvious meaning. This makes the dependence clear and completes the proof of the proposition.

The results above should make it evident that tests on individual coefficients, c_{ti}, or subsets of risk premia coefficients are not unambiguous. To demonstrate this let us assume normality for the error terms so that the test statistics become unambiguously determined in their distribution. Such linear tests involve consideration of quantities like

$$A\bar{c}_{t\cdot}^{*^{0\prime}}$$

where

$$\bar{c}_{t\cdot}^{*^0} = (\bar{c}_{t1}^0, \bar{c}_{t2}^0, \cdots, \bar{c}_{tk}^0).$$

A is a suitable matrix with known elements and $\bar{c}_{t\cdot}^{*^0} = c_{t\cdot}^{*^0}Q'$, $c_{t\cdot}^{*^0}$ being the "true" risk premia vector. The usual test statistic then would obey, for the test of $A\bar{c}_{t\cdot}^{*^{0\prime}} = 0$,

$$\tilde{\bar{c}}_{t\cdot}^* A'(A\Phi_{22}A')^{-1}A\bar{c}_{t\cdot}^{*\prime} = \bar{c}_{t\cdot}^* Q'A'(AQ\Phi_{22}^0 Q'A')^{-1}AQ\tilde{c}_{t\cdot}^{*\prime} \sim \chi_r^2$$

where

$$\Phi_{22} = Q'\Phi_{22}^0 Q \quad \text{and} \quad A \text{ is } r \times k \ (r \leq k) \text{ of rank } r.$$

Since, in general,

$$Q'A'(AQ\Phi_{22}^0 Q'A')^{-1}AQ \neq A'(A\Phi_{22}^0 A')^{-1}A,$$

a test of the hypothesis

$$A\bar{c}_{t\cdot}^{*^{0\prime}} = 0$$

is not equivalent to a test of

$$Ac_{t\cdot}^{*^{0\prime}} = 0. \qquad (20)$$

In the special case, however, when A is the identity matrix of order k (i.e., when we simultaneously test all risk premia), we find that the test statistic reduces to

$$\tilde{c}^*_{t\cdot}(\Phi^0_{22})^{-1}\tilde{c}^{*\prime}_{t\cdot} \sim \chi^2_k$$

which is appropriate for testing the hypothesis in (20).

Thus, in this context the crucial testable hypothesis is how many factors there are and whether none of them is priced, rather than whether some of them are priced and others are not.

III. A Critical Appraisal of the RR and Similar Empirical Tests

The APT model as explained earlier requires the set of securities, to which the (rates of) return generating function in (1) applies, to be large enough so that a SLLN applies. It has the important implication that

$$E_{t\cdot} = c_{t\cdot}B^*.$$

There is no presumption of time stationarity with respect to the vector $c_{t\cdot}$ which describes the dependence of the mean (expected) rate of return vector on the rows of B^*.

It is a practical necessity, and was explicitly assumed earlier, that the distributions of $f_{t\cdot}$ and $u_{t\cdot}$ be time stationary, i.e., it was explicitly assumed that their distribution (or at least their second moments) *did not vary with t*. At least this must be so over a sufficiently long period to permit the estimation of the relevant covariance matrix.[4]

A second important implication of the APT model as exposited above is that, within any degree of (probabilistic) approximation desired, the vector of returns of the m securities in question may be written as

$$r_{t\cdot} = c_{t\cdot}B^* + f_{t\cdot}B + u_{t\cdot}, \qquad t = 1, 2, \cdots, T \tag{21}$$

which means that if we are to subject the model to empirical testing, we ought to treat *all m securities symmetrically.*

It has been a practice initiated in the paper by RR, and by now quite widely adopted by other researchers, to divide the universe of securities into a number of groups (42 in the case of RR) and treat them as "cross-sections" from a population in the manner one treats a sample of households in the context of a consumer expenditures survey. The analogy is, of course, quite appealing, which

[4] One significant limitation that is found in all papers attempting to estimate or test the APT model is that in the estimation of the relevant covariance matrix it is assumed that the mean return process is time invariant. This is so since the (sample) covariance matrix computed by any factor analytic software package will, barring instructions to the contrary, compute the mean of the security returns as if the return generating process had a time stationary mean—in this context, a constant mean. Actually, there is a further logical problem; in the context of the APT model, the justification for the risk premia vector is the presence of the risk factors through the term $f_{t\cdot}B$ in the return generating function. Since the "factors" are assumed to have a time stationary distribution, indeed to be independent identically distributed with mean zero and covariance matrix I, and since B is also assumed to be a matrix of fixed constants, it is difficult to understand, conceptually, why the risk premia vector should not also be time stationary. Thus, the only component of (10) for which the model carries no such implications is the constant term, c_{t0}, which may be interpreted as the risk-free rate.

is the reason for its wide acceptance. It is, however, very misleading. What enables us to use the cross-sectional information of a consumer expenditures survey to infer something about the parameters that characterize that particular universe is that each individual in the cross-section has some fairly well-defined attributes which can be measured unambiguously and independently of how many individuals there are in the cross-section, coupled with a presumption of parametric homogeneity among the entities of the relevant universe.

A reflection on the nature of the model as exhibited in (21) will disclose that if we partitioned the universe into 42 groups as RR do, then for the ith group we should have

$$r_{t\cdot}^{(i)} = c_{t\cdot}^{(i)} B_{(i)}^{*} + f_{t\cdot} B_{(i)} + u_{t\cdot}^{(i)}, \qquad i = 1, 2, \cdots, 42 \tag{22}$$

where $r_{t\cdot}^{(1)}$ consists of the first 30 elements of $r_{t\cdot}$, $r_{t\cdot}^{(2)}$ of the second 30 elements and so on. Similarly, $B_{(1)}$ consists of the first 30 columns of B, $B_{(2)}$ of the second 30 columns, and so on. The same is true of $B_{(1)}^{*}$, $u_{t\cdot}^{(1)}$, $B_{(2)}^{*}$, $u_{t\cdot}^{(2)}$, etc.

The question arises whether each group can be dealt with in isolation with any degree of assurance regarding the reliability of the ensuing results. In their paper, RR and those who have followed their lead, such as, for example, Hughes [10], make the caveat that while only a relatively small number of factors may be identified in each group, one must bear in mind that perhaps it may be different factors that correspond to different groups. The remainder of their discussion appears to ignore this point and proceeds as if the same small number of factors is identified for each group; RR are particularly pleased that the number of significant factors extracted in each of their 42 groups (of alphabetically arranged 30 securities) ranges between three and five.

Unfortunately, the situation is far more grave than the literature has thus far allowed for. Treating each group of 30 securities as a cross-section and looking to the results from such an exercise for confirmatory evidence about the number of factors is not appropriate. Most importantly it should be stressed that, in general, what is the equivalent of the explanatory variables (attributes) for the 30 securities cannot be measured reliably *independently* of the issue of how many securities we treat simultaneously. This is so since those "explanatory variables" are given by the (sub) matrix $B_{(i)}^{*}$ and this cannot be measured reliably in a 30-securities context—for reasons we shall explain below. Contrast this to the consumer expenditures survey context, in which each individual household's income, size, composition, and other relevant socioeconomic attributes can be accurately ascertained independently of how many households there are in the sample (cross-section).

The fundamental reason for this state of affairs is, essentially, that there is no necessary and simple connection between "factors" found in a 30-security context and "factors" to be determined in the context in which APT models may be held to apply. As pointed out in another context by one of the authors (Dhrymes [5]), the "factors" postulated in such models are not *ab initio* tangible concrete entities. Rather, the structure simply represents the researchers' rendition of the well-established pattern of covariation among securities' returns. If, after prolonged empirical investigations, the number of "factors" found is stabilized and an economic/financial interpretation is attached to them, we may, at that stage, think of such risk factors as reflecting fundamental economic forces at work in the securities markets. Thus, the nature of the factors is to be inferred from the observed behavior of security returns—not the other way around. Consequently, since the "theory" indicates that this pervasive pattern of covariation affects certain groups of securities obeying certain requirements, their existence and identification can only be determined in that context.

A simple example from the psychometrics literature may help to put this matter in more intuitive terms. Factor analysis has been often applied to the results of different intelligence tests in order to determine the "common factors" underlying the components of human intelligence. The number of securities in the context of the APT is like the number of tests one administers; the number of trading days is like the number of individuals to whom one administers the tests. If there are too few of them (individuals), the confidence one has in the results is not very strong; if there are very many, then one's confidence in the results of the analysis increases. *The number of tests has nothing to do with sampling variation*; it has something to do with one's universe of discourse. If a specific number of tests elicits a performance governed by the operation of k factors, then one has to analyze all of these test results (on all individuals) simultaneously. Recall that factors are not observed or observable directly; they are inferred only by the performance of individuals on all the tests administered. If only some tests are analyzed (such as using only the test measuring verbal skills while excluding math and other relevant tests), then part of the information on how these factors affect the results is missing and hence the results of the analysis may be misleading. Using an abbreviated environment would necessarily distort the evidence, much in the manner of the fable of the blind man feeling a large elephant.

By way of a logical explanation as to why $B^*_{(i)}$ cannot be measured reliably in the context employed by RR and others, such as Brown and Weinstein [1] for example, consider the model in (10) and suppose $r_{t\cdot}$ is stated in terms of standard deviates, i.e., we subtract from each r_{ti} its mean and divide by its standard deviation, thus conforming to the standard procedures in factor analysis computer software. Making allowance for this construction, the interpretation of Ψ in (6) is now that of a correlation matrix so that its diagonal elements are unity.

Partitioning Ψ in accordance with the RR scheme above we have

$$\Psi = [\Psi_{ij}], \qquad i, j = 1, 2, \cdots, 42 \tag{23}$$

so that Ψ_{ii} is the correlation matrix for the ith group of 30 securities and Ψ_{ij}, $i \neq j$, the "cross-correlation" matrix between securities in the ith and j^{th} groups. If we subject all 1260 securities to factor analysis simultaneously, we shall obtain estimates of B and Ω, say $\tilde{B}$ and $\tilde{\Omega}$, obeying

$$\begin{gathered} \operatorname{diag}(S) = \operatorname{diag}(\tilde{B}'\tilde{B} + \tilde{\Omega}) \\ [\tilde{\Omega}^{-1/2}(S - \tilde{\Omega})\tilde{\Omega}^{-1/2}]\tilde{\Omega}^{-1/2}\tilde{B}' = \tilde{\Omega}^{-1/2}\tilde{B}'(\tilde{B}\tilde{\Omega}^{-1}\tilde{B}'). \end{gathered} \tag{24}$$

where S is the sample correlation matrix. On the other hand, factor analyzing each of the 42 groups we obtain

$$\mathrm{diag}(S_{ii}) = \mathrm{diag}(\hat{B}_i'\hat{B}_i + \hat{\Omega}_i)$$

$$[\hat{\Omega}_i^{-1/2}(S_{ii} - \hat{\Omega}_i)\hat{\Omega}_i^{-1/2}]\hat{\Omega}_i^{-1/2}\hat{B}_i' = \hat{\Omega}_i^{-1/2}\hat{B}_i'(\hat{B}_i\hat{\Omega}_i^{-1}\hat{B}_i') \tag{25}$$

for $i = 1, 2, \cdots, 42$.

In (24) and (25) we impose, respectively, the conditions that $(\tilde{B}\tilde{\Omega}^{-1}\tilde{B}')$ and $(\hat{B}_i\hat{\Omega}_i^{-1}\hat{B}_i')$, $= 1, 2, \cdots, 42$ be *diagonal.* The procedure in (25) is essentially the RR procedure, and it may be rationalized by assuming that there exist orthogonal matrices, Q_i, such that

$$\tilde{B}_i' = Q_i\hat{B}_i', \qquad i = 1, 2, \cdots, 42 \tag{26}$$

and that while the $\hat{B}_i$, $\hat{\Omega}_i$ of (25) do not satisfy (24), there is still a well-defined relationship between them as given by (26). If that is, indeed, the case, then certain aspects of the RR methodology will not be inappropriate, even if the procedure would not be the most efficient possible. *Intuitively, this is not very likely to be true since we seem to be arguing that the characteristic vectors corresponding to the k largest characteristic roots of a matrix and its principal submatrices are related in the manner of (26). We also seem to be arguing that ignoring the off-diagonal blocks constitutes a misspecification that entails no cost.*

Since the impression that (26) is correct is rather widespread, it is appropriate for us to address this issue.[5] A particularly simple way of doing this is by noting that if (26) is correct, then the length (inner product) of the columns of $\tilde{B}_i'$ and $\hat{B}_i'$ must be identical. *This identity is not a matter of statistical significance and departures from it (beyond round-off errors) cannot be attributed to sampling error.* Rather, the equality of the length (inner product) of the two sets of vectors is a simple consequence of the mathematical relationship noted in Equation (26); thus, any discrepancy between the lengths (inner product) of these two sets of vectors can only mean that the *relationship exhibited in (26) is false.* Consequently, there is no such simple relationship linking the "factor loadings" obtained from a set of, say, eight groups each containing 30 securities and the factor loadings obtained when we "factor analyze" these 240 securities as a simple group. In order that we may explore these issues, we extract "five factors" from a group of 240 securities and "five factors" from each of its eight constituent groups of 30 securities each. We present in Table I the length of the columns of $\tilde{B}_i'$ and $\hat{B}_i'$ (five in each case). The first column refers to the case where the $\hat{B}_i'$ have been obtained by the factor analysis of the eight groups of 30 securities each; the second column refers to the case where the $\tilde{B}_i$ are the 5×30 submatrices of the matrix $\tilde{B}$ obtained by factor analyzing the entire group of 240 securities. Although this is not a particularly stringent test, the results show quite unambiguously that no such relation as (26) exists in the current context. It is quite important to realize that factor analyzing 30 security groups *is not equivalent in any way to factor analyzing a 240- or a 1260-security group if we impose the condition of*

[5] In an earlier version of this paper, we had given a counterexample illustrating these issues; in the interest of brevity we have eliminated it from the current version. The counterexample, however, is available from the authors on request.

Table I

Diagonal Elements of $B_i\hat{B}_i'$ and $\tilde{B}_i\tilde{B}_i'$, $i = 1, 4, 5, 8, 9, 10, 11, 41$, Showing Length of Vector of Factor Loadings Extracted for Each of The Eight Groups and Length of Corresponding Subvectors Obtained from the Large (240 Securities) Group

Factor	Subgroups (30's)	Large Group Subvectors	Factor	Subgroups (30's)	Large Group Subvectors
Group 1			Group 9		
1	3.1067	2.83768	1	3.23763	2.97218
2	0.35945	0.096835	2	0.435946	0.064010
3	0.23551	0.198218	3	0.286408	0.349995
4	0.22128	0.221701	4	0.258647	0.167212
5	0.19161	0.052237	5	0.240895	0.228194
Group 4			Group 10		
1	3.02258	2.71746	1	2.94329	2.68487
2	0.24484	0.171007	2	0.306789	0.054957
3	0.25544	0.159556	3	0.905512	0.249841
4	0.22275	0.155994	4	0.233484	0.177722
5	0.18105	0.122979	5	0.180469	0.139429
Group 5			Group 11		
1	3.54568	3.16758	1	2.54230	2.49865
2	0.339056	0.484800	2	0.353051	0.111158
3	0.285417	0.271622	3	0.259849	0.254911
4	0.216376	0.171041	4	0.243409	0.150558
5	0.202698	0.093324	5	0.212725	0.184807
Group 8			Group 41		
1	3.24736	2.93784	1	3.33370	2.93098
2	0.343372	0.051216	2	0.330169	0.460566
3	0.268385	0.249631	3	0.250717	0.261120
4	0.192920	0.146789	4	0.233161	0.115732
5	0.196137	0.136052	5	0.201804	0.075048

Note: In view of Equation (26), corresponding entries in the two columns should be *identical*, allowing for round-off error. *A departure from this identity is not a matter of statistical significance, and its occurrence implies that Equation (26) is false.* The eight groups are numbered following the RR classification scheme.

extracting the same number of factors in the two contexts. Thus, the RR procedure is not equivalent to testing the universe of securities for which the APT is postulated to hold. The number of securities used in testing the APT should be sufficiently large so that the SLLN can be invoked as shown by Ross [17] and Huberman [9].

IV. A Partial Test for the Loss of Information Entailed by the RR Procedures

As indicated in the preceding section, the RR methodology does not use the information contained in the off-diagonal blocks of the matrix (23) (i.e., the covariance matrix of the *entire* set of securities). This methodology can then be justified only as a special case when the information in the off-diagonal blocks of (23) can be ignored. One may therefore interpret the RR methodology as operating on the implicit assumption that the off-diagonal blocks of the matrix in (23) obey

$$\Psi_{ij} = 0, \qquad i \neq j, \qquad i, j = 1, 2, \cdots, 42 \tag{27}$$

and extract five factors from each group (or 210 in all) rather than five from the entire group.

While we cannot actually test the null hypothesis (16) that $\Psi_{ij} = 0$ for the entire set of securities, we can carry out a "test" for a set of 240 securities. The (log) likelihood function (LF) under H_0 as in (27) is given by

$$L_1 = -\frac{30nT}{2}\ln(2\pi) - \frac{T}{2}\sum_{i=1}^{n}\left[\ln|B_i'B_i + \Omega_i| + tr\Psi_{ii}^{-1}S_{ii}\right] \tag{28}$$

where

$$\Psi_{ii} = B_i'B_i + \Omega_i, \quad S_{ii} = \frac{1}{T}\sum_{t=1}^{T} r_{t\cdot}^{(i)\prime} r_{t\cdot}^{(i)}, \quad i = 1, 2, \cdots, n \tag{29}$$

(and as required in most computer software the return on the jth security, r_{tj}, is stated as a standardized deviate), and where n is the number of groups of securities (8 in our case).

Maximizing under H_0, and extracting five "factors" per group yields the RR results. In the particular case under consideration we find

$$\max_{H_0} L_1 = -\frac{30nT}{2}[\ln(2\pi) + 1] - \frac{T}{2}\sum_{i=1}^{n}\ln|\hat{B}_i'\hat{B}_i + \hat{\Omega}_i|. \tag{30}$$

Under the alternative, the LF is

$$L_2 = -\frac{30nT}{2}\ln(2\pi) - \frac{T}{2}\ln|B'B + \Omega| - \frac{T}{2}tr\Psi^{-1}S$$

where now

$$S = \frac{1}{T}\sum_{t=1}^{T} r_{t\cdot}' r_{t\cdot}.$$

Maximizing under the alternative and still extracting five "factors" yields the RR results as would be obtained for the entire set of 240 securities. In particular, we find

$$\max_{H_1} L_2 = -\frac{30nT}{2}[\ln(2\pi) + 1] - \frac{T}{2}\ln|\tilde{B}'\tilde{B} + \tilde{\Omega}|. \tag{31}$$

Now had we extracted only five "factors" from all 240 securities in the likelihood function of (28), as a nested set of hypotheses would require, we would find a maximized value for the LF in (28), say L^*, obeying

$$L_1^* \leq \max_{H_0} L_1.$$

Thus, if we treat

$$\ln \lambda = \max_{H_0} L_1 - \max_{H_1} L_2 = -\frac{T}{2}\left[\sum_{i=1}^{n} \ln |\hat{B}_i'\hat{B}_i + \hat{\Omega}_i| - \ln |\tilde{B}'\tilde{B} + \tilde{\Omega}|\right]$$

as the likelihood ratio test statistic, we would obtain a value for λ which is larger than the correct one. Hence

$$-2 \ln \lambda = T[\textstyle\sum_{i=1}^{n} \ln |\hat{B}_i'\hat{B}_i + \hat{\Omega}_i| - \ln |\tilde{B}'\tilde{B} + \tilde{\Omega}|] \tag{32}$$

would yield a value which is smaller than the correct one. Hence, if we reject on the basis of (32), we would certainly reject on the basis of the correct LR test statistic. Now, in the present case

$$n = 8, \qquad T = 2196$$

$$\textstyle\sum_{i=1}^{8} \ln |\hat{B}_i'\hat{B}_i + \hat{\Omega}_i| = -15.49002$$

$$\ln |\tilde{B}'\tilde{B} + \tilde{\Omega}| = -24.16200.$$

Hence

$$-2 \ln \lambda = 20{,}049 \tag{33}$$

and we remind the reader that, for the correct test, the statistic would be distributed as chi-square with 1050 degrees of freedom, and the number appearing on the right side of (33) would be larger. We could, of course, continue with the formalities and actually carry out the test; but the point is abundantly made by the preceding, viz. that there is an enormous loss of information by dealing, *seriatim*, with groups of 30 securities and consequently that the RR procedure cannot be rationalized in terms of ignoring information of little value. Indeed, if we were to accept the proposition that

$$\Psi_{ij} = 0, \qquad i \neq j,$$

then since the assignment of securities to groups is arbitrary we would conclude that there are no common risk factors, thus denying the *raison d'être* of the APT model.

V. How Many Factors Are There?

Notwithstanding the criticism of the basic RR approach developed in the earlier section, we deem it important to reexamine the results obtained by them with a view to reassessing the evidence presented thus far on behalf of the empirical validity of the APT model. This is done for two reasons. First, it is an important scientific axiom that potentially important new empirical results be subjected to the test of replication; this is particularly important in the case of the work by RR since while their findings are very provocative, their data exhibit a rather vexing missing observations problem. Second, a reexamination of part of the evidence presented by them would certainly permit us to examine, in an empirical context, some of the issues we had raised earlier, and either confirm or raise doubt about certain purported empirical regularities obtained in the basic work by RR.

Table II

Chi-Square Test of the Hypothesis That k Factors Generate Daily Security Returns for Selected Groups

Group	$k = 1$	$k = 2$	$k = 3$	$k = 4$	$k = 5$
1	572.35	435.41	372.63	318.38	269.37
	(0.0001)	(0.0185)	(0.1742)	(0.5209)	(0.8554)
6	873.95	659.04	452.08	362.26	309.89
	(0.0001)	(0.0001)	(0.0001)	(0.0560)	(0.2643)
11	611.09	472.36	399.48	333.67	280.32
	(0.0001)	(0.0005)	(0.0295)	(0.3016)	(0.7214)
16	570.17	455.25	364.93	312.95	273.87
	(0.0001)	(0.0031)	(0.2556)	(0.6157)	(0.8062)
21	692.12	596.79	502.53	444.129	382.87
	(0.0001)	(0.0001)	(0.0001)	(0.0001)	(0.0004)
26	547.99	441.82	377.27	315.79	277.64
	(0.0001)	(0.0107)	(0.1304)	(0.5716)	(0.7586)
31	553.53	466.29	394.49	327.30	288.28
	(0.0001)	(0.0010)	(0.0433)	(0.3923)	(0.5592)
36	606.24	493.53	426.06	369.29	314.41
	(0.0001)	(0.0001)	(0.0027)	(0.0326)	(0.2091)
42	565.53	457.46	404.03	344.85	300.89
	(0.0001)	(0.0025)	(0.0205)	(0.1723)	(0.3942)
Number of times the null hypothesis is accepted at 5% significance level for the entire 42 groups					
	0	1	11	29	36

Note: Number of degrees of freedom for the chi-square test for each group is ½ $[(30 - k)^2 - 30 - k]$. Number of securities in each group is 30. Number of observations for each security is, at most, 2619. No security has more than 110 missing observations. Values in parentheses indicate the p-value associated with the statistic, i.e., the probability that the test statistic (under the null hypothesis) will assume a value at least as large as the statistic obtained in this particular test. Groups are numbered following the RR classification scheme and only results for every fifth group are presented here in the interest of brevity.

The question we shall examine in this section is how many factors can be said to characterize the return generating process for securities traded on the New York and American stock exchanges. This question was raised by RR [16] who assert (Table II, p. 1088) that in about 88% of their groups (about 37 out of 42) "the probability that no more than five factors are needed to explain returns" is higher than 0.5, and (Table III, p. 1092) that when c_{t0} is not taken as known, in 95% of the groups three or fewer factors have associated "risk premium significant at the 95% level."

As we have pointed out in Section II one cannot test unambiguously the "significance" of individual risk premia although one can test unambiguously the null hypothesis

$$c_{t\cdot}^{*} = 0$$

where

$$c_{t\cdot} = (c_{t0}, c_{t\cdot}^{*})$$

i.e., $c_{t\cdot}^{*}$ is the vector of risk premia. Thus, the important issue in this research is how many factors there are rather than how many "priced" factors there are. RR

Description of the Data

Source:	Center for Research in Security Prices, Graduate School of Business, University of Chicago, Daily Stock Returns Files
Selection Criteria:[a]	By alphabetical order of 42 groups with the size of 30 individual securities listed on the New York and American Stock Exchanges
Maximum Sample Size Per Security:	2619 daily returns
Minimum Sample Size Per Security:[b]	2509 daily returns
Number of Selected Securities:	1260
Time Period:	July 3, 1962 to December 31, 1972

[a] Richard Roll was kind enough to give us a complete list of the companies in the RR study. We were not able to find 13 securities in the RR data in the 1982 CRSP Daily Return files due to name changes. We also replaced 11 securities which had more than 110 missing observations. In the RR sample, there are several securities with more than 800, and one with more than 1400, missing observations.

[b] The smallest sample size per group is 2424 days out of a possible 2619 days. There were eight groups with sample size less than 2550 days, and only two groups with less than 2500 days. Note that estimation of the correlation matrix requires simultaneous observations within each group. Therefore, minimum sample size for a group can be less than the minimum size per security.

and others who followed their lead, such as Chen [3] among others, settle on five factors. Apparently, previous researchers, in the process of establishing "the number of factors" by the conventional likelihood ratio test (asymptotically a chi-square test), have not appreciated the connection between how many factors are found and the number of securities one considers.[6] Table II presents chi-square tests on one to five factors for each of the 42 groups in the RR analytical framework. Our results differ appreciably from those obtained by RR ([16], Table II, p. 1088). Thus, if we interpret the "probability that no more than five factors are needed to explain returns" as the *p*-value associated with the statistic involved in testing for a five-factor decomposition, the comparison is as follows:

p-value	0.9	0.8	0.7	0.6	0.5	0.4	0.3	0.2	0.1	0
RR	38.1	16.7	7.1	2.4	12.0	2.4	4.8	4.8	9.6	2.4
Ours	0	12.0	9.5	4.8	16.7	11.9	11.9	9.5	7.1	16.6

In the above, the entry below each *p*-value, say 0.5, is to be interpreted as the percent of groups with *p*-values in the interval [0.5, to 0.6). Thus, for example, our results for *p*-value equal to zero show that seven groups (16.6%) have a *p*-value which indicates that a five-factor decomposition is inadequate at the 10% level of significance, while RR find only one such group (2.4%). The difference in the findings may be attributed either to the very large number of missing observations for some securities in the RR sample or to the greater precision of

[6] Factor analytic methods have been frequently used in the finance literature. In fact, the relation between number of factors and number of securities was noted by Meyers [13] without an explanation. See Elton and Gruber [8], Chapter 6, for a good summary of the applications of factor analysis in finance and for an extensive literature survey.

Table III

Chi-Square Test of the Hypothesis That k Factors Generate Daily Security Returns Using Varying Group Sizes

Number of Factors (k)	Number of Securities in a Group					
	15	30	45	60	90	240
1	132.6	572.4	1246.4	2318.7	5548.9	
	(0.0023)	(0.0001)	(0.0001)	(0.0001)	(0.0001)	
2	78.0	435.4	1065.1	2057.9	4986.59	
	(0.4140)	(0.0189)	(0.0001)	(0.0001)	(0.0001)	
3	54.5	372.6	958.41	1845.6	4501.7	
	(0.7676)	(0.1742)	(0.0094)	(0.0001)	(0.0001)	
4	37.7	318.4	858.6	1697.4	4190.5	
	(0.9165)	(0.5309)	(0.1461)	(0.0023)	(0.0001)	
5	28.5[a]	269.4	776.5	1603.3	3962.8	30756.2[b]
	(0.9132)	(0.6554)	(0.4785)	(0.0133)	(0.0001)	(0.0001)
6		230.3	711.2	1502.1	3776.7	
		(0.9617)	(0.7290)	(0.0762)	(0.0003)	
7		199.3	658.9	1409.4	3606.3	
		(0.9869)	(0.8403)	(0.2301)	(0.0061)	
8		165.6	610.6	1320.7	3460.0	
		(0.9985)	(0.9067)	(0.4735)	(0.0369)	
9		139.7	558.3	1247.4	3321.7	
		(0.9999)	(0.9660)	(0.6377)	(0.1299)	
10		117.4	570.4	1159.88	3188.9	
		(0.9999)	(0.9882)	(0.8691)	(0.3091)	

Note: Figures in the first line are the chi-square values. Figures in the parentheses are computed as $\frac{1}{2}[(n-k)^2 - n - k]$, where n is the number of securities in the group and k is the number of factors. Only five factors are estimated for the group of 240 securities.

[a] It is not possible to extract more than five factors.

[b] Only five factors are estimated due to accelerating computer costs.

our computer software (SAS) or both.[7] The differences in sample coverage between our set and that of RR amount only to 24 firms (see the description of our data on p. 338).

To examine the issue of "how many factors there are," we consider the case of an expanding "universe" of securities and we give these results in Table III. Thus, if one considers groups of, say, 15 securities, then only one or two factors may be "found"; if one considers 30 securities, then two or three may be "found." This becomes plausible if one understands the operational significance of the test, instead of concentrating solely on the purely abstract and synthetic concept of factors. What the test does (see, for example, Morrison [14], p. 269ff) is to test the hypothesis that after the extraction of k roots of the appropriate matrix the remaining roots are equal—and presumably small. Thus, looking at the 15×15 reduced correlation matrix entailed in the use of 15 security groups, it would not be surprising to find only one to two "distinct" characteristic roots; as we enlarge the scope of the investigation by dealing with, say, 30 security, 45 security, 90 security or 240 security groups, we should not be surprised if we encounter more distinct characteristic roots. This is well-illustrated in Table III which gives the

[7] We also used the same software package (EFAP) used by RR. These results are similar to those obtained by the SAS package. In their recent paper, Cho, Elton, and Gruber [4] report results similar to ours.

chi-square statistics and p-values associated with a given number of factors for (overlapping) groups of 15, 30, 45, 60, and 90 security groups. We also give the p-value associated with five factors in the case of a group consisting of 240 securities.

We remind the reader that the p-value[8] is the probability that a (chi-square) statistic at least as large as the one obtained would be realized if the null hypothesis is true, i.e., if there are at most k factors and the remaining $m - k$ characteristic roots are the same. Choosing a level of significance at 0.05, we see from Table III that for the group of 15 securities we have at most a two-factor model; for the group of 30 securities (containing the initial 15) we have a three-factor model; for the group of 45 securities we have a four-factor model; for the group of 60 securities a six-factor model; and for a group of 90 securities a nine-factor model. While these results have been obtained with a certain set of 240 securities, we have no reason to believe that, aside from singularity problems, the same phenomenon will not manifest itself with another group of 240 securities. The interesting question is at what level will the number of factors stabilize so that adding more securities to the universe will not change the number of factors conventional testing procedures will produce. We reserve this line of inquiry for another paper.

We do, however, report in Table IV the estimates of the factor loadings from a group of 240 securities and those obtained if we factor analyzed its eight constituent groups of 30 securities each. Due to space limitations, we only present this comparison for the first 60 securities. Interestingly, for any given security, estimates of the first factor loading do not change erratically as the "universe" expands. Estimates of the factor loadings for the remainder of the factors, however, change dramatically as the "universe" expands.

The import of this aspect of our work, then, is that the empirical finding in RR that the return generating process may be adequately characterized by a five-factor scheme is not supported. It is then still an open question as to how many factors give an adequate characterization, but it is almost certain that there are more than five.

[8] To be precise, let ξ be the test statistic, which is chi-squared with r degrees of freedom. If the level of significance is 10%, then the acceptance region is defined by

$$\text{Probability } (\xi \leq t_{0.10}) = 0.9$$

where $t_{0.10}$ is the boundary of the acceptance region defined by the specified level of significance. Hence

$$\text{Probability } (\xi > t_{0.10}) = 0.1$$

both statements under H_0. The p-value that is associated with *a given statistic s* is then

$$\text{Probability } (\xi \geq s \mid H_0) = p\text{-value}$$

Hence, in order to "accept" a hypothesis at, say, the 10% level of significance, the test statistic obtained must have an associated p-value of at least 0.1. Of course, if the associated p-value is greater than 0.1, it may be the case that the hypothesis accepted contains "redundant" factors. For example, in Table IV and for the case of 15 securities, the p-value associated with one factor is 0.0023, hence the one-factor model should be rejected at the 5% significance level; the p-value for the two-factor model is 0.4140, which means that this should be accepted; the p-value for the three-factor model is 0.7676, which is also to be "accepted." On the other hand, this really contains one "redundant" factor.

VI. How Well Does the APT Model Explain Daily Returns?

In dealing with complex estimation procedures like those entailed by the APT model, it is not straightforward to determine just what is the explanatory power of the model or alternatively what is a measure of the "goodness-of-fit." We have chosen to measure "goodness-of-fit" by the (mean) square of the correlation coefficient between "predicted" and actual rates of return within the sample period for each group. For more details on why this is a useful measure see Dhrymes [6], Chapter 2. We shall first give an account of the procedure and then discuss our findings.

We designate, in the RR methodological context, the estimator of the vector of coefficients, $c_{t\cdot}$, (involving the "risk-free" rate and risk premia) by

$$\tilde{c}_{t\cdot}^{(i)\prime} = (\tilde{B}_i^* \Psi_{ii}^{-1} \tilde{B}_i^{*\prime})^{-1} \tilde{B}_i^* \tilde{\Psi}_{ii}^{-1} r_{t\cdot}^{(i)\prime}, \qquad \begin{array}{l} i = 1, 2, \cdots, 42 \\ t = 1, 2, \cdots, T \end{array} \tag{34}$$

within each "cross-section" or group of 30 securities. Thus, we have a collection of T estimates for such coefficients for each group. Owing to the fact that generalized least squares procedures are employed in the estimators of (34), the usual R^2 is not very useful or meaningful.

Thus, we use the estimates in (34) to "predict" rates of return, by

$$\tilde{r}_{t\cdot}^{(i)\prime} = \tilde{B}_i^{*\prime} (\tilde{B}_i^* \tilde{\Psi}_{ii}^{-1} \tilde{B}_i^{*\prime})^{-1} \tilde{B}_i^* \tilde{\Psi}_{ii}^{-1} r_{t\cdot}^{(i)\prime} = A_i r_{t\cdot}^{(i)\prime} \qquad \begin{array}{l} i = 1, 2, \cdots, 42 \\ t = 1, 2, \cdots, T. \end{array} \tag{35}$$

Then we compute (over T observations) the square of the correlation coefficients between the actual and predicted values within each group, i.e., we compute

$$R_{ij}^2 = [\mathrm{Corr}(r_{ij}^{(i)}, \tilde{r}_{ij}^{(i)})]^2, \qquad j = 1, 2, \cdots, 30.$$

The statistics given in Table V refer to

$$R_i^{*^2} = (1/30) \textstyle\sum_{j=1}^{30} R_{ij}^2. \tag{36}$$

Consequently, what we have in Table V are statistics that give a measure of the mean explanatory power or goodness-of-fit for the 30 securities in the ith group. We have done this in the case where we have used only one factor and where we have used five factors.

Several observations are in order. First, clearly at least one of the remaining four factors contributes importantly to the explanation of returns in the context of the APT model. Thus, the typical $R_i^{*^2}$ for the five-factor case is about twice the corresponding $R_i^{*^2}$ in the one-factor case. Second, the typical correlation is of the order of 0.3 in the case of five factors and about 0.15 in the case of one factor.

VII. Additional Tests of the APT Model

We have carried out two additional tests of the APT which we cannot present in detail here in view of space limitations, but which we shall summarize in view of the importance RR place on them. These two tests consist of (1) an investigation of the relationship between the constant term or intercept in the RR cross-

Table IV

Effect of Group Size on the Estimates of Factor Loading

	Factor 1		Factor 2		Factor 3		Factor 4		Factor 5	
Security	(a)	(b)	(a)	(b)	(a)	(b)	(a)	(b)	(a)	(b)
1	0.34301	0.35724	0.01151	−0.11849	0.08339	−0.15421	−0.10169	−0.09776	0.08887	0.02068
2	0.26761	0.29088	0.01657	0.14466	−0.01217	0.11512	0.14923	−0.06598	−0.02374	−0.04764
3	0.45764	0.45577	0.05844	−0.03549	−0.09902	0.07795	−0.05537	0.00672	0.03867	0.00237
4	0.48656	0.49847	0.09482	−0.15348	−0.21406	0.14236	−0.01419	−0.01614	−0.04208	0.07065
5	0.26938	0.29360	0.01804	0.06250	0.03573	−0.00284	0.03926	−0.03192	0.00914	0.11346
6	0.25149	0.31159	0.07037	0.19731	0.07316	−0.20100	0.07671	0.00950	0.04320	0.08345
7	0.17076	0.19279	−0.00823	0.06214	0.09163	−0.10155	0.00381	0.06930	0.02038	−0.05445
8	0.29154	0.30195	0.03549	−0.03405	0.05869	0.01576	−0.05353	0.08203	−0.00401	0.01626
9	0.14089	0.16681	0.05705	0.14805	0.03437	0.00504	0.14623	−0.00019	0.03386	0.04758
10	0.23886	0.25228	−0.01933	−0.05308	0.07894	−0.05234	−0.05091	0.03391	0.06375	0.07454
11	0.10899	0.14624	0.03967	0.15365	0.07481	−0.01931	0.09424	0.05798	0.00760	−0.03799
12	0.16868	0.18307	0.00971	0.11081	0.07766	0.00805	0.07895	0.00955	0.03468	−0.05260
13	0.28098	0.28760	0.01658	0.02965	0.12869	−0.09825	−0.07218	−0.06310	−0.00477	−0.10965
14	0.34900	0.35310	0.06631	0.09803	0.01324	0.03121	0.12312	−0.00881	0.01049	0.15848
15	0.46722	0.47271	0.05190	−0.03094	−0.15800	0.04911	−0.08409	−0.11453	0.05553	0.06990
16	0.27706	0.27374	0.05516	0.16885	0.00954	−0.02110	0.10702	0.02568	−0.05370	0.01330
17	0.21684	0.26351	0.06742	0.17886	0.05731	0.03293	0.13076	0.01768	0.01336	−0.02118
18	0.26804	0.28819	0.01419	0.01000	−0.02847	0.13687	0.10407	0.12255	0.04402	0.10326
19	0.20803	0.19866	0.01086	0.07676	0.05684	−0.03509	0.06085	0.07363	−0.03545	−0.00995
20	0.38283	0.39971	−0.00874	−0.13148	0.01843	−0.12364	−0.12410	0.05489	0.04228	0.04205
21	0.45467	0.44895	−0.01909	0.00432	0.07669	−0.04804	−0.01463	−0.03987	0.04025	−0.04668
22	0.34498	0.35191	−0.01179	−0.08561	0.02781	−0.02926	−0.08141	0.04670	0.03636	−0.04906
23	0.12078	0.13405	0.02868	0.07965	0.11959	−0.13553	−0.06627	−0.22166	0.02321	0.05291
24	0.20618	0.20640	−0.22441	−0.02853	0.04288	−0.11423	0.02303	0.07416	0.06892	−0.05730
25	0.25661	0.26771	0.01285	0.07071	−0.01387	0.12422	0.07418	−0.19787	0.03214	−0.04322
26	0.50319	0.51228	−0.05831	−0.14862	−0.07452	0.05006	−0.11978	−0.05966	0.01733	−0.10228
27	0.22149	0.24849	−0.02304	0.10345	0.03685	0.06609	0.09502	0.16071	0.06919	0.10227
28	0.39352	0.41647	−0.00137	0.03893	0.03112	0.02107	0.04287	0.06735	−0.05720	−0.17248
29	0.25206	0.25412	−0.03066	0.09717	0.13312	0.04712	0.04144	0.06267	−0.05256	−0.17396
30	0.29395	0.32082	0.00588	−0.16542	−0.00557	−0.09269	−0.07941	0.11322	0.00312	0.01288
31	0.21205	0.21198	0.07090	0.01332	0.06219	0.00521	−0.02153	−0.01223	0.00524	0.05128
32	0.23807	0.25915	0.02371	0.07730	0.03052	0.16568	0.05748	−0.13780	0.01272	−0.07643

Table IV—*Continued*

	Factor 1		Factor 2		Factor 3		Factor 4		Factor 5	
Security	(a)	(b)	(a)	(b)	(a)	(b)	(a)	(b)	(a)	(b)
33	0.26478	0.29668	0.00696	0.18634	0.10602	−0.05850	−0.06638	−0.18642	−0.12960	0.04983
34	0.28912	0.31687	−0.03304	0.14878	0.10592	0.03991	−0.07752	−0.09832	−0.09863	0.02598
35	0.23751	0.27244	0.04911	0.09158	0.04311	0.16671	0.04915	0.13117	0.07946	0.04873
36	0.26254	0.27919	0.03167	0.02980	0.00398	0.05356	0.09937	−0.02001	−0.01669	0.05039
37	0.41241	0.40702	−0.36521	0.08224	−0.00582	−0.08784	0.07546	0.03160	−0.04735	0.06807
38	0.30784	0.29731	0.03028	−0.01583	0.08926	0.01638	−0.03049	0.01053	−0.00577	0.07849
39	0.32584	0.34266	0.02310	0.03574	0.00772	−0.21601	−0.07560	0.00520	−0.09633	0.00079
40	0.23206	0.26257	0.01510	0.11503	0.09286	0.09603	0.02584	0.03050	0.07580	−0.00539
41	0.21193	0.23441	−0.00166	−0.04631	0.07918	0.04014	0.10253	0.03320	0.00698	−0.13417
42	0.34305	0.37291	−0.01505	−0.00766	0.06114	0.07163	0.02607	−0.06447	0.04243	0.11717
43	0.24401	0.24909	0.04142	0.00853	−0.02423	−0.01114	0.13276	0.20230	−0.11286	0.04653
44	0.39762	0.44041	0.05887	0.04047	0.02390	−0.07102	0.04315	0.05332	−0.01232	−0.08036
45	0.28283	0.30192	0.03636	0.09511	0.11662	−0.03135	−0.11473	0.07821	−0.02905	0.06770
46	0.13576	0.12319	−0.03679	0.05422	0.03815	0.01119	0.09924	0.01295	−0.00831	−0.02105
47	0.27812	0.27343	0.01773	−0.06769	−0.00982	0.10950	0.08100	0.05530	0.02230	−0.05773
48	0.16851	0.19681	0.02790	0.02431	0.03237	0.12862	0.04847	0.02383	0.03735	−0.03807
49	0.22462	0.22965	0.00639	0.05360	−0.08456	0.02845	−0.08162	−0.09090	−0.07664	0.07176
50	0.35168	0.39336	−0.00676	0.13158	0.03084	−0.18638	0.06484	0.07740	−0.16676	−0.09556
51	0.19512	0.21469	0.01553	−0.02108	−0.06556	0.15959	−0.00852	0.03851	0.12456	−0.09492
52	0.20396	0.24635	0.03239	−0.0.3913	0.07650	0.09956	0.10694	−0.07547	0.00595	0.01579
53	0.50936	0.51384	0.05390	−0.20767	−0.08883	−0.04232	0.06991	0.05945	−0.02376	0.06582
54	0.51235	0.51515	0.07911	−0.21992	−0.17779	−0.01904	0.07804	−0.07762	−0.02102	0.03670
55	0.14234	0.14788	−0.02987	−0.03820	0.05303	0.03175	0.07368	−0.01377	−0.01225	0.11177
56	0.40374	0.39379	0.01991	−0.05442	−0.00689	−0.07360	−0.04476	−0.11685	0.00627	−0.02960
57	0.32436	0.30144	0.04618	−0.05421	−0.02761	−0.01982	0.00055	0.02976	−0.02102	−0.14782
58	0.40243	0.45506	0.02783	−0.02162	0.07134	0.01922	−0.00680	−0.07177	0.04908	−0.16761
59	0.22556	0.24618	0.02527	−0.02865	0.05926	0.02563	0.08455	0.03755	0.00653	0.10351
60	0.22458	0.28366	0.03544	0.08757	0.12825	0.07710	0.07703	0.16824	0.03885	0.01669

Note: Column (a) contains the estimates of factor loadings for the kth factor, $k = 1, 2, \cdots, 5$, from a group of 240 securities. Column (b) contains the estimates of the corresponding factors from groups of 30 securities, i.e., first 30 rows are the estimates from the first group; second 30 rows are the estimates from the second group, etc. Only the estimates of the factor loadings for the first 60 securities are shown here.

Table V

Summary Statistics for the Squared Correlation Coefficient between Realized Daily Returns and the Forecasts by One- and Five-Factor Models

	One-Factor Model		Five-Factor Model	
Group	Mean	Std. Dev.	Mean	Std. Dev.
1	0.1626	0.0933	0.3069	0.1381
2	0.1802	0.0859	0.3184	0.1833
3	0.1588	0.0809	0.2843	0.2614
4	0.1617	0.0952	0.3013	0.1290
5	0.1789	0.1048	0.3135	0.1650
6	0.1536	0.0681	0.2933	0.2164
7	0.1524	0.0794	0.2960	0.1813
8	0.1734	0.0695	0.3105	0.1259
9	0.1711	0.0925	0.3130	0.1581
10	0.1619	0.0957	0.2994	0.1483
11	0.1482	0.0811	0.2919	0.1329
12	0.1649	0.0816	0.3034	0.1740
13	0.1518	0.0988	0.2883	0.1810
14	0.1637	0.0791	0.3033	0.1493
15	0.1695	0.1236	0.3035	0.1753
16	0.1768	0.0913	0.3126	0.1621
17	0.1903	0.1076	0.2368	0.1453
18	0.1675	0.1023	0.2991	0.1983
19	0.1540	0.0905	0.2928	0.1515
20	0.1529	0.0774	0.2936	0.2423
21	0.1685	0.0814	0.3052	0.1702
22	0.1712	0.0828	0.3081	0.1373
23	0.1533	0.0852	0.2914	0.1754
24	0.1693	0.0911	0.3018	0.1842
25	0.1672	0.0793	0.3056	0.1677
26	0.1612	0.0690	0.3026	0.1007
27	0.1524	0.0897	0.2957	0.1458
28	0.1639	0.0829	0.2959	0.1894
29	0.1508	0.1005	0.2899	0.1695
30	0.1547	0.0791	0.2959	0.1462
31	0.1560	0.0824	0.2943	0.1678
32	0.1496	0.0749	0.2971	0.1571
33	0.1617	0.0841	0.2970	0.1856
34	0.1459	0.0859	0.2882	0.1728
35	0.1655	0.0872	0.3042	0.1480
36	0.1580	0.0866	0.2880	0.2190
37	0.1588	0.0973	0.2957	0.1731
38	0.1460	0.0684	0.2842	0.2041
39	0.1467	0.0822	0.3019	0.1832
40	0.1828	0.1088	0.3212	0.1830
41	0.1720	0.1050	0.3091	0.1634
42	0.1486	0.0825	0.2879	0.1962

Note: Forecasts of daily returns are estimated by $\tilde{r}_{t\cdot}' = \hat{B}^{*\prime}(\hat{B}^{*}\hat{\Psi}\hat{B}^{*\prime})^{-1}\hat{B}^{*}\hat{\Psi}r_{t\cdot}'$. See Equation (35) for definition of variables. Mean is the average of squared correlations between the forecast, $\tilde{r}_{t\cdot}$, and the realized daily return, $r_{t\cdot}$, for 30 securities in each group. Std. Dev. is the standard deviation of the squared correlation for the 30 securities in each group.

section regressions and the theoretically expected risk-free rate or zero-beta return,[9] and (2) an analysis of the pricing of residual variance vs. covariance measures of risk. We should note, however, that the procedures followed in the two tests, like those used by RR, are subject to the basic limitations in the application of factor analysis discussed earlier in this paper.

Our intercept analysis for the 42 groups of 30 securities each does not reject the hypothesis that the intercepts are, on average, the same in all groups, which is consistent with the APT model, but does indicate that the intercepts are insignificantly different from zero and/or significantly different from the risk-free rate for most groups, which is inconsistent with the model.[10] When standard deviation and skewness are introduced into the cross-section asset-return regressions, while generally yielding insignificant coefficients, they turn out to be significant at least as frequently as the factors suggested by RR, which again is inconsistent with the APT model.[11]

VIII. Conclusions

In this paper, we sought to reevaluate the empirical evidence bearing on the relevance of the APT model; although our findings are applicable to several other studies—many still unpublished—we have centered our discussion on the important paper by RR which constitutes the *locus classicus* of this literature.

Certain important conclusions emerge from our analysis. First, the basic methodology of analyzing small groups of securities in order to gather confirmatory or contrary evidence relative to the APT model is seriously flawed. Given the theoretical foundations put forth by Ross [17], we must in our empirical analysis treat all securities symmetrically; if that is not possible because of computer software limitations, then other ways consistent with the basic requirements of the model have to be found. Analyzing small groups of securities produces results whose meaning is unclear and which cannot possibly be what the investigator wishes to accomplish.

Second, because of the indeterminacies of factor analysis, it is not possible to test directly whether a given "factor" is priced, i.e., it is not meaningful to carry out "t-tests" (or other similar tests) of significance on individual risk premia coefficients. We can, however, carry out unambiguously "F-tests" or asymptotic chi-square tests on the significance of the *vector of risk premia.* Thus, the important research issue here is how many factors there are and whether (collectively) they are priced.

Third, the basic conclusion of RR that there are three to five factors does not appear to be robust; our results show that how many factors one "discovers" depends on the size of the group of securities one deals with. For example, when dealing with a 15-security group one "discovers" two factors; when dealing with

[9] Under certain conditions, Ingersoll [11] argues that the intercept in the APT could be a "zero-beta" asset even though a risk-free asset exists. However, this would seem to imply that the market does price risk other than common or factor risk and that arbitrage pricing theory, unlike the CAPM, cannot explain the basic risk premium between risky and risk-free assets.

[10] This finding is inconsistent even with the zero-beta version of the model since the required rate of return on such an asset is presumably in excess of zero.

[11] These additional results are available in a longer version of this paper.

a group of 30 securities, one "discovers" three factors; with a group of 45 securities, four factors; with a group of 60 securities six factors; and with a group of 90 securities nine factors. While this exercise has not been repeated with many groups and thus we cannot put forth the proposition that we tend to "discover" factors equal to 10% of the number of securities in the group analyzed, still it raises grave doubts about the major empirical import of previous research, viz. that three to five factors give an adequate characterization of (common) market risk. This finding also suggests a possible fruitful line for future research.

Finally, we ought to point out that our findings have relevance more to the empirical methodology currently in use for testing the APT, rather than to the validity of arbitrage pricing theory models *per se*.

REFERENCES

1. S. J. Brown and M. I. Weinstein. "A New Approach to Testing Asset Pricing Models: The Bilinear Paradigm." *Journal of Finance* 38 (June 1983), 711–44.
2. Gary Chamberlain and Michael Rothschild. "Arbitrage, Factor Structure, and Mean-Variance Analysis on Large Asset Markets." Unpublished manuscript, University of Wisconsin at Madison, June 1981.
3. Nai-Fu Chen. "Some Empirical Tests of the Theory of Arbitrage Pricing." *Journal of Finance* 38 (December 1983), 1393–1414.
4. D. Chinhyung Cho, Edwin J. Elton, and Martin J. Gruber. "On the Robustness of the Roll and Ross APT Methodology." Unpublished manuscript, Graduate School of Business Administration, New York University, 1982.
5. Phoebus J. Dhrymes. "On The Testability of Arbitrage Pricing Theory Models," Discussion paper No. 184, Department of Economics, Columbia University, February 1983.
6. ———. *Introductory Econometrics.* New York: Springer-Verlag, 1978.
7. Phoebus J. Dhrymes, Irwin Friend, Mustafa N. Gultekin, and N. Bulent Gultekin. "An Empirical Examination of the Implications of Arbitrage Pricing Theory." *Journal of Banking and Finance* (1984), forthcoming.
8. Edwin J. Elton and Martin J. Gruber. *Modern Portfolio Theory and Investment Analysis.* New York: John Wiley and Sons, 1981.
9. Gur Huberman. "A Simple Approach to Arbitrage Pricing Theory." *Journal of Economic Theory* 28 (October 1982), 183–91.
10. Patricia Hughes. "A Test of the Arbitrage Pricing Theory." Unpublished manuscript, University of British Columbia, August 1981.
11. Jonathan E. Ingersoll, Jr. "Some Results in the Theory of Arbitrage Pricing." Unpublished manuscript, University of Chicago, Graduate School of Business, May 1981.
12. J. O. Jobson. "A Multivariate Linear Regression Test for the Arbitrage Pricing Theory." *Journal of Finance* 37 (September 1982), 1037–42.
13. Stephen Meyers. "A Re-examination of Market and Industry Factors in Stock Price Behavior." *Journal of Finance* 28 (June 1973), 695–705.
14. Donald F. Morrison. *Multivariate Statistical Methods.* New York: McGraw-Hill Book Company, 1967.
15. Marc Reinganum. "The Arbitrage Pricing Theory: Some Empirical Results." *Journal of Finance* 36 (May 1981), 313–21.
16. Richard Roll and Stephen A. Ross. "An Empirical Investigation of the Arbitrage Pricing Theory." *The Journal of Finance* 35 (December 1980), 1073–103.
17. Stephen A. Ross. "The Arbitrage Theory of Capital Asset Pricing." *Journal of Economic Theory* 13 (December 1976), 341–60.
18. ———. "Return, Risk and Arbitrage." In Irwin Friend and James L. Brickler (eds.) *Risk and Return in Finance.* Cambridge, MA: Ballinger Books, 1977.
19. J. Shanken. "The Arbitrage Pricing Theory: Is It Testable?" *Journal of Finance* 37 (December 1982), 1129–40.

The empirical relevance of arbitrage pricing models

Their major implications "are not supported by the evidence currently available."

*Phoebus J. Dhrymes**

The standard Capital Asset Pricing Model (CAPM) has been a ubiquitous tool for portfolio analysis in the 1960s and 1970s. While it is still extensively used, there have been, over the years, a number of critical comments regarding its validity. Until the late 1970s, however, there was no credible successor. Recently, arbitrage pricing theory and models associated with it have been proposed as alternatives to CAPM.

The proponents of arbitrage pricing theory models (APTM) claim, on their behalf, several important advantages over CAPM.

Foremost are the extreme simplicity and, consequently, credibility of the assumptions underlying such models; their ability to "explain" returns on securities as "rewards" for different types of risk; and, finally, the lack of ambiguity in their implementation — this, in reference to the issue of how to define the market portfolio in the context of CAPM.

By now, a large amount of theoretical and empirical work has been undertaken on the subject and a number of scholarly papers have appeared in *The Journal of Finance* and similar journals. In this article, I shall explain the meaning of arbitrage pricing theory and models that have sprung from it. I shall also examine the evidence presented by the proponents of APTM, as well as some recent critical work on the subject, supplying citations as needed.

* This work was completed while the author was Visiting Professor of Finance at the Wharton School. The analysis and results quoted in this article are taken from two papers, by Dhrymes et al., that appeared in *The Journal of Finance* and *The Journal of Banking and Finance*, respectively. The author would like to thank Irwin Friend for helpful comments on an earlier draft. *The Journal of Finance* for June, 1984 includes a reply by Roll and Ross and a reply by them to this article will be forthcoming in the Fall, 1984 issue of this *Journal*.

WHAT ARE ARBITRAGE PRICING THEORY MODELS?

Every scientific investigation begins with a number of hypotheses, and work on APTM is no exception. The version exposited by the chief advocates of APTM begins by postulating that the return (or the rate of return) on an asset consists of two components, a *systematic* component and a *random* component.[1] The systematic component, referred to as the expected rate of return, is for the moment left unspecified. Indeed, it is one of the attractive features of APTM that the theory "explains" this systematic or expected rate of return.

In view of the well-known covariation among security returns, we would expect the random components to be correlated, in some form, across assets. On the other hand, every security analyst knows that there are, all too frequently, events peculiar to individual companies that affect the rate of return on their stock. Bringing these two considerations together would justify splitting the random component of the return in two: one subcomponent that accounts for the covariation amongst securities' returns and one that is peculiar or idiosyncractic to a particular security. For technical reasons beyond the scope of this article, it is *necessary to assume that these two subcomponents are mutually independent or uncorrelated.*

This, then, is the basic framework. But how do we explain the composition of the expected rate of return? Well, up to now we have said nothing about how financial markets and their participants operate. The essence of APTM is the assertion that *markets operate in such a way as to rule out profitable riskless arbitrage.* In other words, markets operate in such a way

1. Footnotes appear at the end of the article.

that it is impossible, by simply rearranging one's portfolio (i.e., without using additional wealth), to earn a higher expected rate of return without incurring additional risk, defined as the standard deviation or variance of one's portfolio.

From these premises, and the requirement that there be a sufficient number of assets so that idiosyncratic risk can be rendered negligible, one is able to conclude that *the expected rate of return is equal to the risk-free rate plus a linear combination of the risk premia associated with the "common risks," i.e., with the subcomponent responsible for the covariation amongst the rates of return for all securities.*

One is struck by the enormous power and potential applications of this model. It purports to tell us how the expected rate of return is made up, and it enumerates a number of risks to which the "source" of the return is referred. Thus, two firms, otherwise identical but earning different after-tax profits — say, because of differential managerial functions — would not exhibit different rates of return; rather, the more profitable firm's stock price would rise to equalize the expected (mean) rate of return. This scheme is, of course, directly useful to security analysts, if one were convinced of its validity.

For once a company's earnings are established and its risk characteristics are evaluated, one would immediately establish the appropriate price for the firm's stock. If, in fact, the stock is below this price, we have a "buy" situation; if above, we have a "sell" situation. Note, also, that *the theory makes no allowance for anything else beyond the risk factors and their "premia" in determining the "appropriate" rate of return (over the risk-free rate) for any given asset.*

THE APTM AND ITS EMPIRICAL IMPLEMENTATION

In this section, I present the unavoidable minimum of mathematical model structure that will enable me to explain precisely just what is meant by the various concepts, such as "common" and "idiosyncratic" risk. It will also enable me to discuss more completely the nature of the empirical evidence produced both by those who support APTM and by those who feel that its promise is as yet unfulfilled.

The model essentially states:

$$r_t = E_t + f_t B + u_t, \tag{1}$$

where r_t is a row vector containing the rates of return on the assets to which one wishes to apply the APTM, say, the securities traded on the New York and American Stock Exchanges — let us call this number m; E_t is the expected (mean) rate-of-return vector for the m securities in question; f_t is a k-element vector of random variables; k is a number much smaller than m — the elements of this vector are what are referred to as the "common" risks; and B is a $k \times m$ matrix, whose elements are commonly referred to as "factor loadings," corresponding to the elements of f_t, which are called "factors." Thus, the vector f_t contains the "common risk factors" and B contains the weights attached to these factors in their relation to a given asset's rate of return. Finally, u_t is an m-element vector of random variables; its elements are the "idiosyncratic" risks associated with each asset. It is an intrinsic aspect of "idiosyncracy" that it is peculiar in its own context. This means, in the model above, that the elements of u_t are mutually independent and, moreover, that they are also independent of the "common risk factors," i.e., the elements of f_t.

It is useful to observe that information regarding the covariation amongst assets is contained solely in the matrix B, while both the matrix B and the covariance matrix of the "idiosyncratic risk" vector u_t convey information on the variance of individual assets. Finally, the subscript $_t$ refers to time, so that, for example, r_t contains the rates of return on all stocks traded on the New York and American Stock exchanges as of the close of the tth trading day, or the close of the tth week, or month, or whatever the unit of time happens to be. In most applications, to date, one uses daily returns.

The conclusion of the theory is that the rate of return function, shown earlier, has the more specific form:

$$r_t = c_{t0}e' + c_t B + f_t B + u_t, \tag{2}$$

where e' is a row vector of ones, c_t is the vector of "risk premia," and c_{t0} is the "risk-free" rate. Thus, the mean return for the ith security consists of the risk-free rate plus a reward for the common risks associated with this security; specifically:

$$E_{ti} = c_{t0} + b_{1i}c_{t1} + b_{2i}c_{t2} + \ldots\ldots + b_{ki}c_{tk}. \tag{3}$$

So, in order to make a judgment as to whether a given security is over or undervalued, all that we need are estimates of the factor loadings — the b's; the risk premia — the c's; the risk-free rate, which may be taken as the (appropriate) Treasury bill rate; and the company's earnings.

This immediately poses the question: How do we estimate the factor loadings, the risk premia, and how do we determine how many "common risk" factors there are? Finally, how do we determine whether we should have confidence in this model as a faithful descriptor of the behavior of pricing of risky assets?

These questions form the essence of the "scientific" approach to the problem and they are, by far, the hardest questions to answer. To merely "tell a story," as most models do, is a comparatively easy undertaking. To be sure, formulating a model has its own rules of logical consistency that must be adhered to, but, however logically consistent and attractive or esthetically pleasing a model may be, it is still merely a plaything unless we can convince ourselves that it faithfully describes the aspects of reality to which it addresses itself.

Hence, in order to assess the "validity" of a model, we need not quibble about how reasonable the assumptions are, whether markets "really" behave the way the model requires, or whether the model is clumsy or attractively put together. Rather, once we are convinced of the logical validity of the model, i.e., that it contains no errors in logic in proceeding from its assumptions to its conclusions, we should ask: Does the model contain any implications that can be falsified by observations on the real world phenomena to which it is addressed? If the answer is no, there is no reason to take such a model seriously, in that knowing about it will not enlighten us about the real world. If the answer is yes, then we would want to test as many of these implications as possible. If all implications are consistent with empirical evidence, then we would have great confidence in the model. If only some implications are accepted, while others are rejected, then we cannot have great confidence in the model, although we would agree that it may contain a kernel of truth. If most, or all, of its implications are inconsistent with "best practice" empirical evidence, then the only option we have is to dismiss it as a faithful description of the phenomena to which it is addressed.

Now, what are the implications from APTM which may be potentially falsifiable by empirical evidence?

First, and foremost, APTM alleges the existence of a rather small number of "common risk" factors. If we find a way to determine the number of such factors, and if they remain manageable in their number, this would be evidence favoring APTM.

There will, of course, remain the problem of stability, i.e., if we make a determination of the number of such "common risk" factors on the basis of a sample covering the period 1962-1972, would the number of such factors remain the same over, say, the period 1973-1983? This represents an issue of a somewhat different genre.

Second, do we have a reliable way of estimating the elements of the matrix B?

Third, can we estimate reliably the parameter c_{t0} and the risk premia parameters, the c_{ti}, $i = 1, 2, \ldots, k$? And, if we can, do our estimates support the view that the first is the "risk-free" rate and the remaining are significantly different from zero and positive? For, if all risk premia parameters are insignificantly different from zero or negative, then the APTM is irrelevant, since its main contribution is to explain the mean rate of return as (partly) a reward for the asset's exposure to "common risk" factors. Fourth, it should be the case that no other economic/financial variable plays a role in "explaining" mean returns, since this would run counter to the implication of the theory, which states that the only thing that counts is exposure to "common risk" factors.

Finally, we are entitled to ask: How much of the return to assets do we explain by this model? If, at one extreme, 90% of the variation of returns is explainable in terms of this model, we should be very pleased with it; if, at the other extreme, only 5% of return variation is explained, then we would not consider it particularly useful. We should note, however, that, strictly speaking, the APTM makes assertions about the *mean return*, and how much of the variation of returns is explained by the model has no bearing on whether the model's implications are consistent with the evidence. Nonetheless, if we have a model that explains only 5% of return variation, we should be wary of urging portfolio managers to buy or sell stocks that are undervalued or overvalued according to the APTM criterion, because of the considerable error potential.

EMPIRICAL EVIDENCE TO-DATE ON APTM

The major empirical evidence to-date in favor of the APTM is that of Roll and Ross in the paper cited in footnote 1. Several other papers have also appeared in scholarly journals essentially making use of the same methodology, with results that range from mild agreement to disagreement relative to the early findings, although the Roll and Ross results were not challenged. The main Roll and Ross results state that there are, at most, three to five identifiable common factors and that their associated risk premia are more or less positive, as one would expect from arbitrage pricing theory. There were some inconsistencies in the theory when it came to testing whether the "constant term" of the equation was equal to the risk-free rate, but, by and large, no challenge was mounted on the empirical validity of APTM in 1979, 1980, or 1981.

The first serious questions were raised in the study by Dhrymes et al.,[2] which was prompted by the manner in which the Roll and Ross study was designed. The Roll and Ross paper had argued that, for reasons of inadequacy of the computer software, the securities in the sample (about 1260 of them) would not be analyzed simultaneously but, rather, would be divided into 42 groups of 30 securities each — and each of the groups would be analyzed as a "self contained" universe. The analysis involves determining how many "common risk" factors there are, i.e., in terms of Equation (1) or (2); how many elements the vector f_t has; the estimation of the elements of the matrix B; and, finally, at a second stage, the estimation of the risk premia vector c_t of Equation (2).

The econometric procedure involves the application of factor analysis to the covariance matrix of the securities being examined. But factor analysis is sensitive to the size of the covariance matrix dealt with. To appreciate what is involved, we note that the covariance matrix of the securities vector in (1) is:

$$Cov(r_t) = B'B + \Omega_{uu}. \tag{4}$$

Now, factor analysis — the technique used to estimate B and Ω, the parameters in this context — proceeds by finding the characteristic roots and vectors of a certain transformation of the covariance matrix in (4); note that B is the coefficient matrix for the common risk factors, while Ω is the *diagonal covariance matrix* of the idiosyncratic risks, the u's. Unfortunately, factor analysis is not invariant to the size of the covariance matrix analyzed. Thus, if one seeks to establish the number of "common risk" factors by analyzing 30 securities *(any 30 securities)*, one would arrive at one answer. If one seeks to do the same thing by analyzing any 60 securities, one would get an answer that cannot be simply related to the first answer. So the basic *initial methodology that sought to establish the number of "common risk" factors by analyzing several groups of 30 securities each is seriously flawed*, because these "common risk" factors — at this stage — have no concrete meaning. They are merely the researcher's way of characterizing the correlation among returns on risky assets. Once the existence of the factors is firmly established empirically, we can try to identify their substantive content. It is important to realize that *the existence and identification of these "common risk" factors is to be inferred from the observations of the behavior of the rates of return of the securities to which this model is deemed applicable.* If we look only at a small subset of such securities, then we get a distorted view of what such factors may be, and our inferences could be extremely misleading.

The situation is entirely analogous to a blind man touching an elephant. By touching only a small surface of the elephant's body, he necessarily gets a very distorted impression of what the animal looks like.

Another analogy that will help clarify the problems involved may be found in the original motivation for factor analysis in the area of testing human subjects. We are all familiar with the usual intelligence or IQ tests. Essentially, the procedure involves administering a number of tests to a number of individuals. Translated into our context, the number of individuals is like the number of trading days over which our sample ranges; the number of tests is like the number of securities we analyze. If different "intelligence" factors play different roles in different tests, i.e., if one test calls into play more of factor one than of factor two, then by confining our attention only to a limited number of tests — say, only reading tests — we would get a distorted view of an individual's capabilities and, concomitantly, a distorted view of the "intelligence factors" that govern human intelligence.

Now, the influence of "common risk" factors reveals itself to us only through the rates of return on all securities that constitute the universe being analyzed. Thus, if we confine ourselves to parts of this universe, we cannot hope to get a reliable view of these "common risk" factors and the manner in which they affect the rates of return on financial assets.

The study by Dhrymes et al. focuses on these and related issues, and in what follows I shall outline the main findings. For ease of reading, the statistical tables on which this discussion is based appear in the Appendix.

In Table 1, having arranged the sample in the same manner as in the study by Roll and Ross, I give part of the results on the question of how many "com-

TABLE 1

CHI-SQUARE TEST OF THE HYPOTHESIS THAT k-FACTORS GENERATE DAILY SECURITY RETURNS FOR SELECTED GROUPS

Group	k = 1	k = 2	k = 3	k = 4	k = 5
1	572.35	435.41	372.63	318.38	269.37
	(.0001)	(.0185)	(.1742)	(.5209)	(.8554)
6	873.95	659.04	452.08	362.26	309.89
	(.0001)	(.0001)	(.0001)	(.0560)	(.2643)
11	611.09	472.36	399.48	333.67	280.32
	(.0001)	(.0005)	(.0295)	(.3016)	(.7214)
16	570.17	455.25	364.93	312.95	273.87
	(.0001)	(.0031)	(.2556)	(.6157)	(.8062)
21	692.12	596.79	502.53	444.129	382.87
	(.0001)	(.0001)	(.0001)	(.0001)	(.0004)
26	547.99	441.82	377.27	315.79	277.64
	(.0001)	(.0107)	(.1304)	(.5716)	(.7586)
31	553.53	466.29	394.49	327.30	288.28
	(.0001)	(.0010)	(.0433)	(.3923)	(.5592)
36	606.24	493.53	426.06	369.29	314.41
	(.0001)	(.0001)	(.0027)	(.0326)	(.2091)
42	565.53	457.46	404.03	344.85	300.89
	(.0001)	(.0025)	(.0205)	(.1723)	(.3942)
Number of Times the Null Hypothesis is Accepted at 5% Significance Level for the Entire 42 Groups					
	0	1	11	29	36

Number of degrees of freedom for the chi-square test for each group is $\frac{1}{2}[(30 - k)^2 - 30 - k]$. Number of securities in each group is 30. Number of observations for each security is 2618. No security has more than 110 missing observations. Values in parentheses indicate the p-value associated with the statistic, i.e., the probability that the test statistic (under the null hypothesis) will assume a value at least as large as the statistic obtained in this particular test. Groups are numbered following the RR classification scheme and only results for every 5th group are presented here in the interest of brevity.

mon risk" factors there are. In the original study by Roll and Ross, a number of securities had many missing observations; in order to avoid the problems this entailed, I have replaced them. In addition, some firms in the original study were not available in the current version of the CRSP tapes, either because they had been merged or for other reasons. These firms have been replaced as well. Nonetheless, my sample differs by only 21 firms from that employed in the Roll and Ross study and, so, for all intents and purposes, both studies operate with the same information set. Thus, any differences in the findings of the two studies could hardly be attributed to differences in data.

My findings show that, using the same procedure, i.e., working with groups of 30 securities each (42 groups in all), 11 groups have a *three "common risk" factor* setup, 18 groups have a *four "common risk" factor* setup, 7 groups have a *five "common risk" factor* setup, and 6 groups require more than a five "common risk" factor setup. This is a noticeable departure from the original results and points to the precarious nature of the results favorable to APTM; some proponents of the latter, may, of course, attribute these differences to the 21 "replacement" firms, but this would only reinforce the perception of the initial empirical support for APTM as rather precarious.

In Table 2, we see a set of results that addresses the question: What happens to the number of "common risk" factors if we increase the number of securities in each group? Using conventional tests, one arrives at the conclusion that, at the 5% level of significance, with a group of 15 securities, we have at most *two "common risk" factors;* with a group of 30 securities we have at most *three "common risk" factors;* with a group of 45 securities we have at most *four "common risk" factors;* with a group of 60 securities we have at most *six "common risk" factors;* and with a group of 90 securities we have at most *nine "common risk" factors.*

This is a striking result, in that it implies that, as we increase the number of securities being analyzed, the number of "common risk" factors "discovered" comes to about 10% of the number of securities analyzed. If this relationship persists as we keep on going, then, for 1260 securities, we would "discover" 126 "common risk" factors, hardly a situation that adds to our understanding of the operation of financial markets. It should be made clear that this set of results is established on the basis of a randomly selected group of 240 securities, and thus may be modified if we did the same, repeatedly, with other large groups. But experience indicates that *five "common risk" factors is a wholly inadequate setup for describing the behavior of returns on securities traded on the New York and American Stock Exchanges.*

TABLE 2

CHI-SQUARE TEST OF THE HYPOTHESIS THAT k-FACTORS GENERATE DAILY SECURITY RETURNS USING VARYING GROUP SIZES

Number of Factors (k)	Number of Securities in a Group 15	30	45	60	90	240
1	132.6	572.4	1246.4	2318.7	5548.9	
	(.0023)	(.0001)	(.0001)	(.0001)	(.0001)	
2	78.0	435.4	1065.1	2057.9	4986.59	
	(.4140)	(.0189)	(.0001)	(.0001)	(.0001)	
3	54.5	372.6	958.41	1845.6	4501.7	
	(.7676)	(.1742)	(.0094)	(.0001)	(.0001)	
4	37.7	318.4	858.6	1697.4	4190.5	
	(.9165)	(.5309)	(.1461)	(.0023)	(.0001)	
5	28.5[a]	269.4	776.5	1603.3	3962.8	30756.2[b]
	(.9132)	(.6554)	(.4785)	(.0133)	(.0001)	(.0001)
6		230.3	711.2	1502.1	3776.7	
		(.9617)	(.7290)	(.0762)	(.0003)	
7		199.3	658.9	1409.4	3606.3	
		(.9869)	(.8403)	(.2301)	(.0061)	
8		165.6	610.6	1320.7	3460.0	
		(.9985)	(.9067)	(.4735)	(.0369)	
9		139.7	558.3	1247.4	3321.7	
		(.9999)	(.9660)	(.6377)	(.1299)	
10		117.4	570.4	1159.88	3188.9	
		(.9999)	(.9882)	(.8691)	(.3091)	

Figures in the first line are the chi-squared values. Figures in parentheses are p values computed from a chi-squared distribution with $\frac{1}{2}[(n - k)^2 - n - k]$ degrees of freedom, where n is the number of securities in the group and k is the number of factors. Only five factors are estimated for the group of 240 securities.

[a] It is not possible to extract more than 5 factors.

[b] Only five factors are estimated due to accelerating computer costs.

Table 3 illustrates another peculiarity that is inherent in this methodological setup and was pointed up earlier. The entries under column (a), for each factor, are the "factor loadings," i.e., the rows of the matrix B of Equation (1) or (2), obtained by "factor analyzing" the covariance matrix of a group of 240 securities. The entries under column (b) purport to estimate the same thing, except that they have been estimated by factor analyzing, separately, the covariance matrices of each of the constituent eight groups containing 30 securities each. Due to space limitations I give these results only for the first 60 securities in the group.

Again the results are striking. For the first factor, the loadings appear to be similar, although differences up to 20% in the magnitude of these loadings are not uncommon. For the second, third, fourth, and fifth factors, however, the results are different: They differ both in sign and magnitude. Indeed, one is hard pressed to accept the proposition that they estimate the same quantity from basically the same information!

It is this aspect that I have stressed earlier, namely, that breaking up the "universe" of firms analyzed into small groups is akin to a blind man touch-

TABLE 3

EFFECT OF GROUP SIZE ON THE ESTIMATES OF FACTOR LOADING

Security	FACTOR 1 (a)	FACTOR 1 (b)	FACTOR 2 (a)	FACTOR 2 (b)	FACTOR 3 (a)	FACTOR 3 (b)	FACTOR 4 (a)	FACTOR 4 (b)	FACTOR 5 (a)	FACTOR 5 (b)
1	0.34301	0.35724	0.01151	−0.11849	0.08339	−0.15421	−0.10169	−0.09776	0.08887	0.02068
2	0.26761	0.29088	0.01657	0.14466	−0.01217	0.11512	0.14923	−0.06598	−0.02374	−0.04764
3	0.45764	0.45577	0.05844	−0.03549	−0.09902	0.07795	−0.05537	0.00672	0.03867	0.00237
4	0.48656	0.49847	0.09482	−0.15348	−0.21406	0.14236	−0.01419	−0.01614	−0.04208	0.07065
5	0.26938	0.29360	0.01804	0.06250	0.03573	−0.00284	0.03926	−0.03192	0.00914	0.11346
6	0.25149	0.31159	0.07037	0.19731	0.07316	−0.20100	0.07671	0.00950	0.04320	0.08345
7	0.17076	0.19279	−0.00823	0.06214	0.09163	−0.10155	0.00381	0.06930	0.02038	−0.05445
8	0.29154	0.30195	0.03549	−0.03405	0.05869	0.01576	−0.05353	0.08203	−0.00401	0.01626
9	0.14089	0.16681	0.05705	0.14805	0.03437	0.00504	0.14623	−0.00019	0.03386	0.04758
10	0.23886	0.25228	−0.01933	−0.05308	0.07894	−0.05234	−0.05091	0.03391	0.06375	0.07454
11	0.10899	0.14624	0.03967	0.15365	0.07481	−0.01931	0.09424	0.05798	0.00760	−0.03799
12	0.16868	0.18307	0.00971	0.11081	0.07766	0.00805	0.07895	0.00955	0.03468	−0.05260
13	0.28098	0.28760	0.01658	0.02965	0.12869	−0.09825	−0.07218	−0.06310	−0.00477	−0.10965
14	0.34900	0.35310	0.06631	0.09803	0.01324	0.03121	0.12312	−0.00881	0.01049	0.15848
15	0.46722	0.47271	0.05190	−0.03094	−0.15800	0.04911	−0.08409	−0.11453	0.05553	0.06990
16	0.22706	0.27374	0.05516	0.16885	0.00954	−0.02110	0.10702	0.02568	−0.05370	0.01330
17	0.21684	0.26351	0.06742	0.17886	0.05731	0.03293	0.13076	0.01768	0.01336	−0.02118
18	0.26804	0.28819	0.01419	0.01000	−0.02847	0.13687	0.10407	0.12255	0.04402	0.10326
19	0.20803	0.19866	0.01086	0.07676	0.05684	−0.03509	0.06085	0.07363	−0.03545	−0.00995
20	0.38283	0.39971	−0.00874	−0.13148	0.01843	−0.12364	−0.12410	0.05489	0.04228	0.04205
21	0.45467	0.44895	−0.01909	0.00432	0.07669	−0.04804	−0.01463	−0.03987	0.04025	−0.04668
22	0.34498	0.35191	−0.01179	−0.08561	0.02781	−0.02926	−0.08141	0.04670	0.03636	−0.04906
23	0.12078	0.13405	0.02868	0.07965	0.11959	−0.13553	−0.06627	−0.22166	0.02321	0.05291
24	0.20618	0.20640	−0.22441	−0.02853	0.04288	−0.11423	0.02303	0.07416	0.06892	−0.05730
25	0.25661	0.26771	0.01285	0.07071	−0.01387	0.12422	0.07418	−0.19787	0.03214	−0.04322
26	0.50319	0.51228	−0.05831	−0.14862	−0.07452	0.05006	−0.11978	−0.05966	0.01733	−0.10228
27	0.22149	0.24849	−0.02304	0.10345	0.03685	0.06609	0.09502	0.16071	0.06919	0.10227
28	0.39352	0.41647	−0.00137	0.03893	0.03112	0.02107	0.04287	0.06735	−0.05720	−0.17248
29	0.25206	0.25412	−0.03066	0.09717	0.13312	0.04712	0.04144	0.06267	−0.05256	−0.17396
30	0.29395	0.32082	0.00588	−0.16542	−0.00557	−0.09269	−0.07941	0.11322	0.00312	0.01288
31	0.21205	0.21198	0.07090	0.01332	0.06219	0.00521	−0.02153	−0.01223	0.00524	0.05128
32	0.23807	0.25915	0.02371	0.07730	0.03052	0.16568	0.05748	−0.13780	0.01272	−0.07643
33	0.26478	0.29668	0.00696	0.18634	0.10602	−0.05850	−0.06638	−0.18642	−0.12960	0.04983
34	0.28912	0.31687	−0.03304	0.14878	0.10592	0.03991	−0.07752	−0.09832	−0.09863	0.02598
35	0.23751	0.27244	0.04911	0.09158	0.04311	0.16671	0.04915	0.13117	0.07946	0.04873
36	0.26254	0.27919	0.03167	0.02980	0.00398	0.05356	0.09937	−0.02001	−0.01669	0.05039
37	0.41241	0.40702	−0.36521	0.08224	−0.00582	−0.08784	0.07546	0.03160	−0.04735	0.06807
38	0.30784	0.29731	0.03028	−0.01583	0.08926	0.01638	−0.03049	0.01053	−0.00577	0.07849
39	0.32584	0.34266	0.02310	0.03574	0.00772	−0.21601	−0.07560	0.00520	−0.09633	0.00079
40	0.23206	0.26257	0.01510	0.11503	0.09286	0.09603	0.02584	0.03050	0.07580	−0.00539
41	0.21193	0.23441	−0.00166	−0.04631	0.07918	0.04014	0.10253	0.03320	0.00698	−0.13417
42	0.34305	0.37291	−0.01505	−0.00766	0.06114	0.07163	0.02607	−0.06447	0.04243	0.11717
43	0.24401	0.24909	0.04142	0.00853	−0.02423	−0.01114	0.13276	0.20230	−0.11286	0.04653
44	0.39762	0.44041	0.05887	0.04047	0.02390	−0.07102	0.04315	0.05332	−0.01232	−0.08036
45	0.28283	0.30192	0.03636	0.09511	0.11662	−0.03135	−0.11473	0.07821	−0.02905	0.06770
46	0.13576	0.12319	−0.03679	0.05422	0.03815	0.01119	0.09924	0.01295	−0.00831	−0.02105
47	0.27812	0.27343	0.01773	−0.06769	−0.00982	0.10950	0.08100	0.05530	0.02230	−0.05773
48	0.16851	0.19681	0.02790	0.02431	0.03237	0.12862	0.04847	0.02383	0.03735	−0.03807
49	0.22462	0.22965	0.00639	0.05360	−0.08456	0.02845	−0.08162	−0.09090	−0.07664	0.07176
50	0.35168	0.39336	−0.00676	0.13158	0.03084	−0.18638	0.06484	0.07740	−0.16676	−0.09556
51	0.19512	0.21469	0.01553	−0.02108	−0.06556	0.15959	−0.00852	0.03851	0.12456	−0.09492
52	0.20396	0.24635	0.03239	−0.03913	0.07650	0.09956	0.10694	−0.07547	0.00595	0.01579
53	0.50936	0.51384	0.05390	−0.20767	−0.08883	−0.04232	0.06991	0.05945	−0.02376	0.06582
54	0.51235	0.51515	0.07911	−0.21992	−0.17779	−0.01904	0.07804	−0.07762	−0.02102	0.03670
55	0.14234	0.14788	−0.02987	−0.03820	0.05303	0.03175	0.07368	−0.01377	−0.01225	0.11177
56	0.40374	0.39379	0.01991	−0.05442	−0.00689	−0.07360	−0.04476	−0.11685	0.00627	−0.02960
57	0.32436	0.30144	0.04618	−0.05421	−0.02671	−0.01982	0.00055	0.02976	−0.02102	−0.14782
58	0.40243	0.45506	0.02783	−0.02162	0.07134	0.01922	−0.00680	−0.07177	0.04908	−0.16761
59	0.22556	0.24618	0.02527	−0.02865	0.05926	0.02563	0.08455	0.03755	0.00653	0.10351
60	0.22458	0.28366	0.03544	0.08757	0.12825	0.07710	0.07703	0.16824	0.03885	0.01669

Column (a) contains the estimates of factor loadings for the kth factor $k = 1, 2, \ldots, 5$, from a group of 240 securities. Column (b) contains the estimates of the corresponding factors from groups of 30 securities, i.e., first 30 rows are the estimates from the first group, second 30 rows are the estimates from the second group, etc. Only the estimates of the factor loadings for the first sixty securities are shown here.

ing an elephant. He cannot possibly get reliable information about the nature of the beast by touching only a small area.

It is just not clear what significance we attribute to, and how we should interpret, these results. Are these poor estimates of the "same factor" loadings or estimates of "different factor" loadings? *The question has no meaning since factors are not, at this stage, concrete entities having an independent existence, but, rather, are merely conceptual constructs in search of concrete meaning,* and the results in Table 3 are simply part of the process of assigning meaning to them.

But enough has been said already to establish the conclusion that what we have learned thus far about the structure of "common risk" factors is very limited. Indeed, the whole issue of how many such factors there are and what meaning is to be assigned to them is very much an open question that may be settled only after further, and scrupulously careful, research.

TABLE 4

SUMMARY STATISTICS FOR THE SQUARED CORRELATION COEFFICIENT BETWEEN REALIZED DAILY RETURNS AND THE FORECASTS BY ONE- AND FIVE-FACTOR MODELS

Group No.	1-Factor Model		5-Factor Model	
	Mean	Std. Dev.	Mean	Std. Dev.
1	.1626	.0933	.3069	.1381
2	.1802	.0859	.3184	.1833
3	.1588	.0809	.2843	.2614
4	.1617	.0952	.3013	.1290
5	.1789	.1048	.3135	.1650
6	.1536	.0681	.2933	.2164
7	.1524	.0794	.2960	.1813
8	.1734	.0695	.3105	.1259
9	.1711	.0925	.3130	.1581
10	.1619	.0957	.2994	.1483
11	.1482	.0811	.2919	.1329
12	.1649	.0816	.3034	.1740
13	.1518	.0988	.2883	.1810
14	.1637	.0791	.3033	.1493
15	.1695	.1236	.3035	.1753
16	.1768	.0913	.3126	.1621
17	.1903	.1076	.2368	.1453
18	.1675	.1023	.2991	.1983
19	.1540	.0905	.2928	.1515
20	.1529	.0774	.2936	.2423
21	.1685	.0814	.3052	.1702
22	.1712	.0828	.3081	.1373
23	.1533	.0852	.2914	.1754
24	.1693	.0911	.3018	.1842
25	.1672	.0793	.3056	.1677
26	.1612	.0690	.3026	.1007
27	.1524	.0897	.2957	.1458
28	.1639	.0829	.2959	.1894
29	.1508	.1005	.2899	.1695
30	.1547	.0791	.2959	.1462
31	.1560	.0824	.2943	.1678
32	.1496	.0749	.2971	.1571
33	.1617	.0841	.2970	.1856
34	.1459	.0859	.2882	.1728
35	.1655	.0872	.3042	.1480
36	.1580	.0866	.2880	.2190
37	.1588	.0973	.2957	.1731
38	.1460	.0684	.2842	.2041
39	.1467	.0822	.3019	.1832
40	.1828	.1088	.3212	.1830
41	.1720	.1050	.3091	.1634
42	.1486	.0825	.2879	.1962

Forecasts of daily returns are estimated by $\hat{r}_t' = \hat{B}^{*\prime}(\hat{B}^{*}\hat{\psi}^{-1}\hat{B}^{*\prime})^{-1}\hat{B}^{*}\hat{\psi}^{-1}r_t'$. Mean is the average of squared correlations between the forecast, $\hat{r}_t$, and the realized daily return, r_t, for 30 securities in each group. Std. Dev. is the standard deviation of the squared correlation for the 30 securities in each group.

HOW WELL DOES THE MODEL FIT THE DATA?

Notwithstanding these fundamental objections to the current methodology and its analytical framework, what can we say about the other implications of the APTM and the faithfulness with which such models describe the rate of return and asset valuation mechanisms? Put otherwise, *if we consider the factor analytic approach, as practiced so far, simply as a data transformation scheme,* how well do such models fit the data? How significant are the risk premia? How close does the constant term of the equation come to the risk-free rate? Do unique measures of risk, such as own standard deviation of return, fail to add anything to the explanatory power of these models? Finally, how robust are the results claimed by the Roll and Ross methodology, relative to the size of the sample? In other words, with half the data do we get basically the same answers, or do our findings change as the size of the sample changes?

The answer to the first question is contained in Table 4. This table presents a measure of explanatory power not previously employed in the financial literature, although it is akin to the usual coefficient of correlation in multiple regression. It is designed to answer the following question: If we use the model to estimate and forecast the mean (expected) return and thus, given earnings, the price of the securities we investigate, what is the correlation between what we forecast and what, in fact, takes place within our sample? (The latter contains 2618 trading days' returns over the period July 3, 1962 through December 31, 1972.)

To obtain this measure, we use the estimated parameters, the elements of B and the c's, to "forecast" the daily returns as given in Equation (3). We then obtain, for each security, the (square) of the correlation coefficient between actual returns and predicted returns over the 10-year period. The entry that appears under "Mean" in Table 4 is actually the average of these correlation coefficients for the securities in the given group.

We notice that, if only one factor is being used to "explain" returns, the correlation is of the order of .15, which means (roughly and not precisely) that 15% of the variation in returns, or, more properly, stock price fluctuations, is "explained" by using only one

TABLE 5

SIGNIFICANCE TESTS OF STANDARD DEVIATION OF DAILY SECURITY RETURNS AS AN ALTERNATIVE HYPOTHESIS TO 5-FACTOR APT MODELS

NON-CONTEMPORANEOUS DATA: 7/12/62-12/31/72

	Statistic										
Group	$\bar{c}_0$‡ (1)	$\bar{c}_1$ (2)	$\bar{c}_2$ (3)	$\bar{c}_3$ (4)	$\bar{c}_4$ (5)	$\bar{c}_5$ (6)	$\bar{c}_6$ (7)	$t(c_0)$§ (8)	$t(c_6)$ (9)	X^2¶ (10)	Number of Observations
1	.00099*	−.02411	.00670	−.05770	.15431	−.08796	.00439	1.77	.13	5.306	415
2	.00060	−.00454	.01327	.01530	−.03833	.01432	−.00991	.84	−.30	.398	432
3	.00045	−.17124	.02814	−.12179	.03573	−.02036	.04864	.96	1.61	6.907	431
4	−.00054	−.02213	.09559	.07184	−.11728	−.04389	.02279	−.86	.53	5.704	432
5	.00015	−.09791	.09584	−.11564	.07680	−.04102	.04145	.26	1.32	7.836	429
6	.00007	.00437	.04252	.02140	.02987	.09399	.01407	.14	.35	1.386	404
7	.00089	−.04200	−.04707	−.04845	−.01184	−.10839	−.00322	1.14	−.09	5.212	428
8	.00017	−.02944	.05188	−.05772	.02201	−.00618	.01863	.30	.43	1.967	429
9	.00053	−.07900	−.08816	.01476	.08874	.04990	.00939	1.26	.28	4.987	428
10	.00034	.03434	−.02655	.05775	.06443	−.05139	−.00121	.81	−.04	3.276	425
11	.00020	−.03672	.07978	.06514	.02431	.02649	.00802	.42	.26	2.818	422
12	.00018	−.03591	.05075	.05685	.03812	−.08505	.01022	.41	.29	4.273	432
13	.00003	.12780	.12752	.05378	.04074	.10661	.00283	.07	.10	9.652†	425
14	−.00011	−.11654	.07841	.09985	−.12782	−.05442	.08869	−.21	2.10**	10.767††	428
15	−.00017	−.09831	−.01429	−.03814	.02788	−.10313	.03393	−.31	.85	5.145	426
16	.00052	−.07376	.03307	−.03441	−.15271	.01455	.01728	.90	.49	4.779	433
17	.00058	−.02186	.04008	−.09331	−.02177	−.07517	−.00294	.94	−.09	4.325	433
18	.00044	.08343	.40931	.18353	.15576	.03324	−.10599	.47	−2.26**	17.404††	432
19	−.00021	−.05289	−.02693	−.00581	.00910	−.05837	.04438	−.37	1.10	2.139	433
20	−.00129	−.03907	.03057	−.11749	−.11754	−.12559	.07009	−.22	2.10**	9.117	428
21	.00057	.06336	−.02380	−.02260	−.01822	−.01598	−.00826	1.09	−.24	2.436	424
22	.00073	−.07700	−.09576	.11271	.03082	−.17165	.02698	1.38	.68	11.874††	427
23	−.00050	−.04523	−.06315	.00428	−.02717	−.08207	.07216	−.71	1.66*	1.928	419
24	−.00069	−.07787	.11208	−.02357	.02810	.02198	.05678	−1.37	1.92*	5.660	432
25	−.00015	.04040	−.12453	.01534	−.05517	−.01148	.06603	−.23	1.34	6.495	433
26	.00189**	−.05467	.00439	−.02094	−.02889	.06853	−.05180	2.49	−.99	1.592	430
27	.00013	.05224	.02934	.07143	.11874	−.03272	−.00395	.30	.11	3.743	420
28	.00075	−.03774	.00948	.01466	.09488	.00169	−.00753	1.39	−.19	3.403	428
29	.00018	−.13478	−.13379	−.00940	.03946	.08805	.06431	.45	2.04**	10.367††	429
30	.00019	−.04442	−.02895	−.03361	−.02834	−.01248	.03596	.04	1.01	.930	434
31	.00038	.00842	.00563	−.01885	.10888	.08047	.00268	.73	.07	3.464	427
32	.00003	−.03827	.02999	−.05944	.02771	.00270	.03946	.05	1.25	1.684	422
33	.00111*	−.19078	.01458	−.02095	.04010	−.05740	.03513	1.99	.93	6.305	431
34	−.00044	−.00491	−.03774	−.07499	−.02103	.21029	.05335	−.83	1.53	10.649†	422
35	.00071	−.06688	.04559	.04169	.02055	−.00387	.02911	1.36	.89	2.303	430
36	.00098*	−.01521	−.01726	.11693	.03626	−.01267	.00765	1.90	.22	10.730†	431
37	.00074	.07372	−.03011	.04755	−.01725	.00506	−.03559	.95	−.87	1.214	433
38	.00051	−.09809	−.03131	−.06356	−.00175	−.14972	.02985	1.07	.83	9.464†	435
39	.00100	−.01016	−.14150	.03102	−.14756	.04998	−.01082	1.07	−.18	4.887	433
40	−.00004	.02641	.01499	.02034	.03701	−.01879	.00973	−.08	.32	.601	418
41	.00022	−.14077	−.14295	−.05267	−.03433	.03332	.05317	.38	1.51	10.130††	422
42	.00080*	−.12312	−.00619	.04561	.01546	−.05611	.02817	1.71	.63	3.041	431

‡ $\bar{c}_0$ through $\bar{c}_6$ are the arithmetic means of the daily cross sectional regression estimates using the GLS model $\hat{c}_t' = (B^*\psi^{-1}B^{*\prime})^{-1} B^*\psi^{-1}\tilde{r}_t'$. $B^{*\prime}$ is $[e{:}B'{:}\sigma]$ which is the augmented matrix of factor loadings with unit vector, (e), and standard deviation, σ, of the securities over the sample period:

$$\text{(i.e., for the i}^{\text{th}}\text{ security, } \sigma_i = \left[\frac{1}{T}\sum_{t=1}^{T}(\tilde{r}_{it} - \bar{r}_i)^2\right]^{1/2}\text{).}$$

c_0 is the intercept term, c_1 through c_5 are the regression coefficients for the factor loadings, and c_6 is the coefficient for the standard deviation.

§ $t(c_0)$ is the "t-ratio" for the intercept term and $t(c_6)$ is the "t-ratio" for the coefficient of the standard deviation; the "t-ratio" $\sqrt{T}(\bar{c}_o/s_o)$, where:

$$\bar{c}_o = (1/T)\sum_{t=1}^{T}\hat{c}_{to}$$

and:

$$s_o = \left[(1/T)\sum_{t=1}^{T}(\hat{c}_{to} - \bar{c}_o)^2\right]^{1/2}.$$

* and ** indicate intercept terms that are significantly different from zero at 10% and 5% levels respectively. In the case of the "t-test," this refers to a bilateral test; if a unilateral test is desired the critical points are 1.65 and 1.31 respectively for the 5% and 10% levels of significance tests.

¶ X^2 is the test statistic to test the hypothesis that none of the risk premia is priced. The test statistic is distributed as chi-square with 5 degrees of freedom. The critical values for chi-square distribution with 5 degrees of freedom at 10% and 5% significance levels are 9.24 and 11.10 respectively.

factor. When all five factors are used, this measure of "explanatory power" rises to about .3.

Thus, under the best of circumstances, such models explain about 30% of the variation in security prices. The obverse of this fact is that observed variations in security prices have a large unexplained component amounting to roughly 70% of their variation.

I leave it to the reader to decide whether this is a significant improvement over other means of predicting or forecasting security prices. One must note, however, that although 30% may appear to be a small fraction, there may exist no other means by which *in general* we would be able to predict security price variations, on the average, more accurately.

Answers to the other questions raised above are discussed in some detail in a second paper by Dhrymes et al.[3] The salient features of that work are summarized in Tables 5 and 6.

Before we discuss these tables, we note that the constant term in the expected (mean) rate of return function as estimated in the 42 groups was tested for equality with the risk-free rate; the latter was taken to be the Treasury bill rate, adjusted so as to be compatible with daily returns. The test rejects the hypothesis unambiguously. Thus, an important implication of arbitrage pricing theory turns out to be incompatible with the empirical evidence examined. Table 5 contains a number of interesting but devastating results relative to APTM, in terms of the methodology introduced in the Roll and Ross study. Here, using the Roll and Ross framework, I sought to test the hypothesis that unique risk, in terms of own standard deviation of the rate of return, plays a role in explaining rates of return. Now, arbitrage pricing theory denies this, so what I attempt here is a test of one of the major implications of APTM.

To guard against possible biases due to the correlation between means and standard deviations in such contexts, I have estimated the factor loadings and standard deviation (as well as skewness) from distinct sets of data. This accounts for the smaller number of observations, as indicated in the last column of Table 5.

Having obtained, for each trading day, estimates for the constant term, the risk premia, as well as the coefficient of standard deviation (some 400-odd such estimates), I took the average (mean) of these estimates for each group. These are the numbers that appear in columns (1) through (6). In column (1) I have the constant term; in columns (2) through (6) I have the five risk premia; finally, in column (7), I have the coefficient of (own) standard deviation.

In the case of the constant term in the 42 groups, we have only *four cases* where this coefficient is significant either at the 5% or the 10% level. Since

TABLE 6

EFFECT OF NUMBER OF OBSERVATIONS ON THE FACTOR STRUCTURE

	Number of Times Null Hypothesis is Accepted at 5% Significance Level[a]				
	k = 1	k = 2	k = 3	k = 4	k = 5
Contiguous Observations[b]					
All 2618 daily observations for entire period	0	1	11	29	36
1309 observations for first half of period	1	13	26	34	39
1309 observations for second half of period	0	9	20	32	38
First 436 observations	7	22	36	38	41
Last 436 observations	16	26	36	41	41
Non-Contiguous Observations					
Every other observation for entire period (1309 observations)	0	9	23	33	38
Every ninth observation for entire period (404-434 observations)	11	20	30	38	42

[a] Hypothesis is that k-factors generate daily security returns.

[b] Missing observations do not exceed 90 for each security for the entire period July 3, 1963 – December 31, 1972.

4 out of 42 is well within the 10% limit, it is a fair interpretation of the results to conclude that, in this framework, the constant term cannot possibly be the risk-free rate unless we are prepared to argue that the risk-free rate was zero over the period 1962-1972 in the U.S.!

Turning now to the coefficient of own standard deviation, we find it is significantly different from zero in only 6 out of 42 cases at either the 5% or the 10% level of significance. While this may appear to be evidence in favor of APTM, we shall see presently that this is, indeed, not so at all. But it is undeniable that the evidence supports the view, in this context, that unique risk measures such as own standard deviation do not help explain the process of stock valuation or their rates of return.

We now turn to the central implication of APTM — that "exposure to common risk factors" accounts for the excess of the rate of return over the risk-free rate. We have already seen that, in this framework, the risk-free rate turns out to have been zero! The sensitivity of returns to "common risk factors" is given by the risk premia coefficients. For technical reasons, explained in the paper by Dhrymes et al. (footnote 2), it is not possible to test whether the risk premia coefficients are, individually, significantly different from zero. Rather, we must test them collectively. Consequently, we are now testing, in effect, whether *at least one of the risk premia coefficients in each group is significantly different from zero.*

The results of the test are given in column (10 of Table 5). Here we see that, out of 42 groups, in only 9 do we find that at least one of the risk premia coefficients is significantly different from zero. By implication, therefore, in 33 out of 42 groups, the risk premia coefficients are *not significantly different from zero; in other words, the central implication of APTM is rejected.*

In this light, the earlier result that in only 6 out of 42 cases are unique measures of risk significant is not appreciably worse than the result we obtain with respect to risk premia. It is fair to say, therefore, that the empirical evidence in this context does not support the central implication of APTM.

Finally, we consider the last set of results in Table 6, bearing on the empirical relevance of APTM, and particularly the robustness of the results put forth by its supporters. We recall that one of the basic views held by supporters of APTM is that, at most, five "common risk" factors suffice to "explain" rates of return on risky assets. The relevant statistics in Table 6 show the following: If the entire sample is used (2618 observations), we conclude that five "common risk" factors will suffice for 36 out of 42 groups. If, however, the first half of the sample is used, then five "common risk" factors will suffice for 39 groups, while, if the last half is used, five "common risk" factors will suffice for 38 groups. On the other hand, if only the first 436 observations are used, five "common risk" factors will suffice for 41 (i.e., nearly all groups), and the same will be true if only the last 436 observations are used.

This seems to imply that, the smaller the sample, the smaller the number of "factors" we "discover," in the sense that *a given number of factors suffices for a larger set of groups for a smaller sample than for a larger sample.* I should say, however, that in view of my earlier critique of procedures that operate with small subsets of securities, it is not clear whether we are talking about the same "factors" in all groups, or whether we are simply adding apples and oranges.

I cannot make the following as a statement of fact, but I conjecture that, if Roll and Ross's initial study did not have the problem with missing observations, and had they used groups of, say, 60 securities, the prevailing view among the supporters of APTM today would be that a larger number than five "common risk factors" characterizes the rates of return on securities traded on the New York and American Stock Exchanges.

CONCLUSION

Over the past few years, a new model has been proposed for explaining the pricing of risky assets and, particularly, securities traded on major exchanges. This is the arbitrage pricing theory model (APTM), which many think has already eclipsed the standard tool of security analysts, the capital asset pricing model (CAPM). While CAPM has, indeed, many well-documented difficulties, its proposed replacement is equally plagued with ambiguities and contradictory empirical findings. If pressed to summarize the state of the current empirical evidence on the validity of APTM, one would have to say that its major implications are not supported by the evidence currently available.

Consequently, its use in pricing of securities is problematical and certainly premature. It is too early to say that the APTM as a paradigm of security pricing has failed, but it is also far too early to support its routine application in such matters. The empirical evidence, thus far, is rather murky and, given the technical difficulties in carrying out a rigorous test of this theory, it may be a long time indeed before a verdict is pronounced. The challenges an opponent can mount against APTM are enormous and prospective users ought to be careful in applying it to all the contexts in which it is held to be applicable.

APPENDIX

[1] R. Roll and S. Ross, "An Empirical Investigation of the Arbitrage Pricing Theory," *The Journal of Finance*, vol. 35, 1980, pp. 1073–1103.

[2] P. J. Dhrymes, I. Friend, and N. B. Gultekin, "A Critical Reexamination of the Empirical Evidence on the Arbitrage Pricing Theory," forthcoming, *The Journal of Finance*.

[3] P. J. Dhrymes, I. Friend, N. B. Gultekin, and M. Gultekin, "An Empirical Examination of Arbitrage Pricing Theory," forthcoming, *The Journal of Banking and Finance*.

ERRATUM

In the Casabona, Fabozzi, and Francis article published in Winter 1984 ("How to Apply Duration to Equity Analysis"), the numerator of equation (10) on page 55 should have been "1 + r" not "r". When r was defined on page 56 it should have been ".2" not ".12". The numerical illustrations that followed were correct as shown.

Journal of Banking and Finance 9 (1985) 73–99. North-Holland

AN EMPIRICAL EXAMINATION OF THE IMPLICATIONS OF ARBITRAGE PRICING THEORY

Phoebus J. DHRYMES

Columbia University, New York, NY 10027, USA

Irwin FRIEND and N. Bulent GULTEKIN

The Wharton School, Philadelphia, PA 19104, USA

Mustafa N. GULTEKIN

New York University, New York, NY 10003, USA

Received November 1983, final version received February 1984

This paper presents a comprehensive set of tests of the implications of the Arbitrage Pricing Theory. We find, unlike previously reported results, a very limited relationship between the expected returns and the covariance (factor loadings) measures of risk. Furthermore, unique variance measures of risk, while generally making only small contributions to the explanation of asset returns, turn out to be significant about as frequently as the coveriance measures of risk — which is inconsistent with the Arbitrage Pricing Theory model. The intercept tests are more mixed but provide only limited support to the model.

1. Introduction

The two key implications of arbitrage pricing theory (APT), as developed by Ross (1976, 1977) and subsequently tested by Roll and Ross (1980) and many others, are first that only covariance measures of risk (beta coefficients on different factors) are relevant to the relative pricing of risky assets, and second that the constant term or intercept in the linear relationship of expected returns on these risky assets to their covariance measures (or factor loadings) is either the risk-free rate of return or zero-beta rate.[1] These two implications characterize all modern capital asset pricing theory, including the well-known capital asset pricing model (CAPM).

This paper will present a comprehensive set of tests of both of these implications of the APT, which lead to substantially different conclusions from those drawn by RR. We find a very limited relationship between the

[1]Under certain conditions, Ingersoll (1981) argues that the intercept in the APT could be a 'zero beta' asset even though a risk-free asset exists. However, this would seem to imply that the market does price risk other than common or factor risk and that arbitrage pricing theory, unlike the CAPM, cannot explain the basic premium between risky and risk-free assets.

expected returns and the covariance measures of risk (factor loadings). Furthermore, unique variance measures of risk, while generally making only small contributions to the explanation of asset returns, turn out to be significant about as frequently as the covariance measures of risk — which is inconsistent with the APT model. The intercept tests are more mixed but provide only limited support to the APT.[2]

Before discussing in detail our tests of the covariance and intercept implications of the APT, we should note that the procedures followed in these tests, like those used in virtually all previous tests of the APT, are subject to several basic limitations in the application of factor analysis which we have described in an earlier paper [see Dhrymes, Friend and Gultekin (1983)]. As demonstrated in that paper, there is a general non-equivalence of factor analyzing small groups of securities (customarily limited by computer software to 30 or so) and factor analyzing a group of securities sufficiently large for the APT model to hold. As a result, it is found that as one increases the number of securities in the groups to which the APT/factor analytic procedures are applied, the number of 'factors' determined increases. Moreover, this increase in the number of 'factors' with larger security groups cannot readily be explained away by a distinction between 'priced' and 'non-priced' risk factors. As our earlier paper shows, it is generally impermissible to carry out tests on whether a given 'risk factor is priced' though such tests are invariably found in the standard factor analytic models used to test the APT.

It is interesting to note that just as our earlier paper found that the number of 'factors' determined increases with the number of securities in the groups to which the APT/factor analytic procedures are applied, the analysis in this paper indicates that the number of 'factors' increases with the number of time-series observations used to estimate factor coefficients.

Our paper is organized in five sections. In section 2, we briefly explain the empirical procedures. Section 3 presents the significance tests for the risk premia and for unique variance as a measure of risk. Section 4 is devoted to intercept tests, and section 5 provides summary and conclusions of our results.

2. The APT model and empirical tests[3]

The APT model, orginated by Ross (1976) and extended by Huberman

[2]The unique variance and intercept results in our APT tests are consistent with a number of previous tests of the CAPM [e.g., see Friend and Westerfield (1981), and Blume and Friend (1973)]. However, while virtually all previous tests of the CAPM find an intercept which corresponds to a zero-beta rather than risk-free rate, they differ in their implications for the relative importance of covariance and unique variance measures of risk.

[3]The APT model and its empirical implications are explained in detail in our previous paper, Dhrymes–Friend–Gultekin (1984). The APT model and empirical methodology is summarized here in order to establish our notation and to make the paper as self-contained as possible.

(1982), starts by postulating the return-generating process for securities

$$r_{t.} = E_{t.} + f_{t.}B + u_{t.}, \tag{1}$$

where $r_{t.}$ is an m-element row vector containing the observed rates of returns at time t for the m securities under consideration; E_t is similarly an m-element row vector containing the expected (mean) returns at time t. Furthermore,

$$v_{t.} = f_{t.}B + u_{t.} \tag{2}$$

represents the error process at time t, and the APT model assumes that the error process has two components: the idiosyncratic component

$$u_{t.}, \qquad t = 1, 2, \ldots$$

and the common component

$$f_{t.}B.$$

Finally, the two components are assumed to have the following properties,

$$\{u'_{t.} : t = 1, 2, \ldots\}$$

is a sequence of independent identically distributed (i.i.d.) random vectors with

$$E(u_{t.}) = 0, \qquad \mathrm{cov}(u'_{t.}, f'_{t.}) = 0 \quad \text{and} \quad \mathrm{cov}(u'_{t.}) = \Omega, \tag{3}$$

Ω being a diagonal matrix. Regarding the common component, we specify that[4]

$$\{f'_{t.} : t = 1, 2, \ldots\}$$

is a sequence of k-element i.i.d. random vectors with

$$E(f'_{t.}) = 0, \qquad \mathrm{cov}(f'_{t.}) = I. \tag{4}$$

It is a consequence of the assertions above that

$$\{(r_{t.} - E_{t.})' : t = 1, 2, \ldots\}$$

[4]Note that neither $f_{t.}$ nor B are directly observable. The specification in (4) is to eliminate this problem. B, however, is identified only up to left multiplication by an orthogonal matrix.

is a sequence of i.i.d. random vectors with

$$E[(r_{t.}-E_{t.})']=0, \qquad \mathrm{cov}\,[(r_{t.}-E_{t.})']=B'B+\Omega=\Psi, \tag{5}$$

where B is a $k\times m$ matrix and Ψ is a diagonal matrix of size m. Ross shows that, if the number of securities (m) is sufficiently large, there exists a $(k+1)$-element row vector, $c_{t.}$, such that

$$E_{t.}=c_{t.}B^*, \qquad t=1,2,\dots,T, \tag{6}$$

where

$$B^*=\begin{bmatrix} e' \\ B \end{bmatrix}, \tag{7}$$

e being an m-element column of ones.[5] The result in (6) characterizes the no-arbitrage condition of the APT model, and we can rewrite (1) with any desired degree of approximation as

$$r_{t.}=c_{t.}B^*+f_{t.}B+u_{t.}, \qquad t=1,2,\dots,T. \tag{8}$$

The empirical tests of the APT initiated first by Roll and Ross (1980) are based upon a two-step factor analytic approach. Factor analytic methods, in effect, are suggested by the formulation in (1) and the composition of the covariance matrix (5). In the first step, one determines the number of factors (k) and estimates the elements of B. If T, the number of trading days, is sufficiently large, using factor analysis we estimate B, say by $\tilde{B}$, and Ω by $\tilde{\Omega}$. We thus implicitly estimate

$$\tilde{\Psi}=\tilde{B}'\tilde{B}+\tilde{\Omega}. \tag{9}$$

In the second stage, using $\tilde{B}$ as 'independent variables', one estimates the vector $c_{t.}$, whose elements have the interpretation that c_{ti} is the 'risk premium' attached to the ith factor, $i=1,2,\dots,k$, while c_{t0} is the risk-free rate or possibly the return on a zero-beta asset. Thus in the second step for each

[5]Ross's original formulation of the APT relies on 'diversified or efficient' portfolios. Huberman (1982) provides a more precise definition of the arbitrage condition and shows that the relation in (6) is an approximation. In both approaches, one relies on the strong law of large numbers. Recently, however, a number of authors introduced models under the generic name of 'Arbitrage Pricing Model or Theory'. These authors, see for example Connor (1981) and Dybvig (1983), attempt to derive Ross's APT model in a finite economy. In doing so, however, these authors rely on much more restrictive assumptions than Ross's model. An attractive feature of Ross's model is the minimal assumptions required as in developing demand theory through revealed preferences.

t we may estimate[6]

$$\tilde{c}'_{t.} = (\tilde{B}^* \tilde{\Psi}^{-1} \tilde{B}^{*\prime})^{-1} \tilde{B}^* \tilde{\Psi}^{-1} r'_{t.}, \qquad t = 1, 2, \ldots, T. \tag{10}$$

If the underlying process is normal and if T is sufficiently large, it can be shown that (approximately)

$$(\tilde{c}_{t.} - c_{t.})' \sim N[0,(B^* \Psi^{-1} B^{*\prime})^{-1}].$$

Thus, we may view the $\{\tilde{c}'_{t.}: t = 1, 2, \ldots, T\}$, approximately, as drawings from a multivariate normal distribution with mean

$$c'_{t.}: \quad t = 1, 2, \ldots, T$$

and covariance matrix

$$(B^* \Psi^{-1} B^{*\prime})^{-1}.$$

There are two crucial testable hypotheses implied by the APT model. First, the intercept term c_{t0} in (10) is the risk-free rate.[7] Second, there is a linear relation between the risk measures embodied in B and the expected returns. As we indicated in our paper, one cannot test unambigously the 'significance' of individual risk premia but one can test unambigously the null hypothesis

$$c_t^* = 0 \quad \text{where} \quad c_{t.} = (c_{t0}, c_{t.}^*).$$

In addition to the two testable hypotheses implied by the APT model, general tests also involve the introduction of other explanatory variables and a test of the hypothesis that the corresponding coefficients are zero. The respecified model in this context is

$$r_{t.} = c_{t.} B^* + d_{t.} P + v_{t.}, \tag{11}$$

where P is a matrix of 'extraneous' variables. Recall that the restriction on empirical evidence implied by (8) is that no other (relevant) economic–financial variables have any effect on the determination of expected rates of return. This implies that $d_{t.}$ should not be significantly different from zero.

[6]In the remainder of the paper, we shall group the securities into 42 groups of 30 securities as RR did. In this context, equations should have a superscript indicating the group number. For example, (10) should be rewritten as

$$\tilde{c}_{t.}^{(i)\prime} = (\tilde{B}_i^* \tilde{\Psi}_{ii}^{-1} \tilde{B}_i^{*\prime})^{-1} B_i^* \tilde{\Psi}_{ii}^{-1} r_{t.}^{(i)\prime}, \qquad i = 1, 2, \ldots, 42.$$

We omit the group superscript for simplicity whenever there is no ambiguity.

[7]The implications of the 'zero-beta' version are discussed further in section 3.

In the next section, we investigate whether the risk premia are priced, i.e., whether $d_{t.}$ is a null vector and whether higher-order moments of returns when introduced as 'extraneous' variables as in (11) are priced. The significance tests on the intercept term c_{t0} are presented in section 4.

3. Empirical results: Contribution of covariance measures vs. unique variance to asset returns

The time series of security returns used in this paper (like RR) consists of daily returns for the July 3, 1962–December 31, 1972 period for each of 1260 New York and American Stock Exchange stocks, providing a sample size (number of observations) ranging from 2509 to 2619 daily returns per security. The first step factor analysis and the second step cross-section analysis are based on 42 groups of 30 stocks each, with the stock selection in these groups determined from an alphabetical ordering.

The results of the second step of the analysis, testing whether (any of) the risk premia are priced for the standard five-factor model used by RR and others, are shown in table 1.[8] Columns (1)–(6) show the means of the intercept term and of the vector of risk premia obtained from the 'cross-sectional' GLS regressions for each t for 42 groups separately. Columns (7) and (8) show the significance tests for the intercept term and the vector of risk premia respectively. Row numbers correspond to the forty-two 30-security groups arranged alphabetically. The test statistic for the significance test for the risk premia for each group is given by (for simplicity, we omit the group superscript below)

$$T\bar{c}^* W^{-1}\bar{c}^{*\prime} \sim \chi_5^2 \quad \text{where} \quad \bar{c}^* = \frac{1}{T}\sum_{t=1}^{T} \tilde{c}_{t.}^* \tag{12}$$

and

$$W = \frac{1}{T}\sum_{t=1}^{T} (\tilde{c}_{t.}^* - \bar{c}^*)'(\tilde{c}_{t.}^* - \bar{c}^*).$$

The test statistic is asympototically chi-square with 5 degrees of freedom. Column (8) of table 1 shows that, for the standard five-factor model used by RR and others, in only six (30-security) groups out of 42 (about 14%) is the

[8]The first stage of the analysis, i.e., the determination of number of factors and estimation of factor loadings, and the problems associated with dividing the universe of asset are discussed in great detail in our previous paper. While we carried out most of the analysis presented in this paper using one to five factor models separately, we only present the results for the five factor model for the sake of brevity and to be comparable to those results reported by RR and others for the five factor model. Most conclusions regarding a five factor model in this paper are, however, also true for one to four factor models.

Table 1

Tests of significance for intercepts and risk premia for 5-factor model using alphabetically ranked groups, 7/12/1962–12/31/1972.

Group	Statistic $\bar{c}_0$[a] (1)	$\bar{c}_1$ (2)	$\bar{c}_2$ (3)	$\bar{c}_3$ (4)	$\bar{c}_4$ (5)	$\bar{c}_5$ (6)	$t(c_0)$[b] (7)	χ^2[c] (8)	Number of observations (9)
1	0.00031	0.02906	−0.00777	−0.01885	0.01955	0.03965	1.56	1.987	2468
2	0.00033	0.01406	0.02373	0.04012	0.01230	−0.01387	1.44	2.551	2571
3	0.00015	0.02496	0.02278	0.03118	0.07034	0.04462	0.86	4.594	2568
4	0.00033	0.04338	0.00014	0.02896	0.08462	−0.07534	1.30	9.869†	2575
5	0.00022	0.05741	0.05473	0.04039	0.01538	−0.00236	0.76	6.122	2554
6	0.00046**	0.01674	0.02822	−0.01043	−0.00628	−0.07789	2.79	4.169	2405
7	0.00023	0.06399	0.04183	−0.03783	−0.04399	−0.01042	0.91	8.109	2540
8	0.00043*	0.03022	−0.04610	−0.03291	0.01554	−0.02364	1.77	4.432	2553
9	0.00043**	0.02555	−0.01606	0.02111	0.04431	0.04152	2.21	3.935	2559
10	0.00017	0.07112	0.03367	0.04216	−0.05987	−0.00789	0.70	8.859	2540
11	0.00030*	0.04828	−0.01387	0.01289	−0.03399	0.00652	1.67	4.095	2512
12	0.00022	0.01358	0.07201	−0.04364	−0.00894	0.06428	0.88	11.959††	2575
13	0.00035	−0.01068	0.04991	−0.03986	0.02182	−0.03180	1.46	4.471	2536
14	0.00015	0.09109	−0.04646	−0.01407	0.02251	0.02635	0.91	8.929	2547
15	0.00017	0.00330	0.06522	−0.03195	0.00244	0.00603	0.58	4.329	2560
16	0.00060**	−0.00024	0.09049	−0.00043	−0.02093	−0.00129	2.06	5.970	2565
17	0.00041	0.01352	0.00119	0.03840	0.00874	0.04897	1.60	2.259	2547
18	−0.00011	0.01109	0.15558	0.01691	0.05566	−0.08433	−0.29	10.737†	2416
19	0.00033	0.04910	0.01900	0.01450	−0.00472	−0.02273	1.53	2.517	2562
20	0.00024	0.03398	0.04584	0.05198	0.03330	−0.01970	1.15	4.963	2527
21	0.00041**	0.03279	−0.00245	0.03490	0.00535	−0.04920	2.20	3.588	2506
22	0.00067**	−0.01277	−0.07062	0.10889	−0.08044	0.06094	2.41	9.928†	2559
23	0.00004	0.01680	0.10448	0.04674	−0.06551	−0.08662	1.15	14.250††	2504
24	0.00028	0.02564	0.01924	0.02261	0.01928	−0.06094	1.61	3.426	2575
25	0.00018	0.04813	0.01171	−0.4854	0.02135	−0.01703	0.86	3.202	2563
26	0.00056**	0.03205	−0.07018	0.01329	0.06546	0.02552	2.48	7.448	2561
27	0.00014	0.06678	−0.00318	−0.01892	0.01963	−0.03929	0.72	5.830	2510
28	0.00046**	0.03424	−0.00961	−0.00822	0.00370	−0.07811	2.51	6.057	2561

Continued overleaf

Table 1 (continued)

	Statistic								
	$\bar{c}_0$[a]	$\bar{c}_1$	$\bar{c}_2$	$\bar{c}_3$	$\bar{c}_4$	$\bar{c}_5$	$t(c_0)$[b]	χ^2[c]	Number of observations
29	−0.00014	0.12947	−0.03723	0.06784	0.00819	0.03151	−0.50	12.022††	2544
30	0.00008	0.06412	−0.00678	0.02018	0.00510	0.02009	0.42	3.846	2545
31	0.00037*	0.03452	0.02932	−0.02035	−0.04517	−0.07711	1.67	6.574	2557
32	0.00015	0.08805	−0.02079	0.03852	−0.03136	−0.01862	0.85	7.339	2492
33	0.00031	0.03286	−0.00259	0.02204	0.01301	0.00448	1.53	0.855	2574
34	0.00064**	0.00090	−0.01326	0.05227	0.00233	−0.01953	3.04	1.976	2511
35	0.00028	0.06050	0.00472	−0.03068	0.02146	−0.09301	1.38	7.608	2546
36	0.00037*	0.01042	0.03715	−0.02369	−0.04576	−0.04488	1.85	3.265	2555
37	0.00027	0.04540	0.05001	−0.02108	−0.06003	0.04478	1.01	2.959	2076
38	0.00012	0.07880	0.03941	−0.01249	0.01153	−0.02106	0.68	6.797	2563
39	0.00011	0.07281	−0.00797	−0.02980	−0.07269	0.06763	0.38	7.304	1917
40	0.00044**	0.02028	−0.01039	0.01125	0.00507	0.06808	2.81	3.444	2508
41	0.00032	0.02727	0.03385	0.01141	0.06001	0.02950	1.61	3.476	2542
42	0.00027*	0.01926	0.04634	−0.00777	0.05096	−0.04919	1.50	5.401	2546

[a]$\bar{c}_0$ through $\bar{c}_5$ are the arithmetic means of the daily cross sectional regression estimates using the GLS model $\bar{c}'_{t.} = (\tilde{B}^*\tilde{\Psi}^{-1}\tilde{B}^{*\prime})^{-1}\tilde{B}^*\tilde{\Psi}^{-1}r'_{t.}$. $B^{*\prime}$ is $[e, B]$, which is the augmented matrix of factor loadings with unit vector.

[b]$t(c_0)$ is the 't-ratio' for the intercept term. 't-ratio' is given by $\sqrt{T}(\bar{c}_0/s_0)$, where $\bar{c}_0 = (1/T)\sum_{t=1}^{T}\tilde{c}_{t0}$ and $s_0 = [(1/T)\sum_{t=1}^{T}(\tilde{c}_{t0} - \bar{c}_o)^2]^{\frac{1}{2}}$. * and ** indicate intercept terms which are significantly different from zero at 10 and 5 percent levels, respectively. In case of a 't-test', this refers to a bilateral test; if a unilateral test is desired the critical points are 1.65 and 1.31, respectively, for the 5 and 10 percent level of significance tests.

[c]χ^2 is the test statistic to test the null hypothesis that none of the risk premia are priced. The test statistic is distributed as chi-square with 5 degrees of freedom. The critical values for chi-square distribution with 5 degrees of freedom at 10 and 5 percent significance levels are 9.24 and 11.10, respectively. † and †† indicate groups for which the null hypothesis is rejected at 10 and 5 percent levels of significance respectively.

risk premium vector 'significantly' different from zero (3 groups at the 5% level and 3 groups at the 10% level). The evidence of table 1 suggests a very substantial failure for one of the crucial implications of the APT model.Thus, just how much explanation for asset returns is afforded by the APT model in the RR context is questionable and certainly at variance with the results they present.[9]

Turning now to the question as to whether the use of the (five) factor model exhausts the 'explanation' of the factor return process, the relevant results are in table 2. Previous writers have considered the ability of unique variance to add to the explanation of asset returns provided by common factors to be a critical test of the APT [e.g., RR (1980)].

To determine whether unique variance is priced (or any other variable which is extraneous from the viewpoint of the APT), the obvious procedure which we (and others) have followed is to add that variable to the factor coefficients (loadings) to determine whether it adds in the cross-section explanation of asset returns. The rationale for pursuing this analysis, in spite of the dependence of the results of factor analysis on the size of the groups selected for analysis, is that while it is not possible to determine the true number of factors in the universe of assets from relatively small samples it may still be possible to determine the relative importance of common factors vs. unique variance or other 'extraneous' risk variables in explaining asset returns. There is at least no clear bias in favor of either the factor or other risk variables, and there is no obvious way of avoiding this complication.

In column (12) in table 2, we give the relevant statistics for testing the null hypothesis of zero-risk premia, when the factor premia are estimated in conjunction with other extraneous variables' coefficients — in this instance standard deviation and skewness of own returns. The skewness of returns has been added to these regressions as another 'extraneous' variable because of the well-known complication in estimating the relation between mean returns and standard deviation which may be caused by skewness in the returns'

[9]In the RR paper there is no counterpart to table 1, so a direct comparison is not possible. RR estimated the risk premia by $\bar{c}=(\tilde{B}^*\tilde{\Psi}^{-1}\tilde{B}^{*\prime})^{-1}\tilde{B}^*\tilde{\Psi}^{-1}\bar{r}'$, where $\bar{r}$ is the mean of rates of returns, i.e., $\bar{r}=(1/T)\sum_{t=1}^{T}\tilde{r}_t$ and use the statistic $T\bar{c}^*\bar{W}^{-1}c^{*\prime}\sim\chi_5^2$, where $\bar{W}=\tilde{B}_i\tilde{\Psi}_{ii}^{-1}[\tilde{\Psi}_{ii}-\delta_i ee']\tilde{\Psi}_{ii}^{-1}\tilde{B}_i'$ and $\delta_i=1/(e'\tilde{\Psi}_{ii}^{-1}e)$. In the RR approach, one relies heavily on the 'truth' of one's assertions relating to the distributional aspects of the cross-sectional GLS estimated coefficients. The approach we employ is more robust to departures from underlying RR procedures. We did, however, repeat the analysis presented in table 1 using the mean returns as shown above and using the test statistics employed by RR. Our results show again that risk premia are priced only in six groups. These groups, using the same group numbers in table 1, are 4, 12, 22, 23, 30 and 39. In table 1, on the other hand, groups with priced risk premia are 4, 12, 18, 23 and 29 with an overlap of three groups between the two methods. This result is again in sharp contrast to those by RR who reported that in 88.1% of the groups at least one factor is priced. Also note that the above test statistic is appropriate when there are no extraneous variables; when there are, as in eq. (11), simply replace in the bracketed equation $\tilde{\Psi}_{ii}-\delta_i ee'$ by $\tilde{\bar{\Psi}}_{ii}-P^{*\prime}(P^*\tilde{\Psi}_{ii}^{-1}P^{*\prime})^{-1}P^*$, where $P^*=(e',p')$, and p is the matrix of observations on the extraneous variables shown in eq. (11).

Table 2

Significance tests of standard deviation and skewness of daily security returns as an alternative hypothesis to 5-factor APT model, 7/12/1962-12/31/1972.

	Statistic													
Group	$\bar{c}_0$[a] (1)	$\bar{c}_1$ (2)	$\bar{c}_2$ (3)	$\bar{c}_3$ (4)	$\bar{c}_4$ (5)	$\bar{c}_5$ (6)	$\bar{c}_6$ (7)	$\bar{c}_7$ (8)	$t(c_0)$[b] (9)	$t(c_6)$ (10)	$t(c_7)$ (11)	χ_c^2[c] (12)	$\chi^2_{\sigma,k}$[d] (13)	Number of observations (14)
1	0.00001	−0.03783	−0.07908	−0.01371	−0.00420	0.01427	0.03485	0.00010	0.04	1.41	0.40	2.456	4.192	2468
2	−0.00017	0.00235	−0.00961	0.00857	−0.05965	−0.03645	0.03865*	0.00009	−0.49	1.89	0.41	2.178	5.932†	2571
3	−0.00013	0.03656	0.00776	−0.01452	0.06596	0.01809	0.02348	0.00015	−0.56	1.57	1.02	4.332	3.931	2568
4	0.00016	−0.03912	−0.02668	−0.02482	0.04715	−0.05703	0.02790*	0.00024	0.58	1.75	1.32	2.738	5.349†	2575
5	0.00009	0.00147	0.02431	−0.00108	0.00853	−0.06110	0.03392	−0.00027	0.27	1.38	−1.21	2.245	2.663	2554
6	0.00046**	0.01532	0.02302	−0.01061	−0.00669	−0.07785	0.00296	−0.00003	2.10	0.13	−0.23	3.513	0.054	2405
7	0.00007	0.03959	0.01366	−0.04117	−0.04679	0.01282	0.01653	−0.00005	0.19	0.81	−0.29	3.954	0.686	2540
8	0.00035	0.02473	−0.03681	−0.03594	0.03054	−0.02378	0.00187	0.00019	1.12	0.08	0.78	3.429	0.783	2553
9	0.00049**	0.05007	−0.00188	0.02049	0.04386	0.04296	−0.01380	0.00009	2.19	−0.83	0.88	4.573	1.041	2559
10	0.00016	0.03880	0.01806	0.03115	−0.06601	−0.00243	0.01694	−0.00019	0.57	0.87	−1.11	3.969	1.412	2540
11	0.00011	0.00515	−0.03769	0.00571	−0.03735	−0.01791	0.02288	0.00004	0.53	1.47	0.31	1.936	3.427	2512
12	0.00032	0.02547	0.10158	−0.02315	−0.00638	0.07869	−0.01650	0.00000	1.07	−0.77	0.01	9.546†	0.594	2575
13	0.00006	−0.01529	0.04487	0.00331	−0.00123	0.00330	0.00935	0.00023	0.21	0.51	1.50	1.005	4.807†	2536
14	0.00008	−0.07285	−0.05287	−0.04776	−0.03221	0.03541	0.02288	−0.00045	0.36	0.86	−1.46	6.761	2.251	2547
15	0.00017	−0.00678	0.03384	−0.04442	−0.00291	−0.00194	0.01229	−0.00007	0.58	0.61	−0.25	2.023	0.380	2560
16	0.00028	0.02331	0.05987	0.01510	−0.01345	−0.01167	−0.00049	0.00028	0.67	−0.02	1.12	1.745	1.390	2565
17	0.00047	0.03402	0.03268	0.05450	0.01245	0.05608	−0.01680	0.00022	1.53	−0.79	1.33	2.578	2.213	2547
18	−0.00073*	−0.03615	0.05279	−0.01240	−0.05942	−0.12489	0.07972**	−0.00036	−1.65	2.51	−1.39	8.416	6.311††	2446
19	0.00022	0.05679	0.02509	0.02881	−0.01251	−0.03451	−0.00182	0.00019	0.93	−0.09	1.21	2.803	1.578	2562
20	0.00004	0.02563	0.03358	0.03710	0.01617	−0.04285	0.01242	0.00014	0.15	0.78	0.73	3.753	1.350	2527
21	0.00028	0.01006	−0.02361	0.01270	0.01619	−0.05447	0.02188	−0.00017	1.29	1.40	−0.65	2.393	2.006	2506
22	0.00065*	−0.01383	−0.07108	0.10832	−0.07522	0.05933	0.00049	0.00004	1.88	0.02	0.16	6.974	0.029	2559
23	−0.00005	0.00615	0.07042	0.03423	−0.06484	−0.08953	0.01824	−0.00011	−0.21	1.08	−0.64	8.751	1.272	2504

24	0.00015	0.00961	0.01333	0.02624	0.00522	−0.04448	0.00899	0.00010	0.66	0.56	0.39	1.323	0.751	2575
25	−0.00006	0.02460	0.00649	−0.07010	−0.01240	−0.02746	0.01814	0.00006	−0.19	0.70	0.28	2.675	0.922	2563
26	0.00051	0.09075	−0.06659	−0.00845	0.10648	−0.00803	−0.02824	0.00051**	1.53	−1.02	2.10	11.349††	4.519	2561
27	0.00007	−0.02385	−0.06570	−0.03161	0.01895	−0.02430	0.03354*	−0.00001	0.32	1.87	−0.08	2.605	3.868	2510
28	0.00024	0.00765	−0.07675	−0.03080	0.00530	−0.08602	0.03259	0.00009	1.07	1.53	0.66	5.927	5.926†	2561
29	−0.00011	0.01278	−0.00711	−0.01440	0.05113	−0.01208	0.03532*	0.00001	−0.39	1.69	0.05	1.892	3.722	2544
30	−0.00016	0.03900	−0.03632	0.03584	−0.00207	−0.01693	0.01691	0.00017	−0.57	0.72	0.46	1.091	1.366	2545
31	0.00005*	−0.01467	0.00712	−0.07649	0.02892	−0.12455	0.02882*	0.00021	0.20	1.66	1.34	8.555	7.076††	2557
32	0.00007	−0.05440	0.01843	−0.00050	−0.03638	−0.01186	0.00961	0.00021	0.35	0.48	1.15	2.980	2.013	2492
33	0.00004	−0.05363	−0.07487	−0.00650	0.01200	0.07720	0.03483	0.00030	0.14	1.47	1.40	3.160	6.073††	2574
34	0.00039	−0.04330	0.01769	0.00395	0.01076	−0.02522	0.02099	0.00022	1.51	1.01	0.98	1.089	3.995	2511
35	0.00016	0.00121	−0.03797	−0.04815	−0.01024	−0.12319	0.01615	0.00026	0.55	0.62	1.07	8.427	3.541	2546
36	−0.00001	0.00225	0.02570	−0.01805	−0.02191	−0.07575	0.02822*	0.00004	−0.05	1.86	0.61	3.042	4.697†	2555
37	0.00010	0.02402	0.04291	−0.04103	−0.06405	0.05175	0.01228	0.00010	0.35	0.46	1.15	3.438	3.420	2076
38	−0.00002	0.05644	0.02344	0.00550	0.02246	−0.01185	0.01913	−0.00014	−0.09	1.10	−0.76	2.314	1.418	2563
39	0.00011	0.07328	0.00209	−0.02705	−0.08171	0.00608	−0.00272	0.00010	0.28	−0.09	0.39	7.674	0.219	1917
40	0.00024	−0.00121	−0.01832	0.00615	0.00497	0.03024	0.01898	−0.00001	0.98	1.06	−0.02	0.650	1.267	2508
41	0.00020	0.00574	0.03139	0.00415	0.05180	0.00824	0.01689	−0.00010	0.78	0.98	−0.55	1.477	1.166	2542
42	0.00023	0.01782	0.03529	−0.02173	0.04517	−0.04707	0.00405	0.00004	1.21	0.18	0.19	3.733	0.087	2546

[a] $\bar{c}_0$ through $\bar{c}_7$ are the arithmetic means of the daily cross sectional regression estimates using the GLS model $\tilde{c}_t' = (\tilde{B}^{**}\tilde{\Psi}^{-1}\tilde{B}^{**\prime})^{-1}\tilde{B}^{**}\tilde{\Psi}^{-1}r_t'$, $B^{**\prime}$ is $[e{:}B'{:}\sigma{:}K]$ which is the augmented matrix of factor loadings with unit vector, (e), standard deviation (σ), and skewness (k) of the securities over the sample period (i.e., for the ith security, $\sigma_i = [1/T\sum_{t=1}^{T}(r_{ti}-\bar{r}_i)^2]^{\frac{1}{2}}$), c_0 is the intercept term, c_1 through c_5 are the regression coefficients for the factor loadings, and c_6 and c_7 are the coefficients for the standard deviation and skewness.

[b] $t(c_0)$ is the 't-ratio' for the intercept term and $t(c_6)$ and $t(c_7)$ are the 't-ratios' for the coefficients of the standard deviation and skewness, respectively; the 't-ratio' for the ith coefficient is given by $\sqrt{T}(\bar{c}_i/s_{ii})$, where $\bar{c}_i = (1/T)\sum_{t=1}^{T}\tilde{c}_{ti}$ and $s_{ii} = [(1/T)\sum_{t=1}^{T}(\tilde{c}_{ti}-\bar{c}_i)^2]^{\frac{1}{2}}$. * and ** indicate regression coefficients which are significantly different from zero at 10 and 5 percent significance levels, respectively. In the case of 't-test' this refers to a bilateral test. If a unilateral test is desired, the critical points are 1.65 and 1.31, respectively, for the 5 and 10 percent levels of significance tests.

[c] χ_c^2 is the test statistic to test the null hypothesis that none of the risk premia is priced. The test statistic is distributed as chi-square with 5 degrees of freedom. The critical values for chi-square distribution with 5 degrees of freedom at 10 and 5 percent significance levels are 9.24 and 11.10, respectively.

[d] $\chi_{\sigma,k}^2$ is the test statistic to test the null hypothesis that c_6 *and* c_7 are not different from zero. It is distributed as chi-square with 2 degrees of freedom. The critical values for chi-square distribution with 2 degrees of freedom at 10 and 5 percent significance levels are 4.61 and 5.99, respectively. † and †† indicate the groups for which the null hypothesis is rejected at 10 and 5 percent significance levels, respectively.

distribution. In only two (out of 42) groups is the null hypothesis of zero risk premia rejected at conventional significance levels.[10]

Interestingly enough, column (13) of table 2, which gives the relevant statistics for the test that the coefficients of standard deviation and skewness are zero, shows that the null hypothesis is rejected at the 5% level in three cases (groups) and at the 10% level in five additional cases (groups). Thus, in 34 out of 42 groups standard deviation and skewness cannot be said to have any perceptible influence on the return generating process, while a similar statement can be made in forty out of forty-two groups for factor risk premia.

Overall, the implications of the test results reviewed in this section are not very favorable to the APT model. Our results, also, do not fully accord with those of RR; in testing for extraneous variables, however, they did not use a sample of contiguous days. This is not likely to explain the difference in our results but further investigation of this issue may be warranted.

To minimize the problem of 'spurious' correlation, RR order their daily returns chronologically and estimate mean returns from data for days 1, 7, 13, 19,..., factor loadings from days 3, 9, 15, 21,..., and standard deviations from days 5, 11, 17, 23,.... Following their procedure, we obtain the results presented in table 3, which indicate that the null hypothesis of zero-risk premia is rejected at the ten percent level in only nine of the 42 groups (five at the 0.05 level), while the hypothesis of no effect of own standard deviation on return is rejected in only six groups (four at the 0.05 level).[11] The moderate difference in results from table 2 may represent the use of non-contemporaneous rather than contemporaneous measures of risk and returns, the cut in the number of observations by a factor of about 85% is a reflection of the skipped dates caused by the use of non-contemporaneous measures, and the omission of a skewness variable. There are, however, some peculiarities in the results that should be noted. For example, when we use factor loadings (without the standard deviation) as independent variables using the non-contiguous observations, the risk premia are 'priced' in only six groups.[12] Similarly, when we use the standard deviation as a single inde-

[10]Incidentally, when we introduce standard deviation as the only extraneous variable, the null hypothesis that the coefficient of standard deviation is zero in the GLS regressions is rejected for 13 groups while the hypothesis that the risk premia vector is null is rejected in seven groups. It is not clear whether the changes in these results are due to the dependency among higher moments because of the deviation of the daily stock returns from normality or due to the (high) correlation among standard deviation, skewness and factor loadings when they are all used together as 'independent' variables.

[11]RR use mean returns as dependent variables instead of running the GLS cross-sectional regressions for the trading day $t = 1, 7, 13, \ldots$. If we follow this procedure and employ the test statistics shown in footnote 6, we obtain the following result: Risk premia are priced only in two groups (groups 13 and 29) while standard deviations are 'priced' in eight groups (groups 4, 14, 20, 23, 24, 29, 34 and 39).

[12]These groups generally do not correspond to the same groups with significant risk premia when we use contiguous data shown in table 1. When we use non-contiguous data, groups 13, 14, 18, 22, 34 and 36 have significant risk premia. In table 1, using contiguous data, however, groups with significant risk premia are 4, 12, 18, 22, 23, and 29.

Table 3

Significance tests of standard deviation of daily security returns as an alternative hypothesis to 5-factor APT models; non-contemporaneous data: 7/12/62–12/31/72.

	Statistic										
Group	$\bar{c}_0$[a] (1)	$\bar{c}_1$ (2)	$\bar{c}_2$ (3)	$\bar{c}_3$ (4)	$\bar{c}_4$ (5)	$\bar{c}_5$ (6)	$\bar{c}_6$ (7)	$t(c_0)$[b] (8)	$t(c_6)$ (9)	χ^2[c] (10)	Number of observations (11)
1	0.00099*	−0.02411	0.00670	−0.05770	0.15431	−0.08796	0.00439	1.77	0.13	5.306	415
2	0.00060	−0.00454	0.01327	0.01530	−0.03833	0.01432	−0.00991	0.84	−0.30	0.398	432
3	0.00045	−0.17124	0.02814	−0.12179	0.03573	−0.02036	0.04864	0.96	1.61	6.907	431
4	−0.00054	−0.02213	0.09559	0.07184	−0.11728	−0.04389	0.02279	−0.86	0.53	5.704	432
5	0.00015	−0.09791	0.09584	−0.11564	0.07680	−0.04102	0.04145	0.26	1.32	7.836	429
6	0.00007	0.00437	0.04252	0.02140	0.02987	0.09399	0.01407	0.14	0.35	1.386	404
7	0.00089	−0.04200	−0.04707	−0.04845	−0.01184	−0.10839	−0.00322	1.14	−0.09	5.212	428
8	0.00017	−0.02944	0.05188	−0.05772	0.02201	−0.00618	0.01863	0.30	0.42	1.967	429
9	0.00053	−0.07900	−0.08816	0.01476	0.08874	0.04990	0.00939	1.26	0.28	4.987	428
10	0.00034	0.03434	−0.02655	0.05775	0.06443	−0.05139	−0.00121	0.81	−0.04	3.276	425
11	0.00020	−0.03672	0.07978	0.06514	0.02431	0.02649	0.00802	0.42	0.26	2.818	422
12	0.00018	−0.03591	0.05075	0.05685	0.03812	−0.08505	0.01022	0.41	0.29	4.273	432
13	0.00003	0.12780	0.12752	0.05378	0.04074	0.01661	0.00283	0.07	0.10	9.652†	425
14	−0.00011	−0.11654	0.07841	0.09985	−0.12782	−0.05442	0.08869	−0.21	2.10**	10.767††	428
15	−0.00017	−0.09831	−0.01429	−0.03814	0.02788	−0.10313	0.03393	−0.31	0.85	5.145	426
16	0.00052	−0.07376	0.03307	−0.03441	−0.15271	0.01455	0.01728	0.90	0.49	4.779	433
17	0.00058	−0.02186	0.04008	−0.09331	−0.02177	−0.07517	−0.00294	0.94	−0.09	4.325	433
18	0.00044	0.08343	0.40931	0.18353	0.15576	0.03324	−0.10599	0.47	−2.26**	17.404††	432
19	−0.00021	−0.05289	−0.02693	−0.00581	0.00910	−0.05837	0.04438	−0.37	1.10	2.139	433
20	−0.00129	−0.03907	0.03057	−0.11749	−0.11754	−0.12559	0.07009	−0.22	2.10**	9.117	428
21	0.00057	0.06336	−0.02380	−0.02260	−0.01822	−0.01598	−0.00826	1.09	−0.24	2.436	424
22	0.00073	−0.07700	−0.09576	0.11271	0.03082	−0.17165	0.02698	1.38	0.68	11.874††	427
23	−0.00050	−0.04523	−0.06315	0.00428	−0.02717	−0.08207	0.07216	−0.71	1.66*	1.928	419
24	−0.00069	−0.07787	0.11208	−0.02357	0.02810	0.02198	0.05678	−1.37	1.92*	5.660	432
25	−0.00015	0.04040	−0.12453	0.01534	−0.05517	−0.01148	0.06603	−0.23	1.34	6.495	433
26	0.00189**	−0.05467	0.00439	−0.02094	−0.02889	0.06853	−0.05180	2.49	−0.99	1.592	430
27	0.00013	0.05224	0.02934	0.07143	0.11874	−0.03272	−0.00395	0.30	0.11	3.743	420
28	0.00075	−0.03774	0.00948	0.01466	0.09488	0.00169	−0.00753	1.39	−0.19	3.403	428

Continued overleaf

Table 3 (continued)

Significance tests of standard deviation of daily security returns as an alternative hypothesis to 5-factor APT models; non-contemporaneous data: 7/12/62-12/31/72.

	Statistic										Number of
	$\bar{c}_0$[a]	$\bar{c}_1$	$\bar{c}_2$	$\bar{c}_3$	$\bar{c}_4$	$\bar{c}_5$	$\bar{c}_6$	$t(c_0)$[b]	$t(c_6)$	χ^2[c]	observations
Group	(1)	(2)	(3)	(4)	(5)	(6)	(7)	(8)	(9)	(10)	(11)
29	0.00018	−0.13478	−0.13379	−0.00940	0.03946	0.08805	0.06431	0.45	2.04**	10.367††	429
30	0.00019	−0.04442	−0.02895	−0.03361	−0.02834	−0.01248	0.03596	0.04	1.01	0.930	434
31	0.00038	0.00842	0.00563	−0.01885	0.10888	0.08047	0.00268	0.73	0.07	3.464	427
32	0.00003	−0.03827	0.02999	−0.05944	0.02771	0.00270	0.03946	0.05	1.25	1.684	422
33	0.00111*	−0.19078	0.01458	−0.02095	0.04010	−0.05740	0.03513	1.99	0.93	6.305	431
34	−0.00044	−0.00491	−0.03774	−0.07499	−0.02103	0.21029	0.05335	−0.83	1.53	10.649†	422
35	0.00071	−0.06688	0.04559	0.04169	0.02055	−0.00387	0.02911	1.36	0.89	2.303	430
36	0.00098*	−0.01521	−0.01726	0.11693	0.03626	−0.01267	0.00765	1.90	0.22	10.730†	431
37	0.00074	0.07372	−0.03011	0.04755	−0.01725	0.00506	−0.03559	0.95	−0.87	1.214	433
38	0.00051	−0.09809	−0.03131	−0.06356	−0.00175	−0.14972	0.02985	1.07	0.83	9.464†	435
39	0.00100	−0.01016	−0.14150	0.03102	−0.14756	0.04998	−0.01082	1.07	−0.18	4.887	433
40	−0.00004	0.02641	0.01499	0.02034	0.03701	−0.01879	0.00973	−0.08	0.32	0.601	418
41	0.00022	−0.14077	−0.14295	−0.05267	−0.03433	0.03332	0.05317	0.38	1.51	10.130††	422
42	0.00080*	−0.12312	−0.00619	0.04561	0.01546	−0.05611	0.02817	1.71	0.63	3.041	431

[a] $\bar{c}_0$ through $\bar{c}_6$ are the arithmetic means of the daily cross sectional regression estimates using the GLS model $\tilde{c}'_{t\cdot} = (\tilde{B}^*\tilde{\Psi}^{-1}\tilde{B}^{*\prime})^{-1}\tilde{B}^*\tilde{\Psi}^{-1}r'_{t\cdot}$. $\tilde{B}^{*\prime}$ is $[e\colon B'\colon\sigma]$ which is the augmented matrix of factor loadings with unit vector, (e), and standard deviation (σ), of the securities over the sample period (i.e., for the ith security, $\sigma_i = [(1/T)\sum_{t=1}^{T}(r_{ti}-\bar{r}_i)^2]^{\frac{1}{2}}$). c_0 is the intercept term, c_1 through c_5 are the regression coefficients for the factor loadings, and c_6 is the coefficient for the standard deviation.

[b] $t(c_0)$ is the 't-ratio' for the intercept term and $t(c_6)$ is the 't-ratio' for the coefficient of the standard deviation; the 't-ratio' for the ith coefficient is given by $\sqrt{T}(\bar{c}_0/s_0)$, where $\bar{c}_0=(1/T)\sum_{t=1}^{T}\tilde{c}_{t0}$ and $s_0=[(1/T)\sum_{t=1}^{T}(\tilde{c}_{t0}-\bar{c}_0)^2]^{\frac{1}{2}}$. * and ** indicate intercept terms which are significantly different from zero at 10 and 5 percent levels, respectively. In the case of the 't-test', this refers to a bilateral test; if a unilateral test is desired the critical points are 1.65 and 1.31, respectively, for the 5 and 10 percent levels of significance tests.

[c] χ^2 is the test statistic to test the hypothesis that none of the risk premia are priced. The test statistic is distributed as chi-square with 5 degrees of freedom. The critical values for chi-square distribution with 5 degrees of freedom at 10 and 5 percent significance levels are 9.24 and 11.10, respectively. † and †† indicate the groups for which the null hypothesis is rejected at 10 and 5 percent significance levels, respectively. † and †† indicate the groups for which the null hypothesis is rejected at 10 and 5 percent significance levels, respectively.

pendent group, again six groups have significant coefficients.[13] On the other hand, when both factor loadings and standard deviation are included as explanatory variables, the risk premia are priced in nine groups while standard deviation is significant in six groups. The findings in table 3, therefore, do not provide much evidence to support the argument that factor loadings rather than standard deviation represent the appropriate measure of risk.

To make a more direct comparison of the results of the analysis of contemporaneous and non-contemporaneous measures of returns and risk, the regressions in table 4 include skewness as an additional explanatory variable, thus duplicating the form of the table 2 regressions. However, as in table 3, non-contemporaneous dates are used, with mean return estimated from days 1, 9, 17, 25,..., factor coefficients from days 3, 11, 19, 17,..., standard deviation from days 5, 11, 21, 29,..., and skewness from days 7, 15, 23, 31,.... Now, with eight days skipped between successive measures of return and risk, the number of observations is again reduced by about 25% from that covered by table 3 and by close to 90% from table 2. In this analysis, the hypothesis of zero-risk premia is rejected at the 10% level in only four of the 42 groups (with one group just below the 10% level) while the hypothesis of both zero standard deviation and skewness effects is not to be rejected in any group (with five groups just below the 10% level).

As we pointed out earlier, however, some care should be exercised in interpreting this set of results. For example, when we use the factor loadings as 'independent' variables in a similar fashion to the GLS regression presented in table 1 while using non-contemporaneous measures of returns as in table 4 (i.e., mean returns are estimated from days 1, 9, 25 etc. and factor loadings from 3, 11, 19, 27 by skipping eight days between successive measures of return and risk measures), we find only three groups where risk premia are 'priced': groups 4, 8 and 18. Interestingly enough, when standard deviations (estimated using the days 5, 13, 21, etc.) are used, the null hypothesis of zero-risk premia is rejected in three groups (groups 8, 17 and 18) while the hypothesis of no effect of standard deviation is rejected in two groups (groups 4 and 14).

Combining these results, there is some but not very strong evidence that both common risk factors and residual or unique risk do affect asset returns, without much basis for differentiating between the relative importance of the common and unique risk factors. There is some difference in the results based on the longer time-series of observations and contemporaneous returns and risk measures, and those based on the much smaller number of observations associated with non-contemporaneous measures of returns and risk, but it is not clear which set of results is the more reliable.

[13]These groups are 4, 13, 14, 26, 34 and 39.

Table 4

Significance tests of standard deviation and skewness of daily security returns as an alternative hypothesis to 5-factor APT models; non-contemporaneous data: 7/12/62–12/31/72.

Group	Statistic $\bar{c}_0$[a] (1)	$\bar{c}_1$ (2)	$\bar{c}_2$ (3)	$\bar{c}_3$ (4)	$\bar{c}_4$ (5)	$\bar{c}_5$ (6)	$\bar{c}_6$ (7)	$\bar{c}_7$ (8)	$t(c_0)$[b] (9)	$t(c_6)$ (10)	$t(c_7)$ (11)	χ_c^{2c} (12)	$\chi^2_{\sigma,k}$ (13)	Number of observations (14)
1	−0.00008	−0.04619	0.00425	−0.00876	0.05141	−0.03852	0.02977	−0.00023	−0.13	0.77	−0.81	0.852	1.446	312
2	−0.00048	−0.04117	−0.07897	0.09634	0.01139	−0.02757	0.02444	0.00010	−0.63	0.59	0.30	4.902	0.449	328
3	−0.00013	−0.01304	0.01808	−0.03945	−0.04506	0.04618	0.02409	0.00012	−0.21	0.68	0.71	1.413	0.937	326
4	−0.00165**	0.11777	0.03226	0.13202	0.21100	−0.12113	0.05347	0.00030	−2.51	1.60	0.96	9.687*	4.225	324
5	−0.00061	0.06664	0.00465	−0.03694	0.10578	−0.06371	0.05383	−0.00044	−0.68	1.48	−1.16	3.220	3.055	324
6	0.00041	0.03194	−0.03190	−0.06846	−0.13760	−0.07362	0.01978	0.00005	0.74	0.44	0.15	5.824	0.294	305
7	−0.00012	0.13684	0.03990	0.02068	0.11361	−0.00602	−0.01237	−0.00039	−0.17	−0.35	−1.28	4.740	2.010	318
8	0.01538**	0.10100	−0.04631	−0.15065	−0.09078	−0.25432	−0.04594	0.00046	2.17	−0.86	1.25	13.312**	1.945	324
9	0.00061	−0.06532	0.06192	0.02783	0.07496	−0.04868	0.00750	−0.00033	1.16	0.24	−1.20	4.125	1.444	325
10	0.00061	0.06904	−0.10191	0.03406	0.03583	0.06961	−0.03086	0.00017	0.87	−0.58	0.47	2.441	0.387	319
11	0.00040	0.13101	−0.01571	0.01356	0.10147	−0.11766	−0.04237	0.00043	0.61	−0.90	1.44	6.715	2.219	319
12	−0.00013	0.01798	0.06065	−0.05358	−0.15187	0.03213	0.02995	−0.00030	−0.22	0.64	−0.96	5.908	1.086	326
13	0.00011	−0.01842	0.03414	0.04750	−0.02283	0.02149	−0.00276	−0.00028	0.22	−0.10	−1.02	1.014	1.037	324
14	−0.00086	−0.02420	0.00600	−0.20458	−0.02669	−0.04640	0.06839	−0.00025	−1.63	1.64*	−0.65	7.512	3.060	324
15	−0.00004	0.09089	0.06216	0.01531	0.02127	0.12839	−0.03221	−0.00019	−0.06	−0.58	−0.53	4.263	1.064	324
16	0.00008	−0.07677	−0.10831	0.00788	−0.02945	−0.16867	0.04318	0.00030	0.11	1.14	1.04	5.045	2.153	325
17	−0.00025	0.15655	−0.04481	0.00365	0.10033	−0.15934	0.06459	0.00069	−0.34	−1.56	1.77	10.343*	4.564	321
18	0.00070	−0.12471	−0.16435	0.02881	0.01429	0.07976	0.02621	−0.00089	0.52	0.46	−1.92	10.166*	4.354	186
19	0.00000	−0.01752	0.05483	0.05131	0.09073	0.05009	−0.01578	−0.00026	0.00	−0.37	−0.82	2.877	1.553	325
20	0.00034	−0.00331	−0.00904	0.00191	−0.08533	0.00699	−0.00273	0.00007	0.45	−0.07	0.30	1.036	0.102	320
21	0.00051	−0.01681	0.01832	−0.00501	0.03339	0.07314	−0.00394	−0.00012	0.88	−0.10	−0.59	1.347	0.365	318
22	0.00039	0.06499	−0.01569	0.00563	0.07549	−0.01108	−0.04399	0.00019	0.52	−0.82	0.96	1.461	1.140	323
23	−0.00044	−0.10119	0.04108	−0.01166	0.03031	0.00147	0.03960	−0.00004	−0.65	1.06	−0.07	3.658	1.128	315
24	−0.00059	−0.06228	−0.01757	−0.05986	−0.04411	−0.04452	0.03906	0.00024	−0.94	1.01	0.45	1.703	1.179	327

25	0.00091	−0.07330	−0.00213	0.11166	−0.04898	−0.04000	−0.04826	0.00059	1.34	−1.03	1.97	4.822	4.016	325
26	0.00051	0.14328	0.06086	0.07361	0.02990	0.11212	−0.03829	−0.00012	0.67	−0.79	−0.48	4.840	1.005	322
27	0.00002	−0.14939	0.01273	0.02261	−0.09082	−0.09675	0.07225	−0.00047	0.03	1.71	−1.56	4.576	3.532	316
28	0.00005	−0.00125	−0.09576	−0.05941	0.12718	−0.07014	0.01191	−0.00009	0.09	0.32	−0.23	6.560	0.166	324
29	0.00021	0.11317	0.14355	−0.10060	0.04146	0.20776	−0.04586	−0.00011	0.45	−1.23	−0.39	8.926	1.531	321
30	−0.00024	0.00421	0.02324	−0.07133	0.02542	−0.10280	0.03537	−0.00079	−0.38	0.91	−1.82	3.054	4.001	323
31	0.00032	−0.07273	0.00911	0.04404	0.07365	−0.04567	0.02882	−0.00025	0.55	−0.11	−1.36	2.752	1.952	324
32	0.00086	−0.13213	−0.02647	−0.02951	0.00247	0.03567	0.00776	−0.00026	1.46	0.18	−0.48	2.347	0.228	313
33	0.00104	0.00044	−0.00911	−0.09850	0.01887	0.04268	0.03215	−0.00009	1.49	−0.84	−0.33	2.371	1.026	326
34	0.00054	0.06780	−0.00275	0.11000	0.01987	0.15964	0.01819	−0.00023	0.80	−0.41	−1.03	5.619	1.332	316
35[e]	It is not possible to estimate five factors													
36	−0.00009	−0.06722	−0.00949	−0.11132	0.03269	−0.10251	0.04246	0.00013	−0.15	0.90	0.45	3.603	1.371	321
37	0.00026	−0.01413	−0.14027	0.12121	−0.14495	−0.01567	0.01260	−0.00065	0.40	0.30	−1.24	7.648	1.591	261
38	0.00048	0.09599	−0.07723	0.03458	−0.04648	0.10490	−0.04151	0.00008	0.83	−1.10	0.27	5.154	1.242	324
39	−0.00002	−0.20141	0.06519	−0.12187	0.08570	−0.00921	0.05975	−0.00008	−0.03	1.24	−0.46	6.145	1.703	243
40	0.00054	0.03192	0.02794	−0.01567	−0.11384	0.03250	0.01600	−0.00017	0.98	0.51	−0.57	2.763	0.532	320
41	0.00081	−0.02393	−0.06348	−0.05060	−0.10806	0.10338	0.00334	−0.00030	1.11	0.07	−0.82	3.622	0.687	321
42	−0.00003	0.11003	−0.08287	−0.07542	0.03196	0.10678	0.04398	−0.00033	−0.06	1.22	−1.20	6.717	2.490	322

[a] $\bar{c}_0$ through $\bar{c}_7$ are the arithmetic means of the daily cross sectional regression estimates using the GLS model $\tilde{c}'_{t.}=(\tilde{B}^{**}\Psi^{-1}\tilde{B}^{**\prime})^{-1}\tilde{B}^{**}\Psi^{-1}r'_{t.}$. $B^{**\prime}$ is $[e:B':\sigma:k]$ which is the augmented matrix of factor loadings with unit vector, (e), standard deviation (σ), and skewness (k) of the securities over the sample period, i.e., for the ith security, $\sigma_i=[(1/T)\sum_{t=1}^{T}(r_{ti}-\bar{r}_i)^2]^{\frac{1}{2}}$. c_0 is the intercept term, c_1 through c_5 are the regression coefficients for the factor loadings, and c_6 and c_7 are the coefficients for the standard deviation and skewness.

[b] $t(c_0)$ is the 't-ratio' for the intercept term and $t(c_6)$ and $t(c_7)$ are the 't-ratios' for the coefficients of the standard deviation and skewness, respectively; the 't-ratio' for the ith coefficient is given by $\sqrt{T}(c_i/s_{ii})$, where $\bar{c}_i=(1/T)\sum_{t=1}^{T}\tilde{c}_{ti}$ and $s_{ii}=[(1/T)\sum_{t=1}^{T}(\tilde{c}_{ti}-\bar{c}_i)^2]^{\frac{1}{2}}$. * and ** indicate regression coefficients which are significantly different from zero at 10 and 5 percent significance levels, respectively. In the case of 't-test' this refers to a bilateral test. If a unilateral test is desired, the critical points are 1.65 and 1.31, respectively, for the 5 and 10 percent levels of significance tests.

[c] χ_c^2 is the test statistic to test the null hypothesis that none of the risk premia are priced. The test statistic is distributed as chi-square with 5 degrees of freedom. The critical values for chi-square distribution with 5 degrees of freedom at 10 and 5 percent significance levels are 9.24 and 11.10, respectively. * and ** indicate the groups for which the null hypothesis is rejected at 10 and 5 percent significance levels, respectively.

[d] $\chi_{\sigma,k}^2$ is the test statistic to test the null hypothesis that c_6 *and* c_7 are not different from zero. It is distributed as chi-square with 2 degrees of freedom. The critical values for chi-square distribution with 2 degrees of freedom at 10 and 5 percent significance levels are 4.61 and 5.99, respectively. † and †† indicate the groups for which the null hypothesis is rejected at 10 and 5 percent significance levels, respectively.

[e] Program does not converge for a 5-factor model, therefore it was not possible to estimate the matrix of factor loadings.

An even more interesting difference in results occurs when we carry out the usual kind of factor analysis, assuming a maximum of five factors as RR and many others have done, and obtain the results presented in table 5 based on the same 404–434 observations per group of stocks covered in table 3. Table 5 presents chi-square tests on one to five factors for each of the 42 groups covered. These results differ substantially from those obtained in table

Table 5

Chi-square test of the hypothesis that *k*-factors generate daily security returns.[a]

Group	$k=1$	$k=2$	$k=3$	$k=4$	$k=5$
1	453.70 (0.0473)	402.043 (0.1703)	353.742†† (0.4045)	312.763 (0.6185)	227.363 (0.7622)
2	457.293 (0.0370)	392.832 (0.2647)	333.713 (0.6998)	293.982 (0.8580)	257.117 (0.9457)
3	441.319 (0.1033)	387.114 (0.3352)	336.933 (0.6549)	292.767 (0.8691)	255.158 (0.9548)
4	419.850 (0.2950)	363.311 (0.6713)	312.867 (0.9121)	266.314 (0.9883)	231.355 (0.9975)
5	423.092 (0.2579)	374.163 (0.5171)	331.430 (0.7300)	290.551 (0.8879)	259.333 (0.9338)
6	498.343 (0.0010)	413.097 (0.0910)	351.131 (0.4429)	303.295 (0.7535)	267.543 (0.8728)
7	519.254 (0.0001)	426.983 (0.0355)	376.392 (0.1416)	325.004 (0.4271)	287.528 (0.6113)
8	490.315 (0.0023)	436.133 (0.0174)	391.226 (0.0548)	347.804 (0.1455)	306.496 (0.3104)
9	462.003 (0.0262)	406.805 (0.1317)	352.560 (0.4218)	312.926 (0.6160)	277.505 (0.7603)
10	470.477 (0.0135)	414.257 (0.0846)	366.918 (0.2328)	321.703 (0.4784)	281.716 (0.7012)
11	513.172 (0.0002)	458.534 (0.0023)	408.658 (0.0138)	363.286 (0.0519)	315.512 (0.1968)
12	583.007 (0.0001)	427.877 (0.0332)	371.846 (0.1816)	324.494 (0.4350)	278.030 (0.7533)
13	469.107 (0.0151)	415.323 (0.0791)	364.262 (0.2636)	324.473 (0.4353)	290.120 (0.5693)
14	422.381 (0.2658)	354.756 (0.7780)	300.538 (0.9687)	264.465 (0.9906)	228.555 (0.9984)
15	483.943 (0.0042)	402.347 (0.1677)	249.639 (0.4652)	309.479 (0.6678)	269.182 (0.8572)
16	413.160 (0.3790)	368.261 (0.6025)	323.222 (0.8256)	278.680 (0.9576)	242.120 (0.9891)
17	466.258 (0.0190)	402.390 (0.1673)	347.936 (0.4909)	308.706 (0.6791)	270.165 (0.8473)
18	483.016 (0.0046)	424.365 (0.0430)	378.034 (0.1287)	337.613 (0.2511)	296.657 (0.4619)
19	437.856 (0.1255)	375.290 (0.5006)	331.702 (0.7265)	296.328 (0.8348)	255.297 (0.0541)
20	790.796 (0.0001)	413.251 (0.0901)	330.028 (0.7479)	282.079 (0.9425)	249.456 (0.9746)

Table 5 (continued)

Group	$k=1$	$k=2$	$k=3$	$k=4$	$k=5$
21	563.209	485.505	416.897	367.379	315.921
	(0.0001)	(0.0001)	(0.0065)	(0.0379)	(0.1924)
22	412.645	353.812	307.047	268.916	236.094
	(0.3858)	(0.7885)	(0.9443)	(0.9843)	(0.9951)
23	454.095	399.254	354.161	318.036	281.903
	(0.0462)	(0.1962)	(0.3984)	(0.5362)	(0.6984)
24	467.248	407.925	349.453	305.851	272.172
	(0.0175)	(0.1237)	(0.4680)	(0.7194)	(0.8258)
25	490.444	421.278	361.323	315.734	279.839
	(0.0023)	(0.0534)	(0.3002)	(0.5724)	(0.7283)
26	542.929	479.078	422.721	367.148	315.920
	(0.0001)	(0.0002)	(0.0037)	(0.0386)	(0.1924)
27	521.078	431.653	360.941	307.578	266.674
	(0.0001)	(0.0249)	(0.3051)	(0.6953)	(0.8806)
28	481.667	423.573	369.595	317.919	277.105
	(0.0052)	(0.0455)	(0.2040)	(0.5381)	(0.7656)
29	476.338	420.528	370.799	322.841	279.254
	(0.0083)	(0.0562)	(0.1918)	(0.4606)	(0.7365)
30	463.798	408.864	360.331	315.609	274.218
	(0.0229)	(0.1172)	(0.3131)	(0.5744)	(0.8020)
31	507.081	438.487	380.113	341.525	304.734
	(0.0004)	(0.0144)	(0.1138)	(0.2062)	(0.3359)
32	521.824	443.379	381.277	338.363	296.901
	(0.0001)	(0.0094)	(0.1060)	(0.2421)	(0.4580)
33	486.613	413.938	357.909	309.374	269.358
	(0.0033)	(0.0863)	(0.3456)	(0.6693)	(0.8555)
34	436.848	377.064	327.255	291.020	248.496
	(0.1326)	(0.4748)	(0.7815)	(0.8841)	(0.9771)
35	420.554	339.520	291.750	251.937	223.479
	(0.2867)	(0.9117)	(0.9872)	(0.9983)	(0.9993)
36	403.948	351.977	309.968	273.635	240.091
	(0.5054)	(0.8081)	(0.9295)	(0.9740)	(0.9916)
37	473.172	407.247	365.407	318.935	285.446
	(0.0108)	(0.1285)	(0.2501)	(0.5221)	(0.6443)
38	495.461	438.274	385.492	337.585	291.758
	(0.0014)	(0.0146)	(0.0810)	(0.2515)	(0.5424)
39	467.352	412.639	369.170	329.619	298.123
	(0.0174)	(0.0936)	(0.2084)	(0.3581)	(0.4382)
40	577.196	488.062	421.972	369.508	275.786
	(0.0001)	(0.0001)	(0.0040)	(0.0320)	(0.7827)
41	489.261	421.790	373.552	327.893	283.900
	(0.0026)	(0.0515)	(0.1658)	(0.3835)	(0.6683)
42	440.180	370.691	321.550	275.815	242.491
	(0.1102)	(0.5676)	(0.8422)	(0.9677)	(0.9886)
Number of times the null hypothesis is accepted at 5% significance level					
	11	20	30	38	42

[a]Number of degrees of freedom for the chi-square test for each group is $\frac{1}{2}[(30-k)^2-30-k]$. Number of securities in each group is 30. Number of observations for each security is 434. No security has more than 110 missing observations. Values in parentheses indicate the p-value associated with the statistic, i.e., the probability that the test statistic (under the null hypothesis) will assume a value at least as large as the statistic obtained in this particular test.

1 of our earlier paper based on 2618 observations. It should be pointed out, as noted in our earlier paper, that with 2618 observations we find a larger number of groups for which the five-factor decomposition is inadequate than do RR, which may be attributable either to the very large number of missing observations for some securities in the RR sample or to the greater precision of our computer software (SAS) or both. However, in any case, in a recent independent analysis, Cho, Elton and Gruber (1982) found results similar to ours.

The sensitivity of the factor results to the number of time-series observations used to estimate mean returns and the different risk measures for each stock included in the analysis is indicated by the tabulation below which shows the number of times (out of 42) that the null hypothesis of at most k (1–5) factors is accepted at the 5% significance level based on 404–434 non-contiguous observations contrasted with the number of times for 2618 contiguous observations. (The non-contiguous observations cover the same time period as the contiguous observations but include only data for days 1, 7, 13, 19... or roughly one-sixth of the total number of daily observations.)

Number of times null hypothesis is accepted at 5% significance level.

	$k=1$	$k=2$	$k=3$	$k=4$	$k=5$
404–434 non-contiguous observations	11	20	30	38	42
2618 contiguous observations	0	1	11	29	36

Obviously, more factors are indicated by the analysis based on the larger number of observations. The reason for this disparity in results is not clear but one possible explanation is that sampling error is so large that only with a very large number of observations can we adequately cope with it.[14] Another possible explanation is the type of stationarity assumption implicit in the estimations of factors from two different sets of days. The stationarity assumption is likely to be a less important basis for explaining the difference in results than the size of the sample of observations because both sets of days cover the same overall period. A more definitive determination of the

[14]It might also be noted that the number of Heywood cases (i.e., degenerate cases where one of the 'factors' is perfectly correlated with a security) increases to 22 groups when factor loadings are estimated from non-contiguous data, resulting in the major reduction in the number of observations. When we use all 2618 contiguous observations, we encounter 11 Heywood cases. In order to avoid Heywood cases, we substituted new securities whenever a Heywood case appeared. Results presented so far are materially the same whether one includes the Heywood cases in the regressions or not. Also note that there are no Heywood cases when one extracts only one factor and the number of Heywood cases are far fewer with a smaller number of factors extracted.

relative importance of these two different explanations is provided by the summary data in table 6, which presents an analysis of the number of factors obtained from daily observations covering (1) every other day for the entire period, (2) every day in the first half of the period, (3) every day in the second half of the period, (4) the first 400 or so days in the period, and (5) the last 400 or so days in the period. Clearly, as the number of observations increases from 400 to 1309 to 2618, the number of 'factors' estimated increases markedly. Even with a sample of observations as large as 1309, the number of 'factors' is appreciably lower than with 2618 observations. On the other hand, with the number of observations held constant, the time period covered seems to have less influence on the number of factors estimated. The results are as sensitive to the number of observations used in estimating mean returns and risk as they are to the number of securities used in each group (the latter having been shown in our earlier paper [DFG (1984)].

Table 6
Effect of number of observations on the factor structure.

	Number of Times null hypothesis is accepted at 5% significance level[a]				
	$k=1$	$k=2$	$k=3$	$k=4$	$k=5$
Contiguous observations[b]					
All 2618 daily observations for entire period	0	1	11	29	36
1309 observations for first half of period	1	13	26	34	39
1309 observations for second half of period	0	9	20	32	38
First 436 observations	7	22	36	38	41
Last 436 observations	16	26	36	41	41
Non-contiguous observations					
Every other observation for entire period (1309 observations)	0	9	23	33	38
Every ninth observation for entire period (404–434) observations)	11	20	30	38	42

[a]Hypothesis is that k-factors generate daily security returns. See table 5 for further explanation of this table.

[b]Missing observations do not exceed 90 for each security for the entire period July 3, 1963–December 31, 1972.

3. Testing the intercept in the cross-section APT pricing relationship

Another important implication of the APT, which it shares with other capital asset pricing models, is that the 'constant' term in the relation

$$r_{t.} = c_{t.}B^* + f_{t.}B + u_{t.},$$

i.e., the term c_{t0}, corresponds to the risk-free rate, or at least a zero beta asset. As we pointed out in our earlier paper, the operational procedure for obtaining $c_{t.}B^*$ is time invariant, which would argue strongly that $c_{t.}$ is time invariant. In turn this could imply that the 'risk-free' rate is also time invariant — which is rather far-fetched and questionable. Despite this and the other reservations expressed earlier regarding the testability of the APT, we proceeded to carry out a test of this particular set of implications. We felt it particularly appropriate since RR and others carry out a test on the equality of intercept terms for adjacent groups only, instead of a test on equality of intercept terms for all groups.

Recall from the last section that once the matrix B_i of factor loadings for the ith group has been estimated on the basis of a five-factor model, we obtain GLS estimators by

$$\tilde{c}_{t.}^{(i)\prime} = (\tilde{B}_i^* \tilde{\Psi}_{ii}^{-1} \tilde{B}_i^{*\prime})^{-1} \tilde{B}_i^* \tilde{\Psi}_{ii}^{-1} r_{t.}^{(i)\prime}, \qquad i = 1, 2, \ldots, 42, \tag{13}$$

where

$$\tilde{B}_i^* = \begin{bmatrix} e' \\ \tilde{B} \end{bmatrix}, \qquad \tilde{\Psi}_{ii} = \tilde{B}_i' \tilde{B}_i + \tilde{\Omega}_i, \qquad t = 1, 2, \ldots, T.$$

If daily returns are normal and if the sample size T on the basis of which $\tilde{B}_i$ and $\tilde{\Omega}_i$ are estimated is large — which it is in the present context — then we would expect that, approximately,

$$\tilde{c}_{t.}^{(i)\prime} \sim N[c_{t.}', (\tilde{B}_i^* \tilde{\Psi}_{ii}^{-1} \tilde{B}_i^{*\prime})^{-1}]. \tag{14}$$

The important thing to realize here is that the covariance matrix is time invariant. Hence, we can treat the $\tilde{c}_{t.}^{(i)}$ as 'observations' from a population with mean $c_{t.}$ and a constant covariance matrix. Hence, defining

$$z_{t.}^{(i)} = \tilde{c}_{t.}^{(i)} - \tilde{c}_{t.}^{(1)}, \qquad i = 2, 3, \ldots, 42 \tag{15}$$

we have that under the APT model, approximately,

$$z_{t.}^{(i)\prime} \sim N(0, K_{ii}), \tag{16}$$

where K_{ii} is an appropriate time invariant covariance matrix. Extracting the first element therefore, we find

$$z_{t0}^{(i)} \sim N(0, K_{00,i}), \qquad i = 2, 3, \ldots, 42.$$

In general, $z_{t0}^{(i)}$ is correlated with $z_{t0}^{(j)}$ but their covariance is also time invariant. Thus, let

$$z_{t0}^{*}=(z_{t0}^{(2)},z_{t0}^{(3)},\dots,z_{t0}^{(42)})$$

and observe that

$$z_{t0}^{*\prime}\sim N(0,Q_0),$$

where Q_0 is an appropriate time invariant covariance matrix. Clearly we can estimate the mean vector and covariance matrix by

$$\bar{z}_0^{*\prime}=\frac{1}{T}\sum_{t=1}^{T}z_{t0}^{*\prime},\qquad \tilde{Q}_0=\frac{1}{T}\sum_{t=1}^{T}(z_{t0}^{*\prime}-\bar{z}_{t0}^{*\prime})(z_{t0}^{*}-\bar{z}_0^{*}) \tag{17}$$

and employ the test statistic

$$T\bar{z}_0^{*}\tilde{Q}_0^{-1}\bar{z}_0^{*\prime}\sim\chi_{41}^{2} \tag{18}$$

to test the hypothesis that the intercepts of the 42 groups are equal.[15]

In this instance, the test statistic turns out to be

$$T\bar{z}_0^{*}\tilde{Q}_0^{-1}\bar{z}_0^{*\prime}=34.4$$

and thus the hypothesis is accepted. This accords with the results of RR who interpret this finding as an endorsement of the APT model. In this connection we should point out that applying the same tests for the equality of constant terms in a one-factor model yields the statistic

$$\chi_{41}^{2}=43.30$$

which similarly implies acceptance. The same conlusion is reached when we use a two, three or four factor model.

Now acceptance of such a hypothesis while confirming an implication of the APT model does not tell us very much; for example, this hypothesis would be accepted even if all or nearly all intercepts were zero. Such a situation would cast some doubts on the usefulness of the APT. Thus, next we tested the hypothesis that all intercepts are zero. This is done through the statistic

$$Tc_0^{*}W_0^{-1}\bar{c}_0^{*\prime}\sim\chi_{42}^{2}, \tag{19}$$

[15]Note that the mean of the daily regression coefficients $c_t^{(i)}$ can easily be estimated using mean return data. If one strictly relies on the model and assumes time stationarity, one can also obtain the covariance matrix of the estimators from mean returns. We have chosen to work with the daily regression coefficients, however, since this represents a procedure that is more robust to departures from stationarity.

where

$$\bar{c}_0^* = (\bar{c}_0^{(1)}, \bar{c}_0^{(2)}, \dots, \bar{c}_0^{(42)}), \qquad \bar{c}_0^{(i)} = \frac{1}{T}\sum_{t=1}^{T} \tilde{c}_{t0}^{(i)}, \tag{20}$$

$$\tilde{W}_0 = \frac{1}{T}\sum_{t=1}^{T} (\tilde{c}_{t0}^* - \bar{c}_0^*)'(\tilde{c}_{t0}^* - \bar{c}_0^*), \qquad \tilde{c}_{t0}^* = (\tilde{c}_{t0}^{(1)}, \tilde{c}_{t0}^{(2)}, \dots, \tilde{c}_{t0}^{(42)}). \tag{21}$$

The test statistic in this case is

$$T\bar{c}_c^* \tilde{W}_0^{-1} c_0^{*\prime} = 67.8$$

and thus, the hypothesis is rejected.[16]

However, rejection of such a hypothesis only means that there is at least one coefficient which can be said to be non-zero. To clarify this issue, we examine table 1, which gives the mean intercepts and the corresponding 't-ratios' in the 42 groups. Even a casual perusal of the table shows that at the 0.1 level of significance only 13 of the intercepts can be said to be non-zero with a bilateral test. Using a unilateral test we find 24 'significant' intercepts. Thus, we are not really violating the meaning of the empirical evidence if we state that at best (from the point of view of the APT model) the evidence is ambiguous and at worst that one of the implications of the model is contradicted by the empirical envidence. The (mean) risk free rate computed from the 7th root of weekly Treasury Bill rates is clearly positive and its standard deviation does not support the hypothesis of a zero daily risk free rate. In fact, the mean weekly rate on Treasury Bills over this period is 0.00084166 with standard deviation 0.0002344, which is clearly significantly different from zero. The associated mean daily rate computed as the 7th root of one plus the weekly rate minus one is 0.0001204 and is also significantly different from zero.

We also test directly the hypothesis that the intercept is the risk-free rate using the weekly T-bill rate. The test is identical to the one in eq. (15) except we redefine $z_t^{(i)}$.

$$z_{t0}^{(i)} = \tilde{c}_{t0}^{(i)} - \tilde{r}\tilde{f}_t, \qquad i = 1, 2, \dots, 42,$$

where $\tilde{r}\tilde{f}_t$ is the seventh root of the (one plus) weekly Treasury bill yield observed every Thursday. In this formulation, we assume that the seventh root of the T-bill yield observed on a Thursday is the daily yield on

[16]Since most readers are most familiar with the normal distribution, one may use the normal approximation $(\chi_r^2 - r)/\sqrt{2r} \sim N(0,1)$ This would yield, in the present instance, $(67.8-42)/\sqrt{82} = 2.8$, while in the previous case we have $(34.4-41)/\sqrt{82} = -0.72$. Thus, in the first case we reject and in the second case we accept at the 10% significance level.

Thursday and the next four trading days.[17] This assumption is the least objectionable when one considers the alternatives. There is no clear way of choosing a daily risk-free rate among observable daily rates, such as Federal Funds rates, daily *T*-bill rates, etc. We decide against using daily *T*-bill rates because of the serious measurement errors. Testing directly the hypothesis that the intercept is the risk-free rate when the weekly *T*-bill rate is used for this purpose, we reject this hypothesis. The test statistic, χ^2_{42}, in this case is 48.87.

We also test the same hypothesis by comparing the seventh root of the (one plus) *T*-bill yield on every Thursday with the intercept term for the same day to avoid the assumption that *T*-bill rates are constant for a week. This procedure results in a smaller number of observations (one fifth of the previous case). We reject the hypothesis in this case as well ($\chi^2_{42} = 51.62$).

This result is quite similar to that generally found in tests of the CAPM, where it has generally been concluded that a zero-beta must be substituted for the risk-free rate to explain the empirical results. However, it should be noted that the zero-beta is not a very satisfactory substitute for the risk-free rate since it is simply a statistical construct until economic theory is brought to bear on its meaning. To a substantial extent, this has been done for the CAPM which has been reformulated theoretically to adjust in a statistically testable manner for the effects of inflation and other variables (e.g., human wealth, differences in lending and borrowing rates, etc.), which would be expected to affect the relation between returns and risk, including the intercept. This has not been done for the APT and it is difficult to see how it could be. It is, in any case, not clear how much importance one should attribute to the intercept test results even if they are consistent with a zero-beta version of the APT model since the risk premia vector has empirically been shown in the previous section to yield few significant results.

4. Conclusions

In a previous paper, we pointed out that the factor analytic procedures which have been used to test the APT are seriously flawed for a number of reasons, including notably the dependence of the number of 'factors' found on the number of assets included in the group which is factor-analyzed and the inability to directly test whether a given 'factor' is priced. As a by-product of the present paper, which attempts to test the two key implications of the APT — the irrelevance of unique variances (and other variables uniquely affecting a particular asset) to the explanation of asset returns, and

[17] To be precise, the *T*-bill yield is measured every Thursday on a *T*-bill which matures on the next Thursday. This yield is compared with the intercept terms estimated for Thursday and for the four trading days following the Thursday on which we measure the *T*-bill yield (i.e., Friday, Monday, Tuesday and Wednesday).

the risk-free or zero-beta interpretation of the intercept in the cross-section mean return-risk relationships, we have found that the number of factors determined is a positive function not only for the number of assets factor-analyzed but also of the number of observations used to estimate mean returns and risk. These basic problems create doubt on the testibility of the APT by proper econometric procedures given the present state of the literature.

Setting aside these basic objections, we adopted the general methodology used in previous empirical tests of the APT and sought through more extensive statistical analysis to test one of the important implications of the model, viz., that the intercept terms $c_{t0}^{(i)}$ are, on average, the same in all groups which would be true if the intercepts were either the risk-free or zero-beta rates of return. This implication is not rejected by the empirical evidence; on the other hand, the same evidence suggests that on average $c_{t0}^{(i)}$ is insignificantly different from zero for most groups. This, of course, runs contrary to the interpretation the APT model places on this coefficient. Moreover, these intercepts are significantly different from the risk-free rate interpreted as the appropriate Treasury Bill rate.

Second, and more importantly, we find that the risk premia vector is not significant in most groups (at least 36 out of 42), indicating a lack of linear relationship between the expected rates of return and the measures of risk parameters implied by the APT model. Furthermore, when (own) standard deviation or (own) standard deviation and skewness are introduced into the asset-return function, they turn out to be 'significant' as frequently as the factors suggested by RR and other authors, although generally yielding insignificant coefficients. We conclude that the evidence on the usefulness of the APT model is at best mixed. Further work and a different methodology is needed to probe more deeply into its implications.

References

Blume, Marshall E. and Irwin Friend, 1973, A new look at the capital asset pricing model, Journal of Finance, March.

Cho, C. Chinlyring, Edwin J. Elton and Martin J. Gruber, 1982, On the robustness of the Roll and Ross APT methodology, unpublished manuscript (Graduate School of Business Administration, New York University, NY).

Connor, Gregory, 1981, Asset prices in a well-diversified economy, Working paper (School of Organization and Management, Yale University, New Haven, CT).

Dhrymes, Phoebus J., Irwin Friend and N. Bulent Gultekin, 1984, A critical reexamination of the empirical evidence on the arbitrage pricing theory, Journal of Finance 39, no. 2, 323–346.

Dybvig, Philip, 1983, An explicit bound on individual assets' deviation from APT pricing in a finite economy, forthcoming in Journal of Financial Economics.

Friend, Irwin and Randolph Westerfield, 1981, Risk and capital asset prices, Journal of Banking and Finance 5, no. 3, 291–315.

Huberman, Gur, 1982, A simple approach to arbitrage pricing theory, Journal of Economic Theory 28, no. 1, 133–151.

Ingersoll, Jonathan E., Jr., 1981, Some results in the theory of arbitrage pricing, unpublished manuscript (Graduate School of Business, University of Chicago, Chicago, IL).

Roll, Richard and Stephen A. Ross, 1980, An empirical investigation of the arbitrage pricing theory, Journal of Finance 35, Dec., 1073–1103.

Ross, Stephen A., 1976, The arbitrage theory of capital asset pricing, Journal of Economic Theory 13, Dec., 341–360.

Ross, Stephen A., 1977, Return, risk and arbitrage, in: Irwin Friend and James L. Brickler, eds., Risk and return in finance (Ballinger, Cambridge, MA).

THE JOURNAL OF FINANCE • VOL. XL, NO. 3 • JULY 1985

New Tests of the APT and Their Implications

PHOEBUS J. DHRYMES, IRWIN FRIEND, MUSTAFA N. GULTEKIN, and N. BULENT GULTEKIN*

ABSTRACT

This paper provides new tests of the arbitrage pricing theory (APT). Test results appear to be extremely sensitive to the number of securities used in the two stages of the tests of the APT model. New tests also indicate that unique risk is fully as important as common risk. While these tests have serious limitations, they are inconsistent with the APT.

IN THIS PAPER, WE report on a number of new tests on the empirical relevance of the arbitrage pricing theory (APT). These tests address more comprehensively the question of stationarity, i.e., the ability of risk measures from one period to "explain" returns in another, as well as other issues we have raised in our previous work. Thus, in Dhrymes et al. [1] and Dhrymes et al. [2], we have shown that there is a general nonequivalence between factor-analyzing small groups of securities and factor-analyzing groups of securities sufficiently large for the APT to hold. As one increases the number of securities to which the factor-analytic procedures are applied, the number of factors "discovered" increases, and this result cannot be readily explained by a distinction between "priced" and "non-priced" risk factors; in addition, we have also shown that it is generally impermissible to perform tests on whether a given risk factor is "priced," although such tests are invariably found in the standard factor-analytic literature used to test the APT.

Abstracting from the basic conceptual and empirical limitations of the factor-analytic techniques used to test the APT, our prior analysis performed comprehensive tests of the two key implications of APT—those relating to: (1) the irrelevance of *unique* (variance or standard deviation) *as contrasted with common* (covariance) measures of risk in the pricing of risky assets and (2) the risk-free or zero-beta rate of return interpretation of the constant term or intercept in the (linear) expected return function. Overall, the results obtained are, in large part, inconsistent with the APT model.

In a response to our recent findings, Roll and Ross [4] argue that the relevant point in tests of the APT is not the number of factors found (through factor analysis) but whether these factors are priced in the second stage of the tests. They claim that since a number of factors found to be *significant in the first-stage time-series analysis of individual securities are not significant in the second-stage* cross-return analysis across securities, it is quite likely that these factors are not "priced," and thus the number of "priced" factors might still be invariant to the number of securities factor-analyzed.

* Columbia University, University of Pennsylvania, and New York University, respectively.

In this paper, we have repeated for much larger groups of securities the usual two-stage procedures used by Roll and Ross [5] and other authors, and we find that the number of "priced" factors rises with the size of the group of stocks being factor-analyzed. As we have argued in our previous work, this procedure lacks rigor in that tests of significance on individual risk premia are invalid in this factor-analytic context. Nonetheless, we perform these tests so as to examine the issues raised in our earlier work, and, also, to appraise the response to it in the context advocated by Roll and Ross and those who follow their lead. What we find is that, abstracting from these problems, the number of "priced" factors *is not invariant* to the number of securities factor-analyzed; similarly, *most* of the factors extracted (from the first stage) appear to be "insignificant" at the second stage. The general tenor of our findings is that, as we increase the number of securities in each group, both the number of factors "discovered" at the first stage as well as the number of "priced" factors at the second stage increase, although most factors are not "priced." Needless to say, these findings do not constitute evidence favorable to the empirical relevance of APT.

In addition to updating our earlier results, we further expanded our analysis to pursue several new lines of inquiry, using data over the period July 3, 1962 to December 31, 1981. Three other new results seem worth mentioning. First, when factors (and unique or total standard deviation) estimated from one-half of the period are used to explain returns from the other half, unique or total standard deviation performs as well as or better than the factor loadings. Second, when the number of time-series observations used by us (and earlier writers) to derive the relevant number of factors is increased (nearly doubled), the number of factors discovered also increases; this is consistent with the results we obtained in our earlier work when we broke the period originally covered into two subperiods. Third, tests on the constant term or intercept seem to depend both on the number of observations and the group size of securitiess factor-analyzed.[1]

I. The APT Model and Updating Our Earlier Empirical Tests

The APT model of Ross (1976) starts with the return-generating process for securities

$$r_{t.} = E_{t.} + f_{t.}B + u_{t.}, \tag{1}$$

where $r_{t.}$ is an m-element row vector containing the observed rates of return at time t for the m securities. $E_{t.}$ is an m-element row vector containing the expected (mean) returns, while $f_{t.}$ is a k-element vector of common (but unobservable) factors affecting security returns, both at time t. B is a $k \times m$ matrix of parameters, indicating the sensitivity of securities to the common factors. $u_{t.}$ is the idiosyncratic component of the error term. Ross shows that if the number of securities (m) is sufficiently large, there exists a $(k + 1)$-element row vector $c_{t.}$ such that

$$E_{t.} = c_{t.}B^*, \quad t = 1, 2, \ldots, T, \tag{2}$$

[1] Due to space limitation, most of our results are summarized briefly. A working paper with more detailed results is available from the authors.

where $B^{*\prime} = [e{:}B']$ and e is an m-element column of ones. The empirical tests of the APT model are based upon a two-stage factor-analytic approach.

In the first step, one determines the number of factors (k) and estimates the elements of B, denoted by $\tilde{B}$. In the second stage, using (the rows of) $\tilde{B}$ as "independent variables," one estimates the vector $c_{t\cdot}$, whose elements have the interpretation that c_{ti} is the "risk premium" attached to the ith factor $i = 1, 2, \ldots k$, while c_{t0} is the risk-free rate (or possibly the return on a zero-beta asset). One estimates, at the second stage, the vector $c_{t\cdot}$ by GLS methods as

$$\tilde{c}'_{t\cdot} = (\tilde{B}_* \tilde{\Psi}^{-1} \tilde{B}^{*\prime})^{-1} \tilde{B}_* \tilde{\Psi}^{-1} r'_{t\cdot}, \quad t = 1, 2, \ldots, T. \tag{3}$$

There are two critical testable hypotheses implied by the APT model. First, the intercept term in (3) is the risk-free (or zero-beta) rate. Second, the risk premium vector is not null. In addition to these two hypotheses above, one could also test the APT model alternatively by introducing other explanatory variables in the model implied by (1) and (2). The restriction on empirical evidence implied by APT is that no other (relevant) economic/financial variables should have any effect on the determination of expected rates of return.

The data in this paper consist of daily stock returns from the CRSP tapes for the July 3, 1962 to December 31, 1981 period. Securities with more than 100 missing observations are deleted. This resulted in 900 New York and American Stock Exchange stocks, providing a sample size (number of observations) ranging from 4793 to 4893 daily returns per security. We rank these securities alphabetically to form groups of 30, 60, and 90 securities each.

The results of the first-stage factor-analysis tests are summarized in Table I for the entire sample period and two equal half-periods; we do this separately for each of the three different group sizes. As showed in our earlier papers, *the number of factors determined increases as both the number of observations and number of securities increase.* We determine a 5-factor model for groups of 30

Table I

χ^2 Tests of the Hypothesis That k-Factors Generate the Daily Stock Returns—Summary Results (Number of Times the Null Hypothesis is Accepted at 5% Level)

		No. of Factors for		No. of Groups with Significant χ^2 Value		
Group Size	No. of Groups (1)	Half-Periods (2)	Entire Period (3)	First Period (4)	Second Period (5)	Entire Period (6)
30 stocks	30	5	7	24 (80%)	9 (30%)	24 (80%)
60 stocks	15	8	11	9 (60%)	1 (7%)	6 (40%)
90 stocks	10	13	17	7 (70%)	1 (10%)	5 (50%)

Note: The first half-period covers July 3, 1962 to April 23, 1972, the second half-period covers April 24, 1973 to December 31, 1981, and the entire period is July 3, 1962 to December 31, 1981. Groups are formed from alphabetically ranked 900 securities from the daily CRSP tapes. Each group is then factor-analyzed. The number of groups in columns (4), (5), and (6) indicate that k-factor-generating models shown in columns (2) and (3) for the half- and entire periods, respectively, are adequate at 5% level, i.e., that χ^2 values are significant at 5% level for this many groups out of total number of groups shown in column (1). Figures in parentheses show percent of groups with significant χ^2 in each set.

stocks, an 8-factor model for groups of 60 stocks, and a 13-factor model for groups of 90 stocks for each of the two subperiods. While such representation of security returns is *adequate for the first half-period, more factors are needed for the second half-period for all group sizes*. For the entire period, about 20% of the groups require more than 7 factors for groups of 30 stocks, 66% require more than 11 factors for groups of 60 stocks, and 50% require more than 17 factors for groups of 90 stocks.

The second-stage results are summarized in Table II for the two half-periods and for the entire period. Column (1) of Table II shows that in the first period, at the 5% level, joint χ^2 tests conclude that the risk premium vector is significantly different from zero for only 5 (16.7%) of 30 groups, for one group (3%) in the second period, and for four groups (13.3%) over the entire period [see last row of columns (6) and (12)]. This is in agreement with the results of our earlier papers which were performed essentially for the first of these two periods and show that common risks are "priced" in very few of the groups. In sum, this analysis, based on using the customary groups of 30 stocks each, provides very little support for the key implication of the APT model.

Table II also presents results relevant to the question of whether 5- or 7-factor decomposition exhausts the "explanation" of the expected return process for groups of 30 stocks (using the same methodology as in our previous work but covering a much longer time period). We test this by including (total) standard deviation of stock returns and, separately, the square root of the residual (specific) variance from the first stage as additional explanatory variables in the second stage.[2] Columns (2), (4), (7), (9), (12), and (14) in Table II show the relevant statistics for testing the null hypothesis of zero-risk premia when the factor risk premia are estimated in conjunction with other extraneous variables for subperiods and the entire period. Once (total) standard deviation (σ) or residual standard deviation (Ω) is included, the null hypothesis of a zero-risk premia vector is rejected for only one group at the 5% level over the two subperiods and is uniformly accepted for the entire period. Both extraneous variables, however, are "priced" at least in 5 or 6 groups for the entire period and from 1 to 5 groups in the two subperiods [see columns (3), (5), (8), (10), (13), and (15)]. The results are similar at the 10% level.

Overall, the implications of the updated test results reviewed in this section are similar to those obtained in our earlier papers and are, generally, not in accord with the implications of the APT model.

II. New Tests of Contributions to Asset Returns of Common Versus Unique Measures of Risk

In this section, we report on new tests of the basic implication of the APT model that only common (factor) risks are priced. In Section I, common and unique

[2] Specific variance is the $\tilde{\Omega}$ term in the covariance matrix, $\tilde{\Psi} = \hat{B}'\hat{B} + \tilde{\Omega}$, estimated by factor-analytic methods.

variance measures are estimated within the sample period, in which they serve as "explanatory" variables.

To minimize further the problem of "spurious" correlation between stock returns and risk measures and to test the robustness of such results, we derived the factor and unique measures of risk from the daily time-series observations in the first half-period (1962 to 1972) and used them to "explain" the daily cross-section returns for the second half-period (1972 to 1981). This technique should not only greatly reduce any concern about "spurious" correlations but should also indicate whether either the common or unique risk measures have any predictive value in assessing investors' return requirements in different assets.

The results summarized in Table III for three group sizes again indicate that both the common and unique measures of risk based on the 1962 to 1972 data provide only extremely limited insights into prospective returns.[3] However, they also indicate that either total or residual standard deviation seems to be a more important determinant of stock returns than factor-risk premia. Thus, the null hypothesis that none of the risk premia estimated in the first period is priced in the second period is rejected for only 1 of 30 groups at the 0.05 level of significance [see column (2)]. Moreover, when total or residual standard deviation is added to the risk premia as explanatory variables, it is not possible to reject the null hypothesis for any group [see column (3)]. In contrast, in these last regressions, both own and residual standard deviation are significant for five groups at the 0.05 level [columns (4) and (6)]. The results are qualitatively identical for groups of 60 and 90 stocks.

In separating the 1962 to 1981 period into two halves for estimating risk and returns independently, it is clear why risk measures observed or at least available at the end of the first half are assumed to determine required returns for the second half rather than the other way around. However, we have replicated the analysis summarized in Table III by inverting the two subperiods used to measure risk and returns though the rationale for this procedure would seem to be much weaker than for the results presented above.[4] The new results summarized in Panel B of Table III suggest a somewhat more important (although still relatively weak) role for factor-risk premia in risky asset pricing, but again their effect on expected returns largely disappears when standard deviation is used as an additional explanatory variable [columns (3) and (5)].

To summarize these results on the effect of unique versus common risk on explaining stock returns, unique risks as measured by residual standard deviation seem at least as important as common risks measured by factor risk premia. However, neither measure of risk contributes appreciably in explaining returns on individual securities. These results are inconsistent with the APT (as well as the CAPM), both of which as usually formulated deny any role to unique risk in the pricing of risky assets.

[3] Due to space limitations, we only present the summaries of the tables. Complete tables are available in a working paper. The numbers in Table III correspond to the similar summaries in the last row of Table II.

[4] The rationale would presumably be based on an extremely long-term stationarity of the relative riskiness of stock returns.

Table II

Tests of Significance for Risk Premia Against Specific Alternatives—Standard Deviations and Residual Standard Deviations as Alternatives to APT Model: Summary Statistics for Groups of 30 Stocks

	First Half-Period (7/3/62–4/23/72)					Second Half-Period (4/24/72–12/31/81)					Entire Period (7/3/62–12/31/81)				
	B^a	B & σ^b		B & Ω^c		B^a	B & σ^b		B & Ω^c		B^a	$B = \sigma^b$		B & Ω^c	
Group	χ_1^2 (1)	χ_2^2 (2)	$t(\sigma)$ (3)	χ_3^2 (4)	$t(\Omega)$ (5)	χ_1^2 (6)	χ_2^2 (7)	$t(\sigma)$ (8)	χ_3^2 (9)	$t(\Omega)$ (10)	χ_1^2 (11)	χ_2^2 (12)	$t(\sigma)$ (13)	χ_3^2 (14)	$t(\Omega)$ (15)
1	4.049	1.765	1.30	1.245	1.42	4.379	4.712	1.48	4.779	1.47	6.765	4.532	1.61	5.626	1.60
2	9.329*	3.428	2.10**	3.862	2.11**	3.770	3.512	−.53	3.620	−.62	12.961*	4.856	1.03	7.366	0.90
3	9.661*	1.738	2.12**	1.542	2.11**	4.036	2.309	1.32	2.913	1.30	15.790**	4.682	2.15**	5.953	2.15**
4	8.192	3.667	1.19	3.839	1.15	5.674	5.095	0.45	4.911	0.37	9.854	5.046	1.02	5.403	1.03
5	6.779	3.666	0.41	6.716	0.56	11.233**	7.695	0.13	8.076	0.04	9.757	3.142	0.47	7.222	0.78
6	5.090	3.613	0.18	4.117	0.19	5.078	4.392	0.71	4.143	0.65	6.448	3.669	0.48	4.504	0.29
7	12.398**	5.979	0.57	6.297	0.51	9.426*	7.117	0.58	7.008	0.62	13.848*	6.161	0.52	6.328	0.51
8	8.019	6.786	2.44**	8.627	2.38**	6.388	3.328	0.46	2.557	0.67	14.393**	6.460	1.46	7.749	1.33
9	16.166**	4.091	0.75	4.682	0.76	6.536	5.298	0.42	5.336	0.37	16.083**	5.603	1.05	7.457	0.94
10	10.198*	4.883	0.38	8.120	0.40	5.862	4.975	0.98	4.256	1.00	7.934	0.869	1.02	1.952	0.99
11	8.326	3.663	0.35	6.535	0.22	7.929	6.013	1.22	6.443	1.06	12.717*	6.655	1.59	5.867	1.49
12	4.140	2.800	0.64	3.254	0.51	5.059	2.690	0.63	2.717	0.46	7.325	4.561	1.07	4.393	0.71
13	5.326	1.775	1.16	2.247	1.20	3.475	3.337	0.48	3.444	0.54	6.444	4.038	0.90	6.461	0.91
14	5.499	4.170	0.14	5.550	0.21	6.578	2.588	2.36**	4.520	2.20**	8.979	3.716	1.87*	8.259	1.88*
15	8.052	6.379	1.02	7.177	0.96	2.135	1.666	0.65	1.196	0.69	5.945	3.178	0.66	3.283	0.62
16	14.783**	8.036	0.64	8.624	0.75	4.980	4.875	1.25	4.537	1.32	12.057*	5.870	1.21	5.943	1.20
17	2.699	1.545	0.73	1.093	0.77	7.157	0.838	1.62	1.237	1.61	7.259	0.799	1.73*	1.010	1.77*

Continued overleaf

Table II *continued*

18	6.411	5.145	0.30	5.150	0.24	3.891	3.903	−.22	3.983	−.32	6.411	5.789	0.59	6.882	0.68
19	3.601	0.638	2.51**	0.705	2.47**	10.488*	5.072	1.05	3.402	1.24	10.904	2.117	2.05**	2.563	2.05**
20	16.807**	4.224	1.62	4.611	1.66*	4.324	2.417	2.14**	2.428	2.14**	19.027**	2.300	1.71*	5.903	1.80*
21	7.391	1.279	1.94*	2.576	1.90*	7.753	5.043	0.72	4.570	0.74	13.531*	2.693	1.27	3.270	1.16
22	9.266*	4.002	1.44	4.836	1.49	4.639	3.819	1.02	3.836	0.92	9.560	3.850	1.65*	4.398	1.56
23	4.799	1.766	1.86*	2.575	1.99**	4.594	4.217	−.21	4.030	−.28	6.479	1.623	1.08	2.330	0.85
24	6.647	2.845	2.02**	2.472	2.02**	1.222	0.322	0.49	0.381	0.44	4.346	1.892	2.00**	5.238	2.09**
25	2.886	1.488	1.06	1.372	0.98	9.809*	12.570**	2.83**	12.716**	2.88**	12.087*	9.472	2.78**	11.551	2.66**
26	6.756	3.422	1.60	3.330	1.53	7.479	7.279	1.02	7.667	1.07	6.421	4.922	1.92*	5.483	1.94*
27	5.276	0.530	1.08	0.713	1.13	2.426	1.897	1.64	2.119	1.55	9.433	2.376	1.27	3.260	1.23
28	6.788	2.933	0.46	5.392	0.37	4.753	4.763	−.33	4.551	−.28	8.445	5.437	0.26	7.334	0.18
29	7.805	2.762	0.85	2.675	0.91	5.742	6.041	1.00	5.983	1.09	11.420	6.905	1.17	6.159	1.25
30	16.463**	8.973	1.71*	10.135*	1.72*	8.930	6.892	1.00	5.984	0.89	10.790	3.089	2.25**	3.208	2.19**
						No. of Significant Statistics									
At 10%	9	0	8	1	9	4	1	3	1	3	10	0	10	0	9
At 5%	5	0	5	0	6	1	1	3	1	3	4	0	5	0	5

Note: The number of factors is 5 for the half-periods and 7 for the entire period, respectively, and these numbers should be used for the degrees of freedom for χ^2 tests.

[a] χ^2 values test the null hypothesis that the risk premia vector is null. The risk premia is estimated by the GLS model $\tilde{c}'_{t\cdot} = (\tilde{B}^*\tilde{\Psi}^{-1}\tilde{B}^{*\prime})^{-1}\tilde{B}^*\tilde{\Psi}^{-1}r'_{t\cdot}$. $B^{*\prime}$ is the $[e{:}B]$ matrix of factor loadings with unit vector e.

[b] Own standard deviation of daily stock returns are included as an additional explanatory variable in B^*. χ^2 value tests the nullity of the risk premia vector while $t(\sigma)$ is the t-ratio for the regression coefficient for own standard deviation.

[c] Square root of residual (or specific) variances (Ω) is included as an additional explanatory variable in B^*. Residual variance corresponds to the diagonal elements of $\tilde{\Omega}$ in $\tilde{\Psi} = \tilde{B}'\tilde{B} + \tilde{\Omega}$ from the factor analysis. $t(\Omega)$ is the t-ratio for the regression coefficient for residual variance.

* and ** indicate groups for which nullity of risk premia is rejected at 10 and 5% levels, respectively.

Table III

Tests of Significance for Risk Premia Against Specific Alternatives Using Risk Measures From One Half-Period and Returns from the Other Half

Period: No. of groups with significant test statistics at 5% level[a]

Group Size	No. of Factors (1)	Independent Variables B^{b} (2)	B (3)	σ^{c} (4)	B (5)	Ω^{d} (6)
	A. Risk Measures are Estimated from the First Half-Period[e]					
30	5	1 (3%)	0	5 (17%)	0	5 (17%)
60	8	1 (7%)	0	3 (20%)	0	3 (20%)
90	13	0	0	2 (20%)	2	2 (20%)
	B. Risk Measures are Estimated from the Second Half-Period					
30	5	6 (20%)	0	6 (20%)	0	4 (13%)
60	8	5 (33%)	1 (7%)	7 (47%)	3 (20%)	8 (53%)
90	13	4 (40%)	4 (40%)	6 (60%)	3 (20%)	6 (60%)

[a] These are summary results showing number of groups with significant risk premia using a χ^2 test. These numbers correspond to the similar summaries in the last row of Table I. Detailed tables are available from the authors.

[b] Factor loadings are the only set of explanatory variables.

[c] Own standard deviation is included as an additional independent variable to the factor loadings.

[d] Squared root of the residual variance is added as an additional independent variable (see footnotes b and c in Table II).

[e] Risk measures (i.e., factor loadings, own standard deviation, and residual variance) are estimated from the daily return during the first half of the period (July 3, 1962 to March 23, 1972). These parameters are independent variables in the GLS model in (3) using the daily returns in the second half-period (March 24, 1972 to December 31, 1981). In Panel B, this order is reversed.

III. Effect of Increased Number of Assets on Estimated Number of "Priced" Factors

In this section, we attempt to determine the empirical relationship, if any, between the number of assets factor analyzed and the estimated number of "priced" factors from such a two-stage procedure. The results are presented in Table IV. The first-step factor analysis indicated that generally seven factors were sufficient in explaining individual security returns for groups of 30 securities, 11 factors for groups of 60 securities, and 17 factors for groups of 90 securities (see Table I). The second-stage cross-section GLS regressions for the groups of 30, 60, and 90 securities, respectively, were initially based on the 7, 11, and 17 factors determined from the relevant factor analysis. However, these tests are repeated by constraining the number of factors to 7 in the first-stage factor analysis for all three group sizes.

When we examined the observed percentages of groups with significant risk premia for a given factor, we do not find a monotonic negative relation between the proportions of significant risk premia and the ordering of factors; i.e., it is not always the first factor that is "significant" and the last few that are "insignificant." Rather, the relationship has an inverted U-shape or occasionally a

Table IV

Tests of Significance for Individual Risk Premia Using t-Tests at 5% Level: Summary of Results (7/3/62–12/31/81)

	No. of Factors											
	1	2	3	4	5	6	7	8	9	10	14	17
Expected Percent of Groups with *at Least* This Number of Risk Premia Significant Using 7-Factor Model[a]												
	30.160	4.4360	0.3760	0.02000	0.00125	0.000658	0.00648					
Observed Percent of Groups with *at Least* This Number of Risk Premia Significant Using 7-Factor Model[b,c]												
Groups of 30 stocks	43.33	10.00	0.00	0.00	0.00	0.00	0.00					
Groups of 60 stocks	93.33	13.33	0.00	0.00	0.00	0.00	0.00					
Groups of 90 stocks	100.00	50.00	0.00	0.00	0.00	0.00	0.00					
Percent of Groups with *This* Factor's Risk Premium Significant in Natural Order from Factor Analysis[d]												
Groups of 30 stocks	6.67	10.00	10.00	3.33	13.33	10.00	0.00					
Groups of 60 stocks	13.33	0.00	40.00	33.33	13.33	6.67	6.67					
Groups of 90 stocks	10.00	20.00	40.00	20.00	20.00	20.00	30.00					
Percent of Groups with *At Least* This Number of Risk Premia Significant[c]												
Groups of 60 stocks (11-factor model)												
Expected	43.1199	10.1894	1.5235	0.1552	0.0011	0.0005	0.12×10^{-4}	0.07×10^{-4}	0.1×10^{-6}			
Observed	73.33	40.00	0.00	0.00	0.00	0.00	0.00	0.00	0.00	0.00	0.00	
Groups of 90 stocks (17-factor model)												
Expected	58.1879	20.7772	5.0253	0.8801	0.1164	0.0119	0.0009	0.6×10^{-4}	0.3×10^{-5}	0.1×10^{-6}		
Observed	100.00	60.00	10.00	0.00	0.00	0.00	0.00	0.00	0.00	0.00	0.00	0.00
Percent of Groups with *This* Factor's Risk Premia Significant in Natural Order from Factor Analysis[d]												
Groups of 60 stocks	6.67	0.00	46.67	20.00	13.33	13.33	6.67	0.00	0.00	6.67	0.00	
Groups of 90 stocks	10.00	10.00	10.00	30.00	30.00	20.00	20.00	20.00	10.00	0.00	10.00	10.00

[a] Probability of observing at least this many significant regression coefficients in (3) given that risk premia vector is null.

[b] Number of factors are constrained to seven fro each group at the first stage.

[c] Using t-tests, many of the regression coefficients are significant at 5% level in the GLS model (3).

[d] The factor with this number from the factor analysis has this percent significant t-ratios.

rectangular shape. This is true whether we use a uniform number of factors (7) for each of the groups of 30, 60, and 90 securities or a different number of factors (7, 11, and 17) suggested by the factor analysis.

Greater insight into the nature of the relationship between the number of "priced" factors and the size of the group of assets factor analyzed can be obtained from an examination of the observed percentages of groups of 30, 60, and 90 securities, respectively, with at least a specified number of significant risk premia (either 1, 2, ..., 7 for the groups of 30 securities, 1, 2, ···, 11 for the group of 60 securities, and 1, 2, ···, 17 for the groups of 90 securities, or 1 to 7 for each of the three sets of groups). Table IV shows that when the factors are arrayed in natural order, the second-stage GLS regressions are more likely to yield at least one factor which is "priced" in the 90 stock groups (100% of the group coefficients have significant t-values at the 0.95 level) than is true for the 60 stock groups (73%) or for the 30 stock groups (43%). In the 60 stock groups, like the 30 stock, there are no groups with at least three "priced" factors. However, 10% of the 90 stock groups have at least three "priced" factors. When the cross-section regressions for the 30, 60, and 90 stock groups are based on the same number of seven factors as found for the groups with the smallest number of securities factor analyzed (30), one finds that at least one or two factors are priced for the larger size groups (especially for the 90 stock groups), more than for the 30 stock groups. In fact, there is considerable evidence in this analysis that in the 90 securities groups, we have at least two significant factors at the 0.05 level; the evidence is less compelling that in the 30 security groups we have at least one significant factor.[5] Nevertheless, the number of "priced" factors found in the second-stage cross-section regressions is much smaller than the number of factors determined in the first-stage (factor) analysis.

Clearly, the evidence above suggests a positive relation between the number of "priced" factors and the number of assets in the groups of assets being factor analyzed. There are, however, two qualifications. First, it is conceivable, although not likely, that the difference in the observed results, while systematic and very large, might occur by chance. One, not very satisfactory, test of this explanation is to compare them with the expected number of groups with at least one, two, three, etc., "significant" factor-risk premia on the null hypothesis of no factor effect on returns, using for this purpose a binomial distribution with probability of success $p = 0.05$ and the number of tosses (n) equal to the number of factors.[6] The expected value for the binomial distribution with different values of p and n are presented in Table IV for comparison with the relevant observed results. Such a comparison indicates uniformly that the larger the number of assets factor-analyzed, the more substantial the difference between the observed and expected proportions of groups with at least one, two, or three priced factors.

[5] If one uses 10% level of significance, the number of "priced" factors rises more dramatically with increasing numbers of stocks in a group.

[6] One problem with this test is that the slope coefficients in our second-stage regressions are not statistically independent, but the alternative would be the use of a fairly arbitrary value for the constant term. As a result, it would be necessary to test the sensitivity of results to the constant term selected (presumably some measure of the risk-free rate), and the test would be conditional on the validity of the assumption that the constant term has the value indicated.

Table V

Tests of Significance for Risk Premia Against Specific Alternatives Using Different Group Sizes (Number of Groups with Significant Test Statistics at 5% Level)

Group Size	No. of Factors (1)	B^a (2)	B (3)	σ^b (4)	B (5)	Ω^c (6)
		Independent Variables				
A. Number of Factors is Not Constrained						
I. First Period: 7/3/62–3/23/72						
30	5	5 (17%)	0	5 (17%)	0	6 (20%)
60	8	4 (27%)	1 (7%)	5 (33%)	1 (7%)	5 (33%)
90	13	4 (40%)	1 (10%)	5 (50%)	1 (10%)	5 (50%)
II. Second Period: 3/24/72–12/31/81						
30	5	1 (3%)	1 (3%)	3 (10%)	1 (3%)	3 (10%)
60	8	0	0	2 (13%)	1 (7%)	2 (13%)
90	13	0	0	2 (20%)	0	2 (20%)
III. Entire Period: 7/3/62–12/31/81						
30	7	4 (13%)	0	5 (17%)	0	5 (17%)
60	11	3 (20%)	0	6 (40%)	0	6 (40%)
90	17	5 (50%)	0	4 (40%)	0	4 (40%)
B. Number of Factors Constrained to Seven (entire period)						
30	7	4 (13%)	0	5 (17%)	0	5 (17%)
60	7	7 (47%)	0	9 (60%)	0	9 (60%)
90	7	9 (90%)	0	6 (60%)	2 (20%)	7 (70%)

[a,b,c] See Table III for explanations.

The second and more important qualification is that, for reasons explained in our earlier papers, it is inappropriate to use *t*-tests for the individual slope coefficients derived from the second-stage cross-section analysis as a measure of the significance of individual factor risk premia. A joint χ^2 test, which can be used to determine whether the risk premia vector is null, is the appropriate one to use, although neither it nor the *t*-tests can indicate whether an individual factor-risk premium is significant. The results obtained from such an analysis are summarized in Table V for 30, 60, and 90 security groups. This is done first using the 7, 11, and 17 factors determined without constraint from the time-series analysis of individual securities, and then constraining the number of factors to be the same, viz. seven, for each of the three groups of securities. These results are shown in Panel B.

The analysis based on χ^2 tests again shows a difference in the implications for the "priced" factors when we analyze groups with different numbers of assets. The proportion of 90 stock groups with a significant χ^2 statistic, which indicates that at least one of the risk factors is "priced," was much higher than the corresponding proportion for 60 stock groups, which in turn was higher than the proportion for 30 stock groups. This is true regardless of whether the unconstrained or constrained number of factors from the first-stage factor analysis of individual securities is used in the second-stage cross-section regressions.

These findings provide strong support to the conclusion that there is a positive relation (association) between the number of assets in the groups being factor-analyzed and "priced" factors. Once again, however, when own or residual variance is included, the risk premia vector is not "priced" and these extraneous variables are priced relatively more often [columns (3) to (6)].

IV. Effect of Increased Group Size on Intercept Test

Another important implication of the APT model, which it shares with other capital asset pricing models, is that the constant term in Equation (3) corresponds to the risk-free rate (or at least the return on a zero-beta asset). This section provides tests about this second implication of the APT model and investigates whether intercept tests are affected by the size of the groups of assets. The relevant results are summarized in Table VI.

Using the entire period, we first test whether the intercept terms are jointly significant. Column (1) in Panel A of Table VI indicates that we reject the hypothesis that all intercepts are zero.

Column (2) presents tests for the equality of intercepts to the risk-free rate. We use, as the risk-free rate, the seventh root of the (one plus) weekly Treasury bill yield observed every Thursday. In this formulation, we assume that the seventh root of the Treasury bill observed on a Thursday is the daily risk-free rate for Thursday and the next four trading days. Testing directly the hypothesis that the intercept is the risk-free rate when the weekly Treasury bill rate is used for this purpose, we accept this hypothesis at the 5% level for the groups of 30 and 60 stocks but reject it for groups of 90 stocks at the 10% level. The test statistic in this case is shown in column (2).

We also test whether all intercepts are equal. χ^2 values in column (3) clearly show that we cannot reject this hypothesis.

We finally test the hypothesis that the intercept terms are equal to the risk-free rate using only observations on every Thursday to avoid the assumption that the Treasury bill rates are constant for a week. This procedure results in a smaller number of observations (one-fifth of the previous number). Interestingly, *we reject the hypothesis in this case for groups of 30 and 60 stocks at the 5% level and for all groups at the 10% level.*[7] We also reject the equality of intercepts as well as equality to zero for groups of 30 and 60 stocks at the 10% level, but not for groups of 90 stocks.

As we indicated in our earlier paper (Dhrymes et al. [2]), the intercept tests are somewhat mixed. When we use observations for the entire period with the exception of groups of 90 stocks, results are not inconsistent with the second implication of the APT model. Further work would be required to determine

[7] Similar results are reported by Gultekin and Rogalski [3] using government bonds.

Table VI

Joint χ^2 Tests for the Intercepts (7/3/62–12/31/81)

	Null Hypotheses		
Stocks Per Group	$c_{t0}^{(i)} = 0$[a] (1)	$c_{t0}^{(i)} = r_{f_t}$[b] (2)	$c_{t0}^{(i)} = c_{t0}^{(1)}$[c] (3)
A. Using All Daily Returns			
30	54.523**	24.974	14.706
60	49.336**	21.292	11.609
90	46.809**	17.642*	5.819
B. Using Returns on Every Thursday[d]			
30	43.304*	44.931**	43.258**
60	23.657*	26.720**	23.521*
90	14.261	17.657*	14.017

Note: The degrees of freedom for the χ^2 tests are 30, 15, and 10 for the groups of 30, 60, and 90 stocks in columns (1) and (2). The corresponding numbers are 29, 14, and 9 for column (3).

[a] We jointly test whether all intercepts are equal to zero.

[b] The intercept term is compared to the seventh root of the (one plus) weekly Treasury bill yield observed every Thursday. It is assumed that this daily yield is constant for the next five trading days. The number of observations is 3280.

[c] The equality of intercepts is tested by subtracting the daily intercept for the first group from the rest of the groups and then testing whether the difference is equal to zero jointly.

[d] The intercept term on each Thursday is compared to the seventh root of the (one plus) weekly Treasury bill observed every Thursday. Intercepts for Monday–Wednesday and Friday are deleted. The number of observations is 702.

* Indicates that we reject the null hypothesis at the 10% level.

** Indicates that we reject the null hypothesis at the 5% level.

whether rejection of the risk-free rate interpretation at the 10% level for groups of 90 stocks is a random aberration or reflects the effects of the increased size of the groups factor-analyzed. Similarly, further work is needed to determine whether the rejection of the risk-free rate and the zero-beta interpretation of the intercept when we use observations on every Thursday is merely a result of the diminished number of observations.

V. A Rejoinder to Roll and Ross' Reply and Summary

The purpose of this section is to provide a rejoinder to the "reply" by Roll and Ross [4] appearing in the same issue of the *Journal of Finance* in which our original paper (Dhrymes et al. [1]) was published. In that paper, we made three major points: (a) the procedure used by Roll and Ross in factor-analyzing 30 securities cannot be expected to yield reliable information on the factor loadings and hence on the crucial questions regarding risk premia, risk-free rates, zero-beta rates, and the like; (b) testing for the "significance" of individual risk premia is not meaningful; and (c) that the number of factors "discovered" increases with the size of security groups analyzed. We shall indicate that their response to each of these points is either misleading or incorrect.

In response to (b), Roll and Ross say that they were well aware of this point all along. Now, it is true that Roll and Ross note in many places that the factor loadings one extracts are subject to rotation—a fact found in all textbooks. However, the ancillary consequence that testing individual risk premia is, therefore, meaningless does not appear in such textbooks, and Roll and Ross certainly do not mention this point. In fact, they provide statistics on how many groups had "one significant," "at least two significant," factors; to this effect, see Table III on page 1092. Their confusion on the issue most clearly emerges from the following quote (p. 1091):

> In our case, however, constraining the sample design to the independent case is especially important because the λ's [estimated risk premia] at best are some unknown linear combination of the *true* λ's and testing for the number of *priced factors* or non-zero λ_j's is thereby reduced to a simple t-test.

One wonders how testing that an *unknown linear combination* of parameters is zero gives one information about how many of the underlying parameters are zero.

The same sort of confusion is also evident in other aspects of their reply. For example, in dismissing our finding that as the number of securities analyzed increases the number of factors also increases, as a result "expected" by them, Roll and Ross state (p. 329 in their Reply [4]):

> We want to take this opportunity to emphasize the irrelevance of the point that factor analysis extracts more factors with larger groups of securities or with larger time-series sample sizes.... To illustrate, suppose that a group of 30 securities contains just one cosmetics company. Factor analysis produces, say, three significant factors. If the sample is large enough we would certainly anticipate finding a fourth significant factor, a factor for the cosmetics industry.

If we take this at face value, it is just not clear what becomes of APT in this context. How could one argue for the validity of the model as originally presented and at the same time maintain that the number of "common" factors is indeterminate? If it has been conceded earlier that individual significance tests are meaningless, who is to decide whether with the addition of the "other" cosmetics firm what we are getting as a "significant" risk premium is not for the "irrelevant" cosmetics factor? What if we replace cosmetics by automobiles or oils? A proper procedure in each case would be to allow for the presence of group factors.

One wonders, of course, whether we would have been treated to a different menu if the original paper used 60 security groups; perhaps we would have been told that five to seven factors were significant. What is more difficult to surmise is how they would have reacted to the 17 factors or so which would have resulted if their original paper used 90 security groups.

In this context, their reply also creates an unfortunate obfuscation; see Footnote 2 (p. 349). In discussing the relation of factor loadings obtained from 240 security groups and those obtained from the constituent 30 security groups, we observed that the impression is widespread that the two sets are related by an orthogonal transformation. We pointed out that if the two matrices of factor loadings are related by an orthogonal transformation, then *as a matter of mathematical requirement* the columns[8] of the two matrices must have the same length, since an orthogonal transformation is distance preserving. This is *not a statistical test*, as we explicitly stated in our paper; it was simply an exercise to disabuse those who hold the view that one gets the same information from the two procedures except for the fact that the normalization is a bit different in the two cases. Thus, we certainly are not making an "unbelievable assertion" that this "particular test" has "infinite statistical power."

In their Reply, we also detect a substantial modification, of what is to be meant by APT. In the original paper by Roll and Ross which we had criticized, the model being tested is the very soul of simplicity and parsimony. It claims that the return-generating function is composed of a "systematic" and a "random" component. The random component is then said to be composed of an "idiosyncratic" and a "common" component. Very few objections can be raised against such a framework. It is then the great virtue of the arbitrage pricing hypothesis, in conjunction with other technical requirements, that it yields a very appealing conclusion about the pricing of risky assets. In the process of this reasoning, it is essential that we leave the specification of the systematic component open since it will be the subject of the conclusion from the no-arbitrage hypothesis. If the number of "factors" responsible for the common components is "large," the parsimonious aspect of this model is lost. Alternatively, if we are to claim that these "factors" are *ab initio* concrete variables which the investigator is to specify, then we are straying away from the simplicity (and parsimony) of the original model and into the complexities of the usual multi-index model, where the role of arbitrage pricing is rather tenuous. For, if we are to specify *ab initio* the systematic component, then we are dealing with a situation far different from that addressed by Ross' original paper. We have questioned the empirical methodology in the paper by Roll and Ross, but not the contribution to the literature made by Ross' earlier theoretical contribution.

Finally, we would like to comment on a point made at the end of the Roll and Ross Reply, regarding the presentation of some of our results. In particular, they maintain:

> We cannot fully discuss the tests of Section VII since they are not reported in full, but it is interesting to note that DFG adopted tests "like those used in RR' even though such procedures are 'subject to the basic limitations. . . discussed earlier in the paper' (p. 345). Despite these alleged limitations, however, DFG rely on them to produce results which they interpret as '. . . inconsistent with the APT model,' (p. 345). So having spent their entire paper criticizing the RR test procedures, DFG finally report results for which the tests are apparently satisfactory.

In our work, we stressed that testing for "significant" *individual risk premia parameters* is not meaningful in the context under consideration; if Roll and Ross had not committed this error, we would not have found it necessary to point

[8] Or, alternatively, the rows, depending on one's point of view.

out this fact. Nonetheless, since the Roll and Ross methodology has found wide acceptance, we did provide in our earlier paper (Dhrymes et al. [2]) a number of results based on the Roll and Ross methodology which turn out to be nonsupportive of the implications of APT models—contrary to the assertions of Roll and Ross. In fact, results reported in this paper show that, again in the 30 security context, whether we use a 10-year time-series sample or a 20-year time-series sample, the proper (joint) test of significance for the risk premia vector rejects its nullity in, at most, 10 of 30 groups. When own (total) or residual standard deviation is introduced as an additional variable, then the hypothesis that the vector of risk premia is null is accepted by the proper (joint) test in 30 of 30 groups, i.e., uniformly for the entire sample. It is difficult to imagine a more complete rejection of the crucial implication of such APT models, using the flawed methodology of splitting the universe of assets into 30 security groups.

REFERENCES

1. Phoebus J. Dhrymes, Irwin Friend, and N. Bulent Gultekin. "A Critical Reexamination on the Empirical Evidence on the Arbitrage Pricing Theory." *Journal of Finance* 39 (June 1984), 323–46.
2. Phoebus J. Dhrymes, Irwin Friend, Mustafa N. Gultekin, and N. Bulent Gultekin. "An Empirical Examination of the Implications of Arbitrage Pricing Theory." *Journal of Banking and Finance* (March 1985), forthcoming.
3. N. Bulent Gultekin and Richard J. Rogalski. "Interest Rate Risk and the APT." *Journal of Finance* 40 (March 1985), 43–61.
4. Richard Roll and Stephen A. Ross. "An Empirical Investigation of the Arbitrage Pricing Theory." *Journal of Finance* 35 (December 1980), 1073–1103.
5. ———. "A Critical Reexamination of the Empirical Evidence on the Arbitrage Pricing Theory: A Reply." *Journal of Finance* 39 (June 1984), 347–50.

Studies in Banking and Finance 5 (1988) 27–47. North-Holland

FINANCIAL STRINGENCY AND THE PROBABILITY OF FIRST HOMEOWNERSHIP

Phoebus J. DHRYMES*

Columbia University, New York, NY 10027, USA

This paper deals with the impact that a tight market for money (financial stringency) may exert on the actions of those who contemplate buying a home for the first time (first homeownership).

The data on which this research is based were obtained from the Annual Housing Survey (now termed the American Housing Survey, henceforward AHS) for the years 1978 and 1979 and are in the form of two cross sectional samples.

The results show that while the choice of (first) homeownership is affected by market (mortgage) interest rates, it is even more sensitive to the magnitude of the initial payment (downpayment and points).

1. Introduction

The purpose of this study is to investigate the extent to which recent developments in the housing and mortgage markets have made it increasingly difficult for households to acquire a home, given that they have not owned a home previously.

The barriers to home acquisition for the first time are threefold:

(i) rising mortgage rates which make the servicing of a loan (any loan) more difficult,
(ii) various marketing devices (points) which although raising the effective interest rate only slightly are a substantial burden on the household in that the financial obligations they entail must be met, in full, at closing,
(iii) rising downpayment requirements (and in addition rising housing prices).

Evidently, the same factors are applicable to households who require a home upon selling a previous residence. Moreover, rising income or expectations of rising income, to some extent, offset these considerations, so why concentrate on homeownership for the first time?

The reasons are as follows:

(a) For some time it has been considered a desirable public policy objective to promote homeownership. Hence, impediments to households seeking homeownership for the first time are worthy of study.

*I would like to acknowledge the excellent research assistance of Jaime Howell.

(b) For previous owners – and as a matter of empirical evidence previous owner means (very) recent previous owners – the last two, and particularly the last, barriers (noted in (ii) and (iii) above), are of lesser consequence; this is so since their effects are mitigated by the fact that such households have participated in and benefited by the recent rise in house values and through the proceeds from the sale of their residences have liquid resources to cope with the requirements under (ii) and (iii) above.

Thus, it is not the intention here to examine the general question of whether and when homeownership dominates renter status in relation to one's income tax bracket and the like. On this issue there is a fairly extensive literature – see Rosen (1979a, b), Aaron (1970, 1972), Summers (1981), White and White (1977) and Linneman (1983). Rather, our objective is to concentrate on the formulation, and estimation of the parameters, of the probability function for first homeownership.

There is very little prior study of this topic, save for the author's initial work with the preliminary AHS data files for 1977; on the other hand (purely theoretical) models of tenure choice as part of a 'general equilibrium' allocation of expenditure and wealth are available – see, for example, the studies of David (1962), Kain and Quigley (1975), Lee (1963), Maisel (1966) and Orcutt, et al. (1961).

2. Theoretical underpinnings

Here we shall examine the issues related to the specification of a probability function to be estimated. Our objective is not so much to articulate a complete model of choice, as it is to motivate the type of function to be estimated.

A house is consumer capital; as with any capital goods one has a choice between ownership and leasing or renting. For most consumer durables this is, usually, a trivial problem and in many instances the choice is not even available. But the principle underlying this problem bears repeating, in that its elucidation will determine the proper specification of the probability function for first homeownership. Let

x_t^* = rental cost per time t,
r = household discount factor – taken as its lending rate, e.g., 'long term' certificate of deposit (C.D.) rate or Treasury bond rate,
m_t = maintenance cost per time t,
a = fraction of maintenance costs borne by the renting household.

If T is the horizon for the household's decision then the present discounted value (*PDV*) of housing costs in renter status is

$$C_{\mathrm{R}}=\sum_{t=1}^{T}\frac{x_t}{(1+r)_t}, \qquad x_t=x_t^*+am_t. \tag{1}$$

To purchase the housing unit at 'time zero' and price P suppose the household is required to make a down payment, P_0, and 'finance' the remaining

$$P_{\mathrm{F}}=P-P_0 \tag{2}$$

over a period of also T years, at *its borrowing rate i.*

In this fashion, the household incurs an obligation, say s, per unit of time determined by

$$P_{\mathrm{F}}=s\sum_{t=1}^{T}\frac{1}{(1+i)^t}. \tag{3}$$

Solving this equation we find

$$s=\left|\frac{(1+i)^T}{(1+i)^T-1}\right| iP_{\mathrm{F}}. \tag{4}$$

This consists of a payment of interest, say, s_{t1}, and a repayment of principal, say

$$s_{t2}=s-s_{t1}. \tag{5}$$

How do we now construct an entity that is comparable to the *PDV* of the housing costs in renter status given in (1)? First, we need to enumerate the recurring obligations (costs) associated with homeownership. To this effect let

$(1-\tau)rP_0$ = opportunity cost of down payment,
$(1-\tau)s_{t+1}$ = interest cost of servicing the mortgage,
$(1-\tau)r\sum_{j=1}^{t-1}s_{j2}$ = opportunity cost of increasing equity,
$(1-\tau)v_t$ = real estate taxes and other tax deductible expenses associated with homeownership,
m_t = maintenance costs,
w_t = other non-deductible costs associated with homeownership,
τ = household's (income) tax rate.

Defining

$$z_t=(1-\tau)\left[rP_0+s_{t1}+r\sum_{j=1}^{t-1}s_{j2}+v_t\right]+m_t+w_t, \tag{6}$$

we have that the *PDV* of (net) homeownership costs are

$$C_H=(1-\tau)P_{0c}+\sum_{t=1}^{T}\frac{z_t}{(1+r)^t}-\frac{(1-g)(P_T-P)}{(1+r)^T}, \tag{7}$$

where g is the capital gains tax rate, and P_{0c} are (other) closing costs. Note that under present tax law the last term of (7) is valid only for

$$P_T-P\geqq 0. \tag{8}$$

If (8) does not hold the last term is to be replaced by

$$-\frac{P_T-P}{(1+r)^T}.$$

so that capital losses are to be absorbed by the household. The terms

$$(1-\tau)P_{0c} \quad \text{and} \quad P_0$$

deserve special attention in that they place a burden on the household's liquid resources. In many circles, it is customary to take the closing costs represented by 'points' and use them to obtain a higher effective mortgage rate as follows: find s as in (4) and then determine the interest rate i_* such that

$$P_F-P_{0c}=s\sum_{t=1}^{T}\frac{1}{(1+i_*)^t}. \tag{9}$$

In general,

$$i_*>i, \tag{10}$$

but the larger the maturity, T, the smaller the difference in (10) for a given level of closing costs, P_{0c}. Thus, the procedure is rather deceptive in terms of conveying the magnitude of the barrier represented by P_{0c}.

Finally, although we have taken T to be the horizon of the decision as well as the term of the mortgage, this need not be the case; their divergence does not create any conceptual problems. To this effect let

$T = T_1$ for the decision horizon,
$T = T_2$ for the mortgage maturity (term).

Let $T_2 > T_1$ and let z_t be determined on the basis of T_2. Then the relevant costs are

$$C_R(T_1) = \sum_{t=1}^{T_1} \frac{x_t}{(1+r)^t},$$

$$C_H(T_1, T_2) = (1-\tau)P_{0c} + \sum_{t=1}^{T_1} \frac{z_t}{(1+r)^t} - \frac{(1-g)(P_{T_1} - P)}{(1+r)^{T_1}}. \tag{11}$$

Abstracting from capital gains, the comparison is essentially between z_t and x_t, since if T_1 is at all large converting $(1-\tau)P_{0c}$ into a flow over T_1 years yields

$$(1-\tau)P_{0c} = d \sum_{t=1}^{T_1} \left(\frac{1}{1+r}\right)^t,$$

which implies

$$d = \left|\frac{r}{1-(1+r)^{-T_1}}\right| (1-\tau)P_{0c}. \tag{12}$$

Thus the comparison essentially involves

$$z_t + d - x_t \gtrless 0. \tag{13}$$

If this difference is negative in the foreseeable future then it is advantageous to buy, provided the "barrier",

$$(1-\tau)P_{0c} + P_0,$$

can be overcome; if positive, then it is not. If the difference above is of mixed sign then the decision will crucially depend on the length of the horizon and the expectation of capital gains.

Under the best of circumstances the comparison in (13) is difficult, since beyond the next few months from the origin of the decision, the magnitudes of τ, r, v_t, w_t and x_t are not known. More recently, with the advent of adjustable rate mortgages (*ARM*), s_{t1} and s_{t2} will not be known either.

Notice that the longer the horizon over which the decision is made the more uncertainty there is but, perhaps, the issue of capital gains becomes less important.

Thus, if one concentrates over the very immediate future one can evaluate z_t, more or less precisely, as

$$(1-\tau)(rP_0+s_{t1}+v_t)+w_t+m_t,$$

and the relevant comparison would be

$$d+(1-\tau)(rP_0+s_{t1}+v_t)+w_t+(1-a)m_t-x_t^*\gtrless 0. \tag{14}$$

In addition, the ownership barrier posed by the initial payment is, in effect,

$$(1-\tau)P_{0c}+P_0,$$

relative to the household's (non-human) wealth.

Consequently, one may argue that, for all intents and purposes, the decision involves one's current housing expenditure and, upon moving, the prospective costs of renting versus homeownership, on a flow basis, and the barrier posed by the requisite initial payments.

We formulate the choice problem as a stochastic one as follows. Let

$$U(z,w;\,\theta,\eta)$$

be the (generic) stochastic utility function characteristic of households in a given market, where z is a vector of the sociolocational characteristics of the individual household and/or housing unit, and w is the vector containing the economic variables bearing on the choice problem. Let us also code the problem so that alternative 1 is homeownership, while alternative 0 is renter status. Under alternative 1 we have utility

$$U(z,w;\,\theta_{\cdot 1},\eta_1),$$

while under alternative 0 we have utility

$$U(z,w;\,\theta_{\cdot 0},\eta_0).$$

Without loss of generality we may write

$$\begin{aligned}U(z,w;\,\theta_{\cdot 0},\eta_0)&=u(z,w;\,\gamma_{\cdot 0})+\varepsilon_0,\\ U(z,w;\,\theta_{\cdot 1},\eta_1)&=u(z,w;\,\gamma_{\cdot 1})+\varepsilon_1,\end{aligned} \tag{15}$$

where, generically,

$$u(z,w;\,\gamma)=\mathrm{E}[U(z,w;\,\theta,\eta)\,|\,(z,w)]. \tag{16}$$

Presumably, alternative 1 will be chosen if

$$u(z,w;\,\gamma_{.1})+\varepsilon_1-(u(z,w;\,\gamma_{.0})+\varepsilon_0)\geqq 0, \quad \text{or} \tag{17}$$

$$\varepsilon_0-\varepsilon_1\leqq u(z,w;\,\gamma_{.1})-u(z,w;\,\gamma_{.0}). \tag{18}$$

Thus, the probability of homeownership is given by

$$F(z,w;\,\gamma_{.1},\gamma_{.0})=\int_{-\infty}^{u_1-u_0} f(\xi)\,\mathrm{d}\xi, \tag{19}$$

where $f(\cdot)$ is the density function of the random variable, $\varepsilon_0-\varepsilon_1$, and u_1, u_0 is an abbreviated expression for the conditional expected utilities in the right member of (18).

If the function $U(\cdot)$ is linear or if we employ a Taylor series expansion we will, in effect, have a relationship in (19) which involves the various sociolocational attributes of the household, as well as the economic variables appropriate for this specification, including the most of ownership, the cost of remaining in renter status and possibly the previous costs of housing – the latter as an indication of the ease, or the difficulty, with which the transition can be made.

3. Econometric aspects of the AHS files

In the preceding section we have sought to elucidate the nature of the problem a household faces in making a decision as to whether to continue in renter status or to change to homeowner status (for the first time). Here we shall examine the stochastic properties we can claim for the sample we shall be working with, which is derived from the 1978 and 1979 AHS files.

The reason why an explicit consideration of the stochastic aspects is merited is that, while we seek to model a decision process for households, in fact, our sample consists, basically, of housing units. Thus, the sampling scheme is not one in which we obtain a random sample of households and on the basis of this information we estimate the parameters of (19); rather, we observe a, more or less, fixed set of dwelling units and we take our information from the households that newly occupied them. How can we rationalize this scheme so that it conforms with the standard requirement of Bernoulli trials? More precisely, we wish to say that for the (relevant) ith household the probability of tenure change upon moving is $F(z,w;\,\gamma)$ and consequently the probability of tenure persistence is $1-F(z,w;\,\gamma)$; moreover, one household's decision is independent of another's.

Now, the AHS files cover a (more or less) fixed number of dwelling units that have been chosen so that they are a 'probability' sample of the stock of

U.S. housing. Periodically, dwelling units are taken out, as they cease to exist as such, and other units are added in, to reflect new construction.

The basic principle behind this 'sampling design' is to reflect accurately the U.S. housing stock. What this means is that, having stratified the housing stock in terms of distinct subpopulations – such as by region, standard metropolitan statistical area (SMSA), central city or not, apartment and single family housing units, etc. – and having decided on the total size of the sample, one selects at random – within each stratum – a number of housing units. This number is in the same proportion to the total sample as the housing units in the stratum are to the total U.S. housing stock.

Clearly, in order to *detect change in housing tenure we must first detect a move by a household*. Thus, the set of households experiencing a change in tenure is a subset of the set of households that have moved during a given time period. There are the obvious exceptions of leasing with option to buy and the conversion of apartments to coops. The first case is sufficiently rare so that it may be safely ignored; the second was not yet a common enough phenomenon by 1978 or 1979 so as to cause appreciable distortion in our findings.

The obvious question is: if we sample from moving households do we induce any distortions? Clearly, the set of moving households consists of those deciding to buy instead of renting and those who move for other reasons. At this stage one has little reason to doubt the independence assumption relative to the decision households make. Now, if we condition on moving all we are doing is to restrict the size of the population we wish to study – and this subpopulation, now, becomes our frame of reference. Within this new frame of reference the condition that household decisions be independent of each other's, evidently, continues to hold.

Within this population we have essentially four subpopulations. Actually, the data classification allows for more but we confine it to this for clarity of exposition.

The four subpopulations involve the transitions:

owner → renter
owner → owner
renter → owner
renter → renter

We further restrict our attention to the last two subpopulations, i.e., we further condition on renter status on previous tenure; it is easy to see that the independence of household decisions within this subpopulation is preserved as well. Our final sample selection involves a further conditioning on not having previously owned a home, which again preserves this independence.

The next and final question is: do we get a 'random sample' of moving households from the AHS files? If we begin with the proposition that every household occupies one housing unit, then the answer is clearly yes. This is so since we can gain information by sampling households directly, or *by sampling the housing units and the households occupying them.* The problem is essentially replicated in the following simple construct. We have an urn that contains a mixture of red and green balls. We can obtain information about the proportion of the mixture by sampling the balls from the urn directly. Alternatively, we gain the same information by *first* arranging the balls in boxes, so that each box contains one ball, and then obtaining a random sample of cells (boxes) and examining the balls occuping them.

The only question that might arise is whether the AHS sample of housing units is 'random'. This, however, lies beyond the scope of this paper and will be conceded at the outset.

Now, given that we have a random sample from the decision making process we wish to study, we can write the likelihood function of our observations as

$$L^* = \prod_{i=1}^{T} [F(x_{i.};\gamma)]^{y_i}[1-F(x_{i.};\gamma)]^{1-y_i}, \quad \text{where} \tag{20}$$

y_i =1 if ith household buys (for the first time)
=0 if ith household continues in renter status,
$x_{i.}$=is the relevant set of variables for the ith household.

The logarithm of the function in (20)

$$L=\sum_{t=1}^{T} y_i \ln F(x_{i.};\gamma)+\sum_{i=1}^{T}(1-y_i)\ln[1-F(x_{i.};\gamma)]. \tag{21}$$

To make the problem completely operational we need to specify exactly the cumulative distribution function (cdf), $F(\cdot)$, in (20) and (21). If the basic error terms in (18) are (jointly) normal, then the density function $f(\cdot)$ in (19) is also normal and we have what is known as 'probit' analysis.

If the basic error terms in (18) are *independent* and have the density

$$\varepsilon_i \sim e^{-s}e^{-e^{-s}}, \qquad i=0,1, \tag{22}$$

then the density $f(\cdot)$, in (19), becomes

$$f(\xi)=\frac{e^{-\xi}}{(1+e^{-\xi})^2}. \tag{23}$$

In this particular case the cdf is explicitly obtainable as

$$F(x;\gamma)=\frac{1}{1+e^{-t}}, \qquad t=u_1-u_0. \tag{24}$$

The terms u_1, u_0 are those implicitly defined in (19), and represent (conditional) expected utilities for alterntives 1 and 0 respectively.

Estimators for the parameter vector, γ, can be attained by maximizing (21) with respect to γ; these are the maximum likelihood estimators. In terms of the model offered in (23) and (24) – and in the 'probit' case as well – we may interpret the parameter vector γ in one of two ways:

(i) The conditional utility functions are

$$u_1(x:\gamma_{.1})=x'\gamma_{.1}, \qquad u_0=x'\gamma_{.0}, \quad \text{so that}$$

$$u_1-u_0=x'\gamma, \qquad \gamma=\gamma_{.1}-\gamma_{.0}. \tag{25}$$

(ii) Expand u_1-u_0 as a Taylor series, with linear terms only, to obtain

$$u_1-u_0=x'\gamma. \tag{26}$$

In either case, we do not commit ourselves as to whether the elements of the vector x appear in their natural ('linear') form or as transformations, for example, logarithms.

4. Data selection and definitions

The data employed in this study have been obtained from the Annual Housing Surveys (AHS) of 1978 and 1979, by focussing on households that have moved (changed addresses) between the previous and current surveys. Unfortunately, many observations have been eliminated due to missing items of information that were very crucial to our analysis. A tabulation of most sample characteristics before and after such elimination is available in an appendix; the latter was not included with the paper in the interest of conserving space. It may, however, be obtained from the author on request.

Basically the selection procedure is as follows:

(1) Obtain all movers, i.e., households who are at the current address in 1978 (1979) for the first time.
(2) Given 1; select all movers who in their immediately previous address were renters.
(3) Given 2; select all previous renters who are now owners.

(4) Given 3; select those who indicate they are first time homeowners; and
(3a) Given 2; select those who are currently renters;
(4a) Given 3a; select those who have never owned a home.

Thus, our sample consists of all movers (in a given year) who are first time homeowners and all movers who have never owned a home. Thus, in essence, we have the subpopulations:

renter → renter (never owned a home)
renter → owner (homeowner for the first time).

The type of data needed for our analysis were, in part, alluded to in the preceding discussion, and fall in two general categories.

(1) Sociolocational characteristics of the (head of the) household such as age, sex, schooling, race, number of household members, region, SMSA or not, central city or not and the like.
(2) Economic characteristics, such as income, number of members gainfully employed, the 'cost' of homeownership or rental, previous housing costs, the amount of downpayment, et cetera.

In general, the data were obtained, in the first instance, from the AHS files, but have been supplemented by information in various publications of the Treasury Department and the Federal Home Loan Bank.

Most of the variables are self explanatory, but a few require explanation. The variable *OCP30* indicates ownership costs per capita. It is obtained for homeowners essentially as the variable z_t of (6) (divided by the number of household members) except that the terms $\sum_{i=1}^{t-1} s_{j2}$, w_t are set to zero and v_t, w_t are interpreted as real estate taxes and insurance/utility costs, respectively. For recurring renters, such a variable is not, evidently, directly available; to define the (virtual) homeownership costs they face, we interpolate, by matching income and region for recurring renters and first homeowner households. To be precise, a recurring renter household with income y in region i is assigned homeownership costs equal to the average of such costs for first homeowner households of income y in region i.

The variable *ROCOR* indicates the ratio of current and previous housing costs; the variable *DPPI* for 1978, and *DPORI* for 1979 indicates the downpayment as a percent of the household's income.

The choice of data conforms, by and large, to the guidelines and considerations discussed in section 2, with several unavoidable deficiencies. First, the variable *DPPI* is best defined as downpayment plus 'points and other closing costs' as a percent of the household's wealth. Unfortunately, wealth is not available in the AHS files – which forced the use of household income in the place of wealth. Moreover, points and other closing costs could not be accurately ascertained. It is possible that by exploiting the longitudinal aspect of the files we shall be able to remedy this deficiency in further work – at least partially. As for points, it is possible that auxiliary sources may provide at least regional or SMSA based information so that this may also be taken into account.

Second, capital gains, or the expectation thereof, may be incorporated in the analysis in a more 'dynamic' version of this model – using time series data or the time series dimension of the AHS files. In doing so, we should also have to model 'expectations' of various varieties but, from a practical point of view, this only means incorporating lagged variables into the estimation framework. This is so, since in the absence of any coherent model of expectation formation, the current practice of 'rational expectations' simply asserts that the process generating the 'expected' variable(s) is an autoregressive one. Third, newly formed households play an important role in the process of 'first homeownership' but we have no pertinent information in our files. This is, however, a deficiency that bears more on the interpretation and potential use of our results rather than the econometric 'quality' of our estimates.

To facilitate reading and comprehending the econometric results, we give in table 1 a glossary of the variables used in the two estimated functions. Finally, we close this section by giving the mean characteristics of the sample in table 2.

The preceding is self explanatory, i.e., 70% of the households were headed by males in 1978 and 71% in 1979; 83% heads were white in 1978 and 82% in 1979 and so on.

The only entry that may appear curious to the reader is the last one, which states that downpayment as a percent of household income is of the order of 92%–95%, and this may appear inordinately high. This puzzlement, however, is easily dispelled if we note, first, that this is *not downpayment as a percent of the price of the house* but rather as a percent of household income, and, second, that for recurring renter households this is interpolated by matching recurring renter and homeowner households by region and income as in the case of homeownership costs.

5. Econometric results

The estimated probability of (first) ownership functions for 1978 and 1979 appear in tables 3 and 4. The coefficient estimates appear in the column entitled BETA. Since most readers are not familiar with 'critical points' for chi-square distribution it is preferable to rely on the p-values appearing under the column entitled P. If the p-value exceeds 0.05 then the hypothesis that the corresponding coefficient is zero is to be accepted at the 5% level of

Table 1

Glossary of variables employed.

DSM	=1	if household head is male
	=0	otherwise,
DRW	=1	if household head is white
	=0	otherwise,
DRB	=1	if household head is black
	=0	otherwise,
DNE	=1	if household is located in New England region
	=0	otherwise,
DNC	=1	if household is located in North Central region
	=0	otherwise,
DS	=1	if household is located in South region
	=0	otherwise,
DCC	=1	if household is located in a central city
	=0	otherwise,

DPPI for 1978 and *CDPORI* for 1979 = downpayment as a percent of household income.

For the following variables the prefix *L* indicates that they enter the function in logarithmic form.

PER = number of persons in household,
GRADE 2 = highest educational level attained by head,
ZAGE = age of head of household,
CTINCPC = per capita income of household – from all sources,
OCPC30 for 1978 and *OCOR302* for 1979 = per capita cost of homeownership,
ROCOR = ratio of current to previous housing costs.

Table 2

Mean characteristics of sample.

	1978		1979	
		Log		Log
DSM	0.703		0.710	
DRW	0.831		0.822	
DRB	0.133		0.140	
DNE	0.200		0.185	
DNC	0.220		0.221	
DS	0.279		0.304	
DCC	0.407		0.397	
PER	2.514	0.766	2.511	0.763
GRADE	14.686	2.652	14.664	2.650
AGE	43.958	3.607	44.061	3.618
Per capita income	7,102.51	8.562	7,748.85	8.651
Per capita housing costs	161.457	4.873	173.596	4.955
Ratio of current to previous housing costs	1.225	0.116	1.218	0.099
Downpayment as a fraction of household income	0.920		0.935	

Table 3

Parameter estimates: First homeownership probability function – AHS files, 1978.

Variable	Beta	Standard error	Chi-square	P	D
Intercept	−14.55085775	2.91271555	24.96	0.0000	–
DSM	0.87450302	0.27511796	10.10	0.0015	0.004
DRW	0.28677232	0.46975238	0.37	0.5415	0.000
DRB	0.11674733	0.55015092	0.05	0.8319	0.000
DNE	0.45379442	0.27059413	2.81	0.0935	0.001
DNC	1.01441158	0.25154454	16.26	0.0001	0.007
DS	−0.01275844	0.27246288	0.00	0.9627	0.000
DCC	−0.57779776	0.19124852	9.13	0.0025	0.004
LPER	0.52827463	0.31108366	2.88	0.0895	0.001
LGRADE2	2.77433587	0.55801945	24.72	0.0000	0.010
LZAGE	−0.31622798	0.19188059	2.72	0.0993	0.001
LCTINPC	0.78265838	0.30700559	6.50	0.0108	0.003
LOCPC30	−0.69703574	0.30371272	5.27	0.0217	0.002
LROCOR	2.76236055	0.24114043	131.23	–	0.052
DPPI	−1.41612305	0.40522193	12.21	0.0005	0.005

−2 log likelihood for model containing intercept only	=1452.18
Convergence obtained in 8 iterations	$D=0.161$
Max absolute derivative=0.6815D-03	$-2 \log L=993.51$
Model chi-square=458.67 with 14 D.F.	$P=0.0$

Classification table.

		Predicted: Negative	Positive	Total
True	Negative	2,159	25	2,184
	Positive	167	49	216
	Total	2,326	74	2,400

Sensitivity: 22.7%, Specificity: 98.9%, Correct: 92.0%, False positive rate: 33.8%, False negative rate: 7.2%.

significance; if not, then it should be rejected at the 5% level of significance. Similarly, for 10%, 1% or whatever.

For 1978 and 1979 the tables suggest the following conclusions, at the 5% level of significance:

(1) The relationship is 'significant'; this is evidenced by the likelihood ratio test carried out immediately below the coefficient estimates and other related columns.
(2) The relationship predicts correctly 92% of the cases within the sample;

Table 4

Parameter estimates: First homeownership probability function – AHS files, 1979.

Variable	Beta	Standard error	Chi-square	P	D
Intercept	−14.82602162	2.82585427	27.53	0.0000	–
DSM	1.92572124	0.41268162	21.77	0.0000	0.009
DRW	0.10127212	0.44461146	0.05	0.8198	0.000
DRB	−0.01436404	0.51974075	0.00	0.9780	0.000
DNE	0.81365819	0.24625476	10.92	0.0010	0.005
DNC	0.45265819	0.24087249	3.53	0.0602	0.001
DS	0.30387605	0.23860554	1.62	0.2028	0.001
DCC	−0.48662727	0.19003354	6.56	0.0104	0.003
LPER	0.81899433	0.31366132	6.82	0.0090	0.003
LGRADE2	1.65322166	0.51655083	10.24	0.0014	0.004
LZAGE	−0.11724580	0.19556616	0.36	0.5488	0.000
LCTINCPC	0.98958837	0.31765136	9.71	0.0018	0.004
LOCOR302	−0.64871476	0.31014288	4.38	0.0365	0.002
LROCOR	2.63699244	0.23440574	126.56	–	0.050
CDPORI	−1.40599822	0.38755192	13.16	0.0003	0.005

−2 log likelihood for model containing intercept only = 1459.26
Convergence obtained in 8 iterations $D = 0.164$
Max absolute derivate = 0.1428D-02 $-2 \log L = 987.59$
Model chi-square = 471.67 with 14 D.F. $P = 0.0$

Classification table.

		Predicted		
		Negative	Positive	Total
True	Negative	2,169	27	2,196
	Positive	162	55	217
	Total	2,331	82	2,413

Sensitivity: 25.3%, Specificity: 98.8%, Correct: 92.2%, False positive rate: 32.9%, False negative rate: 6.9%.

on the other hand, it predicts better recurring renter status (specificity: 98.9%, 98.8%) than it does homeownership (sensitivity: 22.7%, 25.3%).

(3) There is no evidence that race per se influences the probability of (first) homeownership. This may be interpreted as providing no evidence for the presence of systematic racial discrimination in (first) home acquisition.

(4) Regional effects are rather weak. From a formal point of view the hypothesis of regional effects is rejected except for the North Central region in 1978 and the New England region for 1979.

(5) Central city households are less likely to be (first) home buyers than others.
(6) Other things being equal, the size of the household is a significant determinant of (first) home acquisition; the coefficient of *LPER* is significant at the 10% level in 1978 and well below the 5% level in 1979.
(7) Educational attainment is a significant factor in both years.
(8) Age of head does not appear to have a bearing on the probability of *first* home acquisition, although it consistently appears in the relation with a negative sign! The latter is understandable by noting that here we are dealing with *first* home acquisition, so that the longer one has made do without owning a house the more likely one will continue to be a renter.
(9) Per capita income (i.e., total household income divided by the number of household members) is a consistent and important determinant.
(10) Ownership costs are also a consistent and important determinant.
(11) The ratio of current to previous housing costs is also consistently significant in a statistical sense. The interpretation of this phenomenon is as follows: if we are told that, upon moving, a household incurs appreciably higher housing costs, then it is more likely that the household has experienced a change in housing tenure, rather than it has remained in renter status.
(12) Finally, the downpayment barrier is a significant one, consistently, as evidenced by the negative and significant coefficient of the last variable, for both 1978 and 1979.

One is struck by the great similarity in the results for 1978 and 1979; the samples involve some 2,400 households in 1978 and 2,413 (totally) different households in 1979. The explanatory power of the model is quite similar in both years and outside the regional variables, we have a very similar pattern in the coefficients in both years.

But what do the results indicate relative to the possible impacts of rising housing values and financial stringency on the probability of first homeownership?

To answer this question we first give the relevant elasticity implications of our results. Evaluating elasticities at the *sample means* we have the following, on a ceteris paribus basis: A 10% increase in mean (per capita) household income leads to a 22.7% increase in the probability of first homeownership in 1978, and a 24.73% increase in 1979. A 10% increase in mean (per capita) homeownership costs leads to a 6.06% decrease in 1978 and a 5.84% decrease in 1979.

A 10% increase in downpayment (or housing values) leads to a 12.52% decrease in 1978 and a 12.23% decrease in 1979.

Thus, the income elasticity of first home acquisition probability is of the order of 2.2 to 2.4; ownership cost elasticity is of the order of (−)0.6, while the downpayment elasticity is of the order of (−)1.2.

If the interest cost is of the order of, say, 70% of homeownership costs, as we define the term in this paper, then a 10% increase in mortgage rates leads to, roughly, a 4.2% (0.7 × 6) reduction in the probability of first home ownership, so that the 'interest' elasticity is of the order of (−)0.4.

This is in accord with the earlier discussion, where we have pointed out that the practice of converting 'points' to an increase in the 'effective' interest rate over the life of the mortgage severely understates the barrier to first homeownership created by these practices. We note, for example, that in a transaction involving a 30-year mortgage for $100,000 and a house value of $120,000, 'charging three points' raises the 'effective' downpayment by 15% ($20,000 versus $23,000) while it raises the effective interest rate from, say, 12% to 12.36% or by less than 4%!

6. Policy implications

In the preceding section we presented the econometric results in broad outline and have obtained the elasticity characteristics of the estimated probability functions, at the sample mean, for key economic variables such as household income, interest and homeownership costs, as well as downpayment requirements.

As is made clear in section 4 a substantial number of observations has been deleted due to missing information. For example, in 1978 931 first ownership households were uncovered; due to missing information the final sample used only 216 of those. The median income in the initial and final samples was about $45,000; what this means is that the cumulative percent of households with income in the class having right boundary at $45,000 exceeds 50% for the first time. Comparison of other (economic) variables is difficult owing to the large number of households classified in the 'not applicable' or 'not answered' category. Sociolocational characteristics are not appreciably distorted except for the regional division of the sample. For example, whites constitute 89% of the original and 89% of the final sample; similarly, blacks are 8.3% of the original and 7.4% of the final sample, while 'other' constitutes 2.57% of the original and 3.24% of the final sample. The results may suggest appreciable distortion for 'other' but this is really a problem with small numbers and expected sampling variations.

In the original sample 91.5% of household heads were male and in the final sample (i.e., after deletions) males were heading 90.7% of households. In regional terms, however, there was appreciable distortion as follows. This shows that there was a disproportionate number of households with missing information in the South and well below average numbers of households with missing information in the North Central region. This will help 'explain'

First homeowner households, 1978.

	North East	North Central	South	West
Original	19.12%	26.85	35.76	18.26
Final	18.98	37.50	25.46	18.06

why in the 1978 cross-section we have a 'significant' regional effect for the North Central region.

For recurring renters the initial sample contained 3,678 households, but after deletions for missing information the final sample contained only 2,184 households. Median income for both was $15,000; median rent was $250 for both. The original sample contained 85.9% households headed by whites while the final sample was 82.5%. For blacks the corresponding statistics are 11.2% and 13.9% respectively. For other, 2.8% and 3.4%.

In the original sample 70.9% of households were headed by male, while in the final sample only 68.3%. Again there was appreciable regional distortion.

Recurring renter households, 1978.

	North East	North Central	South	West
Original	17.42%	21.8	33.52	27.24
Final	20.14	20.55	28.2	31.09

Again, for some unknown reason entirely too many southern households were lost due to missing information. In contrast to the case of first homeowner households, here the North Central has not gained appreciably in its representation within the final sample; rather the North East and West have gained. Basically, the same conclusions are obtained by examining the 1979 sample for first homeowners. As before the major problem is with the regional representation. For the other variables roughly similar medians are found in both the original and final samples.

First homeowner households, 1979.

	North East	North Central	South	West
Original	17.2%	26.9	36.4	19.5
Final	24.4	25.3	27.6	22.6

Again, the South loses disproportionately too many households due to missing information. This time, however, the major 'gainer' is the North East, which again helps to explain why we have a 'significant' regional effect for the North East in 1979.

For recurring renters in 1979 we do not seem to have any appreciable discrepancies in the regional composition of the original relative to the final sample. We also have the rather expected, but still striking result, that rural households are severely underrepresented due to missing information. Thus, the non-SMSA, rural components are as follows:

	Homeowner		Recurring renter	
	1978	1979	1978	1979
Original	56.5%	55.0	47.3	47.0
Final	22.7	20.7	18.8	20.0

The only policy inference to be derived from these results is that the South field operations of the census could conceivably be improved as is the case for rural field operations in general. To what extent there are two distinct phenomena, or it is the case that the South is overwhelmingly more rural than the other regions is also a matter that deserves some further consideration.

The second set of policy issues relates to the implications of our econometric findings relative to various 'barriers' to homeownership.

We have established in the previous section, that at the mean, the income elasticity of the probability of first homeownership is of the order of 2.3; mortgage interest rate elasticity is of the order of (−)0.4 – on the assumption that interest costs are 70% of homeownership cost. One may adjust it accordingly if one feels that this is too high or too low. Finally, the 'down payment' elasticity is of the order of (−)1.2.

Thus, the results leave no doubt that the 'prime mover' in this market is household income – other things being equal. On the other hand, the downpayment 'barrier' is far more significant than the 'interest' barrier – even though our treatment of downpayment is not without deficiencies owing to lack of information on 'points' and other closing costs.

We shall now show how certain marketing practices in the home mortgage market impact on the probability of first homeownership.

Recently, an interesting phenomenon in such markets is the introduction of ARM (adjustable rate mortgage) coupled with a number of 'points'. In many markets the 'points' plus the first year mortgage rate is roughly equal to the interest rate the financial institution would demand for the loan in accord with its stated formula for adjustment. This implies that the 'advertised' rate is well below market when it is offered. This is done, I presume, because financial institutions have 'rules' about determining 'qualified' or credit worthy borrowers that have to do with the 'monthly payment' the borrower will undertake at the *initial* rate. This 'qualifies' more borrowers. For example, in most areas of the North East, the initial rate is of the order of 9 to 9.75% with three to three and a half points. According to the adjustment formula employed, under present market conditions, the rate should be about 12.25%. In many such instruments there is also a 'cap' of 2 percentage points in upward or downward adjustment. Thus, a household borrowing at, say 9.5%, and three points can look forward to an upward adjustment of its interest cost by roughly 21%. The question is: does this practice encourage or discourage first time homeownership, as against, for example, a policy that offers the same terms for the first two years but eliminates the 'points'? This could mean in this hypothetical case offering 12.5% for the first year and 11.5% for the second; or 11.5% for the first two years and only one 'point'. Take the benchmark as 11.5% mortgage rate and one 'point'. This would in effect incorporate more or less realistic rates and more realistic 'closing' costs.

We apply this to the median (1979) house value and mortgage of $50,000 and $40,000 respectively. The 'promotional' package reduces the rate by 17% and hence homeownership costs by about 12%. The extra two points raise downpayment by $800.00 or by 7.7%. The first raises the probability of first homeownership by 6.8%; the latter reduces the probability by 9.2%. Thus, the whole package has the effect of reducing the probability of first homeownership by 2.4%. The import of this discussion is that current practices have two deficiencies:

(a) They hide problems from borrowing households who may not entirely realize that under current market conditions they face very substantial increases in what they perceive to be their housing costs with ARM.
(b) By relying substantially on 'points' rather than interest rates to adjust to market conditions financial institutions may be unnecessarily discouraging first homeownership.

7. Conclusions

We have examined the determinants of the probability of first homeownership using the AHS files for 1978, 1979. These data constitute the best available source and are eminently suitable for such study. Our major conclusions are that:

(i) While there is an inordinately large number of observations that had to be discarded, there was no appreciable distortion of the composition of the sample in terms of economic characteristics – at least this is so when considering only medians.

There is regional distortion in that the South is invariably under-represented in the sample after deletions of observations due to missing information. The same is true for rural (non-SMSA) households.

(ii) The probability of (first) homeownership is particularly sensitive to household income; less so to downpayment (front end payments) and even less so to mortgage interest rates. To be precise, the elasticity for income is of the order of 2.3; for homeownership costs (−)0.6 – and assuming interest costs to be 70% of ownership costs – the interest elasticity is (−)0.4; the downpayment elasticity is (−)1.2

(iii) Lending schemes relying on ARM instruments with below market rates and compensatory 'points' discourage first time homeownership relative to schemes that could offer market rates and deemphasize points.

(iv) The relationships estimated for 1978, 1979 are certainly very significant and the estimated coefficients are remarkably similar as between the two years.

(v) It would appear that it would be highly beneficial to analyze the four cross sections currently available – 1977, 1978, 1979 and 1980 – in a combined time series cross-sectional framework.

References

Aaron, H.J., 1970, Income taxes and housing, American Economic Review, Dec., 798–806.

Aaron, H.J., 1972, Shelter and subsidies: Who benefits from federal housing policies? (Brookings Institution, Washington, DC).

David, Martin, 1962, Family composition and consumption (North-Holland, Amsterdam).

Dhrymes, P.J., 1978, Introductory econometrics (Springer-Verlag, New York).

Dhrymes, P.J., 1981, Limited dependent variables, Mimeo.

Kain, J. and J. Quigley, 1975, Housing markets and racial discrimination (National Bureau of Economic Research, New York).

Lee, T.H., 1963, Demand for housing: A cross section analysis, Review of Economics and Statistics 45, 190–196.

Linneman, P., 1983, An economic analysis of the homeownership decision, Mimeo. (University of Pennsylvania, Philadelphia, PA).

Maisel, S.J., 1966, Rates of ownership, mobility and purchase, In: Essays in urban land economics, Real Estate Research Program (University of California, Los Angeles, CA).

Orcutt, G.H. et al., 1961, Microanalysis of socioeconomic systems (Harper & Row, New York).

Rosen, H.S., 1979a, Owner-occupied housing and the federal income tax: Estimates and simulations, Journal of Urban Economics, April.

Rosen, H.S., 1979b, Housing decisions and the U.S. income tax: An econometric analysis, Journal of Public Economics 11, no. 1, Jan., 1–23.

Summers, L., 1981, Inflation, the stock market and owner-occupied housing, American Economic Review, May.

White, M.J. and L.J. White, 1977, The tax subsidy to owner-occupied housing: Who benefits?, Journal of Public Economics 3, 111–126.

PART VI

TOPICS IN ECONOMIC THEORY

On Optimal Advertising Capital and Research Expenditures under Dynamic Conditions[1]

By PHOEBUS J. DHRYMES

The purpose of this paper is to extend the results obtained by Professors Nerlove and Arrow in their article in the May, 1962, issue of this journal.[2] In particular, it will be shown that an analysis similar to theirs can be employed to study the characterisation of optimal expenditure policies where the firm is permitted to manipulate not only its demand function but also its cost function.

We deal first with the case where the only additional policy variable employed is expenditure on the capital stock. We shall employ assumptions parallel to those of Nerlove and Arrow.

I. FORMULATION OF THE PROBLEM

Consider a firm with demand function

$$q = f(p, A_1, z), f \in C'' \quad \ldots (1)$$

where p is price of output, A_1 is level of " goodwill " and z is an exogenous variable.

The firm's cost function is given by:

$$C = C(q, A_2), C \in C'' \quad \ldots (2)$$

where q is output and A_2 is the capital stock.

It is assumed, if necessary after suitable normalisation, that a dollar's expenditure on the capital stock increments it by one unit, and similarly with respect to advertising expenditure and the level of " goodwill ". If both stocks are assumed to decay exponentially, then we have the relations

$$\begin{aligned} \dot{A}_1 &= a_1 - \delta_1 A_1 \\ \dot{A}_2 &= a_2 - \delta_2 A_2 \end{aligned} \quad \ldots (3)$$

where the a_i denote expenditure on the ith stock and δ_i are positive constants. The initial stocks are given by:

$$\begin{aligned} A_1(0) &= A_{10} \\ A_2(0) &= A_{20} \end{aligned} \quad \ldots (3a)$$

[1] The research on which this article is based was done while the author was a National Science Foundation Post-Doctoral Fellow and was supported in part by Office of Naval Research Contract Nonr-225(50) at Stanford University.

I wish to thank Professor K. J. Arrow and M. Kurz for helpful comments.

[2] Marc Nerlove and Kenneth J. Arrow, " Optimal Advertising Policy under Dynamic Conditions ", *Economica*, May, 1962, pp. 129–42.

The problem now is to choose $p(t)$, $A_1(t)$, $A_2(t)$ so as to maximise

$$V(A_1, A_2, p, z) = \int_0^\infty e^{-\alpha t}\left[pf(p, A_1, z) - C(q, A_2) - \sum_{i=1}^{2} a_i\right]dt - \sum_{i=1}^{2} A_{i0} \quad (4)$$

subject to (3) and (3a). The inclusion of the term $\sum_{i=1}^{2} A_{i0}$ in the maximand of (4) is innocuous since it is a fixed number. If, holding A_1, A_2, z constant, we maximise (4) with respect to p, we shall obtain a solution

$$\hat{p}(t) = P(A_1, A_2, z) \quad \text{(4a)}$$

which gives the optimal time path in terms of A_1, A_2, and z.

Inserting (4) and (3) into (5) and performing an integration by parts yields:

$$S(A_1, A_2, z) = \int_0^\infty e^{-\alpha t}\left[R(A_1, A_2, z) - \sum_{i=1}^{2} (\alpha + \delta_i)A_i\right]dt \quad (5)$$

where $R(A_1, A_2, z) = \hat{p}\, f(p, A_1, z) - C(\hat{q}, A_2)$ and we have assumed

$$\lim_{t \to \infty} e^{-\alpha t}\,[A_1(t) + A_2(t)] = 0 \quad \text{(5a)}$$

for the optimal $A_1(t)$, $A_2(t)$. As will be shown later, this involves little loss of generality.

From (5) we must now deduce the characterisation of the optimal policies $A_1^*(t)$, $A_2^*(t)$.

II. Characterisation of the Solution

Before we proceed, it is necessary to impose some conditions on the function $R(A_1, A_2, z)$, for otherwise it is not possible to say anything about the solution. More specifically:

Assumption 1. For given z, the function $R(A_1, A_2, z)$ is continuous and bounded in A_1, A_2. If z is interpreted as national income, boundedness is indeed a required specification on R since, if not imposed, we could have the profits of this firm exceeding national income.

We have, for given z:

Lemma 2·1. There exist policies $A_i(t)$, $i = 1, 2$, maximising (5) and they are finite.

Proof: Let $\Pi(A_1, A_2, z) = R(A_1, A_2, z) - \sum_{i=1}^{2} (\alpha + \delta_i)A_i$. Now if, for every t, Π is maximised for given z, then so is (5). On the other hand, if (5) is maximised, then $\Pi(A_1, A_2, z)$ must be maximised for each interval of t. Hence we shall merely show that Π assumes its maximum on the finite plane.

Since $R(A_1, A_2, z)$ is bounded, it follows that there exists a pair $(\bar{A}_1, \bar{A}_2)$ such that $\Pi(A_1, A_2, z)$ is decreasing for $A_1 > \bar{A}_1$, $A_2 > \bar{A}_2$. Thus we need consider Π on the rectangle $0 \leq A_1 \leq \bar{A}_1$, $0 \leq A_2 \leq \bar{A}_2$. Since Π is continuous, there exists a pair (A_1^*, A_2^*) such that $\Pi(A_1^*, A_2^*, z) = \max.$ for given z. It is, of course, to be understood that in general A_1^*, A_2^* are functions of z.

Remark 2·2. This shows that the assumption (5a) does not restrict the generality of our result, since the lemma states that for bounded z optimal policies are finite, hence that $e^{\alpha t}$ grows " faster " than they do.

Assumption 2. The function $R(A_1, A_2, z)$ is strictly concave in A_1, A_2 for given z.

Lemma 2·3. The maximum of Lemma 2·1 is absolute and the functions $A_1^*(z)$, $A_2^*(z)$ are continuous in z.

Proof: The first part of the lemma is redundant: we give the proof here in the interest of completeness.

Thus let $X=(A_1, A_2)$, D the domain of Π. Then for any $Y \epsilon D$ and sufficiently small λ,

$$\Pi(X^*) \geq \Pi\,[(1-\lambda)\,X^*+\lambda Y] \geq (1-\lambda)\,\Pi(X^*)+\lambda\Pi(Y)$$

or $$\Pi(X^*) \geq \Pi(Y).$$

For the second part we argue as follows: Let $(z_i: i=1, 2, \ldots)$ be a sequence such that $\lim_{i\to\infty} z_i = z_0$. This defines the sequence $\{X^*(z_i)=(A_1^*(z_i), A_2^*(z_i)): i=1, 2, \ldots\}$. Suppose $\lim_{i\to\infty} X^*(z_i)=X \neq X^*(z_0)$.

Then, since the $X^*(z_i)$ represents maximising policies, we find for sufficiently small λ

$$\Pi(X) \geq \Pi[(1-\lambda)\,X+\lambda X^*(z_0)] \geq (1-\lambda)\,\Pi[X]+\lambda\Pi[X^*(z_0)]$$

or $$\Pi(X) \geq \Pi[X^*(z_0)].$$

But strict inequality is impossible since $X^*(z_0)$ is the maximising set for z_0.

Thus the $A_1^*(z)$, $A_2^*(z)$ are continuous in z.

Lemma 2·4. If (A_1^*, A_2^*) is the maximum for $\Pi(A_1, A_2)$, the optimum expenditure policy for $A_{i0} \leq A_i^*$, $i=1, 2$, $t>0$, is given by

$$a_i^*=\delta_i A_i^* \quad i=1, 2$$

and $$a_i^*=\delta_i A_i^* \text{ if } A_{i0}=A_i^* \quad i=1, 2,\ t=0$$
$$=+\infty \quad A_{i0}<A_i^*.$$

Proof: Since expenditures are not constrained, the assertion for $A_{i0}<A_i^*$, $t=0$, follows from the fact that (A_1^*, A_2^*) is a maximum. The assertion for $t>0$, $A_{i0}=A_1^*$, is an immediate consequence of (3) and Lemma 2·3.

It remains next to deal with the situation where $A_{i0}<A_1^*$ for at least one i. Now the decay of stocks constrains the manner of decumulation, since stocks cannot be decumulated faster than they decay. Let P be the admissible family of decumulation paths. For any path $\Gamma \epsilon P$, let $c(\Gamma)$ be the cost associated with it; note that an admissible path may involve partial maintenance for an otherwise redundant stock.

The problem is then to find a path L^* minimising the line integral

$$\int_\Gamma [\Pi(A_1^*, A_2^*, z)-\Pi(A_1, A_2, z)]-c(\Gamma) \ldots\ldots\ldots\ldots\ldots\ldots (6)$$

with the constraint $\Gamma \epsilon P$. This is itself a problem in the calculus of variations which is too cumbersome to be considered here. Instead we shall show that, by restricting the form of the function Π, we obtain a simple characterisation of the solution affording maximal correspondence with the results of Nerlove and Arrow.

Observe first that for given $\bar{A}_1$, $\bar{A}_2$, the functions $\Pi(\bar{A}_1, A_2)$, $\Pi(A_1, \bar{A}_2)$ are concave in A_2, A_1, respectively. To this we add:

Assumption 3. The function $\Pi(A_1, A_2)$ has a maximum at A_2^* for any fixed A_1, and a maximum at A_1^* for any fixed A_2.

It should be pointed out that while Assumptions 1 and 2 have their direct analogues in Nerlove and Arrow's treatment, Assumption 3 deals with a situation that does not arise in their problem.

We have:

Lemma 2·5. If $A_{i0} > A_i^*$ $i = 1, 2$ then there exist constants τ_i $i = 1, 2$ such that optimal expenditure policies are given by:

$$a_i^* = 0 \qquad \text{for} \quad o \leq t \leq \tau_i \qquad i = 1, 2$$
$$a_i^* = \delta_i A_i^* \qquad t > \tau_i \qquad i = 1, 2$$

Proof: Let $X_0 = (A_{10}, A_{20})$, $X_1 = (A_1^*, A_{20})$, $X_2 = (A_{10}, A_2^*)$, $X_3 = (A_1^*, A_2^*)$ and R_0 be the closed rectangle with vertices X_i, $i = 0, 1, 2, 3$. Since the functions $\Pi(A_1, A_{20})$, $\Pi(A_{10}, A_2)$ are concave in A_1, A_2 respectively, it follows by Assumption 3 that:

$$\Pi(X_0) - \Pi(X_1) \leq \Pi_1(X_1)\,(A_{10} - A_1^*) = 0$$
$$\Pi(X_0) - \Pi(X_2) \leq \Pi_2(X_2)\,(A_{20} - A_2^*) = 0.$$

Hence $\quad \Pi(X_i) \geq \Pi(X_0), \quad i = 1, 2, 3.$

It is, of course, apparent that any optimal policy must remain within R_0.

Since R_0 is a (closed bounded) convex set for any $X \epsilon R_0$, we have

$$\Pi(X) \geq \sum_{i=0}^{3} \lambda_i \Pi(X_i) \geq \sum_{i=0}^{3} \lambda_i \Pi(X_0) = \Pi(X_0)$$

where $\quad 0 \leq \lambda_i \leq 1, \ \sum_{i=0}^{3} \lambda_i = 1.$

This shows that if the firm maintains none of the stocks, its profit does not decline. We next show that it is not optimal to partially maintain either of the two stocks. Consider any sequence of points, $\{X^{(i)}\}$, such that $X^{(i)} \epsilon R_0$, $X^{(o)} = X_0$, $\lim_{i \to \infty} X^{(i)} = X^*$, and let R_i be the (closed) rectangles having opposite vertices, X^* and $X^{(i)}$. We have $R_0 \supset R_1 \supset R_2$ . . . An application of the previous argument shows that if X is any point in R_n, then $\Pi(X) \geq \Pi(X^{(n)})$.

From this it readily follows that partial maintenance of any of the stocks is non-optimal. Thus optimal policy is to decumulate as fast as possible. Because of the constraints, we must have:

$$A_i^{(t)} = A_{i0}\, e^{-\delta_i t} \quad 0 \leq t \leq \tau_i$$

where $A_i(\tau_i) = A_i^*$, $i = 1, 2$. Thereafter Lemma 2·4 applies.

Perhaps an illustration will clarify the method of reasoning (Figure 1). Suppose with partial maintenance of A_2, after the lapse of time $\triangle t$, we arrive at $X^{(1)}$, in Figure 1. Without partial maintenance we arrive at $X^{(2)}$. An application of the previous reasoning shows $\Pi(X^{(2)}) \geq \Pi(X^{(1)})$. Since it is costly to arrive at $X^{(1)}$ and costless to arrive at $X^{(2)}$, the conclusion is clear.

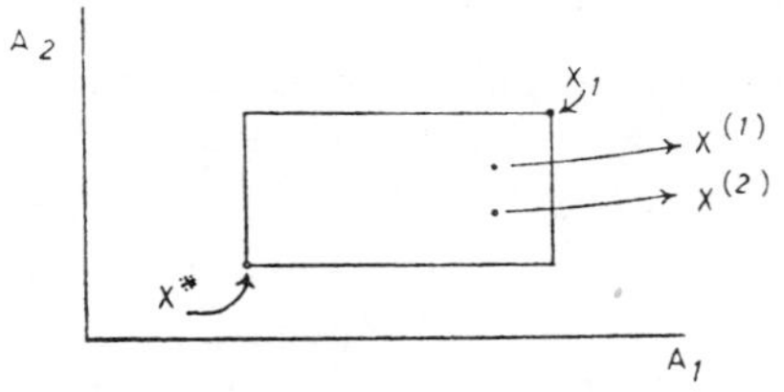

FIGURE 1

It remains now to consider the optimal policy when one of the stocks is above and the other below the optimal level. A construction similar to Figure 1 will show that optimal policy is to increase the deficient stock to its optimal level instantaneously and to let the redundant stock decay at its maximal rate. Details are left for the reader.

III. EXTENSION TO THE CASE OF RESEARCH EXPENDITURES

Let A_3 denote the stock of knowledge or level of efficiency which may be thought of as a kind of integral effect of expenditures on research and development.

If assumptions analogous to (3) are made about A_3, then the preceding formulation shows that the lemmas of Section II still are valid, provided we have an assumption analogous to Assumption 3 for the function $\Pi(A_1, A_2, A_3, z)$.

The variable A_3 enters into the cost function so that now the firm has two alternatives in manipulating its cost structure. However, the qualitative characterisation of the solution will be simplified considerably if we bear in mind that it is very realistic to assume that $\delta_3 = 0$, i.e., that knowledge or efficiency does not decay, or that " we can't forget ". Hence if a solution yields $A_{30}^{*} < A_{30}$, then we ought to treat the level of efficiency as a datum and thus resolve our problem. This is the case where we have friction moving " backward ". On the other hand, it is possible to argue that such initial conditions do not or cannot arise in practice; so we may neglect this case by suitably restricting the class of admissible initial conditions. In this case, the analogues of Lemmas 2·1, 2·3, and 2·4 are easily established and this, in conjunction with Lemma 2·5, is sufficient to characterise the solution.

Stanford University.

INTERNATIONAL
ECONOMIC
REVIEW

September, 1964
Vol. 5, No. 3

ON THE THEORY OF THE MONOPOLISTIC MULTIPRODUCT FIRM UNDER UNCERTAINTY*

BY PHOEBUS J. DHRYMES[1]

THE PROBLEM to be treated in this paper is that of optimal production for a firm that is capable of producing n products, the demand for which is subject to a random component.

The analytical framework is similar to that of portfolio selection and to some extent rests on modern utility theory. The objective is to study the response of the product mix of the firm to changes in the subjective disposition of the entrepreneur toward risk, to changes in the probability characteristics of the demand for the firm's products, and to changes in specific tax rates imposed on the various outputs of the firm.

1. PRELIMINARIES

Consider the monopolistic firm that sells the same product in m markets. Let the respective demand functions be

$$p_i = f_i(Q_i) \, . \tag{1}$$

If the cost function is given by

$$C = c(Q) \, , \tag{2}$$

where

$$Q = \sum_{i=1}^{m} Q_i \, ,$$

then maximization of profit yields the condition

$$\frac{dR}{dQ} = \frac{dC}{dQ} \, , \tag{3}$$

where

$$R = \sum_{i=1}^{m} R_i, \quad R_i = f_i(Q_i)Q_i \, , \quad \frac{dR}{dQ_i} = \frac{dR}{dQ}\frac{dQ}{dQ_i} \, , \text{ and } \frac{dQ}{dQ_i} = 1 \, .$$

* Manuscript received June 30, 1963, revised February 7, 1964.

[1] I should like to thank L. R. Klein for several helpful comments and suggestions.

Thus, the discriminating monopolist equalizes marginal revenue in all markets.

Consider now the monopolist that produces in m locations but sells only in one market. Let the cost of producing in the i-th location be

$$C_i = c_i(Q_i) , \tag{4}$$

where Q_i is the output produced in the i-th location. The total cost of production is

$$C = \sum_{i=1}^{m} c_i(Q_i) . \tag{5}$$

If the demand function for the product is given by

$$p = f(Q) , \tag{6}$$

then profit maximization will yield the condition

$$\frac{dR}{dQ}\frac{dQ}{dQ_i} = \frac{dc_i}{dQ_i} \quad \text{or} \quad \frac{dR}{dQ} = \frac{dc_i}{dQ_i} . \tag{7}$$

Hence, in the absence of transport costs, the monopolist will equalize marginal costs in all locations.

If transport costs are introduced, it no longer follows that the monopolist will equalize marginal costs in all locations. If $t_i(Q_i)$ is the cost of delivering Q_i units from the i-th location to the market, the cost to the monopolist of marketing his output is given by

$$C = \sum_{i=1}^{m} [c_i(Q_i) + t_i(Q_i)] , \tag{8}$$

and profit maximization will yield the condition

$$\frac{dR}{dQ}\frac{dQ}{dQ_i} - \frac{dt_i}{dQ_i} - \frac{dc_i}{dQ_i} = 0 \quad \text{or} \quad \frac{dR}{dQ} = \frac{dt_i}{dQ_i} + \frac{dc_i}{dQ_i} . \tag{9}$$

Thus, the monopolist will equalize the marginal costs of production *and* transport in all localities.

In general, if a monopolist produces in m locations and sells in k markets an otherwise homogeneous good, let the cost of producing in the i-th location be

$$C_i = c_i(Q_i) , \tag{10}$$

the cost of transporting from the i-th location to the s-th market be

$$T_{is} = t_{is}(Q_{is}) , \tag{11}$$

and the demand function in the s-th market be

$$p_s = f_s(V_s) , \tag{12}$$

V_s being the quantity sold in the s-th market.

The problem is now much more complicated and involves maximizing

$$\Pi = \sum_{s=1}^{k} R_s(V_s) - \sum_{i=1}^{m} c_i(Q_i) - \sum_{i=1}^{m}\sum_{s=1}^{k} t_{is}(Q_{is}) , \tag{13}$$

subject to the constraints

$$V_s = \sum_{i=1}^{m} Q_{is} , \qquad Q_i = \sum_{s=1}^{k} Q_{is} , \tag{14}$$

where $R_s(V_s) = V_s f_s(V_s)$.

To this effect, set up the Lagrangean expression

$$\begin{aligned} \Lambda = & \sum_{s=1}^{k} R_s(V_s) - \sum_{i=1}^{m} c_i(Q_i) - \sum_{i=1}^{m}\sum_{s=1}^{k} t_{is}(Q_{is}) \\ & + \sum_{s=1}^{k} \lambda_s\Big[V_s - \sum_{i=1}^{m} Q_{is}\Big] + \sum_{i=1}^{m} \mu_i \Big[Q_i - \sum_{s=1}^{k} Q_{is}\Big] . \end{aligned} \tag{15}$$

First order conditions yield

$$\begin{aligned} & \frac{dR_\alpha(V_\alpha)}{dV_\alpha} + \lambda_\alpha = 0 , && \alpha = 1, 2, \cdots, k , \\ & -\frac{dc_\beta(Q_\beta)}{dQ_\beta} + \mu_\beta = 0 , && \beta = 1, 2, \cdots, m , \\ & -\frac{dt_\gamma\delta}{dQ_\gamma\delta} - \lambda_\delta - \mu_\lambda = 0 , && \gamma = 1, 2, \cdots, m , \\ & && \delta = 1, 2, \cdots, k . \end{aligned} \tag{16}$$

Combining the equations in (16), we obtain

$$\frac{dR_\alpha(V_\alpha)}{dV_\alpha} = \frac{dt_{\beta\alpha}}{dQ_{\beta\alpha}} + \frac{dc_\beta}{dQ_\beta} . \tag{16a}$$

Apart from questions of existence of a solution to the system in (16) and (16a) and the appropriateness of the equality relationship in the constraints (14), the first order conditions as expressed in (16a) simply state that in order for some output to be produced in the β-th location and marketed in the α-th market it is necessary that the marginal revenue in the α-th market be equal to the marginal production cost in the β-th location *plus* the marginal transport cost to the α-th market.

We could further generalize the problem by considering the case of a monopolist producing q different goods in a number of different locations and selling in k markets. The generalization, however, will not yield any radically new conditions; further, such results are reasonably well-known. They are almost textbook material.

Nonetheless there are certain inadequacies in the formulations given above. Either in the case where q different goods are produced, or in the case where the same good is produced in k different locations, it is not enough to allow only for the transport of goods from one locality, to another. We must allow for the fact that certain fixed factors could be moved from one production locality to another, or in the case of q different goods we must allow for the possibility that some fixed factors could be shifted from producing a given good, to producing another. Thus, the results indicated above should be taken as the characterization of equilibrium in the long run, where all factors are freely variable in every location, or for the production of every good.

The problem I propose to treat here is the following. Suppose a firm is capable of producing n products; the firm can buy on the market competitively the (variable) factors $x_1, \cdots, x_k$; in addition, it has at its disposal limited amounts of the (fixed) factors $x_{k+1}, \cdots, x_m$. In general, if x^0_{ij}, $j = k+1, \cdots, m$, is the amount of the j-th (fixed) factor attached to the plant producing the i-th good, then we have the relation

$$X_j = \sum_{i=1}^{n} x^0_{ij} , \qquad j = k+1, \cdots, m . \tag{17}$$

While augmentation of the X_j cannot be accomplished in the short run, some "shifting" can take place, so that the x_{ij}, $j = k+1, \cdots, m$, can be considered variable in a limited sense, i.e., subject to the constraint

$$X_j - \sum_{i=1}^{n} x_{ij} \geqq 0 , \qquad j = k+1, \cdots, m , \tag{18}$$

where x_{ij} is the quantity of the j-th fixed factor actually employed in the production of the i-th good at the equilibrium configuration.

If the firm's demand functions for the n products are subject to random components, then the firm's profit is a random variable, and the firm will wish to guard against the eventuality of suffering large losses. It is, of course, intuitively clear that the earlier conditions that equated marginal revenue to marginal costs, in an appropriate context, will not in general hold here, and the question arises as to the proper characterization of the equilibrium configuration.

2. THE MODEL

a. *Specification of the cost aspect*: This is perhaps the least controversial aspect, since there exists a long tradition and considerable concensus on this score.

By the assumption that the firm buys on a competitive market, the total variable cost is given by

$$V = \sum_{i=1}^{n}\sum_{j=1}^{k} x_{ij} w_j , \tag{19}$$

where w_j is the price of the j-th (variable) factor, given independently of the firm's activity.

In addition to this, there is the cost of shifting (fixed) factors from the production of one commodity to the production of another. This will be called the relocation cost and will be denoted by

$$\begin{aligned} S &= h(x_{1\,k+1}, \cdots, x_{1\,m}; x_{2\,k+1}, \cdots, x_{2\,m}; \cdots; x_{n\,k+1}, \cdots, x_{n\,m}) \\ &= h(x)\,, \end{aligned} \tag{20}$$

where x is to be interpreted as a vector with nm components x_{ij}, $i = 1, \cdots, n$, $j = 1, \cdots, m$. The expression $h(x)$ is introduced only as a matter of convenience, and it is to be understood that h does not depend on x_{ij} for $j = 1, 2, \cdots, k$. More precisely, we have

$$\frac{\partial h(x)}{\partial x_{ij}} \equiv 0 \qquad \text{all } i, \text{ and } j = 1, 2, \cdots, k\,. \tag{21}$$

There is also a fixed element of cost, related to depreciation, obsolescence, etc. Hence the total cost of production to the firm is given by

$$C = V + S + F\,, \tag{22}$$

where F is a constant representing fixed costs.

The function h can be assumed to be (strictly) convex in its arguments. This simply means that relocation can take place only at nondecreasing (increasing) costs.

b. *Specification of the production aspect*: The production of each commodity is assumed to be governed by a production function

$$Q_i = f_i(x_{i1}, x_{i2}, \cdots, x_{ik}; x_{i\,k+1}, \cdots, x_{im}) = f_i(x)\,, \tag{23}$$

where the notation $f_i(x)$ is to have the same interpretation, *mutatis mutandis*, given to the notation $h(x)$ in (20).

Each function $f_i(x)$ is assumed to be (strictly) concave in its arguments. This simply means that production of every commodity takes place under a regime of (diminishing) nonincreasing marginal productivity for each factor.

Recall that if the function f is twice differentiable, then convexity implies that the matrix of second order partial derivatives

$$H = [f_{ij}] \qquad i, j = 1, 2, \cdots, p \tag{24}$$

is positive (semi) definite on X, and concavity that it is negative (semi) definite on X, X being the domain of f.

c. *Specification of the demand aspect*: We shall assume that i-th output of the firm is given by

$$p_i = g_i(Q_1, \cdots, Q_n) + u_i \,, \qquad i = 1, 2, \cdots, n \,. \tag{25}$$

We postulate that $u = (u_1, u_2, \cdots, u_n)'$ has a multivariate distribution with mean vector 0 and convariance matrix $\Sigma = [\sigma_{ij}]$. The profit function of the firm is thus given by

$$\Pi(x, u) = R[Q(x)] - C(x) + \sum_{i=1}^{n} u_i Q_i \,, \tag{26}$$

where $C(x)$ is the cost function, essentially defined in (22), and we define

$$R[Q(x)] = \sum_{i=1}^{n} g_i[Q(x)]Q_i(x) \tag{27}$$

$$Q = (Q_1, Q_2, \cdots, Q_n)' \,.$$

Clearly $\Pi(x, u)$ is a random variable with parameters

$$\begin{aligned} E[\Pi(x, u)] &= R[Q(x)] - C(x) = \Pi(x, 0) \\ \text{Var}\,[\Pi(x, u)] &= Q'\Sigma Q = \sigma_\pi^2 \,, \end{aligned} \tag{28}$$

where we have assumed implicitly that $E[uQ'] = 0$. It is of course evident that if $\sigma_0 = \min_i \sigma_{ii}$, then $\sigma_0 \gtrless \sigma_\pi^2$; so even if the entrepreneur were solely interested in minimizing the variance of his profit he will either specialize in one commodity or diversify. But the specification of the criterion of good performance is yet to be discussed.

d. *Specification of the objective function*: In the case of perfect certainty there is both a tradition and a modicum of empirical relevance in specifying profit to be the quantity to be maximized. In the present case, however, the situation is not very clear. To maximize profit means to maximize the stochastic function (26) with respect to the inputs x_{ij}, hence with respect to the outputs Q_i. This is in general impossible because of the presence of the random vriables u_i. Other criteria must be sought. One frequently proposed criterion is maximization of the expected value of profits, i.e., maximization of $\Pi(x, 0)$ with respect to the inputs x_{ij}. This action, however, will lead to a situation in which the risk of ruin may be too large to be acceptable by the firm, as may be readily seen by using Chebyshev's inequality on (26) in conjunction with (28).

One possible remedy to this may be to maximize expected profit subject to a constraint on the risk incurred, i.e., subject to

$$v \geqq Q'\Sigma Q \,. \tag{29}$$

This is, in fact, the approach followed by Markowitz [7], in a different context. But a still neater approach, suggested by the work of von Neumann and Morgenstern [9], Luce and Raiffa [6], Debreu [3, 4] and

Marschak [8], is to maximize the expected value of an appropriate utility function.

In the present context we shall employ a quadratic utility function (in profit). Since such functions are unique only up to an (increasing) affine transformation, it involves no loss in generality to write the function as

$$U = \Pi(x, u) + \frac{1}{2}\alpha[\Pi(x, u) - \Pi(x, 0)]^2 . \tag{30}$$

This particular form may also be rationalized as an (incomplete) Taylor's series expansion of a more general utility function. The sign of the parameter α may be taken as indicating risk attraction ($\alpha > 0$), or risk aversion ($\alpha < 0$), a terminology to be employed repeatedly below.

In this framework, notice that maximization of expected profit implies that the entrepreneur's utility function is linear in "money," while maximization of expected profit subject to a variance constraint

$$v \geqq Q'\Sigma Q \tag{31}$$

implies that the entrepreneur displays risk aversion.

3. FORMULATION OF THE PROBLEM

Consider an entrepreneur operating a monopolistic firm and characterized by a utility function as given in (30). Suppose that his cost, production and demand specifications are as in (22), (23), and (25), respectively. Then, the problem we are dealing with is of the form

$$\text{Max}\,(\Pi(x) + (1/2)\alpha v) \tag{32}$$

subject to

$$\sum_{i=1}^{n} x_{ij} \leqq X_j , \qquad j = k+1, \cdots, m ,$$

$$x_{ij} \geqq 0 , \qquad \text{all } i \text{ and } j ,$$

where, for simplicity, we have written $\Pi(x)$ instead of $\Pi(x, 0)$. We shall adhere to this practice below.

In general, conditions of stationarity for this type of problem are not known, since we cannot specify that Π is concave in x. The difficulty really lies in our inability to specify that the expected revenue function is concave in x. This is so since it is given by

$$R(Q) = \sum_{i=1}^{n} g_i Q_i = \sum_{i=1}^{n} R_i(Q) . \tag{33}$$

We know that Q is concave in x and that the R_i are concave in Q, so that R is concave in Q. But unless we can also assert that R is increasing, or at least nondecreasing in Q, we cannot easily show that R is concave in x. The fact that R is concave in x, provided R is nondecreasing in Q, is quite easy to establish. Thus, define

$$H(x) = R[Q(x)] \ . \tag{34}$$

Let $x_1, x_2 \in X$, X convex, $X \subset R^{mn}$, where R^{mn} is the mn-dimensional Euclidean space. Then for $\lambda_i \geqq 0$, $\lambda_1 + \lambda_2 = 1$

$$\begin{aligned} H(\lambda_1 x_1 + \lambda_2 x_2) &= R[Q(\lambda_1 x_1 + \lambda_2 x_2)] \geqq R(\lambda_1 Q(x_1) + \lambda_2 Q(x_2)] \\ &\geqq \lambda_1 R[Q(x_1)] + \lambda_2 R[Q(x_2)] = \lambda_1 H(x_1) + \lambda_2 H(x_2) \ . \end{aligned} \tag{35}$$

Since we do not wish to restrict the form of Π unnecessarily, we shall not make the assumption that R is nondecreasing in Q. But this means that we should seek the solution by more devious means. First, note that if outputs were to be specified by, say, $Q = Q^0$, then maximization of expected utility is equivalent to minimization of cost under the constraints

$$Q^0 = f(x) \ , \qquad X_j \geqq \sum_{i=1}^{n} x_{ij} \ , \qquad j = k+1, \cdots, m \ , \tag{36}$$

where f is a vector valued function of x; i.e., it is a vector consisting of the functions f_i, $i = 1, 2, \cdots, n$.

A problem similar to this was treated by Pfouts [10]. Since

$$C(x) = V(x) + h(x) + F \tag{37}$$

and since h is convex in x, V linear in x, and F a constant, it follows that C is convex in x. Moreover, the constraints

$$Q^0 - f(x) = 0 \ , \qquad \sum_{i=1}^{n} x_{ij} - X_j \leqq 0 \ , \qquad j = k+1, \cdots, m \ , \tag{38}$$

are also convex in x.

Thus, the problem is to minimize a convex function subject to convex inequality constraints. This is equivalent to finding the saddle point of the Lagrangean expression

$$L(x, \lambda, \mu) = C(x) + \sum_{i=1}^{n} \lambda_i [Q_i^0 - f_i(x)] + \sum_{j=k+1}^{m} \mu_j \Big[\sum_{i=1}^{n} x_{ij} - X_j \Big] \tag{39}$$

for

$$x_{ij} \geqq 0 \ , \qquad \lambda_i \geqq 0 \ , \qquad \mu_j \geqq 0 \ .$$

Necessary and sufficient conditions are known to be

$$\frac{\partial C}{\partial x_{ij}} - \lambda_i \frac{\partial f_i}{\partial x_{ij}} \geqq 0 \ , \qquad i, j = 1, 2, \cdots, k \ , \tag{40a}$$

$$\frac{\partial C}{\partial x_{ij}} = \mu_j - \lambda_i \frac{\partial f_i}{\partial x_{ij}} \geqq 0 \ , \qquad i, j = k+1, \cdots, m \ , \tag{40b}$$

(40c) $$\sum_{i,j} \frac{\partial L}{\partial x_{ij}}(x^0, \lambda^0, \mu^0)x^0_{ij} = 0 ,$$

(40d) $$\frac{\partial L}{\partial \lambda_i} \leqq 0 , \qquad i = 1, 2, \cdots, n ,$$

(40e) $$\frac{\partial L}{\partial \mu_j} \leqq 0 , \qquad j = k + 1, \cdots, m ,$$

(40f) $$\sum_{i=1}^{n} \frac{\partial L}{\partial \lambda_i}(x^0, \lambda^0, \mu^0)\lambda^0_i = 0 ,$$

(40g) $$\sum_{j=k+1}^{m} \frac{\partial L}{\partial \mu_j}(x^0, \lambda^0, \mu^0)\mu^0_j = 0 .$$

Variables with zero superscripts indicate equilibrium magnitudes.

Various conclusions emerge from these conditions:

i. Since the first constraint in (38) is given by an equality, it follows that (40d) is also an equality;

ii. if we assume that the functions $f_i(x)$ are such that $f_i(x') = 0$ for any x' containing at least one (relevant) zero component—this is the case for Cobb-Douglas functions—and if the vector of output specifications Q^0 is strictly positive, then (40c) implies that the inequality in (40a) is really an equality;

iii. if for some j_0 in (40e), $\partial L/\partial \mu_{j_0} < 0$, then by (40g) $\mu_{j_0} = 0$;

iv. since the partial derivatives of the functions C and f can be safely assumed to be positive, it follows that the λ_i are positive for all i.

Thus, the multipliers λ_i can be interpreted as implicit prices attached to the outputs Q_i, and the μ_i can be interpreted as implicit prices attached to the fixed factors x_j, $j = k + 1, \cdots, m$.

Economically, the following conditions emerge:

a. Factor employment equilibrium is characterized by the familiar equation—marginal rate of substitution equals factor price ratio, appropriately defined. If the price of a factor exceeds its marginal "value" productivity for a given output, then this (variable) factor will not be used in the production of that output, conditions (40a) and (40c).

b. For fixed factors we have that if such factors are not fully utilized, their implicit "price" is zero, and the condition (40b) essentially reads, marginal cost of relocation = marginal value productivity of the relocated input.

The important result to be gleaned from the preceding discussion is that the factor employment equilibrium of the multiproduct firm is essentially similar to that of the uniproduct firm, except that in the former case several aspects are present which are not in the latter. Furthermore, if the equations (40) are solved, we shall obtain the equilibrium factor employment configuration as a function of the specified set of outputs. Thus

$$x_{ij}^0 = k_{ij}(Q) , \qquad \text{all } i \text{ and } j , \tag{41}$$

and we can construct a cost function in terms of the specified outputs,

$$\sum_{i=1}^{n}\sum_{j=1}^{k} w_j k_{ij}(Q) + h(x(Q)) + F = C^*(Q) , \tag{42}$$

where we have dropped the notation Q^0, since the equations (41) will hold for any specified output set.

We shall assume the function C^* to be convex in Q; this is a fairly standard assumption and simply means that marginal costs are rising with output. In terms of the set of assumptions already made concerning the function h, it is sufficient that the functions k_{ij} in (41) be convex in Q and that h be nondecreasing in x, which are certainly reasonable and do not involve any inconsistencies. But now the problem of utility maximization is quite manageable. Essentially we shall view the firm as making the following two-step decision:

i. Decide on the optimum output mix on the basis of expected utility maximization;
ii. Having done so, decide on optimum factor employment.

In order to see that this essentially leads to the same result as maximizing expected utility *ab initio* with respect to factor inputs we state the following:

LEMMA 1: *Let Q_0 be the solution to the problem of maximizing $E[U(\Pi^*)]$, and x^0 the solution to the problem in equation* (39), *Q_0 being the set of specified outputs, then*

$$H(x^0) \geqq H(x)$$

for any $x \in X$, where $H(x) = \Pi(x) + (1/2)\alpha Q'(x)\Sigma Q(x)$ is the maximand of equation (32), *and X is the constraint set of equation* (39) *and hence identical in the relevant dimensions to that of equation* (32).

This Lemma is sufficiently well known so that no formal proof is required here. Thus, the problem as now formulated involves the maximization of the function

$$\Pi^*(Q) + (1/2)\alpha Q'\Sigma Q , \tag{44}$$

subject to the constraint $Q \geqq 0$.

We shall gnore the constraint, however, and we shall assume that the function is such that the solution will always yield nonnegative vectors. First order conditions involve

$$\frac{\partial \Pi^*}{\partial Q_i} + \alpha \Sigma_i Q = 0 , \qquad i = 1, \cdots, n , \tag{45}$$

where Σ_i is the i-th row of Σ.

The question of second-order conditions will be dealt with shortly. In general, in solving the equations (45), we shall determine the optimal output mix in terms of the parameters Σ and α. We are interested in two general problems:

i. What is the effect on the equilibrium configuration of output of a change in the entrepreneur's disposition toward risk;

ii. What is the effect on the equilibrium configuration of output of a change in the parameters of the distribution of price?

Consider first the solution to these problems in the case where $n = 1$. The first order conditions are given by

$$\frac{d\Pi^*}{dQ} + \alpha\sigma_{11} Q = 0 , \tag{46}$$

Differentiating (46) totally with respect to α, we find

$$\left(\frac{d^2\Pi^*}{dQ^2} + \alpha\sigma_{11}\right)\frac{dQ}{d\alpha} = -\sigma_{11}Q , \tag{46a}$$

The expression in parentheses gives, in fact, the second-order conditions and should be nonpositive (negative) for a maximum. In general, the solution to (46) will yield a stationary point which would represent a maximum if $(d^2\Pi^*/dQ^2) + \alpha\sigma_{11} \leqq 0$. Note that the condition is automatically satisfied if the entrepreneur is a risk averter, $\alpha < 0$; if he is, however, attracted to risk, $\alpha > 0$, the solution to (46) may not represent a maximum; indeed second-order conditions, for an interior maximum, require $(d^2\Pi^*/dQ^2) \leqq -\alpha\sigma_{11}$, which may not be satisfied if $\alpha\sigma_{11}$ is large. Thus, in the case of a risk averter, we have unambiguously

$$\frac{dQ}{d\alpha} > 0 . \tag{47}$$

Hence, an increase in risk aversion will increase output; but note that increasing risk aversion means decreasing $|\alpha|$. On the other hand, if $\alpha > 0$, provided an interior maximum exists, then (47) will also hold; in this case, however, it may be that the solution to the problem is a corner solution. Behavior characterized by risk attraction is, however, highly uncommon so that in subsequent discussion we shall analyze carefully the case of risk aversion and shall only interject a few comments concerning risk attraction.

Differentiating the first order conditions (45) with respect to α, we find

$$(48) \qquad (J + \alpha\Sigma)Q_\alpha = -\Sigma Q ,$$

where J is the matrix of second order partial derivatives of $\Pi^*(Q)$. Q_α is the column of partial derivatives of the (equilibrium) outputs Q_i with respect to α. The system will have unique solution if $J + \alpha\Sigma$ is nonsingular. To tackle this problem, we prove the following lemma:

LEMMA 2: *A necessary and sufficient condition for* (48) *to have a unique solution is that α should not be a root of the positive* (*semi*) *definite matrix $R'(-J)R$, where $R'^{-1}R^{-1} = \Sigma$.*

PROOF: $J + \alpha\Sigma$ is singular iff $|J + \alpha\Sigma| = 0$. The latter holds iff $|R'(-J)R - \alpha I| = 0$. But the matrix $R'(-J)R$ is positive (semi) definite since R is nonsingular, and J is negative (semi) definite.

COROLLARY 1: *If the entrepreneur is a risk averter, the solution to the system* (45) *represents a maximum, and the solution to the system* (48) *is unique.*

PROOF: The condition implies that $\alpha < 0$; hence the matrix $J + \alpha\Sigma$ is negative definite. This establishes that the solution to (45) represents a maximum. Since $\alpha < 0$, it cannot be the root of a positive (semi) definite matrix, and $J + \alpha\Sigma$ is nonsingular.

COROLLARY 2: *If the entrepreneur is attracted to risk* ($\alpha > 0$), *the solution to the system* (45) *represents a maximum if and only if the roots of $|\lambda(\alpha\Sigma) - (-J)| = 0$ are greater than unity.*

PROOF: The matrix $J + \alpha\Sigma$ is negative definite if and only if $z'(J + \alpha\Sigma)z < 0$, for all $z \neq 0$; hence if and only if $z'(-J)z > z'(\alpha\Sigma)z$. But $(-J)$ is positive (semi) definite; thus we have the following factorization:

$$(49) \qquad \begin{aligned} \alpha\Sigma &= W'W \\ -J &= W'DW , \end{aligned}$$

where D is a diagonal matrix whose (nonzero) elements are the roots of $|\lambda\alpha\Sigma - (-J)| = 0$, and W is a nonsingular matrix. We may write

$$(49a) \qquad z'W'DWz > z'W'Wz .$$

Thus defining $y = Wz$, the conclusion of the corollary is proved.

Actually, this particular result is somewhat incomplete since one would like to get a condition involving the roots of J and $\alpha\Sigma$ rather than conditions on the roots of $|\lambda(\alpha\Sigma) - (-J)| = 0$, which are incidentally the roots of $W'^{-1}(-J)W^{-1}$ as well. Unfortunately, I have not been able to do so. The following characterization of the effect of a change in the risk attitude of the entrepreneur on the equilibrium configuration of output may be given:

LEMMA 3. *If the entrepreneur is a risk averter, then*

$$\left(\frac{d\Pi^*}{dQ}\right)' \cdot Q_\alpha > 0 , \tag{50}$$

where $d\Pi^*/dQ = (\partial\Pi^*/\partial Q_1, \cdots, \partial\Pi^*/\partial Q_n)'$, $Q_\alpha = (\partial Q_1/\partial\alpha, \cdots, \partial Q_n/\partial\alpha)'$.

PROOF: From (45), we have

$$\frac{d\Pi^*}{dQ}\frac{1}{\alpha} = -\Sigma Q . \tag{50a}$$

Substituting in (48), we find

$$\frac{d\Pi^*}{dQ} = (\alpha J + \alpha^2\Sigma)Q_\alpha . \tag{50b}$$

Premultiplying by Q'_α, we have

$$Q'_\alpha \cdot \frac{d\Pi^*}{dQ} = Q'_\alpha(\alpha J + \alpha^2\Sigma)Q_\alpha > 0 , \tag{50c}$$

since $\alpha J + \alpha^2\Sigma$ is positive definite, and certainly we cannot have identically $Q_\alpha = 0$ by virtue of (48).

The conclusion of the lemma may be expressed also in terms of elasticities. Define by ε_i the (partial) elasticity of profit with respect to the i-th commodity and by η_j the (partial) elasticity of the (equilibrium) output of the j-th commodity with respect to the risk parameter α. Then (50) may be rewritten as

$$\frac{\Pi^*}{\alpha}\left(\frac{d\Pi^*}{dQ}\right)' \cdot Q_\alpha = \sum_{i=1}^{n} \varepsilon_i\eta_i < 0 , \tag{51}$$

since $\alpha < 0$.

The insight gained thus far is not very sharp, however, since we can neither conclude that the partial elasticities of profit with respect to output are positive nor that the partial elasticities of equilibrium output with respect to the risk parameters are all negative. What we can say is that for at least one good the two elasticities must be of opposite sign.

Contrasting this result with the uniproduct case we detect several differences. First, in that case we can state the following:

i. At the equilibrium output the profit function is increasing; this is readily seen from (46); it follows, therfore, that the output elasticity of profit is positive. No similar statement can be made in the multiproduct case; a similar conclusion would require, as a sufficient condition, that the matrix Σ contains all positive elements, or that in some sense the goods produced by the firm are complementary. We shall return to such considerations below.
ii. The elasticity of the equilibrium output with respect to the risk parameter is negative, which, in turn, means that the response of equilibrium output to an increase in the risk parameter is positive. Again no such unambiguous statement can be made in the multiproduct case.

4. SPECIAL CASES

Definition: Two goods Q_i and Q_j will be termed stochastically complementary if $\sigma_{ij} > 0$, stochastically competitive if $\sigma_{ij} < 0$, and stochastically independent if $\sigma_{ij} = 0$, $i \neq j$. The use of the terms conforms very much to their ordinary usage; we have termed goods complementary if they tend to vary in the same direction for given prices, competitive if they tend to vary in opposite directions, etc. Bearing in mind this definition, we have the following:

LEMMA 4: If all goods are stochastically complementary, then

(52) $$\frac{d\Pi^*}{dQ} > 0 ,$$

and

$$Q_\alpha \geqq 0 ,$$

if

(52a) $$\frac{\partial^2 \Pi^*}{\partial Q_i \partial Q_j} \geqq -\alpha\sigma_{ij} , \qquad i \neq j .$$

PROOF: The first part of the Lemma follows immediately from (50a). To prove the second part, it suffices to show that if the condition (52a) holds, then the matrix $(\alpha J + \alpha^2\Sigma)^{-1}$ transforms positive vectors into positive vectors. That this is indeed the case is easily seen from (50b). The proof of this fact is rather simple and is given in the interest of completeness. Let

(53) $$C = -(\alpha J + \alpha^2\Sigma) ,$$

and observe that C is negative definite. All its elements save those on the main diagonal are nonnegative. Define

$$M = \mu I + C \,, \tag{53a}$$

and take μ large enough so that all the elements of the matrix M are nonnegative. Hence M is a Frobenius matrix and has its largest root (in absolute value) positive. If r_0 is the largest root of M, it follows that $r_0 < \mu$, and thus the largest root of M/μ is less than unity in absolute value. It follows that

$$(\alpha J + \alpha^2 \Sigma)^{-1} = -C^{-1} = \frac{1}{\mu}\left(I - \frac{M}{\mu}\right)^{-1} = \sum_{k=0}^{\infty}\left(\frac{M^k}{\mu^{k+1}}\right) . \tag{54}$$

The conclusion of the second part of the lemma is obvious from (54). Thus, although the condition (52a) is only sufficient but not necessary—necessary conditions are very difficult to obtain here—for the nonnegativity of Q_α, it is seen that to obtain a situation analogous to that of the uniproduct case rather severe restrictions have to be imposed, such as those given in (52a). These restrictions not only require the positivity of the second order partial derivatives of the profit function, but impose a strictly positive lower bound on them as well.

Similar results may be obtained for independent goods; this case, however, requires only that the second order partial derivatives be nonnegative. No result of comparable simplicity can be obtained in the case that all goods are stochastically competitive, since then we cannot even obtain simple conditions under which $d\Pi^*/dQ \geqq 0$, at equilibrium. Finally, perhaps something should be said about the intuitive meaning of (52a). We have established that under the conditions of Lemma 4, the (expected) profit function at equilibrium is increasing with respect to all outputs. Hence the requirement that $Q_\alpha \geqq 0$ could only serve to increase expected profit, on the other hand it would also serve to increase the variance; hence the conditions merely insure that the net effect of all these forces does not decrease the expected utility of the entire operation to the entrepreneur.

We must now analyze the impact of a change in the parameters of the distribution of price. As before, differentiating totally the equilibrium conditions (45) with respect to α, we find the response of the equilibrium output configuration to a change in the covariance between the demand for two goods, say, the r-th and the s-th.

Thus we obtain:

$$\sum_{j=1}^{n} \frac{\partial^2 \Pi^*}{\partial Q_i \partial Q_j} \frac{\partial Q_j}{\partial \sigma_{rs}} + \alpha \sum_{j=1}^{n} \sigma_{ij} \frac{\partial Q_j}{\partial \sigma_{rs}} + \alpha(\delta_{ir} Q_s + \delta_{is} Q_r) = 0 \,, \tag{55}$$

$$i = 1, 2, \cdots, n \,,$$

where δ_{ij} is the Kronecker delta, and Q_s, Q_r are the s-th and r-th goods, respectively. In matrix notation, (55) simply reads

(55a) $$(J + \alpha\Sigma)Q\sigma_{rs} = -\alpha(e_r Q_s + e_s Q_r) ,$$

where e_i is the column vector whose components are all zero, save the i-th one, which is unity, and $Q\sigma_{rs} = (\partial Q_1/\partial\sigma_{rs}, \cdots, \partial Q_n/\partial\sigma_{rs})'$.

Hence

(55b) $$Q\sigma_{rs} = -(\alpha J + \alpha^2\Sigma)^{-1}e_r Q_s - (\alpha J + \alpha^2\Sigma)^{-1}e_s Q_r .$$

It is easily seen from (55b) that the same conditions, viz. (52a), that insure the nonnegativity of Q_α will insure the nonpositivity of $Q\sigma_{rs}$. It is convenient to define

(56) $$(v_{ij}) = V = \alpha J + \alpha^2\Sigma .$$

Then apart from any restrictions on the nature of the stochastic relations between the goods, we have

(56a) $$\frac{\partial Q_s}{\partial\sigma_{ss}} = -2Q_s\frac{V_{ss}}{|V|} < 0 ,$$

where V^{ss} is the cofactor of v_{ss}; the inequality holds because V is positive definite. In general, the only clear conclusion to be obtained from (55b) is that if the covariance of demand between any two goods, say the r-th and s-th changes, then the equilibrium magnitude of all goods will be changed, and this irrespective of whether such goods are independent of the r-th and s-th goods or not. This is easily verified, since

(56b) $$\frac{\partial Q_j}{\partial\sigma_{rs}} = -\frac{V^{rj}}{|V|}Q_s - \frac{V^{sj}}{|V|}Q_r ,$$

which need not be zero if $\sigma_{rj} = \sigma_{sj} = 0$.

Finally, it is possible to analyze in this context the response of the equilibrium output mix to the imposition (or change) of a specific tax rate levied on an output(s) of the multiproduct firm.

Let the tax on the i-th commodity be t_i. If the market price is given by p_i, the net price to the firm is $p_i - t_i$. Thus the maximand of equation (44) becomes now

(57) $$\Pi^*(Q) + (1/2)\alpha Q'\Sigma Q - t'Q ,$$
$$t = (t_1, t_2, \cdots, t_n)' .$$

The first order conditions (45) are

(58) $$\frac{\partial\Pi^*}{\partial Q_i} + \alpha\Sigma_i Q - t_i = 0 .$$

Hence differentiating totally (58) with respect to t_k, we have

$$\sum_{j=1}^{n}\left(\frac{\partial \Pi^*}{\partial Q_i \partial Q_j} + \alpha\sigma_{ij}\right)\frac{\partial Q_j}{\partial t_k} = \delta_{ik}, \qquad \begin{matrix} i = 1, 2, \cdots, n, \\ k = 1, 2, \cdots, n, \end{matrix} \tag{59}$$

where δ_{ik} is the Kronecker delta.

In matrix form, (59) reads

$$(J + \alpha\Sigma)Q_t = I, \tag{59a}$$

where

$$Q_t = \left[\frac{\partial Q_j}{\partial t_k}\right], \qquad \begin{matrix} j = 1, 2, \cdots, n, \\ k = 1, 2, \cdots, n; \end{matrix}$$

hence

$$Q_t = (J + \alpha\Sigma)^{-1}. \tag{59b}$$

Employing the notation of (56), we have

$$\frac{\partial Q_i}{\partial t_j} = \alpha\frac{V^{ij}}{|V|}. \tag{60}$$

Clearly

$$\frac{\partial Q_i}{\partial t_j} < 0 \qquad i = 1, 2, \cdots, n, \tag{60a}$$

since $\alpha < 0$.

On the other hand, if (52a) holds as well, then we have, in general,

$$\frac{\partial Q_i}{\partial t_j} < 0, \qquad \text{all } i \text{ and } j. \tag{60b}$$

But from (60) it follows that it is possible for the imposition of a specific tax on commodity j to evoke an increase in the equilibrium output of commodity i for $i \neq j$.

The simple case, $n = 2$,

$$\frac{\partial^2 \Pi^*}{\partial Q_1 \partial Q_2} + \alpha\sigma_{12} < 0,$$

is sufficient to establish this eventuality. This particular example shows that the introduction of uncertainty leads to interesting patterns of reaction that are not available in the certainty case. In the latter instance the example above would hold only if

$$\frac{\partial^2 \Pi^*}{\partial Q_1 \partial Q_2} < 0;$$

in the former instance, however, the example would be valid even if

$$\frac{\partial^2 \Pi^*}{\partial Q_1 \partial Q_2} > 0 \, .$$

Clearly this is the more plausible alternative.

In the uniproduct firm, the corresponding result is, of course,

$$\frac{\partial Q}{\partial t} = \left(\frac{\partial^2 \Pi^*}{\partial Q^2} + \alpha \sigma_{11} \right)^{-1} , \tag{61}$$

which is unambiguously negative.

5. CONCLUSION

We have briefly examined here the theory of the monopolistic multiproduct firm under uncertainty, a subject long neglected in the literature. It was found that the problem of optimization for this firm could be decomposed into two convenient aspects. Thus we could envisage the firm as first deciding on an optimal output mix on the basis of expected utility maximization, and secondly, given this output mix, as deciding on the optimal combination of inputs necessary to carry out its production decisions, on the basis of constrained cost minimization.

While, essentially, the qualitative conclusions drawn from the latter aspect are quite similar to those obtained in the case of the uniproduct firm, it was found that the response of the multiproduct firm to changes in the state of uncertainty, both in terms of its attitude toward risk and changes in the parameters of the relevant distribution, is much more complex than in the case of the uniproduct firm. The same holds true of changes in specific tax rates applied to the firm's products.

It is possible to obtain a special case which exactly duplicates the response of the uniproduct firm, but this is found only at the expense of very severe restrictions on the type of goods produced by the firm and on the cost and demand characteristics of its operation.

University of Pennsylvania, U.S.A.

REFERENCES

[1] BAILEY, M. J., "Price and Output Determination by a Firm Selling Related Products," *American Economic Review*, XLIV (March, 1954), 82–93.

[2] CLEMENS, E. W., "Price Discrimination and the Multiple-Product Firm," *Review of Economic Studies*, XIX (1951–52), 1–11.

[3] DEBREU, G., "Stochastic Choice and Cardinal Utility," *Econometrica*, XXVI (July, 1958), 440–44.

[4] ———, "Topological Methods in Cardinal Utility Theory," *Mathematical Methods in the Social Sciences*, ed. K. J. Arrow, *et. al.* (Stanford: Stanford University Press,

1959), 16-26.

[5] KUHN, H. W. AND A. TUCKER, "Nonlinear Programming," *Proceedings of the Second Berkeley Symposium on Mathematical Statistics and Probability*, ed. J. Neyman, (Berkeley and Los Angeles: University of California Press, 1951) 481-92.

[6] LUCE, R. D., AND H. RAIFFA, *Games and Decisions* (New York: John Wiley and Sons, 1957).

[7] MARKOWITZ, H. M., *Portfolio Selection* (New York: John Wiley and Sons, 1959).

[8] MARSCHAK, J., "Why 'Should' Statisticians and Businessmen Maximize 'Moral Expectation'", *Proceedings of the Second Berkeley Symposium on Mathematical Statistics and Probability*, ed. J. Neyman, (Berkeley and Los Angeles: University of California Press, 1951), 493-506.

[9] NEUMANN, J. V. AND O. MORGENSTERN, *Theory of Games and Economic Behavior*, second edition, (Princeton: Princeton University Press, 1947).

[10] PFOUTS, R. W., "The Theory of Cost and Production in the Multi-Product Firm," *Econometrica*, XXIX (October, 1961), 650-58.

[11] WELDON, J. C., "The Multi-Product Firm," *Canadian Journal of Economics and Political Science*, XIV (May, 1948) 176-90.

Reprinted from THE REVIEW OF ECONOMIC STUDIES, Vol. XXXIV (4), October, 1967, P. J. DHRYMES, pp. 399-408.

On a Class of Utility and Production Functions Yielding Everywhere Differentiable Demand Functions [1]

1. INTRODUCTION

The purpose of this paper is to characterize the class of utility and production functions whose associated demand functions are *everywhere differentiable* in the positive orthant of n-dimensional Euclidean space. To avoid tiresome repetition we shall refer to such functions as *everywhere differentiable*.

The problem is an essential one, since in the usual comparative statics analysis one obtains a number of qualitative results whose derivation depends on the existence of certain derivatives. While it is true that as stated such results require only local differentiability about the equilibrium point, none the less since the price vector and other relevant quantities are taken as arbitrary points in the positive orthant of the appropriate space, in fact the validity of comparative statics analysis requires that the utility and production function employed admit of everywhere differentiable demand functions.

Now, it is possible to find functions which are " nice "[2] by the standards of economic theory and yet their associated demand functions fail to be differentiable, on some open subset of their domain.

The class we shall determine will not be the widest possible, since we shall employ the slightly restrictive

Definition 1. Let $F(.)$ be a function defined on $\bar{E}^n$—the positive orthant of Euclidean n-space. Let it be desired to extremize $F(.)$ under the constraint $g(x) = 0$. We shall say F has a constrained maximum (minimum) at x^0 if $f'h = 0$ and $h'F^{**}h<0(>0)$ for all vectors h such that $\sum_{i=1}^{n} g_i(x^0)h_i = 0$, where f and F^{**} are respectively the gradient and Hessian (evaluated at $x = x^0$) and $g_i(.)$ is the partial of $g(.)$ with respect to its ith argument.

Remark 1. It may be noted that a maximum (minimum) in the sense of definition 1 is what is occasionally referred to as a " regular " or " proper " maximum (minimum) i.e. one in which knowledge of derivatives of higher order than the second is unnecessary in determining whether a given stationary point represents a maximum, a minimum (or a saddle point). Thus we are considering the class of functions which (everywhere) admit of regular maxima (or minima) and hence their associated demand functions are everywhere differentiable. Of course $F(.)$ and $g(.)$ are assumed to be at least twice differentiable and differentiable respectively.

1 The research on which this paper is based was carried out during the author's tenure of a John Simon Guggenheim Memorial Fellowship.

2 For example the utility function $u(x) = x_1^3x_2+x_1x_2^3$ is an infinitely differentiable strictly quasi-concave function with positive first order partials in the positive quadrant of the real plane; yet, its associated demand functions are not differentiable on $\{(p,m); p = 1, m>0\}$ where p is the price ratio and m real income in terms of x_2. See [4].

2. CONSUMER DEMAND FUNCTIONS

Let $u(.)$ be a function defined on the positive orthant of $\bar{E}^n$ and let it serve as an individual's utility index in a competitive context. In the theory of consumer choice it is shown that demand functions can be derived from the solution of the first order conditions to the problem of maximizing the Lagrangean

$$\Lambda = u(x)+\lambda(I-p'x) \qquad \text{...(1)}$$

where $x, p \in \bar{E}^n$ and denote respectively the commodity and price vectors, λ is the Lagrangean multiplier and I the consumer's income.

The question of differentiability of the resulting demand functions is best attacked by obtaining an expression for such derivatives and examining the conditions under which they exist. The first order conditions of the problem in (1) are

$$\begin{aligned} \underline{u}-\lambda p &= 0 \\ I-p'x &= 0 \end{aligned} \qquad \text{...(2)}$$

where $\underline{u}$ is the gradient of $u(.)$. Put $x^* = \begin{pmatrix} x \\ \lambda \end{pmatrix}$ and consider perturbations in (2) under a change in I and a change in p_k. In the first case we obtain

$$DU^*D^* \frac{\partial x^*}{\partial I} = e_{n+1} \qquad \text{...(3)}$$

where

$$U^* = \begin{bmatrix} U^{**} & \underline{u} \\ \underline{u}' & 0 \end{bmatrix}, \; D = \text{diag}\left(1, 1, ..., 1, -\frac{1}{\lambda}\right), \; D^* = \text{diag}\left(1, 1, ..., 1, \frac{1}{\lambda}\right) \qquad \text{...(3a)}$$

U^{**} is the Hessian of $u(.)$ and e_s is a vector all of whose elements are zero except the sth, which is unity. In the second case we obtain

$$DU^*D^* \frac{\partial x^*}{\partial p_k} = \lambda e_k - x_k e_{n+1}. \qquad \text{...(3b)}$$

It is obvious from (3) and (3b) that if a demand function is everywhere differentiable with respect to any of its arguments then it must be so differentiable with respect to all. Thus, we shall confine our attention to (3). But it is apparent that everywhere differentiability is guaranteed if and only if for $x \in \bar{E}^n$

$$| U^* | \neq 0. \qquad \text{...(4)}$$

Employing the so-called formula of Schur [2] we have

$$| U^* | = -(\underline{u}'U^{**-1}\underline{u})| U^{**} |. \qquad \text{...(4a)}$$

Thus, a sufficient condition for (4) is that U^{**} be non-singular (negative definite) everywhere in $\bar{E}^n$. Actually, we can prove a stronger result. Before we do so, however, we need the following.[1]

Theorem 1. *Let A be a symmetric matrix; then, a necessary and sufficient condition that $x'Ax<0$ subject to $B'x = 0$, where B is an arbitrary $n\times k$ matrix is that there exist a number ϕ such that*

$$M = A+\phi BB' \qquad \text{...(5)}$$

is negative definite.

Proof.[2] Sufficiency is obvious.

[1] Theorem 1 may be found in Debreu [1]; the proof given there, however, is not sufficiently illuminating from the point of view of the applications we have in mind. For this reason and for the sake of completeness we give an alternative proof.

[2] The simplicity of this proof owes much to suggestions of an anonymous referee of this paper.

Necessity. Since $x'Ax<0$ for $B'x = 0$ we need only consider x such that $B'x \neq 0$. Thus let us extremize $x'Ax$ subject to

$$x'BB'x = 1. \qquad \text{...(5a)}$$

The first order conditions are

$$Ax-\mu BB'x = 0 \qquad \text{...(5b)}$$

where μ is the Lagrangean multiplier. Moreover, premultiplying by x' we obtain, in view of the constraint,

$$x'Ax = \mu. \qquad \text{...(5c)}$$

Equations (5b) and (5c) show that the quadratic form is maximized when x is chosen as the characteristic vector of A in the metric of BB' corresponding to the largest characteristic root. Let μ_i, $i = 1, 2, ..., n$ be the characteristic roots; let

$$\mu^* = \max_i \mu_i \qquad \text{...(5d)}$$

and choose ϕ such that

$$\phi < -\mu^*. \qquad \text{...(5e)}$$

Note, then, that for any vector y, such that $y'BB'y = 1$

$$y'(A+\phi BB')y = y'Ay+\phi \leqq \mu^*+\phi<0 \quad \text{q.e.d.} \qquad \text{...(5f)}$$

Remark 2. It is clear from the proof that we can choose $\phi<0$; moreover ϕ can be chosen in such a way that $c\phi$, ϕ both satisfy the conclusion of the theorem for $c>0$.

We are now in a position to prove

Theorem 2. *Let $u(.)$ be the utility function of the problem considered above. Then a necessary and sufficient condition for $u(.)$ to yield* everywhere differentiable *demand functions is that a function $\phi(.)$ exist such that*

$$M = U^{**}+\phi \underline{u}\underline{u}' \qquad \text{...(6)}$$

is negative definite (in $\bar{E}^n$).

Proof. Sufficiency; suppose such a function exists, then

$$y'U^{**}y<0 \text{ for } \underline{u}'y = 0 \qquad \text{...(6a)}$$

and hence the solution of (2) yields a maximum. We next show that this implies the non-singularity of U^*. Consider the matrix

$$P = \begin{bmatrix} I & -\dfrac{V^{-1}\underline{u}}{m} \\ \tfrac{1}{2}\phi'\underline{u} & \dfrac{1}{m} \end{bmatrix} \qquad \text{...(6c)}$$

where

$$V = U^{**}+\tfrac{1}{2}\phi\underline{u}\underline{u}', \quad m = (-\underline{u}'V^{-1}MV^{-1}\underline{u})^{\frac{1}{2}} \text{ [1]} \qquad \text{...(6d)}$$

and note that

$$P'U^*P = \begin{bmatrix} M & 0 \\ 0 & 1 \end{bmatrix}. \qquad \text{...(6e)}$$

We therefore have

$$|M| = |P|^2|U^*| = \frac{1}{m^2}\left(1+\frac{\phi}{2}\underline{u}'V^{-1}\underline{u}\right)|U^*| \neq 0 \qquad \text{...(6f)}$$

and indeed sgn $\{|U^*|\}$ = sgn $\{|M|\}$.

[1] Notice that by Remark 2, ϕ can be chosen so that V and M are both negative definite. Hence, $-V^{-1}MV^{-1}$ is positive definite and thus $m^2>0$ as required by (6d).

Necessity. Let $x^0(p, I)$ be a solution to (2) which is a maximum (in the sense of definition 1). Thus we have $y'U^{**}(x^0)y<0$ for all y such that $\underline{u}'(x^0)y = 0$. By Theorem 1 there exists a number ϕ which depends on x^0, thus $\phi(x^0)<0$, such that

$$M(x^0) = U^{**}(x^0)+\phi(x^0)\underline{u}(x^0)u'(x^0) \qquad \text{...(7)}$$

is negative definite. Since x^0 depends on $\begin{pmatrix} p \\ I \end{pmatrix}$ and the latter is an arbitrary vector in $\bar{E}^{n+1}$, it follows that M must be negative definite for any $x \in \{x\colon x = x^0(p, I), (p', I) \in \bar{E}^{n+1}\}$. In general this will be all of $\bar{E}^n$. But if M is thus negative definite in $\bar{E}^n$, then by (6f) U^* must be non-singular there. q.e.d.

3. FIRM DEMAND FUNCTIONS

The theory of the firm viewed as minimizing cost under an output constraint is formally identical with the development of section 1; thus the discussion here will be a brief one.

Let $F(.)$ be the production function and let the firm operate in a competitive factor market. The problem, then, is to maximize the Lagrangean

$$\Lambda = p'x+\lambda[Q^0-F(x)] \qquad \text{...(8)}$$

where p, x are respectively the price and input vectors, λ is the Lagrangean multiplier and Q^0 the fixed output constraint. The first order conditions yield

$$p-\lambda \underline{f} = 0$$
$$Q^0-F(x) = 0 \qquad \text{...(8a)}$$

where $\underline{f}$ is the gradient of $F(.)$.

Let (x^0, λ^0) be a solution of (8a) and consider variations in it given by the vector y. For such variations to be admissible, they must satisfy the constraint. Expanding (8) by Taylor series we have:

$$\Lambda(x^0+y) = \Lambda(x^0)+p'y-\lambda^0\underline{f}'y-\tfrac{1}{2}\lambda^0y'F^{**}y+\text{remainder} \qquad \text{...(8b)}$$

where F^{**} is the Hessian of $F(.)$—evaluated at x^0, as is also $\underline{f}$. From (8a) we conclude

$$\Lambda(x^0+y)-\Lambda(x^0) = -\tfrac{1}{2}\lambda^0y'F^{**}y+\text{remainder}. \qquad \text{...(8c)}$$

Thus for a proper minimum we conclude that F^{**} must be negative definite for

$$y \in \{y\colon \underline{f}'y = 0\}.$$

By Theorem 2 this is so if and only if there exists a function σ such that $N = F^{**}+\sigma\underline{f}\underline{f}'$ is negative definite for $x \in \bar{E}^n$:

Considering perturbations in (8a) with respect to a change in Q^0 and p_k we have

$$BF^*B^*\frac{\partial x^*}{\partial Q^0} = e_{n+1} \qquad \text{...(9)}$$

$$BF^*B^*\frac{\partial x^0}{\partial p_k} = e_k \qquad \text{...(9a)}$$

where

$$B = \text{diag}\,(\lambda, \lambda, ..., \lambda, 1),\ B^* = \text{diag}\left(1, 1, ..., 1, \frac{1}{\lambda}\right),\ x^* = \begin{pmatrix} x \\ \lambda \end{pmatrix} \qquad \text{...(9b)}$$

and

$$F^* = \begin{bmatrix} F^{**} & f \\ f' & 0 \end{bmatrix}. \qquad \text{...(9c)}$$

It is clear from (9) through (9c) that the crucial question of differentiability relates to the non-singularity of F^* in $\bar{E}^n$ and this was dealt with in Theorem 2.

Remark 3. The class of functions $G(.)$ that yield demand functions which are everywhere differentiable in $\bar{E}^n$ are those for which there exists a function $s(x)$ ($\leqq 0$) such that $G^{**}+sgg'$ is everywhere (in $\bar{E}^n$) negative definite, where G^{**}, g are respectively the Hessian and gradient of $G(.)$. It is clear that if G^{**} is everywhere negative definite then such $s(.)$ will always exist; in particular $s(x) \equiv 0$ will do.

It is not, in general, sufficient to specify that $G(.)$ is strictly quasi-concave in order to ensure the everywhere differentiability of the resulting demand functions, as the counter-example (in footnote 2, p. 399, and in [4]) indicates. On the other hand if $G(.)$ has a singular Hessian for some $x \in \bar{E}^n$, this does not rule out the existence of a function $s(.)$ as above. Thus if $G(x) = Ax_1^\alpha x_2^\beta$, $\alpha+\beta = 1$, the choice $s(x) = -1$ will satisfy the conditions of Theorem 2.

4. ALTERNATIVE DERIVATION OF THE SALIENT PROPOSITIONS OF THE THEORIES OF THE FIRM AND CONSUMER BEHAVIOUR

In this section we shall restrict our discussion to production and utility functions possessing negative definite Hessians in $\bar{E}^n$. We shall then derive the usual propositions of micro theory by making extensive use of the properties of such matrices and without reference to the cumbersome apparatus of determinant theory.[1]

Consider again the system (9). Solving we obtain

$$\frac{\partial x^*}{\partial Q^0} = B^{*-1}F^{*-1}B^{-1}e_{n+1} \qquad ...(10)$$

where

$$F^{*-1} = \begin{bmatrix} F^{**-1}\left(I - \frac{ff'F^{**-1}}{\phi}\right) & \frac{F^{**-1}f}{\phi} \\ \frac{f'F^{**-1}}{\phi} & -\frac{1}{\phi} \end{bmatrix}, \quad \phi = f'F^{**-1}f.$$

Proposition 1. At equilibrium marginal costs are rising.

Proof. Using (8a) and the definition of cost, C, we have

$$\frac{\partial C}{\partial Q^0} = p'\frac{\partial x}{\partial Q^0} = \lambda f'\frac{F^{**-1}f}{\phi} = \lambda \qquad ...(10b)$$

$$\frac{\partial^2 C}{\partial Q^{02}} = \frac{\partial \lambda}{\partial Q^0} = -\frac{\lambda}{\phi} > 0. \qquad ...(10c)$$

Proposition 2. If $F_{ij} \geqq 0$, $i \neq j$, i.e. all factors are complementary, then an increase in output will increase the employment of all factors (provided $\frac{\partial F}{\partial x_i} > 0$ all i).

Proof. Define

$$M = \rho I + F^{**}. \qquad ...(11)$$

If ρ is chosen large enough then M is a non-null matrix whose elements are non-negative. Now

$$(-F^{**})^{-1} = (\rho I - M)^{-1} = \sum_{k=0}^{\infty} \frac{M^k}{\rho^{k+1}} \qquad ...(11a)$$

[1] This has a decided pedagogical advantage since such matrices are extensively used in econometric theory. Thus we obtain a unity of formal apparatus in the two areas, a unity that has this far escaped exploitation and perhaps notice.

is a valid expansion since if $\mu(M)$ is any root of M then $|\mu(M)| < \rho$. But since M is a non-null matrix with non-negative elements we conclude that F^{**-1} is a non-null matrix with non-positive elements—indeed its diagonal elements are strictly negative. The conclusion of the proposition follows then, from

$$\frac{\partial x}{\partial Q^0} = \frac{F^{**-1}\underline{f}}{\phi} \qquad \ldots(11b)$$

Remark 4. The condition $F_{ij} \geq 0$, $i \neq j$, holds for members of the CES class of production functions with positive elasticity of substitution.

Let us now consider perturbations in factor prices. Solving (9a) we find

$$\frac{\partial x^*}{\partial p_k} = B^{*-1}F^{*-1}B^{-1}e_k, \quad k = 1, 2, \ldots, n. \qquad \ldots(12)$$

Definition 2. The substitution matrix is given by

$$S = F^{**-1} - \frac{F^{**-1}\underline{f}\underline{f}'F^{**-1}}{\phi}. \qquad \ldots(12a)$$

Remark 5. Strictly speaking the substitution matrix is given by λS and consists of $\left(\frac{\partial x_i}{\partial p_k}\right)$ $i, k = 1, 2, \ldots, n$; however since $\lambda > 0$ it is simpler to deal with the quantity defined in (12a).

Proposition 3. The own substitution term is strictly negative.

Proof. Referring to (9c) and (12a) we see that the ith diagonal element of S is given by

$$S_{ii} = \frac{|F^{*(i)}|}{|F^*|} \qquad \ldots(12b)$$

where the notation $A^{(i)}$ indicates the submatrix of A resulting when we delete its ith row and column. However using (4a) we have

$$|F^{*(i)}| = -(\underline{f}^{(i)'}F^{**(i)-1}\underline{f}^{(i)})|F^{**(i)}| \qquad \ldots(12c)$$

Since F^{**} and $F^{**(i)}$ are both negative definite matrices of dimension n and $(n-1)$ respectively we conclude

$$\operatorname{sgn}(S_{ii}) = \operatorname{sgn}\left\{\frac{|F^{*(i)}|}{|F^*|}\right\} = -1 \qquad \text{q.e.d.} \qquad \ldots(12d)$$

Proposition 4. The substitution matrix is singular.

Proof. We show

$$\underline{f}'S = 0. \qquad \ldots(13)$$

But from (12a) we have

$$\underline{f}'S = \underline{f}'F^{**-1} - \frac{\underline{f}'F^{**-1}\underline{f}\underline{f}'F^{**-1}}{\phi} = \underline{f}'F^{**-1} - \underline{f}'F^{**-1} = 0. \qquad \ldots(13a)$$

Remark 6. Proposition 4 shows that if p is a vector of (positive) prices defining the equilibrium in (8a) and c is any scalar, then

$$q'S = 0, \text{ where } q = cp.$$

Proposition 5. The substitution matrix is negative semidefinite, of rank $n-1$.

Proof. We shall first show that for any $y \in E^n$, $y'Sy \leq 0$. We may write

$$S = \frac{1}{\phi}[\phi F^{**-1} - F^{**-1}\underline{f}\underline{f}'F^{**-1}] = \frac{1}{\phi}[W - Z]. \qquad \ldots(14)$$

It is clear that W is positive definite and Z positive semidefinite. Let the rank of Z be r, and consider the roots of Z in the metric of W, i.e. consider

$$|\mu W - Z| = 0. \qquad \text{...(14a)}$$

Now there exists a non-singular matrix T such that

$$T'T = W, \; T'MT = Z, \; M = \text{diag}\,(\mu_1, \mu_2, \ldots, \mu_n) \qquad \text{...(14b)}$$

where $\mu_1 \geqq \mu_2 \geqq \ldots \geqq \mu_r > \mu_{r+1} \ldots \mu_n$ are the roots of (14a) and $\mu_{r+i} = 0, i = 1, 2, \ldots, n-r$, the rank of Z being r. Hence, the non-zero roots of (14a) are exactly those of

$$|\mu I - T'^{-1}ZT^{-1}| = \left|\mu I - \frac{1}{\phi^2}\, Tff'T'\right| = \mu - \frac{f'T'Tf}{\phi^2} = \mu - 1 = 0. \qquad \text{...(14c)}$$

This shows that the only non-zero root of (14a) is unity. Thus for $x = Ty$ we obtain

$$y'Sy = \frac{1}{\phi}[y'T'Ty - y'T'MTy] = \frac{1}{\phi} \sum_{j=2}^{n} x_j^2 \leqq 0. \qquad \text{...(14d)}$$

Finally, in view of (14*c*) $I - M$ is clearly of rank $n-1$; thus since

$$S = \frac{1}{\phi}[T'T - T'MT] = \frac{1}{\phi}\, T'(I-M)T \qquad \text{...(14e)}$$

we conclude

$$\text{rank}\,(S) = n-1 \quad \text{Q.E.D.} \qquad \text{...(14f)}$$

Remark 7. Since S is a negative semidefinite matrix of rank $n-1$ this implies that every principal submatrix of order $k(\leqq n-1)$ must be negative definite.

The preceding refers to a very restrictive theory of the firm, confining the latter's reaction to changing factor prices to a fixed isoquant. Thus consider the more general version in which the firm is viewed as maximizing profit. If $R(Q)$ is the firm's revenue function, then the problem is to maximize profits, defined by

$$\pi(x) = R(F) - p'x - C_0 \qquad \text{...(15)}$$

where C_0 indicates fixed costs and we assume $R' > 0$. First order conditions are

$$\underline{\pi} = R'\underline{f} - p = 0 \qquad \text{...(15a)}$$

where $\underline{\pi}$ is the gradient of the profit function. We have

Lemma 1. *The Hessian of the profit function,* $\pi^{**} = (\pi_{ij})$, *is negative definite if and only if*

$$R'' < -\frac{R'}{\phi}. \qquad \text{...(16)}$$

Proof. We have

$$\pi^{**} = R'F^{**} + R''ff' = -R'\left[W - \frac{R''}{R'}ff'\right] \qquad \text{...(16a)}$$

where $W = -F^{**}$. Thus, π^{**} is negative definite if and only if $W - \frac{R''}{R'}ff'$ is positive definite. Now since W is positive definite and $\underline{f}\,\underline{f}'$ is positive semi-definite (of rank 1) there exists a non-singular matrix T such that

$$W = T'T, \; T'MT = \underline{f}\,\underline{f}', \; M = \text{diag}\,(\mu, 0, 0, \ldots, 0) \qquad \text{...(16b)}$$

where μ is the (only) non-zero root of

$$|\mu W - \underline{f}\,\underline{f}'| = 0. \qquad \text{...(16c)}$$

Indeed it may be shown that $\mu = -\phi$. Let $y \in E^n$ and note

$$y'\pi^{**}y = -R'\left[y'T'Ty - \frac{R''}{R'}y'T'MTy\right] = -R'\left[\left(1+\frac{\phi R''}{R'}\right)x_1^2 + \sum_{i=2}^{n} x_i^2\right] \quad ...(16d)$$

where $x = Ty$. For the expression in (the last) square brackets to be positive for non-null x it is necessary and sufficient that

$$1+\frac{\phi R''}{R'} > 0 \text{ or } R'' < -\frac{R'}{\phi} \qquad \text{q.e.d.} \quad ...(16e)$$

Remark 8. Lemma 1 imposes a strictly positive upper bound on R'', the bound depending on the characteristics of the productive function. Note also that this condition is identical with the usual constraint $R'' < C''$, where C is the cost expressed as a function of output. To see this note that from (16e), (10b), (10c), and the equilibrium condition $R' = C'$, we have

$$R'' < R'\left(-\frac{1}{\phi}\right) = C'\left(-\frac{1}{\phi}\right) = -\frac{\lambda}{\phi} = C''. \quad ...(16f)$$

Considering now perturbations in (15a) under a change in p_k we find

$$[R'F^{**} + R''\underline{f}\underline{f}']\frac{\partial x}{\partial p_k} = e_k \text{ or } \frac{\partial x}{\partial p_k} = \pi^{**-1}e_k. \quad ...(17)$$

Proposition 6. If the revenue function satisfies (16) then the demand function for the kth factor has an unambiguously negative slope in the direction of its own price.

Proof. From (17) it is evident that $\frac{\partial x_k}{\partial p_k}$ is the (k, k) element of π^{**-1}. By Lemma 1 π^{**} (and hence π^{**-1}) is negative definite and thus $\pi^{**(k,k)} < 0$.

Turning now to the theory of consumer behaviour and solving (3) we find

$$\frac{\partial x^*}{\partial I} = D^{*-1}U^{*-1}D^{-1}e_{n+1} \quad ...(18)$$

where

$$U^{*-1} = \begin{bmatrix} U^{**-1} - \frac{U^{**-1}\underline{u}\underline{u}'U^{**-1}}{\psi} & \frac{U^{**-1}\underline{u}}{\psi} \\ \frac{\underline{u}'U^{**-1}}{\psi} & \frac{1}{\psi} \end{bmatrix}, \quad \psi = \underline{u}'U^{**-1}\underline{u}. \quad ...(18a)$$

The vector of income effects is given by

$$\frac{\partial x}{\partial I} = \frac{\lambda U^{**-1}\underline{u}}{\psi}. \quad ...(18b)$$

Comparing this with (11b) we note that the condition for absence of inferior consumption goods is similar to that needed to establish the absence of inferior factors, viz. that U^{**-1} transform positive vectors into negative (non-positive) ones. If we wish to give sufficient conditions for this result, however, we cannot immediately invoke Proposition 2. This is so since customarily the theory of consumer behaviour operates in a framework in which the utility index is represented as being arbitrary to within a monotone transformation by a function $G(.)$ such that $G' > 0$. Thus, if $u(.)$ is a utility index and $G(.)$ a function as above, then $G(u)$ should give us all the results of traditional theory. On the other hand, note that the Hessian of $G(.)$ can be written as

$$G^{**} = G'U^{**} + G''\underline{u}\underline{u}'. \quad ...(19)$$

By Lemma 1, provided U^{**} is negative definite, G^{**} is negative definite if and only if

$$G'' < -\frac{G'}{\psi}. \qquad \text{...(19a)}$$

Thus, in order to take advantage of the simplicity induced by the fact that the Hessian of the utility function is negative definite we have to restrict the arbitrariness of the transform by (19a). Notice that $G'' \leqq 0$ satisfies (19a). Thus we may prove

Proposition 7. A sufficient condition for the absence of inferior goods is that for *some* utility index $G(.)$

$$G_{ij} \geqq 0 \quad i \neq j. \qquad \text{...(21)}$$

Proof. Let $u(.)$ be a utility index and let $G(u)$ be a transform of this index such that it obeys $G'>0$ and (19a). Let λ and μ be respectively the Lagrangean multipliers associated with $u(.)$ and $G(.)$. Then we have

$$\frac{\partial x}{\partial I} = \lambda \frac{U^{**-1}\underline{u}}{\underline{u}'U^{**-1}\underline{u}} = \mu \frac{G^{**-1}\underline{g}}{\underline{g}'F^{**-1}\underline{g}} \qquad \text{...(21a)}$$

where g is the gradient of G. Since

$$G_{ij} = G'u_{ij} + G''u_i u_j \qquad \text{...(21b)}$$

we observe that even if $u_{ij} \ngeqq 0$ for $i \neq j$, still there may exist a transform $G(.)$ such that $G_{ij} \geqq 0$, all $i \neq j$. But this is the sufficient condition of Proposition 2. q.e.d.

If we now consider perturbations in the equilibrium of the system due to a change in p_k, $k = 1, 2, \ldots, n$, we shall obtain the substitution matrix

$$\Sigma = U^{**-1} - \frac{U^{**-1}\underline{u}\underline{u}'U^{**-1}}{\psi}, \qquad \text{...(22)}$$

which is simply the $n \times n$ principal submatrix of U^{*-1} as given in (18a). Since substitution effects are invariant under a transformation of the utility index by $G(.)$ as in Proposition 7 it follows, by a comparison with (12a), that Propositions 3, 4 and 5 are fully valid in the present case as well. Indeed Proposition 5 and Remark 7 immediately imply the validity of the well-known result of Hicks with respect to composite goods. Thus if x^1 is a (proper) subset of goods whose elements display constant relative prices with respect to each other and if Σ_{11} is the corresponding submatrix of Σ then by Remark 7 Σ_{11} is *negative definite*. The analogue of the substitution effect for x^1 treated as a group will then be a quadratic form in Σ_{11} and thus negative.

Remark 9. Finally it is worth pointing out that the arbitrariness of the utility index does not always have the effect of inhibiting the derivation of strong results. Thus, in the theory of the firm, in order to rule out the absence of inferior factors it is sufficient to have $F_{ij} \geqq 0$, $i \neq j$, $F(.)$ being the production function. If the condition does not hold then we cannot so assert. On the other hand if the utility index does not obey $u_{ij} \geqq 0$, $i \neq j$, then this alone does not prevent our asserting the absence of inferior goods, since there may exist some transform $G(u)$ for which $G_{ij} \geqq 0$, $i \neq j$.

5. CONCLUSION

We have provided in this paper necessary and sufficient conditions for the differentiability of demand functions in the slightly restrictive case where in determining whether a given stationary point is a maximum or minimum one does not require knowledge of derivatives beyond those of the second order. These necessary and sufficient conditions were in the form of a characterization of the Hessian of the production and utility functions.

Beyond that we have developed the salient propositions of the theories of the firm and consumer behaviour using exclusively the properties of positive definite matrices and avoiding the cumbersome conditions involving the alternation of signs of certain determinants, and we have obtained a set of sufficient conditions on the utility and production functions that rule out the case of inferior goods and inferior factors. The proofs of these salient propositions are thus considerably simplified and moreover we obtain a certain unity of formal techniques in dealing with typical problems arising in economic theory, econometrics and mathematical statistics.

University of Pennsylvania P. J. DHRYMES.

REFERENCES

[1] Debreu, G. " Definite and Semi-Definite Quadratic Forms ", *Econometrica*, **20** (1952), 295.

[2] Gantmacher, F. R. *The Theory of Matrices*, vol. I (New York: Chelsea Publishing Co., 1959).

[3] Hicks, J. R. *Value and Capital*, 2nd edition (Oxford: Clarendon Press, 1946).

[4] Katzner, D. " A Note on the Differentiability of Demand Functions " (Mimeographed).

[5] Mosak, J. L. *General Equilibrium Theory in International Trade* (Bloomington, Indiana: The Principia Press Inc., 1944).

[6] Samuelson, P. *The Foundations of Economic Analysis* (Cambridge: Harvard University Press, 1955).

Name index

Economists of the Twentieth Century

Monetarism and Macroeconomic Policy
Thomas Mayer

Studies in Fiscal Federalism
Wallace E. Oates

The World Economy in Perspective
Essays in International Trade and European Integration
Herbert Giersch

Towards a New Economics
Critical Essays on Ecology, Distribution and Other Themes
Kenneth E. Boulding

Studies in Positive and Normative Economics
Martin J. Bailey

The Collected Essays of Richard E. Quandt (2 volumes)
Richard E. Quandt

International Trade Theory and Policy
Selected Essays of W. Max Corden
W. Max Corden

Organization and Technology in Capitalist Development
William Lazonick

Studies in Human Capital
Collected Essays of Jacob Mincer, Volume 1
Jacob Mincer

Studies in Labor Supply
Collected Essays of Jacob Mincer, Volume 2
Jacob Mincer

Macroeconomics and Economic Policy
The Selected Essays of Assar Lindbeck, Volume I
Assar Lindbeck

The Welfare State
The Selected Essays of Assar Lindbeck, Volume II
Assar Lindbeck

Classical Economics, Public Expenditure and Growth
Walter Eltis

Money, Interest Rates and Inflation
Frederic S. Mishkin

The Public Choice Approach to Politics
Dennis C. Mueller

The Liberal Economic Order
Volume I Essays on International Economics
Volume II Money, Cycles and Related Themes
Gottfried Haberler
Edited by Anthony Y.C. Koo

Economic Growth and Business Cycles
Prices and the Process of Cyclical Development
Paolo Sylos Labini

International Adjustment, Money and Trade
Theory and Measurement for Economic Policy, Volume I
Herbert G. Grubel

International Capital and Service Flows
Theory and Measurement for Economic Policy, Volume II
Herbert G. Grubel

Unintended Effects of Government Policies
Theory and Measurement for Economic Policy, Volume III
Herbert G. Grubel

The Economics of Competitive Enterprise
Selected Essays of P.W.S. Andrews
Edited by Frederic S. Lee and Peter E. Earl

The Repressed Economy
Causes, Consequences, Reform
Deepak Lal

Economic Theory and Market Socialism
Selected Essays of Oskar Lange
Edited by Tadeusz Kowalik

Trade, Development and Political Economy
Selected Essays of Ronald Findlay
Ronald Findlay

General Equilibrium Theory
The Collected Essays of Takashi Negishi, Volume I
Takashi Negishi

The History of Economics
The Collected Essays of Takashi Negishi, Volume II
Takashi Negishi

Studies in Econometric Theory
The Collected Essays of Takeshi Amemiya
Takeshi Amemiya

Exchange Rates and the Monetary System
Selected Essays of Peter B. Kenen
Peter B. Kenen

Econometric Methods and Applications (2 volumes)
G.S. Maddala

National Accounting and Economic Theory
The Collected Papers of Dan Usher, Volume I
Dan Usher

Welfare Economics and Public Finance
The Collected Papers of Dan Usher, Volume II
Dan Usher

Economic Theory and Capitalist Society
The Selected Essays of Shigeto Tsuru, Volume I
Shigeto Tsuru

Methodology, Money and the Firm
The Collected Essays of D.P. O'Brien (2 volumes)
D.P. O'Brien

Economic Theory and Financial Policy
The Selected Essays of Jacques J. Polak (2 volumes)
Jacques J. Polak

Sturdy Econometrics
Edward E. Leamer

The Emergence of Economic Ideas
Essays in the History of Economics
Nathan Rosenberg

Productivity Change, Public Goods and Transaction Costs
Essays at the Boundaries of Microeconomics
Yoram Barzel

Reflections on Economic Development
The Selected Essays of Michael P. Todaro
Michael P. Todaro

The Economic Development of Modern Japan
The Selected Essays of Shigeto Tsuru, Volume II
Shigeto Tsuru

Money, Credit and Policy
Allan H. Meltzer

Macroeconomics and Monetary Theory
The Selected Essays of Meghnad Desai, Volume I
Meghnad Desai

Poverty, Famine and Economic Development
The Selected Essays of Meghnad Desai, Volume II
Meghnad Desai

Explaining the Economic Performance of Nations
Essays in Time and Space
Angus Maddison

Economic Doctrine and Method
Selected Papers of R.W. Clower
Robert W. Clower

Economic Theory and Reality
Selected Essays on their Disparity and Reconciliation
Tibor Scitovsky

Doing Economic Research
Essays on the Applied Methodology of Economics
Thomas Mayer

Institutions and Development Strategies
The Selected Essays of Irma Adelman, Volume I
Irma Adelman

Dynamics and Income Distribution
The Selected Essays of Irma Adelman, Volume II
Irma Adelman

The Economics of Growth and Development
Selected Essays of A.P. Thirlwall
A.P. Thirlwall

Theoretical and Applied Econometrics
The Selected Papers of Phoebus J. Dhrymes
Phoebus J. Dhrymes

Innovation, Technology and the Economy
The Selected Essays of Edwin Mansfield (2 volumes)
Edwin Mansfield

Economic Theory and Policy in Context
The Selected Essays of R.D. Collison Black
R.D. Collison Black

Capitalism, Socialism and Post-Keynesianism
Selected Essays of G.C. Harcourt
G.C. Harcourt

Time Series Analysis and Macroeconometric Modelling
The Collected Papers of Kenneth F. Wallis
Kenneth F. Wallis

Foundations of Modern Econometrics
The Selected Essays of Ragnar Frisch (2 volumes)
Olav Bjerkholt

Growth, the Environment and the Distribution of Incomes
Essays by a Sceptical Optimist
Wilfred Beckerman